Handbook of Research on Business Process Modeling

Jorge Cardoso
SAP Research, Germany

Wil van der Aalst
Technische Universiteit Eindhoven, The Netherlands

Information Science REFERENCE

INFORMATION SCIENCE REFERENCE

Hershey · New York

Director of Editorial Content: Kristin Klinger
Senior Managing Editor: Jamie Snavely
Managing Editor: Jeff Ash
Assistant Managing Editor: Carole Coulson
Typesetter: Carole Coulson
Cover Design: Lisa Tosheff
Printed at: Yurchak Printing Inc.

Published in the United States of America by
Information Science Reference (an imprint of IGI Global)
701 E. Chocolate Avenue,
Hershey PA 17033
Tel: 717-533-8845
Fax: 717-533-8661
E-mail: cust@igi-global.com
Web site: http://www.igi-global.com/reference

and in the United Kingdom by
Information Science Reference (an imprint of IGI Global)
3 Henrietta Street
Covent Garden
London WC2E 8LU
Tel: 44 20 7240 0856
Fax: 44 20 7379 0609
Web site: http://www.eurospanbookstore.com

Library of Congress Cataloging-in-Publication Data

Handbook of research on business process modeling / Jorge Cardoso and Wil van der Aalst, editors.
p. cm.
Includes bibliographical references and index.
Summary: "This book aids managers in the transformation of organizations into world-class competitors through business process applications"--Provided by publisher.
ISBN 978-1-60566-288-6 (hardcover) -- ISBN 978-1-60566-289-3 (ebook) 1. Business--Data processing. 2. Management information systems. I. Cardoso, Jorge, 1970- II. Aalst, Wil van der. HF5548.2.H3626 2009 658.4'034--dc22
2008052197

British Cataloguing in Publication Data
A Cataloguing in Publication record for this book is available from the British Library.

List of Contributors

Table of Contents

Preface xx

Section I
Advanced Modeling Methodologies

Chapter I
Business Process Modelling in the jABC: The One-Thing-Approach 1
Tiziana Margaria, Universität Potsdam, Germany
Bernhard Steffen, TU Dortmund, Germany

Chapter II
Modeling Process-Driven SOAs: A View-Based Approach 27
Huy Tran, Distributed Systems Group, Institute of Information Systems, Vienna University of Technology, Austria
Ta'id Holmes, Distributed Systems Group, Institute of Information Systems, Vienna University of Technology, Austria
Uwe Zdun, Distributed Systems Group, Institute of Information Systems, Vienna University of Technology, Austria
Schahram Dustdar, Distributed Systems Group, Institute of Information Systems, Vienna University of Technology, Austria

Chapter III
Process Modeling for Holistic Process Management 49
Stefan Jablonski, University of Bayreuth, Germany

Section II
Modern Business Process Languages

Chapter IV
The Dichotomy of Modeling and Execution: BPMN and WS-BPEL 70
Matthias Kloppmann, IBM Deutschland Research and Development GmbH, Germany
Dieter König, IBM Deutschland Research and Development GmbH, Germany
Simon Moser, IBM Deutschland Research and Development GmbH, Germany

Section IV
Enriching Process Models and Enactment Architectures

Chapter XII
Temporalities for Workflow Management Systems 255
Carlo Combi, Università degli Studi di Verona, Italy
Giuseppe Pozzi, Politecnico Di Milano, Italy

Chapter XIII
The People Integration Challenge 274
Karsten Ploesser, SAP Research CEC, Australia
Nick Russell, Technische Universiteit Eindhoven, The Netherlands

Chapter XIV
Semantic Business Process Management: Applying Ontologies in BPM 299
Dimka Karastoyanova, University of Stuttgart, Germany
Tammo van Lessen, University of Stuttgart, Germany
Frank Leymann, University of Stuttgart, Germany
Zhilei Ma, University of Stuttgart, Germany
Jörg Nitzsche, University of Stuttgart, Germany
Branimir Wetzstein, University of Stuttgart, Germany

Chapter XV
Compiling Business Process Models into Executable Code 318
Cesare Pautasso, University of Lugano, Switzerland

Chapter XVI
Using WfMS to Support Unstructured Activities 338
Hernâni Mourão, Polytechnic Institute of Setúbal, Portugal
Pedro Antunes, University of Lisboa & LaSIGE - Large Scale Informatics Systems Laboratory, Portugal

Section V
Business Process Management in Organizations

Chapter XVII
Business Process Engineering 366
Guillermo Jimenez, Centro de Sistemas Inteligentes Tecnológico de Monterrey, Mexico

Chapter XVIII
B2B and EAI with Business Process Management 384
Christoph Bussler, Merced Systems, Inc., USA

Detailed Table of Contents

The one thing approach is designed to overcome the classical communication hurdles between application experts and the various levels of IT experts. Technically, it is realized in terms of eXtreme Model Driven Design, a technique that puts the user-level process in the center of the development. It enables customers/users to design, animate, validate, and control their processes throughout the whole life cycle, starting with the first requirement analysis, and ending with the demand-driven process evolution over its entire life span. This strict way of top-down thinking emphasizes the primary goal of every development: customer satisfaction.

This chapter introduces a view-based, model-driven approach for process-driven, service-oriented architectures. A typical business process consists of numerous tangled concerns, such as the process control flow, service invocations, fault handling, transactions, and so on. The author's view-based approach

Due to the absence of commonly accepted conceptual and formal foundations for workflow management, and more generally business process management (BPM), a plethora of approaches to process modelling and execution exists both in academia and in industry. The introduction of workflow patterns provided a deep and language independent understanding of modelling issues and requirements encountered in business process specification. They provide a comparative insight into various approaches to process specification and serve as guidance for language and tool development. YAWL (Yet Another Workflow Language) is a novel and formally defined workflow language based on workflow patterns and Petri nets, thus leveraging off both practical and theoretical insights in the field of BPM. This chapter provides an overview of this language and its corresponding open source support environment.

There are many different notations and formalisms for modelling business processes and workflows. These notations and formalisms have been introduced with different purposes and objectives. Later, influenced by other notations, comparisons with other tools, or by standardization efforts, these notations have been extended in order to increase expressiveness and to be more competitive. This resulted in an increasing number of notations and formalisms for modelling business processes and in an increase of the different modelling constructs provided by modelling notations, which makes it difficult to compare modelling notations and to make transformations between them. One of the reasons is that, in each notation, the new concepts are introduced in a different way by extending the already existing constructs. In this chapter, the authors go the opposite direction: showing that it is possible to add most of the typical extensions on top of any existing notation or formalism—without changing the formalism itself. Basically, they introduce blocks with some additional attributes defining their initiation and termination behaviour. This serves two purposes: First, it gives a clearer understanding of the basic constructs and how they can be combined with more advanced constructs. Second, it will help combining different modelling notations with each other. Note that, though they introduce a notation for blocks in this chapter, they are not so much interested in promoting this notation here. The notation should just prove that it is possible to separate different issues of a modelling notation, and this way making its concepts clearer and the interchange of models easier. A fully-fledged block notation with a clear and simple interface to existing formalisms is yet to be developed.

This chapter introduces the basic concepts of information control net (ICN) and its workflow models. In principle, a workflow model is the theoretical basis of a workflow modeling methodology as well as a workflow enactment architecture. Particularly, the workflow model is directly related with how its major components are embodied for implementing the underlying workflow enactment system, too. Accordingly, the authors describe the graphical and formal representations of ICN-based workflow model and its advanced models—role-based model and actor-based model—that can be automatically transformed from the ICN-based workflow model in order to improve their verifiability, maintainability and usability. Conclusively stating, we strongly believe that the ICN-based workflow model and its advanced models be very useful not only for maximizing the quality of workflows but also for strengthening theoretical backgrounds of the recent research issues, such as workflow verification/validation, workflow reengineering, workflow intelligence, workflow mining/rediscovery, and advanced workflow architectures, and so on.

Section III
Process Models in Dynamic Environments

Chapter VIII
Enabling Adaptive Process-Aware Information Systems with ADEPT2 173
Manfred Reichert, University of Ulm, Germany
Peter Dadam, University of Ulm, Germany

In dynamic environments it must be possible to quickly implement new business processes, to enable ad-hoc deviations from the defined business processes on-demand (e.g., by dynamically adding, deleting or moving process activities), and to support dynamic process evolution (i.e., to propagate process schema changes to already running process instances). These fundamental requirements must be met without affecting process consistency and robustness of the process-aware information system. In this chapter the authors describe how these challenges have been addressed in the ADEPT2 process management system. Our overall vision is to provide a next generation technology for the support of dynamic processes, which enables full process lifecycle management and which can be applied to a variety of application domains.

Chapter IX
Modeling Business Process Variability for Design-Time Configuration 204
Marcello La Rosa, Queensland University of Technology, Australia
Marlon Dumas, Queensland University of Technology, Australia, & University of Tartu, Estonia
Arthur H.M. ter Hofstede, Queensland University of Technology, Australia

A reference process model represents multiple variants of a common business process in an integrated and reusable manner. It is intended to be individualized in order to fit the requirements of a specific organization or project. This practice of individualizing reference process models provides an attractive alternative with respect to designing process models from scratch; in particular, it enables the reuse of proven practices. This chapter introduces techniques for representing variability in the context of reference process models, as well as techniques that facilitate the individualization of reference process models with respect to a given set of requirements.

Chapter X
Design of Repairable Processes.. 229
Cinzia Cappiello, Politecnico di Milano – Dipartimento di Elettronica e Informazione, Italy
Barbara Pernici, Politecnico di Milano – Dipartimento di Elettronica e Informazione, Italy

This chapter illustrates the concept of repairable processes and self-healing functionalities and discusses about their design requirements. Self-healing processes are able to monitor themselves, to diagnose the causes of a failure and to recover from the failure, where a failure can be either the inability to provide a given service, or a loss in the service quality. Defining the process as a composition of services, the aim of this chapter is also to provide guidelines for designing services in such a way that they can be easily recovered during their execution. Repair mechanisms are thoroughly described by distinguishing between mechanisms applicable at design time and at run time.

Chapter XI
Web Process Adaptation.. 245
Kunal Verma, Accenture Technology Labs, USA

Adaptation is an important concept for Web processes. The author provides an overview of adaptation with respect to control theory and how it is applied to other contexts. Specifically, the chapter focuses on open loop and closed loop adaptation. Then the current Web process standard WS-BPEL supports open loop adaptation is discussed. Finally, the author discusses an academic research framework METEOR-S, which supports closed loop adaptation.

Section IV
Enriching Process Models and Enactment Architectures

Chapter XII
Temporalities for Workflow Management Systems.. 255
Carlo Combi, Università degli Studi di Verona, Italy
Giuseppe Pozzi, Politecnico Di Milano, Italy

Time is a very important dimension of any aspect in human life, affecting also information and information management. As such, time must be dealt with in a suitable way, considering all its facets. The related literature already considered temporal information management from a pure database point of view: temporal aspects (also known as temporalities) of stored information cannot be neglected and the adoption of a suitable database management system (Temporal Database Management System - TDBMS) could be helpful. Recently, research of the temporal data management area started to consider business processes, extending and enriching models, techniques, and architectures to suitably manage temporal aspects. According to this scenario, the authors discuss here some of the main advantages achievable in managing temporal aspects and we consider temporalities in process models, in exception definition, in the architecture of a Workflow Management System (WfMS), and in the scheduling of tasks and their assignment to agents.

Chapter XIII
The People Integration Challenge.. 274
Karsten Ploesser, SAP Research CEC, Australia
Nick Russell, Technische Universiteit Eindhoven, The Netherlands

This chapter discusses the challenges associated with integrating work performed by human agents into automated workflows. It briefly recounts the evolution of business process support systems and concludes that although the support for people integration continues to evolve in these offerings, in broad terms it has not advanced markedly since their inception several decades ago. Nevertheless, people are an integral part of business processes and integration of human work deserves special consideration during process design and deployment. To this end, the chapter explores the requirements associated with modelling human integration and examines the support for people integration offered by WS-BPEL, which (together with its WS-BPEL4People and WS-HumanTask extensions) currently represents the state of the art when defining and implementing business processes in a service-oriented environment. In order to do this, it utilises a common framework for language assessment, the workflow re-source patterns, both to illustrate the capabilities of WS-BPEL and to identify future technical opportunities.

Chapter XIV
Semantic Business Process Management: Applying Ontologies in BPM 299
Dimka Karastoyanova, University of Stuttgart, Germany
Tammo van Lessen, University of Stuttgart, Germany
Frank Leymann, University of Stuttgart, Germany
Zhilei Ma, University of Stuttgart, Germany
Jörg Nitzsche, University of Stuttgart, Germany
Branimir Wetzstein, University of Stuttgart, Germany

Even though process orientation/BPM is a widely accepted paradigm with heavy impact on industry and research the available technology does not support the business professionals' tasks in an appropriate manner that is in a way allowing processes modeling using concepts from the business domain. This results in a gap between the business people expertise and the IT knowledge required. The current trend in bridging this gap is to utilize technologies developed for the Semantic Web, for example ontologies, while maintaining reusability and flexibility of processes. In this chapter the authors present an overview of existing technologies, supporting the BPM lifecycle, and focus on potential benefits Semantic Web technologies can bring to BPM. The authors will show how these technologies help automate the transition between the inherently separate/detached business professionals' level and the IT level without the burden of additional knowledge acquisition on behalf of the business professionals. As background information they briefly discuss existing process modeling notations like the Business Process Modeling Notation (BPMN) as well as the execution centric Business Process Execution Language (BPEL), and their limitations in terms of proper support for the business professional. The chapter stresses on the added value Semantic Web technologies yield when leveraged for the benefit of BPM. For this the authors give examples of existing BPM techniques that can be improved by using Semantic Web technologies, as well as novel approaches which became possible only through the availability of semantic descriptions. They show how process model configuration can be automated and thus simplified and how flexibility during process execution is increased. Additionally, they present innovative techniques like automatic process composition and auto-completion of process models where suitable process fragments are automatically discovered to make up the process model. They also present a reference architecture of a BPM system that utilizes Semantic Web technologies in an SOA environment.

Chapter XV
Compiling Business Process Models into Executable Code.. 318
Cesare Pautasso, University of Lugano, Switzerland

Model-driven architecture (MDA), design and transformation techniques can be applied with success to the domain of business process modeling (BPM) with the goal of making the vision of business-driven development a reality. This chapter is centered on the idea of compiling business process models for executing them, and how this idea has been driving the design of the JOpera for Eclipse workflow management tool. JOpera presents users with a simple, graph-based process modeling language with a visual representation of both control and data-flow aspects. As an intermediate representation, the graphs are converted into Event-Condition-Action rules, which are further compiled into Java bytecode for efficient execution. These transformations of process models are performed by the JOpera process compiler in a completely transparent way, where the generated executable artefacts are kept hidden from users at all times (i.e., even for debugging process executions, which is done by augmenting the original, high level notation). The author evaluates his approach by discussing how using a compiler has opened up the several possibilities for performing optimization on the generated code and also simplified the design the corresponding workflow engine architecture.

Chapter XVI
Using WfMS to Support Unstructured Activities... 338
Hernâni Mourão, Polytechnic Institute of Setúbal, Portugal
Pedro Antunes, University of Lisboa & LaSIGE - Large Scale Informatics Systems Laboratory, Portugal

In this chapter the authors propose a solution to handle unexpected exceptions in WfMS. They characterize these events deeply and recognize that some of them require immediate reaction and users can not plan their response in advance. Current approaches that handle unexpected exceptions are categorized by their resilience property and it is identified that supporting unstructured activities becomes critical to react to these events. Their proposed system is able to change its behaviour from supporting structured activities to supporting unstructured activities and back to its original mode. They also describe how the system was implemented and we discuss a concrete scenario where it was tested

Section V
Business Process Management in Organizations

In this chapter the author introduces the role of a business process engineer (BPE) and necessary competencies to define, simulate, analyze, and improve business processes. As a minimal body of knowledge for a BPE we propose two complementary fields: enterprise integration engineering (EIE) and business process management (BPM). EIE is presented as a discipline that enriches business models by providing additional views to enhance and extend the coverage of business models through the consideration of additional elements to those that are normally considered by a process model, such as the inclusion of mission, vision, and strategy which are cornerstone in EIE. A BPE is a person who holistically uses principles of BPE, EIE, and associated tools to build business models that identify elements such as information sources involved, the roles which use and transform the information, and the processes that guide end-to-end transformation of information along the business.

This chapter introduces the application of process management to business-to-business (B2B) integration and enterprise application integration (EAI). It introduces several integration examples and a complete conceptual model of integration with a focus on process management. Several specific process-oriented integration problems are introduced that are process-specific in nature. The goal of this chapter is to introduce B2B and EAI integration, to show how process management fits into the conceptual model of integration and to convey solution strategies to specific process-oriented integration problems. The exercises at the end of the chapter continue the various examples and allow the reader to apply their knowledge to several advanced integration problems.

This chapter is devoted to automated support for interorganizational business process management, that is, formation and enactment of business processes that span multiple autonomous organizations. A treatment of intra- and interorganizational business processes is included to provide a conceptual background. It describes a number of research approaches in this area, including the context of these approaches and the design of the systems proposed by them. The approaches are described from early developments in the field relying on dedicated technology to current designs based on standardized technology from the service-oriented context. The chapter thereby provides an overview of developments in the area of interorganizational business process management.

Chapter XX
The Journey to Business Process Compliance.. 426
Guido Governatori, NICTA, Queensland Research Laboratory, Australia
Shazia Sadiq, University of Queensland, Australia

It is a typical scenario that many organisations have their business processes specified independently of their business obligations (which includes contractual obligations to business partners, as well as obligations a business has to fulfil against regulations and industry standards). This is because of the lack of guidelines and tools that facilitate derivation of processes from contracts but also because of the traditional mindset of treating contracts separately from business processes. This chapter will provide a solution to one specific problem that arises from this situation, namely the lack of mechanisms to check whether business processes are compliant with business contracts. The chapter begins by defining the space for business process compliance and the eco-system for ensuring that process are compliant. The key point is that compliance is a relationship between two sets of specifications: the specifications for executing a business process and the specifications regulating a business. The central part of the chapter focuses on a logic based formalism for describing both the semantics of normative specifications and the semantics of compliance checking procedures.

Section VI
Improving Business Processes

Chapter XXI
Business Process Intelligence 456
M. Castellanos, Hewlett-Packard Laboratories, USA
A. K. Alves de Medeiros, Eindhoven University of Technology, The Netherlands
J. Mendling, Queensland University of Technology, Australia
B. Weber, University of Innsbruck, Austria
A. J. M. M. Weijters, Eindhoven University of Technology, The Netherlands

Business Process Intelligence (BPI) is an emerging area that is getting increasingly popular for enterprises. The need to improve business process efficiency, to react quickly to changes and to meet regulatory compliance is among the main drivers for BPI. BPI refers to the application of Business Intelligence techniques to business processes and comprises a large range of application areas spanning from process monitoring and analysis to process discovery, conformance checking, prediction and optimization. This chapter provides an introductory overview of BPI and its application areas and delivers an understanding of how to apply BPI in one's own setting. In particular, it shows how process mining techniques such as process discovery and conformance checking can be used to support process modeling and process redesign. In addition, it illustrates how processes can be improved and optimized over time using analytics for explanation, prediction, optimization and what-if-analysis. Throughout the chapter, a strong emphasis is given to describe tools that use these techniques to support BPI. Finally, major challenges for applying BPI in practice and future trends are discussed.

Chapter XXII
Applied Sequence Clustering Techniques for Process Mining 481
Diogo R. Ferreira, IST – Technical University of Lisbon, Portugal

This chapter introduces the principles of sequence clustering and presents two case studies where the technique is used to discover behavioral patterns in event logs. In the first case study, the goal is to understand the way members of a software team perform their daily work, and the application of sequence clustering reveals a set of behavioral patterns that are related to some of the main processes being carried out by that team. In the second case study, the goal is to analyze the event history recorded in a technical support database in order to determine whether the recorded behavior complies with a predefined issue handling process. In this case, the application of sequence clustering confirms that all behavioral patterns share a common trend that resembles the original process. Throughout the chapter, special attention is given to the need for data preprocessing in order to obtain results that provide insight into the typical behavior of business processes.

Chapter XXIII
A Data-Centric Design Methodology for Business Processes 503
Kamal Bhattacharya, IBM T.J. Watson Research Lab, USA
Richard Hull, IBM T.J. Watson Research Lab, USA
Jianwen Su, University of California at Santa Barbaara, USA

This chapter describes a design methodology for business processes and workflows that focuses first on "business artifacts", which represent key (real or conceptual) business entities, including both the business-relevant data about them and their macro-level lifecycles. Individual workflow services (a.k.a. tasks) are then incorporated, by specifying how they operate on the artifacts and fit into their lifecycles. The resulting workflow is specified in a particular artifact-centric workflow model, which is introduced using an extended example. At the logical level this workflow model is largely declarative, in contrast with most traditional workflow models which are procedural and/or graph-based. The chapter includes a discussion of how the declarative, artifact-centric workflow specification can be mapped into an optimized physical realization.

Chapter XXIV
Measurement and Maturity of Business Processes 532
Laura Sanchez, University of Castilla-La Mancha, Spain
Andrea Delgado, University of the Republica, Uruguay
Francisco Ruiz, University of Castilla-La Mancha, Spain
Félix García, University of Castilla-La Mancha, Spain
Mario Piattini, University of Castilla-La Mancha, Spain

The underlying premise of process management is that the quality of products and services is largely determined by the quality of the processes used to develop, deliver and support them. A concept which has been closely related to process quality over the last few years is the maturity of the process and it is important to highlight the current proposal of Business Process Maturity Model (BPMM), which is based on the principles, architecture and practices of CMM and CMMI for Software and describes the

essential practices for the development, preparation, deployment, operations and support of product and service offers from determining customer needs. When maturity models are in place, it is important not to forget the important role that measurement can play, being essential in organizations which intend to reach a high level in the maturity in their processes. This is demonstrated by observing the degree of importance that measurement activities have in maturity models. This chapter tackles the Business Process Maturity Model and the role that business measurement plays in the context of this model. In addition, a set of representative business process measures aligned with the characteristics of BPMM are introduced which can guide organizations to support the measurement of their business processes depending on their maturity.

Preface

In today's dynamic and competitive business environments, organizations are challenged to meet customers' expectations, reduce time-to-market, optimize resource allocation and improve efficiency. By modeling and analyzing their business processes, enterprises can reduce the time and cost of carrying out important activities, improve effectiveness and conform to regulations. A business process is the configuration by which an organization carries out activities across units or departments to produce value for its customers. Activities are generally ordered across time and place, with a beginning, an end, and clearly defined inputs and outputs. Since business processes are the fundamental building blocks of an organization's success, information technologies that focus on process management and improvement have been good candidates to help organizations to fulfill their corporate visions and to improve their competitive positions. In the past two decades, a special interest has been given to Business Process Modeling (BPM) to leverage the computational power of modern information systems to enable organizations to document, model, understand and improve their business processes. The focus on BPM has resulted in the development of workflow management systems, dedicated analysis tools for verification, simulation, and process mining, and various process standards ranging from BPMN to BPEL.

While BPM is not new, it is still a novel paradigm for many of us and for many people it entails a new mindset to ensure a successful outcome and benefit for organizations. Managers and professionals are looking for literature that guides them in the development of end-to-end applications based on process-aware information systems. A key aspect is re-thinking the approach to process modeling. After many years of experience with BPM and associated systems, we have decided to compile a handbook which will help students, researchers and practitioners to exploit BPM and turn promises into tangible results. With the support and contribution of more than 50 academics and practitioners around the world, the Handbook on Business Process Modeling was shaped having in mind the objective to lay the foundations for understanding the concepts and technologies behind BPM.

This book provides valuable answers to frequent problems that people in both academia and industry commonly face when studying and executing BPM undertakings. In each chapter a key concern of business process modeling is discussed. A variety of relevant topics and solutions are discussed in 25 chapters structured in six sections:

- Advanced modelling methodologies
- Modern business process languages
- Process models in dynamic environments
- Enriching process models and enactment architectures
- Business process management in organizations
- Improving business processes

Section I introduces advanced modeling methodologies. Three approaches are presented. The first approach was designed to overcome the classical communication hurdles between application experts and the various levels of IT experts. It relies on the eXtreme Model-Driven Design (XMDD) and the jABC framework for service-oriented and model-driven development. The second methodology introduces a view-based, model-driven approach for process-driven, service-oriented architectures. This view-based approach separates these concerns into a number of tailored perspectives at different abstraction levels. On the one hand, the separation of process concerns helps reducing the complexity of process development by breaking a business process into appropriate architectural views. On the other hand, the separation of levels of abstraction offers appropriately adapted views to stakeholders, and therefore, helps to quickly react to changes at the business level and at the technical level as well. The last methodology presents a process modeling approach for holistic process management. The main idea behind this methodology is that domain specific process models are required both to capture the contents of a process based application and to present a process model in a user-friendly way. Therefore, the chapter presents how perspective oriented process modeling supports domain specific process model.

Section II presents modern business process languages. The first language presented is YAWL. YAWL (Yet Another Workflow Language) is a novel and formally defined workflow language based on the well-known workflow patterns and Petri nets, thus leveraging on both practical and theoretical insights in the field of BPM. This chapter provides an overview of this language and its corresponding open source support environment. The second chapter explains that a key aspect of the future of Business Process Management is to combine graphical modeling with a precise specification of an executable business process. The chapter describes how the Business Process Modeling Notation (BPMN), the Service Component Architecture (SCA) and WS-BPEL can be used jointly and combined to model, deploy and execute business process choreographies. Based on these specifications, the dichotomy between modeling and execution can be addressed efficiently. The third chapter clarifies that workflow patterns should not be interpreted as a list of constructs that a modeling notation or workflow language should have. Rather, they show what needs to be expressible by a construct or by a combination of constructs. The chapter discusses modeling constructs with a new focus: minimality and orthogonality. Minimality tries to minimize the number of constructs that are needed for expressing all the necessary patterns. Orthogonality means that the constructs are as independent from each other as possible. The last chapter in this second section introduces the basic concepts of Information Control Net (ICN) and its workflow models. The chapter presents the graphical and formal representations of ICN-based workflow model and its advanced models—role-based model and actor-based model—which can be automatically transformed from an ICN-based workflow model in order to improve their verifiability, maintainability and usability.

Section III studies the use of process models in dynamic environments. In dynamic environments it must be possible to quickly implement new business processes, to enable ad-hoc deviations from the defined business processes on-demand (e.g., by dynamically adding, deleting or moving process activities), and to support dynamic process evolution (i.e., to propagate process schema changes to already running process instances). These fundamental requirements must be met without affecting process consistency and robustness of the process-aware information system. The first chapter presents how these challenges have been addressed in the ADEPT2 process management system. The overall vision is to provide a next generation technology for the support of dynamic processes, which enables full process lifecycle management and which can be applied to a variety of application domains. The second chapter introduces techniques for representing variability in the context of reference process models, as well as techniques that facilitate the individualization of reference process models with respect to a given set of requirements. A reference process model represents multiple variants of a common business process in an integrated and reusable manner. It is intended to be individualized in order to fit the requirements of a specific organization or project. The third chapter illustrates the concept of repairable processes and self-healing functionalities and discusses their design requirements. Self-healing processes are able to monitor themselves, to diagnose the causes of a failure and to recover from the failure, where a failure can be either the inability to provide a given service, or a loss in the service quality. Repair mechanisms are thoroughly described by distinguishing between mechanisms applicable at design time and at run time. The last chapter discusses the adaptation of Web processes and provides an overview of adaptation with respect to control theory and how it is applied to other contexts. Specifically, the focus is on open loop and closed loop adaptation. The chapter shows how the current Web process standard WS-BPEL supports open loop adaptation and shows support for closed loop adaptation using METEOR-S, an academic research framework.

Section IV explores how process models can be enriched with additional elements and how enactment architectures can be extended to support new concepts. The first chapter discusses the role of time in workflow management systems. It enumerates some of the main advantages achievable in managing temporal aspects in process models, in exception definition, in the architecture of a workflow management system, and in the scheduling of tasks and their assignment to agents. The second chapter discusses the challenges associated with integrating work performed by human agents into automated workflows. It briefly recounts the evolution of business process support systems and concludes that although the support for people integration continues to evolve in these offerings, in broad terms it has not advanced markedly since their inception several decades ago. The chapter explores the requirements associated with modeling human integration and examines the support for people integration offered by WS-BPEL, which (together with its WS-BPEL4People and WS-HumanTask extensions) currently represents the state of the art when defining and implementing business processes in a service-oriented environment. The third chapter identifies a gap between the business people expertise and the IT knowledge required to carry out a suitable and accurate process modeling. One solution to close the gap is to use technologies developed for the Semantic Web and ontologies. The chapter explains how these technologies help automate the transition between the inherently separate/detached business professionals' level and the IT level without the burden of additional knowledge acquisition on behalf of the business professionals. The fourth chapter presents how model transformation and refinement techniques can be applied to produce executable code out of business process models. Once a business process has been modeled using some language, there are two main alternatives to be considered in order to run the process model using a workflow execution engine. The first involves the direct interpretation of the model. The second alternative is the compilation of the model into a lower-level representation amenable to more efficient execution. The chapter shows how model-driven architecture (MDA) techniques have been applied with success to the domain of business process modeling. As an example case study, the chapter shows how the idea of compiling business process models has been driving the design of the JOpera for Eclipse workflow management tool. The last chapter illustrates how workflow management systems can be extended to support unstructured activities. Workflow systems are based on the premise that procedures are able to define the details of the work carried out in organizations. Original systems were biased by the rationalistic view that organizations follow procedures on a rigid way to achieve their goals. However, organizations also require flexibility when performing their daily operations and procedures since they do not necessarily have all the required information to accomplish their work. This chapter describes a solution developed to address the problem that traditional workflow systems have while coping with unstructured activities. It makes the assumption that there will always be situations where users should be able to decide on what are the most suited activities to fulfill organizational goals, with or without restrictions imposed by the workflow system.

Section V exemplifies how business process management can be used in organizations. The first chapter introduces the notion of business process engineering and the role of a business process engineer. It enumerates the necessary competencies to define, simulate, analyze and improve business processes. A process engineer is considered a person who holistically uses principles of business process engineering, enterprise integration engineering, and associated tools to build business models that identify elements such as information sources involved, the roles which use and transform the information, and the processes that guide end-to-end transformation of information along the business. The second chapter introduces the application of process management to business-to-business (B2B) integration and enterprise application integration (EAI). It introduces several integration examples and a complete conceptual model of integration with a focus on process management. Several specific process-oriented integration problems are introduced that are process-specific in nature. The goal of this chapter is to introduce B2B and EAI integration, to show how process management fits into the conceptual model of integration and to convey solution strategies to specific process-oriented integration problems. The third chapter is devoted to automated support for inter-organizational business process management, that is, formation and enactment of business processes that span multiple autonomous organizations. A treatment of intra- and inter-organizational business processes is included to provide a conceptual background. It describes a number of research approaches in this area, including the context of these approaches and the design of systems. The approaches are described from early developments in the field relying on dedicated technology to current designs based on standardized technology from the service-oriented context. The fourth chapter introduces the concept of business process governance. Process governance provides enterprises with approaches and toolkits to enhance business process management regarding strategy, infrastructure, and enterprise people. Business process governance can be seen from four points of view: business process alignment with its environment, controls and leverages to reach enterprise objectives, business process maturity assessment, and enterprise organizational structure. These perspectives, when analyzed correctly, allow enterprises to retain competitiveness, improve their business processes and make an efficient use of their human resources, and infrastructures. The last chapter addresses the topic of business process compliance. The chapter provides a solution to one specific problem that arises from the lack of mechanisms to check whether business processes are compliant with business contracts. The chapter begins by defining the space for business process compliance and the eco-system for ensuring that process are compliant. The key point is that compliance is a relationship between two sets of specifications: the specifications for executing a business process and the specifications regulating a business. The central part of the chapter focuses on a logic based formalism for describing both the semantics of normative specifications and the semantics of compliance checking procedures.

Section VI of this book studies available solutions to improve business processes. The first chapter explores an emerging area that is getting increasingly popular for enterprises: Business Process Intelligence (BPI). BPI refers to the application of business intelligence techniques to business processes and comprises a large range of application areas spanning from process monitoring and analysis to process discovery, conformance checking, prediction and optimization. This chapter provides an overview of BPI and its application areas and delivers an understanding of how to apply BPI in one's own setting. In particular, it shows how process mining techniques such as process discovery and conformance checking can be used to support process modeling. The second chapter introduces the principles of sequence clustering and presents two case studies where the technique is used to discover behavioral patterns in event logs. In the first case study, the goal is to understand the way members of a software team perform their daily work, and the application of sequence clustering reveals a set of behavioral patterns that are related to some of the main processes being carried out by that team. In the second case study, the goal is to analyze the event history recorded in a technical support database in order to determine whether the recorded behavior complies with a predefined issue handling process. The third chapter describes a design methodology for business processes and workflows that focuses first on the key data objects to be manipulated by the workflow along with their macro life-cycles, and then incorporates the individual workflow services that will operate on those objects and the association of the services to the artifacts. The resulting workflow is specified in an artifact-centric workflow model, which is introduced using an extended example. The last chapter introduces the notion of process maturity. Process maturity is the degree of explicit definition, management, measurement, control and effectiveness that a process has. The chapter describes the current proposal for a Business Process Maturity Model, from OMG, which is based on the principles, architecture and practices from software engineering. A second topic addressed by this chapter is the notion of process measures. The use of measures makes it possible for organizations to learn from the past in order to improve performance and achieve better predictability over time. Therefore, measurement activities are fundamental for the improvement of process, product and service quality, since they provide objective information that can be used for decision making.

This book represents a valuable contribution to the available literature on Business Process Modeling. Thanks to the efforts of the leading experts in the field we managed to compile a comprehensive handbook. The book also shows that there have been many breakthroughs in recent years and highlights the enormous potential of BPM and its supporting systems. Therefore, we invite you to be part of the exciting BPM community and we are looking forward for your comments, ideas and suggestions for upcoming editions.

Jorge Cardoso, SAP Research, Germany
Wil van der Aalst, TU/e, The Netherlands
December 2008

About the Editors

Jorge Cardoso joined SAP Research, Germany, in 2007. Currently he is also assistant professor at University of Coimbra working within the Information System group. He previously gave lectures at the University of Madeira (Portugal), the University of Georgia (USA) and at the Instituto Politécnico de Leiria (Portugal). He has worked at the Boeing Company (USA) on enterprise application integration and at CCG, Zentrum für Graphische Datenverarbeitung on Computer Supported Cooperative Work systems. He has published over 90 refereed papers in the areas of workflow management systems, semantic Web, and related fields. He has edited several books, and organized several international conferences on Semantics and Information Systems.

Wil van der Aalst is a full professor of Information Systems at the Technische Universiteit Eindhoven (TU/e) having a position in both the Department of Mathematics and Computer Science and the Department of Technology Management. Currently he is also an adjunct professor at Queensland University of Technology (QUT) working within the BPM group there. His research interests include workflow management, process mining, Petri nets, business process management, process modeling, and process analysis. Wil van der Aalst has published more than 100 journal papers, 13 books (as author or editor), 200 refereed conference/workshop publications, and 30 book chapters. Many of his papers are highly cited (he has an H-index of more than 55 according to Google Scholar) and his ideas have influenced researchers, software developers, and standardization committees working on process support. He has been a co-chair of many conferences including the Business Process Management conference, the International Conference on Cooperative Information Systems, the International conference on the Application and Theory of Petri Nets, and the IEEE International Conference on Services Computing. He is also editor/member of the editorial board of several journals, including the *Business Process Management Journal*, the *International Journal of Business Process Integration and Management*, the *International Journal on Enterprise Modelling and Information Systems Architectures*, *Computers in Industry, IEEE Transactions on Services Computing, Lecture Notes in Business Information Processing*, and *Transactions on Petri Nets and Other Models of Concurrency*.

Section I
Advanced Modeling Methodologies

Chapter I
Business Process Modelling in the jABC:
The One-Thing-Approach

Tiziana Margaria
Universität Potsdam, Germany

Bernhard Steffen
TU Dortmund, Germany

ABSTRACT

The one thing approach is designed to overcome the classical communication hurdles between application experts and the various levels of IT experts. Technically, it is realized in terms of eXtreme Model Driven Design, a technique that puts the user-level process in the center of the development. It enables customers/users to design, animate, validate, and control their processes throughout the whole life cycle, starting with the first requirement analysis, and ending with the demand-driven process evolution over its entire life span. This strict way of top-down thinking emphasizes the primary goal of every development: customer satisfaction.

WHY "ONE THING": THE CULTURAL GAP

Globalization is a general and inevitable trend. It started with enterprises and politics and is now increasingly characterizing the process landscape: global operations require a global process modelling, global coordination, and, at least since Sarbanes-Oxley Act and Basel II, global transparency. This trend puts enormous pressure on the process management, its efficiency, its compliance, its reliability, and its agility. Especially in large organizations it requires a large amount of automation and standardization, and often radical re-organization, in order to minimize the total cost of ownership, to control risks, and to protect the corresponding investment. These are necessary preconditions for enterprises to be able to consolidate their business leadership by using innovative processes as their distinguishing intellectual property. At the same time, they need to obey new regulations, like the Sarbanes-Oxley Act and Basel II, which ask for just-in-time audits and retraceability of any business-relevant decision and operation.

This need to be flexible yet comply to changing regulations contrasts with the current state of the art in business process development, where essentially:

- Each business process, even if modelled by business developers, requires the manual support of IT experts for their realization,
- The (IT-supported) realization is a totally separate `thing′ from the original model, even though perhaps partially and semi-automatically generated from it, and where
- Changes in one thing (the model or the implementation) typically do not show up at the respective other level, let alone they are automatically taken care of.

We follow instead a holistic approach to close the classical gap between business-driven requirements on one side and IT-based realization on the other. We provide for this a seamless method called the *one thing approach*, described below, and a matching toolset that supports this method along the entire life span. The toolset is based on the jABC Framework (Jörges et al., 2006) to cover the business development phase and the business-to-IT transition, and on Integrated Development Environments (IDEs), like e.g. the popular Eclipse or NetBeans (http://www.netbeans.org), to support the IT development and deployment.

The name 'One-Thing Approach' (OTA) (Steffen & Narayan, 2007) reflects the fact that there is only one artefact during the whole systems' life cycle. This artefact is successively refined in various dimensions in order to add details concerning roles, rights, permissions, performance constraints, simulation code (to animate the models), productive code, pre/post conditions, etc.. The central effect is that all stakeholders, including the application expert, can follow the progress from their own perspective (view): initially, application experts may for instance. only browse the documentation and annotate the models, but as soon as some simulation code is available, they may start playing with the system in order to check and enforce an adequate user experience. The user experience gets the more realistic the further the development progresses. This continuous involvement of the application expert allows one to control the harm of the classical business/IT gap, because misconceptions and misunderstandings become immediately apparent.

Key to our solution for reducing this classical cultural gap is the tight combination of two central principles of software and system design: *service orientation* and *model driven design*.

- **Service-orientation** helps reducing the gap between requirements and implementation in the software development process in a very pragmatic fashion: in service oriented environments, a very high-level kind of programming in terms of orchestration *coordinates and harmonizes* application-level `things′ that are provided as services. Realizing the individual services is a clearly distinct task, which may well follow the classical software engineering practice, but it may also be hierarchical within the service world, in the sense that provided services may well be themselves composed of other services. This approach has the potential to truly include the application expert (typically the business developer and the business analyst) in the early development process: at the level of orchestration-driven service requirement, definition, and early refinement, which are close to the area of expertise. This inclusion of non-IT stakeholders as owners of the artefacts is a promise that object-orientation failed to achieve. Thus service-orientation, seen as a paradigm, has a potential to achieve a far broader corporate and societal penetration and impact than object orientation.

- **Model-driven design** too addresses the same gap reduction. However, while service orientation is very much an engineering and structuring concept, model driven design is highly conceptual. Models, if expressed in terms of well-understood mathematical structures, are the basis from which code (fragments) are (semi-) automatically generated. This should guarantee that the resulting implementations inherit essential properties, characteristics, and features from their source models.

By combining the power of these two paradigms we can play with the requirement/ implementation gap, and turn it into a playground for the stakeholders, who can this way define the range of possible alternative solutions. With adequate tool support, we can regard orchestration graphs as (hierarchical) formal models, and thus we can apply various analysis and verifications techniques, like data flow analyses and model checking, to service orchestrations in order to enforce required policies, technical frame conditions, e.g. for interoperabilities or executability, and compliance.

By choosing an adequate level for the elementary services within the hierarchical modelling, this enables formerly excluded professionals (business developers and business analysts) to perform formally controlled high-level modelling in terms of orchestration graphs or process models. The implementation of such models hinges on elementary services, which themselves virtualize the often complex implementation of their respective functionality. This nicely and effectively decouples the service composition from the basic service realization, in a hierarchical separation of concerns that gives non-IT stakeholders an unprecendented degree of control and ownership, independently of IT.

This combined approach, which we call eXtreme Model-Driven Design (XMDD), is very flexible, since the level of modelling and its granularity can be varied at need during the modelling, design, and development process. This happens for example according to the skills and responsibility of the persons currently in charge, or according to the properties and features one intends to establish for the final product.

One of its major strengths is that it enables non-IT experts to control the whole process life cycle from the process modelling level. In particular, roles and rights or permissions can be controlled (defined, modified, monitored) by business experts without requiring any IT support, on easily understandable models. These models are then successively refined in our jABC-based approach up to a level where the basic functionalities can be implemented as simple services. The code for these services is typically rather small, just combining results of some calls to APIs or Web Services, and can be semi-automatically generated to a large extent. The quality of these services has to be guaranteed by the providers, according to some service-level agreement. Thus typical implementation issues, like e.g., connecting to data bases or executing a transaction on an ERP system, are virtualized for the jABC, and delegated to other parties. Moreover concerns like e.g. high availability, roll back, and the management of session and long running transactions do also not belong to the top-level modelling framework. They are captured by our execution engine, which also comprises the functionality of the popular BPEL engines like Active BPEL (Active BPEL execution engine, 2008).

This radically service-oriented approach puts the emphasis on the business process and hands the control over to the IT only at the level of elementary services. Thus the business side is and remains process owner much longer than in usual model-driven approaches.

Thus changing requirements at the business side can mostly be treated in the business process model, typically without requiring IT support. On the other hand, platform migration may happen simply by exchanging the service implementations, and therefore transparent to the business user.

In this chapter, we illustrate the principles behind the one thing approach, and the means we provide to successfully realize it: the XMDD paradigm and the jABC framework for service oriented, model driven development. It is beyond the scope of this chapter to provide a technical description of the jABC, and of the analyis and verification technologies it offers.

Instead we present an example of use of the one thing approach in practice, and describe how it was used in a joint project with IKEA.

EXTREME MODEL DRIVEN DESIGN: THE ONE THING APPROACH

As Figure 1 shows, across the creation of a new product there are clear zones of responsibility for the different professional profiles: product definition, whereby we consider as product any entity for which there is a market, starts from ideas and suggestions by business and product developers: they capture customer needs and work in a customer and market-driven way, owning the product conception and product placement facets. These professionals are typically unfamiliar with IT issues, and define and refine the "what" of the new product. They have the responsibility of specifying, conceiving, and validating it from a user, marketing, and business point of view.

Similarly, they have again the lead in determining successive releases of the product: modifications, enhancements, variations, and diversifications into product lines all carry the signature of business developers, who consult the IT where necessary.

IT, on the other hand, typically is in charge of the technical realisation, starting from the technical aspects of product design and validation (which correspond to the technical requirements), to the realisation and deployment, followed by testing. In this phase, IT teams have the lead, and resort to the creatives (to which they directly or indirectly still report) for consultations in case technical issues have repercussions at the product conception and product placement level.

EXTREME MODEL-DRIVEN DESIGN (XMDD) CONTRASTS THE CLASSICAL SOFTWARE ENGINEERING PRACTICE

There, entire descriptions or models provided by the business developers are transformed (with loss of information and high potential of misunderstanding) into new kinds of artefacts, accessible to the IT experts and to their tools. These new artefacts include documentation and code skeletons artefacts that constitute the blueprint for the realization but are extraneous to the cultural milieu of the business team. Thus in this heterogeneous collaboration there is no cultural common ground, let alone an agreed tangible format for mutual reviewing or for exchanging information unambiguously. As a consequence, misunderstandings and errors are often introduced at this stage, and their discovery and repair happen much later, at higher cost, if at all.

With XMDD, on the contrary, there exists only *one* heterogeneous hierarchical thing: a service logic model which is successively, hierarchically, and collaboratively refined at two levels:

- At the *modelling level,* the refinement establishes a homogeneous model hierarchy. This hierarchy focusses at its higher levels of abstraction on the business perspective of the resulting product, and it stops as soon as it reaches a granularity where the virtualized

Figure 1. Distribution of competences during product development

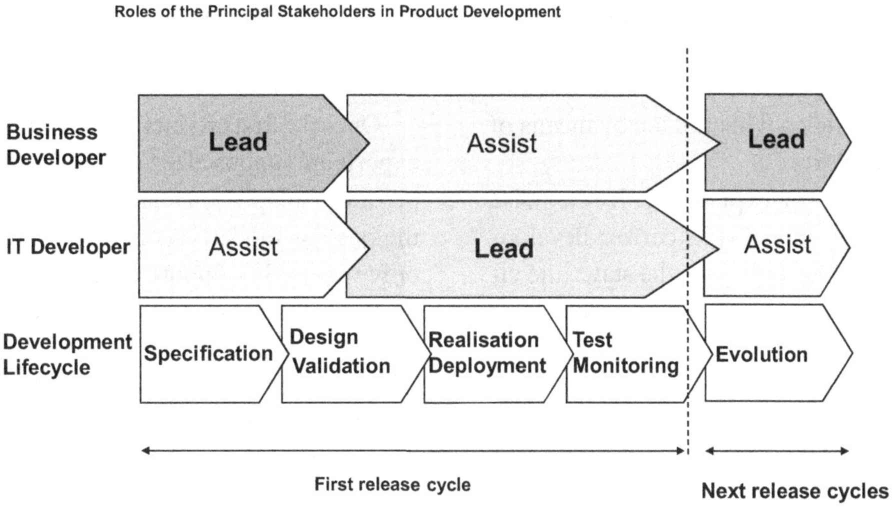

user-level functionalities (the elementary services) are adequately mapped onto code or existing services.

- At the *implementation level,* refinement means delegation to already existing (third party) services or to classical program development, be it direct implementation, or outsourcing, or reuse of available program artefacts (open source or third party products). This delegation is organized and managed (i.e. in particular controlled and supervised) at the granularity decided at the modelling level, thus it remains traceable, controllable, and understandable also for the non-IT responsibles.

The jABC framework already mentioned is a development environment for XMDD. It covers both levels, with an emphasis on the modelling level. Between these two levels, the control of the development is handed over from the jABC, which provides all the means of controlling and guiding the construction of complex models, to an appropriate IDE environment, which provides developers with all the features needed to implement and code. IDEs can be widespread programming platforms like e.g. Netbeans or Eclipse, but also .Net, or specialized frameworks in case of special needs. We have so far integrated services implemented in Prolog, or in other specialized and proprietary platforms, as common in embedded systems. Here, the emphasis is on the openness and ease of communication with the IDE of choice.

We are not aware so far of any other framework or project that combines the features of service-orientation and model driven design in a similarly radical fashion.

Our jABC framework coherently supports this XMDD style by offering a selection of features that help the different stakeholders to master their own responsibilities in an adequate way for their competencies and skills. In particular, our approach takes up and elaborates on the main characteristics that make extreme programming so successful: the tight inclusion of the customer/application expert.

Besides an early, model-based user experience, our environment also integrates and offers business creatives for the first time powerful model-based analysis and verification techniques already at the modelling level:

1. **Early detection of conceptual/logical errors,** i.e. the possibility to challenge already early versions of the models (e.g. before any IT implementation starts) for their essential features, like compliance to required policies. This is done by means of model checking.
2. **Immediate user experience,** by stepwise executing the model at its current development stage. Depending on the stage, the effects of execution may range from document browsing, where the user/application expert follows the documentation along the flow of a particular use case scenario, to animation, simulation, and eventually proper execution of the running code.
3. **Model-based testing:** Like use case scenarios, the developed models also serve as the basis for test generation. This closely resembles the 'test first' idea of agile and test-driven programming, which formulates and collects as early as possible agreements on 'tangible' properties of the final product.
4. **Adaptation and evolution:** The majority of the 'day-to-day' adaptation and evolution steps, especially those concerning the business perspective of the product, can happen at the model level without requiring classical programming skills. Therefore they are now definable and controllable directly by the application experts.

With these four options, XMDD really aims at the direct empowerment of the application expert at the modelling level during the early development process. This goes well beyond the role of a close observer typical for extreme programming, and well beyond the support given by popular business-oriented modelling environments like e.g. ARIS or WebSphere Business Modeller where control is typically lost for good after the handing over to the IT. Extreme model driven design is here in advantage, as the models form a uniform common ground which remains part of the 'one thing' that eventually becomes the running product. This is particularly important for the evolution process later in the product's lifecycle: since evolution is market driven, it is again under the lead of the business experts.

Once the first product is available, the business experts are supposed to take over the control of the product's adaptation and evolution process from the process modelling level. Ideally, this should only require IT support for changes at the lower levels of abstraction, close to the implementation. This empowerment of the application expert, which we consider essential for a truly agile process management, becomes feasible with XMDD because of the harmonic combination of

- The *'one thing' philosophy*, where changing the model directly changes the process and the code all the way down to the deployable product, and conversely, changing the implementation of a component directly becomes operational as part of the overall process,
- The *model-level control via formal methods*, that allows an early and precise control of essential frame conditions at the model level - which, besides others, may be required to guarantee the executability of the modelled process or to obey certain business rules and policies, and
- The *virtualization infrastructure* provided by the underlying IDE, which seamlessly takes over the support of all facets of implementation and deployment.

A major benefit of this approach are the two dimensions of looseness, which allow one to precisely describe the essentials at an abstract level, without being forced by the formalism to take design decision before they become important.

One dimension of looseness is due to the model hierarchy, which allows one to refine parts only on demand and as far as necessary at a time.

The other dimension concerns the orchestration. Using temporal logic constraints, that express in a natural way precedences, causalities, exclusions, global do's and don't, one can impose orchestration structure without being forced to go to the level of concrete process structures. E.g. one can enforce precedences, like "no shipment before payment" or "access only after authentication" for all processes of a certain business unit, just by formulating such constraints once. This layer taps directly into the business knowledge of the stakeholders, and makes it an independent steering wheel for all the models and processes. This is particular beneficial when dealing with product lines, where the individual products are all different but have an essential common kernel, e.g., because they all need to conform to the same business rules. Also the first dimension of looseness, model hierarchy, supports product line management: e.g. in case of an international enterprise, business processes may look identical from a high level managerial perspective, and only become diverse at lower abstraction levels. Our approach allows one to maintain as much similarity as possible, and to reduce the difference only to parts that are really different. In many

Figure 2. Refinement of the model types in terms of orchestrations of enterprise and IT services; the implementation of the single services is either by reuse of legacy or realized in the IDE

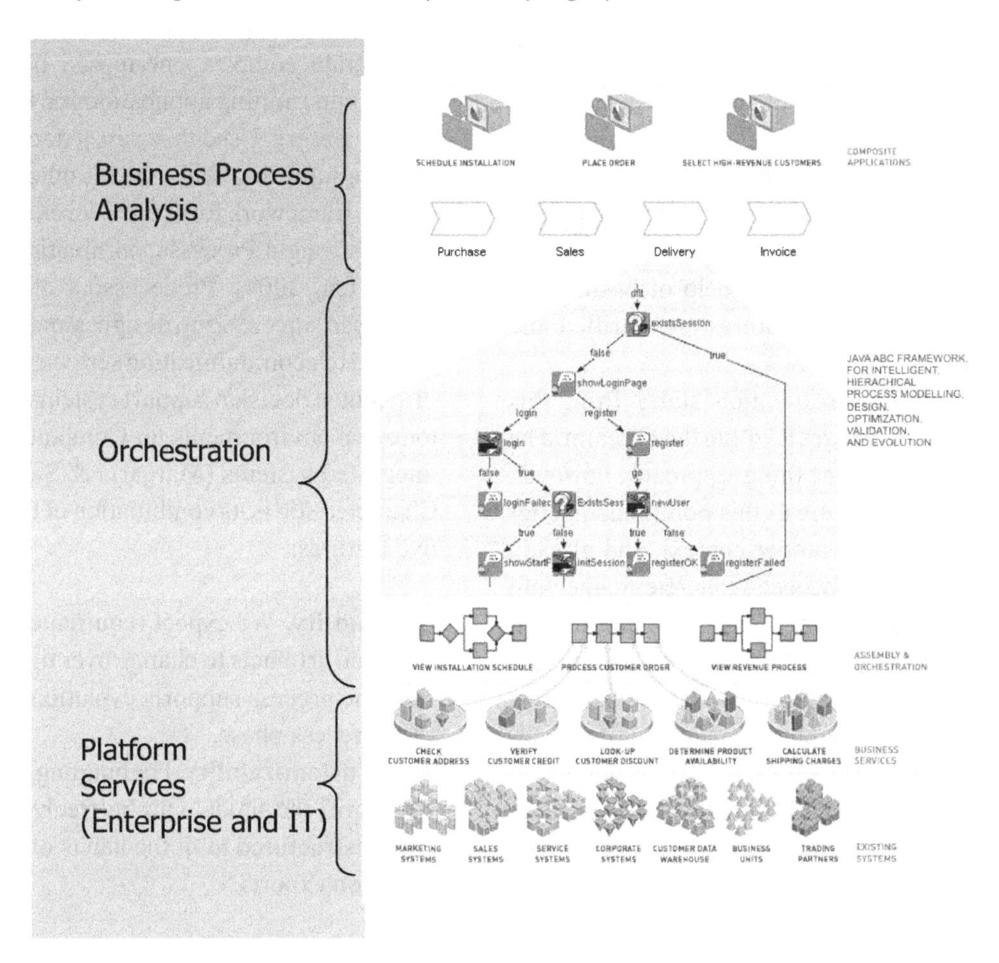

cases this means that high-level modifications of business processes can be done just once at the, e.g. managerial level, without having to touch the corresponding individual processes of the product line.

In the following we sketch our integrated XMDD-based environment for true continuous engineering, which supports consistent propagation of information by bridging the cultural boundaries using the 'one thing' philosophy.

THE jABC FRAMEWORK: AN INTERGRATED ENVIRONMENT FOR EXTREME MODEL DRIVEN DESIGN

The initial product definition (in our case a business process) typically concentrates on the user experience: what are the required capabilities, how should the interaction be organized, and what is an adequate presentation? This high-level view is then refined in terms of processes that provide those capabilities: behavioural models capture the "what happens when..." stories and scenarios, to be checked against desired and undesired behavioural properties, and to be refined successively and cooperatively with the help of business or IT analysts, until the features are clarified and cleared.

The technical realization starts from this model, and concretizes it within the IT realm. The advantage in our 'one thing' approach, however, is that the IT tasks are at this point much better defined, put in the proper context, and already partitioned. Typically, once a concrete architecture and platform has been chosen (e.g. mobile, or web, or embedded, or p2p), the remaining implementation tasks are programming in the small, against the services provided by the platform of choice.

In the XMDD setting, a product is defined in terms of the features and services it provides, those it uses, a behavioural model of their orchestrations/choreography and the policies and constraints it has to fulfil.

The technical realization then concerns (1) the implementation of the missing services, maybe as new components, or their mapping to already available services, and (2) the realization of the underlying business objects in an adequate data model and persistency layer. In our setting, the early phases of product design as well as the platform independent technical refinement and validation/testing are done with the jABC, while the technical development, the support for platform dependent modelling, and the coding are realized with a standard IDE .

jABC: Empowering the Business Developer

jABC (http://www.jabc.de; Jörges et al. 2006) is a flexible framework that supports the whole lifecycle of a business process. It can be used by business and application experts to graphically orchestrate complex end-to-end business processes into running applications on the basis of a service library. Used this way, it does not require any programming skills. On the other hand, it is a mature framework for service development based on Lightweight Process Coordination (Margaria & Steffen, 2004). Predecessors of jABC have been used since 1995 to design, among others, industrial telecommunication services, Web-based distributed decision support systems, and test automation environments for Computer-Telephony integrated systems (Margaria & Steffen, 2006). Characteristic is its combination of the following five features:

- **Agility.** We expect requirements, models, and artefacts to change over time; therefore the process supports evolution as a normal process phase.
- **Customizability.** The building blocks which form the model can be freely renamed or restructured to fit the habits of the application experts.

- **Consistency.** The same modelling paradigm underlies the whole process, from the very first steps of prototyping up to the final execution, guaranteeing traceability and semantic consistency.
- **Verification.** With techniques like model checking and local checks we support the user to consistently develop/modify his model and still guarantee vital frame conditions, like specific requirements or policies. The basic idea is to define local or global properties that the model must satisfy, and to provide automatic checking mechanisms for model compliance to them.
- **Service orientation.** Existing or external features, applications, or services can be easily integrated into a model by wrapping their functionality into building blocks that can be seamlessly used as services inside the models.

The key to this wide range of users and of uses is its support of different model types and its offer of different functionalities depending on the phase of development and on the user group.

Models and Metamodel

jABC models, the Service Logic Graphs (SLGs), are a behavioural counterpart to the SCA - Service Composition Architecture - (Curbera, 2007; SCA Website, 2008) composites and they are architecturally compliant with the coming standard for Service Composition (Jung et al., 2008). As shown in the grey shaded part of Figure2, jABC users easily develop services and applications by graphically composing and configuring reusable building-blocks into (flow-) graph structures. Their handling is very simple, mostly by drag and drop from a collection of functional building blocks. These basic building blocks are called *SIBs* (Service Independent Building Block) in analogy to the original naming of elementary telecommunication services (Margaria, Steffen & Reitenspieß, 2005; Magedanz, Blum & Dutkowski, 2007). SIBs have one ingoing and one or more outgoing edges (*branches*), which depend on the different outcomes of the *execution* of their functionality. The resulting models, that orchestrate SIBs, are called Service Logic Graphs (SLGs). The terminology used in the SIB libraries and in the SLGs is tailored towards the considered target user group, typically the experts of the current application domain, without requiring any IT knowledge. Thus they are adequate to represent the behaviour of a service to business developers, customers, and end users.

Concretely, a SIB is an executable entity, internally realized as a specifically annotated Java class.[1] As such, it intrinsically carries an arbitrarily fine-grained/precise operational semantics. A SIB can be a model placeholder for some functionality or a full implementation of that functionality, as well as any level of refinement/abstraction expressible by the (Java) programming language in between.

SIBs can be arranged into topologies called *Service Logic Graphs* (SLG) which specify process behavior by connecting outgoing SIB branches to the entry points of other SIBs. Inside an SLG, the execution of a SIB starts whenever one of its incoming branches is *active*, which means that the SIB which governs the branch terminated its execution with an outcome associated with that branch. One SIBs inside an SLG can be assigned to be *start SIB*, which means that its execution is started without an incoming active branch; start SIBs are the entry points of the process modelled by the respective SLG.

Figures 6, 7, and 8 show a process from a case study, graphically modeled as SLG. In the basic, sequential case, each SIB terminates with one active branch which determines the next SIB to be executed. Parallel and concurrent structures are likewise possible, as used in the bioinformatics applications (Lamprecht, Margaria & Steffen,

2008; Lamprecht et al., 2008). Hence, an SLG is a graphical, executable, node-action process description.

SLGs can be canonically wrapped into (*graph-*) SIBs to allow for a hierarchical organization of complex process models. Moreover, process models which follow a certain standard defined by jABC can be directly exported into (partial or complete) stand-alone applications, a feature which turns jABC from a modeling into a development tool. Finally, there are SIBs which serve as wrappers for outside functionality (e.g., non-Java applications such as C++, C#, SOAP/WSDL Web services, etc.): this enables modeling and building heterogeneous, distributed, applications.

The service concept as a compositional paradigm is particularly strong in jABC, since all visible business-logic in an SLG boils down to *orchestration* of the functionality abstracted within the SIBs. Each SIB independently and without interruption manipulates the global context, and upon its termination the jABC passes the control to the next SIB. As opposed to a component-oriented approach, SIBs never access or interact with other SIBs through channels or interfaces; instead, their functionality is local and self-contained.

MODELLING VARIABILITY AND ADAPTABILITY

Several kinds of SLGs accompany the entire development. They differ only in their look and feel, and can be drawn, executed and refined in any combination. Figure 2 shows how this is organized.

At the top level, we can start as abstractly as with a **phase diagram SLG** model, as in Figure 2 and 6.

The phases are refined into **process diagram SLG** models, that describe the behaviour of the product (Figures7 and 8). They can include aspects of orchestration (local behaviours) and choreography (distributed behaviour), they support hierarchical refinement, and they can be accompanied by the definition of the data model within the same environment. A rich import/export functionality allows here for example an export of the orchestration as BPEL model, or as UML activity diagram, or as Java, C++, or C# source code, and to support specific applications in finances and bio-informatics, recently even as COBOL and Bioperl.

The team decides how much to refine, establishing this way the granularity of the basic services. Process diagrams can be used all the way down to the **enterprise service** level, where fine grained individual activities meaningful for the business process are defined, the level of abstraction advocated in (Kaiser, 2007). They can be refined even further, to include the **technical services** provided by the technical platform and by the backend systems. This is the case in many of our applications, and typically done concerning telecommunications: the Parlay-X services (Magedanz, Blum & Dutkowski, 2007), and the platform services (Bosch, 2007) mentioned in this issue are examples of this kind: they are themselves of business nature for telecommunication providers, but of technical nature for anybody else, including individual end users but also other enterprises that bind them into their own processes and products as parts of a communication component or service.

Source code can be represented in this style as well: **control flow graph SLG** models are available for example for Java and C/C++, with accompanying import/export functionality, so that the seamless transition to the developer's environment is smooth and can happen at a number levels of abstraction, according to the needs and circumstances.

The jABC framework is flexible enough to also cover other notations in use today, like extended event-driven process chains (eEPCs), BPEL, BPMN, and part of UML. However, in our experience, users had less problems with the intuitive understanding of our notation, despite that fact that it is more concise. In fact, our models allow one to express almost twice as much behaviour as in eEPC notation, which eliminates redundancies and helps understanding and mastering more complex circumstances.

We now describe how all these models can situation-specifically be handled by using adequate plugins. In particular we sketched how the interpretations of the models might change depending on the stage of development.

VARYING POWER FOR DIFFERENT NEEDS AT DIFFERENT TIMES

The development process is supported in jABC by an extensible set of plugins that provide additional features needed along the development lifecycle like animation, rapid prototyping, formal verification, debugging, code generation, monitoring, and evolution. It does not substitute but rather enhance other modelling practices like the UML-based RUP (Rational Unified Process), which we also frequently use for developing individual service components.

Figure 3 shows which of the main plugins support which phases in the lifecycle of Figure1. While several plugins address IT developers, like the retargetable code generator GeneSys, others are specifically targeted at business developers or come with two modes of functioning:

an abstract and definitional one for the business developer, who can for instance sketch a data model in DBSchema, or annotate a SIB with some caveats and restrictions with the Local Checker, or animate the process with the Tracer, which executes whatever activity is linked to the model elements, for example browsing in the corresponding documentation.

The same plugins behave very differently in the subsequent phases of the lifecycle, where they address IT experts:

DBSchema produces ER diagrams and supports the definition, filling of and migration between jDBC compliant databases, as well as bidirectional object/relational mapping via Hibernate, the Local Checker accepts and executes pre-and postconditions expressed in suitable logical lan-

Figure 3. Plugins support the different lifecycle phases in the jABC

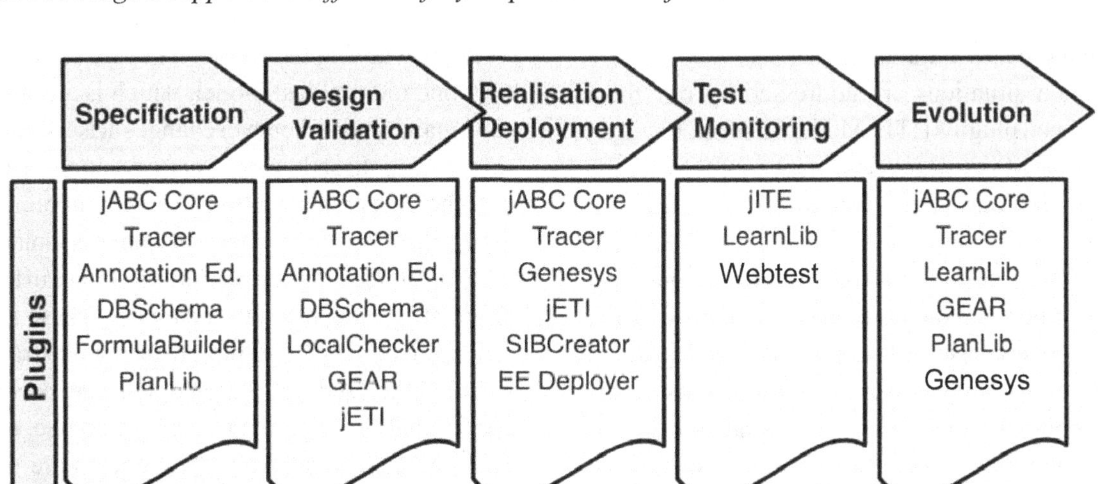

guages, and the Tracer is a full fledged interpreter for SLGs, that provides a multithreaded execution, monitoring, and debugging environment for the SLGs, which can be used to simulate prototypes or as mature runtime environment, with the same dynamicity of languages like Ruby or Python, but on a conceptually more solid footing.

The most innovative features for a business developer address the *evolution* part of the XMDD-supported continuous engineering.

XMDD-BASED CONTINUOUS ENGINEERING

The conceptually more advanced features of the jABC are particularly valuable in the later phases of the product lifecycle. Product evolution requires a delicate balance of maintaining essential parts of the product, yet at the same time modifying erroneous or no longer adequate features and adding totally new functionality. In the course of a product's lifecycle the emphasis thus shifts from modelling and development towards the analysis and validation that guarantee stability and trust: buggy new features are typically accepted to some extent, but customers get angry whenever well-established features are accidentally affected. This becomes even harder when adding legacy components or external services, for which typically no behavioural model exists.

Such situations are addressed by our most advanced plugins (ITE, Model Checker, PlanLib, and LearnLib), which provide the jABC with the following four main features:

- **(Regression) testing:** Given a product and a new candidate release, validate that the new release still supports the vital features of its predecessor. Our model-based approach allows here to go beyond the classical approach, where the test executions of the two releases are required to match precisely. Overcoming this original restriction helped to drastically reduce the number of irrelevant test failures.
- **Verification:** Given a model and the rules of the game, like business rules, policies, governance, or compliance requirements, check whether the model respects the rules. If not, provide detailed diagnostic information – typically in terms of a violating run.
- **Synthesis:** Given (sufficient) knowledge about the collection of available services, and given an abstract description of a business process to be realized with that collection, generate adequate, executable orchestrations/choreographies.
- **Learning:** Given an executable system together with an interface for remote execution, construct a corresponding behavioral model. This feature is invaluable whenever one attempts to integrate third party/legacy components, or to discover a posteriori the effects of some customization on known systems.

For a seamless continuous engineering it is important that these functionalities seamlessly cooperate with the functionalities that support the earlier phases, most importantly the model execution (tracer plugin) and the content editor, that captures documentation and annotations. In the 'one thing approach' this comes essentially for free, since during the whole life cycle there exist only one hierarchical model, which is automatically maintained whenever changes arise. Regression testing directly works on this model, and it uses the tracer for execution. The same applies for the verification: here, when a property is violated, the analysis tool provides counterexamples in form of violating runs through the model. These runs can immediately be explored using the tracer. Also synthesized and learned solution become operational by using the tracer – of course, only as far as their underlying components are realized. The content editor, which organizes the documentation, but may also be used to specify the roles and rights, access policies, and pre- and post conditions, is also part of the 'one thing' that lives along the whole model and product life cycle: it therefore guarantees that the documentation and the implementation of a process-oriented solution stay in synchrony.

The 'one thing approach' requires some discipline: lower level activities should never destroy higher level structure! This is very much in contrast to classical 'many pieces' approaches, where the current structure is handed over and translated or re-coded in new formalisms over and over again while being enriched and completed. These many translation gaps are source of semantic gaps, termed "impedance mismatch" by Steve Vinoski (Vinoski, 2008), which causes irrecoverable information losses.

On the contrary, having just one artefact which is successively refined, there is typically only one level in it where a certain structure is adequately addressed. In particular this means that one should never modify the code that is generated at the very end for a certain platform. What can certainly be modified at the code-level is the implementation of the individual (elementary) services, at least as long as they continue to satisfy their contract. Also, the level for a certain structure may change along the lifecycle, perhaps due to the fact that a previously low ranked functionality enters the focus of the business expert, who wants to get control over its internal structure and properties..

In the following, a concrete case study illustrates how the one-thing-approach was adopted and applied by our project partners in an industrial environment. It concentrates on the business developer view. The IT view has been extensively discussed in many other publications.

CASE STUDY: COLLABORATIVE DEVELOPMENT OF SCM APPLICATIONS

In 2006 we used our one-thing-approach for the model-driven collaborative design of IKEA's

Figure 4. The IKEA IT working method within P3: RUP workflow

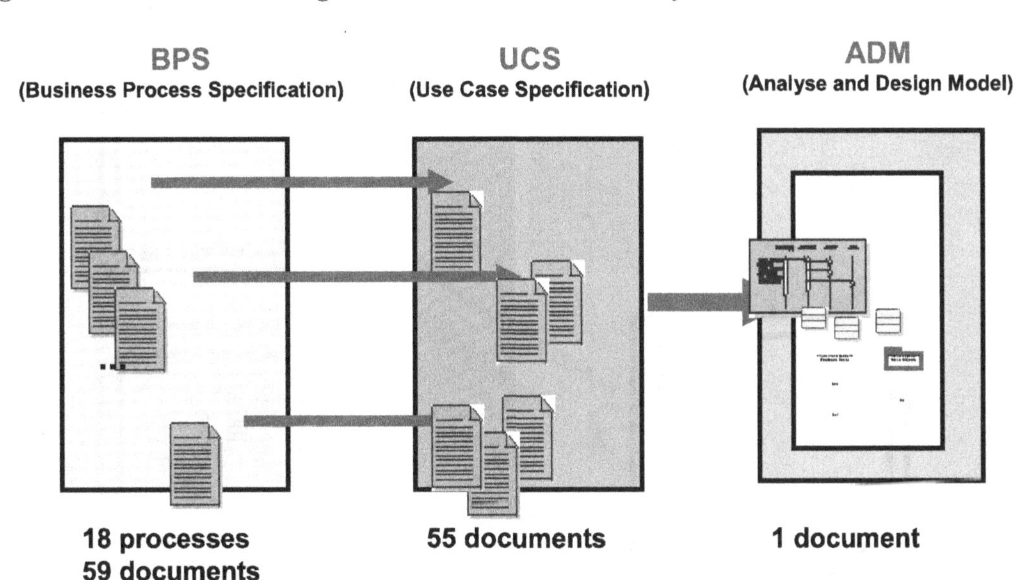

Delivery Management Process, which was to become part of their new worldwide, harmonized IT platform named P3. This joint project was meant to complement the RUP-based (Rational Unified Process) development process already in place in their company.

Over a period of 8 months, an IKEA team used the jABC to model the business-level processes of part of their P3 project that aimed at the complete redesign of the global Supply Chain Management of the company. A substantial part of the design had been already done by then by several loosely collaborating teams. This evaluation concerned the team in charge of describing the new, worldwide, harmonized document management process. This team was flanked within P3 by a number of other teams in charge of tasks among which delivery management (the real shipping), warehouse management, store management.

The task of the joint project was to evaluate:

- Whether and how the one-thing approach elicits cooperation and fosters early consensus between teams operating in parallel and largely independently,
- Whether and how it fosters an improved consistency of the outcome, and
- Whether the jABC way of handling the collaborative design of complex systems is effective and adequate for the cooperation of non-programmers and technical people.

The Setting

Shipping goods beyond country boundaries using various means of transportation in an economy of scale requires an enormous organizational effort. IKEA was redesigning the whole IT landscape around its world-wide delivery management process. This ongoing project involved a major effort by teams distributed world-wide and spanning various corporations: a clear case of global process

Figure 5. (a) Introducing the 'One Thing Approach' for the early, non-IT owned phases

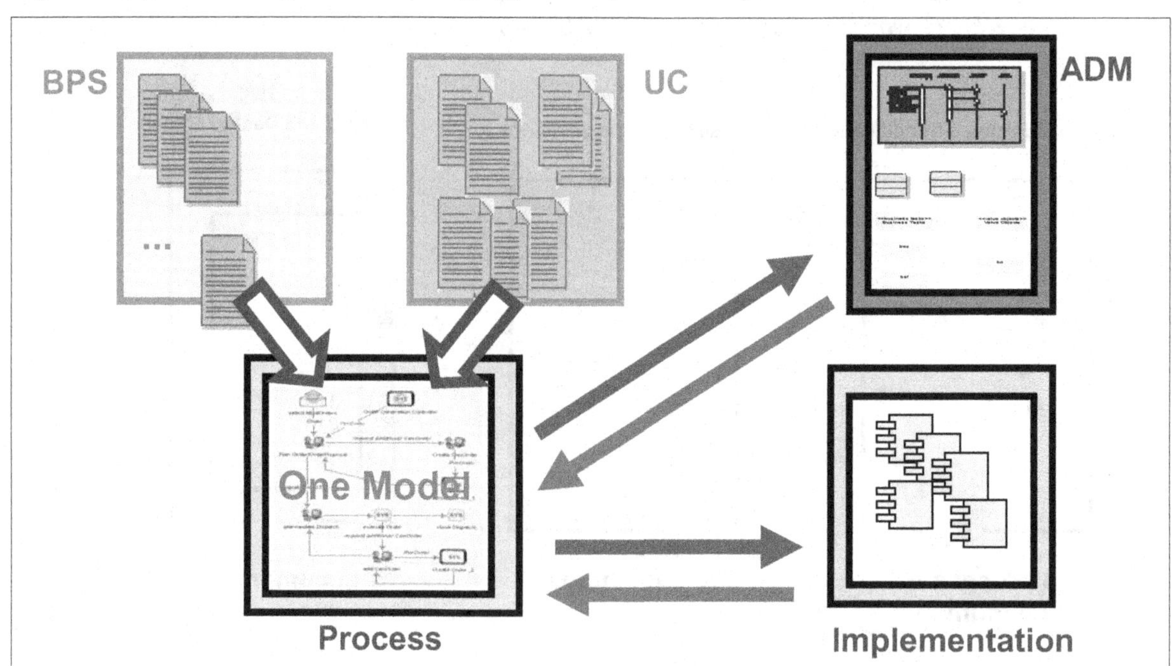

introduction in a context of SCM harmonization for a global player.

The chosen scope of the evaluation addressed the design of an integrated document management system for this new global SCM process, provided by IKEA IT Germany. In this context,

- The document management system sits in the background, essentially as a controller/executor serving the overall delivery process,
- It has strict real time constraints, which are stringent and business critical,
- Kts reliability is business critical. In particular this requires the integration of flexible mechanisms for fault tolerance,
- It is realized as a network of platforms, ranging from pure data management to systems steering the loading and unloading of vehicles or monitoring the progress of a shipment.

The Starting Point

As shown in Figure 4, the development process in use at IKEA was the state-of-the-art Rational Unified Process (RUP - Rational Unified Process, 2008). Requirement modelling tools were Microsoft Word, for a large number of requirement documents produced by non-technical team members, together with Rational products (Rose) for Use cases and for the subsequent analysis and design model. The development modelling language was UML (Unified Modelling Language).

Although a widely recognized development best practice, RUP with UML turned out not to adequately cover the needs of the P3 project in several respects.

The complete RUP requires a complex organization of the team in a large number of roles, covered by single, well identified stakeholders. Here, the team was large, but very loosely organized (in smaller teams distributed over several continents and time zones), and the distribution of topics and responsibility was such that it consisted of loosely coordinated subprojects.

Therefore the RUP flavour implemented was a lightweight, customized and simplified version.

Even then, the whole project addressed processes, while most of the models in the recommended simplified version support primarily a static view instead of a behavioral description. This leads to a number of deficiencies:

- **Vertically,** across the abstraction layers: it fails to consistently connect the different levels of abstraction. E.g., there is no clear connection between the Use cases, which are the entry point to UML, and the Business Process Specifications provided by the business analysts (which, in our case, are spread in 59 word documents describing 18 processes).
- **Horizontally,** within an abstraction level: it fails to consistently connect the different models at the same level. E.g., the mutual dependencies between the many Use cases are not addressed.

As an obvious consequence, the impact of changes to an individual process model remains totally undetected.

Introducing jABC

We introduced the jABC-based process modelling approach to P3 in order to complement the RUP modelling in a way that compensates for the mentioned deficiencies. In the given context, it was essential to be able to support the method with a tool. A pure methodological approach would not have lead to a project, since there was a clear perception of already implementing with the customized RUP a recognized and widely adopted best practice. It was however evident that tool support was lacking and would bring a benefit.

In particular, the industrial partners wished a tool that made it possible to check consistency vertically, horizontally, and over changes. As pictured in Figure 5(a), the task was to create a one-thing model for the first two phases of the definition of the document delivery process. This should happen on the basis of the 18 documents constituting the Business Process Specifications, and referring to (and maintaining consistency with) the 55 documents of the Use case specifications.

jABC (http:// www.jabc.de) convinced the partners since it had already been in industrial use for over ten years, starting back in 1995 with the design of processes for industrial telecommunication services (Margaria, Steffen & Reitenspieß, 2005), and because of its low threshold to adoption for non-IT experts.

From a modeller's point of view, jABC allows users of any background to easily develop behavioural models by graphically composing reusable building-blocks into (flow-) graph structures. This allows business developers and business analysts to directly formulate the processes already described in the many document's prose. The additional benefit is that this graphical modeling process is flanked in jABC by an extensible set of plugins that provide additional desirable functionality: the animation, rapid prototyping, formal verification, debugging capabilities are useful already on the very high-level models. They help business experts to validate their first sketches, their refinements and precisations, and later their evolution.

It this sense, jABC does not substitute but rather enhance other modelling practices like the UML-based RUP already adopted in this context, which may in fact be profitably used in our process to design the single components.

Figure 6. The P3 Business Process Overview designed within the jABC

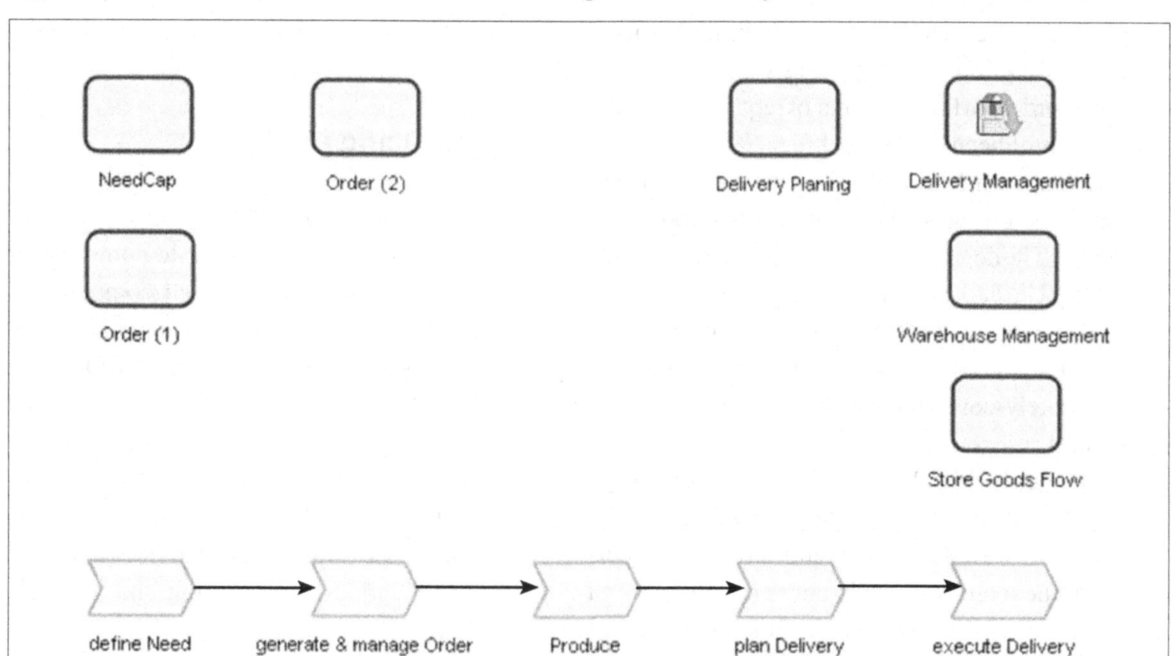

Designing the Document Management Process

A central requirement to the jABC process-oriented models was the capability to bridge the gap between the high-level models of the whole project, typically produced by business analysts with no UML or technical background, and the detailed models usable by programmers and engineers at implementation time.

As shown in Figure 4, we had **a set of 132 distinct** yet interrelated documents that described the high-level requirements and specifications for the new system.

In the course of the projects, these documents were condensed into a single, hierarchical jABC model (see Figure 5), which was annotated with the essential parts of the original documents, and which was immediately animatable and executable. This was done internally at IKEA, and it required decreasing support by the jABC team over the course of the project, as skills and confidence in the use of the different facilities increased.

The Global Workflow

In jABC, every functionality used within an application or service is encapsulated within a Service-Independent Building Block (SIB). In fact, the IKEA team used SIBs to form the global workflow of the entire project within a Service Logic Graph (SLG), jABC's way of defining processes. A SIB could contain a single functionality, or also whole subgraphs (another SLG), thus serving as a macro that hides more detailed and basic steps.

Using graph SIBs we are able to model the big picture workflow exactly as described by the business analysts, and in a familiar notation: as shown in Figure 6, the process flow at the bottom shows the top-level phases of the global supply chain process. Each phase is composed of own processes, which are here drawn vertically on top of it. In particular, to the **Execute delivery** phase are associated the processes **Delivery Management**, which describes the transport of the goods, as well as **Warehouse Management**, and **Store Goods Flow** for the in-store logistics and warehousing. These processes were under the responsibility of other teams. The Delivery Management process is already implemented, as indicated by the graph SIB icon with the diskette and the arrow.

The Delivery Management Workflow

In Figure 7 we see the top-level flow of the Delivery Management process. The Delivery Management SLG shows the typical structure of these processes, which makes explicit their embedded system character. On the left we see a high-level process for the shipment of the ordered goods, and on the right separate functionality for the associated document management, with an event driven communication that is highly deadline-sensitive. The document management runs on an own platform (hardware and software). In fact it is under the responsibility of a distinct group of designers and of a distinct operation team. The document management process executes in parallel with the shipment process, but additionally to producing its own deliverables (the shipment documents), it monitors and controls the shipment process. As such, the shipment process de facto behaves like a business and time critical controlled system, and the document manager as its controller.

The Document Management Workflow

The Document Management process shown in Figure 8 (left) is the basis for the successive implementation of the event driven embedded document management system. It contains functionality to set up and administer the lists of shipment documents associated with each shipment order, it manages the deadlines and the human-in-the-

Figure 7 . The Delivery Management Workflow designed within the jABC

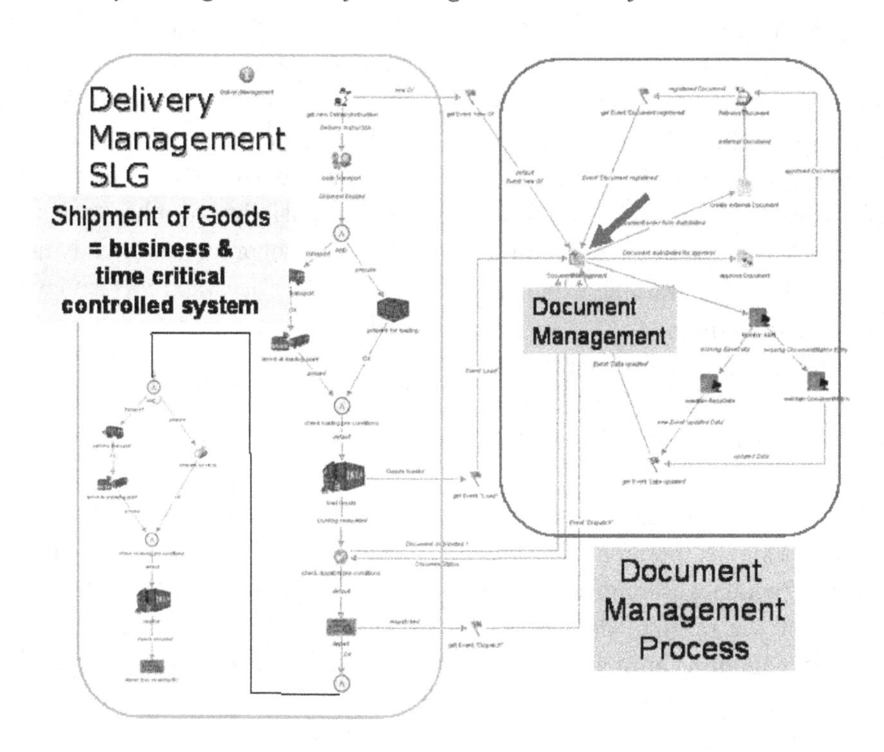

Figure 8. The Document Management and the Execute-Event SLGs

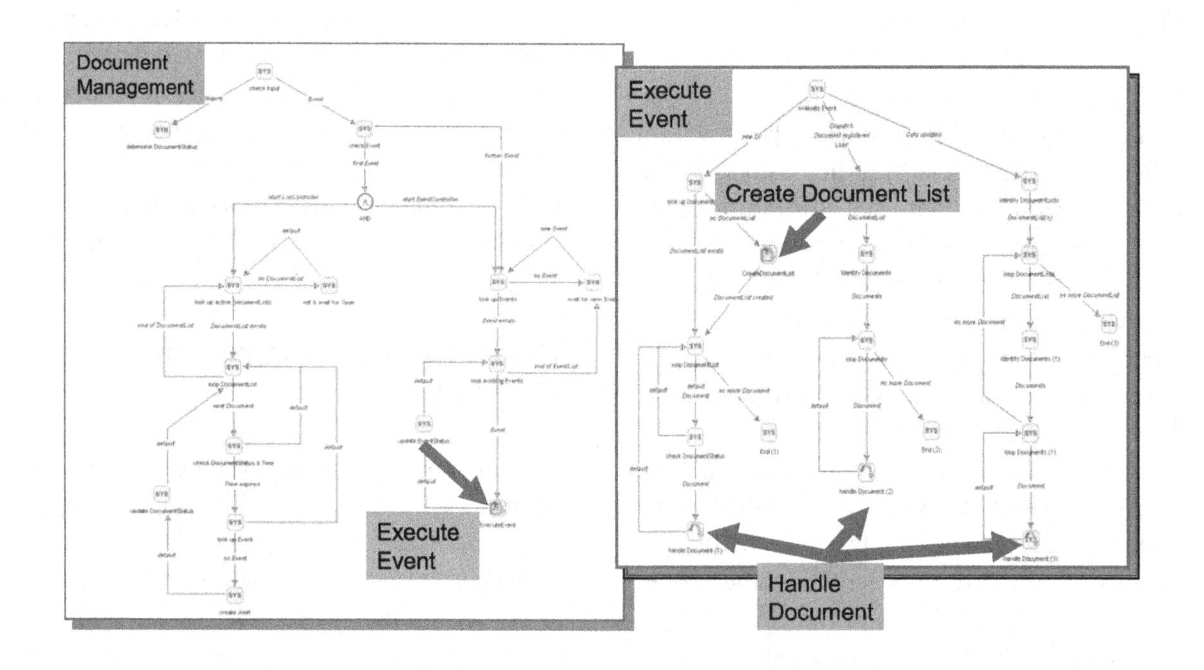

loop functionality and exceptions, and it contains a dedicated event manager, the **Execute Event** SIB, that runs in parallel to this functionality.

The Execute Event SIB, shown in Figure 8(right), is itself still hierarchical: it has a subgraph **Create Document List** for creating the document list, and several occurrences of the **Handle Document** document handler. These more detailed processes are hidden in this subgraph, and can be expanded at need to the required level of detail.

At this early design stage, most SIBs just contain the calls to animation and simulation code. This is sufficient to animate the specifications and to show the interplay of the different functionalities, in particular concerning the interoperability and cooperation of the shipment and document delivery subprocesses, which are under the responsibility of different teams.

Later on these SIBs must be further refined and finally implemented by software components, like Java classes or external web services provided by external systems and applications.

Workflow Granularity

The top-level workflow designed within the jABC shown in Figure 6 is rather simple: it is for instance cycle free. The loops needed by the detailed tasks can be modelled in different ways, mostly depending on the desired abstraction of the workflow:

- They can be modelled within the implementation code of the specific SIBs, e.g., as iterations over variables. This is desirable, if there is no need to reason (or prove anything) about that behaviour at the model level, which is considered an implementation issue.
- If we are interested in analyzing the loop behaviour, we can refine the SLG of the workflow and model the (relevant) loops at the workflow level, either for the whole process, or just inside specific graph SIBs if that portion of the workflow needs specific attention.

In principle, workflows can be refined up to the detail of single statements, if is desired.

Successive analysis of the code can help also in cases where the workflow has not been refined to the very end.

In this case, we ended with a successive refinement of the processes in 5 levels[2]. The overall business logic contained in the many documents was captured and expressed, without one line of code, resulting in the individuation of several shared subprocesses, that were isolated and capsuled in own models and reused several times.

The models, even at intermediate stages of design, were immediately executable as animated traces in the jABC, via the Tracer plugin.

Workflow Validation and Verification

Our approach also supports model checking-based (Clarke, Grumberg & Peled, 2001; Queille & Sifakis, 1982) verification of compliance to business rules at the process level, to guarantee the satisfaction of certain properties. That way we are able to build *certified* business processes. A knowledge base of such properties or constraints greatly improves the overall quality and reliability of the processes.

For this verification purpose, SLGs become mathematical objects, on which formal proofs are carried out. The SLGs are semantically interpreted as Kripke Transition Systems (KTS), a generalization of both Kripke structures and labelled transition systems (Müller-Olm, Schmidt & Steffen, 1999) that allows labels both on nodes and edges. Nodes in the SLG represent activities (or services, or components, depending on the application domain). The edges directly correspond to the SIB branches: they describe how to continue the execution depending on the result of the previous activity. More formally, a KTS is defined as follows:

A KTS (V,AP, Act,→) consists of a set of nodes V and a set of atomic propositions AP describing basic properties for a node. The interpretation function $I : V \rightarrow 2^{AP}$ *specifies which propositions hold at which node. A set of action labels Act is used to designate the edges. The possible transitions between nodes are given through the relation → is contained in* $V \times Act \times V$ (Müller-Olm, Schmidt & Steffen, 1999; Bakera & Renner, 2007).

Model checking (Clarke, Grumberg & Peled, 2001; Queille & Sifakis, 1982) is a powerful approach to automatic verification of models, as it provides an effective way to determine whether a given system model is consistent with a specified property. The jABC framework incorporates this technique via the core plugin GEAR (Bakera & Renner, 2007). Intuitively, any system modelled as SLG can be verified with this plugin: SLGs can be seen as KTS including atomic propositions and actions. Specifcations of a model can be defined using appropriate formalisms, in the case of GEAR these are temporal logics, for example CTL (Computation Tree Logic) or the modal *mu*-calculus (Kozen, 1983).

An example of such business rule is the following:

A truckload can only depart if the Bill of Consignment and the Load Approval are ready. If it is a Non-EU delivery additionally the Custom Documents must be available

not Departure U (BillOfConsignment
^ LoadApproval
^ (NonEUDelivery *implies* CustomDocuments))

In these formulas, Departure, BillOfConsignment, etc. are atomic propositions that hold in particular nodes of the model, while U is the *until* operator. These atomic propositions can be gained in different ways. In the simplest case they are annotated to the nodes manually by the user.

Workflow Execution

After designing the workflow, by means of the tracer plugin we are able to animate, simulate or interpret it. What happens depends on the kind of executable code associated with the SIBs: mock code, simulation code, or real implementation. Already the document browsing, where one can step through the model while investigating the corresponding documentation, turns out to be of enormous help in practice. In fact, it was possible to link every SIB to the documents describing its structure, its behaviour, and its relation with the environment and with other parts of the model. This way it was possible to detect under- and overspecifications, and to take adequate corrective actions in the same or in other teams. Using more advanced features of the content editor, which allows one not only to write documentation or to link toward illustrations, pictures and GUI designs, but also to specify e.g. rules and rights, or pre conditions and post conditions, provides a significant user experience way before any implementation is done. As this user experience is automatically enhanced with the progress of the development in the one thing approach, the tracer, as flexible behavioural execution engine, becomes a powerful means for the application expert to keep track with the progressing (IT-) design, and to check whether the development is in accordance with his understanding. This enables a very close and transparent cooperation between the application experts and the IT team at the process-level, which makes classical auditing and acceptance check procedures almost unnecessary, in the same way as they are unnecessary for extreme programming.

In fact, it was the tracer which very much stood in the center of attention during the IKEA project. Other more advanced features where used much less frequently or not at all. E.g., model checking-based verification was only used with support by the jABC team, and up to now, the project remained at a level of modeling and incomplete design, where the code generation is not yet applicable. This underlines the fact that the jABC environment is beneficial and well accepted during the phases that precede the transition to implementation.

Workflow Evolution

The whole process of designing the solution to the P3 redesign challenge can be solved with little initial coding effort, just by instantiating existing template SIBs provided with the jABC (like the SYS SIB used here) and graphically designing, documenting, and configuring the workflows at the SLGs level. In fact, this is already also sufficient to support a flexible change management, an important requirement for the second project phase.

APPROACH AND LESSONS LEARNED

The project was organized as a do-it-yourself experience for the industrial partner: rather than having the models developed at the university, the jABC team was mostly just covering supporting roles (as tutors, teachers, support when questions arose about the modelling style or the framework), as well as by specializing our modelling framework according to the customer's demands. The modelling and the validation themselves were carried out by the industrial team at IKEA.

What we aimed at was a tool support tailored to the working habits of the business developers at IKEA. We wanted to show the benefits of the one-thing approach as a hands-on experience, and in particular provide a clear understanding of the difference between so-called shelf models, as

Figure 9. The proposed new method: the One-Model built with the 'One Thing Approach' covers through refinement the needs of the early design phases

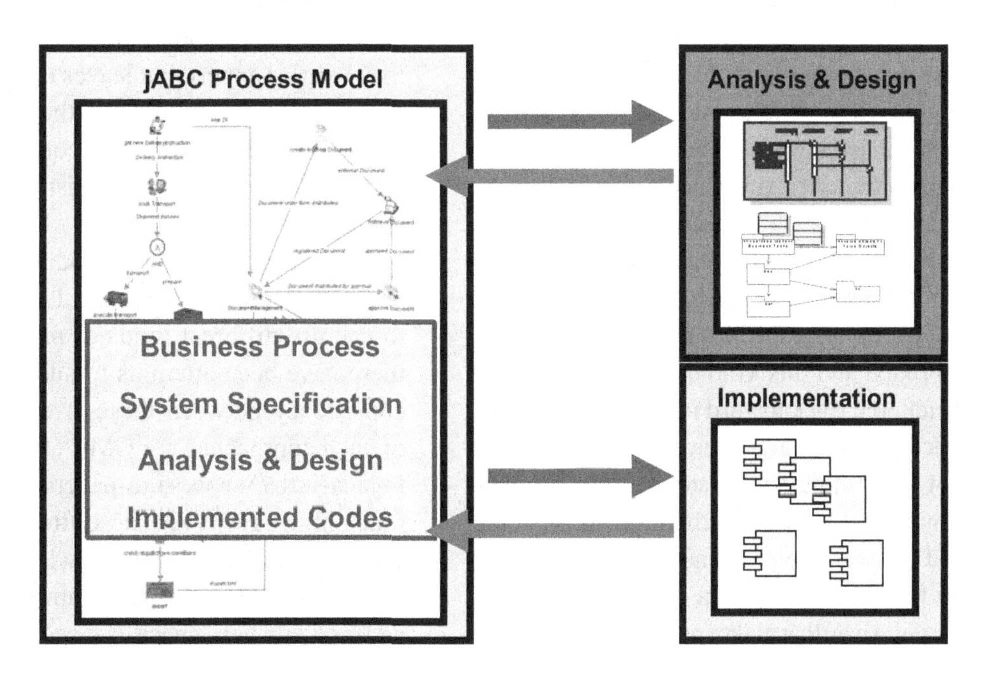

typically offered by classical business modelling tools, and the `living' models within the jABC framework, which can be on demand and by inception walked through, animated, validated, refined, simulated, executed and modified. In fact, the term `living model' was coined by our customers as a result of this experience.

The result of the cooperation, therefore, was not only an adequate modelling within the one thing approach, but also a refined tool support. We learned about the habits of the customer, their natural way of thinking, and we accordingly devised the best way of support within our framework capabilities. Central issues in this phase were for example where does the business expert need which information, what is of primary importance and what rather secondary, what is information which should be printable, which information should be provided in a first walk-through animation, what should be the options for further refinements etc. .

Indeed it where the customers who led us to developing the content editor, and the very simple kind of modelling in terms of dialogue SIBs, which immediately illustrates the decision-driven structure of the intended processes, and makes the use case and word specifications redundant (Figure 9). This nicely pointed us over and over again towards the `less is more' principle: Whereas we may provide complex hidden functionality, accessible at need, we must take utmost care that the immediate user experience remains simple. Thus remarks like "this is simpler to use as VISIO", and the experience that people started to work profitably with the jABC after only a few hours of training are the best indicator for us that this approach and this kind of support is on the right track: the track toward improving software construction in the large - meant not only in the sense of large individual systems, but also in its reach: we hope to address the bulk of process-oriented software (mass) construction.

Key for our solution is the clear separation of concerns, in a way that makes process development "simple for the many, but difficult for the few" - another slogan that has brought up to us in the context of the cooperation with IKEA. We are still continuously looking for adequate technologies and patterns that improve the power of process management and control for non-IT people. This should be reached without lifting, but rather lowering their required level of technical knowledge. Indeed, steering processes from the users' point of view seems to be a natural thing to achieve. It is our experience that putting this perspective at the center of our support significantly simplifies the whole life cycle of process-oriented systems, while at the same time leading to more adequate solutions.

RELATED WORK

There are three large areas of related work, which, in fact, can be seen as the three main facets of our approach: model-driven design, service oriented computing, and business process modelling. The main differences to our jABC-based approach can be sketched quite easily: the first two areas view the world from the technological/IT perspective. They do not (directly) address the applications experts. Business process modelling, in contrast, supports the business expert, but leaves the classical business/IT gap when it comes to the realization. The following elaboration is not comprehensive, but addresses the main characteristics of these three areas.

Numerous techniques, models, and diagrams have been proposed by the UML-community to capture different kinds of requirements, and there have been attempts to address the mutual consistency between these artefacts. Examples of such approaches are GMT (Davis, 2003) and Fujaba (http://wwwcs.uni-paderborn.de/cs/fujaba/index.html). However, these attempts are technically involved, requiring knowledge of technical modelling, UML, and programming, and typically address only very specific aspects. Thus they are not yet ready for a wider systematic use in practice, and require significant computer science knowledge. In particular, they are inadequate for a use by non-IT people, like business analysts because they are tied to the IT perspective. Rather than reflecting the user process, these models specify IT-based solutions. This is true e.g. for the whole Rational suite, also at the platform independent modelling levels.

Service-oriented computing virtualizes platforms and functionality and establishes a new kind of reuse. In particular in combination with standards like e.g. in Web Services, this is rather promising. Still, the methodology is not yet at a level accessible by application experts. The required knowledge about the syntax is awkward, the provided frameworks and tools are still quite unreliable, due to too many layers that must work together perfectly, and are outside of the responsibility of the user and of the developer, and still require too much knowledge about e.g., middleware and interface specification, including formalism like WSDL. This is an agreed result from the experience of two years of Semantic Web Service Challenge: lessons learned that explicitly address this point are summarized in a specific Chapter of the book (Petrie, et al. 2008) and in (Margaria, 2008).

Finally, there exist also many approaches to business process modelling and workflow management, typically supported for analysis by techniques like simulation. However, they lack (intuitive) verification techniques for end-to-end processes, and they are not adequately linked to the realization process: the known cultural gap between business and IT remains unresolved. This is also true for elaborate products like Websphere Business Modeller and supporting products, which in the IBM World provide some means to bridge the cultural gap. However, this typically only works within quite homogeneous (IBM) scenarios, and, in contrast to the 'one-thing approach', it requires multiple handovers between different kinds of artefacts, thereby cutting the business expert off the later phases of the life cycle.

The BPEL (BPEL, 2008) approach looks promising here. It comes with dedicated execution engines which support the execution of the process models themselves - and indeed, this approach is the most similar to ours. However, BPEL engines typically fail in practice (in particular, when cross platform/organizational processes are concerned), as they are focussed on Web Services, and largely proprietary. The focus on the sole Web service technology, e.g. excludes their application in business scenarios comprising the processing of high data volumes, or (legacy) functionality not available as Web Services. Moreover, BPEL (like BPNM) can not really be regarded as a language for non IT people.

CONCLUSION AND PERSPECTIVES

This successful evaluation spawned discussions in the other teams and at headquarters, on aiming at a more global impact that covers as many aspects of the overall delivery process as possible, in order to guarantee a maximum of consistency.

The central contribution of the one-thing approach in this project was the support of the *vertical* consistency of models, e.g. across abstraction layers, as well as of the *horizontal* model consistency, which is needed e.g. across organizational borders within a same abstraction level. In the particular case of IKEA's SCM setting we had to bridge e.g., between various business process specifications provided by business analysts and Use case/ activity diagram views needed by the designers, keeping adequate track of the dependencies.

Scenarios like this are ideal candidates for applying the one-thing-approach for end-to-end processes as described in (Hörmann et al., 2008).. There, horizontal consistency is guaranteed by maintaining the global perspective throughout the refinement process down to the code level, and vertical consistency by the simple discipline for refinement. Thus this holistic approach goes beyond state of the art approaches, as e.g. represented by IDEs like Eclipse and NETBeans, which do not support the business process level, as well as beyond process modelling tools like ARIS and WebsSphere Business Modeller, which fail to capture the later phases of development. Also combinations of these techniques are not sufficient, as they introduce (technological) gaps when moving from one technique to the other, which destroy the direct link between the realization and the modelling level. In contrast, in our one-thing-approach, changes at the business process level are immediately done on the 'one thing', and therefore immediately operational, as long as no new functionality is added that requires coding.

ACKNOWLEDGMENT

We would like to thank the many colleagues and project partners with whom we discussed and refined our views. Ralf Nagel, Sven Jörges, Georg Jung, Wolfgang Schubert, Horst Voigt, Martina Hörmann, Hong Trinh, and many others who co-developed and applied the methodology and the tools here described.

REFERENCES

Active BPEL execution engine (2008). Retrieved August 2008, from http://www.activevos.com/community-open-source.php

Bakera, M., & Renner, C. (2007). *GEAR - A model checking plugin for the jABC framework.* Retrieved May 2008, from http://www.jabc.de/modelchecking/

BPEL specifications website (2008). Retrieved August 2008, from http://www.ibm.com/developerworks/library/specification/ws-bpel/

Bosch, J. (2007). *Towards mobile services: Three approaches.* IEEE Computer

Clarke, E. M., Grumberg, O., & Peled, D.A. (2001). *Model checking.* MIT Press.

Curbera F. (2007). *Policy and service contracts in SOA.* IEEE Computer

Davis, J. (2003). *GME: Generic modeling environment, demonstration session.* OOPSLA 2003 (pp. 82-83). Anaheim, CA, ACM.

Hörmann, M., Margaria, T., Mender, T., Nagel, R., Steffen, B., & Trinh, H. (2008, October). The jABC approach to rigorous collaborative development of SCM applications. In *Proceedings of the ISoLA 2008, 3rd Int. Symp. on Leveraging Applications of Formal Methods, Verification, and Validation, Chalkidiki (GR).* CCIS N.17, Springer Verlag.

Jörges, S., Kubczak, C., Nagel, R., Margaria, T., & Steffen, B. (2006). Model-driven development with the jABC. *In HVC 2006 - IBM Haifa Verification Conference, Haifa, Israel, October 23-26 2006. LNCS 4383.* IBM, Springer Verlag.

Jung, G., Margaria, T., Nagel, R., Schubert, W., Steffen, B., & Voigt, H. (2008, October). SCA and jABC: Bringing a service-oriented paradigm to Web-service construction. In *ISoLA'08, Proc. 3rd Int. Symp. on Leveraging Applications of Formal Methods, Verification, and Validation, Chalkidiki (GR), Oct. 2008.* CCIS N. 017, Springer Verlag.

Kaiser, M. (2007) From composition to emergence - Towards the realization of policy-oriented enterprise management. *IEEE Computer, 40*(11), 57-63. IEEE Press.

Kozen, D. (1983). Results on the Propositional mu-Calculus. *Theoretical Computer Science, 27,* 333-354.

Lamprecht, A.L., Margaria, T., & Steffen, B. (2008). Seven variations of an alignment workflow – an illustration of agile process design/management in Bio-jETI. *In: ISBRA 2008: 4th Int. Symp. on Bioinformatics Research and Applications* (pp. 445–456). LNCS 4983, Springer.

Lamprecht, A.L., Margaria, T., Steffen, B., Sczyrba, A., Hartmeier, S., & Giegerich, R. (2008). Genefisher-p: Variations of genefisher as processes in biojeti. *BioMed Central (BMC) Bioinformatics 2008; Supplement dedicated to Network Tools and Applications in Biology 2007 Workshop (NETTAB 2007)* ISSN 1471-2105. Published online 2008 April 25. 9 (Suppl. 4) S13

Magedanz, T., Blum, N., & Dutkowski, S. (2007). *Evolution of SOA concepts in telecommunications.* IEEE Computer Nov. 2007.

Margaria, T., (2008). The Semantic Web services challenge: Tackling complexity at the orchestration level. *Invited paper ICECCS 2008 (13th IEEE Intern. Conf. on Engineering of Complex Computer Systems), Belfast (UK), April 2008,* (pp.183-189). IEEE CS Press.

Margaria, T., & Steffen, B. (2004). Lightweight coarse-grained coordination: A scalable system-level approach. *STTT,* 5(2-3), 107-123. Springer Verlag.

Margaria, T., & Steffen, B. (2006). Service engineering: Linking business and IT. *IEEE Computer, issue 60th anniv. of the Computer Society, (pp 53–63)*

Margaria, T., Steffen, B., & Reitenspieß, M. (2005). Service-oriented design: The roots. *ICSOC 2005: 3rd ACM SIG-SOFT/SIGWEB Intern. Conf. on Service-Oriented Computing, Amsterdam (NL), Dec. 2005* (pp.450-464). LNCS N. 3826, Springer Verlag.

Müller-Olm, M., Schmidt, D.A., & Steffen, B. (1999). *Model-checking: A tutorial introduction* (pp. 330-354). Proc. SAS, LNCS.

Petrie, C., Margaria, T., Zaremba, M., & Lausen, H. (Eds.) (in press) (2008). *SemanticWeb services challenge: Results from the first year (Semantic Web and beyond),* to appear Nov. 2008. Springer Verlag.

RUP - Rational Unified Process (2008). Retrieved August, 2008, from http://www-306.ibm.com/software/awdtools/rup/

Service Component Architecture Website (2008). Retrieved October 2008, from http://www-128.ibm.com/developerworks/library/specification/ws-sca/

Steffen, B., & Narayan, P., (2007). Full Life-Cycle Support for End-to-End Processes. *IEEE Computer, Vol. 40(11), (pp. 57-63).* IEEE Press.

Vinoski, S. (2008). *Convenience Over Correctness - Internet Computing.* IEEE Volume 12(4), (pp 89-92).

Queille, J.-P., & Sifakis, J. (1982). Specification and verification of concurrent systems in CESAR. *Proc. 5th Colloquium on International Symposium on Programming* (pp.337-351). Springer-Verlag London.

QUESTIONS

What are the main characteristics of the one thing approach?
What does X stands for in XMDD, and why?
What is the application profile for XMDD - in contrast to software development in the large?
Where are the limitations of XMDD?
What are the main weaknesses of RUP?

KEY TERMS

eXtreme Model Driven Design: Combines ideas from service orientation, model driven design und extreme programming to enable application experts to control the design and evolution of processes during the whole life cycle on the basis of Lightweight Process Coordination (LPC)[Margaria and Steffen,2004].

Hierarchical Service Logic Graphs: Form the modelling backbone of the One Thing Approach. All the information concerning documentation, role, rights, consistency conditions, animation code, execution code,....., come here together.

Immediate User Experience is a result of the eXtreme Model driven Design approach, where already the first graphical models are executable, be it as the basis for interactive `what/if games', documentation browsing or animation. This allows one to early detect conceptual errors in the requirement models.

jABC: An extensible framework designed to support the one thing approach and eXtreme Model Driven Design. It provides tools for documentation, graphical modelling, verification, code generation, validation, and adaptation. In particular it supports the idea of immediate user interaction and seamless acceptance [Haifa]

One Thing Approach: It provides the conceptual modelling infrastructure (one thing for all) that enables all the stakeholders (application experts, designer, component experts, implementer, quality insurers,..) to closely cooperate following the eXtreme Model Driven Design Paradigm. In particular it enables immediate user experience and seamless acceptance.

Seamless Acceptance: Is a direct consequence of the One Thing Approach: The fact that all stakeholders work on and modify one and the same thing allows every stakeholder to observe the progress of the development at their level of expertise.

ENDNOTES

1 While jABC is currently implemented in Java, the core concept is independent of the programming language. Previous versions, for example, realized the same model in C++.

2 We are not allowed to expose here more detail on the real concrete processes.

Chapter II
Modeling Process-Driven SOAs: A View-Based Approach

Huy Tran
Distributed Systems Group, Institute of Information Systems
Vienna University of Technology, Austria

Ta'id Holmes
Distributed Systems Group, Institute of Information Systems
Vienna University of Technology, Austria

Uwe Zdun
Distributed Systems Group, Institute of Information Systems
Vienna University of Technology, Austria

Schahram Dustdar
Distributed Systems Group, Institute of Information Systems
Vienna University of Technology, Austria

ABSTRACT

This chapter introduces a view-based, model-driven approach for process-driven, service-oriented architectures. A typical business process consists of numerous tangled concerns, such as the process control flow, service invocations, fault handling, transactions, and so on. Our view-based approach separates these concerns into a number of tailored perspectives at different abstraction levels. On the one hand, the separation of process concerns helps reducing the complexity of process development by breaking a business process into appropriate architectural views. On the other hand, the separation of levels of abstraction offers appropriately adapted views to stakeholders, and therefore, helps quickly re-act to changes at the business level and at the technical level as well. Our approach is realized as a model-driven tool-chain for business process development.

INTRODUCTION

Service-oriented computing is an emerging paradigm that made an important shift from traditional tightly coupled to loosely coupled software development. Software components or software systems are exposed as services. Each service offers its functionality via a standard, platform-independent interface. Message exchange is the only way to communicate with a certain service.

The interoperable and platform independent nature of services underpins a novel approach to business process development by using processes running in process engines to invoke existing services from process activities (also called process tasks or steps). Hentrich and Zdun (2006) call this kind of architecture a process-driven, service-oriented architecture (SOA). In this approach, a typical business process consists of many activities, the control flow and the process data. Each activity corresponds to a communication task (e.g., a service invocation or an interaction with a human), or a data processing task. The control flow describes how these activities are ordered and coordinated to achieve the business goals. Being well considered in research and industry, this approach has led to a number of standardization efforts such as BPEL (IBM et al., 2003), XPDL (WfMC, 2005), BPMN (OMG, 2006), and so forth.

As the number of services or processes involved in a business process grows, the complexity of developing and maintaining the business processes also increases along with the number of invocations and data exchanges. Therefore, it is error-prone and time consuming for developers to work with large business processes that comprise numerous concerns. This problem occurs because business process descriptions integrate various concerns of the process, such as the process control flow, the data dependencies, the service invocations, fault handling, etc. In addition, this problem also occurs at different abstraction levels. For instance, the business process is relevant for different stakeholders: Business experts require a high-level business-oriented understanding of the various process elements (e.g., the relations of processes and activities to business goals and organization units), whereas the technical experts require the technical details (e.g., deployment information or communication protocol details for service invocations).

Besides such complexity, business experts and technical experts alike have to deal with a constant need for change. On the one hand, process-driven SOA aims at supporting business agility. That is, the process models should enable a quicker reaction on business changes in the IT by manipulating business process models instead of code. On the other hand, the technical infrastructure, for instance, technologies, platforms, etc., constantly evolves.

One of the successful approaches to manage complexity is *separation of concerns* (Ghezzi et al., 1991). Process-driven SOAs use modularization as a specific realization of this principle. Services expose standard interfaces to processes and hide unnecessary details for using or reusing. This helps in reducing the complexity of process-driven SOA models. However, from the modelers' point of view, such abstraction is often not enough to cope with the complexity challenges explained above, because modularization only exhibits a single perspective of the system focusing on its (de-)composition. Other - more problem-oriented - perspectives, such as a business-oriented perspective or a technical perspective (used as an example above), are not exhibited to the modeler. In the field of software architecture, *architectural views* have been proposed as a solution to this problem. An *architectural view* is a representation of a system from the perspective of a related set of *concern*s (IEEE, 2000). The architectural view concept offers a separation of concerns that has the potential to resolve the complexity challenges in process-driven SOAs, because it offers more tailored perspectives on a system, but it has not yet been exploited in process modeling languages or tools.

We introduce in this chapter a view-based approach inspired by the concept of architectural views for modeling process-driven SOAs. Perspectives on business process models and service interactions—as the most important concerns in process-driven SOA—are used as central views in the view-based approach. This approach is extensible with all kinds of other views. In particular, the approach offers separated views in which each of them represents a certain part of the processes and services. Some important views are the collaboration view, the information view, the human interaction view and the control flow view. These views can be separately considered to get a better understanding of a specific concern, or they can be merged to produce a richer view or a thorough view of the processes and services.

Technically, the aforementioned concepts are realized using the model-driven software development (MDSD) paradigm (Völter and Stahl, 2006). We have chosen this approach to integrate the various view models into one model, and to automatically generate platform-specific or executable code in BPEL (IBM et al., 2003), WSDL (W3C, 2001) and XML Schema (W3C, 2001). In addition, MDSD is also used to separate the platform-specific views from the platform-neutral and integrated views, so that business experts do not have to deal with platform-specific details. The code generation process is driven by model transformations from relevant views into executable code.

This chapter starts by introducing some basic concepts and an overview of the view-based modeling framework. Then we give deeper insight into the framework which is followed by a discussion of view development mechanisms such as view extension, view integration and code generation mechanisms. A simple case study, namely, a Shopping process, is used to illustrate the realization of the modeling framework concepts. The chapter concludes with a discussion to summarize the main points and to broaden the presented topics with some outlooks.

OVERVIEW OF THE MODELING FRAMEWORK

In this section, we briefly introduce the View-based Modeling Framework (VbMF) which utilizes the MDSD paradigm. VbMF comprises modeling elements such as a meta-model, view models, and view instances (see Figure 1). In VbMF, a view (or a model) is a representation of a process from the perspective of related concerns. Each view instance comprises many relevant elements and relationships among these elements. The appearance of view elements and their relationships are precisely specified in a view model that the view must conform to. A view model, in turn, conforms to the meta-model at layer M2. We devise a simple meta-model, which is based on the meta-model of the Eclipse Modeling Framework (Eclipse EMF, 2006), as the cornerstone for the modeling framework. The framework view models are developed on top of that meta-model.

In our approach, we categorize distinct activities – in which the modeling elements are manipulated (see Figure 2):

- **Design** activities define new architectural view instances or new view models. This kind of activity includes *Extension activities* which create a new view model by adding more features to an existing view model.
- **Integration** activities are done by the View Integrator to combine view instances to produce a richer view or a thorough view of a business process.
- **Transformation** activities are performed by the Code Generator to generate executable code from one or many architectural views.

Figure 1. Layered architecture of view-based modeling framework

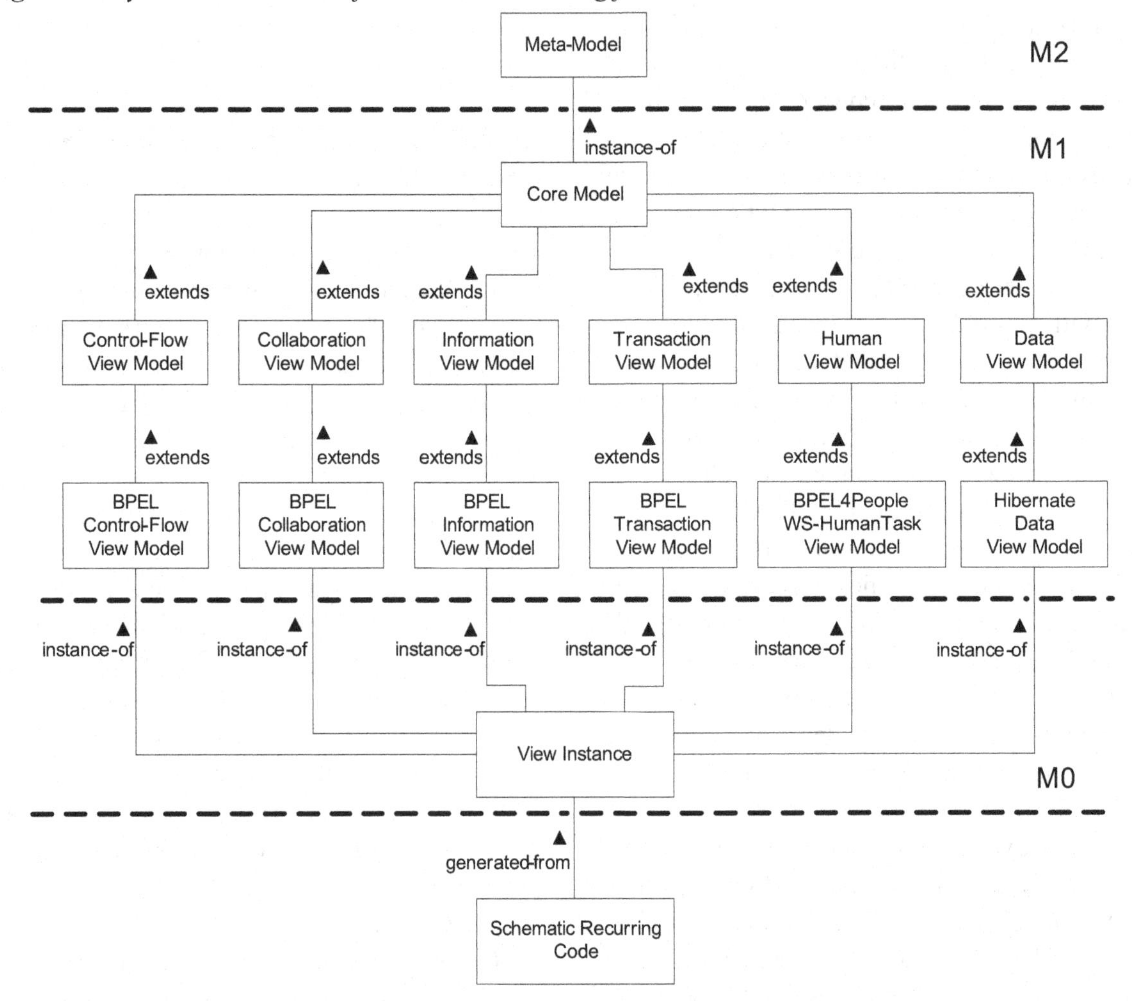

- **Interpretation** activities are used to extract relevant views from existing legacy business process code.

Before generating outputs, the View Integrator validates the conformity of the input views against corresponding view models. *Extension* and *Integration* are the most important activities used to extend our view-based model-driven framework toward various dimensions. Existing view models can be enhanced using the extension mechanisms or can be merged using the integration mechanisms as explained in the subsequent sections.

VIEW-BASED MODELING FRAMEWORK

A typical business process comprises various concerns that require support of modeling approaches. In this chapter we firstly examine basic process concerns such as the control flow, data handling and messaging, and collaboration (see Figure 3). However, the view-based modeling framework is not just bound to these concerns. The framework is fully open and extensible such that other concerns, for instance, transactions, fault and event handling, security, human interaction,

Figure 2. Top-down and bottom-up approach in view-based modeling framework

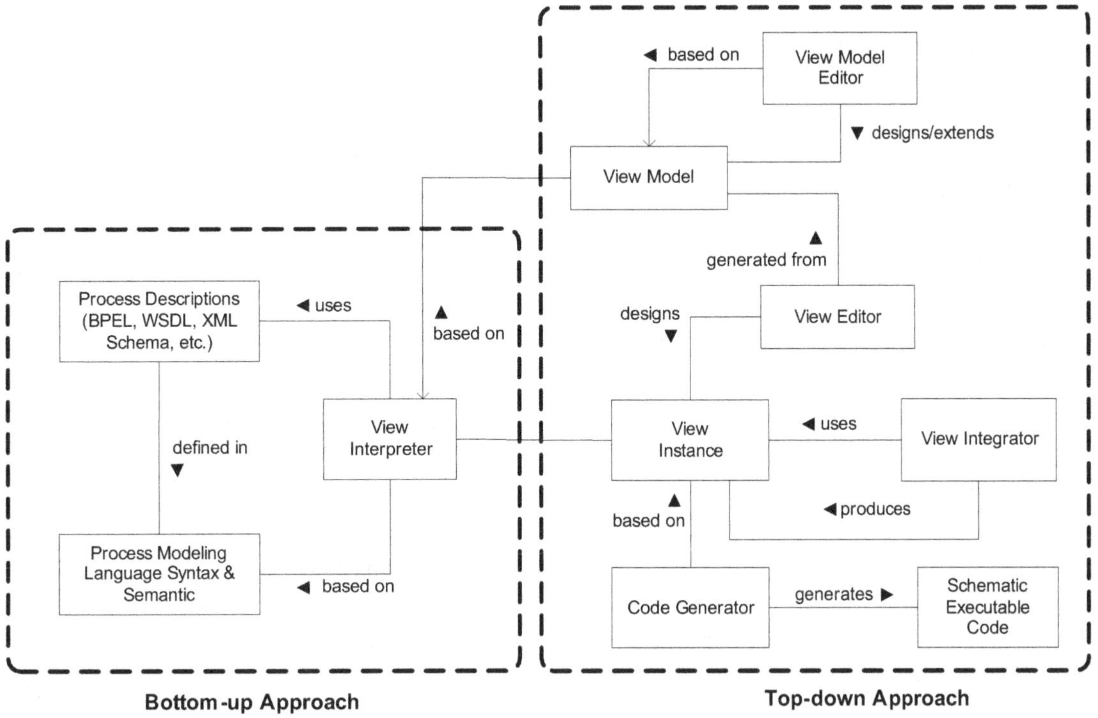

◄ based on
View Model Editor
▼ designs/extends
View Model
▲ generated from
designs ▼
View Editor
Process Descriptions (BPEL, WSDL, XML Schema, etc.)
◄ uses
▲ based on
View Interpreter
View Instance
◄ uses
View Integrator
defined in ▼
▲ based on
◄ produces
Process Modeling Language Syntax & Semantic
◄ based on
Code Generator
generates ►
Schematic Executable Code

Bottom-up Approach

Top-down Approach

Figure 3. The Core model (left-hand side) and the control-flow view model (right-hand side)

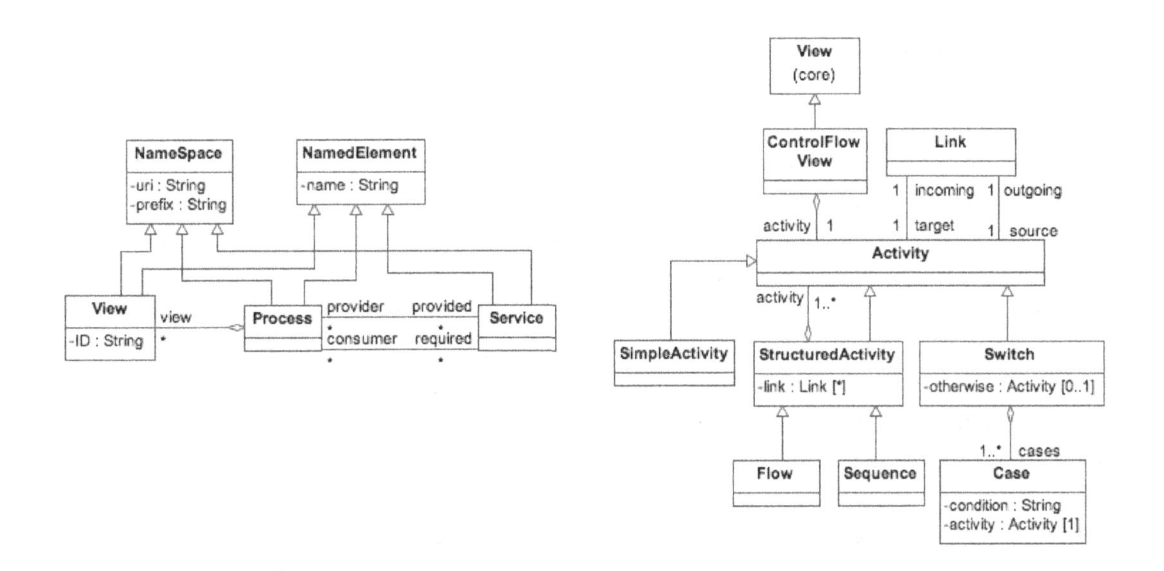

and so on, can be plugged-in using the same approach. In the next sections, we present in detail the formalized representations of process concerns in terms of appropriate view models along with the discussion of the extensibility mechanisms *Extend* and *Integrate.*

The Core Model

Aiming at the openness and the extensibility, we devise a basic model, called the Core model, as a foundation for the other view models (see Figure 3). Each of the other view models is defined by extending the Core model. Therefore, the view models are independent of each other. The Core model is the place where the relationships among the view models are maintained. Hence, the relationships in the Core model are needed for view integrations.

The Core model provides a number of important abstract elements: *View, Process* and *Service.* Each of them can be extended further. At the heart of the Core model is the View element that captures the architectural view concept. Each specific view (i.e., each instance of the View element) represents one perspective on a particular Process. A Service specifies external functions that the Process provides or requires. A View acts as a container for modeling elements representing the objects which appear inside the Process. Different instances of each of these elements can be distinguished through the features of the common superclasses *NamedElement*, defining a name property, and *NameSpace,* defining an URI and prefix based namespace identifier.

The view models that represent concerns of a business process are mostly derived from the Core model. Therefore, these elements of the Core model are important extension points. The hierarchical structures in which those elements are roots can be used to define the integration points used to merge view models as mentioned in the description of the integration mechanisms below.

Control-Flow View Model

The control flow is one of the most important concerns of a SOA process. A Control-flow View comprises many activities and control structures. The activities are process tasks such as service invocations or data handling, while control structures describe the execution order of the activities to achieve a certain goal. Each Control-flow View is defined based on the Control-flow View model.

There are several approaches to modeling process control flows such as state-charts, block structures (IBM et al., 2003), activity diagrams (OMG, 2004), Petri-nets (Aalst et al., 2000), and so on. Despite of this diversity in control flow modeling, it is well accepted that existing modeling languages share five common basic patterns: *Sequence, Parallel Split, Synchronization, Exclusive Choice*, and *Simple Merge* (Aalst et al., 2003). Thus, we adopted these patterns as the building blocks of the Control-flow View model. Other, more advanced patterns can be added later by using extension mechanisms to augment the Control-flow View model. We define the Control-flow View model and semantics of the control structures with respect to these patterns (see Table 1).

The primary entity of the Control-flow View model is the *Activity* element (see Figure 3), which is the base class for other elements such as *Sequence, Flow,* and *Switch.* Another important entity in the Control-flow View model is the *SimpleActivity* class that represents a concrete action such as a service invocation, a data processing task, and so on. The actual description of each SimpleActivity is modeled in another specific view. For instance, a service invocation is described in a Collaboration View, while a data processing action is specified in an Information View. Each SimpleActivity is a placeholder or a reference to another activity, i.e., an interaction or a data processing task. Therefore, every SimpleActivity becomes an integration point that

Table 1. Semantics of basic control structures

Structure	Description
Sequence	An activity is only enabled after the completion of another activity in the same sequence structure. The sequence structure is therefore equivalent to the semantics of the *Sequence* pattern.
Flow	All activities of a flow structure are executed in parallel. The subsequent activity of the flow structure is only enabled after the completion of all activities in the flow structure. The semantics of the flow structure is equivalent to a control block starting with the *Parallel Split* pattern and ending by the *Synchronization* pattern.
Switch	Only one of many alternative paths of control inside a switch structure is enabled according to a condition value. After the active path finished, the process continues with the subsequent activity of the switch structure. The semantics of the switch structure is equivalent to a control block starting with the *Exclusive Choice* pattern and ending by the *Simple Merge* pattern.

can be used to merge a Control-flow View with an Information View, or with a Collaboration View, respectively.

The *StructuredActivity* element is an abstract representation of a group of related activities. Some of these activities probably have logical correlations. For instance, a shipping activity must be subsequent to an activity receiving purchase orders. The *Link* element is used in such scenarios.

Collaboration View Model

A business process is often developed by composing the functionality provided by various parties such as services or other processes. Other partners, in turn, might use the process. All business functions required or provided by the process are typically exposed in terms of standard interfaces (e.g., WSDL portTypes). We captured these concepts in the Core model by the relationships between the two elements Process and Service. The Collaboration View model (see Figure 4) extends the Core model to represent the interactions between the business process and its partners.

In the Collaboration View model, the *Service* element from the Core model is extended by a tailored and specific *Service* element that exposes a number of *Interfaces*. Each Interface provides some *Operations*. An Operation represents an action that might need some inputs and produces some outputs via correspondent *Channels*. The details of each data element are not defined in the Collaboration View but in the Information View. A Channel only holds a reference to a *Message* entity. Therefore, each Message becomes an integration point that can be used to combine a specific Collaboration View with a corresponding Information View.

The ability and the responsibility of an interaction partner are modeled by the *Role* element. Every partner, who provides the relevant interface associated with a particular role, can play that role. These concepts are captured by using the *PartnerLink* and the *PartnerLinkType* elements and their relationships with the Role element. An interaction between the process and one of its partners is represented by the *Interaction* element that associates with a particular PartnerLink.

Information View Model

The third basic concern we consider in the context of this chapter is information. This concern is formalized by the Information View model (see Figure 4). This view model involves the representation of data object flows inside the process and message objects traveling back and forth between the process and the external world.

Figure 4. The collaboration view model (left-hand side) and the information view model (right-hand side)

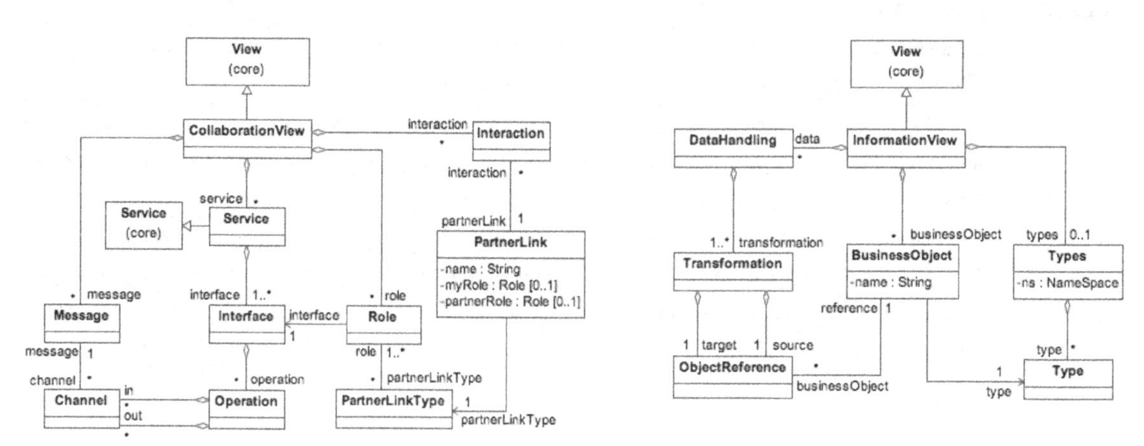

In the Information View model, the *BusinessObject* element, which has a generic type, namely, *Type*, is the abstraction of any piece of information, for instance, a purchase order received from the customer or a request sent to a banking service to verify the customer's credit card, and so forth. Each Information View consists of a number of BusinessObjects. Messages exchanged between the process and its partners or data flowing inside the process might go through some *Transformations* that convert or extract existing data to form new pieces of data. The transformations are performed inside a *DataHandling* object. The source or the target of a certain transformation is an *ObjectReference* entity that holds a reference to a particular BusinessObject.

Human View Model

So far we have examined different perspectives of a business process such as the control flow, the interaction with external process elements as described in the Collaboration View and the Information View. These essential views allow the specification of automated processes. If we are interested in processes that can be automated and that do not require human interaction, we may use these views for designing various processes. However, business processes often involve human participants. Certain process activities need appropriate human interactions. We name such process elements *Tasks*. Tasks, thus, are simple process activities that are accomplished by a person. Tasks may specify certain input values as well as a Task Description and may yield a result that can be represented using output values.

Besides the task as a special process element, the *Human View* as shown in Figure 5 defines human roles and their relationships to the respective process and tasks. *Roles* are abstracting concrete users that may play certain roles. The Human

Figure 5. The human view model

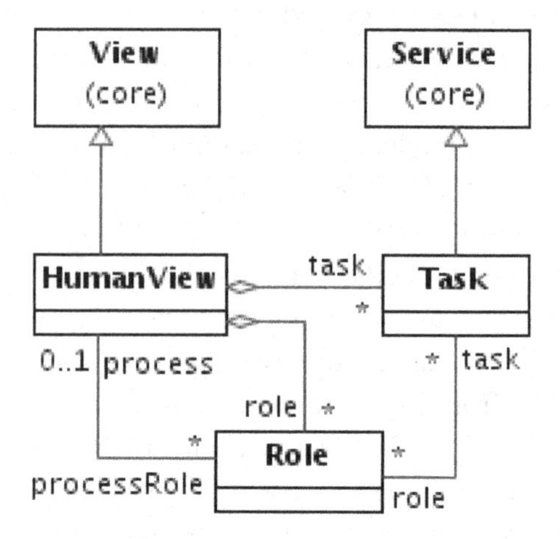

View thus establishes a role-based abstraction. This role-based abstraction can be used for role-based access control (RBAC). RBAC, in general, is administered through roles and role hierarchies that mirror an enterprise's job positions and organizational structure. Users are assigned membership into roles consistent with a user's duties, competency, and responsibility.

Examples for different roles are: Task Owner, Process Supervisor or Escalation Recipient. By binding, for instance, the role of a Process Supervisor to a process, RBAC can define that those users that are associated with this role may monitor the process execution. Similarly, the owner of a task may complete the task by sending results back to the process. He may however not follow up the process.

We can specify an activity as defined within a Control-flow View to be a human Task in the Human View that is bound to for instance an owner, the person who performs the task. Likewise, process stakeholders can be specified for the process by associating them with the human view.

Extension Mechanisms

During the process development lifecycle, various stakeholders take part in with different needs and responsibility. For instance, the business experts - who are familiar with business concepts and methods - sketch blueprint designs of the business process functionality using abstract and high level languages such as flow-charts, BPMN diagrams, or UML activity diagrams. Based on these designs, the IT experts implement the business processes using executable languages such as BPEL, XPDL, etc. Hence, these stakeholders work at different levels of abstraction.

The aforementioned view models for the Control-flow, the Collaboration and the Information Views are the cornerstones to create abstract views. These abstract views aim at representing the high level, domain-related concepts, and therefore, they are useful for the business experts. According to the specific requirements on the granularity of the views, we can gradually refine these views toward more concrete, platform- or technology- specific views using the extension mechanisms.

A view refinement is performed by, firstly, choosing adequate extension points, and consequently, applying extension methods to create the resulting view. An extension point of a certain view is a view's element which is enhanced in another view by adding additional features (e.g., new element attributes, or new relationships with other elements) to form a new element in the corresponding view. Extension methods are modeling relationships such as generalization, extend, etc., that we can use to establish and maintain the relationships between an existing view and its extension. For instance, the Control-flow View, Collaboration View, and Information View models are mostly extensions of the Core model using the generalization relationship. We demonstrate the extensibility of the Collaboration View model by an enhanced view model, namely, the BPEL Collaboration View model (see Figure 6). Similar BPEL-specific view model extensions have also been developed for the Information View and the Control-flow View (omitted here for space reasons).

In the same way, more specific view models for other technologies can be derived. In addition, other business process concerns such as transactions, event handling, and so on, can be formalized by new adequate view models derived from the basic view model using the same approach as used above.

Integration Mechanisms

In our approach, the Control-flow View—as the most important concern in process-driven SOA—is often used as the central view. Views can be integrated via integration points to provide a richer view or a thorough view of the business process. In the scope of this chapter, we utilize named-based

Figure 6. BPEL-specific extension of the collaboration view

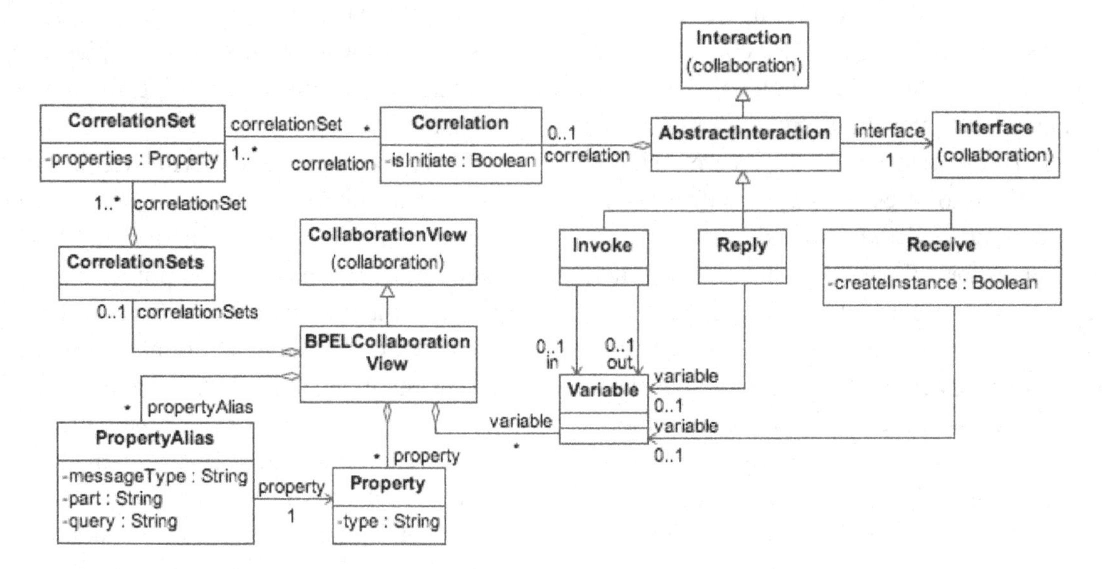

matching mechanism for integrating views. This mechanism is effectively used at the view level (or model level) because from a modeler's point of view, it makes sense and is reasonable to give the same name to the modeling entities that pose the same functionality and semantics. However, other view integration approaches such as those using class hierarchical structures or ontology-based structures are applicable in the view-based modeling framework.

Model Transformations

There are two basic types of model transformations: model-to-model and model-to-code. A model-to-model transformation maps a model conforming to a given meta-model to another kind of model conforming to another meta-model. Model-to-code, so-called code generation, produces executable code from a certain model. In the view-based modeling framework, the model transformations are mostly model-to-code that take as input one or many views and generate codes in executable languages, for instance, Java, BPEL/WSDL, and so on. In the literature, numerous code generation techniques are described, such as the combination of templates and filtering, the combination of template and meta-model, inline generation, or code weaving (Völter and Stahl, 2006). In our prototype, we used the combination of template and meta-model technique which is realized in the openArchitectureWare framework (oAW, 2002) to implement the model transformations. But any other of above-mentioned techniques could be utilized in this framework with reasonable modifications as well.

CASE STUDY

To demonstrate the realization of the aforementioned concepts, we explain a simple but realistic case study, namely, a Shopping process.

The Shopping Process

The Shopping process is initiated when a certain customer issues a purchase order. The purchase order is retrieved via the *ReceiveOrder* activity. The process then contacts the Banking service to validate the credit card information through the *VerifyCreditCard* activity. The Banking service only needs some necessary information such as the owner's name, owner's address, card number, and expiry date. The process performs a preparation step, namely, *PrepareVerify,* which extracts such information from the purchase order. A preparation step is often executed before an interaction on the process takes place in order to arrange the needed input data for the interaction. After validating the customer's credit card, the control flow is divided into two branches according to the validation result. In case a negative confirmation is issued from the Bank service, e.g., because the credit card is invalid, the customer will receive an order cancellation notification along with an explaining message via the *CancelOrder* activity. Otherwise, a positive confirmation triggers the second control branch in which the process continues with two concurrent activities: *DoShipping* and *DoCharging.* The DoShipping activity gets delivery information from the purchase order and sends ordered products to the customer's shipping address, while the DoCharging activity sends a request to the Banking service for the credit card's payment. Finally, the purchase invoice is prepared and sent back to the customer during the last step, *SendInvoice.* After that, the Shopping process successfully finishes.

Figure 7 shows the Shopping process developed using BPEL. VbMF can manage several important process concerns, for example, the control flow and service collaboration, data handling, fault and event handling, and transactions. For the demonstration purpose, in this chapter we only examine the control flow and service collaborations of the Shopping process. Therefore, in Figure 7, we present appropriate BPEL code and omit irrelevant parts.

In the next paragraphs, we present an illustrative case study by the following steps. Firstly, the architectural views of the Shopping process are designed based on our view models and the sample extensions for BPEL constructs presented in the previous sections. These views are presented using the Eclipse Tree-based Editor (Eclipse EMF, 2006). Secondly, some views are integrated to produce a richer perspective. And finally, these views are used to generate executable code in WS-BPEL and WSDL that can be deployed into a BPEL engine.

View Development

Figure 8 shows the Control-flow View instance of the Shopping process. There are no details of data exchanges or service communication in

Figure 7. Case study: The Shopping process developed using BPEL language

```
<?xml version="1.0" encoding="UTF-8"?>
<bp:process name="Shopping"
  xmlns="http://www.shopping.com/"
  xmlns:shop="http://www.shopping.com/"
  xmlns:bank="http://www.banking.com/"
  xmlns:ship="http://www.shipping.com/"
  xmlns:bp="http://schemas.xmlsoap.org/ws/2003/03/business-process/"
  xmlns:xsd="http://www.w3.org/2001/XMLSchema">

  <bp:partnerLinks>
    <bp:partnerLink name="Seller"
      partnerLinkType="shop:SellerPLT" myRole="Seller" />
    <bp:partnerLink name="Approver" partnerRole="Approver"
```

continued on following page

Figure 7. continued

```
      partnerLinkType="shop:ApproverPLT" />
    <bp:partnerLink name="Payer" partnerRole="Payer"
      partnerLinkType="shop:PayerPLT" />
    <bp:partnerLink name="ShippingPartner" partnerRole="ShippingPartner"
      partnerLinkType="shop:ShippingPartnerPLT" />
  </bp:partnerLinks>

  <bp:variables>
    <bp:variable name="order_input" messageType="shop:PurchaseOrder" />
    <bp:variable name="order_output" messageType="shop:OrderResponse" />
    <bp:variable name="verify_input" messageType="bank:VerifyRequest" />
    <bp:variable name="verify_output" messageType="bank:VerifyResponse" />
    <bp:variable name="charge_input" messageType="bank:ChargeRequest" />
    <bp:variable name="charge_output" messageType="bank:ChargeResponse" />
    <bp:variable name="ship_input" messageType="ship:ShippingRequest" />
    <bp:variable name="ship_output" messageType="ship:ShippingResponse" />
  </bp:variables>

  <bp:sequence>
    <bp:receive name="ReceiveOrder"
      variable="order_input"
      partnerLink="Seller"
      portType="shop:Shopping"
      operation="doShopping"
      createInstance="yes" />
    <bp:assign name="PrepareVerify">
      <bp:copy>
          ...
      </bp:copy>
    </bp:assign>
    <bp:invoke name="VerifyCrediCard"
      inputVariable="verify_input"
      outputVariable="verify_output"
      partnerLink="Approver"
      portType="bank:CreditCard"
      operation="verifyCreditCard" />
    <bp:switch>
      <bp:case condition="condition">
        <bp:sequence>
          <bp:assign name="PrepareCancel">
            <bp:copy>
              ...
            </bp:copy>
          </bp:assign>
          <bp:reply name="CancelOrder"
            variable="order_output"
            partnerLink="Seller"
            portType="shop:Shopping"
            operation="doShopping" />
        </bp:sequence>
      </bp:case>
      <bp:otherwise>
```

continued on following page

Figure 7. continued

```
        <bp:sequence>
          <bp:flow>
            <bp:sequence>
              <bp:assign name="PrepareShipping">
                <bp:copy>
                  ...
                </bp:copy>
              </bp:assign>
              <bp:invoke name="DoShipping"
                inputVariable="ship_input"
                outputVariable="ship_output"
                partnerLink="ShippingPartner"
                portType="ship:Shipping"
                operation="doShipping" />
            </bp:sequence>
            <bp:sequence>
              <bp:assign name="PrepareCharging">
                <bp:copy>
                  ...
              </bp:copy>
              </bp:assign>
              <bp:invoke name="DoCharging"
                inputVariable="charge_input"
                outputVariable="charge_output"
                partnerLink="Payer"
                portType="bank:CreditCard"
                operation="chargeCreditCard" />
            </bp:sequence>
          </bp:flow>
          <bp:assign name="PrepareInvoice">
            <bp:copy>
               ...
            </bp:copy>
          </bp:assign>

          <bp:reply name="SendInvoice"
            variable="order_output"
            partnerLink="Seller"
            portType="shop:Shopping"
            operation="doShopping" />
        </bp:sequence>
      </bp:otherwise>
    </bp:switch>
  </bp:sequence>
</bp:process>
```

this view. Hence, the Control-flow View can be used by the stakeholders who need a high level of abstraction, for instance, the business experts or the domain analysts.

Moreover, using the extension view models (e.g., the BPEL-specific extension of the Collaboration View given in Figure 6), the technical experts or the IT developers can develop much richer views for a particular concern. In Figure 9, there are two models side by side in which one is the abstract collaboration model (i.e., the left-hand side view in Figure 9) and another one, which is at the right-hand side in Figure 9, is a view based on the BPEL Collaboration view model.

View Integration

The views also can be integrated to produce new richer views of the Shopping process. At the right-hand side of Figure 9, we present an integrated view which is the result of the combination of the Control-flow View and the Collaboration View of the Shopping process. The SimpleActivity entities in the Control-flow View define the most important integration points with relevant Interaction entities in the Collaboration view. The output view consists of control structures based on the Control-flow View and additional collaboration-related entities such as Roles, Services, etc. Moreover, relevant activities of this view also comprise additional collaboration-specific attributes.

Figure 8. The control-flow view (left-hand side) and an integrated view of the shopping process – the result of integration the control-flow view and the collaboration view (right-hand side).

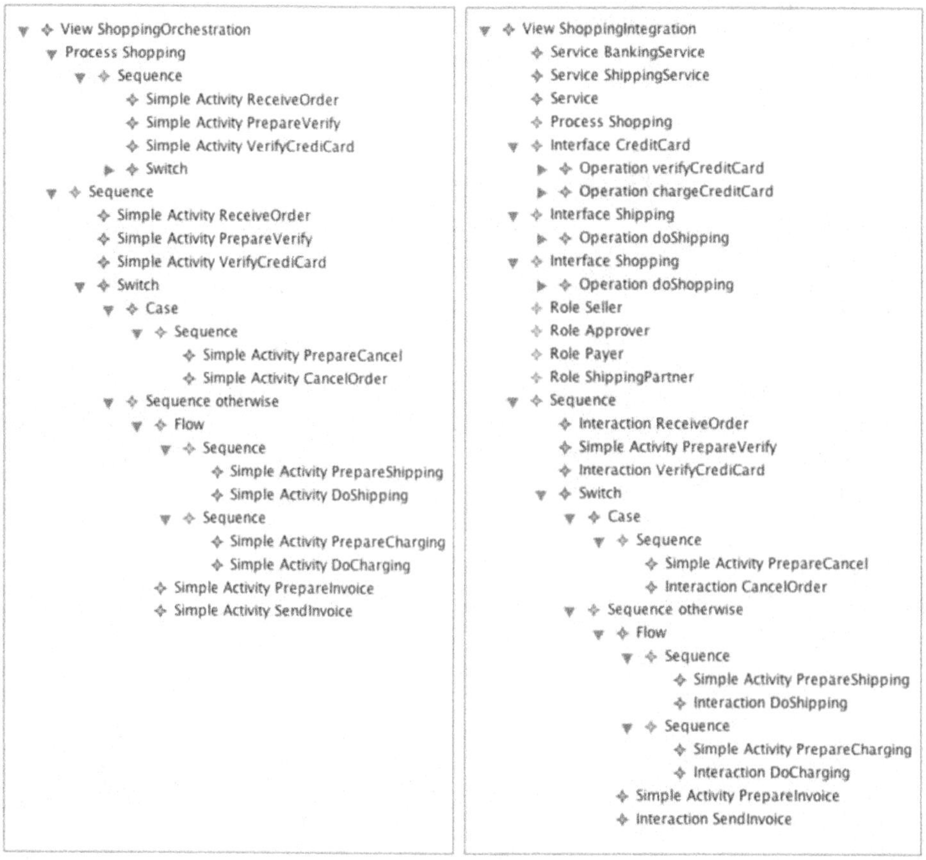

View ShoppingOrchestration
Process Shopping
Sequence
Simple Activity ReceiveOrder
Simple Activity PrepareVerify
Simple Activity VerifyCrediCard
Switch
Sequence
Simple Activity ReceiveOrder
Simple Activity PrepareVerify
Simple Activity VerifyCrediCard
Switch
Case
Sequence
Simple Activity PrepareCancel
Simple Activity CancelOrder
Sequence otherwise
Flow
Sequence
Simple Activity PrepareShipping
Simple Activity DoShipping
Sequence
Simple Activity PrepareCharging
Simple Activity DoCharging
Simple Activity PrepareInvoice
Simple Activity SendInvoice

View ShoppingIntegration
Service BankingService
Service ShippingService
Service
Process Shopping
Interface CreditCard
Operation verifyCreditCard
Operation chargeCreditCard
Interface Shipping
Operation doShipping
Interface Shopping
Operation doShopping
Role Seller
Role Approver
Role Payer
Role ShippingPartner
Sequence
Interaction ReceiveOrder
Simple Activity PrepareVerify
Interaction VerifyCrediCard
Switch
Case
Sequence
Simple Activity PrepareCancel
Interaction CancelOrder
Sequence otherwise
Flow
Sequence
Simple Activity PrepareShipping
Interaction DoShipping
Sequence
Simple Activity PrepareCharging
Interaction DoCharging
Simple Activity PrepareInvoice
Interaction SendInvoice

continued on following page

Figure 9. The collaboration view (left-hand side) and the corresponding BPEL-specific extension view of the collaboration view (right-hand side) of the shopping process.

Code Generation

After developing appropriate views for the Shopping process, we use illustrative template-based transformations to generate executable code for the process in BPEL and a service description in WSDL that represents the provided functions in terms of service interfaces. The modeling framework's models and Shopping process's models are EMF Ecore models (Eclipse EMF, 2006). We used the oAW's Xpand language (oAW, 2002) to define the code generation templates (see Figure 10).

Figure 10 Templates in oAW's Xpand language for generating BPEL code from the control-flow View and the BPEL-specific extension of the collaboration view

```
#
#  Template for the main process
#
«DEFINE BPEL(core::View iv, core::View cv) FOR core::View»
«FILE process.name+".bpel"»
<?xml version="1.0" encoding="UTF-8"?>
<process name="«name»"
     «EXPAND Namespace FOR cv»
     xmlns="http://schemas.xmlsoap.org/ws/2003/03/business-process/"
     xmlns:xsd="http://www.w3.org/2001/XMLSchema">
            ......
     «EXPAND Control(iv, cv) FOR this»
</process>
«ENDFILE»
«ENDDEFINE»

#
# Template for the control structures
#
«DEFINE Control(core::View iv, core::View cv) FOR core::View»
     «LET getActivities(this) AS activities»
          «IF (activities != null && activities.size > 1)»
               <sequence>
               «EXPAND Activity(iv, cv) FOREACH activities»
               </sequence>
          «ELSEIF (activities != null && activities.size > 0)»
               «EXPAND Activity(iv, cv) FOREACH activities»
          «ENDIF»
     «ENDLET»
«ENDDEFINE»

#
# Template for generating code from the SimpleActivity of a Control-flow View

# Use named-based to integrate an appropriate SimpleActivity with an Interac-
tion
# entity in a BPEL CollaborationView
#
«DEFINE Activity(core::View iv, core::View cv) FOR
orchestration::SimpleActivity»
     «EXPAND SimpleActivity(iv, cv) FOR getActivityByName(name, iv, cv)»
«ENDDEFINE»

#
# Template for generating code from the Invoke activity
#
«DEFINE SimpleActivity(core::View iv,core::View cv) FOR
bpelcollaboration::Invoke»
     <invoke name="«name»"
```

continued on following page

Figure 10. continued

```
          «IF (in != null)»
               inputVariable="«getInput().name»"
          «ENDIF»
          «IF (out != null)»
               outputVariable="«getOutput().name»"
          «ENDIF»
          partnerLink="«partnerLink.name»"
          portType="«getRole().interface.name»"
          operation="«getOperation(getInterface(getRole())).name»"/>
«ENDDEFINE»

#
# Template for generating code from the Receive activity
#
«DEFINE SimpleActivity(core::View iv,core::View cv) FOR
bpelcollaboration::Receive»
     <receive name="«name»"
          «IF (variable != null)»
               variable="«getVariable().name»"
          «ENDIF»
          «IF ( createInstance != null) »
               createInstance="«createInstance»"
          «ENDIF»
          partnerLink="«partnerLink.name»"
          portType="«getRole().interface.name»"
          operation="«getOperation(getInterface(getRole())).name»"/>
«ENDDEFINE»

#
# Template for generating code from the Reply activity
#
«DEFINE SimpleActivity(core::View iv,core::View cv) FOR
bpelcollaboration::Reply»
     <reply name="«name»"
          «IF (variable != null)»
               variable="«getVariable().name»"
          «ENDIF»
          partnerLink="«partnerLink.name»"
          portType="«getRole().interface.name»"
          operation="«getOperation(getInterface(getRole())).name»"/>
«ENDDEFINE»
```

We present a model transformation (aka code generation) snippet in oAW's Xpand language that generates executable code in BPEL language for activities such as Invoke, Receive and Reply using the BPEL-specific extension view given in Figure 3. The resulting executable code in BPEL and WSDL has been successfully deployed on the Active BPEL Engine (Active Endpoints, 2006).

CONCLUSION

Existing modeling approaches lack sufficient support to manage the complexity of developing large business processes with many different concerns because most of them consider the process model as a whole. We introduced in this chapter a view-based framework that precisely specifies various concerns of the process model and uses those models to capture a particular perspective of the business process. It not only helps to manage the development complexity by the separation of a business process's concerns, but also to cope with both business and technical changes using the separation of levels of abstraction. The proposed modeling framework can possibly be extended with other concerns of the business process such as security, event handling, etc., to cover all relevant concepts and process development technologies.

ACKNOWLEDGMENT

We would like to thank anonymous reviewers who provide useful feedback on an earlier draft of this chapter. This work was supported by the European Union FP7 project COMPAS, grant no. 215175.

SUGGESTED ADDITIONAL READING

There are several standardization efforts for process modeling languages, such as BPEL (IBM et al., 2003), BPMN (OMG, 2006), XPDL (WfMC, 2005), and so on. They can be categorized into different dimensions, for instance, textual and graphical languages, or abstract and executable languages. Most of these modeling languages consider the business process model as a whole, and therefore, do not support the separation of the process model's concerns. All these modeling languages can be integrated into the view-based modeling approach using extension models.

The concept of architectural views (or viewpoints) has potential of dealing with software development complexity, and therefore, is well-known in literature, for instance, the Open Distributed Processing Reference Model proposed in ISO (1998), or UML modeling language specified in UML (2003), to name a few. However, this concept has not been exploited in the field of business process development, and particularly, in process-driven SOA modeling. Axenath et al., (2005) present the Amfibia framework as an effort on formalizing different aspects of business process modeling, and propose an open framework to integrate various modeling formalisms through the interface concept. Akin to the approach presented in this chapter, Amfibia has the main idea of providing a modeling framework that does not depend on a particular existing formalism or methodology. The major contribution in Amfibia is to exploit dynamic interaction of those aspects. Therefore, the distinct point to VbMF is that in Amfibia the interaction of different "aspects" is only performed by event synchronization at run-time when the workflow management system executes the process. Using extension and integration mechanisms in VbMF, the integrity and consistency between models can be verified earlier at design time.

In this chapter, we also exploit the model-driven software development (MDSD) paradigm, which is widely used to separate platform-independent models from platform-specific models, to separate different levels of abstraction in order to provide appropriate adapted and tailored views to the stakeholders. Völter and Stahl (2006) provide a bigger, thorough picture about this emerging development paradigm in terms of the basic philosophy, methodology and techniques as well. Through this book, readers achieve helpful knowledge on basic terminologies such as meta-modeling, meta-meta-model, meta-model, model, platform-independent and platform-specific models, and modeling techniques such as model transformation, code generation as well.

Human interaction with SOAs have lately been formalized in The WS-BPEL Extension for People (BPEL4People) (Agrawal et al., 2007b). BPEL4-People defines a *peopleActivity* as a new BPEL *extensionActivity* and thus realizes integration of human process activities into BPEL processes. BPEL4People is based on the WS-HumanTask specification that introduces formal definition of human tasks. Various roles for processes and tasks are defined in BPEL4People as well as WS-HumanTask that users can be assigned to for role-based access control.

REFERENCES

Aalst, W. van der, Desel, J., & Oberweis, A. (Eds.). (2000). *Business process management: Models, techniques, and empirical studies - Lecture Notes in Computer Science* (Vol. 1806). Springer-Verlag.

Aalst, W. van der, Hofstede, A. H. M. ter, Kiepuszewski, B., & Barros, A. P. (2003). Workflow patterns. *Distributed and Parallel Databases*, 14 (1), 5–51.

Active Endpoints (2006). ActiveBPEL Open Source Engine. http://www.active-endpoints.com.

Agrawal, A., Amend, M., Das, M., Ford, M., Keller, C., Kloppmann, M., König, D., Leymann, F., Müller, R., Pfau, G., Plösser, K., Rangaswamy, R., Rickayzen, A., Rowley, M., Schmidt, P., Trickovic, I., Yiu, A., & Zeller, M. (2007a). Web Services Human Task (WS-HumanTask), Version 1.0. http://download.boulder.ibm.com/ibmdl/pub/software/dw/specs/ws-bpel4people/WS-HumanTask_v1.pdf.

Agrawal, A., Amend, M., Das, M., Ford, M., Keller, C., Kloppmann, M., König, D., Leymann, F., Müller, R., Pfau, G., Plösser, K., Rangaswamy, R., Rickayzen, A., Rowley, M., Schmidt, P., Trickovic, I., Yiu, A., & Zeller, M. (2007b). WS-BPEL Extension for People (BPEL4People), Version 1.0. http://download.boulder.ibm.com/ibmdl/pub/software/dw/specs/ws-bpel4people/BPEL4People_v1.pdf.

Axenath, B., Kindler, E., & Rubin, V. (2005). An open and formalism independent meta-model for business processes. In *Proc. of the Workshop on Business Process Reference Models* (pp. 45–59).

Eclipse EMF. (2006). *Eclipse Modeling Framework*. http://www.eclipse.org/emf/.

Ferraiolo, D., Barkley, J., & Kuhn, D. R.. (1999). A role-based access control model and reference implementation within a corporate intranet. *ACM Transactions on Information and System Security* (TISSEC), 2(1), 34-64.

Ghezzi, C., Jazayeri, M., & Mandrioli, D. (1991). *Fundamentals of Software Engineering*. Prentice Hall

Hentrich, C., & Zdun, U. (2006). Patterns for Process-oriented integration in Service-Oriented Architectures. In *Proc. of 11th European Con-*

ference on Pattern Languages of Programs (EuroPLoP'06). Irsee, Germany.

IBM, Systems, Microsoft, SAP AG, & Systems Siebel. (2003). *Business Process Execution Language for Web services.* ftp://www6.software.ibm.com/software/developer/library/ws-bpel.pdf.

IEEE. (2000). Recommended Practice for Architectural Description of Software Intensive Systems (Tech. Rep. No. IEEE-std-1471-2000). IEEE.

ISO. (1998). Open Distributed Processing Reference Model (IS 10746). http://isotc.iso.org/.

oAW. (2002) openArchitectureWare Project. http://www.openarchitectureware.org.

OMG. (2004). Unified Modelling Language 2.0 (UML). http://www.uml.org

OMG. (2006). Business Process Modeling Notation (BPMN). http://www.bpmn.org

Völter, M. & Stahl, T. (2006). *Model-Driven Software Development: Technology, Engineering, Management.* Wiley.

W3C. (2001). Web Services Description Language 1.1. http://www.w3.org/TR/wsdl

W3C. (2001). XML Schema Part 1: Structures http://www.w3.org/TR/xmlschema-1/ and Part 2: Datatypes http://www.w3.org/TR/xmlschema-2/

WfMC. (2005). XML Process Definition Language (XPDL). http://www.wfmc.org/standards/XPDL.htm

KEY TERMS

Architectural View: A view is a representation of a whole system from the perspective of a related set of concerns (IEEE, 2000).

Business Process Modelling: Business Process Modelling (BPM) is the representation of current ("as is") and proposed ("to be") enterprise processes, so that they may be compared and contrasted. By comparing and contrasting current and proposed enterprise processes business analysts and managers can identify specific process transformations that can result in quantifiable improvements to their businesses (Business Process Modeling Forum).

Model-Driven Software Development (MDSD) or Model-Driven Development (MDD): A paradigm that advocates the concept of models, that is, models will be the most important development artifacts at the centre of developers' attention. In MDSD, domain-specific languages are often used to create models that capture domain abstraction, express application structure or behavior in an efficient and domain-specific way. These models are subsequently transformed into executable code by a sequence of model transformations (Völter and Stahl, 2006).

Model and Meta-Model: A model is an abstract representation of a system's structure, function or behavior. A meta-model defines the basic constructs that may occur in a concrete model. Meta-models and models have a class-instance relationship: each model is an instance of a meta-model (Völter and Stahl, 2006).

Model Transformation: Transformation maps high-level models into low-level models (aka model-to-model transformations), or maps models into source code, executable code (aka model-to-code or code generation).

Role-Based Access Control (RBAC): Access control decisions are often based on the roles individual users take on as part of an organization. A role describes a set of transactions that a user or set of users can perform within the context of an organization. RBAC provide a means of naming and describing relationships between individuals and rights, providing a method of meeting the secure processing needs of many commercial and civilian government organizations (Ferraiolo et al., 1999).

Separation of Concerns: The process of breaking a software system into distinct pieces such that the overlaps between those pieces are as little as possible, in order to make it easier to understand, to design, to develop, to maintain, etc., the system.

Service Oriented Architecture (SOA): An architectural style in which software components or software systems operate in a loosely-coupled environment, and are delivered to end-users in terms of software units, namely, services. A service provides a standard interface (e.g., service interfaces described using WSDL), and utilizes message exchange as the only communication method.

Stakeholder: In general, stakeholder is a person or organization with a legitimate interest in a given situation, action or enterprise. In the context of this chapter, stakeholder is a person who involved in the business process development at different levels of abstraction, for instance, the business experts, system analysts, IT developers, and so forth.

Web Service Description Language (WSDL): a standard XML-based language for describing network services as a set of endpoints operating on messages containing either document-oriented or procedure-oriented information. The operations and messages are described abstractly, and then bound to a concrete network protocol and message format to define an endpoint. WSDL is extensible to allow description of endpoints and their messages regardless of what message formats or network protocols are used to communicate (W3C, 2001)

EXERCISES

For the exercises completing this chapter, we are using the following scenario:

At a rescue center rescue missions are controlled. Each emergency call is answered by a co-coordinating officer and is recorded by the control center system. If not supplied by the caller, the officer asks for the following information:

- *What happened?*
- *Who is calling? How can the caller be contacted?*
- *Where did the accident happen?*
- *How many people are injured?*

After the call, the officer assigns a rescue team to the mission and sends a short description together with the location via, for instance, a Short Data Service (SDS). The rescue team confirms acceptance of the mission by sending a status code '2'. At arrival it notifies the rescue center with status code '3'. After first aid measures, the team prepares to make the patient transportable. When leaving the location the status code is updated to '4'. At the arrival at the hospital with further medical treatment the status is set to '5'. After the team has prepared for standby the rescue center is notified with a status '6'.

Beginner

Describe the human task of receiving an emergency call. What are the in- and outputs and who may and who may, for example, not perform this task? Define some human roles and describe the relations between them and human tasks as well as the process.

Table 1 lists basic patterns for control flow modeling that have been defined in the Controlflow View meta-model of the VbMF. UML activity diagrams (OMG, 2004) or Petri-nets (Aalst et al., 2000) are approaches to model process control flows. Transform the textual description of the rescue mission into a UML activity diagram for representing and visualizing the corresponding workflow.

Intermediate

During the rescue mission multiple participants are involved. BPMN diagrams can help to distinguish these using pools and lanes that represent responsibilities for activities. Identify the different participants that are involved in the rescue mission and draw a BPMN diagram for the rescue mission where you group the process elements that are associated with a participant accordingly.

Improve the process and provide means for also alerting a fire brigade if necessary. For close collaboration the process itself invokes an external activity by passing the information of the rescue operation to the alarm service of the fire brigade.

Advanced

A company wants to optimize one of its business workflows. Therefore out of a process with about twenty elements a sub-process containing five process elements is being out-sourced. How do the process models change? Using the view-based approach, what views do you need to modify and where do you need to specify additional information?

Practical Exercise

BPEL is specified on top of WSDL and XSD. Therefore the conceptual views of the VbMF need to be bound to appropriate syntax. For the Information View e.g. the messages that are being sent have to be defined in XML schemata. For the example of the rescue mission specify XML schemata for the messages that are being sent and extend them with chronological information.

Chapter III
Process Modeling for Holistic Process Management

Stefan Jablonski
University of Bayreuth, Germany

ABSTRACT

This chapter presents a process modeling approach for holistic process management. The main idea is that domain specific process models are required both to capture the contents of a process based application and to present a process model in a user friendly way. We presents how perspective oriented process modeling supports domain specific process model. Besides we describe how this approach can be implemented by applying a multi level meta modeling approach.

1. FUNDAMENTALS OF PROCESS MANAGEMENT

"Business process management (BPM) is a method of efficiently aligning an organization with the wants and needs of clients." (W3C, 2008). We want to complement this characterization and claim that clients could stem from inside of an enterprise or are external, i.e. customers of an enterprise. Despite the strong emphasis of enterprises, we prefer to talk about process management, neglecting the term "business" in order to indicate that processes are general, i.e. they span the business field, the technical field and many other application domains. We regard a process as a collection of activities that consume some input in order to produce a certain output; hereby, applications (systems, tools, etc.) are used. Agents are necessary to initiate and drive the execution of processes. Often agents are special applications but sometimes agents are human users who are interacting with applications in order to drive a process.

1.1 Process Management Life Cycle

The main idea behind process management is to find out how a certain application should be performed. The assumption is that this application is composed of single activities which have to be executed in a certain order. A process describing this application will be defined and then implemented. Usually a graphical modeling language like BPMN (Object Management Group, 2006a) is chosen to specify a process; the result is a process model depicting the main features of a process.

Figure 1 depicts a sample process describing a clinical path. After a patient is registered, he has to be examined. Then a physician has to be assigned that is performing the surgery. After surgery a follow-up examination has to be performed. The boxes above the process steps illustrate data that are produced and consumed by the process steps. Although we omit to discuss this process model in detail, the graphical representations provides a quite good overview on the whole process. This process will be refined in the following subsections; especially we introduce the notation that is used in Figure 1. The process depicted in Figure 1 is just a small part of the real process; however, this part is sufficient to introduce the main concepts of process management.

The enactment of processes shows many facets. Two extreme enactments are rather important: A first popular enactment strategy is to create a process model (i.e. the schema of a process) from an existing application that describes its function in detail (descriptive enactment). The main usage of such a descriptive enactment is to use the process model for reengineering (i.e. improving) the application. Another important enactment is to create a process model in order to subsequently automate its execution, i.e. a process management system is used that proactively drives and supervises its execution (prescriptive enactment). What kind of enactment will be selected is mainly depending on the purpose and goal of a process model: If the process model is considered to be descriptive, it illustrates how a certain application should be performed. Thus the actual implementation of this application can be tracked and points of improvements can be identified by comparing process model and data from the execution. Prescriptive process models instead define a clear guideline how a process must be performed. Whether this guideline refers to its strict enforcement or to a flexible guidance depends on the characteristics of the application. Activities which determine how a process is modeled and executed are summarized in the process management life cycle (W3C, 2008).

Figure 1. Sample process

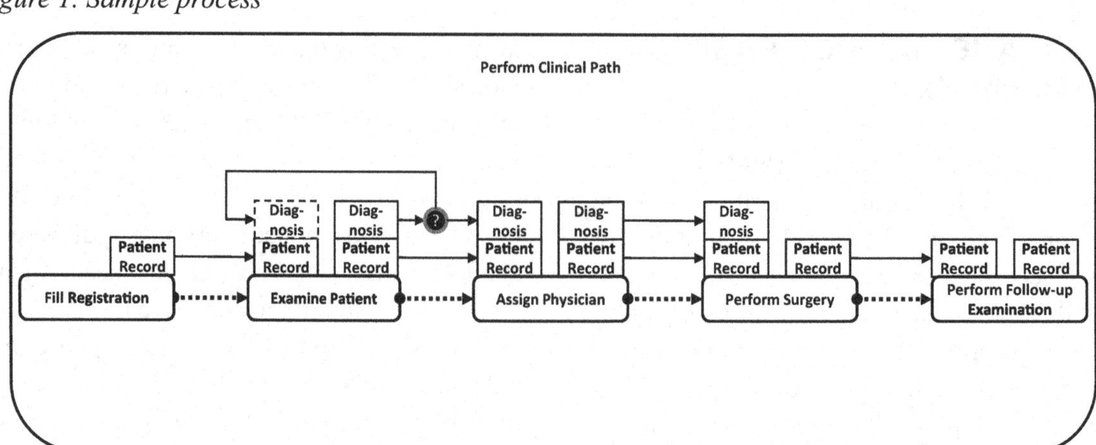

We will detail this life cycle a little bit more in order to clearer identify the purposes of process modeling and process execution.

The process management life cycle is constituted by a set of activities. In the process design phase existing processes have to be identified and target processes must be defined. Also, the modeling method with an accompanying modeling language must be specified. The design phase is tightly coupled with the second phase called process modeling. Here, process models have to be declared. For that, a process modeling language must be available; it is defined according to the requirements identified by the process design. A process model is an informal, semi-formal, or formal representation of a process (Boehm, 2000). If the process should merely depict the principle outline of a process based application then the representation suffices to be informal or semi-formal. If the process should eventually be executed by a process management system then the process model must be formal. Process execution is the third phase of process management. Here, processes are performed, often in an automated manner, i.e. a process management system is interpreting a process model and is proactively offering process steps to be performed. Executed processes might be monitored in order to observe whether they are implemented in an adequate way. Process performance then can be improved in the fifth phase of process management which is called process optimization.

We regard one observation as fundamental. The five phases of the process management cycle can be divided into two groups. Process design and process modeling compose one group, the remaining three phases constitute a second group. Why do we see this division? The first two phases, process design and process modeling, define the groundwork for the three later phases. In the design phase the realm of the process based application is demarcated and it is determined how processes are modeled. For instance, it will be determined that processes are modeled in a fine grained manner in order to be able to execute them eventually automatically. The modeling phase can then be regarded as enactment of the decisions made during the design phase; the process model is defined. The outcome of these two phases is the input for the subsequent three phases. Process execution, process monitoring and process optimization must adopt defined process models and must work on them. Disregarding exceptional cases and special execution features (ad hoc change of processes) a process model cannot be altered within the three last phases of the process management cycle. For instance, if a process is only modeled in an informal, coarse grained manner, it will not be executable by a process management system afterwards. Nevertheless, we do not neglect that there is feedback from the three last to the two first phases: this is why it is called the process management life cycle – it is a cyclic procedure.

Our discussion should not rank the two groups of phases; especially, it should not articulate that process design and process modeling is more important than the remaining three phases. It should merely clarify that the two first phases are decisive for the whole process management life cycle. This is why we want to concentrate on them in this contribution. Our thesis is that process design and process modeling must be supported by more powerful methods and tools in order to gain better process based applications.

1.2 Holistic Approach

Often—and we subscribe to this statement—process management is considered to be a holistic approach. What does that mean? Holism means that a system cannot be explained just by knowing of what components it is composed of; instead a system is defined by means of its own behavior (visible to the outside, i.e. the user) and the behavior of its components. Beyond question it is needed to identify all parts of a system in a complete way; it is not useful just to consider a few components of a system and neglect others. The behavior of a system can therefore only be determined when all components are dealt with. What does this definition mean for process management?

In process management the system is embodied by the process itself. Its components are among other things, activities that are performed, data that are consumed and produced, agents that are involved, tools that are invoked. The process literally spoken glues all these components together.

It is always critical when an approach requires something to be "complete". Thus, we have to discuss completeness in the context of process management. First, completeness is not an absolute concept. That means that there is not a general definition that determines completeness for all application domains. Instead, completeness is relative: each application domain or each application must determine how completeness is interpreted. Referring to the definition of holism completeness has to deal with the components of a system: all components must be identified. For a process that means that all its perspectives (features, properties) which are decisive for its effectiveness and efficiency must be identified. That activities, data, agents, tools are required in (almost) all process based application is doubtless. However, applications differ with respect to the required detail of perspectives and often also need application specific extensions. We call those perspectives domain specific. Domain specific modeling constructs enhance readability of process models for domain experts. Some examples shed some light into this discussion:

Example 1: In banking applications many critical process steps must be performed that are subject to special execution policies. For instance, the transfer of money from one account to another must be implemented in a transactional way, i.e. it must happen completely or must not happen at all. Other steps do not demand such high safety, for example when a newsletter is distributed to the customers. It is vital for a bank to demarcate the various degrees of safety a process step must comply with. Thus, a perspective "safety" must be introduced in this application domain since the domain experts need to recognize safety requirements at a process model in order to better comprehend the process.

Example 2: In an engineering application time is a critical factor. However, it is not sufficient just to specify an execution time for a process step. In order to effectively measure the performance of process execution this application domain requires a fine grained monitoring of time. The following categories of time might be differentiated: setup time, waiting time, execution time, cooling-off time, clearing time etc. Thus, the time perspective of a process model must comprehend all these different categories of time. Recall, the usage of a domain specific terminology also enhances readability of process models for domain experts.

Example 3: In the clinical path depicted in Figure 1 it is most important to assign DRG (Diagnosis Related Groups) to processes if possible. This is relevant for accounting in a clinic. DRG might be assigned to process steps and so extend the functional perspective of a process model (cf. Section 2.1).

What is the consequence of regarding process design and modeling as holistic approach? We discuss these issues with respect to the five phases of process management:

- **Process design:** Those perspectives which are characteristic for a specific application domain must be identified and defined.
- **Process modeling:** The process modeling language must offer modeling construct to describe all relevant perspectives of a process model, including the domain specific ones.
- **Process execution:** The process execution engine must be able to interpret the domain specific perspectives.

- **Process monitoring:** The process monitoring engine must be able to observe the domain specific perspectives.
- **Process optimization:** The domain specific perspectives must be investigated individually.

Since we concentrate on the first two phases of the process management life cycle we focus on the process modeling language. This language must be designed such that all domain specific features are represented. Then processes can be modeled according to these domain specific extensions. Thus, the final goal of holistic process management is to have a process modeling language that can be tailored to domain specific needs. We will present in this contribution, first, how processes are modeled in a comprehensive way, and second, how process modeling languages can be extended to capture domain specific features. We also provide an outlook on the architecture of a process execution engine. In total, this represents a holistic approach to process management.

Domain specific extensibility is also often discussed as flexibility (Clark et al., 2008). However, this is just one aspect of flexibility, namely the adaptation of a process modeling language. Other aspects of flexibility investigate the adaptability of process models (Heinl et al., 1999) or of executing process instances (Object Management Group, 2006b).

1.3 Standards

Before we are going to present an approach to holistic process management we have to tackle the standard question: When we promote domain specific process management we definitely deviate from process standards. Is it worth to abstain from standards in order to support domain specific modeling? In order to respond to this question it is necessary to discuss the pros and the cons of a standard. We will do this from the perspective of an application.

Interoperability and portability are two of the most valuable features of standards (Gray & Reuter, 1993). In the realm of process management it means that a standard process model can be interpreted by all tools that implement the standard. Another advantage of a standard is its publicity: process models defined in a standard language can be interpreted by people easier if they are already acquainted with the standard.

Standard languages are on the other side never complete in the sense of the holistic approach. Since they represent a compromise reflecting most of the requirements identified by the standard body they will not cover all modeling elements of all domains. Therefore, process models might suffer from readability and might not cover all features of a specific application domain.

In order to assess whether an enterprise should prefer a standard process modeling language or should go with a domain specific extension the usage of process models must be analyzed. If process models are frequently exchanged with partners, process management tools (for modeling and/or execution, etc.) are often replaced, and the number of domain specific extensions is very low then a standard should be appropriate. Alternatively, if process models are seldom exchanged, tools are not replaced often and a lot of powerful domain specific extensions are identified, a domain specific language is preferred. A third alternative is to use a domain specific language and filter out domain specific extensions when process models have to be exchanged with partners.

In Section 2 the contents of a process modeling language are outlined. After that the conceptual architecture for implementing process modeling languages is presented (Section 3). Process visualization as an important issue of process management is discussed in Section 4. Section 5 concludes this contribution by summarizing the major issues of process design and modeling.

2. PERSPECTIVE ORIENTED PROCESS MODELING

In this sub-section we present the Perspective Oriented Process Modeling (POPM) approach (Boehm, 2000; Jablonski & Bussler, 1996). Its goal is to provide a skeleton for the definition of a holistic process modeling framework. The main question is how the demanding feature "holistic" can be achieved. We already discussed above that completeness cannot be achieved by simply offering a process modeling language. Thus, the POPM is approach is different: instead of prescribing a process modeling language POPM just offers a methodology for defining process modeling languages which can be adjusted to individual application domains. This methodology encompasses three pillars:

- For each process modeling language a process skeleton is defined. This skeleton is the anchor for the features of the corresponding process modeling language.
- Features of a process modeling language are classified into so-called perspectives. Each perspective describes an important aspect of process models. Perspectives should be orthogonal to each other as far as possible; however, interdependencies will not be avoidable.
- Each perspective is defined by a set of (modeling) features that can be configured individually for each process modeling language that has to be created.

Referring to the examples of Section 1.2 the POPM methodology would mean the following. Besides the usual perspectives—we will explain them subsequently—the application domain would require the introduction of a safety perspective in the first example; in the second example a time perspective must be introduced. This time perspective would show the features setup time, waiting time, etc. Following this methodology a process modeling language can become holistic with respect to the application domain it is provided for.

We are just now referring to the so-called "usual" perspective of a process model. What does that mean? Due to experiences and the analysis of very many use cases the following five perspectives are considered as fundamental for almost all application domains:

- The **Functional Perspective** describes the processes themselves and their structures. Each process can be decomposed into subprocesses.
- The **Data Perspective** describes which data (or documents) a process step consumes or produces. Thus the input and output data of a process is being described. All inputs and outputs together build up the flow of data in the process model.
- The **Behavioral Perspective** describes the order in which processes have to be executed.
- The **Organizational Perspective** defines persons or roles that are responsible for the execution of a given process.
- The **Operational Perspective** defines tools or systems that support the execution of a process.

The identified five basic perspectives will be presented in detail subsequently. Before, the universality of the POPM approach must be deliberated. The POPM approach is universal since it allows creating any process modeling language. Universality is achieved since a process modeling language can be customized with respect to perspectives and features of perspectives. Thus, it is not prescribed a priori which contents a process modeling language must cover.

2.1 Functional Perspective

The functional perspective defines what has to be done, i.e. processes are defined. For example, a process "Fill Registration" is specified. Besides the name (and identification) of a process typically its purpose, goals, etc. are identified. Processes are elementary or composite: an elementary process cannot be decomposed anymore; in contrast, composite processes consist of so-called sub-processes. "Sub-process" is a role name and depicts nothing but another process. Sub-processes directly point to the concept type/usage. This concept borrows the corresponding feature from object oriented modeling. An object, here a process, must be defined first. Then it can be used within another context; in our case it is another process that uses the first process as sub-process. For example, after having defined "Fill Registration" and "Assign Physician" another process "Perform Clinical Path" might use these processes as sub-processes. This means that within a process "Perform Clinical Path" the processes "Fill Registration" and "Assign Physician" will be performed eventually – these are usages of the former process definitions. 0 depicts this situation which uses processes from Figure 1. On the left side of 0 six processes are defined. The process "Perform Clinical Path" is then refined by using the other five processes as sub-processes. Thus, these sub-processes are usages of the process definitions from the left side. This means among other things, that these usages are changing (right side) when the corresponding definitions of the processes (left side) have been changed. The process model "Perform Clinical Path" is a preliminary stage of the final process model in Figure 1. In Figure 2a modeler has already decided that the five sub-processes are executed when "Perform Clinical Path" is performed. However, he has still not decided in which order these processes are executed, what data they need, who has to execute them, and what tools are required. These perspectives will be filled subsequently.

By the way, we name "Perform Clinical Path" the super-process of "Fill Registration", "Assign Physician" etc. Again, "super-process" is just a role name. Consequently, super-processes must be composite, while sub-processes are either elementary or composite. Super-processes which form the upper end of a process hierarchy might also be called top-level-processes (role name). According to this definition "Perform Clinical Path" is the top-level-process in Figure 2. Process decomposition—the creation of process hierarchies – might span arbitrary levels. Experience shows that is quite common to define up to seven process levels as a maximum; however, this is not a strict constraint but rather a recommendation.

When a process is going to be performed (phase process execution) then instances are derived from the process definitions and usages, respectively. Typically, multiple instances are derived from a

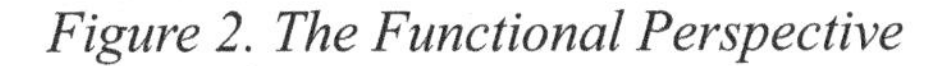
Figure 2. The Functional Perspective

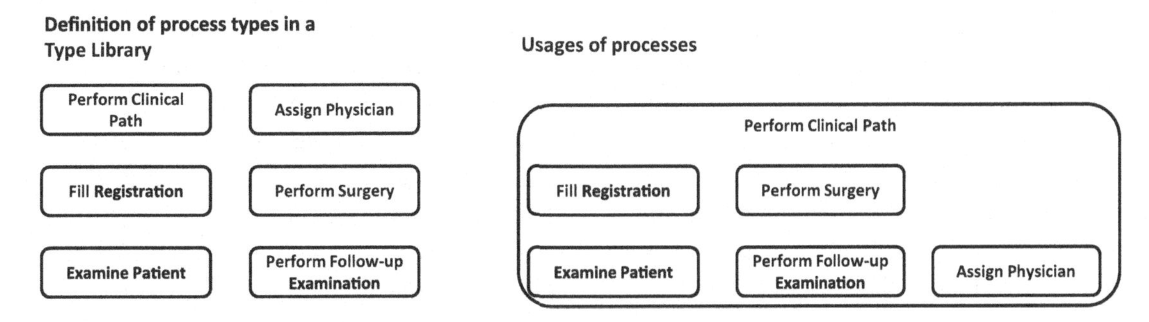

process definition, describing multiple concrete "Perform Clinical Path" processes (i.e. they are under execution) for corresponding patients.

All features of the functional perspective reported so far can be denoted as generally applicable. We now want to introduce some more features which represent potential features of the functional perspective. First, constraints should be discussed. It is possible to specify constraints for processes, indicating that a process cannot be started, continued, terminated, etc. before certain constraints hold. For instance, after 6 pm a routine surgery must not be performed. Besides, a powerful extension of processes is to provide methods for starting, pausing, resuming, recovering, delaying, terminating, etc. Normally, it is just possible to start a process and finally to end it. Additional methods introduce more flexibility to process execution. However, this flexibility might not be needed generally, so this is a typical domain specific extension.

Since in the context of the functional perspective the term "process" will be focused, it is appropriate to discuss often used synonyms here. Often processes are distinguished from workflows. However, we want to use both terms synonymously in this contribution. In fact, we prefer the term "workflow" when we specifically want to point to the fact that it is going to be executed. Also, we might use the term "process step" instead of "process"; but also this is a synonymous usage; process steps are mostly equivalent to elementary processes (Section 2.1).

Due to expressiveness we intentionally avoid to use terms like "activity" which refers to elementary processes. In the same way, we refuse to introduce "top-level-process" as structural notion (like composite or elementary process) instead of a role name. Such usages would drastically delimit modeling power and would increase modeling complexity. If everything is named process it is easy to decompose it by defining new sub-processes. Let's assume an elementary process is refined; nevertheless, it remains a process. If it had been named activity first (without internal sub-structure) this refinement would also have changed its type from activity to process. Alternatively, if a top-level-process would be used as a sub-process under another process definition this new usage does not change its type as long as "top-level-process" is just a role name instead of a structural term.

2.2 Data and Dataflow Perspective

Processes do have parameters. IN, OUT and INOUT parameters are distinguished. Input parameters (IN, INOUT) are consumed by a process i.e. they are read and used within the process; output parameters (OUT, INOUT) are produced by a process. In Figure 1 input parameters are depicted as rectangles sitting left above a process; output parameters are sitting right above a process. INOUT parameters are both sitting on the left and the right side.

Parameters are the most important data for a process. They should be distinguished from production data. The latter are data stemming from the application domain; they exist even if a process management system is not available. Parameters are just known by the process management system and just come into existence because there is a process management system. Nevertheless they normally refer to some production data.

Parameters can be mandatory or optional. In Figure 1 mandatory data are identified by solid lines, optional data are indicated by dotted lines. It is also possible to define local variables for processes. Applying the usual scoping rules, process variables are defined for super-processes; they are available for all sub-processes of such a super-process. Data, i.e. parameters and local variables should be typed.

Through the production and consumption of data, dependencies between processes are defined. For example, a process "Fill Registration" produces a patient record. This record is needed (consumed) by a process "Assign Physician" in order to determine an appropriate physician for the surgery. Through this production / consumption relationship a dependency between the two processes is established. Such dependencies determine a data flow between processes, i.e. they can also determine the execution order of processes.

Data flow can be controlled by flow conditions. For example, it can be decided that data are flowing from "Examine Patient" to "Assign Physician" only if the data item "Diagnosis" is completely filled. If this data item is only partially complete then data flow determines that "Examine Patient" has to be executed again in order to produce a complete patient record. In Figure 1 this behavior is depicted by a decision element (circle with question mark); in this modeling construct the completeness of "Diagnosis" is checked. The two exits of this modeling construct point to the subsequent step "Assign Physician" (if "Diagnosis" is complete) and to "Examine Patient" (if "Diagnosis" is not complete). The dotted rectangle of the input data "Diagnosis" for process "Examine Patient" indicates that this data is optional. Of course, it cannot exist when this process is executed for the first time. But when it has to be re-executed this data item will be there.

Generally data flow can adopt all flow patterns that are usually exclusively assigned to control flow (see Section 2.3 "Behavioral Perspective"); (University of Eindhoven, 2008) summarizes such patterns nicely. However, we postulate that also data flow can show these patterns. We differentiate clearly between data and control flow and consider them as equipollent. We discuss this issue at the end of the next sub-section.

Figure 1 also nicely shows that data elements go through stages. For example, the data item "Patient Record" is used by most of the processes. However, the content of this data item is continuously growing when the diverse processes are executed. For instance, after surgery a report of this surgery will be inserted into the patient record. It would be illustrative to indicate this maturing in the process model. To add an attribute "Stage" to data items would be a domain specific extension of a process model.

2.3 Behavioral Perspective

The behavioral perspective also defines dependencies between processes. However, in contrast to data flow where data embody the dependencies the behavioral perspectives concentrates on modal dependencies between processes; these dependencies form the control flow between processes. We summarize temporal and causal dependencies underneath modal dependencies. Typical examples of temporal dependencies are relative control flow constraints: the start of a subsequent process must be delayed for two hours after the predecessor process has finished (e.g. this models drying time within a production process). A causal dependency expresses that a subsequent process can only be performed if the predecessor process has been performed successfully.

Typical control flow constructs are sequential execution, branching, alternative and loops; refer to (University of Eindhoven, 2008) for a comprehensive collection of control flow constructs. With respect to the determination of flow control, data flow and control flow are equivalent. This means that a subsequent step can only be performed when both data flow and control flow are determining this step as executable. For example, although a metal part is already available for the next process step (i.e. data flow is complete) control flow causes a delay of the start of the subsequent process since control flow demands a two hours cooling-off time.

It is interesting to note that experience indicates that more than 90 percent of flow dependencies are determined by data flow – not through control flow. This is important to consider and to distinguish in process models since its neglect causes many modeling errors. Regard the following scenario. Process A produces data element d that is subsequently consumed by process B. However, the process modeler has misleadingly modeled this dependency as control flow dependency between processes A and B; data flow between A and B is not modeled at all. Due to a change in the application data item d will from now on be delivered by process C (instead of A). This new dependency will be inserted into the process model (hopefully as data flow between processes C and B). However, looking at the process model the modeler does not recognize that the dependency between processes A and B stems from the former exchange of data item d. This is due to the fact that this dependency was not modeled as data flow. Then the dependency between A and B remains in the process and the overall execution of the process becomes suboptimal since B cannot be executed before A has finished although there is no dependency between these steps any more. The precise modeling of this data flow dependency would have most probably avoided this wrong modeling and then would have lead to a more adequate process model.

2.4 Organizational Perspective

A fourth perspective is relevant for almost all application domains, the organizational perspective. Here, the agents responsible and eligible to perform processes are determined. An agent initiates the execution of a process. Typically, agents are human who are selected to execute certain processes. However, also a batch queue can play the role of an agent, when a process has to be performed in batch mode.

The backbone of the organizational perspective is the definition of the organization which defines the context for process execution. The organization consists of the population (including human and non-human agents) on one side and the organizational structure on the other side. Elements of the population have to finally perform a workflow. They are often determined by evaluating so-called organizational policies (Boehm, 2000) which assign agents to processes. Organizational policies often work on organizational structures. For example, when a head physician is intended to perform the surgery, his assistant physician must do the follow-up examination.

In Figure 3 (left) a sample organization is depicted. The organizational structure shows that the Orthopedic Clinic is lead by a Head Physician. Currently, three Assistant Physicians are assigned to him. The grey boxes represent the current population. Especially, it is shown who is assigned to what position of the organization. Taking this sample organization the above example would be interpreted as: when Prof. Dr. Smith is performing a surgery, one of the three Assistant Physicians (Dr. Miller, Dr. Bush, Dr. Snake) is responsible for the follow-up examination.

To use agent names directly in organizational policies is quite an exception. Then, the process

Figure 3. Model of an organization: Assignment of organizational policies

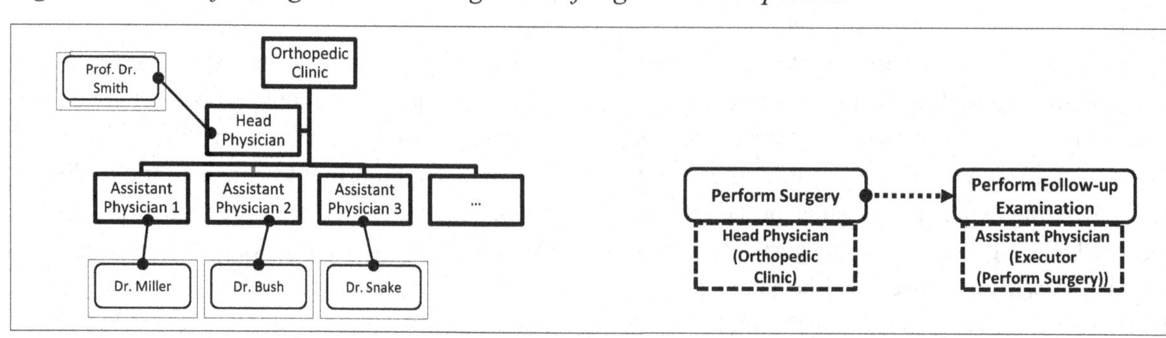

can exclusively be performed by the named agent. If Dr. Bush would be associated to the process "Perform Follow-up Examination" the process is not flexible any more. Namely, if Dr. Bush would not be available (due to holidays or because he quit) the process model must be changed in order to assign another physician to the process step. This is not an adequate solution. In order to provide more flexibility often so-called roles are introduced. For instance, in the example of Figure 1 we could have chosen to assign the role "Assistant Physician" to the process "Perform Follow-up Examination". However, this would not lead to the result intended. In principle, all assistant physicians of the respective clinics would now be eligible to perform the follow-up examination. Recall, that if more than just the Orthopedic Clinics would exist, all Assistant Physicians of all clinics are eligible to perform the process. Of course, this is not the goal of the process definition. Thus, roles have to be replaced by more powerful organizational policies which often make use of :

- Organizational structures on one side (the assistant physician assigned to the head physician) and of
- A back-reference to formerly performed processes (the assistant of the head physician who was performing the former process)

In Figure 3 (right) two processes from the process model in Figure 1 are detailed. Process "Perform Surgery" has to be executed from the Head Physician of the Orthopedic Clinic. This policy assignment makes use of the organizational structure (Figure 3, left). The policy assignment of process "Perform Follow-up Examination" references the executor of the former process "Perform Surgery".

Finally, agents selected to be eligible performing a process must be synchronized. In our example above an Assistant Physician shall perform the follow-up examination. However, in the example of the Orthopedic Clinic three Assistant Physicians are available. In principle, all three will be notified about the work to do. However, it is the intention of the process finally to have one physician who is doing the examination. Synchronization here means that out of the set of selected agents a subset is chosen. In most cases, this means that one agent is determined. However, it might also be the case that – for example – two agents must do the work: a credit assessment process step within a banking application must be performed by two eligible bank clerks.

2.5 Operational Perspective

The operational perspective is the fifth perspective relevant for almost all application domains. Here, the set of tools, systems, etc. is specified which is used when a certain process must be performed. For instance, in the "Fill Registration" process a word processing system is specified meaning that the registration form must be edited with this system. We call these systems process applications. Process applications are called within elementary processes after they are initiated by agents.

It is possible to introduce an abstract specification for process applications. For example, for the "Fill Registration" process not a concrete word processing system is specified but an abstract process application type "MS Word Compatible Text Processing Systems". Such a specification requires that there is a definition of this process application type determining all text processing systems fitting into this class of applications. Then, depending on the actual process applications available one of them can be selected when a concrete process instance must be performed.

Figure 4 shows a detail of the process model from Figure 1. As with the organizational perspective also the operational perspective must make use of references. The process "Perform Surgery" must be executed in the operating room of the Orthopedic Clinic. The follow-up examination takes place in the room of the doctor selected to

Figure 4. Operational Perspective

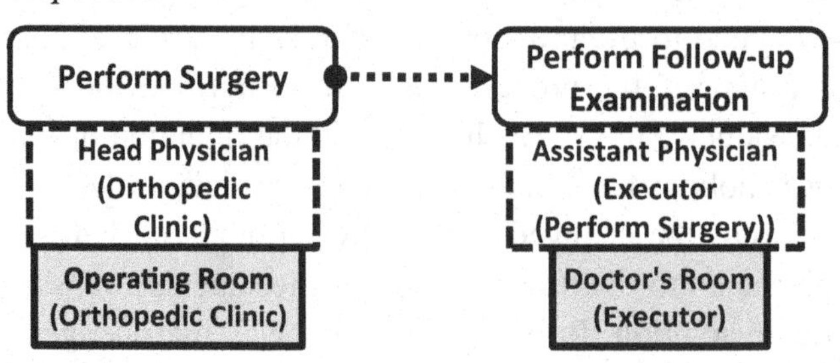

perform the process. From this example it becomes clear that simplified assignments like "Operation Room" are quite ambiguous. However, it has to be distinguished who is the consumer of a process model. If a process model is presented within a clinic it might be sufficient that simplified assignments like "Operation Room" are taken in order to simplify notation and to increase readability. However, when such a process model is made publically available or must be interpreted by a process execution system all these ambiguities must be resolved; otherwise the process models might convey inappropriate information.

Process applications consume and produce data. Thus, data flow must be specified between them and the embedding elementary processes. Normally, process applications are wrapped in order to provide a more general interface to the calling elementary processes. It is most convenient to support a web services interface here (W3C, 2008), in order to be able to integrate arbitrary web services into elementary processes.

2.6 Further Perspectives

As already discussed in Section 1.2 the above collection of perspectives is neither complete nor effective in general. Further perspectives must be added according to domain specific requirements. In 9 the security, the causality, the history, the integrity and failure, the quality, and the autonomy perspectives were shortly introduced. It is beyond the scope of this contribution to discuss these perspectives here. However, it is most important to mention again that holistic process management can only be achieved when perspectives are developed according to domain specific needs. This not just means to add new perspectives, but it also means to adjust the features of perspectives to these individual requirements.

3. IMPLEMENTING PERSPECTIVE ORIENTED PROCESS MODELING

This section shall provide an overview on the \ However, the principle presented here is generally applicable and POPM is merely one example that makes use out of it. The approach we present is a hierarchical meta modeling approach. It provides an ideal method to implement domain specific process modeling languages.

Eventually, process models like "Fill Registration" must be specified. A process modeling language is used to define process models. Such a process modeling language can also be regarded as a model. Thus, it is the meta model of process models. Usually a modeling tool works in the following way: the meta model (here: process modeling language) is implemented, then models (here: process models) can be defined. Since in our special case we do not know what modeling language should be implemented since each application domain might define its individual process modeling language, we have to choose another approach: Instead of implementing one concrete meta model, i.e. process modeling language, we go one step higher in the meta model hierarchy and implement a meta meta model, i.e. a model that facilitates to model process modeling languages. Having this meta meta model available, (arbitrary) process modeling languages could be implemented. Here, one of the characteristics of meta modeling techniques becomes apparent: meta models describe the structure of models (Seidewitz, 2003).

Figure 5 depicts the implementation of the meta model hierarchy (Jablonski et al., 2008). As with OMG's Meta Object Facility (Object Management Group, 2006b) layers of such a stack are named Mx, whereby "x" denotes the level of the layer within the stack. A domain modeler is working on layer M1: he is defining process models (right side). According to the type/usage concept only modeling artifacts that are defined can be referenced in models. Thus, a type library is storing all process types, data types, agent types, etc. that have once been declared. They can be used in new process models (usages). The language used by the domain modeler is defined on layer M2. A Domain Specific Process Meta Model (DSPMM) is representing this process modeling language. Obviously, a conventional modeling tool supports exactly one process modeling language. Thus, M2 is provided with one DSPMM that is fixed.

When we claim that a powerful domain specific tool must support multiple process modeling languages the layer M2 must be made flexible. The goal is to support multiple process modeling languages, i.e. new languages must be definable. In order to support this feature, the same conceptual approach is taken as between layer M1 and M2: in order to specify multiple process models on M1, a process modeling language is provided on M2. Therefore, in order to define multiple process modeling languages on M2, a meta model for these languages must be defined on M3, the Abstract Process Meta Meta Model (APM^2M). A tool for domain specific modeling accordingly must implement this APM^2M in order to finally implement various domain specific modeling languages.

Without going into details we introduce an Abstract Process Meta Model (APMM) on M2; this serves as a library for the domain specific process models on M2. Refer to cf. (Jablonski et al., 2008) for further discussion.

In order to complete the discussion of the meta model stack, the layer M0 must be introduced. On this lowest layer process instances are defined. They are derived from process models on M1 and represent actual process executions.

Finally, we just want to provide an indication of the implementation of a tool suitable for multiple domain specific process models. In (Jablonski et al., 2008) we elaborate that a powerful implementation concept for such a tool is through a so-called linguistic meta model. This specific meta model is used to describe all models depicted in Figure 5. Therefore, the tool is just implementing one model that facilitates the description of all models on the diverse layers in the meta model hierarchy. For such a challenging implementation advanced modeling concepts like powertypes and deep instantiation are required. (Jablonski et al., 2008) comprehensively introduces such an implementation.

Knowing the meta model stack as a foundation for implementing tools for domain specific process models we want to refer back to the process management life cycle, especially we want to revisit the two focused phases process design and process modeling. With respect to the meta model stack one of the main tasks of process design is to develop a domain specific process meta model on M2. This meta model defines the process modeling language for an application domain. The design phase has to identify the main modeling concepts needed for the specific domain. For example, a bubbles-and-arcs notation is determined (i.e. processes are illustrated as "bubbles" and dependencies between processes like data and control flow are illustrated as "arcs"). Besides, swimlanes should be introduced indicat-

Figure 5. The meta layer stack of POPM

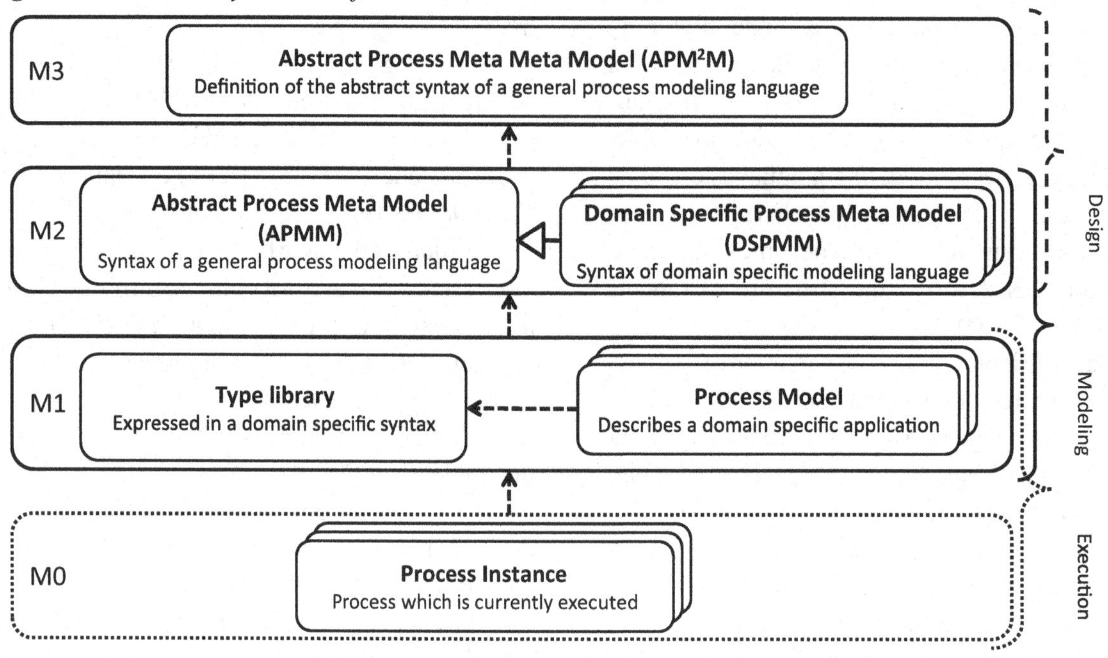

ing the organizational perspective (cf. Section 4). Last but not least process should carry attributes for cost and time measurements.

Having determined the process modeling language in the design phase and having implemented it, process models are constructed in the modeling phase. Process modeling takes place on layer M1. If process models should finally be executed process instances are derived which are located on layer M0. Figure 5 nicely shows that each of the phases design, modeling and execution spans two layers. This stems from the rationale that always on the upper of the two levels the definition is located whereby on the lower levels the derivations are sitting. According to this a domain specific language is an instance of the APM²M, process models are instances of a domain specific process modeling language, and process instances are derived from process models.

3.1 Excursus

Since this is a textbook about modeling and we were stating that our approach is not just applicable for process management we want to discuss another very prominent scenario. Let's assume that we want to define language for data modeling. It should bear features of Entity Relationship Diagrams (ERD) (Elmasri & Navathe, 2006) whereby we want to have two domain specific extensions (whether these extensions are meaningful should not be discussed; it is just of interest that new features have to be integrated): we want to introduce colors for each entity indicating whether they are relevant just internally or are also offered on interfaces to external partners. Another extension should model roles names for entities, describing the names that are used within existing applications; also these applications should be modeled with a separate modeling construct. How would such a model extension be enacted?

The two extensions are identified in the design phase. A designer has to define a new domain specific modeling language. We can assume that a modeling language for conventional ERD is already in place and is defined as APMM. Thus, the new, extended ERD language is derived from that APMM. A modeler then uses this new domain specific language and creates the extended ERD.

4. PROCESS VISUALIZATION

4.1 Models as Communication Means

So far we were concerned with the contents of process models. In this sub-section we focus another aspect of process management, namely process visualization. Most process modeling systems offer some kind of graphical notation. There are also standards like Business Process Modeling Notation (BPMN) (Object Management Group, 2006a) that also define the appearance of such a notation. Although these systems and standards have different notations, they all aim at the visualization of business process models in a manner that modelers and users can better grasp them to improve modeling and decrease misunderstandings. However, conventional tools and methods only support one predetermined way of process visualization. Here, we see a problem. In order to discuss it we have to dig into the rationale of modeling.

One of the primary purposes of a model is to act as a communication means. That means that a model should convey and clarify the structure of the part of reality under consideration. Process models are complex models like for example construction plans. When models get complex—like in the case of a construction plan—it is quite common to provide different views onto such a model. For instance, there is a version of the construction plan showing just the shapes of the wall; another version of the construction plan also includes the run of water pipes and electrical circuits. Having all elements integrated into one single plan would increase complexity, would reduce readability and usability and therefore would drastically lower the benefit of such a plan.

This matured practical experience should also be utilized for process modeling. Consequently, we postulate the following:

- For a process model different views should be provided
- Application domains should be able to define their individual views

The first postulation leads to a 1: n ratio between a process model and its views. Like in the construction plan case, these views should support individual perspectives of a process model. For instance, domain experts who have to manage the assignment of work to people should be supported by a swimlane presentation whereby the swimlanes represent organizational units. Besides, to gain a quick overview over a complex process parameters should be hidden as well as the operational perspective. The second postulation supports domain specific representations. Let's assume that an enterprise has a long tradition in process modeling. During this period they have got used to specific shapes of processes, flows, etc. When a new process modeling tool has to be introduced this tool should allow using the same shapes as before. This would increase the acceptance decisively. In contrast, if the new process modeling language would introduce new shapes for process modeling, both the understanding of these process models and their acceptance would decline.

4.2 Supporting Domain Specific Visualization

Supporting domain specific views for process visualization will drastically increase the complexity of a modeling tool: the latter must support arbitrary visualizations which will be expensive. Recall, in Section 3 we were facing a quite similar problem when arbitrary process modeling languages had to be implemented. Actually, to keep the implementation amount for a process model-

Figure 6. Extension of the meta modeling stack for visualization

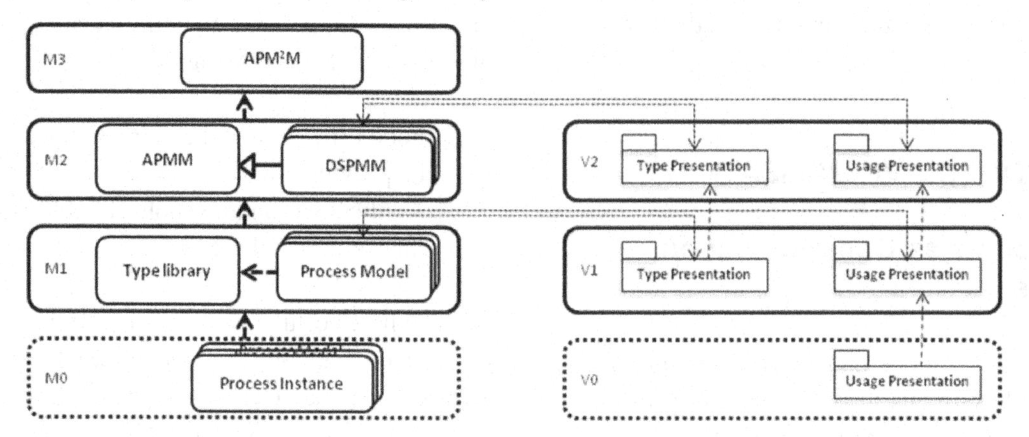

ing tool within a certain limit we extend the meta modeling approach from Section 3 (for a detailed discussion refer to (Jablonski & Götz, 2007); here we summarize and simplify the concept).

In Figure 6 the extension of the meta model stack for visualization is depicted. Two different presentation packages have to be provided: type and usage presentation. Corresponding to meta level M2 a visualization meta level V2 is introduced. V2 contains presentations for types and usages of modeling constructs offered by a domain specific process modeling language on M2. For instance, the following sample presentations are supported:

- **Process definition:** The whole modeling window is regarded as the process definition. For example, Figure 1 presents the process definition; the whole figure corresponds to the modeling window of a process modeler.
- **Process usage:** Process usages are depicted as rectangles with rounded corners in Figure 1.
- **Data usages:** Data usages are depicted as rectangles in Figure 1.

On visualization meta level V1 concrete visualizations for processes, data, organizational units, etc. are defined (Figure 6). It is necessary to represent each process definition and usage individually since it should be possible to alter the general presentations given in layer V2 for a concrete scenario. V0 completes the visualization by providing presentations for process instances.

It is interesting to look into the configuration of the visualization packages within the layer V2, V1 and V0. Figure 7 depicts the principle structure of the packages. A three layer structure can be identified: on the top layer basic shapes are offered; they are used in the middle layer to construct so-called diagram types. The presentation layer then defines concrete presentations.

The package "Basic Shapes" contains basic shapes like rectangle, circle, etc. but also means like "Gluing Point". This set of shapes provides all common modeling artifacts for process models. On the middle layer these basic shapes are configured in such a way that principle graphical presentations are defined. For example, graph structured presentations are defined which allow to derive concrete presentations on the lower layer like a bubble-and-arcs model (Figure 1). Block structured diagrams are also defined on the Diagram Type Layer; they allow to derive for example swimlane presentations on the Presentation Layer.

Figure 7. Configuration of visualization packages

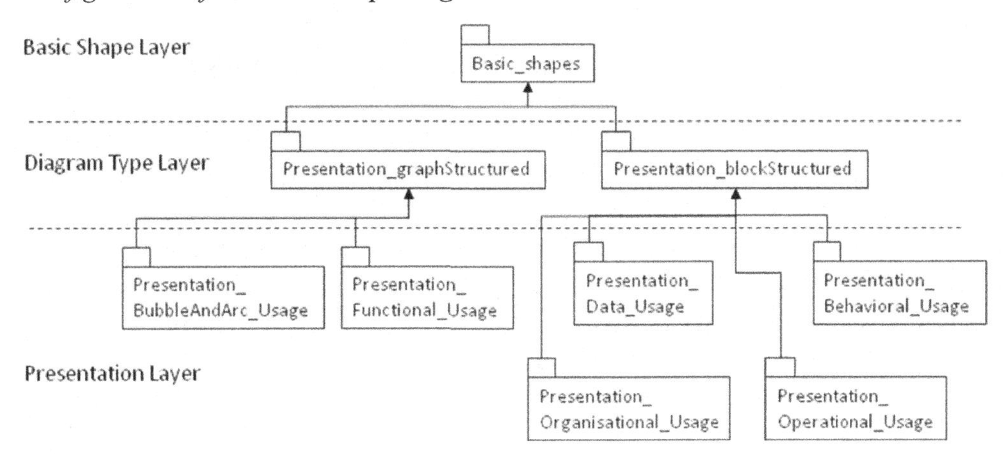

Figure 8 Alternative presentation of a process model: (a) bubbles-and-arcs notation, (b) swimlanes

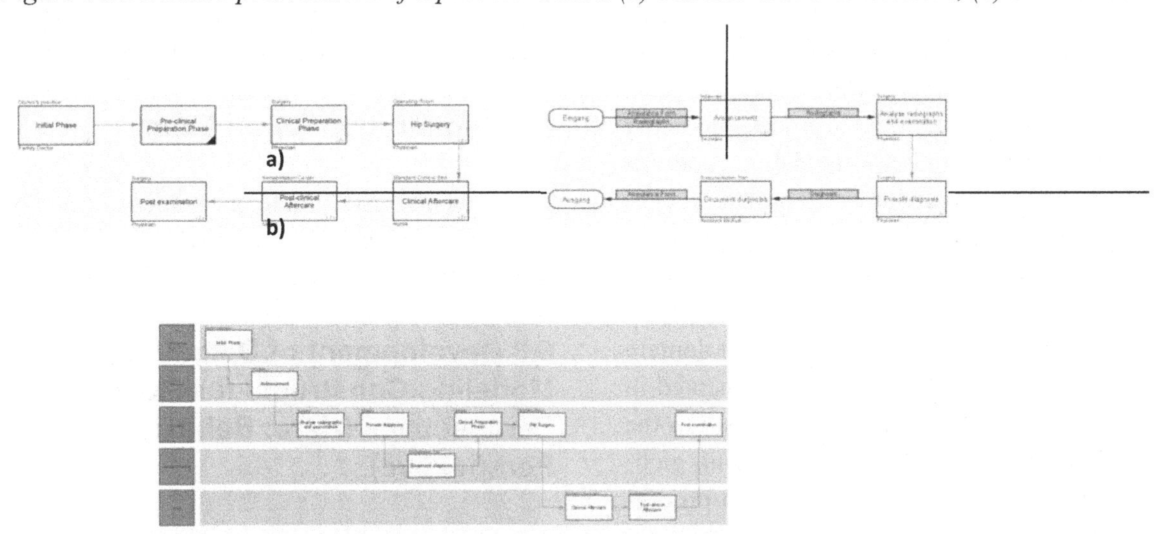

It would be out of the scope of this contribution to go into further details. However, we want to conclude from the presentation so far that through such an extension of the meta model stack, domain specific visualizations could be defined. In Figure 8 the expressiveness of such an approach is shown. Both presentations contain the same process model: The upper left process model describes a hip surgery (bubbles-and-arcs presentation). Its second process step "Pre-clinical Preparation Phase" is a composite one; the upper right process model describes this composite process. The swimlane presentation in the lower part of Figure 8 depicts the same process model. Through the selection of different visualization packages this process model is presented in two alternative ways. Domain experts now can choose what presentations better suites their purposes. The content of the process model depicted is not of importance. However, it is most important that the same process model is presented in different forms.

5. CONCLUSION, SUMMARY, AND OUTLOOK

This contribution focuses on process design and modeling. The main message is to analyze thoroughly the requirements of an application domain in the design phase. This might result in the need for domain specific process modeling constructs. Although such an extension of a process modeling language might cause leaving a standard but the resulting expressiveness of a process model and then its increased usability might balance this deviation. Besides, there are methods to map non-standard process models to standard process models.

Section 2 introduces perspective oriented process modeling. This section conveys some basic modeling principles which can be applied generally. Perspective oriented process modeling fosters a clear separation of modeling concerns which yields into more appropriate process models through modularization, i.e. through a concentration on perspectives. Domain specific process models result from this. Section 3 then acts as a sort of feasibility study: it proves that domain specific process models can be implemented in an efficient way. Besides, it introduces into the domain of meta modeling which is again globally applicable and is not restricted to process modeling. This section demonstrates how process modeling language can be constructed by defining them on a meta layer within a meta model stack. Finally, Section 4 adds that process visualization is as important as the content related design of process modeling languages. Process visualization is an important means that determines whether a process model will be comprehended, i.e. will be accepted by users.

In summary, this chapter contributes general concepts to process modeling. Hereby, the general applicability of these concepts is always emphasized. Coping with process modeling then also means to be able to master other modeling tasks as Section 3.1 shortly indicates.

6. EXERCISES

6.1 Process Design

Collect specific process modeling features that are most relevant for processes from:

- The engineering domain
- The medical domain
- The financial domain.

The three examples in the first section shows some possible features.

If you are not familiar with these domains select another domain that you know better. Classify features with respect to the perspectives you became acquainted with in this chapter.

6.2 Registration for an Exam

Model your registration for an exam at the end of a term. Pay much attention that you regard model perspectives.

6.3 Development of Domain Specific Modeling Constructs for Flow Perspectives (Here: Behavioral Perspective)

Define modeling constructs for the following scenarios:

- Three processes A, B, and C must be executed as fast as possible, i.e. waiting times must be reduced as much as possible. Assume that waiting time is caused by the non-availability of agents that have to perform the processes. Agents agA, agB, and agC are responsible to execute the processes. Their processing must not overlap.
- A process step has to be executed at least m times and at most n times.

6.4 Modeling the Organizational Perspective

The chair for Databases and Information Systems is headed by a full professor. Three research assistants are assigned to the chair. The chair is offering 6 courses (dbis1 to dbis6); each course encompasses a lecture and practical exercises. All lectures are given by the professor. Each assistant is responsible for two practical exercises.

7. SUGGESTED ADDITIONAL READING

Although this book is about process modeling we always recommend getting familiar with data modeling. There are many textbooks about data modeling. We recommend (Elmasri & Navathe, 2006) as a general introduction into Entity Relationship modeling and relational database modeling.

There are not too many textbooks about process management. (Leymann & Roller, 1999) provides a decent insight into workflow management, focusing on production workflow. The BPM (Business Process Management) conference series 2 supplies many research contributions to the business process management.

REFERENCES

Boehm, M. (2000). *Design of workflow types, (in German).* Berlin: Springer-Verlag.

BPM (2008). *Business process management conference series.* Retrieved 2008-04-01, from http://bpm08.polimi.it/

Bussler, C., & Jablonski, S. (1994). An approach to integrate workflow modeling and organization modeling in an enterprise. In *Proceedings 3rd IEEE Workshop on Enabling Technologies: Infrastructures for Collaborative Enterprises (WET ICE).*

Clark, T., Sammut, P., & Willians, J. (2008). *Applied metamodelling – A foundation for language driven development, 2nd Edition.* Retrieved 2008-04-01, from http://www.ceteva.com/book.html

Elmasri, R., & Navathe, S.B. (2006). *Fundamentals of database systems. Fifth Edition.* Amsterdam: Addison Wesley.

Gray, J., & Reuter, A. (1993). *Transaction processing: Concepts and techniques.* Morgan Kaufmann.

Heinl, P., Horn, S., Jablonski, S., Neeb, J., Stein, K., & Teschke, M. (1999). A comprehensive approach to flexibility in workflow management systems. *SIGSOFT Softw. Eng. Notes, 24*(2), 79-88

Jablonski, S. (1994). MOBILE: A modular workflow model and architecture.In *Proc. International Working Conference on Dynamic Modelling and Information Systems.*

Jablonski, S., & Bussler, C. (1996). *Workflow management – Modeling concepts, architecture and implementation.* London: Int. Thomson Computer Press.

Jablonski, S., & Götz, M. (2007) Perspective oriented business process visualization. *3rd International Workshop on Business Process Design (BPD) 5th International Conference on Business Process Management (BPM 2007).*

Jablonski, S., Volz, B., & Dornstauder, S. (2008) A meta modeling framework for domain specific process management. In *Proceedings 1st International Workshop on Semantics for Business Process Management.*

Leymann, F., Roller, D. (1999). *Production workflow: Concepts and techniques.* Pearson Education.

Object Management Group (2006a). *Business process modeling notation specification.*

Object Management Group (2006b). *Meta object facility core specification* (Version 2.0)

Rinderle, S., Reichert, M., & Dadam, P. (2004). Correctness criteria for dynamic changes in workflow systems - A survey. Data and knowledge engineering. *Special Issue, Advances in Business Process Management 50*(1), 9-34.

Seidewitz, E. (2003) What models mean. *IEEE Software, 20*(5), 26-31

Wikipedia (2008). *Business process management.* Retrieved 2008-04-01, from http://en.wikipedia.org/wiki/Business_Process_Management.

University of Eindhoven (2008). *Workflow patterns.* Retrieved 2008-04-01, from http://www.workflowpatterns.com/

W3C (2008). *Web services description language (WSDL) Version 2.0 Part 0: Primer.* Retrieved 2008-04-01, from http://www.w3.org/TR/wsdl20-primer/

KEY TERMS

Behavioral Perspective: Describes the order in which processes have to be executed.

Data Perspective: Describes which data (or documents) a process step consumes or produces. Thus the input and output data of a process is being described. All inputs and outputs together build up the flow of data in the process model.

Domain Specific Process Modeling: Describes a method for process modeling that allows the extension of standard process modeling languages in order to better reflect domain specific features.

Functional Perspective: Describes the processes themselves and their structures. Each process can be decomposed into sub-processes.

Operational Perspective: Defines tools or systems that support the execution of a process.

Organizational Perspective: Defines persons or roles that are responsible for the execution of a given process.

Perspective Oriented Process Modeling: A method to model process which distinguishes several perspectives of a process model: functional perspective, behavioral perspective, data(flow) perspective, organizational perspective, and operational perspective. Through this decomposition of a process model domain specific extensions of process modeling languages can be implemented.

Section II

Modern Business Process Languages

Chapter IV
The Dichotomy of Modeling and Execution:
BPMN and WS-BPEL

Matthias Kloppmann
IBM Deutschland Research and Development GmbH, Germany

Dieter König
IBM Deutschland Research and Development GmbH, Germany

Simon Moser
IBM Deutschland Research and Development GmbH, Germany

ABSTRACT

This chapter introduces a set of languages intended to model and run business processes. The Business Process Modeling Notation 1.1 (BPMN) is a notation used to graphically depict business processes. BPMN is able to express choreographies, i.e. the cooperation of separate, autonomous business processes to jointly achieve a larger scenario. Since BPMN is only a notation, there is no specification for a meta-model that allows rendering BPMN choreographies into an executable form. This chapter describes how the Service Component Architecture (SCA) and the Web Services Business Process Execution Language (WS-BPEL) help to close that gap. BPMN, SCA and WS-BPEL can jointly be used and combined to model, deploy and execute business process choreographies. We will also integrate the related BPEL4People specification, since BPMN allows human 'user tasks', but WS-BPEL focuses only on automated business process. The authors argue that, based on these specifications, the dichotomy between modeling and execution can be addressed efficiently. In this chapter, we will show that a key aspect of the future of Business Process Management is to combine graphical modeling (via BPMN) with a precise specification of an executable business process (via WS-BPEL and related standards).

INTRODUCTION

Automating business processes using an IT infrastructure has three aspects: First, a model of the business process is needed, which is usually authored in a graphical way. When it comes to deploying the business processes to a runtime environment, secondly a deployment model is required. Finally, a standardized execution behavior is necessary in order to ensure portability between process runtime infrastructures. These three aspects are most essential, but do not cover the complete lifecycle of Business Process Management (BPM) yet. As shown in Figure 1, the whole lifecycle consists of four steps: designing and simulating a business process (Model and Simulate), composing the existing services (Assemble), mapping the assembly to a concrete IT infrastructure and using it (Deploy and Execute), and continuously improving the processes (Monitor and Optimize).

In this chapter, we will show how BPMN, SCA and WS-BPEL together address the pieces Modeling, Assembling, Deployment and Execution. In order to better understand the relation between these three languages, two more concepts need to be introduced: *choreography* of services and *orchestration* of services. These terms have an intentional connotation with music: choreography represents a set of services that work together to achieve a larger goal; however, each service acts in an individual way – similar to dancers in a ballet. On the contrary, in an orchestration, a set of services are orchestrated by a "conductor", i.e. a main service that orchestrates, or "conducts", all participating services.

When looking at the individual languages, WS-BPEL is a pure orchestration language. In turn, SCA exhibits certain aspects of a choreography language. BPMN, however, is capable of describing aspects of both concepts.

In the first section of this chapter, the reader will learn about BPMN, SCA, WS-BPEL, and a related specification (BPEL4People, extending WS-BPEL to include tasks performed by humans). The second section shows how to use BPMN for business process modeling and how to map such models to SCA and WS-BPEL for execution. The third section provides recommendations for improving this mapping. Finally, the chapter provides a summary and concludes with future considerations in the last section.

Business Process Modeling Notation

BPMN, the Business Process Modeling Notation 1.1 (OMG, 2008a), is a notation used to graphically depict business processes. The language provides

Figure 1. The BPM lifecycle

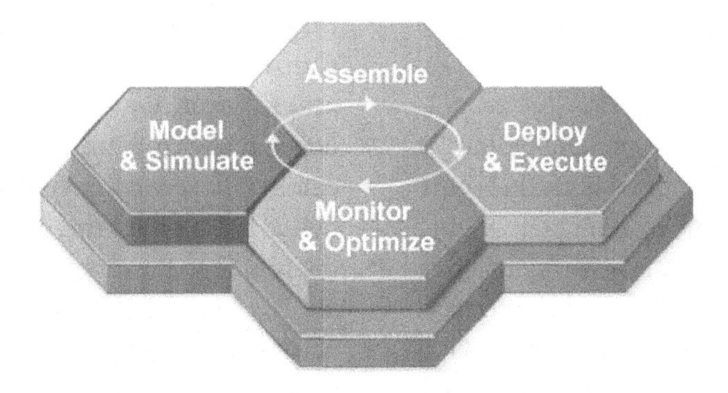

users the capability to capture their internal business procedures in a graphical notation. In other words, BPMN is a graph-oriented visual language that allows to model business processes in a flowchart-like fashion. Such a standardized graphical notation for business processes allows to explain and exchange processes in a standard manner and to better understand collaborations and business transactions between organizations. Basically, the BPMN language consists of four core elements:

- **Flow objects** are the nodes of the BPMN graph. There are three kinds of flow objects: *activities*, *events* and *gateways*.
- **Connecting objects** are the edges of a BPMN graph. BPMN allows three different kinds of connecting objects: *sequence flow*, *message flow* and *association*.
- **Swimlanes** are used to group other modeling elements in two distinct ways: A *pool* represents a process. It can be divided up into multiple *lanes*, where each lane is a sub-partition of that process and is used to organize and categorize activities (e.g. activities that are performed by the same department are grouped in the same lane).
- **Artifacts.** As an example, a data object is an artifact that represents the data that an activity requires before it can be performed, or that an activity produced after is has been performed. For the sake of completeness, there are two more artifacts mentioned in the BPMN standard, *text annotation* and *group*. Both will not be important in the context of this chapter.

In order to get a better understanding of BPMN, we will use the example shown in Figure 2 to explain the elements in greater detail: Figure 2 represents a choreography consisting of three processes: a Buyer process, a seller process and a shipper process. Since each process is a participant in that B2B scenario, each process is represented as its own pool. Within a pool, you see rounded rectangles representing activities. In the buyer process, Send Quote Request, Receive Quote and Receive Fault are activities. Furthermore, you see events in the example in Figure 2. An Event happens during the course of the process, normally having a cause and a result. Events are represented as circles, and there are three types of events: *start events* (in the buyer process, this is the circle at the very left that is connected to the Send Quote Request activity), *end events* (in the buyer process that is e.g. the circle at the very right of the pool), and *intermediate events*. The third main element from the flow objects group is a gateway. *Gateways* split or join the control flow of the process and are represented as diamonds. The split or join behavior depends on the symbol inside the diamond: A "+" for example indicates a parallel AND fork or join, while "x" indicates an exclusive split or merge. No symbol is equivalent to "x". In the buyer process a gateway can be seen after the Send Quote Request activity (in this particular case, it is an *event-based gateway*), or after the Send Order Request activity (where it is a *parallel AND gateway*). For a complete list of possible gateways, refer to the BPMN specification.

Now let's take a look at the second core element of the BPMN specification, the connecting objects. As mentioned earlier, connecting objects represent the arcs inside a BPMN model. The first arc type, the sequence flow, is a solid line that represents the control flow in which the connected activities are executed. When, in the buyer process example from Figure 2, the Send Quote Request activity is connected from the start event, that means that there is a control dependency from the start to Send Quote Request. The second arc type, a message flow, is a dotted line representing a message being sent from the source to the target (which reside in different pools). A message flow is modeled between the activities Send Quote Request (in the buyer process) and Receive Quote Request (in the

Figure 2. BPMN representation of choreography

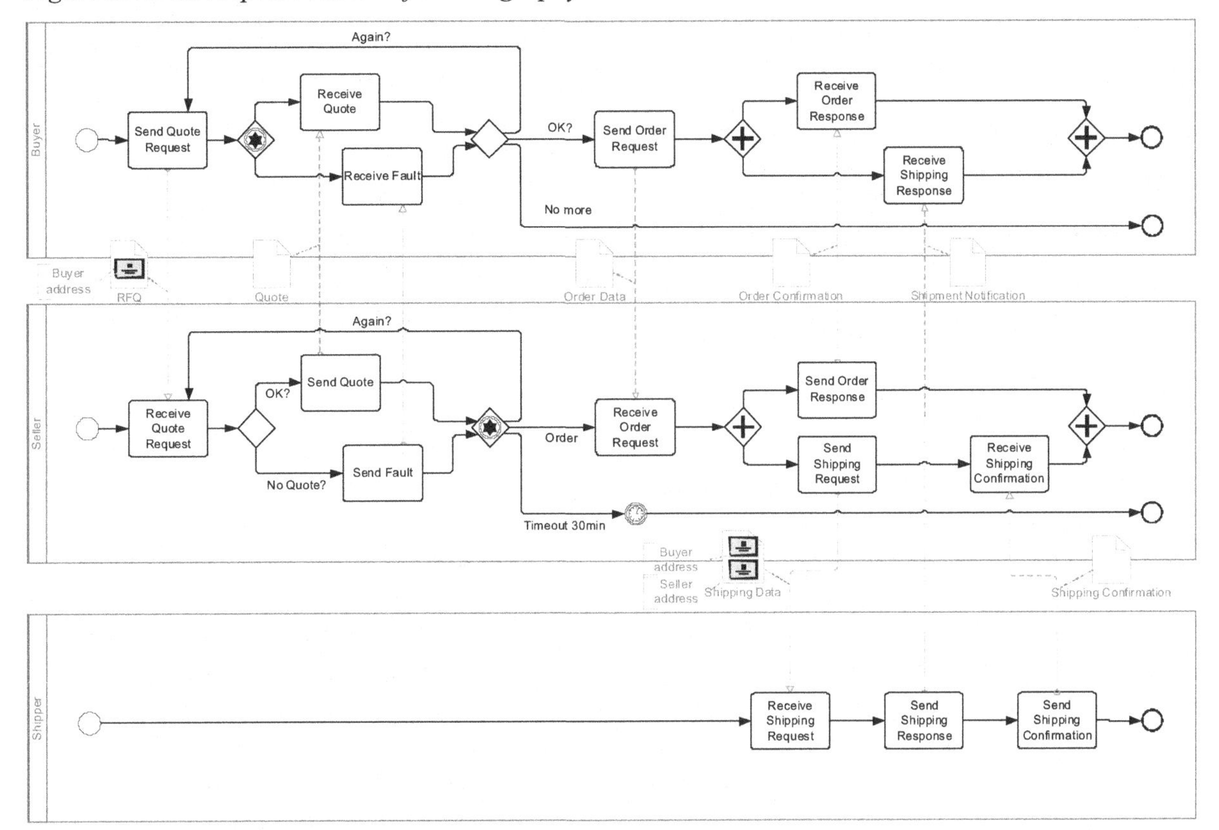

seller process). The third arc type, association, can be seen at the message flow connection just mentioned. In this case, it associates the message flow with the RFQ data object.

Using this last example, we are also able to explain the relevant subset of the fourth core element of BPMN: *artifacts*. RFQ in Figure 2 represents a *data object* artifact. The Receive Quote Request activity in the seller process requires data of type RFQ before it can be performed, so the Send Quote Request activity must provide that information.

WS-BPEL 2.0 and BPEL4People

As it becomes obvious from the previous section, BPMN allows to model business processes (or even complete *choreographies*) graphically. According to the BPMN 1.1 specification, its primary goal is to "provide a notation that is readily understandable by all business users". Although BPMN mentions "token flows" in an abstract way, it lacks precise execution semantics. When it comes to actually executing a business process, WS-BPEL, the Web Services Business Process Execution Language 2.0 (OASIS, 2007), comes into the picture.

WS-BPEL is a Web service-based language to describe executable business processes. A WS-BPEL process implements one Web service by specifying the process' interactions with other Web services, and the logic how these interactions take place. In the example from Figure 2, this means the following: Each of the three processes (where each one was created from a different BPMN pool) will have at least one inbound service interface. Furthermore, they also require other services. Table 1 gives an overview

Table 1. Overview of the process relations

	Provided service interfaces	Required service interfaces
Buyer process	BuyerProcessInterface SellerCallbackInterface ShipperCallbackInterface1	SellerProcessInterface
Seller process	SellerProcessInterface ShipperCallbackInterface2	ShipperProcessInterface SellerCallbackInterface
Shipper process	ShipperProcessInterface	ShipperCallbackInterface1 ShipperCallbackInterface2

of all services interfaces for the processes shown in Figure 2.

This means that each interface that a WS-BPEL process exposes to the outside world is a service interface. This is true both for the service interfaces the process provides (inbound interfaces), as well as service interfaces that the process calls (outbound interfaces). WS-BPEL is a language that allows orchestrating other services, ranging from simply invoking services in a particular order and under particular conditions up to long-running stateful conversations between services. WS-BPEL offers a recursive aggregation model that allows combining existing Web services into higher level Web services.

WS-BPEL consists of seven basic language elements: *Basic activities* and *structured activities* represent the possible instructions of the language. Together they form the building blocks of a BPEL Business process. *Handlers* (Fault, Event, Compensation and Termination Handler) are responsible for dealing with special situations in a process (e.g. faults) and *variables* are responsible for storing data. Language elements related to the communication with other services include *partner links* (to define the communication interfaces with the outside world), *correlation sets* and *properties* (to help correlating the messages sent between process instances), and *message exchanges* (to resolve potential ambiguities in the relationship between inbound and outbound message activities).

We will now introduce the single language elements in greater detail. WS-BPEL consists of the following basic activities:

- **receive:** The receive activity initiates a new process when used at its start, or does a blocking wait for a matching message to arrive when used during a process.
- **reply:** The reply activity sends a message in reply.
- **invoke:** The invoke activity calls a Web service operation of a partner service. This can either be a one-way or a request-response call. One-way means that the called service will not send a response, whereas request-response blocks the process until a response is received.
- **assign:** The assign activity updates the values of variables or partner links with new data.
- **validate:** The validate activity checks the correctness of XML data stored in variables.
- **wait:** The wait activity pauses the process, either for a given time period or until a certain point in time has passed.
- **empty:** The empty activity is a no-op instruction for a business process.

Additionally, there are basic activities that deal with fault situations:

- **throw:** The throw activity generates a fault from inside the business process.
- **rethrow:** The rethrow activity propagates a fault from inside a fault handler to an enclosing scope, where the process itself is the outermost scope.
- **compensate:** The compensate activity invokes compensation on all completed child scopes in default order.
- **compensateScope:** The compensateScope activity invokes compensation on one particular (completed) child scope.
- **exit:** The exit activity immediately terminates execution of a business process instance.

Furthermore, WS-BPEL offers structured activities. Structured activities can have other activities as children, i.e. they represent container activities. WS-BPEL consists of the following structured activities:

- **flow:** The activities contained in a flow are executed in parallel, partially ordered through control links. A flow activity represents a directed graph. Note that cyclic control links are not allowed.
- **sequence:** The activities contained in a sequence are performed sequentially in lexical order.
- **if:** The if activity represents a choice between multiple branches. However, exactly one branch is selected.
- **while:** The contained activity of a while loop is executed as long as a specified predicate evaluates to true.
- **repeatUntil:** The contained activity of a repeatUntil loop is executed until a specified predicate evaluates to true.
- **forEach:** The activity contained in a forEach loop is performed sequentially or in parallel, controlled by a specified counter variable. This loop can be terminated prematurely by means of a completion condition.
- **pick:** The pick activity blocks and waits either for a suitable message to arrive or for a time out, whichever occurs first.
- **scope:** A container which associates its contained activity with its own local elements, such as variables, partner links, correlation sets and handlers. These elements are described in more detail below.

The BPEL 2.0 standard has an explicit placeholder for new (basic or structured) activities introduced by language extensions, known as an *extension activity.* A concrete example of a language extension introducing a new activity type is discussed later (BPEL4People).

To handle exceptional situations, WS-BPEL offers four different handlers:

- **catch and catchAll:** Fault handlers for dealing with fault situations in a process. A fault handler can be compared to the catch-part of a try{}... catch{}-block in programming languages like e.g. Java™.
- **onEvent and onAlarm:** Event handlers for processing unsolicited inbound messages or timer alarms concurrently to the regular control flow.
- **compensationHandler:** A compensation handler undoes the persisted effects of a successfully completed scope.
- **terminationHandler:** A termination handler can be used for customizing a forced scope termination, e.g. caused by an external fault.

Another element of the WS-BPEL language is a variable. WS-BPEL supports both global (i.e. process level) and local (i.e. scope level) variables. BPEL variables may be typed using an XML schema (XSD) type or element, or a WSDL message. For initializing or assigning variables, WS-

BPEL provides the assign activity. Each assign consists of one or more copy statements. In each copy the from element specifies the assignment source for data elements or partner links and the to element specifies the assignment target.

Additionally to concepts introduced already, there are three more concepts for communication: partner links, correlation sets and (variable) properties:

- **PartnerLinks** describe the relationship between a process and its services. A partner link points to a Web service interface the process provides via a myRole attribute. Consequently, a partnerRole attribute points to the Web service interface that is required from the partner. A partner link can only have one myRole attribute (inbound partner), only one partnerRole attribute (outbound partner) as well as both attributes (bidirectional partner).
- **CorrelationSets** are of help in identifying (stateful) process instances. Each process instance will get one or more unique keys based on business data, which are used to correlate a process instance with an incoming message. A correlation set consists of one or more properties.
- A **property** is business data which creates a name that has a semantic meaning beyond an associated XML type, e.g. a social security number versus a plain XML schema integer type. Therefore, properties help to isolate the process logic from the details of a variable definition. Such typed properties are then mapped (aliased) to the parts of a WSDL message or an XSD element.

WS-BPEL Extension for People

As shown in the previous sections, the WS-BPEL standard introduces a language for describing automated business processes. However, in many practical situations, automated service orchestration is not enough and many business process scenarios require human interactions. Since WS-BPEL offers hooks to extend the language, BPEL4People (Active Endpoints, Adobe, BEA, IBM, Oracle, SAP AG, 2007) uses these extension mechanisms to incorporate people as another type of participants in business processes. BPEL4People consists of two specifications – the first one, *WS-HumanTask*, defines the specifics of a single user interaction, whereas the second one, *BPEL4People*, is about invoking such user interactions from a WS-BPEL process.

BPEL4People introduces a number of new concepts for processes, like *generic human roles*. Such a role defines the kind of participation in a business process, e.g. a process initiator or a business administrator. In order to assign actual people to this role, the concept of *logical people groups* is used. A logical people group is an abstract concept that represents an abstract person or an abstract group of persons. For example, a logical people group 'voters' would represent all people with voting rights in a given organization. During deployment, this logical people group can be associated with a set of users, or with a query against a people directory (e.g. LDAP). In the latter case, during execution of the process, that query returns real people's user-IDs. In other words, a process using the logical people group 'voters' might yield different results when deployed into two different enterprises.

In our context, there is another concept worthwhile mentioning: the *people activity,* which is a WS-BPEL extension activity. A people activity is a basic activity used to integrate human interactions within BPEL processes. The human task can be inlined in the people activity, referenced as a standalone artifact, or invoked as a separate service.

This closes an important gap in todays WS-BPEL specification, since humans may also take part in business processes and can influence the process execution.

Service Component Architecture

SCA, the Service Component Architecture (OSOA, 2007), is a family of specifications providing a simplified programming model for the Service Oriented Architecture. It defines

- a core: the component assembly model specification
- client and implementation language specifications, such as SCA-BPEL
- binding specifications for interaction protocols, such as Web services
- a policy framework specification

The assembly model describes a way to assemble and deploy *components*. The difference between a service and a component is that a service is only an interface, whereas a component is an interface with an associated implementation. Thus, a component consists of zero or more inbound interfaces (*services*), zero or more outbound interfaces (*references*) and an implementation. In SCA, a service or a reference can be specified as a Web service interface or as a Java interface. A component implementation can either point to a specific implementation language (such as WS-BPEL) or it can be implemented by a *composite*. SCA composites are used to recursively assemble a set of components, services, references and the wires that interconnect them. Similar to a component, a composite can also have services and references which represent the interfaces of the composite to the outside world. Also, SCA composites can have a set of *properties* which can be used to configure contained components. The top-level composite can be the unit of deployment. The composite is deployed into an SCA *domain*, which is a (potentially distributed) runtime environment typically controlled by a single organization. A component can be considered as an abstract wrapper for a service implementation, e.g. a business process.

Both WS-BPEL and SCA are XML languages describing service compositions, however, note that they are complementary technologies. While WS-BPEL describes the business logic and the service orchestration, SCA describes the structure of an application, i.e. the dependencies between its components. SCA also adds binding and policy aspects, which are out of scope for the WS-BPEL standard.

Each component needs an implementation that does the actual work – the component itself provides just a view on an implementation. The SCA family of specifications allows for all kinds of implementation types, WS-BPEL just being one of them. Other possible implementation types include Java, PHP or C++.

BUSINESS PROCESS MANAGEMENT USING BPMN AND WS-BPEL

This section will show how the mapping from BPMN to executable BPEL and SCA models can be done. The described mappings in this section are based on the BPMN 1.1 and WS-BPEL 2.0 standards and the BPEL4People/WS-HumanTask 1.0 and SCA 1.0 specifications, as submitted to OASIS. Consider the choreography shown in Figure 2, consisting of three processes:

- A buyer process, which issues a price quote request against a seller (potentially multiple times) and, if satisfied with the price, issues an order, which is then delivered.
- A seller process which answers price quotation requests, guaranteeing prices for a certain amount of time. Upon receipt of an order, it issues shipment via a third party.
- A shipper process which is called by the seller to deliver an order. It receives both the buyer address and the seller address. The shipper process then sends a shipping response directly to the buyer process and

a shipping confirmation to the seller process.

From a high-level perspective, the orchestration aspects of BPMN will be mapped to WS-BPEL, whereas choreography aspects of BPMN will be mapped to SCA. Limitations in both mappings will be spelled out in the respective sections.

Mapping from BPMN to WS-BPEL

First, we start with the mapping from BPMN 1.1 to WS-BPEL 2.0. Figure 2 can be mapped to a model of three interacting processes, i.e., each BPMN pool maps to an individual BPEL process. Figure 3 below shows a mapping for the seller process (the most complex of the three

Figure 3. BPEL Representation of Seller Process

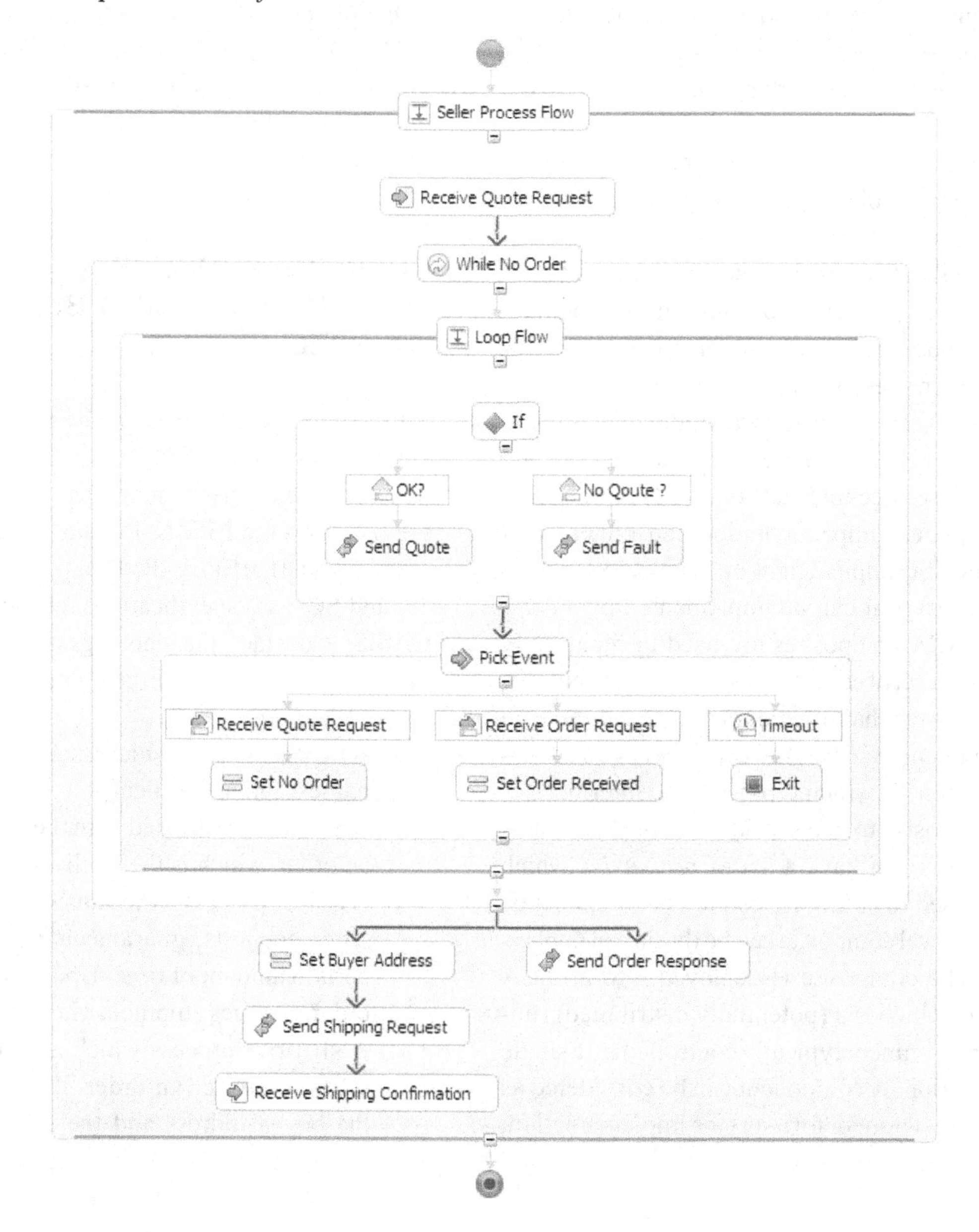

processes). The mapping was developed along the lines of Appendix A of the BPMN specification, which contains a mapping from BPMN 1.1 to BPEL4WS 1.1, a predecessor specification of the WS-BPEL 2.0 standard. The other two processes can be mapped similarly.

The main activity of the WS-BPEL process becomes a flow activity, since the original seller process in BPMN has parallel parts. The communication activities in the BPMN process (e.g. ReceiveQuoteRequest, SendQuote, ReceiveOrderRequest) are mapped to communicating BPEL activities (invoke, receive, reply, and pick) with the same names. Note that the BPMN message flow connections between the pools in Figure 2 were mapped to WS-BPEL partner links, and the resulting communicating BPEL activities are bound to these partner links.

Figure 3 shows the resulting WS-BPEL process, visualized by the Eclipse BPEL Designer (Eclipse Foundation 2008). As it can be seen, the mapping from BPMN to WS-BPEL is not straightforward in the sense that the BPMN graph structure cannot always be preserved in WS-BPEL. This yields a different structure for the process which has several consequences. The different representation of the process model is harder to understand. Also, having a modified structure makes it more complicated to develop a reversible mapping and, if an execution error occurs, it may be hard to correlate that to its original modeling construct.

The backward link "Again?" in the seller process indicates a cycle, which is mapped to a while loop, where the loop body consists of the activities enclosed in the cycle. In general, cyclic BPMN control flows must be mapped onto one of the WS-BPEL loop constructs, that is, while, repeatUntil, or forEach. Note that the path taken inside the pick activity must be indicated through a variable (order) which determines whether the loop is exited or not. This is important since the path out of the Receive Order Request activity, according to the BPMN process, must only be taken if an order has been received and the loop has been exited right after.

The BPMN complex event-based gateway, which models the deferred choice control flow pattern (Russel et al. 2006), is turned into the structured WS-BPEL pick activity named Pick Event.

This is caused by the fact that the WS-BPEL language does not allow expressing these kinds of graphical control flow structures in its flow activity. Having the ability to express structures like these in BPEL would allow mapping the BPMN constructs in a way that preserves the graph structure in a more recognizable fashion. It would make it easier to solve the problem that the mapping to WS-BPEL is not always reversible. Therefore, we will later suggest a couple of WS-BPEL extensions enabling a canonical mapping from BPMN to WS-BPEL.

Introducing Constraints for BPMN

The mapping from BPMN to WS-BPEL 2.0 (adjusted along the lines of the mapping described in the BPMN specification) has been introduced, and some possible areas of improvement have been outlined. In addition to that, in this section, we will give some best practices when it comes to modeling BPMN in order to simplify the mapping and avoid the construction of non-executable process models.

BPMN, using a flowchart like notation form, gives the user a high degree of expressive freedom when it comes to modeling business processes. However, in terms of mapping such processes into executable WS-BPEL processes, this can cause problems. WS-BPEL has very clear semantics in terms of its control flow behavior. Every split of the control flow has a dedicated point where the control flow merges, and the split and merge semantics in these cases are identical (e.g. if the control flow is forked into parallel branches, then there will be a parallel join, too). In a WS-BPEL engine, the runtime environment for a WS-BPEL process, the status of all incoming links must be known before evaluating whether an activity with one or more incoming links gets executed. If a predecessor activity failed, and therefore the outgoing links of this predecessor activity were not navigated, a status can still be guaranteed because of a concept called dead-path elimination (cf. OASIS, 2007). Dead-path elimination guarantees that for such (dead) links an appropriate status is set so it can be used to evaluate whether a successor activity gets executed.

This semantic is different in BPMN with its token flow semantics. In BPMN, it is possible to model a parallel fork with an exclusive merge of control flow or vice versa an exclusive split with a parallel merge. Obviously, such models have control flow errors such as "lack of synchronization" or deadlocks (c.f. Sadiq and Orlowska, 2000), resulting in non-executable process models. Therefore, one necessary constraint for the BPMN model is its structurally correctness in that sense. Vanhatalo et al, 2007 describe a method to automatically decide whether a process model is structurally correct, and therefore executable. This method first divides a process into so-called Single-Entry Single-Exit (SESE) regions, where each region must have exactly one control flow entry point, and one control flow exit point, and no region must overlap with another region. Therefore, any activity in a process belongs to exactly one region. Regions can be nested into each other, yielding the process structure tree (PST). A second step tries to classify each region in the PST as a "sequential", "cyclic" or "parallel" region. If this is possible for all regions, the process is transformable to BPEL.

Second, BPMN also describes the concept of an *ad-hoc process*. In an ad-hoc process, the activities have no pre-definable sequence relationship. This means that these activities can have any arbitrary order at runtime. Additionally, it cannot be determined beforehand how often the activities will get executed. Therefore, when the process should be executed by a BPEL runtime, ad-hoc processes in BPMN should be avoided.

Mapping BPMN Constructs to SCA

BPMN has collaborative aspects, which are modeled as BPMN Pools. The example from Figure 2 shows a choreography of three processes. These three processes would most likely be run by three different companies, and therefore be deployed into three different runtime environments (cf. SCA domains).

Figure 4 shows the SCA composite for the Seller process. It consists of a SellerComposite, which represents the unit of deployment. In other words, the BPMN pool from Figure 2 maps to the SellerComposite. In the given example, the composite only has one component, the SellerProcessComponent which is implemented by the WS-BPEL SellerProcess (as shown in Figure 3). During the mapping from a BPMN pool to a BPEL process, we described how the communication dependencies from one pool to the next, represented as message flow connections in Figure 2, become the partner links in the WS-BPEL process. In the SCA assembly model, BPEL partner links are represented by services (for inbound interactions) and references (for outbound interactions). Specifically, a BPEL partner link with only a "myRole" specification maps to an SCA service, and a partner link with only a "partnerRole" specification maps to an SCA reference. Partner links defining both roles are mapped according to a set of rules provided by the SCA-BPEL specification. Services are shown as green elements in Figure 4 and references are shown as pink elements. Component services and references can be wired to services and references of the composite itself, which has been done in Figure 4, showing the recursive service aggregation model that the SCA language offers.

The example from Figure 2 is a typical B2B interaction. However, imagine a situation where all

Figure 4. SCA Composite containing the Seller Process Component

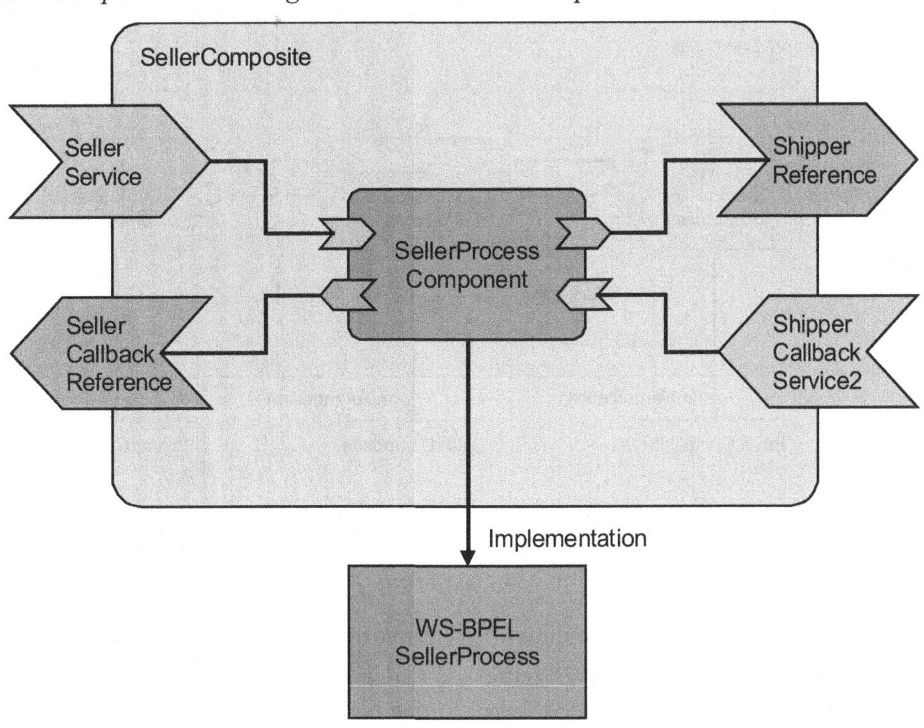

three "partners" belong to the same organization. In this case, the three processes would be deployed into a single SCA domain. The relationship between them could then be described by another, domain-wide SCA composite, which represents the whole choreography. Figure 5 shows the choreography composite of the example from Figure 2. The wired components are implemented by the three composites created from the original BPMN pools (again an example for recursive service aggregation). For example, the SellerComposite in Figure 5 is exactly the composite from Figure 4. In other words, the SellerCompositeComponent is implemented by the SellerComposite from Figure 4.

Again, the components have outbound references (pink) and inbound services (green). References of a component can be wired to services of another component. In order to connect a component's reference to another component's service, it is necessary that the reference and the service have a matching interface. The BuyerCompositeComponent requires a sellerInterface, and the SellerCompositeComponent provides a sellerInterface, so they can be wired. In Figure 5, the solid lines between the composite components are such explicit wires. The dashed lines represent callbacks that are dynamically resolved using endpoint references passed at runtime, instead of being statically wired. For a full list of provided and required interfaces for the components, refer to Table 1. As mentioned above, this works well in the case where all three "partners" belong to the same organization. However, SCA is not well-suited for the case of cross-enterprise choreographies, since wirings crossing enterprise boundaries are not supported today.

Mapping BPMN User Tasks to BPEL-4People

BPMN describes the concept of a *user task* as an activity being performed by a human. In ad-

Figure 5. Domain-level SCA choreography

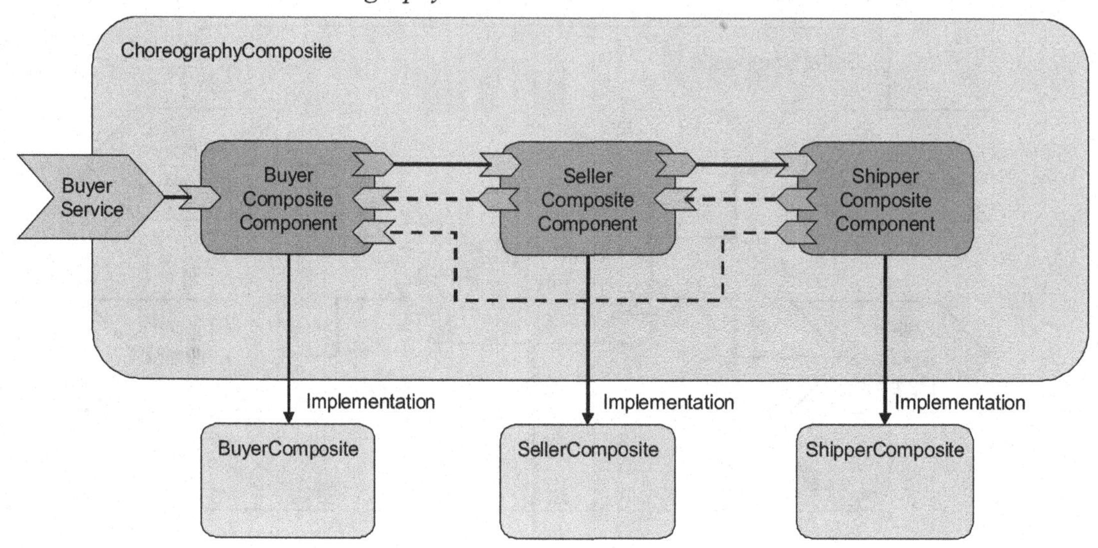

dition to the WS-BPEL mapping already shown in previous sections, user tasks map nicely to WS-BPEL extension elements introduced by BPEL4People. The human interaction is defined by a WS-HumanTask task definition, and its invocation from a WS-BPEL process is defined by a BPEL4People people activity.

Consider the example shown in Figure 6. It shows an enhanced version of the seller process from the initial example. The enhancement basically consists of the fact that the process got two additional user tasks. First, after the price quote request is received, there is a manual step to assess the quote, rendered by the Assess Quote activity. Second, after the order has been received, there is another additional human step to validate the order request for completeness, shown in activity Validate Order Request. These two activities have been modeled in two separate lanes, since, a *lane* is a sub-partition that is used to organize and categorize activities. A categorization is needed here since these two additional manual steps have to be done by different roles within the enterprise: a controller has to assess the proposed quote and might raise or lower it depending on the financial situation of the company and the customer. After the order has been placed, an accountant has to make sure that the order request is correct so it can be put in the books correctly.

In order to map the BPMN process from Figure 6 to WS-BPEL, the lanes associated with certain groups of people within the enterprise are canonically mapped to BPEL4People *logical people groups.* These logical people groups can then be associated with BPEL4People people activities with inlined human tasks. Alternatively, a human task may be defined as a separate definition that is reusable by multiple processes. In this case, either a people activity references the human task definition or the human task is invoked as a service, similar to automatic service activities.

Applying these mappings to the example from Figure 6 yields the following: the Assess Quote activity is associated with the logical people group controllers, and the Validate Order Request activity with the logical people group accountants, since these are the logical people groups associated with the lanes. The user task assessQuote (and also the user task validateOrderRequest) can be mapped to BPEL4People in two ways, either using an inline BPEL4People peopleActivity, or using

Figure 6. Enhanced Seller Process including multiple lanes

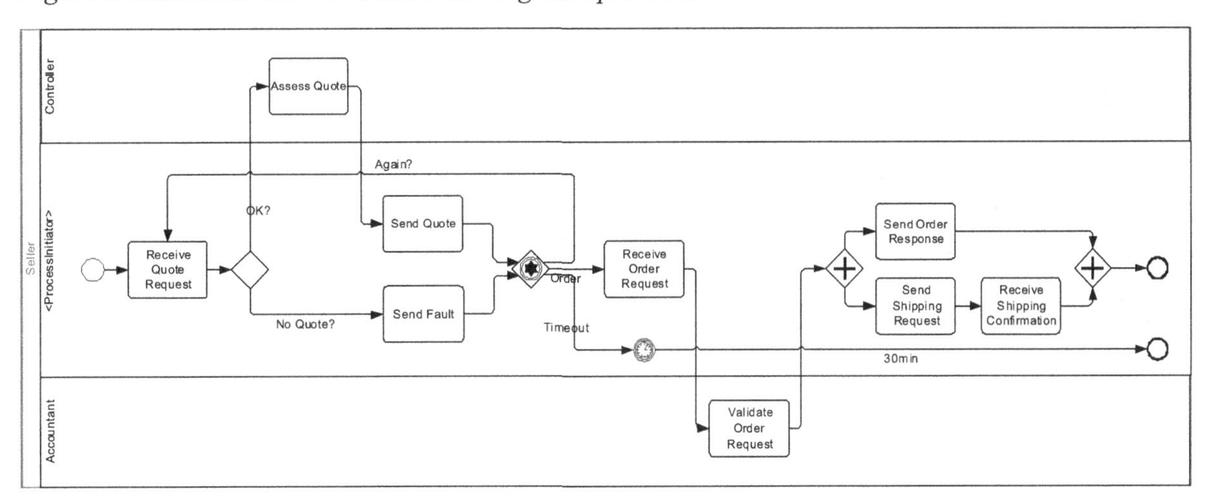

a regular WS-BPEL invoke activity bound to a standalone WS-HumanTask definition. These two options are different from a deployment perspective, thus the corresponding SCA would look a little different: For the inline task option, there would be just one composite with a process component containing the entire process. For the second alternative, the assembly diagram would also contain a process component, but additionally a WS-HumanTask component for each BPMN user task that got transformed into a standalone WS-HumanTask definition. The process component and the human task component would then be wired appropriately.

Whether to do it one way or the other depends on the actual usage scenario. As a rule of thumb, it makes sense to map user tasks to inline BPEL-4People peopleActivities if the task needs access to the surrounding process context. In case that the activity is a service currently implemented by a human, and possibly needs to be exchanged by an automatic service in the future, it is preferably mapped to a standalone WS-HumanTask so it can benefit from the flexibility that loose coupling of services offers.

REMAINING PAIN POINTS AND SUGGESTED IMPROVEMENTS

In this section, we will show open gaps that exist today in the languages introduced. This includes certain recommendations for BPMN, possible extensions for WS-BPEL that would allow an improved mapping and some further recommendations that are currently not addressed by any of the languages presented in this chapter.

Modeling, assembling, deploying and executing have already been discussed in this chapter, whereas monitoring has not been covered yet. In section "Recommendations for BPMN", we will argue that augmenting BPMN with *Key Performance Indicators* (KPIs) will help to support the complete BPM lifecycle (see Figure 1).

In section "Recommendations for BPEL" possible enhancements for WS-BPEL are introduced. Since BPMN allows graphical notations that can contain cycles, a great improvement would be if WS-BPEL's flow activity would allow for a straightforward mapping. While this is not part of the WS-BPEL 2.0 standard, vendors have introduced appropriate language extensions to handle such cases.

Finally, we will discuss the issue of a global choreography model. We will describe why, in the authors' opinion, neither SCA nor other proposed choreography approaches such as WS-CDL (Kavantzas et al., 2005) are well suited to fill the gap of a good model for describing choreographies. We will also share some thoughts on how the situation could be improved.

Recommendations for BPMN

Monitoring is an essential part of the BPM lifecycle. It is important to monitor the execution of a business process, since this runtime information should be used as feedback in order to improve the business process model (see the backward connection from Monitor and Optimize to Model and Simulate in Figure 1).

Such runtime information is usually described as Key Performance Indicators (KPIs). KPIs are abstract entities that help an enterprise defining and measuring progress towards organizational goals. The cost of an activity is an example for a KPI. It is associated with a concrete metric, such as a currency unit. In the simulation phase of the process, the cost of the activity has been estimated with e.g. 500 Euros. While executing and monitoring the process it has been found that the actual cost of the activity exceeds the estimated cost. In order to achieve the overall cost goals of the process, the process model must be improved. Therefore, the process could be changed such that the activity in question is executed less often.

In the languages presented so far (BPMN, SCA and WS-BPEL), there is no possibility to model Key Performance Indicators. Supporting KPIs closes another important gap in the BPM lifecycle.

Recommendations for BPEL

As we've seen, looking at the mapping from BPMN models to WS-BPEL process definitions, many elements of a BPMN diagram map nicely to WS-BPEL's flow activity, containing activities that are connected with control links. Other elements, however, have no direct representation in a WS-BPEL flow, requiring the mapping to make use of structured activities and handlers in WS-BPEL processes. Although this is a completely valid approach, the resulting WS-BPEL process definition is often difficult to understand as its structure is not directly recognizable, compared to the original BPMN diagram, complicating reverse mapping or problem determination.

To illustrate this, we take a closer look at three concrete cases arising from typical BPMN scenarios: cyclic flows, deferred choices and faults.

Cyclic control dependencies are disallowed for activities in a WS-BPEL flow activity. As a result, any repeating sequence of steps, modeled as BPMN sequence flow diagrams with a cyclic graph structure, must be mapped to one of WS-BPEL's loop activities (while, repeatUntil, forEach). Moreover, when cyclic graph structures and parallelism are mixed in BPMN, it is possible that the result is not structurally correct and therefore cannot be mapped to WS-BPEL.

The "Deferred Choice" control flow pattern models a situation where a choice is triggered by an external event. In BPMN, it is represented as an event-based exclusive gateway followed by a number of message or wait events. This has no direct representation in a WS-BPEL flow and must be mapped to a WS-BPEL pick activity, which again does no longer preserve the original graph structure.

BPMN also allows handling faults via a sequence flow to an activity dealing with the exceptional situation. WS-BPEL concepts do now allow a direct continuation of the control flow via a link representing the exceptional situation. Instead, modeling BPMN exception flows requires a mapping to fault handlers associated with WS-BPEL scopes.

The following sections illustrate what WS-BPEL extensions allowing a more direct mapping of the above mentioned BPMN scenarios might look like.

WS-BPEL Extension for Cyclic Flows

The concepts introduced for the SESE region analysis mentioned earlier provide the foundation for the introduction of a BPEL flow extension allowing for control flow cycles. This WS-BPEL extension for cyclic flows also supports the explicit specification of split and join semantics in the same way as BPMN's parallel (AND), inclusive (IOR) or exclusive (XOR) gateways. It addresses most real-world scenarios and avoids such semantic difficulties.

Supporting cyclic control dependencies in a WS-BPEL flow activity does not imply allowing arbitrary flow graphs: their structural correctness is still required. Consider a cyclic flow graph containing a fork where one branch leaves the loop but the other does not. This is a situation also called a "lack of synchronization", as reported in (Sadiq and Orlowska, 2000) – one example for a structurally incorrect flow graph.

To validate structural correctness of extended flow graphs, region analysis is used to decompose the graph into regions with either control cycles (cyclic region), parallel processing (parallel region), or none of the two (sequential region). Extended flow graphs containing a region that is both cyclic and parallel are structurally incorrect. Regions can be recursively nested, allowing to arbitrarily combine cyclic, parallel and sequential behavior in extended flow graphs. Figure 7 shows a standard WS-BPEL flow graph with fork/join semantics which is acyclic (left) and extension flow graphs with split/merge semantics for which cycles are allowed (right).

WS-BPEL Extension for Deferred Choices

We saw that the "Deferred Choice" control flow pattern can be mapped to a standard WS-BPEL pick activity, with the drawback of losing the graph structure of the original BPMN diagram. In order to support a "Deferred Choice" properly in a BPEL flow activity, one must distinguish two cases.

First, the deferred choice may be taken at the beginning of a flow activity. In other words, the event causing the choice to be made is a start event creating a new process instance. In this case, it is sufficient to indicate that multiple BPEL receive activities belong to a group for which the exclusive

Figure 7. Control Cycles and Fork/Join vs. Split/Merge Semantics

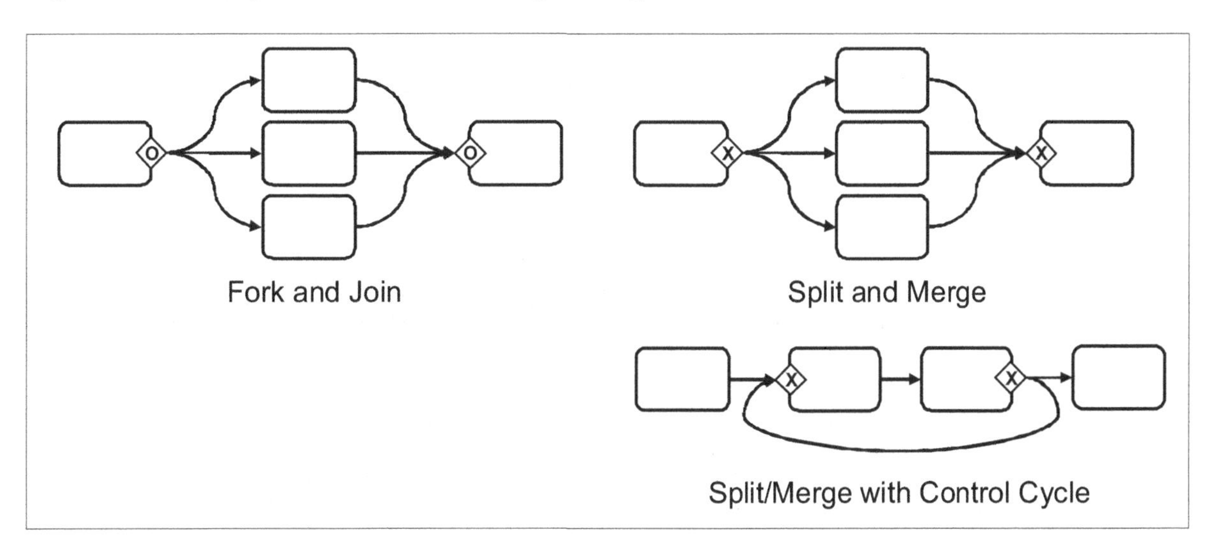

choice is made. When a message event occurs then the remaining receive activities can be "disabled" such that only one path is taken.

Second, the deferred choice may be taken within a flow activity, i.e. the process instance already exists, then the corresponding BPEL flow definition needs to provide a choice between a number of given message or timer events. For this purpose, BPEL receive and wait activities can be modeled as targets of links with a common source activity. Again, the receive/wait activities form a group for which an exclusive choice is made and remaining receive/wait activities are disabled.

Figure 8 shows two flow graphs implementing the Deferred Choice control flow pattern, one case where the message event instantiates a new process instance (left) and one case where the message or timer event occurs in an existing process instance (right).

WS-BPEL Extension for Fault Links

Links in a WS-BPEL flow activity are only taken during regular control flow navigation. In case of a fault, instead of terminating all running activities in a scope and invoking a fault handler, it is proposed that a special kind of link may be used for faults. Similar to associating a link with a transition condition (refer to the WS-BPEL standard for more information), a link could alternatively be associated with a fault name and optional fault data. Instead of resuming navigation in a fault handler, a fault then causes the fault link to be navigated.

Figure 9 shows a flow graph with standard BPEL links associated with transition conditions (both p_1 and p_2) and links associated with faults – the first fault link is taken when fault f_1 occurs and the second fault link is taken when fault f_2 occurs. The links are evaluated in the order of appearance, i.e. like for BPEL fault handlers, the first matching fault link is taken. If a fault occurs then the regular links are not navigated.

The benefit of introducing fault links as an extension to WS-BPEL is a preservation of the BPMN flow graph structure when mapping a BPMN process model containing exception flows to WS-BPEL. Furthermore, this extension also offers a WS-BPEL flow designer the capability for dealing with exceptional situations in a more local fashion. In other words, a fault can be handled where it occurs, without leaving the flow activity.

Improved Mapping and Further Considerations

Using the proposed WS-BPEL language extensions outlined above, the BPMN example from

Figure 8. Flow implementing the Deferred Choice Control Flow Pattern

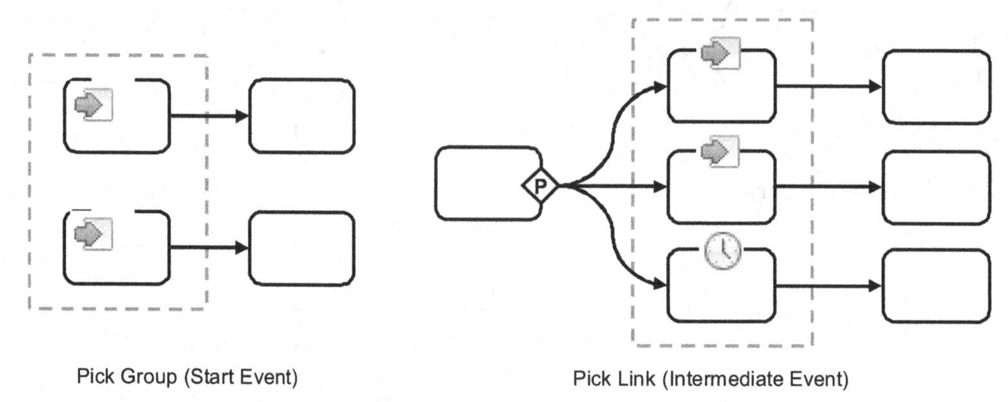

Figure 9. Flow Links Associated with Faults

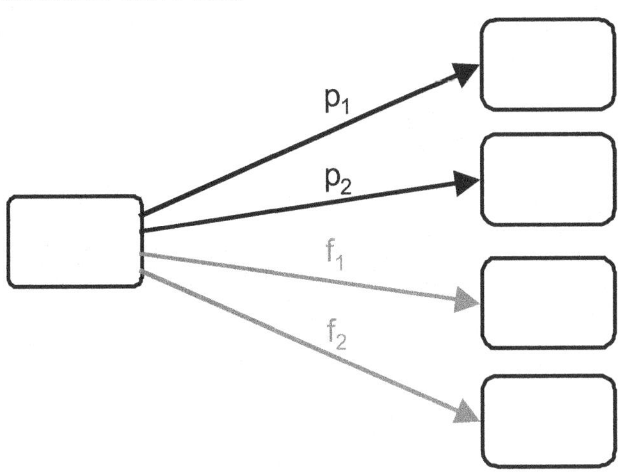

Figure 2 could be mapped in a more straightforward fashion. Figure 10 shows a generalized flow activity containing a control cycle, created by the "back link" to activity "While No Order". It also shows "pick links" (as green arrows) implementing the Deferred Choice pattern, leaving the activity "Pick Event". A SESE region analysis would identify an outer region, identical to the "Generic Seller Process" itself, which has no parallelism but a cyclic graph structure, and an inner region, identical to the "Parallel Flow" activity, which allows parallelism but no cycles.

Note that two empty activities ("While No Order" and "Pick Event") have been inserted in place of BPMN gateways, which is sometimes a convenient approach for achieving an even better preservation of the original BPMN graph structure. The second "Receive Quote Request" activity has been introduced for two reasons: first, the generalized flow activity needs a unique starting point; second, it preserves the BPEL rule that a start activity (which instantiates the process) is not the target of a link. Finally, the "Pick Event" activity has been introduced such that the "pick links" have one common source activity.

So far, it has been shown how existing languages can help to achieve Business Process Management solutions, and some extensions to these existing languages have been proposed to further simplify existing weaknesses. However, one gap remains to be addressed: the lack of a global description of a service choreography. As pointed out earlier, SCA can only address certain aspects of it: By restricting itself to a SCA domain, an SCA definition is only valid within an organization, and hence not capable of addressing a global choreography model addressing multiple B2B partners.

The Web Services – Choreography Description Language (WS-CDL) (Kavantzas et al., 2005) has promised to solve this problem; however, the authors see several issues with that. WS-CDL introduces concepts that overlap with the WS-BPEL 2.0 standard, such as a number of activity types, the ordering of activities, partner links, or exception handling. WS-CDL lacks modularity and therefore composability with other Web services standards by reinventing type definitions (already addressed by XML Schema) and its relationship to WS-Policy is left unspecified. Moreover, WS-CDL does not address the important choreography aspect of behavioral compatibility (Martens and Moser, 2006).

Behavioral compatibility describes the property whether messages produced by one process can be consumed by another process in such a way

Figure 10. BPEL Mapping revisited

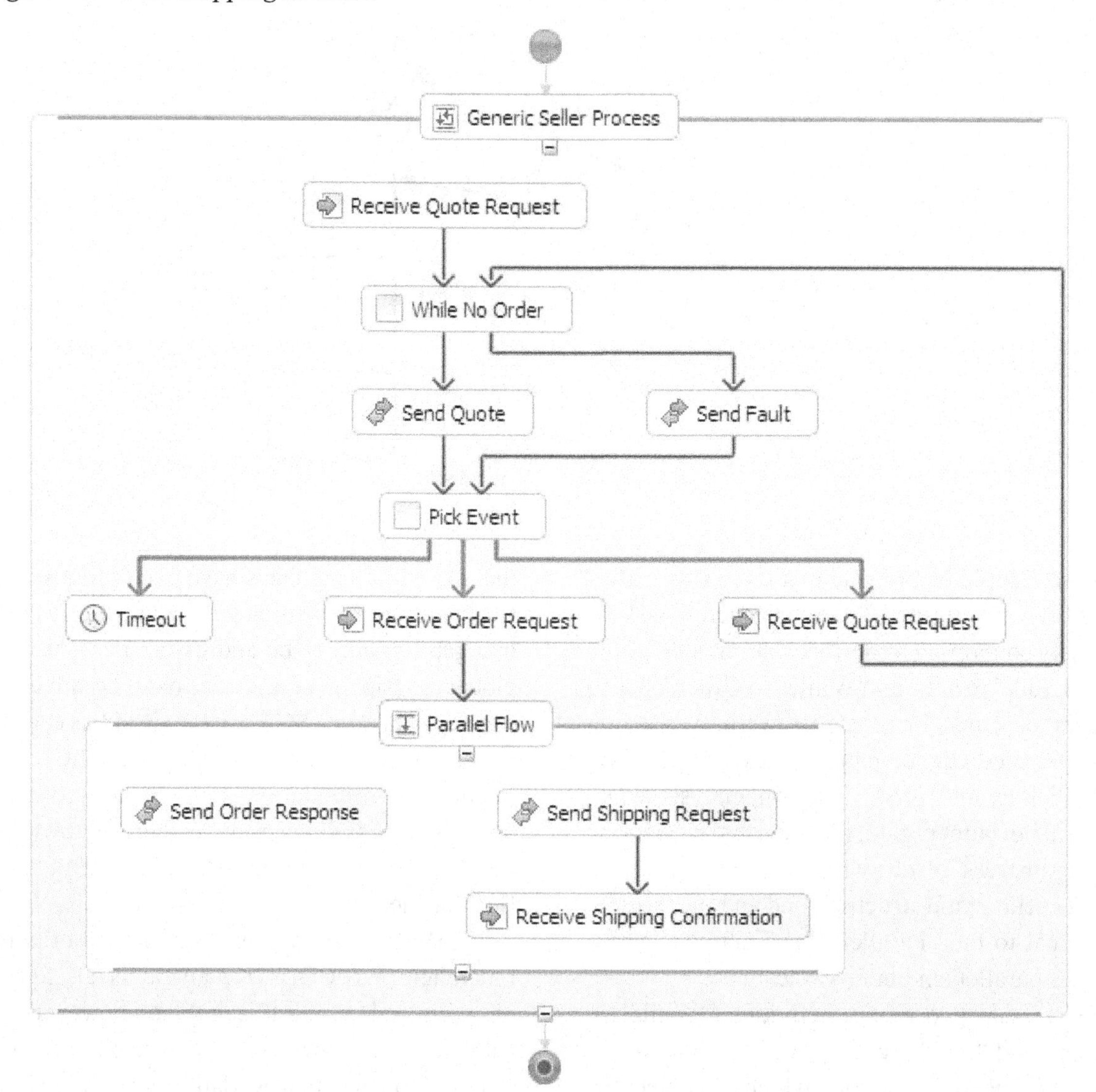

that the interaction does not cause a deadlock.

A better approach is provided a language called BPEL4Chor (Decker et al., 2007). BPEL4Chor offers a means to describe choreographies by extending WS-BPEL 2.0 in three aspects.

- The first extension is a description for each participant's behavior. It defines the control flow dependencies between WS-BPEL activities, in particular between communication activities, for a given participant in the choreography.
- Second, the topology between participants is described. A participant topology defines the structural aspects of a service choreography by specifying participant types, participant references, and message links (used to interconnect the participants).
- The third extension is a participant grounding. Participant groundings define the actual

technical configuration of the choreography, which becomes Web service-specific. In other words, concrete configurations for data formats and port types for each participant are established.

WS-BPEL itself remains unchanged, and the extensions support a better integration between service choreographies and orchestrations. By having participant behavior descriptions, it also enables checking behavioral compatibility.

BPEL4Chor, on the other side, is not using the concepts of WS-BPEL Abstract Processes but introduces a similar participant behavior description. It limits itself to choreographies containing only BPEL processes and also has some overlap with SCA Assembly Model. Thus, BPEL4Chor can be considered a step in the right direction; however, in order to cover real-world choreographies, further work remains to be done to reconcile concepts from SCA and BPEL4Chor, as an open standard.

CONCLUSION AND OUTLOOK

In this chapter, we have shown how the dichotomy between modeling and execution can be addressed by a set of well-known standards. BPMN provides a graphical notation suitable for a non-technical audience to describe business processes and choreographies. First, we have been enhancing an existing mapping from BPMN to WS-BPEL, showing how certain improvements could help achieving an even smoother mapping between the two. Second, we have also introduced new mappings from BPMN, targeting SCA and BPEL4People.

This set of existing standards and proposed improvements allows targeting the whole stack of modeling, deployment and execution of (interacting) business processes. To fully cover the entire BPM life-cycle, it has been shown that extensions for monitoring are still required. Finally, various approaches for models describing global choreographies have been discussed. Additional work is needed to address aspects not covered in this chapter, e.g., mapping of BPMN timer start events, or BPMN rule-based events.

After summarizing this chapter and giving some ideas for future work, we will conclude this section with an outlook: Currently, there is an ongoing effort at the OMG standardization body to create BPMN 2.0 (OMG, 2008b). This effort aims at a version 2.0 of BPMN, renaming the acronym to Business Process Model and Notation. This emphasizes that BPMN 2.0 will focus not only on the notation, but also on the model, including its semantics and including its serialization, to allow for model interchange with well-defined semantics. Also, work on WS-BPEL and its extensions progresses at OASIS to provide a fuller set of business process execution capabilities. Through their evolution, BPMN and WS-BPEL have benefitted from each other and continue to do so. In the foreseeable future we expect versions of BPMN and WS-BPEL that in their combination truly cover the entire BPM life-cycle.

EXERCISES

Beginner:

a. Outline the differences between a service choreography and a service orchestration. Describe which of the three languages BPMN, SCA and BPEL covers which aspects. Explain why SCA in its current form is not suited to describe choreographies.
b. Use BPMN notation to model a travel reservation process consisting of the following steps:
   - A reception activity that receives a travel request
   - A human task that validates the request (executed by user role "clerk")

- Another human task for searching the cheapest airline (executed by user role "travel agent"). Note that the human tasks must be grouped in appropriate lanes.
- A set of parallel activities for booking a flight, a hotel, and a car
- A cycle for looping back to the airline search if any of the bookings failed
- A reply activity that delivers the travel confirmation to the client

Intermediate:

c. Take the process modeled in exercise (b), and appropriately transform it to standard BPEL 2.0 (without extensions) and SCA.
d. BPEL 2.0 in its current form is not capable of describing cyclic BPMN diagrams in a graphical way. Why? Name (at least) two concepts by which BPEL has to be extended in order to allow such a transformation.
e. Take the process modeled in exercise b) and transform it to extended BPEL.

Advanced:

f. Create the SESE regions for the process created in e), and identify for each region whether the region has parallel, cyclic or sequential (neither parallel nor cyclic) behavior.

SUGGESTED ADDITIONAL READING

In this chapter, we have been given short introductions to the relevant standards. However, in detail knowledge of these standards is crucial. Therefore, the authors suggest getting an in depth understanding of the WS-BPEL 2.0 standard (OASIS, 2007) as well as the BPMN standard (OMG, 2008a). The SCA standards are still under construction (OSOA, 2007), however it might be worth keeping an eye on the progress in this area. Very relevant for the understanding of BPMN user tasks and the corresponding WS-BPEL extensions is the BPEL4People whitepaper (Active Endpoints et al., 2007), which is currently also undergoing standardization. Due to the issues discussed in BPMN to BPEL section, the method described by Vanhatalo, Völzer and Leymann (2007) to detect and classify regions in process models is highly recommended for additional studies, since in the opinion of the authors it offers the most promising approach to decide whether a BPMN model has a correct executable semantic.

REFERENCES

Active Endpoints, Adobe, BEA, IBM, Oracle, SAP AG (2007): *WS-BPEL Extension for people.* Retrieved March 30, 2008 from IBM's Web site: http://www.ibm.com/developerworks/webservices/library/specification/ws-bpel4people/

Decker, G., Kopp, O., Leymann, F. and Weske, M.(2007, July) BPEL4Chor: Extending BPEL for Modeling Choreographies. In *Proceedings of the IEEE 2007 International Conference on Web Services* (ICWS), Salt Lake City, Utah. IEEE Computer Society.

Eclipse Foundation. (n.d.). *The Eclipse BPEL designer.* Web Site: http://www.eclipse org/bpel

Kavantzas, N., Burdett, D., Ritzinger, G., Fletcher, T. and Lafon, Y.(2005). *Web Services Choreography Description Language* Version 1.0, W3C Candidate Recommendation. Web Site: http://www.w3.org/TR/ws-cdl-10/

Martens, A., Moser, S.(2006, September). Diagnosing SCA components using WOMBAT. In P*roceedings of BPM'06, 4th International Conference on Business Process Management,* Vienna, Austria (LNCS 4102).

OASIS (2007): *Web Service Business Process Execution Language (WS-BPEL)* Version 2.0, OASIS Standard, April 2007, OASIS Technical Committee, http://docs.oasis-open.org/wsbpel/2.0/OS/wsbpel-v2.0-OS.pdf

OMG (2008a). *Business Process Modeling Notation (BPMN),* Version 1.1, OMG Available Specification, January 2008, http://www.omg.org/spec/BPMN/1.1/PDF

OMG (2008b). *Business Process Modeling Notation (BPMN),* Version 2.0, Request For Proposal, February 2008, http://www.bpmn.org/Documents/BPMN%202-0%20RFP%2007-06-05.pdf

OSOA (2007). *Service Component Architecture Specifications - Open SOA collaboration.* Retrieved March 21, 2007 from OSOA's Web Site: http://www.osoa.org/display/Main/Service+Component+Architecture+Specifications

Russel, N., ter Hofstede, A.H.M., van der Aalst, W.M.P et al (2006). *Workflow Control-Flow Patterns: A Revised View,* BPM Center Report BPM-06-22, BPMcenter.org, 2006, Web Site: http://www.workflowpatterns.com/documentation/documents/BPM-06-22.pdf

Sadiq, W. and Orlowska, M.E. (2000). Analysing process models using graph reduction techniques. *Information Systems 25*(2), pp. 117–134

Vanhatalo, J., Völzer, H., and Leymann, F. (2007): *Faster and more focused control-flow analysis for business process models through SESE decomposition,* Service-Oriented Computing (ICSOC 2007), (Lecture Notes in Computer Science, 4749). Springer.

Chapter V
Yet Another Workflow Language:
Concepts, Tool Support, and Application

Chun Ouyang
Queensland University of Technology, Australia

Michael Adams
Queensland University of Technology, Australia

Arthur H. M. ter Hofstede
Queensland University of Technology, Australia

ABSTRACT

Due to the absence of commonly accepted conceptual and formal foundations for workflow management, and more generally Business Process Management (BPM), a plethora of approaches to process modelling and execution exists both in academia and in industry. The introduction of workflow patterns provided a deep and language independent understanding of modelling issues and requirements encountered in business process specification. They provide a comparative insight into various approaches to process specification and serve as guidance for language and tool development. YAWL (Yet Another Workflow Language) is a novel and formally defined workflow language based on workflow patterns and Petri nets, thus leveraging off both practical and theoretical insights in the field of BPM. This chapter provides an overview of this language and its corresponding open source support environment.

INTRODUCTION

There exists an abundance of approaches to business process modelling and execution. This is partly due to the lack of commonly accepted conceptual and formal foundations. Standardisation efforts over time, while significant in number and level of industry support, have not (fully) succeeded in providing such foundations. In order to provide a deeper insight into constructs used in business process specification and execution, a collection of workflow patterns was introduced (van der Aalst, ter Hofstede, Kiepuszewski & Barros, 2003). Note that the word "patterns" here refers to components within business processes that have generic applicability and are recurrent in form.

The original patterns collection focussed on control-flow specification only and derived from an analysis of a number of commercially available systems and research prototypes. Over time, this pattern collection was revised (Russell, ter Hofstede, van der Aalst & Mulyar, 2006) and extended with patterns for the data perspective (Russell, ter Hofstede, Edmond & van der Aalst, 2005), the resource perspective (Russell, van der Aalst, ter Hofstede & Edmond, 2005), and exception handling (Russell, van der Aalst & ter Hofstede, 2006). The original control-flow patterns have been used for comparing process modelling languages, tool selection and as a basis for language development.

While Petri nets have a number of distinct advantages for the specification of executable processes (van der Aalst, 1996), they lack sufficient support for a number of the originally identified workflow control-flow patterns (van der Aalst & ter Hofstede, 2002). This observation led to the development of YAWL (Yet Another Workflow Language) (van der Aalst & ter Hofstede, 2005), a formally defined language that took Workflow nets (van der Aalst, 1997), which are based on Petri nets, as a starting point and introduced a number of constructs directly supporting those patterns. As such, YAWL provides powerful support for control-flow specification, and over time an open source support environment was developed which also provided support for the specification of data aspects, resource aspects and exception handling.

It is worthwhile noting that when it comes to the derivation of executable process models, two fundamentally different approaches can be observed. In the first approach emphasis is on the specification of intuitive models, easily understood by the various stakeholders, using an informal language. These models are subsequently to be transformed to models captured in an executable language. A typical example of this approach is BPMN (OMG, 2006) combined with BPEL (Jordan & Evdemon, 2007) (mappings from BPMN to BPEL are, for example, described in (Ouyang, Dumas, van der Aalst, ter Hofstede & Mendling, 2008)).

In the second approach, process models are captured in a formal language of which the models are directly executable. YAWL falls in the latter category and in this chapter this language and its support environment are examined in some depth. Firstly, the workflow patterns are elaborated upon and a brief overview of approaches to process specification is presented. Secondly, the specification of the various aspects involved in business process modelling using YAWL is studied. Thirdly, the support environment of YAWL is examined. Fourthly, we present a case study of the application of the YAWL environment in the film and TV domain. Finally, we conclude the paper briefly listing, among others, a number of current research topics in BPM.

BACKGROUND

Workflow Patterns

To gain a better understanding of the fundamental concepts underpinning business processes, the Workflow Patterns Initiative (www.workflowpatterns.com) was conceived in the late 1990s with the goal of identifying the core architectural constructs inherent in process technology. After almost a decade of research, more than 120 workflow patterns have been identified in the control-flow, data, and resource perspectives. The control-flow perspective captures aspects related to execution order of various tasks in a process, e.g. sequence, choice, parallelism and synchronization. The data perspective describes how data elements are defined and utilised during the execution of a process. The resource perspective deals with the overall organisational context in which a process functions and the issue of resource to task allocation. In addition to these, the exception handling perspective deals with the various causes of exceptions and the various actions that need to be taken as a result of exceptions occurring. In the following we outline the patterns in each of these perspectives.

Control-flow patterns describe structural characteristics of a business process and the manner in which the thread of execution flows through the process model. Originally 20 control-flow patterns were proposed (van der Aalst, ter Hofstede, Kiepuszewski & Barros, 2003), but in the latest review this has grown to 43 patterns (Russell, ter Hofstede, van der Aalst & Mulyar, 2006). These patterns can be classified into eight categories:

1. **Basic control-flow patterns.** These capture elementary aspects of process control such as sequential, parallel and conditional routing, and are similar to the definitions of these concepts initially proposed by the Workflow Management Coalition (1999). Examples are *Exclusive Choice* (XOR-split) and *Simple Merge* (XOR-join) patterns.
2. **Advanced branching and synchronization patterns.** These characterise more complex branching and merging concepts that arise in business processes. Examples are the *Multi-Choice* (*OR-split*) pattern, which supports selection of a number of branches based on their conditions, and the *Synchronising Merge* (*OR-join*) pattern, which performs simple merging, partial synchronisation, or full synchronisation depending on the context.
3. **Multiple instance patterns.** These describe situations where there are multiple threads of execution active in a process model related to the same activity.
4. **State-based patterns.** These reflect situations that are most easily modelled in process languages with an explicit notion of state. An example is the *Deferred Choice* pattern which captures the scenario when the choice among a set of alternative conditional branches is delayed until the processing in one of these branches is actually started.
5. **Iteration patterns.** These capture repetitive behaviour in a process, such as looping.
6. **Trigger patterns.** These deal with external signals required to initiate certain work items.
7. **Cancellation patterns.** These categorize the various cancellation scenarios that may be relevant to certain work items.
8. **Termination patterns.** These address the issue of when the execution of a process is considered to be finished.

Data patterns aim to capture a series of data characteristics that occur repeatedly in business processes. In total 40 patterns were defined (Russell, ter Hofstede, Edmond & van der Aalst, 2005), which can be divided into four distinct groups. Firstly, *data visibility patterns* identify the potential contexts of a process in which a data element is defined and can be reused, e.g. to capture *production* information, or to manage *monitoring* data or to capture *interaction* with the external environment. Secondly, *data interaction patterns* describe the various ways in which data elements can be passed between active components (e.g. tasks and sub-processes) within a process (i.e. *internal data interaction*) and also between those components and the external environment with which the process interacts (i.e. *external data interaction*). Thirdly, *data transfer patterns*, which can be seen as an extension to the data interaction patterns, focussing on the manner in which the *actual* transfer of data elements occurs between process components, that is, how data elements can be passed across the interface of a process component. Lastly, *data-based routing patterns* characterise the manner in which data elements can influence the operation of other process perspectives.

Resource patterns aim to capture the various ways in which resources are represented and utilized in business processes. In total 43 patterns were identified (Russell, van der Aalst, ter Hofstede & Edmond, 2005), which can be classified into seven categories mostly based on the typical work item lifecycle (which includes states such as *offered, allocated* and *started*). These are: *creation patterns,* which correspond to design-time work allocation directives for individual work items; *push patterns,* in which the system proactively distributes work items to human resources; *pull patterns,* in which resources proactively identify and commit to executing specific work items; *detour patterns,* which involve the re-routing of work items which have already been distributed to one or more resources, either at the instigation of the resource(s) or the system; *auto-start patterns,* which describe the automated commencement of individual work items based on various criteria; *visibility patterns,* which deal with the configuration of the visibility of unallocated and allocated work items for certain participants; and *multiple resource patterns,* which correspond to work allocations involving multiple participants or resources.

Finally, *exception patterns* form a classification framework for dealing with exceptions that occur during the execution of a process. In general, an exception relates to a specific work item in an instance of a process (or *case*) being executed. The exception handling strategies are proposed respectively at work item level (e.g. re-allocating a work item to a different resource due to the unavailability of the resource that the work item was allocated to) and at case level (e.g. removing all remaining work items in the current case). Consideration is given to what recovery action needs to be taken to remedy the effects caused by an exception occurring (e.g. to *compensate* for the effects of the exception). Based on the above, and taking into account the various alternatives identified for each of these aspects, *135* possible patterns were conceived (Russell, van der Aalst & ter Hofstede, 2006) which provide support for a range of exception types including work item failure, deadline expiry and resource unavailability.

Approaches to Process Modelling and Execution

The workflow patterns have been used to evaluate a wide range of existing workflow products and standards in terms of the control-flow, data, resource, and exception handling perspectives. They have been found to be especially useful for the comparison of process languages, for tool selection, and also for the identification of specific strengths and weaknesses of individual tools and languages. Details of these evaluation results and impact the workflow patterns have made in the past few years can be found on the web site of the Workflow Patterns Initiative.

The original 20 control-flow patterns were used to evaluate workflow systems such as Staffware Process Suite, IBM's WebSphere, and the case handling system FLOWer. The results of these evaluations showed that workflow systems at the time typically provided limited support for these patterns. Later, established process modelling techniques such as Petri nets, EPCs, UML Activity Diagrams (both versions 1.4 and 2.0) and BPMN were also subjected to a patterns-based analysis. Petri nets have at least three distinct advantages for being used as a workflow language: 1) they have a formal foundation; 2) they are state-based instead of (just) event-based, hence they can make a proper distinction between the execution of tasks and moments where the process is awaiting further execution-related decisions; and 3) the existence of an abundance of analysis techniques (van der Aalst, 1996). Petri nets can also be extended with colour (i.e. data), time, and hierarchy, which makes them quite expressive compared to many process languages, e.g. they offer direct support to all state-based patterns. Nevertheless, there are serious limitations in Petri nets (as in other languages) when it comes to capturing three categories of patterns: (1) patterns involving multiple instances (a concept which supports situations where multiple instances of the same task in the same case are active at the same time); (2) advanced synchronisation patterns (specifically the so-called OR-join which waits if some of its not-yet-activated branches can be activated sometime in the future); and (3) cancellation patterns. This observation triggered the development of a new language, YAWL, which took Petri nets as a starting point and introduced mechanisms that provide direct support for the control-flow patterns, especially the above three categories of patterns.

YAWL supports both process modelling and execution. Each YAWL construct has both a graphical representation and an executable semantics, and thus a process model written in YAWL is directly executable. Some existing process languages such as BPMN and EPC (Keller, Nüttgens & Scheer, 1992) take a different approach and focus on the specification of intuitive models that can be easily understood by the various stakeholders. For process automation, these models need to be transformed to models specified in an executable language such as BPEL or YAWL. A typical example of this approach is the use of BPMN in conjunction with BPEL. However, there are obvious drawbacks to this separation of modelling and execution, especially when both languages are based on different paradigms or when the modelling language contains potentially complex concepts and little consideration was given to their precise meaning. For example, BPMN is graph-oriented, which means that a model captured in BPMN can have an arbitrary topology, whilst most BPEL constructs are block-structured, which means that if a segment of a BPEL model starts with a branching construct it ends with the corresponding synchronisation construct[1]. A mapping from BPMN to BPEL such as the one proposed in (Ouyang, Dumas, van der Aalst, ter Hofstede & Mendling, 2007) needs to handle the above mismatches properly and may still result in BPEL code that is hard to understand.

CONCEPTS

YAWL, although inspired by Petri nets, is a completely new language with its own semantics and is specifically designed for workflow specification. Initially, to overcome the limitations of Petri nets, YAWL was extended with features to facilitate patterns involving multiple instances, advanced synchronisation patterns, and cancellation patterns. Moreover, YAWL allows for hierarchical decomposition and handles arbitrarily complex data. Over time, YAWL has also been extended to support resource management, exception handling, evolving workflows, and process verification.

Control-Flow Perspective

As a formally defined language, YAWL took Workflow nets (van der Aalst, 1997), which are based on Petri nets (Murata, 1989), as a starting point to capture control-flow specification in workflows. Given that YAWL has its roots in Petri nets and Workflow nets we will first introduce these formal languages before introducing YAWL.

Petri Nets

A classical Petri net is a directed bipartite graph which consists of two types of nodes referred to as *places* (drawn as circles) and *transitions* (drawn as rectangles). Hence the nodes are connected via directed *arcs* and connections between two nodes of the same type are not allowed. A place p is called an input place of a transition t if there is a directed arc from p to t. Place p is called an output place of transition t if there is a directed arc from t to p.

Places may contain zero or more *tokens* (drawn as black dots). The state, often referred to as *marking*, is the distribution of tokens over places. A transition *t* is said to be *enabled* if each input place of *t* contains at least one token, and an enabled transition *t* may *fire*, which consumes one token from each input place of *t* and produces one token for each output place of *t*. Intuitively, if a transition *t* is used to model a task or an action, the firing of *t* resembles the occurrence of that task or action. Upon the firing of a transition, a Petri net can move from one state (i.e. marking) to another.

To give an illustrative example, we consider a simplified process of buying a house (Figure 1 shows a Petri net that models the process). First, the buyer submits a purchase offer (task *submit offer*), and waits for the result. If the offer is accepted, the buyer will be notified about the acceptance (task *notify of acceptance*), and will then receive a purchase contract (task *receive purchase contract*). Otherwise the buyer will be notified of the rejection of the offer (task *notify of rejection*), and must then decide whether to revise or to withdraw the offer. If task *revise offer* is executed, the buyer will have to wait again for notification of whether the offer is accepted or rejected. Otherwise, when task *withdraw offer* is executed the process will terminate. Upon receiving the purchase contract, the buyer carries out, in parallel, loan procurement and *house inspection*. The loan procurement involves a number of tasks. Firstly, the task *loan application* is executed. Next, task *check loan amount* is performed to find out if the loan amount exceeds 80% of the contracted purchase price. If so, the buyer needs to *buy loan insurance* to protect him/herself in case that he/she happens to suffer financially during the term of the loan. At the end of the loan procurement, the buyer will *receive loan contract* with the granted loan amount. Finally, after both loan procurement and house inspection are completed, *settle*ment can be carried out, where the buyer (with the loan provider) pays the contracted purchase price and takes possession of the house.

In Figure 1, all tasks are modelled by transitions. In addition, the transitions *exceeds 80%* and *does not exceed 80%* are added to model the two possible outcomes of executing task *check loan amount*. Places capture the states between tasks (in YAWL places will be referred to as *conditions*). For example, the output place of transition *submit offer* corresponds to the state where the potential buyer is waiting to learn whether the offer is accepted or rejected. Place *i* models the start condition and place *o* models the end condition. Initially, place *i* is marked (with a token), indicating that the process is ready to start.

Workflow Nets

A workflow process definition specifies a number of *tasks* to be executed in a specific order. There are *conditions* that correspond to causal

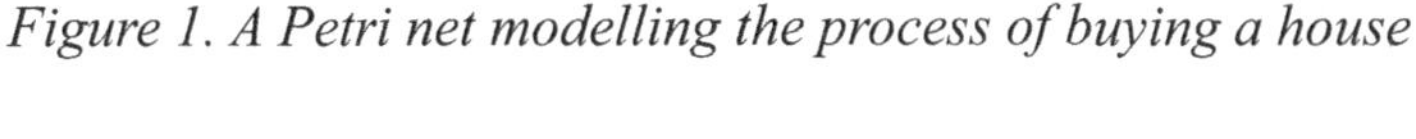

Figure 1. A Petri net modelling the process of buying a house

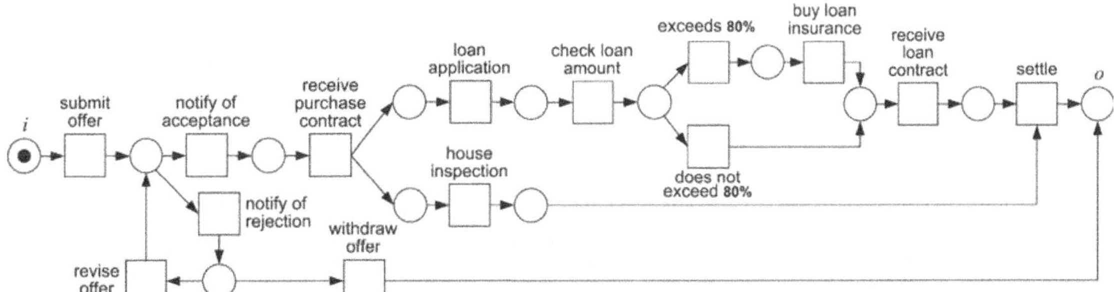

dependencies between tasks. Each task has *pre-conditions,* which should hold before the task is executed, and *post-conditions,* which should hold after execution of the task. A Petri net that models a workflow process definition is called a Workflow net (WF-net). A WF-net satisfies two requirements. First of all, there is exactly one input place (*i*) and one output place (*o*) in a WF-net. A token in place *i* represents a case (e.g. an insurance claim, a tax declaration, a purchase order, or a request for information) that needs to be handled, and a token in place *o* represents a case that has been handled. Secondly, in a WF-net there are no dangling tasks and/or conditions. Since tasks are modelled by transitions and conditions by places, this requirement implies that all transitions and places should be located on a path from the input place to the output place in a WF-net (van der Aalst, 1997). Based on the above, it can be proven that the Petri net model of the process of buying a house in Figure 1 is a WF-net.

Figure 2 shows the six routing elements for workflow modelling as they exist in WF-nets. Special notations are used to denote the fact that a task is an AND-split/join or an explicit XOR-split/join. The AND-split and the AND-join capture parallel routing and both correspond to the normal behaviour of a transition in Petri nets. The implicit XOR-split and XOR-join are modelled by places. The explicit XOR-split is modelled by a transition which produces one token in one of its output places, and the explicit XOR-join by a transition which is enabled if one of the input places contains a token. The explicit XOR-split corresponds to the Exclusive Choice pattern, and the implicit XOR-split to the Deferred Choice pattern. These patterns allow one to distinguish between a choice made by the system and a choice made by the environment. In general, there is no compelling need to distinguish between implicit and explicit XOR-joins as both capture the Simple Merge pattern.

Using the above routing elements, the WF-net modelling the previous house buying process can be re-drawn as shown in Figure 3. For example, there are two implicit XOR-splits: one corresponds to the state where the buyer is waiting for the outcome of the offer; the other corresponds to the

Figure 2. WF-net routing elements

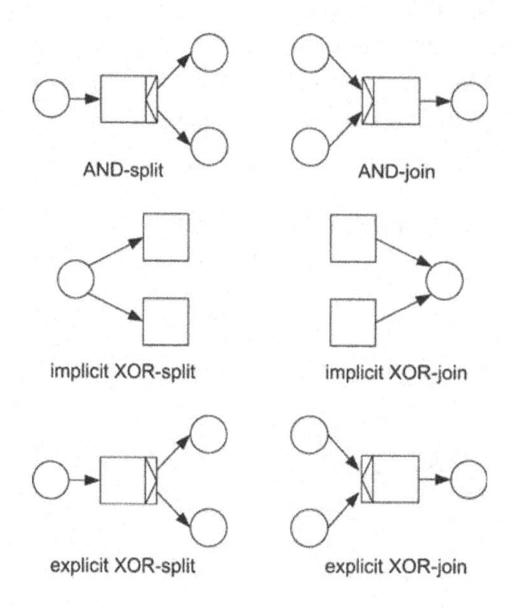

Figure 3. A WF-net modelling the house buying process in Figure 1 using routing elements

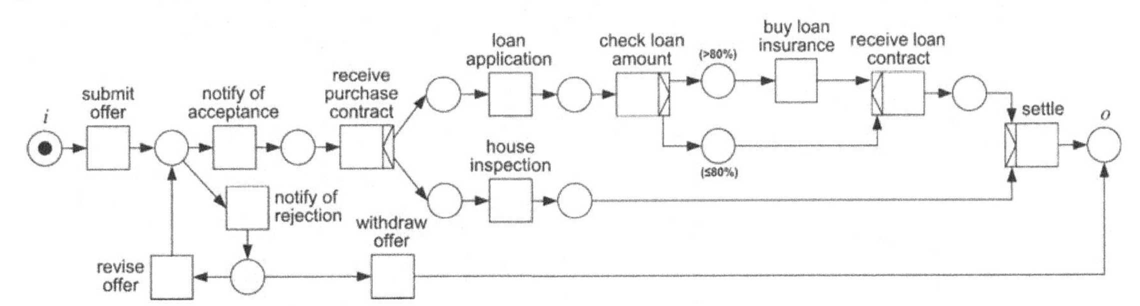

state where the buyer is deciding whether to revise or to withdraw the offer upon receipt of a rejection. In both scenarios, the choices are not made by the workflow system, but are delayed until the processing in one of the alternative branches is actually started. For example, the choice between the revision and the withdrawal of the offer is delayed until the buyer makes the decision, and at the moment when the buyer decides to withdraw the offer, the task *revise offer* is disabled.

YAWL

YAWL extends the class of WF-nets with multiple instance tasks, composite tasks, OR-joins, and cancellation regions. In contrast to Petri nets and WF-nets, YAWL's visual representation allows tasks to be directly connected as this can help compress a diagram (note this can only be done when the place in-between had one input task and one output task; the removed place formally still exists). Figure 4 shows the modelling elements of YAWL. A process definition in YAWL consists of *tasks*, which are transition-like objects, and *conditions*, which are place-like objects. Each process definition starts with a unique *input condition* and a unique *output condition*.

A workflow specification in YAWL is a set of workflow nets which forms a directed rooted graph (the root is referred to as the main or root net). There are *atomic tasks* and *composite tasks*. Atomic tasks correspond to atomic actions, i.e. actions that are either performed by a user or by a software application. Each composite task refers to a child or sub-net that contains its expansion. Both types of tasks can also be *multiple instance* tasks and thus have multiple concurrent instances at runtime.

Also, as shown in Figure 4, YAWL adopts the notations of AND/XOR-splits/joins used in WF-nets. Moreover, it introduces *OR-splits* and *OR-joins* which correspond to the Multi-Choice pattern and the Synchronising Merge pattern respectively. Finally, YAWL provides a notation for *removing tokens* from a specified region upon completion of a certain task. This is denoted by associating a dashed lasso to that task that contains the conditions and tasks from which tokens need to be removed or that need to be cancelled. This region is known as a *cancellation region* and this notion provides a generalisation of the Cancel Activity and Cancel Case patterns.

We re-consider the process definition of buying a house in Figure 1 and extend it to include sub-processes, multiple instances, advanced synchronisation, and cancellation. Figure 5 shows a YAWL net of the resulting process definition. Both *loan procurement* and *house inspection* are modelled by composite tasks that are linked to the corresponding sub-processes (shown within dot-dashed rounded boxes), respectively. Task *loan application* can have multiple instances, capturing the fact that the buyer may apply for a loan with more than one financial institution at

Figure 4. Modelling elements in YAWL (taken from (van der Aalst & ter Hofstede, 2005))

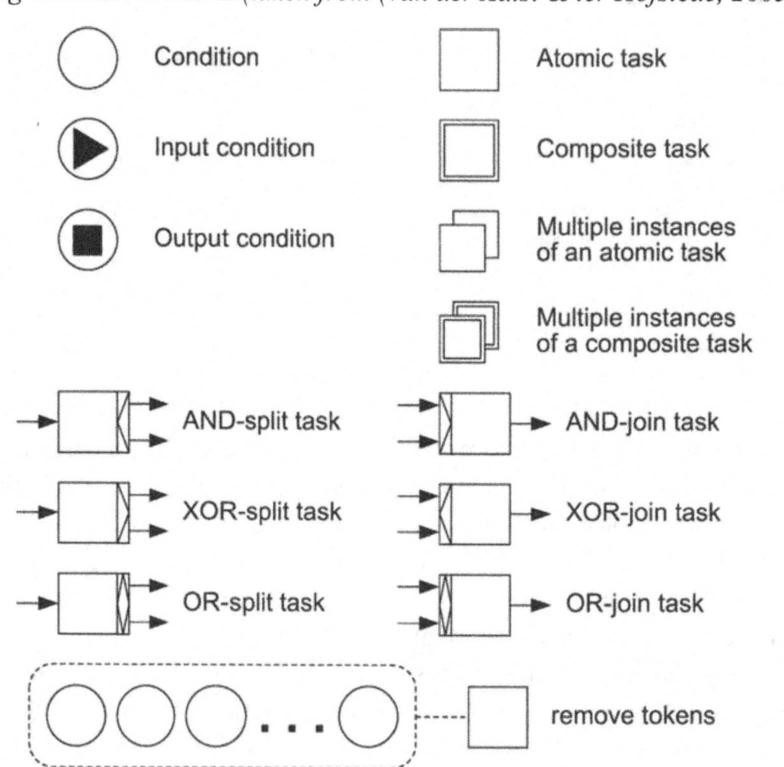

Figure 5. A YAWL net modelling the extended process of buying a house in Figure 1

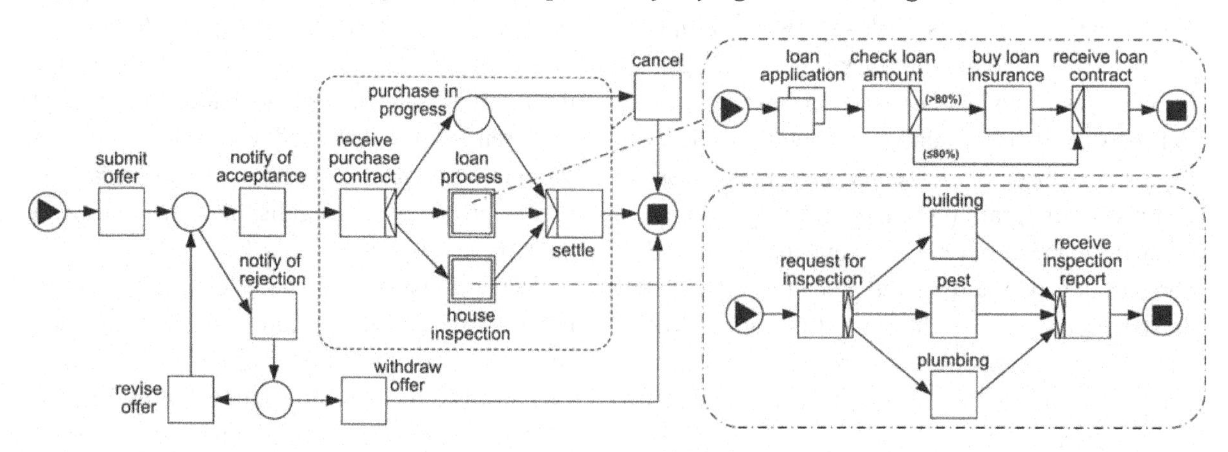

the same time to increase the chance of obtaining a loan by the due date.

In the sub-process of *house inspection*, task *request for inspection* has OR-split behaviour and task *receive inspection report* has OR-join behaviour. After a request for inspection is made, it is possible that a set of inspection tasks (*building*, *pest* and *plumbing*) are executed, possibly all, possibly one or two. The OR-join synchronises only if necessary, i.e. it will synchronise only the inspection tasks that were actually selected. In general, the semantics of OR-joins are more difficult. The synchronisation decision cannot be made *locally*, that is, just by inspecting its input places. It requires awareness of the current state of the workflow and the ability to find out whether more tokens can reach the OR-join from the current state on input branches that have not yet received a token. The definition of a suitable semantics of the OR-join within the context of YAWL can be found in (Wynn, Edmond, van der Aalst & ter Hofstede, 2005).

The process definition shown in Figure 5 also allows the withdrawal of an ongoing purchase through the execution of the task *cancel*. This task is enabled if there is a token in the place *purchase in progress*. If the environment (e.g. the buyer) decides to cancel the purchase, all tokens inside the cancellation region linked to task *cancel* will be removed.

Data Perspective

YAWL was initially designed with a focus on control-flow but has since been extended to offer full support for the data perspective. In YAWL, data values are represented as XML documents and data types are defined using XML Schema. The YAWL environment is one of the few workflow systems that completely rely on XML-based standards for handling data.

Like most programming languages, data elements are stored in variables in YAWL. There are *net variables* for storing data that can be manipulated by any individual task in a net, and *task variables* for storing data that can be used or modified only within the context of individual execution instances of a certain task. In the case of a composite task, its task variables are conceptually the net variables of the corresponding subnet linked to that task. Data passing between tasks is achieved by passing values between a net and its tasks where XQueries may be used for transformation purposes. It is not possible to directly pass data between tasks, since each task variable is local to its task (i.e. it is not accessible by other tasks). The variables of a composite task serve as intermediate variables for passing data from a higher level to a lower level of a process definition. YAWL also supports exchange of information between a process and its environment (i.e. workflow engine users and Web services). When data is required from the environment at run time, either a Web form will be generated requesting the data from the user or a Web service will be invoked that can provide the required data. In addition to the above, data elements can be defined and used for conditional routing and for the creation of multiple instances. If a task is an OR-split or XOR-split, its branching conditions are specified as XPath Boolean expressions over certain variable(s) associated with the task. The data carried by the variable(s) may determine the evaluation results of the expressions and thus determine which branch(es) will be chosen.

For example, Figure 6 depicts the data definitions associated with the OR-join task *request for inspection* in the process shown in Figure 5. There are five task variables: *PropertyInfo* (input only); *InspectDate* (output only); *needBuildingInspection* (output only); *needPestInspection* (output only); and *needPlumbingInspection* (output only). The values of input task variables are determined by the contents of the net variables through a set of inbound mappings. An example of the data obtained by the inbound mappings is shown inside the task *request for inspection*. The values of output task variables are obtained from the user input and are used to update the net variables through a set of outbound mappings. Both inbound and outbound mappings are defined using XQueries. Three Boolean variables *needBuildingInspection*, *needPestInspection* and *needPlumbingInspection* indicate respectively whether or not to take the corresponding inspection tasks, and their values are checked using XPath expressions.

For a multiple instance task, it is possible to specify a number of parameters which include: the *maximum* and *minimum* number of instances allowed, a *threshold* for completion (this can be useful to capture situations where the task can be considered complete even though not all its instances have completed), and a flag indicating whether the number of instances is fixed upon initiation of the task (*static*) or may be increased after it has started (*dynamic*). For example, in Figure 5 task "*loan application*" has its minimum set to *one* and its maximum set to *unbounded.* If the buyer wants to proceed to the next task as soon as one instance of the application completes, the value of threshold can be set to *one*. The flag is set to *static* if the buyer must decide how many loan applications to submit before submitting any, while if he/she wishes to keep the option open to submit loan applications at a later stage, the flag should be set to *dynamic*. Handling of multiple instances is far from trivial and space restrictions prevent us from providing more detail. However, it should be mentioned that the start of a multiple instance task requires the presence of instance-specific data to be assigned to each of the instances that are to be started and that its completion requires the aggregation of such data.

Resource Perspective

The third key perspective of a process, after control-flow and data, is the resource perspective. The YAWL resource perspective provides direct support for 38 of the 43 identified resource patterns – the five remaining being particular to the case-handling paradigm. In YAWL, a human resource is referred to as a *Participant*. Each participant may perform one or more *Roles*, hold one or more *Positions* (each of which belongs to an *Org Group*) and possess a number of *Capabilities*. Workflow tasks that, at runtime, are required to be performed by a participant have their resourcing requirements specified at design time concomitantly with the design of the process control-flow and data perspectives, using the YAWL process editor. Conceptually, a task has three *interaction points* (places in a task lifecycle where distribution decisions can by made by the system and/or participants):

Figure 6. Data perspective of task request for inspection in the process shown in Figure 5

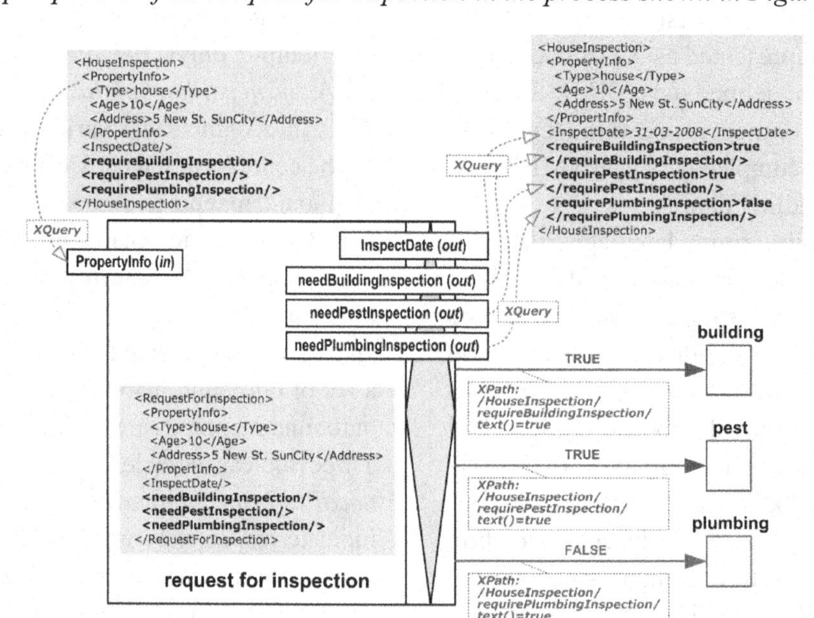

- **Offer:** A task may be offered to one or more participants for execution. There is no implied obligation (from a system perspective) for the participant to accept the offer.
- **Allocate:** A task may be allocated to a single participant, so that the participant is committed (willingly or not) to performing that task. If the task was previously offered to several other participants, the offer is withdrawn from them; and
- **Start:** A task is allocated to a participant and started (enters executing state).

Correspondingly, each participant may have, at any particular time, tasks in any of three personal work queues, one for each of the interaction points (a fourth, *suspended*, is a derivative of the *started* queue). A process designer must specify that each of the three interaction points be either user- or system-initiated. If an offer is user-initiated, it is passed to an administrator so that it can be manually offered or allocated at a later time. If an offer is system-initiated, the designer must also provide details of a *distribution set* of resources to which the offer should be made. A distribution set may consist of the union of zero or more individual participants, zero or more roles, and zero or more dynamic variables (which at runtime will be supplied with details of participants and/or roles to which the task should be offered). The resultant distribution set may be further *filtered* by specifying that only those participants with certain capabilities, occupying certain positions and/or being members of certain org groups, be included.

If an allocation is user-initiated, the task is placed on the offered queue of each of the participants in the distribution set, from which one of the participants may manually choose to allocate the task to him/herself, at which point the task is removed from the offered queues of all offered participants. If the allocation is system-initiated, an *allocation strategy* (e.g. random choice, round robin, shortest queue) is invoked that selects a single participant from the distribution set, and the task is placed on that participant's allocated queue.

Finally, if a start is user-initiated, a participant must select the task from their allocated queue to start execution of the task. If a start is system-initiated, the task is automatically started and placed in the participant's started queue for action.

A designer may also specify certain *constraints* to apply, for example that a certain task must not be performed by the same participant who completed an earlier task in a process (*Separation of Duties*), or that if a participant who is a member of the distribution set of a task is the same participant who completed a particular previous task in the process, then they must also be allocated the new task (*Familiar Task*).

At runtime, a participant, having the required *privileges* (or authorizations), can further affect the allocation and execution of tasks. If a task is allocated to them, he/she may: *deallocate* it (pass the task to an administrator for manual reallocation); *delegate* it (to a member of their 'team' – those who occupy positions that ultimately report to the participant's position); or *skip* the task (complete it immediately without first starting it). If the task has been started, a participant may *reallocate* it (to a member of their team), and in doing so may preserve the work done within the task thus far (*stateful reallocation*), or to reset the task data to its original values (*stateless reallocation*).

Further, at runtime a participant with the necessary privileges may choose to *pile* a task, so that all instances of the task across all cases of the process are directly allocated to the participant, overriding any design time resourcing specifications; and/or *chain* a task, which means that for all future tasks in the same process instance where the distribution set specified includes the participant as a member, each of those tasks are to be automatically allocated to the participant and started.

Finally, an administrator has access to a worklisted queue, which includes all of the currently active tasks whether offered, allocated or started, from which a task can be manually reoffered, reallocated or restarted.

Exception Handling

Ideally, cases are handled following the process description as it was prepared at design time. However, it is possible that unexpected events occur during execution. Deviations from normal execution are often termed *exceptions*[2]. Below, we discuss the notion of a *workflow exception* (or exception for short) at the business process level and the various ways in which they can be triggered and handled. We also describe a generic workflow exception handling language and how it is used to specify exception handling strategies. For illustrative examples, we use process models in YAWL. The discussion is based on the work presented in (Russell, van der Aalst & ter Hofstede, 2006).

An exception is a distinct, identifiable event which occurs at a specific point of time during the execution of a workflow. Exception events can be classified into five groups: *work item failure*; *deadline expiry*; *resource unavailability*; *external trigger*; and *constraint violation*. For example, *resource unavailability* refers to a problem with work item allocation that arises when no resource can be found that meets the specified allocation criteria.

In general an exception relates to a specific work item in a case of a process being executed. The exception handling strategies are thus proposed at both work item level and case level. At work item level, how to handle an exception that occurs for a specific work item depends on the current state of execution of the work item. For example, consider that a work item has been *allocated* to a specific resource. This resource could become unavailable and a strategy that could be chosen is to *re-allocate* the work item to a different resource; it could also be *re-offered* to a number of resources. Based on the execution lifecycle for a work item, *fifteen* strategies for exception handling at work item level are proposed, and details can be found in (Russell, van der Aalst & ter Hofstede, 2006). At the case level the issue arises as to what to do with the case itself when an exception occurs. There are three alternative strategies for handling workflow cases that involve exceptions: (1) *continue the workflow case* and not interfere with the execution of work items not associated with the exception that occurred; (2) *remove the current case* and remove all associated work items; and (3) *remove all cases* of the affected process and remove all work items associated with any case of the process involved. After exception handling has occurred at the work item and the case level, consideration needs to be given to what recovery action needs to be taken to remedy the effects caused by the occurrence of the exception. There are three alternate courses of action: *no action* (i.e. do nothing); *rollback* the effects of the exception; or *compensate* for the effects of the exception.

The action taken in response to an exception can be specified as a pattern that succinctly describes the form of recovery that will be attempted. An exception pattern is represented in the form of a tuple comprising three elements: (1) how the work item associated with the exception should be handled; (2) how the case and other related cases of the process model in which the exception is raised should be handled; and 3) what recovery action (if any) is to be undertaken. From the various alternatives identified for each of these elements (see above) *135* combinations were identified as meaningful (Russell, van der Aalst & ter Hofstede, 2006). For example, the pattern (*reallocate*, *continue workflow case*, *no action*) may be specified for a *resource unavailability* exception for the *pest inspection* task in the house buying process shown in Figure 5. It indicates that if a work item corresponding to the *pest inspection* task has been allocated to a specific resource that is unavailable, then the work item is *reallocated* to a difference resource. Other than this, the current workflow case continues and no specific recovery action is undertaken.

Figure 7 provides an overview of suggested graphical notations for exception handling primitives, which are for the most part realised in the YAWL environment. The YAWL environment provides comprehensive support for exception handling based on the framework presented in this section, though it should be pointed out that the current implementation does not provide full support (e.g. it does not support rollbacks nor does it yet deal with the resource unavailable exception). It also offers a further case-handling strategy not covered by the framework, as one can indicate that upon the occurrence of a certain exception all *ancestor* cases of a certain case need to be removed. For reasons of space we refer the interested reader to (Adams, ter Hofstede, van der Aalst & Edmond, 2007) for a detailed treatment of exception handling in the YAWL environment.

Dynamic Workflow

Workflow management systems are used to configure and control structured business processes from which well-defined workflow models and instances can be derived. However, the proprietary process definition frameworks imposed make it difficult to support: (i) dynamic evolution (i.e. modifying process definitions during execution) following unexpected or developmental change in the business processes being modelled; and (ii) deviations from the prescribed process model at runtime.

Without support for dynamic evolution, the occurrence of a process deviation requires either suspension of execution while the deviation is handled manually, or an entire process abort. However, since most processes are long and complex, neither manual intervention nor process termination are satisfactory solutions. Manual handling incurs an added penalty: the corrective actions undertaken are not added to "organisational memory", and so natural process evolution is not incorporated into future iterations of the process.

The YAWL system provides support for flexibility and dynamic exception handling through the concept of *worklets*, (Adams, ter Hofstede, Edmond & van der Aalst, 2006), an extensible repertoire of self-contained sub-processes and

Figure 7. Exception handling primitives (Taken from (Russell, van der Aalst & ter Hofstede, 2006))

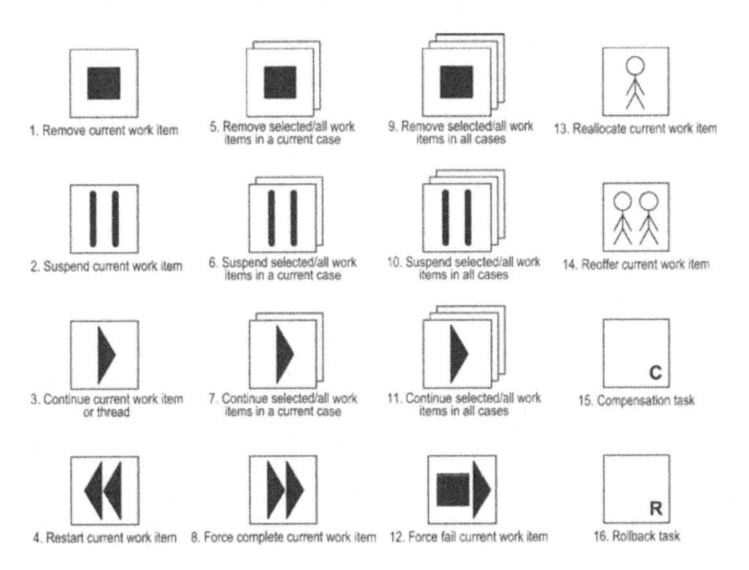

associated selection rules, grounded in a formal set of work practice principles derived from Activity Theory (Leontiev, 1978). This approach directly provides for dynamic change and process evolution without having to resort to off-system intervention and/or system downtime.

Flexibility is supported by allowing a process designer to designate certain workitems to each be substituted at runtime with a dynamically selected worklet, which contextually handles one specific task in a larger, composite process activity. Each worklet is a complete extended workflow net (EWF-net) compliant with Definition 1 of the YAWL semantics in (van der Aalst & ter Hofstede, 2005). An extensible repertoire of worklets is maintained for each task in a specification. When a task is enabled, a choice may be made from the repertoire based on the contextual data values available to the task, using an extensible set of ripple-down rules to determine the most appropriate substitution. The task is checked out of the YAWL engine, the corresponding data inputs of the original task are mapped to the inputs of the worklet, and the selected worklet is launched as a separate case. When the worklet has completed, its output data is mapped back to the original task, which is then checked back into the engine, allowing the original process to continue.

The worklet executed for a task is run as a separate case in the engine, so that, from an engine perspective, the worklet and its parent are two distinct, unrelated cases. The worklet service tracks the relationships, data mappings and synchronisations between cases. Any number of worklets can form the repertoire of an individual task, and any number of tasks in a particular specification can be associated with a worklet. A worklet may be a member of one or more repertoires, i.e. it may be re-used for several distinct tasks within and across process specifications.

The worklet concept extends to dynamic exception handling by allowing designers to define exception handling processes (called *exlets*) for parent workflow instances, to be invoked when certain events occur and thereby allowing execution of the parent process to continue unhindered. It has been designed so that the enactment engine, besides providing notifications at certain points in the life cycle of a process instance, needs no knowledge of an exception occurring, or of any invocation of handling processes. Additionally, exlets for unexpected exceptions may be added during the runtime of a process instance, and such handling methods automatically become an implicit part of the process specification for all current and future instances of the process, which provides for continuous evolution of the process while avoiding any need to modify the original process definition.

Exception handling, when enabled, will detect and handle up to ten different kinds of process exceptions. As part of the exlet, a process designer may choose from various actions (such as cancelling, suspending, completing, failing and restarting) and apply them at a task, case and/or specification level. And, since exlets can include compensatory worklets, the original parent process model only needs to reveal the actual business logic for the process, while the repertoire of exlets grows as new exceptions arise or different ways of handling exceptions are formulated.

An extensible repertoire of exlets is maintained for each type of potential exception within each workflow specification. If an exlet is executed that contains a compensation action (i.e. a worklet to be executed as a compensatory process) it is run as a separate case in the YAWL engine, so that from an engine perspective, the worklet and its 'parent' (i.e. the process that invoked the exception) are two distinct, unrelated cases. Since a worklet is launched as a separate case, it may have its own worklet/exlet repertoire.

Any number of exlets can form the repertoire of an individual task or case. An exlet may be a member of one or more repertoires. The exception handling repertoire for a task or case can be added to at any time, as can the rules base used, including while the parent process is executing. Worklets and exlets can be used in combination within particular case instances to achieve dynamic flexibility and exception handling simultaneously.

SYSTEM

Architecture

To support the YAWL language introduced in the previous section, we have developed a system using state-of-the-art technology. In this section, we describe the overall architecture of this system, which is depicted in Figure 8. Workflow specifications are designed using the YAWL designer and deployed into the YAWL engine which, after performing all necessary verifications and task registrations, stores these specifications in the YAWL repository, which manages a collection of "runable" workflow specifications.

Once successfully deployed, workflow specifications can be instantiated through the YAWL engine, leading to workflow instances (or *cases*). The engine handles the execution of these cases, i.e. based on the state of a case and its specification, the engine determines which events it should offer to the environment. The environment of a YAWL system is composed of so-called YAWL services. Inspired by the "web services" paradigm, end-users, applications, and organizations are all abstracted as services in YAWL. Figure 8 shows the three standard YAWL services: (1) YAWL Resource Service, with integrated worklist handler and administration tool; (2) YAWL web services invoker; and (3) YAWL worklet service, which provides dynamic flexibility and exception handling capabilities.

The YAWL worklist handler corresponds to the classical worklist handler (also named "inbox") present in most workflow management systems. It is the component used to assign work to users of the system. Through the worklist handler users are offered and allocated work items, and can start and signal their completion. In traditional workflow systems, the worklist handler is embedded in the workflow engine. In YAWL however, it is considered to be a service completely decoupled from the engine. The YAWL web

Figure 8. YAWL system architecture

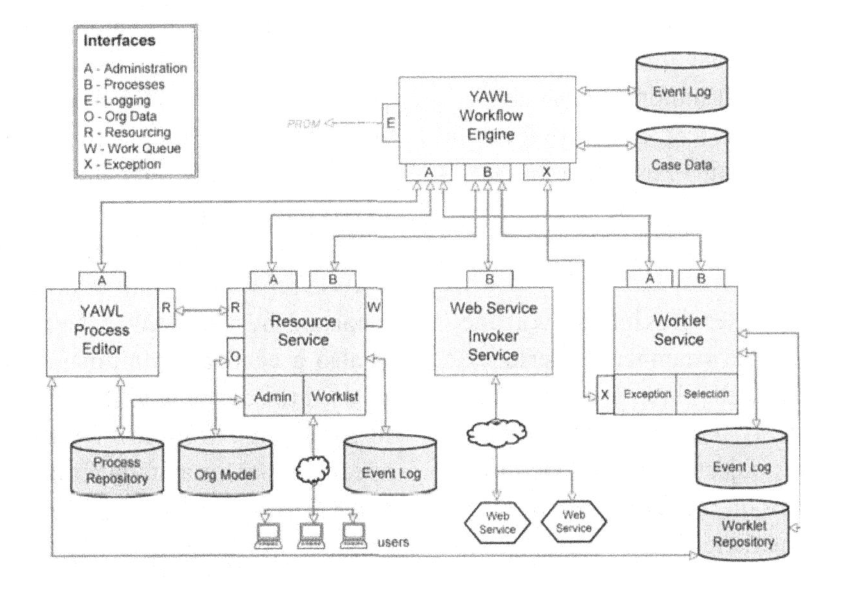

services invoker is the glue between the engine and other web services. Note that it is unlikely that web services will be able to directly connect to the YAWL engine, since they will typically be designed for more general purposes than just interacting with a workflow engine. Similarly, it is desirable not to adapt the interface of the engine to suit specific services. Otherwise, this interface will need to cater for an undetermined number of message types. Accordingly, the YAWL web services broker acts as a mediator between the YAWL engine and external web services that may be invoked by the engine to delegate tasks (e.g. delegating a *payment* task to an online payment service). The YAWL interoperability broker is a service designed to interconnect different workflow engines. For example, a task in one system could be subcontracted to another system where the task corresponds to a whole process.

Each service shown in Figure 8 conforms to the architecture of a so-called custom YAWL service, and any number of custom services can be implemented for particular interaction purposes with the YAWL engine. A custom service connects the engine with an entity in the environment. For example, a custom YAWL service could offer communication with mobile phones, printers, assembly robots, etc. Note that it is also possible that there are multiple services of the same type, e.g. multiple worklist handlers, web services brokers, and exception handling services. For example, there may exist multiple implementations of worklist handlers (e.g. customized for a specific application domain or organization) and the same worklist handler may be instantiated multiple times (e.g., one worklist handler per geographical region).

As alluded to earlier, services interact with the engine and each other via a number of interfaces, which provide methods for object and data passing via HTTP requests and responses. All data are passed as XML; objects are marshaled into XML representations on the server side of each interface and reconstructed back to objects on the client side. The YAWL engine provides four interfaces:

- **Interface A:** Which provides endpoints for process definition, administration and monitoring;
- **Interface B:** Which provides endpoints for client and invoked applications and workflow interoperability, and is used by services to connect to the engine, to start and cancel case instances, and to check workitems in and out of the engine;
- **Interface E:** Which provides access to archival data in the engine's process logs; and
- **Interface X:** Which allows the engine to notify custom services of certain events and checkpoints during the execution of each process instance where process exceptions either may have occurred or should be tested for.

The resource service also provides three interfaces to allow developers to implement other worklist handlers and administration tools while leveraging the full functionality of the service. Interface R provides organizational data to external (authorized) entities such as the YAWL Process Editor; Interface W provides access to the internal work queue routing functionalities; and Interface O allows organizational data to be provided from any data source. In addition, the service's framework is fully extendible, allowing further constraints, filters and allocation strategies to be "plugged in" by developers.

Workflow specifications are managed by the YAWL repository, and workflow instances are managed by the YAWL engine. Clearly, there is also a need for administration tool that can be used to control workflow instances manually (e.g. deleting a workflow instance or a workflow specification), manually allocate resources to tasks, and provide information about the state of running workflow instances and details or aggregated data about completed instances. This is the role of the administration tools integrated into the resource service.

Design Environment

The YAWL Editor provides a GUI design environment for the specification and verification of YAWL workflows. It is an independent tool that interacts with the YAWL Engine via Interface A and with the Resource Service via Interface R. Below we briefly show by means of examples how the Editor supports the modelling of control-flow dependencies, data passing, and resource management.

Figure 9 shows a screenshot of the control-flow aspects of a YAWL model of the house buying process (depicted in Figure 5) in the editor. Modelling elements such as tasks and conditions can be selected from the left panel. Routing constructs, i.e. splits and joins, can be added to tasks and tasks can be decorated with an icon to indicate whether it is be performed manually, automatically, or whether it is purely used for routing purposes. This latter option exists solely for readability purposes and does not have any formal meaning.

Figure 10 shows an example of a dialog for specifying the data mapping between the variables of a task and those of a net in the YAWL Editor. There are definitions of task variables and net variables, data mappings from net variables to task variables (*input* parameters), and a data mapping from a task variable to a net variable (an *output* parameter). Both task and net variables are XML elements and mappings are specified using XQuery as in some cases one may wish to pass on the result of the application of an operation on the values of parameters rather than the values themselves.

The YAWL Editor supports the specification of resourcing aspects via a 5-step wizard dialog. Figure 11 shows a screenshot of the second step where the process analyst needs to specify to which resources are to be offered work items of a certain task. This can be specified as a combination of roles, users, and variables (which may contain user or role data at runtime).

The YAWL Editor also offers functionality in relation to syntactical validation of process models, design-time verification (e.g. will every case of the model always reach the output condition), user-defined data types, and exporting of

Figure 9. Control-flow specification in the YAWL Editor

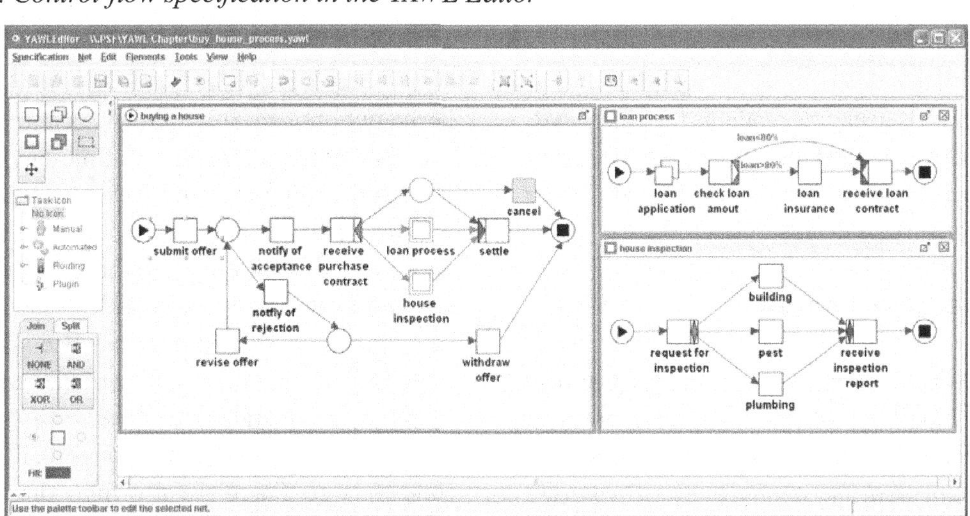

Figure 10. Data specification in the YAWL Editor

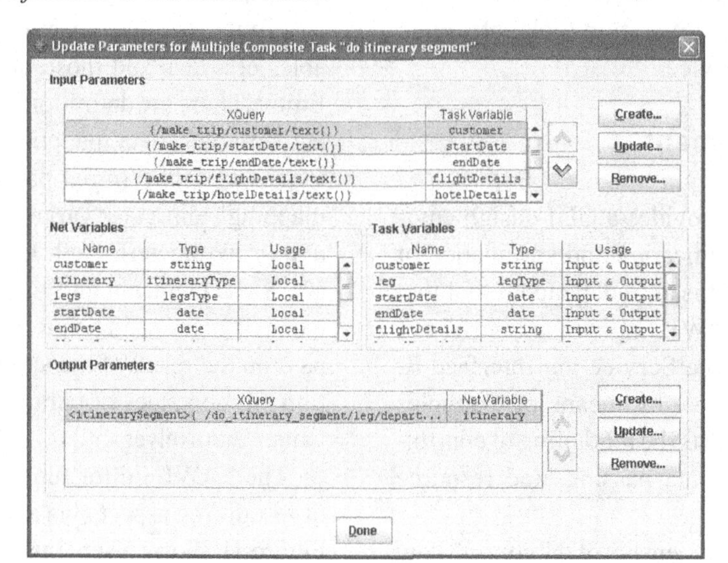

Figure 11. The second step in configuring the resource specification in the YAWL Editor

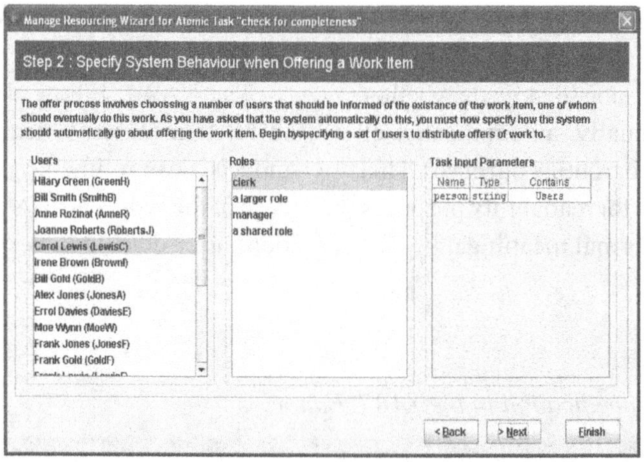

process models to engine readable files (i.e. XML files that can be loaded into the engine for execution). The reader is referred to the YAWL Editor manual for further details.

Runtime Environment

The YAWL runtime environment supports worklist handling where each work item is handled based on the three interaction points, i.e. *offered*, *allocated*, and *started* (with *suspended* a derivative of *started*), within a work item lifecycle. The user interface in the runtime environment is presented by means of Web pages and forms within a browser. Figure 12 depicts a screen of an allocated work queue in the YAWL runtime environment. The screen displays the information about a work item that has been allocated, including the process specification, the identifier of the process instance (i.e. the *case number*), and the task that the work item belongs to, its creation time and age. There are also functionalities that

Figure 12. Screen of an allocated work queue in the YAWL runtime environment

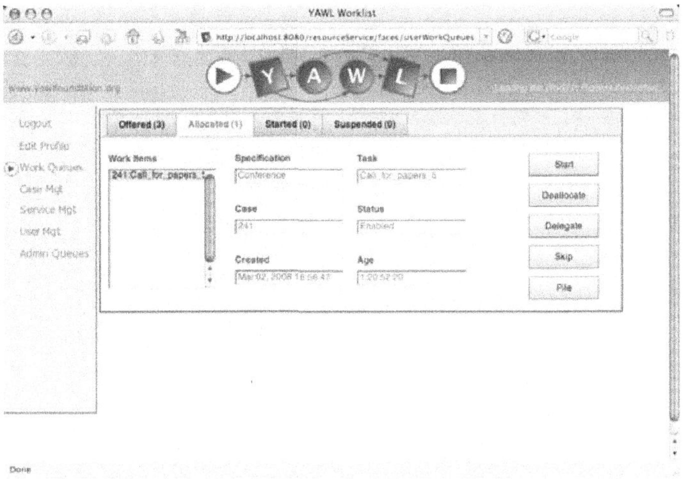

Figure 13. Dynamically generated form for work item with user-defined data types

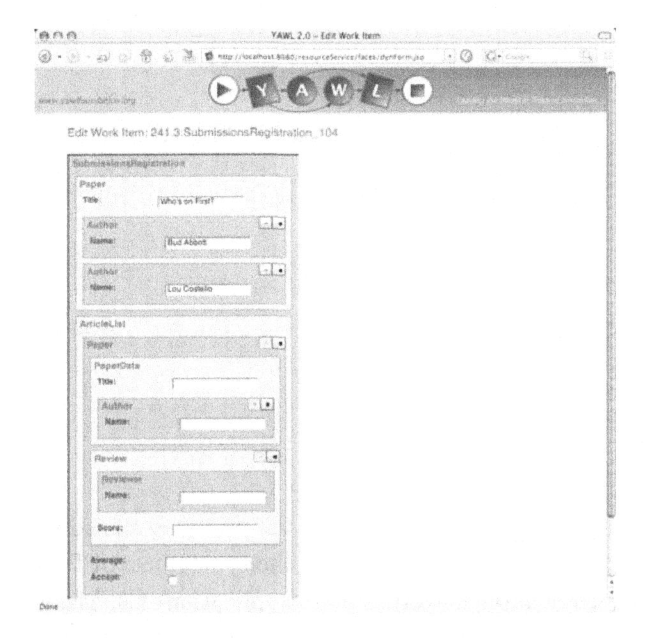

support different operations associated with the work item, e.g. to delegate the work item to another participant.

YAWL supports automatic form generation for each work item. Figure 13 shows an example of a dynamically generated form for a work item with user-defined data type.

YAWL also supports administrative operations such as management, maintenance and monitoring capabilities. A participant who has been assigned administrative privileges has access to perform these operations. Figure 14 shows an administration form for maintaining organisation data in terms of individual users. Figure 15 shows an

Figure 14. Admin screen for organisation data maintenance

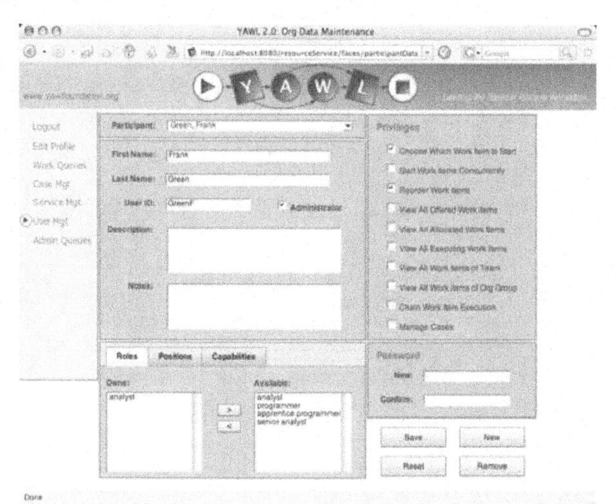

Figure 15. Admin screen for management of work queues

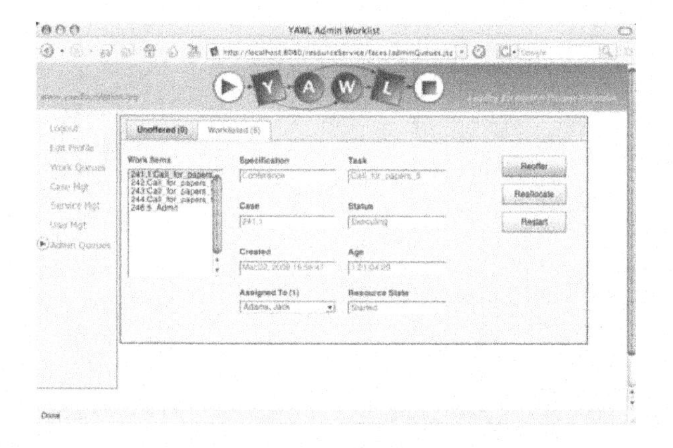

administration form for managing and monitoring work queues. In addition, administrators can upload/unload a process specification as well as launch and cancel process instances using a case management administration form.

CASE STUDY: YAWL4FILM

Background and Overview

As part of the Australian Research Council Centre of Excellence for Creative Industries and Innovation (www.cci.edu.au), we move well beyond the typical use of BPM and investigate how the application of BPM and workflow technology can deliver benefits to the field of *screen business.* The screen business comprises all creative and business related aspects and processes of film, television and new media content, from concept to production and finally distribution. For example, a film production lifecycle consists of four phases: *development*, *pre-production*, *production*, and *post-production* (Clevé, 2006). The production phase is generally the most expensive since the majority of cast and crew are contracted and the majority of equipment and resources are utilised in this period. A film production process, which refers to a process in the production phase, includes daily shooting activities such as acting, camera and sound recording over a period varying from days to years. It involves handling large amounts of forms and reports on a daily basis and coordinating geographically distributed stakeholders. Traditionally the forms and reports are purely paper-based and the production of these documents is a highly manual process. Not surprisingly, such a process is time-consuming and error-prone, and can easily increase the risk of delays in the schedule.

Within the above context YAWL was applied to the automation of film production processes. This led to the development of a prototype, namely YAWL4Film, that exploits the principles of BPM in order to coordinate work distribution with production teams, automate the daily document processing and report generation, ensure data synchronisation across distributed nodes, archive and manage all shooting related documents systematically, and document experiences gained in a film production project for reuse in the future. YAWL4Film consists of a YAWL model capturing the control-flow, data, and resource aspects of a film production process. It also extends the general YAWL system with customised user interface to support templates used in professional filmmaking.

Process Model

Figure 16 depicts the YAWL model capturing a film production process. An instance of the process model starts with the collection of specific production documents (e.g. *cast list*, *crew list*, *location notes*, and *shooting schedule*) generated during

Figure 16. A film production process model in YAWL

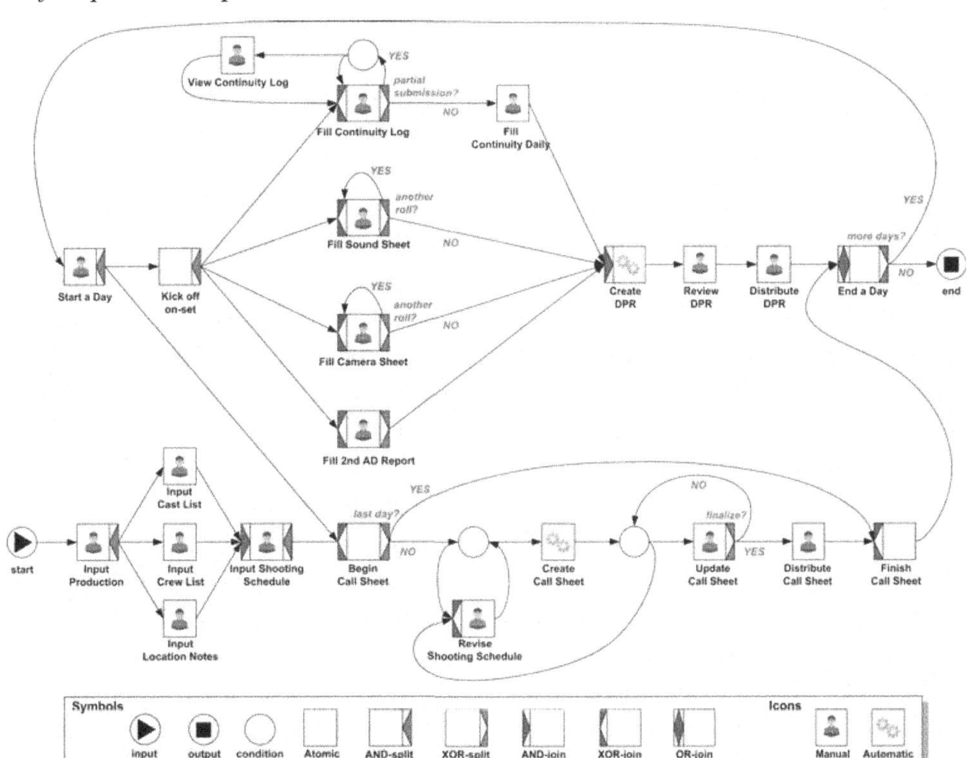

the pre-production phase. Next, the shooting starts and is carried out on a daily basis.

Each day tasks are performed along two main parallel streams. One stream focuses on the production of a *call sheet*. It starts from task *Begin Call Sheet* and ends with task *Finish Call Sheet*. A call sheet is a daily shooting schedule for a specific day. It is usually maintained by the production office and is sent out to all cast and crew the day prior. A draft call sheet can be created from the shooting schedule. It may go through any number of revisions before it is finalized, and most of the revisions result from the changes to the shooting schedule. The other stream specifies the flow of onset shooting activities and supports the production of a DPR. It starts with task *Kick Off on-set* and ends with task *Distribute DPR*. At first, tasks are executed to record the logs and technical notes about individual shooting activities into a number of documents. These are *continuity log* and *continuity daily*, which are filled by the Continuity person, *sound sheet* by a Sound Recordist, *camera sheet* by a Camera Assistant, and *2nd Assistant Director (AD) Report* by the 2nd AD. It is possible to interrupt filling in the continuity log and the 2nd AD report, e.g. for a meal break, and then to resume the work after the break. Also, there can be many camera and sound sheets to be filled in during a shooting day. Upon completion of these on-set documents, a DPR can be generated and passed onto the Production Manager for review. After the review is finished, the DPR is circulated to certain crew members such as Producer and Executive Producer.

In this process model, it is interesting to see how the OR-join associated with task *End a Day* behaves. Before the first shooting day starts, an instance of the call sheet branch is executed for producing the first day's call sheet. Since it is the only active incoming branch to task *End a Day*, the task will be performed once the call sheet has completed, without waiting for the completion of a DPR. In this case, the OR-join behaves like an XOR-join. On the other hand, if both call sheet and DPR branches are active (which is the case for the rest of the shooting days) the OR-join behaves like an AND-join.

User Interface

Most tasks in the film production process are manual (annotated with an icon of a human) and require users to fill in forms. While the YAWL environment supports automatic generation of screens based on input/output parameters and their types, in order to support templates used in professional filmmaking custom-made Web forms were created and linked to the worklist handler of YAWL. Figure 17 for example depicts the Web form for task *Update Call Sheet* (see Figure 16) as seen by a production office crew member e.g. Production Coordinator.

The custom forms and their links to YAWL were developed using standard Java technology. Each form can load an XML file (complying with the schema of the work item), save the user input into a local XML file, and submit the form back to the worklist handler once it has been completed by the user. Upon submission a backup copy is stored on the server. Moreover, each form provides data validation upon save and submission to prevent the generation of invalid XML documents that would block the execution of the process. Finally, a print function allows the user to generate a printer-ready document from the Web form, which resembles the hard copy format used in practice in this business. This function relies on XSLT transformations to convert the XML of the form to HTML.

Pilot Projects

YAWL4Film was deployed on two film production projects at the AFTRS in October 2007. Project 1, *Rope Burn*, was a three-day shoot in studio with 30 onset crew, 6 cast and 6 production office crew. The office was run by a professional Production Manager and supervised by a student Producer.

Project 2, *Family Man*, was a three-day shoot on location and in studio with 35 crew, 5 cast and 4 production office crew. A semi-professional Production Manager was contracted and supervised by a student Producer. In both projects YAWL4Film shadowed the process of call sheet generation, DPR generation, and cast and crew database updates. For *Rope Burn* the system was used on-set alongside the traditional paper method of data capture, and later for *Family Man* the

Figure 17. An example of custom Web form – call sheet

ROPE BURN

DIRECTOR: MELVIN MONTALBAN I PRODUCER: ADAM BISHOP

TUES, 9-10-2007 Shoot Day 1 of 3

Production Managers: ALICE WHITE 0402022022
1st AD: CHERYL SMITH 0413105790
Police: Eastwood Police Station ph (02) 9858 5944
Fire/Ambulance: 000
Hospital: Ryde Hospital 1 Denistone Road Eastwood NSW 2212 ph (02) 9874 0199

Production Office

Address: Australian Film Television and Radio School: Corner Epping and Balaclava Roads, North Ryde, NSW

Phone: +61.2.9805 6676 Fax: +61.2.9887 1030 Email: ropeburnproduction@gmail.com

Weather

Sunrise: 05:24:00 Sunset: 18:02:00
Forecast:
Partly Cloudy Min 14 Max 21

Call Times

Calls	Time	Location
Crew	08:00:00	AFTRS

Shooting Schedule

Start of Day Notes: ABSOLUTELY NO FOOD OR DRINK (EXCEPT FOR WATER BOTTLES) IN STUDIO

Sc: 9 Pages: 4/8 Timing: 00:00:25 Night / INT Set: DRESSING ROOM
Synopsis: Charlie's not going to Europe with them

Character	Artist	PU	M/UP	WR	On Set
CHARLIE	Eloise Oxer	0630	0745	0715	0815
SIMONE	Amelia Best	0620	0715	0845	0815

Insert Row | Delete Row

Shoot Times: 09:00-11:15
Scene Notes: BLOCK-THROUGH 0815-0830 THEN LIGHT/COMPLETE M/UP AND WR 0830-0900

Sc: 2 Pages: 1 2/8 Timing: 00:01:07 Night / INT Set: DRESSING ROOM
Synopsis: Simone and Charlie get it on but are interrupted.

Partial Submission Final Submission

Print Preview | Print | Save | Submission | Upload

ROPE BURN PRODUCTION OFFICE

ROPE BURN

DIRECTOR: MELVIN MONTALBAN I PRODUCER: ADAM BISHOP

TUES 9 October 2007 Shoot Day 1 of 3

AFTRS STUDIO 1

SC	PAGE TIMING	D/N INT/EXT	SET/LOCATION	CHARACTER	ARTIST	PU	WR	M/UP	ON SET
9	0 4/8 00:00:25	Night INT	DRESSING ROOM @ AFTRS Studio 1	CHARLIE	Eloise Oxer	0630	0745	0715	0815
				SIMONE	Amelia Best	0620	0715	0845	0815
2	1 2/8	Night	DRESSING ROOM @ AFTRS Studio 1	CHARLIE	Eloise Oxer	CLD	CLD	CLD	CLD

system totally replaced the paper-based method for the two crew members.

From the feedback for the two projects, it was clear that the system would save time and create more precise documentation:

I have managed over a dozen productions offices, and the amount of time this tool could save is incredible. Seeing the system up and running makes me realize how manual and laborious many of the activities are in any production office.
- Production Manager in *Rope Burn*

I found the electronic form simple and easy to fill in. It was really just the same as using a paper form, but much cleaner and neater, e.g., no messy handwriting, smudges or crumpled paper.
- 2nd AD in *Family Man*

EPILOGUE

In this section we will point the reader to some current and associated areas of research.

Business process executions are generally logged and may provide valuable information about what is happening in an organisation, e.g. where the bottlenecks are. The log files of the YAWL environment may be exported via Interface E to the ProM (www.processmining.org) environment for further analysis. This powerful open source environment has more than 190 plug-ins and supports mining of process-related information, various forms of analysis and even conversions between different process languages (van der Aalst et al, 2007). The use of ProM in combination with YAWL provides real opportunities for process analysis and subsequent improvement. Recent work was conducted to also exploit ProM for the purposes of process simulation where the current state of a process is taken as a starting point to provide the potential to do a what-if analysis for the immediate future (Rozinat et al, 2008).

In order to exploit similarities between models capturing best practices in different but related domains, the area of configurable reference process models came into existence, see e.g. (Rosemann & van der Aalst, 2007). Variation points are explicitly defined in a configurable process model and constraints are specified that govern what types of settings are possible for a model. A configurable reference model allows one (in principle) to quickly generate a model that applies to a specific context. In (Gottschalk, van der Aalst, Jansen-Vullers & La Rosa, 2008) an approach for configurable YAWL models, referred to as C-YAWL, is described. In this approach variations are expressed through the concepts of hiding and blocking. Hidden concepts act as silent steps, while blocked concepts rule out certain paths at runtime.

YAWL currently does not provide support for loosely coupled workflows at the conceptual level. These workflows may reside in different organisational settings and are hence fairly autonomous. As they may need to interact with each other it is beneficial if these interactions could be made explicit and expressed as part of a YAWL specification. An example of an interaction could be one workflow starting a case of another workflow or sending information to and requesting information back from another already running workflow. A first exploration of this area in the context of YAWL can be found in (Aldred, van der Aalst, Dumas & ter Hofstede, 2007). Further work is required to concretise this work and introduce language elements into the YAWL language to directly support aspects of inter-process communication.

In (Russell, 2007), newYAWL was proposed and defined based on the latest collections of patterns for the control-flow, data and resource perspectives. The semantics of this language was formally defined in terms of CPN Tools (resulting in 55 models), hence is executable, and it provides direct support for 118 of 126 workflow patterns across the three perspectives (and one pattern partially supported). This formalisation provided a blueprint for new resourcing support in YAWL 2.0 Beta, which was briefly discussed in this chapter.

Finally, it is worthwhile mentioning that research has been conducted or is ongoing to relate YAWL to other process languages. For example, a mapping from BPEL to YAWL has been studied by (Brogi & Popescu, 2006) and the ProM framework supports a mapping from Petri nets to YAWL models. Currently the mapping from BPMN to YAWL is studied and a support component is expected to be released sometime soon.

EXERCISES

1. List the three main perspectives of a business process. Do these perspectives influence each other? If so, illustrate relationships between these perspectives using examples.
2. Select three existing software systems and three modelling languages in the field of business process and workflow management. Find evaluations of these offerings in terms of the control-flow patterns and provide a comparative summary based on these evaluations.
3. For each of the statements below determine whether they are true or false. Provide a brief motivation for each of your answers.
   (1) Petri nets are workflow nets.
   (2) YAWL models can be seen as workflow nets.
   (3) The control-flow of a process may be affected by data.
   (4) The XOR-split concept in YAWL is used to capture the Deferred Choice pattern.
4. Consider the YAWL process model shown in Figure 5 in this Chapter. Is it possible to cancel a running instance of the process before the buyer is notified of the offer acceptance result? Explain your answer.
5. Redraw the sub-process for *house inspection* by replacing the OR-split and OR-join tasks with other split(s)/join(s). The resulting process should exhibit the same process behaviour as the original process.
6. Consider a complaint handling process. First the complaint is registered, then in parallel a questionnaire is sent to the complainant and the complaint is processed. If the complainant returns the questionnaire in two weeks, task process questionnaire is executed. Otherwise, once two weeks are passed, the result of the questionnaire is discarded. In parallel the complaint is evaluated. Based on the evaluation result, the processing is either done or continues to check processing. If the check result is not OK, the complaint requires re-processing. Finally, the complaint processing result is archived.
   (1) Create a YAWL model to capture this process and use at least 10 data elements to capture data associated with the various tasks.
   (2) Extend the model with the resource perspective.
   (3) Draw the process model in the YAWL Editor and execute it in the YAWL Engine. Provide screenshots of an offered work item, an allocated work item, a work item being worked on, and a started work item.
7. Consider the following abstract YAWL model. Please provide all possible execution scenarios of this model. Is it possible to reach the end of the process (i.e. the output condition) in each execution scenario? Are there any problems with this model? If so, please propose a remedy for any problem(s) that you may detect.

Exhibit 1.

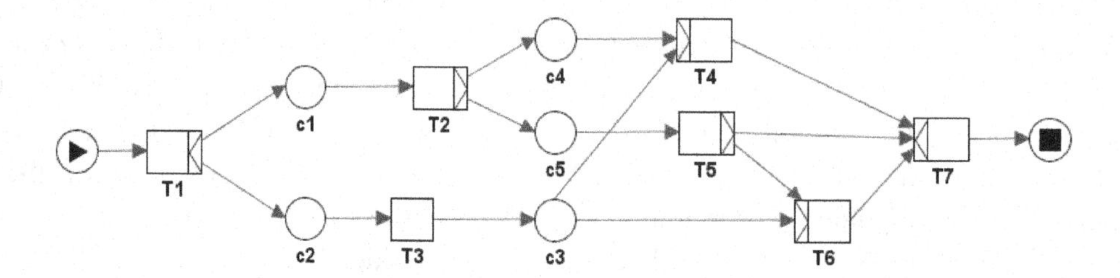

REFERENCES

van der Aalst, W.M.P. (1996). Three good reasons for using a Petri-net-based workflow management system. In S. Navathe & T. Wakayama (Eds.), *Proceedings of the International Working Conference on Information and Process Integration in Enterprises* (pp. 179-201), Cambridge, MA: Kluwer Academic Publisher.

van der Aalst, W. M. P. (1997). Verification of Workflow nets. In *Proceedings of the 18th International Conference on Application and Theory of Petri Nets* (pp. 407-426). Springer.

van der Aalst, W. M. P., van Dongen, B. F., Günther, C. W., Mans, R. S., Alves de Medeiros, A. K., Rozinat, A., Rubin, V., Song, M., Verbeek, H. M. W., & Weijters, A. J. M. M. (2007). ProM 4.0: Comprehensive Support for Real Process Analysis. In *Proceedings of the 28th International Conference on Applications and Theory of Petri Nets and Other Models of Concurrency* (pp. 484-494). Springer-Verlag.

van der Aalst, W. M. P. & van Hee, K. M. (2002). *Workflow Management: Models, Methods, and Systems.* Cambridge, MA: MIT Press.

van der Aalst, W. M. P., & ter Hofstede, A. H. M. (2002). Workflow patterns: On the expressive power of (Petri-net-based) workflow languages (invited talk). In *Proceedings of the 4th Workshop on the Practical Use of Coloured Petri Nets and CPN Tools* (pp. 1-20). Denmark: University of Aarhus.

van der Aalst, W. M. P., & ter Hofstede, A. H. M. (2005). YAWL: Yet another workflow language. *Information Systems, 30*(4), 245-275.

van der Aalst, W. M. P., ter Hofstede, A. H. M., Kiepuszewski, B., & Barros, A. P. (2003). Workflow patterns. *Distributed and Parallel Databases, 14*(1), 5-51.

Adams, M., ter Hofstede, A. H. M., van der Aalst, W. M. P., & Edmond, D. (2007). Dynamic, extensible and context-aware exception handling for workflows. In R. Meersman & Z. Tari et al. (Eds.), *Proceedings of the 15th International Conference on Cooperative Information Systems* (pp. 95-112), Vilamoura, Portugal: Springer- Verlag.

Adams, M., ter Hofstede, A. H. M., Edmond, D., & van der Aalst, W. M. P. (2006). Worklets: A service-oriented implementation of dynamic Flexibility in workflows. In R. Meersman & Z. Tari et al. (Eds.), *Proceedings of the 14th International Conference on Cooperative Information Systems* (pp. 291-308). Montpellier, France: Springer-Verlag.

Aldred, L., van der Aalst, W. M. P., Dumas, M., & ter Hofstede, A. H. M. (2007). Communication abstractions for distributed business processes. In *Proceedings of the 19th International Conference on Advanced Information Systems Engineering* (pp. 409-423). Springer-Verlag.

Brogi, A., & Popescu, R. (2006). From BPEL Processes to YAWL workflows. In M. Bravetti, M. Nunez, & G. Zavattaro (Eds.), *Proceedings of the 3rd International Workshop on Web Services and Formal Methods* (pp. 107-122). Springer-Verlag.

Casati, F., & Cugola, G. (2001). Error handling in process support systems. In A. Romanovsky, C. Dony, J. Lindskov Knudsen, & A. Tripathi (Eds.), *Advances in exception handling techniques*, (LNCS, 2022, pp. 251-270). Springer-Verlag.

Clevé, B. (2006). *Film production management*. Burlington, Oxford.

Gottschalk, F., van der Aalst, W. M. P., Jansen-Vullers, M. H., & La Rosa, M. (2008). Configurable workflow models, *International Journal of Cooperative Information Systems 17*(2), 177-221.

Leontiev, A. N. (1978). *Activity, consciousness and personality*. Englewood Cliffs, NJ: Prentice Hall.

Jordan, D., & Evdemon, J. (2007). *Web services business process execution language (WS-BPEL) – version 2.0*. Committee Specification. OASIS WS-BPEL TC. Available via http://www.oasis-open.org/committees/download.php/22475/wsbpel-v2.0-CS01.pdf

Keller, G., Nüttgens, M., & Scheer, A. W. (1992). *Semantische Prozessmodellierung auf der Grundlage "Ereignisgesteuerter Prozessketten (EPK)"*. Technical Report 89, Institut für Wirtschaftsinformatik Saarbrücken, Saarbrücken, Germany.

Murata, T. (1989). Petri nets: Properties, analysis and applications. *Proceedings of the IEEE*, *77*(4), 541–580.

Ouyang, C., Dumas, M., van der Aalst, W. M. P., ter Hofstede, A. H. M., & Mendling, J. (2008). From business process models to process-oriented software systems. Accepted for publication. *ACM Transactions on Software Engineering and Methodology*.

OMG. (2006). *Business process modeling notation (BPMN) - Version 1.0*. OMG Final Adopted Specification. Available via http://www.bpmn.org/

Rosemann, M., & van der Aalst, W. M. P. (2007). A configurable reference modelling language. *Information Systems, 32*(1), 1-23.

Rozinat, A., Wynn, M., van der Aalst, W. M. P., ter Hofstede, A. H. M., & Fidge, C. (2008). Workflow Simulation for Operational Decision Support using YAWL and ProM. In *Proceedings of the 6th International Conference on Business Process Management*. Milan, Italy: Springer-Verlag.

Russell, N. (2007). *Foundations of process-aware information systems*. Doctoral Thesis, Queensland University of Technology, Brisbane, Australia.

Russell, N., van der Aalst, W. M. P., & ter Hofstede, A. H. M. (2006). Workflow exception patterns. In *Proceedings of the 18th International Conference on Advanced Information Systems Engineering* (pp. 288-302). Springer-Verlag.

Russell, N., van der Aalst, W. M. P., ter Hofstede, A. H. M., & Edmond, D. (2005). Workflow resource patterns: Identification, representation and tool support. In *Proceedings of the 17th International Conference on Advanced Information Systems Engineering* (pp. 216-232). Springer-Verlag.

Russell, N., ter Hofstede, A. H. M., van der Aalst, W. M. P., & Mulyar, N. (2006). *Workflow control-flow patterns: A revised view*. BPM Center Report BPM-06-22, BPMcenter.org

Russell, N., ter Hofstede, A. H. M., Edmond, D., & van der Aalst, van der, W. M. P. (2005). Workflow data patterns: Identification, representation and tool support. In *Proceedings of the 24th International Conference on Conceptual Modeling* (pp. 353-368). Springer-Verlag.

Workflow Management Coalition (1999). *Terminology and glossary*. Technical Report Document Number WFMC-TC-1011, Issue 3.0. Available at http://www.wfmc.org/standards/

docs/TC-1011_term_glossary_v3.pdf (Latest access: 08 September 2008)

Wynn, M. T., Edmond, D., van der Aalst, W. M. P., & ter Hofstede, A. H. M. (2005). Achieving a general, formal and decidable approach to the OR-join in workflow using reset nets. In *Proceedings of the 26th International conference on Application and Theory of Petri nets and Other Models of Concurrency* (pp. 423-443). Springer-Verlag.

SUGGESTED ADDITIONAL READING

W.M.P. van der Aalst and K. van Hee. *Workflow Management: Models, Methods, and Systems.* MIT press, Cambridge, MA. 2002. *This book provides an overview of the field of workflow management and an in-depth treatment of WF-nets.*

M. Weske. *Business Process Management: Concepts, Languages, Architectures.* Springer, Berlin, Heidelberg. 2007. *This book provides an overview of more technically focussed areas in the field of Business Process Management and includes treatments of the original workflow control-flow patterns, WF-nets, YAWL, and BPMN.*

M. Dumas, W.M.P. van der Aalst, and A.H.M. ter Hofstede. *Process Aware Information Systems: Bridging People and Software Through Process Technology.* Wiley-Interscience. 2005. *This book covers a fairly broad range of topics in the area of Process-aware Information Systems ranging from concepts and techniques to standards and tools. The book contains a discussion of the orginal control-flow patterns and Petri nets and UML* Activity Diagrams.

N. Russell. *Foundations of Process-Aware Information Systems.* PhD Thesis, Queensland University of Technology, Brisbane, Australia, 2007. *This thesis provides a comprehensive treatment of the latest definitions of the workflow patterns and introduces newYAWL.*

M. Adams. *Facilitating Dynamic Flexibility and Exception Handling for Workflows.* PhD Thesis, Queensland University of Technology, Brisbane, Australia, 2007. *This thesis provides a comprehensive treatment of exception handling and dynamic workflow in YAWL and covers conceptual foundations, formalisation and implementation.*

M. Wynn. *Semantics, Verification, and Implementation of Workflows with Cancellation Regions and OR-joins.* PhD Thesis, Queensland University of Technology, Brisbane, Australia, 2006. *This thesis provides an in-depth treatment of the OR-join in YAWL, both definition and implementation, as well as of a verification approach to YAWL models based on their mapping to Reset nets.*

H. M. W. Verbeek, W.M.P. van der Aalst, and A.H.M. ter Hofstede. Verifying workflows with cancellation regions and OR-joins: An approach based on relaxed soundness and invariants. *The Computer Journal.* 50(3): 294-314. 2007. *This article provides the theoretical foundations of additional verification methods that have been implemented for the YAWL environment.*

T. Murata. Petri nets: Properties, analysis and applications. *Proceedings of the IEEE,* 77(4), 541–580. 1989. *Classical article providing an overview of the field of Petri nets.*

J. Desel and J. Esparza. Free Choice nets. *Cambridge Tracts in Theoretical Computer Science.* Volume 40. 1995. *Comprehensive book on Free Choice nets. This subclass of Petri nets has particular relevance to the area of workflow due to the fact that many concepts of existing workflow languages can be mapped to a free choice Petri net.*

KEY TERMS

Petri Net: A Petri net is the description of a process in terms of places (capturing conditions), transitions (capturing tasks), and arcs (capturing relation between conditions and tasks). The semantics is always formally defined.

Process: The definition of a process indicates which tasks must be performed and in what order to successfully complete a case. A process consists of tasks, conditions, and sub-processes.

Process Automation: Process automation is the application of software applications, tools and infrastructure to manage routine activities in order to free up employees to handle exceptions or perform more creative work.

Process Execution: Process execution is to enact a process according to the process definition (e.g. in format of a process model) using certain software or tools (e.g. a process execution engine or a workflow engine).

Process Modelling: Process modelling is the use of information and graphics to represent processes in a consistent way.

Workflow: A workflow comprises cases, resources, and triggers that relate to a particular process.

Workflow Engine: The workflow engine takes care of the actual management of the workflow. Among other things, it is concerned with task-assignment generation, resource allocation, activity performance, case preparation and modification, the launching of applications, and the recording of logistical information.

Workflow Pattern: A workflow pattern is a specialized form of a design pattern as defined in the area of software engineering. Workflow patterns refer specifically to recurrent problems and proven solutions related to the development of workflow applications in particular, and more broadly, process-oriented applications.

Workflow System: A workflow system is one that supports the workflows in a specific business situation. It usually consists of a workflow management system (e.g. a workflow engine) plus process and resource classification definitions, applications, a database system, and so on.

YAWL: YAWL stands for Yet Another Workflow Language. It is a process modelling and execution language based on the workflow patterns and Petri nets. YAWL is also the name of the corresponding workflow system that implements the YAWL language.

ENDNOTES

1 Although BPEL provides control links that can be used to connect various constructs, it imposes a number of constraints on the usage of control links (e.g. they cannot form a loop nor cross the boundary of a loop) so that the support for a graph-based modelling is restricted.

2 Generally, there is a clear distinction between *exceptions* at the business process level, and system level *failures*, which include situations such as database malfunctions or network failures (see, for example, Casati & Cugola, 2001). Workflow systems typically rely on the recovery mechanisms of the underlying operating systems and application interfaces, or the transactional properties of the underlying database platform to handle system failures, using methods such as retries and rollbacks. Since system level failures occur below the business process layer, they are considered to be outside the scope of this chapter.

Chapter VI
Modelling Constructs

Ekkart Kindler
Denmark's Technical University, DTU Informatics, Denmark

ABSTRACT

There are many different notations and formalisms for modelling business processes and workflows. These notations and formalisms have been introduced with different purposes and objectives. Later, influenced by other notations, comparisons with other tools, or by standardization efforts, these notations have been extended in order to increase expressiveness and to be more competitive. This resulted in an increasing number of notations and formalisms for modelling business processes and in an increase of the different modelling constructs provided by modelling notations, which makes it difficult to compare modelling notations and to make transformations between them. One of the reasons is that, in each notation, the new concepts are introduced in a different way by extending the already existing constructs. In this chapter, the authors go the opposite direction: showing that it is possible to add most of the typical extensions on top of any existing notation or formalism—without changing the formalism itself. Basically, they introduce blocks with some additional attributes defining their initiation and termination behaviour. This serves two purposes: First, it gives a clearer understanding of the basic constructs and how they can be combined with more advanced constructs. Second, it will help combining different modelling notations with each other. Note that, though they introduce a notation for blocks in this chapter, they are not so much interested in promoting this notation here. The notation should just prove that it is possible to separate different issues of a modelling notation, and this way making its concepts clearer and the interchange of models easier. A fully-fledged block notation with a clear and simple interface to existing formalisms is yet to be developed.

1. INTRODUCTION

Today, there are many different notations for modelling *business processes* and their different aspects. These *modelling notations* have evolved over time in a more or less systematic way. Though these notations sometimes are very different syntactically, the underlying ideas and the concepts share some common understanding and have many similarities. Due to the syntactic differences, however, it is often difficult to compare the concepts and the expressive power of modelling notations for business processes.

One approach to compare and evaluate modelling notations and workflow management tools is the definition of *workflow patterns*, which distil situations that were found in existing workflow models or as constructs in existing notations and tools. Up to now, over hundred workflow patterns have been identified by the *Workflow Patterns initiative*[1], which is a joint effort of Eindhoven University of Technology and Queensland University of Technology. And many others have contributed or identified their own patterns. These patterns are used for the evaluation of existing tools and business process modelling notations.

The workflow patterns, however, should not be interpreted as a list of *workflow constructs* that a modelling notation should have. Rather, they show what needs to be expressible by a construct or by a combination of constructs. In this chapter, we will discuss modelling constructs with a new focus: minimality and orthogonality. Minimality, in contrast to many existing approaches, tries to minimize the number of constructs that are needed for expressing all the necessary patterns. Orthogonality means that the constructs are as independent from each other as possible. In particular, we show how to add some of the more advanced constructs on top of, basically, any existing formalism. The main idea is to add blocks with some specific features for initiating and terminating them, where each block can have a model of, basically, any formalism.

Before discussing the actual patterns and the modelling constructs in Sect. 4, we will give some more background on the concepts of business process modelling in Sect. 2. And we will discuss some basic principles that underlie different modelling notations in Sect. 3.

2. BACKGROUND AND MOTIVATION

In this section, we give a more detailed motivation for our fresh look at modelling constructs and the research direction we are heading at. Actually, the general idea behind this work is summarized in a motto coming from the bible:

For the letter kills, but the Spirit gives life.
2. Corinthians 3:6b (NIV)

Our endeavour is to understand the spirit of business processes and what is needed to model them—unspoilt by the letter of a particular modelling notation. Only in the end, we try to capture this spirit in letters, i. e. in concrete modelling constructs—in order to prove that the proposed concepts can be made work.

2.1 Business Processes Modelling

Before going into a detailed motivation, we introduce the most important concepts of business processes and their aspects, and introduce our terminology, which follows the lines of AMFIBIA [Axenath, Kindler, and Rubin, 2007], which in turn was inspired by terminology from [Hollingsworth, 1995; van der Aalst and van Hee, 2002; Leymann and Roller, 1999] and is roughly compatible with it.

A *business process* involves a set of *tasks* that are executed in some enterprise or administration according to some rules in order to achieve certain *goals*. Though the *goals* and objectives are very important for developing and understanding process models, the goals are, typically, modelled only very informally or not modelled at all. A *business process model* is a more or less formal and more or less detailed description of the persons and artifacts involved in the execution of a business process and its task and the rules governing their execution.

Any distinct execution of a business process model is an *instance* of the business process. Often, an instance of a business process is also called a business process. But, this easily results in confusion. Therefore, we use the term business process model for the model and the term *case* for the instance. The same distinction, applies for tasks: The term task refers to a task in the model; an instances of a task in a particular case is called an *activity*. Note that, even within the same case, a task can be executed, i. e. instantiated, many times.

There are many different ways how to actually model a business process. We call each of them a business process modelling notation; and if the meaning[2] of a notation is precisely defined, we call the notation along with that meaning a business process modelling formalism. Note that the same notation can have different interpretations, which, strictly speaking, makes them different formalisms based on the same notation. Event Driven Process Chains (EPCs) [Keller, Nüttgens, and Scheer, 1992] are a good example for such a notation, and we give some reasons for the plethora of different interpretations of EPCs later in this chapter.

Independently of the concrete modelling notations or formalisms, it is well accepted that there are three main aspects of business processes that need to be defined for a business process: *control*, *information*, and *organization*. The control aspect defines the order in which the different tasks of a business process are executed, where concurrent or parallel execution of different tasks is allowed. The organization aspect defines the organization structure and the resources and agents that are involved in the business process, and in which way they may or must participate in the different tasks. The information aspect defines the information and documents that are involved in a business process, how it is represented, and how it is propagated among the different tasks. Actually, there are many more aspects that could be considered, e.g. transactionality and security, but these are beyond the scope of this chapter.

Most modelling notations cover more than one aspect. Still most modelling notations started out at or were focused on one aspect, and constructs for modelling other aspects where later added as extensions. The historical evolution of a notation has an impact on its modelling constructs and how they look like. In principle, however, we have shown in the AMFIBIA approach [Axenath, Kindler, and Rubin, 2007] that it is possible to define the different aspects of a business process independently of each other and even independently from a concrete modelling notation. Though this might not be important for practically modelling business processes, this separation provides a clearer understanding of the underlying concepts and their relation.

2.2 Business Processes and Workflows

Up to now, we did not make much of a difference between a *business process model* and a *workflow model*. There is, however, a very significant difference: In our terminology, a *workflow model* is a business process model that is made for being executed by a workflow management system [Hollingsworth, 1995; Workflow Management Coalition, 1999]. This means that a workflow model must cover many IT-specific details and is much more technical than a business process model. In particular, workflow models need to be *operational* (see Sect. 3.2) and, this way, any workflow modelling notation is a formalism by definition.

There are good reasons to make business process models that are not workflow models. One reason could be to get a better understanding of the process going on in a company or in some piece of existing software (see Sect. 3.1 for some more details). Some business process modelling notations have been defined for exactly this purpose; and there was no need for a precisely defined meaning of such notations. This, actually, was the original intention of EPCs [Keller, Nüttgens, and Scheer, 1992]. Other notations such as the one from MQSeries [Leymann and Roller, 1999] have been devised as a workflow notation.

2.3 Problems with Existing Notations

Sometimes, however, the actual intention of a newly devised notation is not made explicit. In that case, the notation lacks a *methodology* that defines its purpose and how to properly achieve that purpose with the notation (and maybe some tools). And sometimes the objective of an existing modelling notation changes over time. An initially informal notation might be assigned a precise meaning. In that case, there are models in a notation that never was meant to have a precise meaning; in these models, some things might have been left open for interpretation, either on purpose or just because the notation did not allow the modeller to make it more precise. Now, with the new meaning assigned to the notation, all these models will have a precise meaning. The question, however, is whether this is the intended one for all already existing models. Typically, it requires some intellectual work to make informal models more precise. This is called a *design decision* or an *implementation decision*. And these decisions cannot be made for all existing models by just giving a more precise semantics to a yet informal notation. That is why defining a precise semantics for an informal notation does not solve problems for already existing models. Still, there are notations where this happened. One example are EPCs [Nüttgens and Rump, 2002]. Today, many different semantics for EPCs have been proposed and a complete overview of existing semantics for EPCs would be a separate chapter.

Actually, one of the reasons for the many different semantics for EPCs are constructs that left some freedom in interpretation, which made it easier to come up with an initial rough model of a business process. For example, there are many interpretations of the non-local OR-join operator [van der Aalst, Desel, and Kindler, 2002; Kindler, 2004).

In many other examples, the change of the objective of a notation might not be that extreme. Still, it often happens that the objective of a modelling notation are not made explicit, change over time or even change with different people or enterprises developing or contributing to a notation. This in itself is not a problem, and getting views from different angles can really improve a notation, formalism, or methodology. Sometimes, however, it results in false compromises, or in inconsistent philosophies or redundant constructs. One example are different interpretations of the OR-join construct in different tools: stakeholders on the workflow-management side who might want to implement a workflow-management system will interpret the non-local behaviour more "local" since they must implement it efficiently; analysts who are just interested in a rough understanding and analysis of a business process, will give it a much more "non-local" semantics in order to obtain simpler models. But since it is the "same notation", we just do not see the difference anymore.

Likewise other notations grew out of other languages that, originally, were made for a quite different purpose (e. g. batch processing). Later, the notations are extended by adding new constructs, but the ones that are there already cannot be revised or removed—even if not appropriate anymore. Therefore, the new constructs tend to be more and more artificial. This way, the notation is not what actually would be needed, but something slightly different. Initially, this might not even be a problem; but over time, the gap might become bigger. This way, existing notations might block the view on what actually would be needed.

Therefore, it is a worthwhile task to have a look at existing models, then step back and find out what the actual idea of the underlying business process was—ignoring the specific notation. And then find a way to appropriately model it. This chapter takes the initiative to start that work.

2.4 Workflow Patterns

Actually, the above problems have been at least some of the stimulating factors for the research on *workflow patterns* [van der Aalst, ter Hofstede, Kiepuszewski, and Barros, 2002 & 2003; Russell, ter Hofstede, van der Aalst, and Mulyar, 2006]. Workflow patterns were introduced in order to better understand what needs to be covered by notations for business processes modelling, for comparing modelling notations and the constructs of existing workflow management systems. This greatly helps in evaluating different technologies and tools. Originally [van der Aalst, ter Hofstede, Kiepuszewski, and Barros, 2002], the workflow patterns focused on the control aspect, but meanwhile there are many other patterns concerning other aspects of business process models. In this chapter, we will focus on the control patterns.

The workflow patterns as proposed in [van der Aalst, ter Hofstede, Kiepuszewski, and Barros, 2002] and later extended in [Russell, ter Hofstede, van der Aalst, and Mulyar, 2006] greatly advances the understanding of modelling notations and formalisms for business process models. And it certainly has an effect on the design of new languages.

Some of the workflow patterns are quite close to workflow constructs of most modelling notations, and other patterns have immediate counterparts in workflow constructs in at least some modelling notations. Therefore, workflow patterns are sometimes confused with workflow constructs. But, this is not their intension. The actual question is: how can the workflow patterns (or a relevant subset of them) be supported by an adequate subset of modelling constructs without introducing a construct for every pattern. This, in a nutshell, is the objective of this chapter.

2.5 Objectives of this Chapter

As pointed out above, there are many notations and formalisms for modelling business processes. But, it is not so clear which of the provided modelling constructs are really needed; and, if needed, for which purpose they are needed. The workflow patterns partially improve the situation. Still, a list of workflow patterns is easily interpreted in a "more is better mentality", obfuscating the view on what is really needed for *adequately* modelling business process models.

Here, we start stepping back a bit and have a look at business processes, unspoilt by a specific modelling notations, and investigate which modelling constructs are really needed and how they should be combined with each other for a specific purpose. Actually, this endeavour goes much beyond the scope of this chapter. This chapter, will provide just some first analysis and ideas, in order to trigger or even provoke research in this direction and, eventually, coming up with a careful study (see advanced exercises).

The goals of this endeavour are:

- A clear understanding of the different objectives of modelling,
- A clear understanding of what needs to be modelled, and the different aspects,
- Conceptually clear ideas of modelling constructs and their meaning,
- A clear distinction between principles, patterns, and constructs, and
- Clear interfaces of the modelling constructs and a way for combining them.

Note that this does not necessarily mean that yet another new workflow language is developed. This would be premature now, and would not have much impact on existing notations and tools. But the ideas contribute to a better understanding and what is really needed and—only in the long run—have an impact on existing systems.

This chapter provides a basis for a discussion and, hopefully, points out the importance of this endeavour. The concrete proposal should provide an idea how this could work, and provide a first heading.

3. PRINCIPLES

Before discussing modelling constructs and how they could be defined, let us have a brief look at the motivation for making models and at different modelling philosophies.

3.1 Modelling Objectives

There are many different reasons why people working on business processes make all kinds of models or, at least, some graphical sketches of the processes. Obviously, the purpose of a model, has a huge impact on the chosen notation. Here, we give an overview of different objectives. Very often, the same model serves different purposes; therefore, the following objectives are not really disjoint.

One objective is to bring some structure in what an analyst learns about a process. In this case, the model is used to develop some *understanding* of what is going on or should go on in a business process. To this end, the models will be used in a highly interactive way, driven by an analyst using them in interaction with the participants and the managers of a process. Later, these models might be used and refined for other purposes, but even getting some rough understanding of a process is an objective in its own right. Therefore, such notations often do not have a precise meaning.

Another objective of a model is *communication and documentation*. This objective is actually part of the first objective. But, it can go much further. A model can help to teach different people what they should do, or help a manager to communicate with the staff, what they are doing. And a model can be used to communicate to a software engineer or IT-expert what he should implement or how existing processes need to be changed, customized, or tailored. Actually, a model alone will almost never be enough. The model needs to be explained by a text or by a personal explanation—how much explanation is needed, of course, depends on the quality of the chosen modelling notation.

Another objective of modelling is to *make things precise and complete*. An appropriate modelling notation forces the modeller to think of all the relevant details and problems, ask the right questions, and then come up with a precise and complete model covering all relevant aspects. A good notation should force the modeller to think about all relevant issues, and look at things from different angles.

Another objective is the *analysis*, *optimization*, and *verification* of the processes. The analysis can be more syntactic like checking that all relevant concepts occur in the processes. Or the analysis could concern the behaviour. This could concern performance measures. Or it could be checking that there are no deadlocks (this would typically be called *verification*). Optimization, typically, is an analysis followed by making some modifications, i. e. making changes to the model. Note, however, that some analysis and verification is not in the interest of the actual process itself, but just helps in making the model correct and complete. In this case, the analysis and verification is actually part of the modelling effort itself; this is often called *validation*. This should not be confused with the actual purpose of making the model; getting the model right cannot be the purpose of the model.

A last objective, is the *execution* of the process, e. g. by a workflow engine. Since the models are directly executed, this allows us to change a process in a very flexible way; in an extreme case the model can be even changed at runtime.

Due to this variety of objectives, it is not too surprising that there are so many different modelling notations. It would be more surprising, if there was a single notation or formalism that is good for all these objectives.

3.2 Criteria for Models

In addition to the different objectives of modelling, there are different modelling principles and philosophies. Though these principles and philosophies are correlated to the objectives, they are often more a matter of belief and personal background. And these philosophies are often made criteria for whether a language or notation is called a modelling notation or not.

One of the most obvious criteria is whether the notation is *graphical* or *textual*. Probably, many people working in business process modelling or modelling in general would not even consider a textual notation to be a modelling notation. This point of view, however, overstates the importance of graphical notations. In this chapter, textual notations are considered to be models too. Being graphical is one criterion for a notation to be a modelling notation, but other criteria are equally important.

Another criterion is the *level of formality*, which means how precisely is the notation defined. This, actually, concerns the precise definition of its syntax as well as the definition of its semantics. We pointed out already that it very much depends on the purpose of making a model, how formal its notation needs to be. Actually, we even made the difference between a notation and a formalism to allow for notations that do not come with a precise semantics. Therefore, also the level of formality should not be overstated as a criterion for being a modelling notation. This depends very much on the objective.

Another criterion is whether the notations are *operational* or not. That means: Can the models be somehow executed or not? First of all, this requires that a notation has a precise semantics; but, even if it has a precise semantics, it is not necessarily executable (or at least not efficiently executable). Actually, a model might exactly define what needs to be achieved, but not how exactly it is achieved. Again, it depends on the purpose of a model, what is necessary. But, at least in the context of workflow management, we would like to end up with operational models.

Maybe, the most important criterion for being a modelling notation is *abstraction*. Does the notation allow for abstracting from irrelevant details and still capture all the relevant details? Again, what is relevant or not depends of the objective. And clearly a workflow modelling notation needs to be more detailed than a business process modelling notation. But, even in the case of a workflow, we would not like to be forced to deal with the bits and bytes and technical details of an operating system etc. We want to deal with and focus on the stuff that is conceptually relevant.

Altogether, this discussion shows that even the criteria for being a modelling notation vary with the objective. In the end, it boils down to that the notation allows (or even forces) the modeller to *adequately* represent all the relevant concepts of a business process for his purpose on the right level of abstraction, not forcing him to introduce artifacts that are irrelevant for his purpose or just there since the notation demands for it in some way (for syntactical reasons or due to the lack of expressive power). We do not believe that all objectives can be achieved with a single notation. But it might be possible to devise a set of related notations that support all objectives and allow for a smooth transition between the different models—starting from the model for the initial understanding up to the workflow model that is executed in the end. But, we should not expect that the transitions between these models can be performed fully automatically. The design decisions taken at these transitions need some intellectual effort.

4. MODELLING CONSTRUCTS

In this section, we discuss some patterns that occur in business processes, and we discuss some ideas on how they could be captured by simple modelling constructs. As discussed earlier, we will focus on the control flow aspect. Only in the end, we will briefly touch on some other aspects—mainly to show that the provided modelling constructs can be combined and extended with modelling concepts from other aspects.

4.1 Patterns and Concepts

In this section, we briefly discuss what needs to be modelled for business processes from the control point of view. We do this by briefly rephrasing and discussing the main workflow patterns and modelling concepts (where the numbers refer to the resp. number of the workflow pattern of [Russell, ter Hofstede, van der Aalst, and Mulyar, 2006]).

Basic Patterns

First of all, for modelling the coordination among or the order of the execution of the tasks of a business process, we need the standard control flow constructs as we have them in programming languages: *sequence* (WCP-1), *choice* (WCP-4 and WCP-5), and *iteration* (WCP-21). Note that [Russell, ter Hofstede, van der Aalst, and Mulyar, 2006] splits up the choice pattern in two parts already: making the choice (WCP-4) and joining the control flow after the choice again (WCP-5). Since we believe that this is already a decision towards specific modelling constructs for realizing such patterns, we consider a choice a single pattern—at least in the *basic* patterns.

We would be tempted to believe, that these three basic patterns are or should be supported by any modelling notation. But, there are modelling notations that do not support iteration. And there are application areas where there is no need for explicit iteration. In these application areas, iteration is rather an exception and should be dealt with as such. If a modelling notation for a workflow system in this area does not support iteration, this could rather be considered as an advantage than a disadvantage—maybe, in combination with a pattern that we call *start over*, which will be discussed at the end of this subsection.

Actually, some of the other patterns that will be discussed below become a problem only in the presence of iteration. Then not having iteration has advantages; at least iteration should be introduced in a more controlled way.

Concurrent Execution and Dependencies

Typical business processes will require that different activities can be executed in parallel to each other since people can work on them independently of each other. We call this pattern *concurrent* execution. In [Russell, ter Hofstede, van der Aalst, and Mulyar, 2006], this pattern is split up in two: the *parallel split* (WCP-2) and the *synchronization* (WCP-3). Again, we believe that this separation is already taking a step towards workflow constructs.

With the introduction of concurrency, everything becomes much more complicated. The reason is that, typically, not all the activities that are executed concurrently can be executed at any time. There are some *dependencies* between them: Some activities can be started only if some others are finished. And there are many different ways in which modelling notations deal with that. As long as there is no iteration, there is a simple solution: we can have explicit dependencies between the activities (resp. the tasks) which tells which activity needs to wait for the termination of others. In the absence of iteration, each activity is executed only once. Therefore, these dependencies have a clear interpretation. As soon as there is some form of iteration, there are many different ways of how such dependencies could be interpreted; the dependencies loose their simple and straightforward interpretation. In this case, a clear and simple interpretation can be achieved by properly nesting the concurrent execution and the other constructs of sequence, choice, and iteration. In that case, however, some dependencies cannot be expressed anymore. Both ways exclude some processes from being properly modelled.

Altogether, these simple solutions, i.e. no iteration or proper nesting, are too restrictive, and therefore many different notations have been introduced. It is the combination of *concurrency* and *iteration* and the need for some form of *dependency* which causes all the trouble and results in the plethora of many different workflow constructs. There are many nice and powerful notations for modelling such concurrent behaviour, but the modelling constructs and the way in which the control is split and joined again is very different among them. Even worse, due to their expressive power, most of them result in problems when combined with some of the more sophisticated patterns discussed below.

Multiple Instances

As discussed above, some parts of a business process are concurrent. Now, an interesting question is how these different parts can be started and later be synchronized again. Often, the same part of a process needs to be executed multiple times concurrently to itself; typically by different people working on different data, which will be combined only after all these concurrent parts are finished. The general name for that pattern is *multiple instances* (WCP-12–WCP-15) and there are many different variants of that. The variants concern questions like: at which time do we know the number of instances that will run concurrently (modelling time WCP-13, run-time WCP-14, or no a priori knowledge WCP-15), or whether or how are the threads synchronized in the end (no synchronization WCP-12, full synchronization of all threads WCP-13/14, or the first *m* finished instances trigger the subsequent task even if not all instances are finished yet WCP-34). Another issue is, whether and how instances can be cancelled.

This shows that there are many different options and constructs that might be needed.

External Choice

Now, let us come back to the basic construct of choice again. The question is who makes the choice if there is one. The first and, from the point of view of a programming language, most natural possibility is that it is made by the workflow system by evaluating the exact conditions. In that case, the people executing a workflow would never be "offered" a choice at the worklist. Therefore, this is called an *internal choice*.

The second possibility is to show both possible choices on the worklist; then the choice would be made by a user selecting one of them. Therefore, this is called *external choice*[3]. Actually, it is not even necessary that the user makes the choice, it could also be that a choice is selected by some incoming event (e. g. a letter from a customer) or the other choice is selected by a timeout (when the expected letter from the customer did not arrive by some deadline). From the view of the control aspect, both of the choices are similar: they are external.

Non-Local Synchronization

Another pattern, which corresponds to a construct, is the non-local OR-join: it synchronizes all potentially incoming threads of control at that point. This is called *structured synchronizing merge* (WCP-7) in [Russell, ter Hofstede, van der Aalst, and Mulyar, 2006]. The problem with that construct is in the term "potentially" incoming thread, which means one needs to find out whether there is the potential for incoming threads or not. This requires a complete analysis of the model, which might be inefficient, undecidable, or even result in an inconsistent semantics (see [Kindler 2006] for a more detailed discussion). Though, there are many problems with this construct, this construct has its purposes: if used in the informal phase, it leaves room for some interpretation and results in much simpler models, by using the "magic" of the non-local OR-join. And even later, the non-local OR-join is not a problem if it is used in a controlled way, i. e. if it is exactly know from where the potential threads of control could come or if their number is known beforehand.

Actually, if used in that controlled way, the non-local OR-join coincides with another pattern, which will be discussed next.

Explicit and Implicit Termination

One important question when devising a modelling notation is: when does a process resp. a case terminate. Basically, there are two choices. The first choice, called *explicit termination* (WCP-43), is termination by executing a designated termination activity[4]. Once this termination activity is finished, the resp. case is also finished. The second choice is that the process is finished, when it is not possible to start any activity anymore. This is called *implicit termination* (WCP-11).

Both philosophies have their advantages and disadvantages. The advantage of explicit termination is that the modeller needs to say explicitly when the process terminates, and that he is forced to think about that. And later, there can be all kinds of analysis techniques to verify whether the model terminates correctly. For example, it could be checked whether there is no work left (there are no other enabled tasks any more), when the process terminates. This is for example done when checking proper termination of a workflow net [van der Aalst, 1998]. The advantage of implicit termination is that there is no need for this kind of analysis, since when the process terminates, it is properly terminated by definition; but of course we loose the chance for a second look for getting our model right. With implicit termination, we cannot distinguish between an unintended deadlock and proper termination.

Actually, the idea of implicit termination can also be applied to parts of a process, e. g. some multiple instances that were started earlier or some selected set of activities, which could be called an *area* or *scope*. In that case, the implicit termination of an area is exactly what we need for the non-local OR-join (restricted to that area). We believe that this was one of the intentions of the non-local OR-join—but the area was not made explicit. In the informal use, this is no problem. When used with an exact semantics, the use of the OR-join and its exact semantics needs careful considerations.

Sub-Processes

Often a task of a process is so complex that it makes sense to start a separate *sub-process* for that purpose. Though this pattern is important, it is not explicitly captured in [Russell, ter Hofstede, van der Aalst, and Mulyar, 2006]. But, pattern *recursion* (WCP-22) shows that it should be there, since recursion is a special case of sub-processes.

Start Over

At last, we would like to discuss another pattern not explicitly covered by [Russell, ter Hofstede, van der Aalst, and Mulyar, 2006]. The reason might be, that it cannot be easily combined with iteration. Another reason might be that it could be considered another aspect, e. g. in the transaction aspect. Since we feel it belongs to the control aspect, we discuss it here. The idea of the start over pattern is the following: Even if the normal execution of a process does not require iteration, we often have situations, where some things decided in earlier activities need to be reconsidered and possibly changed. Note that this is considered as an exception, and it is typically difficult to foresee all the possibilities when such "reconsiderations" could occur; therefore, modelling this control flow by normal control constructs is very tedious and introduces many artifacts. The *start over* pattern allows that a user goes back to that activity (even without having an explicit loop construct there), makes the necessary changes, and then re-executes all intermediate activities again. Of course, this can be done in a more intelligent way, so that only the affected activities need to be revisited again. And the model might also forbid to go back beyond certain milestones and make explicit which tasks may be subject to reconsiderations and which are not. A detailed discussion of this pattern, however, is beyond the scope of this chapter.

4.2 Constructs

Finally, let's have a look at the modelling constructs for business processes from the control point of view. What is more important, we will have a look on how "special purpose constructs" can be combined with an underlying set of basic constructs in a simple and concise way. Actually, that is the main purpose of this chapter.

Basic Formalism

In order to support the basic patterns, we need a basic formalism or some basic constructs. Actually, we can use any formalism for that purpose that provides us with some basic properties, which will be discussed below. In our examples, we use Petri nets, and we can keep Petri nets in the back of our minds, since a concrete modelling notation for the basic constructs might help to better understand the idea. But, we could use any other formalism instead. In the Petri net, we will distinguish some start transitions and some termination transitions. Later, we will show how such a formalism, resp. our Petri nets, can be used in combination with some other constructs that provide the modelling power needed for a specific purpose.

The interface to this formalism should be in such a way that we do not need to talk about it's internal structure, and in particular, its internal states. This is why we suggest initiating and terminating them by initial and terminal tasks instead of defining an initial state and terminal states. But, the formalism of course will have a concept of *state*, and we assume that when creating a new instance of a model, it is in some initial state (which might be explicitly modelled or implicit). The formalism must have some distinguished *initial tasks*. And it must be possible to start an initial task any time, i. e. in any state—though we might not want that to happen, which will be discussed later. For any possible state, the formalism must define which tasks are *enabled*, i. e. which tasks could be instantiated to an activity. For any enabled task, it must be possible to *start* the task. The start of the task will result in a change of the state, and this way, also changes the set of enabled tasks. Moreover, a started task can be *terminated*; this must be possible in any state (provided that the task was started before and was not yet terminated). Then the termination of the task results in another state change.

Note that by splitting the start and the termination of a task in this interface, the formalism can take care of the fact that several tasks can be executed concurrently without forcing the formalism to be truly concurrent. Moreover, the start of a task can disable another one. This way, this interface provides the possibility to support external choice.

Actually, these concepts of the control aspect of workflow models have been already identified in AMFIBIA [Axenath, Kindler, and Rubin, 2007]. And the implementation of AMFIBIA has demonstrated that it is possible to plug-in different kinds of control formalisms for modelling the control flow of a business process. Here, we use the very same concepts for adding the more sophisticated constructs on top of any basic formalism.

Blocks

We assume that the basic formalism provides all the basic coordination mechanisms that are needed, such as sequence, choice, iteration, and concurrency with any kind of dependencies we wish for. Next, we show, how any such formalism can then be enhanced with some more modelling power for multiple instances, their synchronization, cancellation, and even for a controlled way of non-local OR-joins.

Actually, we need to introduce only one additional concept for that purpose: *blocks*. A block refers to a model in some basic formalism that supports the interface defined above. We call the tasks occurring in that formalism the tasks of that block. In addition, a block may contain other blocks, which are called its *sub-blocks*. The tasks of the block may trigger or start sub-blocks by pointing to initial tasks of the sub-blocks. In turn, the tasks of the block may be triggered by the termination of its sub-blocks, and there are different modes for starting a sub-block and how the termination of a sub-block can trigger tasks of the block.

Figure 1. A simple example of using blocks

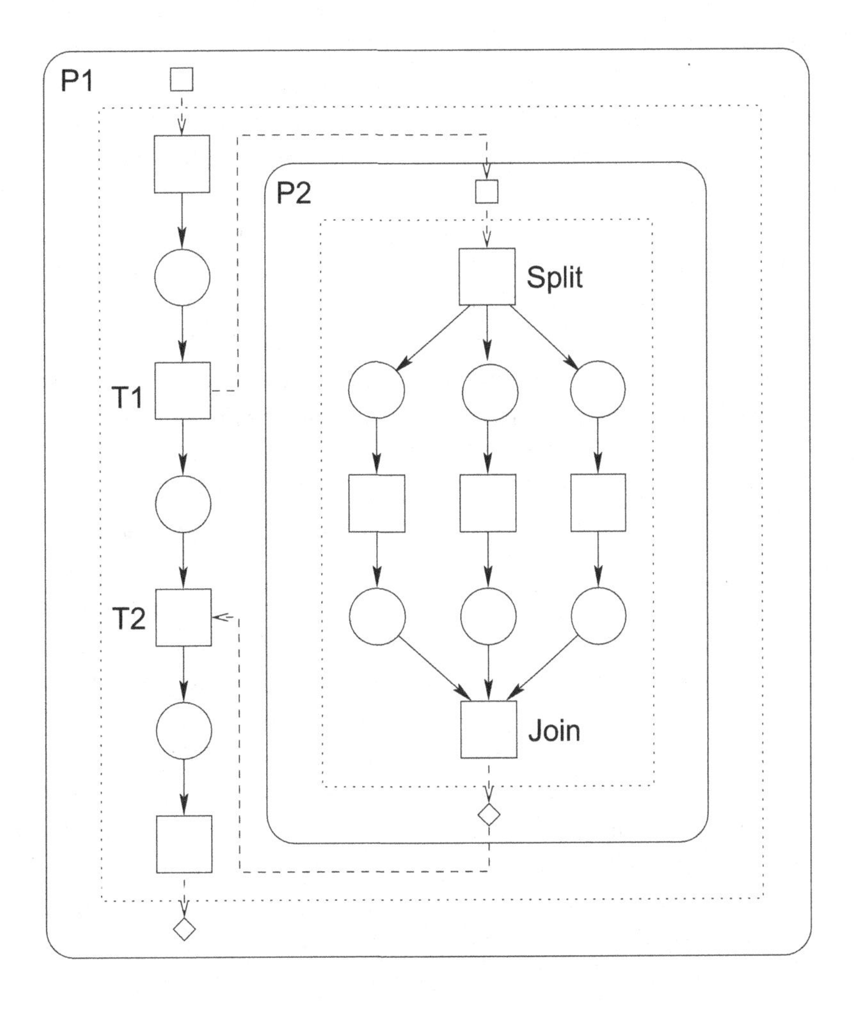

Before discussing these details, we illustrate the general idea by the help of an example, which is shown in Fig. 1. This example consists of one process **P1**, represented as a main block. This block has a sub-block **P2**. The model of the main block is a Petri net consisting of a sequence of four transitions. The start transition is indicated by the additional square at the top of the block with a pointer to that transition, and the termination transition has a pointer to a diamond at the bottom of the block. The sub-block **P2** looks similar, but shows some concurrent behaviour. Now, the idea is that transition **T1** triggers the execution of the sub-block, and then transition **T2** waits for the sub-block to terminate. These triggers are represented by the dashed arcs. Note that these arcs do refer to the interface of the sub-block only; they do not directly go to the formalism within the block. This is actually the key to make this concept independent from the basic formalism.

The basic idea is that a task of the block can trigger the start of the execution of a sub-block, and the termination of a sub-block can be used to trigger a task of the block. The different modes of starting a sub-block and of terminating a sub-block and triggering other tasks will cover many of the patterns mentioned above. Moreover, the sub-blocks will be used for defining an exact scope for non-local operations. And, since sub-blocks refer to models again, blocks provide a straightforward way of sub-processes and even recursion.

Block Entry Modes

Now, let us discuss the different options on how a block can be triggered, which we call *block entry modes*.

First of all, we need to know whether the same sub-block may be triggered and started again, when it is active already (i. e. if it was started already, but did not yet terminate). In analogy to the terminology used in [Russell, ter Hofstede, van der Aalst, and Mulyar, 2006], we call a sub-block *blocking*, if it cannot be started when it is active already. In that case, a task that triggers the execution of the sub-block would also be blocked until the block is not active anymore. This is what we assumed (without saying) in our example of Fig. 1, but it is not relevant there since the sub-block **P2** is triggered only once by the Petri net of the main block.

If a sub-block is not blocking, it may be triggered while active. In this case, we have two major choices. One choice would be to create a new and independent instance every time the sub-block is triggered. This would implement the multiple instance pattern. Therefore, we call this a *multiple instance* block (see example of Fig. 3, which will be discussed later). Another choice is that the sub-block may be triggered while active, but this does not create a new instance of that sub-block. Rather, the triggered initial task of that sub-block will be started in the existing instance[5], resulting in a state change of the existing instance. We call this a *multiple entry* block (see example of Fig. 2, which will be discussed later). Note that such a block might be triggered many times, but it still terminates only once. Only if it is triggered again once after is has terminated, it will be terminate again. But at any time, there will be at most one active instance of a multiple entry block. Since multiple entry blocks and blocking blocks have this property in common, we call both types also *single instance* blocks.

Block Termination Modes

Above, we have already tipped on the termination of a block. And as discussed earlier, the termination of a sub-block may trigger another task of the block. The question now is: When does a sub-block terminate and signal its termination?

For single instance blocks there is not much of a choice. They terminate when the block terminates. The only choice would be whether it terminates explicitly or implicitly. Therefore, it needs to be defined for each sub-block whether it is an implicitly terminating block or not. For the graphical representation of implicit termination, we use a black diamond in the bottom right corner of the block (as shown in Fig. 2); this way, it is possible to use the same sub-block with explicit and implicit termination, and the super-block may even exploit the knowledge on how the sub-block terminated.

Actually, the combination of a multiple entry block with implicit termination provides a controlled form of a non-local OR-join, which, we believe, is close to its original intention. Since we exactly know the scope of the threads and where the threads are, this can easily and efficiently be implemented. Figure 2 shows the idea: The sub-block **P2** is now a multi-entry block, which says that, whenever one of the initial transitions are triggered, new tokens will be added by these transitions to the existing instance of the Petri net, where the inner details of this Petri net are not shown in this figure. The Petri net in the main block triggers the start tasks of the sub-block in an arbitrary way. So, we do not know beforehand which threads need to be synchronized. Once the Petri net in the main block decides not to trigger sub-blocks anymore, it waits for the sub-block to terminate. Since it waits for implicit termination (black diamond in the bottom right corner), it waits for the termination of all activities within the sub-blocks, which is very similar to the be-

Figure 2. Synchronizing all potential threads

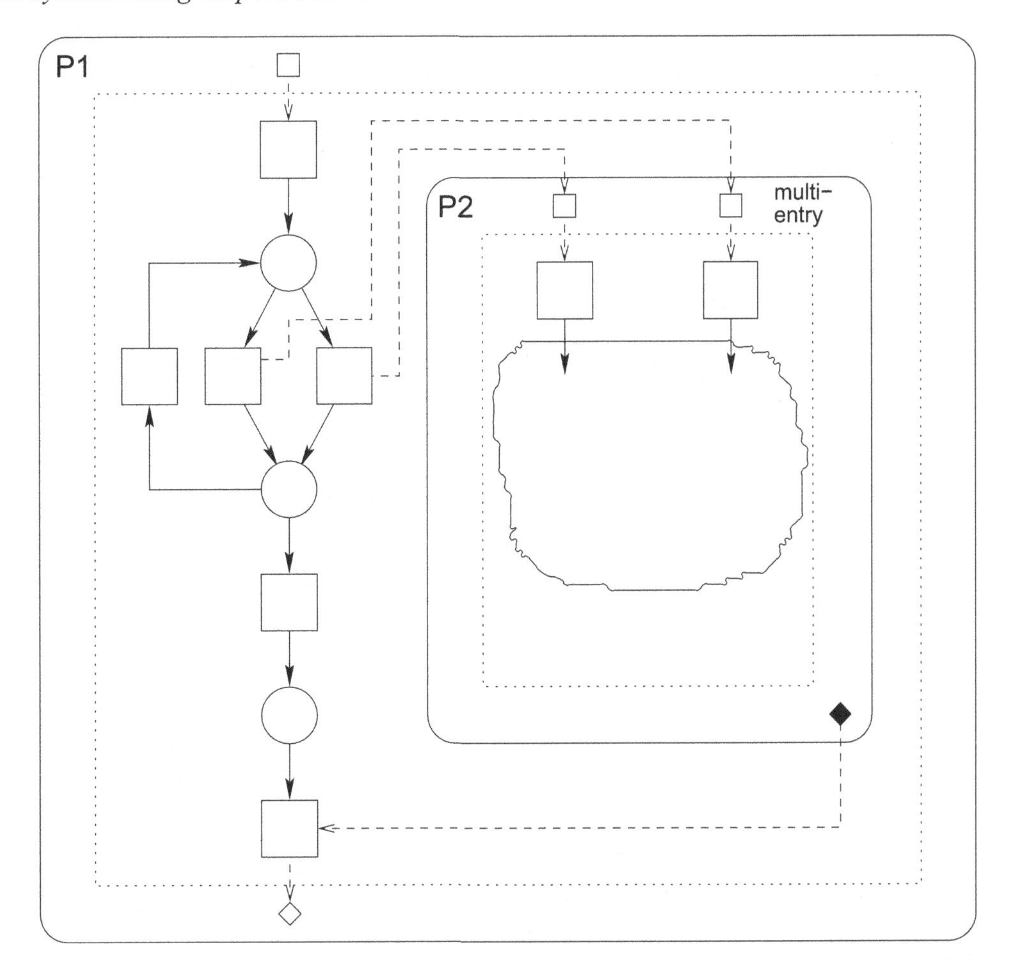

haviour of an OR-join—just in a slightly more controlled way.

For multiple instance blocks, there are more choices on how the termination could trigger the super-block. Of course, we have the choice between every instance terminating implicitly or explicitly. The more interesting question is: If we have several instances running, when do we signal the termination of the sub-block? There are two choices: Either, we signal the termination of every instance, which we call *instance termination.* Or we signal the termination only when the last active instance terminates. We call this *collective termination.* The second case implements the most general *multiple instance with synchronization pattern* (WCP-15). Since it is under the control of a sub-block, however, it is not a problem implementing it.

Figure 3 shows another example, which is structurally similar. But now, the sub-block is a multi-instance block. This means that, whenever the main block triggers the sub-block, a new instance is created. And all these instances run independently of each other. And, just for variety, we indicated that actually there could be two different models running in the sub-block. Which of them are triggered is up to the main-block.

In this example, we decided to use explicit termination of the individual instances again (indicated by the white diamonds). But, we chose collective termination for the sub-block. This way, the main process, after starting some instances, will wait until all instances have terminated explicitly.

Actually, there is one further choice for signalling the termination of a multiple instance block: when the first or the first *m* instances of the block

Figure 3. Multiple instances with synchronization

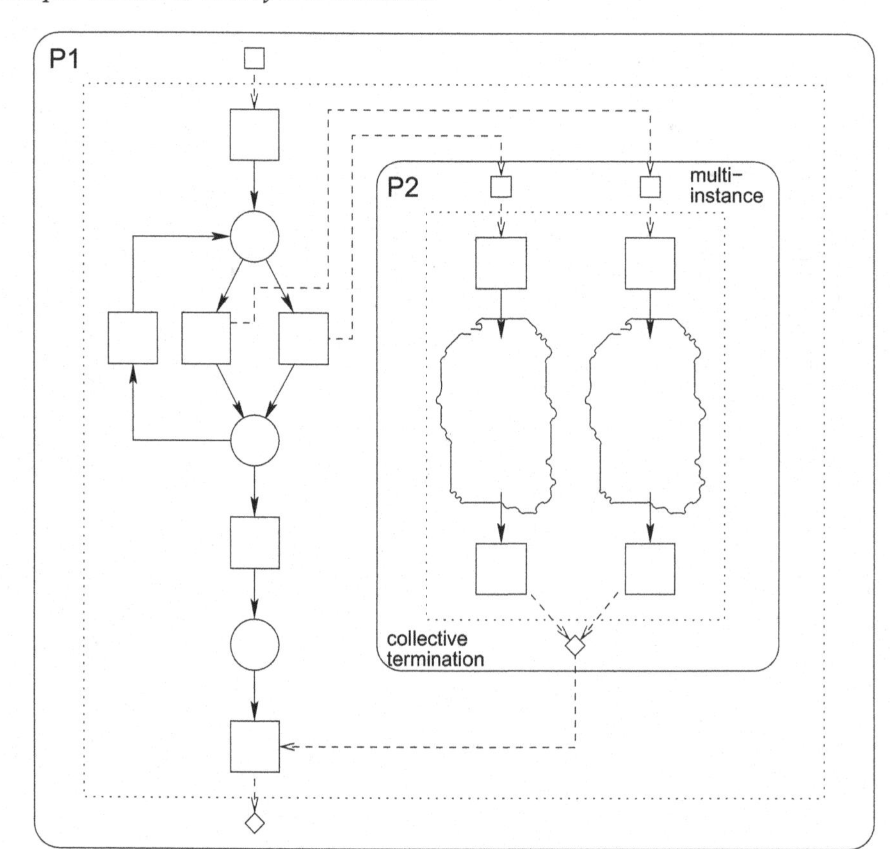

are terminated, the block signals its termination. Still the other instances will be completing their execution; the super-block is just not aware of them anymore and not waiting for them anymore. This realizes the *static partial join for multiple instances* (WCP-34) pattern.

The important feature for realizing this feature it is not so much signalling the termination after the termination of *m* instances. The important feature is that a block is allowed to continue its execution even after it signalled its termination (see Exercise 2). But, for different reasons, this feature is a bit problematic; one reason is related to exception handling, which will be discussed later. Therefore, we are not sure whether this *continue execution after signalling termination* should be introduced.

Cancellation

The concept of blocks can be used for many more purposes and for introducing new modelling constructs for any basic modelling formalism. We show this by the workflow patterns for cancellation (mainly WCP-19, WCP-20, WCP-25, and WCP-26).

Cancellation means, that the execution of an activity (WCP-19), a complete case (WCP-20), or some part (a scope) of the executed process (WCP-25) can be aborted. Again, a block can be used for explicitly defining the scope of the abort. This way, we need only one construct for an abort, and dependent on whether it contains a single task, the complete business process, or only a part, this concept can be used to realize all the patterns. The cancellation of a sub-block will be triggered by a cancellation signal, which could either come from the sub-block itself (when the block wants to cancel itself) or from the outside of the block. We indicated such possibilities in the schema shown in Figure 4 by black squares on the left-hand side of a block.

Cancellation can have all kinds of side effects and could or should also have an effect on other aspects such as the information aspect or the transaction aspect. The information aspect deals with how data are propagated among different activities within a case, and thus needs to make sure that the data of a cancelled block do not affect other activities any more. For the transaction aspect, the situation is even more complicated: It must make sure that, dependent on the exact

Figure 4. The general schema for blocks

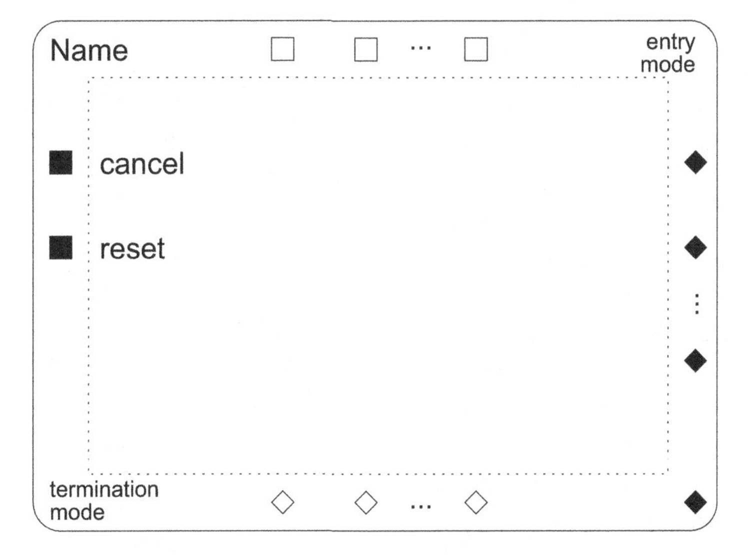

requirement for transactionality, all the data are ignored in a consistent way or are made persistent in a consistent way. Achieving these side effects is much easier, if the scope of cancellation is not coming from some specific scoping construct of some modelling notation for the control flow, but if there is a single and unified concept of blocks for all the aspects.

Exceptions

Note that it is also possible to deal with exceptions ofblocks. A block terminates when an exceptional situation is encountered. This termination, of course, needs to be distinguished from normal termination, so that the block that started the sub-block can properly react to this exception, e. g. terminate with an exception itself or just proceed as normal. In the schema of Fig. 4, the exceptions have been indicated on the right-hand side as black diamonds[6].

The details of this idea need to be worked out. But, we would like to point out one problem already with the *static partial join for multiple instances* (WCP-34) pattern. Remember that this pattern means that a multiple instance sub-block might signal its proper termination, when still some instances are running. Then, the block is not aware of these sub-blocks anymore. In that case, it is not clear, how to react on an exception of one of these running instances.

5. CONCLUSION

In this chapter, we have discussed a block concept for modelling notations of business processes. Blocks themselves are nothing new and occur in other modelling notations, e. g. in BPEL [Andrews, Cubera, et al. 2003]. Here, we have shown that it is possible that virtually any formalism for control flow can be equipped with a concept of blocks. For these blocks, we defined some features concerning entry and termination modes, as well as cancellation and even exceptions completely independently of the basic modelling formalism. The blocks plus the constructs from the basic modelling formalism then support the major workflow patterns as proposed in [Russell, ter Hofstede, van der Aalst, and Mulyar, 2006]—even some tricky patterns like the non-local OR-join, multiple instances with synchronization, or implicit termination. The only requirement for making that work is that the basic formalism supports a very basic interface, which is the one proposed in AMFIBIA.

One reason why this works is that blocks provide an explicit scope for non-local constructs and for multiple instances. Due to the explicit scope, the constructs can be efficiently implemented.

Note that the goal of this chapter was not to introduce yet another workflow notation. Actually, we did introduce only a kind of ad-hoc notation for graphics here. One reason is that the notation as well as the concepts are still a bit premature. Another reason is that the concepts presented here, are clearly on the formal and operational side—ignoring a bit the objectives behind more informal notations. We hope that there could be a less formal notation without a strict concept of blocks. The blocks could then be introduced later in the design process as design decisions in order to make the models executable. This, however, needs further analysis.

The main message of this chapter is that much of the modelling power can be achieved with a single construct, which can be combined with virtually any basic modelling notation. This way, we hope to have proved that sometimes it might help to strip a modelling notation from some of its constructs, instead of adding more and more and more constructs to it.

And we hope to eventually find some people who would be willing to find out what is really needed in business process modelling—independently from a fixed notation. Thinking about solutions to some of the exercises might be a start.

REFERENCES

Andrews, T., Cubera, F., Dholakia, H., Goland, Y., Klein, J., Leymann, F., Liu, K., Roller, D., Smith, D., Thatte, S., Trickovic, I., & Weerawarama, S. (2003). *Business process execution language for web services specification*. Technical Report Version 1.1, May 5.

Axenath, B., Kindler E., & Rubin, V. (2007). AMFIBIA: A meta-model for the integration of business process modelling aspects. *International Journal on Business Process Integration and Management, 2*(2), 120-131.

Hollingsworth, D. (1995, January). *The workflow reference model.* (Technical Report TC00-1003). The Workflow Management Coalition (WfMC).

Keller, G., Nüttgens, M., & Scheer, A.-W. (1992, January). *Semantische Prozessmodellierung auf der Grundlage Ereignisgesteuerter Prozessketten (EPK).* (Technical Report Veröffentlichungen des Instituts für Wirtschaftsinformatik (IWi), Heft 89). Universität des Saarlandes.

Kindler, E. (2004, June). On the semantics of EPCs: Resolving the vicious circle. In J. Desel, B. Pernici, & M. Weske (Eds.), *Business Process Management, Second International Conference, BPM 2004*, (*LNCS*, 3080 pp. 82–97). Springer.

Kindler, E. (2006, January). On the semantics of EPCs: Resolving the vicious circle. *Data and Knowledge Engineering, 56*(1), 23-40.

Leymann, F., & Roller, D. (1999). *Production workflow: Concepts and techniques*. Upper Saddle River, NJ: Prentice-Hall PTR.

Nüttgens, M., & Rump, F. J. (2002). Syntax und Semantik Ereignisgesteuerter Prozessketten (EPK). In *PROMISE 2002, Prozessorientierte Methoden und Werkzeuge für die Entwicklung von Informationssystemen*, volume P-21 of *GI Lecture Notes in Informatics*, (pp. 64–77). Gesellschaft für Informatik.

Russell, N., ter Hofstede, A. H. M., van der Aalst, W. M. P., & Mulyar, N. (2006). *Workflow control-flow patterns: A revised view.* (Technical Report Report BPM-06-22). BPM Center, BPMcenter.org.

van der Aalst, W. (1998). The application of Petri nets to workflow management. *The Journal of Circuits, Systems and Computers, 8*(1), 21-66.

van der Aalst, W., Desel, J., & Kindler, E. (2002, November). On the semantics of EPCs: A vicious circle. In M. Nüttgens & F. J. Rump (Eds.), *EPK 2002, Geschäftsprozessmanagement mit Ereignisgesteuerten Prozessketten*, (pp. 71–79).

van der Aalst, W., & van Hee, K. (2002). *Workflow management: Models, methods, and systems*. Cooperative Information Systems. The MIT Press.

van der Aalst, W. M. P., ter Hofstede, A. H. M., Kiepuszewski, B., & Barros, A. P. (2002). *Workflow Patterns.* (QUT Technical report, FIT-TR-2002-02, Queensland University of Technology, Brisbane). (Accepted for publication in Distributed and Parallel Databases, also see http://www.tm.tue.nl/it/research/patterns.).

van der Aalst, W. M. P., ter Hofstede, A. H. M., Kiepuszewski, B., & Barros, A. P. (2003, July). Workflow patterns. *Distributed and Parallel Databases, 14*(3), 5-51.

Workflow Management Coalition: Terminology & glossary. (1999, February). (Technical Report WFMC-TC-1011). The Workflow Management Coalition (WfMC).

EXERCISES

Here are four exercises that should help better understanding the ideas and concepts of this chapter, and to work them out in more detail. The effort for solving them is increasing: starting from about 15 minutes (Exercise 1) up to the equivalent of a student project (Exercise 4), the results of which could actually be a small publication.

1. The IBM workflow system MQ-Series (WebSphere) does not provide an explicit construct for iteration. But, this can be realized by making use of sub-processes with exit conditions. How can this idea be represented with blocks?
   Hint: Use a block that has two different exits.
2. The workflow-pattern *static partial join for multiple instances* (WCP-34 of [Russell, ter Hofstede, van der Aalst, and Mulyar, 2006]) starts a number n of instances of a sub-processes; subsequent activities can be started if at least a fixed number m out of these n sub-processes have terminated. How can this be modelled with the termination modes defined in this chapter and the feature of blocks that are allowed to continue their execution even after signalling their termination?
3. This chapter presented the idea of some concepts only! Many subtleties and problems have not been addressed. Think on solutions and answers to the following questions:
   a. In the examples, the start and exit events of a sub-block were connected to exactly one transition of the super-block. But, this is not necessary. How exactly could the meaning of an exit event be defined, that is connected to several events of the super-block? What should happen, when the sub-block terminates, but the corresponding transition in the super-block is not enabled? Discuss the choices!
   b. Blocks can be nested. What does implicit termination of a block mean then? We discussed that it is possible that a sub-block signals termination, but still is running (without the super-block being aware of that). What does that imply for implicit termination?
   c. If a sub-block raises an exception, it terminates and the corresponding event triggers a transition in the super-block. What should happen if no such transition is enabled in the super-block when the exception occurs? Think of exception-handling in some programming language.
4. Show that the ideas of blocks can be made work by
   a. Implementing a simple simulator for this block concept, with an implementation of Petri nets that have the interface for a formalism or by
   b. Defining a precise semantics for this framework.

KEY TERMS

Block: Blocks are a way of structuring a business process model in disjoint parts. In the context of this chapter, they are also used as the scope for certain modelling constructs such as non-local synchronization. They are independent of a particular modelling formalism and can be used for integrating models for different aspects of the same business process.

Business Process Model: A business process model is a more or less formal and more or less detailed description of the persons and documents involved in the execution of a business process and its task and the rules governing their execution.

Modelling Construct: A modelling construct is the basic syntactical units provided by a modelling notation for building a model.

Modelling Notation / Formalism: A modelling notation defines the rules according to which a model is built. It defines the textual or graphical syntax of a model. A modelling notation is called a modelling formalism if, along with the syntax, a precise meaning is defined.

Non-Local Synchronization: Synchronization means that two or more threads of control wait for each other. A synchronization is called non-local when the exact kind and number of the different threads one waits for is not know locally at a workflow construct. A typical example is the non-local OR-join construct.

Workflow Pattern: Workflow patterns were introduced in order to better understand what needs to be covered by notations for business processes modelling and for comparing modelling notations. They distil typical situations in business processes that need to be modelled.

ENDNOTES

1 See http://www.workflowpatterns.com/

2 Note that we do not use the term semantics here, since it is typically used only for a mathematical definition of the meaning of the notation. By using the more general term "meaning", we accept that a precise text explaining the meaning of a notation or an implementation executing it makes a notation a formalism.

3 In [Russell, ter Hofstede, van der Aalst, and Mulyar, 2006], it is called *deferred choice* (WCP-16) which puts the focus more on the time when choices are made.

4 Explicit termination could also be formulated in a way that a specific termination state (or one of a set of designated termination states) is reached. This, actually, is the definition given in [Russell, ter Hofstede, van der Aalst, and Mulyar, 2006]. Since the concept of a state is a concept not strictly necessary for talking on business processes, we prefer to define termination by designated termination activities.

5 In order to do this, we have required in our interface for the basic formalism that it must be possible to start all the initial tasks in any state.

6 Actually, implicit termination was also shown as a black diamond in the bottom right corner. We have chosen that notation since implicit termination could be considered as kind of an exception: a deadlock without explicit termination.

Chapter VII
ICN-Based Workflow Model and its Advances

Kwanghoon Kim
Kyonggi University, South Korea

Clarence A. Ellis
University of Colorado at Boulder, USA

ABSTRACT

This chapter introduces the basic concepts of information control net (ICN) and its workflow models. In principle, a workflow model is the theoretical basis of a workflow modeling methodology as well as a workflow enactment architecture. Particularly, the workflow model is directly related with how its major components are embodied for implementing the underlying workflow enactment system, too. Accordingly, the authors describe the graphical and formal representations of ICN-based workflow model and its advanced models—role-based model and actor-based model—that can be automatically transformed from the ICN-based workflow model in order to improve their verifiability, maintainability and usability. Conclusively stating, we strongly believe that the ICN-based workflow model and its advanced models be very useful not only for maximizing the quality of workflows but also for strengthening theoretical backgrounds of the recent research issues, such as workflow verification/validation, workflow reengineering, workflow intelligence, workflow mining/rediscovery, and advanced workflow architectures, and so on.

INTRODUCTION

In general, a workflow management system consists of two components—modeling component and enacting component. The modeling component allows a modeler to define, analyze and maintain all of the workflow-related information which is necessary to describe a workflow procedure[2], and the enacting component supports users to play essential roles of invoking, executing and monitoring the workflow model defined by the modeling component. In other words, the logical foundation of the modeling component is the so-called workflow model that is represented by a set of entities and their relationships in order to describe a specific workflow. Therefore, the expressiveness of a workflow is decided by the underlying workflow model and its modeling system. Also, the conceptual methodology of the enacting component is called workflow architecture that is used to describing an internal structure of the workflow enacting component and characterizing its architectural style focusing on capabilities to create, manage and execute the workflow model.

In result, the workflow model and the workflow architecture become the theoretical bases on the design and implementation of a workflow management system. Of course, there may be several different types of the workflow model and different styles of the workflow architecture. According to which type of the workflow model, the underlying workflow management system may have a different way of representation and different features in modeling a workflow procedure. Likewise, different styles of the workflow architecture may show different ways of executing workflow procedures and different efficiencies as well. Therefore, the workflow model and the workflow architecture have to incorporate the advanced technological and organizational features so that the corresponding workflow management system not only displays an efficient way of modeling work and effective supports of executing performance, but also acclimates itself to a new technological and organizational environment. As the important technological trends that may affect the innovation of workflow model and architecture, we consider the powerful networked personal computing facilities like Grid/P2P computing environment, and the increasingly large and complex workflow applications; The advanced workflow models and their architectures introduced in this chapter are the outcomes of those research activities trying to improve the expressiveness of the traditional workflow model and architecture for acclimating the recent technological trends.

In this chapter, we introduce a typical workflow modeling methodology, the so-called information control net abbreviated to ICN, and describe the basic concept of ICN-based workflow model and its formalism through graphical notations and their

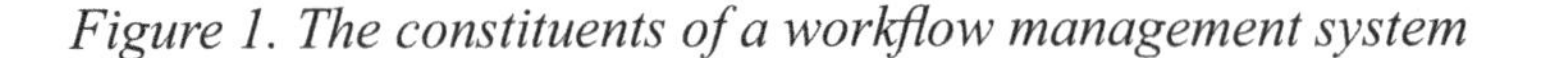

Figure 1. The constituents of a workflow management system

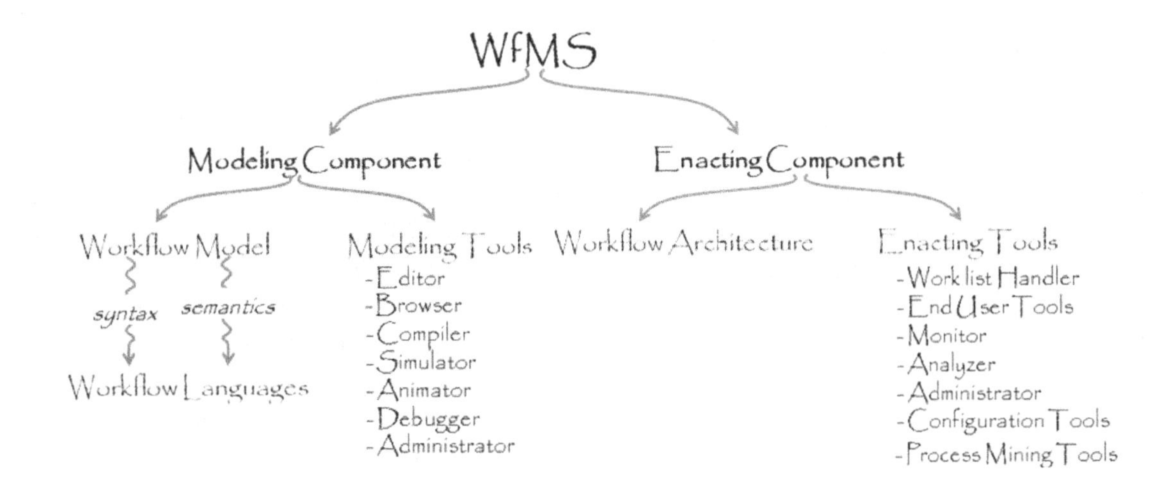

formal expressions. Based upon the methodology, we also explain the detailed descriptions of the advanced workflow models and their formalisms through defining graphical and formal notations. Finally, we summarize with suggesting a list of future research and development issues related with the advanced workflow models.

BACKGROUND

As shown in Figure 1, which is slightly modified from (Ellis & Nutt, 1993), a workflow management system is based upon two conceptual supports as well as two sets of functional supports; the former is workflow model and workflow architecture, and the latter is a set of modeling-related tools and another set of enacting-related tools. The modeling-related tools used to contain those graphical tools for a modeler to define, analyze, and maintain all the information necessary to describe a workflow procedure. In other words, in order to efficiently modeling a workflow procedure it is necessary to be supported by several tools, such as graphical editor and browser, simulator, animator, debugger and administrating tool. The workflow editor and browser take in charge of graphical editing supports to the specifications of workflow procedures, and the workflow language and its verification tools are to check the integrity of the specified workflow models. Particularly, the simulator and animator are used to checking up the pragmatical properties of the specified workflow models. Last of all, a defined and verified workflow model through those tools' supports is translated into one of the workflow languages like WPDL[3] or XPDL[4].

So far, several types of workflow models have been introduced in the literature. Almost all of the currently available workflow management systems are based upon the following types of workflow model:

- **Communication-based model (Bair, 1990).** This model stems from Winograd/Flores' "Conversation for Action Model". It assumes that the objective of office procedure reengineering is to improve customer satisfaction. It reduces every action in a workflow for four phases based on communication between a customer and a performer: Preparation, Negotiation, Performance, and Acceptance phase. But this model is not appropriate for modeling and supporting the development of workflow implementations which have some objectives such as minimizing information system cost(not customer satisfaction), because it has some limitations in supporting the development of workflow management; For example, it is not able to indicate which activities can occur in parallel, in conditional, or in alternative.
- **Activity-based model (Ellis, 1983).** This model focuses on modeling the work instead of modeling the commitments among humans. Unlike communication-based model, activity-based model does not capture objectives such as customer satisfaction. Many commercial workflow management systems provide activity-based workflow models. The ICN-based workflow model, which is the major part of this chapter, is one of the activity-based models. Also, there are several extensions such as procedure-based model, document-based model, goal-based model, and object-oriented model. Especially, the goal-based model is a typical example that combines the communication-based model and the activity-based model.
- **Perspective-based model (Kim & Ellis, 2001).** The model supports the specification of workflows through several perspectives: the functional (the functional units of workflow processing), the behavior (the control flow of workflow), the information(the data flow of workflow), the operational(the applications deployed in workflow), and the

organizational(the organizational structure and actors who perform the workflow) perspective. This model focuses on the open aspects to support the integration of additional perspectives such as the history perspective and transactional perspective.

- **Transactional model (Kim & Ellis, 2001).** This model involves the specification of the extended transaction management that consists of a set of constituent transactions corresponding to the workflow activities, and a set of transaction dependencies between them corresponding to the workflow structure and correctness criterion. Thus, the model focuses on the system-oriented workflows, not the human-oriented workflows. The system-oriented workflow involves computer systems that perform computation-intensive operations and specialized software tasks. That is, while the human-oriented workflow often controls an coordinates human tasks, the system-oriented workflow controls and coordinates software tasks.

The execution of a workflow model is an essential task of the enacting component. The conceptual basis of the enacting component is workflow architecture, and also its functional basis is supported by a set of enacting tools, such as worklist handler, end user (client) tools, monitoring tools, analyzer, and others. Basically, the workflow architecture is directly related with the conceptual idea in terms of how to implement an enactment controller (workflow engine) handling the execution of a workflow model, while the enacting tools have something to do with how to provide graphical and functional interfaces to the users and the invoked applications that are associated with the workflow model. The enactment controller's essential functionality is made up of information managing component and scheduling component. The information managing component's primary function is to manage the controller's database schema and also it may be strengthened with additional functions like recovering from failures without losing data or logging all execution trails and events. The scheduling component is to control the execution flow of a workflow model and to provide the communication channels among active components of the underlying workflow architecture. The control flow part is the most important factor in deciding a style of workflow architecture, and can be a decisive criterion for classifying types of workflow architecture. The followings are the important considerations characterizing the control flow part of a workflow architecture:

- What entity types of a workflow model are concretized in a workflow architecture: activity, role, actor, workcase or others
- Which of them are realized as active software modules (objects) of the workflow architecture: passive components vs. active components
- How they are communicating and interacting with each other: method invoking vs. message queueing

Similarly, the enacting tools primarily support two types of interactions—interactions with the end users and interactions with invoked application programs. The former is the interface with the end users through worklists assigned to each of the users, and the latter is the interface with application programs representing the specific tasks to be performed by the user. The user interface and the application program interface appear in the WfMC's reference model as worklist and invoked applications, respectively. As a result, the workflow architecture of a workflow management system is decided by the approaches that the functional supports and their interaction mechanisms are implemented. That is, the implementation architecture implies an execution infrastructure for workflow models. Also, the implementation architecture for a workflow management system can be differently configured by considering the requirements like reliability, scalability, robustness and manageability. Therefore, it is no exaggeration to say that the efficiency of a workflow management system is determined by its underlying workflow architecture.

So far, several workflow architectures for a workflow management system have been proposed and implemented. Each of these architectures reflects a specific workflow model and contrives its own optimal implementations to satisfy various requirements from document management, imaging, application launching, and/or human coordination, collaboration, and decision making arena. However, there have been a lot of changes and evolutions in the technological computing environments and in the business circumstances as well; workflow architectures should be able to cope with not only those evolving technological trends changing from the centralized computing or the homogeneous distributed computing environments to the heterogeneous distributed computing environments without loss of performance and scalability capabilities, but also those swiftly changing business requirements from the process automation issues to the process intelligence, business activity monitoring, process agility, and the realtime enterprise architecture issues.

Conclusively, considering those advanced workflow requirements require workflow management systems to be enriched by dynamic changes, goal-based, and heterogeneous distributed and large scaled, which mean that a workflow model should provide a way to effectively represent flexibility, distribution and scalability concerns of workflow procedures; according to what workflow model is used, its workflow architecture should reflect dynamically evolving workflow procedures, distributed enactment controllers and an increasing number of actors and roles, too. However, the previous workflow models and architectures lack for supports for these advanced requirements. Therefore, in this chapter we introduce several advanced workflow models that can be feasible resolutions of those advanced requirements. We strongly believe that the advanced workflow models can be more effective and efficient if the concepts of actor, role and workcase orientations rather than activity orientation are embedded into workflow models and their workflow architectures at the same time. This chapter peculiarly addresses the Information Control Net (ICN) that is a formal methodology to systematically and formally describe the advanced workflow models, and describes their

Figure 2. The workflow meta-model

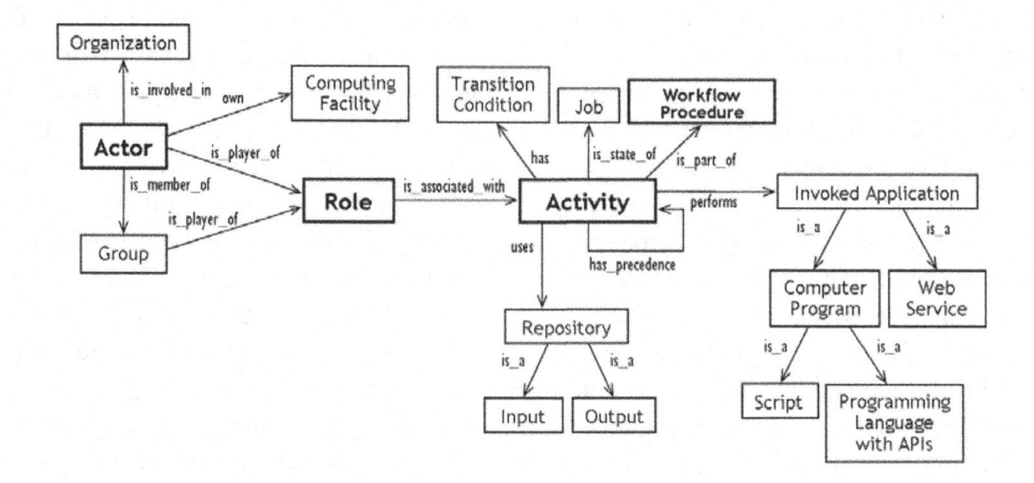

implications to be expected from incorporating the advanced concepts into the advanced workflow architectures. In the following sections, we precisely state the ICN-based workflow model through an example, its meta-model and advanced workflow models. At the end, we summarize the chapter with stating the architectural implications of the ICN-based workflow model and its advanced workflow models.

ICN-Based Workflow Model

This section describes the basic concept of ICN-based workflow model (Ellis, 1983), and its advanced workflow models role-based model, and actor-based model—to be the theoretical bases for their advanced workflow architectures. In describing the ICN-based workflow model, we define its graphical notations and their formal representations. Additionally, we try to define the advanced workflow models through graphical notations and their formal representations too, and finally we specify the algorithms that are able to automatically generate the advanced workflow models from the ICN-based workflow model.

Workflow Meta-Model

In describing a ICN-based workflow model, we would use the basic workflow terminology—workflow procedure, activity, job, workcase, role, actor/group, and invoked application including web services. These terms become the primitive entity types to be composed into ICN-based workflow models, and also they have appropriate relationships with each other as shown in Figure 2. The followings are the basic definitions of the primitive entity types:

- A **workflow procedure** is defined by a predefined or intended set of tasks or steps, called activities, and their temporal ordering of executions. A workflow management system helps to organize, control, and execute such defined workflow procedures. Conclusively, a workflow procedure can be described by a temporal order of the associated activities through the combinations of sequential logics, conjunctive logics (after activity A, do activities B and C), disjunctive logics (after activity A, do activity B or C), and loop logics.
- An **activity** is a conceptual entity of the basic unit of work (task or step), and the activities in a workflow procedure have precedence relationships, each other, in terms of their execution sequences. Also, the activity can be precisely specified by one of the three entity types—compound activity, elementary activity and gateway activity. The compound activity represents an activity containing another workflow procedure, which is called subworkflow. The elementary activity is an activity that can be realized by a computer program, such as application program, transaction, script, or web service. And the gateway activity implies an activity that is used to controlling execution sequences of elementary/compound activities. The types of gateway activities consist of conjunctive gateway (after activity A, do activities B and C), disjunctive gateway (after activity A, do activity B or C), and loop gateway. Particularly, both the disjunctive gateway and the loop gateway need to be set some specific **transition conditions** in order to select one of the possible transition pathes during the execution time. The transition condition itself can be defined by using the input/output relevant data on the **repository**. Additionally, each activity has to be associated with a real performer, such as organizational staff (role, participant) and system, who possesses all ownerships over that activity.
- A **role**, as an logical unit of the organizational structure, is a named designator for one or more participants, which conveniently acts

as the basis for participating works, skills, access controls, execution controls, authority, and responsibility over the associated activity.

- An **actor** is a person, program, or entity that can fulfill roles to execute, to be responsible for, or to be associated in some way with activities and workflow procedures. Multiple instances of a workflow procedure may be in various stages of execution. Thus, the workflow procedure can be considered as a class (in object oriented terminology), and each execution, called a **workcase**, can be considered an instance. A workcase is thus defined as the locus of control for a particular execution of a workflow procedure.
- An **invoked application program** that automatically performs the associated activity, or provides automated assistance within hybrid activities are called **scripts**. If an activity is executed in automatic or hybrid mode, this means that whole/part of the invoked application program associated with the activity is automatically launched by an workflow enactment service.
- Finally, a **repository** is a set of input and output relevant data of an activity. Eventually, the repository provides a communication channel between the workflow enactment domain and the invoked application programs domain. That is, the input and the output repositories are used to realizing the input parameters and the output parameters of the associated invoked application program, respectively.

Information Control Net

An ICN-based workflow model can be defined by capturing the notations of workflow procedures, activities and their control precedence, invoked applications, roles, actors, and input/output repositories, as explained in the previous section of the workflow meta-model. In this section, we define the basic concept of workflow model with respect to the formal and graphical descriptions of ICN-based workflow model. The following [**Definition 1**] is a formal definition of ICN-based workflow model, and its functional components to be used for retrieving workflow-related information, such as activity precedence(control flow), activity-role association, activity-relevant data association(data flow), activity-invoked application association, activity-transition condition association, and role-actor association information. Based upon these types of information, it is possible to retrieve several types of derived workflow-related information like activity-actor association, relevant data-invoked application association, role complexity, actor complexity information, and so forth.

Definition 1. Information Control Net (ICN) *for formally defining workflow model. A basic* ***ICN*** *is 8-tuple* $\Gamma = (\delta, \rho, \lambda, \varepsilon, \pi, \kappa, \boldsymbol{I}, \boldsymbol{O})$ *over a set* ***A*** *of activities (including a set of group activities), a set* ***T*** *of transition conditions, a set* ***R*** *of repositories, a set* ***G*** *of invoked application programs, a set* ***P*** *of roles, and a set* ***C*** *of actors (including a set of actor groups), where*

- ***I*** *is a finite set of initial input repositories, assumed to be loaded with information by some external process before execution of the ICN;*
- ***O*** *is a finite set of final output repositories, perhaps containing information used by some external process after execution of the ICN;* $\delta = \delta_i \cup \delta_o$ *where,* $\delta_o : A \rightarrow \wp(\wp(A))$ *is a multi-valued function mapping an activity to its sets of (immediate) successors (subset of the powerset of* ***A****) and* $\delta_i : A \rightarrow \wp(\wp(A))$ *is a multi-valued function mapping an activity to its sets of (immediate) predecessors (subset of the powerset of* ***A****);*

$\rho = \rho_i \cup \rho_o$

where $\rho_o : A \rightarrow \wp(R)$ *is a multi-valued function mapping an activity to its set of output repositories, and* $\rho_i : A \rightarrow \wp(R)$ *is a multi-valued function mapping an activity to its set of input repositories;*
$\lambda = \lambda_a \cup \lambda_g$
where $\lambda_g : A \rightarrow \wp(G)$ *is a single-valued function mapping an activity to its invoked application program, and* $\lambda_a : G \rightarrow \wp(A)$ *is a multi-valued function mapping an invoked application program to its set of associated activities;*
$\varepsilon = \varepsilon_a \cup \varepsilon_p$
where $\varepsilon_p : A \rightarrow \wp(P)$ *is a single-valued function mapping an activity to a role, and* $\varepsilon_a : P \rightarrow \wp(A)$ *is a multi-valued function mapping a role to its sets of associated activities;*
$\pi = \pi_p \cup \pi_c$
where, $\pi_c : P \rightarrow \wp(C)$ *is a multi-valued function mapping a role to its sets of associated actors, and* $\pi_p : C \rightarrow \wp(P)$ *is a multi-valued function mapping an actor to its sets of associated roles;*
$\kappa = \kappa_i \cup \kappa_o$
where $\kappa_i : A \rightarrow \wp(T)$ *is a multi-valued function mapping an activity to a set of control-transition conditions,* ***T****, on directed arcs,* $(\delta_i(\alpha), \quad \alpha \in A)$ *between* $\delta_i(\alpha)$ *and α; and* $\kappa_o : A \rightarrow \wp(T)$ *is a multi-valued function mapping an activity to a set of control-transition conditions,* ***T****, on directed arcs,* $(\alpha \in A, \delta_o(\alpha))$ *between α and* $\delta_o(\alpha)$

Starting and Terminating Nodes. Additionally, the execution of a workflow model commences by a single χ transition-condition. So, we always assume without loss of generality that there is a single starting node ($\nabla\nabla\nabla\nabla\nabla\nabla : \alpha_I$). At the commencement, it is assumed that all input repositories in the set **I** have been initialized with data by the external system:

$\alpha_I \in A | \delta_i(\alpha_I) = \{\emptyset\} \wedge \kappa_o(\alpha_I) = \{\{\chi\}\}.$

The execution is terminated with any one λ output transition-condition. Also we assume without loss of generality that there is a single terminating node ($\nabla\nabla\nabla\nabla\nabla\nabla : \alpha_F$). The set of output repositories **O** is data holders that may be used after termination by the external system:

$\alpha_F \in A | \delta_o(\alpha_F) = \{\emptyset\} \wedge \kappa_i(\alpha_F) = \{\{\chi\}\}.$

Control Flow: Temporal Ordering of Activities. Given a formal definition, the temporal ordering of activities in a workflow model can be interpreted as follows: For any activity α, in general,

$$\delta(\alpha) = \{ \{\beta_{11}, \beta_{12}, \ldots, \beta_{1m(1)}\}, \{\beta_{21}, \beta_{22}, \ldots, \beta_{2m(2)}\}, \ldots \{\beta_{11}, \beta_{12}, \ldots, \beta_{1m(1)}\}, \},$$

means that upon the completion of activity α, a transition that simultaneously initiates all of the activities β_{i1} through $\beta_{im(i)}$ occurs, which is called a parallel transition; otherwise only one value out of $i(1 \leq i \leq n)$ is selected as the result of a decision made within activity *α*, which is called a decision transition. Note that if $n = 1 \wedge m = 1$, then neither decision nor parallel is needed after completion of activity *α*, which means that the transition is a sequential transition. Additionally stating to make sure, if $m(i) = 1$ for all *i*, then no parallel processing is initiated by completion of *α*.

Based on the interpretation, we graphically define these primitive transition types as shown in Figure3. The former, that an activity has a conjunctive (or parallel) transition, is represented by a solid dot(•), and the latter, that an activity has a disjunctive (or decision) transition, is represented by hollow dot(○). Besides, as defined in the previous section, these special types of activities are called gateway activities, and in order to be syntactically safe, it is very important for these gateway activities to keep the structured properties—proper nesting and matched pair properties. Therefore, not only each of the gateway activities always keeps matched pair with split and join types of gateway activity in a workflow procedure, but also multiple sets of the gateway activities keep in a properly nested pattern. Summarily, the following is to formally describe for the basic transition types modeled by the exclusive-OR and AND gateway activities depicted in Figure 3.

Sequential Transition between activities *incoming* $\rightarrow \delta_i(\alpha_B) = \{\{\alpha_A\}\}$; *outgoing* $\rightarrow \delta_o(\alpha_B) = \{\{\alpha_C\}\}$;

Exclusive OR Transition through *xor-gateway* *xor-split* $\rightarrow \delta_o(\alpha_A) = \{\{\alpha_B\}, \{\alpha_C\}\}$; *xor-join* $\rightarrow \delta_i(\alpha_D) = \{\{\alpha_B\}, \{\alpha_C\}\}$;

AND Transition through *and-gateway* *and-split* $\rightarrow \delta_o(\alpha_A) = \{\{\alpha_B, \alpha_C\}\}$; *and-join* $\rightarrow \delta_i(\alpha_D) = \{\{\alpha_B, \alpha_C\}\}$;

Loop Transition: Block Activity. Especially, we have to take care of an iterative (loop) transition that is the most essential as well as common construct in modeling the temporal ordering of activities. We do need to graphically define the iterative (loop) transition type as a pair of double-hollow dots of gateway activities shown in Figure 3. At a glance, it can be interpreted as a special type of disjunctive transition type; however, if we replace this transition type with a disjunctive transition type, it is very hard to maintain the structured properties—matched pair and proper nesting—of workflow model. Therefore, we introduce a concept of block[5] activity in order to keep the structured properties in modeling a workflow procedure and for the sake of the simplification of modeling work, as well. The block activity contains two gateway—loop-begin and loop-end—activities, and modeling the temporal ordering of the activities inside of the two gateway activities is done by an exactly same way of the ICN-based workflow modeling approach; justly on the gateway activities we have to specify the loop's exit conditions in the modeling time. Accordingly, the formal definition of a block activity's gateway activities shown in Figure3 is as the following:

loop-begin Gateway
$\rightarrow \delta_i(\alpha_{loop-begin}) = \{\{\alpha_A\}\}$; $\delta_o(\alpha_{loop-begin}) = \{\{\alpha_B\}\}$;

loop-end Gateway
$\rightarrow \delta_i(\alpha_{loop-end}) = \{\{\alpha_C\}\}$; $\delta_o(\alpha_{loop-end}) = \{\{\alpha_D\}\}$;

Assigning Roles and Actors. For any activity α, $\varepsilon_p(\alpha) = \{\eta_1, \eta_2, \ldots, \eta_n\}$, where n is the number

Figure 3. The information control net primitives

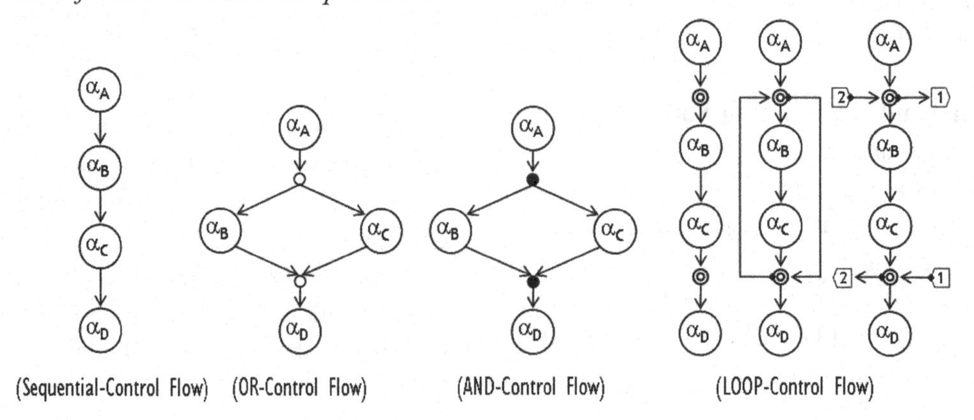

of roles, $\forall \eta \in P$, involved in the activity, means that an activity α is performed by one of the roles; Also, $\varepsilon_a(\eta) = \{\alpha_1, \alpha_2, ..., \alpha_m\}$, where m is the number of activities performed by the role, means that a role η is associated with several activities in a workflow procedure. Typically one or more participants are associated with each activity via roles. A role is a named designator for one or more participants which conveniently acts as the basis for partitioning of work skills, access controls, execution controls, and authority / responsibility. An actor is a person, program, or entity that can fulfill roles to execute, to be responsible for, or to be associated in some way with activities and procedures.

An Example : The Hiring Workflow Model

In order to clarify the ICN-based workflow model formally defined in the previous section, we show how a workflow procedure is transformed into the ICN-based workflow model through a hiring workflow procedure as an example. The hiring workflow procedure consists of 18 elementary activities having precedence with each other and 12 gateway activities, 10 types of roles—applicant(η_1), hiring clerk(η_2), hiring manager(η_3), personnel clerk(η_4), employment clerk(η_5), medical clerk(η_6), personnel manager(η_7), medical manager(η_8), employment manager(η_9), and computer(η_{10}), and 5 relevant data—applicant information(γ_1), decision result(γ_2), checkup done(γ_13), checkup resultγ_4 s(), and review results(γ_5)—as depicted in Figure 4. The detailed description of the elementary activities are the followings:

Elementary Activities

- The APPLY activity(α_1) is accessed by an applicant. The applicant fills out an application form through the employment page on the World Wide Web or the employment interfaces. This entails creating a workcase of the hiring procedure and starting the workcase's execution. Applicants should give the following information: personnel data, security data, affirmative action data including working preference, education, employment experience, etc.
- The NEW APPLICANT INFO activity(α_2) validates the application information written by an applicant, stores it in the database, and prepares and distributes the information for the medical screening, the security checking, and the background checking activities
- The DECISION activity(α_3) reviews and evaluates the applicant's information and decides whether the applicant is eligible and appropriate for the requirements of an open position.
- The REJECTING activity(α_4) receives the applicants who failed in the employment procedure, composes a rejection letter, and sends it to them.
- The DATABASE UPDATE activity-Rejecting(α_5) updates the employment database automatically.
- The HIRING activities$[(\alpha]_6, \alpha_7, \alpha_8)$ physically consist of three activities: request compensation(α_6), offer letter(α_7), and hiring activity(α_8). It receives the applicants who passed in the employment procedure, composes a job offer letter, and sends it to them after deciding the applicant's salary.
- The SECURITY SCREENING LOOP activities$[(\alpha]_9, \alpha_{13})$consist of checking activity(α_{10}) and reviewing activity(α_{10}), which validates the security information written by the applicants through iterations of checking and reviewing activities. After checking the information, the actor writes the checking results with comments. Then after reviewing the results, the security manager continues the security testing loop activities until the results satisfy the organization's rules and regulations.

Figure 4. The hiring workflow model: ICN's control and data flow

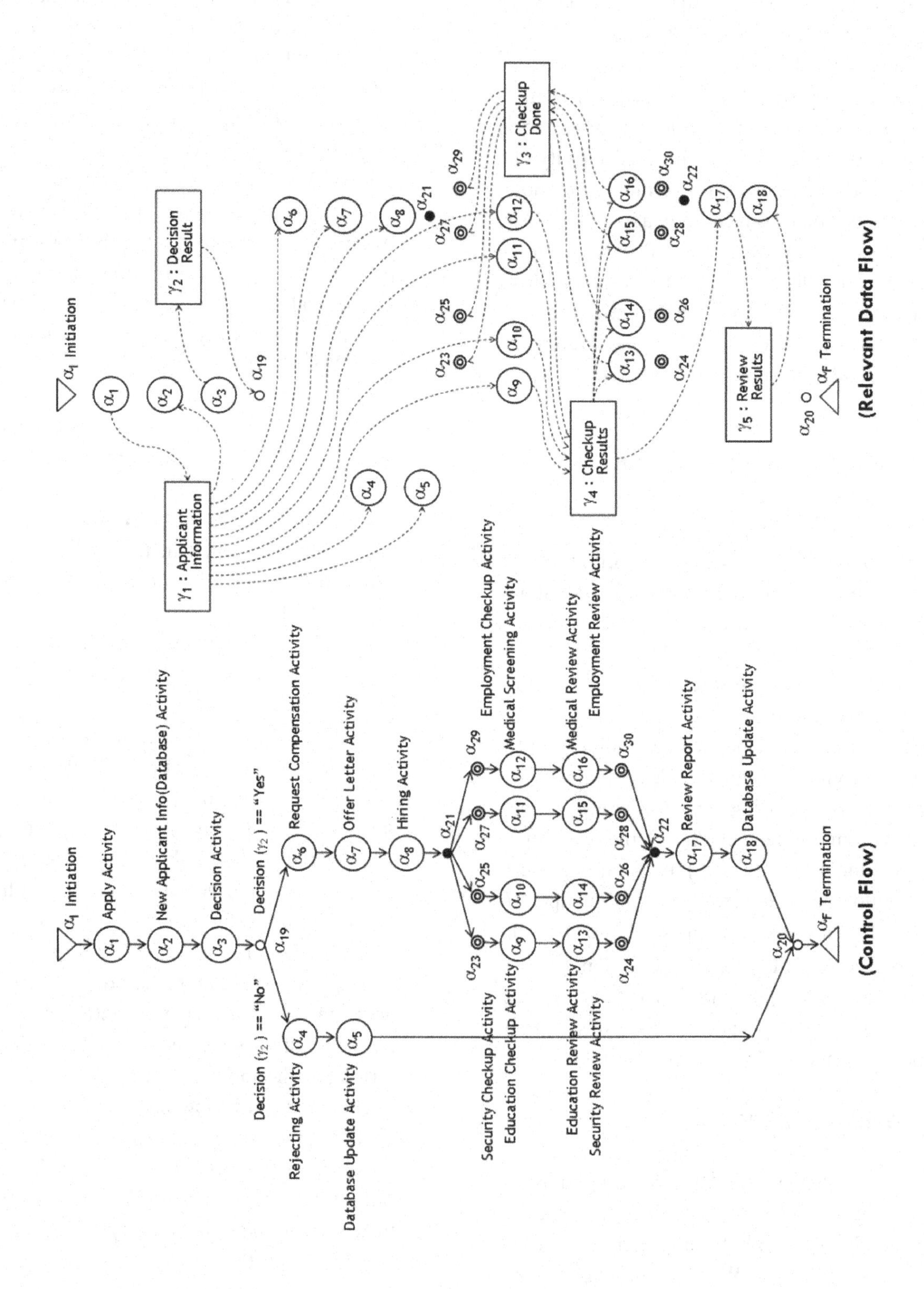

Figure 5. The hiring workflow model: ICN's role and actor assignments

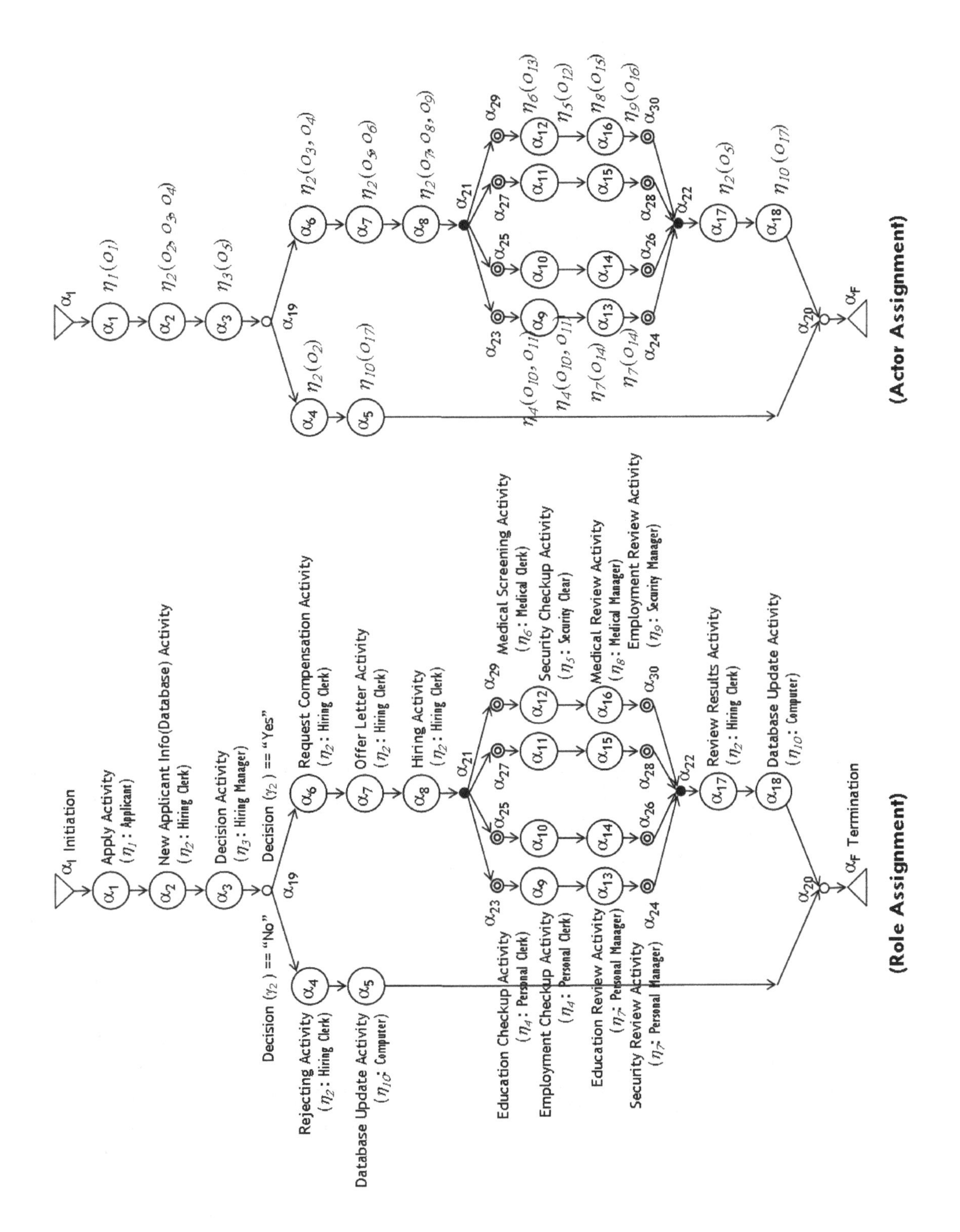

Table 1. Formal representation of the ICN-based hiring workflow model

Definition	Description
$\Gamma = (\delta, \rho, \lambda, \varepsilon, \pi, \kappa, \mathbf{I}, \mathbf{O})$ over $\mathbf{A}, \mathbf{R}, \mathbf{P}, \mathbf{C}, \mathbf{T}$	The ICN-based Hiring Workflow Model
$\mathbf{A} = A_{elementary} \cup A_{gateway} \cup A_{block}$	Activities
$A_{elementary} = \{\alpha_1, \alpha_2, \alpha_3, \alpha_4, \alpha_5, \alpha_6, \alpha_7, \alpha_8, \alpha_9, \alpha_{10}, \alpha_{11}, \alpha_{12}, \alpha_{13}, \alpha_{14}, \alpha_{15}, \alpha_{16}, \alpha_{17}, \alpha_{18}, \alpha_I, \alpha_F\}$	Elementary Activities
$A_{gateway} = \{\alpha_{19}, \alpha_{20}, \alpha_{21}, \alpha_{22}, \alpha_{23}, \alpha_{24}, \alpha_{25}, \alpha_{26}, \alpha_{27}, \alpha_{28}, \alpha_{29}, \alpha_{30}\}$	Gateway Activities
$A_{block} = \{block_1(\alpha_{23} \rhd \alpha_{24}), block_2(\alpha_{25} \rhd \alpha_{26}), block_3(\alpha_{27} \rhd \alpha_{28}), block_4(\alpha_{29} \rhd \alpha_{30})\}$	Block Activities
$\mathbf{R} = \{\gamma_1, \gamma_2, \gamma_3, \gamma_4, \gamma_5\}$	Repositories
$\mathbf{P} = \{\eta_1, \eta_2, \eta_3, \eta_4, \eta_5, \eta_6, \eta_7, \eta_8, \eta_9, \eta_{10}\}, \eta_2 = \{\eta_{2.1} \cup \eta_{2.2} \cup \eta_{2.3} \cup \eta_{2.4} \cup \eta_{2.5} \cup \eta_{2.6}\}$	Roles
$\mathbf{C} = \{o_1, o_2, o_3, o_4, o_5, o_6, o_7, o_8, o_9, o_{10}, o_{11}, o_{12}, o_{13}, o_{14}, o_{15}, o_{16}, o_{17}\}$	Actors
$\mathbf{G} = \{\tau_1, \tau_2, \tau_3, \tau_4, \tau_5, \tau_6, \tau_7, \tau_8, \tau_9, \tau_{10}, \tau_{11}, \tau_{12}, \tau_{13}, \tau_{14}, \tau_{15}, \tau_{16}, \tau_{17}\}$	Invoked Applications
$\mathbf{T} = \{d(default), tc_1(\gamma_2 =' No'), tc_2(\gamma_2 =' Yes'), tc_3(\gamma_3 =' No'), tc_4(\gamma_3 =' Yes')\}$	Transition Conditions
$\mathbf{I} = \{\emptyset\}$	Initial Input Repositories
$\mathbf{O} = \{\emptyset\}$	Final Output Repositories

$\delta = \delta_i \cup \delta_o$ /* Control Flow */	$\delta_i(\alpha_I) = \{\emptyset\};$	$\delta_i(\alpha_1) = \{\alpha_I\};$	$\delta_o(\alpha_I) = \{\alpha_1\};$	$\delta_o(\alpha_1) = \{\alpha_2\};$
	$\delta_i(\alpha_2) = \{\alpha_1\};$	$\delta_i(\alpha_3) = \{\alpha_2\};$	$\delta_o(\alpha_2) = \{\alpha_3\};$	$\delta_o(\alpha_3) = \{\alpha_4, \alpha_6\};$
	$\delta_i(\alpha_4) = \{\alpha_3\};$	$\delta_i(\alpha_5) = \{\alpha_4\};$	$\delta_o(\alpha_4) = \{\alpha_5\};$	$\delta_o(\alpha_5) = \{\alpha_F\};$
	$\delta_i(\alpha_6) = \{\alpha_3\};$	$\delta_i(\alpha_7) = \{\alpha_6\};$	$\delta_o(\alpha_6) = \{\alpha_7\};$	$\delta_o(\alpha_7) = \{\alpha_8\};$
	$\delta_i(\alpha_8) = \{\alpha_7\};$	$\delta_i(block_1) = \{\alpha_8\};$	$\delta_o(\alpha_8) = \{block_1, block_2, block_3, block_4\};$	
	$\delta_i(block_2) = \{\alpha_8\};$		$\delta_o(block_1) = \{\alpha_{17}\};$	
	$\delta_i(block_3) = \{\alpha_8\};$		$\delta_o(block_2) = \{\alpha_{17}\};$	
	$\delta_i(block_4) = \{\alpha_8\};$		$\delta_o(block_3) = \{\alpha_{17}\};$	
	$\delta_i(\alpha_{17}) = \{block_1, block_2, block_3, block_4\};$		$\delta_o(block_4) = \{\alpha_{17}\};$	
	$\delta_i(\alpha_{18}) = \{\alpha_{17}\};$		$\delta_o(\alpha_{17}) = \{\alpha_{18}\};$	
	$\delta_i(\alpha_F) = \{\{\alpha_5\}, \{\alpha_{18}\}\};$		$\delta_o(\alpha_{18}) = \{\alpha_F\};$	$\delta_o(\alpha_F) = \{\emptyset\};$
	$\mathbf{A}_{\text{block1}}$:		$\mathbf{A}_{\text{block1}}$:	
	$\delta_i(\alpha_{23}) = \{\alpha_8\};$	$\delta_i(\alpha_9) = \{\alpha_{23}\};$	$\delta_o(\alpha_{23}) = \{\alpha_9\};$	$\delta_o(\alpha_9) = \{\alpha_{13}\};$
	$\delta_i(\alpha_{13}) = \{\alpha_9\};$	$\delta_i(\alpha_{24}) = \{\alpha_{13}\};$	$\delta_o(\alpha_{13}) = \{\alpha_{24}\};$	$\delta_o(\alpha_{24}) = \{\alpha_{17}\};$
	$\mathbf{A}_{\text{block2}}$:		$\mathbf{A}_{\text{block2}}$:	
	$\delta_i(\alpha_{25}) = \{\alpha_8\};$	$\delta_i(\alpha_{10}) = \{\alpha_{25}\};$	$\delta_o(\alpha_{25}) = \{\alpha_{10}\};$	$\delta_o(\alpha_{10}) = \{\alpha_{14}\};$
	$\delta_i(\alpha_{14}) = \{\alpha_{10}\};$	$\delta_i(\alpha_{26}) = \{\alpha_{14}\};$	$\delta_o(\alpha_{14}) = \{\alpha_{26}\};$	$\delta_o(\alpha_{26}) = \{\alpha_{17}\};$
	$\mathbf{A}_{\text{block3}}$:		$\mathbf{A}_{\text{block3}}$:	
	$\delta_i(\alpha_{27}) = \{\alpha_8\};$	$\delta_i(\alpha_{11}) = \{\alpha_{27}\};$	$\delta_o(\alpha_{27}) = \{\alpha_{11}\};$	$\delta_o(\alpha_{11}) = \{\alpha_{15}\};$
	$\delta_i(\alpha_{15}) = \{\alpha_{11}\};$	$\delta_i(\alpha_{28}) = \{\alpha_{15}\};$	$\delta_o(\alpha_{15}) = \{\alpha_{28}\};$	$\delta_o(\alpha_{28}) = \{\alpha_{17}\};$
	$\mathbf{A}_{\text{block4}}$:		$\mathbf{A}_{\text{block4}}$:	
	$\delta_i(\alpha_{29}) = \{\alpha_8\};$	$\delta_i(\alpha_{12}) = \{\alpha_{29}\};$	$\delta_o(\alpha_{29}) = \{\alpha_{12}\};$	$\delta_o(\alpha_{12}) = \{\alpha_{16}\};$
	$\delta_i(\alpha_{16}) = \{\alpha_{12}\};$	$\delta_i(\alpha_{30}) = \{\alpha_{16}\};$	$\delta_o(\alpha_{16}) = \{\alpha_{30}\};$	$\delta_o(\alpha_{30}) = \{\alpha_{17}\};$

- The EDUCATIONAL BACKGROUND SCREENING LOOP activities$(\alpha_{10}, \alpha_{14})$, validates the educational background information submitted by the applicant. After checking the information, the actor prepares the checking results with some comments. Then after reviewing the results, the manager continues the educational background testing loop activities until the results satisfy the organization's rules and regulations.
- The MEDICAL SCREENING LOOP activities$(\alpha_{11}, \alpha_{15})$ do a series of medical tests, such as drugs, venereal diseases, and geriatric diseases. After testing, the actor prepares the test results with some comments, and send them to the personal department. Then after reviewing the results, the manager continues the medical screening loop activities until the results satisfy the organization's rules and regulations.
- The EMPLOYMENT EXPERIENCE SCREENING LOOP activities$(\alpha_{12}, \alpha_{16})$ validates the employment experience information submitted by the applicant. After checking the information, the actor prepares the checking results with some comments. Then after reviewing the results, the manager continues the employment experience testing loop activities until the results satisfy the organization's rules and regulations.
- The REVIEW APPLICANT INFO activity(α_{17}) reviews the results sent by the previous activities, and decides whether the applicant should be failed or passed, based

Table 2. Continuing: Formal representation of the ICN-based hiring workflow model

$\rho = \rho_i \cup \rho_o$ /* Data Flow */	$\rho_i(\alpha_I) = \{\emptyset\}; \quad \rho_i(\alpha_1) = \{\emptyset\};$ $\rho_i(\alpha_2) = \{\gamma_1\}; \quad \rho_i(\alpha_3) = \{\gamma_1\};$ $\rho_i(\alpha_4) = \{\gamma_1\}; \quad \rho_i(\alpha_5) = \{\gamma_1\};$ $\rho_i(\alpha_6) = \{\gamma_1\}; \quad \rho_i(\alpha_7) = \{\gamma_1\};$ $\rho_i(\alpha_8) = \{\gamma_1\}; \quad \rho_i(\alpha_9) = \{\gamma_1\};$ $\rho_i(\alpha_{10}) = \{\gamma_1\}; \quad \rho_i(\alpha_{11}) = \{\gamma_1\};$ $\rho_i(\alpha_{12}) = \{\gamma_1\}; \quad \rho_i(\alpha_{13}) = \{\gamma_4\};$ $\rho_i(\alpha_{14}) = \{\gamma_4\}; \quad \rho_i(\alpha_{15}) = \{\gamma_4\};$ $\rho_i(\alpha_{16}) = \{\gamma_4\}; \quad \rho_i(\alpha_{17}) = \{\gamma_4\};$ $\rho_i(\alpha_{18}) = \{\gamma_5\}; \quad \rho_i(\alpha_{19}) = \{\gamma_2\};$ $\rho_i(\alpha_{20}) = \{\emptyset\}; \quad \rho_i(\alpha_{21}) = \{\emptyset\};$ $\rho_i(\alpha_{22}) = \{\emptyset\}; \quad \rho_i(\alpha_{23}) = \{\gamma_3\};$ $\rho_i(\alpha_{24}) = \{\emptyset\}; \quad \rho_i(\alpha_{25}) = \{\gamma_3\};$ $\rho_i(\alpha_{26}) = \{\emptyset\}; \quad \rho_i(\alpha_{27}) = \{\gamma_3\};$ $\rho_i(\alpha_{28}) = \{\emptyset\}; \quad \rho_i(\alpha_{29}) = \{\gamma_3\};$ $\rho_i(\alpha_{30}) = \{\emptyset\}; \rho_i(\alpha_F) = \{\emptyset\};$	$\rho_o(\alpha_I) = \{\emptyset\}; \quad \rho_o(\alpha_1) = \{\gamma_1\};$ $\rho_o(\alpha_2) = \{\emptyset\}; \quad \rho_o(\alpha_3) = \{\gamma_2\};$ $\rho_o(\alpha_4) = \{\emptyset\}; \quad \rho_o(\alpha_5) = \{\emptyset\};$ $\rho_o(\alpha_6) = \{\emptyset\}; \quad \rho_o(\alpha_7) = \{\emptyset\};$ $\rho_o(\alpha_8) = \{\emptyset\}; \quad \rho_o(\alpha_9) = \{\gamma_4\};$ $\rho_o(\alpha_{10}) = \{\gamma_4\}; \quad \rho_o(\alpha_{11}) = \{\gamma_4\};$ $\rho_o(\alpha_{12}) = \{\gamma_4\}; \quad \rho_o(\alpha_{13}) = \{\gamma_3\};$ $\rho_o(\alpha_{14}) = \{\gamma_3\}; \quad \rho_o(\alpha_{15}) = \{\gamma_3\};$ $\rho_o(\alpha_{16}) = \{\gamma_3\}; \quad \rho_o(\alpha_{17}) = \{\gamma_5\};$ $\rho_o(\alpha_{18}) = \{\emptyset\}; \quad \rho_o(\alpha_{19}) = \{\emptyset\};$ $\rho_o(\alpha_{20}) = \{\emptyset\}; \quad \rho_o(\alpha_{21}) = \{\emptyset\};$ $\rho_o(\alpha_{22}) = \{\emptyset\}; \quad \rho_o(\alpha_{23}) = \{\emptyset\};$ $\rho_o(\alpha_{24}) = \{\emptyset\}; \quad \rho_o(\alpha_{25}) = \{\emptyset\};$ $\rho_o(\alpha_{26}) = \{\emptyset\}; \quad \rho_o(\alpha_{27}) = \{\emptyset\};$ $\rho_o(\alpha_{28}) = \{\emptyset\}; \quad \rho_o(\alpha_{29}) = \{\emptyset\};$ $\rho_o(\alpha_{30}) = \{\emptyset\}; \rho_o(\alpha_F) = \{\emptyset\};$
$\lambda = \lambda_g \cup \lambda_a$ /* Invoked Applications Assignments */	$\lambda_g(\alpha_I) = \{\emptyset\}; \quad \lambda_g(\alpha_1) = \{\tau_1\};$ $\lambda_g(\alpha_2) = \{\tau_2\}; \quad \lambda_g(\alpha_3) = \{\tau_3\};$ $\lambda_g(\alpha_4) = \{\tau_4\}; \quad \lambda_g(\alpha_5) = \{\tau_5\};$ $\lambda_g(\alpha_6) = \{\tau_6\}; \quad \lambda_g(\alpha_7) = \{\tau_7\};$ $\lambda_g(\alpha_8) = \{\tau_8\}; \quad \lambda_g(\alpha_9) = \{\tau_9\};$ $\lambda_g(\alpha_{10}) = \{\tau_{10}\}; \quad \lambda_g(\alpha_{11}) = \{\tau_{11}\};$ $\lambda_g(\alpha_{12}) = \{\tau_{12}\}; \quad \lambda_g(\alpha_{13}) = \{\tau_{13}\};$ $\lambda_g(\alpha_{14}) = \{\tau_{14}\}; \quad \lambda_g(\alpha_{15}) = \{\tau_{15}\};$ $\lambda_g(\alpha_{16}) = \{\tau_{16}\}; \quad \lambda_g(\alpha_{17}) = \{\tau_{17}\};$ $\lambda_g(\alpha_{18}) = \{\tau_5\}; \lambda_g(\alpha_F) = \{\emptyset\};$	$\lambda_a(\tau_1) = \{\alpha_1\}; \quad \lambda_a(\tau_2) = \{\alpha_2\};$ $\lambda_a(\tau_3) = \{\alpha_3\}; \quad \lambda_a(\tau_4) = \{\alpha_4\};$ $\lambda_a(\tau_5) = \{\alpha_5, \alpha_{18}\}; \quad \lambda_a(\tau_6) = \{\alpha_6\};$ $\lambda_a(\tau_7) = \{\alpha_7\}; \quad \lambda_a(\tau_8) = \{\alpha_8\};$ $\lambda_a(\tau_9) = \{\alpha_9\}; \quad \lambda_a(\tau_{10}) = \{\alpha_{10}\};$ $\lambda_a(\tau_{11}) = \{\alpha_{11}\}; \quad \lambda_a(\tau_{12}) = \{\alpha_{12}\};$ $\lambda_a(\tau_{13}) = \{\alpha_{13}\}; \quad \lambda_a(\tau_{14}) = \{\alpha_{14}\};$ $\lambda_a(\tau_{15}) = \{\alpha_{15}\}; \quad \lambda_a(\tau_{16}) = \{\alpha_{16}\};$ $\lambda_a(\tau_{17}) = \{\alpha_{17}\};$
$\varepsilon = \varepsilon_p \cup \varepsilon_a$ /* Role Assignments */	$\varepsilon_p(\alpha_I) = \{\emptyset\}; \quad \varepsilon_p(\alpha_1) = \{\eta_1\};$ $\varepsilon_p(\alpha_2) = \{\eta_{2.1}\}; \quad \varepsilon_p(\alpha_3) = \{\eta_3\};$ $\varepsilon_p(\alpha_4) = \{\eta_{2.2}\}; \quad \varepsilon_p(\alpha_5) = \{\eta_{10}\};$ $\varepsilon_p(\alpha_6) = \{\eta_{2.3}\}; \quad \varepsilon_p(\alpha_7) = \{\eta_{2.4}\};$ $\varepsilon_p(\alpha_8) = \{\eta_{2.5}\}; \quad \varepsilon_p(\alpha_9) = \{\eta_4\};$ $\varepsilon_p(\alpha_{10}) = \{\eta_4\}; \quad \varepsilon_p(\alpha_{11}) = \{\eta_5\};$ $\varepsilon_p(\alpha_{12}) = \{\eta_6\}; \quad \varepsilon_p(\alpha_{13}) = \{\eta_7\};$ $\varepsilon_p(\alpha_{14}) = \{\eta_7\}; \quad \varepsilon_p(\alpha_{15}) = \{\eta_8\};$ $\varepsilon_p(\alpha_{16}) = \{\eta_9\}; \quad \varepsilon_p(\alpha_{17}) = \{\eta_{2.6}\};$ $\varepsilon_p(\alpha_{18}) = \{\eta_{10}\}; \varepsilon_p(\alpha_F) = \{\emptyset\};$	$\varepsilon_a(\eta_1) = \{\alpha_1\};$ $\varepsilon_a(\eta_2) = \{\alpha_2, \alpha_4, \alpha_6, \alpha_7, \alpha_8, \alpha_{17}\};$ $\varepsilon_a(\eta_{2.1}) = \{\alpha_2\}; \quad \varepsilon_a(\eta_{2.2}) = \{\alpha_4\};$ $\varepsilon_a(\eta_{2.3}) = \{\alpha_6\}; \quad \varepsilon_a(\eta_{2.4}) = \{\alpha_7\};$ $\varepsilon_a(\eta_{2.5}) = \{\alpha_8\}; \quad \varepsilon_a(\eta_{2.6}) = \{\alpha_{17}\};$ $\varepsilon_a(\eta_3) = \{\alpha_3\}; \quad \varepsilon_a(\eta_4) = \{\alpha_9, \alpha_{10}\};$ $\varepsilon_a(\eta_5) = \{\alpha_{11}\}; \quad \varepsilon_a(\eta_6) = \{\alpha_{12}\};$ $\varepsilon_a(\eta_7) = \{\alpha_{13}, \alpha_{14}\};$ $\varepsilon_a(\eta_8) = \{\alpha_{15}\}; \quad \varepsilon_a(\eta_9) = \{\alpha_{16}\};$ $\varepsilon_a(\eta_{10}) = \{\alpha_5, \alpha_{18}\};$
$\pi = \pi_p \cup \pi_c$ /* Actor Assignments */	$\pi_p(o_1) = \{\eta_1\};$ $\pi_p(o_2) = \{\{\eta_2, \eta_{2.1}, \eta_{2.2}\}\};$ $\pi_p(o_3) = \{\{\eta_2, \eta_{2.1}, \eta_{2.3}\}\};$ $\pi_p(o_4) = \{\{\eta_2, \eta_{2.1}, \eta_{2.3}\}\};$ $\pi_p(o_5) = \{\{\eta_2, \eta_{2.4}, \eta_{2.6}\}, \{\eta_3\}\};$ $\pi_p(o_6) = \{\{\eta_2, \eta_{2.4}\}\};$ $\pi_p(o_7) = \{\{\eta_2, \eta_{2.5}\}\};$ $\pi_p(o_8) = \{\{\eta_2, \eta_{2.5}\}\};$ $\pi_p(o_9) = \{\{\eta_2, \eta_{2.5}\}\};$ $\pi_p(o_{10}) = \{\eta_4\}; \quad \pi_p(o_{11}) = \{\eta_4\};$ $\pi_p(o_{12}) = \{\eta_5\}; \quad \pi_p(o_{13}) = \{\eta_6\};$ $\pi_p(o_{14}) = \{\eta_7\}; \quad \pi_p(o_{15}) = \{\eta_8\};$ $\pi_p(o_{16}) = \{\eta_9\}; \pi_p(o_{17}) = \{\eta_{10}\};$	$\pi_c(\eta_1) = \{o_1\};$ $\pi_c(\eta_2) = \{o_2, o_3, o_4, o_5, o_6, o_7, o_8, o_9\};$ $\pi_c(\eta_{2.1}) = \{o_2, o_3, o_4\};$ $\pi_c(\eta_{2.2}) = \{o_2\};$ $\pi_c(\eta_{2.3}) = \{o_3, o_4\};$ $\pi_c(\eta_{2.4}) = \{o_5, o_6\};$ $\pi_c(\eta_{2.5}) = \{o_7, o_8, o_9\};$ $\pi_c(\eta_{2.6}) = \{o_5\}; \quad \pi_c(\eta_3) = \{o_5\};$ $\pi_c(\eta_4) = \{o_{10}, o_{11}\}; \pi_c(\eta_5) = \{o_{12}\};$ $\pi_c(\eta_6) = \{o_{13}\}; \quad \pi_c(\eta_7) = \{o_{14}\};$ $\pi_c(\eta_8) = \{o_{15}\}; \quad \pi_c(\eta_9) = \{o_{16}\};$ $\pi_c(\eta_{10}) = \{o_{17}\};$
$\kappa = \kappa_i \cup \kappa_o$ /* TC Assignments */	$\kappa_i(\alpha_I) = \{\emptyset\}; \quad \kappa_i(\alpha_1) = \{d\};$ $\kappa_i(\alpha_2) = \{d\}; \quad \kappa_i(\alpha_3) = \{d\};$ $\kappa_i(\alpha_4) = \{tc_1\}; \quad \kappa_i(\alpha_5) = \{d\};$ $\kappa_i(\alpha_6) = \{tc_2\}; \quad \kappa_i(\alpha_7) = \{d\};$ $\kappa_i(\alpha_8) = \{d\}; \quad \kappa_i(\alpha_9) = \{tc_3\};$ $\kappa_i(\alpha_{10}) = \{tc_3\}; \quad \kappa_i(\alpha_{11}) = \{tc_3\};$ $\kappa_i(\alpha_{12}) = \{tc_3\}; \quad \kappa_i(\alpha_{13}) = \{d\};$ $\kappa_i(\alpha_{14}) = \{d\}; \quad \kappa_i(\alpha_{15}) = \{d\};$ $\kappa_i(\alpha_{16}) = \{d\}; \quad \kappa_i(\alpha_{17}) = \{tc_4\};$ $\kappa_i(\alpha_{18}) = \{d\}; \quad \kappa_i(\alpha_{19}) = \{d\};$ $\kappa_i(\alpha_{20}) = \{d\}; \quad \kappa_i(\alpha_{21}) = \{d\};$ $\kappa_i(\alpha_{22}) = \{tc_4\}; \kappa_i(\alpha_{23}) = \{d, tc_3\};$ $\kappa_i(\alpha_{24}) = \{d\}; \quad \kappa_i(\alpha_{25}) = \{d, tc_3\};$ $\kappa_i(\alpha_{26}) = \{d\}; \quad \kappa_i(\alpha_{27}) = \{d, tc_3\};$ $\kappa_i(\alpha_{28}) = \{d\}; \quad \kappa_i(\alpha_{29}) = \{d, tc_3\};$ $\kappa_i(\alpha_{30}) = \{d\}; \kappa_i(\alpha_F) = \{d\};$	$\kappa_o(\alpha_I) = \{d\}; \quad \kappa_o(\alpha_1) = \{d\};$ $\kappa_o(\alpha_2) = \{d\}; \quad \kappa_o(\alpha_3) = \{d\};$ $\kappa_o(\alpha_4) = \{d\}; \quad \kappa_o(\alpha_5) = \{d\};$ $\kappa_o(\alpha_6) = \{d\}; \quad \kappa_o(\alpha_7) = \{d\};$ $\kappa_o(\alpha_8) = \{d\}; \quad \kappa_o(\alpha_9) = \{d\};$ $\kappa_o(\alpha_{10}) = \{d\}; \quad \kappa_o(\alpha_{11}) = \{d\};$ $\kappa_o(\alpha_{12}) = \{d\}; \quad \kappa_o(\alpha_{13}) = \{d\};$ $\kappa_o(\alpha_{14}) = \{d\}; \quad \kappa_o(\alpha_{15}) = \{d\};$ $\kappa_o(\alpha_{16}) = \{d\}; \quad \kappa_o(\alpha_{17}) = \{d\};$ $\kappa_o(\alpha_{18}) = \{d\}; \kappa_o(\alpha_{19}) = \{tc_1, tc_2\};$ $\kappa_o(\alpha_{20}) = \{d\}; \quad \kappa_o(\alpha_{21}) = \{d\};$ $\kappa_o(\alpha_{22}) = \{d\}; \kappa_o(\alpha_{23}) = \{tc_3, tc_4\};$ $\kappa_o(\alpha_{24}) = \{tc_3, tc_4\};$ $\kappa_o(\alpha_{25}) = \{tc_3, tc_4\};$ $\kappa_o(\alpha_{26}) = \{tc_3, tc_4\};$ $\kappa_o(\alpha_{27}) = \{tc_3, tc_4\};$ $\kappa_o(\alpha_{28}) = \{tc_3, tc_4\};$ $\kappa_o(\alpha_{29}) = \{tc_3, tc_4\};$ $\kappa_o(\alpha_{30}) = \{tc_3, tc_4\}; \kappa_o(\alpha_F) = \{\emptyset\};$

on the organization's employment policy. If the results satisfy the policy, then the actor prepares and informs so that the clerks can proceed continuously to the internal hiring procedure.

- The DATABASE UPDATE activity-Hiring (α_{15}) updates the employment database automatically.

Actors and Roles

There are ten roles—applicant, hiring clerk, hiring manager, personnel clerk, personnel manager, medical clerk, medical manager, employment clerk, employment manager and computer—and seventeen actors in the hiring workflow procedure. The basic principle of role-actor association is many-to-many association; an actor may be involved in several roles at the same time and *vice versa*. The left-hand side of Figure 5 presents the ICN-based hiring workflow model and its role and actor assignments. In the role assignments function($\varepsilon = \varepsilon_p \cup \varepsilon_a$), as you can recognize that the role of hiring cler(η_{15})k has 6 subgroups ($\eta_2 = \{\eta_{21} \cup \eta_{22} \cup \eta_{23} \cup \eta_{24} \cup \eta_{25} \cup \eta_{25}\}$) it is possible for a role to be made up of several subgroups.

Relevant Data

There are typically five relevant data within the hiring workflow model: application information, decision result, checkup done, checkup results, and review results. In fact, there are other relevant data for processing applications, but we do not specify the details here to simplify the model. The right-hand side of Figure 4 depicts the relevant data flows and assignments (access mode : read or write) on each of the activities.

According to the formal definition of the ICN-based workflow model, we try to graphically define the hiring workflow procedure as shown in Figure 4 and Figure 5. Figure 4 shows the control flow (temporal orders) and data flow (input/output relevant data on repository) among the activities in the hiring workflow procedure, and Figure 5 graphically presents the activity-role association and the role-actor association in the hiring workflow procedure. Based upon the graphical definition of the ICN-based workflow model, we also give a formal representation of the hiring workflow procedure as shown in Table 1 and Table 2, which is made up by the execution results of the functional components, such as δ, ρ, λ, ε, π where δ, ρ, λ, ε, π and κ represent control flows, data flows, invoked application program associations, role associations, actor associations and transition condition associations, respectively.

ADVANCED WORKFLOW MODELS

In the previous section, we defined the ICN-based workflow model and showed how it works through graphical and formal representations of the hiring workflow procedure as an example. Once we define a workflow procedure by an ICN-based workflow modeling tool, the defined model is interpreted into one of the standard forms of process definition languages such as WPDL[6] and XPDL[7], and eventually it will be stored onto a database organized by a workflow process schema based on the workflow meta-model. From the database, we are able to derive various sorts of workflow-related knowledge and information. These derived knowledge and information can be effectively used for embodying advanced workflow architectures which are sophisticatedly implementable for the advanced computing environments like a grid computing environment, and the special domains of workflow applications, such as collaborative and scientific workflow applications. Therefore, in this section, we introduce two advanced workflow models—role-based model and actor-based model—that are automatically derived from the original ICN-based workflow model, and we show that these two advanced models are fitted very well into organizing role-based workflow architecture as well as actor-based workflow architecture, respectively.

Role-Based Workflow Model

In this subsection, we define the basic concept of role-based workflow model and its graphical and formal representations. Basically, the primary goal of role-based workflow model is to make a reasonable workflow model to be applied into a workflow architecture that is appropriate to the recent working behaviors as well as the newly emerging computing environments. In terms of the working behaviors, the traditional workflow management systems support the so-called *uni-casting* work item delivery because of delivering a work item to an exact actor through pushing mechanism of the workflow engine, while on the other the recent working behaviors require the so-called *any-casting* work item delivery as well as the *multi-casting* work item delivery, which mean that not only anyone out of a group of actors is able to voluntarily pull a work item, but also all actors of the group of actors are able to collaboratively work on a single work item at the same time. The role-based workflow model is able to efficiently describe these working behaviors. Also, the grid computing environment is one of the newly emerging computing environments, and the role-based workflow model can be a reasonable theoretical basis for workflow architectures deployed over a grid computing environment.

The formal definition of the role-based workflow model is described in [**Definition 2**], and its graphical primitive is illustrated in Figure 6. The model represents two types of information— role flows and acquisition activities of roles— through which we are able to get precedence (predecessor/successor) relationships among roles as well as acquired activities of each role in a workflow procedure. The activities on the incoming directed arcs, such as $\alpha_A, \alpha_B, \alpha_C, \alpha_D, \alpha_F,$ are the previously performed activities by the predecessor of the role, η, and the activities on the outgoing directed arcs, such as $\alpha_E, \alpha_C, \alpha_D,$ are the acquisition activities of the role, η. And besides, the activities, α_C, α_D, on the transitive directed arc imply not only the acquired activities of the role but also the previous activities of the role, itself. As stated in the figure, the characteristics of the role flow graph are multiple-incoming arcs, multiple-outgoing arcs, cyclic, self-transitive, and multiple-activity associations on arc.

Definition 2. Role-based Workflow Model *A role-based workflow model is formally defined as* $\mathfrak{R} = (\xi, \vartheta, \mathbf{S}, \mathbf{E})$, *over a set* **P** *of roles and a set* **A** *of activities, where,*

- **S** *is a finite set of the initial roles connected from some external role-based workflow models;*
- **E** *is a finite set of the final roles connected to some external role-based workflow models.*

Figure 6. The primitive of role-based workflow model

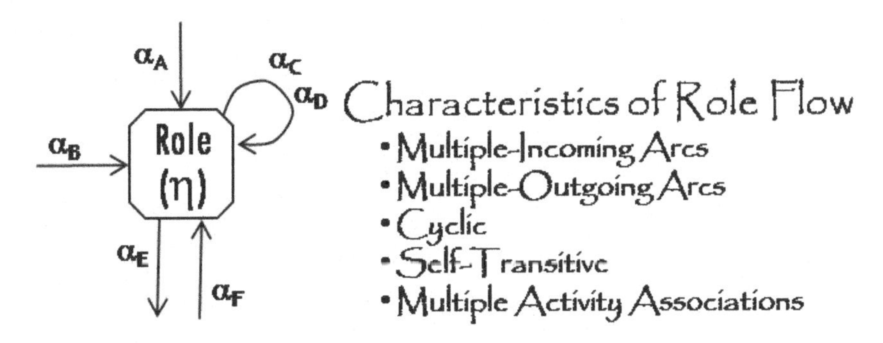

- $\xi = \xi_i \cup \xi_o$ /* *Role Flow: successors and predecessors* */ *where* $\xi_o : P \rightarrow \wp(P)$, *is a multi-valued function mapping a role to its sets of (immediate) successors, and* $\xi_i : P \rightarrow \wp(P)$ *is a multi-valued function mapping a role to its sets of (immediate) predecessors;*
- $\vartheta = \vartheta_i \cup \vartheta_o$ /* *previous worked and acquisition activities* */ *where,* $\vartheta_i : P \rightarrow \wp(P)$ *is a multi-valued function returning a set of previously worked activities,* $J \subseteq A$ *, on directed arcs,* $(\xi_i(\eta), \eta), \eta \in P$, *from* $\xi_i(\eta)$ *to* η*; and* $\vartheta_o : P \rightarrow \wp(P)$ *is a multi-valued function returning a set of acquisition activities,* $J \subseteq A$ *, on directed arcs,* $(\eta, \xi_o(\eta)), \eta \in P$, *from* η *to* $\xi_o(\eta)$*;*

In terms of designing and modeling a workflow procedure, it is definitely inconvenient for us to design the workflow procedure by using the role-based workflow model. In other words, it is very important to provide a modeling methodology based upon the conventional workflow modeling approaches. Therefore, we conceive an automatic modeling methodology for the role-based workflow model, which algorithmically constructs a role-based workflow model from an ICN-based workflow model. The following is the algorithm automatically extracting a role-based workflow model from an ICN-based workflow model.

The Construction Algorithm for Role-Based Workflow Model. A sketch of the algorithm is given as the following:

Input An ICN, $\Gamma = (\delta, \rho, \lambda, \varepsilon, \pi, \kappa, I, O)$;
Output A Role-based Workflow Model, $\Re = (\xi, \vartheta, S, E)$;
Begin Procedure
  For $(\forall \alpha \in A)$ **Do**
    Begin
      /* $\xi = \xi_i \cup \xi_o$ */
      Add *all members of* $\varepsilon_p(\alpha)$ **To** $\xi_i(\varepsilon_p(\delta_o(\alpha)))$;
      Add *all members of* $\varepsilon_p(\delta_o(\alpha))$ **To**

Figure 7. A role-based model of the hiring workflow procedure

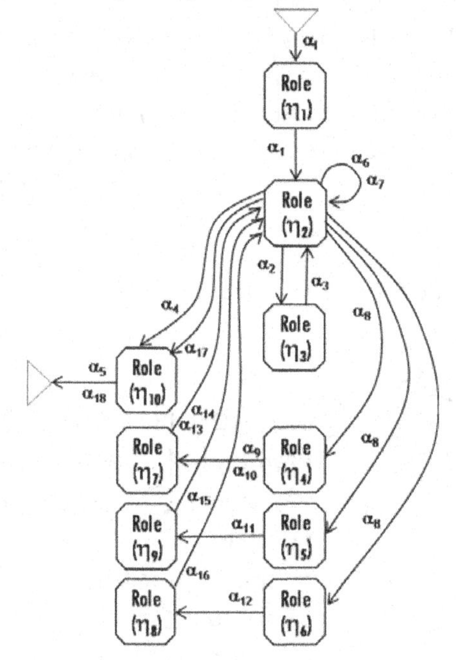

Table 3. Formal representation of the role-based hiring workflow model

$\Re = (\xi, \vartheta, \mathbf{S}, \mathbf{E})$ over $\mathbf{A}, \mathbf{P}$	The Role-based Hiring Workflow Model	
$\mathbf{A} = \{\alpha_1, \alpha_2, \alpha_3, \alpha_4, \alpha_5, \alpha_6, \alpha_7, \alpha_8, \alpha_9, \alpha_{10}, \alpha_{11}, \alpha_{12}, \alpha_{13}, \alpha_{14}, \alpha_{15}, \alpha_{16}, \alpha_{17}, \alpha_{18}, \alpha_I, \alpha_F\}$	Elementary Activities	
$\mathbf{P} = \{\eta_I, \eta_1, \eta_2, \eta_3, \eta_4, \eta_5, \eta_6, \eta_7, \eta_8, \eta_9, \eta_{10}, \eta_F\}$ $\eta_2 = \{\eta_{2.1} \cup \eta_{2.2} \cup \eta_{2.3} \cup \eta_{2.4} \cup \eta_{2.5} \cup \eta_{2.6}\}$	Roles	
$\mathbf{S} = \{\emptyset\}$	Initial Roles from some external role-based workflow models	
$\mathbf{E} = \{\emptyset\}$	Final Roles to some external role-based workflow models	
$\xi = \xi_i \cup \xi_o$	ξ_i:**Predecessors**	ξ_o:**Successors**
	$\xi_i(\eta_I) = \{\emptyset\}$;	$\xi_o(\eta_I) = \{\eta_1\}$;
	$\xi_i(\eta_1) = \{\eta_I\}$;	$\xi_o(\eta_1) = \{\eta_2\}$;
	$\xi_i(\eta_2) = \{\eta_1, \eta_2, \eta_7, \eta_8, \eta_9\}$;	$\xi_o(\eta_2) = \{\eta_2, \eta_3, \eta_4, \eta_5, \eta_6, \eta_{10}\}$;
	$\xi_i(\eta_3) = \{\eta_2\}$;	$\xi_o(\eta_3) = \{\eta_2\}$;
	$\xi_i(\eta_4) = \{\eta_2\}$;	$\xi_o(\eta_4) = \{\eta_7\}$;
	$\xi_i(\eta_5) = \{\eta_2\}$;	$\xi_o(\eta_5) = \{\eta_9\}$;
	$\xi_i(\eta_6) = \{\eta_2\}$;	$\xi_o(\eta_6) = \{\eta_8\}$;
	$\xi_i(\eta_7) = \{\eta_4\}$;	$\xi_o(\eta_7) = \{\eta_2\}$;
	$\xi_i(\eta_8) = \{\eta_6\}$;	$\xi_o(\eta_8) = \{\eta_2\}$;
	$\xi_i(\eta_9) = \{\eta_5\}$;	$\xi_o(\eta_9) = \{\eta_2\}$;
	$\xi_i(\eta_{10}) = \{\eta_2\}$;	$\xi_o(\eta_{10}) = \{\eta_F\}$;
	$\xi_i(\eta_F) = \{\eta_7\}$;	$\xi_o(\eta_F) = \{\emptyset\}$;
$\vartheta = \vartheta_i \cup \vartheta_o$	ϑ_i:**PreviousWorked**	ϑ_o:**AcquisitionWork**
	$\vartheta_i(\eta_I) = \{\emptyset\}$;	$\vartheta_o(\eta_I) = \{(\alpha_I, \eta_1)\}$;
	$\vartheta_i(\eta_1) = \{(\alpha_I, \eta_I)\}$;	$\vartheta_o(\eta_1) = \{(\alpha_1, \eta_2)\}$;
	$\vartheta_i(\eta_2) = \{(\alpha_1, \eta_1), (\alpha_3, \eta_3), (\alpha_6, \eta_2), (\alpha_7, \eta_2), (\alpha_{13}, \eta_7), (\alpha_{14}, \eta_7), (\alpha_{15}, \eta_9), (\alpha_{16}, \eta_8)\}$;	$\vartheta_o(\eta_2) = \{(\alpha_2, \eta_3), (\alpha_4, \eta_{10}), (\alpha_6, \eta_2), (\alpha_7, \eta_2), (\alpha_8, \eta_4), (\alpha_8, \eta_5), (\alpha_8, \eta_6), (\alpha_{17}, \eta_{10})\}$;
	$\vartheta_i(\eta_3) = \{(\alpha_2, \eta_2)\}$;	$\vartheta_o(\eta_3) = \{(\alpha_3, \eta_2)\}$;
	$\vartheta_i(\eta_4) = \{(\alpha_8, \eta_2)\}$;	$\vartheta_o(\eta_4) = \{(\alpha_9, \eta_7), (\alpha_{10}, \eta_7)\}$;
	$\vartheta_i(\eta_5) = \{(\alpha_8, \eta_2)\}$;	$\vartheta_o(\eta_5) = \{(\alpha_{11}, \eta_9)\}$;
	$\vartheta_i(\eta_6) = \{(\alpha_8, \eta_2)\}$;	$\vartheta_o(\eta_6) = \{(\alpha_{12}, \eta_8)\}$;
	$\vartheta_i(\eta_7) = \{(\alpha_9, \eta_4), (\alpha_{10}, \eta_4)\}$;	$\vartheta_o(\eta_7) = \{(\alpha_{13}, \eta_2), (\alpha_{14}, \eta_2)\}$;
	$\vartheta_i(\eta_8) = \{(\alpha_{12}, \eta_6)\}$;	$\vartheta_o(\eta_8) = \{(\alpha_{16}, \eta_2)\}$;
	$\vartheta_i(\eta_9) = \{(\alpha_{11}, \eta_5)\}$;	$\vartheta_o(\eta_9) = \{(\alpha_{15}, \eta_2)\}$;
	$\vartheta_i(\eta_{10}) = \{(\alpha_4, \eta_2), (\alpha_{17}, \eta_2)\}$;	$\vartheta_o(\eta_{10}) = \{(\alpha_5, \eta_F), (\alpha_{18}, \eta_F)\}$;
	$\vartheta_i(\eta_F) = \{(\alpha_5, \eta_{10}), (\alpha_{18}, \eta_{10})\}$;	$\vartheta_o(\eta_F) = \{\emptyset\}$;

$\xi_i(\varepsilon_p(\alpha))$;

/* $\vartheta = \vartheta_i \cup \vartheta_o$ */

Add *arc* $(\alpha, \varepsilon_p(\alpha))$ **To** $\vartheta_i(\varepsilon_p(\delta_o(\alpha)))$

Add *arc* $(\alpha, \varepsilon_p(\delta_o(\alpha)))$ **To** $\vartheta_i(\varepsilon_p(\alpha))$

End

End Procedure

As a result, we show a role-based workflow model of the hiring workflow procedure in Figure 7, which is automatically generated by applying the algorithm to the ICN-based hiring workflow model. As you can see, the role-based hiring workflow model shows the role flow information and each role's acquition activities based upon 10 roles and 18 elementary activities. Note that we did not handle the subgroups $(\eta_{2.1}, \eta_{2.2}, \eta_{2.3}, \eta_{2.4}, \eta_{2.5}, \eta_{2.6})$ of the role, η_2, in this case, for the sake of simplification. However, without any revisions of the algorithm, the role-based hiring workflow model can be modified if the subgroups are taken into the algorithm as input. Also the algorithm ignores the gateway activities including block activities, because role assignments have nothing to do with these special types of activities. Accordingly, Table. 3 is the final outcomes of execution of the algorithm by inputting the ICN-based hiring workflow model, and finally we summarize them as the formal representation of the role-based hiring workflow model.

Actor-Based Workflow Model

In this subsection, we introduce the basic concept and definition of actor-based workflow model as the second one out of the advanced workflow models. The conceptual background of the actor-based workflow model comes from the fact that it should be able to incorporate the advanced technological and organizational trends into workflow model in order for the underlying workflow management system to effectively acclimate itself to a new technological and organizational environment. That is, the recent technological trends in workflow area can be characterized by increasingly powerful networked personal computing facilities (P2P[8] computing environments) and increasingly large and complex workflow applications. And, if the concept of actor orientation can be embedded into a workflow model, then the workflow model ought to be more effective and efficient in these evolving technological trends. Therefore, we define an actor-based workflow model so as to effectively model and design coordination among humans (actors) who handle activities associated in a workflow procedure. This subsection addresses the actor-based workflow model by systematically and formally formulating a way to describe and incorporate the concept of actor orientation into workflow models and architectures.

Basically, the actor-based workflow model represents the behaviors of acquisitioning activities among actors associated in a workflow procedure. The formal definition of the actor-based workflow model is given in [**Definition 3**], and its graphical primitive construct is illustrated in Figure 8. The behaviors of the model are revealed through incoming and outgoing directed arcs labeled with activities associated with each of actors. The directed arcs imply two kinds of behaviors—actor flows and acquisition activities of actors—through which we are able to get precedence (candidate-predecessor/candidate-successor) relationships among actors as well as acquisition activities of each actor in a workflow procedure. In terms of defining actor's predecessors and successors, we would use the prepositional word, "**candidate**", because, unlike in the role-based workflow model, in actor-based workflow model a role-actor mapping is an one-to-many relationship, and the actor selection mechanism will choose one actor out of the assigned actors mapped to the corresponding role during the workflow model's runtime.

The activities on the incoming directed arcs, such as $\alpha_A, \alpha_C, \alpha_E, \alpha_F$, are the previously performed activities by the predecessors of the actor, *O*, and the activities on the outgoing directed arcs, such as $\alpha_B, \alpha_C, \alpha_D$, are the activities acquired by the actor, itself. And besides, the activity, α_C, on the transitive directed arc implies not only the acquisitioning activities of the actor but also the previously performed activities by the actor, itself. As stated in the figure, the characteristics of the actor flow graph are multiple-incoming arcs, multiple-outgoing arcs, cyclic, self-transitive, and multiple-activity associations on arcs.

Definition 3. Actor-Based Workflow Model. *An actor-based workflow model is formally defined as* $\Lambda = (\sigma, \psi, \mathbf{S}, \mathbf{E})$, *over a set* **C** *of actors, and a set* **A** *of activities, where*

- **S** *is a finite set of coordinators or coordinator-groups connected from some external actor-based workflow models;*

Figure 8. The hiring of actor-based workflow model

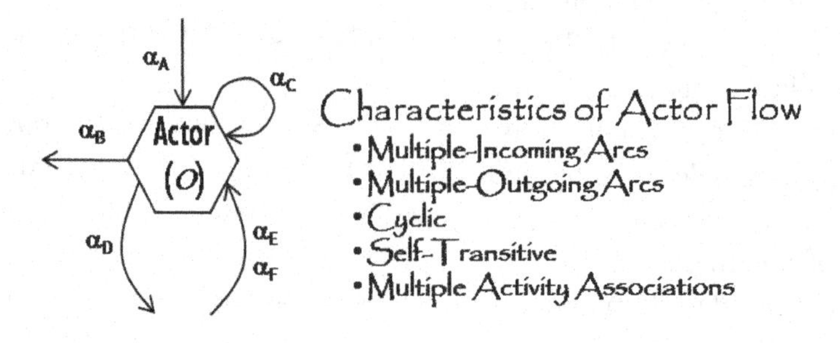

- **E** *is a finite set of coordinators or coordinator-groups connected to some external actor-based workflow models;*
- $\sigma = \sigma_i \cup \sigma_o$ */* Actor Flow: successors and predecessors */ where,* $\sigma_o : P \rightarrow \wp(P)$ *is a multi-valued function mapping an actor to its sets of (immediate) candidate-successors, and* $\sigma_i : P \rightarrow \wp(P)$ *is a multi-valued function mapping an actor to its sets of (immediate) candidate-predecessors;*
- $\psi = \psi \cup \psi_o$ */* acquisition activities */ where,* $\psi_i : P \rightarrow \wp(P)$ *is a multi-valued function returning a bag of previously worked activities,* $(K \subseteq A)$*, on directed arcs,* $(\sigma_i(o), o), o \in C$ *, from* $\sigma_i(o)$ *to o; and* $\psi_o : P \rightarrow \wp(P)$ *is a multi-valued function returning a set of acquisition activities,* $(K \subseteq A)$ *, on directed arcs,* $(o, \sigma_o(o)), o \in C$ *from o to* $\sigma_o(o)$*;*

Likewise, the actor-based workflow modeling methodology might not be a convenient work in terms of designing and modeling a workflow procedure, too. In other words, it is very important for the actor-based workflow model to provide an effective modeling tool with keeping the conventional workflow modeling approaches. Therefore, we conceive an automatic modeling methodology for the actor-based workflow model, which algorithmically constructs an actor-based workflow model from an ICN-based workflow model. The following is the construction algorithm for automatically extracting an actor-based workflow model from an ICN-based workflow model. Particularly, in order to construct an actor-based workflow model, it needs, as inputs, the sets of δ_o (control flow information), ε_p (activity-role mapping information) and π_c (role-actor mapping information) in an ICN-based workflow model. Additionally, we have to remind that a group of actors can cooperatively and simultaneously perform

Figure 9. An actor-based model of the hiring workflow procedure

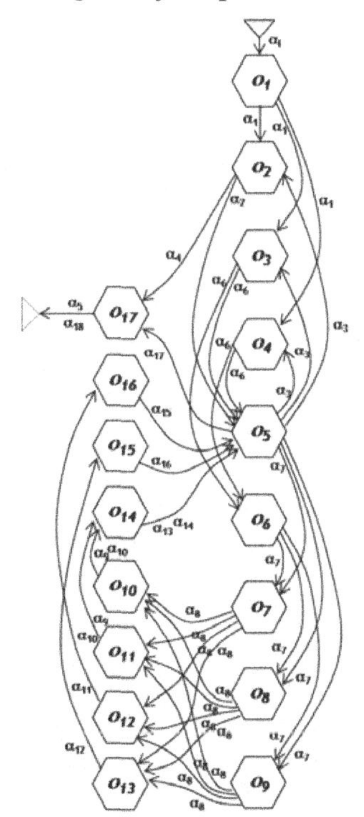

an activity, which is called a realtime groupware activity, and almost all current available workflow models do not support such realtime groupware activities. Therefore, the actor-based workflow model is able to provide a feasible solution for supporting such realtime groupware activities, which is one of the cutting-edge workflow features to be required in the future-generation workflow management systems.

The Construction Algorithm for the Actor-based Workflow Model. An actor-based workflow model is constructed from an ICN-based workflow model through the following algorithm:

Input An ICN, $\Gamma = (\delta, \rho, \lambda, \varepsilon, \pi, \kappa, \mathbf{I}, \mathbf{O})$;
Output A Actor-based Workflow Model,
$\Lambda = (\sigma, \psi, \mathbf{S}, \mathbf{E})$;
Begin Procedure
For $(\forall\alpha \in A)$ **Do**
Begin
/* $\sigma = \sigma_i \cup \sigma_o$ */
Add *all members of* $\pi_c(\varepsilon_p(\alpha))$ **To**
$\sigma_i(each\ member\ of\ [\pi_c(\varepsilon]_p(\delta_o(\alpha))))$;

Table 4. Formal representation of the actor-based hiring workflow model

$\Lambda = (\sigma, \psi, \mathbf{S}, \mathbf{E})$ over $\mathbf{A}, \mathbf{C}$	The Actor-based Hiring Workflow Model
$\mathbf{A} = \{\alpha_I, \alpha_2, \alpha_3, \alpha_4, \alpha_5, \alpha_6, \alpha_7, \alpha_8, \alpha_9, \alpha_{10}, \alpha_{11}, \alpha_{12}, \alpha_{13}, \alpha_{14}, \alpha_{15}, \alpha_{16}, \alpha_{17}, \alpha_{18}, \alpha_1, \alpha_F\}$	Elementary Activities
$\mathbf{C} = \{o_I, o_1, o_2, o_3, o_4, o_5, o_6, o_7\ o_8, o_9, o_{10}, o_{11}, o_{12}, o_{13}, o_{14}, o_{15}, o_{16}, o_{17}, o_F\}$	Actors
$\mathbf{S} = \{\emptyset\}$	Initial Actors from some external actor-based workflow models
$\mathbf{E} = \{\emptyset\}$	Final Actors to some external actor-based workflow models

$\sigma = \sigma_i \cup \sigma_o$	σ_i:**CandidatePredecessors**	σ_o:**CandidateSuccessors**
	$\sigma_i(o_I) = \{\emptyset\}$;	$\sigma_o(o_I) = \{o_1\}$;
	$\sigma_i(o_1) = \{o_I\}$;	$\sigma_o(o_1) = \{o_2, o_3, o_4\}$;
	$\sigma_i(o_2) = \{o_2, o_5\}$;	$\sigma_o(o_2) = \{o_5, o_{17}\}$;
	$\sigma_i(o_3) = \{o_1, o_5\}$;	$\sigma_o(o_3) = \{o_5, o_6\}$;
	$\sigma_i(o_4) = \{o_1, o_5\}$;	$\sigma_o(o_4) = \{o_5, o_6\}$;
	$\sigma_i(o_5) = \{o_2, o_3, o_4, o_{14}, o_{15}, o_{16}\}$;	$\sigma_o(o_5) = \{o_2, o_3, o_4, o_7, o_8, o_9, o_{17}\}$;
	$\sigma_i(o_6) = \{o_3, o_4\}$;	$\sigma_o(o_6) = \{o_7, o_8, o_9\}$;
	$\sigma_i(o_7) = \{o_5, o_6\}$;	$\sigma_o(o_7) = \{o_{10}, o_{11}, o_{12}, o_{13}\}$;
	$\sigma_i(o_8) = \{o_5, o_6\}$;	$\sigma_o(o_8) = \{o_{10}, o_{11}, o_{12}, o_{13}\}$;
	$\sigma_i(o_9) = \{o_5, o_6\}$;	$\sigma_o(o_9) = \{o_{10}, o_{11}, o_{12}, o_{13}\}$;
	$\sigma_i(o_{10}) = \{o_7, o_8, o_9\}$;	$\sigma_o(o_{10}) = \{o_{14}\}$;
	$\sigma_i(o_{11}) = \{o_7, o_8, o_9\}$;	$\sigma_o(o_{11}) = \{o_{14}\}$;
	$\sigma_i(o_{12}) = \{o_7, o_8, o_9\}$;	$\sigma_o(o_{12}) = \{o_{16}\}$;
	$\sigma_i(o_{13}) = \{o_7, o_8, o_9\}$;	$\sigma_o(o_{13}) = \{o_{15}\}$;
	$\sigma_i(o_{14}) = \{o_{10}, o_{11}\}$;	$\sigma_o(o_{14}) = \{o_5\}$;
	$\sigma_i(o_{15}) = \{o_{13}\}$;	$\sigma_o(o_{15}) = \{o_5\}$;
	$\sigma_i(o_{16}) = \{o_{12}\}$;	$\sigma_o(o_{16}) = \{o_5\}$;
	$\sigma_i(o_{17}) = \{o_5, o_2\}$;	$\sigma_o(o_{17}) = \{o_F\}$;
	$\sigma_i(o_F) = \{o_{17}\}$;	$\sigma_o(o_F) = \{\emptyset\}$;
$\psi = \psi_i \cup \psi_o$	ψ_i:**PreviousWork**	ψ_o:**AcquisitionWork**
	$\psi_i(o_I) = \{\emptyset\}$;	$\psi_o(o_I) = \{(\alpha_I, o_1)\}$;
	$\psi_i(o_1) = \{(\alpha_I, o_I)\}$;	$\psi_o(o_1) = \{(\alpha_1, o_2), (\alpha_1, o_3), (\alpha_1, o_4)\}$;
	$\psi_i(o_2) = \{(\alpha_1, o_1), (\alpha_3, o_5)\}$;	$\psi_o(o_2) = \{(\alpha_2, o_5), (\alpha_4, o_{17})\}$;
	$\psi_i(o_3) = \{(\alpha_1, o_1, (\alpha_3, o_5)\}$;	$\psi_o(o_3) = \{(\alpha_6, o_5), (\alpha_6, o_6)\}$;
	$\psi_i(o_4) = \{(\alpha_1, o_1, (\alpha_3, o_5)\}$;	$\psi_o(o_4) = \{(\alpha_6, o_5), (\alpha_6, o_6)\}$;
	$\psi_i(o_5) = \{(\alpha_2, o_2), (\alpha_6, o_3), (\alpha_6, o_4), (\alpha_{13}, o_{14}), (\alpha_{14}, o_{14}), (\alpha_{15}, o_{16}), (\alpha_{16}, o_{15})\}$;	$\psi_o(o_5) = \{(\alpha_3, o_2), (\alpha_3, o_3), (\alpha_3, o_4), (\alpha_7, o_7), (\alpha_7, o_8), (\alpha_7, o_9), (\alpha_{17}, o_{17})\}$;
	$\psi_i(o_6) = \{(\alpha_6, o_3), (\alpha_6, o_4)\}$;	$\psi_o(o_6) = \{(\alpha_7, o_7), (\alpha_7, o_8), (\alpha_7, o_9)\}$;
	$\psi_i(o_7) = \{(\alpha_7, o_5), (\alpha_7, o_6)\}$;	$\psi_o(o_7) = \{(\alpha_8, o_{10}), (\alpha_8, o_{11}), (\alpha_8, o_{12}), (\alpha_8, o_{13})\}$;
	$\psi_i(o_8) = \{(\alpha_7, o_5), (\alpha_7, o_6)\}$;	$\psi_o(o_8) = \{(\alpha_8, o_{10}), (\alpha_8, o_{11}), (\alpha_8, o_{12}), (\alpha_8, o_{13})\}$;
	$\psi_i(o_9) = \{(\alpha_7, o_5), (\alpha_7, o_6)\}$;	$\psi_o(o_9) = \{(\alpha_8, o_{10}), (\alpha_8, o_{11}), (\alpha_8, o_{12}), (\alpha_8, o_{13})\}$;
	$\psi_i(o_{10}) = \{(\alpha_8, o_7), (\alpha_8, o_8), (\alpha_8, o_9)\}$;	$\psi_o(o_{10}) = \{(\alpha_9, o_{14}), (\alpha 10, o_{14})\}$;
	$\psi_i(o_{11}) = \{(\alpha_8, o_7), (\alpha_8, o_8), (\alpha_8, o_9)\}$;	$\psi_o(o_{11}) = \{(\alpha_9, o_{14}), (\alpha 10, o_{14})\}$;
	$\psi_i(o_{12}) = \{(\alpha_8, o_7), (\alpha_8, o_8), (\alpha_8, o_9)\}$;	$\psi_o(o_{12}) = \{(\alpha_{11}, o_{16})\}$;
	$\psi_i(o_{13}) = \{(\alpha_8, o_7), (\alpha_8, o_8), (\alpha_8, o_9)\}$;	$\psi_o(o_{13}) = \{(\alpha_{12}, o_{15})\}$;
	$\psi_i(o_{14}) = \{(\alpha_9, o_{10}), (\alpha_{10}, o_{10}), (\alpha_9, o_{11}), (\alpha_{10}, o_{11})\}$;	$\psi_o(o_{14}) = \{(\alpha_{13}, o_5), (\alpha_{14}, o_5)\}$;
	$\psi_i(o_{15}) = \{(\alpha_{12}, o_{13})\}$;	$\psi_o(o_{15}) = \{(\alpha_{16}, o_5)\}$;
	$\psi_i(o_{16}) = \{(\alpha_{11}, o_{12}\}$;	$\psi_o(o_{16}) = \{(\alpha_{15}, o_5)\}$;
	$\psi_i(o_{17}) = \{(\alpha_4, o_2), (\alpha_{17}, o_5)\}$;	$\psi_o(o_{17}) = \{(\alpha_5, o_F), (\alpha_{18}, o_F)\}$;
	$\psi_i(o_F) = \{(\alpha_5, o_{17}), (\alpha_{18}, o_{17})\}$;	$\psi_o(o_F) = \{\emptyset\}$;

Add *all members of*
$\llbracket \pi_{\downarrow}C\ (\varepsilon \rrbracket\ _{\downarrow}p\ (\delta_{\downarrow}o\ (\alpha)\ )))(\delta_{\downarrow}o\ (\alpha)\ ))$ **To**
$\sigma_o(\textit{each member of } \llbracket \pi_C(\varepsilon \rrbracket_p(\alpha)))$;
/* $\psi = \psi_i \cup \psi_o = \psi_i \cup \psi_o$ */
Add *all pairs of* $(\alpha, o), \forall o \in \pi_C(\varepsilon(\alpha))$ **T**
$\psi_{\downarrow}i$ *each member of* $\pi_{\downarrow}C\ (\varepsilon_{\downarrow}p\ (\delta_{\downarrow}o\ (\alpha)\ )))$
;
Add *all pairs of* $(\alpha, o), \forall o \in \pi_C(\varepsilon_p(\delta_O(\alpha)))$
To $\psi_{\downarrow}O$ *each member of* $\pi_{\downarrow}C\ (\varepsilon_{\downarrow}p\ (\alpha)))$;
End
End Procedure

As an example, we apply the algorithm to the hiring workflow procedure; the input of the algorithm is the information sets of the ICN-based hiring workflow model, and its output is the actor-based hiring workflow model graphically represented in Figure 9 as well as formally specified in Table 4. Unlike the role-based workflow model in which an activity is mapped to just a single role (one-to-one relationship), the actor-based workflow model has one-to-many relationships in the mappings of activities and actors. Because of the one-to-many relationships between activities and actors, an actor node may have several outgoing directed arcs that have the same activity as their labels. Therefore, during the runtime of an actor-based workflow model, each actor node having the same activity labeled on outgoing arcs needs to have a selection mechanism choosing one of the neighbor actors that have the same activity labeled on arcs so as to assign the activity to the chosen actor. On Figure 9, for example, the actor node, o_1, has three outgoing directed arcs labeled with the same activity, α_2, and so o_1 has to select one of the neighbor actors, o_2, o_3, o_4, so as to proceed to the selected actor after performing α_2 during runtime. There should be several actor selection mechanisms, such as random, sequential, heuristic selection mechanism and so on. Of course, it is possible for each actor node in a workflow procedure to have a different selection mechanism.

IMPLICATIONS ON WORKFLOW ARCHITECTURES

Workflow Architectural Complexity

As stated in the previous sections, the goal of a workflow management system is to orchestrate the enactment of workflow procedures, which is however becoming more and more complicated work according to rapidly scaling up the complexities of workflow procedures in terms of structure, size and workload. Accordingly, the higher degree of complexities in workflow procedures requires the architectural renovations of workflow management systems. As a consequence of this atmosphere, we need to be concerned about the advanced workflow architectures based upon the advanced workflow models presented in the previous sections. At the same time, it is necessary to make some criteria, which is called the degree of workflow architectural complexity, in order to effectively characterizing them; the workflow architectures can be classified based on the degree of workflow architectural complexity consisting of three perspectives and dimensions—Workflow Engagement, Workflow Structure and Workflow Instantiation. We describe the meanings of them as the followings:

- **Workflow engagement:** This dimension of the workflow architectural complexity has to do with the sizes of workflow's physical components that are served and engaged for a workflow management system. The physical components are directly related with the components of workflow models, such as actors, roles, activities, workflow procedures, business processes, and organizations. So, the degree of workflow commitment can be decided by the sizes of these components, and it also becomes an essential criterion that is able to characterize the system's scalability and performance - How well the workflow and business process management system handles, commits, and serves for a huge number of requests coming out of a large number of actors, procedures and organizational compartments, which are involved in one or even more organizations.

- **Workflow structure:** This dimension of the workflow architectural complexity has something to do with interactional complexities between activities within a workflow procedure and between collaborative activities that are involved in interactions between workflow procedures in collaboration. In a large scale workflow procedure, several hundreds of activities might be co-associated with each other in diverse types of complex relationships, such as subworkflow, conjunctive, disjunctive, massively parallel, and cooperative relationships. Also, the recent e-Commerce, e-Logistics and e-Government marketplaces require more complicated relationships for supporting the inter-organizational workflow services like collaborative workflows, choreographical workflows, orchestrated workflows, and chained workflows. So, these structural complexity ought to be a critical criterion for deciding the degree of workflow architectural complexity.
- **Workflow instantiation:** This dimension of the workflow architectural complexity has directly related with measurement of the system's performance. In a large scale workflow application domain, the number of workcases instantiated from a workflow procedure may be from several hundred-thousands of workcases to several millions of workcases. Also, the large number of workflow procedures can be managed and maintained in a workflow management system. Specially, this dimension is inflicting heavy effect on the fundamental infrastructures of the workflow management systems. That is, the systems can be extensively deployed on distributed computing environments, such as clustered, grid, and peer-to-peer computing architectures, in order to handle those large scale workcases without any further performance degradation. So, this dimension should be the most important criterion in deciding the degree of workflow architectural complexity.

The workflow architectural renovations should be accomplished by supporting the highest levels of services in all three dimensions. Particularly, in order to be satisfied with the highest levels of services in both the workflow engagement dimension and the workflow structure dimension, it is necessary for the system to be completely renovated from the fundamental and philosophical reformations, whereas the highest level of the workflow instantiation can be renovated only through the software architectural reformations. We would expect that the role-based workflow model and the actor-based workflow model presented in this chapter ought to be the theoretical basis for the architectural renovations satisfying the higher levels of complexities in the workflow engagement dimension and the workflow structure dimension.

Workflow Architectural Framework

In order to systematically support the workflow architectural renovations, we conceived an architectural framework in [34]. The architectural framework suggests that there are some overriding elements that generically characterize any workflow system. These elements are captured in the generic level of the architectural description, and include elements of workflow execution, control, and data. At a more detailed level, every workflow system deals with some set of conceptual objects such as workcases, activities, actors, and roles. These objects, and their representation are dealt with in the conceptual level of the architectural description. Finally, the lowest, most detailed level of our framework is concerned with the physical components of a workflow system. At this level we specify the details of processors, workstations, and networks. This level is concerned with implementation details of concrete elements, their functionality, and their inter-connectivity. Conclusively, the framework has the three levels of considerations—generic level, conceptual level, and implementation level.

Generic Level of Consideration. At the generic level, a common high-level framework from which to view the entire architectural style of a workflow system is defined. This architectural style is characterized by distribution choices selected for the execution component, the control component, and the data component of a workflow system. the structural categories possible for each component are centralized, decentralized, and dispersed. Note that the terms decentralized and dispersed refer to replicated and partitioned systems respectively.

- **Centralized:** Control, application data and / or execution scripts are kept at a single site. A site is a node of the workflow network.
- **Decentralized (replicated):** Full copies of control, application data, and / or execution scripts are distributed to more than one site.
- **Dispersed (partitioned):** Control, application data, and / or execution scripts are divided into multiple partitions, and the various partitions are kept, in a non-replicated fashion, at different sites.

Conceptual Level of Consideration. The conceptual level of our framework elucidates a taxonomy based upon the workflow concepts of activities, roles, actors, and workcases. At the generic level, we dealt with elements that are indeed generic (control, data, execution), and generally applicable to all distributed systems. While on the other, at the conceptual level, we will deal with concepts that are not generic, but specific to workflow systems. The choice of concepts follows the standards recommendation of the workflow management coalition (WfMC). The concepts will be introduced with respect to the control dimension of the generic architecture, but, as we shall see, the same concepts also serve to partition the possibilities for data and scripts. In result, at the conceptual level, an architectural framework needs to deal with issues of concept embodiment, relationships among concepts, concept communication, and conceptual responsibility distribution.

The notion of workflow concept embodiment is related to the recent notions of software architectures that argue that careful choices concerning implementation of active entities as processes, threads, or active agents has tremendous influence upon performance of a system. Recent literature has shown that these software choices are equally as important for performance as hardware choices. All workflow systems must keep data, or some representation of concepts such as activities and actors. A few modern architectures have recently implemented some of these concepts as active processes rather than as passive data. We argue that there are a plethora of unexplored workflow architectures that are radical in that they embody activities, roles, actors, and / or workcases as active processes. We specifically capture this notion of active versus passive in our conceptual level taxonomy.

Relationships among concepts: There are numerous relationships between these workflow concepts that must be supported within a workflow architecture. The precedence relationship exists among activities; the performer relation exists between roles and activities; the part-of relationship exists between activities and procedures; etc. Some of these relationships can be specified (bound) at system creation time; others may be fixed (bound) on a per workcase basis at the time of workcase creation; still others need to be changed in various dynamic timeframes. For example, when a new application needs administrative processing in the hiring workflow procedure, a choice must be made of which secretary will do the work. This is a binding of actor to activity that, in many environments is best done (by a workflow scheduler or a manager) as a dynamic late binding. It depends upon who is available, who is best qualified, who dealt with this application in the past, and other factors as well. In our taxonomy, we specifically capture notions of relationships, and there binding time, recognizing that there is a spectrum of binding choices ranging from static fixed, through periodic binding, opportunistic binding, up to last minute dynamic binding.

Responsibility distribution: There exist numerous options and decisions about placement and movement of data, scripts, and control information; many of these options remain unexplored in today's workflow products. Within all workflow architectures, there must be entities responsible for answering questions such as "what activity should be executed next?" and "when should this application data be moved to another site?" and "where is the most efficient site to execute this script?" Again we note that in the majority of today's workflow products, the static answer to many of these questions is "at the workflow server." In the large scale workflow systems of the near future, this answer is inadequate. There is a pressing need to explore workflow solutions that are much more distributed. One of the areas needing research is the communication between concepts once placement and movement are not simply always at the server. For example, within the JOIN operation when several activities must all finish before a successor activity can commence, how do we efficiently implement a distributed join? If the server is a bottleneck, how do we open up communication between activity entities, which can greatly decrease traffic to the server? As the size of workflow applications grows larger and larger, these issues become more pressing.

Based upon those architectural considerations, we can derive our conceptual taxonomy as shown in Figure 10, in which there are three dimensions—process embodiment, process representation and process creation—corresponding to the four relevant concepts of workcase, activity, role, and actor. We would suggest that further dimensions can and should be added in the future. In each dimension, we can choose to implement control of the concept passively as data available on the server or elsewhere, or we can implement control actively with one active agent for each instance, or with one active agent for each class, or with both (dual active). The processes that are

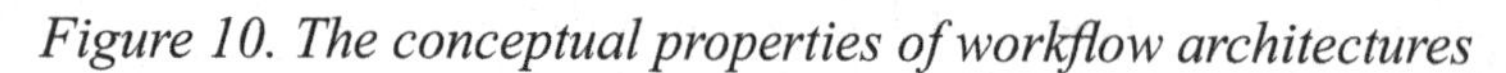
Figure 10. The conceptual properties of workflow architectures

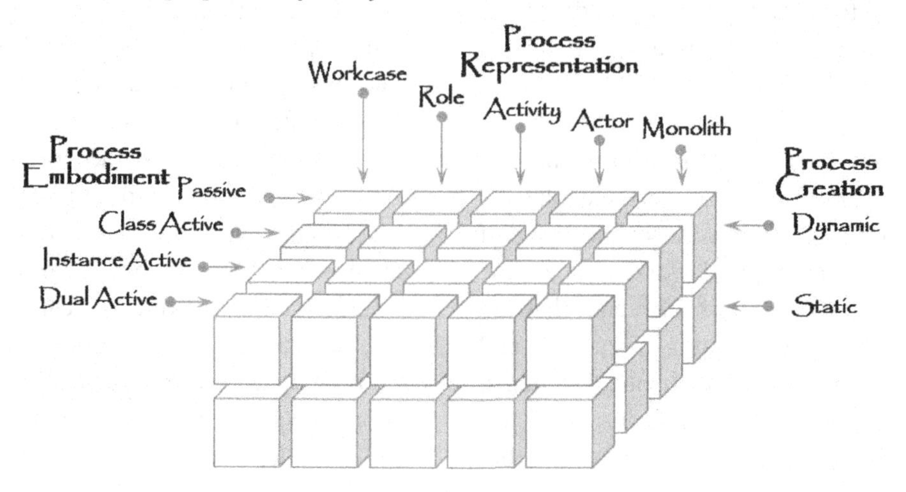

created, manipulated, and destroyed in the active schemes can be static or dynamic. Note that replicated or partitioned or hybrid schemes can be used, and the same dimensions can be used for data and scripts.

Implementation Level of Consideration. The implementation level is the lowest level of the architectural framework. Components at this level include processors, networks, and memories. If there are questions concerning the performance of an architecture, then this level must be involved in the answer. Specifications of processor speeds, memory sizes, and network parameters are given at this level. In the previous levels, we were concerned with generic and conceptual entities, but not with where those entities reside in the network. Pragmatic questions of actual distribution are answered at this level. Thus, the question of which memory module contains our application data, or which processor executes a script, are implementation level details. This level can be modeled or implemented in great detail or little detail. Issues of caching, multiprocessing, threads versus process, network protocols, etc, may all be of potential concern at this level. Additionally, a complex and important consideration is the internetwork configuration. Fully connected networks have very different performance characteristics from store and forward. Broadcast media such as Ethernet are very different from point to point systems with switches. Satellite speeds for bulk transfer are very different from coaxial cable telephone line speeds.

Advanced Workflow Architectures

Based upon the conceptual taxonomy of Figure 10, we can selectively extract several advanced workflow architectures chosen from the boxes of each process embodiment dimension (concept) —workcase, role, activity, and actor. Particularly, we remind that the role-based workflow model and the actor-based workflow model introduced in the previous sections of this chapter become the theoretical bases for the role-based workflow architecture and the actor-based workflow architecture, respectively. The followings are the details of the advanced workflow architectures that are possibly derived from the conceptual workflow taxonomy:

The active workcase dimension implies that architectures can be created in which the workcase is not simply represented as data, but as a software process that actively guides the workcase from activity to activity helping to find and select actors, roles, data, etc, for each activity. Class active, workcase centric architecture means that there is one workcase process that supervises all of the workcase instances. Tasks of this process include maintenance of all workcase histories, scheduling tasks, and up-to-date knowledge of the state of each workcase. External queries of the current status of any workcase instance are directed to this process. Instance active, workcase centric architecture means that there is one workcase process for each workcase instance. Again, this process maintains state and history, and performs other tasks. It can also act as an active negotiator for the workcase with the goal of expeditiously completing the task. It can thus help to perform activities, and perform negotiation on behalf of the workcase. This abstraction supports architectures of migrating intelligent forms.

The active activity dimension suggests an architecture in which each activity type, or each activity instance, is represented by a process. We call these architectures activity centric architectures. The five dashed ovals in figure 1 each represent the domain of a class active, activity centric process. In an instance active architecture, each of the 15 activities in figure 1 would posses its own dedicated process. Since each dimension is independent of the others, it is possible to simultaneously have software processes for all workcases, and for all activities. This implies that when a particular workcase is enabled to perform a particular activity, a coupling operation is performed in which the two (or more) processes can very efficiently share data, and work together to perform the activity. Note that there may be workcase specific goals and data and scripts controlled by the workcase process; and activity specific goals and data and scripts controlled by the activity process. The coupling can be an efficient and elegant means of effectively performing the activity.

Role processes do the work of selecting which roles will be chosen to perform (or supervise, or otherwise participate in) which activities. In general this may require the evaluation of a complex network. Selection of the class active, role centric architecture implies that there is a role server process somewhere on the network. Note that it can be replicated or partitioned. This process also maintains the history of all roles, and is able to answer queries concerning all role assignments. Note that certain roles may be privileged to access certain sensitive data (e.g. management salaries or customer credit) that is not available to the workflow system in general. In this case, it can be quite useful to implement an instance active role centric architecture that features one role process for each role instance. Thus, the manager role can have access to, and protect, different data than the credit clerk role.

The actor centric architecture is similar to the role centric architecture except that, in the instance active case, there can be one for each person in the system although several people may be assigned to the same role. Actor processes do the work of selecting which actors will be chosen to play which roles, and perform which activities. In general this may require the evaluation of a complex network. These active agents maintain history and current actor status, do scheduling, and reply to relevant external queries. Selection of the class active, actor centric architecture implies that there is an actor server process somewhere on the network. At the conceptual level, we do not specify where this process resides. It could be on a dedicated actor server machine, or elsewhere, or migrating. There can also be a mixture of instance active processes and class active processes which all couple to perform a complex activity. We present an example of this later. We do not specify how the coupling is accomplished. This depends upon the network interconnection parameters, and other details, which are properly the domain of the implementation level architecture.

SUMMARY

The expressiveness of a workflow management system is determined by the content of its underlying workflow model. That is, a workflow model gives a lot of influences on design workflow procedures and implementation of a workflow management system as well. Depending on workflow model, the corresponding workflow management system may have not only different features but different methodologies. Therefore, the workflow model should incorporate the advanced technological and organizational trends so that its corresponding workflow management system enables to be effective and acclimatizes itself to a new technological and organizational working environment.

The recent trends in working environments require new types of workflow management systems that provide cooperative working facilities, by which group of people works together simultaneously, and that are equipped by increasingly large and complex workflow applications. The recent trend in technological environments in term of implementing a workflow management system is undoubtedly the object orientation. The international standard organization for object orientation, OMG (Object Management Group), has announced the workflow management facility as a standard architecture of workflow management systems. The object oriented architecture stemmed from the joint team's proposal for workflow management facility is based on activity entities. The activity based object orientation should not be suitable for straightforwardly accommodating the recent trends in terms of the working environments supporting not only cooperative group works which are represented by the multi-cast workflow, but also pull-based works that are represented by the any-cast workflow. We strongly believe that role based workflow model is the best solution for realizing the multi-cast workflow as well as the any-cast workflow. Based on the role-based model, we can derive a design methodology for prescribing role oriented workflow procedures, and at the same time, a role oriented workflow management system. This chapter specifically addresses the Information Control Net (ICN). The ICN can be used systematically and formally to formulate a way to describe and incorporate the concept of role orientation into workflow models and architectures.

In order for a workflow process to be deployed through a workflow enactment engine, it is eventually represented by a set of activity precedence data (representing control flows), their relevant data (representing data flow), and others including their roles, actors and invoked applications, which are standardized as WPDL (Workflow Process Definition Language) or XPDL (XML Process Definition Language) by WfMC. And then the workflow enactment engine uses the activity-driven information to enact the workflow process. This is quite normal and reasonable under the traditional computing environment, because it is reflecting the way of office works in the real-world. So we call it activity-driven workflow framework. However, this should not be true if the activity-driven workflow framework without any further modification is applied into the Grid or P2P computing environment, because the Grid/P2P's resource configuration is quite inapt to the scheme of the activity-driven workflow framework. Under the Grid/P2P, the workflow process's data has to be disseminated into each of workstations and PCs—Peers. But each of the peers is owned by each of actors involved in the workflow process. Therefore, we need to reorganize the workflow process's data from the activity-driven information to actor-driven information. In other words, the actor-based workflow model ought to be the impeccable theory for accomplishing a high-level of efficiency in enacting workflows over Grid/P2P computing environment.

REFERENCES

Ferraiolo, D. F., & Kuhn, D. R. (1992). Role-based access controls. *Proceedings of the 15th NIST-NSA National Computer Security Conference.*

Ferraiolo, D. F., et al. (1995). *An introduction to role-based access control.* NIST/ITL Bulletin.

Ferraiolo, D. F., Cugini, J. A., & Kuhn, D. R. (1995). Role-based access control: Features and Motivations. *Proceedings of the 11th Annual Computer Security Applications.*

Ellis, C. A., & Nutt, G. J. (1980). Office information systems and computer science. *ACM Computing Surveys, 12*(1).

Ellis, C. A., & Nutt, G. J. (1993). The modeling and analysis of coordination systems. *University of Colorado/Dept. of Computer Science Technical Report, CU-CS-639-93.*

Ellis, C. A. (1983). Formal and informal models of office activity. *Proceedings of the 1983 Would Computer Congress.*

Bair, J. H. (1990). Contrasting workflow models: getting to the roots of three vendors. *Proceedings of International CSCW Conference.*

Kim, K., et al. (1996). Practical experience on workflow: hiring process automation by FlowMark. *IBM Internship Report, IBM/ISSC Boulder Colorado.*

Kim, K., & Paik, S. (1996). Practical experiences and requirements on workflow. *Lecture Notes Asian '96 Post-Conference Workshop: Coordina-*

tion Technology for Collaborative Applications, the 2nd Asian Computer Science Conference.

Park, M., & Kim, K. (2008). Control-path oriented workflow intelligence analyses. *Journal of information science and engineering, 34*(3).

Kim, K., & Ra, I. (2007). e-Lollapalooza: a process-driven e-Business service integration system for e-Logistics services. *KSII Transactions on Internet and Information Systems, 1*(1), 33-52.

Kim, K. (2007). Signal-Algorithm: structured workflow process mining through amalgamating temporal workcases. *Lecture Notes in Artificial Intelligence, 4426,* 119-130.

Kim, K. (2007). A layered workflow knowledge Grid/P2P architecture and its models for future generation workflow systems. *Future Generation Computer Systems, 23*(3), 304-316.

Kim, K. (2006). Beyond Workflow Mining. *Lecture Notes in Computer Science, 4102,* 49-64.

Kim, K. (2006). A XML-based workflow event logging mechanism for workflow mining. *Lecture Notes in Computer Science, 3842,* 132-136.

Kim, K. (2006). An enterprise workflow Grid/P2P architecture for massively parallel and very large scale workflow systems. *Lecture Notes in Computer Science, 3842,* 472-476.

Kim, K. (1999). Actor-oriented Workflow Model. *Proceedings of the 2nd international symposium on Cooperative Database Systems for Advanced Applications.*

Kim, K. (2005). A process-driven e-business service integration system and its application to e-logistics services. *Lecture Notes in Computer Science, 3762*, 485-494.

Kim, K. (2005). A Process-Driven Inter-organizational Choreography Modeling System. *Lecture Notes in Computer Science, 3762*, 485-494.

Wainer, J., Kim, K., & Ellis, C. A. (2005). A workflow mining method through model rewriting. *Lecture Notes in Computer Science, 3706,* 184-191.

Kim, K., & Ahn, H. (2005). An EJB-based very large scale workflow system and its performance measurement. *Lecture Notes in Computer Science, 3739*, 526-537.

Kim, K., & Kim, H. (2005). A Peer-to-Peer workflow model for distributing large-scale workflow data onto Grid/P2P. *Journal of digital information management, 3*(2), 64-70.

Kim, K., Ahn, H., & Kim, C. (2005). SCO control net for the process-driven SCORM content aggregation model. *Lecture Notes in Computer Science, 3483,* 38-47.

Kim, K., Won, J., & Kim, C. (2005). A fragment-driven process modeling methodology. *Lecture Notes in Computer Science, 3483,* 817-826.

Kim, K., Lee, J., & Kim, C. (2005). A real-time cooperative swim-lane business process modeler. *Lecture Notes in Computer Science, 3483,* 176-185.

Kim, K., Yoo, H., & Won, J. (2004). The e-Lollapalooza global workflow modeler: a registry-based e-Logistic. *Lecture Notes in Computer Science,* (pp. 419-430).

Kim, K. (2004). Cooperative fragment-driven workflow modeling methodology and system. *WfMC Workflow Handbook,* (pp. 189-207).

Kim, K., et al. (2003). Role-based model and architecture for workflow systems. *International Journal of Computer and Information Science, 4*(4).

Kim, K. (2003). Workflow dependency analysis and its implications on distributed workflow systems. *Proceeding of the AINA*, (pp. 677-682).

Kim, K. (2003). Workflow reduction for reachable-path rediscovery. *IEEE Proceeding of the ICDM Workshop.*

Kim, K., & Kim, I. (2002). The Admon-Time workflow client: why do we need the third type of workflow client designated for administration and monitoring services? *Lecture Notes in Computer Science, 2419,* 213-224.

Kim, K., & Ellis, C. A. (2001). Performance analytic models and analyses for workflow architectures. *Journal of Information Systems Frontiers, 3*(3), 339-355.

ENDNOTES

1 The work was supported by the Contents Convergence Software Research Center, 2007-81-0, funded by the GRRC Program of Gyeonggi Province, South Korea.

2 In terms of the terminological usage, workflow procedure can be interchangeably used with business process. We prefer workflow procedure to business process in this chapter.

3 Workflow Process Definition Language

4 XML-based Process Definition Language, Version 1.0 and 2.0 are available in the international standardization organization, workflow management coalition.

5 The terminology and concept of block was firstly used in the workflow modeling system of FlowMark Workflow Management System of IBM.

6 Workflow Process Definition Language

7 XML-based Process Definition Language

8 P2P stands for Peer-to-Peer grid computing environment.

Section III
Process Models in Dynamic Environments

Chapter VIII
Enabling Adaptive Process-Aware Information Systems with ADEPT2

Manfred Reichert
University of Ulm, Germany

Peter Dadam
University of Ulm, Germany

ABSTRACT

In dynamic environments it must be possible to quickly implement new business processes, to enable ad-hoc deviations from the defined business processes on-demand (e.g., by dynamically adding, deleting or moving process activities), and to support dynamic process evolution (i.e., to propagate process schema changes to already running process instances). These fundamental requirements must be met without affecting process consistency and robustness of the process-aware information system. In this chapter the authors describe how these challenges have been addressed in the ADEPT2 process management system. Their overall vision is to provide a next generation technology for the support of dynamic processes, which enables full process lifecycle management and which can be applied to a variety of application domains.

INTRODUCTION

In today's dynamic business world the economic success of an enterprise increasingly depends on its ability to quickly and flexibly react to changes in its environment. Generally, the reasons for such changes can be manifold. As examples consider the introduction of new regulations, the availability of new medical tests, or changes in customers' attitudes. Companies and organizations therefore have recognized business agility as prerequisite for being able to cope with changes and to deal with emerging trends like business-on-demand, high product and service variability, and faster time-to-market (Weber, Rinderle, & Reichert, 2007).

Process-aware information systems (PAISs) offer promising perspectives in this respect, and a growing interest in aligning information systems in a process-oriented way can be observed (Weske, 2007). As opposed to data- or function-centered information systems, PAISs separate process logic and application code. Most PAISs describe process logic explicitly in terms of a *process template* providing the schema for handling respective *business cases*. Usually, the core of the *process layer* is built by a process management system which provides generic functions for modeling, configuring, executing, and monitoring business processes. This separation of concerns increases maintainability and reduces cost of change (Mutschler, Weber, & Reichert, 2008a). Changes to one layer often can be performed without affecting other layers; e.g., changing the execution order of process activities or adding new activities to a process template can, to a large degree, be accomplished without touching the application services linked to the different process activities (Dadam, Reichert, & Kuhn, 2000). Usually, the process logic is expressed in terms of executable *process models*, which can be checked for the absence of errors already at buildtime (e.g., to exclude deadlocks or incomplete data flow specifications). Examples for PAIS-enabling technologies include workflow management systems (van der Aalst & van Hee, 2002) and case handling tools (van der Aalst, Weske, & Grünbauer, 2005; Weske, 2007).

The ability to effectively deal with process change has been identified as one of the most fundamental success factors for PAISs (Reichert & Dadam, 1997; Müller, Greiner, & Rahm, 2004; Pesic, Schonenberg, Sidorova, & van der Aalst, 2007). In domains like healthcare (Lenz & Reichert, 2007; Dadam et al., 2000) or automotive engineering (Mutschler, Bumiller, & Reichert, 2006; Müller, Herbst, Hammori, & Reichert, 2006), for example, any PAIS would not be accepted by users if rigidity came with it. Through the described separation of concerns PAISs facilitate changes. However, enterprises running PAISs are still reluctant to adapt process implementations once they are running properly (Reijers & van der Aalst, 2005; Mutschler, Reichert, & Bumiller, 2008b). High complexity and high cost of change are mentioned as major reasons for not fully leveraging the potential of PAISs. To overcome this unsatisfactory situation more flexible PAISs are needed enabling companies to capture real-world processes adequately without leading to mismatches between computerized business processes and those running in reality (Lenz & Reichert, 2007; Reichert, Hensinger, & Dadam, 1998b). Instead, users must be able to deviate from the predefined processes if required and to evolve PAIS implementations over time. Such changes must be possible at a high level of abstraction and without affecting consistency and robustness of the PAIS.

Changes can take place at both the *process type* and the *process instance* level. Changes of single process instances, for example, become necessary to deal with exceptional situations (Reichert & Dadam, 1998a; Minor, Schmalen, Koldehoff, & Bergmann, 2007). Thus they often have to be accomplished in an ad-hoc manner. Such *ad-hoc changes* must not affect PAIS robustness or lead to errors; i.e., none of the execution guarantees ensured by formal checks at buildtime must be violated due to dynamic process changes. *Process type changes*, in turn, are continuously applied to adapt the PAIS to evolving business processes (Casati, Ceri, Pernici, & Pozzi, 1998; Rinderle, Reichert, & Dadam, 2004b; Pesic et al., 2007). Regarding long-running processes, *evolving process schemes* also require the migration of already running process instances to the new schema version. Important challenges emerging in this context are to perform *instance migrations* on-the-fly, to guarantee *compliance* of migrated instances with the new schema version, and to avoid performance penalties (Rinderle, Reichert, & Dadam, 2004a).

Off-the-shelf process management systems like *Staffware*, *WebSphere Process Server* and

FLOWer do not support dynamic structural process changes or offer restricted change features only (Weber et al., 2007). Several vendors promise flexible process support, but are unable to cope with fundamental issues related to process change (e.g., correctness). Most systems completely lack support for ad-hoc changes or for migrating process instances to a changed process schema. Thus, application developers are forced to realize workarounds and to extend applications with respective process support functions to cope with these limitations. This, in turn, aggravates PAIS development and PAIS maintenance significantly.

In the ADEPT2 project we have designed and implemented a process management system which allows for both kinds of structural changes in a flexible and reliable manner (Reichert, Rinderle, Kreher, & Dadam, 2005). The design of such a process management technology constitutes a big challenge. First, many trade-offs exist which have to be dealt with. For example, complexity of dynamic process changes increases, the higher expressiveness of the used process modeling formalism becomes. Second, complex interdependencies between the different features of such a technology exist that must be carefully understood in order to avoid implementation gaps. Process schema evolution, for example, requires high-level change operations, schema versioning support, change logging, on-the-fly migration of running process instances, and dynamic worklist adaptations (Weber et al., 2007). Thus the integrated treatment of these different system features becomes crucial. Third, even if the conceptual pillars of adaptive process management technology are well understood, it still will be a quantum leap to implement respective features in an efficient, robust and integrated manner.

This chapter gives insights into the ADEPT2 process management system, which is one of the few systems that provide integrated support for dynamic structural process changes at different levels. Using this next generation process management technology, new processes can be composed in a plug & play like fashion and be flexibly executed during run-time. ADEPT2 enables support for a broad spectrum of processes ranging from simple document-centred processes (Karbe & Ramsperger, 1991) to complex processes that integrate distributed application services (Khalaf, Keller, & Leymann, 2006). We illustrate how ad-hoc changes of single process instances as well as process schema changes with (optional) propagation of the changes to running process instances can be supported in an integrated and easy-to-use way.

The remainder of this chapter is structured as follows: We first give background information needed for the understanding of the chapter. Then we show how business processes can be modeled and enacted in ADEPT2. Based on this we introduce the ADEPT2 process change framework and its components. Following these conceptual considerations we sketch the architecture of the ADEPT2 system and give insights into its design principles. We conclude with a summary and outlook on future work.

BACKGROUNDS AND BASIC NOTIONS

When implementing a new process in a PAIS its logic has to be explicitly defined based on the modeling constructs provided by a *process meta model*. More precisely, for each business process to be supported, a *process type* represented by a *process schema* is defined. For one particular process type several process schemes may exist representing the different *versions* and the *evolution* of this type over time.

Figure 1 shows a simple example of a process schema (in ADEPT2 notation). It comprises seven activities which are connected through control edges. Generally, control edges specify precedence relations between activities. For example, activity *order medical examination* is

Figure 1. Example of a process schema (in ADEPT2 notation)

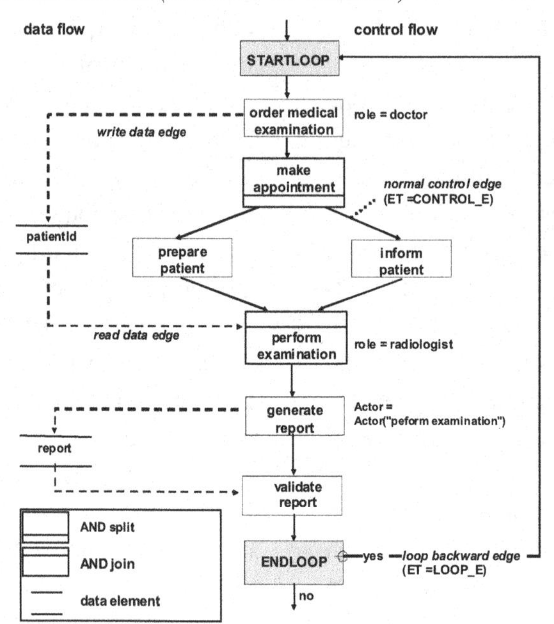

followed by activity *make appointment*, whereas activities *prepare patient* and *inform patient* can be executed in parallel. Furthermore, the process schema contains a loop structure, which allows for the repetitive execution of the depicted process fragment. Finally, data flow is modeled by linking activities with data elements. Respective data links either represent a read or a write access of an activity to a data element. In our example, for instance, activity *perform examination* reads data element *patientId*, which is written by activity *order medical examination* before.

Based on a process schema new *process instances* can be created and executed. Each of these process instances logically corresponds to a different *business case*. The PAIS orchestrates the process instances according to the logic defined by their process schema. Generally, a large number of process instances, being in different states, may run on a particular process schema.

To deal with evolving processes, exceptions and uncertainty, PAISs must be flexible. This can be achieved either through *structural process changes* (Reichert & Dadam 1998a; Rinderle et al., 2004a) or by allowing for *loosely specified process models* (Sadiq, Sadiq, & Orlowska, 2001; Adams, ter Hofstede, Edmond, & van der Aalst, 2006). In the following we focus on structural schema adaptations and show how they can be accomplished in a PAIS during runtime. Loosely specified process models, in turn, enable flexibility by leaving parts of the process model unspecified at build-time and by allowing end users to add the missing information during run-time. This approach is especially useful in case of uncertainty as it allows for deferring decisions from build- to run-time, when more information becomes available. For example, when treating a cruciate rupture for a patient we might not know in advance which treatment will be exactly performed in which execution order. Therefore, this part of the process remains unspecified during build-time and the physician decides on the exact treatment at run-time. For additional information we refer to the approaches followed by Pockets of Flexibility (Sadiq et al., 2001) and Worklets (Adams et al., 2006).

In general, structural adaptations of a process schema can be triggered and performed at two levels, the *process type* and the *process instance level*.

Process schema *changes at the type level* (in the following denoted as *process schema evolution*) become necessary to deal with the evolving nature of real-world processes (Rinderle et al., 2004b); e.g., to adapt the process schema to legal changes or to a redesigned business process. In PAISs process schema evolution often requires the dynamic propagation of the corresponding changes to related process instances, particularly if these instances are long-running. For example, assume that in a patient treatment process, due to a new legal requirement, patients have to be educated about potential risks of a surgery before this intervention takes place. Let us further assume that this change is also relevant for patients for which the treatment has already been started. In such a scenario, stopping all ongoing treatments, aborting them and re-starting the treatments is not a viable option. As a large number of treatment processes might be running at the same time, applying this change manually to all ongoing treatment processes is also not a feasible option. Instead system support is required to add this additional activity to all patient treatments for which this is still feasible; i.e., for which the surgery has not yet started.

Ad-hoc changes of single process instances, in turn, are usually required to deal with exceptions or unanticipated situations, resulting in an instance-specific process schema afterwards (Reichert & Dadam, 1997). In particular, such ad-hoc changes must not affect other process instances. In a medical treatment process, for example, the current medication of a particular patient might have to be discontinued due to an allergic reaction of this patient.

PROCESS MODELING AND ENACTMENT IN ADEPT2

When designing an adaptive process management system several trade-offs exist which have to be carefully considered. On the one hand, as known from discussions about workflow patterns (van der Aalst, ter Hofstede, Kiepuszewski, & Barros, 2003), high expressiveness of the used process meta model allows to cover a broad spectrum of processes. On the other hand, with increasing expressiveness of the used process meta model, dynamic process changes become more difficult to handle for users (Reichert, 2000). When designing ADEPT2 we kept this trade-off in mind and we found an adequate balance between expressiveness and runtime flexibility. Though ADEPT2 uses a block-structured modeling approach, it enables a sufficient degree of expressiveness due to several modeling extensions and relaxations; for a detailed discussion we refer to (Reichert, 2000) and (Reichert, Dadam, & Bauer, 2003a).

Process Modeling in ADEPT2

The ADEPT2 process meta model allows for the integrated modeling of different process aspects including process activities, control and data flow, actor assignments, organizational, semantical, and temporal constraints, and resources. Here we focus on the basic concepts available for modeling control and data flow, and we sketch how new processes can be composed in a plug & play like fashion. We refer to reading material covering other aspects at the end of this section.

Basic Concepts for Control Flow Modeling

In ADEPT2 the control flow of a process schema is represented as attributed graph with distinguishable node and edge types (Reichert et al., 2003a). This allows for efficient correctness checks and eases the handling of loop backs. Formally, a control flow schema corresponds to a tuple (N,E, ...) with node set N and edge set E. Each control edge e ∈ E has one of the edge types CONTROL_E, SYNC_E, or LOOP_E: CONTROL_E expresses a normal precedence relation, whereas SYNC_E allows to express a wait-for relation between activities of parallel branches. The latter concept is similar to *links* as used in WS-BPEL. Regarding Figure 2, for example, a necessary pre-condition for enabling activity H is that activity E either is completed or skipped before (see below). Finally, LOOP_E represents a loop backward edge.

Similarly, each node n ∈ N has one of the node types STARTFLOW, ENDFLOW, ACTIVITY, STARTLOOP, ENDLOOP, AND-/XOR-Split, and AND-/XOR-Join. Based on these elements, we can model sequences, parallel branchings, conditional branchings, and loop backs. ADEPT2 adopts concepts from block-structured process description languages, but enriches them by additional control structures in order to increase expressiveness. More precisely, branchings as well as loops have exactly one entry and one exit node. Furthermore, control blocks may be nested, but are not allowed to overlap (cf. Figure 2). As this limits expressive power, in addition, the aforementioned synchronization edges can be used for process modeling (see Reichert & Dadam, 1998a; Reichert, 2000).

We have selected this relaxed block structure because it is quickly understood by users, allows to provide user-friendly, syntax-driven process modeling tools (see below), enables the realization of high-level change patterns guaranteeing soundness, and makes it possible to implement efficient algorithms for process analysis. Note that we provide relaxations (e.g., synchronization edges and backward failure edges) and extensions (e.g., temporal constraints, actor assignments), respectively, which allow for sufficient expressiveness to cover a broad spectrum of processes from different domains. We already applied the ADEPT1 technology in domains like healthcare, logistics, and e-commerce, and the feedback we received was very positive (Müller et al., 2004; Bassil, Keller, & Kropf, 2004; Bassil, Benyoucef,

Figure 2. Block-structuring of ADEPT2 process models

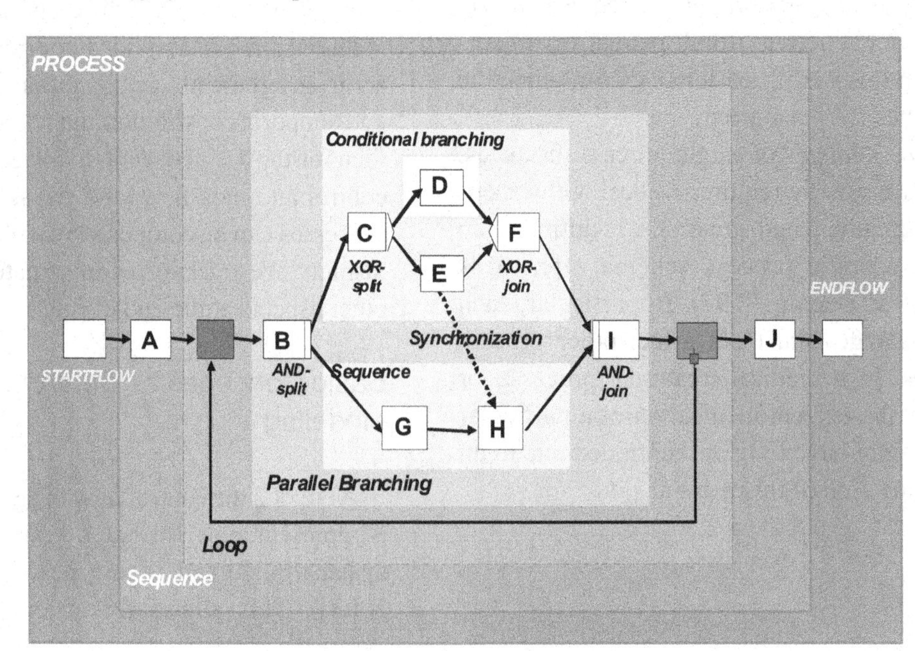

Keller, R., & Kropf, 2002; Golani & Gal, 2006). In particular, the expressiveness of our meta model was considered as being sufficient in most cases. We are currently applying ADEPT2 in other domains like construction engineering and disaster management, and we can make similar observations here.

Basic Concepts for Data Flow Modeling

Data exchange between activities is realized through writing and reading (global) process variables (denoted as *data elements* in the following). In this context, ADEPT2 considers both basic and complex data types. In addition, user-defined types are supported. Data elements are connected with input and output parameters of process activities. Each input parameter of a particular activity is mapped to exactly one data element by a *read data edge* and each activity output parameter is connected to a data element by a *write data edge*. An example is depicted in Figure 1. Activity *order medical examination* writes data element *patientID* which is then read by the subsequent activity *perform examination*.

The total collection of data elements and data edges constitutes the *data flow schema*. For its modeling, a number of constraints must be met. The most important one ensures that all data elements mandatorily read by an activity X must have been written before X becomes enabled; in particular, this has to be ensured independently from the execution path leading to activation of X (Reichert, 2000). Note that this property is crucial for the proper invocation of activity programs without missing input data.

Process Composition by Plug & Play of Application Components

Based on the described modeling concepts a new process can be realized by creating a process template (i.e., process schema). Among other things such a template describes the control flow for the process activities as well as the data flow between them. It either has to be defined from scratch or an existing template is chosen from the process template repository and adapted as needed ("process cloning").

Afterwards application components (e.g., web services or Java components) have to be assigned to the process activities. Using the ADEPT2 process editor these components can be selected from the component repository and be inserted into the process template by drag & drop. Following this, ADEPT2 analyzes whether the application functions can be connected in the desired order; e.g., we check whether the input parameters of application functions can be correctly supplied for all possible execution paths imposed by the process schema. Only those process templates passing all correctness checks may be released and transferred to the runtime system. We denote this feature as *correctness by construction.*

When dragging application components from the repository and assigning them to particular activities in the process template, the process designer does not need to have detailed knowledge about the implementation of these components. Instead the component repository provides an integrated, homogeneous view as well as access to the different components. Internally, this is based on a set of wrappers provided for the different types of application components. Our chosen architecture allows to add new wrappers if new component types have to be supported. Currently, ADEPT2 allows to integrate different kinds of application components like electronic forms, stand-alone executables, web services, Java library functions, and function calls to legacy systems.

Process Enactment in ADEPT2

Based on a given process schema new *process instances* can be created and started. State transitions of a single activity instance are depicted in Figure 3. Initially, activity status is set to

Figure 3. Internal state transitions of a process activity

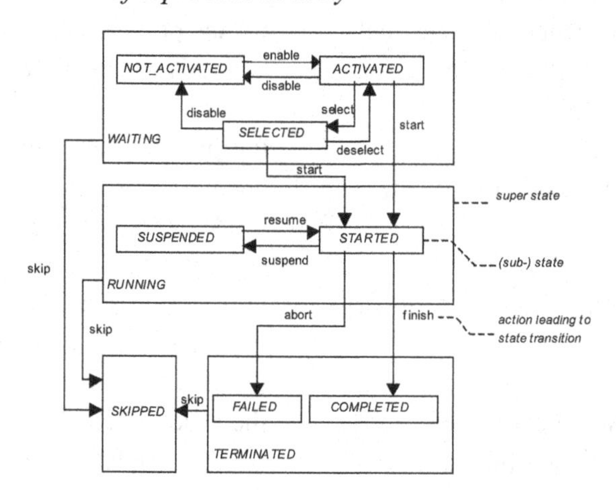

NOT _ ACTIVATED. It changes to ACTIVATED when all preconditions for executing this activity are met. In this case corresponding *work items* are inserted into the *worklists* of authorized users. If one of them selects the respective item from his worklist, activity status changes to RUNNING and respective work items are removed from the worklists of other users. Furthermore, the application component associated with the activity is started. At successful termination, activity status changes to COMPLETED.

To determine which activities are to be executed next, process enactment in ADEPT2 is based on a well-defined operational semantics (Reichert & Dadam, 1998a; Reichert, 2000). For each process instance we further maintain information about its current state by assigning markings to its activities and control edges respectively. Figure 4 depicts an example showing two process instances in different states.

Similar to Petri Nets, markings are determined by well defined marking and enactment rules. In particular, ADEPT2 maintains markings of already passed regions (except loop backs). Furthermore, activities belonging to non-selected paths of a conditional branching are marked as SKIPPED. Note that this allows to easily check whether certain changes may be applied in the current status of a process instance or not (see later). As aforementioned, ADEPT2 ensures dynamic properties like the absence of deadlocks, proper process termination, and reachability of markings which enable the activation of particular activity. The described block structuring as well as the used node and edge types help us to accomplish this in an efficient manner. Deadlocks, for example, can be excluded if the process schema (excluding loop backs) does not contain cycles (Reichert & Dadam, 1998a).

For each data element ADEPT2 stores different versions of a data object during runtime if available. In more detail, for each write access to a data element, always a new version of the respective data object is created and stored in the runtime database; i.e., data objects are not physically overwritten. This allows us to use different versions of a data element within different branches of a branching with AND-Split and XOR-Join. As shown in (Reichert et al., 2003a) maintaining data object versions is also important to enable correct rollback of process instances at the occurrence of semantical errors (e.g., activity failures).

Figure 4. Examples of two process instances running on the process schema from Figure 1

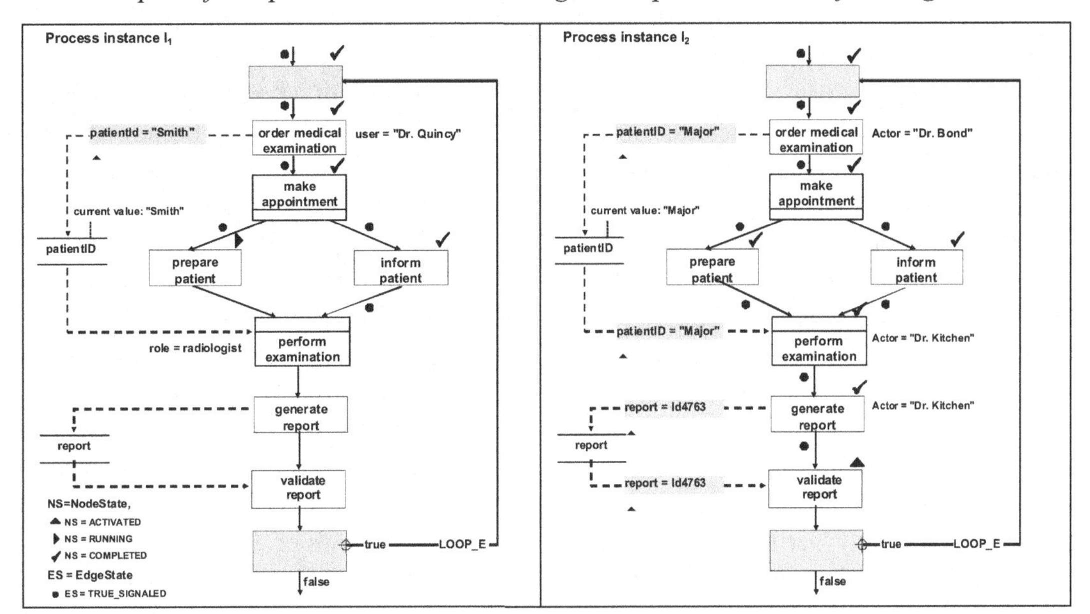

Other Process Aspects Covered in ADEPT2

Activities and their control as well as data flow are not the only viewpoints supported in our approach. ADEPT2 also considers organizational models (Rinderle & Reichert, 2007a), actor and resource assignments (Rinderle & Reichert, 2005b; Rinderle-Ma & Reichert, 2008c), and application components. In related projects, we have further looked at temporal constraints (Dadam, Reichert, & Kuhn, 2000), partitioned process schemes with distributed enactment (Reichert, Bauer, & Dadam, 1999; Bauer, Reichert, & Dadam, 2003), and configurable process visualizations (Bobrik, Bauer, & Reichert; 2006; Bobrik, Reichert, & Bauer, 2007). All these viewpoints are not only relevant for process modeling, but have to be considered in the context of (dynamic) process changes as well (Reichert & Bauer, 2007; Rinderle & Reichert, 2005b, 2007a; Dadam et al., 2000). On the one hand, each of the aspects can be primary subject to (dynamic) change. On the other hand, the different aspects might have to be adjusted due to the change of another aspect (e.g., adaptation of temporal constraints when changing the control flow structure). To set a focus, however, in this chapter we restrict ourselves to control and data flow changes. The above given references provide further information on the other aspects.

Note that we consider process correctness only at the syntactical level in this chapter (e.g., absence of deadlock-causing cycles and correctness of data flow). Respective checks are fundamental for both process modeling and process change. However, errors may be still caused at the *semantical* level (e.g., due to the violation of business rules) though not affecting the robustness of the PAIS. Therefore, the integration and verification of domain knowledge flags a milestone in the development of adaptive process management technology. In the SeaFlows project, we are currently developing a framework for defining *semantic constraints* over processes in such a way that they can express real-world domain knowledge on the one hand and are still manageable concerning the effort for maintenance and semantic process verification on the other hand (Ly, Göser, Rinderle-Ma, & Dadam, 2008). This viewpoint can be used to detect semantic conflicts (e.g., drug incompatibilities) when modeling process schemes, applying ad-hoc changes at process instance level, or propagating process schema changes to already running process instances, even if they have been already individually modified themselves; i.e., SeaFlows provides techniques to ensure semantic correctness for single and concurrent changes which are, in addition, minimal regarding the set of semantic constraints to be checked. Together with further optimizations of the semantic checks based on certain process meta model properties this allows for efficiently verifying processes. Altogether, the SeaFlows framework provides the basis for process management systems which are *adaptive* and *semantic-aware* at the same time; note that this is a fundamental issue when thinking of business process compliance. For further details we refer to (Ly et al., 2008; Ly, Rinderle, & Dadam, 2008).

ADEPT2 PROCESS CHANGE FRAMEWORK

This section deals with fundamental aspects of dynamic process changes as supported by ADEPT2. Though we illustrate relevant issues along the ADEPT2 process meta model, it is worth mentioning that most of the described concepts can be applied in connection with other process modeling formalisms as well; see (Reichert, Rinderle, & Dadam, 2003b) and (Reichert & Rinderle, 2006) for examples.

Requirements

In order to adequately deal with process changes during runtime users need to be able to define them at a high level of abstraction. Several fundamental requirements, which will be discussed in the following, exist in this context:

1. **Support of structural adaptations at different levels.** Any framework enabling dynamic process changes should allow for structural schema adaptations at both the process type and the process instance level. In principle, the same set of change patterns should be applicable at both levels.
2. **Enabling a high level of abstraction when defining process changes.** It must be possible to define structural process adaptations at a high level of abstraction. In particular, all complexity associated with the adjustment of data flows or the adaptation of instance states should be hidden from users.
3. **Completeness of change operations.** To be able to define arbitrary structural schema adaptations a complete set of change operations is required; i.e., given two correct schemes it must be always possible to transform one schema into the other based on the given set of change operations.
4. **Correctness of changes.** The ultimate ambition of any change framework must be to ensure correctness of dynamic changes (Rinderle, Reichert, & Dadam, 2003). First, structural and behavioral soundness of the modified process schema should be guaranteed independent from whether the change is applied at instance level or not. Second, when performing structural schema changes at instance level, this must not lead to inconsistent process states or errors. Therefore, an adequate *correctness criterion* is needed to decide whether a given process instance is *compliant* with a modified process schema. This criterion must not be too restrictive, i.e., no process instance should be needlessly excluded from being migrated to the new schema version.
5. **Change efficiency.** We must be able to efficiently decide whether a process instance is

compliant with a modified schema. Furthermore, when migrating compliant instances to the modified schema, state adaptations need to be accomplished automatically and in an efficient way.

We show how ADEPT2 deals with these fundamental requirements. There exist additional challenges not treated here, but which have been considered in the design of the ADEPT2 framework as well: change authorization (Weber, Reichert, Wild, & Rinderle, 2005a), change traceability (Rinderle, Reichert, Jurisch, & Kreher, 2006b; Rinderle, Jurisch, & Reichert, 2007b), change annotation and reuse (Weber, Wild, & Breu, 2004; Rinderle, Weber, Reichert, & Wild, 2005a; Weber, Rinderle, Wild, & Reichert, 2005c; Weber, Reichert, & Wild, 2006), and change mining (Günther, Rinderle, Reichert, & van der Aalst, 2006; Günther, Rinderle-Ma, Reichert, van der Aalst, & Recker, 2008; Li, Reichert, & Wombacher, 2008b). The given references provide additional reading material on these advanced aspects.

Support of Change Patterns in ADEPT2

Two alternatives exist for realizing structural adaptations of a process schema (Weber et al., 2007). A first option is to realize the schema adaptations based on a set of change primitives like add node, remove node, add edge, and remove edge (Minor et al., 2007). Following such a low-level approach, the realization of a particular change (e.g., to move an activity to a new position) requires the combined application of multiple change primitives. To specify structural adaptations at this low level of abstraction is a complex and error-prone task. Furthermore, when applying a single change primitive, soundness of the resulting process schema cannot be guaranteed by construction; i.e., it is not possible to associate formal pre-/post-conditions with the application of single change primitives. Instead, correctness of a process schema has to be explicitly checked after applying the respective set of primitives.

Another, more favorable option is to base structural adaptations on high-level change operations (Weber et al., 2007), which abstract from the concrete schema transformations to be conducted; e.g., to insert a process fragment between two sets of nodes or to move process fragments from their current position to a new one (Reichert & Dadam, 1998a). Instead of specifying a set of change primitives the user applies one or few high-level change patterns to define a schema adaptation. Following this approach, it becomes possible to associate pre-/post-conditions with the respective change operations. This, in turn, allows the PAIS to guarantee soundness when applying the patterns (Reichert, 2000). Note that soundness will be crucial if changes have to be defined by end users or—even more challenging—by intelligent software agents (Müller et al., 2004; Golani & Gal, 2006; Bassil et al., 2004). In order to meet this fundamental goal ADEPT2 only considers high-level change patterns. Of course, the same patterns can be used for process modeling as well, enabling the already mentioned "correctness by construction". A similar approach is provided in (Gschwind, Koehler, & Wong, 2008).

ADEPT2 provides a complete set of change patterns and change operations respectively based on which structural adaptations at the process type as well as the process instance level can be expressed. In particular, this can be accomplished at a high level of abstraction. Furthermore, the change patterns are applicable to the whole process schema; i.e., the region to which the respective change operation is applied can be chosen dynamically (as opposed to late modeling of loosely specified process models where changes are usually restricted to a predefined region). This allows to flexibly deal with exceptions and to cope with the evolving nature of business processes. Furthermore, the application of a change pattern to a sound process schema results in a sound schema again, i.e., structural and behavioral soundness of the schema are preserved.

We do not present the complete set of change patterns supported by ADEPT2 (Weber et al., 2007; Weber, Reichert, & Rinderle, 2008b), but only give selected examples in the following:

- **Insert process fragment:** This change operation can be used to add process fragments to a given process schema. One parameter of this operation describes the position at which the new fragment is embedded in the schema; e.g., ADEPT2 allows to serially insert a fragment between two succeeding activities or to insert new fragments between two sets of activities (Reichert, 2000). Special cases of the latter variant include the insertion of a process fragment in parallel to another one (parallel insert) or the association of the newly added fragment with an execution condition (conditional insert). Figure 5a depicts an example of a parallel insertion.
- **Delete process fragment.** This change operation can be used to remove a process fragment. Figure 5b and Figure 5c depict two simple examples.
- **Move process fragment.** This change operation allows users to shift a process fragment from its current position in the process schema to a new one. One parameter of this operation specifies the way the fragment is re-embedded in the process schema afterwards. Though the move operation could be realized by the combined use of the insert and delete operation, ADEPT2 introduces it as separate operation since it provides a higher level of abstraction to users.

Other examples of ADEPT2 change operations include the embedding of a process fragment in a conditional branch or loop construct, and the addition or deletion of synchronizations between parallel activities. When applying such high-level changes, ADEPT2 automatically reduces complexity through simple schema refactoring

Figure 5. Insertion and deletion of process activities in ADEPT2

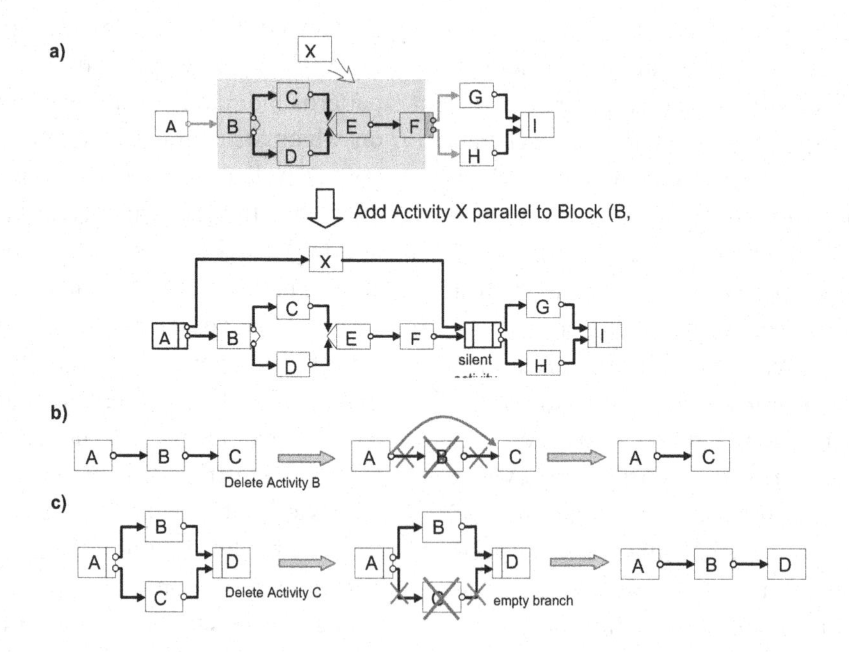

(Reichert & Dadam, 1998a); e.g., empty branches or unnecessary nodes are removed after change application (cf. Figure 5). Generally, the change patterns offered by ADEPT2 can be also used for a large variety of behavior preserving process refactorings (Weber & Reichert, 2008a).

Generally, structural adaptations of a control flow schema have to be combined with adjustments of the data flow schema in order to preserve soundness. As simple example consider Figure 6 where activity B shall be deleted from the depicted process schema. To preserve schema correctness we must deal with the data dependencies activities D and E have on activity B. Figure 6 shows four basic options supported by ADEPT2 in this context: (a) cascading deletion of data-dependent activities; (b) insertion of an alternate activity which writes the respective data element; (c) insertion of an auxiliary service (e.g., an electronic form) which is invoked when deleting B, or insertion of an auxiliary service which is invoked when starting the first data-dependent activity (D in our example). Which of these four options is most favorable in a given context depends on the semantics of the activity to be primarily deleted. It therefore has to be chosen by the process designer at buildtime or by the user requesting the deletion at runtime. Regarding the example from Figure 1, for instance, deletion of activity *generate report* should be always accompanied by deletion of activity *validate report* since the second activity strongly depends on the first one; i.e., option (a) has to be applied. ADEPT2 allows to explicitly specify such strong dependencies at buildtime, which enables the runtime system to automatically apply option (a) if required. By contrast, option (c) might be favorable when deleting automated activity *make appointment* in Figure 1; e.g., in case the appointment is exceptionally made by phone and therefore can be manually entered into the system.

In summary, ADEPT2 provides a complete set of high-level change operations which can be used for specifying structural adaptations as well as for accomplishing structural comparisons of process schemes (Li, Reichert, & Wombacher, 2008a). In particular, these high-level operations cover most of the change patterns described in (Weber et al. 2007; Weber et al., 2008b). Finally, the application of ADEPT2 operations to a correct process schema results in a correct schema again. Basic to the latter is the formal semantics defined

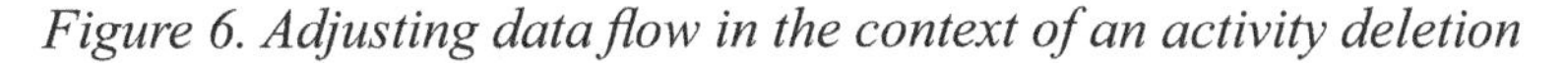

Figure 6. Adjusting data flow in the context of an activity deletion

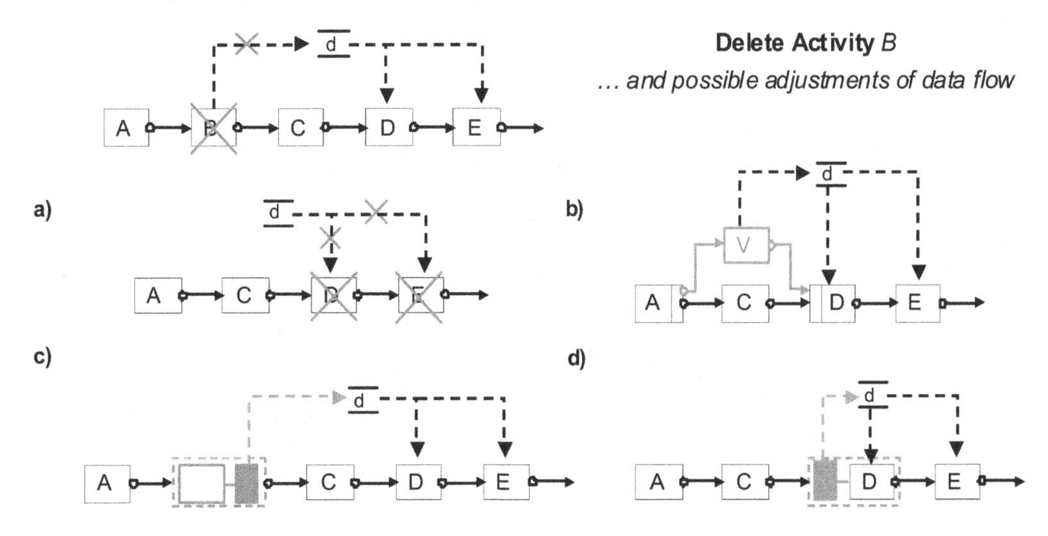

for the supported change patterns (Rinderle-Ma, Reichert, & Weber, B.; 2008b).

Ensuring Correctness of Dynamic Changes

So far, we have only looked at structural schema adaptations without considering the state of the process instances running on the respective schema. In this subsection we discuss under which conditions a structural schema change can be applied at the process instance level as well. Obviously, structural adaptations have to be restricted with respect to the current state of an instance. As example consider Figure 7a. Activity X is serially added between activities A and B resulting in a correct process schema afterwards. Consider now process instance I from Figure 7b. When applying the schema change to this instance, an inconsistent state would result; i.e., activity B would have state COMPLETED though its preceding activity X would still be in state ACTIVATED.

To avoid such inconsistencies we need a formal foundation for dynamic changes. In the following, let I be an instance running on process schema S and having marking M_S. Assume further that S is transformed into another correct process schema S' by applying change Δ. Then the following two issues arise:

1. Can Δ be correctly propagated to process instance I, i.e., can Δ be applied to I without causing inconsistencies? For this case, I is denoted as being compliant with the modified schema S'.
2. How can we migrate a compliant instance I to S' such that further execution of I can be based on S'? Which state adaptations become necessary and how can they be automatically accomplished?

Both issues are fundamental for any adaptive process management system. While the first one concerns *pre-conditions* on the state of the respective instance, the second one is related to *post-conditions* to be satisfied after the dynamic change. We need an efficient method allowing for automated compliance checks and instance migrations. Intuitively, instance I would be compliant with the modified schema S' if it could have been executed according to S' as well and had produced the same effects on data elements (Rinderle et al., 2004b; Casati et al., 1998). Trivially, this will be always the case if instance I has not yet entered the region affected by the change. Generally, we need information about the previous execution of instance I to decide on this and to determine a correct follow-up marking when structurally adapting it. At the logical level we make use of the *execution history* (i.e., trace) kept for each process instance. We assume that this execution history

Figure 7. Schema change and inconsistency due to uncontrolled change propagation at instance level

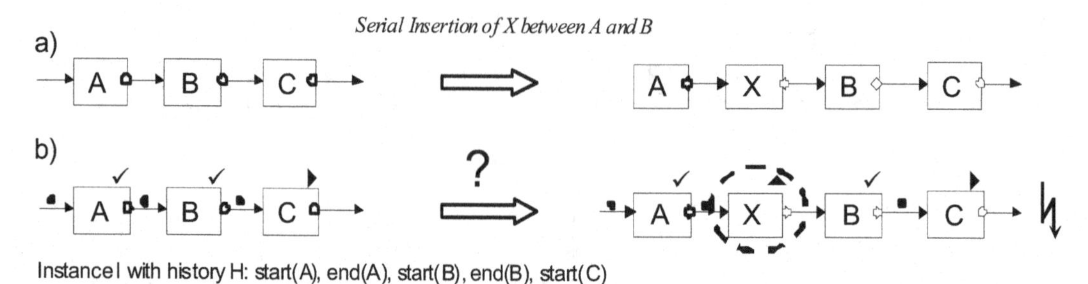

logs events related to the start and completion of activity executions. Obviously, an instance I with history H will be compliant with modified schema S′ and therefore can migrate to S′ if H can be produced on S′ as well. We then obtain a correct new state (i.e., marking) for instance I by "replaying" all events from H on S′ in the order they occurred.

Taking our example from Figure 7b this property does not hold for instance I. Therefore the depicted schema change must not be applied to this instance. As another example consider the process instance from Figure 8a and assume that activity C shall be moved to the position between activities A and B resulting in schema S′. Since the execution history of I can be produced on S′ as well the instance change will be allowed (cf. Figure 8b). Note that we have to deactivate activity B and activate activity C in this context before proceeding with the flow of control. Similar considerations hold for the instance from Figure 8a when moving activity C to a position parallel to activity B resulting in process schema S″. Again this change is valid since the execution history of I can be produced on S″ as well (cf. Figure 8c).

Note that the described compliance criterion is still too restrictive to serve as general correctness principle. Concerning changes of a loop structure, for example, it might needlessly exclude instances from migration, particularly if the loop is its nth run (n>1) and previous iterations do not comply with the new schema version. We refer to (Rinderle et al., 2004b) for relaxations provided in this context.

Generally, it would be no good idea to guarantee compliance and to determine follow-up markings of compliant instances by accessing the whole execution history and by trying to replay it on the modified schema. This would cause a performance penalty, particularly if a large number of instances were running on the schema to be modified (see below). ADEPT2 therefore utilizes the semantics of the applied change operations as well as information on the change context to efficiently check for compliance and to adapt state markings of compliant instances when migrating them to the new schema version (Rinderle et al., 2004b). For example, an activity in state COMPLETED or RUNNING must be not deleted from a process instance. Or when adding a new activity to a process instance or moving an existing one, the corresponding execution history must not contain any entry related to successor activities of the added or shifted activity. This would be the case, for example, if the successor nodes had marking NOT _ ACTIVATED or ACTIVATED. Obviously, this does not hold for the scenario depicted in Figure 7.

In summary, the ADEPT2 change framework is based on a well-defined correctness criterion, which is independent of the ADEPT2 process meta model and which is based on an adapted notion of trace equivalence (Rinderle et al., 2004a). This compliance criterion considers control as

Figure 8. Process instance I and two possible changes (Movement of activity C)

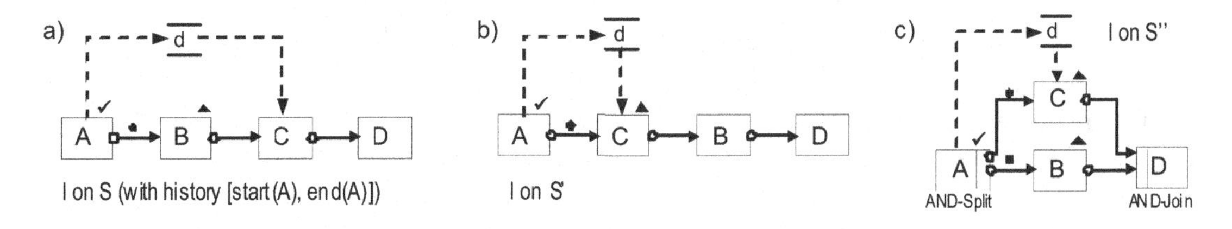

well as data flow changes, ensures correctness of instances after migration, works correctly in connection with loop backs, and does not needlessly exclude instances from migrations. To enable efficient compliance checks, precise and easy to implement compliance conditions have been defined for each change operation. ADEPT2 automatically adapts the states of compliant instances when migrating them to an updated schema. Finally, we are currently working on the relaxation of the described compliance criterion in order to increase the number of process instances that can be dynamically and automatically migrated to a new process schema version (Rinderle-Ma, Reichert, & Weber, 2008a).

Scenarios for Dynamic Process Changes in ADEPT2

After having introduced the basic pillars of the ADEPT2 change framework we now sketch how ADEPT2 supports dynamic process changes at different levels.

Ad-Hoc Changes of Single Process Instances

Figure 9 a – h illustrate how the interaction between the ADEPT2 system and the end user looks like when performing an ad-hoc change. In this example, we assume that during the execution of a particular process instance (e.g., the treatment of a certain patient under risk) an additional lab test becomes necessary. Assume that this medical test has not been foreseen at buildtime (cf. Figure 9a). As a consequence, this particular process instance will have to be individually adapted if the change request is approved by the system. After the user has pressed the "exception button" (cf. Figure 9b), he can specify the type of the intended ad-hoc change (cf. Figure 9c). If an insert operation shall be applied, for example, the system will display the tasks that can be added in the given context and for which the user has respective authorization (cf. Figure 9d). As aforementioned, these tasks can be based on simple or complex application components (e.g., *write letter* or *send email*), or even be complete processes.

Generally, authorized users can retrieve the task to be dynamically added to a particular process instance from the ADEPT2 activity repository. This repository organizes the tasks in different categories, provides query facilities to retrieve them, and maintains the information necessary to plug the tasks into an instance schema (e.g., interface specification and task attributes). We restrict access to exactly those tasks that can be added in the given context; i.e., selectable tasks depend on the profile of the current user, the process type, the process instance, etc. For details we refer to (Weber et al.; 2005a). Finally, ADEPT2 also allows for the reuse of ad-hoc changes previously applied in a similar problem context. Basic to this reusability are case-based reasoning techniques (Weber, Reichert, Wild, & Rinderle-Ma, 2008c).

Following this task selection procedure, the user simply has to state after which activities in the process the execution of the newly added activity shall be started and before which activities it shall be finished (cf. Figure 9e). Finally, the system checks whether the desired structural adaptation is valid in the given state of the instance (cf. Figure 9f and Figure 9g). In this context, the same checks are performed as during buildtime (e.g., to ensure for the absence of deadlocks). In addition, the current process instance state is taken into account when modifying the instance.

As already discussed, such adaptations can be specified at a high level of abstraction (e.g. "Insert Step X between activity set A1 and activity set A2"), which eases change definition significantly. All change operations are guarded by pre-conditions which are either automatically checked by the system when the operation is invoked or which are used to hide non-allowed changes from users. Post-conditions guarantee

Figure 9. Ad-hoc change in ADEPT2 (User view)

a) An exception occurs

b) User presses the "exception button"

c) User selects type of the ad-hoc change

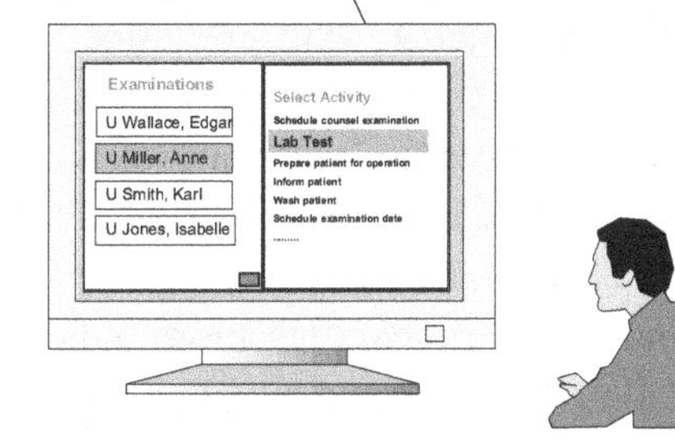

d) User selects step to be inserted

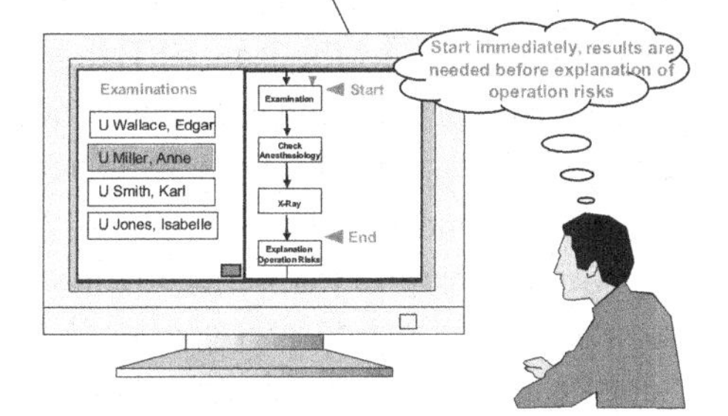

e) User specifies where to insert the step

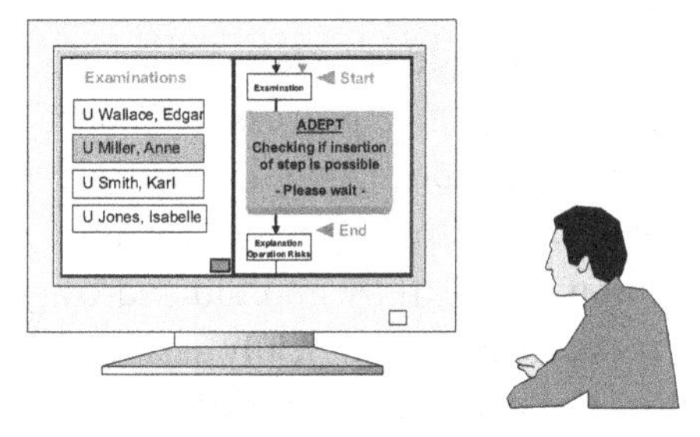

f) System checks validity of the change

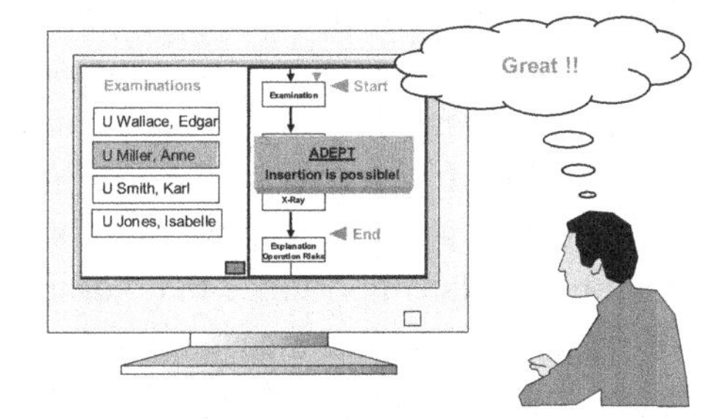

g) Change can be applied

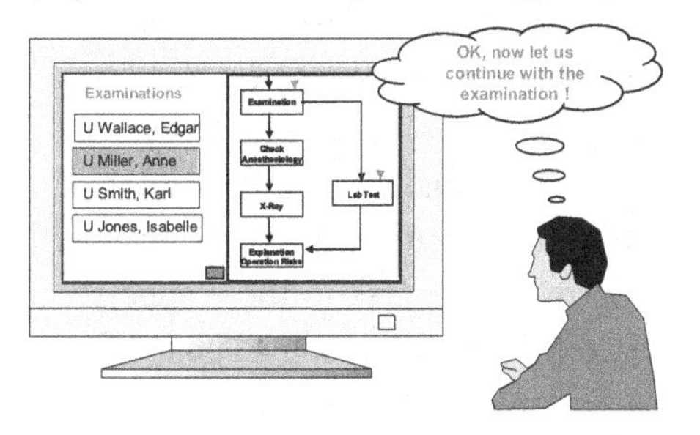

h) User continues work

that the resulting process instance is correct again. Furthermore, all change operations and change patterns respectively are made available via the ADEPT2 API (*application programming interface*) as well. The same applies for the querying interface of the ADEPT2 repository. This allows for the implementation of sophisticated end user clients or even automated agents (Müller et al., 2004).

To enable change traceability ADEPT2 stores process instance changes in change logs (Rinderle et al., 2006b, 2007b). Together with execution logs, which capture enactment information of process instances, the structure and state of a particular process instance can be reconstructed at any time. Both change and execution log are also valuable sources for process learning and process optimization (Günther et al., 2008; Li et al., 2008b).

By performing the described ad-hoc deviation inside the PAIS the added task becomes an integral part of the respective process instance. This way full system support becomes possible relieving the user from handling the exception; i.e., task execution can be fully coordinated by the PAIS, the task can be automatically assigned to user worklists, its status can be monitored by the PAIS, and its results can be analyzed and evaluated in the context of the respective process instance. By contrast, if the exception had been handled manually, i.e. outside the PAIS, it would be the intellectual responsibility of the end user to accomplish task execution, monitoring and analysis, and to relate the task to the respective process instance (e.g., by attaching a "post-it" to his screen). As we know from healthcare the latter approach unnecessarily burdens users resulting in organizational overload and omissive errors (Lenz & Reichert, 2007).

Process Schema Evolution

Though the support of ad-hoc modifications is very important, it is not yet sufficient. As motivated, for long-running processes it is often required to adapt the process schema (from which new instances can be created afterwards) due to organizational changes. Then process instances currently running on this process schema can be affected by the change as well. If processes are of short duration only, already running instances can be usually finished according to the old schema version. However, this strategy will not be applicable for long running processes. Then the old process schema version may no longer be applicable, e.g., when legal regulations have changed or when the old process reveals severe problems.

One solution would be to individually modify each of the running process instances by applying corresponding ad-hoc changes (as described above). However, this would be too inefficient and error-prone if a multitude of running process instances had been involved. Note that the number of active process instances can range from dozens up to thousands (Bauer, Reichert, & Dadam, 2003); i.e., compliance checking and change propagation might become necessary for a large number of instances.

An adaptive process management system must be able to support correct changes of a process schema and their propagation to already running process instances if desired. In other words, if a process schema is changed and thus a new version of this schema is created, process instances should be allowed to migrate to the new schema version (i.e., to be transferred and re-linked to the new process schema version). In this context, it is of particular importance that ad-hoc changes of single process instances and instance migrations do not exclude each other since both kinds of changes are needed for the support of long-running processes (Rinderle, Reichert, & Dadam, 2004c + 2004d).

The ADEPT2 technology implements the combined handling of both kinds of changes. Process instances which have been individually modified can be also migrated to a changed process schema if this does not cause inconsistencies or errors in the following. All correctness checks (on the schema and the state of the instances) needed and all adaptations to be accomplished when migrating the instances to the new process schema version are performed by ADEPT2. The implementation is based on the change framework and the formal foundations described before. ADEPT2 can precisely state under which conditions a process instance can be migrated to the new process schema version. This allows for checking the compliance of a collection of process instances with the changed schema version in an efficient and effective manner. Finally, concurrent and conflicting changes at the process type and the process instance level are managed in a reliable and consistent manner as well.

Figure 10 a – c illustrate how such a process schema evolution is conducted from the user's point of view in ADEPT2. The process designer loads the process schema from the process template repository, adapts it (using the ADEPT2 process editor and the change patterns supported by it), and creates a new schema version (cf. Figure 10a). Then the system checks whether the running process instances can be correctly migrated to the new process schema version (cf. Figure 10 b+c). These checks are based on state conditions and structural comparisons (in order to ensure compliance and soundness respectively). Furthermore, the system calculates which adaptations become necessary to perform the migration at the process instance level. The ADEPT2 system analyzes all running instances of the old schema and creates a list of instances which can be migrated as well as a list of instances for which this is not possible (together with a report which explains the different judgments). When pressing the "migration button" ADEPT2 automatically conducts the migration for all selected process instances (see Figure 10d).

In ADEPT2, the on-the-fly migration of a collection of process instances to a modified process schema does not violate correctness and consistency properties of these instances.

Figure 10. Process schema evolution in ADEPT2 (User perspective)

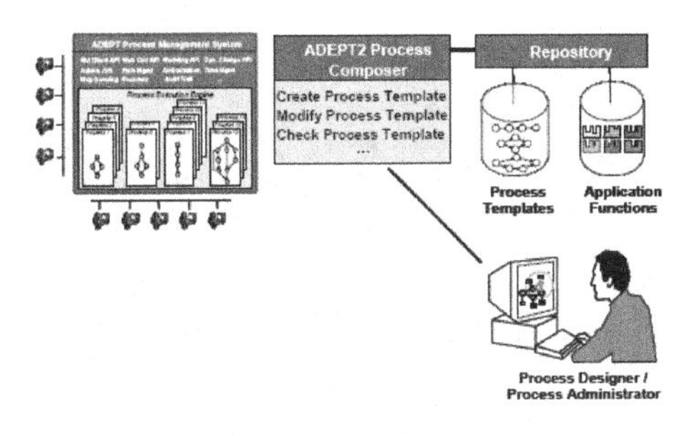

a) Process schema change

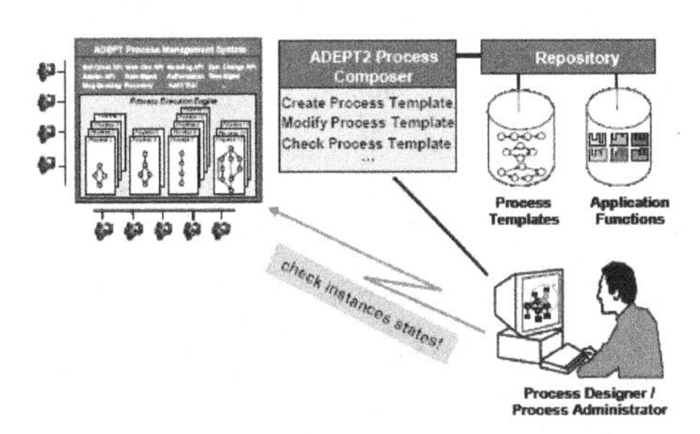

b) Check state of running process instances

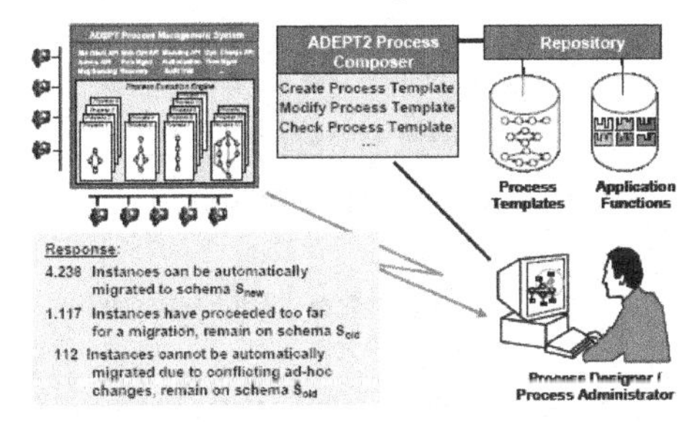

c) Result of checks

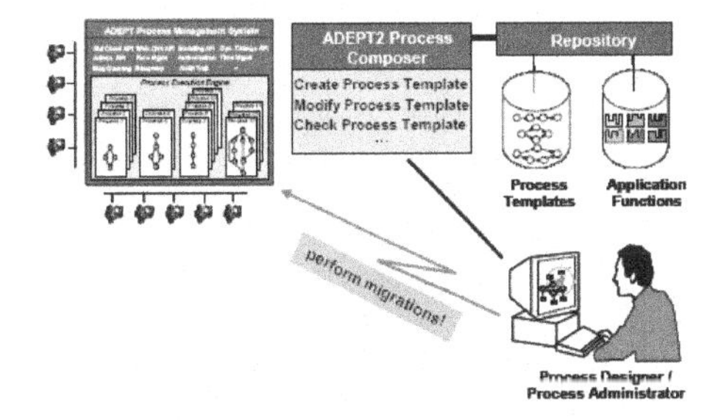

d) Execute instance migration

At the system level this is ensured based on the correctness principle introduced in the previous section. As example consider Figure 11 where a new schema version S' is created from schema S on which three instances are running. Instance I1 can be migrated to the new process schema version. By contrast, instances I2 and I3 cannot migrate. I3 has progressed too far and is therefore not compliant with the updated schema. Though there is no state conflict for I2 this instance can also not migrate to S'. I2 was individually modified by a previous ad-hoc change conflicting with the depicted schema change at the type level. More precisely, when propagating the type change to I2 a deadlock-causing cycle would occur. The ADEPT2 change framework provides efficient means to detect such conflicts. Basic to this are sophisticated conflict tests (see Rinderle, Reichert, & Dadam, 2004d). In summary, we restrict propagation of a type change to those instances for which the change does not conflict with instance state or previous ad-hoc changes.

Full Process Lifecycle Support Through Adaptive Processes

As shown, adaptive process management technology like ADEPT2 extends traditional PAISs with the ability to deal with dynamic structural changes at different process levels. This enables full life cycle support as depicted in Figure 12 (Weber, Reichert, Rinderle, & Wild, 2005b).

At build-time an initial representation of a process is created by explicitly modeling its template from scratch (based on analysis results), by cloning an existing process template and adapting it, or by discovering a process model through the mining of execution logs (1). The first two options have been described earlier in this chapter; the latter one requires support by a sophisticated process mining tool like ProM (van Dongen, de Medeiros, Verbeek, Weijters, & van der Aalst, 2005).

At run-time new process instances can be derived from the predefined process template (2).

Figure 11. Process schema evolution in ADEPT2 (System perspective)

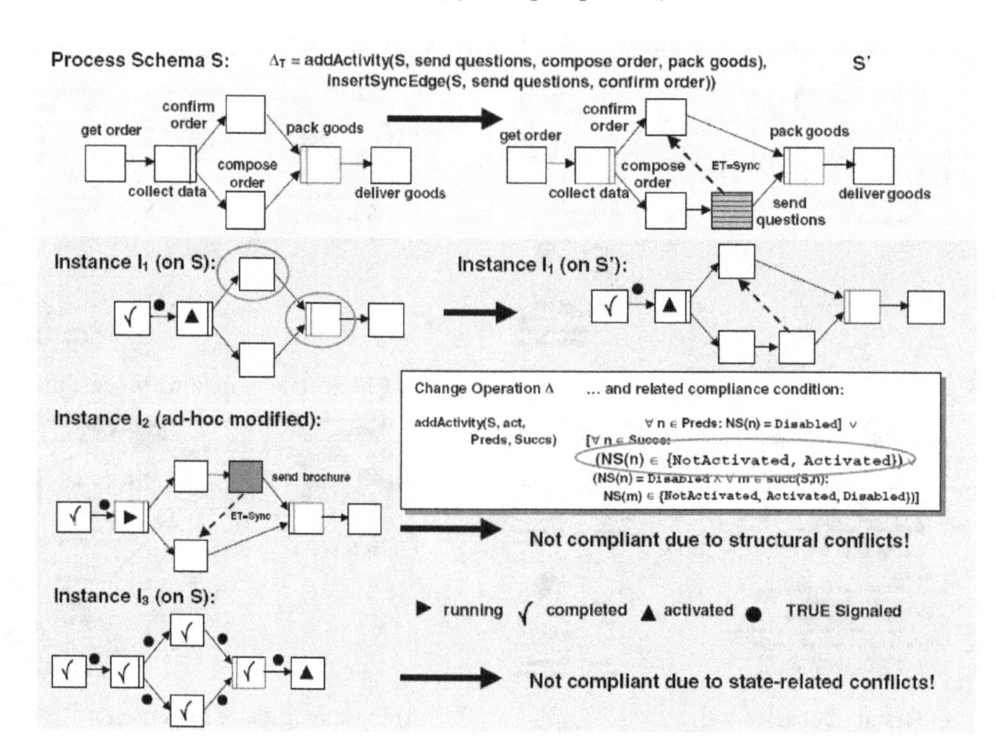

In general, an instance is enacted according to the process template it was derived from. While automated activities are executed without user interaction, non-automated activities are assigned to the worklists of users to be worked on (3). The latter is based on actor assignment rules associated with the non-automated activity.

If exceptional situations occur during runtime, process participants may deviate from the predefined schema (4). ADEPT2 balances well between flexibility and security in this context; i.e., process changes are restricted to authorized users, but without nullifying the advantages of a flexible system by handling authorizations in a too rigid way. In (Weber, Reichert, Wild, & Rinderle, 2005a) we discuss the requirements relevant in this context and propose a comprehensive access control (AC) model with special focus on adaptive PAISs. We support both the definition of user dependent and process type dependent access rights, and allow for the specification of access rights for individual change patterns. If desired, access rights can be specified at an abstract (i.e., coarse-grained) level (e.g., for a whole process category or process template). Fine-grained specification of access rights (e.g., concerning the deletion of a particular process activity) is supported as well, allowing context-based assistance of users when performing a change. Generally, the more detailed the respective specifications, the more costly their definition and maintenance becomes. Altogether our AC approach allows for the compact definition of user dependent access rights restricting process changes to authorized users only. Finally, the definition of process type dependent access rights is supported to only allow for those change commands which are applicable within a particular process context. For further details we refer to (Weber et al., 2005a).

While execution logs record information about the start and completion of activities as well as their ordering, process changes are recorded in change logs (5). The analysis of respective logs by a process engineer and by business process intelligence tools, respectively, allows to discover malfunctions or bottlenecks (Li, Reichert, & Wombacher, 2008c). In (Li, Reichert, & Wombacher, 2008b) we additionally provide an

Figure 12. Process lifecycle management in ADEPT2 (See Weber et al., 2005b)

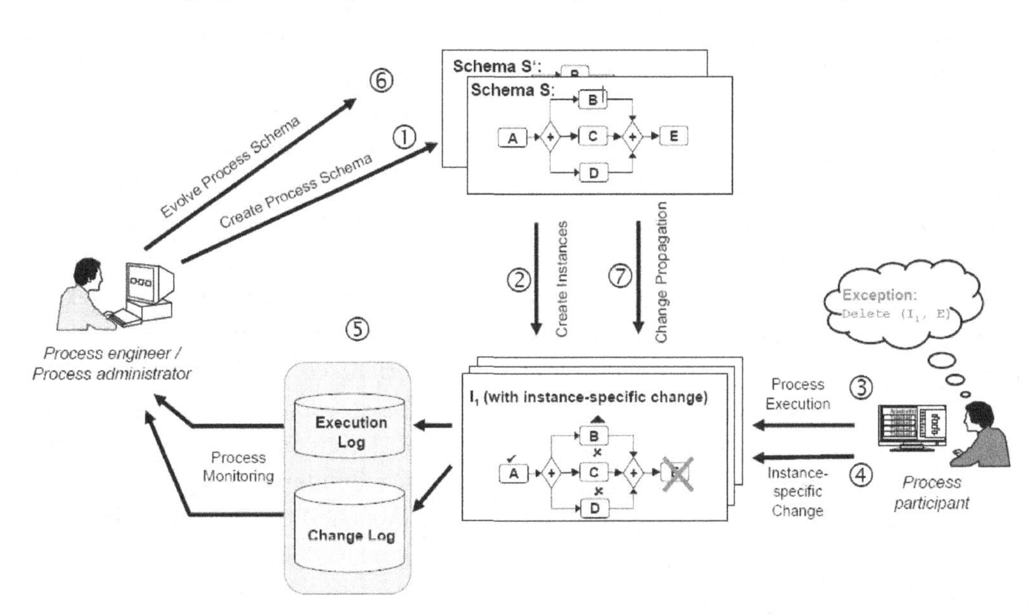

approach which fosters learning from past ad-hoc changes; i.e., an approach which allows for mining instance variants. As result we obtain a generic process model for which the average distance between this model and the respective instance variants becomes minimal. By adopting this generic model as new template in the PAIS, need for future ad-hoc adaptation decreases; i.e., mining execution and change logs can result in an evolution of the process schema; i.e., an updated process schema version (6). In addition, it becomes possible to provide recommendations to users about future process enactment based on execution logs (e.g., Schonenberg, Weber, van Dongen, & van der Aalst, 2008).

If desired and possible, running process instances migrate to the new schema version and continue their execution based on the new schema (7).

ARCHITECTURE OF THE ADEPT2 PROCESS MANAGEMENT SYSTEM

The design of the ADEPT2 system has been governed by a number of principles in order to realize a sustainable and modular system architecture. The considered design principles refer to general architectural aspects as well as to conceptual issues concerning the different system features. Our overall goal was to enable ad-hoc flexibility and process schema evolution, together with other process support features, in an integrated way, while ensuring robustness, correctness, extensibility, performance and usability at the same time. This section summarizes major design principles and gives an overview of the developed system architecture.

High-end process management technology like ADEPT2 has a complexity comparable to database management systems. To master this complexity a proper and modular system architecture has been chosen for ADEPT2 with clear separation of concerns and well-defined interfaces. This is fundamental to enable exchangeability of implementations, to foster extensibility of the architecture, and to realize autonomy and independency of the system components to a large extent. The overall architecture of ADEPT2 is layered (cf. Figure 13). Thereby, components of lower layers hide as much complexity as possible from upper layers. Basic components are combinable in a flexible way to realize higher-level services like ad-hoc flexibility or process schema evolution. To foster this, ADEPT2 system components are reusable in different context using powerful configuration facilities.

To make implementation and maintenance of the different system components as easy as possible, each component is kept as simple as possible and only has access to the information needed for its proper functioning. Furthermore, communication details are hidden from component developers and independency from the used middleware components (e.g., database management systems) has been realized. Two important design goals concern avoidance of code redundancies and system extensibility:

- **Avoidance of code redundancies.** One major design goal for the ADEPT2 system architecture was to avoid code redundancies. For example, components for process modeling, process schema evolution, and ad-hoc process changes are more or less based on the same set of change operations. This suggests to implement these operations by one separate system component, and to make this component configurable such that it can be reused in different context. Similar considerations have been made for other ADEPT2 components (e.g., visualization, logging, versioning, and access control). This design principle does not only reduce code redundancies, but also results in better maintainability, decreased cost of change, and reduced error rates.

- **Extensibility of system functions.** Generally, it must be possible to add new components to the overall architecture or to adapt existing ones. Ideally, such extensions or changes do not affect other components; i.e., their implementations must be robust with respect to changes of other components. As example assume that the set of supported change operations shall be extended (e.g., to offer additional change patterns to users). This extension, however, must not affect the components realizing process schema evolution or ad-hoc flexibility. In ADEPT2 we achieve this by mapping high-level change operations internally to a stable set of low-level change primitives (e.g., to add/delete nodes).

Figure 13 depicts the overall architecture of the ADEPT2 process management system, which features a layered and service-oriented architecture. Each layer comprises different components offering services to upper-layer components. The first layer is a thin abstraction on SQL, enabling a DBMS independent implementation of persistency. The second layer is responsible for storing and locking different entities of the process management system (e.g., process schemes and process instances). The third layer encapsulates essential process support functions including process enactment and change management. The topmost layer provides different buildtime and runtime tools to the user, including a process editor and a monitoring component.

Components of the ADEPT2 architecture are loosely coupled enabling the easy exchange of component implementations. Furthermore, basic infrastructure services like storage management or the techniques used for inter-component communication can be easily exchanged. Additional plug-in interfaces are provided which allow for the extension of the core architecture, the data models, and the user interface.

Implementation of the different components of the ADEPT2 architecture raised many challenges, e.g., with respect to storage representation of schema and instance data: Unchanged instances are stored in a redundant-free manner by referencing their original schema and by capturing instance-specific data (e.g., activity states). As example consider instances I1, I3, I4, and I6 from Figure 14. For changed ("biased") instances, this approach is not applicable. One alternative would be to maintain a complete schema for each biased instance, another to materialize instance-specific schemes on-the-fly. ADEPT2 follows a hybrid

Figure 13. Basic Architecture of ADEPT2 (BT: Buildtime; RT: Runtime)

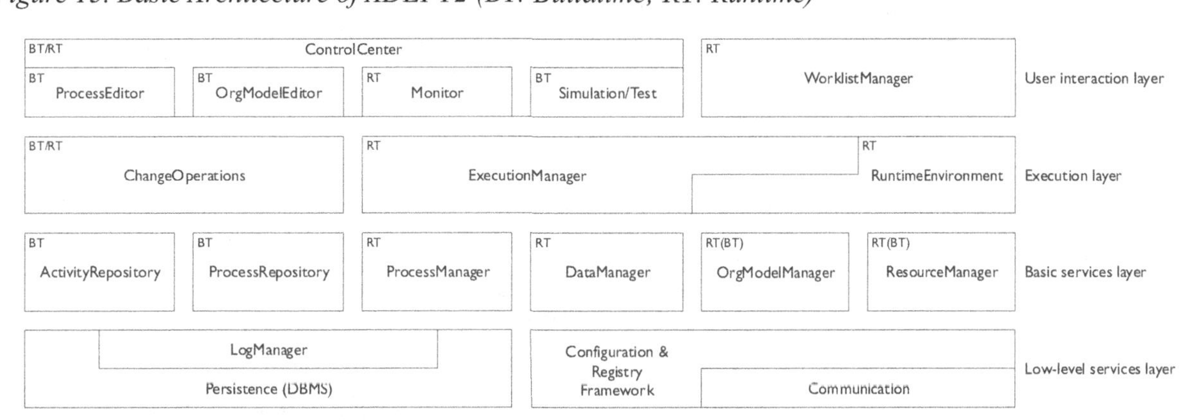

approach: For each biased instance we maintain a minimal substitution block that captures all changes applied to it so far. This block is then used to overlay parts of the original schema when accessing the instance (I2 and I5 in our example from Figure 14).

ADEPT2 provides sophisticated buildtime and runtime components to the different user groups. This includes tools for modeling, verifying and testing process schemes, components for monitoring and dynamically adapting process instances, and different worklist clients (incl. Web clients). Many applications, however, require adapted user interfaces and functions to integrate process support features the best possible way. On the one hand, the provided user components are configurable in a flexible way. On the other hand, all functions (e.g., ad-hoc changes) offered by the process management system are made available via programming interfaces (APIs) as well.

We have implemented the described architecture in a proof-of-concept prototype in order to demonstrate major flexibility concepts and their interplay. Figure 15 shows a screen of the ADEPT2 process editor, which constitutes the main system component for modeling and adapting process schemes.

This editor allows to quickly compose new process templates out of pre-defined activity templates, to guarantee schema correctness by construction and on-the-fly checks, and to integrate application components (e.g., web services) in a plug-and-play like fashion. Another user component is the ADEPT2 Test Client. It provides a fully-fledged test environment for process execution and change. Unlike common test tools, this client runs on a light-weight variant of the ADEPT2 process management system. As such, various execution modes between pure simulation to production mode become possible.

SUMMARY AND OUTLOOK

The ADEPT2 technology meets major requirements claimed for next generation process management technology. It provides advanced functionality to support process composition by plug & play of arbitrary application components, it enables ad-hoc flexibility for process instances

Figure 14. Managing Template and Instance Objects in the ProcessManager (Logical View)

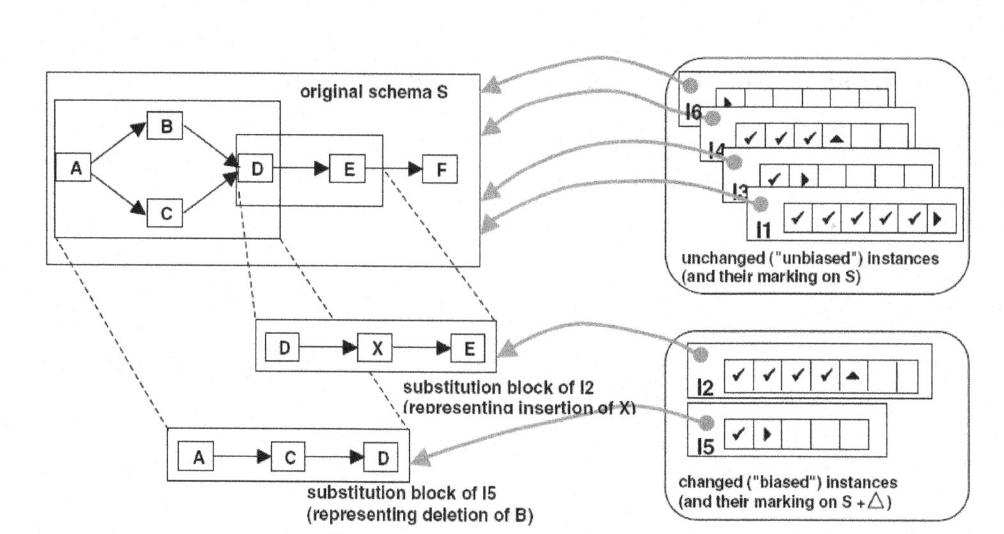

Figure 15. Screenshot of ADEPT2 Process Editor

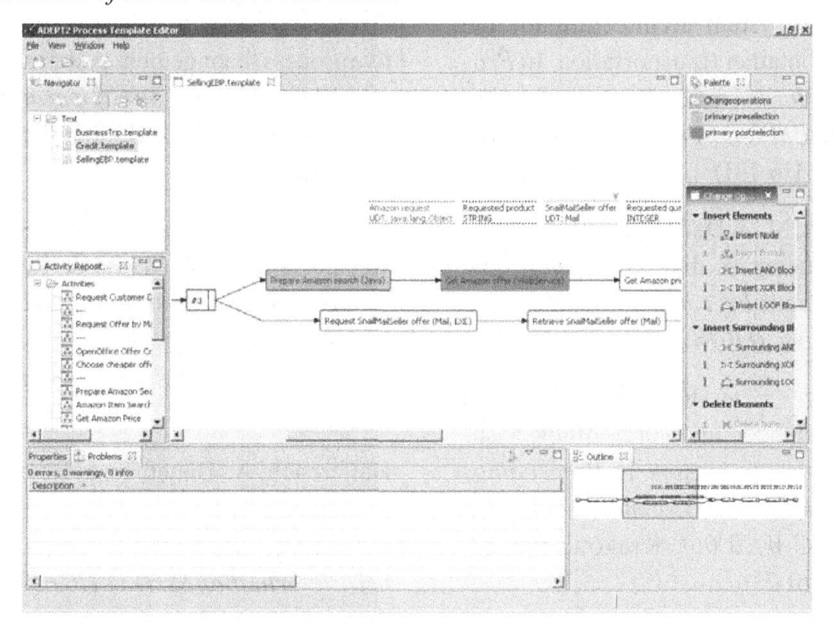

without losing control, and it supports process schema evolution in a controlled and efficient manner. As opposed to many other PAISs all these aspects work in interplay as well. For example, it is possible to propagate process schema changes to individually modified process instances or to dynamically compose processes out of existing application components. All in all such a complex system requires an adequate conceptual framework and a proper system architecture. ADEPT2 considers both conceptual and architectural issues in the design of a next generation process management system.

Challenges on which we are currently working include the following ones: dynamic changes of distributed processes and process choreographies (Reichert & Bauer, 2007; Rinderle, Wombacher, & Reichert, 2006c), data-driven modeling, coordination and adaptation of large process structures (Rinderle & Reichert, 2006a; Müller, Reichert, & Herbst, 2007 + 2008), process configuration (Hallerbach, Bauer, & Reichert, 2008; Thom, Reichert, Chiao, Iochpe, & Hess, 2008), process variants mining (Li et al., 2008b), process visualization and monitoring (Bobrik et al., 2006, 2007), dynamic evolution of other PAIS aspects (Rinderle & Reichert, 2005b and 2007; Ly, Rinderle, Dadam, & Reichert, 2005), and evaluation models for (adaptive) PAISs (Mutschler, Reichert, & Rinderle, 2007; Mutschler & Reichert, 2008c). All these activities target at full process lifecycle support in process-aware information systems (Weber, Reichert, Wild, & Rinderle-Ma, 2008c).

REFERENCES

Adams, M., ter Hofstede, A., Edmond, D., & van der Aalst, W.M.P. (2006). A service-oriented implementation of dynamic flexibility in workflows. In *Proceedings of the 14th Int'l Conf. on Cooperative Information Systems (CoopIS'06)*, Montpellier, France, (LNCS 4275, pp. 291-308).

Bassil, S., Benyoucef, M., Keller, R., & Kropf, P. (2002): Addressing dynamism in e-negotiations by workflow management systems. In *Proceedings DEXA'02 Workshops*, (pp. 655-659).

Bassil, S., Keller, R., & Kropf, P. (2004). A workflow-oriented system architecture for the management of container transportation. In *Proceedings of the 2nd Int'l Conf. on Business Process Management (BPM'04)*, Potsdam, Germany, (LNCS 3080, pp. 116-131).

Bauer, T., Reichert, M., & Dadam, P. (2003). Intra-subnet load balancing in distributed workflow management systems. *Int'l Journal Cooperative Information Systems (IJCIS)*, *12*(3), 295-323.

Bobrik, R., Bauer, T., & Reichert, M. (2006) Proviado – personalized and configurable visualizations of business processes. In *Proceedings 7th Int'l Conf. on Electronic Commerce and Web Technologies (EC-WEB'06)*, Krakow, Poland, (*LNCS 4082*, pp. 61-71).

Bobrik, R., Reichert, M., & Bauer, T. (2007). View-based process visualization. In *Proceedings of the 5th Int'l Conf. on Business Process Management (BPM'07)*, Brisbane, Austalia. (LNCS 4714, pp. 88-95).

Casati, F., Ceri, S., Pernici, B., & Pozzi, G. (1998). Workflow evolution. *Data and Knowledge Engineering*, *24*(3), 211-238.

Dadam, P., Reichert, M., & Kuhn, K. (2000). Clinical workflows - the killer application for process-oriented information systems? In *Proceedings of the 4th Int'l Conf. on Business Information Systems (BIS'2000)*, (pp. 36-59),Poznan, Poland. Springer, .

Golani, M. & Gal, A. (2006). Optimizing exception handling in workflows using process restructuring. In *Proceedings of the 4th Int'l Conf. Business Process Management (BPM'06)*, Vienna, Austria, (LNCS 4102, pp. 407-413).

Gschwind, T., Koehler, J., & Wong, J. (2008). Applying patterns during business process modeling. In *Proceedings of the 6th Int'l Conf. Business Process Management (BPM'08)*, Milan, Italy, (*LNCS 5240*, pp. 4-19).

Günther, C.W., Rinderle, S., Reichert, M., & van der Aalst, W.M.P. (2006). Change mining in adaptive process management systems. In *Proceedings of the 14th Int'l Conf. on Cooperative Information Systems (CoopIS'06)*, Montpellier, France. (LNCS 4275, pp. 309-326).

Günther, C. W., Rinderle-Ma, S., Reichert, M., van der Aalst, W. M. P., & Recker, J. (2008). Using process mining to learn from process changes in evolutionary systems. *Int'l Journal of Business Process Integration and Management*, *3*(1), 61-78.

Hallerbach, A., Bauer, T., & Reichert, M. (2008). Managing process variants in the process lifecycle. In: *Proceedings of the 10th Int'l Conf. on Enterprise Information Systems (ICEIS'08)*, Barcelona, Spain, (pp. 154-161).

Karbe, B.. & Ramsperger, N. (1991). Concepts and implementation of migrating office processes. *Wissensbasierte Systeme*, (pp. 136-147).

Khalaf, R., Keller, A., & Leymann, F. (2006). Business processes for web services: Principles and applications. *IBM Systems Journal*, *45*(2), 425-446.

Lenz, R., & Reichert, M. (2007). IT support for healthcare processes – premises, challenges, perspectives. *Data and Knowledge Engineering*, *61*(1), 39-58.

Li, C., Reichert, M., & Wombacher, A. (2008a). On measuring process model similarity based on high-level change operations. In *Proceedings of the 27th Int'l Conf. on Conceptual Modeling (ER'08)*, Barcelona, Spain. Springer, (LNCS, 2008).

Li, C., Reichert, M., & Wombacher, A. (2008b). Discovering reference process models by mining process variants. In *Proceedings of the 6th Int'l Conference on Web Services (ICWS'08)*, Beijing, China. IEEE Computer Society Press.

Li, C., Reichert, M., & Wombacher, A. (2008c). Mining based on learning from process change logs. In *Proceedings BPM'08 workshops – 4th Int'l Workshop on Business Process Intelligence (BPI'08)*, Milan, Italy. LNBIP (to appear).

Ly, L.T., Rinderle, S., Dadam, P., & Reichert, M. (2005) Mining staff assignment rules from event-based data. In *Proceedings of the BPM'05 workshops*, Nancy, France. Springer (LNCS 3812, pp. 177-190.

Ly, L.T., Göser, K., Rinderle-Ma, S., & Dadam, P. (2008). Compliance of semantic constraints – A re-quirements analysis for process management systems. In *Proceedings 1st Int'l Workshop on Governance, Risk and Compliance - Applications in Information Systems (GRCIS'08)*, Montpellier, France.

Ly, L.T., Rinderle, S., & Dadam, P. (2008). Integration and verification of semantic constraints in adaptive process management systems. *Data and Knowledge Engineering, 64*(1), 3-23.

Minor, M., Schmalen, D., Koldehoff, A., & Bergmann, R. (2007). Structural adaptation of workflows supported by a suspension mechanism and by case-based reasoning. In *Proceedings of the WETICE'07 workshops*, (pp. 370-375). IEEE Computer Press.

Müller, R., Greiner, U., & Rahm, E. (2004). AgentWork: A workflow system supporting rule-based workflow adaptation. *Data and Knowledge Engineering, 51*(2), 223-256.

Müller, D., Herbst, J., Hammori, M., & Reichert, M. (2006). IT support for release management processes in the automotive industry. In *Proceedings of the 4th Int'l Conf. on Business Process Management (BPM'06)*, Vienna, Austria. (LNCS 4102, pp. 368-377).

Müller, D., Reichert, M., & Herbst, J. (2007). Data-driven modeling and coordination of large process structures. In *Proceedings of the 15th Int'l Conf. on Cooperative Information Systems (CoopIS'07)*, Vilamoura, Algarve, Portugal (LNCS 4803, pp. 131-149).

Müller, D., Reichert, M., & Herbst, J. (2008). A new paradigm for the enactment and dynamic adaptation of data-driven process structures. In *Proceedings of the 20th Int'l Conf. on Advanced Information Systems Engineering (CAiSE'08)*, Montpellier, France (LNCS 5074, pp. 48-63).

Mutschler, B., Bumiller, J., & Reichert, M. (2006). Why process-orientation is scarce: an empirical study of process-oriented information systems in the automotive industry. In *Proceedings of the 10th Int'l Conf. on Enterprise Computing (EDOC '06)*, Hong Kong,433-440. IEEE Computer Press.

Mutschler, B., Reichert, M., & Rinderle, S. (2007). Analyzing the dynamic cost factors of process-aware information systems: a model-based approach. In *Proceedings of the 19th Int'l Conf. on Advanced Information Systems Engineering (CAiSE'07)*, Trondheim, Norway (LNCS 4495, pp. 589-603).

Mutschler, B., Weber, B., & Reichert, M. (2008a). Workflow management versus case handling: results from a controlled software experiment. In *Proceedings of the 23rd Annual ACM Symposium on Applied Computing (SAC'08)*, Fortaleza, Brazil, (pp. 82-89).

Mutschler, B., Reichert, M., & Bumiller, J. (2008b): Unleashing the effectiveness of process-oriented information systems: problem analysis, critical success factors and implications, *IEEE Transactions on Systems, Man, and Cybernetics, 38*(3), 280-291.

Mutschler, B., & Reichert, M. (2008c). On modeling and analyzing cost factors in information systems engineering. In *Proceedings of the 20th Int'l Conf. on Advanced Information Systems Engineering (CAiSE'08)*, Montpellier, France (LNCS 5074, pp. 510-524).

Pesic, M., Schonenberg, M., Sidorova, N., & van der Aalst, W.M.P. (2007). Constraint-based workflow models: change made easy. In *Proceedings of the 15th Int'l Conf. on Cooperative Information Systems (CoopIS'07)*, Vilamoura, Algarve, Portugal (LNCS 4803, pp. 77-94).

Reichert, M., & Dadam, P. (1997). A framework for dynamic changes in workflow management systems. In *Proc. 8th Int'l Workshop on Database and Expert Systems Applications*, Toulouse, (pp. 42-48).

Reichert, M., & Dadam, P. (1998a). ADEPTflex – supporting dynamic changes of workflows without losing control. *Journal of Intelligent Information Systems, 10*(2), 93-129.

Reichert, M., Hensinger, C., & Dadam, P. (1998b). Supporting adaptive workflows in advanced application environments. In *Proceedings of the EDBT Workshop on Workflow Management Systems (in conjunction with EDBT'98 conference)*, Valencia, Spain, (pp. 100-109).

Reichert, M., Bauer, T., & Dadam, P. (1999). Enterprise-wide and cross-enterprise workflow-management: challenges and research issues for adaptive workflows. In *Proceedings of the Informatik'99 Workshop on Enterprise-wide and Cross-enterprise Workflow Management*, CEUR Workshop Proceedings, *24*, 56-64.

Reichert, M. (2000). Dynamische Ablaufänderungen in Workflow Management Systemen. *Dissertation*, Universität Ulm, Fakultät für Informatik.

Reichert, M., Dadam, P., & Bauer, T. (2003a). Dealing with forward and backward jumps in workflow management systems. *Int'l Journal Software and Systems Modeling, 2*(1), 37-58.

Reichert, M., Rinderle, S., & Dadam, P. (2003b). On the common support of workflow type and instance changes under correctness constraints. In *Proc. 11th Int'l Conf. Cooperative Information Systems (CoopIS '03)*, Catania, Italy (LNCS 2888, pp. 407-425).

Reichert, M., Rinderle, S., Kreher, U., & Dadam, P. (2005). Adaptive process management with ADEPT2. In *Proceedings of the 21st Int'l Conf. on Data Engineering (ICDE'05)*, Tokyo.

Reichert, M., & Rinderle, S. (2006). On design principles for realizing adaptive service flows with BPEL. In *Proceedings EMISA'06*, Hamburg (Lecture Notes in Informatics (LNI), P-95, pp. 133-146).

Reichert, M., & Bauer, T. (2007): Supporting adhoc changes in distributed workflow management systems. In *Proceedings of the 15th Int'l Conf. on Cooperative Information Systems (CoopIS'07)*, Vilamoura, Algarve, Portugal (LNCS 4803, pp. 150-168).

Reijers, H., & van der Aalst, W. M. P. (2005). The effectiveness of workflow management systems: predictions and lessons learned. *Int'l Journal of Information Management, 5*, 457–471.

Rinderle, S., Reichert, M., & Dadam, P. (2003). Evaluation of correctness criteria for dynamic workflow changes. In *Proceedings of the 1st Int'l Conf. on Business Process Management (BPM '03)*, Eindhoven, Netherlands. Springer (LNCS 2678, pp. 41-57).

Rinderle, S., Reichert, M., & Dadam, P. (2004a). Correctness criteria for dynamic changes in workflow systems - a survey. *Data and Knowledge Engineering, 50*(1), 9-34.

Rinderle, S., Reichert, M., & Dadam, P. (2004b). Flexible support of team processes by adaptive workflow systems. *Distributed and Parallel Databases, 16*(1), 91-116.

Rinderle, S., Reichert, M., & Dadam, P. (2004c). Disjoint and overlapping process changes - challenges, solutions, applications. In *Proceedings of the 12th Int'l Conf. Cooperative Information Systems (CoopIS'04)*, Agia Napa, Cyprus (LNCS 3290, pp. 101-120).

Rinderle, S., Reichert, M., & Dadam, P. (2004d). On dealing with structural conflicts between process type and instance changes. In *Proceedings of the 2nd Int'l Conf. Business Process Management (BPM'04)*, Potsdam, Germany (LNCS 3080, pp. 274-289).

Rinderle, S., Weber, B., Reichert, M., & Wild, W. (2005a). Integrating process learning and process evolution - a semantics based approach. In *Proceedings of the 3rd Int'l Conf. Business Process Management (BPM'05)*, Nancy, France (LNCS 3649, pp. 252-267).

Rinderle, S., & Reichert, M. (2005b). On the controlled evolution of access rules in cooperative information systems. In *Proceedings of the 13th Int'l Conf. on Cooperative Information Systems (CoopIS'05)*, Agia Napa, Cyprus. Springer (LNCS 3760, pp. 238-255).

Rinderle, S., & Reichert, M. (2006a). Data-driven process control and exception handling in process management systems. In *Proceedings of the 18th Int'l Conf. on Advanced Information Systems Engineering (CAiSE'06)*, Luxembourg (LNCS 4001, pp. 273–287).

Rinderle, S., Reichert, M., Jurisch, M., & Kreher, U. (2006b). On representing, purging and utilizing change logs in process management systems. In *Proceedings of the 4th Int'l Conf. Business Process Management (BPM'06)*, Vienna, Austria (LNCS 4102, 241-256).

Rinderle, S., Wombacher, A., & Reichert, M. (2006c). Evolution of process choreographies in DYCHOR. In *Proceedings of the 14th Int'l Conf. on Cooperative Information Systems (CoopIS'06)*, Montpellier, France (LNCS 4275, pp. 273-290).

Rinderle, S., & Reichert, M. (2007a). A formal framework for adaptive access control models. *Journal on Data Semantics,* IX, (LNCS 4601) 82-112.

Rinderle, S., Jurisch, M., & Reichert, M. (2007b). On deriving net change information from change logs – the DELTALAYER algorithm. In *Proceedings of the 12th Conf. on Database Systems in Business, Technology and Web (BTW'07)*, Aachen, (Lecture Notes in Informatics, LNI-103, pp. 364-381).

Rinderle-Ma, S., Reichert, M., & Weber, B. (2008a). Relaxed compliance notions in adaptive process management systems. In *Proceedings of the 27th Int'l Conference on Conceptual Modeling (ER'08)*, Barcelona, Spain. Springer, LNCS.

Rinderle-Ma, S., Reichert, M., & Weber, B. (2008b). On the formal semantics of change patterns in process-aware information systems. In *Proceedings of the 27th Int'l Conference on Conceptual Modeling (ER'08)*, Barcelona, Spain. Springer, LNCS.

Rinderle-Ma, S. & Reichert, M. (2008c) Managing the lfe cycle of access rules in CEOSIS. In *Proceedings of the 12th IEEE Int'l Enterprise Computing Conference (EDOC'08)*, Munich, Germany.

Sadiq, S., Sadiq, W., Orlowska, M. (2001). Pockets of flexibility in workflow specifications. In *Proceedings of the 20th Int'l Conference on Conceptual Modeling (ER'01)*, Yokohama, Japan, *(LNCS 2224, pp.* 513-526).

Schonenberg, H., Weber, B., van Dongen, B., & van der Aalst, W.M.P. (2008). Supporting flexible processes by recommendations based on history. In *Proceedings of the 6th Int'l Conf. on Business Process Management (BPM'08).* Milan, Italy (LNCS 5240, pp. 51-66).

Thom, L., Reichert, M., Chiao, C., Iochpe, C., & Hess, G. (2008). Inventing less, reusing more and adding intelligence to business process modeling. In *Proceedings of the 19th Int'l Conference on Database and Expert Systems Applications (DEXA '08)*, Turin, Italy (LNCS 5181, pp. 837-850).

Van der Aalst, W. M. P., & van Hee, K. M. (2002). *Workflow management: models, methods, and systems.* MIT Press.

Van der Aalst, W. M. P., ter Hofstede, A., Kiepuszewski, B., & Barros, A. (2003). Workflow patterns, *Distributed and Parallel Databases, 14* (1), 5–51.

Van der Aalst, W. M. P., Weske, M., & Grünbauer, D. (2005). Case handling: A new paradigm for business process support. *Data and Knowledge Engineering, 53*(2), 129-162.

Van Dongen, B., de Medeiros A., Verbeek, H., Weijters, A., & van der Aalst, W. M. P. (2005). The ProM framework: A new era in process mining tool support. In *Proceedings 26th Int'l Conf. on the Applications and Theory of Petri Nets (ICATPN'05)*, Miami, FL (LNCS 3536, pp. 444-454).

Weber, B., Wild, W., & Breu, B. (2004). CBRFlow. enabling adaptive workflow management through conversational case-based reasoning. In *Proceedings of the ECCBR'04 conference*. Madrid, Spain (LNCS 3155, pp. 434-448).

Weber, B., Reichert, M. Wild, W., & Rinderle, S. (2005a). Balancing flexibility and security in adaptive process management systems. In *Proceedings of the 13th Int'l Conf. on Cooperative Information Systems (CoopIS'05)*, Agia Napa, Cyprus (LNCS 3760, pp. 59-76).

Weber, B., Reichert, M., Rinderle, S., & Wild, W. (2005b). Towards a framework for the agile mining of business processes. In *Proceedings of the BPM'05 Workshops*, Nancy, France (LNCS 3812, pp. 191-202).

Weber, B., Rinderle, S., Wild, W., & Reichert, M. (2005c) CCBR–driven business process evolution. In Proceedings of the 6th Int'l Conf. on Case-Based Reasoning (ICCBR'05), Chicago (LNCS 3620, pp. 610-624).

Weber, B., Reichert, M., & Wild, W. (2006) Case-base maintenance for CCBR-based process evolution. In Proceedings of the 8th European Conf. on Case-Based Reasoning (ECCBR'06), Ölüdeniz/Fethiye, Turkey (LNCS 4106, pp. 106-120.

Weber, B., Rinderle, S., & Reichert, M. (2007). Change patterns and change support features in process-aware information systems. In *Proceedings of the 19th Int'l Conf. on Advanced Information Systems Engineering (CAiSE'07)*, Trondheim, Norway (LNCS 4495, pp. 574-588).

Weber, B. & Reichert, M. (2008a). Refactoring process models in large process repositories. In *Proceedings of the 20th Int'l Conf. on Advanced Information Systems Engineering (CAiSE'08)*, Montpellier, France (LNCS 5074, pp. 124-139).

Weber, B., Reichert, M., & Rinderle-Ma, S. (2008b). Change patterns and change support features – enhancing flexibility in process-aware information systems. *Data and Knowledge Engineering, 66*(3), 438-466.

Weber, B., Reichert, M., Wild, W., & Rinderle-Ma, S. (2008c). Providing integrated life cycle support in process-aware information systems. *Int'l Journal of Cooperative Information Systems (IJCIS)*, World Scientific Publ. (to appear).

Weske, M. (2000). *Workflow management systems: Formal foundation, conceptual design, implementation aspects.* University of Münster, Germany, Habilitation Thesis.

Weske, M. (2007). *Business process management.* Berlin: Springer.

KEY TERMS

Adaptive Process: Refers to the ability of the process-aware information system to dynamically adapt the schema of ongoing process instances during runtime.

Ad-Hoc Process Change: Refers to a process change which is applied in an ad-hoc manner to a given process instance. Usually, ad-hoc instance changes become necessary to deal with exceptions or situations not anticipated at process design time.

Change Pattern: Allows for a high-level process adaptation at the process type as well as the process instance level. Examples include high-level changes like inserting, deleting and moving process fragments. Change patterns can be also used to assess the expressiveness of a process change framework.

Compliance Criterion: Refers to a well-established correctness criterion that can be applied to check whether a running process instance is compliant with a modified process schema or not (i.e., whether it can dynamically migrate to this schema or not). For example, compliance will be always ensured if the execution log of the respective process instance can be produced on the new schema as well.

Dynamic Process Change: Refers to a (structural) change that is applied to the schema of a running process instance during runtime. After the change, process execution continues based on the new schema version of the process instance.

Process Schema Evolution: Refers to the continuous adaptation of the schema of a particular process type to cope with evolving needs and environmental changes. Particularly for long-running processes, it then often becomes necessary to migrate already running process instances to the new schema version.

EXCERCISES

1. Which advantages do block-structured process models offer with respect to process change?
2. Why is it important to adjust the data flow schema as well when inserting, deleting or moving activities in a control flow schema?
3. Which other process aspects, besides data flow, may have to be adapted when applying a change pattern to a process schema and process instance respectively?
4. Consider the process schema resulting from the change depicted in Figure 5 a). Assume that activity G shall be deleted from this schema. Draw the new schema version resulting from this change. Try to avoid the use of silent activities in this context.
5. Give examples of real-world processes where ad-hoc deviations from the pre-defined business process may become necessary during process enactment!
6. Consider the process schema from Figure 1 and the corresponding instances from Figure 4. Assume that new activity *prepare examination* shall be serially inserted between activities *make appointment* and *perform examination.*
    a. Draw the new process schema version resulting from this change!
    b. Which of the instances could migrate to the new schema afterwards? Explain your answer!
7. What are commonalities between the migration of process instances to a new schema version (due to the evolution of the corresponding process type schema) and the ad-hoc change of a single process instance? What are major differences?
8. In which respect does the ability of a PAIS to adapt process instances during runtime foster process lifecycle management?
9. How can unchanged as well as changed (i.e., biased) process instances be efficiently stored in a PAIS? Give an example!

Chapter IX
Modelling Business Process Variability for Design-Time Configuration

Marcello La Rosa
Queensland University of Technology, Australia

Marlon Dumas
Queensland University of Technology, Australia
& University of Tartu, Estonia

Arthur H.M. ter Hofstede
Queensland University of Technology, Australia

ABSTRACT

A reference process model represents multiple variants of a common business process in an integrated and reusable manner. It is intended to be individualized in order to fit the requirements of a specific organization or project. This practice of individualizing reference process models provides an attractive alternative with respect to designing process models from scratch; in particular, it enables the reuse of proven practices. This chapter introduces techniques for representing variability in the context of reference process models, as well as techniques that facilitate the individualization of reference process models with respect to a given set of requirements.

INTRODUCTION

Some business processes tend to recur in different organizations or even in different industries. For example, process analysts often use the term *order-to-cash* to refer to a business process that starts from the moment a purchase order is received by a supplier, to the moment this purchase order has been fulfilled (and the supplier has received the corresponding payment). Virtually all order-to-cash processes include activities related to invoicing, delivery and payment. However, variations can be observed across order-to-cash processes. For example, an order-to-cash process for the delivery of goods (e.g. delivery of office supplies) is different from an order-to-cash process for the delivery of services (e.g. delivery of consultancy services). In the first case, there is a physical delivery that happens at a discrete point in time and the condition of the goods can be checked upon receipt. On the other hand, the delivery of a service may occur over a long period of time (say 6 months). Over this period, several invoices may be issued for the same original purchase order. Also, checking the quality of a consultancy service is often trickier than checking the quality of a box of reams of paper. Not surprisingly, the corresponding order-to-cash process models will have many differences.

But despite such differences, companies have a lot to learn from each other when it comes to analysing and re-designing their order-to-cash processes. It would be inefficient if every time a company wants to model its order-to-cash, it did so completely from scratch, without consideration for how other companies perform their order-to-cash process. In this setting, this chapter deals with the following question: *How to model business processes that are similar to one another in many ways, yet differ in some other ways from one organization, project or industry to another?* If we can do so, it then becomes possible to capture multiple order-to-cash processes in a single model. This combined order-to-cash process model can then be used as a starting point to derive order-to-cash process models for specific companies.

This idea is captured by the concept of *reference process model.* A reference process model combines a family of similar process models together. A reference process model is designed in a generic manner and is intended to be configured to fit the requirements of specific organizations or projects. Thus, it is an alternative to designing process models from scratch.

In this chapter, we will use examples taken from the film industry, in particular from the *post-production* phase of a screen project. Figure 1 shows two process models for screen post-production: *shooting on Tape* and *shooting on Film*. The modeling language used in this figure is BPMN (cf. Chapter X). These process models share some commonalities, represented by the first

Figure 1. A reference process model is an integrated representation of several variants of a process model

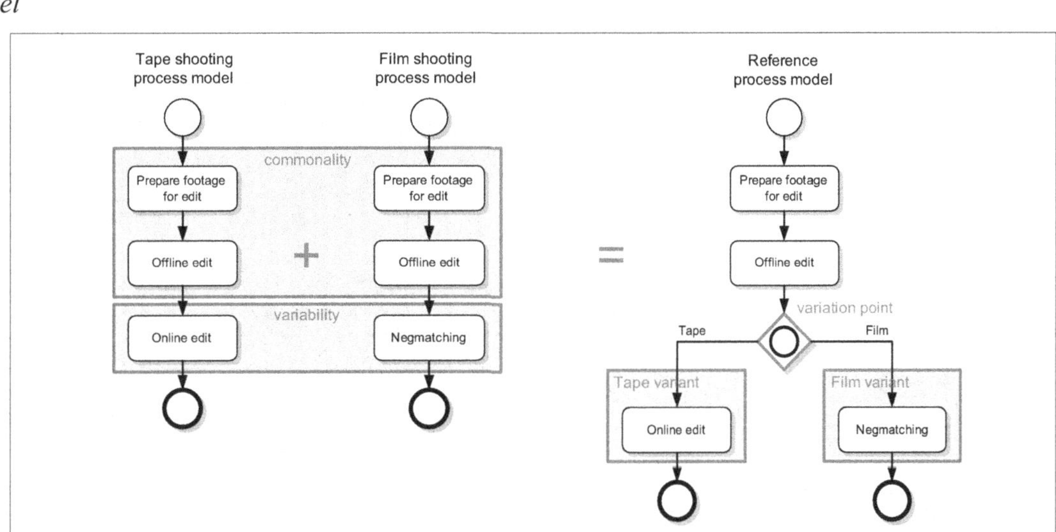

two activities. Whether the movie is shot on Tape or on Film, post-production always starts with the preparation of the footage for edit, followed by the Offline edit. After this activity, the two practices differ in the way the edit is completed - Online if the footage is Tape, or Negmatching if the footage is Film. Online edit is a cheap editing procedure that well combines with low-budget movies typically shot on Tape. On the other hand, if the movie is shot on Film on a high-budget production, it is preferable to carry out a Negmatching instead of an Online edit, as the former offers better quality results, although it requires higher costs. This represents a variability in post-production. Depending on the type of project, one option or the other will be used.

A reference process model for screen post-production may combine both of these options, by merging the commonalities and capturing the variability by means of *variation points*. A variation point, depicted by a special OR-gateway on the right-hand side of Figure 1, is a point in the process model in which multiple variants exist and a decision needs to be taken of which variant to use. The selection of the most suitable variant is called *configuration*. Once all the variation points have been configured, the reference process model can be transformed into a derived model (e.g. by dropping the variants that are no longer needed), through a process called *individualization*.

The decision of the variants to be assigned needs to be taken before deploying and executing the derived process model. Hence, to leverage reference process models in the process lifecycle (cf. Chapter **X**), the design phase essentially needs to be split into two phases: one where the reference model is designed (and variability is captured), and another where the reference model is configured and individualized to fit a particular organizational context. This *configuration & individualization* phase precedes the implementation phase, where the derived models are deployed for execution, as shown in Figure 2.

Figure 2. Reference process models are intended to be configured and individualized to the needs of a specific setting. The configuration & individualization of a reference process model follows the design of the reference model, and precedes the deployment of the derived model for execution (implementation time).

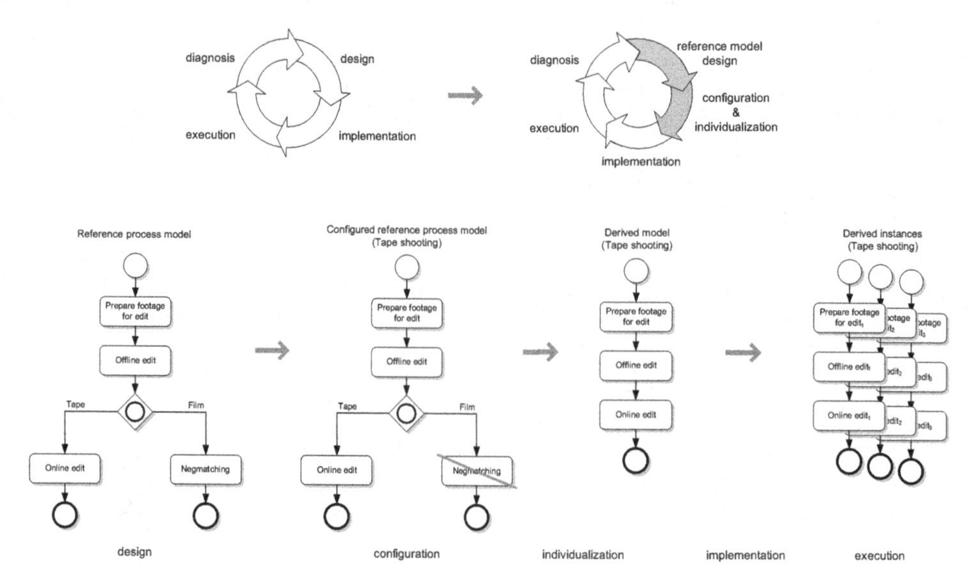

Note that the configuration and individualization of reference process models is still a design-time activity. It is not based on data that would only be available at run-time (i.e. when the process is executed), but rather on the requirements of the project or organization for which the reference process model is being configured. Workflow management systems often have to deal with deviations and changes not anticipated at design-time. For example, people may stop performing certain roles or may take roles that normally they do not take. Similarly, deviations with respect to what a process model dictates may occur as a result for example of deadline violations or emergencies (for example a task may be skipped or fast-tracked because of a special situation). This kind of run-time flexibility is supported by systems such as YAWL (cf. Chapter V) and ADEPT (cf. Chapter VIII). This chapter is not concerned with the modelling of workflows that need to be adapted during the execution phase.

Nowadays reference process models are widespread in industry. Examples of commercial products for specific domains are ITIL[1] - for IT service management, and SCOR[2] (Stephens, 2001) - for supply chain management. The most comprehensive example is probably the SAP Reference Model[3] (Curran and Keller, 1997), incorporating a collection of common business processes which are supported by the SAP's Enterprise Resource Planning system.

Unfortunately, reference process models in commercial use tend to be captured in natural language (e.g. ITIL), or in existing general modeling languages. For example, the SAP reference process model is based on the Event-Driven Process Chains (EPCs) notation. The unavailability of a dedicated reference process modeling language, with an explicit representation of variation points and variants, leads to limitations. Firstly, it is not clear which model variants exist and how they can be selected. Secondly, no decision support is provided for the actual selection of the variants, so it is difficult to estimate the impact of a configuration decision throughout the reference process model. As a result, the individualization is entirely manual and error-prone. Analysts take the reference process models merely as a source of inspiration, but ultimately, they design their own model on the basis of the reference process model, with little guidance as to which model elements need to be removed or modified to address a given requirement.

This chapter provides an overview of current research proposals aiming to address the above shortcomings. The purpose of the chapter is to show how to: (i) capture reference process models using different techniques, and (ii) capture the parameters that affect the way a reference process model will be individualized to meet specific requirements.

Accordingly, the first part presents several approaches for the representation of variability in business process models, based on extensions to current process modeling notations, such as EPC, YAWL and BPMN. The second part deals with techniques to model the variability of the domain in which the reference process model has been constructed, in a way independent from the underlying process. Questionnaire models, Feature Diagrams and Adaptive Mechanisms are introduced in this part. These approaches can be used to facilitate the communication of the variability to subject-matter experts, who are usually not proficient in process modeling notations. The chapter concludes with a summary and an overview on future research trends in this field, followed by pointers to suggested readings and exercises.

LANGUAGES FOR BUSINESS PROCESS VARIABILITY MODELING

In order to capture reference process models in a reusable manner, we somehow need to represent the points in which the reference process model will differ when it is individualized. Below we present three different approaches to capture this variability. The first one is based on the concept of configurable nodes (whereby special nodes in the process can have multiple variants). In the second approach, it is rather the arcs (or edges) of the process model that are made configurable, in the sense that they can be hidden or blocked. Finally, in the third approach annotations are attached to elements of the process model to indicate in which ways they can vary during individualization.

Configurable Nodes

An approach to capture variability in process models is represented by Configurable Event-driven Process Chains (C-EPCs) (Rosemann and Aalst, 2007). C-EPCs extend EPCs by providing a means to explicitly represent variability in EPC reference process models. This is achieved by identifying a set of variation points (*configurable nodes*) in the model, to which variants (*alternatives*) can be assigned, as well as constraints to restrict the combination of allowed variants. By configuring each configurable node to exactly one alternative among the ones allowed, it is possible to derive an EPC model from the starting C-EPC.

Any function or connector can become a configurable node if it is highlighted with a thicker border in the model. Figure 3 shows a more elaborate example of the post-production reference process model in C-EPC (trivial events are omitted). Here we can identify 4 configurable functions and 5 configurable connectors. All the non-configurable nodes represent the commonalities in the reference process model. For example, function Offline edit denotes a commonality, as it is not configurable. In fact, whether the project is shot on Tape or on Film, this function will always be performed.

Configurable functions have three alternatives: included (ON), excluded (OFF) or conditionally skipped (OPT). The first two alternatives allow one to decide a priori whether to keep the function in or permanently discard it from the process; the last option permits the deferral of this choice to run-time, where the execution of the function can be skipped on an instance-by-instance basis. For example, if we are not interested in releasing the movie on Tape, we simply need to set function Tape finish to OFF. When a function is excluded, it is removed from the process and its incoming and outgoing nodes are connected. In our case, function Telecine transfer would be directly connected to the OR-join_5. If a function is configured to be conditionally skipped, an XOR-split and an XOR-join are inserted in the derived model (before and after the function) to allow the user to bypass it at run-time.

A *configurable connector* can only be configured into an equally or less restrictive connector. In other words, the model resulting from a configuration step should have the same or less traces than the original model. Consequently, a configurable OR can be left as a regular OR (no restriction is applied), or restricted to an XOR, to an AND or to one of its outgoing/incoming sequences of nodes SEQ_n (where *n* is the node starting the SEQuence). If the connector is of type split, *n* must be one of its outgoing nodes; if the connector is of type join, *n* must be one of its incoming nodes. For example, the choice of the medium is modelled in the C-EPC of Figure 3 by configuring the OR-join_1. This connector can be set as its left-hand side branch - SEQ_{1a} if the choice is Tape (this results in branch SEQ_{1b} being removed), to its right-hand side branch - SEQ_{1b} for Film (this results in branch SEQ_{1a} being removed), or to an AND-join if the project supports both the media. Moreover, if the connector is configured as an OR-join, the decision of the medium is postponed to run-time, when the movie is actually shot. A configurable XOR can be set to a regular XOR or to an outgoing/incoming sequence of nodes. An AND connector can only be mapped to a regular AND, therefore not allowing any restriction. These options are summarized in Table 1.

Figure 3. The post-production reference process model in C-EPC

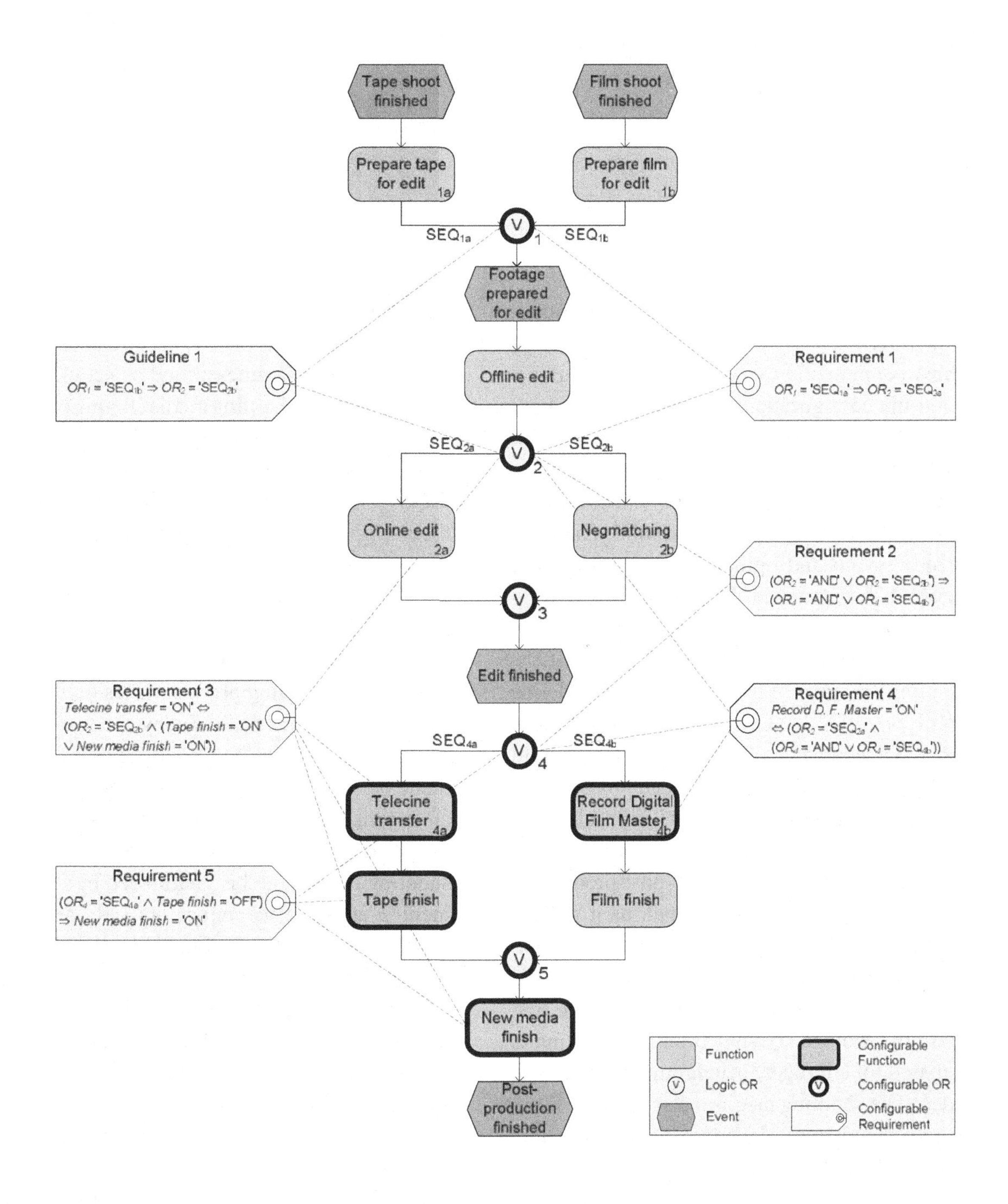

Table 1. Configurable connectors can be configured to equally or less expressive types (Rosemann and Aalst, 2007)

Config. connector \ Connector type	OR	XOR	AND	SEQ_n
OR	X	X	X	X
XOR		X		X
AND			X	

Configuration requirements formalize constraints over the alternatives of configurable nodes, whilst *configuration guidelines* express advice to aid the configuration process. They are both expressed in the form of logical predicates and depicted as notes attached to the involved nodes. Only requirements are mandatory and must hold in order for a configuration to be valid. There are 5 requirements and 1 guideline in the process of Figure 3. For example, Requirement 1 (OR_1 = 'SEQ_{1a}' $\Rightarrow$ OR_2 = 'SEQ_{2a}') refers to tape shooting, which implies to perform an Online edit if the medium if Tape. On the other hand, Guideline 1 (OR_1 = 'SEQ_{1b}' $\Rightarrow$ OR_2 = 'SEQ_{2b}') suggests to perform a Negmatching if the shooting medium if Film, as this is the recommended procedure to get best results when the medium if Film, although an Online edit is still possible in this case.

Let us now examine the post-production reference process model in detail, as it will be used as working example throughout the chapter. Post-Production aims at the creative and technical editing of a screen business project. In the first phase the footage arriving from the shooting is prepared for editing by synchronizing audio and video. The shooting medium can be Tape, Film, or both the media. Of the two, Film results in a more costly operation as special treatments are required for making it visible and permanent. Once the footage is ready, the project is edited on a low-resolution format in the Offline edit. The editing decisions are then transferred to a high-resolution format in the cut stage. The cut can be done through an Online edit and/or Negmatching, according to the shooting media (Requirement 1). This choice is modeled by configuring the OR-split$_2$ and the OR-join$_3$ to one of the two branches (SEQ_{2a}, SEQ_{2b}) or to both (AND), and is bound to the configuration of the OR-join$_1$ via Requirement 1.

After the cut stage, the project can be finished for delivery on Tape, Film, New medium (e.g. DVD, QuickTime) or any combination thereof. The overall finishing process varies on the basis of the delivery media and may involve further tasks, according to the configuration choices made before. For example since Negmatching is an expensive activity, if performed, it must lead to at least a finish of Film. This is the case of a shooting on film, and is guaranteed by Requirement 2 attached to connectors OR_2 and OR_4. Accordingly, if Negmatching is enabled by OR_2, function Film finish is always executed by forcing OR_4 to be configured to SEQ_{4b} or to an AND. On the other hand, if only Online edit is executed and the finish is on Film, function Record Digital Film Master is needed to transfer the editing results to Film. This constraint is enforced by Requirement 4. Analogously, function Telecine transfer is used only if Negmatching is performed and if a finish on Tape or New medium is expected. This is enforced by Requirement 3. Finally, Requirement

5 guarantees that at least one finish medium is selected, as function New medium finish must be set to ON, if no Film nor Tape finish is desired (i.e. if OR_4 = 'SEQ_{4a}' and Tape finish = 'OFF').

Once all the configurable nodes have been assigned an alternative that complies with the requirements, an algorithm (Rosemann and Aalst, 2007) can be used to derive an EPC from the C-EPC model. If the starting C-EPC is syntactically correct (i.e. if each node is properly connected), the algorithm ensures the preservation of the correctness in the derived model.

Let us assume we want to produce a medium budget movie on Tape, thus performing an Online edit, with a finish on Film. The corresponding configuration will be OR_1 = 'SEQ_{1a}', OR_2 = OR_3 = 'SEQ_{2a}', OR_4 = OR_5 = 'SEQ_{4b}', Telecine transfer = Tape finish = New medium finish = 'OFF', and Record digital film master = 'ON'. By applying this configuration to the C-EPC of Figure 3, we can obtain the derived model shown in Figure 4. Here the connectors have been removed as a consequence of being configured to a sequence of nodes.

Hiding and Blocking

Another approach to capturing variability in process models in presented in (Aalst et al., 2006, Gottschalk et al., 2007a). This approach is motivated by the need for a more language-independent representation of choices in a configurable process model. In the light of this, the authors apply the operators of *hiding* and *blocking* from the concept

Figure 4. The derived EPC process model from the C-EPC for a project shot on tape, edited online and delivered on film

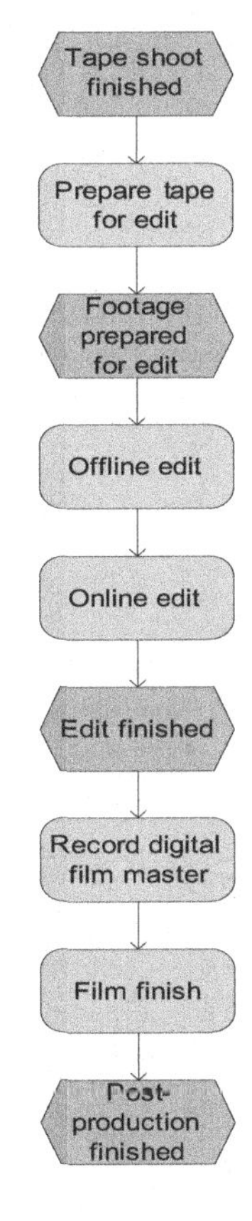

of inheritance of workflow behaviour (Aalst and Basten, 2002) to Labelled Transition Systems (LTSs). LTSs are a formal abstraction of computing processes, therefore any process model with a formal semantics (e.g. Petri Nets or YAWL) can be mapped onto an LTS.

An LTS is a graph composed by *nodes*, representing states, and *directed edges* between nodes, representing labelled transitions, where the label can denote some event, activity or action. A traditional choice (i.e. the (X)OR in EPC or BPMN) is modelled as a node with two or more outgoing edges. Figure 5.a shows a simplified version of the post-production reference process model as an LTS, where transitions capturing the parallel execution of activities have been omitted for simplicity. For example, a choice between the edges labelled Prepare tape for edit and Prepare film for edit must be made after the first node.

Hiding and blocking can be applied to configure the edges, which are the active elements of an LTS. According to the inheritance of workflow behaviour,[4] blocking corresponds to *encapsulation*, i.e. the execution of an atomic action is disabled. In the LTS this means that a blocked edge cannot be taken anymore, and the process flow will never reach a subsequent node. Blocking an edge implies the removal of the edge from the LTS, together with all the edges and nodes following the blocked edge, until a node with other incoming edges (i.e. a join) is reached. Hiding corresponds to *abstraction*, i.e. the execution of an atomic action becomes unobservable. In the LTS an hidden edge is skipped, but the corresponding path is still possible (the edge's label is no longer relevant). This implies the merge of the surrounding nodes.

The reference process model in Figure 5.a can be configured by selecting the desired parts through the application of hiding and blocking. Figure 5.b shows this model configured for a project shot on Tape and delivered on Film, where 3 edges have been blocked and 1 edge has been hidden. Figure 5.c shows the derived model, after the removal of the irrelevant parts and the merge of the affected nodes. The edges Offline edit, Online edit and Negmatching on the right-hand side of the LTS have not been explicitly blocked, as these

Figure 5. Three LTSs: (a) the reference process model for post-production, (b) the configured model for a project shot on Tape, edited Online and delivered on Film, and (c) the derived model.

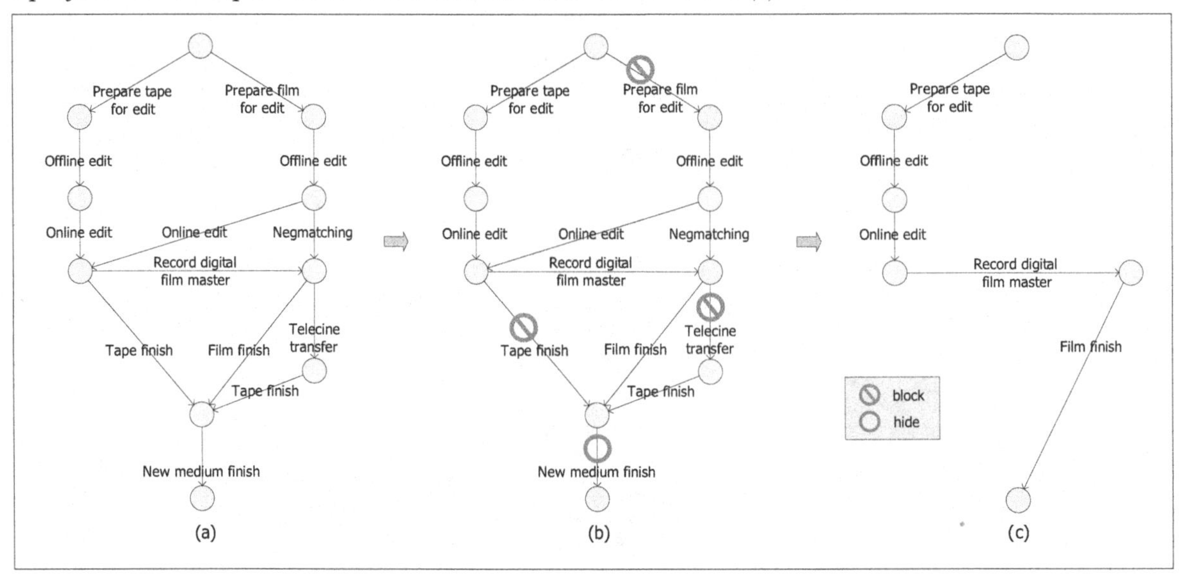

edges and the nodes in-between are removed as a consequence of blocking the edge Prepare film for edit. Similarly, the edge Tape finish has been removed after blocking Telecine transfer. On the other hand, hiding the edge New medium finish implies the merge of its surrounding nodes.

The option to defer decisions to run-time can be achieved using *optional blocking* and *optional hiding* (Gottschalk et al., 2007), which can be enabled at run-time.

A configurable process modelling language should allow the specification of which edges / labels can be blocked and hidden. To prove its feasibility, this approach has been applied to the executable languages of Petri Nets, YAWL, BPEL and SAP WebFlow. In this chapter we present the extension to the YAWL language, namely Configurable YAWL (C-YAWL) (Gottschalk et al., 2008).

C-YAWL extends YAWL with so-called *ports* to capture variation points (for a lexicon of the YAWL language, the reader is referred to chapter X). A task's join has an *input port* for each combination of arcs through which the task can be triggered, whilst a task's split has an *output port* for each combination of subsequent arcs that can be triggered after the task's completion. For example, let us consider the case of a join with 2 incoming arcs and a split with 2 outgoing arcs. If the join (split) is of type XOR, it will have 2 ports. This is because an XOR-join can be activated by each incoming branch, while an XOR-split will put a token only in one of its outgoing branches. If the join (split) is of type AND, it will only have 1 port. In fact, an AND-join is activated when there is a token in both the incoming branches, while an AND-split simultaneously puts a token in all its outgoing branches. If the join is of type OR, it will only have 1 port, as the OR-join is considered as an AND-join from a configuration perspective, due to its synchronizing merge behaviour. On the other hand, an OR-split will have 3 ports - one for each combination of the outgoing arcs, as it can generate tokens for each combination of the outgoing branches.

In C-YAWL, the hiding and blocking operators are applied to input and output ports. An input port can be configured as *enabled* to allow the triggering of the task via this port, as *blocked* to prevent the triggering, or as *hidden* to skip the task's execution without blocking the subsequent process. An output port can be enabled to allow the triggering of paths leaving the port, or blocked to prevent their triggering. In C-YAWL all the ports are configurable and are enabled by default.

Figure 6.a depicts the post-production process in C-YAWL with a sample port configuration for a project shot on Tape, edited Online and finished on Film. Figure 6.b shows the YAWL model derived by applying a cleaning-up algorithm.

The first task of the model, τ_1, is used to route the process flow according to the shoot media. This task has only one incoming arc from the input condition. Therefore, its join has only one input port which always needs to be enabled (in YAWL, a task with no join/split decoration has an XOR behaviour by default). The task's OR-split has three output ports: one to trigger the path to condition 0a (leading to the preparation of the Film), one to trigger the path to condition 0b (leading to the preparation of the Tape) and one to trigger both paths. Of the three, the only port to be enabled is the one that leads to the preparation of the Tape for edit. The input port of the OR-join of the task Offline is configured as enabled as this task is always executed. Since the project is edited Online, the output port of the task Offline that triggers the condition 2b is the only one to be enabled. Similar considerations to the OR-join of Offline also hold for the OR-join of task τ_2. The project is finished on Film, so the output port of the OR-split of τ_2 that triggers 4b is the only one to be enabled. Finally, although New Medium finish is not required, the process needs to complete (a YAWL process has a unique input and output condition). Therefore, its input port is hidden.

C-YAWL allows the definition of configuration requirements to restrict the values each port can take, based on the configuration of other ports. These requirements are expressed as boolean conditions over the ports configuration, similarly to the requirements in a C-EPC model. For example, the following requirement for the post-production model binds the outgoing ports of tasks τ_1 and Offline edit, by implying to prepare the Film medium if Negmatching is to be executed: (output, (Offline edit), {2a}, enabled) $\Rightarrow$ (output, (τ_1), {0a}, enabled).

The hiding and blocking operators can also be applied to the configuration of elements specific to the YAWL language, such as cancellation regions and composite tasks. For example, it is possible to configure the cancellation region of a task by blocking the region, or to restrict the number of worklets assigned to a composite task, by blocking or hiding them. The same approach is followed for the configuration of multiple instance tasks, where the values of their parameters can be restricted, e.g., by decreasing the maximum number of allowed instances.

Figure 6. (a) the post-production reference process model in C-YAWL and its port configuration for a project shot on tape, edited online and delivered on film; (b) the derived YAWL model

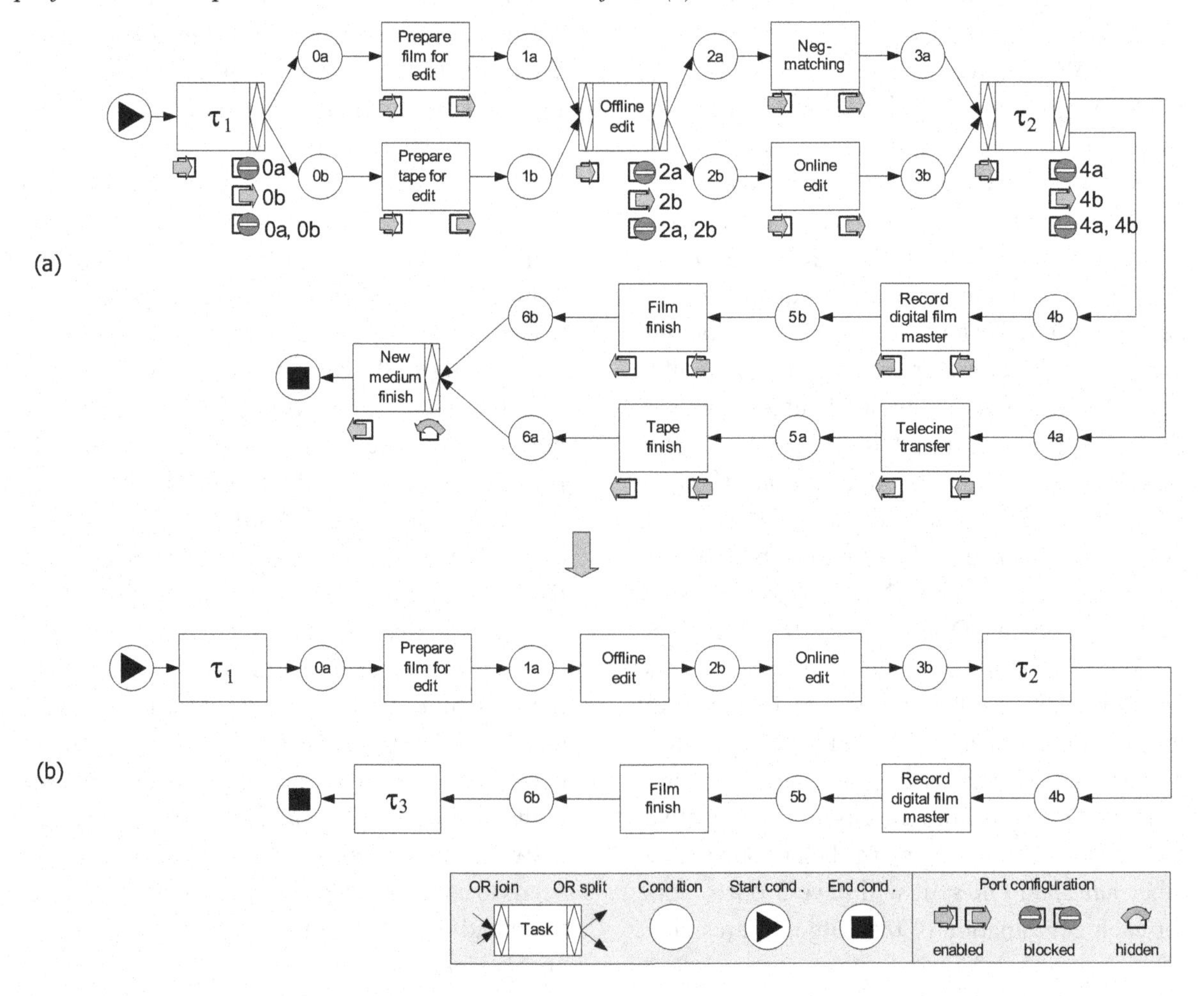

Annotation-Based Process Variability

The idea of capturing variability in process models has also been explored in (Puhlmann et al., 2005, Schnieders and Puhlmann, 2006). The aim of this approach is not to provide a language for representing and configuring reference process models, but rather to improve the customization of process-oriented software systems, i.e. of systems that are developed from the specification of process models.

Accordingly, if the variability of a software system can be directly represented in the underlying process model, it is possible to generate code stubs for the system from the individualization of the process model itself. The purpose of this proposal is outside the topic of the chapter, so we only focus on the way the authors represent process variability.

According to this approach, a "variant-rich process model" is a process model extended with stereotype annotations to accommodate variability. Stereotypes are an extensibility mechanism borrowed from UML, that allows designers to extend the UML vocabulary with new model elements. These elements, derived from existing ones (e.g. a process activity), have specific properties that are suitable for a specific context (e.g. configuration).

A variant-rich process model can be defined in UML Activity Diagrams (ADs) or BPMN. The places in a process model where variability can occur are marked as variation points with the stereotype «VarPoint». A variation point represents an abstract activity, such as Prepare medium for edit, which needs to be realized with a concrete variant («Variant») among a set of possible ones. For example, Prepare medium for edit is an abstract activity which can be realized with the variant Prepare Tape for edit, or Prepare Film for edit, or both of them.

It is possible to annotate the default variant for a variation point with the stereotype «Default». Figure 7.a shows the reference process model for post-production in annotated BPMN. Here, for example, Prepare Tape for edit is the default variant for Prepare medium for edit, as this corresponds to the most common choice in this domain.

If the variants are exclusive, i.e. if only one variant can be assigned to a given variation point, the stereotype «Abstract» is used instead of «VarPoint». In Figure 7.a we assume that the variants Online edit and Negmatching are exclusive, so their variation point Picture cut has been annotated with the tag «Abstract». As a shortcut, when the variants are exclusive, the default resolution can be depicted directly on the variation point with the stereotype «Alternative».

A variation point annotated with the stereotype «Null» indicates optional behaviour. It can only be associated to one variant and its resolution is not mandatory. This is the case of the variation point Transfer tape to film which may be resolved with the variant Record digital film master, or be completely dropped from the process model. A shortcut for a «Null» variation point and its variant is achieved by depicting the variant straight on the variation point, with the stereotype «Optional». This is the case of Telecine transfer, which subsumes the variation point Transfer film to tape.

Through a configuration, each variation point is realized with one or more variants according to its type. Figure 7.b shows the derived process model for a project shot on Tape, edited Online and finished on Film.

DOMAIN-ORIENTED PROCESS CONFIGURATION

The previous section has shown different approaches to modeling variability in business processes. The purpose was to capture multiple process variants in a same artefact – the *reference process model*, which can then be configured to fit

Figure 7. (a) The post-production reference process model in annotated BPMN; (b) the derived process model

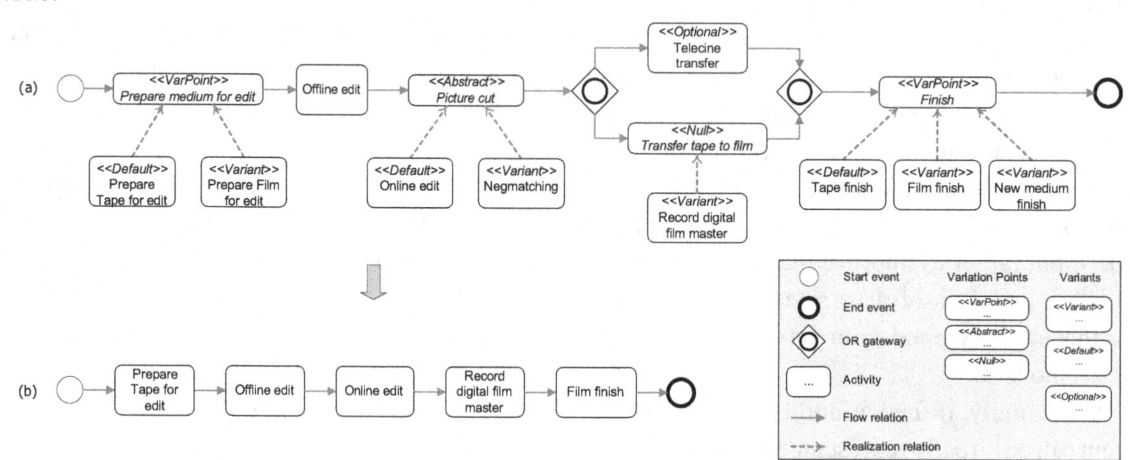

the characteristics of a specific setting. We have also seen that some approaches, such as C-EPC and C-YAWL, go beyond this by capturing the dependencies among the various process variants, by means of a set of boolean expressions.

However, an aspect that is neglected by all these approaches, is the provision of support during the actual configuration of the reference process model. In other words, either there is no restriction in the number of allowed configurations (and derived models) one can obtain, or the user is left with the burden of checking the interdependencies manually. In real configuration scenarios, made up of numerous process variants (e.g. in the ITIL or SAP reference models), these interdependencies can be very complex and intricate, making the whole configuration process complex and error-prone.

Another important aspect is the relation between the reference process model and the domain in which it has been constructed. For example, in these approaches it is not clear which variation points in the reference process model are affected by a high-level decision in the context domain, e.g. shooting the project on a low budget.

Moreover, the stakeholders involved in the configuration are required to have a thorough understanding of both the application domain and the modeling notation. While it is normal to assume that the modellers who produce the reference process model are familiar with the notation in question, it is less realistic to assume that those who provide input for configuring these models (e.g. a screen director) are sufficiently proficient with the notation.

In the light of this, this section introduces three main research proposals aiming at addressing these shortcomings. These proposals provide an independent representation of the variability in the context domain, and can be used to complement the above approaches.

Questionnaire Models

The issue of representing the variability of a given domain independently of specific notations or languages has been dealt with in (La Rosa et al., 2007, La Rosa et al., 2008). Here the authors propose a framework based on the use of questionnaires as interfaces to configure reference process models.

In this framework, the variability of a domain is captured by a set of *domain facts*, which form the answers to a set of *questions* expressed in natural language. Each fact is a boolean variable representing a feature of the domain that can vary, i.e. that may be enabled or disabled depending on a specific application scenario. For instance, "Tape shoot" is a variant for the post-production domain, as there are projects in which this variant is enabled and others in which it is disabled (e.g. when the shooting medium is only film).

Questions group facts according to their content, so that all the facts of a same question can be set at once by answering the question. For example, the question "Which shooting media have been used?" groups the facts "Tape shoot" and "Film shoot", and allows a user to answer.

Each fact has a *default* value, which can be used to identify the most common choice for that fact. Since the majority of production projects are shot on tape, which is less expensive than film, we can assign a default value of *true* to "Tape shoot", and of *false* to "Film shoot". Moreover, a fact can be marked as *mandatory* if it needs to be explicitly set when answering the questionnaire. If a non-mandatory fact is left unset, i.e. if the corresponding question is left unanswered, its default value can be used to answer the question. In this way, each fact will always be set, either explicitly by an answer or by using its default value.

Questions and their facts are organized in a questionnaire model. Figure 8 shows one such a model for the post-production domain, where all questions and facts have been assigned a unique identifier and a description.

Some questions refer to high-level decisions in post-production: question q_1 enquires the estimated budget for the project, with facts f_1 to f_3 referring to typical budget ranges for a Post-Production project. Meanwhile, question q_2 refers

Figure 8. A possible questionnaire model for the post-production domain

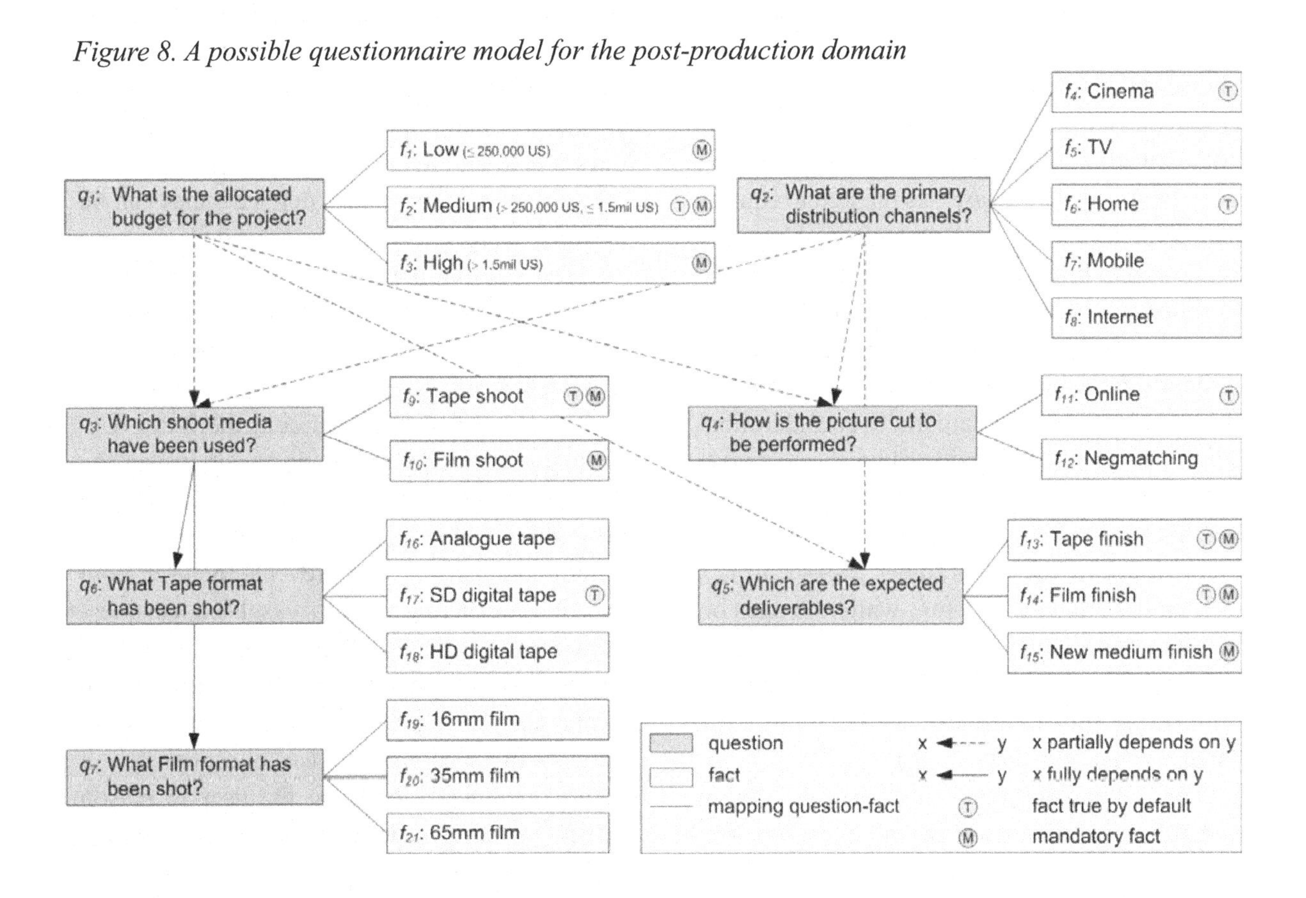

to the distribution channel, which can be Cinema, TV, Home, Mobile and/or Internet (each one specified by a fact). Other questions refer to the shooting media used (q_3), the type of picture cut (q_4) and the type of finish (q_5). Some other questions refer to very specific aspects of the project, such as the format of the tape (q_6) and of the film (q_7) used for the shooting.

Clearly, the facts of these two questions are related to the ones of question q_3, as it would make no sense to ask for the tape format if tape is not chosen in q_3. Similarly, there is a relation between the film formats and the choice of film in q_3. Another interplay is the one between q_3 and q_4, i.e. between the shooting medium and the picture cut. In fact, Negmatching is a costly operation and can be chosen only if the project is at least shot on film, i.e. if f_{10} is enabled in q_3. All these choices are also related to the level of budget and to the distribution channel. For low budget productions (f_1 = *true*), shooting on film (f_{10}) and finishing on film (f_{14}) are not allowed, hence their facts need to be disabled. In turn, if shooting on film is not allowed (f_{10} = *false*), Negmatching must be denied (f_{12} = *false*). Furthermore, if finishing on film is not allowed (f_{14} = *false*), distributing on Cinema must be denied (f_4 = *false*), as the latter requires a finish on film. For a medium budget, although it is allowed to finish on film, it is still not possible to shoot on film and cut with Negmatching.

These interactions among the facts of a questionnaire model indeed refer to constraints over the elements of the domain under consideration. They can be modelled with *domain constraints* in the form of boolean expressions. For example, the interactions depending on low budget can be modelled by the constraints $f_1 \Rightarrow \neg(f_{10} \vee f_{14})$, $\neg f_{10} \Rightarrow \neg f_{12}$ and $\neg f_{14} \Rightarrow \neg f_4$, while the ones on medium budget by the constraints $f_2 \Rightarrow \neg f_{10}$ and $\neg f_{10} \Rightarrow \neg f_{12}$. Since only one level of budget is allowed per project, we also need to impose the further constraint $xor(f_1, f_2, f_3)$.

A stakeholder needs to allow for these constraints while answering the questionnaire. Therefore, a *domain configuration* is a valuation of facts as a result of completing a questionnaire, which does not violate the constraints.

In the model of Figure 8, some of the facts have been identified as mandatory to force the user to explicitly answer the questions these facts belong to. For instance, this is done for q_1, as the choice of the budget is rather important and cannot be neglected by the user. Moreover, default values have been assigned in order to reflect the typical choices made in a medium budget project, with Cinema and Home video distribution.

A questionnaire model also establishes an order relation for posing questions to the user. This is done via order dependencies. A *partial dependency* (represented by a dashed arrow) captures an optional precedence between two questions: e.g. q_3 can be posed after q_1 or q_2 have been answered. A *full dependency* (full arrow) captures a mandatory precedence: e.g. q_6 is posed after q_3 only. The dependencies can be set in a way to give priority to the most discriminating questions, i.e. q_1 and q_2, so that subsequent questions can be (partly) answered by using the constraints. If, e.g., we answer q_3 with "Film shoot" only, the question about the tape formats (q_6) becomes irrelevant, and so on. These dependencies can be arbitrary so long as cycles are avoided.

The questionnaire model, constructed by a team of modellers in collaboration with domain experts, can be linked to the variation points of a reference process model with the purpose of configuring and individualizing the latter. Users (e.g. a subject-matter expert) can answer the questionnaire by means of an interactive tool that poses the questions in an order consistent with the order dependencies, and prevents the user from entering conflicting answers to subsequent questions by dynamically checking the constraints. In this way the user is not left with the burden of manually checking the constraints among the variants of the domain. Also, questions are in natural language, fostering the user to reason directly in terms on domain concepts, rather than modeling elements. Once the questionnaire has been completed, the answers can be collected and used to automatically individualize the reference process model, as shown in Figure 9.

The idea is that each variation point and its variants in a reference process model can be associated with boolean expressions over the facts of a questionnaire model. Such expressions embody the requirements of the configurable process and the constraints of the domain. Thus, an alternative is selected whenever the corresponding boolean expression evaluates to *true*, triggering the execution of an action to configure the variation point with the selected variant, and to remove the irrelevant variants.

The approach has been implemented in an interactive tool called *Quaestio*[5] and tested with reference process models defined in the C-EPC and C-YAWL languages.

Let us see how the link between a questionnaire model and a reference process model works, by considering the C-EPC example for post-production shown in Figure 3. We can notice that a mapping can be established between question q_4: "How is the picture cut to be performed", and the variants of the configurable node OR_2. This mapping should be defined in a way that i) when both f_{11} ("Online cut") and f_{12} ("Negmatching") are enabled, the node is configured as an AND, ii) when only f_{11} is enabled, the node is configured with its left-hand side branch, and iii) when only f_{12} is enabled, the node is configured with its right-hand side branch. Therefore, we need to link a boolean expression over the facts f_{11} and f_{12} to the variants of the OR_2, in order to capture the relation depicted in Figure 10. The mapping we are looking for is presented in Table 2.

The above is an example of direct mapping between one question and one variation point. More complex mappings can however be defined. For example, there can be questions affecting a number of variation points. In general, the most discriminating questions have a huge impact on a reference process model. This is the case of q_1. For instance, if we set the budget level to low, a number of configurable nodes in the C-EPC model would need to be configured. These are OR_1, which would be configured to SEQ_{1a} (preparation of the tape for edit), OR_2 with SEQ_{2a} (Online edit), OR_4 with SEQ_{4a} (to deny a finish of film) and Telecine transfer to OFF. Some other nodes, e.g. the configurable functions Telecine transfer and Record digital film master, are not directly affected by a specific question. Their configuration

Figure 9. The questionnaire-based framework for reference process models configuration

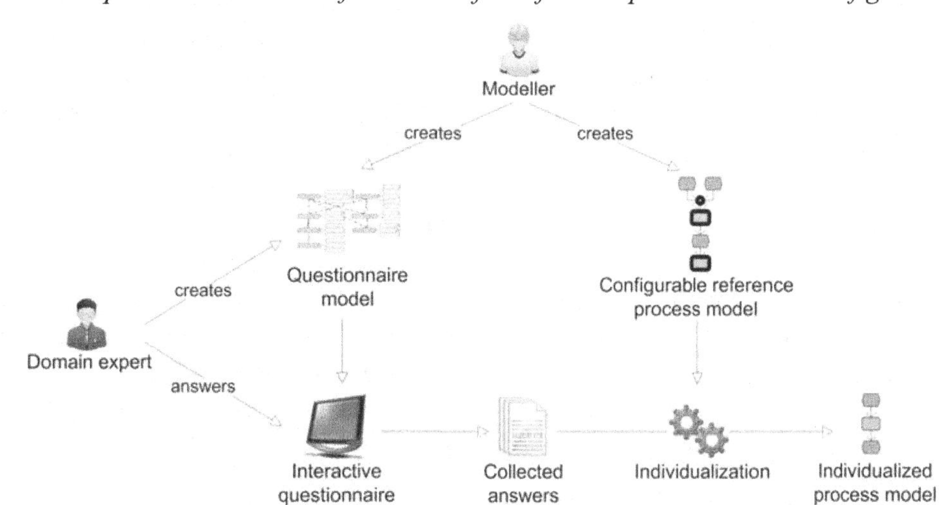

Figure 10. The relation between the facts of question q_4 and the configurable node OR_2

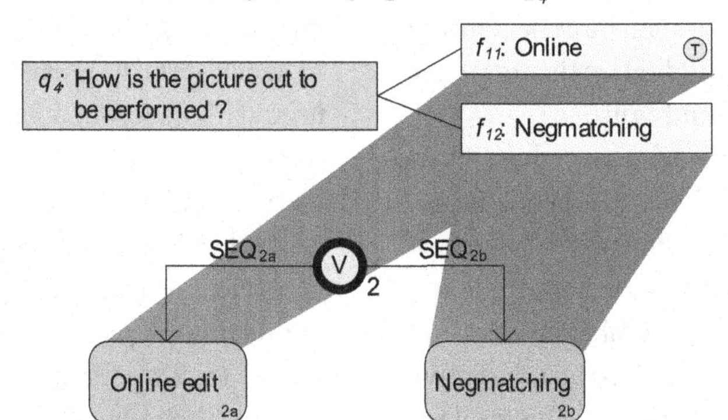

Table 2. The mapping between q_4 and OR_2

Configurable node	Alternative	Boolean expression
OR_2	AND	$f_{11} \wedge f_{12}$
	SEQ_{2a}	$f_{11} \wedge \neg f_{12}$
	SEQ_{2b}	$\neg f_{11} \wedge f_{12}$
	OR	*false*
	XOR	*false*

in fact depends on the answers given to questions q_4 and q_5. Record digital film master is set to ON if the cut is only done Online (f_{11} = *true* and f_{12} = *false*) and a film finish is required (f_{14} = *true*). Telecine transfer is set to ON if the cut is only done with Negmatching (f_{11} = *false* and f_{12} = *true*) and the project is finished on tape (f_{13} = *true*) and/ or on new medium (f_{15} = *true*).

Feature Diagrams

Another research stream has led to techniques for capturing domain variability in terms of the supported features. A number of feature modeling languages have been proposed in this field; for an overview, the reader is referred to (Schobbens et al., 2006).

These languages view feature models as tree-like structures called *feature diagrams*, with high-level features being decomposed into sub-features. A *feature* represents a domain property that is relevant to some stakeholder and is used to capture a commonality or discriminate among different domain scenarios. For example, in post-production, the feature "Edit" can be modelled with two sub-features: "Offline" and "Cut", which represent the two stages that are needed to accomplish the edit of a movie. In particular, "Offline" represents a commonality, i.e. an aspect of the domain that does not vary, while "Cut" can be further decomposed into two sub-features: "Online" and "Negmatching", representing the two possible variants for this activity.

A *feature model* consists of one or more feature diagrams and includes a set of *attributes* such as feature descriptions, constraints and mandatoriness/optionality. Constraints are arbitrary propositional logic expressions over the values of features, specified by means of a proper grammar. Constraints among the sub-features of a same feature can be graphically represented to model restrictions in the number of sub-features the feature can have. These relations can be: AND (all the sub-features must be selected), XOR (only one sub-feature can be selected) and OR (one or more can be selected). OR relationships can be further specified with an n:m cardinality, where n indicates the minimum and m indicates the maximum number of allowed sub-features. For example, the sub-features of "Cut" are bound by an OR relation (it is possible to have more that one type of cut), while the sub-features of "Budget", which are "Low", "Medium" and "High", have an XOR relation.

Figure 11 shows a possible feature diagram for the post-production domain, using the notation proposed in (Batory, 2005). There are features related to the options for budget, shooting, type of edit and transfer, finish and distribution channel.

Some features have been identified as *mandatory* (with a full circle on top of them) if they are required, while some others have been identified as *optional* (with an empty circle), if they can be excluded. The feature "Transfer" and its sub-features "Telecine" and "Digital film mastering" are optional. Their inclusion depends on the selection of the sub-features of "Edit" and "Finish", by means of proper constraints. If an optional feature always represents a variability, on the other hand, a mandatory feature does not necessarily represent a commonality. In fact, a mandatory feature can still be excluded if it has an XOR/OR relation with the sibling features. This is the case of the sub-features of "Budget", which are all mandatory (a choice on the budget is required), but only one can be included at a time, due to their XOR relation.

A *configuration* specifies a valid scenario in terms of features selected/deselected, viz. a scenario that complies with the constraints. Although the initial aim of feature-based approaches was to facilitate the configuration of software product families, a feature diagram can also be used for the configuration of reference process models. For example, in (Puhlmann et al., 2005) the authors link a feature diagram to a variant-rich process

Figure 11. A possible feature diagram for the post-production domain

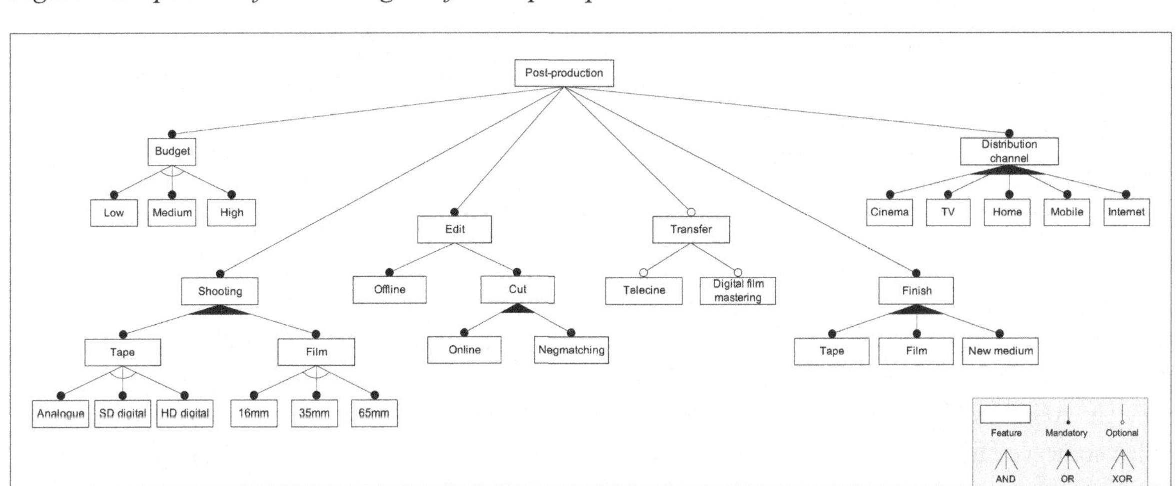

Figure 12. The relation between the variation point Prepare medium for edit and the sub-features of "shooting"

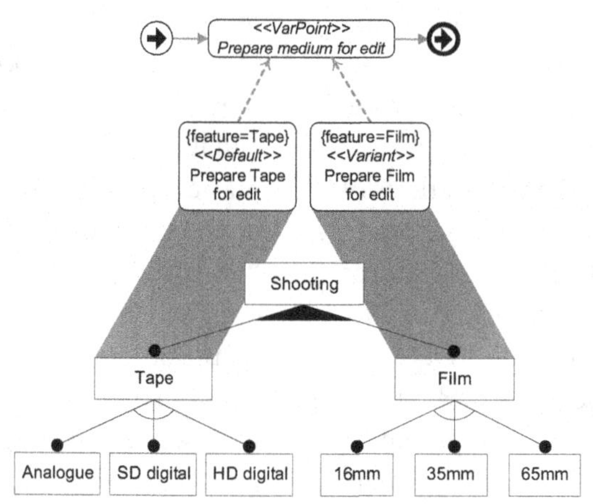

model in UML ADs or BPMN, by tagging each process variant with the name of a feature. In this way, the realization of variation points with variants is done via the evaluation of a feature configuration. Figure 12 shows an example of "tagged" variants for the BPMN model in Figure 7, in relation to the features of Figure 11.

Adaptive Mechanisms

The separation of process configuration from the context domain has also been investigated in (Becker et al., 2004, Becker et al., 2006). This approach is based upon the principle of model projection. Since the reference process model contains information for multiple application scenarios, it is possible to create a projection for a specific scenario, by fading out those process branches that are not relevant to the scenario in question.

Business characteristics can be used to determine the available application scenarios. For example, in the case of post-production, we can identify the business characteristic 'Budget Level' (BL) yielding the following scenarios: 'Low budget' (L), 'Medium budget' (M) or 'High budget' (H). Another example is the 'Shooting type', which can be 'Tape shooting' or 'Film shooting'.

The business characteristics are linked to the elements of a reference process model by means of adaptation parameters, defined in the form of simple attributes or logical terms. The language chosen by the approach to capture reference process models is (plain) EPC. Figure 13.a shows the post-production example, where each function and event is associated with a logical term referring to the project's budget. For example, the event Film shoot finished and the function Prepare film for edit are linked to the term NOT BL (L), meaning that these elements are not suitable for a low budget project, while the function Online edit has the term BL (L | M | H), meaning that it is suitable to any type of budget (where | stands for the logical OR).

The projection of the reference process model to a specific scenario is done by removing those elements whose parameters evaluate to false. Figure 13.b shows the projection of the post-production model for a low budget project.

SUMMARY AND OUTLOOK

Reference process models constitute a promising approach to achieve reuse during process modelling. The idea is that instead of designing process

Figure 13 (a) The post-production reference process model in EPC, with logical terms for the budget levels; (b) the model projection for a low budget project

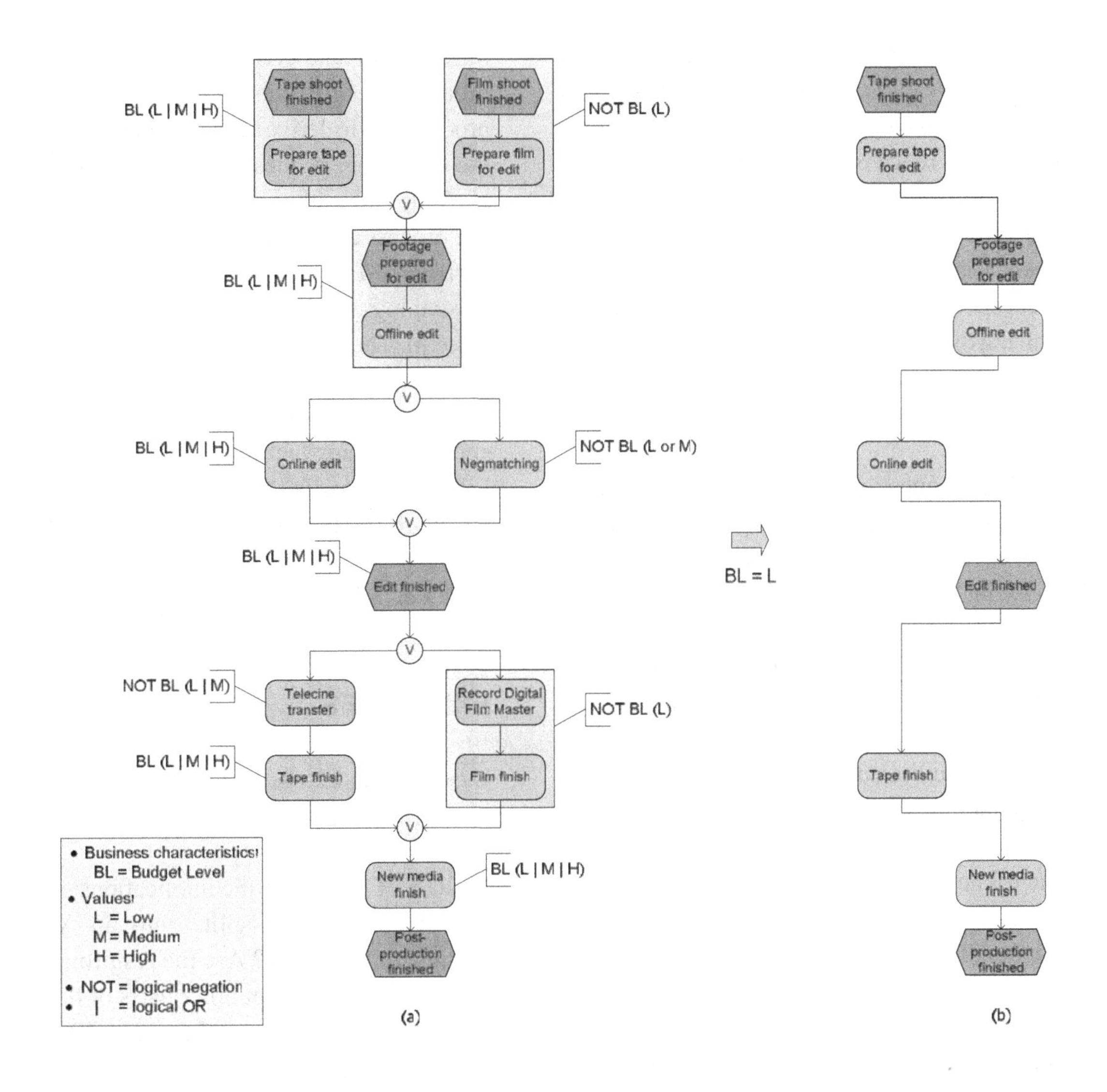

models from scratch, we can take a reference process model and manipulate it to meet specific requirements. However, in current mainstream practice, reference process models tend to focus on the commonalities within a family of process models (e.g. the activities that are common to multiple order-to-cash process models). Also, existing reference process models need to be individualized manually, and they provide little guidance to modellers regarding which model elements need to be removed or modified to address a given requirement.

This chapter provided an overview of recent research proposals that aim to address these limitations in existing reference process models. On the one hand, the chapter described three techniques for capturing variability in a reference process model, so that it becomes possible to represent (in an integrated manner) which elements are common to all individualizations of a reference process model, and which elements differ (and how they differ). This basically tells us "how the reference process model varies", but not "why it varies". The second part of the chapter described techniques to capture the domain parameters that affect the variability (and therefore the configuration) of a reference process model. This is a key component of a reference process model since it provides a basis for a user to decide how the reference process model should be individualized to meet specific requirements. Three methods for capturing this domain variability were presented: one based on feature models, the other based on questionnaires, and the last based on adaptive mechanisms.

One key question that has perhaps not been sufficiently well addressed in the literature on reference process models is *how do we come up with the reference process model in the first place?* One possible starting point is to collect a number of related process models from different (preferably successful) process design projects, and to merge them together. But how can this merger be facilitated is an open question. Since process models are usually represented as graphs, techniques from the field of graph matching could come to the rescue (Bunke, 2000). For example, there exist graph matching algorithms that take as input collections of graphs and compute their similarities and differences. These techniques could be employed to identify elements that are common to all models in a collection of similar models (i.e. a common denominator) and to identify variations with respect to such a common denominator. These variations can then be captured as configurable nodes. The output of these techniques could be taken as a starting point in the design of a reference process model, but of course, further information would need to be added, especially information related to the domain parameters and how these domain parameters relate to the configurable nodes in the reference process model.

Another direction for automating the construction of reference process model is by using process mining techniques. The idea of process mining is to take event logs related to a business process (e.g. all events related to an order-to-cash process) and to derive a process model that matches the event log in question. In (Jansen-Vullers et al., 2006) the authors discuss extensions to existing process mining techniques that allow one to derive a C-EPC from a regular EPC and one or several logs (extracted for example from an SAP system). The authors also show how to automate the individualization of C-EPCs using process mining techniques. Specifically, given a C-EPC and a log, their technique can derive a regular EPC corresponding to an individualization of the C-EPC. Further research is required to refine these techniques and to validate their applicability in practice.

EXERCISES

Describe the key benefits of configurable reference process models.

In a C-EPC, what are the implications of turning a "configurable OR-split" into an XOR-split during configuration? Are the resulting changes local, or do they affect other parts of the model? What about turning a configurable OR-split into an AND-split?

Download the Quaestio interactive tool from www.processconfiguration.com. The Quaestio tool distribution includes a screen post-production C-EPC similar to the one presented in this chapter. This C-EPC is captured as an EPC Markup Language file (extension `.epml`), and can be viewed using a toolset known as iEPCTools (also available at: www.processconfiguration.com).

The Quaestio tool distribution also includes a questionnaire model corresponding to the post-production C-EPC (see file with extension `.qml`). Load this questionnaire model into the Quaestio tool and follow the questions to individualize the configurable process model according to the following parameters:

- High budget,
- Shooting on film,
- Distribution on cinema and home.

After responding to all relevant questions you will obtain a *configuration*, i.e. an assignment of values to each domain fact. This configuration can then be saved (`.cml`) and *applied* to the post-production C-EPC using the corresponding menu options in the Quaestio tool. The result will be an individualized EPC (a new `.epml` file) that can be displayed using iEPCTools.

What differences do you observe between the original C-EPC and the individualized EPC? Which tasks or branches have been removed? Compare these changes with the specification of the mapping between the questionnaire model and the C-EPC, which can be found in the file with extension `.cmap`.

Consider the process of travel applications in a university consisting of Faculties X and Y. In Faculty X staff members obtain a quote for the trip and provide justification in the form of supporting documentation (e.g. a letter of invitation or notification of acceptance of a conference article). They then approach their group leader for approval followed by the Dean of the Faculty. A similar process occurs in Faculty Y except that the Dean can approve the travel application before the group leader. In Faculty X if the duration of the trip exceeds 10 working days, a Faculty-based committee also needs to approve the trip and requires further information, e.g. the applicant needs to provide details of other trips they made in the last three years and be more detailed in terms of benefits that the trip may bring to the Faculty. This again is similar in Faculty Y except that this process only applies in case the trip exceeds 15 working days and no details are requested from the applicant of previous trips as the system of the Faculty provides this information automatically. Can you model both processes in a single configurable process model (e.g. as a C-EPC or C-YAWL model)? What are the features or domain facts that affect the configuration of the resulting configurable process model? What would be the benefits of representing the processes at both Faculties together in a single configurable reference process model as opposed to representing them as two completely separate process models?
In this chapter, we focused on the representation of variability of control-flow elements in a process model, such as optional tasks and configurable control-flow connectors. Can you provide examples where the variability of a process model affects data-flow elements (e.g. a task that may or may not produce certain data objects as outputs), or resources (e.g. a task that may be performed by one role or by another depending on the variant being considered)?

This chapter described three different techniques to capture variability in business processes. Some of these techniques allow the modeller to represent a greater spectrum of variability, while others are less fine-grained (e.g. some work at the level of activities while others work at the level of individual control-flow dependencies). In light of these considerations, which technique would be best at communicating process variation requirements to stakeholders (e.g. a business analyst or a process owner)? Which one would be more adequate to define variations in executable specifications? Which one would clutter the model the least?

ADDITIONAL READINGS AND RESOURCES

Configurable Nodes

Michael Rosemann and Wil M. P. van der Aalst: A configurable reference modelling language. Information Systems 32(1): 1-23, 2007. *This is the main article on C-EPCs. It describes the C-EPC notation and provides a technique to individualize C-EPCs.*

M. La Rosa, M. Dumas, A. ter Hofstede, J. Mendling, F. Gottschalk, Beyond Control-Flow: Extending Business Process Configuration to Roles and Objects. In Proceedings of the 27th International Conference on Conceptual Modeling (ER 08), Springer-Verlag 2008. *In this article configuration of organizational roles and objects participating in a process model is discussed. The process modelling notation used is C-iEPC - an extension of C-EPC, in which configurable nodes are extended to cater for variability of objects and roles.*

Hiding & Blocking

F. Gottschalk, W. van der Aalst, M. Jansen-Vullers, M. La Rosa. Configurable Workflow Models. International Journal on Cooperative Information Systems, Vol. 17 No. 2 June 2008. *In this article, the approach based on the hiding & blocking operators is applied to executable process languages such as C-YAWL, BPEL and SAP Web Flow.*

W.M.P. van der Aalst, M. Dumas, F. Gottschalk, A.H.M. ter Hofstede, M. La Rosa and J. Mendling. Correctness-Preserving Configuration of Business Process Models. In Proceedings of Fundamental Approaches to Software Engineering (FASE 2008), Lecture Notes in Computer Science 4961, pages 46–61, Budapest, Hungary, 2008. Springer-Verlag. *In this article focus is on the issue of correctness of configured process models and it is shown under which circumstances a process model that results from a configuration can be guaranteed to be correct, from a syntactic and semantic perspective. The process models are represented as Petri nets and configuration is carried out by using the hiding & blocking operators.*

Annotation-Based Process Variability

Process Family Engineering in Service-Oriented Applications (PESOA) at www.pesoa.de. *This web-site contains links to research in the area of annotation-based process variability. An Eclipse plugin can be downloaded from this tool, to configure feature diagrams and link their result to variant-reach process models.*

F. Puhlmann, A. Schnieders, J Weiland and M. Weske Variability Mechanisms for Process Models. Process Family Engineering in Service-Oriented Applications (PESOA). BMBF-Project. Technical report. 2005. *This is the technical report on the outcomes of the PESOA project.*

Questionnaire Models

Process Configuration home page at www.processconfiguration.com. *This web-site contains links to research in the area of process configuration. The Quaestio tool is also available for download from this web-site, as part of the Synergia configuration toolset.*

M. La Rosa, Wil M.P. van der Aalst, M. Dumas and A. ter Hofstede. Questionnaire-based Variability Modeling for System Configuration, Software and Systems Modeling, 2009. *This article introduces the use of questionnaires for the configuration of process models. The article also compares the approach to the area of variability management in the field of software engineering.*

M. La Rosa, J. Lux, S. Seidel, M. Dumas and A. ter Hofstede. Questionnaire-driven Configuration of Reference Process Models. In Proceedings of the 19th International Conference on Advanced Information Systems Engineering (CAiSE 2007), Lecture Notes in Computer Science 4495, pages 424-438, Trondheim, Norway, 2007. Springer-Verlag. *This article provides a discussion of the application of the questionnaire-based approach to the configuration of C-EPCs.*

Krzysztof Czarnecki and Michal Antkiewicz: Mapping Features to Models: A Template Approach Based on Superimposed Variants. In Proceedings of the 4th International Conference on Generative Programming and Component Engineering, Lecture Notes in Computer Science 3676, pages 422-437, Tallinn, Estonia, 2005. Springer. *This paper shows another approach to link feature diagrams to process models represented as UML ADs.*

REFERENCES

van der Aalst, W. M. P., & Basten, T. (2002) Inheritance Of Workflows: An Approach To Tackling Problems Related To Change. *Theoretical Computer Science, 270*, 125-203.

van Der Aalst, W. M. P., Dreiling, A., Gottschalk, F., Rosemann, M. & Jansen-Vullers, M. H. (2006) Configurable Process Models As A Basis For Reference Modeling. *Bpm 2005 Workshops (Workshop On Business Process Reference Models)*, Lncs 3812, 512-518.

Baeten, J. C. M., & Weijland W. P. (1991) Process Algebra, Cambridge University Press, New York, Ny.

Batory, D. S. (2005) Feature Models, Grammars, And Propositional Formulas. *Proceedings Of The 6th International Conference On Software Product Lines (Splc), 3714*, 7-20.

Becker, J., Delfmann, P., Dreiling, A., Knackstedt, R., & Kuropka, D. (2004) Configurative Process Modeling - Outlining An Approach To Increased Business Process Model Usability. *Proceedings Of The 15th Irma International Conference.*

Becker, J., Delfmann, P., & Knackstedt, R. (2006) Adaptive Reference Modeling: Integrating Configurative And Generic Adaptation Techniques For Information Models. *Reference Modeling Conference 2006.*

Bunke, H. (2000) Recent Developments In Graph Matching. *International Conference On Pattern Recognition (Icpr).* Barcelona, Spain, Ieee Computer Society.

Curran, T., & Keller, G. (1997) *Sap R/3 Business Blueprint: Understanding The Business Process Reference Model*, Upper Saddle River.

Gottschalk, F., Aalst, Van Der W. M. P., & Jansen-Vullers, M. H. (2007) Configurable Process Models - A Foundational Approach. *Reference Modeling. Efficient Information Systems Design Through Reuse Of Information Models*, (pp. 59-78).

Gottschalk, F., Van Der Aalst, W. M. P., Jansen-Vullers, M. H., & La Rosa, M. (2008) Configurable Workflow Models. *International Journal Of Cooperative Information Systems, 17*, 2.

Jansen-Vullers, M. H., Van Der Aalst, W. M. P., & Rosemann, M. (2006) Mining Configurable Enterprise Information Systems. *Data And Knowledge Engineering, 56*, 195-244.

La Rosa, M., Van Der Aalst, W. M. P., Dumas, M., & Ter Hofstede, A. H. M. (2008) Questionnaire-Based Variability Modeling For System Configuration. *International Journal On Software And Systems Modeling.*

La Rosa, M., Lux, J., Seidel, S., Dumas, M., & Ter Hofstede, A. H. M. (2007) Questionnaire-Driven Configuration Of Reference Process Models. *19th International Conference On Advanced Informa-*

tion Systems Engineering (Caise). Trondheim, Norway, Springer-Verlag.

Puhlmann, F., Schnieders, A., Weiland, J., & Weske, M. (2005) Variability Mechanisms For Process Models. Process Family Engineering In Service-Oriented Applications (Pesoa). Bmbf-Project.

Rosemann, M., & Aalst, W. M. P. V. D. (2007) A Configurable Reference Modelling Language. *Information Systems, 32*, 1-23.

Schnieders, A., & Puhlmann, F. (2006) Variability Mechanisms In E-Business Process Families. *Proceedings Of The 9th International Conference On Business Information Systems (Bis'06)*, (pp. 583-601).

Schobbens, P.-Y., Heymans, P., Trigaux, J.-C., & Bontemps, Y. (2006) Feature Diagrams: A Survey And A Formal Semantics. *14th International Conference On Requirements Engineering.* Minneapolis, Minnesota, Usa.

Stephens, S. (2001) The Supply Chain Council And The Scor Reference Model. *Supply Chain Management - An International Journal,* 1, 9-13.

KEY TERMS

Business Process Modeling Notation: A standard notation for modelling business processes defined by the Object Management Group.

Configurable Node: A specific mechanism for representing variation points in graph-oriented modelling notations. In these notations, models are composed of nodes and arcs, and variation points may be captured by designating some of the nodes in the model as being configurable.

Configurable Process Model: A model that represents multiple variants of a business process in a consolidated manner. For example, a configurable order-to-cash process model is a model that captures different ways in which an order-to-cash process can be performed in practice. Configurable process models are intended to be individualized in order to derive process models that meet the requirements of a specific organization or project.

Domain Model: A model that represents key concepts, dependencies and decisions in a given domain of activity, such as accounting, logistics, manufacturing, banking or insurance.

Event-Driven Process Chains: A notation for modelling business processes based on the concepts of events, functions and connectors.

Model Configuration: The process of deriving an individualized model from a configurable model by resolving each of the variation points in the configurable model.

Reference Process Model: A business process model that is intended to serve as a reference in a given domain. A reference process model generally encodes best-practices in a given domain. A reference process model may be represented in the form of a configurable process model.

Variation Point: A point in a model (or other artifact) where a choice needs to be made between multiple possible variants. This choice is made during the configuration of the model.

ENDNOTES

1. www.itil-officialsite.com
2. www.supply-chain.org
3. www.sap.com/solutions/business-suite/erp
4. The inheritance of workflow behaviour borrows the concepts of *blocking* and *hiding* from Process Algebra (Baeten and Weijland, 1991). These concepts should not be confused with *blocking* and *hiding* in Object Oriented programming.
5. The tool can be downloaded from www.processconfiguration.com

Chapter X
Design of Repairable Processes

Cinzia Cappiello
Politecnico di Milano – Dipartimento di Elettronica e Informazione, Italy

Barbara Pernici
Politecnico di Milano – Dipartimento di Elettronica e Informazione, Italy

ABSTRACT

This chapter illustrates the concept of repairable processes and self-healing functionalities and discusses about their design requirements. Self-healing processes are able to monitor themselves, to diagnose the causes of a failure and to recover from the failure, where a failure can be either the inability to provide a given service, or a loss in the service quality. Defining the process as a composition of services, the aim of this chapter is also to provide guidelines for designing services in such a way that they can be easily recovered during their execution. Repair mechanisms are thoroughly described by distinguishing between mechanisms applicable at design time and at run time.

INTRODUCTION

New technologies, such as Web services and the semantic Web, are currently available for the development of information systems, where processes may be defined as a composition of services which can be selected dynamically to provide advanced personalized value added services and reactive/proactive systems. In order to employ the full potential of Web services, appropriate models and methods for service-based information systems and for workflows are being developed.

When considering service design and development, first of all the goals of designing a service need to be clarified, as several alternatives are possible [Pernici 2005]:

- **Integration (EAI):** In this case the goal is to integrate different information systems in order to create new cooperative applications. It is important to define the granularity at which services are considered, and how existing systems are wrapped to offer their functionalities in a cooperative information system through a service-oriented approach [Papazoglou and Van den Heuvel 2006].

- **Redesign (e.g., in mobile, multi-channel applications):** The goal is to modify existing functionalities in order to offer them in a variable environment setting, for instance allowing users to interact with the system from a variety of different devices and from different places. To provide the requested functionality, redesign has to take into consideration quality of service parameters and their variability and to manage the services dynamic selection and binding.
- **New added-value services:** New services are created as a composition of existing services. Composition allows reusing services in several contexts and for different applications. Composition may be performed following a fixed process schema, or designing the composition structure dynamically.

The service oriented approach introduces some new issues in the process design strategies in comparison with the traditional software design. For example, the granularity of the service has to be defined and the interface of the service should clearly state all the functional and non functional properties. Possible solutions to some design problems have been proposed by using reference models and ontologies. Regarding models, the need for models with a rich set of elements as a basis for the design process is a clear prerequisite for all design methodologies. Models should include a variety of aspects, and in particular:

- Business services modeling
- Service composition and coordination
- Interaction between clients and providers
- Service modeling with its Quality of Service (QoS) properties
- Transactional properties
- Self description (metadata).

For each model element, a modelling language should be defined. Existing background in the area, which can be a basis for modelling Web services include the WS-stack, UML2, BPMN, EPC, Aris, and so on. No clear and unique background still emerges.

In order to better understand the complexity of Web services design and of the corresponding processes design, the classical life cycle is represented in Figure 1 [Pernici 2005]. Here, the typical phases are:

- **Analysis:** This phase aims at defining the process goals in order to guide the composition of existing services and to base design (or redesign) on QoS requirements.
- **Logical design:** It should define functionalities and behaviour of the single services that compose the business process and in particular, it is necessary to describe:
  - interface
  - composition of services
  - selection of components
  - coordination design (and possibly distributed orchestration)
  - interaction paradigms
  - adaptivity
- **Physical design:** There is some debate on whether physical design should be a specific issue of service design. Relevant topics are optimization, aimed at improving service performance, and selective reuse.
- **Deployment:** For the deployment phase, deployment criteria should be specified during the design of services.
- **Monitoring:** The issue of this phase is to design the right level of information for monitoring by providing selective visibility of QoS for a given service (depending on consumer, context, costs involved, . . .) and identifying observable elements in order

Figure 1. Service design phases

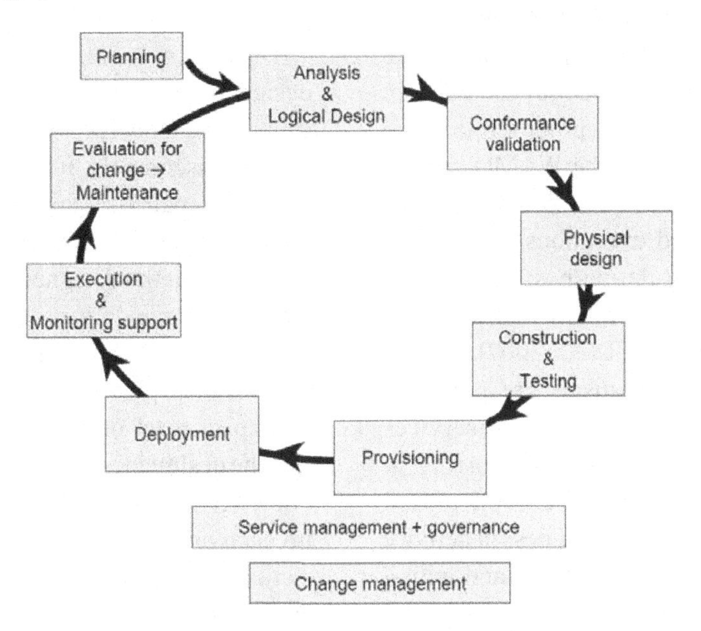

to diagnose faults out of symptoms, and in general, to interpret system events to infer the system state and correct/incorrect behaviour.

- **Testing:** Testing should be performed both on functional and non-functional characteristics of services. A contract with the users should be provided as a basis for the testing phase. In fact, atomic services (i.e., services providing a single function) should be tested along the users' requirements. A language for specifying testing should be also designed.

The design approach shows how service-oriented architectures are already addressing different issues and increasing the value that IT brings to companies by (i) improving and assuring interoperability and adaptivity and (ii) providing the flexibility that makes business change easier to implement. The latter is an important aspect since the dynamic nature of the business world shows the continuous pressure to reduce expenses, increase revenues, and remain competitive. This calls for a rapid reaction to the market trends, a rapid handling of user needs, and a rapid understanding of forthcoming challenges. To better support businesses in the process of reaching these goals, Web services in process-based service compositions would also need to be self-aware of the environment in which they operate, repairable in case of failure, and possibly self-healing so they can recover to normal levels of operation after disturbances. In fact, nowadays, complex systems are often required to have a high level of autonomy, even in faulty situations. Self-healability is an additional property obtainable through the combination of diagnosability and repairability [Console et al., 2007]. In fact, a system is self-healing if each occurrence of faults recognized by a diagnosis automatically raises a suitable repair plan. In order to guarantee the self-healability of a system, it is necessary to modify the process workflow with the insertion of suitable components for diagnosis and repair actions [WS-Diamond, Deliverable 5.1]. The analysis of exception management mechanisms have to be added at the logical design phase of the traditional approach depicted in Figure 1.

Note that the problem of exception modeling and handling has been studied extensively in the workflow literature and in particular in the WIDE project [Casati et al., 2000] the concept of exception pattern has been proposed to make exception design easier. In the WAMO system [Eder and Liebhart, 1995] a constructive approach to handle unanticipated exceptions at run time has been proposed, to define possible process repair plans according to predefined rules. In WS-BPEL [OASIS WSBPEL TC, 2007], several exception handling mechanisms are proposed to support the design of sophisticated services able to manage faulty situations occurring at run time. However, modeling of exceptions and repair rules might also become a design activity with costs which cannot be justified and with a severe impact on comprehensibility, violating the feasible comprehensibility requirement [Lindland et al., 1994a].

Different repair strategies can be adopted. Each repair strategy is characterized by its complexity and its functional and non functional properties. Along the process context and goals, a repair strategy can be can more suitable than another and this calls for appropriate methods as described in this chapter. In Section 2, the main types of repair strategies are compared. More details of all the listed design time and run time repair strategies are provided in Section 3 and Section 4 respectively. Section 5 proposes a methodology that supports the selection of repair actions and methods to apply to the process at run time or design time.

TYPES OF REPAIR

As described above, applications may incur in situations which are not anticipated in the developed models. A first distinction needs to be done between expected exceptions, which are part of the models, and unexpected exceptions, which cannot be anticipated at design time or for which the additional cost for considering them at design time would not be justified [WS-Diamond, Deliverable 4.1]. Also for unanticipated exceptions, process design should consider possible alternatives to support ad hoc recovery from failures at run time. Consequently, it is possible to distinguish between repair strategies to adopt at *design time* or at *run time.* The former are pre-defined repair methods that the designer provides together with the workflow model in order to increase the process reliability. These mechanisms are very important and designer provides them in order to enable a system to react on some exceptional situations that the designer can predict. Each method covers one activity or a fixed group of activities and is invoked under some a-priory known conditions. Actually, such repair strategies may be considered just as a part of the whole workflow model: a repair strategy is just a scope of activities that are invoked at a given time moment if some condition is fulfilled.

The main disadvantage of this type of repair is that it can not cover all cases and all exceptional situations. They do not depend on the environment in which an activity was executed. The condition specifying when the repair action should be executed depends only on the internal objects within the handled scope. It never depends on the environment variables within the whole workflow or on other scopes. However, the system should be able to react on some group of faults automatically, not only using pre-defined handlers. Automatically generated run time repair plans or, in alternative, ad hoc manually performed repair actions, must be able to bring the system state into a normal mode by executing a set of simple repair actions in a given order.

Repair strategies are also distinguished on the basis of the type of repair: *functional repair* and *non-functional repair.* To the class of functional repair belong all exceptional situations where the internal business-logic of workflow activities is somehow corrupted and the activity produces wrong, abnormal results. Faults in this case are hidden inside the realisation of activities. To the class of non-functional faults belong all faults that are not related to the internal business logic which workflow partners provide in form of operations. These faults are related to the properties of the workflow process, not to some activities or their scopes. The main group of such faults are QoS faults.

Finally, repair strategies are also distinguished on the basis of the level of their application: *instance level, class level, infrastructural level.* Instance level repair strategies correct the single instance that fails at a certain time instant. Class level repair strategies extend their action to several instances of the same process. Furthermore, some faults are caused by the environment in which activities are started. Workflow management systems and web services execution containers have their own parameters and requirements. When these constraints are violated, we say that the repair action is at an infrastructural level. Reasons of violations may be found in the workflow design: activities' parameters depend often on the concrete workflow where they are used. In one workflow they are correct, but in other one they may violate some requirements and constraints. We can say that infrastructural faults (i) are mostly QoS faults; (ii) may be caused by wrong values of the workflow process' parameters; (iii) are, possibly, consequences of class or instance faults and repair shall go to the corresponding level.

In the following sections, we introduce possible repair strategies, as listed in Table 1. The considered repair strategies are classified along the properties discussed above. In the next sections, we discuss first design time repair strategies, then run time strategies.

Table 1. Repair strategies

Repair strategy	*Functional*	*Non functional*	*Instance level*	*Class level*	*Infrastructural level*
Insertion of functional monitors	X		X		
Exception handlers	X		X		
Service redundancy	X			X	
QoS constraints monitors		X	X	X	X

(a) Design time repair strategies

Repair strategy	*Functional*	*Non functional*	*Instance level*	*Class level*	*Infrastructural level*
Redo/Retry the invocation of a failed service	X		X		
Compensation actions	X		X		
Service substitution	X		X		
Architectural reconfiguration		X		X	X

(b) Run time repair strategies

DESIGN TIME REPAIR STRATEGIES

Predefined management mechanisms are used at design time in order to modify the process flow and enable the service repairability. It is important to underline that the techniques employed to realize this kind of recovery are strictly dependent on the model used to describe Web services. Some models describe how Web services act internally (i.e., orchestration), while other models only describe how different Web services collaborate (i.e., choreography) [Pelz, 2003]. While both choreography and orchestration are exploited to detect faults, design time repair actions only rely on the orchestration model of the service by controlling the execution of its internal process.

Design alternatives to improve self-healability are the following:

- Insertion of functional monitors
- Exception handlers
- Service redundancy
- QoS constraints monitors

Insertion of Functional Monitors

The first mechanism that it is possible to use in the process design is the insertion of monitors. They improve both service diagnosability and repairability since monitoring activities analyze messages exchanged between modules in order to detect anomalies to prevent faults or to detect failures. In this section, we focus, in particular, on quality of information in the process, and data quality blocks are described as an example of a monitoring mechanism. They are inserted in the process flow to evaluate data quality dimensions associated with exchanged data. Data quality aims at evaluating the suitability of data involved in a specific process [Wand and Wang, 1996]. The most important dimensions are accuracy, completeness, consistency, and timeliness. Accuracy, completeness, and consistency assess data along their numerical extension and correctness [Redman, 1996] [Wang and Strong, 1996]. Timeliness evaluates the validity of data along time [Ballou et al. 1998]. These dimensions are objective dimensions and, therefore, are suitable for a quantitative evaluation and constitute a minimal set that provides sufficient information to evaluate the data quality level.

Along the presented data quality dimensions, it is possible to classify faults along two categories: value mismatch and missing data.

The value mismatch can be derived by:

- **Typos:** e.g., Jhon instead of John
- **Different format:** e.g., date expressed as dd/mm/yyyy instead of mm/dd/yyyy
- **Conflict in data values:** e.g., Residence city: London Country: Italy
- **Delay in update operations**

Typos are related to data accuracy while conflicts in data values are related to data consistency. A case of different format can be related to both accuracy, because the value is not a right representation of real-world value, and to representation consistency. Delay in update operations between two databases that contain the same values can be related to both timeliness, since the out-of-date value is not valid anymore, and accuracy since that the out-of-date value is a incorrect representation of the real world value. Missing data can be caused by value unavailability or by a delay in update operations. The former is related to the completeness dimension. Delay in update operations between two databases that contain the same values can be related to the timeliness dimension but in this case the update operation would create new tuples in a database. The conformity of quality of service dimensions with respect to users expectations is checked. When data quality values are below specified thresholds, alarms are sent to the systems manager.

Anyway, repair actions for data quality at design time require the identification of the causes of data errors and their permanent elimination through an observation of the whole process where data are involved. Data tracking methods are required in order to determine the exact stage or steps in information process where the causes of data quality decreasing occur [Ballou et al. 1998]. In the literature several methods exist that allow the representation of a process and the associated information flow in order to detect errors and facilitate data quality improvement. An example is the Information Product Map (IP-MAP) methodology [Shankaranarayan et al., 2000] which graphically describes the process by which the information product is manufactured. There are different types of construct blocks that form the IP-MAP but the most important innovative feature is the introduction of data quality block that is used to represent the checks for data quality that are essential in producing a defect-free information product. Therefore, a list of the data quality checks that are being performed on the specified component data items is associated with this block.

Each data quality block relies on a model of the system itself to interpret a set of measurements, to detect the presence of faults and to identify the specific causes of the fault. It is necessary to model the Web service execution and the role of data in it considering both the data flow and structure. In this scenario, for each activity a_{ik}, it is not sufficient to consider only input and output information flows, but it is also necessary to consider data that are used by the activity but do not derive from previous activities executed in the process. We refer to external data identifying all data that belong to this category.

According to this model an error in the output data can be consequence of:

- An error generated by the activities that precede the analyzed one
- An error generated by the analyzed activity. This type of error can be classified as self-generated error

In this case, for example, the detection and correction of errors due to value mismatch can be performed using different methods:

- **Data cleaning by manual identification:** Comparison between the value stored in the database and the correct value in the real world
- **Data bashing (or Multiple sources identification):** Comparison of the values stored in different databases in order to detect inconsistencies; in this case certified databases (e.g., dictionaries, syndicated data) are often used to check the correctness of the data values that flow in the process activities
- **Cleaning using Data edits:** Automatic procedures that verify that data representation satisfies specific requirements

In case a self-generated error occurs, the causes can also be related to the data structure or external processes. In fact, it is necessary to consider that the activity can be influenced not only by the previous activities but also by other external processes that for example might use the same data sources.

Exception Handlers

Broadly defined, an exception is an error or fault condition that affects a program's results. Exception handlers improve both diagnosability and repairability since they detect and correct service faults occurring in a single instance.

Considering the de-facto standard for Web-Service Orchestration,WS-BPEL [OASIS WSPEL TC, 2007], it provides standard patterns for managing exceptions. Specific handlers (fault, compensation, event and termination) are associated with a single action, with a scope, that is, a set of actions, or with a process. The following basic handlers are provided:

- **Fault handler:** To explicitly catch errors and to handle them by executing specified subroutines.Its aim is to undo the partial and unsuccessful work of a scope. The first thing it does is to terminate all the activities contained within the scope. Sources of faults can be: (i) invoke activity responding with a fault WSDL message,(ii) a programmatic throw activity (iii) standard fault that pertains to the engine. If a fault is not consumed in the current scope it is recursively forwarded to the enclosing ones. If the termination of instance has not be invoked, after consuming the exception the normal flow restarts at the end of the scope associated with the fault.
- **Compensation handler:** While a business process is running, it might be necessary to undo one of the steps that have already been successfully completed. The specification of these undo steps are defined using compensation handlers that can be defined at the scope level. Each handler contains one activity which is run when a scope needs to be compensated. A compensation handler is available only after the related scope has been completed in a correct way. This can happen in either of two cases: explicit or implicit compensation. Explicit compensation occurs upon the execution of a compensate activity. This activity may occur anywhere, and refers to the name of the scope that it wants compensated. When a compensate activity is reached, it runs the compensation handler on the specified scope. On the other hand, implicit compensation occurs when faults are being handled and propagated. Consider the scenario in which a scope A contains a compensable scope B that has completed normally, but then another nested activity in A throws a fault. Implicit compensation ensures that whatever happened in scope B gets undone by running its compensation handler. Therefore, implicit compensation of a scope goes through all its nested scopes and runs their compensation handlers in reverse order of completion of those scopes.
- **Event handler:** The whole process as well as each scope can be associated with a set of event handlers that are invoked concurrently if the corresponding event occurs. The actions taken within an event handler can be any type of activity, such as a sequence or a flow. Event handler is considered as a part of the normal processing of the scope, i.e., active event handlers are concurrent activities within the scope. Events can be: i) incoming messages; ii) temporal alarms.
- **Termination handler:** Forces termination of a scope by disabling the scope's event handlers and terminating its primary activity and all running event handler instances. Forced termination for a scope applies only if the scope is in normal processing mode. If the scope has already invoked fault handling behaviour, then the termination handler is uninstalled, and the forced termination has no effect. The already active fault handling is allowed to complete. If the fault handler itself throws a fault, this fault is propagated to the next enclosing scope. A fault in a termination handler must cause all running contained activities to be terminated.

The major problems that handlers create are about their lack of flexibility. Those handlers are enabled at different time during execution: fault, event, and termination handlers are enabled only during execution time (of a task or scope); compensation handler is enabled when the status is "completed" and therefore the execution point is ahead of the scope.

Using these handlers as they are, it is possible to realize very basic "recovery" patterns. In fact WS-BPEL provides the four handlers as standard patterns and leaves to designer any other specification about the tasks actually executed when a handler is fired. For example, designers could use the exit activity to interrupt a service execution or define generic runtime exceptions during service implementation. Runtime exceptions represent problems that are detected by the runtime system. This includes arithmetic exceptions (such as when dividing by zero), pointer exceptions (such as trying to access an object through a null reference), and indexing exceptions (such as attempting to access an array element through an index that is too large or too small). Runtime exceptions can occur anywhere in a program and in a typical program can be very numerous. Typically, the cost of checking for runtime exceptions exceeds the benefit of catching or specifying them. Therefore more powerful and flexible instruments could be built, but this effort is currently fully in charge of the designer [WS-Diamond, Deliverable 3.1].

To choose or define a suitable language, possibly Web-Service based, supporting a good range of recovery actions, three different approaches can be followed: to define a totally new workflow language and workflow engine, to start from an existing language defining an extension and the corresponding extended engine or to use the concepts of annotation and preprocessing for enhancing the language at design time without modifying the workflow engine. The most effective and generally applicable approach is the third one. For example, in [Modafferi and Conforti 2006] five new patterns enabling specific recovery actions are described. They cover a wide range of possibility:

- **External variable setting:** The ability of modifying the value of process variables by means of external messages. A common typology of errors during Business Process execution are related to data. Actual recovery actions in this field are often performed outside the process by human actors. Even if it is performed out of the process, this kind of recovery usually produces the need for an update for several process variables. This pattern allows the designer to simply identify which variables can be set from incoming messages, and associate with an event handler the activity of suspending the process and modifying the corresponding variables.
- **Timeout:** The specification of a time deadline associated with a task. In a communication between two Web services one problem is the time that one actor can wait before the message arrival. We need a pattern to manage, at process level, timeout in the communication. The designer specifies a timeout for each chosen Receive activity and the corresponding recovery actions, that is the set of activities performed if the timeout happens. In WS-BPEL time-out can be realized using a *pick* activity with an alarm to abort waiting for a message. In fact, the pick activity combines the use of an onMessage handler that manages the reception of the client's response to the inquiry embodied by a one-way invoke and of an onAlarm handler that specifies the timeout.
- **Redo pattern:** The ability of redoing a single Task or an entire scope of a stateful service. The action of Redo is not related to the concept of rolling back a process or part of it. According to [Hamadi and Benatallah, 2004], it is assumed that concurrently with a running process, at a time, the system can ask for redoing a Task or a scope without any relationship with the current point in the execution flow.
- **Future alternative behaviour:** The possibility of specifying alternative paths to be followed, in the prosecution of the execution, after the reception of an enabling message. The typical example is when a given (and not vital) service during the process execution becomes not available and an incoming message carries this information, each operation related to this service will be skipped until the situation does not change. The idea behind this pattern is to have some

alternative behaviours available along the process and related to several portions of it. The preprocessing phase uses a condition block to store all the possible alternative behaviours in the corresponding places, and a specific variable drives one and only one of this kind of conditions. Each alternative behaviour is fired (or killed) by a specific message. This approach assumes that default and alternative behaviours are mutually exclusive and that the incoming message fires the associated behaviour along all the process. If for a single scope more than one alternative behaviour has been defined, the last incoming message will decide the actual behaviour.

- **Rollback and conditionally re-execution of the flow:** The possibility of going back in the process to a point defined as safe for redoing the same set of tasks or for performing an alternative path. By using the simple compensation handler provided by standard WS-BPEL it is possible to compensate a scope, but the execution flow could proceed only ahead and no "jump" or "go to" construct are provided. The only way to go back is to use a loop in a proper way. It is possible to define, by considering the solution presented in [Modafferi et al, 2005], a more general pattern that allows the rollback of the process until a safe point and then to execute the same or a possibly different behavior. The concept of safe points is derived from [Grefen et al, 1999] and their identification is in charge of the designer. Safe points can be also called "migration points" because each point can be the "starting point" for migrating to an alternative behavior.

Service Redundancy

In the process design, it is possible to insert redundant elements in order to reduce the probability of failure in the process execution and to increase the process availability. The adoption of this repair strategy modifies the process flow in order to assure the correctness of multiple instance of the same process. This is classifiable as a class level repair strategy. In [Jaeger and Ladner, 2005] three patterns are proposed (see Figure 2). In all the three arrangements actions are linked by an AND split followed by an "1 service out of n-services join": the join condition synchronizes only the first finishing service. For the other part of the parallel arrangement we consider three sub-structures: (a) the best alternative candidate is put into an redundant AND-split with an 1-out-of-n-join arrangement (b) the quickest of alternative candidates is synchronized by an AND-split followed by an 1-out-of-join (c) an alternative candidate is synchronized by a XOR split followed by an XOR join (RP3). The first arrangement that suggests alternative candidates improves the execution time if the alternative candidate provides a quicker execution time than the original candidate. The actions are linked by an AND split followed by a 1-out-of-n join that means that from a parallel arrangement all n tasks are started, but at least one task is required to finish for the synchronization. The cost raises by the cost of the additionally executed task.

The availability improves because every additionally invoked service raises the probability for the successful execution of the arrangement.

The reputation can be reduced if the alternative service offers a lower reputation than the original one. The first arrangement that suggests alternative candidates improves the execution time if the alternative candidate provides a quicker execution time than the original candidate. The actions are linked by an AND split followed by a 1-out-of-n join that means that from a parallel arrangement all n tasks are started, but at least one task is required to finish for the synchronization. The cost raises by the cost of the additionally executed task. The reputation can be reduced if the alternative service offers a lower reputation than the original one. The availability improves because every additionally invoked service raises the probability for the successful execution of the arrangement.

The second solution arranges the original service in a parallel structure containing the alternative candidates in a parallel AND-split with 1-out-of-n-join structure. Both joining elements will synchronize upon the first candidate end. This arrangement reduces the execution time if one of the alternative candidates provides a quicker execution time than the original service. The cost raises by the sum of all additionally executed tasks. Like before, the reputation can be reduced if an additional candidate offers a lower reputation. And the availability improves because every additionally invoked service raises the probability for the successful execution of the arrangement.

Finally, the third solution is different from the previous replacement structures: this structure invokes only one of the available alternative candidates. It is assumed that the probability of executing the individual candidates is equally partitioned. Thus, the execution time improves if the selected candidate executes quicker. For a high number of executions, the cost raises by the mean value of the individual costs. Again, the reputation may lower for this arrangement if alternative candidates show a lower reputation than the original service.

QoS Constraints Monitors

In order to avoid failure, it is possible to define QoS constraints that have to be satisfied during the service execution. QoS constraints can be classified in local and global constraints. Local constraints define quality of Web services to be invoked for a given task in the process i.e., candidate Web services are selected according to a desired characteristic, e.g., the price of a single Web service invocation is lower than a given threshold. Global constraints specify requirements at process level, i.e., constraints posing restrictions over the whole composed service execution can be introduced, e.g. the price of the composed service execution is lower than a fixed budget. Constraints may be specified on a set of N pre-defined quality dimensions. They are monitored and, if they cannot be satisfied, before a service execution fails, suitable negotiation mechanisms are performed in order to determine new quality values for Web service invocations. For example, if the data quality global constraints cannot be fulfilled, then it could be possible to improve the data quality of service invocations

Figure 2. Redundancy actions [Jaeger and Ladner, 2005]

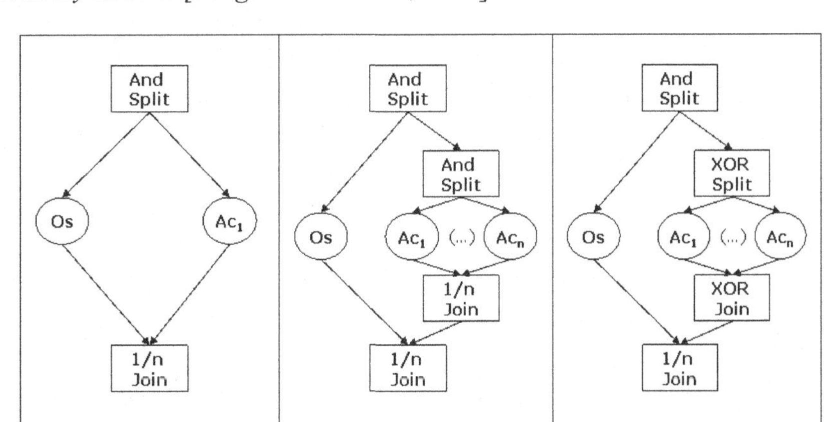

e.g., by performing data cleaning procedures. If the negotiation succeeds, an agreement on the new price and quality parameters for a given operation invocation is achieved. If the negotiation fails, a relaxation of the problem is performed in order to identify the largest set of global constraints specified by the user which could be fulfilled. Subsequently, the quality parameters of the operation invocations which lead to constraints violation are negotiated.

RUN-TIME REPAIR STRATEGIES

Run time repair actions do not modify the process flow, but they are procedures that require additional components that have to be activated when a failure occurs. Run time actions can be also implemented as semi-automatic procedures. This kind of recovery actions are performed by the service management infrastructure.

Run time actions can consider the failed service with the re-invocation, the compensation of a process activity and the substitution of the whole service, or with the re-allocation of the service resources. In order to retry or substitute a service, a registry in which the services are described along their functional and non-functional requirements is needed.

The following repair actions are considered:

- **Redo:** Re-execute the service with possibly new values of input parameters.
- **Retry Web services invocation:** This recovery action is applied when faults point out a temporary unavailability of one or more services that compose the internal process of the analyzed Web service. In this case, the solution is to suspend the execution of the process and retry the invocation of the unavailable services until they return available. This solution is quite simple and does not require any sophisticated methodologies to manage the service invocation. Note that the repair action Retry is applicable for example in case when Web service wraps a human activity. This action differs from Redo activity, because a) it uses the same input objects in the same state as it was on executing the activity without correcting/changing/adjusting them b) it can be done several times and depends on how many times it was invoked – an amount of execution times may be calculated.
- **Compensation:** This is the most complicated repair action. It has some specific requirements, characteristics and needs to be described in more details. We consider the compensation mechanism as follows. Each activity may have an associated compensation action. This action reverses the internal behavior of activity. Main goal of compensation action is to delete the side effects on the world that were caused by activity (changes in databases, removing created items etc.) and restore the effects of executing of this activity within the workflow (changes in states of objects). It means, that state of objects, affected by the activity will be the same as it was before executing this activity. Not each activity may have the compensation action.
- **Substitute Web services:** A more complex situation is the case where one or more services are considered as definitely unavailable and, in order to complete the process execution, it is necessary to substitute each failed service. The Substitute repair action allows us to change the provider of the service. For example, users can book a flight ticket at some other flight agency. They need to substitute the service with another one that has the same operation. This requires an analysis of partners' descriptions to find the equivalent operations at different partners. A possibility is to describe semantic links between operations e.g.: operation o1 at partner A is equivalent to operation o5

at partner B, which means that they have the same sets of outputs, and the same or similar set of inputs. Having such a library of "similar" operations we can apply the substitute action.

- **Architectural reconfiguration (Reallocate Web services):** This type of recovery action is very useful for the particular subset of QoS violation faults that derives from a lack of hardware or software resources on the service provider side. In this situation, reallocating and executing the service on different machines or application servers can solve the problem. Reallocation is possible only if Web services are provided with an ad-hoc management interface and the recovery manager has free access to all the resources (e.g., the recovery manager can determine the load balancing or the application priority in the operating system). Reallocation may be performed as reactive actions, when QoS violations are detected, but also as proactive actions, when optimization of service execution plans is performed using predictive techniques on future states of the execution environment. As discussed for substitution, the mechanisms are the same as those used for infrastructure repair, where additional constraints have to be considered when the service is executed within a process.

Other actions may be needed to support run time the above repair actions [WS-Diamond, Deliverable 4.4], such as:

- **Inform:** It informs the provider of Web service about which operation was faulty, and provides all necessary information: when it was faulty, states of input objects, etc. This action requires the provider to accept such messages using some interface or protocol. As soon as this repair action was applied, workflow manager has to know in which time functionality is available.
- **Completion of missing parameters:** Service invocation may fail when the input message structure is correct but some of the message parameters are missing, that is they are associated with a null value. Possible recovery actions may be based on knowledge of the role of parameters. [De Antonellis et al., 2006] describes a technique to dynamically evaluate message composition of invoked Web service operations and look for missing information when parameters are necessary for message execution, while optional parts are ignored. The technique is based on an adaptive service invocation infrastructure.

REPAIR STRATEGIES EVALUATION

As discussed in the previous sections, a significant number of repair strategies are available to support the design of repairable processes. Repair strategies are characterized by different properties (e.g., objectives, complexity, applicability) and a repair strategy can be more suitable than another along a specific process context and goals. Thus, in complex scenarios, it could be necessary to adopt a systematic approach to support the repair plan selection. For example, a thorough analysis of the processes should be conducted to identify the relevant tasks, the actors within their roles and their requirements. The most suitable repair strategy may also depend on the process stakeholders requirements, where the stakeholders include both the end users and the process owners.

For each task of the processes, repair strategies should be evaluated along functional and non functional constraints. Note that among all the criteria that can be defined and that are relevant for repair strategies selection in case of failure, it is important to consider the following quality dimensions:

- **Availability:** Consider the property of the system to be continuously operational,

- **Execution cost and time:** Consider the computational cost and the related time of an activity,
- **Failure risk:** Consider the risk associated with the activity to fail during the execution.

These dimensions are some of the main drivers for the selection of the suitable repair strategy. Users can also specify the relevance of each quality dimension along the specific context. For example, for a crucial task, availability can be considered more important than the execution time and thus a complex repair strategy that increases the response time but assures high availability could be selected (e.g., redundancy). Note that execution cost, execution time, and failure risk are variables the importance of which can be evaluated only by the stakeholders. However, it is necessary to consider that providers have their own requirements in provisioning services. In fact, considering that sometimes the provision of a perfect service can raise costs significantly, providers should consider the benefits that such improvement activities would produce. Benefits are estimated in the process analysis by considering the importance of the user for a specific service.

Furthermore, providers have to consider dimensions such as:

- **Reputation:** Measure the trustworthiness of the service provider.
- **Fidelity:** Consider relationship between the alternative service providers and the process owner.

Considering that a process can involve the orchestration and composition of different services, a process can be executed by using services provided by different providers. The process owner should always care about its own reputation that could be decreased with a service fail for its fault or another provider's fault. In the same way, if process owners always contact the same providers, and thus have a strong relationship with them, fidelity can be a relevant driver for the selection of the suitable repair strategy. For example, the service of a trusted provider might not be substitutable with a service of another provider to avoid breakdowns in diplomatic relations.

The evaluation of both stakeholders' and providers' constraints defines the set of the viable repair strategies.

CONCLUDING REMARKS

In this chapter process repair has been analyzed. Two different strategies are being proposed to improve process reliability and repair: to anticipate possible failures at design time, modifying the structure of the process to provide alternatives to execution in case of failure, and strategies for recovery at design time, where some repair actions that can be executed at run time in case of failures are provided when designing the process, but their actual use is decided at run time. Recent research work is focusing on supporting repair of unanticipated failures, leveraging on available repair actions at run time. In particular, this approach has been investigated in the WS-Diamond EU Project, where repair is supported by two main types of functionalities: *diagnostic tools*, which allow monitoring the process and the identification of the causes of failures, and *planning tools*, which allow the construction, at run time, of a repair plan, based on the available repair actions and the current state of the process. The research on self-healing mechanisms is still in its initial stages, and possible directions include the adoption of learning mechanisms to improve the selection of repair strategies based on past repair decisions performed with manual intervention, in order to minimize human intervention [Pernici and Rosati 2007], and also on optimization mechanisms to select the best possible strategy among the available ones based on the stakeholders' preferences and the process and service structure.

ACKNOWLEDGMENT

Part of this work has been performed within the FET Open EU Project WS-Diamond (Web site: http://wsdiamond.di.unito.it/). It has also been partially supported by the MIUR TEKNE National project and the Network of Excellence S-Cube.

REFERENCES

Ballou, D. P., Wang, R. Y., Pazer, H. L., & Tayi, G.K. (1998). Modelling information manufacturing systems to determine information product quality. *Management Science, 44*(4), 462–533.

Casati, F., Castano, S., Fugini, M.G., Mirbel, I., & Pernici, B. (2000). Using patterns to design rules in workflows. *IEEE Trans. Software Eng.*, *26*(8), 760-785.

Console, L., Fugini, M. G., & the WS-Diamond Team (2007). WS-DIAMOND: An approach to Web Services – DIAgnosability, MONitoring and Diagnosis. In *Proceedings of the E-Challenges Conference.*

De Antonellis, V., Melchiori, M., De Santis, L., Mecella, M., Mussi, E., Pernici, B., & Plebani, P. (2006). A layered architecture for flexible Web service invocation. *Software – Practice and Experience, 36*(2), 191-223.

Eder, J., & Liebhart, W. (1995). The Workflow Activity Model WAMO. In *Proceedings of CoopIS* (pp. 87-98).

Grefen, P., Pernici, B., & Sanchez, G. (Eds.) (1999). *Database support for workflow management: The WIDE Project.* Kluwer Academic Publishers.

Hamadi, R., & Benatallah, B. (2004). Recovery nets: Towards self-adaptive workflow systems. In *Proceedings of the International Conference on Web Information Systems Engineering (WISE)*, (LNCS 3306, pp. 439-453). Springer.

Jaeger, M. C., & Ladner, H. (2005). Improving the QoS of WS compositions based on redundant services". In *Proceedings of the International Conference on Next Generation Web Services Practices.*

Lindland, O. I., Sindre, G., & Sølvberg, A. (1994). Understanding quality in conceptual modelling. *IEEE Software, 11*(2), 42-49.

Modafferi, S., Benatallah, B., Casati, F., & Pernici, B. (2005). A methodology for designing and managing context-aware workflows. In *Proceedings of IFIP TC 8 Working Conference on Mobile Information Systems (MOBIS).*

Modafferi, S., & Conforti, E. (2006). Methods for enabling recovery actions in WS-BPEL. In *Proceedings of OTM Conferences (1)*, 219-236.

OASIS WSBPEL Technical Committee (2007). *Web Services Business Process Execution Language v2.0.* OASIS Standard.

Papazoglou, M., & Van den Heuvel, W.-J. (2006). Service-oriented design and development methodology. *Int. J. on Web Engineering and Technology,* 412-442.

Pelz, C. (2003). Web services orchestration and choreography. *IEEE Computer, 36*(8), 46-52.

Penker, M., & Eriksson, H. (2000). *Business modeling with UML: Business patterns at work.* Wiley.

Pernici, B (2005) *Report on "Service design and development".* Dagstuhl seminar no. 05462 on Service Oriented Computing

Pernici, B., & Rosati, A. M. (2007). Automatic learning of repair strategies for web services. In *Proceedings of the European Conference on Web Services (ECOWS)*, (pp. 119-128).

Redman, T. C. (1996). *Data quality for the information age.* Artech House.

Shankaranarayan, G., Wang, R. Y., & Ziad, M. (2000). Modeling the manufacture of an information product with IP-MAP. In *Proceedings of the 6th International Conference on Information Quality.*

Wand, Y., & Wang, R. Y. (1996). Anchoring data quality dimensions in ontological foundations. *Communication of the ACM, 39*(11), 86-95.

Wang, R. Y., & Strong, D. M (1996). Beyond accuracy: What data quality means to data consumers. *Journal of Management Information Systems, 12*(4), 5-34.

WS-Diamond Deliverable 3.1. *Specification of execution mechanisms and composition strategies for self-healing Web services.* Technical report, WS-DIAMOND European project, 2006. Available on line at: http://wsdiamond.di.unito.it/

WS-Diamond Deliverable 4.1.*Characterization of diagnosis and repair for Web services.* Technical report, WS-DIAMOND European project, 2006. Available on line at: http://wsdiamond.di.unito.it/

WS-Diamond Deliverable 4.4. *Specification of repair/reconfiguration algorithms for Web Services.* Technical report, WS-DIAMOND European project, 2006. Available on line at: http://wsdiamond.di.unito.it/

WS-Diamond Deliverable 5.1. *Characterization of diagnosability and repairability for self-healing Web Services. Technical report,* WS-DIAMOND European project, 2006. Available on line at: http://wsdiamond.di.unito.it/

Chapter XI
Web Process Adaptation

Kunal Verma
Accenture Technology Labs, USA

ABSTRACT

Adaptation is an important concept for Web processes. The author provides an overview of adaptation with respect to control theory and how it is applied to other contexts. Specifically the author focuses on open loop and closed loop adaptation. Then the cahpter discusses the current Web process standard WS-BPEL supports open loop adaptation. Finally, the author discusses an academic research framework METEOR-S, which supports closed loop adaptation.

INTRODUCTION

Adaptation refers to a system's ability to react to certain erroneous conditions or changes in the environment. In the context of a Web process, adaptation refers to the process's ability to react to errors that may occur during the execution of the process or some changes in the environment of the process that may prevent the process from fulfilling its goals. During the execution of a Web process, here are some examples of errors: (1) the supplier service may fail before the order is placed, (2) the supplier may be unable to deliver the order on time after the order is placed, (3) the supplier may be unable to deliver the order at all after the order is placed. Here are some potential changes to the environment during the execution of the process: (1) The currency of the supplier's country changes making previous order sub-optimal (2) Some other supplier offers a new discount. In all these cases, the Web process should be able to adapt.

Control theory has been to create adaptive systems that vary from highly sophisticated applications such as flight controllers and cruise control to simple appliances such as washing machines and sprinkler systems. In this chapter, we will cover some of the basics of control theory, in particular open-loop and closed-loop controllers. The main difference between open and closed loop controllers is that open loop controllers do not monitor the environment, whereas closed loop controller do. This is particularly relevant to Web processes, because for intelligent adaptation, the Web process must monitor the environment, however current standards like WS-BPEL do not provide direct support for that. We will also discuss an academic research effort, METEOR-S that enhances WS-BPEL infrastructure to provide support for closed loop adaptation.

CONTROL THEORY BASICS

In this section, we will briefly define some basic concepts in control theory – system, controller, open and closed feedback.

System

A system is defined as an abstraction that represents a set of real world objects (shown in Figure 1). For example, you can have a system that represents an airplane. A system can consist of set of systems. For example, an airplane system consists of the navigation system, the propeller system and the cargo system. We determine a system by choosing the relevant interactions we want to consider plus choosing the system boundary or, equivalently, providing membership criteria to determine which objects are part of the system, and which objects are outside of the system and are therefore part of the environment of the system. A boundary is used to separate the system from its environment.

Controller

A controller (shown in Figure 2) is a device which monitors the system and/or environment and affects the behaviour of the system. For example, the heating system of a house can be equipped with a thermostat (controller) for sensing the air temperature of the house (environment) which can turn the A/C on or off when the air temperature becomes too low or too high. The controller affects the behaviour of the system based on a set of system or environment control variables. In this case, the desired temperature is the control variable.

Open and Closed Loop Controllers

An open-loop controller is a type of controller which uses only the current state and its model

Figure 1. System and boundary

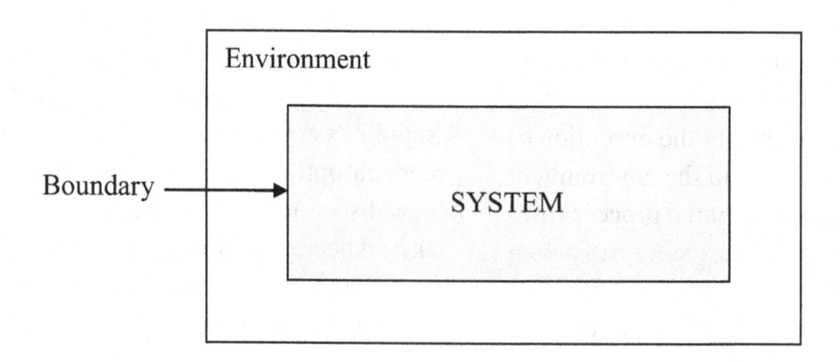

Figure 2. A controller monitors and controls a system's behaviour

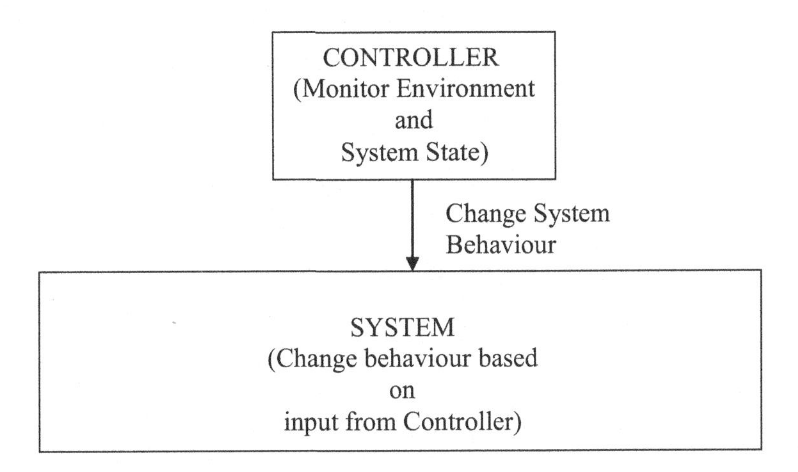

of the system. It does not use a model of the environment. For example, consider a sprinkler system, which is programmed to turn on every Wednesday. The sprinkler system would activate every Wednesday, even if it is raining, leading to wastage. An open loop controller is very simple to implement, however it does not have optimal behaviour.

Open-loop control is useful in cases where there are not too many changes and all events are predictable. For example, determining the voltage to be fed to an electric motor that drives a constant load, in order to achieve a desired speed would be a good application of open-loop control.

A closed loop controller uses the environment, in addition to the current state and model of the system. Consider the example of the cruise control, where a sensor monitors the speed of vehicle and uses that to control the behaviour of the vehicle. In addition, feedback on how the system is actually performing allows the controller to dynamically compensate for disturbances to the system, such as changes in slope of the ground or wind speed.

An open loop controller is far more complex to implement, but if properly implemented it typically will have close to optimal behaviour.

ADAPTATION CONTROLLER FOR WEB PROCESSES

With respect to control theory, the Web process engine is the system and the adaptation controller (Figure 3) is responsible for helping the Web process adapt to errors in execution or changes in the environment. The environment includes the Web services that the process interacts with and any other factor that affect the services or the process. In case of open loop control, the adaptation controller will only consider the state of the executing process, where in open loop control, the adaptation controller will consider both the environment and the state of the executing process.

Adaptation in WS-BPEL: Open Loop Adaptation

In WS-BPEL, the adaptation controller can only have a pre-defined set of adaptation flows. That means that the process reacts to an event the same way, regardless of environment. This is open loop adaptation, because the process has the same reaction to the same event regardless of the condition of the environment.

Figure 3. Web process controller

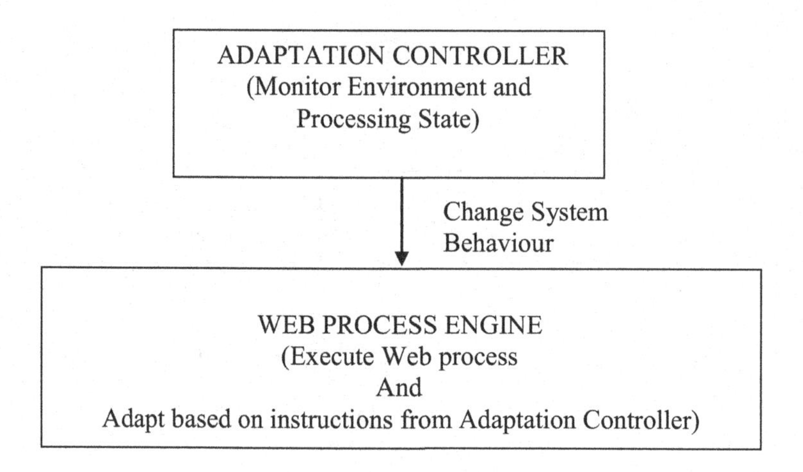

Figure 4. Open Loop Adaptation in WS-BPEL based on pre-defined flows

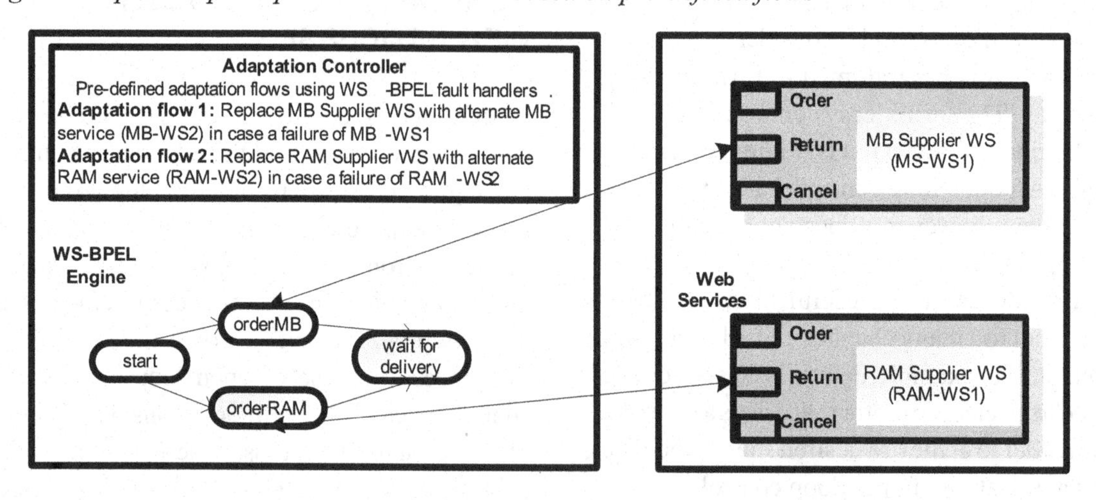

This can be illustrated with the help on an example. Consider a supply chain process of a computer parts manufacturer shown in Figure 4. This process is used by the computer parts manufacturer to order both RAM and motherboard (MB) from the corresponding supplier Web services (RAM-WS1 and MB-WS1). Then the process waits for delivery of the parts. Consider the case, where RAM-WS1 is not available when the order is being placed. WS-BPEL provides a construct to deal with such failures the computer manufacturer can provide an alternate RAM provider service (RAM-WS2) using the fault handler. Similarly, an alternate service can also be provided for another motherboard supplier (MB-WS2). Since, the adaptation flows have to be pre-defined, we refer to this type of adaptation as open-loop adaptation.

There are the following this disadvantages of using open loop adaptation:

- Since, the alternate services are pre-defined before the process starts, if there are any changes to environment, like another motherboard service (say MB-WS3) offering a new discount, then they will be missed by the process engine and it will choose MB-WS2 regardless, whenever MB-WS1 fails.
- One can imagine an even more reactive system, which replaces MB-WS1 with MB-WS3, if there are cost savings. However, that is not possible to model using open loop adaptation approach, since the complete state of the process and the environment are not considered for adaptation.
- Consider an even more complicated case of adaptation, where one of the suppliers is unable to deliver the order on time. In such a case, the adaptation decision is far more complex, as a number of environment factors such as promised customer SLA and priority, inventory levels and manufacturing capacity will have to be considered before a decision can be made. That is not possible with an open-loop approach. The next section will discuss a research prototype which attempts to augment the current adaptation capabilities of WS-BPEL with closed loop adaptation.

Adaptation in METEOR-S: Closed Loop Adaptation

The METEOR-S (Verma 2006; Verma et al., 2006) project provides an evolutionary approach for closed loop adaptation by creating a model of the environment as well as the process. It achieves that by creating a system that can be seen as a layer between a WS-BPEL process engine and the Web services. This is shown in Figure 5. This layer decouples the Web services from the Web processes and allows selection of the services at runtime. It also allows adapting the process to errors that may occur during execution. The architecture consists of the following components: (1) process managers, (2) service managers and (3) adaptation module. For each executing process, there is a process manager that maintains both a global view and process-level optimization criteria controls each process instance. There is a service manager that controls the interaction of the process with each service. The adaptation module provides support for decision-making based on run-time events with the help of a Markov Decision Process based framework.

In METEOR-S, the general approach of adaptation is to model the relevant states and events of the process across various points of its execution. If the process executes normally the state machine

Figure 5. Closed looped adaptation in METEOR-S based on external events

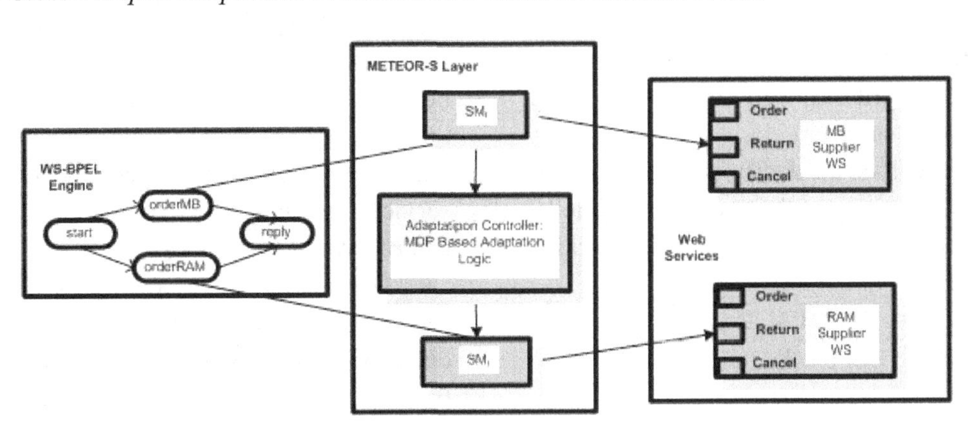

transitions effortlessly from the start state to the goal state. If, however, there is an unexpected event and exception, the process transitions to an error state. The process adaptation mechanism should ideally find an optimal path from the error state to the goal state. Such problems are characterized as sequential decision-making problems in decision theory literature. The field that deals with the uncertainties that are often part of the process, such as about the model or transitions, is called stochastic decision making. Markov decision processes provide a comprehensive model for stochastic decision making; they have been used to control agents and robots in uncertain environments. A Web process execution environment should be able to deal with events and uncertainty in the same was as an agent or robot in an unpredictable environment by taking the next action, in response to an event that would lead toward a goal state.

Let us look at adaptation problem in the context of the supply chain scenario. Each supplier Web service has three relevant operations for this interaction: order, cancel, and return. In addition, there are two events related with service: received and delayed. In a normal execution of the process, the service manager would invoke the order operation of supplier Web service and get a timely received event, signifying that the ordered goods from that supplier have been received on time. However, if the ordered goods are delayed, the service manager must decide whether to cancel the order and change the supplier. This requires a decision-making framework that takes into account the costs associated with not reacting or cancelling the order as well as the reliability of the alternative supplier

In METEOR-S, the decision-making process of a service manager (SM), which is modelled as a Markov decision process (MDP) called SM-MDP.

SM-MDP = <S, A, PA, T, C, OC>, where

- S is the set of states of the service manager. The state is updated with each interaction of the service manager with the service it manages.
- A is the set of actions of the service manager. The actions are the operations of the Web service.
- PA:S → A is a function that gives the permissible actions of the service manager from a particular state.
- T:S × A × S → [0, 1] is the Markovian transition function. The transition function gives the probability of ending in a state j by performing action a in state I.
- C:S × A →R is the function that gives the cost of performing an action from some state of the service manager.

For the supply chain scenario, the actions are the following: = {**Order (O), Return(R), Cancel (C), Wait (W)**}. The action, **Order** denotes the invocation of the *order* operation of the supplier that will be chosen if the supplier has to be changed and the actions **Return** and **Cancel** signify the invocation of the Web services to cancel the order or return it (if received). While the other actions are from the *semantic* template, please note that **Wait** is a special virtual action, which allows the Service Manager to perform a no-operation (NOP), if that is the optimal action. Then the relevant events that will change the state of the service manager are identified. In this case, the events are *E* = {**Received (Rec), Delayed (Del)**}. **Received** signifies the goods' being received and **Delayed** signifies the goods' being delayed. Events correspond to messages that the services send to their respective service managers. Each process specifies the events the services can generate and an endpoint where it can *r*eceive the messages.

The state transition showing the state, actions and events are shown in Figure 6. The transitions due to actions are depicted using solid lines. The transitions due to the events are shown dashed.

The events allow us to model the potential non-determinisms processes. For example, in our scenario when an order is placed, there are three possibilities – (1) it is delayed and the service provider sends a notification, (2) it is received and the service provider sends a notification and (3) it is either of the two and no notification is sent.

Solution of the service manager's model described in Section 6.1 results in a *policy*. The *policy* is a prescription of the optimal action to be performed by each service manager given the state of the Web process and the number of steps to go. Formally, a policy is $\pi: S \times N \rightarrow A$, where S and A are as defined previously, and N is the set of natural numbers denoting number of steps. The advantage of a policy-based approach is that regardless of the current state of the service manager, the policy will always prescribe the optimal action. In order to compute the policy, we associate each state with a value that represents the long-term expected cost of performing the optimal policy from that state. Let $V: S \times N \rightarrow R$ be the function that associates this value to each state. The value function can be computed using the value iteration algorithm developed by Bellman (Bellman, 1958) that utilized dynamic programming. Please note γ ε [0, 1] and is called the discount factor. It represents the significance that is given to the future in decision making. As shown in equation (1), if γ is 0, then only the current state is considered.

$$V_n(s_i) = \min_{a \in PA(s_i)} Q_n(s_i, a)$$

$$Q_n(s_i, a) = C(s_i, a) + \gamma \times \sum_{s'} T(s_j \mid s_i, a) \times V_{n-1}(s_j) \quad (1)$$

The optimal action from each state is the one that optimizes the value function and is stored in the policy,

$$\pi_n = \arg\min_{a \in PA(s_i)} Q_n(s_i, a) \quad (2)$$

We note that the dynamic programming formulation presented above is not the sole method for generating policies for MDPs. Linear programming based formulations also exist for solving the process manager's model.

From the context of the example, the policy would represent the optimal action for the service manager and would depend on the cost associated with different actions and the probabilities of events. Consider state *S3* from Figure 6, the generated policy would depend on the various costs and the probability of future delays:

Figure 6. Generated state transition diagram

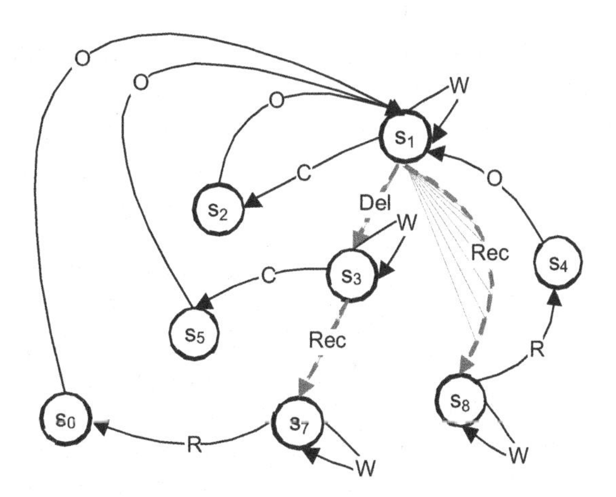

- If the cost and probability of delay is high, then the optimal action for the service manager, when it enters the state *S3* would be cancel, signifying that it is better for the service manager to cancel to order.
- If the cost and probability of delay is low, then the optimal action for service manager, when it enters the state *S3* would be wait, signifying that it is better for the service manager to wait out the delay.

OTHER EXAMPLES OF CLOSED LOOP WEB PROCESS ADAPTATION

Typically, work in this category can be divided into two groups – work that deals with application level events and work that deals with system-level events. In both application and system level event based adaptation, different modelling paradigms such as ECA rules or temporal logic are used to model and enforce the adaptation. The difference is in the kind of events that are handled. AGENTWORK (Muller et al., 2004) used ECA rules to make changes in running instances of patient care in the healthcare domain; VEMS (Davulcu et al., 1999) utilized temporal logic to make changes to workflow instances. JOpera (Pautasso et al., 2005) discusses a self-adapting distributed architecture for executing Web processes based on system level events. It provides a framework for reconfiguring process engines in a distributed environment. In another work, (Baresi et al., 2003) discuss an approach for context-aware composition of e-Services based on an abstract description of both e-Services and context. Adaptation rules are specified as ECA rules. Contexts describe channels, the various ways in which a service can be accessed. Further, channels are associated with QoS metrics such as Round trip time and cost. When a service defaults on a QoS guarantee, adaptation is achieved by changing the channel. ECA rules are used to represent the adaptation rules.

CONCLUSION

In this chapter, we covered some basics of control theory and how it is relevant to Web process adaptation. We briefly discussed how WS-BPEL only allows for open looped adaptation and how the METEOR-S approach extends current WS-BPEL infrastructure to provide support for closed loop adaptation. Then we provided an overview of how Markov Decision Processes can be used model decision making for adaptation. Finally, we discussed some other approaches that also provide support for closed loop adaptation.

REFERENCES

Baresi, L., Bianchini, D., Antonellis V.D., Fugini, M.G., Pernici, B., & Plebani, P. (2003). Context-aware composition of e-services. In *Proceedings of the Third VLDB Workshop on Technologies for E-Services.*

Bellman, R. (1958). *Dynamic programming and Stochastic Control Processes Information and Control, 1*(3), 228-239.

Davulcu, H., Kifer, M., Pokorny, L. R., Ramakrishnan, C. R., Ramakrishnan, I. V., & Dawson S. D. (1999). Modeling and Analysis of Interactions in Virtual Enterprises. In *Proceedings of the Ninth International Workshop on Research Issues on Data Engineering: Information Technology for Virtual Enterprises.*

Muller, R., Greiner, U., & Rahm, E. (2004) AGENTWORK: A workflow system supporting rule-based workflow adaptation. *Journal of Data and Knowledge Engineering, 51*(2), 223-256.

Pautasso, C., Heinis, T., & Alonso, G. (2005) Autonomic execution of Web service compositions.

In *Proceedings of the Third IEEE International Conference on Web Services.*

Verma, K. (2006, August). *Configuration and adaptation of Semantic Web processes.*Unpublished doctoral thesis, Department of Computer Science, The University of Georgia.

Verma, K., Doshi, P., Gomadam, K., Miller, J. A., & Sheth, A. P. (2006). Optimal adaptation in Web processes with coordination constraints. In *Proceedings of the Fourth IEEE International Conference on Web Services,* Chicago, IL.

EXERCISES

1. What is closed-loop adaptation?
2. What is open-loop adaptation?
3. What are the advantages and disadvantaged of open-loop vs. closed-loop adaptation? When would you choose one vs. the other?
4. What kind of adaptation does WS-BPEL support? Give an example of a process adaptation that can be modeled using WS-BPEL? Given an example of a process that cannot be modeled using WS-BPEL?
5. Give an example of a process adaptation that can be supported using METEOR-S.

Section IV

Enriching Process Models and Enactment Architectures

Chapter XII
Temporalities for Workflow Management Systems

Carlo Combi
Università degli Studi di Verona, Italy

Giuseppe Pozzi
Politecnico di Milano, Italy

ABSTRACT

Time is a very important dimension of any aspect in human life, affecting also information and information management. As such, time must be dealt with in a suitable way, considering all its facets. The related literature already considered temporal information management from a pure database point of view: temporal aspects (also known as temporalities) of stored information cannot be neglected and the adoption of a suitable database management system (Temporal Database Management System - TDBMS) could be helpful. Recently, research of the temporal data management area started to consider business processes, extending and enriching models, techniques, and architectures to suitably manage temporal aspects. According to this scenario, the authors discuss here some of the main advantages achievable in managing temporal aspects and consider temporalities in process models, in exception definition, in the architecture of a Workflow Management System (WfMS), and in the scheduling of tasks and their assignment to agents.

INTRODUCTION

Time features any aspect of human life, being associated or associable with any fact or information or event. The need for supporting temporal information, as well as storing, reasoning about, and representing data and facts, has been recognized for a long time (Snodgrass & Ahn, 1985), showing that a proper management of temporal information is required. The literature presents an analysis of the current status and sketches about future trends on storing (Jensen & Snodgrass, 1999, Khatri et al., 2004), representing and reasoning (Chittaro & Montanari, 2000) on temporal information: other papers consider these trends in several application domains, e.g. in medicine (Adlassnig et al., 2006, Combi & Pozzi, 2006b).

Time is thus relevant for any human activity, either if managed in a "traditional" way or with the support of ICT (Information and Communication Technology) tools. Workflow Management Systems - WfMS – (Aalst & van Hee, 2004, Grefen et al., 1999, Weske, 2007) can help in managing activities and/or business processes, and can be even more helpful if such systems can properly manage time and related temporal dimensions (i.e., temporalities). As an example, changes in the managed information, in the organization, in the process model, as well as deadlines, constraints on the activation or completion of a task or of the entire process, temporal synchronization of tasks can be easily defined, monitored, and detected by a suitable WfMS (Marjanovic & Orlowska, 1999a, Marjanovic & Orlowska, 1999b).

Since most of the information managed by a WfMS is stored by a database management system (DBMS), it can be easily observed that a suitable management of temporalities by the DBMS itself, which could result in a temporal DBMS (TDBMS), could be helpful. Unfortunately, and to the best of our knowledge, very few TDBMSs are available: despite this, we shall consider throughout the paper that some temporalities can be managed at the DBMS level: as an example, we shall assume that the valid time dimension, which is one of the relevant elements in managing temporalities, is available and manageable by the DBMS.

The chapter is organized as follows. The first section is entitled *Temporalities in Workflow Models* and it considers the main models and the related temporalities used in a workflow system: the process model, describing the single atomic work units and their coordination; the information model, describing all the information of the process instances (i.e., cases) by the workflow system; the organizational model, describing the agents (i.e., participants, which can be human or not, of an organization), and the structure of the organization where process instances will be executed.

The second section is entitled *Temporalities in Expected Exceptions* and it considers the abnormal events, also known as exceptions, which may occur during the execution of process instances. The section focuses on expected exceptions, i.e. those exceptions which must be considered at process design time, may occur at any time during the execution of the process, may deviate the "normal" flow of execution, and include a not negligible semantics.

The third section is entitled *Temporal Scheduling* and it considers the scheduler of a workflow management system, its policies for assigning tasks to agents and for fulfilling the defined temporal constraints. The section also includes the description of one possible algorithm for a temporal scheduler of a WfMS.

The fourth section is entitled *Temporal Architectures for WfMSs* and it considers both the general architecture of a WfMS and the changes that can be applied to such architecture, enriching it to suitably managing temporalities. The section discusses the pros and cons of three different architectures, depending on the availability of a full-fledged temporal database management system or not.

Finally, the last section entitled *Conclusions* provides an overview of the chapter and sketches out some possible research topics in the area.

TEMPORALITIES IN WORKFLOW MODELS

When considering a business process and its enactment via a Workflow Management System (WfMS), the main models to be considered relate to the process model (i.e., the schema of the considered process), to the information model (i.e., the information managed by the process and those generated by the WfMS for internal purposes like tracking the activities), and to the organizational model (i.e., the description of hierarchies and skills of the agents inside the organization where the process is executed). Other models can be defined as well, to consider expected exceptions which may occur during the enactment of the instances (cases) of the defined processes, or to consider transactional aspects of the process identifying savepoints, rollbacks, and—possibly—compensating tasks (Grefen et al., 1999).

Temporalities in the Process Model

The responsible for defining the structure of the business process model, aka workflow designer, by a graphical tool designs the workflow schema: this schema is generally stored by suitable database files, mostly on top of a relational DBMS (RDBMS) or, more seldom, by XML files.

As an example, consider the process of Figure 1, which describes the activities of a bookstore receiving from Web-customers some orders of purchase of rare books. The notation herein described comes from the BPMN (Business Process Modeling Notation) (The Business Process Management Notation, 2008): obviously several different notations exist, or can be defined (Russell et al., 2006).

With respect to the process of Figure 1, if the book is in stock, it is immediately delivered; otherwise the production of the book is started and the book will be delivered later on. While several solutions are possible, the schema of the process can be mapped on tables of a RDBMS like in the following (Casati et al., 1996a):

- `WorkFlow`, with attributes `WfName` (unique name of the schema) and `StartTask` (name of the first task to be executed and belonging to that schema);
- `WorkTask`, with attributes `WfName` (name of the schema) and `WTName` (name of the task, unique for every schema);
- `RoutingTask`, with attributes `WfName` (name of the schema), `RoutingTaskName` (name of the routing task, unique for every schema), `RoutingTaskType` ("and split", "or split" to activate parallel execution; "and join", "or join" to resynchronize after parallel execution of two or more branches);
- `NextTask`, with attributes `WfName` (name of the schema), `WorkTask` (name of the task, unique for every schema), `NextTask` (name of the successor task or routing task, which must belong to the same schema);
- `AfterFork`, with attributes `WfName` (name of the schema), `ForkTask` (name of the routing task from the `RoutingTask` table), `NextTask` (name of the task, belonging to he same schema, to be activated after the fork), `Condition` (logical condition to

Figure 1. The customer sends in the order and the system checks if the requested book is in stock: if yes, the payment is received and the book is sent out. If the book is not in stock, the book is produced, the payment is received, and finally the book is shipped.

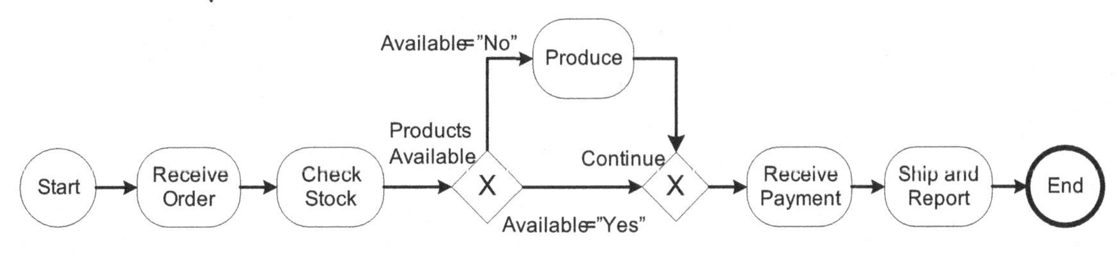

selectively activate any of the outgoing arcs from `ForkTask` to `NextTask`).

Table 1 depicts the table of a relational DBMS describing the schema of the process of Figure 1. Insofar, please disregard the attribute VT.

Let us now assume that this workflow schema has been defined on October 15, 2007. On November, the bookstore managers decide to improve the process, releasing a new version of the same process model on November 12, 2007. From now on, the schema will be the one depicted in Figure 2. Whenever the production of the requested book is needed, the customer is informed about the expected delay of the delivery.

Figure 2 depicts the new version of the schema. Due to several reasons, like keeping track of all the previous versions of a schema, completing the running cases according to the schema that was respectively valid at case start time or identifying some ad-hoc policies to migrate from one version to another (Casati et al., 1996b, Casati et al., 1998), identifying the latest version of the schema for the cases to be started from scratch, a suitable temporal DBMS (TDBMS) will be helpful.

A TDBMS is a DBMS where the temporal aspect of stored data is managed directly by the DBMS. In such a case, the DBMS usually provides two temporal dimensions for data: valid time and transaction time (Jensen & Snodgrass, 1999). Valid time (VT) is the time when the fact is true in the real word; transaction time (TT) is the time when the fact is current in the DBMS. Other temporal dimensions can be added, if needed (Combi et al., 2007b). VT and TT are often associated with each tuple, i.e., the VT and TT of a tuple are unique and refer to any attribute of that tuple. VT and TT are intervals, having a lower bound as the beginning instant and an upper bound as the ending instant: an upper bound set to $+\infty$ means that the interval is not finished yet, and thus the information can be still valid and/or still current inside the database.

By VT and TT, the TDBMS enables one to reconstruct the status of the database and of the considered real word domain at any previous instant, thus fulfilling the previously defined requirements. Let us now consider the VT attribute introduced for tables representing workflow schemata in Table 1. By introducing the VT, the tables describing the process model are able to represent both the old version of the workflow schema (valid up to November 11, 2007) and the new one, still valid.

After storing and managing the valid time of data, suitable temporal extensions are needed even for the query language, which allows us to retrieve the required information about workflow schemata. In the following we shall discuss some simple temporal extensions to the well-known query language SQL and its application on workflow data.

As an example, if we want to obtain the list of the work tasks of the process as defined last (this

Figure 2. A change with respect to the schema of Figure 1 is applied. If the book is not in stock, the customer is informed about the delay in the delivery, the book is produced, the payment is received and, finally, the book is shipped.

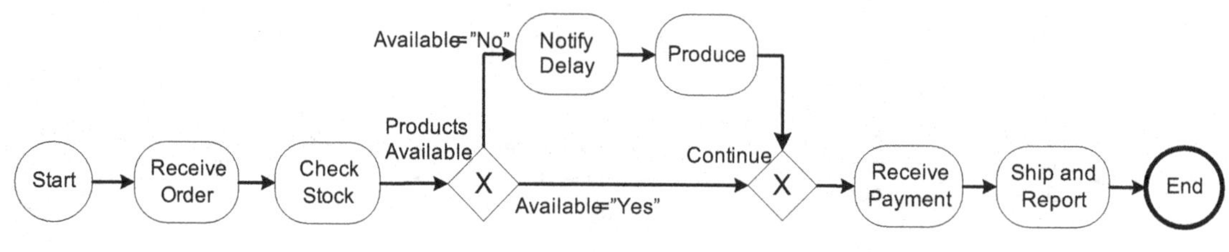

Table 1. These tables completely describe the process model of a workflow. The attribute VT (Valid Time) is defined, as usual, as an interval: if the upper bound of the interval is set to +∞, the tuple is still valid.

WorkFlow	WfName	StartTask	VT
	E-BookShop	ReceiveOrder	[10-15-2007 - +∞]
	LoanMgmt	GetApplicantData	[11-10-2007 - +∞]

WorkTask	WfName	WTName	VT
	E-BookShop	ReceiveOrder	[10-15-2007 - +∞]
	E-BookShop	CheckStock	[10-15-2007 - +∞]
	E-BookShop	ReceivePayment	[10-15-2007 - +∞]
	E-BookShop	Produce	[10-15-2007 - +∞]
	E-BookShop	ShipAndReport	[10-15-2007 - +∞]
	E-BookShop	NotifyDelay	[11-12-2007 - +∞]
	LoanMgmt	GetApplicantData	[11-10-2007 - +∞]

RoutingTask	WfName	RuotingTaskName	RoutingTaskType	VT
	E-BookShop	ProductsAvailable	OR Split	[10-15-2007 - +∞]
	E-BookShop	Continue	OR join	[10-15-2007 - +∞]

NextTask	WfName	WorkTask	NextTask	VT
	E-BookShop	ReceiveOrder	CheckStock	[10-15-2007 - +∞]
	E-BookShop	CheckStock	ProductsAvailable	[10-15-2007 - +∞]
	E-BookShop	Produce	Continue	[10-15-2007 - +∞]
	E-BookShop	Continue	ReceivePayment	[10-15-2007 - +∞]
	E-BookShop	ReceivePayment	ShipAndReport	[10-15-2007 - +∞]
	E-BookShop	ShipAndReport	EndWf	[10-15-2007 - +∞]
	E-BookShop	NotifyDelay	Produce	[11-12-2007 - +∞]

AfterFork	WfName	Forktask	NextTask	Condition	VT
	E-BookShop	ProductsAvailable	Continue	Available="Yes"	[10-15-2007 - +∞]
	E-BookShop	ProductsAvailable	Produce	Available="No"	[10-15-2007 – 11-11-2007]
	E-BookShop	ProductsAvailable	NotifyDelay	Available="No"	[11-12-2007 - +∞]

is what we need whenever we have to start a new case, and we shall start new cases according to the schema defined last), the query over the table `WorkTask` sounds like:

```
SELECT WTName
FROM WorkTask WT
WHERE WT.WfName = "E-BookShop" AND
VALID(WT) CONTAINS CURRENT DATE
```

If, instead, we want to obtain the list of the work tasks of the process as it was at the schema creation time, e.g. to execute the case according to the schema valid at the timestamp of the creation of the case, the same query sounds like:

```
SELECT WTName
FROM WorkTask WT, WorkFlow WF
WHERE WF.WfName = WT.WfName AND
    WT.SchemaName = "E-BookShop"
    AND VALID(WT) STARTS VALID(WF)
```

The above mentioned criteria have been described over a temporal relational DBMS: however, their validity spans in general, even if the adopted data model is different from the relational one (e.g., XML data model, like for the X-PDL process definition language standardized by the Workflow Management Coalition), on condition that temporal dimensions can be suitably managed.

The workflow designer may also enrich the process model by defining some temporal constraints related to the duration of every single task. As an example, the table `WorkTask` may also include two attributes referring to the expected task duration (`ExpectedTaskDuration`, i.e., an average value of durations for the execution of a task as foreseen a priori as in Casati et al., 1999) and to the maximum task duration (`MaxTaskDuration`, i.e., the duration for the execution of a task believed as the maximum acceptable as foreseen a priori). Should the duration of a task at run time exceed these values (or other durations defined starting from these durations such as 2*`ExpectedTaskDuration`), the exception management unit or the scheduler may take interventions to suitably compensate the constraint violation.

Constraints on the duration of a task can be easily extended to a group of tasks or to a couple of tasks connected via a straight connection, defining the `MaxTaskDuration` or the `ExpectedTaskDuration` for the group or for the couple of tasks. Such extensions deal with the group of tasks as one unique piece: thus the constraint includes also the time required for the scheduling of tasks belonging to the group over which the constraint has been defined.

Figure 3. After the completion of task A, tasks B and C (total fork, i.e. AND split) are scheduled. A constraint asserts that C must be opened within a maximum delay δ after B has been opened.

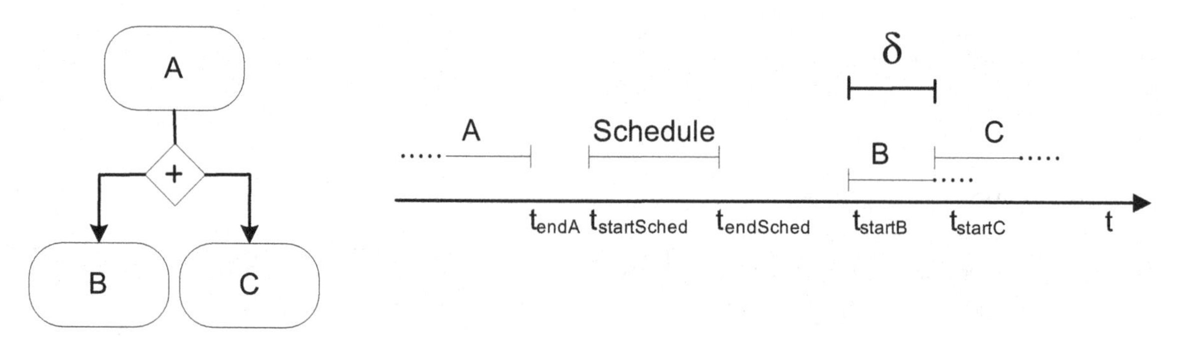

Some more constraints, involving two or more tasks, can be defined. As an example (Figure 3), the workflow designer may want to define a constraint saying that task `C` must be activated within a maximum delay of δ after task `B` has been activated; the delay δ includes all the time that may be required to schedule activity `C`, to assign it to the executing agent, and to let the agent actively start the task.

Temporalities in the Information Model

The information model describes two types of data: data from the log files and data from the managed processes. Log files include data about all the cases and tasks, their executing agent, start time and end time for execution, and so on: the structure of these data is fixed and independent from the managed process. Data from processes are strictly related to the considered application, managed by the WfMS, and entered/updated/deleted directly via the WfMS: data stored by an information system external to the WfMS or managed by suitable external applications are traditionally not considered as belonging to the information model.

The information model, as well as the process model and the organizational model, stores data via the DBMS coupled to the WfMS. While the structure of the tables storing the process models (see above), the organizational model (see below), and the log files are not process dependent, i.e. we have one unique structure of tables regardless of the considered processes and organizations, the structure of tables storing process specific data have no fixed structure. A suitable compiler of the process definition language reads the process definition with the definition of workflow variables, populates the tables of the process model as discussed in the previous section, and creates suitable tables to store the workflow variables of the considered process (see table `E_BookShopData` of Table 2).

As an example, if we consider the process model of the bookstore from above, a reasonable structure of the workflow variables may include: `CustomerName`, `OrderedBook`, `Amount`, `OrderDate`, `ExpectedDeliveryDate`.

Temporal aspects of these data are relevant. As an example, assume that the `ExpectedDeliveryDate` was originally set to February 20th: due to a technical problem in producing the book, a delay of 2 weeks was introduced and the new delivery date set to March 5th. The use of a temporal information model helps us to keep track of the changes. Let us focus in this case only on TT: the update of the information is mapped onto a

Table 2. The upper bound of the TT interval asserts that the first tuple has been cancelled on Feb 18th, while the lower bound of the TT interval asserts that the second tuple has been stored since February 18th and it is still current (the upper bound is set to $+\infty$).

E_BookShopData	Case_Id	CustomerName	Ordered Book	Amount	Order Date	Expected Delivery Date	TT
	101	Ely Culbertson	Contract Bridge	19.99	02-01-2008	02-20-2008	[02-01-2008 -02-18-2008]
	101	Ely Culbertson	Contract Bridge	19.99	02-01-2008	03-05-2008	[02-18-2008 -$+\infty$]

TDBMS by setting the upper bound of the interval of the TT to the timestamp when the tuple has been updated (or removed), thus formally saying that the tuple is no longer current in the database, and by inserting a new tuple whose lower bound of the TT interval is set to the timestamp when the update (or insert) took place.

Thus if we assume that the case was started on February 1st, the original `ExpectedDeliveryDate` was set to February 20th, on February 18th the new `ExpectedDeliveryDate` was set to March 5th, the resulting tuples for the case are those depicted in Table 2.

Temporalities in the Organizational Model

The organizational model describes the structure of the organization where the WfMS enacts cases. Figure 4 provides a temporally enhanced ER (Entity-Relationship) schema of the organizational model: a watch in the graphical notation corresponding to entities and relationships stands for a construct having a valid time dimension. For sake of clarity the relationships between `Actor`, `Function`, `Team`, and `Group` are not depicted: temporalities are considered for `Agent` and `Performs`. Further details can be found in (Combi & Pozzi, 2006a).

Information stored within the organizational model considers agents' data like name, e-mail address, hiring date, role, name of the manager. An agent is a participant of the organization, and can be human or not. Relevant temporal information is provided by entities `Availability` and `Unavailability`. `Availability` describes the normal availability of the agent, i.e. the normal working hours and working days for the agent. `Unavailability` describes when the agent is not available: this may happen during the normal availability time for several reasons (e.g., illness, family reasons...) or during local or nation-wide holidays, or when the agent left under authorization (e.g., during an external mission). `Availability` and `Unavailability` represent a set of intervals (instants) where an agent can be available or unavailable, respectively. Valid times for these entities refer to the interval during which the given availabilities/unavailabilities hold. We want to stress the concept that the set of instants that belong to the availability is different from the set of instants that do not belong to unavailability: indeed, unavailability refers to the fact that an agent can be unavailable during his/her

Figure 4. Organizational model: temporal information is associated with the agent and to his/her/its relationship with roles.

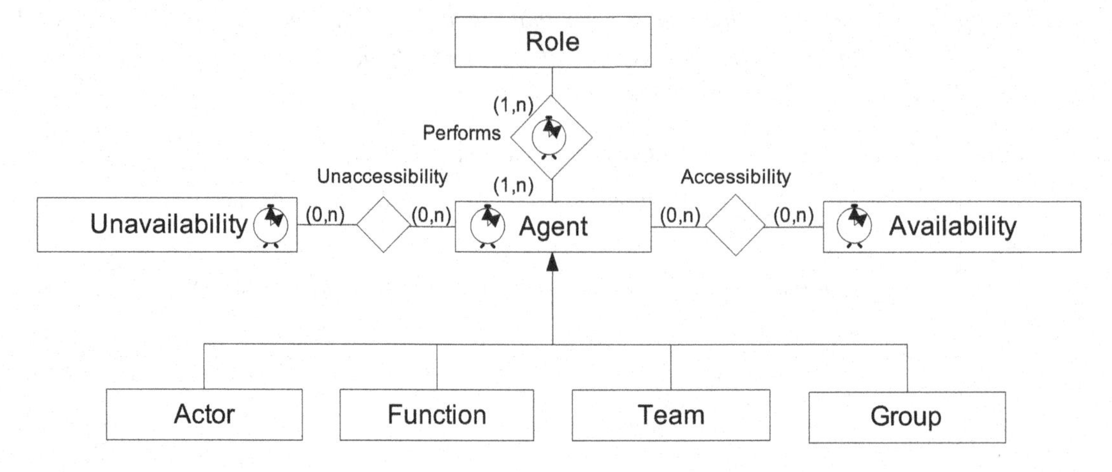

Table 3. The Table depicts information about agents. Agent Thomas Stern is available every day from 9:00 a.m. to 12:30 p.m., starting from October 15th, 2007 which was his hiring date: the same agent is also available on Mondays from 1:30 pm. To 5:00 p.m. The agent Hermann is available every day from 9:00 a.m. to 12:30 p.m., starting from November 10th, 2007 which was his hiring date.

Agent	Agent_Id	Name	e-mail	Role	VT
	101	Thomas Stern	eliot@bookstore.com	clerk	[10-15-2007 - +∞]
	102	Hermann	melville@bookstore.com	clerk	[11-10-2007 - +∞]

Accessibility	Agent_Id	Availability
	101	1
	101	2
	102	1

UnAccessibility	Agent_Id	UnAvailability
	102	3
	...	...
	...	...

Availability	Av_Id	StartTime	EndTime	TimeAvail	VT
	1	9:00 a.m.	12:30 p.m.	DailyTime	[10-15-2007 - +∞]
	2	1:30 p.m.	5:00 p.m.	PeriodicTime	[10-15-2007 - +∞]

PeriodicTime	Id	Type	ExpressionName
	2	Available	1/Days_In_Week
	...	...	...

normal availability time, e.g. because of one of the above mentioned reasons.

The availability/unavailability of an agent may look like "every Monday 8:30 a.m. to 5:30 p.m."; "the first Friday of every month 1:45 p.m. to 6:00 p.m."; "every day 9:00 a.m. to 5:00 p.m.". The literature presents some proposals on how to express periodical times and workday calendars (Liu et al., 2008, Leban et al, 1986): in the following we adopt a notation based on Leban et al., 1986. This notation has the shape, for example, of *1/Days_In_Week* to refer to every Monday (i.e., the first day of every week), or *2/Weeks_In_Month* to refer to the second week of every month, or *1..5/Days_In_Month* to refer to the first 5 days of every month.

The availability/unavailability is expressed by two types of expressions: `DailyTime` represents a temporal interval of hours for every day, e.g. from 9:00 a.m. to 12:30 p.m.; `PeriodicTime` represents an interval of hours during the days specified by a periodic expression, e.g. every Monday. As an example Table 3 depicts information about an agent who is available every day from 8:30 a.m. to 12:30 p.m. and every Monday (*1/Days_In_Week* of the `PeriodicTime` table) afternoon from 1:30 p.m. to 5:00 p.m.

TEMPORALITIES IN EXPECTED EXCEPTIONS

During the normal execution of processes, several exceptions may occur (Eder & Liebhart, 1995) such as hardware, software, network, or power failures, to mention few of them. Some of these exceptions are not strictly related to the process we consider and enacted by the WfMS, even if the effects of the occurrence of such exceptions are relevant over the considered process. On the other hand, other exceptions are strictly related to the considered process, and they can be modeled within the process itself: we refer to these exceptions by the term of "expected exception" (Eder et al., 1999). The semantics of these exceptions is not negligible, for a correct execution of the process.

Expected exceptions are classified according to the respective triggering event (Casati et al., 1999); after an event has been detected, a related condition can be checked and, in case, the specified action can be executed, typically to manage the exception or to inform an agent about its occurrence. Exceptions can be described by triggers (also known as rules) according to the *ECA* paradigm: whenever an *E*xception occurs (i.e. the trigger is fired), a *C*ondition is checked and, possibly, the *A*ction is executed. Triggering events can be: data event (e.g., a change in a workflow variable); workflow event (e.g., the start or completion of a task instance or of a case); external event (e.g., the customer calling to cancel his/her reservation); temporal event (e.g., on February 19th, 2008 at 4:56 p.m.). We focus here on temporal events.

Temporal events can, in turn, be classified as (Casati et al. 1999):

- **Timestamp:** This exception is fired at a given timestamp, like February 19th, 2008 at 4:56 p.m. This means that an internal alarm is set, typically managed by the operating system, and when the current timestamp of the local system reaches the specified deadline, the event is captured. Next, the system will check the condition and, possibly, execute the respective action.
- **Interval based:** This exception is fired when the specified temporal interval elapsed since the occurrence of another event, known as anchor event. Typically, anchor events are the start or completion of a task instance or of a case: thus, the interval based exception is fired after the specified interval elapsed from the start or completion of the task instance or of the case. As an example, we may define a temporal trigger saying that the event is the elapsing of 20 minutes after the start of the task `GetCustomerData`: this trigger can be useful to monitor the duration of the execution of task (or cases), enabling the user to check the status of the task (or of the case) at a temporal interval from the specified anchor.
- **Periodic timestamp:** This exception is fired whenever the periodical temporal condition occurs. As soon as the first occurrence of the periodic timestamp is reached, the trigger is fired and the next occurrence of the same periodic timestamp is evaluated: in this way, the operating system sets up a new alarm, to capture the next occurrence of the timestamp. As an example, we may define a trigger that is fired every day at 6:00 p.m., remembering to all the employees that the working day has ended. We may also define some more complex periodic conditions, by expressing them according to some notation similar to that of Leban et al., 1986.

As an example of a language useful to define and manage exceptions, we consider here the Chimera-Exception language (Casati et al., 1999). This language adopts the ECA paradigm and assumes that data about the process, organizational, and information models are stored by suitable database tables (whose name is quite intuitive).

Example 1: The following trigger is an example of a timestamp trigger. By the `notify` action it sends e-mail messages to the agents that are executing tasks (i.e., the status of the task is "running") on December 25th, 2008 at midnight.

```
define trigger ChristmastDay
   events timestamp("25-Dec-08")
     at 12:00:00 a.m.
   condition task(T),
     agent(A),  A=T.  executor,
```

```
      T.status="running"
    actions notify (T.executor,
       "Merry Christmas")
end
```

Example 2: The following trigger is an example of an interval-based trigger, which assumes that, for every task defined by the process model, a suitable attribute `ExpectedTaskDuration` describes the expected duration for the execution of the task. The anchor event is the workflow event `TaskStart` applied to the task instance `GetCustomerData`. Let us assume that the attribute `ExpectedTaskDuration` assumes the value of "10 minutes". If the execution of the task `GetCustomerData` started on February 19th, 2008 at 1:23 p.m., the trigger is fired on February 19th, 2008 at 1:43 p.m., i.e. exactly 20 minutes after the start of the task. After the trigger is fired, the performed action is that of sending an e-mail to the agent responsible of the case.

```
define trigger slowTaskExecution
  events event1:elapsed (2
    expectedTaskDuration) since
    taskStart("GetCustomerData")
  condition task(T),
          temporalEvent(E),
    occurred (event1, E),
    E.dependsOnTask=T,
  actions notify(T.executor,
    "Slowexecution for task"+
    oIdToString(T))
end
```

Example 3: The following trigger is an example of a periodical trigger, where – as usual - periodicities are expressed according to a notation similar to that of Leban et al., 1986. Everyday at 6.00 p.m. the trigger is fired: all the agents executing tasks which are still running will be sent an e-mail message remembering them to go home (should they need it!).

```
define trigger stopWork
   events [18,18]/hour:during:day
   condition task(T),
           T.status="running"
   actions notify (T.executor,
           "Time to go home!")
   order 10
end
```

Another way of dealing with expected exceptions is that of defining event nodes inside the process model (The Business process Management Notation, 2008). An event node corresponds to an activity that is sensitive to the occurrence of a particular event: such an activity remains silent within the process model till the event occurs. After capturing the event, the event node starts a suitable task to manage that event. Event nodes provide a suitable way to manage asynchronous exceptions, i.e. those exceptions whose time of occurrence is not know at process design time. Event nodes can be as well used to manage temporal exceptions (Casati & Pozzi, 1999).

TEMPORAL SCHEDULING

The scheduler of a WfMS is the component that reads from the process model, selects the next task(s) to be activated, reads from the organizational model, selects the available agents, and couples any task to be activated to the respective executing agent (Chen & Yang, 2008, Liu et al., 2007, Combi & Pozzi, 2006a). The coupling is performed according to the required role (as from the process model) and to the work list of agents, distributing the work load among the several agents.

In order to work suitably, the scheduler must consider the temporalities of the managed information (process model, organizational model, workload balancing). Thus the temporal scheduler must consider the real `Availability` of the agent, as well as the `Unavailability` of the agent, and the *presence* of the agent at task start time: periodical times must be considered, too (Liu et al., 2007, Leban et al. 1986). In fact, if an agent currently is on holiday and he/she will be back to work at time t_{btw}, any task assigned to that agent will remain unserved in the worklist at least till time t_{btw}. Moreover, if the deadline for the completion of the task is $t_{deadline}$, and the following relationship holds

$$t_{btw} + \text{ExpectedTaskDuration} > t_{deadline}$$

the scheduler can know well in advance that the deadline could be missed and the constraint will be violated.

As a further example, consider an agent whose work list includes items according to a `FIFO` priority (Bierbaumer et al., 2005), and the sum of the `ExpectedTaskDuration` for the tasks of that work list is t_{sum}. It is reasonable to assume that any new work item inserted in the list of that agent will be completed within an interval of t_{sum}+ `ExpectedTaskDuration` from the current timestamp.

The temporal scheduler has to consider several aspects, as the expected start time for task execution (i.e. when the selected agent will effectively start the execution), and also the `MaxTaskDuration`, to check whether the availability of the agent may suffice for the completion of the task: if no agent is found, the scheduler considers the `ExpectedTaskDuration`, to estimate whether the considered agent could be able to complete the task within this second duration. In this latter case, we cannot say for sure if the agent will complete the task even in its worst case.

If no agent is available according to the currently owned role or selectable in order to obtain a correct work load distribution, an alternate agent must be found. The main difference of a temporal scheduler with respect to a traditional scheduler is that a temporal scheduler hierarchically escalates the task assignment policy to find the agent whose *past* role is nearest to the currently required role and whose availability complies with the temporal requirements. This search can be easily performed exploiting the temporal database which represents the organizational model as in Figure 4 and Table 3.

The Algorithm

The algorithm for task assignment considers tasks to be assigned and sorts them according to their priority. The priority is evaluated according to the expected deadline, as read from the process model, for completion of the task (a task whose deadline is the nearest comes first) and, secondly, according to the expected duration of the task (a task whose duration is the shortest comes first): in this way, tasks whose deadline for completion is the nearest will be scheduled first.

The task assignment policy considers the selection criteria in the following order: role, effective availability, workload, number of unavailabilities, presence at task start and task completion times.

- **Role:** The selectable agents must own the role defined by the process model.
- **Effective availability:** The selectable agents are those who can complete the task within the specified deadlines, with respect to the effective working time of agents.
- **Workload:** The workload of task executions must be balanced among the agents; agents whose recent history presents a lower workload will be selected first.
- **Number of unavailabilities:** Agents with a lower number of unavailabilities over the expected interval of execution of the task will be selected first.
- **Presence at task start and task completion times:** The selectable agents are those who can guarantee their availability during the expected execution time for the task.

The first check on agents verifies the role of the selectable agent. The second check on agents verifies the temporal availability of the selectable agent: this latter function aims at verifying the real availability of the agent and considers all the involved temporalities. Actually, the algorithm checks whether the selectable agent is available for a span of time that guarantees the completion of the task within the defined constraints: the span of time obtained by considering both the `availability` and the `unavailability` of that agent must be greater than the `MaxTaskDuration` of the task under consideration plus the amount of time required by the agent to execute all the tasks that already are inside the work list of that agent.

In other words, the algorithm checks whether the following property holds for the agent *j*, candidate for the execution of task *k*, and whose work list includes all the *i* tasks:

$$\texttt{effAvailability}_j > \texttt{maxTaskDuration}_k + \sum_{i=1}^{n} \texttt{maxTaskDuration}_i$$

where $\texttt{effAvailability}_j$ (i.e., the effective availability) is a span of time (i.e., a duration) obtained by considering the intervals of availability and unavailability of the agent *j*, within the time constraints for the completion of the task.

If two or more agents are selectable, the scheduler compares the workload of the selectable agents: the task will be assigned to the agents whose work load is the smallest. If two or more agents still share the same workload, the scheduler compares these agents and selects the agent whose available working time is greater if considered over the lifespan of the task. The available working time is evaluated by considering the `availability` and the `unavailability` over the lifespan of the task.

The last check is on the presence of the agents at the expected start and completion times of the tasks; eventually, if two or more agents still persist at the same level, the *head or tail* mechanism is invoked.

If, instead, the function returns no agent available, the best alternative is that of consulting the temporal organizational model to retrieve a substitute agent whose *past* role complies with the role actually required for the task under assignment. If at the end some agents remain as selectable, the scheduler inserts the task in the work list of one of them and completes the assignment.

TEMPORAL ARCHITECTURES FOR WFMSS

In the above of the current chapter, we assumed that the WfMS relies on top of a temporal DBMS. This enables one to have an automatic management of temporal dimensions for stored data (valid time and transaction time), without having to consider an explicit management of VT and TT: queries over the process models can be directly performed as depicted in the section above, e.g., exploiting the STARTS operator of the above query, and the developers of the workflow engine do not need to code very complex queries managing VT and TT. Figure 5.A depicts the architecture of such a WfMS, taking all the advantages from the TDBMS.

If, instead, the adopted DBMS has no facility to manage the temporal dimensions, the developers of the workflow engine must take into account and directly manage VT and TT. The WfMS must include all the required management of temporal aspects, resulting in a more challenging effort. Including the management of temporal aspects means that, for instance, the `STARTS` operator of the above query is not available: the developers must then explicitly code the query by using standard SQL statements. As an example, if we consider the `STARTS` operator of the `SQL` snippet `VALID(WT) STARTS VALID(WF)`, it must be translated saying that the interval of validity of the tuple of the `WorkTask` table must start together with and finish before the interval of validity for the tuple of the `WorkFlow` table. The query must be expressed in SQL in a way like the following, where we assume we have the attributes `BeginValid` and `EndValid`:

```
WT.BeginValid = WF.BeginValid AND
WT.EndValid <= WFEndValid
```

Figure 5.B depicts such a situation.

To the best of our knowledge, no commercial DBMS can be said to be a TDBMS. The architecture of Figure 5.A remains at a pure theoretical level. On the other hand, several efforts have been done in order to enrich the existing atemporal (timeless) DBMSs, empowering them by a suitable temporal layer that emulates the behavior of a TDBMS. We cite here the TimeDB layer (Steiner, 1999), which has been successfully used in the development of the prototype of a temporal WfMS described in (Combi & Pozzi, 2004). The temporal layer of TimeDB can be added to almost any DBMS which provides an ODBC connectivity, resulting in a good compromise in terms of temporal dimension management and of performances.

Figure 5. The Figure describes the several architectures of a generic WfMS exploiting the temporal dimensions of data. The architecture on the left-hand side features a temporal DBMS; the architecture in the middle features a plain (atemporal, or timeless) DBMS, and the temporal features must be embedded and implemented into the WfMS; the architecture on the right-hand side features a temporal layer which interfaces the WfMS to an atemporal (timeless) DBMS and simulates the use of a full-fledged TDBMS.

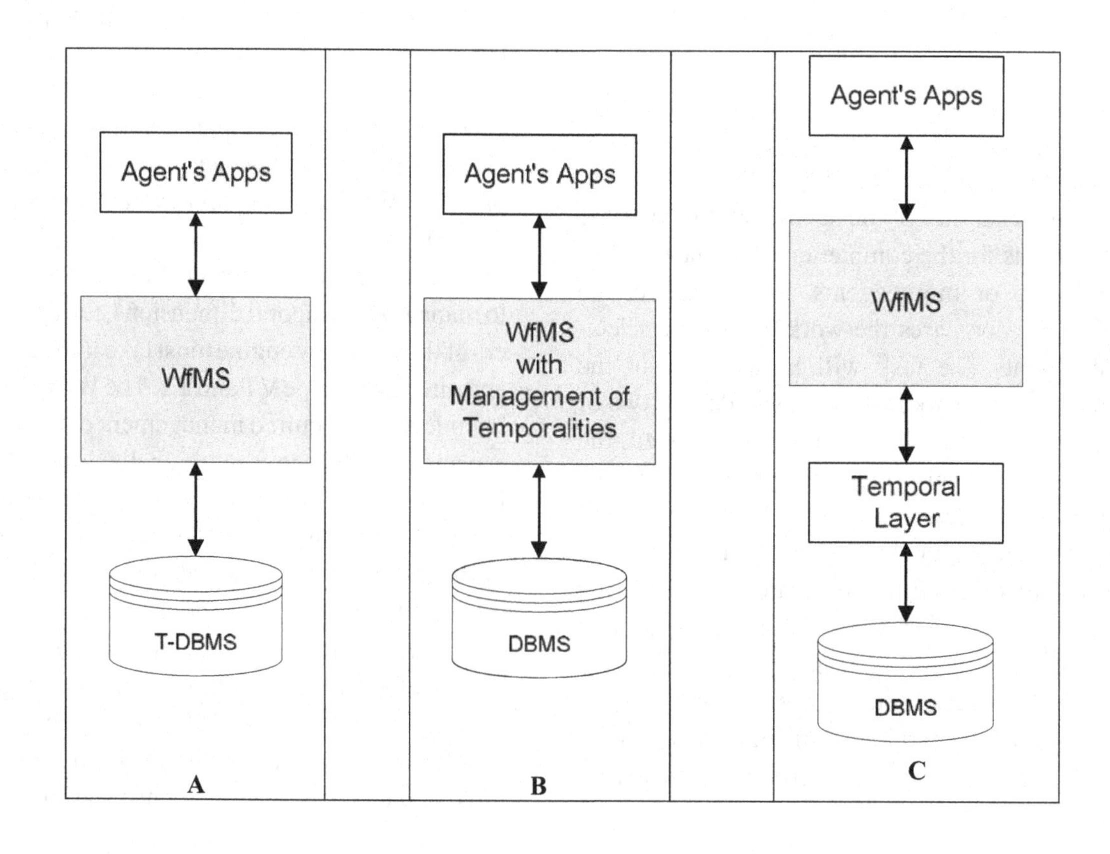

Figure 5.C depicts the architecture achieved by exploiting a temporal layer. If we want any other application to take advantages from the temporal layer, connections to the DBMS must go through such a temporal layer: if, instead, we already have legacy systems which connect to the atemporal DBMS, they will interact directly with the DBMS itself, without taking any advantage form the temporal layer.

CONCLUSION

This chapter considered some of the most important temporal aspects when managing a business process by a WfMS. These aspects influence several components: the workflow models, i.e. the process model, the information model, the organizational model; the exception management unit; the scheduler and its scheduling algorithms and policies; the architecture of the WfMS, which could take several advantages from a proper management of temporalities.

A unified management of temporal data, e.g. by a temporal database management system (TDBMS), could be helpful for all of these components. However, to the best of our knowledge, at present very few DBMSs support facilities to deal with temporal information, and even fewer WfMSs can take advantages from these features.

As future research direction in the area of temporalities for a WfMS, we foresee both more extensions of the models (process model, particularly) to formally consider temporal aspects in a more detailed way, and more powerful underlying software (e.g., DBMS), that could provide suitable tools for the complete management of temporalities. Moreover, we also expect to have more efforts in providing real portability of process definitions and interoperability among several WfMSs, without neglecting the several temporal aspects.

REFERENCES

van der Aalst, W. M. P., & van Hee, K. (2004). *Workflow Management Models, Methods, and Systems*. Boston (MA): MIT Press.

Adlassnig, K. P., Combi, C., Das, A. K., Keravnou, E. T., & Pozzi, G. (2006). Temporal representation and reasoning in medicine: Research directions and challenges. *Artificial Intelligence in Medicine, 38*(2), 101-113.

Bierbaumer, M., Eder, J., & Pichler, H. (2005). Calculation of delay times for workflows with fixed-date constraints. In *Proceedings of the CEC (Conference on E-Commerce Technology)* (pp. 544-547).

The Business Process Modeling Notation, http://www.bpmn.org, accessed April 4th, 2008.

Cardoso, J. (2005). How to measure the control flow complexity for Web processes and workflows. In Layna Fisher (Ed.), *2005 workflow handbook*, (pp. 199-212). Light Point, FL: Future Strategies Inc.

Casati, F., Ceri, S., Pernici, B., & Pozzi, G. (1996a). Deriving production rules for workflow enactment. Database and expert systems applications (pp. 94-115).

Casati, F., Ceri, S., Pernici, B., & Pozzi, G. (1996b). *Workflow evolution*. ER (pp. 438-455).

Casati, F., Ceri, S., Pernici, B., & Pozzi, G. (1998). Workflow evolution. *Int. Journal Data and Knowledge Engineering, 24*(1), 211-239.

Casati F., Ceri S., Paraboschi S., & Pozzi G. (1999). Specification and implementation of exceptions in workflow management systems. *ACM Transactions on Database Systems, 24*(3), 405-451.

Casati, F., & Pozzi, G. (1999). *Modeling exceptional behaviors in commercial workflow management systems*. CoopIS, (pp. 127-138).

Chen, J., & Yang, Y. (2008). *Temporal dependency based checkpoint selection for dynamic verification of fixed-time constraints in grid workflow systems.* ICSE, (pp. 141-150).

Chittaro, L., & Montanari, A. (2000). Temporal representation and reasoning in artificial intelligence: Issues and approaches. *Ann. Math. Artif. Intell., 28*(1-4), 47-106.

Combi, C., & Pozzi, G. (2002). Towards temporal information in workflow systems. *ER Workshops,* (pp. 13-25).

Combi, C., & Pozzi, G. (2003). Temporal conceptual modeling of workflows. *ER,* (pp. 59-76).

Combi, C., & Pozzi, G. (2004). Architectures for a temporal workflow management system. *ACM SAC,* (pp. 659-666).

Combi, C., Daniel, F., & Pozzi, G. (2006). A Portable approach to exception handling in workflow management systems. *OTM Conferences,* (1), 201-218.

Combi, C., & Pozzi, G. (2006a). Task scheduling for a temporal workflow management system. *TIME,* 61-68.

Combi, C., & Pozzi, G. (2006b). Temporal representation and reasoning in medicine. *Artificial Intelligence in Medicine, 38*(2), 97-100.

Combi, C., Gozzi, M., Juàrez, J. M., Oliboni, B., & Pozzi, G. (2007a). Conceptual modeling of temporal clinical workflows. *TIME,* (pp. 70-81).

Combi, C., Montanari, A., & Pozzi, G. (2007b). The T4SQL temporal query language. *CIKM,* (pp. 193-202).

Combi, C., Daniel, F., & Pozzi, G. (2008). XPDL Enabled Cross-Product Exception Handling for WfMSs. In L. Fisher (Ed.), *2008 BPM and workflow handbook.* Light Point, FL: Future Strategies Inc. in collaboration with Workflow Management Coalition.

Eder, J., & Liebhart, W. (1995). The Workflow activity model WAMO. *CoopIS,* (pp. 87–98).

Eder, J., Panagos, E., & Rabinovich, M., (1999). Time constraints in workflow systems. *CAISE,* (pp. 286-300).

Eder, J., & Pichler, H. (2005). Probabilistic calculation of execution intervals for workflows. *TIME,* (pp. 183-185).

Eder, J., Eichner, H., & Pichler, H. (2006a). A Probabilistic approach to reduce the number of deadline violations and the tardiness of workflows. *OTM Workshops,* (1), 5-7.

Eder, J., Pichler, H., & Vielgut, S. (2006b). An architecture for proactive timed Web service compositions. *Business Process Management Workshops,* (pp. 323-335).

Grefen, P., Pernici, B., & Sanchez Gutierez, G. (Eds.), 1999 *Database support for workflow management: The Wide Project.* Dordrecht, The Netherlands: Kluwer Academic Publisher.

Jensen, C., & Snodgrass, R. T. (1999). Temporal data management. *TKDE, 11*(1), 36-44.

Khatri, V., Ram S., & Snodgrass, R. T. (2004). Augmenting a conceptual model with geospatiotemporal annotations. *TKDE, 16*(11), 1324-1338.

Leban, B., McDonald, D., & Forster, D. (1986). A representation for collections of temporal Intervals. *AAAI86,* (pp. 367-371).

Liu, J., Zhou, C., Chen, J., Liu, H., Wen, Y. (2007). A job scheduling optimization model based on time difference in service grid environments. *GCC (Grid and Cooperative Computing),* 283-287.

Liu, J., Zhou, C., & Chen, J. (2008). WdCM: A workday calendar model for workflows in service grid environments. *Concurrency and Computation: Practice and Experience, 20*(4), 377-392.

Marjanovic, O., & Orlowska, M. E. (1999a). On modeling and verification of temporal constraints in production workflows. *Knowl. Inf. Syst., 1*(2), 157-192.

Marjanovic, O., & Orlowska, M. E. (1999b). Time management in dynamic workflows. *CODAS,* (pp. 138-149).

Russell, N., van der Aalst, W. M. P., ter Hofstede, A. H. M., & Wohed, P. (2006). On the suitability of UML 2.0 Activity diagrams for business process modeling. *APCCM (Asia-Pacific Conference on Conceptual Modeling),* (pp. 95-104).

Snodgrass, R. T. (Ed.) (1995). *The TSQL2 Temporal Query Language.* Boston: Kluwer Academic Publisher.

Snodgrass, R. T., & Ahn, I. (1985). A taxonomy of time in databases. *SIGMOD Conference,* (pp. 236-246).

Steiner, A. (1999). TimeDB, Timeconsult. *http://www.timeconsult.com.* accessed April 4th, 2008

Weske, M. (2007). *Business process management: Concepts, languages, architectures.* Berlin, Heidelberg, Germany: Springer-Verlag

KEY TERMS

Conceptual Modeling: A model which describes a part of the real world at a very high level, without considering any implementation issue.

Exception: Any abnormal event which may occur during the execution of a process. Exceptions can deviate the main flow of execution defined for a business process: expected exceptions can be managed by suitably defined exception manager units.

Scheduler: A software module which sorts activities and prepares them for execution according to several criteria, such as the required skill the executor must own, the priority of the activity, the time that activity has already been waiting for to be executed.

Temporal Database Management System (TDBMS): A database and its related database management system (DBMS) which can directly manage temporal dimensions of data, without requiring the developer to manage them explicitly. A TDBMS generally makes available some temporal dimensions such as the valid time and the transaction time.

Temporal Dimension: The temporal aspect, o temporality, of any fact or information. Several temporal dimensions can be defined, such as valid time, describing when the fact or the information is true in the real word, and transaction time, describing when the fact or the information is current in the database management system (DBMS).

Workflow Management System (WfMS) Architecture: A description of the several software modules, and their respective interconnections, which set up a complex software systems, e.g. a workflow management system (WfMS).

EXERCISES

Exercise 1

(This exercise relates to the subsection Temporalities in the Process Model)

Consider the following process. A car rental company receives reservation requests. The task `GetRentalData` collects customer's data and pick-up and return date and place. Next, the task `ChooseCar` specifies the type of car the customer prefers. The task `CheckCarAvailability` queries the database and verifies whether the specified car is available by defining a value for the workflow variable Available: according to the result of the query, the routing task `R1` leads to the task `RejectReservation`, informing the customer about the failure in reserving the car: otherwise, the task `MakeReservation` performs the reservation and the task `Send-`

Confirmation sends the customer a mail with reservation details.

Formally describe the process and map it onto the above defined relational tables, without considering the temporal dimensions VT and TT.

A solution for a situation similar to that in the exercise is available in the paper (Combi & Pozzi, 2002).

Exercise 2

(This exercise relates to the subsection Temporalities in the Process Model)

After having implemented the schema of Exercise 1, consider the following improvement of the same process.

Let us assume that the previous schema was valid since May 24th, 2007. After March 1st, 2008, the CEO of the car rental company proposes to improve the process as follows. If the reservation succeeds, the customer is no longer sent a confirmation: on the other hand, if instead the reservation fails, the customer is informed and an apologizing mail is sent along with some advertising flyers (task SendApologies).

Formally describe the process and map it onto the above defined relational tables, exploiting the management of the temporal dimensions VT and TT.

A solution to a problem similar to the exercise is available in the paper (Combi & Pozzi, 2002).

Exercise 3

(This exercise relates to the subsection Temporalities in the Information Model)

After having implemented the schema of Exercise 2, describe the information model storing information about the customer, the required car, the pick up and return dates, the availability. Enrich the model considering the two temporal dimensions VT and TT

A situation similar to the solution for the exercise is described in the paper (Combi & Pozzi, 2002).

Exercise 4

(This exercise relates to the subsection Temporalities in the Organizational Model)

Extend the table of Table 3 to consider unavailability of agents, preserving the concepts expressed by the ER diagram of Figure 4 (as answers, take a look at the paper of Combi & Pozzi,2006a); Extend the organizational model of Figure 3, considering the relationships (and their related temporalities) between Actor, Function, Team, Group and Role.

A solution of the exercise is available in the paper (Combi & Pozzi, 2006a).

Exercise 5

(This exercise relates to the subsection Temporalities in Expected Exceptions)

Consider the trigger of Example 2. Find a way on how to map that trigger, i.e., obtain a behavior similar to that achievable by the trigger, in a WfMS that has no exception management unit. Hint: the only way is that of introducing suitable tasks inside the process model, each task monitoring a specific event.

Suggestions for the solution of the exercise could be found in the paper (Casati & Pozzi, 1999).

Exercise 6

(This exercise relates to the subsection Temporal Scheduling)

With reference to the described scheduling algorithm, describe it by a pseudo code, basing the description on the tables of Table 3.

Suggestions for the solution of the exercise can be found in the paper (Combi &Pozzi, 2006a).

Exercise 7

(This exercise relates to the subsection Temporal Architectures for WfMSs)

Discuss pros and cons of extending the described architectures to consider active DBMSs, i.e., database systems having some active behaviour through triggers.

Some suggestions for the solution of the exercise could be found in the paper (Combi & Pozzi, 2004).

SUGGESTED ADDITIONAL READINGS

Suggested additional readings are classified according to the subsections of the current chapter they refer to.

Temporalities in the Process Model

The papers (Snodgrass, 1995) and (Jensens and Snodgrass, 1999) contain full details about the management of temporal information by a DBMS and the temporal query language TSQL2, which extends SQL to manage temporal dimensions.

The paper (Combi & Popzzi, 2002) contains a comprehensive description of some temporal aspects which are relevant for WfMSs. Further details concerning the definition of constraints over groups of tasks, constraint monitoring, and a more detailed description of the state of the art can be found in (Combi & Pozzi, 2003, Casati et al, 1999).

An example of use of conceptual modeling on a real application domain can be found in (Combi et al., 2007a).

Beyond the above methodology, workflow processes can also be modeled by Petri's nets. Additional readings can be found in (van der Aalst & van Hee, 2004).

Temporalities in the Organizational Model

More details concerning some topics about unavailability and the notation for periodic events can be found in (Combi & Pozzi, 2006a, Liu et al, 2008).

Temporalities in Expected Exceptions

The interested reader can find details about the Chimera-Exception language in (Casati et al., 1999), about the mapping of the triggers on top of commercially available WfMSs in (Casati & Pozzi, 1999, Combi et al., 2006, Combi et al., 2008).

Furthermore, information about the evaluation of the complexity of a schema can be found in (Cardoso, 2005): this suggests a way on how to measure the incremental complexity of the schema itself, as introduced by the mapping of exception as defined in (Casati & Pozzi, 1999).

Temporal Scheduling

Further details about scheduling policies in a temporal WfMS are available in (Combi & Pozzi, 2006a, Bierbaumer et al., 2005, Eder & Pichler, 2005). The paper (Eder et al., 2006a) describes the usage of such policies for Web service composition.

Temporal Architectures for WfMSs

Further details about the temporal architectures of a WfMS, also including some practical aspects of Java programming, are available in (Combi & Pozzi, 2004).

Other related architectural issues can be found in (Eder et al., 2006b).

Chapter XIII
The People Integration Challenge

Karsten Ploesser
SAP Research CEC, Australia

Nick Russell
Technische Universiteit Eindhoven, The Netherlands

ABSTRACT

This chapter discusses the challenges associated with integrating work performed by human agents into automated workflows. It briefly recounts the evolution of business process support systems and concludes that although the support for people integration continues to evolve in these offerings, in broad terms it has not advanced markedly since their inception several decades ago. Nevertheless, people are an integral part of business processes and integration of human work deserves special consideration during process design and deployment. To this end, the chapter explores the requirements associated with modelling human integration and examines the support for people integration offered by WS-BPEL, which (together with its WS-BPEL4People and WS-HumanTask extensions) currently represents the state of the art when defining and implementing business processes in a service-oriented environment. In order to do this, it utilises a common framework for language assessment, the workflow resource patterns, both to illustrate the capabilities of WS-BPEL and to identify future technical opportunities.

INTRODUCTION

Processes don't do work, people do.– John Seely Brown, Former Chief Scientist, Xerox

Inspired by the work of Hammer and others (Hammer and Champy, 1993; Davenport, 1993) on business process reengineering, modern corporations are increasingly adopting process-orientation and Business Process Management (BPM), as the fundamental rationale for structuring and managing their organisations. Integrating people both within and outside of the organisation into the enactment of these business processes is a crucial aspect of BPM. This trend coincides with the service enablement of enterprise systems, an architectural approach commonly referred to as the Service-oriented Architecture (SOA). While techniques for the composition and orchestration of enterprise services have considerably advanced in recent years, the challenge of integrating people into these automated processes has mostly been overlooked.

This applies in particular to service orchestration languages such as the Web Service Business Process Execution Language (Alves et al. 2007). While WS-BPEL promises easy integration of enterprise systems exposed via Web Services, it initially did not accommodate human-performed activities, an issue later remedied by two language extensions, WS-BPEL Extension for People (Agrawal et al. 2007a) and Web Services Human Task (Agrawal et al. 2007b). The purpose of this chapter is to provide a compelling case for people integration. It examines the common requirements and challenges of people integration documented in the literature. Given the priority of service enablement on the agenda of organisations, it proceeds to assess the capability of web service technology to effectively deal with people integration in a manner which is generically applicable.

Furthermore, we will explore the reasons why people integration deserves special consideration during business process design. Process-orientation and the division of labour have led to a high degree of specialisation in the individuals that make up an organisation. It is of paramount importance that in this context, the individual units of work that are part of a business process are routed to the right individual such that they can be executed on a timely and efficient basis. Indeed, many commercial systems have not markedly advanced in their support of the wide range of ways in which humans may wish or be required to interact with a business process. To this end, we will discuss patterns frequently observed in people-centric business processes and the implications of these when modelling human integration. On a general level, these encompass patterns observed in Process-aware Information Systems (PAIS) such as case handling, delegation, escalation and reallocation. Recent research has led to the classification of these requirements into a comprehensive catalogue of *resource patterns*.

From an industry perspective, WS-BPEL4People and WS-HumanTask constitute the state of the art in regard to people integration in a service-enabled environment. Although the specifications target a particular application domain, namely Web Services, they provide insights into the general, technological challenges of integrating people into automated business processes and provide a basis for an assessment of contemporary systems. We will examine the lessons that have been learnt in this area and explore the recent architectural and technological challenges associated with integrating human resources in automated business process solutions. In this light, the section introduces and discusses concepts underpinning WS-BPEL4People and WS-HumanTask. We conclude by giving an outlook on future challenges for people-centric process management that go beyond the technical integration of human tasks and put forward several recommendations that may help to improve the way humans interact with automated processes in the future.

THE CASE FOR PEOPLE INTEGRATION

The notion of the business process can be traced back to the Industrial Revolution when the advent of large-scale mechanisation allowed many processes that were previously conducted on an individual basis by hand to be done in bulk by machine. In doing so, processes that had previously been conducted from beginning to end under the auspices of a single person were now undertaken as a series of repetitive tasks, each of which was carried out by a different individual. As a consequence, workers changed from being generalists to specialists, and the process itself rather than an individual resource, became the means of coordinating the sequence of activities leading to the desired production outcome.

These concepts were formalised by Frederick Taylor (Taylor, 1911) as part of his *scientific management* approach which advocated a more rigorous approach to defining and conducting business processes. Key themes of this work included the establishment of rules and procedures to ensure that process outcomes were predictable, the division of large-scale processes into a sequence of individual activities, the identification of the *standard method* denoting the best way to undertake each activity based on detailed study of various possible approaches, the matching of individual workers to activities based on ability and the recording of statistics about the conduct of a process to provide a scientific basis for further refinement.

These concepts have been extremely influential in modern management theory and have characterised the contemporary notion of the business process and its operation. One of the most significant criticisms of scientific management was that it did not consider the potential opportunities that might result from the application of technology to a business process. This view was challenged in the early nineties, when it was recognised that disruptive technologies, especially information technology, actually created new possibilities for conducting business processes. Indeed, rather than simply using technology to automate existing processes, figures such as Hammer and Champy (Hammer and Champy, 1993) advocated the notion of *business process redesign*, where technology was actively utilised as a means of radically changing existing processes in order to eliminate non-productive work and "achieve dramatic improvements in critical contemporary measures of performance, such as cost, quality, service, and speed".

One of the key drivers for these changes was the emergence of configurable technology to support complex, cross-organisational business processes involving multiple resources. Commonly known as workflow systems, this technology had its genesis in early research efforts to automate office activities and had some early successes in specific application domains such as document management and image transport that involved the trafficking of complex information between various parties. By the early nineties, it was available in various configurable forms ranging from groupware that supported unstructured interactions between a group of individuals relating to a specific objective, through to production workflow systems that facilitated high volume, repetitive processes involving multiple activities in accordance with a strictly enforced process model. One of the fundamental commonalities across all of these forms of the technology was the fact that it involved the coordination of a series of activities in conjunction with a group of human resources who actually undertook the associated work requirements.

The rise of workflow technology also triggered a concomitant rise in the use of business process modelling notations as a means of documenting business process requirements. Many of these notations had their roots in process modelling and consequently focused on the control-flow aspects of process execution, describing the individual activities making up a business process and the manner in which the thread of control should be routed between them. Over time there has been significant convergence of modelling approaches and Event-driven Process Chains (Keller, Nüttgens, and Scheer, 1992), the Business Process Modeling Notation (Object Management Group/ Business Process Management Initiative [OMG/ BPMI], 2006), and UML Activity Diagrams (OMG, 2005) have emerged as the forerunners in this domain and are widely used for describing business processes.

These modelling notations operate at a conceptual level and do not focus on defining a business process in sufficient detail that it can be directly executed. In an effort to establish a common language that would support the interchange of workflow specifications between distinct offerings, the WfMC proposed the XML Process Definition Language (XPDL) (Workflow Management Coalition, 2002). However the need to integrate a wide variety of offerings with fundamentally different conceptual and technological underpinnings ultimately resulted in the initial version of XPDL becoming the lowest common denominator between systems rather than the Tower of Babel it had initially promised to be.

In recognition of the enormity of the task, the subsequent version of XPDL 2.0 (Workflow Management Coalition, 2005) took the form of an XML serialization of BPMN. In neither case, was a precise definition of the various language constructs provided hence there remain ambiguities in how specific language elements should be interpreted in an operational context. Moreover, the XPDL initiatives have only had a cursory impact on the workflow execution languages used in practice, and these continue to differ in both format and content for individual workflow offerings.

With the advent of the service-oriented architecture, WS-BPEL, which operates in the context of a distributed web services environment, has come to the fore as a first step toward a standard execution language and it is achieving relatively broad acceptance by vendors, however like the current modelling notations, it too tends to focus on control-flow and (to a lesser degree) data issues.

The question of what factors should be captured when defining a business process is now something that is increasingly open to debate. A good description of a business process is provided by Pall (Pall, 1987) who defines it as "the logical organization of people, materials, energy, equipment, and procedures into work activities designed to produce a specified end result (work product)". Implicit in this definition is the proposition that business processes involve the coordination of factors in a number of distinct perspectives. One area that does give some guidance to these factors is that of *enterprise modelling* or *business modelling*. These disciplines focus on providing comprehensive descriptions of business enterprises and include consideration of the processes that operate within individual organisations. The table below gives an indication of the range of perspectives that three common business/enterprise modelling techniques consider.

Table 1. Perspectives in common enterprise modelling techniques

CIMOSA (Vernadat, 1996)	**Zachman** (Zachman, 1987)	**ARIS** (Scheer, 2000)
Function	Function	Function
Information	Schedule	Control
Resource	Data	Data
Organization	Organization	Organization
	Network	
	Strategy	

It is clear that for each of these techniques, in addition to control-flow and data considerations, the organizational or resource perspective plays a major role. Moreover, when we consider the majority of contemporary workflow systems, it's evident that the definition of an executable process includes the necessity not only to specify control-flow and data-flow but also to describe how the resultant work activities will be routed to individual resources. This observation is consistent with the historical development of the concept of a business process which fundamentally centres on the coordination of a group of human resources and materials in order to deliver a specific production outcome.

FROM WORKFLOW TO SERVICE ORCHESTRATION

Process support technology has been discussed in the scientific community and industry as early as the 1970's. While production planning and control systems led to huge productivity gains in manufacturing processes, office workers did not achieve the same increases in productivity despite the large scale deployment of information technology. Inspired by the manufacturing successes, several research projects studied the application of process technology to office environments. Most early process support technologies focused on specific application verticals such as image management or work group support. These concepts eventually evolved into workflow management. Indeed, Jablonski et al. point out office automation, database management, and document management as the conceptual ancestors of workflow management (Jablonksi and Bussler, 1996). Over the past decade, academic research as well as commercial development of workflow management and related technologies has established a plethora of automation options. Many of the initial challenges of office automation remain valid to this day: in particular the challenge of integrating people into automated work procedures in an efficient and non-obtrusive way. In the following section, we will briefly recount the more recent history of process support technology and discuss whether these technologies provide adequate support for human integration.

Increasingly widespread interest in workflow management solutions motivated business software vendors to integrate this technology into their business applications. Workflow environments typically shipped as part of larger offerings, such as enterprise resource planning (ERP) software. They enabled the extension and adaptation of the highly standardised business processes encoded in an ERP system to the specific requirements of an organisation. The main focus of workflow was sequencing repetitive activities and managing the document flow of a typical office environment, for example in payroll and leave management processes. This was typically motivated by larger initiatives in the areas of business process definition and conformance. Workflow technology helped drive down lead time and fostered increased transparency of work procedures through performance measurement. However, workflow management systems were frequently criticised for being inflexible and constraining in many situations. Rather than empowering the knowledge worker in clerical work, rigid process structures and the inability to deal with out-of-band situations presented serious limitations.

The widespread adoption of ERP systems led to the emergence of new classes of enterprise applications such as customer relationship (CRM) and supply chain management (SCM). These applications extended the reach of business software beyond that of back office automation as introduced by ERP into more significant areas that were increasingly cross-organisational in focus. Moreover these deployments often integrated applications from differing functional area, in contrast to previous systems, which were generally limited to a single application area. As a consequence, these systems required extensive integration with other systems not only within a single organisation but also across multiple organisations. Process technology in this context was mainly concerned with enterprise application integration (EAI). EAI middleware architectures utilised process technology to orchestrate business functions across applications, but did not provide any support for human integration. Only much later did the question arise as to how workflows embedded in local business applications could be connected through EAI middleware.

The advent of Web Services technology marked the beginning of a paradigm shift towards a *service-oriented architecture* (SOA). At its core, SOA promises reuse, interoperability and composition of enterprise application assets based on the use of standardised protocols and interface description languages. The common technological layer lowers the cost of integration and facilitates the consumption of enterprise services. But can it help connect individual business activities into business processes? Several proposals have been put forward, most notably the Business Process Modeling Language (BPML) backed by the Business Process Management Initiative, IBM's Web Services Flow Language (WSFL), and the orchestration language underlying Microsoft's BizTalk server (XLANG). The latter two proposals were subsequently merged into the Web Service Business Process Execution Language (WS-BPEL) and submitted to the standards body OASIS[1] for ratification. Essentially, WS-BPEL allows the orchestration of business activities to be wrapped as Web Services. In its initial version, WS-BPEL did not contain support for human integration, an omission that marked it apart from other process technologies which incorporated a modicum of support for human resources in the conduct of business processes. However, this situation has been remedied by the recent extensions WS-BPEL Extension for People (WS-BPEL4People) and Web Service Human Task (WS-HumanTask). The capacity to seamlessly combine both application systems as well as humans through a common Web Service layer provides a powerful integration framework for the implementation of workflows in a service-enabled environment.

MODELLING THE HUMAN PROCESS INTERFACE

Although human work is an integral part of business process design, modelling the complex interactions between humans that result from the division of labour in large organisations has received relatively little attention. Traditionally, the focus of business process modelling has been the description of the routing or *flow* of work in a business process. This is commonly referred to as the *control-flow* perspective of process modelling. Flowcharts that describe task routing often serve as a first draft design, but additional layers of information are needed to fully document and potentially automate the workflow. Thus most process modelling languages support other perspectives in addition to the control-flow perspective that for instance allow the specification of the flow of data (and documents) in the business process and the assignment of tasks to organisational units (cf. Table 1). In fact, several prominent process modelling notations provide artefacts to integrate organisational entities and specify the resources a business process requires to achieve its prescribed outcome. This information is commonly used for the purpose of process documentation and dissemination of process manuals as well as for cost analysis based on practices such as activity-based costing.

In flowcharting languages such as UML Activity Diagrams (OMG, 2005) and Business Process Modelling Notation (OMG/BPMI, 2006), organisational responsibility is generally depicted by *swimlanes*. These are referred to as *partitions* in UML ADs and *pools* and *lanes* in BPMN. Swimlanes can be decomposed into subdivisions to specify responsibility on an actor level. In BPMN, pools typically represent an organisational unit. Lanes can be used as subdivisions and refer to roles or a specific individual within the organisational unit. By placing tasks into pools or lanes, one can specify the allocation of tasks to the respective organisational entity. A similar approach is supported by UML ADs. Event-driven process chains (Keller et al., 1992) is another example of a notation widely used in the business process modelling community. In EPCs, roles and resources are denoted by a special symbol that can be attached to any task. One may thus annotate who assumes responsibility for a particular unit of work at task level.

Although the notation proposed by UML ADs, BPMN, and EPCs provides sufficient support for the static, direct assignment of units of work to organisational entities, it falls short of capturing the dynamics and constraints of a real world business environment. This is of particular importance if the process model should later on serve as a blueprint for process automation. While this chapter deals mainly with notational expressiveness required to model human-centric business processes, the interested reader may refer to the respective chapters in this book that deal with runtime issues such as scheduling in workflow systems. In a business process, allocations must often be resolved in the context of a concrete case. Furthermore, static assignment cannot describe constraints between tasks in a given case. The broad range of situations that arise when describing resources and work distribution in the context of PAIS have been the subject of significant research. Most notably, Russell et al. (2005) have developed a comprehensive classification of these requirements in the form of a catalogue of *resource patterns*.

Distribution or *creation* patterns deal with the assignment of work items to organisational resources. In general, creation patterns express the potential range of actors able to perform a unit of work in a given workflow case. Role-based allocation is one of the most widely supported patterns. This approach to work distribution is commonly utilised in the process modelling notations discussed earlier. Roles are introduced as an indirection mechanism for task distribution. The concept of roles allows the definition of the specific population to whom a task might be assigned to be deferred to runtime. Thus, one avoids issues such as continual changes to a process model in case of employee turnover. Often business requirements demand far more complex workflow models. Common examples of such scenarios include case handling and separation of duties.

Case handling assigns all work items within a workflow case to the same actor in order to maximise work efficiency. It is often applied on the basis that the group of tasks which make up the process are so interrelated that they are most effectively executed under the auspices of a single individual.

Separation of duty is a quintessential control mechanism typically employed in environments that demand high levels of security and accountability. In its most basic form, it excludes the agent of one task from executing another, related task. By way of example, an applicant for a line of credit would obviously be excluded from its approval. Separation of duty scenarios can often not solely be defined on the basis of workflow case data, but might require data from other cases of the same type if not all related cases running in an organisation. In summary, business process execution languages need to be able to support the dynamic and flexible evaluation of work assignments based on current as well as historic data. Furthermore they should be capable of expressing the interdependencies between tasks and enforcing the necessary associated constraints.

Push, pull and visibility patterns describe how human participants gain awareness of work items assigned to them and the level of visibility a task has among a group of users. Work distribution can be either user-initiated, i.e. a user actively pulls the latest work items assigned to them from the process engine, or proactively pushed to them by the process engine in accordance with a distribution algorithm for the purpose of workload balancing.

Detour patterns describe situations where the resource to which a task is assigned actively seeks to vary how the task is performed (or who it is performed by) from the approach prescribed in the process model. Common examples of this include personal task management methods such as suspending and skipping. Resources may involve others in finding a solution through forwarding tasks, defining substitutes in the event of annual leave or requesting clarifications from the task initiator or previous processors of the task. They may choose to delegate work in order to balance their workload or manage the late assignment of tasks. These patterns are generally not encoded at workflow type level but are case-specific. However, they should be supported by the process or task execution environment. Business process execution languages should furthermore provide the ability to disable certain features for security reasons.

SERVICE-ENABLING HUMAN TASKS

Information systems in real world environments are seldom homogenous from a technological point of view. On the contrary, it is generally the case that a plethora of technologies and protocols need to be integrated in accordance with an organisation's business requirements. It is the principal objective of standardisation to achieve interoperability and portability across diverse components. In recent years, several standards initiatives such as the Workflow Management Coalition[2] (WfMC) aimed to provide standards for workflow management systems, but paid little attention to the specific requirements of people integration in heterogeneous environments. This section builds on the discussion of the principal requirements of people integration in the section on modelling the *human process interface*. In this section, we will investigate the issues inherent to people integration in heterogeneous environments by looking at two industry standardisation efforts as a concrete example. Conceptual gaps found in these efforts are then addressed in the next section dedicated to potential further enhancements.

The WS-BPEL standard initiative has achieved broad mindshare by industry stakeholders and practitioners as it specifies both a language and execution environment for distributed business processes. It is mostly used for the orchestration and composition of Web Services in large-scale, distributed environments and is now widely supported in the business process tool chains of principal IT vendors. Its success notwithstanding, core WS-BPEL failed to address several key requirements in business processes. In particular it did not provide support for human tasks as first class citizens or the componentisation of processes by means of subprocesses. Recent language extensions to the WS-BPEL standards family (of which WS-BPEL4People and WS-HumanTask are arguably the most important) have largely remedied these difficulties. The modelling and automation of business processes coincides with a general trend in organisations towards reuse and componentisation of existing IT assets through Web Service technology and service-oriented architectures (SOA). In fact, SOA has evolved into a mainstream development approach supporting the lightweight assembly of business processes from a pool of service-enabled components.

WS-BPEL4People and WS-HumanTask introduce the concepts of people activity and human task to standardise the automated creation of human tasks by WS-BPEL processes and the allocation of such tasks to resources in the organisation. Furthermore, WS-HumanTask specifies a number of operations for client applications to provide access to and manipulation of business tasks by human users. One of the fundamental differences in WS-HumanTask when compared with traditional approaches to Web Services is that it assumes that tasks are stateful entities.

This is in line with more recent approaches that try to enable stateful Web Service invocation by keeping the service definition and state information separate[3]. On this basis, there are two distinct strategies for the service-enablement of tasks. One corresponds to the traditional notion of stateless service invocation and involves the definition of a task manager interface responsible for controlling the lifecycle of tasks. The other approach is based on the idea of stateful invocation and allows the specification of dedicated task interfaces for each task type, e.g. a dedicated purchasing or voting task interface as opposed to a generic task manager interface.

The benefit of utilising a task manager interface is that no extensions to the underlying process language and Web Service stack are required. Lifecycle functions can be invoked through regular WS-BPEL invoke statements. A clear disadvantage is that this multiplies the number of invoke and receive statements required to actually control the lifecycle. Consequently, process definitions tend to become verbose and bloated with technical statements that are difficult to maintain and extend in the future. Exposing tasks through Web Service wrappers and providing a dedicated activity to control the lifecycle results in more concise process definitions and allows for a tight coupling of process and task. WS-BPEL4People adopts this approach and introduces a people activity based on the WS-BPEL 2.0 extension mechanism and a coordination protocol for handling lifecycle messages which can be negotiated through WS-Policy. The downside of the latter approach is that it creates dependencies on other layers in the Web Service stack such as WS-Policy.

Architectural Constellations

The separation of the people activity and human task concepts discussed in the previous section was undertaken for a number of reasons. First, business task management and process management are often considered as separate technological components. Many business applications and groupware products come with business task support, but do not have an explicit notion of process management. Through the separation of processes and tasks and the service-enablement of the latter, an organisation may leverage its existing IT assets. Another consideration is the reuse of task definitions across several process defini-

Figure 1. Alternative constellations of processes and task in WS-BPEL4People

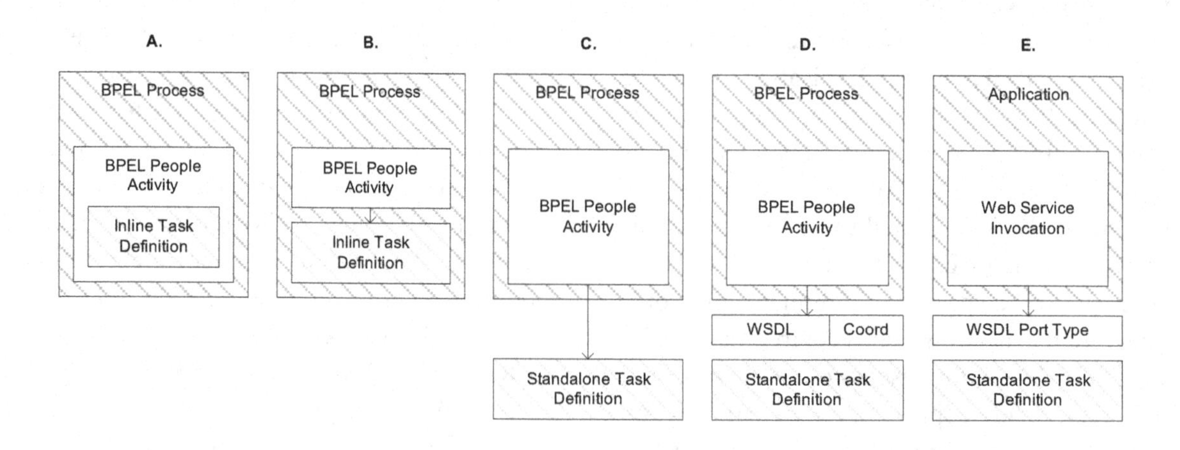

tions. Tasks often have fairly generic attributes that makes them suitable candidates for reuse. For example, a purchasing task may often be required in more than one process within an organisation. Both specifications have a dedicated section in which this rationale and the ensuing technical considerations are discussed, albeit from slightly different viewpoints. All in all, WS-BPEL4People introduces four distinct architectural approaches to people integration. This is complemented by a fifth scenario in WS-HumanTask targeted at utilising standalone tasks in the context of Web Service enabled applications. The constellations are illustrated in Figure 1 and will be explained in more detail in the following paragraphs.

- Embedding a task in an activity
- Definition of a task at scope or process level,
- Integration of stand-alone tasks through proprietary protocols at runtime,
- Integration of stand-alone tasks through a standardised coordination protocol
- Usage of tasks external to processes, e.g. through generic Web Service clients

The specifications refer to tasks in constellations A and B as *inline tasks*. This has two implications. On the one hand, the tooling environment will store the task definition with the process model. As a result, the task definition cannot be reused in other process models. However, this allows tasks to reference data elements defined in the process model, or more precisely the immediate scope. References to data are recursive, i.e. expressions in the task definition may refer to variables in the surrounding as well as parent scopes. On the other hand, these tasks are considered to be invoked in the same runtime environment as the process itself, i.e. task management is embedded in the workflow runtime. Thus, interoperability concerns do not play a role.

At design time, constellation C supports the specification of tasks in a separate definition and references them from a people activity, thus enabling reuse across several process models. Constellation C is similar to A and B to the extent that tasks are invoked through a proprietary protocol. This allows for the coupling of separate workflow runtime and task management components of the same vendor. From a standards point of view, it is irrelevant whether the workflow runtime and task management component are embedded or coupled by means of a proprietary protocol, as interoperability across vendors is not a key concern.

Constellation D ultimately enables full reuse of tasks both at design time and runtime. Similar to constellation C, tasks can be specified as part of a separate definition and then deployed into task management environments separate to the workflow execution environment. Accordingly, this constellation supports architectures with workflow and task management components from different vendors supporting WS-BPEL4People and WS-HumanTask. For instance, this allows the integration of legacy task management systems into business processes via a WS-HumanTask wrapper. At runtime, the lifecycle of tasks is coupled with that of the process through a standardised Web Service coordination protocol. As a result, the constellation fully satisfies the criteria of portability and interoperability.

Through the service-enablement of human tasks, it is conceivable that processes may not only orchestrate tasks, but that they may also be invoked by a regular Web Service client. Constellation E is not explicitly mentioned alongside the other constellations, but is implicitly described in the WS-HumanTask specification. It describes two scenarios integrating tasks into regular applications in a service-enabled environment. A loosely coupled integration with coordination protocol agnostic applications is achieved through regular Web Service invocation of the task. If tight lifecycle integration is required, applications must negotiate the coordination protocol with the task component.

The WS-HumanTask Lifecycle Model

As outlined before, one of the key standardisation concerns in heterogeneous, distributed environments is the compatibility of design, deployment, and runtime artifacts in a scenario. The concept of interoperability requires that every component participating in a scenario must exhibit a steady, observable behaviour and needs to adhere to mutually agreed communication protocols in order to seamlessly integrate with its peers. Of similar importance is the concept of portability. Portability demands that definitions produced in one tooling environment can be read and correctly deployed in another environment. Both concepts can be understood as the common denominator for a range of possible implementation strategies and often standards allow vendor specific extensions through well-defined extension points. In this section, we will look primarily at the common task lifecycle model put forward by the WS-HumanTask specification (illustrated in Figure 2), which plays a pivotal role in facilitating interoperability between process and task engines. A detailed discussion of the WS-HumanTask task metamodel can be found in the work of Russell et al. (2008).

A task lifecycle model describes the states that discrete work items transition through during the course of task execution. In general, every task management implementation provides a task lifecycle model to manage the states of individual work items. Perhaps the most widely referenced definitions of process and activity instance lifecycles are those proposed in the WfMC Reference Model (Workflow Management Coalition (1995)). In the academic literature, Russell et al. (2005) provide a comprehensive discussion of the states required in a task lifecycle model. Each transition may enable or disable a set of actions and thus restrict what users may do with a task in a given situation. Furthermore, the lifecycle model defines initial and valid final states. Thus regardless of whether a task is actually a legacy helpdesk application wrapped by WS-HumanTask or a business task infrastructure, the task will always exhibit a common observable behaviour. The specification distinguishes between the normal processing of a task and deviations from the normal course of actions instigated by events in the business environment. This results in different interactions between the requesting application, typically a WS-BPEL process engine requesting task creation, the task infrastructure, and client applications such as a task list client. The task instance lifecycle is synchronised with the people activity lifecycle in the requesting application through a coordination protocol and protocol handlers standardised by WS-HumanTask. The protocol enables overriding of certain attributes, passing of context data and synchronisation of the principal initial and final states.

From the perspective of a WS-HumanTask aware *requesting application*, the task commences in an initial state and transitions either to the principal final state *Completed* (successful completion) or *Failed* (unsuccessful completion). Deviations from the normal course of action can lead to three alternative final states. The *Error* state is set in case an unrecoverable technical error forces the task environment to prematurely terminate task execution. This is considered to be an unsuccessful outcome of task execution and no result is returned. The task transitions into the state *Exited* if the task environment was notified by the requesting application to immediately terminate task execution. In general, the termination of a process instance entails the termination of all task instances it requested. The state *Obsolete* is reached when the executor of the task decides to skip it, e.g. because outcomes of the task are no longer relevant in the enclosing case. The task is considered to have "successfully" completed, but an empty result message is returned to the requesting application. Note that the task can only be skipped if its definition explicitly enables this feature.

From the perspective of a WS-HumanTask aware *task environment*, normal processing commences when a request for the creation of the task is received. This request may override certain attributes of the task, such as the potential owners and priority of the task. Once the potential owners, priority and other task properties are resolved, the task transitions to the *Created* state. The task will remain in this state until the activation deadline, if specified, is reached. It then proceeds to the state *Ready*, implying that the task is ready for processing. Tasks with exactly one potential owner however are immediately tunnelled to the *Reserved* state. In all other cases, a member of the potential owners set will need to claim the task, to set it to *Reserved.* This state prevents other potential owners from claiming the task, by assigning the user who claimed the task as its actual owner. The user can now work on the task, transitioning it to the state *In Progress* at a time of their choosing. Ultimately, the user will reach an outcome of the unit of work, which may be either successful or unsuccessful. Depending on the user decision, the task either transitions to the final state *Completed* or *Failed* to indicate a successful or unsuccessful conclusion of the task.

Several deviations from the normal course of action are specified by WS-HumanTask. If during instantiation of the task the resolution of people assignments fails, the task would permanently remain in state *Created.* In such situations, a business administrator can be asked to nominate potential owners, transitioning the task to state *Ready.* Note that WS-HumanTask requires compliant implementations to ensure the assignment of at least one person to the business administrator role during runtime. Furthermore, the operations

Figure 2. Task lifecycle model of WS-HumanTask

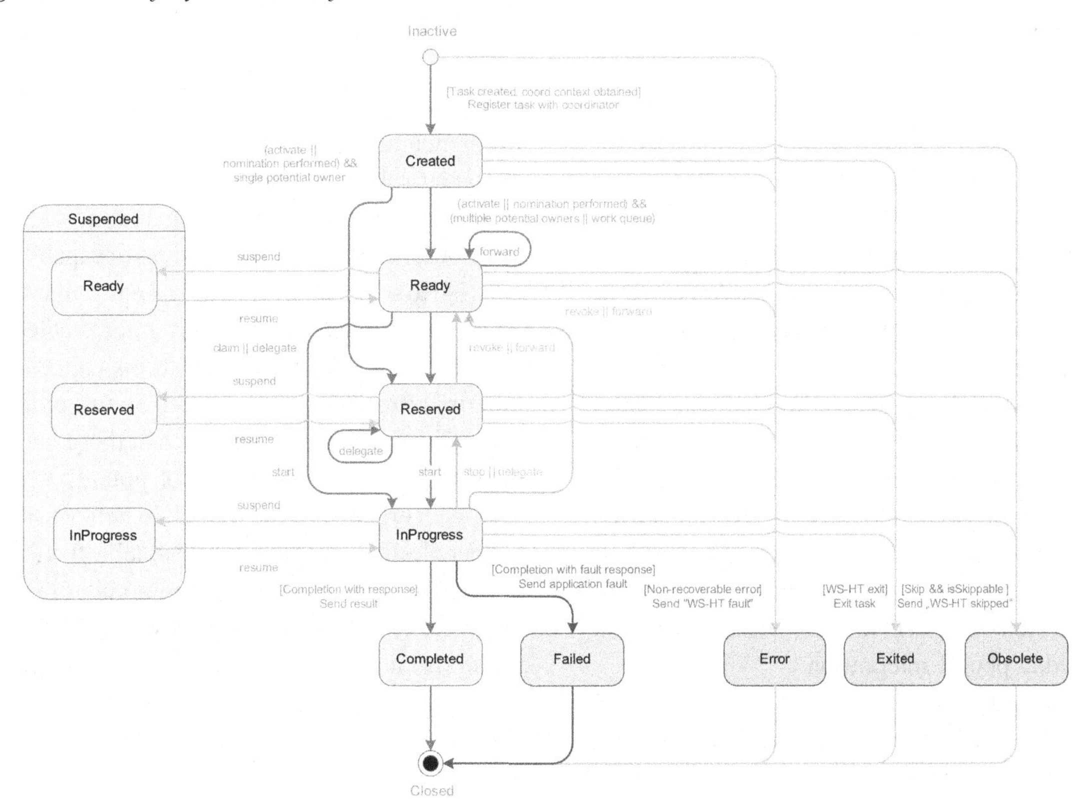

of delegation and releasing entail state transitions from an active state to the *Reserved* state in the former case and from an active state to the *Ready* state in the latter case. If in an active state, a task may be suspended and subsequently resumed.

Suspension of a task is considered to be motivated by business reasons, e.g. a customer files bankruptcy while a sales order is still in process. As per WS-HumanTask, a task may transition into the complex state *Suspended* from any of the active states. The substates *Suspended.Ready*, *Supended.Reserved*, and *Suspended.InProgress* reflect the original state in which the task was suspended. As outlined before, skipping a task sends it automatically to the final state *Obsolete*, assuming that task completion was "successful" because the task outcome is no longer required.

Roles and Role Resolution

A workflow is of little use unless one specifies how the tasks it prescribes are to be enacted by resources. So what exactly are resources? In the context of workflow management, a resource is generally considered to be an actor performing a distinct unit of work, i.e. a task. The allocation of a task to resources is dynamic, as we will outline further into the section. Resources may be characterised as *human*, e.g. specialists performing a unit of work that demands certain skills, or *non-human*, e.g. equipment required to produce a certain artefact. We will focus on human resources in the following as knowledge of their behaviour has practical implications on the design of workflows. Human resources are generally members of organisations. In the remainder of this section, we relate the notion of a resource in workflow management to concepts derived from the practice of organisational modelling and discuss their support in the WS-BPEL extensions targeted at people integration.

Effectively, an organisation forms the pool from which the executor of a task can be selected. Organisations are typically structured in an organic fashion, forming a number of organisational units, with each unit potentially comprising several units of smaller size. A unit is made up of positions, that are responsible for certain functions and can be characterised by the skills, capabilities, and authorisations associated with a particular type of work. Positions form a hierarchical structure, linked by reporting lines, with increasing accountability on higher levels in the hierarchy. Moreover, we may associate tasks with a function or position to express that the individual(s) assuming this position is responsible for certain recurring units of work. Together, these elements form the organisational structure or model of an enterprise. Zur Muehlen (1999) documents a number of meta-models for organisational modelling in workflow systems. Russell et al. (2005) propose a comprehensive meta-model for the specification of both human and non-human resources.

Organisational models often evolve independently of workflow models. Separating these two into distinct models allows for a more robust workflow design that is independent of organisational changes. The concept of the role is the connecting piece between the two. Roles are a fundamental aspect of workflow management. By using roles, we may refer to certain aspects of the organisational model, e.g. the individuals, positions, functions, authorisations or capabilities we wish to select for performing a particular task. As a simple example, we may refer to George Washington as an individual, to his capacity as the (first) President of the United States, or to his capability for passing bills. Each of these options provides for differing levels of potential reuse within an organisational model. In lieu of assigning people directly to tasks, roles enable flexibility through indirection. This accommodates the fact that roles tend to be stable entities whilst people regularly change roles and assume new positions. A role will remain constant, whereas the individual assuming the role may change.

There are different types of roles one can utilise when specifying assignments in a workflow. On the one hand, there are the generic, dynamic roles individuals may assume in the context of a workflow, such as the *process initiator, process administrator* and *stakeholder*. These assignments vary from case to case. On the other hand, there are the relatively static, functional roles that are derived from the organisational structure. The two role types are often used in conjunction. For instance, we may assign a particular organisational role such as *brand manager* to the generic role *process stakeholder* to express that brand managers are stakeholders of processes that deal with the creation of new products. In WS-BPEL4People and WS-HumanTask terminology, the generic process roles are called *generic human roles* and they correspond to the roles *initiator, administrator, stakeholder*, and *owners* in the case of tasks. Generic human roles (as per the above terminology) can be specified at both process and task level. Additional generic human roles are conceivable and can in fact be introduced as vendor specific extensions through the extension mechanism provided by the specifications.

Traditionally roles were bound to the human resource management component of an enterprise application, in which the workflow was embedded. However, in the heterogeneous service-oriented environment of WS-BPEL4People, this is far less likely to be the case. A number of distinct organisational directories (that vary both in protocol and structure) may coexist and need to be integrated. Unfortunately, the Web Service stack to date does not provide a standardised organisational query language and unique resource identifier mechanism across directories. WS-HumanTask bridges this gap by introducing a layer of abstraction, the *logical people group*. Logical people groups are design-time artefacts, which are bound to concrete *people queries* against specific organisational directories at configuration-time. This approach has the ability to integrate a vast number of directories with very different features and structures. Because of their generic character, logical people group cannot accommodate many of the advanced features of directories. For instance, they do not directly support the specification of role hierarchy, role inheritance, nor the description of the capabilities of an individual role as this is generally not supported by many of the currently available people directories.

Accordingly, more complex allocations based for instance on role hierarchy need to be pushed to the people query layer. WS-HumanTask introduces role parameterisation to facilitate the development of queries. To find the manager of a specific individual or the key account manager for a product and region, one may pass variables from the workflow context to the role resolution mechanism. In this case, we may pass the individual's name or the product number and region

Table 2. Generic human roles supported in BPEL4People and WS-HumanTask

Generic Human Role	WS-BPEL4People	WS-HumanTask
Initiator	The person that initiates a process or on whose behalf the process is initiated.	The person that initiates a task or on whose behalf the task is initiated.
Administrator	A person allowed to perform administrative actions on a process such as deadline resolution.	A person allowed to perform administrative actions on a task such as nomination.
Stakeholder	A person accountable for the outcome of the process who may influence its progress.	A person accountable for the outcome of a task with the privilege to influence its progress.
Owner	N/A	Persons that play a role in the execution of a task, being either authorised to or excluded from undertaking it.

code to yield the proper assignments. However, the specification remains silent on how to enforce authorisation in people queries.

Workflow introduces an element of dynamism to the resolution of roles. Roles can be resolved in accordance with the context of a workflow case to yield more appropriate assignments. For instance, an auditor may be prevented from participating in the auditing case of one company if he is already participating in another case. This is achieved at workflow and task level by the definition of three actor sets. A modeller restricts the set of authorised owners, i.e. actors which have the required privileges to perform this task, by assigning tasks to functions and positions in the organisational hierarchy. Moreover, the modeller may determine a set of potential actors who are entitled to perform a task in a concrete workflow case. This set ideally is a subset of the authorised owners. Finally, out of the set of potential owners, one actor will pick the task and thus become the executing resource. Figure 3 relates the sets to one another. In general, it is prohibited that a non-authorised actor may pick a task, even if they are a potential owner. In fact, under these circumstances, the actor needs to be excluded from task execution for security and audit reasons.

Note that WS-HumanTask does not have an explicit notion of authorised owners, as some directories do not support the provisioning of tasks as part of the organisational structure. To achieve the same effect, the specification introduces the generic role of excluded owners which can be set to prevent certain actors from performing a given task.

The assignment of users to one of the actor sets can depend on any number of attributes assigned to them, their function or position within the enterprise. Table 3 lists the allocation strategies found in workflow scenarios and relates them to the Workflow Resource Patterns introduced by Russell et al. (2005). Support for each pattern is briefly indicated based on an evaluation of the WS-BPEL extensions by Russell et al. (2007). Note that not all of the strategies can directly be implemented through features of WS-BPEL4People or WS-HumanTask. As outlined above, this is due to the generic nature of logical people groups.

Deadline and Escalation Management

Unlike regular Web Service invocation, task invocation does not follow a strict command-

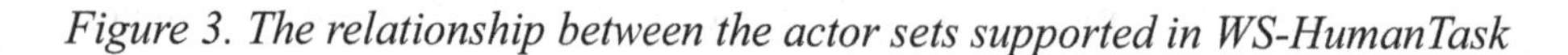

Figure 3. The relationship between the actor sets supported in WS-HumanTask

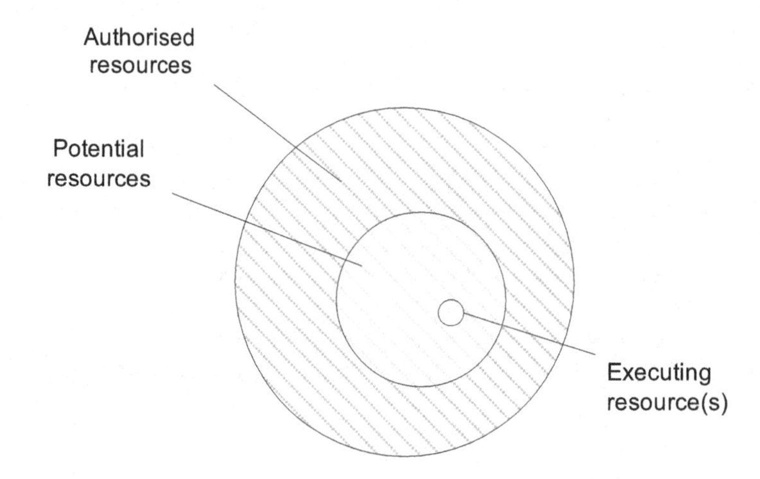

Table 3. Task creation patterns support in BPEL4People and WS-HumanTask

Creation Patterns	Workflow Resource Pattern	Rationale	
Direct Distribution	R-DA	The static assignment of an individual or group to a task. Supported via literal assignment of potential or actual owners.	+
Role-based Distribution	R-RBA	The task is assigned to individuals or groups corresponding to a particular role. Supported via assignment of logical people groups.	+
Deferred Distribution	R-FBA	Resolving the resource assignment for a task is deferred to runtime. Supported via assignment based on expressions.	+
Authorisation	R-RA	The assignment of a task to resources possessing a certain authorisation. Limited support through generic human role privileges, but no general mechanism.	+/–
Separation of Duty	R-SOD	The resource assignments for two tasks must be mutually exclusive. Supported via the excluded owners set.	+
Case Handling	R-CH	All tasks within a case are allocated to the same resource. Pattern not supported.	–
Retain Familiar	R-RF	Where several resources are available, assign the task to the resource having processed a previous work item. Supported via assigning the actual owner to the same value as a preceding task.	+
Capability-based Distribution	R-CBA	The assignment of the task to resources that possess a certain capability or skill set. No support for specification of capabilities.	–
History-based Distribution	R-HBA	The offering of a task to resources based on execution history. Partly supported through the `getMyTasks` function.	+/–
Organisational Distribution	R-OA	The assignment of a task to resources based on their position within the organisational hierarchy. Only group membership can be identified.	+/–
Automatic Execution	R-AE	The execution of a task not under the auspices of a resource. Directly supported via standard WS-BPEL.	+

and-control approach. In fact, the expectation that human participants perform a work item immediately upon assignment and within a given timeframe is arguably simplistic. A number of factors weigh against this assumption such as the current workload of the agent and situations typically not considered during process design, an obvious example being annual leave of the assignee. Still, a workflow designer expects a certain level of control over the cycle time of individual tasks as well as the overarching process if workflows are to improve the efficiency of repetitive work procedures. Deadline and escalation management is the instrument of choice to meet these organisational objectives. Van der Aalst et al. (2007) identify three principal stages in escalation: *detecting* an overdue unit of work, *deciding* on an escalation strategy, and *executing* the escalation strategy.

WS-HumanTask supports the definition of two types of task deadlines for the *detection* of overdue work items. Activation deadlines specify by what time work on the task must have commenced whereas completion deadlines describe by which time work on the task must be complete. The former is typically used to avoid long idle times prior to task commencement. By way of example, we can imagine a call centre where incoming tasks should be commenced within a given timeframe to allow for constant throughput. The latter type of deadline provides control over the allotted task processing time. If within this timeframe the task does not reach a final state, certain recovery actions may be triggered such as the notification of an executive at a higher level in the organisational hierarchy. This is particularly useful where organisations have arranged service level agreements with clients and guarantee low cycle times.

Van der Aalst et al. (2007) suggest that the detection step is to be followed by a decision on the applicable escalation strategy. The authors identify three mechanisms to accomplish this decision: manual, automatic, and semi-automatic selection. WS-HumanTask supports the automated selection of escalations based on a set of conditions or *rules*. The process designer may model several escalation strategies and define a condition under which the strategy may be applied. Depending on the result of evaluation, the escalation is either executed or ignored. Escalations can be implemented in WS-HumanTask in two ways. One is the cancellation of the current task assignment and the reallocation to another agent or group of agents. Another strategy is the notification (possibly in combination with task reassignment) to a more senior person. This typically involves notification of the superior of the task assignee or dedicated escalation managers that streamline work for important clients of the organisation and ensure that service level agreements are met. Escalations do not occur in isolation. In fact, it is not uncommon that an overdue task triggers a number of escalations throughout its lifecycle, which may run sequentially or concurrently. By way of example, the line manager and an escalation manager could be informed at the same time about the delay of a work item assigned to a subordinate.

In a distributed environment such as the one targeted by WS-BPEL4People and WS-HumanTask, the question arises as to which component monitors deadlines and triggers escalations. The specifications suggest that in certain architectural constellations, the task and process execution environment may be realised through two distinct components. Under such circumstances, there needs to be a clear decision as to what component assumes control. This is particularly important to avoid synchronisation issues that may occur when both environments handle deadlines concurrently. The following scenarios illustrate race conditions that could arise in such a situation.

1. The process cancels a task after a deadline set by it was exceeded, while the task environment has independently identified an exceeded deadline and has triggered an escalation.
2. The process escalates a task that has returned to normal processing after an escalation triggered by the task environment was successfully completed.

Thus, only one component should be in control as a general design principle. WS-BPEL4People and WS-HumanTask suggest that the lifecycle of tasks is tightly coupled with that of the process. Accordingly, it should be up to the process to decide to cancel or escalate a task. Consequently, more complicated escalation patterns are pushed to the process layer, avoiding the synchronisation issues outlined above.

Building Task List Clients

Process automation has its limits. At some stage, there will need to be a human in the loop taking decisions and performing units of work which are not able to be automated. While the preceding sections have dealt with issues intrinsic to workflow design, the focus of this section is on the human participant. In particular, we will discuss how humans gain awareness of work assigned to them, how task workers may interact with one another through workflow, and how ultimately they influence the overall sequence of the tasks in the workflow.

Workflow environments generally provide at least three key runtime components: the process engine, the task component and a task list client. Most notably, these components are reflected in the WfMC reference model (Workflow Management Coalition [WfMC], 1995), an established reference architecture for workflow systems. In WS-HumanTask, these concepts correspond to the notion of *requesting application*, *supporting application*, and *task list client*. Figure 4 illustrates the components as specified in the proposal. A task list client represents the user interface (UI) component on top of the task runtime and is often also referred to as the work list or task inbox.

Task list clients can be implemented in many different ways using diverse UI technologies. By way of example, they could be realised through hypertext forms embedded in a Web browser, rich clients with processing logic, or as mobile clients with offline synchronisation capabilities. However, two basic patterns emerge, push-based clients and pull-based clients. Although the difference between them may appear subtle, it has implications with respect to the supporting architecture. The former type of client requires the task runtime to push updates regarding task status to registered clients. The latter type of client pulls information regarding task status at regular intervals from the task runtime environment. As the latter variant is generally easier to implement and represents the lowest common denominator in distributed environments, WS-HumanTask seeks to enable pull-based clients. The specification remains silent on the approach to supporting push-oriented work distribution strategies. However, it is conceivable that vendor-specific extensions could implement a push-based protocol between the task infrastructure and task list client.

Actors in an organisation form a complex, dynamic system and are required to adapt to external as well as internal change. Thus, work practices may deviate from the path suggested by the workflow designer. For instance, in a typi-

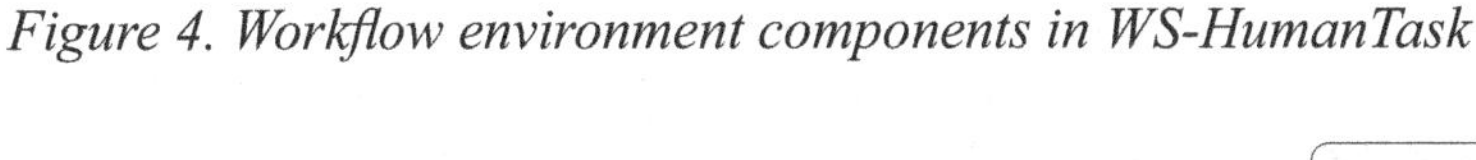

Figure 4. Workflow environment components in WS-HumanTask

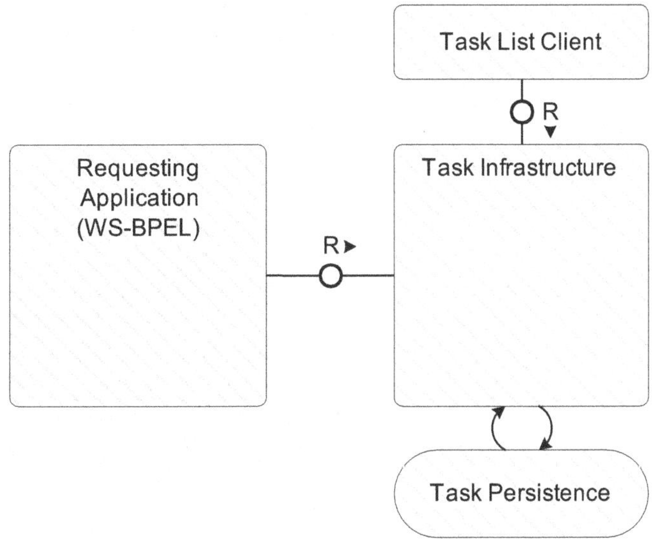

cal work setting, situations may arise that force the assigned agent of a task to interrupt work, discontinue a task or reallocate it by suggesting other suitable agents that might take it over. A task environment should allow the flexible handling of such situations in order to avoid dissatisfaction amongst the participating actors. A number of common scenarios have been classified by Russell et al. (2005) into a comprehensive list of detour patterns. Table 4 discusses each pattern and briefly indicates whether it is supported in WS-BPEL4People and WS-HumanTask based on the assessment of Russell et al. (2007).

Other common scenarios require the collaboration of multiple users consecutively assigned to a task. By way of example, a claims processing agent may append supportive evidence to a task, but then decide to forward the task to another, more experienced agent for further assessment. This is captured by the concept of ad hoc attachments in WS-HumanTask. According to the specification, task list clients should provide a mechanism for adding and retrieving arbitrary, named attachments at runtime without prior design time knowledge. Another feature commonly found in collaborative environments is the ability for participants in a case to document progress and comment on the entries of others. This corresponds to the notion of comments in WS-HumanTask, a chronologically ordered list of textual notes attached by agents working on a task. In summary, WS-HumanTask provides the necessary building blocks for the implementation of rich, collaborative task list clients.

OPPORTUNITIES FOR FURTHER ENHANCEMENT

The WS-BPEL4People proposal is a significant step forward for the WS-BPEL initiative and provides a comprehensive range of facilities for

Table 4. Detour patterns support in BPEL4People and WS-HumanTask

Detour Pattern	Workflow Resource Pattern	Rationale	
Delegation	R-D	Delegation of a work item by one resource to another. Supported via the delegate function.	+
Escalation	R-E	Reallocation of a work item by the task environment to resources other than the currently assigned ones to expedite completion. Supported via the specification of escalation deadlines.	+
Deallocation	R-SD	Ability for a resource to release a work item allocated to it. Supported via the release function.	+
Stateful Reallocation	R-PR	Forwarding a work item by one resource to another without losing state. Supported via the forward function.	+
Stateless Reallocation	R-UR	Forwarding a work item by one resource to another without retaining state. Not supported.	-
Suspension/Resumption	R-SR	Ability for a resource to suspend and resume a work item allocated to it. Supported via the suspend/resume functions.	+
Skipping a Task	R-SK	Ability for a resource to skip a work item allocated to it, marking it as completed. Supported via the skip function	+
Redo a Task	R-REDO	Ability for a resource to recommence working on a work item that has been completed. Not supported.	–
Pre-do a Task	R-PRE	Ability for a resource to commence working on a work item ahead of time. Not supported.	–

integrating human resources in the automation of business processes. It continues the incremental approach taken by WS-BPEL to provide enhanced support for business processes in an SOA environment. In doing so, it leverages a wide range of underpinning technologies and standards developed during the WS-BPEL initiative in areas such as web service security, transaction management and reliability.

Notwithstanding these advances however, much of the focus of the WS-BPEL4People proposal tends to be at the level of technical integration rather than on the broader opportunities that the integration of human resources offer for. In this section, we will consider four areas of opportunity for further development of the WS-BPEL4People initiative.

Enhancing the Notion of the Organisational Model

Although WS-BPEL4People recognises human resources as a key part of a business process, it does so in isolation from the broader organisational context in which they exist. Human resources are denoted as a set of actors who can undertake activities but other than basic mechanisms for grouping on the basis of roles, there is no differentiation between them or any consideration of their place within the broader organisational hierarchy. Details of the unique characteristics of individual resources, the job(s) they hold, the departments to which they belong and the relationships that they have with other resources both in terms of responsibility and reporting are omitted and cannot be used for the purposes of distributing work items.

The expectation proffered by the WS-BPEL-4People extension is that the organisational model corresponding to a business process will be described elsewhere and that the information contained within it will be accessible via the queries that assign task instances to resources at runtime. However the query language provided for this purpose lacks the range of operators that allow for the specification of realistic work assignments such as "assign this task to Mark's manager" or "offer this task to all members of the sales department".

As a means of addressing this issue, we can expect that either a richer organisational model will be incorporated within the WS-BPEL environment or the capabilities of the WS-BPEL4People query language will be significantly extended in order to support more complex queries against externally held organisational models.

Integrating External Resource Repositories

Although WS-BPEL4People assumes the existence of external repositories of organisational information which identify individual resources and their relative position in an organisational context, it does so in an abstract way. Moreover, it does not consider the specific characteristics or capabilities of individual resources when making work allocation decisions. These details are assumed to be handled by potential extensions to the query language.

These abstractions serve to simplify the notion of resources in a WS-BPEL4People context, however they mitigate against the direct usage of established repositories of resource information that are widely deployed by many organisations. WS-BPEL4People could play a prominent role here were it able to directly utilise and mediate more detailed resource definitions held in distinct systems (e.g. X.500 style directory services, ERP/HR systems) for work distribution purposes.

Supporting Complex Work Distribution Strategies

Much of the detail of work distribution in WS-BPEL4People is delegated to the query language which retrieves the identity of the resources to whom a task instance will be assigned. The execution of these queries is assumed to occur in the context of an organisational database for a given process instance. Whilst this approach is effective for simple distribution strategies, it does not allow more complex approaches to work distribution to be effected. In particular, distribution decisions based on execution history, the state of other process instances or the workload of available resources are not possible.

Another area for potential enhancement of the WS-BPEL4People extension is to provide a means of accessing execution history and current state information for all executing process instances and available resources when making work distribution decisions. This could be effected either via defining suitable extensions to the query language or by making these details available within executing process instances.

Extending Security and Authorisation Capabilities

There is consideration of a number of common distribution constraints within the WS-BPEL-4People extension such as the 4-eyes principle where two tasks in the same process instance must be executed by different resources and the retain familiar requirement where two tasks must be completed by the same resource. However the extension as a whole lacks a broad security framework. Although individual tasks have distribution queries associated with them, there is no mechanism to stop one of these resources delegating a task to another resource at runtime or for preventing unintended resources from executing specific tasks.

Another notable absence is the ability to specify privileges defining what actions a resource can undertake. Ideally it should be possible to specify these on a per-task basis in order to restrict the range of actions that a resource can initiate in regard to that task (e.g. delegation, reallocation etc.). Although these considerations may not fall into the ambit of the WS-BPEL4People extension, it may be necessary to further extend related proposals such as WS-Security, WS-Authorisation and WS-Policy to take these issues into account.

SUMMARY AND OUTLOOK

After reading the chapter, the reader will be able to understand the key architectural considerations for the implementation of business process support systems that facilitate the integration and scheduling of human work. These considerations are reflected in contemporary systems to a varying degree. Using an example from the Web service domain, the WS-BPEL4People and WS-HumanTask proposals, the chapter explores the extent to which these patterns are supported and realised in a contemporary language. The chapter concludes by identifying white spots of the WS-BPEL extensions, which culminates in the proposition of several enhancements. A number of issues remain to improve the support for people integration in commercial process support systems, most notably systems based on a Web-service infrastructure. Some of these questions have been answered by academic research. Nevertheless, there remains a large potential for future research.

FURTHER READING

This chapter assumes familiarity with the underlying concepts of languages for Web Service orchestration. The interested reader may find it helpful to review the following references as an introduction to the general issues of implementing business processes by means of Web Services.

Most notably, the authors of the Web Service Business Process Execution language specification (Alves et al. 2007) specify the syntax and operational semantics required to realise business processes using Web Services. In its second revision, the standard is now widely supported by the offerings of major software vendors.

Weerawarana, Curbera, Leymann, Storey, and Ferguson (2005) provide an excellent introduction to the general concepts of the Web Service stack of standards. The technologies discussed cover a wide range of use cases from security, quality of service, and the modelling of business processes. The authors provide sufficient insight into the practical aspects of applying these technologies.

A recent addition to the WS-BPEL technology stack, the WS-BPEL Extension for People (Agrawal et al. 2007a) standardises language extensions to support the integration of human work into automated business processes. Based on common notions from workflow systems, the proposal introduces concepts such as the *people activity* to integrate human tasks into the automated flow of control in a WS-BPEL process.

The Web Services Human Task (Agrawal et al. 2007b) proposal complements WS-BPEL4People by specifying a common language for *human tasks*. This incorporates the definition and reuse of human tasks, roles and rendering mechanisms for the display of work related information. Together, the two proposals form the basis for human workflow support in the Web Service orchestration domain.

REFERENCES

Agrawal, A., Amend, M., Das, M., Keller, C., Kloppmann, M., König, D., Leymann, F., Müller, R., Pfau, G., Ploesser, K., Rangaswamy, R., Rickayzen, A., Rowley, M., Schmidt, P., Trickovic, I., Yiu, A., & Zeller, M. (2007). *WS-BPEL extension for people (WS-BPEL4People), Version 1.0*. http://download.boulder.ibm.com/ibmdl/pub/software/dw/specs/ws-bpel4people/BPEL4People_v1.pdf

Agrawal, A., Amend, M., Das, M., Keller, C., Kloppmann, M., König, D., Leymann, F., Müller, R., Pfau, G., Ploesser, K., Rangaswamy, R., Rickayzen, A., Rowley, M., Schmidt, P., Trickovic, I., Yiu, A., & Zeller, M. (2007). *Web services human task (WS-HumanTask), Version 1.0*. http://download.boulder.ibm.com/ibmdl/pub/software/dw/specs/ws-bpel4people/WS-HumanTask_v1.pdf

Alves, A., Arkin, A., Askary, S., Barreto, C., Bloch, B., Curbera, F., Ford, M., Goland, Y., Guizar, A., Kartha, N., Liu, C.K., Khalaf, R., Koenig, D., Marin, M., Mehta, V., Thatte, S., van der Rijn, D., Yendluri, P., & Yiu. A. (2007). *Web Services Business Process Execution Language - Version 2.0*. OASIS.

Davenport, T. H. (1993). *Process innovation: Reengineering work through information technology*. Boston: Harvard Business School Press.

Hammer, M., & Champy, J. (1993). *Reengineering the corporation – A manifesto for business revolution*. New York: Harper Business.

Jablonski, S., & Bussler, C. (1996). *Workflow management. Modeling concepts, architecture and implementation*. London: International Thomson Computer Press.

Keller, G., Nüttgens, M., & Scheer, A.W. (1992) *Semantische Prozess-modellierung*. Veröffentlichungen des Instituts für Wirtschaftinformatik, Nr 89, Saarbrücken, Germany.

Object Management Group (2005). *Unified modeling language: Superstructure version 2.0 formal/05-07-04*. Technical report, http://www.omg.org/cgi-bin/doc?formal/05-07-04

Object Management Group/Business Process Management Initiative (2006). *BPMN 1.0: OMG Final adopted specification*. http://www.bpmn.org

Pall, G. A. (1987). *Quality press management*. Eaglewood Cliffs, NJ: Prentice-Hall.

Russell, N., van der Aalst, W. M. P., ter Hofstede, A. H. M., & Edmond, D. (2005). Workflow resource patterns: Identification, representation and tool support. In O. Pastor & J. Falcão e Cunha,

(Eds.), *17th International Conference CAiSE 2005, Proceedings,* (LNCS, 3520, pp. 216-232).

Russell, N., & van der Aalst, W. M. P. (2007). *Evaluation of the BPEL4People and WS-HumanTask Extensions to WS-BPEL 2.0 using the Workflow Resource Patterns.* BPM Center Report BPM-07-10, http://www.bpmcenter.org

Russell, N., & van der Aalst, W. M. P. (2008). Work Distribution and Resource Management in BPEL4People: Capabilities and Opportunities. *20th International Conference CAiSE 2008, Proceedings,* (LNCS, 5074, pp. 94-108).

Scheer, A. W. (2000). *ARIS - Business process modelling.* Berlin: Springer

Taylor, F. W. (1911). *The principles of scientific management.* New York: Harper Bros..

van der Aalst, W. M. P., Rosemann, M., & Dumas, M. (2007). Deadline-based escalation in process-aware information systems. *Decision Support Systems 43*, 492-511.

Vernadat, F. B. (1996). *Enterprise modeling and integration.* London: Chapman and Hall.

Weerawarana S., Curbera, F., Leymann, F., Storey, T., & Ferguson D. F. (2005). *Web services platform architecture: SOAP, WSDL, WS-Policy, WS-Addressing, WS-BPEL, WS-Reliable Messaging, and More.* Upper Saddle River, NJ: Prentice Hall PTR.

Workflow Management Coalition (1995). *Reference model - The workflow reference model.* Technical Report WFMC-TC-1003, 19-Jan-95, 1.1, http://www.wfmc.org/standards/docs/tc003v11.pdf

Workflow Management Coalition (2002). *Workflow standard: Workflow process definition interface – XML process definition language (XPDL) WFMCTC-1025).* (Tech. Rep.). Lighthouse Point, FL: Workflow Management Coalition.

Workflow Management Coalition (2005). *Process Definition Interface - XML Process Definition Language Version 2.00.* WFMC-TC-1025, (Tech. Rep.). Lighthouse Point, FL: Workflow Management Coalition. Available at http://www.wfmc.org/standards/docs/TC-1025_xpdl_2_2005-10-03.pdf

Zachman, J. A. (1987). A framework for information systems architecture. *IBM Systems Journal, 26*(3), 276-292.

zur Muehlen, M. (1999). Resource modeling in workflow applications. In *Proceedings of the Workflow Management Conference,* (Münster, 1999), (pp. 137-153). University of Münster, .

EXERCISES

1. Identify the main constituents of an organisation model and the relationships that exist between them.
2. There are five possible constellations for implementing a task using WS-BPEL4People. Illustrate the implementation of three of these describing their operation on a comparative basis.
3. Draw the work item lifecycle for WS-HumanTask work items. Explain the situation each of the states corresponds to from the perspective of the human resource(s) who are involved.
4. There are a number of generic human roles supported by the WS-BPEL4People and WS-HumanTask extensions. What is the purpose of these roles? Identify three of them and discuss their operation in the context of a task.
5. Review the WS-HumanTask proposal, then show how the *separation of duties* and *retain familiar* patterns can be implemented using WS-HumanTask. Include any relevant XML fragments that may assist in illustrating these patterns.

6. Review the WS-HumanTask proposal, then show how the *delegation* pattern might be implemented.

KEY TERMS

Human Role: The organizational or process-related role (or roles) that a human agent assumes in a particular business process. Roles are typically used as a grouping mechanism for individual agents with similar capabilities or responsibilities. They increase the flexibility of process definitions by providing a means of specifying work distribution that is independent of individual resources and allow individual work items to be directed suitable resources on a dynamic basis at runtime rather than requiring their identification in the design-time process model.

Human Task: A defined unit of work undertaken by a human agent in the context of a business process. Human tasks typically relate to activities for which there is no potential or requirement for automation. Individual human tasks are often composed into workflows that document a broader organizational process and in doing so identify the division of labor between the various organizational agents and groups that undertake the constituent human tasks.

Service Enablement: An architectural paradigm that advocates the encapsulation of functions into reusable components by means of a platform-independent interface description language. Such components can be freely assembled into new solutions, promoting both the flexibility and reuse of existing IT assets.

Web Service Business Process Execution Language for People: A language extension for the Web Service Business Process Execution Language (WS-BPEL), an industry standard for the automation of business processes in a service-oriented environment. Initially, WS-BPEL lacked support for creating and scheduling tasks to be performed by human resources. This was perceived as a major impediment to its adoption in a broader context and an industry consortium formed to develop the Web Service Business Process Execution Language for People (WS-BPEL4People) proposal. The proposed extension standardizes the invocation and coordination of service-enabled human tasks (cf. Web Service Human Task) via a WS-BPEL process.

Web Service Human Task: A Web Service standard that is independent of, but often used in conjunction with, the Web Service Business Process Execution Language for People (WS-BPEL). Web Service Human Task (WS-HumanTask) defines a common metamodel for the description of human tasks and standardized interfaces as well as a coordination protocol for their invocation by Web Service clients. The standard thus facilitates the deployment of human task as services, enabling the reuse of existing business task management components in a service-oriented environment.

Work Distribution: The distribution of individual work items to agents in an organization based on both static criteria specified as part of the design-time process model and also on dynamic criteria (also contained in the process model) evaluated at runtime on the basis of the current process state, resource characteristics and preceding execution history.

Workflow Resource Patterns: A comprehensive collection of patterns identifying desirable work distribution and resource management capabilities in workflow management systems. They are part of a larger framework that includes coverage of related workflow perspectives, such as control flow, data flow, and exception handling. The patterns are frequently used as a reference against which workflow systems, web service composition standards and business process modeling languages can be evaluated and compared.

ENDNOTES

[1] The Organization for the Advancement of Structured Information Standards, cf. http://www.oasis-open.org

[2] The coalition's homepage can be found at http://www.wfmc.org/

[3] See the WS-Resource primer at http://docs.oasis-open.org/wsrf/wsrf-primer-1.2-primer-cd-02.pdf

Chapter XIV
Semantic Business Process Management:
Applying Ontologies in BPM

Dimka Karastoyanova
University of Stuttgart, Germany

Tammo van Lessen
University of Stuttgart, Germany

Frank Leymann
University of Stuttgart, Germany

Zhilei Ma
University of Stuttgart, Germany

Jörg Nitzsche
University of Stuttgart, Germany

Branimir Wetzstein
University of Stuttgart, Germany

ABSTRACT

Even though process orientation/BPM is a widely accepted paradigm with heavy impact on industry and research the available technology does not support the business professionals' tasks in an appropriate manner that is in a way allowing processes modeling using concepts from the business domain. This results in a gap between the business people expertise and the IT knowledge required. The current trend in bridging this gap is to utilize technologies developed for the Semantic Web, for example ontologies, while maintaining reusability and flexibility of processes. In this chapter the authors present an overview of existing technologies, supporting the BPM lifecycle, and focus on potential benefits Semantic Web technologies can bring to BPM. The authors will show how these technologies help automate the transition between the inherently separate/detached business professionals' level and the IT level without the burden of additional knowledge acquisition on behalf of the business professionals. As background information they briefly discuss existing process modeling notations like the Business Process Modeling Notation (BPMN) as well as the execution centric Business Process Execution Language (BPEL), and their limitations in terms of proper support for the business professional. The chapter stresses on the added value Semantic Web technologies yield when leveraged for the benefit of BPM. For this the authors give examples of existing BPM techniques that can be improved by using Semantic Web technologies, as well as novel approaches which became possible only through the availability of semantic descriptions. They show how process model configuration can be automated and thus simplified and how flexibility during process execution is increased. Additionally, they present innovative techniques like automatic process composition and auto-completion of process models where suitable process fragments are automatically discovered to make up the process model. They also present a reference architecture of a BPM system that utilizes Semantic Web technologies in an SOA environment.

1. INTRODUCTION

Business Process Management (BPM) has gained an extraordinary acclaim in the last decades and is being successfully applied for business process enactment in enterprises as well as for scripting integration logic [We07]. A multitude of both commercial and non-commercial tools supporting all or some of the life cycle phases of a process exists. Nowadays, mergers and acquisitions of companies are commonplace and typically they require splitting and merging of the IT support and integration of the business processes and the domain models of the affected companies. While IT infrastructure is easier to integrate, in particular using the SOA [Bu00] paradigm, it is extremely complicated to reconcile differences on the business level, especially business processes and domain model. To enable this reconciliation business people depend on the assistance of IT personnel. Due to the differences in terminologies and background the collaborative work of technical personnel and business experts is tedious and error-prone. Definitely there is a lack of support on a significant scale for this collaborative endeavor. The need for comprehensive support that narrows the gap between IT and businesses, i.e. domain experts, is obvious and has been proven by multiple case studies and reports.

Semantic Web Services [CDM+04] is a technology based on approaches and techniques from the Semantic Web [BJO01, HBM02]. They use ontologies as underlying conceptual framework to describe functional and non-functional properties of service in a machine-understandable manner. The technology has been created to facilitate the shift from human-to-application interactions to human-to-application-to-human interactions which in turn is needed in order to automate the daily tasks of human aided by computers. The same techniques can be applied to automate interactions among applications that are by design not interoperable, since they have been created using different domain models. A similar approach can be applied in order to address the above mentioned differences in terminology and domain knowledge between IT and business experts.

In this chapter we motivate the need of semantic information in the field of BPM and use the business process lifecycle to structure the discussion and show during which phases of this life cycle semantic information can be used to achieve improvements. We give an overview of the existing Semantic Web Services technologies and we stress on the added value Semantic Web and Semantic Web Service technologies yield when leveraged for the benefit of BPM [HLD+05]. For this we give an overview of common BPM techniques that can be improved by using Semantic Web technologies, as well as present novel approaches which became possible only through the availability of semantic descriptions. We show for instance how process model configuration can be automated and thus simplified and how flexibility during process execution is increased. Additionally, we present innovative techniques like automatic process composition and auto-completion of process models where suitable process fragments are automatically discovered to make up the process model. We also present a reference architecture of a BPM system that has been devised as part of our work in the project SUPER[1]. This architecture utilizes Semantic Web technologies in an SOA environment and is designed and devised to be independent of application domains. It has been tested in applications from the telecommunications domain [SBC+08]. The presented approaches and the architecture can be applied to other domains like scientific computing, e-government, healthcare and others, and can be extended to grid applications. Based on the presented approaches and techniques it is possible to address another pressing need identified by business experts, namely the ability to query the process space of an enterprise using the terminology natural for the domain experts rather then terms inherent to IT.

The remainder of the chapter is structured as follows. Section 2 provides background information about business process management in general, the BPM lifecycle and technologies used in the different phases. The new technologies and techniques developed and envisioned for semantic BPM (SBPM), as well as the improvements that can be achieved by using them, are introduced in Section 3. The reference architecture for SBPM is presented in Section 4; section 5 concludes the chapter and gives directions for future work.

2. BACKGROUND INFORMATION OVERVIEW: EXISTING TECHNOLOGIES, NOTATIONS AND APPROACHES

In this section we provide background information about the lifecycle of business processes. We also give an overview of the existing Semantic Web Service frameworks used to describe the semantics of services by means of ontologies as the underlying paradigm and motivate the need for the use of semantics in the context of BPM.

2.1 BPM Lifecycle

A business process goes through four major phases throughout its lifecycle: (i) modeling, (ii) configuration, (iii) execution and (iv) analysis. In business process modeling, process models are created which may on the one hand serve as documentation of the processes of a company and on the other hand may serve as a template for the execution of multiple process instances of a single model. There are at least three dimensions that need to be represented in a process model [LeRo00]. The business logic ("what") describes the sequence of steps (control flow) that need to be executed in order to reach a desired outcome and the data used for carrying out these steps and that may be shared with external participants (data flow). Tasks can be executed by human participants or automatically by applications. The "who" dimension of a workflow assigns human participants to tasks in the control flow in a declarative manner to be flexible and independent of organizational models. For this purpose, so called staff queries make out this dimension and are used during process execution to assign concrete staff members playing a particular role to a particular task in a process instance. The "what with" dimension is used to assign applications to tasks in a process model; these applications are executed automatically or aid humans during the fulfillment of a task. Additional dimensions may also be identified and specified. However, the common agreement is that a process model needs to implement at least the three dimensions described above. Therefore, the meta model for business processes contains mandatory constructs for describing these three dimensions.

Processes are created and used by people playing different roles in enterprises. These roles include strategists that define the overall strategy of the organization, business analysts that define coarse grained steps in a business process and process developers that create executable artifacts. The level of detail used for process modeling by these users differs significantly due to the different purposes these artifacts serve.

In order to accommodate the needs of each user role several *process modeling* notations have evolved that can be grouped into two major groups: graphical and text-based notations; some notations are proprietary some have made it to public standards. The most prominent graphical notation for instance is the Business Process Modeling Notation (BPMN) [BPMN]. It is used by strategists and business experts to model an overall conceptual view of a business process even in a cross-organizational setting ignoring technical details. Although considered a de facto standard, BPMN still doesn't have an explicit operational semantics which makes it difficult to use since it is not an unambiguous modeling notation. Process developers use an absolutely different notation for representing process models, the de facto standard for service based processes, WS-BPEL [BPEL]. It is an XML-based language that uses Web Services as activity implementations and can be mapped to various proprietary graphical notations. Since process developers in fact need to *implement* the business processes created by business analysts on a technical level there is a need for a mapping between these different notations to facilitate and automate the process implementation step. The mapping between the two de facto standards is still incomplete and makes for an impedance mismatch between conceptual and executable process models and hampers automation. The automation is further hindered by the fact that business experts omit details in the process model needed for the representation on the technical level. Naturally, nowadays for each of the notations tailor-made modeling tools exist. Typically, they utilize a process library that stores the corresponding modeling artifacts; a library may enable sophisticated versioning strategies [Le06].

The executable processes are run on so-called process engines; for example there are multiple commercial and non-commercial BPEL implementations. The BPEL process models are used for the step-wise execution (navigation) of process instances. The engine interacts with a piece of middleware, called the service bus [Ch04, Le05], for the execution of interaction activities; interaction activities stand for the execution of a task by a Web Service [WCL05]. The discovery of services and binding to them is either deployment driven, in which case concrete services (static assignment) or their abstract descriptions are provided during process deployment, or declarative, where only the needed functional and non-functional properties of services are provided in terms of their WSDL [WSDL] port type and policies respectively. In the latter case, the service bus is responsible for discovering concrete service ports and binding to them dynamically. The discovery of services is aided by a service registry, which is exposed as a service on the bus [Le05, KLN+07], too. During process execution an engine may publish events notifying the discrete navigation steps [KLN+06, Wu06]. These events may be used to notify external components like monitoring tools [Ni06] and auditing components. There are already existing formats for representing events in an audit trail, for example MXML which is utilized by mining tools like for instance ProM [WAD+07]. Audit data typically grow to significant size; these data are used as input for process *mining and analysis* algorithms. In case of predefined control flows that are executed using a workflow engine the applicability of process mining is limited to proving deviations in services bound or exception handling, as well as compliance checking [SOX], e.g. when human participants are involved and they had to follow certain rules like the "four eyes principle". Process reengineering and discovery, however, is extremely useful in the situation where case handling tools have been used for process support, or there is no predefined control and data flow for a business process, or the implementation of the business process is done in a non-process based technique and the documentation is sparse.

2.2 Applying Ontologies in Service Modeling and Execution

Process orientation has been discussed for many years but with the emergence of Web Services (WS), which is the most popular implementation of service oriented architecture (SOA), workflow technology and BPM got established to a great extent. In an SOA high-level business concepts [KBS04] are identified and encapsulated as agnostic, self-contained services. When leveraged for BPM, these services serve as activity implementations of a process, i.e. a process orchestrates services. The latest trend in SOA is to add semantic annotations, i.e. ontological concepts, to services to make service discovery more precise, to enhance flexibility and to increase the degree of automation.

Since the discovery of appropriate services that implement a task is also a major challenge when implementing a conceptual process model, semantic technologies are considered to have a high potential to bridge the gap between the IT view and the technical view on business processes.

There are three major initiatives towards Semantic Web Services (SWS). The early frameworks OWL-S [OWLS] and WSMO [WSMO] follow a top down approach. They define their own conceptual model of services expressed in an ontology and define how these models can be mapped to WSDL. Hence they can be considered a layer on top of Web Services. Whereas OWL-S concentrates on describing only services in terms of the message exchange they can involve in (service model), the real world effect they cause (service profile) and the grounding (service grounding), i.e. mapping to WSDL, WSMO provides a more comprehensive framework as it also describe a service requester. Therefore, WSMO distinguishes between a *Web Service* and a so called *goal*. Both are described in terms of the message exchange they can get involved in (choreography), and the real world effect they cause or require respectively (capability). For the purpose of communication, both, WSMO Web Service descriptions as well as Goal descriptions can be grounded to WSDL in a fashion that enables both, synchronous, i.e. blocking, as well as asynchronous, i.e. non-blocking, (WS-*) standards based interaction between service requester and service provider [NLK+07a] which is compliant with the Basic Profile [BEF+04] of the WS-Interoperability Organization[2]. The Semantic Execution Environment [SEE] technical committee (SEE TC) is currently working on a reference architecture for WSMO implementations of which the two most prominent are the Web Service Model eXecution environment (WSMX) [WSMX] and the Internet Reasoning Service (IRS III) [IRS]. Since OWL-S only defines one of two interacting parties, the service provider, OWL-S frameworks only support conversational interactions between requester and service in terms of a sequence of remote procedure calls [OWLS].

The latest approach towards adding semantic annotations to Web Services is SAWSDL [SAWSDL] - it follows a bottom up approach and has become a W3C recommendation in 2007. SAWSDL defines an extension to WSDL which takes the conceptual model of WSDL as basis instead of inventing a new conceptual model for services and allows annotating WSDL. Each element of WSDL, e.g. messages and operations, can be annotated with an ontological concept by means of a `modelReference` attribute. Additionally, it can be defined how XML data can be transformed into ontological instances and vice versa, which is called lifting or lowering, by means of transformation rules referenced by the `liftingSchemaMapping` or `lowering-SchemaMapping` attributes, respectively.

3. ENHANCING BPM WITH SEMANTICS

Despite of increasing software support for BPM, there is still a need for better support for human involvement throughout the BPM life cycle. In particular, there are substantial difficulties when it comes to bridge the gap between the business view and the IT view on business processes. One of the main problems is the translation of the high-level business process models, which are created by business users, to workflow models, which are executable IT representations of the business processes. These difficulties result in significant time delays between design and execution phases of the process, thus having a negative impact on the performance of process redesign and process agility. They are caused partly by the lack of understanding of the business needs by IT experts and of technical details by business/domain experts, a phenomenon often referred to as the Business-IT gap.

The vision of Semantic Business Process Management (SBPM) is to close the Business-IT gap by using semantic technologies [HLD+05]. Similarly to how Semantic Web Services achieve improved automation in discovery and mediation as compared to conventional Web services, the goal of SBPM is to combine BPM with Semantic Web related technologies, in particular ontologies and Semantic Web Services (SWS), in order to achieve automation in the BPM lifecycle and to provide more convenient features to business users and IT engineers. In the SUPER project existing BPM standards and notations, amongst others BPMN, BPEL and MXML, are extended with semantic features.

3.1 SBPM Lifecycle

The usage of semantic technologies does not affect the main phases of the BPM lifecycle, but attempts to increase the automation degree within and across the phases, and adds new or enhances existing BPM functionalities. The SBPM lifecycle thus contains the following phases: SBP Modeling, SBP Configuration, SBP Execution, and SBP Analysis. Figure 1 depicts the SBPM lifecycle and

Figure 1. SBPM lifecycle

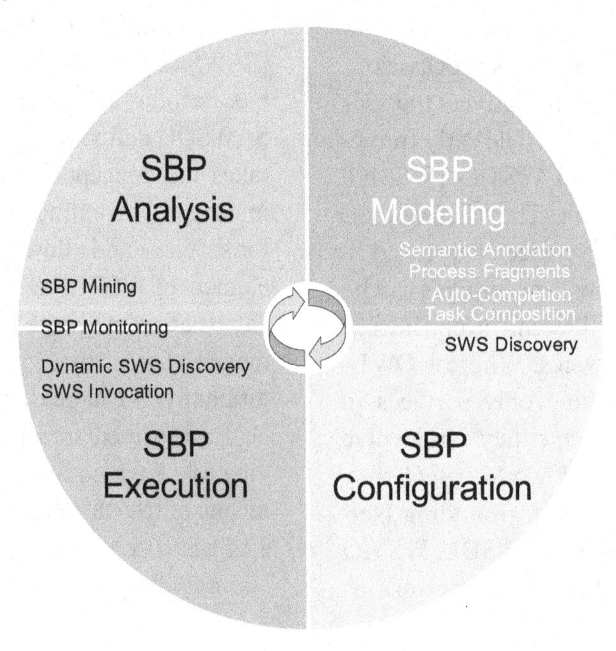

lists the functionalities related to each of these life cycle phases.

In the following sections, we describe ongoing work on how semantic technologies are used in BPM for each of the four phases and depict the benefits of their usage.

3.2 Modeling

Semantic business process (SBP) modeling exploits modern Semantic Web [HBM02] technology in conventional business process modeling aiming at facilitating the modeling work of business users (i.e. strategists and analysts). In contrast to conventional business process modeling, SBP modeling adopts well-defined ontologies. Ontologies establish a consistent and unambiguous vocabulary for the knowledge within a domain. They provide a representation of a set of concepts in a domain and the relations among these concepts in a machine-readable manner. The ontologies developed in SUPER for SBP modeling can be classified into two categories: an ontology stack for process modeling and domain-specific ontologies. The ontology stack comprises ontologies for modeling different aspects of a business process, namely process modeling ontologies, business organization ontologies, business resource ontologies, business data ontologies, business function ontologies and so on. Process modeling ontologies include for instance an ontological representation of extended BPMN [AFK+07] and BPEL [NWL07]. These ontologies are used to model business processes and to capture essential aspects of the business process, e.g. control flow, organization-related information, needed resources, data flow, the business function of each activity and their real world effect in terms of WSMO capabilities. It is usually necessary to complement the ontology stack with domain-specific ontologies, which refine and extend the standard ontologies [HeRo07] by defining concepts (business data and business function definitions) of a certain domain, e.g., telecommunications or supply-chain management domain. For example, a supply-chain domain ontology would define business data concepts such as "purchase order", "invoice", and "shipment", and business functions such as "Process Purchase Order", or "Ship Order to Customer". The business expert would then use these concepts to annotate his process model and thus specify its semantics explicitly.

The ontological description and annotation of business process models increases the power of querying process modeling artifacts and fosters using process fragments in business process modeling. A process fragment is a part of a business process which has been identified as potentially reusable in other business process models. A business process may combine multiple fragments, some of which may encompass self-contained business logic. These identified process fragments can be treated as reusable building blocks for future modeling work. In the conventional approach for querying process models or process fragments, queries target on the structural, the syntactic, and the linguistic aspects of process models. However, such approaches do not take the ontological meaning into account, which leads to imprecise results. For example, two business processes may have exactly the same control flow, but implement complete different business logic. With help of the ontological description and annotation, the query capacities have been extended in SBPM by one further dimension, namely the semantic dimension. As ontologies define a consistent and unambiguous vocabulary for modeling and annotating process artifacts in a certain domain, more precise match-making of the semantics of these artifacts is enabled. Furthermore, by adopting modern reasoning technologies, new knowledge can be derived according to pre-defined axioms and relations, which are not explicitly specified in the process modeling artifacts. All these benefits enable a more powerful and precise search of process modeling artifacts. These new querying capabilities can for instance be applied during auto-completion. Auto-completion is a feature that assists modelers with suggestions how to complement an incomplete process model created by the user. The suggested alternatives are represented by already modeled process fragments.

Another technique that profits from semantically annotated process models is composition. Composition ensures that implementations are available for each task in the conceptual process model. Therefore the composition first uses the semantic task descriptions to check whether there exists a corresponding implementation, i.e. service, for each task. In the next step for all tasks where no direct implementation exists, composition tries to synthesize a process fragment by composing several services, which implement the desired functionalities collectively, by using AI planning techniques [WMD+07]. Since each service invocation becomes a task in the conceptual model, i.e. a coarse grained task is split into several fine grained tasks, this step can be considered as a refinement step of the conceptual process model. An implementation of this approach has been presented in [BHK+08].

In addition, the ontological description and annotation of business process models lays the foundation for enhanced functionalities in configuration, implementation, execution, analysis and optimization of business processes, which will be explained in the following sections in this chapter.

3.3 Configuration

The configuration phase aims at mapping a semantically enriched conceptual process model to an executable model that is bound to a concrete service, in particular Web Service and Semantic Web Service, technology and process implementation. That is, the process model has to be translated from the formalism used by business experts to a formalism that can be executed for instance by an execution engine and the semantic descriptions of tasks have to be mapped to concrete implementations, e.g. services.

Given the conceptual model is sufficiently well described and no errors occur, the configuration phase could be performed mostly automated. There are for instance several approaches that deal with the translation from BPMN to BPEL. SBPM complements these approaches by introducing an approach that represents BPMN and BPEL process models using ontologies and translates between them via ontology mediation.

In SUPER, WSMO is used to describe the functionality a (set of) task(s) of a process requires and the functionality services provide. BPEL4SWS [NLK+07b] (BPEL for Semantic Web Services) (see section 3.1.3) is used to implement processes. Given this setting there are several strategies for binding implementations to executable process models during configuration:

- **WSDL services as activity implementations.** As WSMO describes existing (WSDL) services it provides a grounding mechanism to WSDL for both goals and Web Services. A grounding in the goal is only required to describe a call back endpoint needed when implementing asynchronous communication in a WS-I complaint manner [NLK+07a]. Given that both WSMO goals and WSMO Web Services describe WSDL endpoints, during configuration the WSMO descriptions can be resolved to WSDL services that can be directly used in the process model. Interaction activities representing the tasks of the conceptual process model reference the WSDL operations the WSMO descriptions are grounded to. This configuration strategy results in a conventional BPEL process that runs on a conventional BPEL engine which invokes traditional Web Services. The endpoint of the actual implementation can be either extracted from the discovered WSMO service and determined during deployment (design time binding) or discovered during runtime (runtime binding).

- **WSMO goals as descriptions of activity implementations.** Using WSMO goals as activity implementations implies the existence and usage of a middleware that implements the WSMO model following the SEE [SEE] reference architecture. Goals can be used with and without a restriction on services that might be used. The restriction might be a single service (which corresponds to design time binding of WSDL services) or a (ranked) list of functionally equal services that were discovered during design time. Even more flexibility is achieved by using a goal without any restrictions on services that might be used. In this case any WSMO Web Service that meets the functional requirements can be discovered and invoked during runtime.

A thorough explanation of the configuration phase has been presented in [WHM+07].

3.4 Execution

In the execution phase ontologies are used for several purposes: (i) to facilitate discovery of services that implement tasks independent of interface definitions, (ii) to enable use of mediators that make use of the semantic descriptions to perform data manipulation tasks, (iii) to enable reasoning over ontological knowledge for evaluating conditions in a process and (iv) to enable generating events that contain not only raw data but data that is well-defined using ontologies.

These features are captured by two specifications: BPEL4SWS [NKL+07b] which is an extension of the Business Process Execution Language (BPEL 2.0) and the Events Ontology (EVO) [PDM08].

BPEL4SWS extends BPEL with a WSDL-less interaction model [NLK+07c] and allows describing activity implementations semantically, i.e. using Semantic Web Service frameworks like OWL-S or WSMO, instead of referring to WSDL port types and operations directly. For communication purposes, however, both the SWS frameworks as well as BPEL4SWS process models make use of WSDL descriptions in a decoupled manner. The WSDL-less interaction model of BPEL4SWS is based on the concept of a conversation that is formed by a set of WSDL-less interaction activities. Therefore several new elements were specified:

- A `<conversation>` element that plays the role of a WSDL-less `<partnerLink>`,
- An `<interactionActivity>` that can be configured such that it behaves like a `<receive>`, `<reply>` or `<invoke>` activity,
- A `<pick>` activity that also allows for WSDL-less `<onMessage>` elements and does not require at least one traditional `<onMessage>`,
- An `<eventHandler>` that also allows for WSDL-less `<onEvent>` elements and
- A `<partner>` element that facilitates grouping several conversations to express that they have to take place with one and the same partner (service).

Additionally, the messages a BPEL4SWS process sends and receives are annotated with ontological concepts using SAWSDL *modelReferences.* A conversation maps to Semantic Web Service frameworks as follows: The messages sent and received during a conversation and their ordering can be described for instance in an OWL-S service model or a WSMO choreography [RSN07]. SWS frameworks additionally enable describing the real world effects in terms of a service profile in OWL-S or a capability in WSMO respectively. This enables discovery of services implementing tasks in a much more flexible manner without the need of knowing the port types of these services prior to execution as it is in traditional BPEL. BPEL itself provides a recursive aggregation model for services, i.e. it uses and combines services to achieve a higher level business value which is again exposed as a service. Since WSMO does not solely focus on describing services but also enables describing the requirements of a requester it is better suited for use in combination with BPEL than OWL-S. Conversations on which a process provides functionality to partner services are described using a WSMO Web Service, whereas conversations on which the process requests functionality are described using a WSMO goal.

BPEL4SWS also defines extension to enhance data processing in BPEL processes. While traditional BPEL allows specifying data manipulation embedded in the process model by means of `<copy>` operations in `<assign>` activities which are based on XML data processing e.g. XPATH, BPEL4SWS defines a new `<extensionAssignOperation>` called `<mediate>`. The mediate operation only defines which data is provided as input and what is the required output in terms of its ontological meaning and relies on the infrastructure to discover an appropriate mediation service to mediate between them. This is, in contrast to the assign activity, where data manipulation has to be defined each time a process is modeled, the mediate operation allows reusing predefined transformation rules.

The ontological meaning of data is also useful when evaluating conditions in a BPEL4SWS process. BPEL allows defining the `expressionLanguage` that is used within a process, scope or even in single elements to evaluate an expression. Thus it is possible to define new expression languages like for instance WSML4BPEL [KLL+08a] that takes a set of variables and a WSML logical expression as input. The set of variables define the knowledge base the expression is applied to.

The Event Ontology (EVO) is an ontology that extends the Core Ontology for Business Process Analysis (COBRA) [PDM08] in order to allow monitoring and analyzing business processes based on the events that are generated by heterogeneous execution environments. EVO is based on a state model that captures different states in the lifecycles of processes and their activities. EVO contains two subclasses of events, namely Process Monitoring Event and Activity Monitoring Event. Process monitoring events capture state transitions of process instances during execution, e.g. instantiated, started, suspended, resumed, completed, aborted and terminated, while activity monitoring events capture the scheduling of activities, e.g. assignment, reassignment, relief, aborted and withdrawn.

3.5 Analysis and Monitoring

Semantic Business Process Analysis comprises the following functionalities [APA+07]: (i) Process monitoring in near-real-time which evaluates key performance indicators (KPIs) of business processes during SBP execution, alerts the responsible business people in case of deviations from target values, and displays KPI values in dashboards; (ii) Ad-Hoc-Queries, which are posed by business people to evaluate business questions considering the performance of executed business processes; (iii) Process mining which operates on the execution histories of finished processes that are logged during SBP execution, and tries to discover explicit process models for conformance checking and optimization of processes.

An approach to SBP Monitoring has been presented in [WML08]. Thereby, a business analyst defines KPIs based on ontology concepts which are part of semantic annotations of semantic business processes. Semantic business processes explicitly specify the semantics of process activities by modeling their inputs, outputs, preconditions and postconditions, in terms of business objects (e.g., “purchase order”) and their state changes (e.g., “purchase order received”) [BDW07]. As KPIs are also based on business objects (e.g., “percentage of purchase orders which were delivered successfully and on time”), semantic annotations of processes can be exploited for the definition of KPIs in the SBP modeling phase. In the next step, the KPI model is transformed to a monitor model, which supports evaluation of KPIs based on events published by the BPEL4SWS process engine at process execution time. As the KPIs are defined on an ontological level, machine reasoning can exploit implicit knowledge for their evaluation during process monitoring.

While SBP monitoring evaluates the KPIs in near-real-time, and allows automatic notification of business people in case of deviations, ad-hoc-queries enable analysis of processes after their execution. They in particular allow analyzing process performance issues beyond predefined KPIs. Queries are therefore executed against the execution history that contains the events collected during process execution. These events are semantically annotated, i.e. the semantics of the concepts of the event are explicitly defined by referencing ontology entities. Based on the semantic annotation of events, reasoning mechanisms can be employed for querying of events.

Process mining focuses on the discovery of models, the conformance between models and event logs, and extension of models based on information derived from event logs. Usage of ontologies allows developing process mining techniques that analyze the event logs and process models at the conceptual level rather than the syntactical level. In case event logs and process models link to ontologies, mining techniques can reason over the concepts the events in the log point to. In the non-semantic case, the actual semantics of these concepts remain in the head of the business analyst who has to interpret them manually.

4. ARCHITECTURE

To realize the requirements described above, an appropriate architecture is needed. As there are multiple agnostic and self contained services involved to achieve the overall goal of SBPM, the architecture features an enterprise service bus (ESB) which integrates the needed set of tools and platform components that support the functionalities throughout all phases of the SBPM lifecycle.

The SBPM reference architecture [KLL+08b] contains four main parts. The execution components are in charge to execute semantic business process models (using the *SBP Execution Engine*

Figure 2. The SBPM reference architecture [KLL+08b]

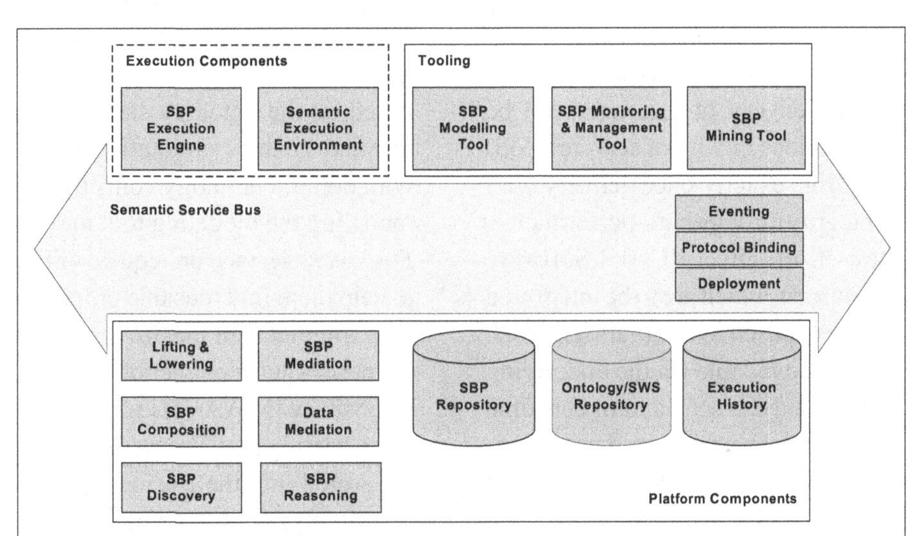

[LND+07]) and to discover and invoke Web Services using semantic descriptions (*Semantic Execution Environment*). The tooling consists of the *SBP Modeling Tool*, which allows for creating and modifying conceptual business process models, the *SBP Monitoring and Management Tool* for observing and steering the running infrastructure and finally the *SBP Mining Tool* that allows for analysis and for detecting deviations between process models and process executions after processes are run. Some services provide key functionalities that are required by multiple consumers. Those services are collected and exposed as *platform components*. The Lifting and Lowering component for instance is capable of translating between XML data and their ontological representation which is needed by both, the SBP Execution Engine as well as the Semantic Execution Environment. Finally the storage layer completes the overall architecture. The *SBP Repository* can store business process models in different ontological representations. The *Ontology/SWS Repository* stores domain ontologies (to describe data instances) and WSMO Web Service descriptions as well as WSMO Goals and the *Execution History* stores all events published during process execution.

The *Semantic Service Bus* (SSB) [KLN+07] provides the communication infrastructure for all SBPM system components. The core of the SSB is a distributed asynchronous scalable messaging backbone that leverages message-oriented middleware. The delivery of messages can be configured with various quality of service (QoS) options ranging from exactly-once delivery with transactional integrity through high-performance, low-latency best-effort delivery [Ch04]. Software components (services), which are to be integrated using the SSB, are exposed as internal endpoints. These endpoints are available via the underlying message backbone and can send and/or consume messages in a unified, transport- and encoding-neutral message format (so called Normalized Messages). The SSB also allows for registering multiple implementations of the same service interface to the same abstract endpoint. It is then up to the routing logic of the bus to which concrete service (i.e. to which concrete endpoint) a message is delegated. When internal services should be accessible from the out side, they must be exposed as external services. Therefore, so called Binding Components are configured to expose a certain service interface using a particular transport protocol, e.g. SOAP/HTTP, SOAP/JMS, WS-ReliableMessaging [WSRM] to get into and out of the SSB. Such binding components can be wired either with concrete service implementations or with abstract endpoints, i.e. a set of implementations. This makes a powerful mechanism to virtualize services and allows for a pluggable architecture. These mechanisms can also be used to mediate data and protocols by adapting the routing logic to place mediation services in the message flow without changing the actual deployment of services which leads to a loosely coupled architecture.

The SBP modeling environment comprises components that enable SBP modeling and SBP configuration. The core component is the *SBP Modeling Tool* which provides the graphical user interface for all functionalities related to modeling and configuration. The SBP modeling tool uses platform services for implementing discovery and composition functionalities. It also acts as a front-end to the semantic business process repository. The SBP modeling tool supports process modeling based on the ontology stack for process modeling and enables annotation of process models with domain ontology concepts. During process modeling the modeling tool may invoke the *SBP Discovery* service on request of business experts to help them find reusable process models or process fragments in the *SBP repository* e.g. for the purpose of auto completion. The Business Process Repository [MWA+07] serves as the back-end of the modeling tool. Process models and fragments are stored into the Business Process Repository in terms of their ontological representations. Additionally, this repository provides functionalities for manipulation of process modeling artifacts providing CRUD (Create, Retrieve, Update, Delete) operations and other standard repository features like versioning, locking, notification, concurrency control, security, support of long-running transactions and so on. One very important difference to conventional repositories is the use of a reasoning component, like the Intelligent Reasoning for Integrated Systems (IRIS) [IRIS] applied for query answering. The use of a reasoner in combination with the repository enhances the expressiveness of the queries that can be run against the repository to discover appropriate process models and enable search not only based on structural characteristics of the models, but rather also on behavioral properties. The result sets become much more precise. Support for auto-completion is enabled in addition to improved discovery of process artifacts.

The SBP model created by the business expert specifies for each activity which functionality is to be performed, by defining its inputs, outputs, preconditions and post-conditions [BDW07]. It, however, does not yet specify which (Semantic) Web Services are to be used to implement the functionality of the activity. This functionality is provided by the composition service [WMD07]. For each activity of the process model, the composition service tries to find a (collection of) SWSs that implement(s) that activity by querying the SWS repository.

The Semantic Web Services Repository is designed to support storage, search, retrieval and management of Semantic Web Services, as well as the ontologies used for describing them, their non-functional properties, their visible/public interfaces and mapping to existing Web Services. In general, Semantic Web Services may be described using any Semantic Web Services framework. Note that the different frameworks follow different approaches to modeling Semantic Web Services. For example, WSMO [WSMO] distinguishes among Semantic Web Services, which are the descriptions a service provider defines for his services and goals, which are meant for use by service requesters and express the user requirements. In case WSMO is used as the underlying framework, this repository should store the Semantic Web Service descriptions, the ontologies used, goal descriptions and the available mediators. The Semantic Web Services Repository is used during modeling for the purpose of composition, during configuration phase where tasks are assigned a description in a service technology or choice, e.g. WSMO or WSDL, and during the execution phase where the Semantic Web Services repository acts as a service registry for dynamic service discovery.

After each task is composed, i.e. assigned an appropriate service description, and the composition is validated by the user, the business process model has to be translated to an executable process model description which is understood by the process engine. The translation is performed by the *transformation service*. The result of the translation is a deployable process model based on BPEL4SWS [KLL+08a], which is an extension of BPEL [BPEL] and enables orchestration of Web Services and Semantic Web Services.

In order to deploy semantic process models to the SBP infrastructure, they are packaged to so-called Semantic Process Artifact Bundles (SPABs) and are subsequently deployed using the SSB's deployment component. It can consume SPABs both locally and remotely, unpacks it and deploys it then to the respective components. The set of components involved in the execution phase of SBPM consists of an enhanced BPEL engine that is capable to execute BPEL4SWS, an execution environment for Semantic Web Services (e.g. IRS-III or WSMX), a lifting and lowering component that can translate messages according to a given translation definition and binding components that can consume and expose external services.

Once a SPAB has been deployed, the semantic business process is able to consume messages. Similar to BPEL processes, BPEL4SWS processes are not explicitly instantiated but rather get started when a message arrives that fits to the signature of the first receiving activity of the process model. When the process model has been instantiated, the process navigator walks though the control flow defined by the model and discharges the activities accordingly. These activities perform mainly data manipulation and service invocation tasks. Beside conventional Web Service invocations, BPEL4SWS can also invoke SWS natively. Such an SWS invocation consists of two steps that are performed by the SEE: Discovery and Invocation. The service discovery is started by the SBP Execution Engine which passes the WSMO Goal as defined in the activity and the call parameters to the SEE. The call parameters must be available in an ontological representation. If this is not the case, the engine calls the Lifting and Lowering component to derive the needed data representation. With the aid of the WSMO Goal, which describes the functional and non-functional properties of the sought-after service, the SEE discovers a matching service candidate from a set of registered WSMO Web Services. Once an appropriate service implementation has been discovered the service gets invoked and the result is returned to engine. The result of the invocations is, before being further processed, lowered again to the XML representation.

To support the analysis phase of the lifecycle the SSB provides a publish-subscribe infrastructure to capture execution events. Each component involved in the execution phase publishes events to a specific messaging topic. Analysis and monitoring tools can subscribe to this topic to get notified when execution events occur. This enables real time monitoring of the whole infrastructure. The Execution History is registered as a fixed subscriber to all events. It is part of the storage layer and serves as audit trail to gather and persist all events occurred during execution. The event format is in contrast to traditional BPM systems serialized as instances of an events ontology (EVO) [PDM08]. As these event instances maintain links to the originating process models, to (semantically described) data models and to business entities [PDM08], novel mining techniques can be leveraged. Execution histories tend to grow in size very fast. For the purposes of analysis a snapshot containing only set of relevant event types for a certain period in time is taken and transformed into a format appropriate for running mining and analysis algorithms. One example of such a format is SA-MXML [MAP08], on which process mining and analysis tools like ProM [MAP08] can operate. The information stored into the execution history can also be used to support the process engine in performing compensation of finished activities, as well as for running compliance test that are needed to proof that processes have been executed according to the imposed regulations.

5. CONCLUSION AND FUTURE RESEARCH DIRECTIONS

With the advent of SOA, the support for BPM has been improved. The major difficulties ensuing from integration problems have been reduced while experts were provided with additional support to focus on the business problems at hand, rather than being forced to deal with integration issues as well. In spite of these improvements in the integration on the technical level, there are still differences in domain models and proprietary business processes as well as in the different terminology used by technical staff and business experts. We identify the need for improved support for business experts in their endeavor to enabling business processes. The barrier to entry needs to be reduced in order to enable the experts (also in other domains apart from business) to apply their knowledge and insights of their domain without being hampered by insufficient or too complex to use IT support.

In this work, we presented an approach to enabling better support using semantics based on ontological descriptions of services, domain models, as well as on a comprehensive ontology stack (covering processes modeling, process-related events, etc.). Additionally, we introduced an architecture of a semantically enhanced BPM system centered around a Semantic Service Bus. This reflects the research results achieved in the project SUPER where semantics has been utilized to enable enhancements in the support of experts during all phases of the process life cycle.

The results have been tested using case studies from the telecommunication domain [SBC+08]. The applicability of these generic approaches (i.e. we devised them so that they are independent of domain) in other application domains is not hindered in any way.

Potential problems are performance and scalability and they need to be addressed in future to enable an enterprise-strength solution. Additionally, the approaches for process auto-completion, service composition, process mining, and ad-hoc semantic-based querying of the process space can further be improved and are part of future work.

ACKNOWLEDGMENT

The work published in this chapter was partially funded by the SUPER project (http://ip-super.org) under the EU 6th Framework Programme Information Society Technologies Objective (contract no. FP6-026850).

REFERENCES

Abramowicz, W., Filipowska, A., Kaczmarek, M., & Kaczmarek, T. (2007, June). Semantically enhanced business process modelling notation. In *Proceedings of the Workshop on Semantic Business Process and Product Lifecycle Management (SBPM-2007)*, (CEUR-WS, 251), ISSN 1613-0073.

Alves de Medeiros, A. K., Pedrinaci, C., ., von der Aalst, W. M. P., ., Domingue, J., ., Song, M., ., Rozinat, A., ., Norton, B., ., & Cabral, L. (2007). An outlook on semantic business process mining and monitoring. In *Proceedings of the 3rd International IFIP Workshop On Semantic Web & Web Semantics (SWWS '07) at On The Move Federated Conferences and Workshops.*

Born, M., ., & Doerr, F., & Weber, I. (2007). User-friendly semantic annotation in business process modeling. In *Proceedings of the Workshop on Human-friendly Service Description, Discovery and Matchmaking (Hf-SDDM) held in conjunction with the 8th International Conference on Web Information Systems Engineering (WISE 2007).*

Ballinger, K., Ehnebuske, D., Ferris, C., Gudgin, M., Liu, C., Nottingham, M., & Yendluri, P. (2004). *Basic Profile Version 1.1.* WS-I Specification. http://www.ws-i.org/Profiles/BasicProfile-1.1.html

Berners-Lee, T., Hendler, J., & Lassila, O. (2001). The Semantic Web. *Scientific American -American Edition, 284,* 28-37.

Born, M.,Hoffmann, J.,Kaczmarek, T., Kowalkiewicz, M., Markovic, I., Scicluna, J.,Weber, I., & Zhou, X. (2008, June 1-5). Semantic annotation and composition of business processes with maestro. In *Proceedings of the 5th Annual European Semantic Web Conference* (ESWC 2008), (LNCS, 5021). Springer.

OASIS WS-BPEL TC: Web Services Business Process Execution Language Version 2.0, OASIS Standard (2007). http://docs.oasis-open.org/wsbpel/2.0/OS/wsbpel-v2.0-OS.html

Business Process Modeling Notation Specification (2006). *OMG final adopted specification.* Retrieved February 6, 2006, from http://www.bpmn.org/Documents/OMG%20Final%20Adopted%20BPMN%201-0%20Spec%2006-02-01.pdf

Burbeck, S. (2000). *The Tao of e-business services: The evolution of Web applications into service-oriented components with Web services.* IBM developerWorks. Available at http://www.ibm.com/developerworks/webservices/library/ws-tao/

Cabral, L., Domingue, J., Motta, E., Payne, T., & Hakimpour, F. (2004, May 10-12). Approaches to Semantic Web services: An overview and comparisons. In *Proceedings of the 1st European Semantic Web Symposium,* Heraklion, Greece.

Chappell, D. A.(2004). *Enterprise service bus: Theory in practice.* O'Reilly Media.

Hendler, J., Berners-Lee, T., & Miller, E. (2002, October). Integrating applications on the Semantic Web. *Journal of the Institute of Electrical Engineers of Japan, 122*(10), 676-680.

Hepp, M., & Roman, D.(2007, Feb. 28-March 2). An ontology framework for semantic business process management. In *Proceedings of Wirtschaftsinformatik*, Karlsruhe, Germany.

Hepp, M., Leymann, F., Domingue, J., Wahler, A., & Fensel, D. (2005, Oct. 18-25). Semantic business process management: A vision towards using Semantic Web services for business process management. In *Proceedings of the IEEE International Conference on e-Business Engineering* (ICEBE 2005), (pp. 535-540), Beijing, China.

Intelligent Reasoning for Integrated Systems (IRIS)http://rsws.deri.org/index.html

Internet Reasoning Service http://kmi.open.ac.uk/projects/irs/

JSR 208: Java™ Business Integration (JBI) http://www.jcp.org/en/jsr/detail?id=208

Krafzig, D., Banke, K., Slama, D. (2004). *Enterprise SOA. Service oriented architecture best practices.* Prentice Hall International.

Karastoyanova, D., van Lessen, T., Leymann, F., Nitzsche, J., & Wutke, D. (2008). *WS-BPEL Extension for Semantic Web services* (BPEL4SWS), Version 1.0.

Karastoyanova, D., van Lessen, T., Leymann, F., Ma, Z., Nitzsche, J., Wetzstein, B., Bhiri, S., Hauswirth M., Zaremba M. (2008, Feb. 26-28). A Reference Architecture for Semantic Business Process Management Systems. Track "Semantic Web Technology in Business Information Systems". In *Proceedings of the Multikonferenz Wirtschaftsinformatik. (MKWI 2008).* Munich, Germany.

Karastoyanova, D., Leymann, F., Nitzsche, J., Wetzstein, B., & Wutke, D. (2006, September). Parameterized BPEL processes: Concepts and implementation. In *Proceedings of the Fourth International Conference on Business Process Management (BPM 2006),* Vienna, Austria. Springer-Verlag.

Karastoyanova, D., van Lessen, T., Nitzsche, J., Wetzstein, B., Wutke, D., & Leymann, F. (2007, April 16). Semantic service bus: Architecture and implementation of a next generation middleware. In *Proceedings of the 2nd International Workshop on Services Engineering (SEIW) 2007, in conjunction with ICDE 2007.* Istanbul, Turkey.

Leymann, F. (2005, December 13-16). The (service) bus: Services penetrate everyday life. In *Proceedings of the 3rd International. Conference on Service Oriented Computing ICSOC'2005,* Amsterdam. (LNCS, 3826), Berlin/Heidelberg: Springer-Verlag.

van Lessen, T. (2006). *Konzipierung und Entwicklung eines Repository für Geschäftsprozesse,* Diplomarbeit, Universität Stuttgart.

Leymann, F., & Roller, D. (2000). *Production workflow.* Prentice Hall.

van Lessen, T., Nitzsche, J., Dimitrov, M., Konstantinov, M., Karastoyanova, D., Cekov, L., &

Leymann, F. (2007, September). An Execution Engine for Semantic Business Process. In *Proceedings of the 2nd International Workshop on Business Oriented Aspects concerning Semantics and Methodologies in Service-oriented Computing (SeMSoC), in conjunction with ICSOC.* Vienna, Austria.

Alves de Medeiros, A. K., van der Aalst, W. M. P., & Pedrinaci, C. (2008). Semantic process mining tools: Core building blocks. In *Proceedings of the 16th European Conference on Information Systems,* Galway, Ireland.

Ma, Z., Wetzstein, B., Anicic, D., Heymans, S., & Leymann. F. (2007, June). Semantic Business Process Repository. *Proceedings of the Workshop on Semantic Business Process and Product Lifecycle Management (SBPM-2007),* (CEUR-WS, 251).

Nitzsche, J. (2006). *Entwicklung eines Monitoring-Tools zur Unterstützung von parametrisierten Web Service Flows*, Diplomarbeit, Universität Stuttgart.

Nitzsche, J., Lessen, T. van; Karastoyanova, D., & Leymann, F. (2007). WSMO/X in the context of business processes: Improvement recommendations. *International Journal on Web Information Systems (ijWIS*).

Nitzsche, J., van Lessen, T., Karastoyanova, D., & Leymann, F. (2007, November). BPEL for Semantic Web services. In *Proceedings of the 3rd International Workshop on Agents and Web Services in Distributed Environments* (AWeSome'07).

Nitzsche, J., Lessen, T. van, Karastoyanova, D., & Leymann, F. (2007, September). BPEL^{light}. In *Proceedings of 5th International Conference on Business Process Management (BPM 2007),* Brisbane, Australia, 24-28 September 2007

Nitzsche, J., Wutke, D., & Lessen, T. van (2007, June 7). An Ontology for Executable Business Processes. *Workshop on Semantic Business Process and Product Lifecycle Management (SBPM 2007), in conjunction with ESWC 2007.* Innsbruck, Austria.

OWL-S (2004). *Semantic markup for Web services.* W3C Member Submission, 22 November 2004http://www.w3.org/Submission/OWL-S/

Pedrinaci, C., Domingue, J., & Alves de Medeiros, A. K. (2008). A core ontology for business process analysis. In *Proceedings of the 5th European Semantic Web Conference.*

Roman, D., Scicluna, J., & Nitzsche, J. (2007). *D14v1.0. Ontology-based choreography.* WSMO Final Draft, 15 February.

Semantic Annotations for WSDL and XML Schema, W3C Recommendation, 28 August 2007http://www.w3.org/TR/sawsdl/

Schreder, B., Bhiri, S., Cekov, L., Konstantinov, M., & Evenson, M. (2008). *Use-case based component integration.* D7.4 of EU-Project SUPER.

Semantic Execution Environment http://www.oasis-open.org/committees/tc_home.php?wg_abbrev=semantic-ex

Sarbanes-Oxley Act of 2002, Public Law 107-204, 107th Congress, Senate and House of Representatives of the United States of America in Congress, 2002. http://frwebgate.access.gpo.gov/cgi-bin/getdoc.cgi?dbname=107_cong_public_laws&docid=f:publ204.107

Weijters, A. J. M. M., van der Aalst, W. M. P., van Dongen, B., Günther, C., Mans, R., Alves de Medeiros, A. K., Rozinat, A., Song, M., & Verbeek, E. (2007). Process mining with ProM. In M. Dastani, & E. de Jong(Eds.), *Proceedings of the 19th Belgium-Netherlands Conference on Artificial Intelligence (BNAIC*).

Weerawarana, S., Curbera, F., & Leymann, F. (2005). *Web services platform architecture: Soap, WSDL, WS-Policy, WS-Addressing, WS-BPEL*

WS-Reliable Messaging and More. Prentice Hall International.

Weske, M. (2007). *Business process management: Concepts, languages, architectures.* Berlin/Heidelberg: Springer-Verlag. ISBN: 978-3-540-73521-2.

Weber, I., Hoffmann, J., Mendling, J., & Nitzsche, J. (2007, September). Towards a methodology for semantic business process modeling and configuration. In *Proceedings of the 2nd International Workshop on Business Oriented Aspects concerning Semantics and Methodologies in Service-oriented Computing.*

Weber, I., Markovic, I., & Drumm, C. (2007). A Conceptual framework for composition in business process management. In *Proceedings of the 10th International Conference on Business Information Systems.*

Wetzstein, B., Ma, Z., & Leymann, F. (2008, May). Towards measuring key performance indicators of semantic business processes. In *Proceedings of 11th International Conference on Business Information Systems (BIS 2008)*, Innsbruck, Austria.

Web Services Description Language (WSDL) 1.1, W3C Note 15 March 2001http://www.w3.org/TR/wsdl

Web Service Modeling Ontology (WSMO), WSMO Final Draft 2, October 2006 http://www.wsmo.org/TR/d2/v1.3/#goals

Web Service Modelling eXecution environment. http://www.wsmx.org/

Web Services Reliable Messaging (WS-ReliableMessaging) (2007). *OASIS Web Services Reliable Messaging (WSRM) TC.*http://www.oasis-open.org/committees/tc_home.php?wg_abbrev=wsrm

Wutke, D. (2006). *Erweiterung einer Workflow-Engine zur Unterstützung von parametrisierten Web Service Flows*, Diplomarbeit, Universität Stuttgart.

KEY TERMS

BPEL for Semantic Web Services (BPEL4SWS) is comprised of a set of specifications that in combination facilitate the orchestration of both, Web Services and semantic Web Services. It uses an extension of BPEL that provides for an interaction model that is independent of WSDL, semantic Web Service description frameworks like OWL-S and WSMO to specify the capabilities the process provides and the capabilities a process requires from its partners. Additionally it defines a grounding format to enable Web Service based communication with partner (semantic) Web Services.

Ontology is one of the essential ingredients in the layered technologies of the Semantic Web. An ontology provides a vocabulary of consolidated concepts arranged in types and categories in well-defined structure for unambiguous use in a specific domain. An ontology in computer science is normally accompanied with a language, usually in an XML representation, for defining the vocabulary and specifying the relationships between the concepts in the vocabulary, e.g. Web Ontology Language (OWL), and Web Services Modeling Language (WSML).

Semantic Web Services (SWS) is an approach to combine (in particular WSDL-based) Web services with Semantic Web technologies (in particular ontologies), in order to achieve more automation in discovery, selection, and invocation of Web services. Web service interface descriptions are described semantically using ontologies, thus specifying their interface in a machine-readable manner. Popular SWS approaches are OWL-S, WSMO, and SA-WSDL.

Semantic Business Process Management combines BPM and Semantic Web technologies (in particular ontologies and SWS). Based on ontological descriptions of BPM artifacts such as process models, data models, and event logs,

SBPM aims to achieve more automation in process modeling, process discovery, service composition, service discovery, and process monitoring and analysis.

The Semantic Service Bus (SSB) is the key integration middleware in semantically enabled SOAs. Similar to an Enterprise Service Bus (ESB) it provides a communication and virtualization platform for services. In addition it introduces platform services fostering the use of semantic web techniques for data mediation, data transformation, process composition, discovery and reasoning. It provides a physically distributed but logically united entry point for semantic web services and semantic business processes and employs deployment strategies for such components.

Service-Oriented Architecture (SOA) is the architectural style for service-oriented computing. By identifying agnostic, self-contained services that encapsulate high-level business concepts it achieves a high degree of reusability. The key concepts of an SOA are "service consumers", "service providers" and a "service discovery" which enable loose coupling between components.

ENDNOTES

1. http://ip-super.org/
2. http://ws-i.org/

Chapter XV
Compiling Business Process Models into Executable Code

Cesare Pautasso
University of Lugano, Switzerland

ABSTRACT

Model-driven architecture (MDA), design and transformation techniques can be applied with success to the domain of business process modeling (BPM) with the goal of making the vision of business-driven development a reality. This chapter is centered on the idea of compiling business process models for executing them, and how this idea has been driving the design of the JOpera for Eclipse workflow management tool. JOpera presents users with a simple, graph-based process modeling language with a visual representation of both control and data-flow aspects. As an intermediate representation, the graphs are converted into Event-Condition-Action rules, which are further compiled into Java bytecode for efficient execution. These transformations of process models are performed by the JOpera process compiler in a completely transparent way, where the generated executable artefacts are kept hidden from users at all times (i.e., even for debugging process executions, which is done by augmenting the original, high level notation). The author evaluates his approach by discussing how using a compiler has opened up the several possibilities for performing optimization on the generated code and also simplified the design the corresponding workflow engine architecture.

INTRODUCTION

The goal of this chapter is to present how model transformation and refinement techniques can be applied to produce executable code out of business process models. The chapter shows how model-driven architecture (MDA) techniques have been applied with success to the domain of business process modeling. More in detail, once a business process has been modeled using some language, there are two main alternatives to be considered in order to run the process model using a workflow execution engine (Figure 1). The first involves the direct interpretation of the model, the second the compilation of the model into a lower-level representation amenable to more efficient execution.

As an example case study, the chapter shows how the idea of compiling business process models has been driving the design of the JOpera for Eclipse workflow management tool. JOpera presents users with a simple, graph-based process modeling language with a visual representation of both control and data-flow aspects. As an intermediate representation, the graphs are converted into Event-Condition-Action rules, which are further compiled into Java bytecode for execution.

These transformations have been fully implemented in the JOpera process compiler in a completely transparent way, where the generated Java executable artifacts are kept hidden from users at all times (i.e., even for debugging process executions, which is done using the original, high level notation). We evaluate our approach by discussing how using a compiler has opened up the several possibilities for performing optimization on the generated code and also simplified the design and positively impacted the quality of the corresponding workflow engine architecture.

This chapter introduces with an example a hierarchy of business process meta-models, leading from abstract, high level and graphical representations suitable for human consumption, down to lower-level languages geared towards efficient execution by a machine. Whereas for didactical purposes (and space limitations) the example presented in this chapter is focused on representations for modeling control-flow aspects, JOpera follows a similar approach with respect to the data flow and the resource perspective of the workflow models. We define relationships and transformations between the representations, in order to support the automatic refinement, optimization and compilation of models in one direction. We also present the abstraction operations required in the reverse direction in order to provide support for "source-level" monitoring and interactive debugging of the execution of business process models.

The rest of this chapter is structured as follows. A motivation for introducing process com-

Figure 1. Interpreted (left) vs. compiled (right) process execution

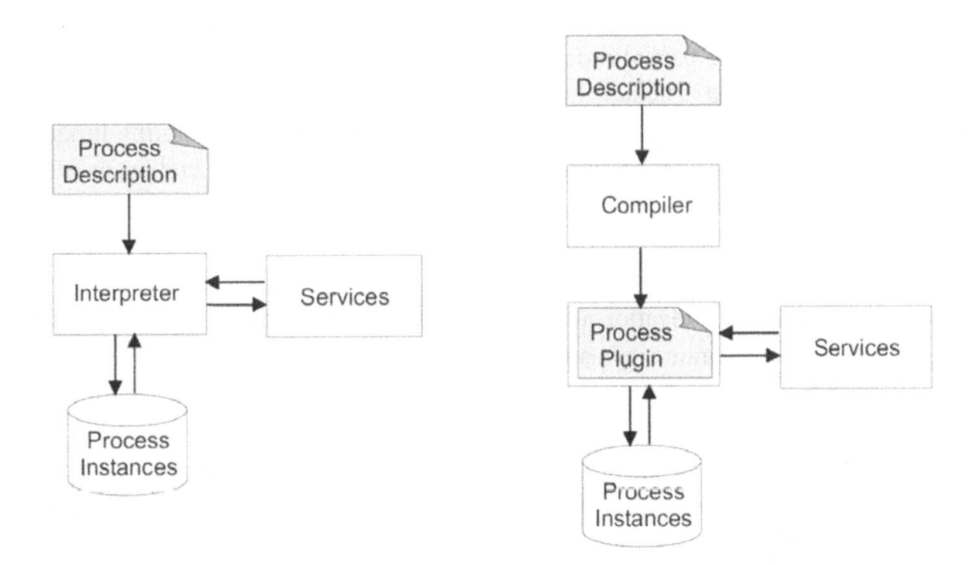

pilation (as opposed to interpretation and model refinement) is presented in the following Section. We then briefly enumerate in Section 'Process Representations' different abstraction levels and viewpoints that can be used to represent a process model that is meant to be compiled for execution using JOpera. In the following section, we show a concrete example of how a process model can be transformed between these representations. In the 'Architecture' Section, we present the design of the architecture of the JOpera workflow engine, emphasizing the role played by its compiler. Before drawing some conclusions, we evaluate the benefits and limitations of our approach in the 'Discussion' Section.

MOTIVATION

Workflow engines traditionally play the role of business process language interpreters. Why should a compiler be used instead of an interpreter? Direct interpretation of process descriptions is the typical approach of most workflow execution engines. In the simplest case, the model description as it is specified by the process modeler is directly fed into the workflow engine, which uses it to initialize the state of a new workflow instance (e.g., stored in a database) and navigate over (or analyze) the control flow dependencies between tasks to determine the partial order in which tasks should be executed. The advantage of this approach lies in the portability of the process models (which can be interpreted by engines running on different hardware/operating system/database platforms). As with most interpreted languages, however, the disadvantage lies in the higher runtime overhead of the execution and in the complexity of the runtime engine infrastructure featuring support for exception handling, late binding, and flexible, ad-hoc execution.

Compiled execution of processes opens up the possibility of transforming process models into a form more suitable for efficient execution. This idea resonates with existing research that applies model-driven engineering techniques to business process management. However, when it comes to compiled workflow execution, it is not feasible to use some kind of vertical transformation (from "business" models to "IT" models) which typically would entail a semi-automatic refinements of models (i.e., not because of the mismatches between the languages used at each level of abstraction, but because developers are required to manually enter missing information and details that are needed to make the workflow models become executable in the first place). Compiled execution instead requires a fully automatic transformation of the models, thus the model fed as input into the compiler must have enough information for it to be already executable.

Another important feature concerns the need of performing debugging and monitoring of the processes being executed by an engine that uses a process compiler. As we are going to discuss later in the chapter, it is important that the user debugging a process execution works in the context of the original model, even if this has been subject to several transformations in order to be compiled. Thus, an approach based on reverse engineering of process models based on lower-level artifacts would only be applicable if it would guarantee that the resulting models are identical with the original source model to be debugged. In practice, this is very challenging to achieve. Thus, we propose a simpler, more pragmatic approach based on establishing and maintaining links between the source process model and the artifacts produced by the compiler.

PROCESS REPRESENTATIONS

In this section we introduce a set of representations for representing the control flow perspective of business process models. These simplified representations are introduced to show how to perform compilation to execute business processes. As

Figure 2. Process representations across the lifecycle of process models

		Process Lifecycle		
		Design-time	**Compile-time**	**Run-time**
Target	**Human**	Control flow Data flow Graphs	N/A	Augmented Control flow Data flow Graphs
	Machine	XML	FSM+ECA	Java Bytecode

shown in Fig. 2, they fulfill different purposes and also target different actors (i.e., human process modelers and their tools) taking part in the whole lifecycle of a workflow model (from design-time, compile-time, to run-time). A similar approach can be applied using more complex transformations to standardized representations featuring more expressive notations.

- **At design-time:** graphical representation – suitable for visualizing the control flow between tasks so that it can be specified and understood by human process modelers;
- **At design-time:** XML-based representation – needed to store a serialization of the workflow model that can be easily parsed by tools and to enable the interoperability of the entire process modeling and execution toolchain;
- **At compile-time:** Finite State Machine (FSM), Event Condition Action (ECA) rule-based representation – the intermediate representation within the compiler;
- **At run-time:** byte-code representation – produced by the compiler, suitable for efficient execution by a Java virtual machine;
- **At run-time:** graphical representation – targeted for human operators that would like to visualize, monitor, and debug the current state of the execution of a process model

It can be observed that these representations could not be more different regarding their syntax (i.e., textual/XML, graphical notation, vs. executable bytecode). Still, they share the same "semantic" model of the process they represent. Thus, it should be possible to transform a process model among all of these representations in a fully automatic way.

As shown in Figure 3, the five representations are linked together by the compiler, which transforms the design-time XML into the executable bytecode, but also by a renderer, which – at design-time – displays the graphical representation of the process flow (which is also stored in the XML). As process modelers view and edit the control flow and data flow graphs in the visual process design environment, their changes are stored in the XML representation, which is kept hidden from users at all times. At run-time, the renderer displays the current state of the execution of the process bytecode by appropriately augmenting (e.g., by using colors) the same graphical representation that was used at design-time.

In the context of the JOpera case study, the control flow and data flow graphs are shown at

Figure 3. Relationship among different process representations

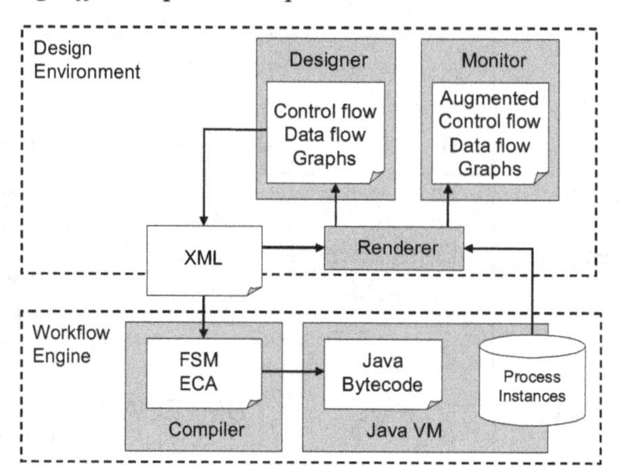

design-time and at run-time using the visual notation of the JOpera Visual Composition Language. These are stored using a specific kind of XML, the Opera Modeling Language (OML), an XML-based version of the Opera Canonical Representation. We will give a concrete example of how both can be used with the example presented in the following section. More information about these research-oriented languages and how they differ from existing standardized representations can be found in the suggested further reading.

EXAMPLE

To show a concrete example of the interplay of the different representations introduced in the previous section, we use a process model from an e-commerce scenario similar to the one of Chapter IV.

Design-Time Control Flow Graphs

The example contains three processes, representing the interaction between a Buyer, a Seller and a Shipping company. The control flow graph of each of the processes is shown in the graphs of Figure 4. The nodes of the graph represent the tasks of a process (whose execution involves sending messages into queues, receiving messages from queues as well as performing local computation), which should be uniquely identified. The edges of the graph represent control flow dependencies, i.e., the partial execution order between the tasks. Tasks linked by an edge are executed sequentially. Tasks not linked by a path in the graph do not have any control flow dependency and may be executed in parallel. Tasks labeled with a '?' icon are subject to conditional activation rules, which are evaluated based on the run-time values of the data parameters associated with the tasks and are stored as attributes of the task nodes.

More in detail, the structure of the Buyer process models a sequence of tasks. The Buyer first sends a request for a quote on a product, waits for a response (which contains the offered price), and makes a decision whether the product should be bought. If so, the Buyer will send the corresponding order request and wait for a confirmation. If the confirmation is positive, the Buyer will also wait to receive a shipment notification.

The control flow graph of the Seller process is the most complex, as it has to deal with the possibility that offers are not accepted by clients within a certain timeframe. The process begins by receiving a quote request from Buyers, then it looks up the price for the requested product in a database and it sends the result in the response

Figure 4. Design-time control-flow graphs

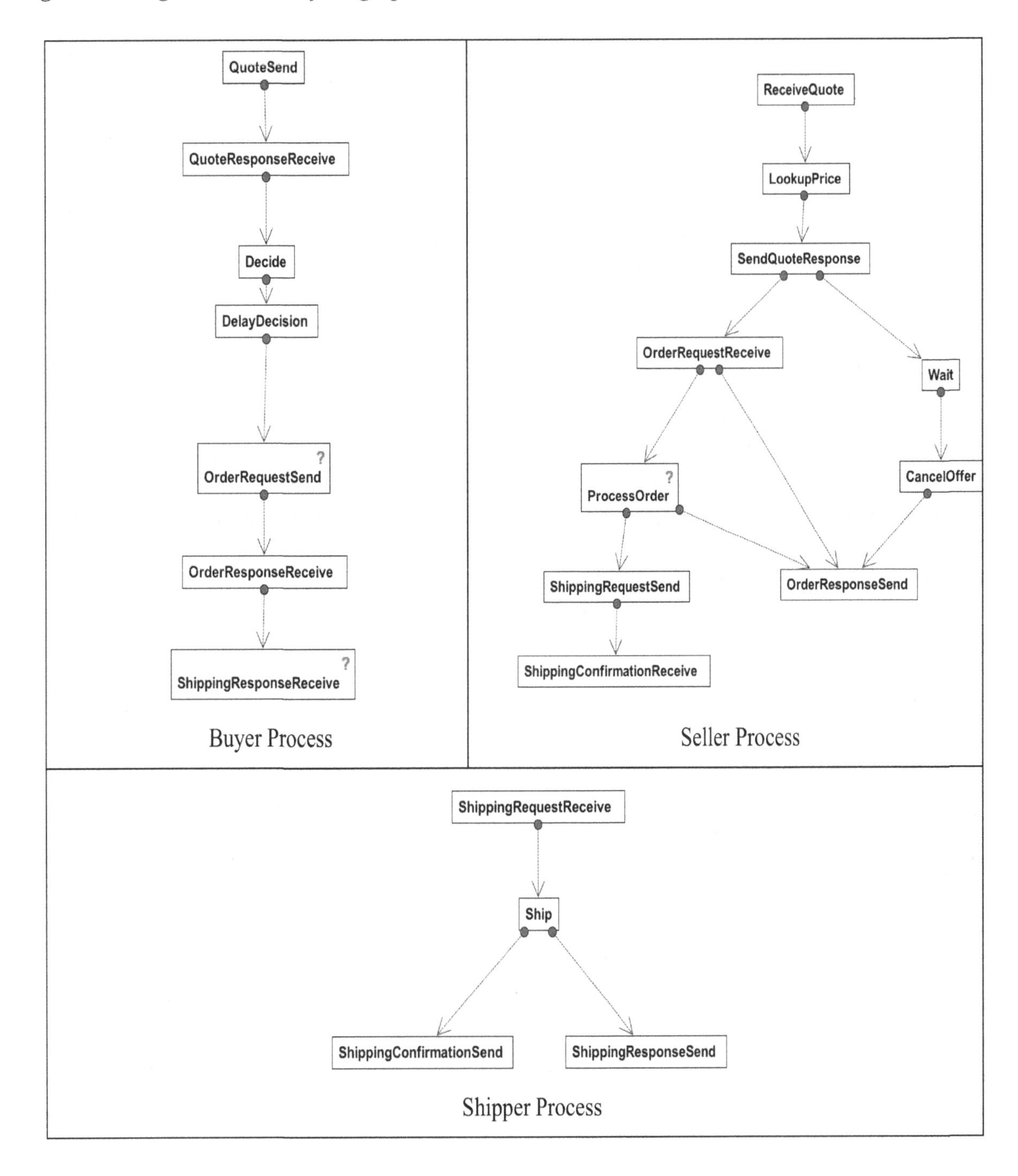

quote to the Buyer. Then, the Seller begins to wait for an order from the Buyer. Once the order arrives, it is processed. If this step is successful, a confirmation response is sent to the Buyer and a request to proceed with the shipment is sent to the Shipper. The Seller process concludes as the confirmation message from the Shipper is received. If the order does not arrive within a certain time (such timer is modeled by the Wait task, which is started at the same time as the OrderRequestReceive task) the offer will be canceled. In case the order from the Buyer arrives late, the order will be answered with a negative acknowledgement (using the same OrderResponseSend task as in the case the order is accepted).

The control flow graph of the Shipper process is also non sequential, as once a request to perform a shipment is received and the shipment task has finished, the messages to confirm the shipment will be sent in parallel to both the Buyer and the Seller processes. Parallel execution after a task has completed is represented by having multiple control flow edges leave the task (i.e., introducing a forking/AND branch in the control flow) to connect it to all tasks that have to be started and executed in parallel after it has finished. Alternative (i.e., XOR and OR) branches in the execution are modeled by associating conditions with the tasks that follow the split in the control flow graph.

Run-Time Control Flow Graphs

Figures 6, 7, and 8 show the same graphical notation for the design-time control flow augmented with colors (and labels) as it is used to monitor the run-time state of the execution of the Buyer and Seller processes. The goal of this augmented notation is to enable users to track in real-time the progress of the process execution as it is superimposed on the original model of the process. Also, it is important to distinguish the outcome of the process execution and give users a clear indication of the tasks that could not be successfully executed.

At run-time, the tasks follow the state machine shown in Figure 5. Tasks that are still waiting to be executed are in the Initial state (white). Currently active tasks are in the Running state (yellow). We distinguish tasks that complete their execution with success using the Finished state (blue) from tasks with a failed execution (Failed state, shown in red). Tasks may also become Unreachable (gray) if their starting condition was not satisfied, or because they were not reached by an active control flow path.

Design-Time XML Serialization

The XML serialization represents the control flow graph of a process as a list of boxes (representing the tasks of the process) followed by a list of arrows (representing the edges of the control flow graph). Since the same tasks can be shown in different graphs (e.g., control and data flow), additional information defining how the tasks are to be executed is listed separately and only referenced from the box displaying the task in the graph.

The example in Listing 1. partially shows the XML representation used in JOpera to store the Shipper Process model: the smallest one, with only four tasks and three control flow edges.

In the example, most XML element have the OID attribute, which contains a unique identifier that can be referenced by other elements. Thus, the graph can be easily reconstructed by following the references found in the (SOURCE, DESTINATION) attribute pair of the ARROW elements. The name of the tasks to be shown inside the boxes is stored as an attribute of the ACTIVITY elements referenced by the boxes, as the same task may be

Figure 5. State machine of a task execution

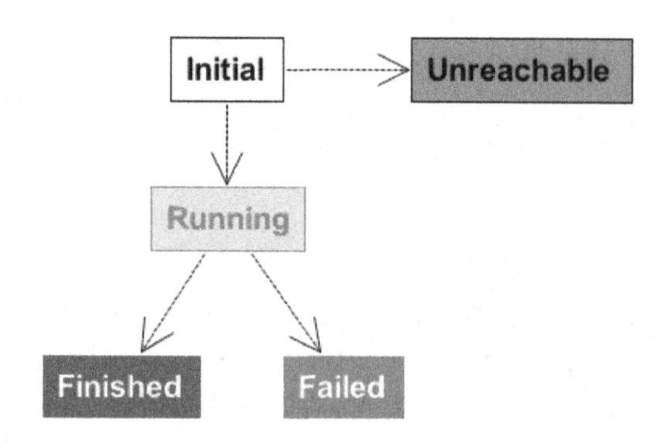

Figure 6. Run-time control flow graphs – Monitoring the execution of the Buyer Process: (a) Receipt of a Quote Response message from the Seller; (b) Delay after the decision; (c) Completed execution upon cancellation of the order by the Seller so that no Shipping Response needs to be received.

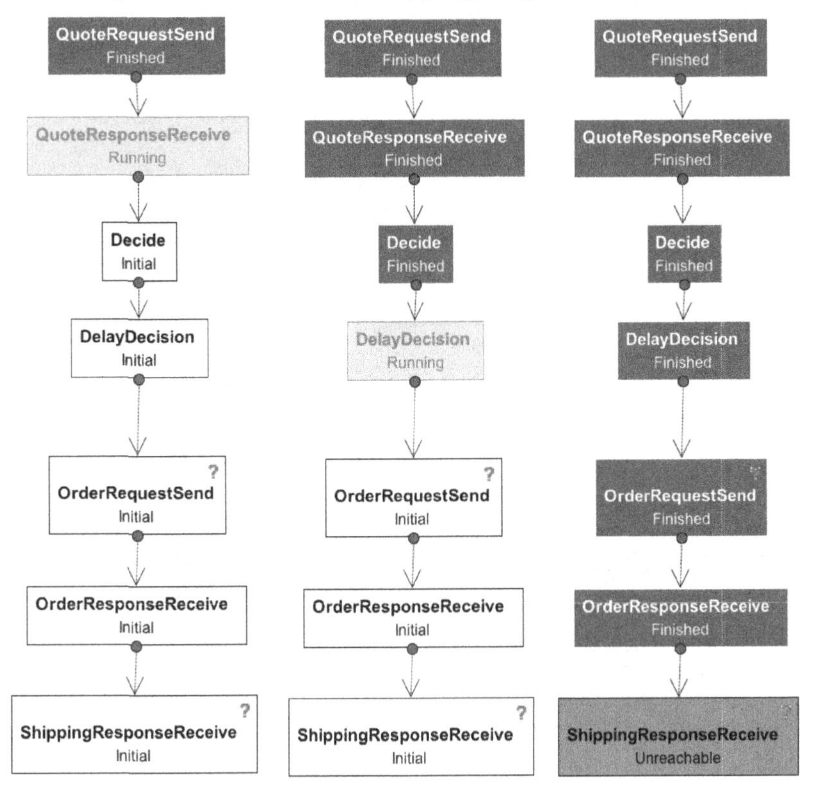

Figure 7. Run-time control flow graphs –the Seller is waiting to receive an order from the Buyer

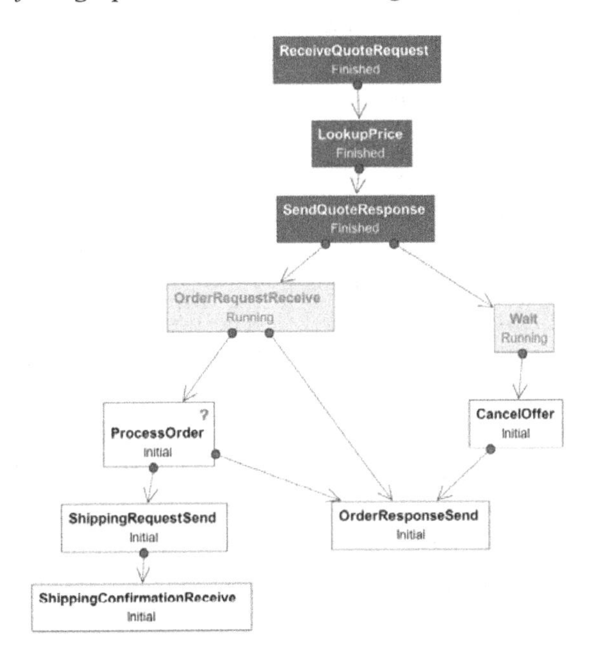

Figure 8. Run-time control flow graphs – Inspecting the completed execution of the Seller Process when the offered quote has been canceled due to the delay of the Buyer in sending the Order message

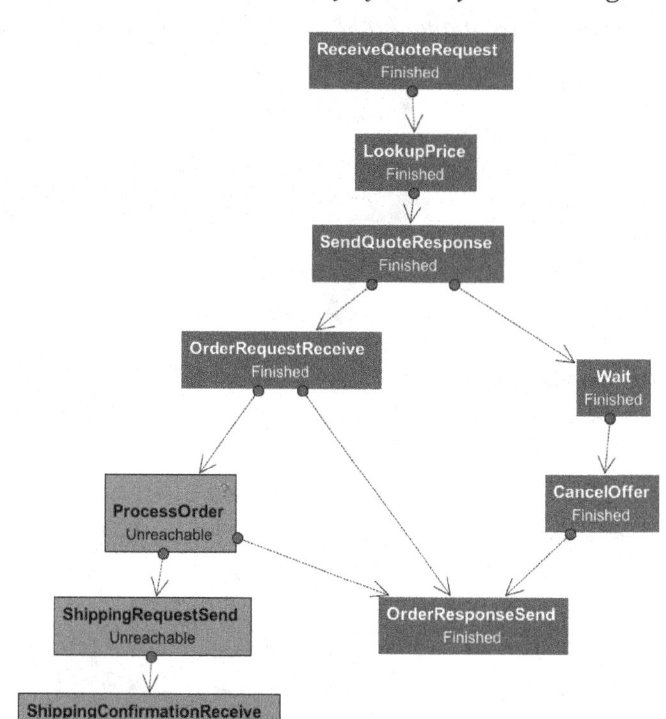

displayed in different graph views (not shown in the example).

From this example it can be seen that the XML code is merely used as a serialization data format which is not meant to be edited by human process modelers (as it would be rather tedious to manually enter unique identifiers for each task and make sure these are correctly referenced across the various elements as well as to specify the location of the boxes). Instead, a graphical editor should be used to render the XML into a visual representation that can be directly edited by the human process modeler.

Also, the particular structure of the XML is not suitable to be fed to an interpreter for direct execution. In order to determine which task should be executed first, the whole set of tasks needs to be searched for tasks that do not have an incoming control flow edge. To activate the next tasks after one has completed, the whole set of edges needs to be scanned to retrieve the successor tasks. As we are going to show next, this structure instead can be fed to the compiler, which will analyze it and produce a more suitable executable representation.

Run-Time Control Flow Graphs

The control flow graph of the process is first translated to a set of rules. These play the role of intermediate representation that can be then analyzed and used to emit executable code. These rules follow the well-known Event Condition Action (ECA) form. In our case, the event refers to a change of the execution state of a task; the condition is a boolean predicate over the values of

Listing 1. XML serialization of the control flow graph of the shipper process

```
<PROCESS OID="Process192" NAME="Shipper" VERSION="1.0" PUBLISHED="true">
    <TASKS>
        <ACTIVITY OID="Activity392" NAME="ShippingRequestReceive" .../>
        <ACTIVITY OID="Activity397" NAME="ShippingResponseSend" ... />
        <ACTIVITY OID="Activity402" NAME="ShippingConfirmationSend" ... />
        <ACTIVITY OID="Activity408" NAME="Ship" ... />
    </TASKS>
    <VIEWS>
     <VIEW OID="View193" NAME="ControlFlow">
      <BOXES>
       <BOX OID="RefBox394" X="260.0" Y="103.0" REF="Activity392" />
       <BOX OID="RefBox399" X="347.0" Y="256.0" REF="Activity397" />
       <BOX OID="RefBox404" X="167.0" Y="256.0" REF="Activity402" />
       <BOX OID="RefBox410" X="311.0" Y="170.0" REF="Activity408" />
      </BOXES>
      <ARROWS>
       <ARROW OID="Arrow415" SOURCE="RefBox394" DESTINATION="RefBox410" />
       <ARROW OID="Arrow424" SOURCE="RefBox410" DESTINATION="RefBox399" />
       <ARROW OID="Arrow427" SOURCE="RefBox410" DESTINATION="RefBox404" />
      </ARROWS>
     </VIEW>
 </VIEWS>
</PROCESS>
```

data flow parameters; and the action corresponds to starting the actual execution of a task.

Before we discuss how the graph can be mapped to the ECA rules, we list the rules corresponding to the control flow graph of the three processes of the running example.

From the example, it can be seen that the Event part of the rule is specified with references to the state of a task (e.g., Finished(Wait) refers to the task Wait becoming Finished). Whereas the example mostly shows references to the Finished state, it is also possible to refer to other states (i.e., Running, Failed, or Not-Reached). Also, the Event to start the first tasks (which do not depend on any other task) of a process is specified by referring to the state of the process itself (e.g., Initial(Shipper) means that the rule is triggered when a new instance of the Shipper process is created).

In the mapping from the control flow graph into the set of ECA rules, one rule will be produced for each task. In general, each edge of the graph corresponds to a reference to the state of the source task. Multiple outgoing edges from a task correspond to multiple rules with events referring to the same task (e.g., the Finished(Ship) event is used in two rules, each starting the execution of a different task: ShippingResponseSend and ShippingConfirmationSend). Multiple incoming edges into a task correspond to a single rule, where the event combines the references to the state of the

Table 1. Rules for the buyer process

Event	Condition	Action/Task
Initial(Buyer)	TRUE	QuoteRequestSend
Finished(QuoteRequestSend)	TRUE	QuoteResponseReceive
Finished(QuoteResponseReceive)	TRUE	Decide
Finished(Decide)	TRUE	DelayDecision
Finished(DelayDecision)	Decide.Decision = "Buy"	OrderRequestSend
Finished(OrderRequestSend)	TRUE	OrderResponseReceive
Finished(OrderResponseReceive)	OrderResponseReceive.Canceled = "No"	ShippingResponseReceive

Table 2. Rules for the Shipper Process

Event	Condition	Action/Task
Initial(Shipper)	TRUE	ShippingRequestReceive
Finished(ShippingRequestReceive)	TRUE	Ship
Finished(Ship)	TRUE	ShippingResponseSend
Finished(Ship)	TRUE	ShippingConfirmationSend

Table 3. Rules for the Seller Process

Event	Condition	Action/Task
Initial(Seller)	TRUE	ReceiveQuoteRequest
Finished(ReceiveQuoteRequest)	TRUE	LookupPrice
Finished(LookupPrice)	TRUE	SendQuoteResponse
Finished(SendQuoteResponse)	TRUE	OrderRequestReceive
Finished(SendQuoteResponse)	TRUE	Wait
Finished(Wait)	TRUE	CancelOffer
Finished(OrderRequestReceive)	CancelOffer.Cancel = "No"	ProcessOrder
Finished(ProcessOrder)	TRUE	ShippingRequestSend
Finished(ShippingRequestSend)	TRUE	ShippingConfirmationReceive
(Finished(ProcessOrder) OR Finished(CancelOffer)) AND Finished(OrderRequestReceive)	TRUE	OrderResponseSend

tasks into a boolean expression (by default, using AND – synchronization – operators)

In the example, this merge is only applied to produce the event of the OrderResponseSend task of the Seller process. In the control flow graph, this task is used to reply to the Buyer that has sent an order request message to the Seller. A reply should be sent after an order has been received (i.e., Fini shed(OrderRequestReceived)). If the offer is still valid, it is also important to wait for the order to be successfully processed (Finished(ProcessOrder)). However, if the offer has been canceled because the Buyer did not reply within the offer's validity time, then the ProcessOrder task will be skipped (as specified by its condition: CancelOffer.Cancel = "No" means the task should be activated only if the offer has not been canceled). Thus this example shows how to use boolean operators to appropriately combine individual changes to the state of the predecessor tasks into a suitable composite event expression. For such expressions, it is not possible to automatically produce them by analyzing the control flow graph. Thus, only in this case, the rule must be specified using a textual syntax by attaching it to the task before the compiler is invoked.

In general, the ECA rule representation can be seen as an "assembly-level" representation of the workflow, giving fine-grained control over the dependencies between tasks. The syntax of these rules can still be understood by process modelers (as opposed to the Java bytecode) that use it only if it becomes necessary to model complex synchronization events. In all other cases, the rules are generated automatically as the control flow graph is edited in the visual environment.

Thus, manual input to annotate the control flow graph by the process modeler is only required for complex dependencies, as the graphical representation (a true sub-language of ECA rules) has not been kept enough expressive[1]. Also, in case the rules are modified directly, it is possible to ensure that the control flow graph is updated to reflect them in a consistent way. To do so, the boolean operators and the structure of the expression are ignored and edges are added to the graph to represent the state references only (As shown in the control flow graph of the Seller process, for the OrderResponseSend task three incoming edges are shown even if the synchronization semantics is not a simple "and-join"). Thanks to this reverse transformation, users are not required to deal with a large number of ECA rules to understand the global structure of the control flow. Instead, they can still rely on the graphical notation to show the overall control flow dependencies of a process model and only need to read individual rules to understand local synchronization constraints.

Run-Time Java Code

From the previously discussed ECA rules, the compiler produces Java code structured as following example. For brevity, we only show the subset of code dedicated to run the control flow of the Shipper process example. The final executable bytecode is generated by sending the Java source code to a standard Java compiler.

Each process model is translated into a separate Java class identified by the process name and version. The class contains several methods. In Listing 1 we show only the method with the code generated from the control flow graph and the corresponding ECA rules.

This first code block is used to retrieve an image of the current state of the execution of a process and its tasks from persistent storage (the Memory). This way, the generated code can be used to run multiple process instances (identified by the TID Context parameter) as their state is managed separately from the state of the generated Java object. The code declares two types of variables. The first (type TID) stores context identifiers, used to refer to specific tasks (Context_TASK) and to a particular instance of the whole process (Context_PROC). The second (type State) stores a temporary copy of the current execution state of tasks and processes. Once the state of the process instance has been reconstructed, the code continues with the execution of a navigation step, used to determine which tasks should be started next based on the current state of the process instance.

The code pattern in Listing 2 is repeated for all tasks that are started at the beginning of the execution of a new process instance and corresponds to the Initial(Shipper) rule. Once the initial tasks are started (asynchronously, through the Exec interface), the state of the whole process transitions to Running.

The following code is used to continue navigation over the control flow graph of the process, once the initial tasks have finished their execution. The expressions evaluated before a task execution is started make sure that the task still needs to be executed (i.e., if its state is initial, the corresponding ECA rule has not fired yet) and then, that the corresponding event (Finished(Ship); Finished(S hippingRequestReceive)) is satisfied. After each task has been started, its state transitions to Run-

Listing 1.

```
public class Process _ Shipper _ 1 _ 0 implements WorkflowTemplate {

public void NavigateControlFlow(TID Context) {
// Read the state of the current workflow instance context

TID Context _ PROC = PROC(Context);
State State _ PROC = Memory.getState(Context _ PROC);
TID Context _ TASK _ ShippingRequestReceive = TASK(Context, "ShippingRequestReceive");
TID Context _ TASK _ ShippingResponseSend = TASK(Context, "ShippingResponseSend");
TID Context _ TASK _ ShippingConfirmationSend = TASK(Context, "ShippingConfirmationSend");
TID Context _ TASK _ Ship = TASK(Context, "Ship");
State State _ ShippingRequestReceive = Memory.getState(Context _ TASK _ ShippingRequestRe-
ceive);
State State _ ShippingResponseSend = Memory.getState(Context _ TASK _ ShippingRespons-
eSend);
State State _ ShippingConfirmationSend = Memory.getState(Context _ TASK _ ShippingConfirma-
tionSend);
State State _ Ship = Memory.getState(Context _ TASK _ Ship);
```

Listing 2.

```
// Activate tasks based on the state of their predecessors

if (State _ PROC == State.INITIAL) {

// TASK: ShippingRequestReceive

if (State _ ShippingRequestReceive == State.INITIAL) {
        Exec.Start(Context _ TASK _ ShippingRequestReceive);
        State _ ShippingRequestReceive = State.RUNNING;
    }
    Memory.setState(Context _ PROC, State.RUNNING);
}
```

ning. Once the task execution completes, the state of the task will be set to Finished (or Failed), thus triggering the repeated execution of the control flow navigation code. (Listing 3).

After a navigation step has been taken to determine which tasks should be activated (if any), the code in Listing 4 infers the state of the overall process based on the newly updated state of its tasks. With this, JOpera supports the implicit termination control-flow pattern. In particular, a process finishes successfully if all of its tasks have either been executed successfully (Finished state) or they have been not reached by the active control flow (Unreachable state)[2]. A process will fail if at least one of its tasks has failed. The code for these rules could be omitted to switch the semantics of the language to explicit termination. However, these final state transitions of the process instance would have to be triggered as part of the execution of special termination tasks to be manually included in the process model.

Listing 3.

```
if (State _ PROC == State.RUNNING) {

// TASK: ShippingResponseSend

    if (State _ ShippingResponseSend == State.INITIAL) {
        if ((State _ Ship == State.FINISHED)) {
                Exec.Start(Context _ TASK _ ShippingResponseSend);
                State _ ShippingResponseSend = State.RUNNING;
}
}

// TASK: ShippingConfirmationSend

    if (State _ ShippingConfirmationSend == State.INITIAL) {
        if ((State _ Ship == State.FINISHED)) {
                Exec.Start(Context _ TASK _ ShippingConfirmationSend);
                State _ ShippingConfirmationSend = State.RUNNING;
        }
}
// TASK: Ship

    if (State _ Ship == State.INITIAL) {
        if ((State _ ShippingRequestReceive == State.FINISHED)) {
                Exec.Start(Context _ TASK _ Ship);
                State _ Ship = State.RUNNING;
        }
}
```

Listing 4.

```
// Detect successful completion of the process

if (((State _ ShippingRequestReceive == State.FINISHED) || (State _ ShippingRequestReceive
== State.UNREACHABLE))
&& ((State _ ShippingResponseSend == State.FINISHED) ||(State _ ShippingResponseSend == State.
UNREACHABLE))
&& ((State _ ShippingConfirmationSend == State.FINISHED) ||(State _ ShippingConfirmationSend
== State.UNREACHABLE))
&& ((State _ Ship == State.FINISHED) || (State _ Ship == State.UNREACHABLE))) {
    Memory.setState(Context _ PROC, State.FINISHED);
}

// Detect failed execution of the process

if ((State _ ShippingRequestReceive == State.FAILED)
|| (State _ ShippingResponseSend == State.FAILED)
|| (State _ ShippingConfirmationSend == State.FAILED)
|| (State _ Ship == State.FAILED)) {
    Memory.setState(Context _ PROC, State.FAILED);
}

// Finalize the execution of the process instance context

if ((State _ PROC == State.FINISHED) || (State _ PROC == State.FAILED)) {
Completed(Context _ PROC);
}
```

Once the code determines that a process has reached a finished or failed state, the execution of the process can be completed (e.g., clients waiting for its results can be notified; the outcome and the execution time can be logged; the state information for the finished process instance discarded).

The code shown in this Section only corresponds to the ECA rules for the process control flow graph. The complete compiled code to execute a JOpera process model is obtained by weaving together this code with the one corresponding to the data flow and resource perspectives of the model. We leave it to the reader as an exercise to identify each by analyzing the full output of the JOpera process compiler.

ARCHITECTURE

As with most compiled languages, also in JOpera the resulting executable code must be linked together with a run-time library. The code shown in the previous section is designed to run within a certain run-time environment and relies on the services provided by the JOpera run-time library (such as persistent state storage, dynamic late binding of tasks, and flexible task invocations). In this section we briefly discuss different deployment scenarios for the process code and present the interface architecture of the infrastructure to support the execution of the generated code. Once workflow models are translated to Java executable code, we consider the following deployment scenarios:

- **Standalone Java program.** The generated code can be directly executed as a Java program. The input of the workflow is read from the command line arguments and the results of the workflow printed out to the standard output. To support this scenario, the compiler also generates a Java main method, which can be invoked to start the process. The Java virtual machine exits once the process completes. Such "pure generation" approach is conceptually simple to understand and easy to implement: the state of the workflow is kept in main memory and the run-time infrastructure required by the generated code is delivered in a small .jar library. However, in typical usage scenarios, more than one workflow should be executed concurrently and starting one dedicated Java virtual machines for each new workflow instance is rather wasteful. Thus, in our experience, compiling workflows to standalone Java programs is not one of the most scalable solutions.
- **Engine container.** The generated code is deployed into a container that plays the role of the traditional workflow engine. It supports the concurrent execution of multiple workflow instances, delivers persistent storage of their execution state and allows running tasks that require a variety of heterogeneous service invocation adapter mechanisms. The main advantage of this "extruded" approach lies in the possibility of reusing the existing infrastructure provided by a workflow engine and simply replacing the interpreter for the process modeling language with the Java code generated by the compiler.
- **Embedding in larger Java programs.** Another interesting deployment scenario involves the linkage of the generated workflow code within existing Java applications. This "embedded" approach opens up the possibility of using workflow languages and programming languages side by side. Since both kinds of languages share the same runtime representation, in JOpera the barriers that make it difficult to efficiently invoke a workflow from a Java program and viceversa disappear.

In all deployment scenarios the interface between the generated code and the corresponding run-time library, engine container, or main program does not change, making the compiler independent from the final deployment environment architecture. As it can be seen, the compiled code is found in a Java class that implements the WorkflowTemplate interface so that the functionality provided by the generated code to its clients is well defined. In the example, this amounts to the NavigateControlFlow method, used to perform each step of the navigation over the control flow graph of the process and initiate the execution of the tasks that become active. To do so, the generated code requires two kinds of services from the environment into which it is deployed. The first enables it to access the state of a particular workflow instance (the Memory load/store interface). The second is used to asynchronously initiate the execution of a task (the Exec interface). With this architecture, the generated code remains decoupled from the actual mechanisms used both to store the state of the execution of a process instance and to execute tasks. Thus, the same workflow code can run using persistent storage but also faster, volatile storage, to manage the state of the corresponding workflow instances. Also, the same workflow code can be bound to tasks executed using a variety of service invocation mechanisms, ensuring the technology independence of the process modeling language and its compiler.

DISCUSSION

Compiling workflow models to executable code brings several benefits to the overall quality of the architecture of a workflow management system. In our experience with JOpera, we have observed that using different representations for process models helps to optimize each to best fulfill their purpose. For example, the XML serialization is not meant to be visualized nor executed, and thus can provide a compact representation to store process models shared along a process-driven development toolchain. Also, the graphical notation helps users to grasp the control flow (and data flow) dependencies and the order of execution of tasks in a more intuitive way compared to reading the XML (or the corresponding ECA rules and Java code). The generated Java code is compiled into Java bytecode, which nowadays can be efficiently executed while still fulfilling the important requirement of portability across multiple hardware and operating system platforms.

Another architectural advantage of a solution based on compilation lies in the possibility of simplifying the workflow engine architecture. The run-time complexity of using a process language interpreter component can be shifted into the compiler. Thus, the size and complexity of the resulting "engine" is reduced, since, as we have shown, it plays more the role of a run-time library, for the execution of the workflow code is performed directly by the Java virtual machine.

Producing Java code out of workflow models has the additional advantage of enabling the efficient embedding of code snippets often used to implement the functionality of certain fine-grained tasks and to express complex conditional execution rules. Such code snippets can be directly injected into the generated code and invoked with the overhead comparable to the one of a local Java method call. Likewise, external Java programs can easily invoke the workflow code.

One known problem of process compilation is due to the limitations of the Java .class file format. For large process models (with hundreds of tasks) it is possible that the size of the generated code goes beyond the maximum allowed size for Java methods. This problem can be addressed by refactoring large processes, splitting them across multiple sub-processes. Also, the compiler could be extended to perform a similar partitioning of the generated Java code, by splitting it into multiple methods or classes.

Concerning the requirement for monitoring and debugging the execution of processes in the context of the original modeling language, we observe that it is possible to project the current execution state of a workflow instance to color (and label) the control flow graph without resorting to any reverse transformation from generated code back to the source model. Thus, by ensuring that a link between the original source model and the generated artifacts is established, this link can be kept in the code and traversed at run-time in the opposite direction to enable source-level debugging of compiled process models. This solution is similar to the approach taken by programming language compilers, which emit so-called "debugging metadata" into the generated executable code and likewise assumes that the source code is available during debugging.

A typical argument in favor of workflow interpretation lies in the possibility of supporting the dynamic evolution of workflows, where the model of a workflow is changed during the execution of a specific instance. If an interpreter is used, it is apparently much easier to evolve the workflow model: as changes are applied, there is no need to regenerate the compiled artifacts and the execution of the workflow can immediately continue over the updated workflow model. Since not all Java virtual machines support hot code replacement, it would seem impossible to modify a running workflow once it is compiled. However, we believe that the idea of dynamic workflows is not incompatible with the one of process compilation, if also process versioning and state migration techniques are applied. In the JOpera architecture presented in this chapter, there is a clear separation between the state of workflow instances and the compiled code of the process model (which remains stateless). Also, the codes of multiple versions of the same process model can co-exist in the same Java VM at the same time. Therefore, if changes are made to the structure of a workflow instance, a new version of the corresponding process can be compiled and the execution state of the running instance can be projected onto the new process structure so that its execution may seamlessly continue with the newer version of the code. By default, all existing workflow instances using the previous version of the code shall remain unaffected by the change. Still, also these can be migrated, depending on the nature of the change and the choice of the user.

CONCLUSION

In this chapter we have presented JOpera for Eclipse, an example of a process support system centered on the idea of compiling business process models before executing them. In JOpera, workflow models are visualized and edited using a graphical representation of both control flow and data flow (not shown in this chapter), which are stored using an XML serialization. At compile-time, the control flow graph is converted into ECA rules, which are used as an intermediate representation before the executable Java bytecode is generated. It is worth noting that such compilation step is kept completely hidden from the users of the tool. Users never see (and are not supposed

Figure 9. Screenshot of the monitoring perspective of JOpera for Eclipse

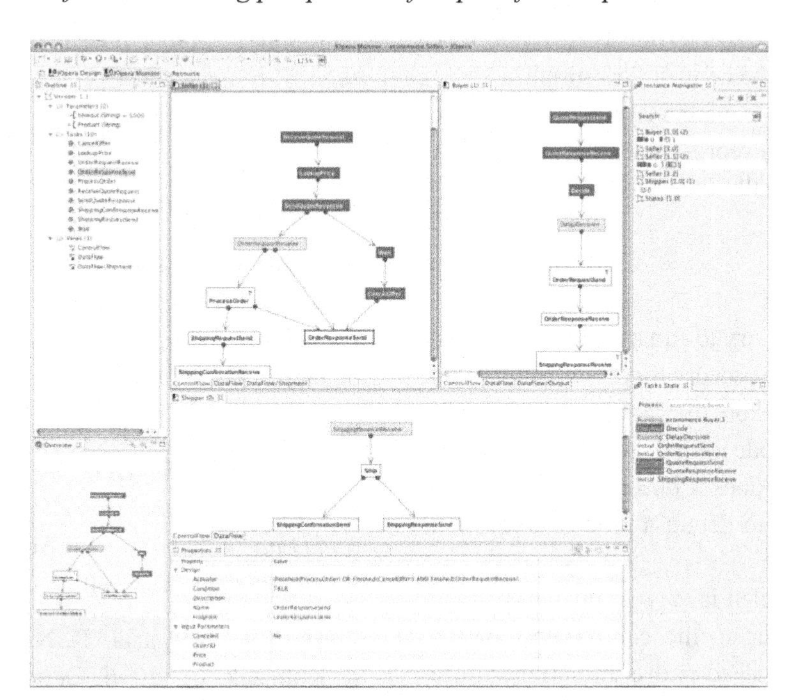

to see) the generated Java executable code and can monitor and debug processes in the original graphical notation used to model them (Fig. 9). Additionally, thanks to the automatic recompilation features of the Eclipse platform, users do not even notice that compilation and deployment are taking place, as they can seamlessly switch from the design-time modeling perspective directly to the execution monitoring perspective within the same integrated environment.

EXERCISES

Beginner

Download and install JOpera (www.jopera.org) and look for the "ecommerce.oml" example. Run it setting different delays for the Buyer decision task and the Seller offer timeout task. What happens if both delays are set to the same duration?

Intermediate

Suppose the ProcessOrder task fails: Should the order be confirmed by the client? Modify the rule associated with the CancelOffer task to reflect this. What happens to the control flow graph?

Why can the transformation between the control flow graph representation and the ECA rules only be partially inverted?

Advanced

Download JOpera, try to run a few examples: do you notice that the process models are compiled to Java bytecode before they are executed? Try to look for the bytecode in the .java (hidden) folder of the workspace: does it make sense to inspect the code in order to debug a process execution problem?

Read the compiled Java code and identify the code corresponding to the control flow of the process. How is the dead-path elimination feature implemented?

ACKNOWLEDGMENT

The author would like to thank Luigi Liquori and the anonymous reviewers for their invaluable feedback to an early draft of this chapter. Many thanks also to Gustavo Alonso, Win Bausch, Biörn Biörnstad, Andreas Bur, and Thomas Heinis for their support, inspiration and help to develop the idea of compiled process execution into the JOpera kernel.

SUGGESTED ADDITIONAL READING

Czarnecki, K., & Helsen, S. (2003, October). Classification of model transformation approaches. In *Proc. of the OOPSLA'03 Workshop on Generative Techniques in the Context of Model-Driven Architecture,* Anaheim, California.

Hauser, R., & Koehler, J. (2004, October). Compling process graphs to executable code. In *Proc. of the 3rd Int'l Conf. on Generative Programming and Component Engineering (GPCE2004)*, (pp. 317-336).

Pautasso, C. *JOpera: Process support for more than Web services.* http://www.jopera.org

Pautasso, C., & Alonso, G. (2004). The JOpera Visual Composition Language. *Journal of Visual Languages and Computing, 16*(1–2), 119-152.

Pautasso, C., & Koehler, J. (2008, September). *Proc. of the 1st Int'l BPM Workshop on Model-Driven Engineering for Business Process Management*, Milan, Italy. (LNBIP). Springer.

Perez, J. M., Ruiz, F., Piattini, M. (2006, September). MDE for BPM: A systematic review. *Proceedings of the 1st Int'l Conf. on Software and Data Technologies (ICSOFT 2006),* Setúbal, Portugal, (pp. 118-124).

Steffen, B., Margaria, T., Nagel, R., Jörges, S., & Kubczak, C. (2006, October). Model-driven development with the jABC. *In Proc. HVC'06, IBMHaifa Verification Conference,* Haifa (Israel), (LNCS, 4383), Springer.

KEY TERMS

Compiler: A software tool which transforms programs written in a source language into executable code for a target platform/architecture. Compilation may occur before a program is executed, but also—in the case of just-in-time compilers—during the execution of a program.

Control Flow: The flow of control defines a partial order relationship between the activities of a business process model, specifying in which temporal order they will be executed.

Data Flow: Activities of a business process may exchange data during the execution of the process. The data flow graph of the process connects activities that exchange data and -- in some notations -- may also represent which input/output parameters of the activities are involved.

Event-Condition-Action Rules: The "ECA" structure for specifying rules originates from active databases, where actions on the data are triggered by the occurrence of particular events subject to the satisfaction of the associated condition (a logical test on properties of the event itself).

Model-Driven Engineering: This software development methodology is centered around the notion of modeling (as opposed to coding) to be the primary activity in the software development process. Model refinement, transformation and code generation techniques are then applied to produce executable software artifacts in a semi-automatic way.

Process Monitor: A software tool used to watch the progress of the execution of one or more business processes.

XML Serialization: A machine-processable, persistent, representation of a process model that uses the XML syntax to store the model's information.

ENDNOTES

1. Alternatively, the graphical notation could become more complex to be able to visualize such arbitrary boolean expressions. However, this would conflict with the minimalistic approach followed to define the syntax of the JOpera visual language. Instead, the JOpera modeling environment gives users the ability to enter arbitrary Boolean expressions using a textual syntax to define properties associated with each task. A similar problem can be found in BPMN, where the synchronization semantics of complex gateways cannot be inferred from the visual notation itself and must be specified using a different representation.
2. This follows the dead path elimination semantics. The generated code to determine whether tasks may be skipped and to set their state to Unreachable is not shown.

Chapter XVI
Using WfMS to Support Unstructured Activities

Hernâni Mourão
Polytechnic Institute of Setúbal, Portugal

Pedro Antunes
University of Lisboa, & LaSIGE - Large Scale Informatics Systems Laboratory, Portugal

ABSTRACT

In this chapter the authors propose a solution to handle unexpected exceptions in WfMS. They characterize these events deeply and recognize that some of them require immediate reaction and users can not plan their response in advance. Current approaches that handle unexpected exceptions are categorized by their resilience property and it is identified that supporting unstructured activities becomes critical to react to these events. Their proposed system is able to change its behaviour from supporting structured activities to supporting unstructured activities and back to its original mode. They also describe how the system was implemented and we discuss a concrete scenario where it was tested.

1. INTRODUCTION

Workflow Management Systems (WfMS) are based on the premise that procedures are able to define the details of the work carried out in organizations. Since procedures and control data emerge from the overall system, the WfMS is much more flexible than traditional information systems, and any change to the procedure or control data may be easily accomplished. Using a WfMS, the organization is released from the task of routing the process and all related information through the different tasks and affected actors.

This original development of WfMS was biased by the rationalistic view that organizations follow procedures on a rigid way to achieve their goals (Suchman, 1983). However, organizations also require flexibility when performing their daily operations and procedures do not necessarily contain all the required information to accomplish the work. This clash between the original objectives of WfMS and the concrete organizational requirements lead to a difficult acceptance of these systems by their target market during the nineties (van der Aalst and Berens, 2001).

It has been shown by various ethnographic studies that the idealistic smooth procedural work is not always followed (Suchman, 1983; Bowers et al., 1995). Often, procedures are only used as guidance, since users adapt to the peculiarities of the situations not completely reflected in procedures. We thus have two different scenarios usually referred as *unstructured,* when users perform unrestricted activities eventually guided by an available procedure, and *structured* when procedures determine the user actions.

These two scenarios should be taken into account when supporting organizational activities. However, WfMS are traditionally algorithm-based and developed with a special focus on the structured scenario. One of the main disadvantages of this approach is the lack of flexibility to adjust to concrete user demand (Abbott and Sarin, 1994). An *exception* is therefore a situation where the WfMS is not able to support the users performing organizational activities.

Various researchers have addressed this lack of flexibility. However, the majority of the proposed solutions are still biased by the rationalistic approach, where more primitives are inserted on the WfMS to handle exceptions but always under any sort of an algorithm-based control. Even when primitives are inserted to increase adaptability, they have their roots on the original workflow model and therefore do not support totally unstructured activities.

In this chapter we describe a solution developed to address the problem that traditional WfMSs have coping with unstructured activities. We assume there will always be situations where users should be able to decide on what are the most suited activities to fulfill organizational goals, with or without restrictions imposed by the system.

2. ADJUSTING THE WFMS TO ORGANIZATIONS

The work processes carried out by organizations have been identified to belong to a continuum ranging from totally unstructured to completely structured (Sheth et al., 1996). It is interesting to note that the majority of the available organizational information systems tend to fall close to both sides of the spectrum boundaries (Sheth et al., 1996), thus leaving a significant gap in between. Unfortunately, traditional WfMS fall into the highly structured boundary and thus contribute to this gap. WfMS emphasize the execution of work models and thus have a normative engagement (Schmidt, 1997). Closer to the other end of the spectrum limits, Suchman (1987) proposes the notion of maps, which position and guide actors in a space of available actions, providing environmental information necessary to decision making but avoiding the normative trait. Email systems, the newly developed collaborative Web platforms sharing information among users and group support systems are examples of systems that fall close to the unstructured limits of the spectrum. Usually these systems promote interaction and do not have a normative engagement.

Since traditional WfMS fall close to the structured limits of the spectrum, they are inadequate to cope with unstructured processes. To support the continuum of organizational needs, WfMS should cope with the whole spectrum of structured and unstructured activities. This requirement has been identified by different authors (Ellis and Nutt, 1993; Abbott and Sarin, 1994). In our solution, we propose a system that is able to switch its behavior from model guidance to map guidance, back and forth. We start this section by discussing the limitations of two definitions of

WfMS and propose an extension to the WFMC reference model.

Sheth et al. (1996) enhance the various facets of a WfMS in their definition. The definition starts with the business process: a collection of activities tied together by a set of precedence relations and having a common organizational objective. This involves distributing, scheduling, controlling and coordinating work activities among humans and computers. This definition also embraces the organizational perspective of business processes as a collection of tasks pursuing a common goal, and the system perspective, where the tasks must be coordinated, distributed, scheduled and controlled.

Therefore, Sheth et al. (1996) define workflow management as the automated coordination, control and communication of work task, both of people and computers, as it is required to carry out business processes. This is performed by a workflow enactment service, which is controlled by a computerized representation of the organizational processes and provides the required services on a computing network.

The WFMC's definition (WfMC, 1999) states that a WfMS consists of software components to store and interpret process definitions, create and manage workflow instances as they are executed, and control their interaction with workflow participants and applications.

Both definitions emphasize the computer control of the workflow execution governed by a representation of the organizational processes. This characteristic is inline with our previous discussion of the structured characteristics of the WfMS. However, we established as one of the objectives of WfMS to be able to support unstructured activities, where users should be able to decide on the most suited activity without being restricted by any system contingency. This requirement implies that the system should be able to transfer execution control to the user.

The WFMC reference model (Hollingswoorth, 1995) is also biased by the rationalistic approach

Figure 1. Extended WfMC's reference mode

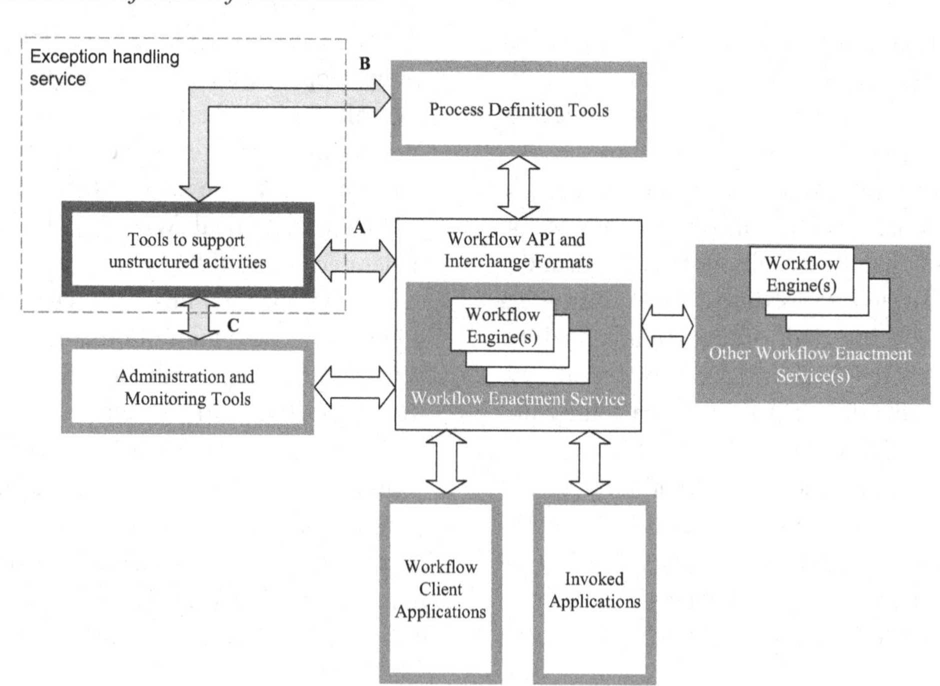

and does not foresee any mechanism of transferring control to the users. To account for unstructured activities, we extended the reference model defined by the WFMC with the model represented in Figure 1. The main idea behind this extension is not to specify the interface details for WfMS interoperability, as in the WFMC reference model, but to identify the new architecture required to support unstructured activities in a traditional WfMS. Therefore, the interfaces are identified here, but the functionality will be described throughout the chapter. The major goal behind this extension is that the system must be able to switch from model guidance to map guidance. This functionality requires direct interaction with the enactment services of WfMS, represented by interface A. Another required functionality is the capacity to implement model changes on the running instances. These changes require access to the process definition tools (interface B) and to the enactment services (interface A) in order to identify the instances on which the change is to be applied.

In some situations it may also be necessary to suspend the execution of a process model, to reallocate a task or to monitor system evolution using the standard WfMS functions. These features are implemented using interface C with the Administering and Monitoring Tools.

3. EXCEPTIONS IN WFMS

There are several ways to classify exceptions in WfMS according to the different perspectives that are applied to the problematic situation. In the related literature, some orthogonal criteria for exceptions classification can be found (Saastamoinen, 1995; Eder and Liebhart, 1995; Casati, 1998; Mourão and Antunes, 2003). Section 3.1 considers a system perspective and classifies exceptions according to the impact of the event on the system behavior. In Section 3.2 we describe a taxonomy that adopts an organizational perspective. Finally, in Section 3.3 we conclude with a proposal for a new taxonomy that classifies exceptions in a set of dimensions helping users deciding on the most adequate strategy to handle the event.

3.1 Systems Perspective on Failures and Exceptions

Eder and Liebhart (1995) characterize failures and exceptions according to a single dimension, encompassing two types of failures and two types of exceptions:

- **Basic failure:** Associated with failures in the systems underlying the WfMS (e.g., operating system, database management system and network)
- **Application failures:** Failures on the applications invoked to execute tasks (e.g., unexpected data input);
- **Expected exceptions:** Events that can be predicted during the modeling phase but do not correspond to the "normal" behavior;
- **Unexpected exceptions:** When the semantics of the process is not accurately modeled by the system (e.g., changes in business rules or a change in the order processing of an important client.)

The Eder and Liebhart's (1995) classification distinguishes two major types of deviations from the standard execution of a WfMS: failures and exceptions. The former result from system malfunctions either within the WfMS and the systems that support it or within the applications that implement the various tasks, where the latter result from semantic discrepancies between the model and the application environment. The authors recognize that the currently available techniques to solve system and application failures do not overcome every situation and therefore suggest an escalating concept to transform into exceptions the failures that cannot be resolved in the level where they occur.

As defined above, expected exceptions may be predicted during the modeling stage but do not correspond to the "normal" process behavior. These situations are usually excluded from the work model in order to reduce complexity. However, some authors posit that mechanisms should be implemented to handle these situations because they may occur frequently (Eder and Liebhart, 1995; Casati, 1998; Chiu et al., 2001; Sadiq, 2000; Luo, 2001) and cause a considerable amount of work to handle. For example, consider the example of a client reporting an accident to a car rental company; the company has to reschedule future rentals for that specific car until the car is repaired. The "normal" behavior should have been the car returning to the company, as planned, while the accident corresponds to a deviation or an "occasional" behavior: an expected exception.

Chiu et al. (2001) combine the above view with another orthogonal characteristic described as *exception source*. The exception source can be internal, when the exception is triggered by the system, or external when a user reports the exception.

Another taxonomy, classifying the type of event that originated the expected exception, was developed by Casati (1998)[1]. We have enriched it distinguishing these classes:

- **Workflow:** Triggered when a task or process is started or ended, it refers to the execution of the workflow itself. E.g., a deadlock situation or a loop being executed more times than expected;
- **Data:** Identified within the task that generates an error condition. The data events, even though identified within a particular instance can affect a collection of instances (e.g., a trip being booked twice for the same client). These exceptions refer only to workflow relevant data used for workflow evolution. If the error refers to application data operations, they will result into an application failure that is not considered by this class;
- **Temporal:** Triggered on the occurrence of a given time stamp (e.g., a rented car not delivered on time);
- **Non-compliance events:** Triggered whenever the system cannot handle the intended process due to differences between the tasks and goals.
- **System/application events:** Triggered when the system is not able to recover from lower level failures, such as database, network or application failures (lower level failures are propagated as semantic failures (Eder and Liebhart, 1995)).

Finally, the definitions found in the literature for unexpected exceptions state that they result from inconsistencies between process modeling in the workflow and the actual execution (Casati, 1998); they are mentioned to be consequences of incomplete or design errors, improvements or changes in the business maneuver, and issues unknown during the modeling stage (Heinl, 1998). From our point of view, any situation that is not predicted in the model and requires out of the box activities (unstructured activities) is an unexpected exception.

3.2 Organizational Perspective on Exceptions

Saastamoinen (1995) proposed a taxonomy based on the organizational semantics associated to exceptions. The taxonomy defines a set of base concepts necessary to construct a consistent conceptual framework that fundaments the characterization of organizational exceptions. Then, the taxonomy was developed using these concepts as well as empirical studies carried out in an organization, with a special attention to the social and financial impacts of exceptions.

Six different criteria were proposed to classify exceptions. However, four of these dimensions can only be established after the handling procedure is finished and can not be used to guide the operators overcoming the situation. The two relevant dimensions are:

- **Exceptionality:** Difference between the exceptional and "normal" event
- **Organizational influence:** Number of people involved in the exception

Three classes of exceptions were identified according to exceptionality: established exceptions, otherwise exceptions and true exceptions. Established exceptions occur when the handling procedure for the event is defined but the rules in the organization do not support users identifying the correct one. Otherwise exceptions occur when the organization has rules to handle the normal event but do not apply completely to the case. Finally, true exceptions occur when the organization has no rules.

According to the organizational influence criteria, exceptions can also be classified at employee, group and organizational level. Employee exceptions are situations that affect only the work of one person. Group exceptions affect a group of people working within the same process, in the same kind of job or on the same project. Organization exceptions affect the work of persons in more than one department or project in the organization.

3.3 New Exception Classification

In this section we discuss an extended exception classification focused on the knowledge about the situation processed by the organization and on the planning capacity. We start by the former dimension and finish with the latter.

Figure 2 shows the expected-unexpected continuum in the Eder and Liebhart's (1995) taxonomy (cf. Section 3.1) below the line. Our taxonomy is shown above the line. In our taxonomy, we propose three exception types. The definition of these types is based on the similarity of the situation with the complete set of rules and past experience that exists in the organization. *True expected* exceptions are at the expected limits of the spectrum and are those for which the handling procedures are entirely defined. For *extended expected* exceptions, which initiate close to the expected limits and extend into the spectrum, some guiding behavior may be drawn from rules and past experience even though some adjustments are required. Finally, *effective unexpected* exceptions are those for which the organization can not derive any guiding behavior from the organizational knowledge base. Since the system may not obtain any handling procedure, the user involvement is mandatory. Even further, some exceptional situations can represent a strategic opportunity that will not be recognized by the system. (E.g., a sales representative may identify new opportunities in some minor changes to an existing process.)

A new dimension will now be used to further classify effective unexpected exceptions: the planning capacity for the handling procedure. In this dimension two classes are identified:

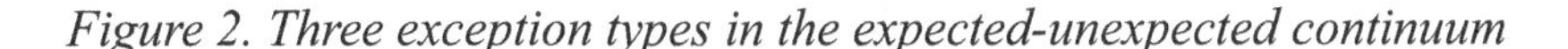
Figure 2. Three exception types in the expected-unexpected continuum

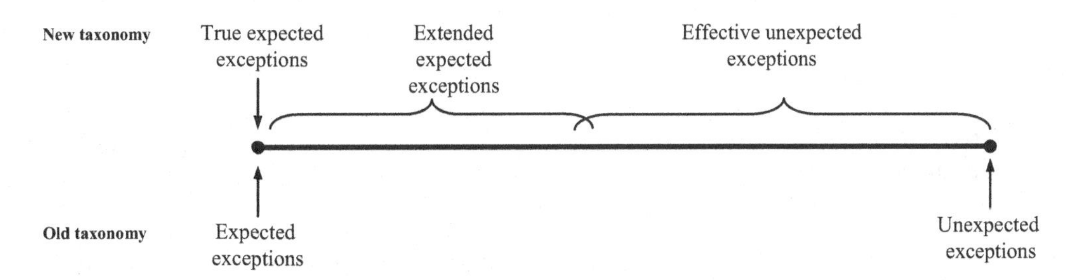

- Planned effective unexpected exceptions
- Ad hoc effective unexpected exceptions

For *planned effective unexpected exceptions*, a reaction plan can be established before the reaction starts. It usually means the organization has enough knowledge about the situation to establish a reaction plan. (E.g., a new legislation that the company has to comply within a period of time.) For *ad hoc effective unexpected exceptions* no plan can a priori be established. The reason may be that there is not enough knowledge about the event that enables advanced planning of reaction procedures, or the environmental conditions vary so much that no plan can robustly be defined. In these cases the situated characteristics of actions should prevail over prescribed ones and the reaction must be implemented in an ad hoc way (unstructured activities) involving problem solving among participants both for situation diagnosis and recovery. For example, if a truck with a very important delivery is stuck on a traffic jam, the users can not define a priori what is the best action to overcome the situation. It may be the case that traffic just starts to flow and no reaction is necessary, while in some situations another delivery by a different road may be the best solution. Users should collect as much information as they can and react as the situation evolves.

Therefore, ad hoc effective unexpected exceptions require human intervention and an innovative posture from the organization to deal with the situation. As no plan is available, human reaction should be map guided, according to Suchman's definition (1987). This exception type is the main focus of the present chapter. From now on, they will be referred as *ad hoc effective unexpected exceptions* or simply *unexpected exceptions* when no distinction is necessary.

4. OPENNESS AND COMPLETENESS

This section describes the two requirements we consider mandatory to support unstructured activities: openness and completeness.

The openness requirement states that the system should be able to collect environmental and workflow status information to support users on their map guided activities. Users should then be able to look for the most relevant information to understand the situation and decide on the most adequate activities to carry out.

On the other hand, users should not be restricted to the services provided by the exception handling system. The challenge is to manage awareness and consistency with the exception handling activities carried outside the WfMS scope. Our solution integrates environmental information about external activities but will not assume control of those activities. The main idea is that unstructured activities characterize human reactions to ad hoc effective unexpected exceptions.

Since some operations are carried outside system boundaries, it should be possible to maintain information on such activities and register any information useful to the involved actors. This requirement is also important to maintain an update history log of the implemented activities carried out during the exception handling procedure.

The completeness requirement states that an exception handling system should consent users to carry out recovery actions without restrictions, i.e., the flexibility of the exception handling system should be on par with the flexibility actors have on their daily activities when working without system control.

This definition is based on the notion that people tend to solve their problems with all the available means. If any system restrictions are imposed to the users' primary goals, they will overcome the system (Strong and Miller, 1995).

It is important to note that the flexibility implied by the completeness requirement should be supported by the WfMS enactment service. When the system is running, the enactment service is responsible for instantiating the work models and guaranteeing the processes run according to what is defined. Therefore, any deviations from the standard procedures must be implemented at this component.

The consequences of this open perspective on WfMS are profound. For instance, the restrictions to the common model changes found in the literature for adaptive and dynamic systems (see Section 5.2) must be relaxed. These restrictions are only applicable if one wants to keep the execution under the specified work models. However, if the objective is, for instance, to graciously abort a workflow instance, no consistency check is necessary. Even further, if the user decides to implement a recovery action that deliberately inserts structural conflicts in the work model, s/he should be advised on potential problems and allowed to proceed.

5. RESILIENCE IN WFMS

Since WfMS support business processes, it is very important they keep operational during business operations even under unpredictable situations. Their ability to adjust to actual businesses solicitations and to react to different hazardous conditions such as failures and exceptions is a core property for a WfMS to actually support organizations:

The resilience property of a WfMS concerns its ability to maintain a coherent state and continue supporting business processes after being subject to any hazardous situations that affect its execution.

It should be emphasized this is a runtime property of the WfMS, because predicting any possible cause of failure or exception during design is considered very difficult or even impossible and makes the system very complex and hard to manage (Casati, 1998). The strategy to manage failures and exceptions is to increase system resilience. Resilience requires both robustness, to avoid system crashes due to failures, and flexibility to adjust to deviations on the user and organizational conditions.

This section focuses on the existing techniques to increase robustness and augment flexibility: resilience. Section 5.1 is dedicated to analyze the systemic approaches to resilience. The systemic techniques assume the objective to provide the WfMS with the necessary mechanisms to react to basic and application failures, and expected exceptions. The systems handling expected exceptions fall in this group because they do not increase flexibility when users face a new exception at runtime.

Section 5.2 proceeds with the human oriented approaches to increase resilience. The various research lines were grouped in two classes according to their approach to the problem (classification inspired by (Han et al., 1998)): metamodels and open-point. Some other approaches to support unstructured activities are also mentioned. Finally, Section 5.3 compares the different approaches to augment resilience and draws conclusions to use in the remainder of the chapter.

5.1 Systemic Approaches to Increase Resilience

We have previously distinguished (cf. Section 3.1) between system and application failures, where system failures result from malfunctions either within the WfMS and the systems that support it and application failures result from errors in the applications that implement the workflow tasks. Systemic approaches aim to handle this type of events and are defined as:

Systemic approaches are designed to handle failures and exceptions without human intervention.

However, it has been recognized that in some situations it is not possible to handle the event without human intervention (Eder and Liebhart, 1995; Casati, 1998; Chiu et al., 2001). A propagation mechanism must be foreseen to transform these situations into unexpected exceptions so they can be handled with human support. Systemic approaches are therefore conditioned by the limited capacity of WfMS to overcome problems without human intervention.

Usually, WfMS use a database management system (DBMS) to persist the workflow relevant data. Transaction processing techniques, developed in the DMBS field, guarantee data integrity and consistency on system failures. In fact, most of the commercially available DBMS on the market implement the necessary transaction processing mechanisms to react in case of failure, returning the system to a coherent state and enabling forward execution (Casati, 1998). Therefore, on the event of a system failure, the DBMS implements a standard failure handling task by restoring a previous coherent state. The WfMS is then able to proceed with forward execution.

A wide variety of work has been developed to increase the system capacity to recover in the case of an application failure. Advanced transition models with relaxed Atomicity, Consistency, Isolation and Durability (ACID) properties were one of the most adopted research lines. This line tries to handle the long-running characteristics of WfMS activities by relaxing the ACID properties of the transactions and defining compensation activities to recover the system to a coherent state. Nevertheless, as mentioned before, researchers in this field recognize that it will always be necessary to escalate the failure to an exception when the system is not able to handle it.

The systems designed to handle true expected exceptions are supported on special constructs triggered by conditions that identify the presence of an expected exception. These constructs initiate the execution of the procedure designed to handle the expected event. The systems developed by Casati (1998), Chiu et al. (2001) and by Adams et al. (2007) are examples developed within this group.

Researchers have tried to increase the applicability of these approaches by applying artificial intelligence techniques and exception mining. The idea behind these approaches is to augment the matching mechanism between the detected event and the existing exception description to verify if the defined procedure can be used in the event handling.

5.2 Human-Oriented Approaches to Increase Resilience

As mentioned at the beginning of this section, resilience is a system's runtime property. Therefore human-oriented approaches to increase flexibility may be defined as:

Human-oriented approaches are designed to support human interventions in business processes at runtime, and increase the systems' resilience by increasing its flexibility.

Flexibility is related to the operations not predicted in the model that users carry out to accomplish work (Agostini and De Michelis, 2000; van der Aalst and Basten, 2002; Ellis and Nutt, 1993; Casati, 1998; Mourão and Antunes, 2004). I.e., when a process is instantiated, the user may implement some operations not predicted in the model but made available by the workflow enactment service. When the intervention requires model adaptation, the process definition tools may be used to design the new model, while the enactment service replaces the old model by the new and continues operation.

Two main research streams can be identified in this area (Han et al., 1998): metamodel and open-point. Metamodel approaches take into major consideration the structural and dynamic constraints to model adaptations, while open-point approaches define special points in the workflow model where the adaptations can be made. Metamodel approaches offer higher intervention latitude since they are not limited by special points in the model where the intervention can be made. However, they require model consistency checks, while in the open-point approaches the consistency checks are not necessary due to the restrictions in the allowed interventions.

Metamodel approaches are usually referred in the literature as producing dynamic and adaptive WfMS and are actually one of the most important research streams to increase flexibility in WfMS. On the occurrence of exceptions, users should be able to change workflow models at runtime, adapting them to the new situation and migrating running instances to the new model without stopping or breaking the system (Ellis et al., 1995; Reichert and Dadam, 1998; Agostini and De Michelis, 2000; Casati, 1998; Sadiq, 2000; van der Aalst and Basten, 2002; Weske, 2001). Two types of interventions are identified in the related literature (van der Aalst and Basten, 2002; Rinderle et al., 2004): ad hoc changes and evolutionary changes.

These interventions may be defined as:

Ad hoc changes are typically applied to a small set of instances and are a reaction to a particular situation that affects some specific processes.

And,

Evolutionary changes result in a new version of the workflow model and result from changes in the business processes that the organization is required to implement.

Both ad hoc and evolutionary changes must be executed under the system control to keep correctness, avoiding the insertion of deadlocks, unreachable states or inconsistencies in the data dependency model. These solutions define *a set of change rules enabling automated correctness checks*. Two correctness criteria must be taken into consideration: structural and state related. The former concerns schema changes and assures the new model is consistent. The state related criterion concerns the state of the instances to be migrated and verifies if they can be propagated to the new model.

It should be emphasized these approaches require that a new model is issued and instances migrated to this new model. Even when ad hoc interventions are allowed, and users may implement special actions in the model they are always restricted by a model, either the original or the changed one. Therefore, users should plan the intervention before any recovering mechanism is started. However, in some situations, especially in ad hoc unplanned effective unexpected exceptions, users are not able to issue any plan and they should start the recovery as soon as they identify the situation.

Recent development on these approaches (Weber et al., 2008) have suggested change patterns and change support features to assess WfMS ability to deal with workflow changes. These are relevant studies to establish a solid framework aiming to support flexibility during runtime operations. In the open point area, the system developed by Adams (2006) enables biding activities to worklets (units of work) at runtime. The system selects the most adequate worklet to the specific case from a set of available worklets. Users can even develop worklets for a particular instance.

Some other approaches deserve being mentioned here because they handle the same problem we identified. The system developed by Agostini and De Michelis (2000) is one of the few approaches having the objective of supporting users in a way similar to our approach, allowing collaboration between the involved actors. However, the model limits interventions and users should not insert any inconsistencies.

Guimarães et al. (1997) proposed an integrated architecture of formal coordinated processes with informal cooperative processes. (Saastamoinen,

1995) presents an approach focused on organizational semantics. Another important research in this area was proposed by Bernstein (2000), who developed a system to support processes in the whole spectrum from structured and unstructured.

5.3 Discussion

From the above discussion it is important to realize that systemic approaches are crucial to increase the WfMS robustness regarding failures and expected exceptions. However, when effective unexpected exceptions are raised (cf. Section 3.3), human intervention is required.

On the systems aiming to augment flexibility, the metamodel approaches rely on modeling formalisms to support operators implementing changes to the model and migrating the running instances to the new model, while open-point approaches define specific points in the model where interventions are allowed. Open-point approaches are easier to implement because they do not require consistency checks but they have lower latitude for user interventions. Metamodel approaches allow a higher degree of interventions but the users should plan new models before starting the interventions. Even further, the interventions are limited to maintain model consistency.

Figure 3 positions the systemic approaches, metamodel and open-point approaches according to the type of control and planning capacity. The arrow below indicates the direction for increasing flexibility and shows how the approaches are positioned within the same control type. Three classes were identified in this dimension: systemic, restricted humanistic and unrestricted humanistic. Systems designed to handle failures and expected exceptions have systemic control and planed reaction. In fact, the reaction to these events is pre-planned. Expected exception handling offers higher flexibility because it is easier to plug-in and change the pre-planned reaction to events. Humanistic approaches augment the operators' latitude of intervention and may be applied at runtime, increasing the flexibility to react to unforeseen events. Humanistic approaches were split in the figure into restricted humanistic and unrestricted humanistic. Open point and metamodel approaches are able to support users on both ad hoc and planned interventions. However, they are not able to support unstructured activities because of their limited latitude for interventions (restricted by model consistency).

Figure 3. Classification of approaches according to control and planning capacity

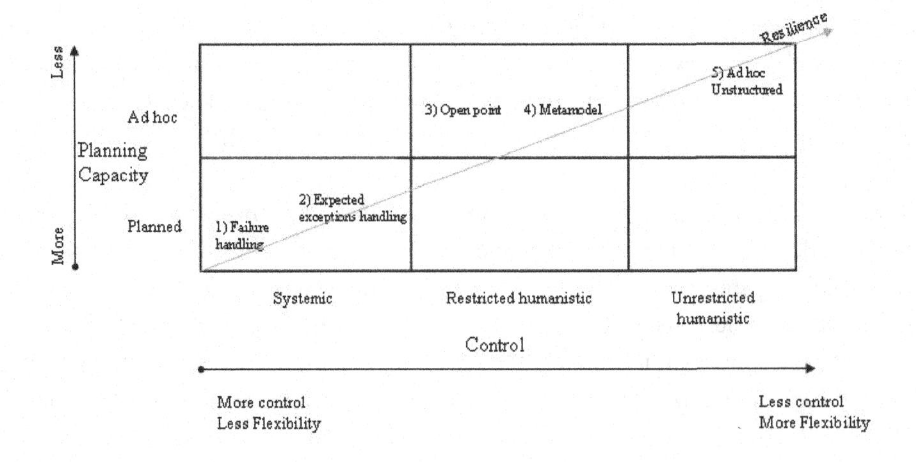

The arrow Resilience in Figure 3 is mainly qualitative and indicates the direction of increasing resilience of a system. A system positioned at some point of the line should be able to support all operation modes from the origin. That means that a metamodel system should implement all features of an open point, expected exception handling and failure handling. Such a system is therefore robust because it reacts to low level failures and expected exceptions, and exhibits some degree of flexibility because it allows restricted humanistic interventions.

The characteristics of our system place it on the top right of the figure, identified as *ad hoc unstructured.* Here, flexibility is at its maximum degree and interventions are fully ad hoc since the planning capacity is very low. They are also unrestricted by model consistency.

From Figure 3 we may realize that systemic approaches rely on the stage (1) and (2) on the resilience axes and they only provide systemic support. Metamodel and open-point are at stage (3) and (4) since they do not provide unrestricted support to unstructured activities.

6. A SOLUTION TO SUPPORT THE WHOLE SPECTRUM OF ORGANIZATIONAL ACTIVITIES

This section introduces our proposed solution to support the whole spectrum of organizational activities. The system should be able to work under model guidance and adopt map guidance when an unexpected exception is detected. Map guidance support for Unstructured Activities is based on the notion that maps position operators on the space of available actions (cf. Section 2). Unstructured activities are carried out until the system is back into a coherent state. Then, the user will either place affected instances under model guidance or abort them. The overall system behavior is modeled by the state diagram in Figure 4.

In our solution, we implement the extended WfMC reference model (cf. Section 2). The developed functionality supporting unstructured activities runs on a workflow engine. A dedicated model implements the components to support unstructured activities.

Figure 4. Solution's state diagram

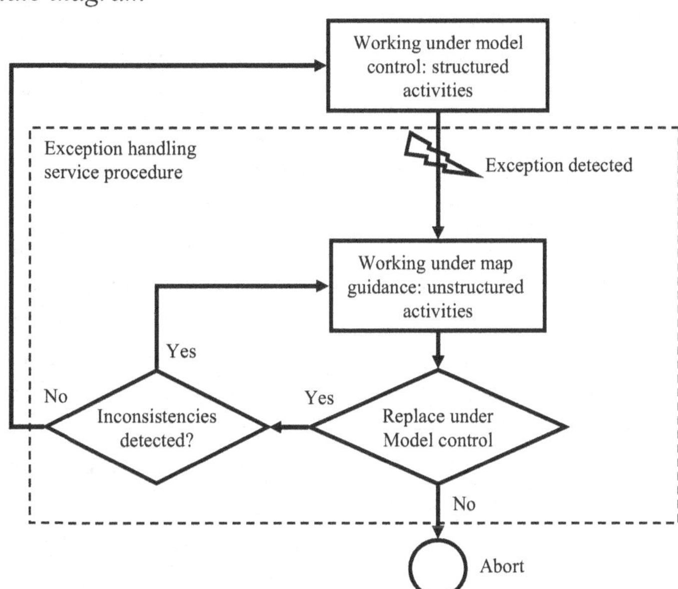

After this brief introduction, in Section 6.1 we present our conceptual approach. The basic exception handling functions are identified in Section 6.2: detection, diagnosis, recovery and monitoring. Section 6.3 discusses the exception diagnosis and in Section 6.4 we discuss the recovery and monitoring functions.

6.1 Conceptual Approach

Figure 1 is our proposal for the extended WfMC reference model. When the system is supporting structured activities, the traditional WfMS has control over activities and the exception handling service is inactive. When an exception is detected, the exception handling service interrupts the WfMS execution and the system starts supporting unstructured activities.

While supporting unstructured activities, the system offers the following functionality:

i. Escalation
ii. Monitoring
iii. Diagnosis
iv. Communication
v. Collaboration
vi. Recovery
vii. Coordination
viii. Tools to determine the best solution
ix. History log

The relevant organizational actors may have to be involved in the exception handling activities. The organizational levels with adequate decision authority should participate in decision making and action implementation. The *escalation* mechanism allows the involvement of organizational members in this process. On the other hand, to support the group of involved users overcoming the exceptional situation the system must also:

1. Support users understanding the situation – diagnosis
2. Support users deciding the most adequate actions to overcome the situation – recovery

To facilitate *diagnosis*, users should be fed with quality information about the peculiarities of the situation at hand. Since information and knowledge about the event are spread throughout the organization and the environment, our solution implements *monitoring* mechanisms to collect relevant data and enable knowledge sharing among the participants (cf. openness requirement in Section 4). This shared effort is supported by *collaboration* and *communication* mechanisms facilitating common situation awareness. *Diagnosis* is also supported by a situation description component used to classify the event according to several dimensions. Since the situation may evolve over time, users may change the description.

The recovery process may be characterized as a mutual adjustment and coordination effort. The *collaboration* and *communication* mechanisms support mutual adjustment. (Mutual adjustment requires combined communication, coordination and collaboration). It should be emphasized that during unstructured activities support, the coordination facet implemented by the WfMS is relaxed since users gain control over orchestrating their activities. This unavoidable characteristic of the solution imposes a special focus: users should coordinate their activities under map guidance.

The functionality *tools to determine the best solution* accounts for application environments where special tools may be used to support both the understanding of the situation and the decision process. (E.g., operations research algorithms in a lot manufacturing company may support users calculating the lots that should be manufactured when reacting to an unexpected change in demand.)

Finally, our solution maintains a *history log* for the situation description and all of the implemented activities. When new values are defined for the situation description, the old values are stored in the historical log.

6.2 Basic Functions

As mentioned before, unexpected exception[2] handling is a problem solving activity that requires understanding the situation and implementing the required activities to overcome the exceptional situation. We distinguish four functions in the process:

- Exception detection
- Situation diagnosis
- Exception recovery
- Monitoring actions

Since detection is only important for triggering the handling procedure and is independent from the other functions, we will not describe it here. This section only describes the other three functions.

The majority of authors identify the first three functions (Sadiq, 2000; Dellarocas and Klein, 1998). However, as it was discussed before (cf. the openness requirement in Section 4) and will be further developed below, we posit that monitoring actions play a key role in unexpected exception handling.

In our solution, we advocate an intertwined play between diagnosis, recovery and monitoring until the exception is resolved. That is to say, the diagnosis is not considered complete on the first approach but rather through an iterative process where different actors may collaboratively contribute and information collected from monitoring and recovery actions is used to improve it. It should also be stressed that both the exceptional situation and perception of the situation may change along this iterative process, as new information is made available and processed by humans. Therefore, monitoring actions support this cognitive process.

After diagnosis, users may carry out recovery actions. The open nature of the proposed solution suggests that the recovery actions do not always run in the inner system context and thus some linking mechanism is necessary to bring environmental information to the system.

6.3 Situation Diagnosis

A good understanding of the exceptional situation is crucial for users to take the right decisions on which recovery actions to adopt. As already mentioned, providing rich context information is critical for convenient map guidance. This information should also support the diagnosis and decision on the best handling strategies. The diagnosis is mostly dependent on a detailed and accurate assessment of the exceptional event.

Using the classifications described in Section 3 and some new added characteristics, we propose the following dimensions:

1. **Scope:** *Process specific* when only a set of instances is affected; or *cross specific* when various sets of instances are affected;
2. **Detection:** *Automatic* if the exception is automatically detected by the system; or *manually* if the exception is manually triggered;
3. **Event type:** Refers to the event that generates the exception (cf. Section 6.2): *data*, *temporal*, *workflow*, *external events*, *non-compliance* or *system/application*;
4. **Organizational impact :** *Employee*, *group* or *organizational,* according to Section 3.2;
5. **Difference to the organizational rules:** *Established exceptions*, *otherwise exceptions* or *true exceptions* (cf. Section 3.2);
6. **Complexity of the solution:** Refers to the complexity associated to obtain an optimal solution: *easy* or *hard.* If the complexity is hard users should consider using a tool to determine the best solution (cf. Section 6.1);

7. **Reaction time:** Defines the time frame for user's reaction to the event: quick, relaxed or *long*. Duration periods associated to this values are context dependent but they should be established because they can be used to select the communication mechanisms with involved actors (e.g., mobile messaging or email);
8. **Time frame to achieve solution:** Possible values include: *quick*, *relaxed* or *long*. As in reaction time, duration periods are context dependent. However, in this dimension they may also be used to guide actors during their recovery operations.

The information listed above is a general characterization of the exceptional event. It is complemented with some specific information identifying the concrete scenario, e.g., the affected instances and the responsible person. Since the information used to classify the exception should be as complete as possible and even be adjusted to a particular implementation, we do not further develop this issue here. The main concept associated to this facet of our solution is that rich information classifying the situation is required and must be used during the exception handling activities.

6.4 Exception Handling Strategies

The following dimensions to classify exception handling strategies are identified (Mourão and Antunes, 2005):

i. **Objective of the intervention:** Describes the general goal for the intervention, e.g., to abort the instance;
ii. **Communication type:** *Synchronous* or *asynchronous*. This dimension classifies the way people exchange information to share the situation knowledge/understanding;
iii. **Collaboration level:** *One person* solves the situation; several persons solve the situation in a *coordinated mode*; or several persons solve the situation in a *collaborative mode*. The involved actors may implement recovery actions in a coordinated mode, meaning that they are aware of each other's activities, while in collaboration mode they only know a general description of the intended objective agreed during the last collaborative session;
iv. **External monitoring:** There is either *enough information* to achieve the best solution or *additional information* must be collected from the environment;
v. **Tools to determine the best solution:** Either *no external decision aids* are required or there is a need for *advanced support* to achieve the best solution.

This classification affords linking the high-level handling strategies with a specific set of tasks available at the system level. The *communication type* expresses how the collaboration support component will interconnect the persons involved in the handling process. Two types of communication are differentiated: synchronous and asynchronous. In synchronous communication, the involved actors exchange information in real time (in face-to-face interactions or using some electronic means to transfer information), whereas in asynchronous communication information is exchanged in deferred time.

As mentioned in Section 6.1, coordinating activities among users is an important aspect of our solution because the coordination facet of traditional WfMS is relaxed. The two modes of operation identified in the *collaboration level* strategy reflect the concern with coordination. In a coordinated mode, users may choose any available tool to coordinate their activities. In a collaborative mode, the coordination aspects are not relevant since users implement their activities in a concerted way.

7. SOLUTION ARCHITECTURE AND IMPLEMENTATION

In this section we start by describing the solution's architecture and its integration with the environment, the WfMS and the actors involved in the exception handling process. In Section 7.2 the solution implementation by a dedicated workflow is discussed. Section 7.3 describes the recovery and monitoring operations that users may implement during unstructured activities.

7.1 Architecture

To introduce the solution's architecture, we detail in Figure 5 our extended reference model. The figure has been reorganized to place the Exception Handling Service at the top. Other components were readjusted in conformity. Additional detail was also added to the figure. In the architecture design, we have mainly focused on the interface with Workflow Enactment Service because our objective is to control the system behavior at run-time. We will assume the existence of primitives to implement interfaces C and B in the figure.

Figure 6 gives more detailed on the model components, comprising the Exception Handling Service, Workflow Enactment Services (represented by the workflow engine), Exception Detection Component, workflow client and invoked applications. Interface A and E are also illustrated. Dashed lines represent information flows whereas uninterrupted lines represent control flows.

Four components are identified as belonging to the exception handling service: *Exception Description*, *WF Interventions*, *Collaboration Support* and *Exception History*. Two distinct interfaces are also identified: interface A and E. The External Facilities, illustrated at the top, represent any exception handling activity carried outside

Figure 5. Detailed version of the extended reference model reorganized; the external interface E and an exception detection component placed close to the enactment services were added

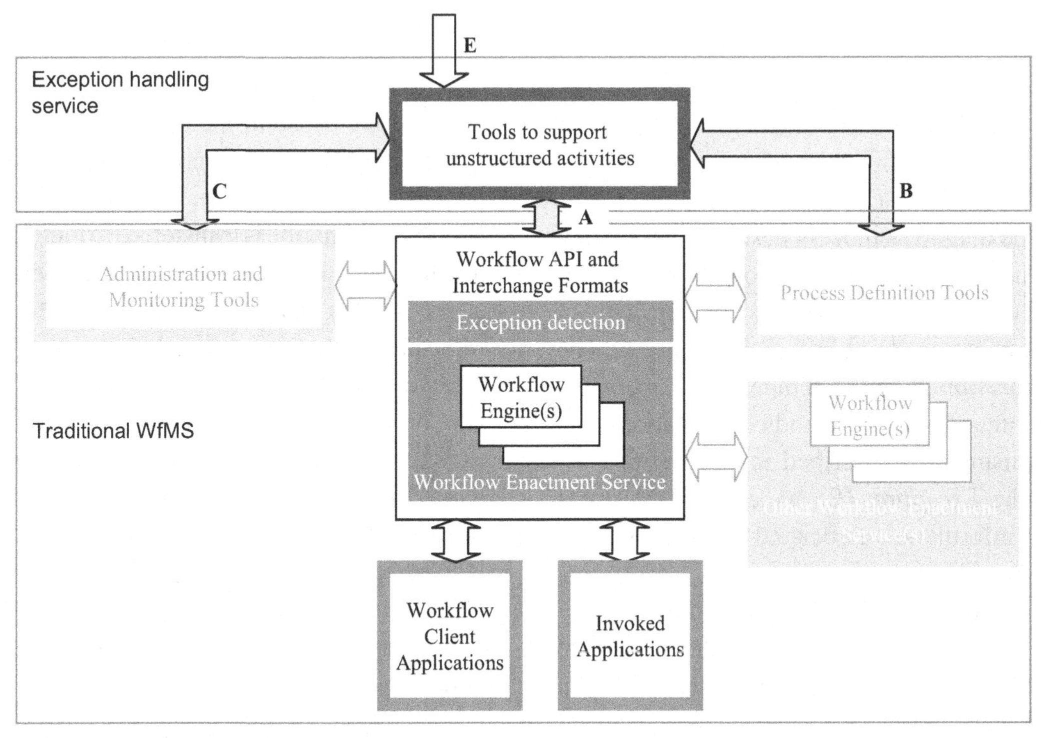

Figure 6. The solution's detailed architecture and its integration with the WfMS and the environment

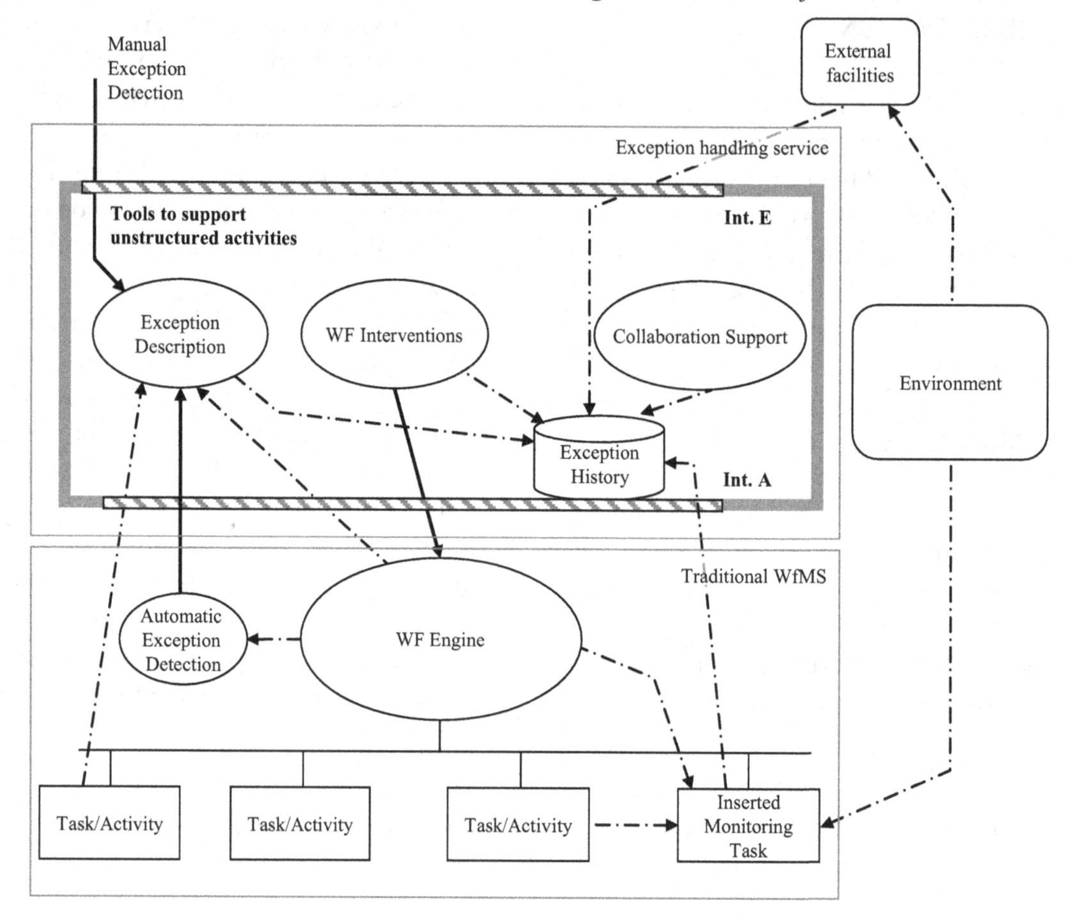

the solution's boundary and will be discussed below together with the interfaces.

The *Exception Description* component supports the diagnosis process described in Section 6.3. The *WF Interventions* component implements the functions associated to objective of the intervention described in Section 6.4. The *Collaboration Support* component implements the communication type and collaboration level mechanisms also described in Section 6.4. Finally, the *Exception History* component stores all log information associated to the exception handling cycles.

The traditional WfMS supported by the proposed solution is represented at the bottom of Figure 6. Naturally, the workflow engine plays a central role. Close to the engine, the *Automatic Exception Detection* component collects information from it and, when an exception is detected, control information is transferred to the exception handling service. The *Inserted Monitoring Task* at the bottom right represents a task to collect information that users decided to insert during the exception handling activities.

Concerning interfaces, the interface A links the exception handling components with the WfMS, while interface E links these components with the users and external environment. Interface A is used to collect information about the WfMS status, to implement low level recovery actions (launch/suspend tasks, etc.), and to automatically detect and signal exceptions.

Interface E connects the exception handling service with users to enable manual exception detection and interaction during exception handling activities. Interface E also supports environmental information gathering about the operations carried outside the framework's scope (cf. Section 6.2).

In Figure 7, the three remaining operator's basic functions (cf. Section 6.1) are added: diagnosis, recovery and monitoring. The diagnosis, recovery, and monitoring functions are carried out by the involved actors with support and orchestration from the components available at Tools to Support Unstructured Activities. Figure 7 represents the information and control flow through interface E between the operators and the system and between External Facilities and the system.

7.2 Exception Handling Workflow

We also claim it is better to cope with ad hoc effective unexpected exceptions in work models using work models (Sadiq, 2000). We implemented our solution using the OpenSymphony suite of components (The OpenSymphony project, 2005).

The project OSWorkflow within the OpenSymphony suite implements a workflow engine that was used to implement our solution. The suite was selected because it implements the core functions of a workflow engine and is easily plugged to the components that exist in the suite and to other projects that exist in the Open Source world. Other projects in the suite implement user validation to passwords and roles, a timer component, persistence store of workflow application

Figure 7. Solution's architecture and its integration with the WfMS, environment and operators' basic functions

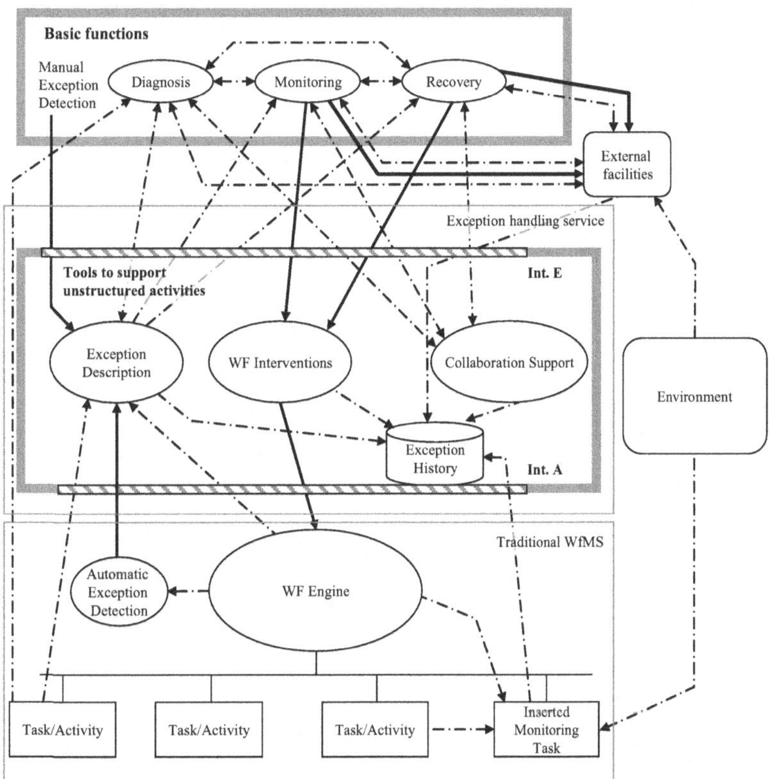

data and Web interfaces. All the components are developed in Java and run over a servlet container. Workflow models are stored in Extended Markup Language (XML) files. Even though Petri Nets are not used by the OpenSymphony project, we choose this formalism because of the solid formalism they allow and it's acceptance by the WfMS community.

When an exceptional event is triggered, the system instantiates the exception handling workflow process represented in Figure 8 and initializes some of the exception description parameters mentioned in Section 6.3. There are two alternative ways to instantiate this process: either by system (interface A) or by user detection (interface E). Then, using the Edit Info task, available right after detection, users may refine the exception information that was issued at detection.

After this task the system activates four components:

- Collaboration support;
- Exception description;
- WF Interventions;
- Insert external info.

The *WF Interventions* component is implemented by independent recovery and monitoring threads. The interface E, identified in Figure 7, is implemented by the thread External Info.

The *Collaboration Support* component supports users specifically collaborating within the scope of an exceptional event. The tasks implemented by this component (see Figure 8) enable involving more actors in exception handling and implement the collaboration mechanism. The *Collaborate* task implemented by this component may be synchronous or asynchronous and at any time the users may choose which type to use.

The *WF Interventions component* is implemented with two threads: implement recovery actions and insert monitoring tasks. The specific actions implemented by this component enable users to implement recovery activities to bring the system back into a coherent state. They will be described in Section 7.3. The monitoring thread affords users to insert monitoring tasks that store exceptional relevant information in the *Exception History*.

Figure 8. Exception handling workflow

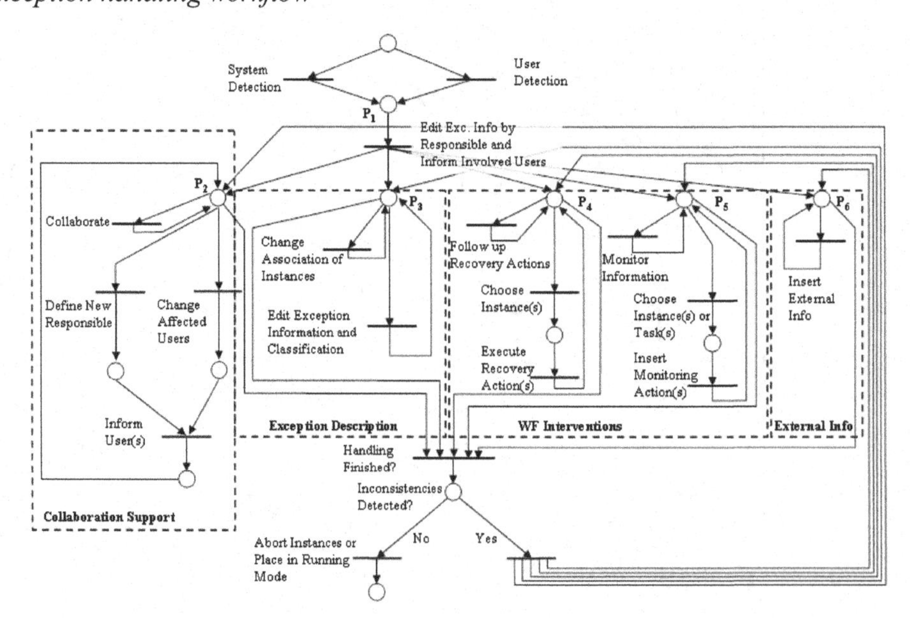

The component *Insert external info* implements interface E, allowing users to insert information associated to the event, either environmental information collected or information about tasks executed outside the workflow scope.

When users identify that coherence has been achieved, they execute the task Handling Finished? (at the bottom of Figure 8), removing the marks from places P_2 to P_6 and suspending the support to unstructured activities. Before finalizing the exception handling process, it is necessary to verify whether inconsistencies were inserted into the affected instances (cf. Section 6).

7.3 Recovery Actions, Monitoring Actions and Support Users Removing Inconsistencies

In Section 6.4 the high level objectives of the intervention were integrated into the handling strategies. To support users implementing these objectives, a set of quasi-atomic recovery actions are available. The Recovery Actions thread shown in Figure 8 affords operators to implement this functionality on the selected workflow instance(s).

The following list of actions is currently available in the implemented solution (Eder and Liebhart, 1995; Agostini and De Michelis, 2000; Reichert et al., 2003; Chiu et al., 2001; Sadiq, 2000):

- **Suspend/resume instance:** This action involves suspending or resuming instance execution;
- **Abort instance:** Abort the instance;
- **Backward jump:** Jump to a previous executed location in the work model;
- **Forward jump:** Jump forward to a task in the work model;
- **Jump:** Jump to another location in the model (this location is neither in the previous executed tasks nor in the upcoming tasks);
- **Move operation:** Move one task to another location in the model;
- **Ad hoc refinement:** Execute one action from a pre-defined list;
- **Ad hoc extension:** Choose a new path or change the model.

Since the *ad hoc refinement* operation inserts threads executing in parallel to the actual instance execution it may also be used in monitoring actions.

8. EVALUATION

We have been able to test our solution in a concrete organization: a Port Authority. During the system tests, we were able to follow an exception since it was detected until it got solved. In this section we discuss this event.

The Port Authority has the responsibility to manage all business activities within its jurisdiction that includes the river and the shore side. The Port Authority manages all vessels and cargo transfers to and from ships. All commercial activities installed on the shore are also under the jurisdiction of the Port Authority that issues licenses and contracts for the rented places.

The business process modeled by the Port Authority refers to managing space rentals. Companies and individuals rent spaces for their business activities for which they pay a fixed amount in a regular basis. For each rented space, there is a contract between the client and the Port Authority expressing all the conditions governing the business agreement. A department with about 10 employees negotiates all contracts, manages client related information and assures clients pay on time. These administrative processes were modeled using the workflow platform. At the end of every month, the system automatically instantiates a process for every rented space that is supposed to pay its fee. A list of debts and free/ occupied zones must be generated at any moment.

To describe the exceptional event, user names were changed to preserve anonymity.

Assume that Henry is updating the client's information when he is informed that the client has bankrupted. Figure 9 shows the Web page for the client editing task, where the link to manually signal an exception is shown at the top.

After selecting the "Report new exception" link, a new instance of the Exception Handling Workflow (EHW) is created (cf. Figure 8) and the user is prompted with the EHW page shown in Figure 10. This corresponds to a mark in place P1 of Figure 8. From there, the exception classification must be accomplished, as shown in Figure 11. Henry realizes that time is not critical and classifies it as relaxed. He also affects John, his direct supervisor, to the exception handling process. He does not define John as responsible because he wants to talk with him first. He inserts a brief description and classifies the exception as an external event with departmental impact. He also defines the exception as a true exception, since it never happened before. The dimensions scope, affected instances, and responsible were automatically defined by the system.

By following the *Start handling* link shown in Figure 10, Henry starts handling the exception. An email is generated to John with the exception handling information inserted by Henry and a link to the EHW shown in Figure 12.

John may then look at the situation in the EHW page and start a collaboration *task* with Henry. He decides using instant messaging. During the conversation, John realizes another company is requesting the space occupied by the company. He also recognizes that the client's debt is 50.000€. John tells Henry to insert this alert in the EHW (cf. Figure 13) and involves Philip, from the lawyer department, in the exception handling process.

Figure 9. Web page for the client edit workflow

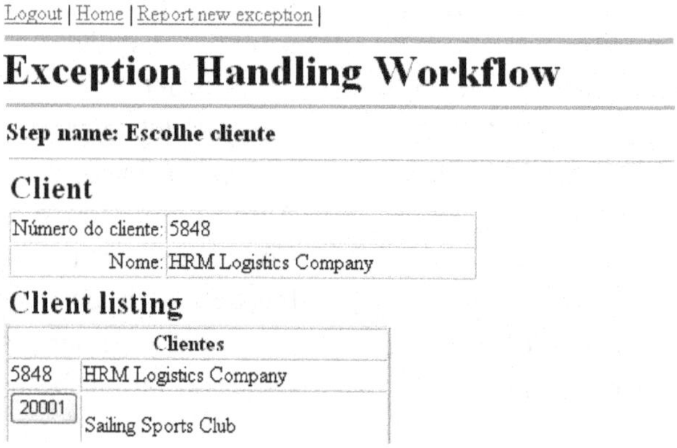

Logout | Home | Report new exception |

Exception Handling Workflow

Step name: Escolhe cliente

Client

Número do cliente:	5848
Nome:	HRM Logistics Company

Client listing

Clientes	
5848	HRM Logistics Company
20001	Sailing Sports Club

Figure 10. Exception handling workflow page (EHW)

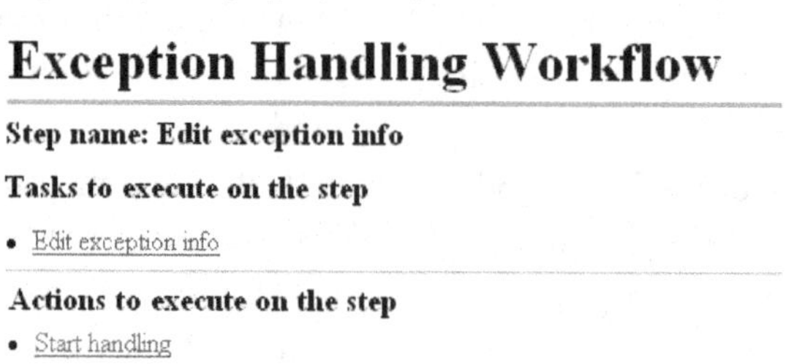

Exception Handling Workflow

Step name: Edit exception info

Tasks to execute on the step

- Edit exception info

Actions to execute on the step

- Start handling

Figure 11. Exception related information

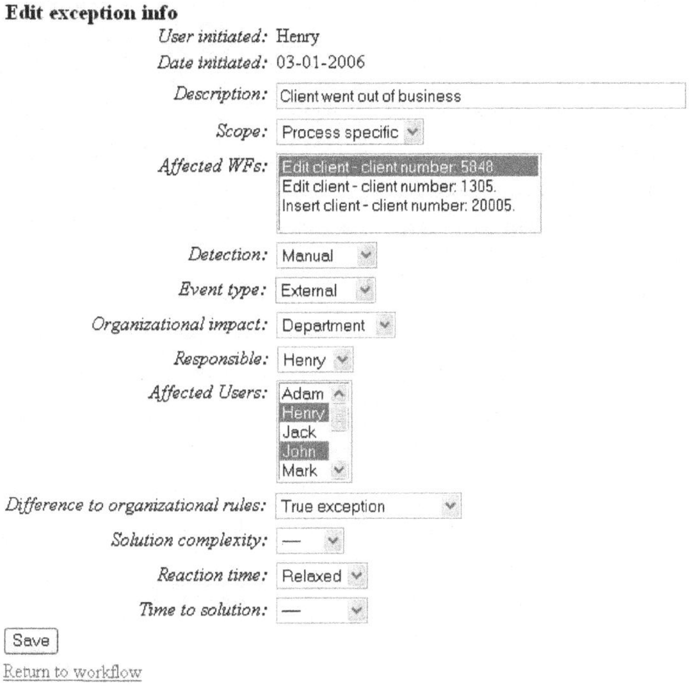

Edit exception info
User initiated: Henry
Date initiated: 03-01-2006
Description: Client went out of business
Scope: Process specific
Affected WFs: Edit client - client number: 5848
Edit client - client number: 1305.
Insert client - client number: 20005.
Detection: Manual
Event type: External
Organizational impact: Department
Responsible: Henry
Affected Users: Adam
Henry
Jack
John
Mark
Difference to organizational rules: True exception
Solution complexity: —
Reaction time: Relaxed
Time to solution: —
Save
Return to workflow

Figure 12. EHW page handling the 5 parallel branches of the exception handling workflow

Exception Handling Workflow
Description: Client went out of business
Step name: Collaboration support
Tasks to execute on the step
Collaborate
Actions to execute on the step
Define new responsible
Change affected users
Step name: Exception description
Tasks to execute on the step
Change association of instances
Edit exception classification
Step name: Recovery actions
Tasks to execute on the step
Follow up recovery actions
Actions to execute on the step
Execute a recovery action
Step name: Monitoring actions
Tasks to execute on the step
Monitoring information
Actions to execute on the step
Insert monitoring action
Step name: External info
Actions to execute on the step
Insert external information

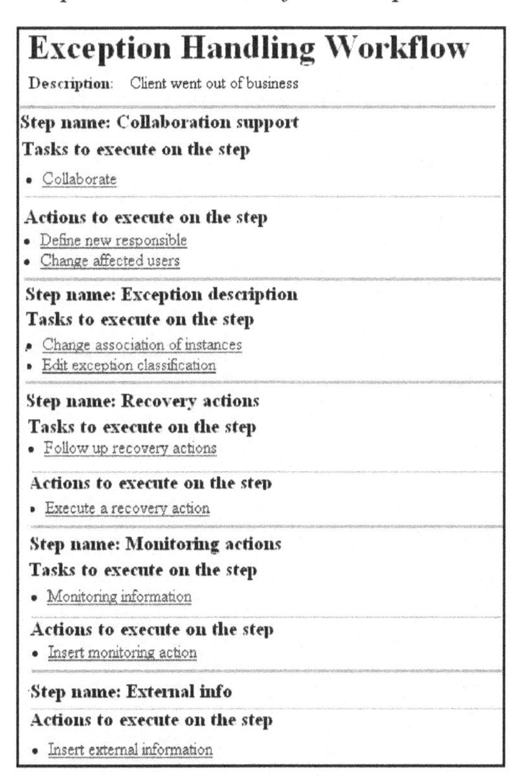

John also decides to insert a monitoring task to identify whether the client has any other debts.

Philip is informed about the situation by email. After reading the email message, he decides to phone Henry to discuss the details. During the phone conversation, they decide Philip will consult an external expert. Philip inserts a comment about this decision in the external information UI shown in Figure 14. Henry will wait for any news.

Philip finds out from the expert that the Port Authority should notify the client by standard mail, giving 5 days to pay the debt. Obtaining no response, they should start a lawsuit action. Philip writes a letter draft and attaches it to the workflow as an entry message in the "edit exception classification" *action*. He then uses the "collaboration support" *step*, to discuss with Henry and John who will send the letter and who will follow this external action. The email mechanism is adopted for that purpose.

Henry will be in charge of the external recovery action. If Henry finds out the company pays the older debts they have to reanalyze the situation. Again, Philip and John are notified about the new events. If the client pays all the old debts they will close the exception handling process.

The system managed the interactions among users to handle this particular case. It was easy to involve an expert from another department in the handling process. Relevant decisions and event related information were easily spread through the involved users improving their knowledge about the situation details and their evolution. The relevant information related to the situation was also attached to the event so it can be used in future events.

8.1 Exercises

1. Consider a situation where a truck with a very important delivery is stuck on a traffic

Figure 13. EHW displaying alert messages at the top

Exception Handling Workflow

Description: Client went out of business

Critical info:
- Amount in debt: 50.000 €

Important info:
- New customer waits space availability

Figure 14. Inserting external decision-making information

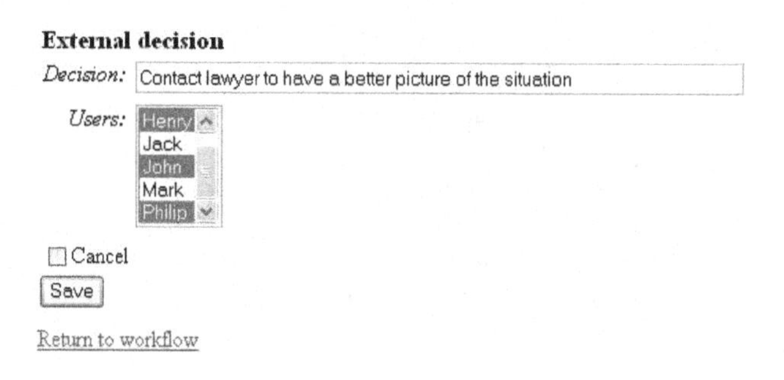

jam. Any delay on the material delivery is charged heavily on the company: it is more expensive than getting a new delivery sent by an airplane.

2. What challenges to the workflow system emerge from this situation?
3. What tasks should the operators initiate to follow up the situation and try to get the most adequate solution?

A sales representative receives a complaint from a customer about a non-implemented functionality in a good that the company produces during a contact visit requested by the client wanting to by those goods. He then realizes that the functionality is very important and that some of the company most important competitors already implement it. What actions should the sales representative initiate regarding this process instance? Who should be involved if the production department does not agree on time with the request?

A manufacturing company receives an alteration to an already placed order. The company is interested in satisfying the customer because it is a very important one. Nevertheless, the company has to calculate the minimum costs associated to the change and all the production departments must be involved. Describe the tasks that the marketing director responsible for the customer has to develop to satisfy the client.

9. SUGGESTED ADDITIONAL READING

Worah and Sheth (1997) present a good overview about systems to handle failures. On the area of expected exceptions the reader may consult the work by Casati et al. (Casati et al., 1999; Casati, 1998) or by Chiu et al. (2001). Interesting work on the area of extended expected exceptions where Case Base Reasoning is used to extend the matching capabilities for the event identification has been developed by Luo (2001). Exception mining techniques are explored by Grigori (2001) and Hwang (1999).

A good survey on metamodel approaches is presented by Rinderle et al. (2004). The work developed by Ellis et al. (1995) is an important milestone because it establishes the notion of dynamic change bug. Relevant readings on this subject are the works from Aalst and Basten (2002), Agostini and De Michelis (2000), Casati (1998), Reichart and Dadam (1998), Sadiq (2000) and from Weske (2001).

On the open point systems there are relevant works from Deiters and Gruhn (1994) and Hsu and Kleissner (1996). Finally, further details on the proposed solution including an implementation description can be consulted in (Mourão, 2008).

REFERENCES

Abbott, K. R., & Sarin, S. K. (1994). Experiences with workflow management: Issues for the next generation. In *CSCW'94 (USA), Chapel Hill, 1994,* (pp.113-120).

Adams, M., Hofstede, A., Edmond, D. Worklets, & van der Aalst, W (2006). A service-oriented implementation of dynamic flexibility in workflows. In *Proceedings of the 14th International Conference on Cooperative Information Systems (CoopIS 2006)*, (pp. 291-308_.

Adams, M., Hofstede, A., van der Aalst, W., & Edmond, D. (2007). Dynamic, extensible and context-aware exception handling for workflows. In *Proceedings of the OTM Conference on Cooperative information Systems (CoopIS 2007)*, (pp. 95-112).

Agostini, A., & De Michelis, G. (2000). A light workflow management system using simple process models. *Computer Supported Cooperative Work*, *9*(3-4), 335-363.

Bernstein, A. (2000). How can cooperative work tools support dynamic group process? Bridging the specificity frontier. In *CSCW '00 (USA), Philadelphia,* (pp. 279-288).

Bowers, J., Button, G., & Sharrock, W. (1995). Workflow from within and without: Technology and cooperative work on the print industry shopfloor. In *ECSCW'95, (Sweden), Stockholm,* (pp. 51-66).

Casati, F. (1998). Models, semantics, and formal methods for the design of workflows and their exceptions. Unpublished doctoral thesis. Politecnico di Milano, Italy.

Casati, F., Ceri, S., Paraboschi, S., & Pozzi, G. (1999). Specification and implementation of exceptions in workflow management systems. *ACM Transactions on Database Systems, 24*(3), 405-451.

Chiu, D. K., Li, Q., & Karlapalem, K. (2001). WEB interface-driven cooperative exception handling in ADOME workflow management system. *Information Systems, 26*(2), 93-120.

Deiters, W., & Gruhn, V. (1994). The Funsoft Net approach to software process management. *International Journal of Software Engineering and Knowledge Engineering, 4*(2), 229-256.

Dellarocas, C., & Klein, M. (1998). A knowledge-based approach for handling exceptions in business processes. In *WITS'98, Helsinki, Finland.*

Eder, J., & Liebhart, W. (1995). The Workflow Activity Model WAMO. In P*roceedings of the Int. Conf. on Cooperative Information Systems, Vienna, Austria.*

Ellis, C., Keddara, K., & Rozenberg, G. (1995). Dynamic change within workflow systems. In *Proc. of conf. on Organizational computing systems,* Milpitas, USA, (pp. 10-21).

Ellis, C., & Nutt, G. J. (1993). Modeling and enactment of workflow systems. In *Application and Theory of Petri Nets, Chicago, USA,* (pp. 1-16). Springer-Verlag.

Grigori, D., Casati, F., Dayal, U., & Shan, M. C. (2001). Improving business process quality through exception understanding, prediction, and prevention. In *VLDB'01,* Rome, Italy.

Guimarães, N., Antunes, P., & Pereira, A. P (1997). The integration of workflow systems and collaboration tools. In *Advances in Workflow Management Systems and Interoperability, Istanbul, Turkey.*

Han, Y., Sheth, A. P., & Bussler, C. (1998). A taxonomy of adaptive workflow management. In *Proceedings of the CSCW'98, Seattle, WA.*

Heinl, P. (1998). Exceptions during workflow execution. In *Proceedings of the EDBT'98, Valencia, Spain.*

Hollingswoorth, D. (1995). *Workflow management coalition - The reference model TC00-1003. WFMC.*

Hsu, M., & Kleissner, K. (1996). ObjectFlow: Towards a process management infrastructure, *Distributed and Parallel Databases,* 2, 169-194.

Hwang, S. Y., Ho, S. F., & Tang, J. (1999). Mining exception instances to facilitate workflow exception handling. In *Proceedings of the 6th Int. Conf. on Database Systems for Advanced Applications, Hsinchu, Taiwan.*

Luo, Z. (2001). Knowledge sharing, coordinated exception handling, and intelligent problem solving for cross-organizational business processes Unpublished doctoral thesis, Dep. of Computer Sciences, University of Georgia.

Mourão, H. R. (2008). *Supporting effective unexpected exception handling in workflow management systems within organizational contexts.* Unpublished doctoral thesis, University of Lisbon.

Mourão, H. R., & Antunes, P. (2003). Supporting direct user interventions in exception handling in workflow management systems. In *Proceedings of CRIWG 2003,* Autrans, France, (pp. 159-167). Springer-Verlag.

Mourão, H. R., & Antunes, P. (2004). Exception handling through a workflow. In *CoopIS 2004,* Agia Napa, (pp. 37-54). Springer-Verlag.

Mourão, H. R., & Antunes, P. (2005). A collaborative framework for unexpected exception handling. In *Proceedings of CRIWG 2005,* Porto de Galinhas, Brasil, (pp. 168-183). Springer-Verlag.

The OpenSymphony project. (2006), Retrievel November 11, 2006, from Http://www.opensymphony.com

Reichert, M., & Dadam, P. (1998). ADEPTflex - Supporting dynamic changes of workflows without losing control. *Journal of Intelligent Information Systems, 10*(2), 93-129.

Reichert, M., Dadam, P., & Bauer, T. (2003). Dealing with forward and backward jumps. *Workflow Management Systems, Software and Systems Modeling, 2*(1), 37-58.

Rinderle, S., Reichert, M., & Dadam, P. (2004). Correctness criteria for dynamic changes in workflow systems - a survey. *Data and Knowledge Engineering, 50*(1), 9-34.

Saastamoinen, H. (1995). On the handling of exceptions in information systems. Unpublished doctoral thesis, University of Jyväskylä.

Sadiq, S. W. (2000). On capturing exceptions in workflow process models. In *Proceedings of the 4th International Conference on Business Information Systems,* Poznan, Poland.

Schmidt, K. (1997). Of maps and scripts - The status of formal constructs in cooperative work. In *GROUP '97,* Phoenix, USA, (pp. 138-147).

Sheth, A. P., Georgakopoulos, D., Joosten, S. M., Rusinkiewicz, M., Scacchi, W., Wileden, J., & Wolf, A. L. (1996). *ACM SIGMOD Record, 25*(4), 55-67.

Strong, D. M., & Miller, S. M. (1995). Exceptions and exception handling in computerized information systems. *ACM Transactions on Information Systems, 13*(2).

Suchman, L. A. (1983). Office procedure as practical action: Models of work and system design. *ACM TOIS, 1*(4), 320-328.

Suchman, L. A. (1987). *Plans and situated actions.* MIT Press.

Van der Aalst, W., & Basten, T. (2002). Inheritance of workflows: An approach to tackling problems related to change. *Theoretical Computer Science, 270*(1), 125-203.

van der Aalst, W., & Berens, P. (2001). Beyond workflow management: Product-driven case handling. In *GROUP 2001, Boulder, USA.*

Weber, B., Reichert, M., & Rinderle-Ma, S (2008). Change patterns and change support features – Enhancing flexibility in process-aware information systems. *Data & Knowledge Engineering, 66,* 438-466

Weske, M. (2001). Formal foundation and conceptual design of dynamic adaptations in a workflow management system. In *International Conference on System Sciences,* 2579-2588.

Worah, D., & Sheth, A. P. (1997). Transactions in Transactional Workflows. In S. Jajodia & K. Larry (Eds.), *Advanced transaction models and architectures.* Kluwer Academic Publishers.

WFMC (1999). *Workflow Management Coalition - Terminology & Glossary* TC00-1011.

KEY TERMS

Exception Handling: Activities carried out by the involved actors to overcome an exceptional situation and to replace the system into a coherent state.

Exceptions in WfMS: Exceptions are situations that the WfMS is not designed to handle. Some of these events could have been foreseen during system design but designers did not include them.

Structured Activities: When procedures determine user's actions having a normative engagement.

Unexpected Exceptions: Situations that where not foreseen during systems design. These events usually are not known by the organization when the system is being designed.

Unstructured Activities: Users performing unrestricted activities eventually guided by and available procedure and rich contextual information. Even though a procedure may be used it does not have an engagement role and users may choose their actions freely.

WfMS Flexibility: The ability a WfMS shows to adjust to concrete user demand.

WfMS Resilience: The resilience property of a WfMS concerns its ability to maintain a coherent state and continue supporting business processes after being subject to any hazardous situations that affect its execution.

ENDNOTES

[1] This classification was developed for expected exceptions, because it assumes that the detection of an unexpected exception is always external to the system. However, any of the above classes may result from an unpredicted situation even though the symptoms are expected.

[2] Remember that we use the term "unexpected exceptions" to refer to ad hoc effective unexpected exceptions whenever it is not necessary to distinguish them.

Section V
Business Process Management in Organizations

Chapter XVII
Business Process Engineering

Guillermo Jimenez
Centro de Sistemas Inteligentes Tecnológico de Monterrey, Mexico

ABSTRACT

In this chapter the authors introduce the role of a business process engineer (BPE) and necessary competencies to define, simulate, analyze, and improve business processes. As a minimal body of knowledge for a BPE we propose two complementary fields: enterprise integration engineering (EIE) and business process management (BPM). EIE is presented as a discipline that enriches business models by providing additional views to enhance and extend the coverage of business models through the consideration of additional elements to those that are normally considered by a process model, such as the inclusion of mission, vision, and strategy which are cornerstone in EIE. A BPE is a person who holistically uses principles of BPE, EIE, and associated tools to build business models that identify elements such as information sources involved, the roles which use and transform the information, and the processes that guide end-to-end transformation of information along the business.

INTRODUCTION

Business process modeling is aimed at the identification and documentation of core business processes. Core business processes are those who provide significant value to the operation of a business. Such value could be achieved by cost reductions and/or performance enhancement. Cost reduction could be a result of limiting resource utilization or introduction of information technologies. Normally resources are human operators or machines involved in the process. Information technologies could enhance resource utilization in many ways, such as providing real-time data of business operations and detailed information on machine operation.

Core business processes are particularly important for a business; identifying and enhancing these processes could result in a significant increased return (for both stakeholders and clients) for an enterprise. Return here is associated with many aspects such as decreased costs, time reduction in operations, limited number of involved resources, or quality improvements.

A business process engineer (BPE) would be a person responsible for assessing and describing operational aspects of businesses including business processes, organizational culture and structure, facilities, and other resources. A main question that BPE should answer is how to identify core business processes. Other questions are how model these core business processes and how one can justify them as goals for increasing return for the business. There exist several proposals for business process modeling, being the standard notation BPMN (business process modeling notation) the one that is being implemented my most business process modeling tool vendors. However, equally importantly to how to model, are what to model and which models would be necessary. This chapter explores these issues.

The following sections in this chapter explain why a BPE requires more knowledge than that normally associated with business process management. Enterprise integration engineering is introduced as an important ingredient for the identification, analysis and evaluation of core business processes. BPMN is introduced as a convenient notation for business processes and a framework for conducting business process engineering is proposed. It is important to note that any particular business has peculiar goals, identifying and achieving them would be the responsibility of any business process engineer. The framework is just a generic reference of what to consider, provide general guidelines and notations to assist a business process engineer to better perform her tasks in identifying and modeling core business processes. The BPE person is cable of adapting the framework to the specific environment and needs of a particular business.

The importance of a process engineering framework is twofold. First, it helps the business process engineer in identifying core business processes. Second, it helps the business process engineer to decide how core business processes should be documented for its appropriate simulation and analysis.

It is important to note also that successful deployment of business processes involves many other issues such as cultural change. These issues are not considered here. However, the business process engineer should be aware of their importance for a successful implementation of any business process improvement effort in an enterprise.

Sections in this chapter are as follows. The next section introduces business process management (BPM) and its expectations. Another section presents a detailed explanation of enterprise integration engineering (EIE) and its goals. Special attention is assigned to introduce EIE and its role in identifying mission, vision and strategy as sources to identify core business processes. After that, other section analyzes BPM, its status and aims. BPM modeling is the core aspect of this book, thus BPMN is presented as a standard for business modeling standard. Finally, the role of a business process engineer and its basic body of knowledge is suggested as a profession for successful implementation of business process management in an enterprise to produce the business value expected by both clients and stakeholders as a result of the successful operation of the enterprise.

BUSINES PROCESS MANAGEMENT

A business is a complex organization whose operation is the responsibility of several departments or business units. To be considered as successful, a business should create profit to its stakeholders. The equation for profit is defined as the result of subtracting operation costs from revenue. According to this definition, there are two not necessarily independent ways to increase profit. The first one is decreasing operation costs which include salaries, facilities, services (such as electricity), among others. The second way is increasing revenue, whose main source are customers.

Revenue increase could be achieved by applying different strategies. Strategies could be for instance: increment market share, selling differentiated goods or services, and offering goods or services at lower costs than competitors. All these strategies are characterized by needing substantial investments from enterprises. For instance, incrementing market share may require the construction of new facilities in other markets and perform intensive marketing campaigns. Producing differentiated goods or services require investment in research. Lowering the cost of offered goods and services requires improving internal operations to reduce the cost associated to production. A common aspect in all these strategies is that implementing them requires the careful definition of a process describing how they will be defined, analyzed, and performed. Every business will need to identify the best strategy or set of strategies to implement. This task will also need to define a process to define strategies, evaluate them and chose the most appropriate.

A common aspect in the successful implementation of a strategy is the need of defining a process. This could create the sense that process definition is present in most of the aspects to successfully create good results. Indeed this is the case. If tasks are performed without a guide, the final results are difficult to predict. This characteristic permeates to all aspects of the operation of an enterprise. As many persons have recently realized, business processes are necessary in every part of the enterprise to guide how to proceed to produce expected results (Smith and Fingar, 2003).

From the previous discussion, it may be simple to understand the necessity of defining business processes for successfully conducting many of the aspects related to enterprise operations. However, this has not been the case in business management in the past. The first efforts to increase the results of an enterprise were addressed to increase the individual competency of labor. The subjacent idea was that if workers were more qualified and their work was limited to cover only those parts where their expertise could be directly applied, they would be more productive (Harrington, 1991). This way of business management was prevalent for many years. The main goal was increasing the productivity of workers.

More recently, mainly in the 1990's the approach changed. In these years, quality improvement programs followed a different approach. The world economy was changing from local and controlled markets to global competition. In this new environment, customers had an increasing number of available choices for goods or services. Quality was the dominating factor guiding customer decisions. Many different approaches for quality improvement were suggested and standardization bodies were created (e.g., ISO9000, six sigma). The concept of business process re-engineering (BPR) was created: re-design all aspects of an enterprise to implement best practices in business operations (Hammer and Champy, 2005). Under BPR, enterprises had to perform drastic changes on resources involved in their operation.

Many enterprises successfully implemented BPR programs. However, there were also many failed programs of BPR implementation. Failures could be attributed to many issues, perhaps the main issue was that many enterprises did not correctly identified the adaptation required for successfully implement BPR. In some cases, the changes required to perform by enterprises were so invasive that it was impossible for them to make all necessary arrangements. In other cases, the re-engineering group failed in fully understanding the enterprise and proposed changes were not appropriate. The final lesson was clear, BPR was not for everyone.

At the same time that BPR concepts were developed, information technologies evolved in many different ways. Computational platforms made possible the development of new software packages with capabilities to link information technology infrastructures. Operational data necessary for decision making by enterprises was readily available. Business managers were able to make decisions based on fresh information from operational data, commonly arriving from different and incompatible systems. Interoperability among previously incompatible systems created a new opportunity of data interchange for decision making. Interoperability set the landmark for integrating the information sources in many different ways to have real-time information of business operation (Jimenez and Espadas, 2007).

One of the tools that information systems interoperability made possible was the creation of workflow systems. A workflow defines the activities that involve several business actors in performing a business task, usually when a business form or template has to be filled by the actors at different stages. The business actors are business people who review the form and authorize it according to special business rules thus it can flow to the following business actor involved in the workflow. However, despite the possibilities brought out by workflow technologies, their use was limited by not taking into account the experience and advance in other areas of business operation. Among other issues, these helped the introduction of a new proposal aimed at business improvement that was necessary to compete in the new world economy.

Many businesses were facing the wall because of the new competitive environment, lack of guarantee of BPR efforts, and workflow approach not considering non-form fulfilling activities as something that needed to be managed. This scenario gave birth to a new proposal for business improvement, the concept of business process management (BPM). A business process could be considered as similar to a workflow. However, a business process does not restrict to form fulfillment activities, a business process could involve any enterprise process directly related to successful business operation.

BPM combines experience from many earlier efforts aimed at improvement of business operations for profit creation and increase. For BPM, not every business process is equally important, only these processes directly related with strategy are the ones that should be considered. Processes that directly relate to strategy are called core business processes. The successful execution of a core business process could be evaluated against attainment of one or more of the business strategies. Similarly to workflows, business processes define the activities necessary to perform a complete business task. Ordinarily, a business process involves the participation of business personnel from various business units. The business process is thus a way to evaluate business unit collaboration to achieve business strategy.

The last remark sets a difference to old business management approaches. Instead of focusing just on individual improvements to business units, BPM relates to how successful collaboration among business units could result in value added goods or services. The following discussions present BPM from perspectives of different people that helped to set out BPM as a new proposal for business improvement.

According to Jeston and Nelis (2006), the goals of BPM are identification, modeling, and implementation of core business processes for the successful operation of a business (see Figure 1). BPM relies upon the consideration that a successful conduction of every activity is essential to the consideration of the core business processes, its correct modeling, and careful implementation. The identification step consists in finding the most important or core processes of a business and how they contribute to the successful operation of the business. The modeling step deals with the representation of the activities that should be performed to produce the outcomes as expected by the business and customers. Finally, implementation concerns to the inclusion of appropriate information technologies to automate the operation of business processes (Jimenez et al., 2006).

The framework for business process management in Figure 1 shows the steps involved in from identifying core process to their final deployment. Every step is equally important for a successful BPM project. Core processes are tightly associated to successful business operation for achieving business goals. How business processes are represented or described could be important for their correct evaluation by involved stakeholders. Successful implementation is highly dependent on core process identification and modeling.

The business process model provides information for discussions by business analysts, chief process officers, and information technologists, to agree upon the best way that business processes support the successful operation of a business (Smith and Fingar, 2003). Understanding a business and how it operates requires a representation that could be understood by all parties. It is thus very important to define which models should be designed and how they could be used by all participants.

Businesses are complex organizations established to produce value to customers through products or services, at the same time they generate revenue to stakeholders. Business are successful only if their operation costs are keep under control to ensure profitability, at the same time that high quality is provided to customers. Successful operation of a business requires the correct identification of its core processes (Burlton, 2001). A core process it one whose incorrect execution produce negative results both to customers and stakeholders. The incorrect execution of a core process may induce customers to look for another supplier for the product or service they need. The aim of business process management and modeling is documenting in an understandable way the core processes of a business (Harmon,

Figure 1. Steps for business process management

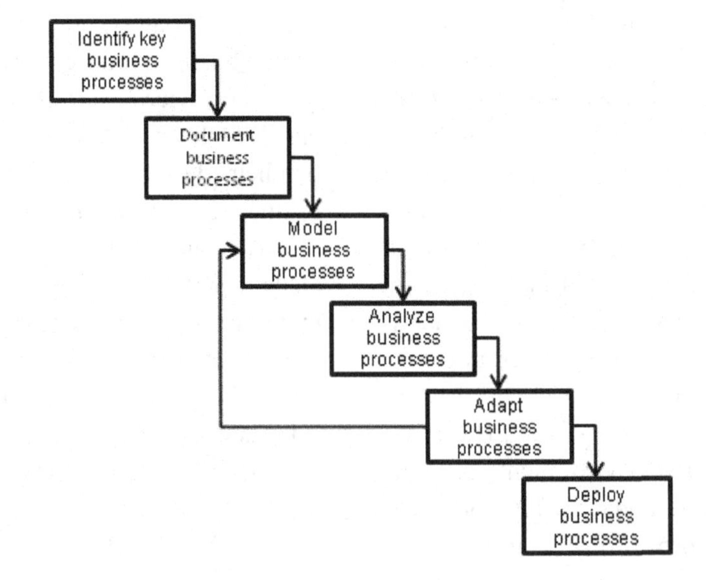

2003). To be effective, business process modeling should consider as a very important part the identification of the core business processes, provide information to their correct implementation, and ideally be useful to help in process improvement. Process modeling is thus an important part for the successful implementation and operation of business processes. However, the identification of core business processes and information for their implementation is equally important (Ould, 2005).

Among other business approaches for business performance improvement, BPM is an evolution of BPR (business process re-engineering) which dealt with radical changes to already defined business processes (Hammer and Champy, 2005). While BPR produced important results, it also was responsible for many disasters (Harmon, 2003). As a consequence, BPM searches for continual improvement of business processes. This is the goal of the new proposal of business process engineering. To avoid the lethal consequences of BPR, processes need to be carefully engineered at the first step, rather than consider that the initial step on a BPM project is to incorporate significant changes to a business process. If the business processes are correctly engineered in the first place, future changes will not need significant changes.

As cleverly as the last affirmation could be, its realization is not simple because too much of the business processes defined and performed are not correctly aligned to the enterprise goals. Process alignment needs to be performed in accordance with enterprise's clear identification of stakeholders and customers. Process alignment and re-definition is generally referred as business process improvement (Harmon, 2003).

To characterize the definition of business process improvement as an engineering activity, we need to understand what engineering means. First of all, it must be clear that many branches of engineering exist (e.g., mechanical, chemical, aerospace, etc.). Any of these branches or specialties deals with the development of some model to analyze a problem and use different approaches to evaluate proposed solutions. One of the approaches to evaluate a proposal is simulation. Simulation usually consists in using some software tool to describe the proposed model and analyze how it performs. If the model does not perform as expected, the model or several parameters are adjusted to run new simulations and analyzing results. Running simulation on software is usually chosen because of its inherent cost savings against building physical prototypes.

Currently, tens of software packages support business process modeling and simulation. Although these packages use different notations and simulation capabilities, they are generally recognized as business process management systems.

A business process engineer would be a person with domain software tools knowledge for modeling and simulation of business processes. Nowadays, the role is recognized as business process analyst, but this characterization limits his or her knowledge and experience to the business domain. Extending the knowledge and experience of a business analyst to be able to use software to simulate her models will extend her capabilities to be able to adapt business models after they are simulated.

BPM has been considered as the third wave for business operation improvement (Smith and Fingar, 2003). However, to be able to produce expected results the following section describes how BPM principles and approaches could be enhanced and improved by extending the coverage of traditional BPM.

ENTERPRISE INTEGRATION ENGINEERING

Enterprise Integration Engineering (EIE) is a discipline whose aim is the development of business architectures (Bernus, Nemes, and Williams,

1996). Business architecture defines several views of a business important to describe elements, roles, information, and processes necessary to fulfill the mission, vision, and strategy of an organization. The views are helpful to provide a broad understanding of business elements and their relationships for a better understanding of the elements that should be considered for a successful implementation of core business processes (Lankhorst et al., 2005). Implementing business processes require the identification of the information sources involved, the roles which use and transform the information, and the processes that guide end-to-end transformation of information (Jimenez and Espadas, 2007).

The main contribution that can be obtained from EIE to business process modeling is enforcement of the inclusion of business strategy for identification of core processes. In the EIE perspective, core processes should be aligned to mission, vision, and strategy. The roots of EIE were established during the 1990s. Several EIE frameworks describe which models or views should be designed (e.g., PERA, CIMOSA, GERAM) (Vernadat, 1996). A common element in EIE frameworks is the inclusion of mission, vision, and strategy for business modeling (Millern and Berger 2001). The last incarnation of an EIE framework is GERAM, and is the one that will be considered here to show how EIE could represent an important contribution to business process modeling, by helping in the identification of core processes, their design, and identification of information technologies necessary for business process implementation, execution and analysis.

An important point to mention is that EIE frameworks do not suggest particular modeling standards; they suggest only what should be modeled to serve as communication tools. Specific modeling tools or approaches could be used as long as all required models are designed. The framework prescribes what needs to be done and is just a guideline to how conducting a business process modeling project; which standards and tools are to be used is open, thus different modeling standards and tools could be selected for specific projects.

GERAM consists of 9 components recommended in enterprise engineering and integration. It thereby sets the standard for the collection of tools and methods from which any enterprise would benefit to more successfully tackle initial integration design, and the change processes which may occur during the enterprise operational lifetime. It does not impose any particular set of tools or methods, but defines the criteria to be satisfied by any set of selected tools and methods. GERAM views enterprise models as an essential component of enterprise engineering and integration; this includes various formal (and less formal) forms of design descriptions utilized in the course of design—as described in enterprise engineering methodologies—such as computer models, and text and graphics based design representations.

The nine components of GERAM (Generalized Enterprise Reference Architecture Method) are the following:

- **GERA (Generalized Enterprise Reference Architecture):** Identifies concepts of enterprise integration
- **EEM (Enterprise Engineering Methodology):** Describe process of enterprise engineering
- **EMLs (Enterprise Modeling Languages):** Provide modeling constructs for modeling of human role, processes and technologies
- **PEMs (Partial Enterprise Models):** Provide reusable reference models and designs of human roles, processes and technologies
- **GEMCs:** (Generic Enterprise Modeling Concepts) (Theories and Definitions): Define the meaning of enterprise modeling constructs

- **EETs (Enterprise Engineering Tools):** Support enterprise engineering
- **EMs (Enterprise Models):** Enterprise designs, and models to support analysis and operation
- **EMOs (Enterprise Modules):** Provide implementable modules of human professions, operational processes, technologies
- **EOS (Enterprise Operational Systems):** Support the operation of the particular enterprise

Relationships among components in GERAM in as follows: 1 employs 2; 2 utilizes 3; 2 and 3 are implemented in 6, which is supported by 4 and 5; 6 is used to build 7; 7 and 8 are used to implement 9. These relationships could be represented in a dependency chart as shown on Figure 2.

The result of applying EIE based on a framework such as GERAM are depicted on Figure 3. As Figure 3 shows, the final model of EIE is an enterprise architecture showing core business processes, information systems and information technologies that support them.

Figure 2. Dependency chart of GERAM components

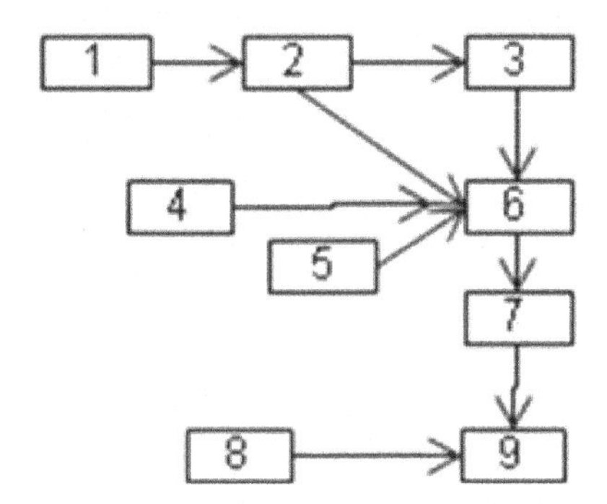

Figure 3. Enterprise architecture produced by applying EIE (Adapted from Lankhorst et al., 2005)

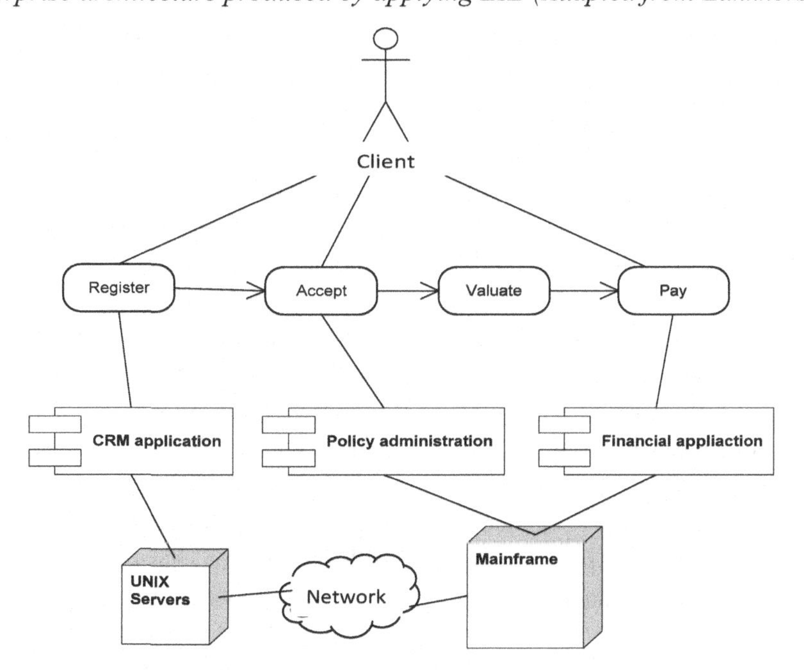

The enterprise architecture as described in Figure 3 shows that the implementation of business processes should consider more than the business models. It will be necessary to show how the business model should be integrated and supported by information systems and technologies. A business process model usually represents roles and activities. The enterprise architecture adds more information that becomes useful for business process implementation and deployment.

Figure 3 shows only part of the contributions of EIE to business process modeling. Business process modeling by itself is a complex task that requires core processes identification and documentation. However, business process implementation requires knowledge on the available information systems and technologies. EIE could help to identify that additional information.

BUSINESS PROCESS ENGINEERING

The mindset of a business process engineer has to be addressed to push business change by innovation. This means that change does not have to start from the current organizational state. Instead, the organization should look at new ways of doing business operations. Creating a healthy organization is as implementing a diet, substantial changes are necessary. This doesn't mean that changes have to be drastic from start. Changes should be planned and continuous improvements implemented based on results. The important thing for a BPE is to define improvement trends in the organization.

Careful attention has to be addressed to process improvement. Individual persons need a special dietary program based on an evaluation. It is a mistake to apply a best practice to every individual to improve her health. Organizations should proceed in a similar way. Implementing 'best practices' puts competitiveness at risk; competitiveness is a differentiating factor for producing value added goods and services. If every organization performs the same processes in the same way, they will not be creating competitiveness, it then would be impossible for customers to distinguish among organizations to whom make business with. A BPE should work to design dietary programs appropriate for particular organizations. Such as a person with high blood pressure needs a different dietary program from a person with high level blood sugar, the program to put an organization in a healthy situation requires designing a specific business improvement program.

Above all, customers have to be the central focus in designing the process improvement program. BPEs will assist the organization in creating differentiating and sustaining processes for organizational competitiveness. Enterprise integration engineering (EIE) provides additional support in designing a process improvement program. A BPE should understand how such support could be applied in a correct way to define value added networks in the way of business processes. Figure 4 shows the influences of EIE to the business process framework.

Mission, vision, and strategy needs to be considered for identifying key business processes (KBP). A KBP is a process directly related to strategy addressed to customers. A correct alignment of processes to strategy would help to achieve vision and make possible the mission of the organization.

What and how to document in business processes could be aided by EIE. Process documentation should be done using standard notations and templates. While every organization could design its own templates, the notation used in process documentation should be in a way that many people understand and for which software process documentation tools exist. With its limitations, BPMN has gained widespread acceptance as the standard notation for business processes modeling, and for which many software tools exist. A BPE professional has to understand BPMN and be able to apply it in modeling business processes.

Figure 4. Steps to business process engineering

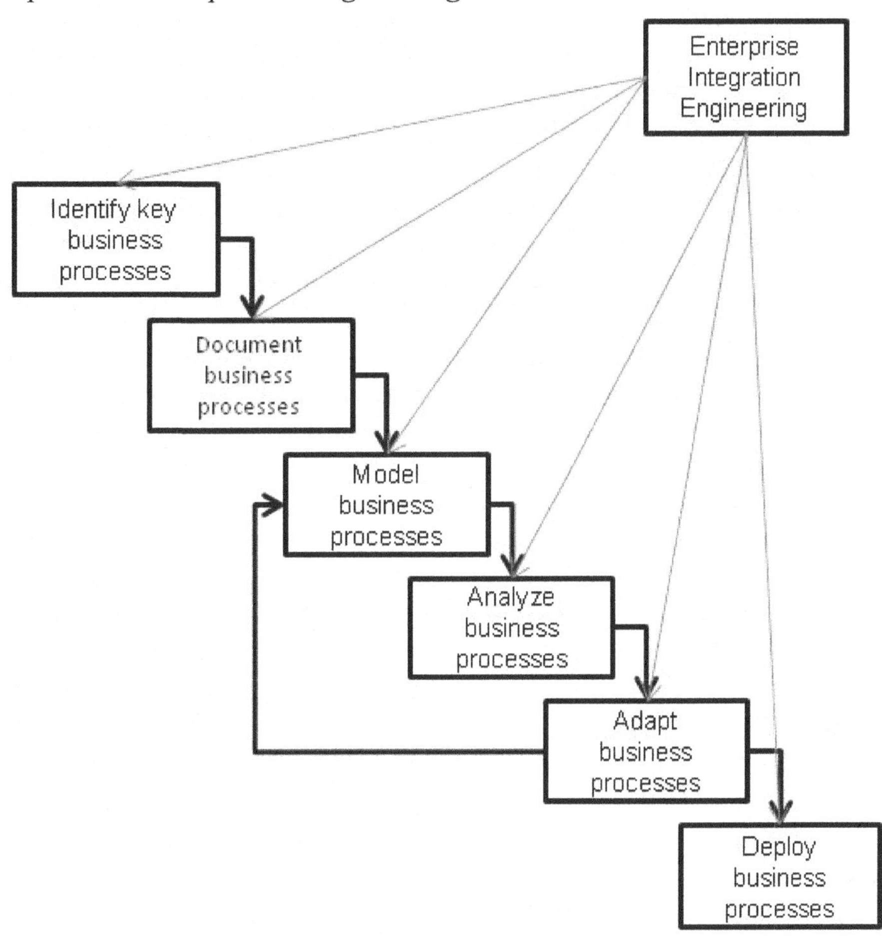

Likewise, the BPE person has to be able to apply different approaches to gather information for process documentation. From documents review to on field observation, people interviews and meeting with process owners, a BPE has to have many approaches for information gathering for business process documentation.

EIE is also useful in business process analysis (BPA). BPA could be performed with the collaboration of process owners and the assistance of simulation tools. EIE could help in identifying involved application systems and roles involved in a business process. As key business processes are normally end-to-end, EIE would provide support for identifying that all involved parties are considered.

Once business process analysis has been conducted, business processes could be adapted to meet expected business goals. Again, here EIE could be important to help in process adaptation. Process adaptation may consist in changes to the process model, including any missing role, defining new roles, or defining new process indicators for assessing the processes.

The final step in the process framework is business process deployment. Here EIE could help in identifying involved application systems, and roles and processes that will be related to a process. In this step, the information technology department will be in charge of the implementation. The BPE should be able to communicate business processes needs for integration to application systems. EIE assists in the identification of the appropriate application systems thus making this step easier to be conducted.

As could be derived from discussions on last paragraphs, it is clear the importance of EIE in assisting the work of the BPE in performing the steps defined by a business process framework. It is also more clear the body of knowledge that a BPE should have. By combining ideas from EIE and BPM, a BPE could perform its job in an easier way. From business process alignment to organizational competiveness, joining EIE and BPM concepts creates a synergistic framework for business process improvement. The following sections present two examples of combining EIE and BPM produce results of great value for enterprises.

MULTIPLE FACILITY CONSTRUCTION MANAGEMENT

An organization in charge of facility construction achieved great success in its processes. The organization was confronting the necessity of increasing its capability in facility construction, moving from managing 10 projects a year to be able to manage more than 20 simultaneous projects. However, the organization lacked from availability of highly trained facility construction managers. To face this new challenge for growing operation needed a careful revision and changes in its processes. Facility construction involved three main stages: civil engineering, mechanical engineering, and electrical engineering. Every facility construction project was assigned a project manager. Depending on the construction stage, the domain engineer was responsible, under the project manager supervision, to control the assigned stage. For instance, an expert civil engineer was responsible of managing civil engineering tasks which should be reported to the project manager, the mechanical engineering stage responsibilities were of the mechanical engineer, and so on.

The success of the organization in performing facility construction increased its operations. As mentioned before, with its available process management resources, the organization was able to conduct as many as ten simultaneous projects. The increased demand required that at least twenty projects be conducted at the same time. A problem that the organization faced was that highly trained project managers in facility construction projects were not available. It thus was necessary to modify the process to make it possible that a single project manager was able to control several construction projects in different countries at the same time. It was necessary that the organization performed facility construction projects around the world. Local country constraints made difficult standardized operations because regulations and local availability of resources to assign building contracts. If building contracts were possible, the domain engineers were responsible to control the project. If contracting companies were not available, the domain engineer has to contract professionals to perform the needed tasks.

This situation describes how an established business process that was successfully applied in the past could not be applicable to the current goal. For the facility construction enterprise, its mission, vision, and strategy needed to be changed to successfully cover the new demands. It was necessary to redefine the organization from single project management to multi-project management with the same human resources. Institutionalized business processes were unable for the new challenge. A new end-to-end business processes definition was necessary.

EIE played a paramount role in assisting new process definition. It helped in the development of new mission, vision, and strategy. It was determined that the organizational chart needed to be modified to be able to cope with the new requirements. It was determined that in most of the cases, domain experts were unable to bring with them a team of trained experts. Thus a practical solution was to hire experts at the country where every project has to be developed. Additionally, new application systems needed to be developed for project control. This made possible for a single project manager to be able to control projects in globally separated countries.

A BPE was in charge of assisting the facility building enterprise in the definition of new processes and determining application systems that needed to be developed. The knowledge of the BPE in project management was decisive for a successful definition and implementation of the new business processes. The application systems were developed, thus currently, the organization is able to perform multi-project management of facility construction projects.

The organization is now able to conduct multi-project facility construction on time and within allotted time and resources, with minimal variance in meeting the goals (i.e., cost and time). This case demonstrates that synergistic combination of EIE and BPM, carefully conducted by a BPE could result in high benefits for an organization.

It needs to be emphasized that the knowledge and experience of the BPE in engineering processes highly contributed to the success in this case. This is an important issue to be considered in other business process improvement efforts. A BPE needs both knowledge on BPM and domain. Or at least have available and be able to use experience from domain experts. Keep in mind that domain experts are both processes operators and their managers.

Other important issue was that involved domain experts needed to be aware of their role in an end-to-end process. In the case presented here, civil, mechanical, and electric engineers were aware of their role and how everyone contributed to the successful operation of the facility. If every role concentrates only on performing his or her job without considering it as a contribution to an end-to-end process, the final result could be different.

STARTEGIC INTELLIGENCE AS SUPPORT FOR SUCESSFUL BUSINESS OPERATION

The successful operation of many businesses is continuously threatened by different aspects. Something common in business analysis is the use of a SWOT (Strengths, Weaknesses, Opportunities, and Threats) model. However, this model is usually applied when a new business unit or product is being planned. Once the decision has been taken and the product or unit has being launched, no formal additional analyses are performed. This could be a mistake, as new threats emerge, or the environment changes. Businesses continuously worried about their successful operation are aware of this necessity. Here is where strategic intelligence could be used. Strategic intelligence addresses the continuous analysis of the business environment, in order to identify potential risks (e.g., threats) and opportunities for their business.

Threats could come from many sources; such as competence in the market, economic changes, political changes, just to name a few. Opportunities could also present in many ways; some of them could be the installment of new potential providers in the region of operation, new rules created by governments, etc. Business should be continuously observing and analyzing their environment to identify these threats and opportunities in their field of operations.

The creation of a strategic intelligence unit is thus essential for the successful operation of a business in a competitive market. The question is how to set such a unit in a business, thus it can be able to provide the essential information to the strategic unit, so actions could be taken when necessary. The information sources need to be identified and information channels need to be created. These information channels will need the support of information technology to provide the back bone for information flow.

EIE and BPM play an important role to identify and define all elements that are important for the definition and implementation of the business processes and information technology infrastructure necessary for creating a strategic intelligence unit. The following paragraphs explain in more detail how EIE and BPM could be helpful.

First of all, EIE will assist in identifying all information sources. End-to-end processes should be defined to describe how the information will flow from sources to the strategic intelligence unit, and the decisions that should be taken to decide if the information is really important. Only the important information should be part of the report being sent to the strategic unit in the enterprise.

This is a clear example in which EIE and BPM leverage each other. BPM assist in the definition of the core processes important for the strategic intelligence unit. The identification of current and new systems necessary to support the information flows are supported by the application of EIE concepts.

The combined use of EIE and BPM were applied to assess the operation of a strategic intelligence unit in a global enterprise. The enterprise has business units around the world, making difficult a careful definition of roles and processes to operate with a minimal amount of resources. The findings in the study are described in the following paragraphs.

The first result of EIE was the identification of the information sources, some of which have been not considered previously as important. For these results, it was important the link between business strategy and the necessary information for making it possible. Several mismatches were found in which helpful information was not provided, although the information sources already existed in the business units.

A second result was that by applying BPM, it was easier to define the information flows from the sources to the strategic intelligence unit and from it to the business strategy unit.

We can conclude this analysis by emphasizing that neither EIE nor BPM played a main role in this project. Instead, the correct application of both, were paramount to a successful identification and definition of all elements and roles important to the definition of the core business processes and information technologies that would be necessary to keep the business operating successfully.

BODY OF KNOWLEDGE FOR BUSINESS PROCESS ENGINEERING

The notion of body of knowledge (BoK) has been suggested in many professional domains as a way to identify the fundamental knowledge of individuals, necessary for defining a professional discipline. A BoK defines the knowledge of a discipline necessary for individuals to perform their job in a standardized way, which at the same time guaranties that obtained outputs fully comply with what was expected. This section proposes a body of knowledge for a discipline of business process engineering, whose responsibilities will be the definition, analysis, and deployment of core business processes within organizations. In this context, an organization could be a business or a non-for profit organization (e.g., government agencies). A business process engineer should be able to work with any organization to assist it in identifying, modeling, analyzing, and deploying core business processes. While any organization is very different to each other, the BoK should cover capabilities necessary for a business process engineer to conduct process improvement projects in a similar and standardized way.

The business process engineer (BPE) should be able to play many roles while assisting an organization in business process alignment to business strategy. This requires broad knowledge in many fields (depicted on Figure 5). These fields constitute our proposal of a BoK for a BPE professional. Fields on Figure 5 provide basic knowledge for the BPE. Enterprise Integration Engineering (EIE) provides models for helping the design of end-to-end business processes. Business Process Management (BPM) is fundamental to guide the process alignment project. Information Technology (IT) knowledge allows the BPE participation in identifying proper technology for business process implementation and deployment. Group Management techniques allow the BPE in organizing project participants towards realization of the goal. Business Analysis is essential for assessing business processes.

While the central focus is on BPM, designing and deploying the correct business models is a multidimensional task. Dimensions are depicted on Figure 5; specific tasks should be managed by the BPE. A BPM project will involve the participation of many persons from the organization. Group management provides necessary skills for organizing and conducting the collaboration of the BPM project participants. The project participants should collaborate along the identification, design and deployment of core business processes. Interpersonal skills will simplify and make effective the effort of the group while working towards identification of core business processes and their latter deployment. Group management is also concerned with change management, necessary for process owners to play their new process related responsibilities with conviction and knowledge of how they collaborate to the successful deployment the core business processes.

Information technologies have undergone a remarkable progress for simplifying business process deployment. For instance, a current trend is the definition of application systems interaction trough interfaces known as services (Jimenez et al, 2006). Business processes interact with application systems requesting information or sending new information. Every interaction is defined by a service. Application systems could define multiple services making thus possible their collaboration with multiple business processes. When all application systems collaborate with business processes through services, it is said that a serviced oriented architecture (SOA) has been defined.

Figure 5. Body of knowledge for a business process engineering discipline

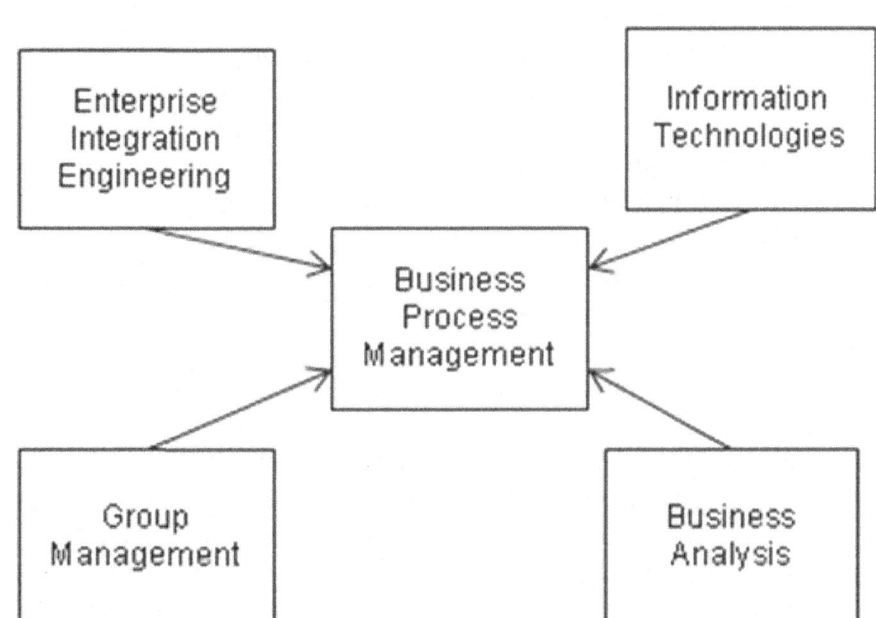

Organizations will require designing their SOA by identifying all the necessary points of interaction with application systems. An enterprise service bus (ESB) is a technological infrastructure that could simplify services publication and consumption by business processes. The BPE should know the possibilities of both SOA and ESB to simplify business process deployment.

There are several software tools that can help the BPE in performing business process analysis. Process analysis could be performed previous or after deployment. Simulators help in analyzing a proposed business process prior to deployment, thus adjustments could be identified and performed. After deployment, business process execution engines tools keep logs of operations. These logs could be analyzed to identify potential improvements for the business processes, after the business processes have been executed for a period of time (usually a few months). The BPE should know the availability of these tools and use them appropriately to adapt the business processes as necessary.

The definition of a business process engineering body of knowledge is important for a profession aimed at assisting organizations in the definition, modeling, analysis, and deployment of core business processes. While the main responsibility of a BPE would be in BPM, knowledge from other areas is important for helping the BPE in conducting BPM projects in a successful way. The areas of knowledge suggested here could be considered as a starting point to the definition of a business process engineering body of knowledge.

One area that would be important for the job of a BPE, and which was not considered here, is quality improvement. While quality improvement programs (e.g., six sigma, ISO 9000) are important for performance improvement, several authors consider them constrained to internal improvement, that is making things right. However, BPM should be addressed, as many authors consider, to making the right things right. Said in other words, BPM should concentrate on how value is generated to goods and services provided to customers. BPM should identify core business processes that increase value to customers. Concentrating efforts to internal improvement without consideration how these improvements add value to goods and services provided to customers could result in a loss of competitiveness for the organization. This does not mean that quality improvement programs are useless. What authors emphasize is that quality improvement program should be linked to end-to-end business processes aimed at providing customers with the added value of the goods and services they demand.

CONCLUSION

Business process modeling is an important step in designing the core processes of a business. Business models are a communication tool for business analysts, chief process officers, and information technologists. The chapter suggested enterprise integration engineering as a complementary approach that can provide additional support to the description of business process models and their alignment to strategy. Enterprise integration engineering includes as an important ingredient the consideration of mission, vision, and strategy for the identification of core business processes thus extending the models that should be part of a business modeling effort. By doing this, enterprise integration engineering contributes to provide more information regarding the elements that should be part of process models; enterprise architecture is the result of enterprise integration engineering. It is still pending a broader evaluation of how the contributions of enterprise integration engineering is really an important aggregate to produce more successful business process models as means of communication and implementation. The chapter shows how business process modeling could be improved through the inclusion of enterprise integration engineering. However, both enterprise integration engineering and business process management are evolving, how their findings, models and frameworks could be combined to define a body of knowledge for a professional on business process engineer may require time. The synergy created by joining EIE and BPM could just be part of the evolution of BPM and was on the past. BPM is currently the focus for improving enterprise operation, it still remain an issue how other trends aimed at similar goals could contribute to set BPM as the main player for achieving successful enterprise operations. Our proposal of defining a body of knowledge for a professional on business process engineering is just one of the many ideas for increasing the possibilities that a BPM effort could help achieve the goals of enterprises to become competitive in a globalized spectrum.

ACKNOWLEDGMENT

This document is result of research partly supported by grant number CAT030 from Tecnológico de Monterrey and CEMEX.

REFERENCES

Bernus, P., Nemes, L., & Williams, T. J. (Eds.) (1996). *Architectures for enterprise integration.* Chapman & Hall.

Burlton, R. T. (2001). *Business process management: Profiting from processes.* Sams Publishing.

Hammer, M., & Champy, J. (2005). *Reengineering the corporation: A manifest for business revolution.* Collins Business Essentials.

Harmon, P. (2003). *Business process change: A manager's guide to improving, redesigning, and automating processes.* Morgan Kaufmann Publishers.

Harrington, H. J. (1991). *Business process improvement: The breakthrough strategy for total quality, productivity, and competitiveness.* Mc Graw Hill.

Jeston, J., & Nelis, J. (2006). *Business process management: Practical guidelines to successful implementations.* Elsevier.

Jimenez, G., Ocampo, M.,Galeano, N.,& Molina, A. (2006). "Business process based integration of dynamic collaborative organizations. In W. Shen (Ed.), *Information technology for balanced manufacturing systems.* Springer.

Jimenez, G., & Espadas, J. (2007). Visual Environment for Supply Chain Integration Using Web Services. In W. Lam & V. Shankararaman (Eds.), *Enterprise architecture and integration: Methods, implementation, and technologies.*Hershey, PA: Information Science Reference.

Lankhorst, M. et al., (2005). *Enterprise architecture at work: Modeling, communication, and analysis.* Springer.

Miller, T., E. & Berger, D. W. (2001). *Totally integrated enterprises: A framework and methodology for business and technology improvement.* St. Lucie Press.

Ould, M. A. (2005). *Business process management: A rigorous approach.* Meghan-Kiffer Press.

Smith, H., & Fingar, P. (2003). *Business process management: The third wave.* Mehan-Kiffer Press.

Vernadat, F. (1996). *Enterprise modeling and integration: Principles and applications.* Chapman & Hall.

EXERCISES

- **Beginner:** Define the three roles of a business process engineer.
- **Intermediate:** Explain why the role of business process engineer is important
- **Advanced:** Describe the proposed role of a business process engineer and her necessary

knowledge to work as a business process engineer.

Practical Exercise

Potential customers of a bank are suffering from delays in opening new accounts. The bank established kiosks along the country to attend new clients. Clients fill their applications for opening accounts at the kiosks. However, kiosks don't have inline access to the bank, thus applications should be filled on paper and are missed at some point on their way to the bank, requiring clients to call the main bank for information regarding their applications. Clients are disappointed with the service, which provokes many of them to drop their intention of opening new accounts. The bank is thus missing the opportunity of incorporating many new clients.

- Describe how a business process engineer should proceed.
- Describe two core business processes.
- Describe how a BPE could help the bank in implementing the necessary processes.

SUGGESTED ADDITIONAL READING

Although most of the following resources are included in the list of references, a recommendation for readers is to review them in detail. They provide information on the main issues discussed in this chapter.

Bernus P., Nemes L., & Williams T. J. (Eds.) (1996) *Architectures for enterprise integration*, Chapman & Hall.

Burltonm R, T. (2001), *Business process management: Profiting from processes*, Sams Publishing.

Harmonm P. (2003). *Business process change: A manager's guide to improving, redesigning, and automating processes.* Morgan Kaufmann Publishers.

Jeston J., & Nelis, J. (2006). *Business process management: Practical guidelines to successful implementations.* Elsevier.

Smith, H., & Fingar, P. (2003). *Business process management: The third wave.* Mehan-Kiffer Press.

White, S. A. (n.d.). *Introduction to BPMN.* IBM Corporation. http://www.bpmn.org/Documents/Introduction to BPMN.pdf

Vernadat, F. (1996). *Enterprise modeling and integration: Principles and applications.* Chapman & Hall

IFIP-IFAC Task Force (1999). *GERAM: Generalized enterprise reference architecture and methodology, Version 1.6.3.*

KEY TERMS

Business Process Management (BPM): A managerial approach whose most important goals and concerns are business process definition, implementation, and improvement. BPM is addressed to how enact the core business processes, supervise their behavior and suggest improvements to achieve the strategy defined by the business.

Business Process Modeling: This consists in describing a business process normally using a graphic notation to show how all process activities are linked in a time frame to produce the expected result. A process model could show the participants and activities each of them perform, times for every activity, decisions that should be taken, parallel paths of activities, and many other important information for a process.

Business Process Modeling Notation (BPMN): BPMN is a standard notation whose evolution is currently managed by the Object Management Group (www.omg.org). BPMN includes many symbols that help build process diagrams to describe business processes in a graphical way. Currently, many software modeling tools support BPMN, and others will do in the future. BPMN is important because it will serve as a standard language for simplifying communication among all participants in describing, designing, implementing, analyzing, and improving business processes.

Business Strategy: A description of how a business will proceed in order to put himself in an improved state, according to its current position. The strategy may be addressed to increase market share, increase its competition by introduction of a new product or improvement of an already produced one, etc.

Core Business Processes: Enterprise operation is conducted (conscious or unconsciously) by business processes. A core business process is that which adds more value to a product or service. Core business processes are normally linked to the business strategy, and are thus paramount for the sustainability of the enterprise. A business process improvement effort will normally be focused to enhance core business processes.

Enterprise Integration Engineering (EIE): A research field whose main interest has been the definition of frameworks for linking business functional areas. The more important findings in EIE are the identification that several models are necessary to describe the operation of an enterprise: data model, organizational model, process model, and resources model. An integrated enterprise is one in which all functional areas know how they contribute to add value to the products or services from the enterprise.

Process Engineering Framework: A framework could be presented in many different flavors. Normally, frameworks come in a graphical model notation to describe the set of elements and their relationships that are important to help create specific models. For process engineering, a framework is relevant to show how business process management should be conducted thus all important steps and work products could be identified.

Value Added Activity: Any activity in a business process in which the enterprise adds some characteristic that is important to a customer or customer segment. These activities are very important in order to identify the total value that is delivered to customers along a business process.

Chapter XVIII
B2B and EAI with Business Process Management

Christoph Bussler
Merced Systems, Inc., USA

ABSTRACT

This chapter introduces the application of process management to business-to-business (B2B) integration and enterprise application integration (EAI). It introduces several integration examples and a complete conceptual model of integration with a focus on process management. Several specific process-oriented integration problems are introduced that are process-specific in nature. The goal of this chapter is to introduce B2B and EAI integration, to show how process management fits into the conceptual model of integration and to convey solution strategies to specific process-oriented integration problems. The exercises at the end of the chapter continue the various examples and allow the reader to apply their knowledge to several advanced integration problems.

INTRODUCTION

The times when organizations implement their individual application systems are definitely over. So is the time where all for the business relevant functions are implemented in-house and where only sales activities require the cooperation of organizations. Instead, application systems like enterprise resource management (ERP) systems can be bought from software vendors and installed within the information technology (IT) department. Once installed, they can be used by the organization's employees. In addition, accounting, supplier interactions, payment processing and other important business functions require automated interactions with the respective organizations that provide the business functions as outsourced functionality.

From an IT perspective this means that application systems need to be integrated with each other as well as those with business partner's IT systems. The integration of application systems within organizations is called enterprise application integration (EAI) and the integration with business partners' IT systems over networks is called business-to-business (B2B) integration. Both, EAI and B2B integration have to work hand in hand in order to provide a seamless business process implementation across the trading partners.

Historically, the two types of integration were subject to software development themselves, however, in the meanwhile packaged software systems, often called middleware, provide this functionality. This book chapter introduces the specific concepts of EAI and B2B integration. It gives an overview of the requirements as well as specific underlying principles that are relevant for integration. As integrations require many processing steps in the general case, process management technology is utilized for integration. In context of this book the role of process management in integration is emphasized and at the center of the discussion. Furthermore, many examples are provided that show how to put the integration concepts to work to solve various specific integration problems.

This chapter starts with introducing two very common examples, one for B2B integration and one for EAI integration in order to show the complexity of integration as well as some of the major requirements. The examples also level set the terminology as well as the meaning of the two forms of integration. After the examples an important abstraction is introduced that shows that from a process management perspective the two types integrations can be abstracted into a single conceptual integration model. Afterwards the most important concepts are listed, discussed and explained using small examples along the way. A series of fundamental integration scenarios follows showing the use of the integration concepts. At the end of the chapter several exercises follow. The interested reader is encouraged to solve them for developing a better understanding in the space.

INTEGRATION EXAMPLES

EAI integration and B2B integration, as shown later in this chapter, are really two specializations of a common abstraction from a process management viewpoint (and other viewpoints as well that are not discussed in more detail in this chapter, see (Bussler, 2003) for a more comprehensive discussion). In order to motivate the common abstraction of EAI and B2B integration as well as to substantiate the integration concepts discussed in the next section, two examples are introduced here that will serve as prototypical use cases throughout the book chapter. The first example is a typical B2B integration from the supply chain domain and the second example is a typical EAI integration from the company-internal IT domain.

B2B Example: RFQ Process

The request for quotation (RFQ) process is a process common to many enterprises. The RFQ process is a communication between two or more companies across a public or private network. The goal of this process is to establish an agreement between a buyer and a seller: A buyer needs a certain product and needs to find out from one or more potential sellers if they can provide the required product. Typical purchasing parameters are price, quality, quantity or availability. The buyer asks several sellers using a request for quote (RFQ) about the desired product and each seller sends back at most one quote (Q) containing the specifics of their offer. This process can iterate several times until a satisfying agreement is reached. Buyers, after receiving quotes, might adjust their purchasing parameters and ask for a revised quote. If a buyer and a seller agree on the parameter settings, the buyer might send a purchase order to the seller to order the products as specified in the seller's quote. The decision to actually buy from a specific seller is done by the buyer after evaluating the various quotes from different sellers. A buyer can of course buy from several sellers at the same time.

Looking at the example from a process perspective, three intertwined processes are necessary to define and to execute the exchange of the business data. Figure 1 show the process from a buyer's viewpoint. A buyer sends out a request for quote (RFQ) (step 1), then receives a quote (Q) (step 2) and decides if the quote is acceptable (step 3). If not, the purchase parameter settings are changed by the buyer and the process starts over. The decision if the received quote is acceptable or not is a buyer-internal process step as no communication with the seller is performed in this step.

What is not described in the process is the underlying implementation, like ensuring that messages between buyer and seller are sent exactly once, error handling as well as waiting for responses. It is assumed that the underlying infrastructure can not only deal with the non-process details but also abstracts nicely from it so that the non-functional implementation details remain invisible at the process level.

The seller's process for the B2B integration is the complement of the buyer's process in the sense that a request from a buyer has to be matched by the response of the seller and vice versa. Figure 2 shows the process from a seller's viewpoint. The first step is receiving the request for quote. The second step is an internal step putting together the quote; the buyer does not see this step at all. The third step is sending back the quote to the buyer who requested the quote. The seller has to make sure that the quote is sent back to exactly the same buyer who sent the original request.

Another important aspect is that in this example the seller's process does not have a loop corresponding to the one of the buyer's process. For the seller each request is treated as independent request. The buyer decided to operate differently. However, as the loop is an internal aspect of the buyer, this matches perfectly. Of course, a seller could decide to also implement the loop in order to track the changes a buyer might make in the purchasing parameter settings. Figure 3 shows the two combined processes. The dashed arrows represent the communication between the buyer and the seller. While business documents are sent

Figure 1. Buyer's implementation of request for quote process

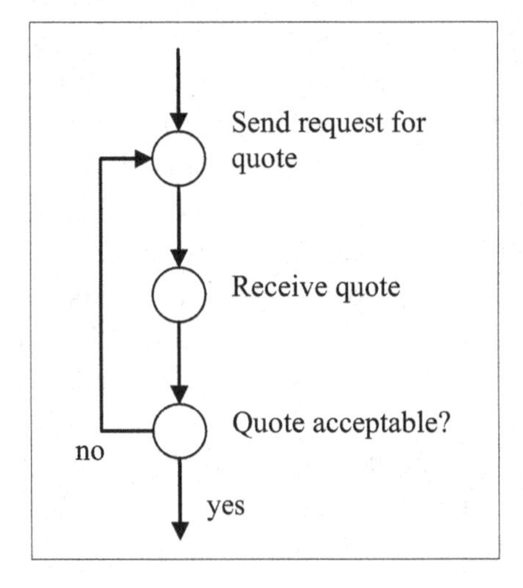

Figure 2. Seller's implementation of the request for quotation process

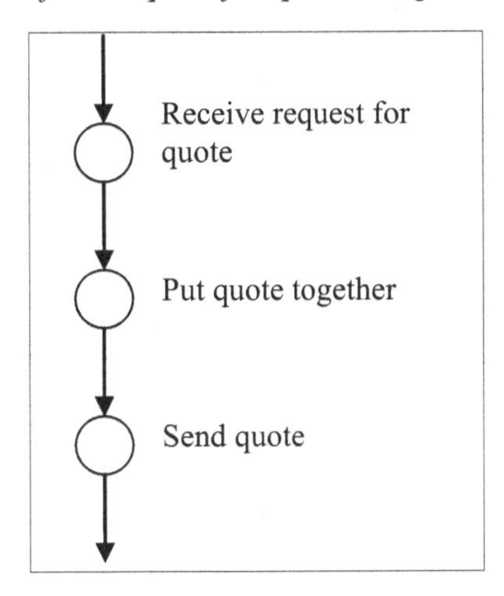

Figure 3. Buyer's and seller's processes combined

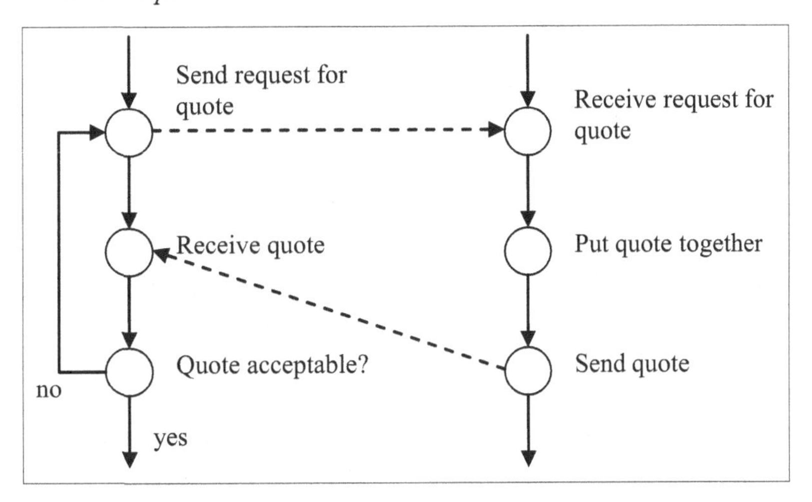

as data messages (request for quote and quote), the data flow also imposes implicit control flow dependencies as the processes cannot advance unless the data arrives.

This figure also shows the third process, namely, the process that represents the message exchange between the buyer and seller (represented as dashed arcs). If only that process were of interest it would contain the steps involved in the sending and receiving of messages.

The contents and representations of the involved data is by itself interesting and has to be discussed. However, since we approach B2B and EAI integration from a process perspective, the precise data definitions are not further elaborated here and the reader is referred to RosettaNet (RosettaNet, 1998), EDI (UN/CEFACT, 1996), or Open Applications Group (Open Applications Group, 1994) instead for standardized definitions of hundreds of business documents.

Figure 4 shows the system and security boundaries of the buyer and seller explicitly. The dashed boxes define those processes that are defined and executed within the domain of the buyer and the seller. The dashed arcs going across the boundaries show the data exchange that crosses the organization's boundaries, establishing the integration as B2B integration.

Figure 4. System boundaries for buyer and seller

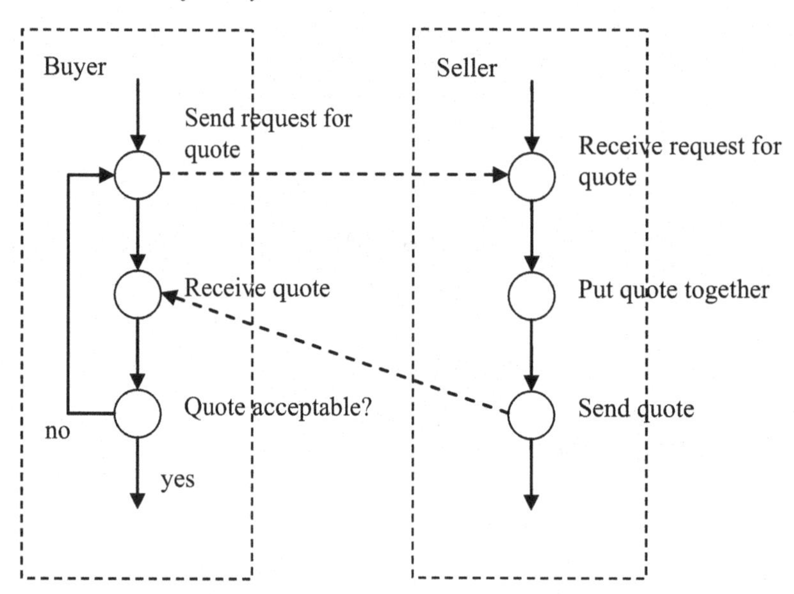

The request for quote process is not executed in isolation. Before a buyer sends out a request the decision to buy has to be made. After the process completed the buyer has to send out a purchase order request to the selected seller in case the buyer decided to make a purchase. However, these upfront and subsequent processes are not further discussed here.

Another important aspect that is not discussed here is the situation that a buyer can decide to abort the process. For example, after having sent the request for quote, the buyer could change his mind. In this case the buyer can either wait for the quote and not get back to the seller or send an abort message. The seller can decide not to send a quote if he is not interested in selling to the requesting buyer. In this case the buyer has to have a time out mechanism so that he does not wait forever for the quote. These situations are further discussed in the exercises at the end of the chapter.

EAI Example: Process Integration

Typical IT departments of larger companies face the challenge of implementing business functionality invoking application systems. Application systems might be provided by software companies as installed products or they might have been implemented in-house by their own IT department. In a typical IT situation there are several application systems, up to several hundred. They have to cooperate in order to provide the business functionality and EAI integration is the means of integrating them.

The example is in the area of purchase order management from a seller's perspective. Once a purchase order is received (possibly after a RFQ process), two validations are performed (in reality there are a lot more, though). One is the buyer's address validation to establish that the address is indeed the buyer's address and that the buyer is not from a restricted country into that selling is prohibited. The second check is to establish that the order matches a quote sent out earlier in case the buyer refers to one. The first check is to avoid shipping problems and that products are illegally shipped into restricted countries. The second check is to avoid that the buyer states cheaper prices than he was quoted earlier in the process.

Any error is forwarded to an error handling process step as in both cases human intervention is necessary to resolve the issue. The error handling process step can decide how to resolve the error. In many error situations it means contacting the buyer and asking for clarification or to resend the purchase order. In the former case the human dealing with the error updates the data with the correct information directly. In the latter case the received purchase order is deleted and the new one processed (sometimes a purchase order update is appropriate, too, depending on the particular situation).

Figure 5 shows the process. All process steps interact with application systems like a system managing addresses or a system managing quotes that have been sent out. As this process interacts with application systems it is categorized as EAI integration. As in the B2B integration example, the specific data passed between the process steps and to and from the application systems are not shown in detail as the focus is on process management in this chapter.

These two examples are very common examples of integration solutions. The exercises at the end of the chapter are extensions of these examples and represent very common integration requirements that have to be implemented often in context of EAI and B2B integration. Since examples are only specific solutions and cannot characterize integration as a whole, more general and comprehensive concepts are discussed later in order to provide a complete characterization of integration.

In reality, B2B and EAI integration scenarios are a lot more complex and touch many more external systems, up to several hundreds running up to several thousands of steps. However, companies are reluctant to document these integration scenarios for publication to non-employees for competitive reasons. This is the reason why it is not easily possible to reference existing publications that contain complex and real scenarios. Somewhat more complex and more detailed examples are in (Bussler 2003) and the reader is referred to that for an additional level of complexity.

Figure 5. Purchase order process

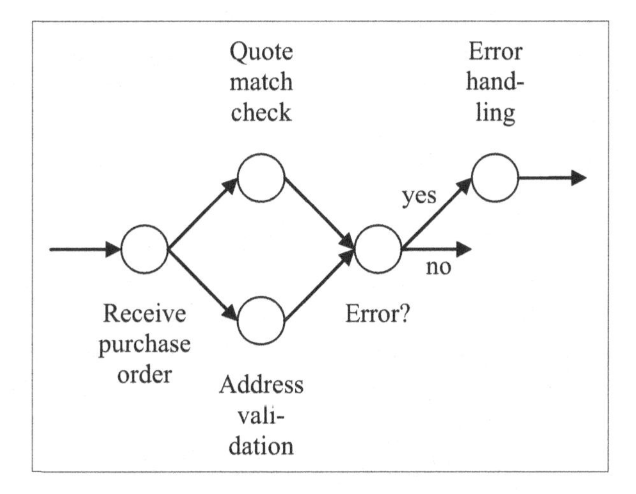

INTEGRATION ABSTRACTION

Before discussing the details of the integration concepts an important abstraction has to be established. As a first approximation, the process representations of the examples earlier show no difference at all for either the B2B integration or the EAI integration case. In both cases there are process steps that are linked with each other and define the particular process logic. The necessary software implementation for sending messages between companies or invoking application systems are invisible at the process level as the process deals with the data from those interactions without having to know how those interactions are actually executed at run time.

A process step that receives data from a B2B interaction with a trading partner or a process step that receives data from an application system is not aware of the difference in sources from where it receives the data. In both cases the data is received by the process step and in case of any error the process step receives the system encoding of the cause of the error (and has to react appropriately).

When the implementation details of interacting with application systems or trading partners are not considered, the process management concepts are the same for B2B and EAI integration. This means that at a process management level, the same process management concepts can be used for either form of integration. The integration concepts that are discussed in the next section ensure and implement this abstraction.

One argument against this abstraction is that in B2B integration a specific pattern of message exchange has to be implemented that ensures that the correct message sequence is achieved: in this case a process must be aware of the message protocol. While this is true, the same applies for application systems. Application systems also expect their interfaces to be called in a specific sequence and any mistake in the sequence will result in error situations. Again, there is no conceptual difference between the two situations.

Another argument against this abstraction is that B2B integration is based on XML while application systems use programming interfaces. Again, this is not true as most of the B2B integration to date is based on non-XML data, like e. g. EDI transmissions. And application systems have also XML-based interfaces that allow exchanging data in XML format.

While this argumentation establishing the integration abstraction is not exhaustive, it gives a clear idea that both, B2B and EAI integration are very similar from a process management perspective and both can be abstracted into a common set of integration concepts. The next section introduces the conceptual model for integration based on this abstraction.

CONCEPTUAL MODEL OF INTEGRATION

The B2B and EAI examples earlier gave a first glimpse into the complexity of applying process management as a solution to integration problems. Based on these examples as well as real world implementations this section outlines the major concepts of EAI and B2B integration that are relevant in the context of process management. While the pictorial representations of the processes earlier appear as rather simple, in real world implementations the complexity is high because of the many systems involved as well as the usually complex process logic itself. Every individual integration utilizes most of the following concepts.

Integration

Often references are made to 'the' integration as opposed to integration as a technology area or approach in general. When integration is used as a concept, it means the set of all processes, data structures, application systems, trading partners and other concepts that are involved in specific processing. For example, an integration can implement the request for quotation integration between trading partners where one trading partner sends a request for quotation and waits for the other one to send back a quotation. Since integrations can be executed multiple times, possibly concurrently in relation to each other, they are typed and every execution is an instance of a specific integration (in the sense of a 'classical' type – instance model).

The temptation is very high to equate an integration with a business process or process model. However, this is not possible and the reason for this is that process models do not recognize all of the integration specific concepts and therefore do not provide specific language constructs for them. For example, data mediation, protocol definition, or canonical data format management are typically not parts of a process model and cannot be defined by the process model. Therefore, if an integration requires a process, the process is "part of" the integration in addition to all the other definitions needed. And, analogously, if an integration interacts with a trading partner, a reference to this trading partner definition is "part of" the integration. Looking at it from another viewpoint, an integration contains every definition and all references to every definition necessary to execute it. Figure 6 provides an overview of the main concepts.

Endpoint

A first integration concept is that of an endpoint. An endpoint represents an application system or trading partner with the goal to exchange data as required by the integration. The concept of an application system is to be interpreted in a wider sense since it can include any type of software, like databases, file systems, queues, in addition to higher-level software like enterprise resource planning systems that implement business semantics. Every application system endpoint needs to be accessible and many forms exist, including programming language APIs, database interface tables, queues, emails, to name a few. The most important distinction is that the interface of an application system is synchronous or asynchronous. In the former case there is a direct synchronous invocation relationship between the process step and the application system. In the latter case a communication technology like a queue is between the process step and the application system that makes them being asynchronous with each other.

The concept of trading partner represents a remote communication over public networks like the Internet or private networks like EDI networks. At

Figure 6. Integration concepts

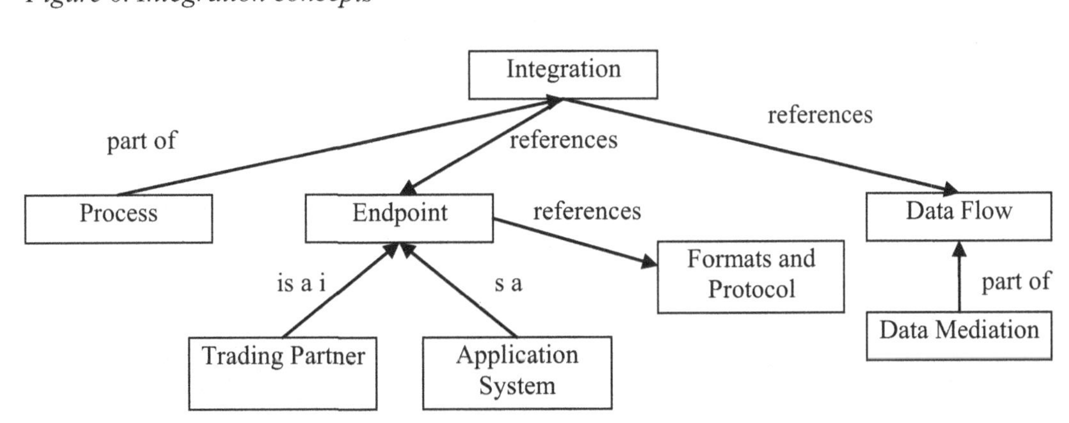

the end of the day the communication infrastructure of a trading partner is a software system, too. However, the style of interaction is different from application systems as trading partners require secured message transfer, preplanned interactions for load control as well as a trust relationship in the sense that no communication will be successful unless a trust relationship exists.

In summary, the concept of endpoint represents non-process management software that an integration has to interact with in order to implement the integration logic.

Formats and Protocols (FAP)

All endpoints (application systems as well as trading partners) have technical interfaces, as already indicated earlier. Endpoints send and receive specific instances of data types and expect a certain call sequence of their functions according to their implementation. It is not relevant for the process management aspect of integration that the implementation of the interfaces is diverse in their technical implementation (e.g., a programming API *vs.* an XML message exchange). From an integration perspective these are implementation details at very low system levels. The relevant part for integration is that in both cases data types (synonym: data structures) have to be clearly defined and the invocation sequence is specified completely, including error cases. An interface in this sense is therefore the sequence of exchanges or invocations together with the relevant data types (synonym: formats) as well as an enumeration of the error states. Ideally, compensating actions are defined, too, in order to be able to cleanly terminate an erroneous protocol execution.

There are many different ways to defining the formats and protocols and several standards exist, too. Figure 7 shows an example protocol of an application system that must be obeyed in order for any integration to work.

The dotted parts of the figure represent the protocol; the solid arcs represent the invocations that are possible. As the figure shows, a certain sequence of the steps has to be obeyed. Also, a loop is shown that allows the repeated retrieval of a purchase order followed by a quote. However, it

Figure 7. Example protocol

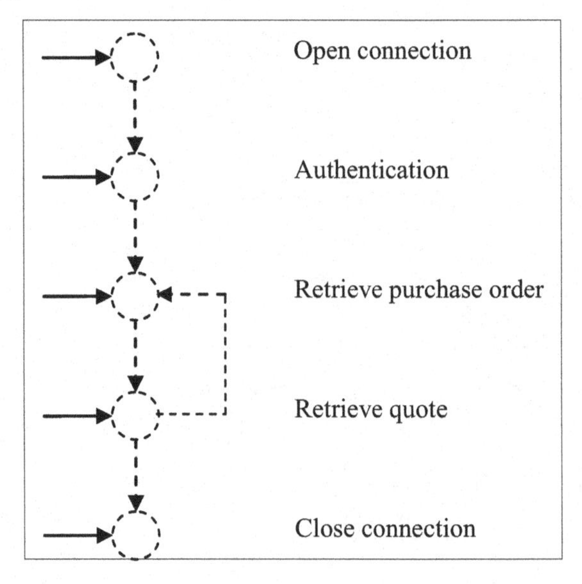

is not possible to retrieve only several purchase orders, it always has to be a pair of purchase order and quote.

Process

A major concept in the integration space is the definition and execution of processes (Jablonski & Bussler, 1996) (Leymann & Roller, 1999) (van der Aalst & van Hee, 2004). Processes are part of integration and are used to define the sequence of interactions with endpoints. As outlined later in the book, processes are defined by connecting process steps with control flow and sometimes data flow constructs in order to derive to a specific sequence amongst the process steps. Control flow defines that a process step can only be executed after another process step finished successfully. Conditional control flow constructs are available, too, that allow conditional process step execution. Depending on the particular process meta model, the available process modeling constructs vary a lot.

Data flow defines the availability of data for each given process step and is used to ensure that process steps have the necessary data to interact with endpoints. Depending on the particular process meta model the data flow is defined explicitly or implicitly.

Since later on in the book process models and process meta models are discussed in a lot more detail no extensive discussion takes place here for the general case. Specifically, however, it is important to emphasize that integration cannot be defined with a single process, but requires several processes that are coordinated. Figure 8 shows the request for quotation example in more detail than Figure 4 (buyer side only). The process is shown on the left in solid lines; the protocol used to communicate with the trading partner is shown in dotted lines. Both are connected for accomplishing the correct data flow, however, the protocol has additional steps for dealing with the acknowledgements that are not important for the business process and hence they are not linked.

In this case a clear separation was achieved by modeling the particular interaction with an endpoint independently of the business process logic dealing with the business data content. Both processes are linked in order to coordinate their control and data flow.

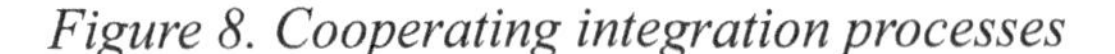

Figure 8. Cooperating integration processes

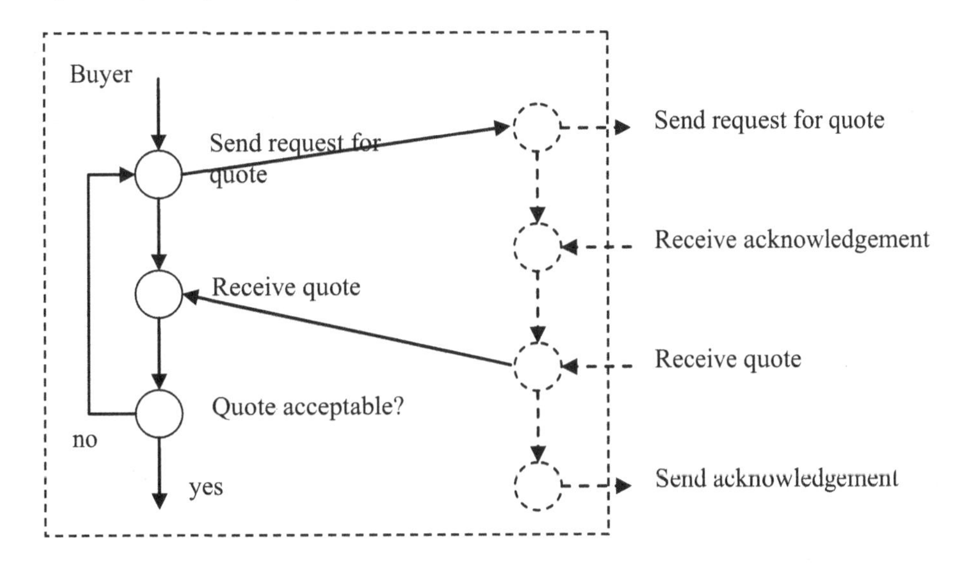

The reason for this separation is that the process representing the endpoint interaction can be reused independently of the business process and vice versa. An implication of this is that the execution of these processes is concurrent in the sense that steps, that are not directly related, can be executed independently of each other.

The ability to model different processes and coordinate them as shown in Figure 8 is an important feature required for a process model to be useful in context of integration for the reason of reuse and concurrency. However, there are additional reasons that are discussed later in context of process mediation which are even more relevant and significant.

Data Flow

Data plays a big role in context of integration. Data is exchanged every time a trading partner or application system is part of an integration. Data is either sent or retrieved from an endpoint and so it is important to define the flow of data between an integration and the endpoints. Furthermore, as an integration is a series of invocations of endpoints, the flow of data must be defined between the various process steps that define the particular order.

The structure and complexity of data varies a lot, from very simple items like an acknowledgement to very complex items like a purchase order. Complexity in data structures is a minor aspect for integration as the current data management technology is capable of handling it.

A bigger topic around data is data heterogeneity. Data that is expected by endpoints or provided by endpoints might not be compatible between the endpoints. For example, an address in one endpoint is a structured data type while an address in another endpoint might be a long string. Figure 9 show this example in more detail. Two address types are shown as well as the data mediation function that transforms the structured address into an address in string form. An example with a concrete address is given, too.

Whenever data types mismatch the two data structures must be converted into each other in order for the data flow to work. If endpoint El sends addresses according to the left address structure, but endpoint E2 expects the address structure on the right, a data transformation (synonym: data mediation) needs to take place that transforms one into the other. As can be seen, the data transformation function contains a lot of knowledge about the string representation as from the data type description it would not be possible

Figure 9. Data heterogeneity

```
AddressType1: structure {            Address: AddressType1;
        City: string;                String (Address.Street + ", " +
        Street: string;      --->    Address.City + ", " +            --->   AddressType2: string
        Zip: natural                 toString(Address.Zip))
}

Address1: AddressType1 = {
        "San Jose",
        "First Street",                                                      Address2: AddressType2 =
        95112                                                                "First Street, San Jose, 95112"
}
```

to know the order of the various address elements. The next section will discuss how data mediation takes place in context of integration.

Data flow is one of the most important aspects of integration as the data passed between the endpoints must be semantically correct in order for an integration to succeed successfully and terminate in such a way that the internal data state of all endpoints is correct and consistent. It is therefore very important to model all aspects around data in an integration very carefully.

Data Mediation

Data mediation, as discussed earlier, is necessary in case the data structures of the endpoints differ when they refer to the semantically same data and are used in the same integration. The latter point is important. If endpoints with different data structures are not used in the same integration, there will be not data flow between them and so no data mediation is necessary. However, if they are used in the same integration, data mediation is necessary. Figure 10 shows two process steps that connect to different endpoints. An address is retrieved in the first step from an endpoint and a transformed address is given to a second endpoint by the third process step. As data flows from one to the other (dotted lines) and the data mismatches (see Figure 9) data mediation has to take place between the process steps.

In the example in Figure 10 the data mediation is modeled as the second process step. This is a convenient approach as process steps can invoke any type of software, including software that specializes in performing the data mediation.

However, this is not the only possible approach of performing data mediation. An alternative exists that is discussed in the next section and this is based on the following argumentation. Process steps communicate with endpoints. Endpoints have their particular way of defining data structures and as endpoints cannot be changed easily, the integration must deal with the data structures as they are defined by the endpoints. If the integration is modeled as in Figure 10 then the process steps themselves have to understand the data structures of the endpoints. This by itself is a challenge as process management systems have their own data type systems and if the data type systems do not match with those of the endpoint implementations this mismatch has to be overcome, too.

If many endpoints are integrated into one integration, many different data structures

Figure 10. Data mediation

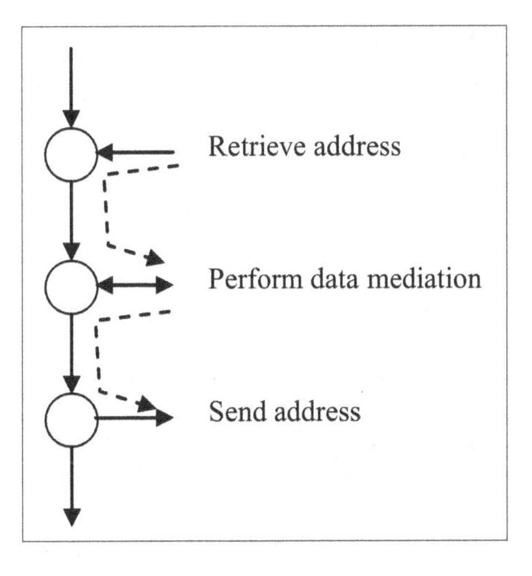

have to be modeled in process steps, as many as required in order to communicate with the endpoints. This is a lot of modeling work, and since the modeling is a human activity it is error prone, too. It would be desirable if process steps would be independent of the data structures of the endpoints. This would reduce the number of data structures significantly and would improve the quality of the integration. The approach that achieves this is discussed next.

Canonical Data Definition

The fundamental idea of making the data types used in the integration independent of the data types defined by the endpoints is to push the data mediation to the boundary of the integration. Instead of performing the data mediation between the process steps, it is done between the endpoints and the process steps. Figure 11 show the approach for the address example shown above.

As can be seen in the figure, the mediation happens between the process steps and the endpoints. A new symbol is introduced for data mediation as this is not a process step since the mediation happens before the process step. This means that the process steps are not aware any more of the data structures as defined by the endpoints. The benefits of this approach are clear: all process steps can operate on a homogeneous set of data structures as all use the same data structures to refer to the same data item. Furthermore, as data mediation does not take place any more inside the process model itself, the process modeler does not have to understand all possible data types of all possible endpoints to model the data mediation. Furthermore, the process model has fewer process steps as all mediations are outside the process model. A lot more benefits are discussed in (Bussler, 2003).

Compensation

While all concepts so far are concepts that are necessary for defining an integration, the concept of compensation is orthogonal to it. Compensation is the definition of actions that are necessary to deal with a failure that might happen during the execution of an integration (Wächter & Reuter, 1992). Sometimes a failure can be addressed by

Figure 11. Canonical data mediation

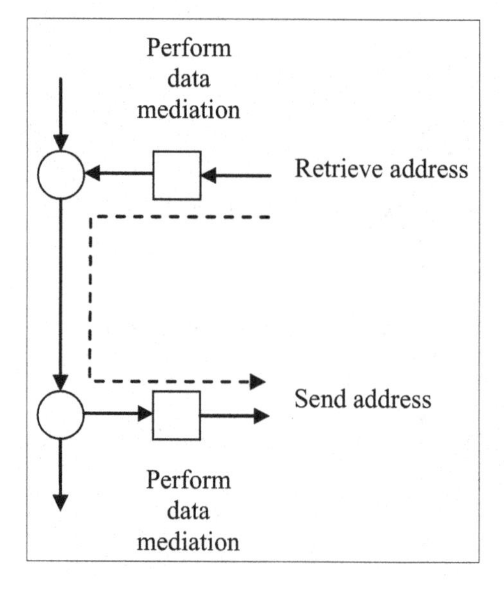

aborting an ongoing transaction and retry its execution. For example, if a quote is to be retrieved and the quoting system is offline. In this case the retrieval of a quote will be aborted and retried later. However, as integrations are long-running, sometimes transactions are already committed and their effect needs to be undone. For example, a buyer might have sent a purchase order and the seller released a manufacturing order fulfilling the purchase order. If then the buyer calls stating that he does not need the products after all, the already committed manufacturing order has to be undone. In this case the compensation cannot be achieved by aborting a transaction as the manufacturing order was already committed. Instead, it has to be marked invalid or it has to be removed from the system, which really is another transaction. In this case the compensation is achieved by executing another transaction.

In fundamental terms, for each process step that modifies data of endpoints compensation has to be define for the case that a failure occurs while the process step is executed as well as after the process step committed its action. This then allows the integration to compensate for failures during process step execution as well as after process step execution.

INTEGRATION SCENARIOS

Integration, independent of it being EAI or B2B integration, can take many forms depending on the specific set of application systems or trading partners that have to be integrated. However, there are some basic patterns that can be found in many settings. Some of those are shown next to illustrate the integration concepts in more detail. In general, canonical data mediation is modeled in all scenarios as this is the preferable approach to the data transformation problem.

Data Copying

An important pattern is the copying of data from one application system to one or more application systems. The data is retrieved from one and passed on to those that need the copied data for their internal processing. In general, several application systems can be the recipient, so the integration

Figure 12. Data copying integration

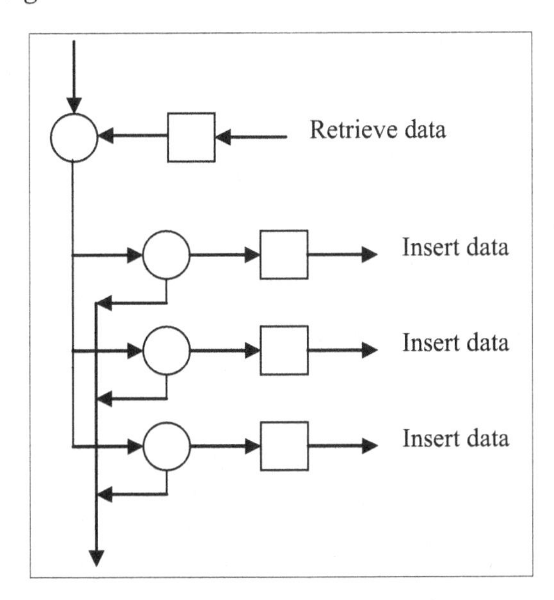

for achieving the copying is generalized. Figure 12 shows the integration for copying data from one to three endpoints.

A first process step retrieves the data that is to be copied and subsequent to this all application systems are updated concurrently (one process step for each application system). After all endpoints are updated, the process completes. This is ensured by the synchronization of all three process steps that send data to endpoints through the confluence of the control flow. Following the canonical data mediation approach, the data mediation takes place between each endpoint and its corresponding process step.

An important modeling decision has to be made. If the data, that is copied, is not yet within the application systems, then a true insertion or creation of new data takes place. The target application systems have not seen this data before and it is new data for them. The second case is the data update. In this case a version of the data is already in the application systems and these data will be updated, i.e., changed. Therefore, in a more elaborate version of the data copying integration pattern, a distinction has to be made if a true creation or an update takes place (or both, for a combined functionality).

In addition, this pattern can be extended towards an all or nothing semantics where it guarantees that all insertions or updates happen or none of them. For example, if one application system returns an update error, the updates of all the other application systems should not happen, either. If all endpoints are transactional, a distributed transaction could be one possible approach. If the endpoints do not allow distributed transactions or if they are not transactional at all (not even locally), a compensation strategy is necessary to possibly undo any already successfully performed data copy or update.

Integration Expansion

The number of integrated application systems or trading partners is not static. Both change over time, either becoming larger by adding endpoints or being removed from the various integrations they participate in. Every time a new application system is added or removed (or changes its interface) and every time a trading partner is added, removed or changes its interface, all integrations that refer to the application system or trading partner have to be changed and revalidated as necessary.

In order to isolate the change and make the change management easier, it is possible to encapsulate the endpoints and make them accessible as a set instead of individually dealing with them. In the following, the data copy integration is revisited. Instead of modeling each application system as a separate step in the "update data" process, the endpoints are collected in a separate process and this is then invoked from the "update data" process.

Figure 13 shows the new model of the integration. The process "update data" ensures that data is retrieved and passed on to the process "update endpoints". The latter contains the actual update invocation of the application systems, including the data mediation for each of the systems. If application systems are added, changed or removed, this change is local to the "update endpoints" process and any process invoking this one does not depend on the change directly. The same type of abstracting can be achieved for endpoints as well as other functionality in addition to the data copy or data update functionality.

Business Process

The easiest integration process implements a business process where different endpoints contribute to its execution. Issues like data copying, replication and the change of endpoints is abstracted from it. In the following a more elaborate version of the business process shown in Figure 5 is discussed and a pattern is extracted from it.

The pattern is like this. Data is retrieved by the integration, prepared for validation and one

Figure 13. Endpoint abstraction

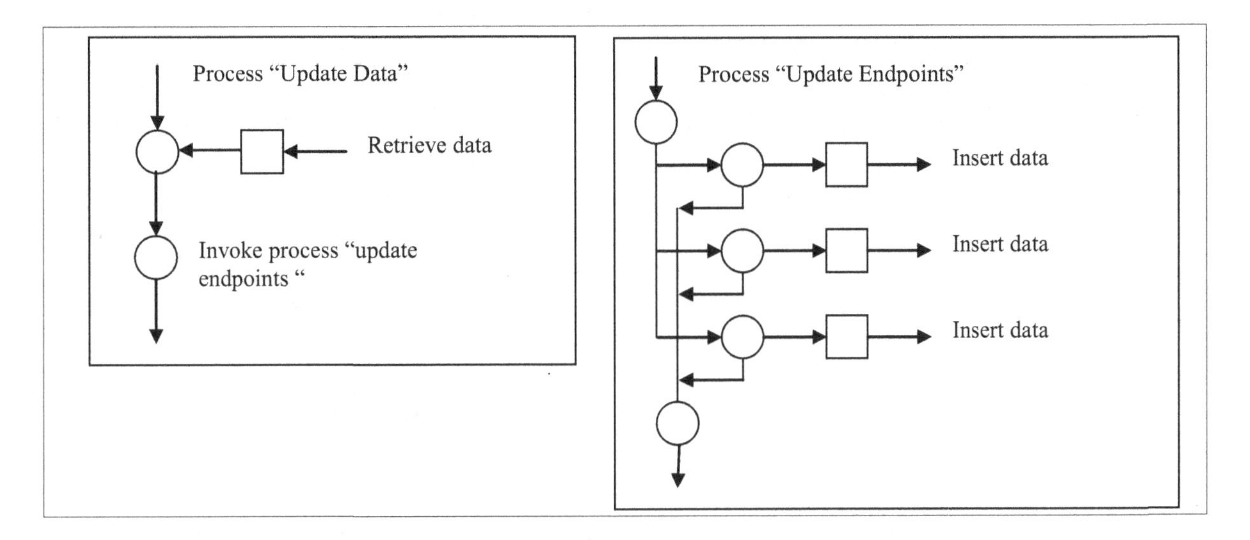

Figure 14. Business process receiving and validating data

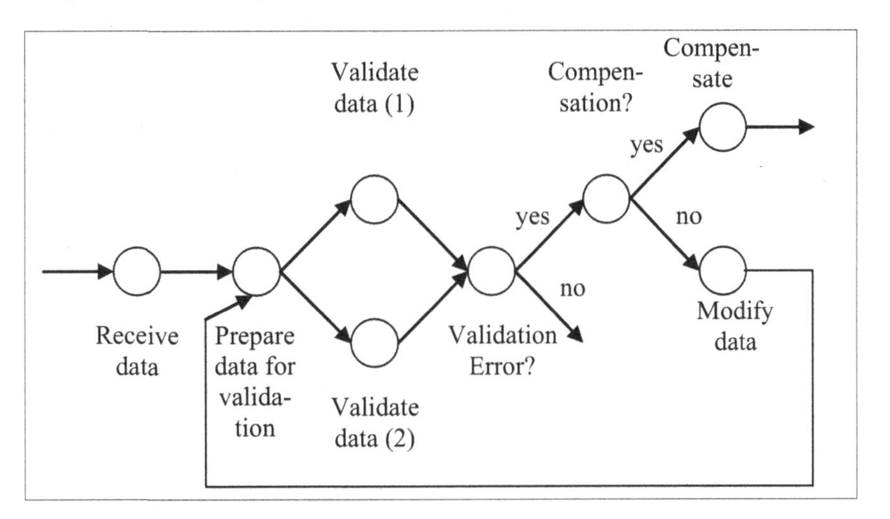

or more validations are performed. Afterwards a check takes place testing if all validations are successful. If they are, the process is done. If at least one validation failed, error handling takes place in either of two forms: either the state of the process is compensated and the process is finished, or the data is updated as part of the error handling and the validation/error handing is repeated.

Figure 14 shows this process pattern. The number of validations changes from situation to situation. Also, the particular compensation changes depending on the logic. For example, in the purchase order receiving case, the compensation could be sending back the rejection of the purchase order.

This pattern is a very common pattern whenever data is received and has to be checked for correctness and consistency.

SUMMARY

This chapter introduces the two areas of integration, business-to-business (B2B) integration and enterprise application integration (EAI). It provides a common abstraction across those two areas from the viewpoint of a conceptual model. The conceptual model of integration is introduced with the emphasis on process management. The chapter clearly shows that process management is an important part of integration in order to define and to execute the behavioral aspects of integration. Several examples introduce specific integration problems and solutions. Exercises from a beginner level to a very advanced level go beyond the examples and introduce the reader to even more complex integration scenarios.

EXERCISES

The following exercises start from a beginner level getting more complex and realistic over time. They are extensions of the discussion in the previous sections and are intended to provide more insight into the complexity of using process management in context of integration.

Hotel Room Availability Inquiry (Beginner)

Define an integration between two travel sites that consists of a B2B protocol as well as and EAI integration for the internal integration of application systems. One site is sending an inquiry to another one asking for available rooms including their availability. The asking site itself posts only 'rooms' for rent, the asked site offers rooms distinguishing between 'standard rooms' and 'deluxe rooms'. In addition, the site offering the rooms insists that rooms are booked for at least 2 days.

Customer Address Update (Intermediate)

Define an EAI integration where the update of a customer address is propagated to two other systems within a single organization. Extend the integration so that any number of trading partners can be added when the same customer address has to be propagated to them, too. This is for example relevant when subsidiaries have to be kept informed.

Error Handling (Intermediate)

Extend the previous EAI integration that adds one more software system that logs errors (error log system). If any of the involved application systems or trading partners encounters an error, log the error as well as the state of the integration at the time of the error into this new error log system. Also, ensure that once an error happens, the integration stops completely and that this is the state that is logged in the error log system as well so that the particular stopped instance of an integration can be found by inspecting the error log system.

Master-Slave Replication (Advanced)

Define a master-slave replication in an EAI integration context so that every application system or trading partner can take the role of the master and every of the remaining application systems or trading partners can take the role of a slave to implement the replication of any type of data.

Consistent Data Update (Advanced)

Define a process that receives a purchase order, checks its validity, sends the order to an ERP system and passes it on to manufacturing in four steps. Then, add another independent process that receives purchase order change requests and updates the involved systems with the changed purchase order data. Ensure that an overall correct system state is preserved at any time.

Data Replication (Most Advanced)

In general, a misunderstanding between the copying of data and the replication of data exists. Replication means that data, which is residing in several places, has always the same value. If the data is updated in any of the places, the others have to be updated, too, without any other software being able to observe different data values in the different locations while the replication takes place. Define a data replication process that replicates a data item across several endpoints. Please remember that any of the endpoints can initiate the change of the data item and while the replication is ongoing, no intermediate data state must be visible.

SUGGESTED ADDITIONAL READING

Alonso, G., Casati, F., Kuno, H., & Machiraju, V. (2003). *Web services.* New York: Springer

Enterprise integration patterns. Retrieved August 30, 2008. Web site: http://www.eaipatterns.com/

Euzenat, J., & Shvaiko, P. (2007). *Ontology matching.* New York: Springer-Verlag

Hohpe, G., & Woolf, B. (2003). *Enterprise integration patterns: Designing, building, and deploying messaging solutions.* New York: Addison Wesley

Kashyap, V., Bussler, C., & Moran, M. (2008). *The Semantic Web - Semantics for data and services on the Web.* New York: Springer

Wikipedia entry for *Business-to-Business Integration.* Retrieved August 30, 2008. Web site: http://en.wikipedia.org/wiki/Business-to-business

Wikipedia Category: *Enterprise Application Integration.* Retrieved August 30, 2008. Web site: http://en.wikipedia.org/wiki/Category:Enterprise_application_integration

REFERENCES

van der Aalst, W., & van Hee, K. (2004). *Workflow management: Models, methods, and systems.* New York: The MIT Press

Bussler, C. (2003). *B2B integration. Concepts and architecture.* New York: Springer

Jablonski, S., & Bussler, C. (1996). *Workflow management - Modeling concepts, architecture and implementation.* New York: International Thomson Computer Press

Leymann, F., & Roller, D. (1999). *Production workflow: Concepts and techniques.* New York: Prentice Hall

Open Applications Group (1994). *Open applications group.* Retrieved April 15, 2008. Web site: http://www.openapplications.org/

RosettaNet (1998). *RosettaNet.* Retrieved April 15, 2008. Web site: http://www.rosettanet.org/cms/sites/RosettaNet/

UN/CEFACT (1996). *United Nations Centre for Trade Facilitation and Electronic Business.* Retrieved April 15, 2008. Web site: http://www.unece.org/cefact/

Wächter, H., & Reuter, A. (1992): The ConTract Model. In Ahmed K. Elmagarmid (Eds.), *Database transaction models for advanced applications* (p. 219-263). San Francisco: Morgan Kaufmann

KEY TERMS

Business-to-Business (B2B) Integration: The exchange of messages between organizations for the purpose of exchanging business information, requests as well as contractual obligations.

Compensation: The actions required to semantically undo an achieved data state in order to neutralize an earlier state change for the purpose of correcting errors.

Control Flow: Concept to define causal dependency between process steps to enforce a specific execution order.

Data Flow: Data dependency and data movement between process steps to ensure that required data is available to a process step at execution time.

Data Mediation: Semantic transformation of data structure and data content to establish semantic equivalence of different representations.

Enterprise Application Integration (EAI): The exchange of messages between software systems for purposes of data replication as well as business process execution.

Formats and Protocols (FAP): Definition and sequence of messages and invocations required by an organization or application system to communicate meaningfully.

Process Management: The definition of process types and the execution of process instances.

Chapter XIX
Systems for Interorganizational Business Process Management

Paul Grefen
Eindhoven University of Technology, The Netherlands

ABSTRACT

This chapter is devoted to automated support for interorganizational business process management, that is, formation and enactment of business processes that span multiple autonomous organizations. A treatment of intra- and interorganizational business processes is included to provide a conceptual background. It describes a number of research approaches in this area, including the context of these approaches and the design of the systems proposed by them. The approaches are described from early developments in the field relying on dedicated technology to current designs based on standardized technology from the service-oriented context. The chapter thereby provides an overview of developments in the area of interorganizational business process management.

INTRODUCTION

In the past, many organizations operated their business processes in a rather stand-alone mode. Although cooperation scenarios with other organizations obviously existed, these scenarios were mostly based on the exchange of physical goods and information (e.g., on the basis of electronic data interchange) – not on the execution of integrated business processes by the collaborating partners. A number of developments has changed the context in which organizations collaborate, however. In the first place, products and services produced have become far more complex, thus requiring more business capabilities and hence larger networks of collaborating organizations.

The fact that competition forces organizations to retract to core business activities only amplifies this development. Secondly, both product specifications and market circumstances have become much more dynamic, thereby requiring business networks to become more dynamic too. Thirdly, market paradigm changes like mass customization and demand chain orientation require much tighter synchronized business processes across individual organizations in a business chain. Fourthly, time pressure has become much greater in the setup and execution of collaborations between organizations. These four developments are forcing organizations to pay much more attention to *how* they cooperate, not only to *what* they exchange. In other words: organizations are forced to operate in business processes that span business chains and take part in the design and management of these interorganizational business processes.

To deal with the complexity of interorganizational business processes and obtain the required efficiency in setting them up and executing them, automated systems are required for interorganizational business process management. These automated systems should support a number of tasks. They should provide support for the design or configuration of interorganizational business processes. As we will see in the sequel of this chapter, support may be in the form of interactive design tools, but may also go into the direction of fully automatic configuration of interorganizational business processes, based on predefined subprocesses within participating organizations. These automated systems should support the automated management of the execution of interorganizational business processes, i.e., that process logic that actually links the internal business processes of multiple autonomous organizations. Then, these systems should support the synchronization of interorganizational business processes with the internal business processes of the organizations.

This chapter discusses the development of systems for interorganizational business process management. It first provides a background by discussing the differences between intraorganizational and interorganizational business processes. A three-level framework is explained that shows how to relate these two kinds of processes. Then, it discusses early approaches towards interorganizational business process management. Next, approaches, architectures and technologies are presented of three major projects from the research experience of the author: CrossFlow, CrossWork and XTC. In doing so, attention is paid to both business process specification and business process enactment, including contractual and transactional aspects. The discussion in this chapter explicitly shows the development from 'traditional' workflow management via advanced interorganizational structured business process management to service-based, highly dynamic business process interaction. The chapter ends with a conclusion presenting main observations from the past and highlighting major trends in current developments.

INTERORGANIZATIONAL BUSINESS PROCESSES

In this section, we explain what interorganizational business processes are. We first discuss the concept of a business process within one organization: an intraorganizational business process. Then, we move to the concept of a business process across multiple organizations: an interorganizational business process. We will see how control flow interfaces are important here. To explain how intra- and interorganizational processes are related, we discuss a three-level framework. In the last part of this section, we add the aspect of dynamism to interorganizational business processes, i.e., the aspect of collaboration networks that change over time. One thing is important to understand here: when we speak of 'organizations', these may be autonomous business entities (like commercial organizations) but also autonomous departments of a single business entity.

The Concept of Intraorganizational Business Processes

An intraorganizational business process is completely run from the process point of view within the boundaries of a single organization (or autonomous part of an organization). The process may call business services (which may be implemented by business processes) of other organizations, but does not 'see' the structure or status of these other services explicitly. We can hence define the concept of intraorganizational business process as follows:

An intraorganizational business process is a business process the process logic of which is enacted by one single organization, but which may call black-box business services of other autonomous organizations.

An intraorganizational business process typically has a number of characteristics:

- It has a single point of process control from a conceptual point of view (it may be technically controlled by a distributed system, but this is transparent to the users).
- There are no reasons for explicit hiding of structure or status details of the parts of the process to other parts of the process.
- The process is run in an environment of which the heterogeneity is controlled, both in terms of languages (syntax and semantics) and protocols used, as in terms of the technical infrastructure (like workflow management systems and middleware). Often, one finds a homogeneous environment within a single organization, i.e., one choice has been made for business process support technology.

The Concept of Interorganizational Business Processes

After having discussed intraorganizational business processes, we turn to the concept of interorganizational business processes. We use the following definition of interorganizational business process:

An interorganizational business process is a business process the process logic of which is enacted by two or more autonomous organizations, of which at least one organization exposes a non-black box projection of the explicit control flow structure of a process to the other organization(s).

This definition states that in an interorganizational business process, at least one party must make a non-trivial (consisting of more than one single activity) process structure accessible to its collaborator(s). This process structure is typically a projection of an intraorganizational business process (we will see more of this projection relation in the sequel of this chapter). In the 'more traditional' interorganizational service invocation (as found in the basic service-oriented computing paradigm), we don't see explicit control flow sharing between organizations (control flow of a service implementation is encapsulated by the service specification).

As such, we can distinguish between various classes of process coupling modes (Grefen et al. 2006). Two classes are illustrated in Figure 1, where the open circles in the center levels indicate control flow interfaces, the filled circles in the top and bottom levels indicate local processes that implement what is offered in the interfaces. The process coupling classes range from black box coupling (left hand side of the figure) to explicit two-way control flow sharing, which is called open box coupling (right hand side). The black box class does actually not comply with our definition of interorganizational workflow, as

Figure 1. Black box processes and shared control flow

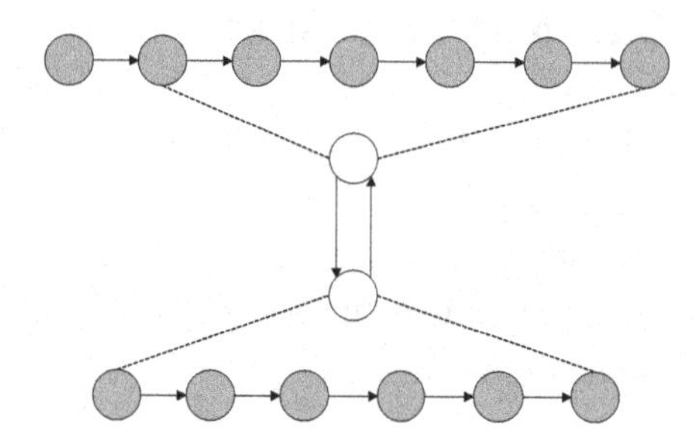

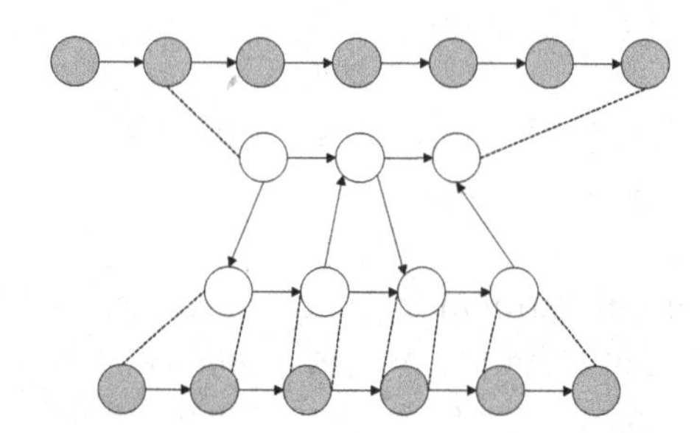

it is in principle no more than a call-and-return service scenario – the fact that the two services at the interface are implemented by processes is completely invisible to the other party.

In (Grefen at al. 2006), also glass box coupling and half-open box coupling are discussed, which are in between black box and open box coupling. Glass box coupling allows one party to observe the status of the process of the other party, but does not allow interference with it. Half-open box coupling does allow one-way interference (we will see in the sequel of this chapter that this coupling mode is relevant for the process-oriented service outsourcing paradigm).

An interorganizational business process differs in characteristics from an intraorganizational business process:

- It explicitly has several points of control, as it is run by multiple autonomous organizations.
- There are two explicit reasons for hiding process details: the fact that some details are private to an organization (for reasons of competition) and the fact that some details are irrelevant to other organizations (as they pertain only to internal matters of a single organization).
- The process is run in a heterogeneous environment. The fact that multiple autonomous organizations collaborate implies that different local choices have been made with respect to languages, protocols and infrastructures for business process management.

Levels in Interorganizational Business Processes

As we have seen above, interorganizational business processes run across multiple autonomous parties, interconnecting intraorganizational business processes of these parties. To clarify the relation between these two types of processes, the three-level process framework has been proposed (Grefen et al. 2003). This framework is shown in Figure 2 with two collaborating parties shown as the two large boxes (but can be trivially extended to more parties): one party initiates the process-based collaboration, the other responds by engaging in the collaboration (the two roles are shown in the figure). At both parties, process specifications exist on three levels, as explained below.

The middle level of the framework is the conceptual level for business process models. At this level, business processes are designed, i.e. their intended functionality is specified in abstract terms. The conceptual level is independent from both (internal) infrastructural specifics and (external) collaboration specifics. It does specify the main aspects of intraorganizational processes, taking collaboration in interorganizational business processes into account in an abstract way.

The bottom level is the internal level, at which process models are directly interpreted by process

Figure 2. Three-level business process framework

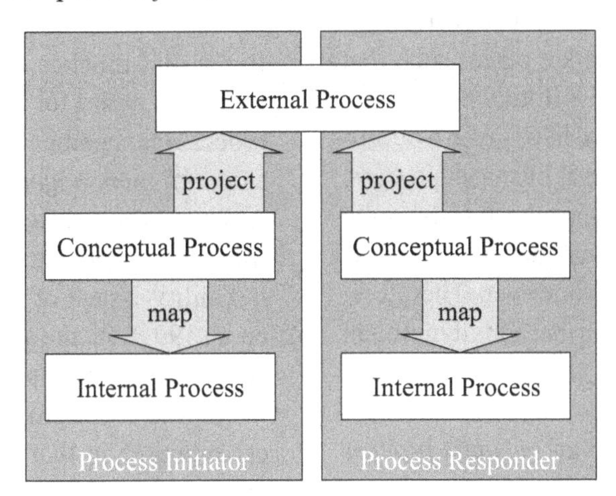

management systems. Hence, process models at this level are in general technology-specific, e.g., described in the specification language of a specific workflow management system. The internal level is of an intraorganizational nature. Models at the conceptual level are mapped to the internal level for process enactment (e.g. by workflow management systems or other process-aware information systems). For details of this mapping see (Grefen et al. 2003). Note that the mapping is not always trivial, as the functionality of the internal level process management systems may be limited: not all constructs used at the conceptual level may be supported. In that case, it may be possible to map 'missing constructs' to a (sometimes complicated) combination of constructs that are supported.

The top level is the external level, at which process interaction with external parties is modeled for use in interorganizational business processes. At this level, process models are market-specific, i.e., have to conform to standards and/or technology used in a specific electronic market. Models at the conceptual level are projected to the external level for integration with processes of partner organizations to form interorganizational business process. Note that projection is used here, since only relevant parts of the conceptual model are of interest at the external level. In the projection, process details are hidden by aggregation/abstraction of process steps.

Note that some authors use the terms 'public process model' and 'private process model', where we use the terms 'external process model' and 'internal process model'.

Static vs. Dynamic Interorganizational Business Processes

So far in this section, we have looked at the characteristics of interorganizational business process management. We have, however, not yet looked at the functionality required for the *dynamic* formation of collaborations. As we have seen in the introduction, this is essential in modern business – thus, this last point is addressed here.

Dynamic formation of collaborations implies that an organization prepares for interorganizational business process management (the *what* and the *how*), without yet knowing which the collaboration parties will be (the *who*). These parties are selected during the execution of a case or set of cases (business process instances), where selection takes place on the basis of characteristics of the case(s) under execution and current market conditions. To allow so, potential collaborators (process responders in terms of the three-level framework shown in Figure 2) expose their process offerings (at the external level) in market places such that they can be found by process initiators.

Earlier in this section, we have given a definition of an interorganizational business process. This definition does not yet take the dynamic nature of interorganizational business process management into account, however. Therefore, we present another definition that adds dynamism to the previous definition:

A dynamic interorganizational business process is an interorganizational business process that is formed dynamically by (automatically) integrating two or more external processes provided by the involved organizations. Here dynamically means that collaborator organizations are found at or just before process run-time by searching business process marketplaces based on the characteristics of (a set of) business process cases and market conditions.

Note that the above definition is formulated in terms of *(near) run-time dynamism*, i.e., the formation of an interorganizational business process instance right before or during the execution of that process instance (or limited set of instances). In this approach, dynamism is not obtained by redesigning the process specification. This is different from *design-time dynamism*, in which flexibility is achieved by explicitly redesigning the process specification at specific points of time. There is extensive work on various approaches to achieve flexibility in business processes (Weber et al. 2008, Schonenberg et al. 2008).

After the conceptual discussion of interorganizational business process management in this section, we turn to concrete approaches and systems for this purpose in the next section.

EARLY DEVELOPMENTS

In the mid-nineties of the previous century, automated support for intraorganizational business process management (at that time usually labeled as *workflow management*) entered a mature stage. Attention was paid to advanced aspects like transaction management, exception management, and flexibility issues of business processes (Grefen en al. 1999). At the same time, collaboration between organizations was changing (as explained in the introduction), also fueled by the rise of e-commerce in that time frame. These two developments together gave way to research interest into automated support for interorganizational business process management.

Below, we first give a brief overview of research efforts in the context of interorganizational business process management. Then, we discuss one project (WISE) in a bit more detail.

Brief Overview of Projects

The FlowJet project at Hewlett-Packard aimed at coupling various types of workflow systems in E-business contexts (Shan 1999). The system was designed with modularity as a starting point to provide *feature on demand* capabilities (Shan et al. 1997). Dynamic resource brokering is within the scope of the project, but explicit contracts for detailed service specification are not considered.

The WISE project is comparable to FlowJet as it uses interorganizational workflow management technology for business-to-business E-commerce scenarios (Alonso et al. 1999, Lazcano 2001). WISE is further discussed in the next subsection.

MariFlow follows a similar approach to the WISE project but is specifically targeted at the marine industry (Cingil et al. 1999). The project aims at providing process management capabilities comparable to the WISE system, enhanced by an advanced marketplace for service contracts.

The COSMOS project developed an architecture that allows organizations to offer and search for services in a catalogue, a negotiation platform, and facilities for contract signing (Griffel et al. 1998). Once the contract is signed, workflow specifications are derived from the contract or encapsulated in the contract constituents of the offering party and a new workflow instance is started.

WISE

The WISE project (Workflow based Internet SErvices) at ETH Zürich aims at providing a software platform for process based business-to-business electronic commerce (Alonso et al. 1999, Lazcano 2001). In doing so, the project focuses on support for networks of small and medium enterprises. The software platform used in WISE is based on the OPERA kernel (Alonso et al. 1997).

WISE relies on a central workflow engine to control interorganizational processes (called virtual business processes). As we will see in the discussion of CrossFlow in the next section, a distributed engine approach has been used elsewhere. A virtual business process in the WISE approach consists of a number of black-box services linked in a workflow process (Alonso et al. 1999). A service is offered by an involved organization and can be a business process controlled by a workflow management system local to that organization – but this is completely orthogonal to the virtual business process.

Specification of virtual business processes in WISE is performed using the Structware/IvyFrame tool (Lienhard 1998), which is internally based on Petri Nets. This tool and its specification technique are used to construct both the conceptual structure of interorganizational processes and the specifications of services exchanged between organizations in a virtual enterprise. Hence, it can be placed both at the conceptual and at the external levels of our three-level framework (see Figure 2).

The Structware/IvyFrame tool has, however, also characteristics related to the internal level, as it not only supports process creation, but also configuration management of underlying enactment platforms (Lazcano 2001).

The graphical representation produced by the Structware/IvyFrame process definition tool is compiled into a language called Opera Canonical Representation (OCR) (Hagen 1999). This language is used internally by WISE to create process templates. As OCR is focused towards process enactment in the context of a specific platform, we can place it at the internal level of our framework. Note, however, that OCR is used for interorganizational coordination, so has external level characteristics too. Further information can be found in the chapter 'Compiling Business Process Models to Executable Code' of this book, where more details on the OCR language and the current version of the OPERA kernel (called JOpera) are given.

CROSSFLOW: DYNAMIC SERVICE OUTSOURCING

As discussed in the introduction, many organizations nowadays focus on their core business processes and buy processes from partners in the market to perform the additional parts of the process required to reach their business goals. We call this the service outsourcing paradigm. In this paradigm, the outsourcing organization (initiator in terms of the three-level framework) is referred to as service consumer, the service implementing organization (responder) as service provider. The details of service outsourcing are specified in a contract between both parties. The combination of service consumer and service provider can be seen as a virtual enterprise that presents itself to a third party (for example a customer) as a single entity.

Traditionally, these virtual enterprises have a more or less stable character over time, i.e., the combinations of service consumer and provider are fixed over long periods of time (e.g., several years). As discussed before, in dynamic e-business settings, however, players in a market and competitive situations change that fast that a more dynamic approach is required to service outsourcing to create or retain a competitive position. This means that in service outsourcing, service consumers dynamically determine which service providers to use in the enactment of their business processes. We call this business model dynamic service outsourcing, the temporary organization formed by service consumer and service provider a dynamic virtual enterprise. Depending on the business domain and the specific interorganizational business process, a dynamic virtual enterprise can have a life span ranging from a few minutes to a few months.

The European CrossFlow project has developed information technology for advanced process support in dynamic virtual enterprises (Grefen et al. 2000). Below, we first discuss the CrossFlow approach to interorganizational business process management. Then, we pay attention to the architecture of the CrossFlow system. We show that the architecture is of a dynamic kind, following the life cycle of a dynamic virtual enterprise.

The CrossFlow Approach

The CrossFlow approach to interorganizational business process management is characterized by four main aspects (Grefen et al. 2000):

- Dynamic service outsourcing
- Contract-based service specification
- Fine-grained, advanced interaction
- Contract-dependent generation of enactment infrastructure

Below, we elaborate these four aspects. Note that the trading-based approach to service outsourcing means that CrossFlow can be considered a project investigating the intersection of workflow management and electronic commerce technology.

Dynamic Service Outsourcing

As indicated above, the CrossFlow approach to interorganizational workflow management is based on a dynamic service consumer/provider paradigm. This means that an organization that wants a service to be performed on its behalf (the service consumer) outsources this service to an organization that can perform this service (the service provider). This outsourcing is performed dynamically, which means that the decision to outsource is taken during the execution of the process instance (case) requiring the service and that the provider is chosen dynamically.

The dynamic search for compatible business partners is performed through a matchmaking facility, which plays the role of a service marketplace. Service providers advertise their services in this facility. Service consumers query the facility for required services. Matchmaking of services is based on the fact that in many markets standard business practices, standard languages and ways of describing services, and standard legal forms and processes have evolved, resulting in common contract templates.

The interaction between service consumers and providers is based on contracts, as described below. Service providers advertise their services in contract templates, which are completed to individual contracts by service consumers.

Contract-Based Service Specification

In the CrossFlow approach, the interaction between service consumer and service provider is completely specified in a contract. The contract defines all relevant details of the service provision (Koetsier et al. 2000). Traditionally, this is limited to an identification of the service and all parameters required to execute the service. CrossFlow contracts, however, also entail a specification of the process used to execute the service. Specification of this process allows for further integration of consumer and provider processes than a mere black-box process would allow. This high level of integration is essential for the close partnerships found in virtual organizations.

In virtual organizations, however, a partner does not require full operational details of other partners. Rather, a well-defined abstraction of their operation should be used to obtain an effective view on both data and processes. As partners in a virtual organization often have different IT platforms, a heterogeneous environment exists. This heterogeneity should be addressed by abstraction of technical details of partners. For both reasons, CrossFlow contracts define the interaction between organizations not in terms of their workflow management systems, but on an abstraction level above these systems (i.e., the external level in the three-level framework).

Fine-Grained, Advanced Interaction

The CrossFlow approach is focused on tightly integrated service consumer and provider processes. For this reason, a common service process specification is included in CrossFlow contracts. To support the tight coupling of processes, additional advanced notions of interaction are required. These notions are operationalized in so-called cooperation support services (CSSs). A broad spectrum of CSSs is relevant for interorganizational workflow management, like remote process monitoring and control, interorganizational transaction management, automatic service remuneration, trust and security management, etc. The design of these services should be such, that they can be selected and combined in a modular way, depending on the application context.

In the context of the CrossFlow project, three areas of advanced cooperation support services are addressed. The selection of these three areas is based on the interest and background of the project partners. Quality of Service monitoring allows tracking the progress of outsourced services, both online during service execution and offline to provide aggregate information. Level of Control enactment provides means for high-level, interorganizational transaction management and consumer-controlled process control over outsourced services. Flexible Change Control allows dynamic changes to execution paths of outsourced processes during their execution.

Contract-Dependent Generation of Enactment Infrastructure

The enactment infrastructure that connects the information systems of service provider and consumer is dynamically set up according to the contract and a specification of the way the contracted service is to be implemented and supervised. To allow this, the cooperation support services are mapped to modular system building blocks and a message-based integration mechanism is used to provide the required level of flexibility. The mechanism uses a subscribe mechanism to cater for flexibility. We will see details of the infrastructure generation in the description of the architecture below.

The CrossFlow System

Now we turn to the architecture of the CrossFlow system, which handles contract-based interorganizational workflow management. The CrossFlow architecture supports both contract making and contract (service) enactment. The architecture is based on commercial workflow management system technology, shielded from the CrossFlow technology by an interface layer. In the project, IBM's MQSeries Workflow (formerly known as FlowMark) product is used.

The lifecycle of a service outsourcing consists of four phases: contract establishment, dynamic infrastructure configuration, contract enactment, and dynamic infrastructure disposal. We describe each of the four phases below. We conclude this section with a discussion of technical details of the prototype implementation. More information on the architecture can be found in (Hoffner et al. 2000).

Contract Establishment

The following describes a typical sequence of events that leads to the establishment of a contractual relationship between the provider and consumer organizations – illustrated in Figure 3.

When the provider WFMS is ready to receive requests for enactment of a process on behalf of a consumer organization, it notifies its Contract Manager of its readiness. A Workflow Module (WM) acts as an interface layer to shield the Contract Manager from details of specific WFMSs. It does so by providing a bi-directional activation interface to the Contract Manager. The Contract Manager selects a pre-existing Contract Template that describes the service and its associated quality of service (QoS) guarantees, work schedule, monitoring and control points as provided by the service, etc. Appropriate values for these service guarantees including the cost of the service must then be determined. These will be decided according to the capabilities of the enactment infrastructure, the resources that the provider is willing to assign to the enactment, and the price associated with the resources. In addition, the requirements that the provider places on the consumer within the terms of the Contract Template are also specified. The service description and the demands are translated into the property and constraint language of the matchmaking facility. The result is then advertised into the trader that serves the specific market. In a competitive market, several provider organizations will advertise the same service with the same associated service contract but with different values describing QoS, scheduling and other guarantees, and the price of the service.

When the consumer WFMS reaches a task that it wishes to have enacted on its behalf externally, it notifies its Contract Manager (again through a Workflow Module). The consumer Contract Manager selects a pre-existing Contract Template that describes the service it is looking for in terms of

Figure 3. CrossFlow architecture in contracting phase

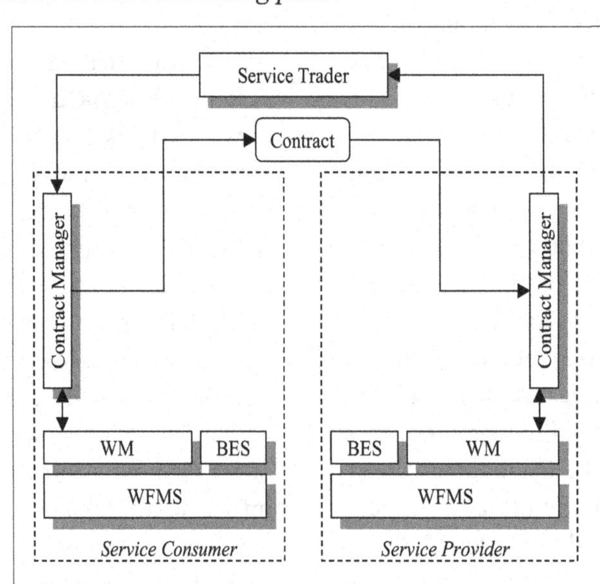

the QoS guarantees, work schedule, monitoring, and control points it wishes to have associated with the provided service. Unlike the provider who specified those parameters as properties, the consumer can place demands in terms of the speed by which it wishes to have the work completed and the maximum price it is willing to pay for it, for example. The consumer must also describe what it offers in terms of its willingness to pay and the means by which it can pay, for example. The consumer's promises and demands are translated into the property and constraint language of the trader. The result is then sent as a search query into the trader serving the market.

The trader compares the promises and demands made by the consumer against the offers previously posted in it by market providers. The matching offers are then sent back to the consumer. The consumer Contract Manager can then compare the offers and select the one that suits its requirements best. By notifying the selected provider, the consumer in effect makes a counter-offer that the provider can accept or reject. The acceptance of the counter-offer signifies an agreement between the two organizations and an electronic contract is established.

Dynamic Infrastructure Generation

Once a contract has been made between service consumer and provider, a dynamic contract and service enactment architecture is set up in a symmetrical way for both partners, as illustrated in Figure 4. For this purpose, the Contract Manager activates the Configuration Manager. The configuration of this enactment infrastructure is based on the contract and requires a number of components:

- **Cooperation support Service** (CSS) modules implement the advanced cooperation support functionalities. Level of Control, Quality of Service, and Flexible Change Control were chosen in the CrossFlow project, but other CSS modules are possible (as we have seen before).
- **Proxy-Gateways** (PG) deal with the crossing of domain boundaries by facilitating the interaction between the organizations' systems, by translating between the internal-external and organizational differences on a syntactical level, and by monitoring and controlling exit-entry to protect the organization's integrity and security.

Figure 4. CrossFlow architecture in configuration phase

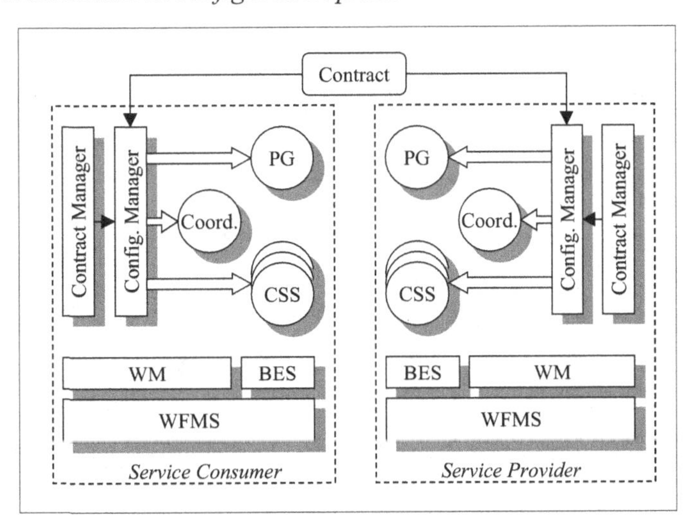

- **Coordinators** (Coord.) are used at each site to connect the various components such as the CSSs, the PG, and the WFMS through the WM.

The functionality of contract and service enactment components is largely dependent on the contents of the contract and the manner in which each organization sees fit to carry out their part of the enactment.

The Internal Enactment Specification (IES) is the organization-specific blueprint that specifies how the contract is to be enacted. It defines which internal resources can be used in which way. For this purpose, the IES describes which components are needed to enact the service and, in addition, it describes the contract implementation policy for each of the deployed CSS components. It also provides the mapping between the workflow process specified in the contract and the workflow process as actually enacted internally by the service provider and similarly the mapping of the data related to the workflow enactment.

Using the contract and the corresponding IES, the Configuration Manager instantiates, and configures a coordinator, a proxy-gateway and a set of CSS components to enact the contract. These components are next linked to each other and to the WM and BES components that provide interfaces to systems at the internal level during contract enactment (shown in Figure 5 and described next).

Contract Enactment

When the set-up described above is ready, the consumer can initiate the actual enactment of the outsourced business process by contacting the provider. The enactment takes place using the dynamically constructed infrastructure as illustrated in Figure 5 (in a simplified way).

Any monitoring information agreed upon in the contract to be provided from the provider to the consumer can either be sent as a notification or requested by the consumer. As a result of the progress update, the consumer may wish to request the provider to modify the enactment of the business process. This may include a change of parameters or a change in the process direction or structure, depending on the contract. Further monitoring information may pass as a result and more changes may be initiated where necessary. Ultimately, an indication of the completion of the process and its results will be passed to the consumer.

Where appropriate, the enactment infrastructure can access the Back End Systems (BES) interface for specific services. These systems

Figure 5. CrossFlow architecture in execution phase

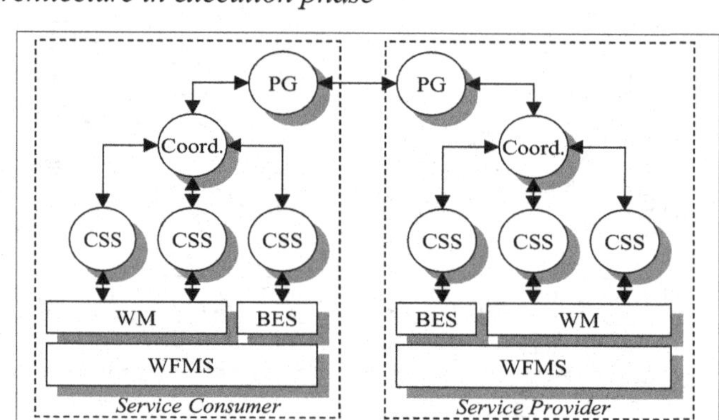

offer CrossFlow services on a permanent basis (not related to the enactment of a single contract) and other more general services.

Dynamic Infrastructure Disposal

When all the administrative processes have been completed and both sides are satisfied with the provision and consumption of the service, the infrastructure created earlier can be dismantled. This means that coordinator, CSS modules, and proxy gateways relating to the service can be deleted.

CrossFlow in Retrospective

The CrossFlow project application scenarios are in the logistics and insurance markets. For the logistics market, a highly dynamic scenario was developed for the distribution of mobile phones to customers, in which a telecom company is the service consumer and logistics providers are service providers. For the insurance market, a scenario was elaborated for damage claim assessment for motor vehicle insurance. Here, the insurance company is the service consumer and assessment expertise firms are the service providers. Both scenarios presented huge steps forward with respect to dynamism in interorganizational business process management at that time. The CrossFlow approach does have two important limitations though.

Firstly, CrossFlow is limited to one-to-one service outsourcing process topologies. Though complex networks can be built by combining multiple service outsourcing scenarios, direct collaboration of more than two partners in one global business process is not possible in the CrossFlow approach. In the next section, we will see how the CrossWork approach lifts this limitation.

Secondly, CrossFlow is based on dedicated technology. Although CrossFlow uses a commercial workflow management system as its basis and a service broker based on CORBA standards, the heart of the system is dedicated technology directly realized in Java. The languages and protocols developed in the CrossFlow project are of a dedicated nature too. An example of a dedicated language is the CrossFlow contract language. Later in this chapter, we will see how the XTC project is positioned in a SOA context from the very start.

CROSSWORK: DYNAMIC PROCESS COMPOSITION

In the previous section, we have seen how CrossFlow supports the bilateral service outsourcing paradigm. Where direct, peer-to-peer interaction between more than two business partners is required, a more general collaboration paradigm is required, however. In the CrossWork project (Grefen et al. 2007), these general interorganizational business process topologies are addressed, which are called *business network processes* (BNPs).

Below, we first discuss business process management in these general, peer-to-peer business topologies. We show how these are centered around the concept of *instant virtual enterprise*, which is a variation of the *dynamic virtual enterprise* concept of the CrossFlow project. After that, we turn to the CrossWork system and its architecture. We end the section again with placing the approach into retrospective.

Business Processes in Instant Virtual Enterprises

Many business domains nowadays rely on tight collaboration between (possibly large numbers of) autonomous business organizations, such that each of these organizations can fulfill a subgoal of an overall business goal. Such a collaboration is commonly called a virtual enterprise (VE). Tight collaboration in a VE implies that the local business processes of the collaborating business organizations need to synchronize at a possibly detailed level. This means that local business processes are actually 'woven' into a global business process (the *business network process*).

Figure 6 shows an example of a VE in a business market consisting of a set of possible business partners (here, seven are shown, but in practice the number is usually much greater). Four business organizations have organized into a VE. Each organization has its local business process, shown inside the ellipses. The local business processes of the partners in the VE are organized into a global VE business process by adding the business process links between the ellipses in such a way that process dependencies are taken into account and overall process quality requirements (such as throughput times) are met.

Operating in frequently changing markets implies that virtual enterprises cannot have a stable character over time: changing market demands require that new business competences are added, existing business competences may become useless, or different selection criteria are used with respect to quality of service parameters. The consequence of this is that VEs must be created in a dynamic way: based on circumstances at a specific point in time, a VE must be set up quickly for a limited amount of operating time. This highly dynamic version of VE is the instant virtual enterprise (IVE). An IVE is mainly determined by the selection of the partners that collaborate in it and by the interorganizational process links that are woven between the partners. The local business processes of the individual partners usually remain stable over time, as they heavily depend on investments made by these partners. Required flexibility in IVE process definition is obtained by the flexible composition of the global process.

IVEs have a dynamic character, i.e., they are created and dismantled in the course of time. The trigger for the creation of an IVE is a new business opportunity in a specific market, observed by an organization operating in that market. The business opportunity is, for example, an order coming in from a party to which the market supplies products. The opportunity is translated into a concrete, high-level business goal first. Then, the IVE goes through four phases:

1. The high-level business goal is decomposed into operational business goals. This decomposition is based on generally accepted knowledge about the domain in

Figure 6. example instant virtual enterprise in market

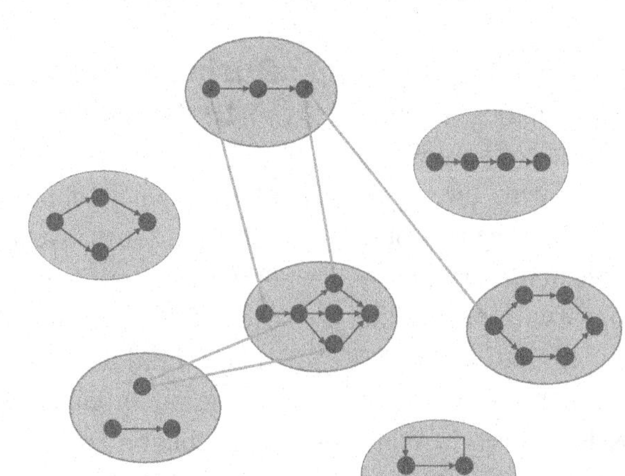

which the market is operating. In an industrial construction market, for example, this knowledge can be contained in an extended bill-of-materials.

2. For each identified operational business goal, a collaboration partner is identified in the market that can fulfill this operational business goal (possibly the organization itself that initiated the IVE creation). The identification is based on the capabilities of potential partners, but also on location and quality of service (QoS) attributes.
3. The external-level projections of the local business processes of the selected partners are retrieved. These projections are abstractions from the actual processes in these organizations, such that sensitive or irrelevant details are hidden (Grefen et al. 2003). The local business processes are next composed into a global business process by weaving interorganizational control flows between them (as illustrated in Figure 6).
4. The composed global business process is mapped onto the distributed infrastructure of the IVE and enacted (executed) there. One of the partners in the IVE will perform the task of the global process coordinator. This may be the initiator of the IVE, depending on available local infrastructure. All partners in the IVE contribute by executing their respective local business processes.

The four phases are the elements in the IVE life cycle (as shown in Figure 7). The life cycle is not strictly linear, however, as problems may be encountered in each phase. For example, it may not be possible to form an acceptable team in the team formation phase on the basis of the specified goal decomposition. Likewise, it may not be possible to construct an acceptable global business process based on the local business processes of selected team members. In these cases, it is necessary to revert to the previous phase in the life cycle and redo the work there. This is illustrated by the dashed backward arrows in Figure 7.

The CrossWork System

The architecture of the CrossWork system is closely related to the IVE lifecycle structure discussed above: each of the four phases of the life cycle is explicitly supported by modules in the architecture. The high-level architecture is shown in Figure 8. In this figure, each of the vertical columns coincides with a phase in the life cycle.

The first three columns together form the front-end of the CrossWork architecture, aimed at support for IVE construction (one could say that this is the IVE build-time environment). Each of the three modules relies on knowledge used for automated reasoning, as depicted by the three knowledge bases coupled to the modules. As complete automation is not feasible for arbitrarily complex situations, each module is linked to a user interface to communicate with business process engineers.

Figure 7. IVE lifecycle phases

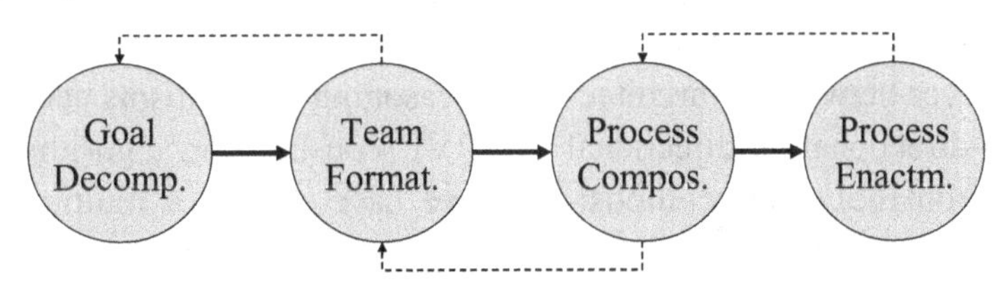

Figure 8. CrossWork architecture

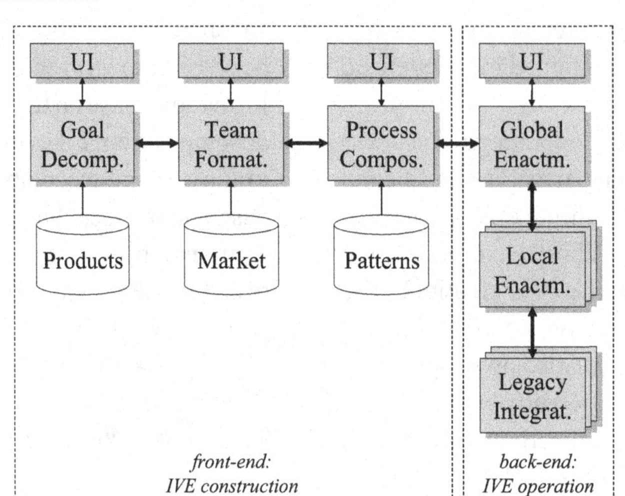

The fourth and right-most column forms the back-end of the CrossWork architecture, aimed at support for IVE operation, i.e., enactment (execution) of global business processes. The back-end is comprised of three main modules. The Global Enactment module is responsible for process management at the IVE level, i.e., for the interorganizational process synchronization. It is equipped with a user interface for global process monitoring. The Local Enactment module is responsible for the enactment of local processes within the boundaries of a single IVE member. This means that there are multiple copies of the Local Enactment module in an IVE (as suggested by the figure). The Local Enactment module drives the user interfaces of the human workers in an IVE member (i.e., is a server to workflow clients). Finally, the Legacy Integration module is aimed at providing interfaces to legacy systems run by individual IVE members. Again this implies that there are multiple copies within an IVE. Typically, one Local Enactment module is linked to one Legacy Integration module.

Note that the interfaces between all architecture components are bi-directional. Bi-directional interfaces in the 'line' from the Goal Decomposition to the Global Enactment modules are chosen to support the life cycle back-tracking as discussed before: if a module cannot fulfill its task, it calls back to the previous module and request a rework. The bi-directional interfaces in the right-most column are needed for synchronization during process enactment.

Obviously, automated support for an IVE must be highly distributed, for the simple reason that the IVE itself consists of possibly many distributed, autonomous parties with local systems that must be integrated into the global process enactment infrastructure. Therefore, the CrossWork system has a distributed nature as well. The bottom-level communication infrastructure layer for the CrossWork system is internet-based. Using internet standards like HTTP as a basic infrastructure allows free choice of higher layers to implement the CrossWork application functionality.

When looking at the application level of CrossWork, we see different requirements for front-end and back-end platforms. On the one hand, the front-end has main requirements in the fields of goal-orientation and support for reasoning mechanisms needed to implement the IVE construction algorithms. For this reason, we have chosen a multi-agent system (MAS) platform as a basis for the front-end application layer, more specifically the JADE platform (Tilab 2008). On the other hand, the back-end has main requirements with respect to portability and interoperability to support IVE process enactment in a distributed, heterogeneous environment as dictated by the existing infrastructure at IVE members. To comply with contemporary system integration practice, we have chosen the back-end application layer to be based on service-oriented computing (SOC), employing technology from the Web service stack.

Global process orchestration is performed by the Global Enactment module (see Figure 8). The basis for this module is a standard BPEL engine – we use Active BPEL (ActiveBPEL 2008) in our prototype system. We use a *paradigm bridge* module to 'decouple' the CrossWork front-end and back-end subsystems. This means that we can use dedicated process manipulation technology in the front-end modules and standard, off-the-shelve process enactment technology in the CrossWork back-end modules.

CrossWork in Retrospective

The CrossWork approach and prototype system have been applied in a test bed scenario in the automotive industry domain (Grefen et al. 2007). The CrossWork technology allows the formation of IVEs in a much shorter time span than the manual approach that is common practice in the domain. The technology also allows the effective handling of more complex business networks and IVEs – by automating domain knowledge, by semi-automatic generation of possible IVE scenarios, and by support for validation of scenarios.

Although CrossWork is aimed at a more general interorganizational business process topology than CrossFlow, it is also more limited in two ways. Firstly, there are no explicit contracts in the approach that underpin the existence of an IVE. Secondly, there is no extensible set of cooperation support service modules – CrossWork focuses on 'core' business process management. It would, however, be possible to infuse these additional CrossFlow ingredients into the CrossWork approach.

Though the CrossWork system uses standard technology (from the MAS and SOC technology domains), the use of standard technology was not the main starting point of CrossWork. We will see in the next section how the XTC project takes a standard technology paradigm (service-oriented architecture) as the basis for interorganizational business process support.

XTC: TRANSACTIONAL PROCESS SERVICE INTEGRATION

In the previous two sections, we have seen two approaches that are firmly rooted in workflow management technology: both CrossFlow and CrossWork rely on underlying workflow management modules to realize their enactment functionality and use other technology classes to cover the entire spectrum of required functionality. The XTC project takes another approach: here the service-oriented paradigm is a starting point taken to address the issue of reliable, interorganizational business process management. Reliability is interpreted in terms of explicit contracting of subprocesses and explicit treatment of transactionality aspects of these subprocesses.

Below, we first discuss the main ingredients of the XTC approach to business process management. Then, we turn to the XTC architecture. As in the previous two sections, we end the section with a retrospective on the approach.

The XTC Approach to Business Process Management

The XTC approach to interorganizational business process management relies on three main choices: the explicit treatment of process reliability, the combination of a service-oriented point of view with a process-oriented point of view, and a modular, service-oriented approach to process composition. We discuss these three main choices below.

Explicit Treatment of Process Reliability

To allow business organization to rely on the automatic management and execution of their business processes, it is necessary that the execution of these processes is performed in a reliable way. To achieve reliability, the support of business-level transaction management functionality is indispensable. Transaction management ensures reliability and robustness in the execution of business processes, both for intraorganizational processes (Grefen et al. 1999) and interorganizational processes (Vonk & Grefen 2003, Grefen & Vonk 2006).

In a service-oriented context, business services are the point of cooperation between organizations. To obtain reliable business services, transactional support for them must be specified in business terminology that is understood by all involved parties. This means that transaction support is specified at the same level (same business terminology) as the service specification itself. Because of explicit business agreements between the involved parties, the transactional agreements should also be included in the electronic contract established between the parties. The agreed transactional semantics is related to a specific service and is therefore specified in the service level agreement (SLA) that is part of the contract and prescribes the quality of service (QoS) of the aspect under consideration (transactional quality of service in this case, denoted by TxQoS).

The TxQoS specified in an SLA concerns high-level business transaction semantics. In XTC, the following transactional properties have been chosen at this level (Wang et al. 2007):

1. **Fluency:** The amount of process interruptions that is allowed;
2. **Interference:** The possibilities to influence the process execution;
3. **Alternation:** The possibilities to use alternative execution paths;
4. **Transparency:** The level of visibility of process status details.

These properties have been abbreviated as the *FIAT* properties. The actual implementation of the transaction support is again an internal matter for an organization. However, a two-way relation exists between the TxQoS offered and the internal underlying systems. First, specification refinement means that the high-level business TxQoS specifications have to be mapped to the low-level technical TxQoS specifications. Second, transaction dependency determines the possible high-level TxQoS, based on the low-level transaction support of the existing systems.

Dual View on Processes and Services

Relating the process view with the service view, it becomes clear that they are 'two sides of the same coin', i.e., they both model the same real world entity but from a different point of view. So, we have a dual view on the concepts that represent the work (processes and services) that is carried out by organizations (Vonk et al. 2007). This dual view is illustrated in Figure 9. Processes specify what has to be done (and in what order), while services are a way to implement (part of) processes. In Figure 9, the thick dashed line illustrates the duality in the model. On the left-hand side is the process view and on the right-hand side the service view. The relation between both is described as follows. Local processes can be implemented as internal or external services, while activities can only be implemented as internal services. Because activities are not visible on the external process level, they are inherently internal (Grefen et al. 2003). In the figure, TxQoS corresponds to the high-level Business TxQoS specifications, while Tx corresponds to both the low-level technical TxQoS specifications and (transactional) systems and applications.

Figure 9. dual view on processes and services

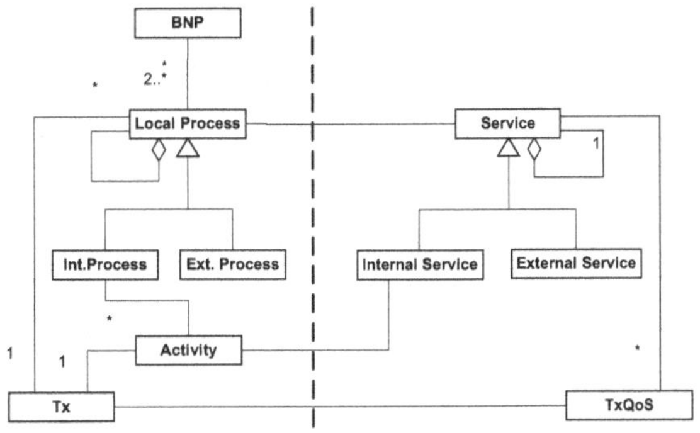

BNP
2..*
Local Process
Service
1
Int.Process
Ext. Process
Internal Service
External Service
Activity
1
1
Tx
TxQoS

Modular, Service-Oriented Business Process Composition

In the XTC approach, processes are composed from subprocesses. Each subprocess is coupled to a service module that describes its transactional behavior. Such a service module is based on an *abstract transactional construct* (ATC) that specifies an abstract transactional behavior based on an abstracted transaction model. In XTC, a library is developed that contains a taxonomy of ATCs. An ATC is parameterized based on the specifics of a subprocess.

Multiple parameterized ATCs are composed into a *composed business transaction* (CBT), which describes the transactional behavior of a composed process – this can be a complex subprocess or a complete process.

The way ATCs can be designed, parameterized and composed into CBTs is governed by the *business transaction framework* (BTF), a conceptual framework that describes the manipulation of ATCs. An ingredient of the BTF that is being developed is a combined algebra and logic called XTraCalm that formally specifies the manipulation of ATCs.

The XTC Architecture

The XTC architecture is based on three phases in the ATC/CBT life cycle (definition, composition an execution) and three levels that distinguish BTF management, ATC/CBT creation, and ATC/CBT management. The XTC architecture can hence be depicted in a 3x3 grid, as shown in Figure 10.

Among all the components, the 'BTF Manager' is the coordinator which coordinates and controls the activities of other modules. It communicates with the underlying systems, like DBMS, WFMS, etc., through the IT infrastructure such as Enterprise Service Bus (ESB). Also it works with other heterogeneous organizations using the open communication standards like SOAP or HTTP. We specify three phases along the BTF life cycle. During the definition phase, the ATC templates are designed based on the classic and widely-adopted transaction models. After the design, one can easily make use of these constructs to build a transaction scheme for a complex process in the composition phase. Also it is flexible to adjust the transaction scheme to accommodate the changes that often take place in a dynamic business context. Instantiated from the transaction scheme composed in the previous phase, concrete business transactions are executed during the execution phase.

Figure 10. XTC architecture

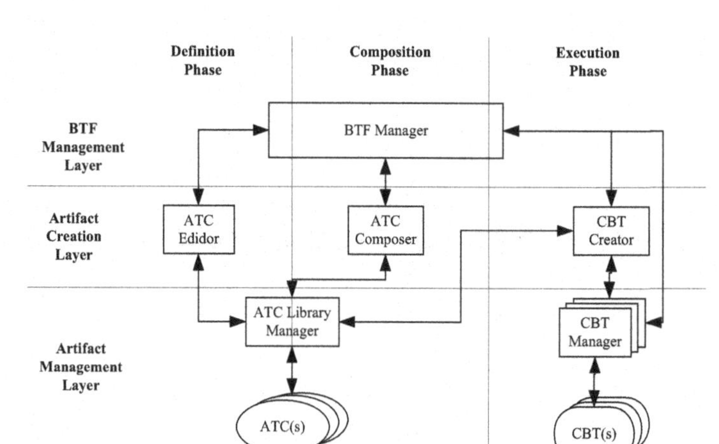

XTC in Retrospective

In the XTC project, healthcare has been chosen as the prototyping application domain. The healthcare domain has very complex processes in which many autonomous parties need to collaborate. Obviously, process reliability is of major importance in this domain. In an elaborate case study, a complex medical process in a hospital is object of analysis (Vonk et al. 2008). Based on required reliability characteristics of this process, explicit contractual and transactional elements are infused into the process.

Like CrossFlow, XTC pays explicit attention to contracting and transactions. Unlike CrossFlow, XTC places both topics in an open context. CrossFlow does consider extensibility through the use of contract clauses and cooperation support modules, but within a dedicated language and technology context.

XTC focuses heavily on the service-oriented integration of business process support with an emphasis on transactional aspects, as well as a conceptual framework around this support (centered on the BTF discussed before). Consequently, less emphasis has been put on details with respect to interfaces towards specific workflow management technology for the enactment of subprocesses encapsulated in ATCs (where CrossFlow and CrossWork did explicitly include this aspect).

CONCLUSION AND OUTLOOK

In this chapter, we have presented the development of interorganizational business process management from the viewpoint of a number of projects. The aim of the chapter is not to be complete, but rather to discuss and relate a number of research efforts from the experience of the author. Consequently, there are many more research projects that could have been placed in this chapter.

The chapter shows a development from static interorganizational business processes (like in the WISE project) via dynamic processes with limited topologies (like in the CrossFlow project) to interorganizational processes with arbitrary topologies (like in the CrossWork and XTC projects).

The chapter also shows a move from dedicated technology (as used for example in WISE and CrossFlow) via a use of standardized technology (like MAS and SOC technology in CrossWork) to the use of standardized technology as a starting point (SOC technology in XTC). Clearly, the use of standardized technology allows the reuse of platforms and enhances interoperability potential.

On the other hand, the use of standards is also dictated to deal with the complexity of advanced interorganizational business process management: not all can be designed from scratch.

As discussed before, CrossWork is more general than CrossFlow in the process topology dimension and the explicit treatment of domain knowledge, but also misses some important CrossFlow ingredients like explicit contracts and a set of extensible support modules. XTC does rely on a well-accepted notion of service-oriented architecture and does place process reliability very central on the basis of explicit contracts, but is less strongly rooted in 'traditional' workflow management technology than CrossFlow and CrossWork. Obviously, an 'ideal' solution to interorganizational business process management requires a 'blend' of ingredients from several approaches. The inherent complexity of this 'blend' is the reason for the fact that an 'ideal' solution has not yet been realized.

ACKNOWLEDGMENT

All colleague researchers of the CrossFlow, CrossWork and XTC projects are thanked for their work, which has provided input for this chapter. Jochem Vonk is thanked especially for his help in preparing this chapter.

EXERCISES

1. Explain the main differences in characteristics between intraorganizational and interorganizational business processes.
2. Given the projects described in this chapter, summarize the main trends that have taken place in the development of interorganizational business process management systems, both from a business and from a technology perspective.
3. Take a business process example that could be integrated into an interorganizational business process from one of the other chapters of this book. Consider this process as being at the conceptual level according to the three-level framework. Determine an appropriate external level specification for this process by aggregating and omitting activities.

REFERENCES (SUGGESTED FURTHER READING)

ActiveBPEL (2008). Active BPEL Web Site. www.activebpel.org.

Alonso, G., Hagen, C., Schek, H. J., & Tresch, M. (1997). Distributed processing over stand-alone systems and applications. In *Proceedings of the 23rd International Conference on Very Large Databases* (pp. 575-579).

Alonso, G., Fiedler, U., Hagen, C., Lazcano, A., Schuldt, H., & Weiler, N. (1999). WISE: Business to business e-commerce. In *Proceedings of the 9th International Workshop on Research Issues on Data Engineering* (pp. 132-139).

Cingil, I., Dogac, A., Tatbul, N., & Arpinar, S. (1999). An adaptable workflow system architecture on the Internet for electronic commerce applications. In *Proceedings of the International Symposium on Distributed Object Applications.*

Grefen, P., Pernici, B., & Sánchez, G. (1999). *Database support for workflow management: The WIDE Project.* Kluwer Academic Publishers.

Grefen, P., Aberer, K., Hoffner, Y., Ludwig, H. (2000). CrossFlow: Cross-organizational workflow management in dynamic virtual enterprises. *Computer Systems Science & Engineering, 15*(5), 277-290. CRL Publishing.

Grefen, P., Ludwig, H., & Angelov, S. (2003). A Three-level framework for process and data management of complex e-services. *International Journal of Cooperative Information Systems, 12*(4), 487-531. World Scientific.

Grefen, P., & Vonk, J. (2006). A taxonomy of transactional workflow support. *International Journal of Cooperative Information Systems, 15*(1), 87–118.

Grefen, P., Mehandjiev, N., Kouvas, G., Weichhart, G., & Eshuis, R. (2007). Dynamic business network process management in instant virtual enterprises. *Beta Technical Report WP198*. Eindhoven University of Technology.

Griffel, F. et al. (1998). Electronic contracting with COSMOS - How to establish, negotiate and execute electronic contracts on the Internet. In *Proceedings of the 2nd International Enterprise Distr. Object Comp. Workshop* La Jolla.

Hagen, C. (1999). *A Generic kernel for reliable process support.* (Doctoral dissertation, Swiss Federal Institute of Technology Zürich). ETH Nr. 13114 .

Hoffner, Y., Ludwig, H., Gülcü, C., & Grefen, P. (2000). Architecture for cross-organisational business processes. In *Proceedings of the 2nd International Workshop Adv. Issues of E-Commerce and Web-Based Information Systems.*

Koetsier, M., Grefen, P., & Vonk, J. (2000). Contracts for cross-organizational workflow management. In *Proceedings 1st International Conference on Electronic Commerce and Web Technologies.* (pp. 110-121). London.

Lazcano, A., Schuldt, H., Alonso, G., & Schek, H. (2001). WISE: Process based e-commerce. *IEEE Data Engineering Bulletin, 24*(1), 46-51.

Lienhard, H. (1998). IvyBeans - Bridge to VSH and the project WISE. In *Proceedings of the Conference of the Swiss Priority Programme Information and Communication Structures,* Zürich, Switzerland.

Schonenberg, H., Mans, R., Russell, N., Mulyar, N., & van der Aalst, W. (2008). Process flexibility: A survey of contemporary approaches. In *Proceedings CIAO!/EOMAS Workshop.* (pp. 16-30).

Shan, M-C., Davis, J., Du, W., & Huang, Y. (1997). *HP Workflow research: Past, present, and future.* (Technical Report HPL-97-105). HP Labs.

Shan, M. (1999). FlowJet: Internet-based e-Service Process Management. In *Proceedings of the Int. Process Techn. Workshop*, Villard de Lans, France.

Tilab (2008). *Java agent development framework.* http://jade.tilab.com/

Vonk, J., & Grefen, P. (2003). Cross-organizational transaction support for e-services in virtual enterprises. *Distributed and Parallel Databases, 14*(2), 137-172.

Vonk, J., Wang, T., & Grefen, P. (2007). A dual view to facilitate transactional QoS. In *Proceedings of the 16th IEEE International Workshops on Enabling Technologies: Infrastructure for Collaborative Enterprises* (pp. 381-382). Paris, France.

Vonk, J., Wang, T., van Aarle, J., Brugmans, S., & Grefen, P. (2008). *An analysis of contractual and transactual aspects of a cardiothoracic surgery process.* Beta Technical Report, Eindhoven University of Technology.

Wang, T., Vonk, J., & Grefen, P. (2006). *Building a business transaction framework based on abstract transaction constructs.* Beta Technical Report WP187, Eindhoven University of Technology.

Wang, T., Vonk, J., & Grefen, P. (2007). TxQoS: A contractual approach for transaction management. In *Proceedings of the 11th IEEE International EDOC Enterprise Computing Conference* (pp. 327-338). Annapolis, MD.

Weber, B., Reichert, M., & Rinderle-Ma, S. (2008). Change patterns and change support features - Enhancing flexibility in process-aware information systems. *Data and Knowledge Engineering, 66*(3), 438-466.

KEY TERMS

Business Network Process: Interorganizational business process established to specify and enact the collaboration of a number of autonomous parties in a peer-to-peer fashion.

Dynamic Business Network Process: Dynamic interorganizational business process established to specify and enact the collaboration of a number of autonomous parties in a peer-to-peer fashion.

Dynamic Interorganizational Business Process: Interorganizational business process that is formed dynamically by (automatically) integrating two or more external processes provided by the involved organizations, where dynamically means that collaborator organizations are found at or just before process run-time by searching business process market places based on the characteristics of (a set of) business process cases and market conditions.

Dynamic Service Outsourcing: The replacement of a part of an internal business process by a business process that is enacted by an external service provider, where the external service provider is selected dynamically, i.e., in a just-in-time fashion.

Dynamic Virtual Enterprise: Formalized collaboration between two or more autonomous organizations with a well-defined temporary character for the achievement of a specific business goal.

Instant Virtual Enterprise: Dynamic virtual enterprise.

Interorganizational Business Process: Business process the process logic of which is enacted by two or more autonomous organizations, of which at least one organization exposes a non-black box projection of the explicit control flow structure of a process to the other organization(s).

Intraorganizational Business Process: Business process the process logic of which is enacted by one single organization, but which may call black-box business services of other autonomous organizations.

Virtual Enterprise: Formalized collaboration between two or more autonomous organizations for the achievement of a specific business goal.

Chapter XX
The Journey to Business Process Compliance

Guido Governatori
NICTA, Queensland Research Laboratory, Australia

Shazia Sadiq
The University of Queensland, Australia

ABSTRACT

It is a typical scenario that many organisations have their business processes specified independently of their business obligations (which includes contractual obligations to business partners, as well as obligations a business has to fulfil against regulations and industry standards). This is because of the lack of guidelines and tools that facilitate derivation of processes from contracts but also because of the traditional mindset of treating contracts separately from business processes. This chapter will provide a solution to one specific problem that arises from this situation, namely the lack of mechanisms to check whether business processes are compliant with business contracts. The chapter begins by defining the space for business process compliance and the eco-system for ensuring that process are compliant. The key point is that compliance is a relationship between two sets of specifications: the specifications for executing a business process and the specifications regulating a business. The central part of the chapter focuses on a logic based formalism for describing both the semantics of normative specifications and the semantics of compliance checking procedures.

1. INTRODUCTION

The term compliance is applied in many disciplines such as management, standards development, regulations, medical practice and so on. It is often used to denote and demonstrate adherence of one set of rules (we refer to them as 'source rules' hereafter) against other set of rules (we refer to them as 'target rules' hereafter). Typically, target rules represent an established or agreed set of guidelines, norms, laws, regulations, recommendations or qualities which, if obeyed, will deliver certain effect or value to those to whom they can apply, or to those with whom they interact. In some way, the target rules are intended for a global or broad community of participants in a specific universe of discourse. On the other hand, source rules are developed to apply to participants and their behaviours in certain local contexts, and adherence of source rules to the target rules then ensures that both local and global expectations or requirements can be met.

In management for example, target rules represent policies that need to be obeyed by companies, their staff or executives, while undertaking their normal course of actions to meet their goals. Examples of such rules are the US regulations such as Sarbanes-Oxley Act[1] or Health Insurance Privacy Act (HIPPA)[2]. In standards development, compliance requirements are stated to ensure necessary consistency of one set of requirements with some broader set of requirements, e.g., a compliance of the ODP Enterprise Language with ODP-RM[3]. Note that in standards communities, the term conformance has a different meaning: it is used to relate an implementation to a standard specification. Finally, in health sector, compliance is referred to a patient's (or doctor's) adherence to a recommended course of treatment.

Similarly, we apply this interpretation of compliance as a metaphor to discuss adherence or consistence of a set of rules in business processes against a set of rules regulating a particular business. This set of rules can stem from different sources, legislation, standards, best practices, internal guidelines and policies, contracts between the parties involved in the process and so on. We will refer to the source of these as normative documents, and to the rules themselves as norms or normative specifications. So, ensuring compliance of business processes with a normative document means ensuring consistency of norms stated in normative documents and rules covering the execution of business processes. In other words, to check that the specification of a business process complies with a normative document regulating the domain of the process, one has to verify that all execution paths of the process, possible according to the specification of the business process, comply with the normative specification. This means that no execution path is in breach of the regulation. This consistency, for example, is necessary to satisfy commitments that parties typically state in their agreements or business contracts while carrying out their mutually related internal business activities. Such compliance also leads to benefits to both parties, e.g., minimisation of costs or damages to either party whether these are associated with potentially inadvertent behaviour or deliberate violations while seeking more opportunistic engagements.

1.1 Compliance Space

Compliance of business processes with normative documents is thus important to ensure establishing better links between these two traditionally separate universes of discourse, i.e., legal and business process spaces (see Figure 1).

Firstly, the source of the normative specifications and the business specifications (i.e., the design of the process to meet the objectives of a business) will be distinct both from an ownership and governance perspective, as well as from a timeline perspective. Where as businesses can be expected to have some form of business objectives, normative specifications will be dictated by mostly external sources and often the various

Figure 1. Compliance space

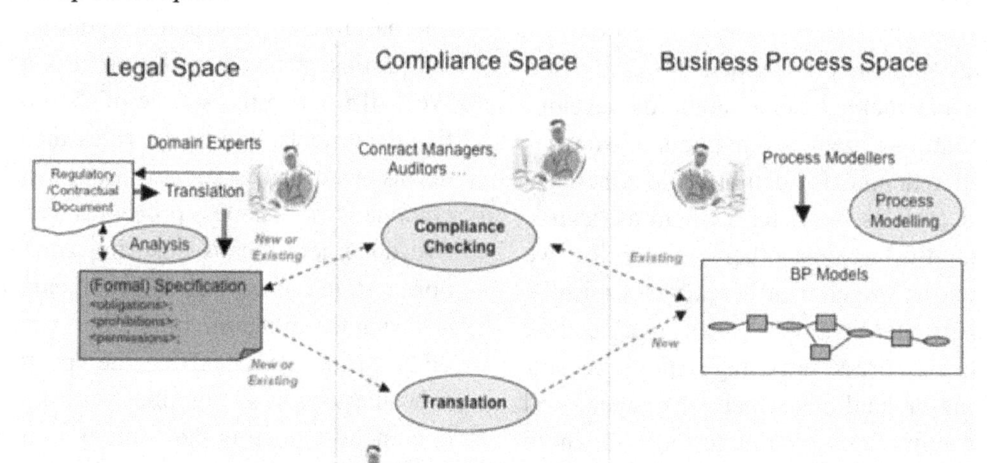

norms regulating a business are created at different times and are subject to evolution over time to accommodate changes in the business and in the society.

Secondly, the two have differing concerns, namely business objectives and normative objectives. Thus the use of business process languages to model normative specifications may not provide a conceptually faithful representation. The focus in the legal space is to describe what processes have to do, what should be avoided in the execution of a process. Thus the major concern in the legal space is on *what* a business has to do. Accordingly, in this space we have a declarative perspective of the objectives of processes, indicating what needs to be done (in order to comply). The business process space, on the other hand, has been the focus of management science, such as various business process re-engineering approaches. This is a domain of business process modellers and business architects involved in enterprise architecture developments. These professionals have typically been involved in identifying business requirements and then designing business processes to satisfy these requirements. Accordingly, business process specifications are fundamentally prescriptive in nature, i.e., detailing how business activities should take place. There is evidence of some developments towards descriptive approaches for BPM, but these works were predominantly focused on achieving flexibility in business process execution, see e.g. (Pesic and van der Aalst, 2006; Sadiq et al., 2005).

Thirdly, there is likelihood of conflicts, inconsistencies and redundancies within the two specifications. Thus the intersection of the two needs to be carefully studied. This is where the compliance space plays its role. The compliance space however, is a new area of interest and endeavour, in particular driven by recent regulative and legislative acts, which require the establishment of stronger and more enforceable compliance requirements against the target set of rules. Some of the largest scandals in corporate history, such as Enron, have led to an increased importance of compliance and related initiatives within organisations. Therefore this new space has led to the development of new roles such as compliance auditors, or requirements for new skills to be developed by existing roles, such as contract managers, business analysts or business architects, for the contract/compliance management domain.

1.2 Managing Compliance

Ensuring compliance of business processes with normative documents is a complex problem involving a number of alternatives. Currently there are two main approaches towards achieving compliance. The first one is *retrospective reporting*, wherein traditional audits are conducted for "after-the-fact" detection, often through manual checks by expensive consultants. With increasing pressures and penalties for non-compliance, this approach is rather limited.

A second and more recent approach is to provide some level of automation through *automated detection*. The bulk of existing software solutions for compliance follow this approach. The proposed solutions hook into variety of enterprise system components (e.g. SAP HR, LDAP Directory, Groupware etc.) and generate audit reports against hard-coded checks performed on the system. These solutions often specialise in certain class of checks, for example the widely supported checks that relate to Segregation of Duty violations in role management and user provisioning systems. Such monitoring capability assists in checking for compliance against the hard-coded checks and consequently in the remediation and/or mitigation of control deficiencies. However, this approach still resides in the space of "after-the-fact" detection.

We believe that a sustainable approach for achieving compliance should fundamentally have a *preventative* focus. As such, we describe an approach that provides the capability to capture compliance requirements through a generic requirements modelling framework, and subsequently facilitate the propagation of these requirements into business process models and enterprise applications, thus achieving *compliance by design*.

The approach we describe in this chapter can be applied to problems common to many enterprises, i.e., there are many existing processes that were designed in the absence of any knowledge of specific regulations, opening possibilities for violations. This requires checking compliance of processes against norms. This can be either against the existing norms, to fix possible inconsistencies that have not been detected yet, or against new regulations to detect whether existing business processes can lead to conflicts with new norms, either in terms of incompatible rules or in terms of unrealistic resource expectations that new legislation may require (see Figure 1).

1.3 Organisation of the Chapter

In this chapter we describe an approach to business process compliance based on (semantic) annotations, where the annotations are written in the formal language chosen to represent the normative specifications. The idea is that business processes are annotated and the annotations provide the conditions a process has to comply with. Annotations can be defined at different levels. For example, we can annotate a full process or a single task in a process. In addition, we can have different types of annotations. Annotations can range from the full set of rules (norms) specific to a process or a single task to simple semantic annotation corresponding to one effect of a particular task, e.g., after the successful execution of task A in a process B the value of the environment variable C is D.

In order to support the above technique based on annotations we first need a formal representation of normative specifications. We will address this issue in the next section where we describe a formalism able to capture the notions need for the representation of normative specifications.

2. NORMATIVE SPECIFICATIONS

Compliance is a relationship between two sets of specifications: the normative specifications that prescribe what a business has to do, and the process modelling specification describing how a business performs its activities. Accordingly to properly verify that a process/procedure complies with the norms regulating the particular business one has to provide conceptually sound representations of the process on one side and the norms on the other, and then check the alignment of the formal specifications of the process and the formal specifications for the norms. This means that the normative specifications tell us what obligations, permissions, prohibitions a process is subject to. A normative document often contains many norms regulating a business. Thus a normative document can be seen as a normative system. Normative systems can be modelled with the help of Deontic Logic. Deontic Logic is the branch of logic that studies the formal properties of normative notions (also called normative positions) such as obligations, permissions, prohibitions. In particular, Deontic Logic can be used to investigate the mutual relationships among the various normative positions, how complex normative positions (e.g., delegation, empowerment, rights and so) can be expressed using simpler one, and the relationships between the norms in a normative system.

Standard Deontic Logic (SDL) is a starting point for logical investigation of the basic normative notions and it offers a very idealised and abstract conceptual representation of these notions but at the same time it suffers from several drawbacks given its high level of abstraction (Sartor, 2005). Over the years many different deontic logics have been proposed to capture the different intuitions behind these normative notions and to overcome drawbacks and limitations of SDL. One of the main limitations in this context is its inability to reason with violations, and the obligations arising in response to violations (Carmo and Jones, 2002). Very often normative statements pertinent to business processes, and in particular contracts, specify conditions about when other conditions in the document have nor been fulfilled, that is when some (contractual) clauses have been violated. Hence, any formal representation, to be conceptually faithful, has to been able to deal with this kind of situations.

In the rest of the section we introduce the basic notions of Deontic Logic and then we present a particular deontic logic that addresses the issue discussed above and that is suitable for checking compliance of business processes.

2.1 Formalising Deontic Constraints

Deontic logic extends first order logic with the deontic operators O, P and F denoting obligations, permissions and prohibitions. The deontic operators satisfy the following equivalence relations:

$$OA \equiv \neg P \neg A \qquad \neg O \neg A \equiv PA \qquad O \neg A \equiv FA \qquad \neg PA \equiv FA.$$

The operators also satisfy the following relationship $OA \rightarrow PA$, meaning that if A is obligatory, then A is permitted. This relationship can be used to ensure checking of the internal consistency of the obligations in a set of norms it is possible to execute obligations without doing something that is forbidden. We extend the notation to cover the subject to whom a normative position applies to. In case of obligation, this can be denoted using the expression $O_s A$ to be read as 's has the obligation to do A', or 'A is obligatory for s'. Where A represents a factual statement. Thus, for example, where A is the proposition 'payTaxes', $O_s A$ means that "s has the obligation to pay the taxes" or that 'paying the taxes is obligatory for s'. Similarly for the other operators.

In case of certain breaches of norms, special norms/policies may be included to express the respective obligations for the actors involved in a process. These policies can vary from pecuniary penalties to the termination of a contract and so on. In deontic logic, this type of expression, namely the activation of certain obligations in case of other obligations being violated, is referred to as contrary-to-duty obligations (CTD) or reparation obligations (because they are intended to 'repair' or 'compensate' violations of primary obligations).

The reparation obligations are in force only when normative violations occur and are meant to 'repair' violations of primary obligations. Thus a reparation policy is a conditional obligation arising in response to a violation, where a violation is signalled by an unfulfilled obligation. The expression of violation conditions and the reparation obligations is an important requirement for formalising norms, design subsequent business processes to minimise or deal with such violations and also to determine the compliance of a process with the relevant norms.

There are a number of different approaches in deontic logic to formalise CTD obligations, but in this paper we use a simple logic of violation, to avoid danger of logical paradoxes that some other approaches may involve (Carmo and Jones, 2002). This logic is also suitable to model chains of violations as described next.

2.2 Formalising Violations of Deontic Constraints

In addition to using the logic based approach to specifying core deontic constraints, we thus provide a simple logic of violation.

The violation expression consists of the primary obligation, its violation conditions, an obligation generated upon the violation condition occurs, and this can recursively be iterated, until the final condition is reached. We introduce the non-boolean connective $\otimes$ whose interpretation is such that $OA \otimes OB$ is read as "OB is the reparation of the violation of OA". In other words the interpretation of $OA \otimes OB$, is that A is obligatory, but if the obligation OA is not fulfilled (i.e., the obligation expressed by OA is violated, i.e., we have $\neg A$), then the obligation OB is activated and becomes in force until it is satisfied or violated. If $OA \otimes OB$ appears in a longer chain of obligations/reparations, e.g., $OA \otimes OB \otimes OC$, then the violation of the OB activate a new obligation, i.e., OC. Similarly for longer chains.

2.3 Formal Contract Logic (FCL)

We now provide a formal account of the idea presented in Section 2.2 which we will refer to as Formal Contract Logic (FCL). FCL was introduced in (Governatori, 2005) for the formal analysis of business contracts. FCL is a combination of an efficient non-monotonic formalism (defeasible logic (Antoniou et al., 2001; Antoniou et al., 2006)) and a deontic logic of violations (Governatori and Rotolo, 2006). This particular combination allows us to represent exceptions as well as the ability to capture violations, the obligations resulting from the violations, and the reparations. In addition FCL has good computational properties: the extension of a theory (i.e., the set of conclusions/normative positions following from a set of facts can be computed in time linear to the size of the theory).

The ability to handle violation is very important for compliance of business processes. Often business processes are deployed in dynamic and somehow unpredictable environments. As a consequence, in some cases, maybe due to external circumstances, it is not possible to operate in the way specified by the norms, but the norms prescribe how to recover from the resulting violations. In other cases, the prescribed behaviour is subject to exceptions. Finally, in other cases, one might not have a complete description of the environment. Accordingly the process has to operate based on the available input, but if more information was available, then the task to be performed could be a different one (this is typically the case of the *due diligence* conditions, where one has to act in a 'reasonable' way based on the available information, but if a more complete description the behaviour might be different). A conceptually sound formalisation of norms (for assessing the compliance of a process) should take into account all the aspects mentioned above. FCL is sound in this respect given the combinations of the deontic component (able to represent the fundamental normative positions and chains of violations/

reparations) and the defeasible component that takes care of the issue about partial information and possibly conflicting provisions.

The language of FCL consists of the following set of atomic symbols: a numerable set of propositional letters $p, q, r, \ldots$, intended to represent the state variables and the tasks of a process. Formulas of the logic are constructed using the deontic operators O (for obligation), P (for permission), negation $\neg$ and the non-boolean connective $\otimes$ (for the contrary-to-duty operator). The formulas of FCL will be constructed in two steps according to the following formation rules:

- Every propositional letter is a literal;
- The negation of a literal is a literal;
- If X is a deontic operator and l is a literal then Xl and $\neg Xl$ are deontic literals.

After we have defined the notions of literal and deontic literal we can use the following set of formation rules to introduce $\otimes$-expressions, i.e., the formulas used to encode chains of obligations and violations.

- Every deontic literal is an $\otimes$-expression;
- If $Ol_1,..., Ol_n$ are deontic literals and l_{n+1} is a literal, then
  - $Ol_1 \otimes \cdots \otimes Ol_n$ and
  - $Ol_1 \otimes \cdots \otimes Ol_n \otimes Pl_{n+1}$

  are $\otimes$-expressions (we also refer to $\otimes$-expressions as obligation chains or simply chains).

The connective $\otimes$ permits combining primary and contrary-to-duty obligations into unique regulations. The meaning of an expression like $O_sA \otimes O_sB \otimes O_sC$ is that the primary obligation for s is A, but if A is not done, then s has the obligation to do B. But if event B fails to be realised, then s has the obligation to do C. Thus B is the reparation of the violation of the obligation O_sA (to have violation of an obligation such as O_sA we must have that A does not hold; this mean that the negation of A, i.e., $\neg A$, holds). Similarly C is the reparation of the obligation O_sB, which is force when the violation of A occurs.

The formation rules for $\otimes$-expressions allow a permission to occur only at the end of such expressions. This is due to the fact that a permission can be used as a reparation of a violation, but it is not possible to violate a permission, thus it makes no sense to have reparations to permissions.

Each condition or norm of a normative document is represented by a rule in FCL, where a rule is an expression

$$r: A_1,..., A_n \Rightarrow C$$

where r is the name/id of the norm, $A_1,..., A_n$ –the *antecedent* of the rule– is the set of the premises of the rule (alternatively it can be understood as the conjunction of all the literals in it) and C is the conclusion of the rule. Each A_i is either a literal or a deontic literal and C is an $\otimes$-expression.

The meaning of a rule is that the normative position (obligation, permission, prohibition) represented by the conclusion of the rule is in force when all the premises of the rule hold. Thus, for example, suppose we have a contract for the provision for a service where we have the following clause:

5.1 *the supplier (S) shall refund the purchaser (P) and pay a penalty of $1000 in case she does not replace within 3 days a service that does not conform with the published standards*

This clause can be represented as:[4]

$$r: \neg a, \neg b \Rightarrow O_sC$$

where the propositional letter a means "a service has been provided according to the published standards", b stands for the event "replacement occurred within 3 days", and c represents the event "refund the customer and pay her the penalty". The norm is activated, i.e., the supplier is obliged to refund the customer and pay a penalty of $1000, when the condition $\neg a$ is true (i.e., we have a faulty service), and the event "replacement occurred within 3 days" lapsed, i.e., its negation ($\neg b$) occurred.

FCL is equipped with rule set. The superiority relation ($\prec$) determines the relative strength of two rules, and it is used when rules have potentially conflicting conclusions. For example given the rules r_1: $A \Rightarrow B \otimes C$ and r_2: $D \Rightarrow \neg C$. $r_1 \prec r_2$ means that rule r_1 prevails over rule r_2 in situation where both fire and they are in conflict (i.e., rule r_2 fires for the secondary obligation C).

2.4 Normal Forms

We introduce transformations of an FCL representation of a normative document to produce a normal form of the same (NFCL). A normal form is a representation of a normative document based on an FCL specification containing all conditions that can generated/derived from the given FCL specification. The purpose of a normal form is to "clean up" the FCL representation of a normative document, that is to identify formal loopholes, deadlocks and inconsistencies in it, and to make hidden conditions explicit.

In the rest of this section we introduce the procedures to generate normal forms. First (Section 2.4.1) we describe a mechanism to derive new contract conditions by merging together existing normative clauses. In particular we link an obligation and the obligations triggered in response to violations of the obligation. Then, in Section 2.4.2, we examine the problem of redundancies, and we give a condition to identify and remove redundancies from the formal normative specification.

2.4.1 Merging Norms

One of the features of the logic of violations is to take two rules, or norms, and merge them into a new clause. In what follows we will first examine some common patterns of this kind of construction and then we will show how to generalise them.

Let us consider a norm like (in what follows Γ and Δ are sets of premises)

$$\Gamma \Rightarrow O_s A$$

Given an obligation like this, if we have that the violation of $O_s A$ is part of the premises of another norm, for example,

$$\Delta, \neg A \Rightarrow O_{s'} C$$

then the latter must be a good candidate as reparational obligation of the former. This idea is formalised is as follows:

$$\frac{\Gamma \Rightarrow O_s A \qquad \Delta, \neg A \Rightarrow O_{s'} C}{\Gamma, \Delta \Rightarrow O_s A \otimes O_{s'} C}$$

This reads as follows: given two policies such that one is a conditional obligation ($\Gamma \Rightarrow O_s A$) and the antecedent of second contains the negation of the propositional content of the consequent of the first ($\Delta, \neg A \Rightarrow O_{s'} C$), then the latter is a reparational obligation of the former. Their reciprocal interplay makes them two related norms so that they cannot be viewed anymore as independent obligations. Therefore we can combine them to obtain an expression (i.e.,$\Gamma, \Delta \Rightarrow O_s A \otimes O_{s'} C$) that exhibits the *explicit reparational obligation* of the second norm with respect to the first. Notice that the subject of the primary obligation and the subject of its reparation can be different, even if very often they are the same.

Suppose that a contract includes the rules

r: $Invoice \Rightarrow O_p PayWithin7Days$
r': $\neg PayWithin7Days \Rightarrow O_p PayWithInterest$

From these we obtain

r'': $Invoice \Rightarrow O_p PayWithin7Days \otimes O_p PayWithInterest$

We can also generate chains of CTDs in order to deal iteratively with violations of reparational obligations. The following case is just an example of this process.

$$\frac{\Gamma \Rightarrow O_s A \otimes O_s B \quad \neg A, \neg B \Rightarrow O_s C}{\Gamma \Rightarrow O_s A \otimes O_s B \otimes O_s C}$$

For example we can consider the situation described by the hypothetical clause 5.1 discussed in the previous pages, whose formal representation is given by the rules

r: $Invoice \Rightarrow O_S QualityOfService \otimes O_S Replace3days$
r': $\neg QualityOfService, \neg Replace3days \Rightarrow O_S Refund\&Penalty$

from which we derive the new rule

r'': $Invoice \Rightarrow O_S QualityOfService \otimes O_S Replace3days \otimes O_S Refund\&Penalty$

The above patterns are just special instances of the general mechanism described in details in (Governatori and Rotolo, 2006; Governatori, 2005).

2.4.2 Removing Redundancies

Given the structure of the inference mechanism it is possible to combine rules in slightly different ways, and in some cases the meaning of the rules resulting from such operations is already covered by other rules in the contract. In other cases, the rules resulting from the merging operation are generalisations of the rules used to produce them, consequently, the original rules are no longer needed in the specifications. To deal with this issue we introduce the notion of subsumption between rules. A rule subsumes a second rule when the behaviour of the second rule is implied by the first rule.

We first introduce the idea with the help of some examples and then we show how to give a formal definition of the notion of subsumption appropriate for FCL.

Let us consider the rules:

r: $Service \Rightarrow O_S QualityOfService \otimes O_S Replace3days \otimes O_S Refund\&Penalty$
r': $Service \Rightarrow O_S QualityOfService \otimes O_S Replace3days$.

The first rule, r, subsumes the second r'. Both rules state that after the supplier has provided the service she has the obligation to provide the service according to the published standards, if she violates such an obligation, then the violation of *QualityOfService* can be repaired by replacing the faulty service within three working days ($O_S Replace3days$). In other words, $O_S Replace3days$ is a secondary obligation arising from the violation of the primary obligation $O_S QualityOfService$. In addition r prescribes that the violation of the secondary obligation $O_S Replace3days$ can be repaired by $O_S Refund\&Penalty$, i.e., the seller has to refund the buyer and in addition she has to pay a penalty.

As we discussed in the previous paragraphs, the conditions of a normative document cannot be taken in isolation in so far as they exist in the document. Consequently, the whole normative document determines the meaning of each single clause (norm) in it. In agreement with this holistic view of norms we have that the normative content of r' is included in that of r. Accordingly, r' does not add any new piece of information to the contract, it is redundant and can be dispensed from the explicit formulation of the norms.

Another common case is exemplified by the rules:

r: $Invoice \Rightarrow O_P PayWithin7Days \otimes O_P PayWithInterest$

r': *Invoice*, $\neg$*PayWithin7Days* $\Rightarrow$ O_P*PayWithInterest*.

The first rule says that after the seller sends the invoice the buyer has one week to pay, otherwise the buyer has to pay the principal plus the interest. Thus, we have the primary obligation O_P*PayWithin7Days*, whose violation is repaired by the secondary obligation O_P*PayWithInterest*, while, according to the second rule, given the same set of circumstances *Invoice* and $\neg$*PayWithin7Days* we have that the primary obligation is O_P*PayWithInterest*. However, the primary obligation of r' obtains when we have a violation of the primary obligation of r. Thus, the condition of applicability of the second rule includes that of the first rule, which then is more general than the second and we can discard r' from the formal representation of the specifications.

The intuitions we have just exemplified is captured by the following definition.

Definition 1. *Let* r_1: $\Gamma \Rightarrow A \otimes B \otimes C$ *and* r_2: $\Delta \Rightarrow D$ *be two rules, where* $A = A_1 \otimes \cdots \otimes A_m$, $B = B_1 \otimes \cdots \otimes B_n$ *and* $C = C_1 \otimes \cdots \otimes C_p$.

Then r_1 *subsumes* r_2 *iff*

1. $\Gamma = \Delta$ *and* $D = A$; *or*
2. $\Gamma \cup \{\neg A_1,\ldots, \neg A_m\} = \Delta$ *and* $D = B$; *or*
3. $\Gamma \cup \{\neg B_1,\ldots, \neg B_n\} = \Delta$ *and* *either* $D = A$ or $D = A \otimes C_1 \otimes \cdots \otimes C_k$, for $k \leq p$.

The intuition is that the normative content of r_2 is fully included in r_1. Thus, r_2 does not add anything new to the system and it can be safely discarded.

Conflicts often arise in normative systems. What we have to determine is whether we have genuine conflicts, i.e., the norms are in some way flawed or whether we have *prima-facie* conflicts. A prima-facie conflict is an apparent conflict that can be resolved when we consider it in the context where it occurs and if we add more information the conflict disappears. For example let us consider the following two rules:

r: *PremiumCustomer* $\Rightarrow$ O_S*Discount*
r': *SpecialOrder* $\Rightarrow$ $O_S\neg$*Discount*

saying that premium customers are entitled to a discount (r), but there is no discount for goods bought with a special order (r'). Is a premium customer entitled to a discount when she places a special order? If we only have the two rules above there is no way to solve the conflict just using the contract and there is the need of a domain expert to advise the knowledge engineer about what to do in such case.[5] The logic can only point out that there is a conflict in the contract. On the other hand, if we have an additional provision

r'' : *PremiumCustomer*, $\neg$*Discount* $\Rightarrow$ O_S*Rebate*

Specifying that if for some reasons a premium customer did not received a discount then the customer is entitled to a rebate on the next order, then it is possible to solve the conflict, because the contract allows a violation of rule r to be amended by r''.

We can now introduce the mechanism for making explicit conflicting norms (contradictory norms) within the system:

$$\frac{\Gamma \Rightarrow A \quad \Delta \Rightarrow \neg A}{\Gamma, \Delta \Rightarrow \bot}$$

where

- There is no rule $\Gamma' \Rightarrow X$ such that either $\neg A \in \Gamma'$ or $X = A \otimes B$;
- There is no conditional rules $\Delta' \Rightarrow X$ such that either $A \in \Delta'$ or $X = \neg A \otimes B$;
- For any formula B, $\{B, \neg B\} \not\subseteq \Gamma \cup \Delta$.

The meaning of these three conditions is that given two rules, we have a conflict if the normative content of the two rules is opposite, such that none of them can be repaired, and the states of affairs/ preconditions they require are consistent.

Once conflicts have been detected there are several ways to deal with them. The first thing to do is to determine whether we have a *prima-facie* conflict or a genuine conflict. As we have seen we have a conflict when we have two rules with opposite conclusions. Thus, a possible way to solve the conflict is to create a superiority relation over the rules and to use it do "defeat" the weaker rule. In Section 2.5 we will examine how to reason with norms, and we will see how to use the superiority relation to solve conflicts.

2.4.3 Normalisation Process

We now describe how to use the machinery presented in Section 2.4.1 and Section 2.4.2 to obtain FCL normal forms. The FCL normal form of a normative document provides a logical representation of normative specifications in format that can be used to check the compliance of a process. This consists of the following three steps:

1. Starting from a formal representation of the explicit clauses of a set of normative specifications we generate all the implicit conditions that can be derived from the normative document by applying the merging mechanism of FCL.
2. We can clean the resulting representation of the contract by removing all redundant rules according to the notion of subsumption.
3. Finally, we use the conflict identification rule to label and detect conflicts.

In general, the process at step 2 must be done several times in the appropriate order as described above. The normal form of a set of rules in FCL is the fixed-point of the above constructions. A normative document contains only finitely many rules and each rule has finitely many elements. In addition it is possible to show that the operation on which the construction is defined is monotonic (Governatori and Rotolo, 2006), thus according to standard set theory results the fixed-point exists and it is unique. Notice that the computation of the fixed-point depends on the order in which the operations of subsumption and merging are performed (subsumption fixed and merging after). Changing the order of these operations, i.e. merging first and subsumption after, or interleaving the two operations does not produce the same result. Specifically, some rules might be excluded from the computation.

2.5 Reasoning with Norms

In the previous section we have examined the mechanism to obtain a set of rules covering all possible (explicit) norms for obligations, permissions and prohibitions that can arise from an initial set of norms. In this section we focus on the issue of how to determine what obligations are in force for a specific situations. Thus taking the well known distinction between schema and instance. The previous section defines the procedure to obtain the full (normalised) schema corresponding to a normative document. Here we study how to get the normative positions active for a specific instance of a business process. The reasoning mechanism of FCL is an extension of Defeasible Logic.

Defeasible logic, originally created by Donald Nute (1994) with a particular concern about efficiency and implementation, is a simple and efficient rule based non-monotonic formalism. Over the year, the logic has been developed and extended, and several variants have been proposed to model different aspects of normative reasoning and encompassed other formalisms to for normative reasoning.

The main intuition of the logic is to be able to derive "plausible" conclusions from partial and sometimes conflicting information. Conclusions are *tentative* conclusions in the sense that a conclusion can be withdrawn when we have new pieces of information.

The knowledge in a Defeasible Theory is organised in *facts* and *rules* and superiority *relation*.

- Facts are indisputable statements.
- Defeasible rules are rules that can be defeated by contrary evidence.
- The superiority relation in a binary relation defined over the set of rules. The superiority relation determines the relative strength of two (conflicting) rules.

The meaning of a defeasible rule, like

$$A_1,...,A_n \Rightarrow C$$

is that normally we are allowed to derive C given $A_1,...,A_n$, unless we have some reasons to support the opposite conclusion (i.e., we have a rule like $B_1,...,B_m \Rightarrow \neg C$.

Defeasible Logic is a "skeptical" non-monotonic logic, meaning that it does not support contradictory conclusions. Instead, Defeasible Logic seeks to resolve conflicts. In cases where there is some support for concluding A but also support for concluding $\neg A$, Defeasible Logic does not conclude either of them (thus the name skeptical). If the support for A has priority over the support for $\neg A$ then A is concluded.

A defeasible conclusion is a tentative conclusion that might be withdrawn by new pieces of information, or in other terms it is the 'best' conclusion we can reach with the given information. In addition, the logic is able to tell whether a conclusion is or is not provable. Thus, it is possible to have the following 2 types of conclusions:

- Positive defeasible conclusions: meaning that the conclusions can be defeasible proved;
- Negative defeasible conclusions: meaning that one can show that the conclusion is not even defeasibly provable.

A defeasible conclusion A can be derived if there is a rule whose conclusion is A, whose prerequisites (antecedent) have either already been proved or given in the case at hand (i.e., facts), and any stronger rule whose conclusion is $\neg A$ (the negation of A) has prerequisites that fail to be derived. In other words, a conclusion A is (defeasibly) derivable when:

1. A is a fact; or
2. There is an applicable defeasible rule for A, and either
   a. All the rules for $\neg A$ are discarded (i.e., not applicable) or
   b. Every applicable rule for $\neg A$ is weaker than an applicable strict or defeasible rule for A.

A rule is applicable if all elements in the body of the rule are derivable (i.e., all the premises are positively provable), and a rule is discarded if at least one of the element of the body is not provable (or it is a negative defeasible conclusion).

2.5.1 Defeasible Logic at Work

We illustrate the inferential mechanism of Defeasible Logic with the help of an example. Let us assume we have a theory containing the following rules:

r_1: *PremiumCustomer(X)* $\Rightarrow$ *Discount(X)*
r_2: *SpecialOrder(X)* $\Rightarrow$ *¬Discount(X)*
r_3: *Promotion(X)* $\Rightarrow$ *¬Discount(X)*

where the superiority relation is thus defined: $r_1 \prec r_3$ and $r_2 \prec r_1$. The theory states that services in promotion are not discounted, and so are special orders with the exception of special orders placed by premium customers, who are normally entitled to a discount.

Consider a scenario where the only piece of information available is that we have received a special order. In this case we can conclude that the price has to be calculated without a discount since rule r_1 is not applicable (we do not know whether the customer is a premium customer or not). In case the special order is received from a premium customer for a service not in promotion, we can derive that the customer is entitled to a discount. Indeed rule r_1 is now applicable and it is stronger than rule r_2, and r_3, which is stronger than r_2, is not applicable (i.e., the service is not in promotion).

2.5.2 Adding Reparation Chains

FCL is an extension of defeasible logic with the reparation operator (⊗). Accordingly the reasoning mechanism to derive conclusion is an extension of that for defeasible logic. In defeasible logic the conclusions of a rule is a single literal and not a reparation chain. Thus, the condition that *OA* appears in the conclusion of a rule means in defeasible logic that *OA* is the conclusions of the rule. FCL extends defeasible logic with reparation chains, thus, we have to extend the reasoning mechanism of defeasible logic to accommodate the additional construction provided by FCL. To prove *OA*, we have to consider all rules with a reparation chain for *OA*, where for all elements before *OA* in the chain, the negation of the element is already provable. Thus to prove *A* given a rule

$$P_1,\ldots,P_n \Rightarrow OC_1 \otimes \cdots \otimes OC_m \otimes OA \otimes OD_1 \otimes \cdots \otimes OD_{k'}$$

we have that $P_1,\ldots,P_n$ must be all provable, and so must be $\neg C_1,\ldots,\neg C_m$. For the full details see (Governatori, 2005).

Consider a process governed by the following rule

$$r\text{: } Invoice \Rightarrow O_P PayWithin7Days \otimes O_P PayWithInterest$$

and a situation where an invoice has been received. Thus, we have *Invoice*. According to the rule the obligation in force is $O_P PayWithin7Days$. Suppose now that, for some reasons, the invoice has not been paid until the tenth day after the reception. The facts of the case at hand are *Invoice* and $\neg PayWithin7Days$. Here, according to the rule and the reasoning mechanism of FCL, we obtain that the obligation in force is $O_P PayWithInterest$.

2.6 Summary

In this section we have argued about the need of conceptual model of normative specifications and we have illustrated how extensions of (Standard) Deontic Logic provide sound conceptual specifications suitable for applications related to business process modelling.

We have introduced the notions of obligation, permission, prohibition and violation and we have shown how to represent them in a rule based formalism. A rule based formalism gives a representation close to the representation of norms in a normative system. Essentially, every norm is mapped to a rule.

A close and faithful representation is the first step for successful modelling. The second step is reasoning. In the framework presented in this chapter reasoning is done in two phases. In the first phase we use a normalisation procedure to generate all and only (maximal) reparation chains (norms) corresponding to all implicit norms that can be obtained from a given, explicit set of norms: the norms a process has to comply with given in a normative document. The output of the normalisation is the compliance schema for a process. In the second reasoning phase, the task is given a activity (or task) in an instance of a process what normative positions apply to the activity? This part is examined in Section 2.5 where we also gave the rationale for the inference mechanism behind FCL.

3. PROCESS MODELLING

We use BPMN notation[6] as our target process description language for a number of reasons. Firstly, graphical business process modelling have a growing acceptance in industry, and BPMN is steadily increasing its span of adoption. Secondly, BPMN models are conducive to translation to executable process models (e.g., BPEL). Finally, BPMN provides a suitable environment for supporting interactions defined by business contracts because it allows for support of process descriptions that range from internal processes to complex cross-organisational processes, involving several parties. Namely, using BPMN it is possible to describe abstract (or public) processes between parties, where the focus is on exchange of messages between them. In this case, it is possible to either abstract away the internal processes of both parties or to abstract away the internal processes of the other partner only, depending on the circumstances. In the last case, the aim is to provide description of interactions from the point of view of one party. In the most detailed form, BPMN allows for the description of internal processes for all parties, along with the messages between them. In BPMN terms this is called a collaboration (global) process.

3.1 Execution Semantics

The basic execution semantics of the control flow aspect of a business process model is defined using token-passing mechanisms, as in Petri Nets. The definitions used here extend the execution semantics for process models given by (Vanhatalo et al., 2007) with semantic annotations in the form of effects and their meaning.

A process model is seen as a graph with nodes of various types –a single start and end node, task nodes, XOR split/join nodes, and parallel split/join nodes– and directed edges (expressing sequentiality in execution). The number of incoming (outgoing) edges are restricted as follows: start node 0 (1), end node 1 (0), task node 1 (1), split node 1 (>1), and join node >1 (1). The location of all tokens, referred to as a *marking*, manifests the state of a process execution. An execution of the process starts with a token on the outgoing edge of the start node and no other tokens in the process, and ends with one token on the incoming edge of the end node and no tokens elsewhere (cf.

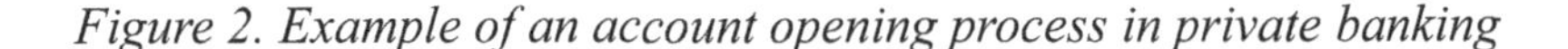

Figure 2. Example of an account opening process in private banking

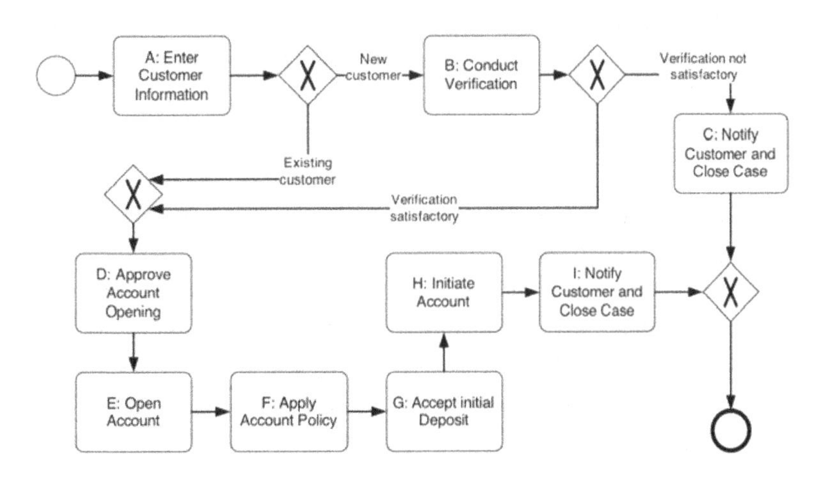

Table 1. Control objectives for the process in Figure 2

Control Objective	Internal Control
Customer due diligence	All new customers must be scanned against provided databases for identity checks.
	Accounts must maintain a positive balance, unless approved by bank manager, or for VIP customers.
Record keeping	Retain history of identity checks performed.

Table 2. Annotations for the process in Figure 2

Task	Semantic Annotation
A	*newCustomer(x)*
B	*checkIdentity(x)*
C	*checkIdentity(x), recordIdentity(x)*
E	*owner(x,y), account(y)*
F	*accountType(y,type)*
G	*positiveBalance(y)*
H	*¬positiveBalance(y)*
I	*accountActive(y)*
J	*notify(x,y)*

soundness, e.g., Wynn et al. (2007)). Task nodes are executed when a token on the incoming link is consumed and a token on the outgoing link is produced. The execution of a XOR (parallel) split node consumes the token on its incoming edge and produces a token on one (all) of its outgoing edges, whereas a XOR (parallel) join node consumes a token on one (all) of its incoming edges and produces a token on its outgoing edge.

3.2 Annotation of Processes

A process model is extended with a set of annotations, where the annotations describe (i) the artefacts or effects of executing a task and (ii) the rules describing the obligations (and other normative positions) relevant for the process.

As for the semantic annotations, the vocabulary is presented as a set of predicates P. There is a set of process variables (x and y in Table 2), over which logical statements can be made, in the form of literals involving these variables. The task nodes can be annotated using *effects* (also referred to as *post-conditions*) which are conjunctions of literals using the process variables. The meaning is that, if executed, a task changes the state of the world according to its effect: every literal mentioned by the effect is true in the resulting world; if a literal l was true before, and is not contradicted by the effect, then it is still true (i.e., the world does not change of its own accord).

The obligations for this example are motivated by the following scenario: A new legislative framework has recently been put in place in Australia for anti-money laundering. The first phase of reforms for the *Anti-Money Laundering and Counter-Terrorism Financing Act 2006* (AML/CTF) covers the financial sector including banks, credit unions, building societies and trustees and extends to casinos, wagering service providers and bullion dealers. The AML/CTF act imposes a number of obligations which include: customer due diligence (identification, verification of identity and ongoing monitoring of transactions), reporting (suspicious matters, threshold transactions and international funds transfer instructions), and record keeping. AML/CTF does not dictate specific conditions but sets out principles businesses have to obey to. Hence businesses need to determine the exact manner in which they will fulfil the obligations, which comprises the design of internal controls specific to the organisation.

Table 1 contains a natural language description of the control objectives and corresponding internal controls for this process; Table 2 shows the semantic effect annotations of the process activities. In this case, the control objectives describe the principles the business is subject to, and the internal controls are the resulting "norms" implementing the control objectives. Control objectives and internal controls are the typical way in which enterprises implement norms regulating they business, processes and procedure.

The control objectives in Table 1 can be expressed by the following FCL rules to create the compliance rule base:

- All new customers must be scanned against provided databases for identity checks.

  r_1: *newCustomer*(*x*) $\Rightarrow$ *OcheckIdentity*(*x*)

  The predicate *newCustomer*(*x*) means that the input data with $Id = x$ is a new customer, for which we have the obligation to check the provided data against provided databases *checkIdentity*(*x*). The obligation resulting from this rule is a non-persistent obligation, i.e. as soon as a check has been performed, the obligation is no longer in force.
- Retain history of identity checks performed.

  r_2: *checkIdentity*(*x*) $\Rightarrow$ *OrecordIdentity*(*x*)

  This rule establishes that there is a permanent obligation to keep record of the identity corresponding to the (new) customer identified by *x*. In addition this obligation is not fulfilled by the achievement of the activity (for example, by storing it in a database). We have a violation of the condition, if for example, the record *x* is deleted from the database.
- Accounts must maintain a positive balance, unless approved by a bank manager, or for VIP customers.

  r_3: *account*(*x*) $\Rightarrow$ *OpositiveBalance*(*x*) $\otimes$ *OapproveManager*(*x*)

  The primary obligation is that each account has to maintain a positive balance *positive-Balance*; if this condition is violated (for any reason the account is not positive), then we still are in an acceptable situation if a bank manager approves the account not to be positive. In this case, the obligation of approving persists until a manager approves the situation; after the approval, the obligation is no longer in force.

  r_4: *account*(*x*), *accountType*(*x, VIP*) *owner* (*x, y*) $\Rightarrow$ *P* $\neg$*positiveBalance*(*x*)

  This rule creates an exception to rule r_3. Accounts of type VIP are allowed to have a non positive balance and no approval is required for this type of accounts (this is achieved by imposing that rule r_4 is stronger than rule r_3, $r_4 \prec r_3$). Notice that the normative position associated to r_4 is a permission.

3.3 Summary

In this section we argued about the advantages about the graphical notation for business processes and we have given an overview of the execution semantics of business processes. However, this is not enough for compliance. While graphical notation can be used to check the structural compliance of a process (i.e., whether task are executed in a prescribed order), graphical notation must be supplemented by annotations. For compliance one has to have two different types of annotations: on one hand we need to know how data is affected by the different task, thus we annotate the single node in a process graph (and eventually the arcs) with the effects produced by the nodes. On the other hand, we have to know the rules (control objectives and internal controls) a process is subject to. Thus, we annotate processes with set of FCL rules describing the normative part regulating the process.

4. COMPLIANCE CHECKING

As stated, our aim in the compliance checking is to figure out (a) which obligations will definitely appear when executing the process, and (b) which of those obligations may not be fulfilled.

In a way, FCL constraint expressions for a normative document define a behavioural and state space which can be used to analyse how well different behaviour execution paths of a business process comply with the FCL constraints. Our aim is to use this analysis as a basis for deciding whether execution paths of a business process are compliant with the FCL and thus with the normative document modelled by the FCL specifications. The central part of this compliance checking is given by the notions of ideal, sub-ideal, non-ideal and irrelevant situations which will be introduced and defined after two simple motivating examples are given.

Consider the following FCL obligation rule:

$service_1$: *WeekDay, FaultMessageEvent* $\Rightarrow$ O_s*Repair24hours*

stating that on a week day, when a fault message occurs, the service provider is obliged to repair the fault within 24hrs.

Assume now that one possible execution path from a process is:

1. A *FaultMessageEvent* is received from a premium customer on a week day
2. The service provider reacts by (in the order):
   a. Sending an apology message,
   b. Repairing the fault within 24 hours and
   c. Sending a reparation confirmation message

When checking compliance of this execution path with the obligation it is obvious that the obligation is fulfilled because the fault is fixed within 24 hours. Notice that the execution path also includes additional conditions such as sending of two additional messages (an apology message, and a reparation confirmation message) which are not critical for the obligation.

Consider another example:

$service_2$: *WeekDay, PremiumCustomer, FaultMessageEvent* $\Rightarrow$ O_s*Repair12hours*

This reflects the requirement for a faster reaction time for premium customers. Assume we have the following situation:

WeekDay, FaultMessageEvent

Obviously, this situation is not sufficient for the O_s*repair12hours* to be activated.

4.1 Ideal Semantics

We now introduce the concepts of ideal, sub-ideal and non-ideal situations to describe various degrees of compliance between execution paths and FCL constraints. We will also provide a semantic interpretation of FCL rules in terms of ideal, sub-ideal, non-ideal and irrelevant situations, which we refer to as Ideal Semantics. In this context, a situation is the state of a process after the execution of a task. Thus, a situation corresponds to the set of effects (literals) obtained after the execution of a task.

Intuitively, an *ideal* situation is a situation where execution paths do not violate FCL expressions, and thus the execution paths (which will then correspond to processes that are related to the contract) are fully compliant with the normative specifications. A *sub-ideal* situation is a situation where there are some violations, but the norms relevant for the situation at hand establish means to recover from the violation, and the compensatory measures have been taken. In other terms there is at least a reparation chains where the primary obligation has not been fulfilled but some of the secondary obligation have been fulfilled. Accordingly, processes resulting in sub-ideal situations are still compliant to a normative document even if they provide non-optimal performances of the normative specifications. A situation is *non-ideal* if it violates a normative document (and the violations are not repaired). In this case, a process resulting in a non-ideal situation does not comply with the normative specifications. There are two possible reasons for a process not to comply with the normative specifications: (1) the process executes some tasks which are prohibited by the normative specifications (or equivalently, it executes the opposite of obligatory tasks); (2) the process fails to execute some tasks required by the normative specifications. Finally, a situation is irrelevant for a normative document if no rule is applicable in the situation. Irrelevant situations correspond to states of affairs where a normative document is silent about them.

As discussed in Section 2.4, for every FCL representation of a contract its normal form contains all conditions that can be derived from the normative specifications and redundant clauses are removed. Thus, normal forms are the most appropriate means to determine whether a process conforms with a normative document. We now define conditions under which we are able to determine whether a situation complies with a set of normative specifications or if it represents a violation of some clauses.

First of all, we define when a situation (set of literals) is either ideal, sub-ideal, non-ideal or irrelevant with respect to a contract rule.

Definition 2:

- *A situation S is* ideal *with respect to a rule* $\Gamma \Rightarrow A_1 \otimes \cdots \otimes A_n$ *iff* $\Gamma \cup \{A_1\} \subseteq S$
- *A situation S is* sub-ideal *with respect to a rule* $\Gamma \Rightarrow A_1 \otimes \cdots \otimes A_n$ *iff* $\Gamma \cup \{A_i\} \subseteq S$, *for some* $1 < i \leq n$ *such that* $\forall A_j, j < i, A_1,\ldots, A_j \notin S$
- *A situation S is* non-ideal *with respect to a rule* $\Gamma \Rightarrow A_1 \otimes \cdots \otimes A_n$ *iff* $\Gamma \subseteq S$ *and S is neither ideal nor sub-ideal, i.e.,* $A_1,\ldots, A_n \notin S$
- *A situation S is* irrelevant *with respect to a rule* $\Gamma \Rightarrow A_1 \otimes \cdots \otimes A_n$ *iff it is neither ideal nor sub-ideal nor non-ideal, i.e.,* $\Gamma \nsubseteq S$

Returning to our first example of the previous section, rule $service_1$, we have that

$\Gamma = \{WeekDay, FaultMessageEvent\}$

Accordingly, for the situation:

$S = \{WeekDay, FaultMessageEvent, SendApologyMessage, Repair24hours, SendReparationConfirmationMessage\}$

we have that $\Gamma \cup \{Repair24hours\} \subseteq S$, thus the situation is classified as ideal. As we have seen in the previous section, for the second rule, i.e., $service_2$, Γ is not a subset of S, thus S is irrelevant for the rules concerning premium customers.

According to Definition 2, a situation is ideal with respect to a norm if the rule is not violated;

sub-ideal when the primary obligation is violated but the rule allows for a reparation, which is satisfied; non-ideal when the primary obligation and all its reparations are violated, and irrelevant when the rule is not applicable. Definition 2 is concerned with the status of a situation with respect to a single rule, while a contract consists of many rules, thus we have to extend this definition to cover the case of a set of rules. In particular we will extend it considering all rules in the normal form for a normative document containing all rules inherent to the document.

Definition 3

- *A situation S is* ideal *with respect to a set of rules R iff for every rule in R, either S is irrelevant or ideal for the rule.*
- *A situation S is* sub-ideal *with respect to a set of rules R iff there is a rule in R for which S is sub-ideal, and there is no rule in R for which S is non-ideal.*
- *A situation S is* non-ideal *with respect to a set of rules R iff there is a rule in R for which S is non-ideal.*
- *A situation S is* irrelevant *with respect to a set of rules R iff for all rules in R the situation S is irrelevant.*

Definition 3 follows immediately from the intuitive interpretation of ideality and the related notions we have provided in Definition 2. On the other hand, the relation between a normal form and the normative specifications from which it is obtained seems to be a more delicate matter. A careful analysis of the conditions for constructing an FCL normal form allows us to state the following general criterion:

Definition 4 *A situation S is ideal (sub-ideal, non-ideal, irrelevant) with respect to a set of FCL rules if S is ideal (sub-ideal, non-ideal, irrelevant) with respect to the normal form of the set of FCL rules.*

It is worth noting that Definition 4 shows the relevance of the distinction between a set of normative specifications and its normal form. This holds in particular for the case of sub-ideal situations. Suppose you have the following set of FCL rules

$\Rightarrow OA \quad \neg A \Rightarrow OB$

The corresponding normal form is

$\Rightarrow OA \otimes OB$

While the situation with $\neg A$ and B is sub-ideal with respect to the latter, it would be non-ideal for the former. In the first case, even if $\neg A \Rightarrow OB$ expresses in fact an implicit reparational obligation of the rule $\Rightarrow A$, this is not made explicit. The key point here is that there was no link between the primary and reparation obligations in the original set of rules, but this is made explicit in the normal form. So, there exists a situation which apparently accomplishes a rule and violates the other without satisfying any reparation. This conclusion cannot be accepted because it is in contrast with our intuition according to which the presence of two rules like $\Rightarrow OA$ and $\neg A \Rightarrow OB$ must lead to a unique regulation. For this reason, we can evaluate a situation as sub-ideal with respect to a set of FCL rules only if it is sub-ideal with respect to its normal form.

4.2 Checking Compliance

The ideal semantics allows us to relate business processes and FCL expression, thus it enable us to determine whether a business process is compliant with a set of regulations. What we have to do now is to look at the details of how to relate the two domains. The idea is as follows:

1. We traverse the graph describing the business process and we identify the sets of effects (sets of literals) for all the tasks (nodes)

in the process according to the execution semantics specified in Section 3.1.

2. For each task we use the set of effects for that particular task to determine the normative positions (obligations, permissions, prohibitions) triggered by the execution of the task. This means that effects of a task are used as a set of facts, and we compute the conclusions of the defeasible theory resulting from the effects and the FCL rules annotating the process (see Section 2.5). In the same way we accumulate effects we accumulate (undischarged) obligations from one task in the process to the task following it in the process.
3. For each task we compare the effects of the tasks and the obligations accumulated up to the task. If an obligation is fulfilled by a task, we discharge the obligation, otherwise if the obligation is violated we signal the violation. Finally, if an obligation is not fulfilled nor violated, we keep the obligation in the stack of obligations and we propagate the obligation to the successive tasks.

Here, we assume that the obligations derived from a task should be fulfilled in the remaining of the process. Variations of this schema are possible. For example, one could stipulate that the obligations derived from a task should be fulfilled by the tasks immediately after the task[7]. In another approach one could use a schema where for each task one has both preconditions and effects. Then the obligations derived from the preconditions must be fulfilled by current task (i.e., the obligations must be fulfilled by the effects of the task), and the obligations derived from the effects are as in our basic schema.

In the rest of the section we discuss in details step 2 (Section 4.3) and 3 (Section 4.4) above.

4.3 From Tasks to Obligations

The second step to perform when we have to determine whether a process is compliant is to determine the obligations derived by the effects of a task. Given a set of rules R and a set of literals S (plain literals and deontic literals), we can use the inference mechanism of defeasible logic (Section 2.5) to compute the set of conclusions (obligations) in force given the set of literals. These are the obligations an agent has to obey to in the situation described by the set of literals. However, the situation could already be sub-ideal, i.e., some of the obligations prescribed by the rules are already violated. Thus, given a set of literals describing a state-of-affairs one has to compute not only the current obligations, but also what reparation chains are in force given the set.

For example consider a scenario where we have the rules $A \Rightarrow OB$ and $\neg B \Rightarrow OC$, and the effects are A and $\neg B$. The normal form of the rules is $A \Rightarrow OB \otimes OC$ and $\neg B \Rightarrow OC$. The only obligation in force for this scenario is OC. Since we have a violation of the first rule ($A \Rightarrow OB$ and $\neg B$), then we know that it is not possible to have an ideal situation here. Hence, computing only the current obligation does not tell us the state of the corresponding business process. What we have to do is to identify the chain for the ideal situation for the task at hand. To deal with this issue we have to identify the *active* reparation chains.

A reparation chain C is *active* given a set of literals S, if

- There is a rule $\Gamma \Rightarrow C$ such that $\Gamma \subseteq S$, i.e., the rule is triggered by the situation, and
- For all rule for conflicting chains[8], either
    - The chain is not triggered by the situation or
    - The negation of an element before the conflicting element is not in the situation.

Let us examine the following example. Consider the rules

$r_1 : A_1 \Rightarrow OB \otimes OC,$
$r_2 : A_2 \Rightarrow O\neg B \otimes OD,$
$r_3 : A_3 \Rightarrow OE \otimes O\neg B.$

The effects describing the situation are A_1 and A_3. In this scenario the active chains are $OB \otimes OC$ and $OE \otimes \neg OB$. The chain $OB \otimes OC$ is active since r_2 cannot be used to activate the chain $O\neg B \otimes OD$. For r_3, and the resulting chain $OE \otimes O\neg B$, we do not have the violation of the primary obligation OE of the rule (i.e., $\neg E$ is not one of the effects), so the resulting obligation $O\neg B$ is not entailed by rule r_3.

Consider, again, the scenario described at the end of Section 2.5. Given the rule

r: $Invoice \Rightarrow O_p PayWithin7Days \otimes$
$O_p PayWithInterest$

and the case data *Invoice* we have that the active chain is

$O_p PayWithin7Days \otimes O_p PayWithInterest,$

and $O_p PayWithin7Days$ is the current obligation in force. In case of a late payment of the invoice, i.e., when the case data consists of both *Invoice* and $\neg PayWithin7Days$, the active chain is still the same, and $O_p PayWithInterest$ is the obligation in force. In the first case, to obey the current obligation (i.e., to pay the invoice in time) results in an ideal situation. In the second case, the best one can do is to end up in a sub-ideal situation.

4.4 Obligation Propagation

A reparation chain is in force if there is a rule of which the reparation chain is the consequent and a set of facts (effects of a task in a process) including the rule antecedents. In addition, we assume that, once in force, a reparation chain remains as such unless we can determine that it has been violated or the obligations corresponding to it have all been obeyed to (these are two cases when we can discharge an obligation or reparation chain). This means that it is not possible to have two instances at the same time of the same reparation chain. Accordingly, a reparation chain in force is uniquely determined by the combination of the task T when the chain has been derived and the rule R from which the chain has been obtained.

The procedure for compliance checking is based on two algorithms, *ComputeObligations* and *CheckCompliance*. *ComputeObligations* is the algorithm to determine the active chains presented in Section 4.3. Given a set of literals S, corresponding to effects of a task T in a process model, we use the algorithm *ComputeObligations* to determine the current set of obligations for the process *Current*. The set of the current obligations includes the new obligations triggered by the task, as well as the obligations carried out from previous tasks. The algorithm *CheckCompliance* scans all elements of *Current* against the set of literals S, and determines the state of each reparation chain ($C = A_1 \otimes A_2$) in *Current*. *CheckCompliance* operates as follows:

if $A_1 \Rightarrow OB$, then
  if $B \in S$, then
    remove($[T, R, A_1 \otimes A_2]$, *Current*)
    remove($[T, R, A_1 \otimes A_2]$, *Unfulfilled*)
    if $[T, R, B_1 \otimes B_2 \otimes A_1 \otimes A_2] \in$ *Violated* then
      add($[T, R, B_1 \otimes B_2 \otimes A_1 \otimes A_2]$,
        Compensated)
  if $\neg B \in S$, then
    add($[T, R, A_1 \otimes A_2, B]$, *Violated*)
    add($[T, R, A_2]$, *Current*)
  else
    add($[T, R, A_1 \otimes A_2]$, *Unfulfilled*).

Let us examine the *CheckCompliance* algorithm. Remember the algorithm scans all active reparation chains one by one. Then for each of them reports on the status of it. For each chain in

Current (the set of all active chains), it looks for the first element of the chain and it determines the content of the obligation (so if the first element is OB, the content of the obligation is B). Then it checks whether the obligation has been fulfilled (B is in the set of effects), or violated ($\neg B$ is in the set of effects), or simply we cannot say anything about it (none of B and $\neg B$ is in the set of effects). In the first case we can discharge the obligation and we remove the chain from the set of active chains (similarly if the obligation was carried over from a previous task, i.e., it was in the set *Unfulfilled*). In case of a violation, we add the information about it in the system. This is done by inserting a tuple with the identifier of the chain and what violation we have in the set *Violated*. In addition, we know that violations can be compensated, thus if the chain has a second element we remove the violated element from the chain and put the rest of the chain in the set of active chains. Here we take the stance that a violation does not discharge an obligation, thus we do not remove the chain from the set of active chains[9]. Finally, in the last case, the set of effects does not tell us if the obligation has been fulfilled or violated, so we propagate the obligation to the successive tasks by putting the chain in the set *Unfulfilled*. The algorithm also checks whether a chain/obligation was previously violated but it was then compensated.

Definition 5

- *A process is* compliant *iff for all* $[T, R, A] \in Current$, $A = OB \otimes C$, *for every* $[T, R, A, B] \in Violated$, $[T, R, A, B] \in Compensated$ *and* $Unfulfilled = \varnothing$.
- *A process is* fully compliant *iff for all* $[T, R, A] \in Current$, $A = OB \otimes C$, $Violated = \varnothing$ *and* $Unfulfilled = \varnothing$.

The above definition relates the state of a process base on the report generated by the *Check-Compliance* algorithm and the ideal semantics for FCL expressions. In particular, a process is compliant if the situation at the end of the process is at least sub-ideal (it is possible to have violations but these have been compensated for). Similarly a process is fully compliant if it results in an ideal situation.

According to Definition 5, a process is not compliant if the set of unfulfilled obligations (*Unfulfilled*) is not empty. Consider, for example the rule

$$r_3: account(x) \Rightarrow OpositiveBalance(x) \otimes OapproveManager(x)$$

relative to the process of Figure 2 with the annotation as in Table 2. After task E we have, among others, the effect $account(x)$. This means that after task E we have the chain

$$[E, r_4, OpositiveBalance(x) \otimes OapproveManager(x)]$$

in *Current* for task F. After task F, the above entry for the chain obtained from rule r_4 is moved to the set *Unfulfilled*. Suppose now that tasks G and H do not have any annotation attached to them. In this case at the end of the process we still have the active chain, but the resulting situation is not ideal: the antecedent of the rule is a subset of the set of effects, but we do not have the first element of the chain as one of the effects. Thus something the process were required to do was not done; hence, the process is not compliant.[1]

4.5 Summary

In this section we have first introduced a semantics to evaluate a set of literals given a set of FCL expressions determining whether obligations relative to a situation (state-of-affairs) where met or not. Accordingly, a state can be ideal, if all (primary) obligations are fulfilled, sub-ideal, if some obligations are not fulfilled but they are repaired, and non-ideal if there are violations which are not compensated.

Then, we discussed a mechanism to determine whether a process is compliant or not based on the ideal semantics. In particular, first we have to gather the effects for a task (and propagate effects from one task to tasks after it), then we have to determine the active obligations as well as the situation is ideal, sub-ideal or non-ideal with respect to the effects of the current task. However, a task could introduce some degree of non-compliance that could be resolved in successive tasks. We have show how to propagate obligations and the compliance status across task. We also have discussed some variants of the main schema.

5. RELATED WORK

Governance, risk and compliance (GRC) is an emerging area of research which holds challenges for various communities including information systems, business software development, legal, cultural, behavioural studies and corporate governance.

In this chapter, we have focused on compliance management from an information systems perspective, in particular the modelling and analysis of compliance requirements. Both process modelling as well as modelling of normative requirements are well studied fields independently, but until recently the interactions between the two have been largely ignored (Desai et al., 2005; Padmanabhan et al., 2006). In particular, zur Muehlen et al. (2007) provide a valuable representational analysis to understand the synergies between process modelling and rule modelling.

It is obvious that the modelling of controls will be undertaken as rules, although the question of appropriate formalism is still under studied. A plethora of proposals exist both in the research community on formal modelling of rules, as well as in the commercial arena through business rule management systems.

Historically, formal modelling of normative systems has focused on how to capture the logical properties of the notions of the normative concepts (e.g., obligations, prohibitions, permissions, violations, ...) and how these relate to the entities in an organisation and to the activities to be performed. Deontic logic is the branch of logic that studies normative concepts such as obligations, permissions, prohibitions and related notions. Standard Deontic Logic (SDL) is a starting point for logical investigation of the basic normative notions and it offers a very idealised and abstract conceptual representation of these notions but at the same time it suffers from several drawbacks given its high level of abstraction (Sartor, 2005). Over the years many different deontic logics have been proposed to capture the different intuitions behind these normative notions and to overcome drawbacks and limitations of SDL. One of the main limitations in this context is its inability to reason with violations, and the obligations arising in response to violations (Carmo and Jones, 2002). Very often normative statements pertinent to business processes, and in particular contracts, specify conditions about when other conditions in the document have nor been fulfilled, that is when some (contractual) clauses have been violated. Hence, any formal representation, to be conceptually faithful, has to been able to deal with this kind of situations.

As we have discussed before compliance is a relationship between two sets of specifications: the normative specifications that prescribe what a business has to do, and the process modelling specification describing how a business performs its activities. Accordingly to properly verify that a process/procedure complies with the norms regulating the particular business one has to provide conceptually sound representations of the process on one side and the norms on the other, and then check the alignment of the formal specifications of the process and the formal specifications for the norms.

In this chapter, we have proposed a formal modelling of controls through the Formal Contract Language (FCL). FCL has proved effective due to its ability to express reparation chains and consequently ability to reason with violations.

There have been some other notable contributions from research on the matter of control modelling. Goedertier and Vanthienen (2006) presents a logical language PENELOPE, that provides the ability to verify temporal constraints arising from compliance requirements on effected business processes. Küster et al. (2007) provide a method to check compliance between object life-cycles that provide reference models for data artefacts e.g. insurance claims and business process models. Giblin et al. (2006) provide temporal rule patterns for regulatory policies, although the objective of this work is to facilitate event monitoring rather than the usage of the patterns for support of design time activities. Furthermore, Agrawal et al. (2006) presented a workflow architecture for supporting Sarbanes-Oxley Internal Controls, which include functions such as workflow modelling, active enforcement, workflow auditing, as well as anomaly detection.

Another line of investigation studies compliance based on the structure of business processes. Ghose and Koliadis (2007) consider an approach where the tasks of a business process model, written in BPMN, are annotated with the effects of the tasks, and a technique to propagate and cumulate the effects from a task to a successive contiguous one is proposed. The technique is designed to take into account possible conflicts between the effects of tasks and to determine the degree of compliance of a BPMN specification. Chopra and Sing (2007), on the other hand, investigate compliance in the context of agents and multi-agent systems based on a classification of paths of tasks. Roman and Kifer (2007) proposed Concurrent Transaction Logic to model the states of a workflow and presented some algorithms to determine whether the workflow is compliant. The major limitation of these approaches to compliance is that they ignore the normative aspects of compliance.

There has been some complementary work in the analysis of formal models representing normative notions. For example, Farrell et al. (2005) study the performance of business contract based on their formal representation. Desai et al. (2008) seek to provide support for assessing the correctness of business contracts represented formally through a set of commitments. The reasoning is based on value of various states of commitment as perceived by cooperative agents. Research on closely related issues has also been carried out in the field of autonomous agents (Alberti et al., 2006).

As discussed previously, modelling the controls is only the first step towards compliance by design. The second essential step is the enrichment of process models with compliance requirements (i.e., the modelled controls). Clearly this cannot take place without a formal controls model (as proposed by above mentioned works), or at least some machine readable specification of the controls. There have been recently some efforts towards support for business process modelling against compliance requirements. In particular, the work of zur Muehlen and Rosemann (2005) provides an appealing method for integrating risks in business processes. The proposed technique for "risk-aware" business process models is developed for EPCs (Event-Driven Process Chains) using an extended notation. Sadiq et al. (2007) propose an approach based on control tags to visualise internal controls on process models. Liu et al. (2007) takes a similar approach of annotating and checking process models against compliance rules, although the visual rule language, namely BPSL is general purpose and does not directly address the deontic notions providing compliance requirements.

Lastly, although this section has primarily focused on preventative approaches to compliance, it is important to identify the role of detective approaches as well, where a wide range of supporting technologies are present. These include several commercial solutions such as business activity monitoring, business intelligence etc. Noteworthy in research literature with respect to compliance monitoring, is the synergy with process mining techniques (van der Aalst et al., 2003) which provide the capability to discover runtime process behaviour (and deviations) and can thereby assist in detection of compliance violations.

6. CONCLUSION

The growing importance of governance, risk and compliance for various industries, has created an evident need to provide supporting tools and methods to enable organisations seeking compliance, which may ranging from safeguards against enforceable undertakings to being champions of corporate social responsibility. The challenges that reside in this topic warrant systematic approaches that motivate and empower business users to achieve a high degree of compliance with regulations, standards, and corporate policies.

Process and control modelling represent two distinct but mutually dependent specifications in current enterprise systems. In this chapter, we take the view that the two specifications, will be created somewhat independently, at different times, and by different stakeholders, using their respective conceptually faithful representation schemes. However the convergence of the two must be supported in order to achieve business practices that our compliant with control objectives stemming from various regulatory, standard and contractual concerns. This convergence should be supported with a systematic and well structured approach if the vision of compliance by design is to be achieved.

We have proposed a means of achieving so called compliance by design through an overall methodology that can be summarised into three main steps of control modelling; process enrichment; and compliance checking through analysis and feedback for compliance aware process (re)design. Figure 3 summarises the overall methodology that provides a structured and systematic approach to undertaking changes in the process model in response to compliance requirements.

The proposed language for control modelling, namely FCL (section 2), provides a conceptually

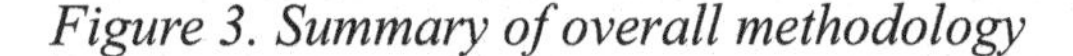

Figure 3. Summary of overall methodology

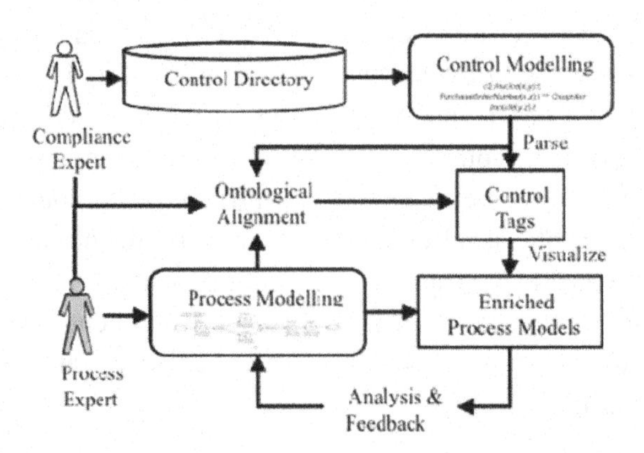

faithful representation of the compliance requirements. In addition FCL offers two reasoning modules: (1) a normaliser to make explicit rules that can be derived from explicitly given rules by merging their normative conclusions, to remove redundancy and identify conflicts rules; and (2) an inference engine to derive conclusions given some propositions as input (Governatori, 2005). The rigour introduced by FCL enables a systematic establishment of control models with process models. As outlined in section 3, process enrichment can be realised as a result through structured control annotations. These annotations can not only provide a means of visualising the impact of compliance controls on process models (Sadiq et al., 2007), but also assist in compliance checking (section 4) and analysis and feedback for subsequent (re)design of the process models.

One of the biggest challenges facing the compliance industry is the measurement of adequacy of controls (KPMG Advisory, 2005). The methodology proposed provides the added benefit of providing the capability for diagnostics. That is provide a means of understanding what needs to be done in order to achieve (an acceptable degree of) compliance (Lu et al., 2007). This has the potential to create a more holistic approach to compliance management, by not only providing preventative and detective techniques, but also corrective recommendations. This allows organisations to better respond to the changing regulatory demands and also reap the benefits of process improvement. We recommend that future research endeavours in this area should strive towards compliance management frameworks that provide a close integration of the process and control modelling perspectives.

ACKNOWLEDGMENT

NICTA is funded by the Australian Government as represented by the Department of Broadband, Communications and the Digital Economy and the Australian Research Council through the ICT Centre of Excellence program and the Queensland Government.

REFERENCES

Agrawal, R., Johnson, C. M., Kiernan, J., & Leymann, F. (2006). Taming compliance with Sarbanes-Oxley internal controls using database technology. In L. Liu, A. Reuter, K.-Y. Whang, & J. Zhang (Eds.), *ICDE*, (pp. 92). IEEE Computer Society.

Alberti, M., Gavanelli, M., Lamma, E., Chesani, F., Mello, P., & Torroni, P. (2006). Compliance verification of agent interaction: a logic-based software tool. *Applied Artificial Intelligence, 20*(2-4), 133–157.

Alonso, G., Dadam, P., & Rosemann, M. (Eds.) (2007, September 24-28). In *Proceedings, Business Process Management, 5th International Conference, BPM 2007, Brisbane, Australia,* (LNCS, 4714). Springer.

Antoniou, G., Billington, D., Governatori, G., & Maher, M. J. (2001). Representation results for defeasible logic. *ACM Transactions on Computational Logic, 2*(2), 255–287.

Antoniou, G., Billington, D., Governatori, G., & Maher, M. J. (2006). Embedding defeasible logic into logic programming. *Theory and Practice of Logic Programming, 6*(6), 703–735.

Carmo, J., & Jones, A. J. (2002). Deontic logic and contrary to duties. In D. Gabbay & F. Guenther (Eds.), *Handbook of philosophical logic, 2nd Edition, 8*, (pp. 265–343). Dordrecht: Kluwer.

Chopra, A. K., & Sing, M. P. (2007, May 8, 2007). Producing compliant interactions: Conformance, coverage and interoperability. In M. Baldoni & U. Endriss (Eds.), *Declarative agent languages and technologies IV*, (LNAI, 4327, pp. 1–15). Berlin Heidelberg. Springer-Verlag.

Desai, N., Mallya, A. U., Chopra, A. K., & Singh, M. P. (2005). Interaction protocols as design abstractions for business processes. *IEEE Trans. Software Eng., 31*(12), 1015–1027.

Desai, N., Narendra, N. C., & Singh, M. P. (2008). Checking correctness of business contracts via commitments. In L. Padgham, D. C. Parkes, J. Müller, & S. Parsons (Eds.), *AAMAS 2008*, (pp. 787–794). IFAAMAS.

Farrell, A. D. H., Sergot, M. J., Sallé, M., & Bartolini, C. (2005). Using the event calculus for tracking the normative state of contracts. *International Journal of Cooperative Information Systems, 14*(2-3), 99–129.

Ghose, A., & G. Koliadis (2007). Auditing business process compliance. In *Service Oriented Computing, ISOC 2007*, (LNCS, pp. 169-180). Springer.

Giblin, C., Müller, S., & Pfitzmann, B. (2006, October). *From regulatory policies to event monitoring rules: Towards model driven compliance automation.* (Technical report, IBM Research Report). Zurich Research Laboratory.

Goedertier, S., & Vanthienen, J. (2006). Designing compliant business processes with obligations and permissions. In *Business Process Management (BPM) Workshops*, (pp. 5–14).

Governatori, G. (2005). Representing business contracts in RuleML. *International Journal of Cooperative Information Systems, 14*(2-3), 181–216.

Governatori, G., Hulstijn, J., Riveret, R., & Rotolo, A. (2007). Characterising deadlines in temporal modal defeasible logic. In *20th Australian Joint Conference on Artificial Intelligence, AI 2007*, (pp. 486–496).

Governatori, G., & Rotolo, A. (2006). Logic of violations: A Gentzen system for reasoning with contrary-to-duty obligations. *Australasian Journal of Logic, 4*, 193–215.

KPMG Advisory (2005). *The Compliance Journey: Balancing Risk and Controls with Business Improvement.* KPMG Advisory.

Küster, J. M., Ryndina, K., & Gall, H. (2007). *Generation of business process models for object life cycle compliance.* See DBLP:conf/bpm/2007, (pp. 165–181).

Liu, Y., Müller, S., & Xu, K. (2007). A static compliance-checking framework for business process models. *IBM Systems Journal, 46*(2), 335–362.

Lu, R., Sadiq, S. W., & Governatori, G. (2007). Compliance aware business process design. In *Business Process Management Workshops*, (pp. 120–131).

Nute, D. (1994). Defeasible logic. In *Handbook of Logic in Artificial Intelligence and Logic Programming, 3.*

Padmanabhan, V., Governatori, G., Sadiq, S., Colomb, R. M., & Rotolo, A. (2006). Process modelling: The deontic way. In M. Stumptner, S. Hartmann, & Y. Kiyoki (Eds.), *Conceptual Modelling 2006. Proceedings of the Thirds Asia-Pacific Conference on Conceptual Modelling (APCCM2006)*, (pp. 75–84). Australian Computer Science Communications.

Pesic, M., & van der Aalst, W. M. P. (2006). A declarative approach for flexible business processes management. In J. Eder & S. Dustdar (Eds.), *Business Process Management Workshops*, Volume 4103 of *Lecture Notes in Computer Science*, (pp. 169–180). Springer.

Roman, D., & Kifer, M. (2007). Reasoning about the behaviour of semantic web services with concurrent transaction logic. In *VLDB*, (pp. 627–638).

Sadiq, S., Governatori, G., & Naimiri, K. (2007). *Modelling of control objectives for business process compliance.* See DBLP:conf/bpm/2007, (pp. 149–164).

Sadiq, S. W., Orlowska, M. E., & Sadiq, W. (2005). Specification and validation of process constraints for flexible workflows. *Inf. Syst., 30*(5), 349–378.

Sartor, G. (2005). *Legal reasoning.* Dordrecht, THe Netherlands: Springer.

van der Aalst, W. M. P., van Dongen, B. F., Herbst, J., Maruster, L., Schimm, G., & Weijters, A. J. M. M. (2003). Workflow mining: A survey of issues and approaches. *Data Knowl. Eng., 47*(2), 237–267.

Vanhatalo, J., Völzer, H., & Leymann, F. (2007). Faster and more focused control-flow analysis for business process models though SESE decomposition. In *5th International Conference on Service-Oriented Computing (ICSOC)*, (pp. 43–55).

Wynn, M. T., Verbeek, H., van der Aalst, W. M., ter Hofstede, A. H., & Edmond, D. (2007). Business process verification - finally a reality! *Business Process Management Journal.*

zur Muehlen, M., Indulska, M., & Kemp, G. (2007). Business process and business rule modeling languages for compliance management: A representational analysis. In *Proc ER 2007: Tutorials, Poster, Panels, and Industrial Contribution.*

zur Muehlen, M., & Rosemann, M. (2005). Integrating risks in business process models. In *Proceedings of 16th Australasian Conference on Information Systems.*

KEY TERMS

Business Process Model: A business process model (BPM) describes the tasks to be executed (and the order in which they are executed) to fulfil some objectives of a business. BPMs aim to automate and optimise business procedures and are typically given in graphical languages. A language for BPM usually has two main elements: tasks and connectors. Tasks correspond to activities to be performed by actors (either human or artificial) and connectors describe the relationships between tasks.

Compliance: Compliance, also know as regulatory compliance, is the process by which an organisation ensures that the specifications for implementing business processes, operations and practise are in accordance with a prescribed and/or agreed set of norms.

Defeasible Logic: Defeasible logic is a simple and efficient rule based non-monotonic formalism. The key idea of the logic is to derive (tentative) conclusions, i.e., conclusions that can be retracted when new piece of information become available, with a minimum amount of information.

Deontic Logic: Deontic logic is the branch of logic that studies the formalisation and properties of normative notions such as obligation, permission, prohibitions, violations and so on. Typically a deontic logic is an extension of classical propositional logic with modal (deontic) operators modelling normative concepts, i.e., obligations, permissions, prohibitions.

Formal Contract Logic (FCL): Formal Contract Logic is obtained from the combination of Defeasible logic (extended with deontic operators) and a Deontic logic of violation. The logic offers two main reasoning mechanisms, one mechanism to combine and to derive new norms (rules) from existing ones, and the second mechanism to derive the normative position in force for a particular case.

Normative Position: A normative position regulates the (prescribed) behaviour of a group of actors in an institution (described by a set of norms). A one-agent normative position regulates the act of one actor; a two-agent normative positions regulate the (possibly joint) acts of two agents, and so on. Typically, obligations, permissions, prohibitions are basic normative positions, complex normative positions, e.g., delegation, power, are obtained by combination of simplex normative positions and actions.

ENDNOTES

1. Sarbanes-Oxley Act of 2002, US Public Law 107-204.
2. Health Insurance Portability and Accountability Act of 1999. US Public Law 104-191.
3. ITU-T Rec X.902, ISO/IEC 10746-2: Foundations, RM-ODP.
4. In the remaining of the chapter we will use O_S and P_S for the obligation and permission operators relative to the *Supplier*, and O_P and P_P for the *Purchaser*. O_s and P_s will be used for a generic subject.
5. As we have seen in Section 2.3 FCL has a superiority relation over rules to handle situations like this one.
6. http://www.bpmn.org.
7. This approach can be used to check the compliance of the flow of tasks.
8. Given a chain $A_1, ..., A_n$ conflicting chain is any containing $\neg A_i$, for some $1 \leq i \leq n$.
9. Governatori et al. (2007) propose a more fine grained classification of obligations. Accordingly it is possible to have obligations that are discharged when are violated, as well as obligations that persist in case of a violation. The above algorithm can be easily modified to deal with the different types of obligations examined by Governatori et al. (2007).
10. What about a situation where after task F we have a task producing the annotation *approveManager*(x) but no task with effect *positiveBalance*(x)? Is the resulting process compliant? In this case we the reparation of the violation, but not the violation. The issue here is that we could have that a sanction is enforced before the violation the sanction was supposed to compensate occurred. Thus we are in a situation similar to that described in footnote 9 where the way to address the issue depends on the types of the obligations we have to deal with. Anyway, (i) it is easy to modify algorithm *CheckCompliance* to account for this type of cases, (ii) if one accepts pre-emptive reparations one can change the definition that classifies a process as compliant by replacing the condition that *Unfulfilled* $= \varnothing$ with the condition: let S be the set of effects for the end task of a process, $\forall[T, R, OA_1 \otimes \cdots \otimes OA_n] \in Unfulfilled$, $\exists A_i \in S$

Section VI

Improving Business Processes

Chapter XXI
Business Process Intelligence

M. Castellanos
Hewlett-Packard Laboratories, USA

A. K. Alves de Medeiros
Eindhoven University of Technology, The Netherlands

J. Mendling
Queensland University of Technology, Australia

B. Weber
University of Innsbruck, Austria

A. J. M. M. Weijters
Eindhoven University of Technology, The Netherlands

ABSTRACT

Business Process Intelligence (BPI) is an emerging area that is getting increasingly popular for enterprises. The need to improve business process efficiency, to react quickly to changes and to meet regulatory compliance is among the main drivers for BPI. BPI refers to the application of Business Intelligence techniques to business processes and comprises a large range of application areas spanning from process monitoring and analysis to process discovery, conformance checking, prediction and optimization. This chapter provides an introductory overview of BPI and its application areas and delivers an understanding of how to apply BPI in one's own setting. In particular, it shows how process mining techniques such as process discovery and conformance checking can be used to support process modeling and process redesign. In addition, it illustrates how processes can be improved and optimized over time using analytics for explanation, prediction, optimization and what-if-analysis. Throughout the chapter, a strong emphasis is given to describe tools that use these techniques to support BPI. Finally, major challenges for applying BPI in practice and future trends are discussed.

1. INTRODUCTION

Business Process Intelligence (BPI) refers to the application of Business Intelligence (BI) techniques to business processes (Grigori et al., 2004). In this context, BI refers to technologies, applications, and practices for the collection, integration, analysis, and presentation of business information and also sometimes to the information itself. The purpose of BI is to support better business decision making (Power 2007). The data source for BI is a so-called data warehouse, i.e., a special data base where an organization stores important historical data. Most of the time the data is collected from different information systems as used in an organization. Data analysis and data mining can be performed using this data. The goal is to translate the data to useful business information that can support the decision making process of the organization. If the data warehouse also contains information about the processes within an organization it is called a process data warehouse (Casati at al., 2007) and can be used as source for BPI analysis.

BPI is an emerging area, that is quickly gaining interest due to the increasing pressure companies are facing to improve the efficiency of their business processes and to quickly react to market changes in order to be competitive in this highly dynamic Internet era. In addition, the need to meet regulatory compliance has recently strengthened this trend (e.g., Sarbanes-Oxley (Sarbanes-Oxley Act 2002)). The large number of buzzwords like Business Activity Monitoring (BAM), Business Operations Management (BOM), Business Process Intelligence (BPI), Process Mining, and Business Operations Intelligence (BOI) is a good indication of the interest of vendors to monitor and analyze business activities to gain insight into the operation of their business and ultimately on their effect on the business goals. In the past the focus of workflow tools has been mostly on process modeling and automation. However, today most vendors of business process management (BPM) suites have extended their portfolio with BPI functionality (e.g., IBM, SAP, Tibco, Oracle, Pallas Athena, Lombardi, webMethods).

Process-aware information systems (PAIS) such as WFM, ERP, SCM and CRM systems are recording business events occurring during process execution in event logs (Dumas et al., 2005). Typically, event logs contain information about start and completion of activities and the resources that executed them. In many cases relevant data (like the values of data fields linked to tasks) is recorded too. Sometimes, there is no, or only a very primitive process model available. However, in many situations it is possible to gather information about the processes as they take place. For instance, in many hospitals, information about the different treatments of a patient are registered (date, time, treatment, medical staff) for reasons like financial administration. This kind of information in combination with appropriate (mining) techniques can also be used to get more insight in the health care process.

BPI exploits this process information by providing the means for analyzing it to give companies a better understanding of how their business processes are actually executed. It supplies support in the discovery of malfunctions and bottlenecks and helps identifying their causes. Therefore, BPI often triggers process improvement or reengineering efforts. BPI not only serves as a tool for improving business processes performance, but also fosters changes by facilitating decision-making. In addition, BPI is used to monitor the alignment of operational business processes with strategic business goals and to give the visibility that regulatory compliance requires. Furthermore, BPI is not restricted to the analysis of historical data, but can also be used to optimize future efforts (e.g., through predicting future problems). To provide for the above, BPI comprises several application areas, which are detailed in the following.

Process analysis: Refers to the analysis of past and sometimes even current process executions. Process analysis can lead to different kinds of models: explanatory, prognosis and decision models. On the explanatory category, process analysis is helpful for business analysts to find correlations between different workflow aspects and performance metrics (e.g., unproportionally high cost occurs whenever goods are shipped to a particular country). In addition, analysts are supported in identifying the causes of malfunctions or bottlenecks (e.g., waiting times at first level customer support result in costly service level agreement violations). These explanatory models help in identifying opportunities for process **optimization** (Castellanos et al., 2005a) whose aim is the generation of decision models that optimize some aspect(s) of the operation of a process. For example, optimizations may include changes in the sizing of resource pools or resource assignment rules. In addition to the analysis of historical data to understand past process behavior (explanatory models) and the identification of opportunities for process optimization (decision models), BPI also aims at building prognosis (a.k.a. prediction) models by **predicting** critical situations and undesired behavior (e.g., exceptional situations or delays on a running process instance that bear the risk of an SLA violation). This enables companies to either prevent the occurrence (or at least minimize the damage) of these critical situations by taking corrective actions proactively, or prepare a plan for handle them after they occur.

Process discovery: Refers to the analysis of business events recorded in event logs to discover process, control, data, organizational, and social structures (Aalst et al., 2007b). Like process analysis, process discovery allows users to gain insight into their operations and can be the first step when implementing business processes with a workflow tool. While process analysis primarily focuses on the analysis of business processes in respect to performance metrics, process discovery aims at constructing process models from historical data. This information can be used together with performance metrics to identify malfunctions or bottlenecks.

Process monitoring: Refers to the monitoring of running process instances (e.g., their progress, bottlenecks and times spent in each activity) and their analysis results (e.g., percentage of instances not completing successfully) to inform users about unusual or undesired situations (i.e., alerts) (Grigori et al., 2004). Process dashboards or reporting features provide information about process performance characteristics like average cycle time or number of processes not meeting a Service Level Agreement (SLA). For example, notifications are automatically sent to individuals if critical events can be detected, enabling them to take immediate action (e.g., process instances with long cycle time raise the likelihood of SLA violation).

Conformance checking: While process monitoring analyses running process instances, conformance checking can be applied to analyze whether a log conforms to a process model and to identify undesired behavior a-posteriori (Rozinat and Aalst, 2008). For instance, (Aalst and de Medeiros, 2005) describes the application of conformance checking to detect security violations (e.g., violations of the separation-of-duty principle) in event logs.

Although the application of business process intelligence can provide companies with substantial benefits and case studies like (Aalst et al., 2007b) clearly show that these techniques have gained a level of maturity that makes them applicable to real-world business processes, the practical use of BPI is still limited. Companies are facing several challenges when applying BPI, and these need to be solved in a practical way before BPI will become mainstream.

In this chapter we first describe the process mining techniques that aid the modeling of business process (cf. Section 2). Then an overview on process optimization including analytics for explanation and prediction, business impact analysis and resource allocation is presented (cf. Section 3). Major challenges for applying BPI in practice are discussed briefly (cf. Section 4).

Finally, a conclusion and an outlook close the chapter (cf. Section 5).

2. PROCESS MINING FOR MODELING

Process mining targets the discovery of information based on an event log. As explained in Section 1, nowadays organizations usually are able to register in some log what events have being carried out during the execution of their business processes. Such logs are the starting point of process mining techniques. These techniques assume event logs to minimally contain data about (i) which events belong to the execution of a same process instance and (ii) the ordering of execution for these events. Additionally, some process mining techniques also require data about the event timestamps, performers and data fields. In general, the more information a log contains, the more different process mining techniques can be used.

The analysis provided by current process mining techniques can be seen as from three types: *discovery*, *conformance* and *extensions* (cf. Figure 1). The techniques that focus on *discovery* mine information based on data in an event log only. This means that these techniques do not assume the existence of pre-defined models to describe aspect of processes in the organization. Examples of such techniques are *control-flow mining* algorithms (Aalst et al., 2004, Cook et al., 2004, de Medeiros, 2006, de Medeiros et al., 2007b, Dongen, 2007, Dongen and van der Aalst, 2005, Greco et al., 2006, 2007, Günther and van der Aalst, 2007, Herbst and Karagiannis, 2004, Pinter and Golani, 2004, Schimm, 2004, Wen et al., 2007) that extract a process model based on the dependency relations that can be inferred among the tasks in the log. Another example are social network mining algorithms (Aalst et al., 2005b, Ly et al., 2005) that discover the relations between the performers of certain tasks, like a graph that shows who is handing over work to whom. The algorithms for *conformance* verify if

Figure 1. Perspectives on process mining

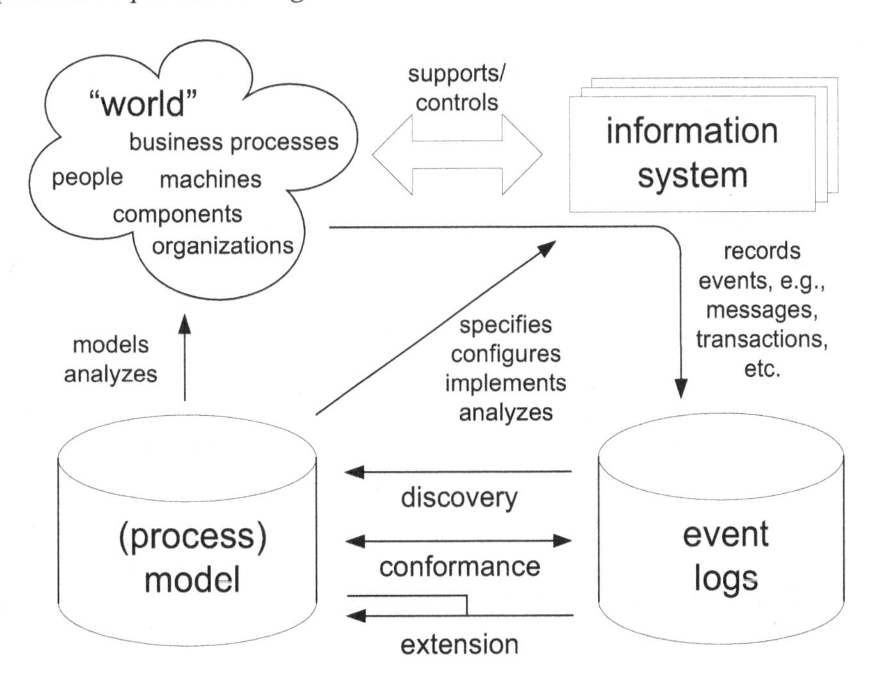

the executions registered in logs follow *prescribed* behaviors and/or rules. Therefore, besides a log, such algorithms also receive as input a model that captures the desired property or behavior to check. Examples are the algorithms that assess how much the behavior expressed in a log matches the behavior defined in a model and points out the differences (Rozinat and Aalst, 2008), and algorithms used for auditing of logs (in this case, the model is the property to be verified) (Aalst et al., 2005a). The *extension* algorithms enhance existing models based on information discovered in event logs. Examples include algorithms that automatically discover business rules for the choices in a given model (Rozinat and van der Aalst, 2006).

The remainder of this section describes the *main process mining techniques that aid the modeling of business process.* Other than providing details of given techniques, we focus on *giving an overview of the possibilities and indicating pointers* where the reader can find more details. The descriptions are based on a running example inspired in a real-life situation (cf. Section 2.1). Relevant discovery, conformance and extension techniques are respectively introduced in Sections 2.2, 2.3 and 2.4. All the illustrated techniques (and many other techniques) are implemented in the process mining tool ProM, an open-source tool available at *www.processmining.org.*

2.1 Running Example

The running example is inspired on processes of the Dutch rental housing organizations. These organizations rent houses at cheaper prices than in the private sector. They have many processes, like registration, personal information update, complaints handling, etc. In this section we will focus on the *process to handle requests (or complaints) for house repairs.* The process starts when a tenant contacts the company to file a complaint. If the complaint indeed involves a repair in the house, a ticket is created and an appointment is made to inspect the house such that the actual problem can be detected/confirmed. Additionally, the inspector estimates how much time will be needed to fix the problem. Easy fixes are usually performed together with the inspection. More complicated fixes require a new appointment and can be performed by an internal or external team. When the repair has been performed, the client is informed and the ticket number is communicated to the financial administration so that they can take care of the payment to the appropriate institutions. The process completes whenever the payment is in place.

The next sections show how a designer could use process mining techniques to get more insight about how complaints are actually handled. The results are based on a simulated event log for the running example.

2.2 Discovery Techniques

When (re-)designing business processes models, two aspects are particularly relevant: the *control-flow structure* (i.e., which tasks precede/follow others and how frequently) and the *organizational structure* (i.e., which teams/roles perform which tasks and how they cooperate). These two structures are important because they define the core elements necessary to execute business processes.

Current *discovery* process mining techniques mine information that helps in modeling both the control-flow and the organizational structure. For instance, have a look at figures 2, 3 and 4. Figure 2 shows the EPC (Event-Driven Process Chain) (Keller et al., 1992) model for an event log of our running example. The mined EPC is shown on the right pane. Note that this discovered model, which captures the control-flow structure of the process in our running example, is a very good starting point for the designer because it objectively summarizes the *real behavior* during process execution (as registered in a log). For instance, by looking at the selected part of the mined model (cf. left pane), it is possible to see that, according to the registered behavior, (i) the tasks `SendTicketToFinAdmin` and `ReadyInformClient` can be executed in any order after the task `Repair Ready` has being completed, and (ii) the two branches containing the respective tasks `TicketReady` and `InformClientWrongPlace` are alternative ones. In a similar way, figures 3 and 4 illustrate how the designer can respectively get feedback about how people are cooperating in the organization and possible roles for tasks. The works in (Aalst

Figure 2. Screenshot containing the result of the ***Multi-phase Macro*** *plug-in for a log of the running example*

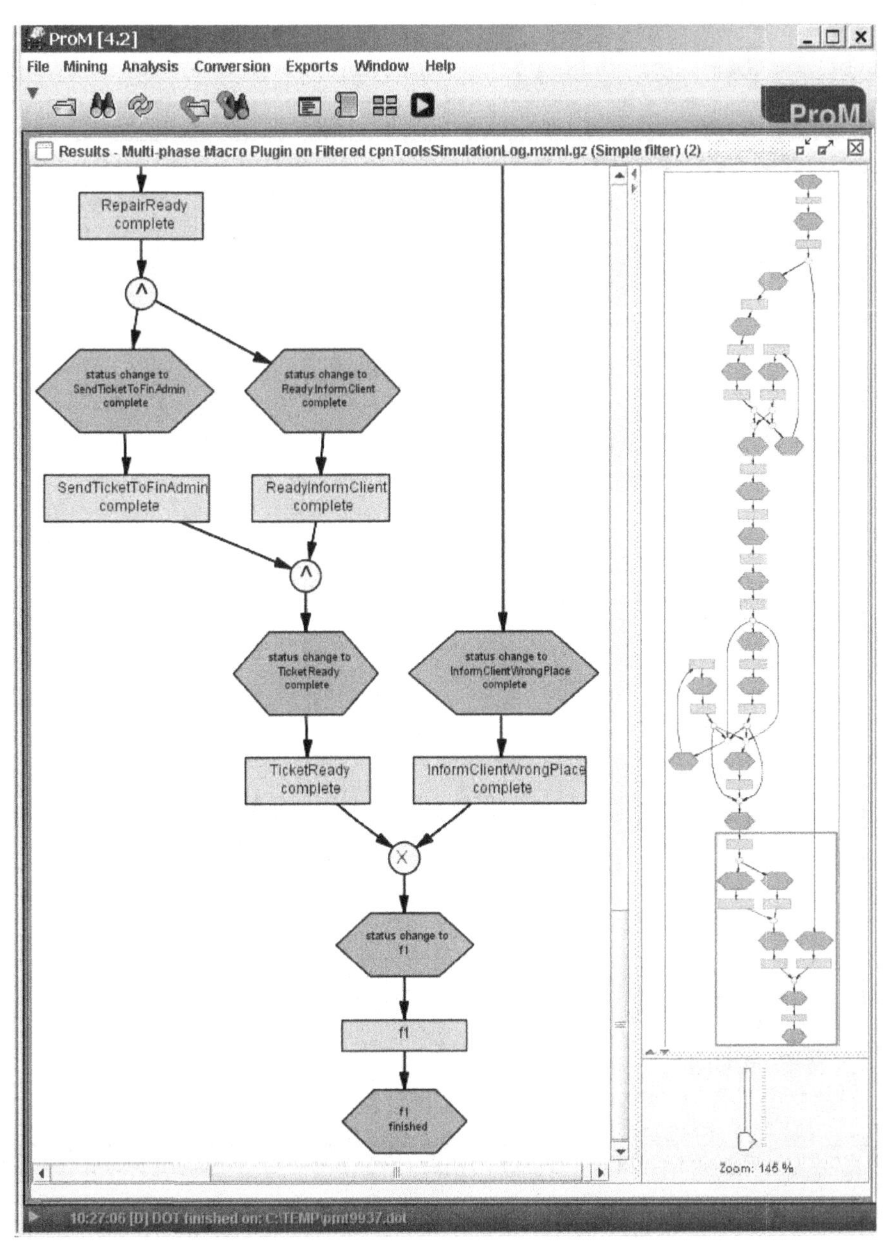

*Figure 3. Screenshot showing the **Analyze Social Network** plug-in in action. The illustrated social network presents the mined handover of work for a log of the running example. Every circle represents a performer (or user). The area of a circle (or "Vertex Size") indicates how often users execute tasks, the stretching direction of a node (horizontally or vertically) indicates the relation between its in (receiving work) and out (handing over) degrees. For instance, note that some performers (like "System") collaborate with many others, while others (like "Monica" and "Dian") collaborate with fewer ones. Furthermore, some users never hand over work (like the external repair companies "DoIt" and "FixIt"). Graphs like this one give the designer insights about how people work together and who are the team players in the organization. This may be useful feedback when defining the scheduling for the distribution of work.*

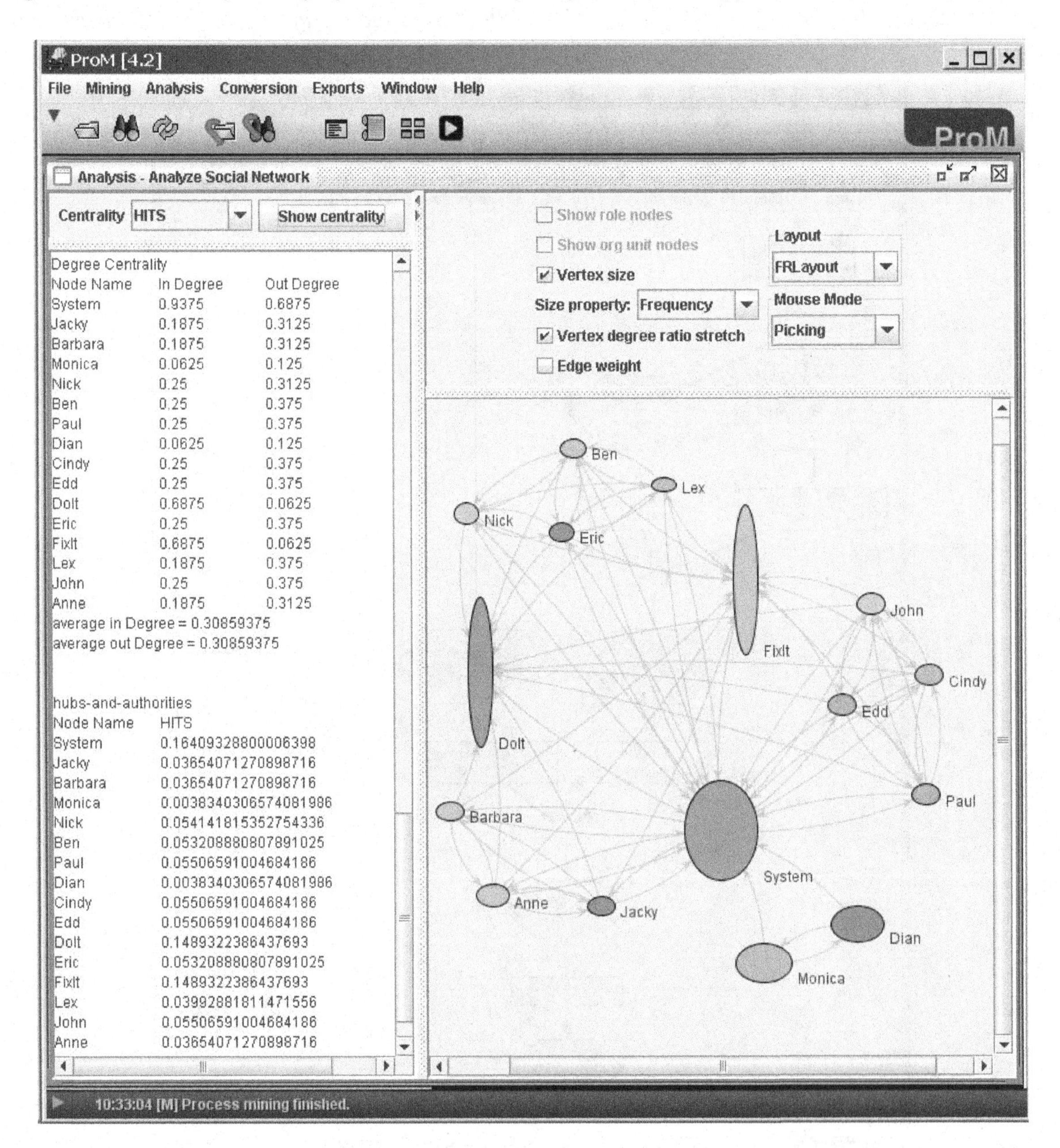

*Figure 4. Screenshot with the result of the plug-in **Organizational Miner**. In this case, four roles have been automatically discovered containing the following users: (a) "System", (c) "Dian" and "Monica" (i.e. front office employees), (d) "FixIt" and "DoIt"' (i.e. external repair companies), and (b) the remaining users (i.e. the technical employees). Note that each mined role relates users to tasks. For instance, the role in the left-pane refers to the task* **ExternRepair.**

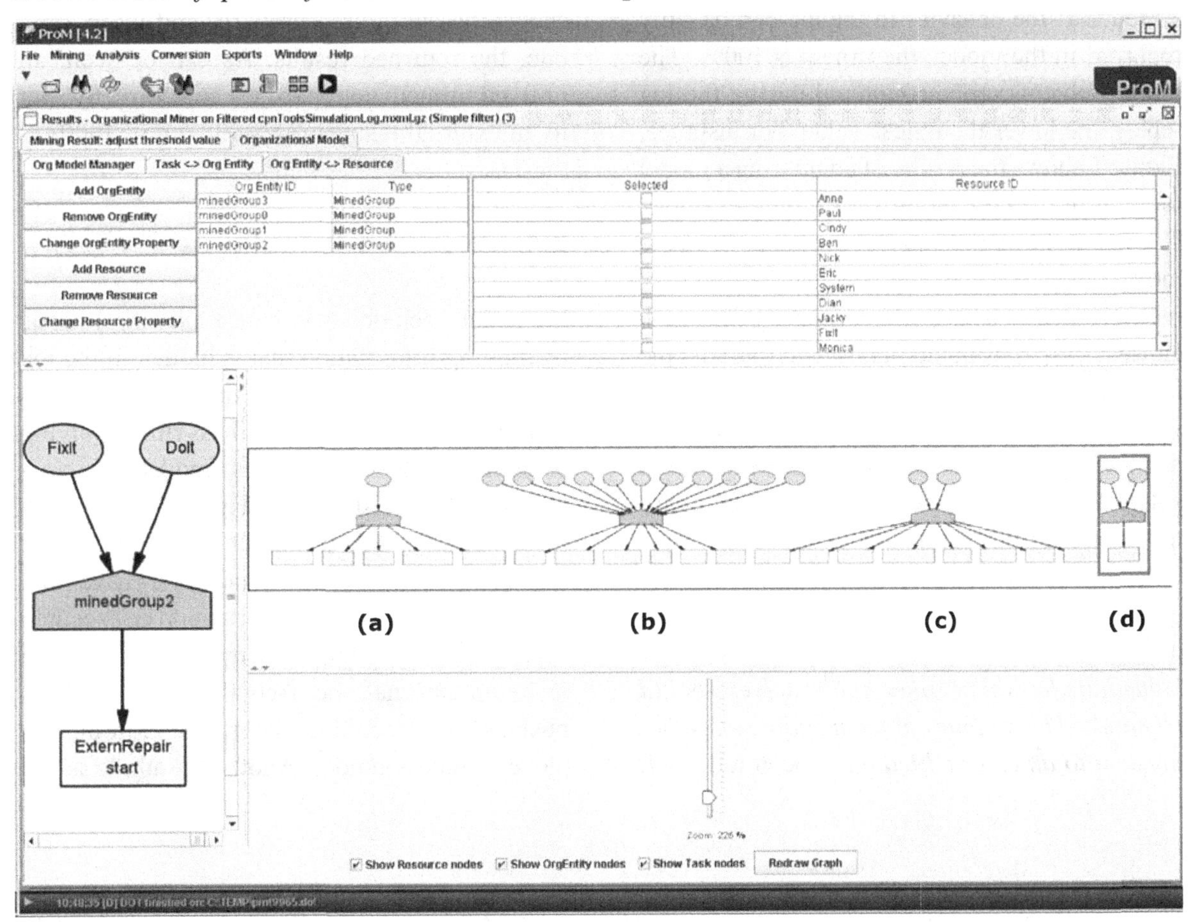

et al., 2004, Cook et al., 2004, de Medeiros, 2006, de Medeiros et al., 2007b, Dongen, 2007, Dongen and van der Aalst, 2005, Greco et al., 2006, 2007, Günther and van der Aalst, 2007, Herbst and Karagiannis, 2004, Pinter and Golani, 2004, Schimm, 2004, Wen et al., 2007) provide details of different existing control-flow mining techniques. For organizational related techniques, the reader is referred to (Aalst et al., 2005b, Song and van der Aalst, 2007).

2.3 Conformance Techniques

The conformance techniques compare the behavior expressed in models with the one registered in logs. They are useful to check compliance in companies. In a nutshell, conformance techniques focus on two aspects: (i) assessing how much a log matches a model and highlighting the points of discrepancy, like the Conformance Checker (Rozinat and Aalst, 2008), and (ii) verifying if certain properties hold in a log, like the LTL Checker[1] (Aalst et al., 2005a).

Conformance Checker is helpful when comparing prescribed behavior with enacted one. The technique basically measure how much a log fits a model. If the behavior in the log can be fully replayed in the model, the fitness is 100%. The more problems are encountered during the log replay, the lower the fitness value. For instance, Figure 5 shows the results of comparing a model to a log in the context of our running example. The result shows that most of the behavior in the model (about 94%, as indicated by the "Fitness" metric) matches what has been actually executed. However, there are points of mismatch because the model defines that the task InformClientSurvey should happen between the tasks ArrangeSuvey and Survey, but this task has not been executed a single time in the log (see value "0" in the input/output arcs of this task).

LTL Checker is mainly used for auditing purposes. For instance, in the setting of our running example one could inspect if the rule that *immediate fixes that could not be solved should be handled by an internal team again before being sent to an external team* has been followed. Figure 6 shows the result of verifying this property for a given log. In this case, the traces in the log have been pre-processed to keep only the tasks `ImmediateRepair`, `InternRepair`, and `ExternRepair`. The top window in this figure shows the configured property and the bottom one, the returned results. As can be seen, an unfixed immediate repair has been directly sent to an external team in 3.8% (38 out of 1000) of the cases.

2.4 Extension Techniques

Extension techniques enhance existing models by making information that is hidden in the log explicit. A good example is the process mining technique that mines the business rules applying to points of choice in process models (Rozinat and van der Aalst, 2006). Figure 7 shows the results of using this technique to a model of our running example. Note that three rules have been mined to determine if a repair should be executed during the inspection, later by an internal team or by an external one. Actually, these *de facto* business rules could be incorporated in the deployed process model. Another example is the

*Figure 5. Screenshot showing a result of the **Conformance Checker** plug-in. In this case, the "Model" perspective is being illustrated. The task **`InformClientSurvey`** should happen between the tasks **`ArrangeSuvey`** and **`Survey`**, but this task has not been executed a single time in the log.*

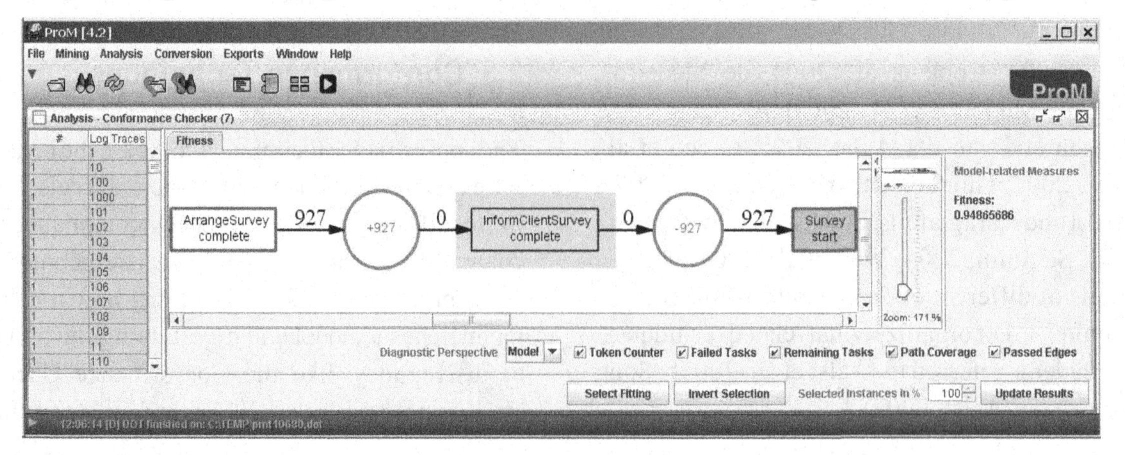

*Figure 6. Screenshot illustrating both interfaces of the **LTL Checker** plug-in. The top window shows the main user interface. The bottom one contains the results of checking the formula "eventually_activity_A_next_B" for a log of the running example*

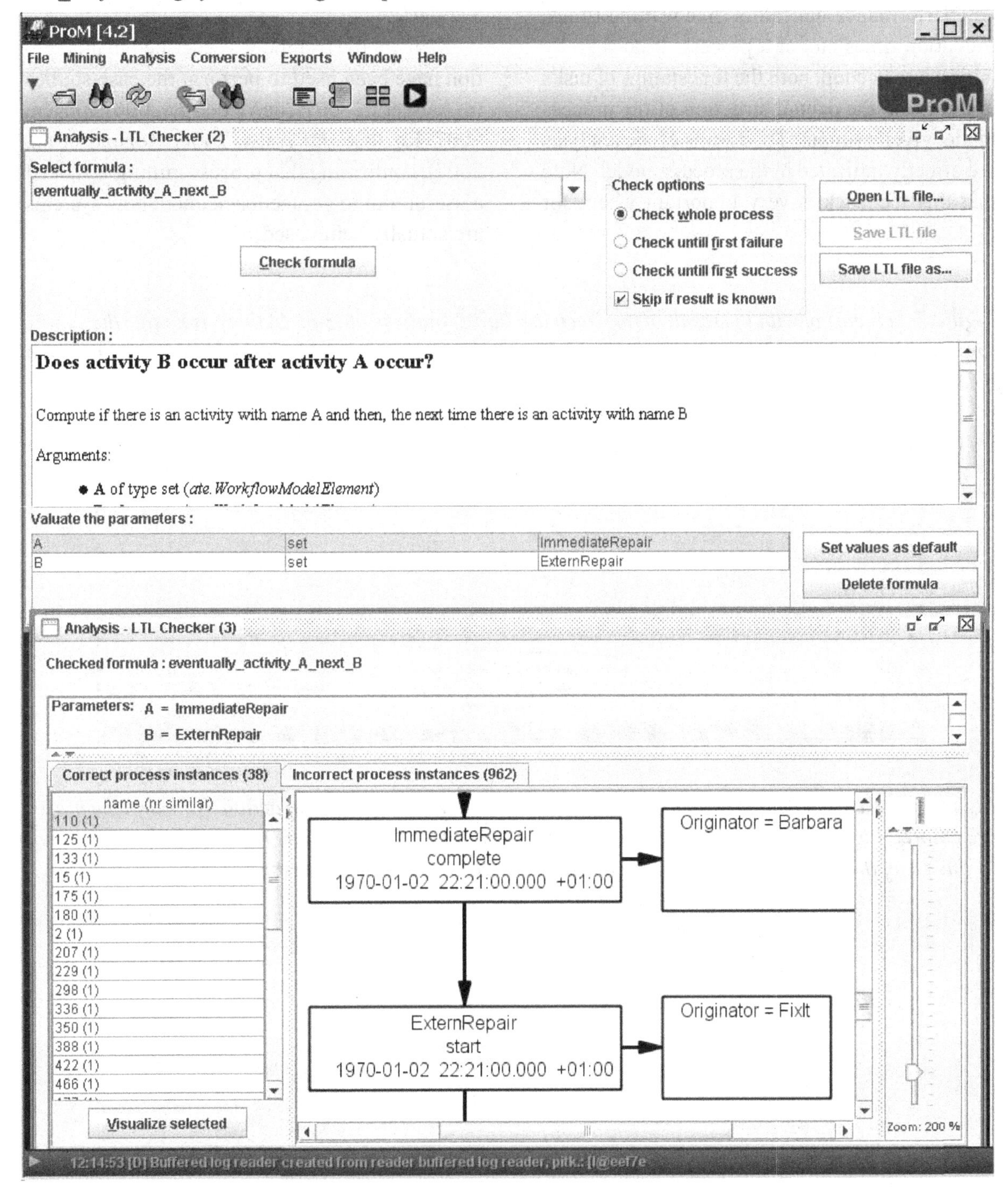

process mining technique that detects bottlenecks in processes (Hornix, 2007). This technique automatically mines upper bounds for different key performance indicators (like waiting times, execution times etc) of a process. It does so by taking into account both the timestamps of tasks in a log and the overall structure of the process model given as input. The results of the analysis are directly indicated in the process model. Note that this feedback is very important when, for instance, trying to optimize throughput times of processes based by re-design. Figure 8 illustrates a bottleneck point for a model of our running example.

Many of the techniques described in this section have been used to perform the case studies in (Aalst et al., 2007a, de Medeiros, 2006, Dongen, 2007, Rozinat and Aalst, 2008, Rozinat et al., 2007), confirming that process mining is indeed a useful tool to get feedback about how systems are actually being used.

Figure 7. Screenshot with the result of the ***Decision Point Analysis*** *plug-in. In this case, after the survey (or inspection) has been completed, a choice is made on how to proceed. The mined rules indicate which fields values determine this choice.*

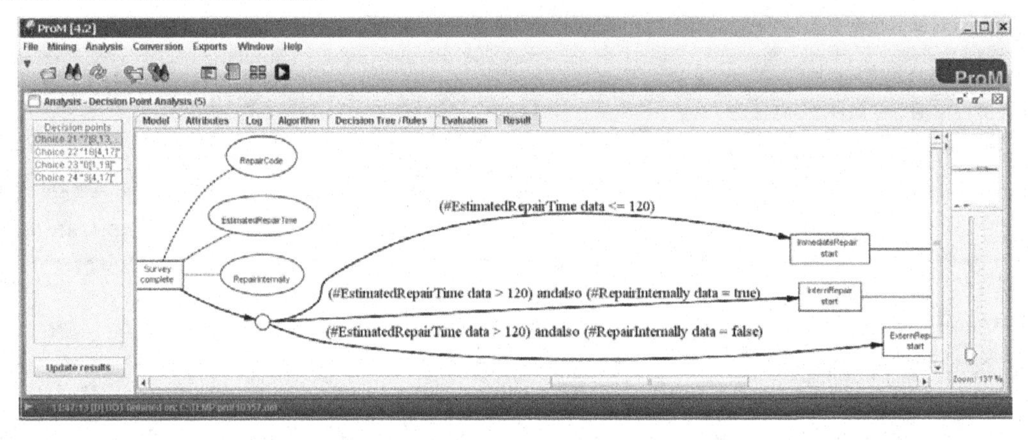

Figure 8. Screenshot of the ***Performance Analysis with Petri Nets*** *plug-in in action. Note that the places are colored based on waiting time thresholds (cf. "Waiting time:" box at the right of the bottom pane). In this case, there is a high waiting time between the tasks* **`InformClientSurvey`** *and* **`Survey`.**

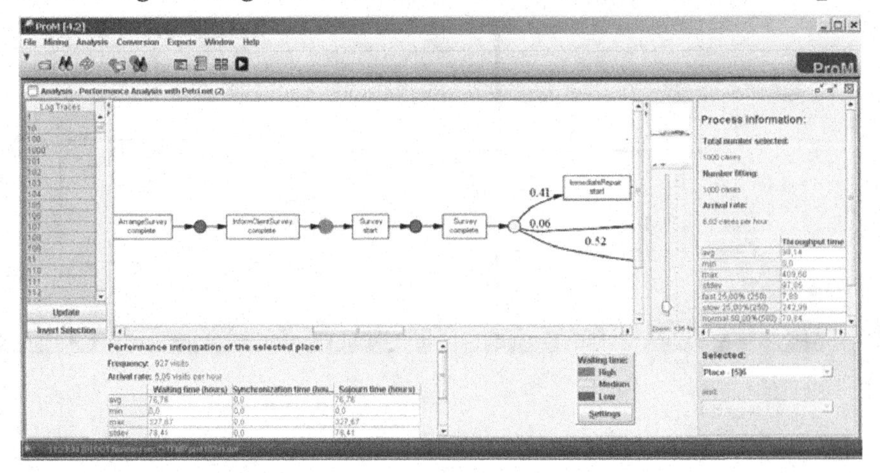

3. PROCESS OPTIMIZATION

In addition to supporting improved modeling (cf. Section 2), Business Process Intelligence also equips companies with functionalities that facilitate the optimization of different quality aspects of their business processes (Casati et al., 2002), either in terms of metrics meaningful to internal operations of the enterprise, or to the external customer perception. Again, process logs are exploited to derive useful information but in this case it is not for modeling purposes, instead it is to compute quality metrics (Casati et al., 2006) and mine process behavior related to them. For example, the performance metric of an order process could be derived from the start and end times of execution of orders processed during a given period of time. By warehousing (Casati et al., 2007) the execution data and the metrics, the business process can be monitored, analyzed and optimized with different kinds of techniques relying on data mining, statistics, simulation, and optimization, among others (Castellanos et al., 2005a, 2005b). There are many opportunities and challenges for analysis and optimization of business processes. Here we give a brief overview of four challenging areas: explanation, also called critical factor analysis (Section 3.1), prediction (Section 3.2), proactive optimization and business impact analysis (Section 3.3), and resource allocation (Section 3.4). The illustrated techniques have been implemented in Business Cockpit, a BPI platform built at HP Labs.

3.1 Critical Factor Analysis

The capability of defining and monitoring metrics (Casati et al., 2006) on a business process can be leveraged by process mining techniques that produce explanatory models to help understand the behavior of a process given by its metrics. In particular, getting insight into the critical factors determining the abnormal behavior of a metric. For example, users may want to know the characteristics of invoices and of the invoice management procedure (the cash out process) that cause a slow execution (*duration* SLA violation). In Figure 9 we observe that when the process (flow) execution starts after 17:30 or when the invoice amount is equal or greater than 10,000 and the

Figure 9. Critical factor tree cash out process duration

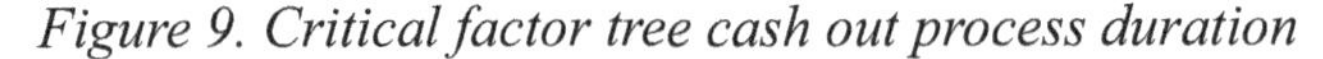

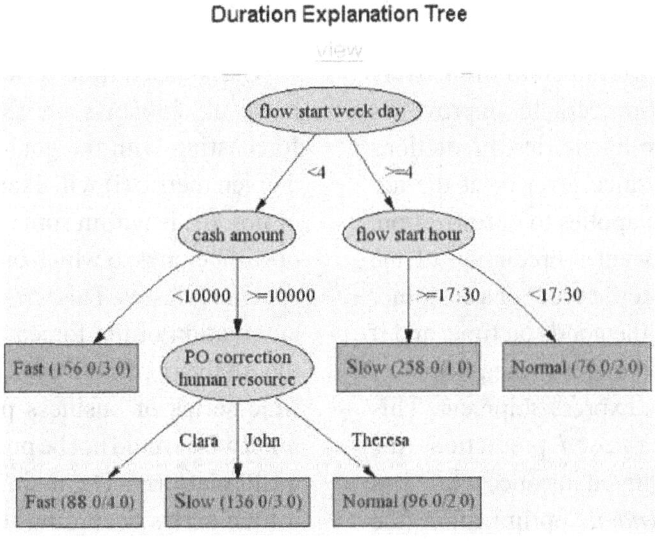

person executing the *purchase order correction* step is John, the process execution is *slow* in general. To obtain this functionality, models are mined as soon as a metric has been defined and computed for all the completed process instances in the process data warehouse[2] (Casati et al., 2007). It is important that the models explaining the critical factors affecting metric behaviors be easily interpretable by the business analysts. In Business Cockpit such models take the form of decision trees (Figure 9) that are automatically mined from process execution data labeled with classes corresponding to metric values (e.g., *slow, normal, fast*). To this end, a solution for each step of the data mining lifecycle had to be tailored to business processes and built into the engine. This analysis functionality is readily available to the users without requiring them to write any code. This implied a compromise between generality and ease of use on one hand, and accuracy on the other. The reader is referred to (Castellanos et al., 2005b) and (Grigori et al., 2004) for further details.

3.2 Prediction

Monitoring and explanations on metric values provide valuable visibility into current and past behavior of business processes but equally important is to provide visibility into future behavior. The ability to predict metrics and performance indicators gives the opportunity to proactively optimize the business process to improve its behavior with respect to its metrics. Predictions can be done at the instance level or at the aggregate level. The same applies to optimization. For example, we may want a prediction of the duration metric for a specific order of a customer to see if we will deliver the goods on time, and if not then we may want to increase the priority of the order so that it uses express shipment. This is referred as *instance-based* prediction (the prediction is done for a given instance while it is being executed) and *dynamic* optimization (the optimization is done during the instance execution), respectively. Instead, we may want to know if the average duration of orders on a certain day of next week will exceed the promised 24 hours delivery time (SLA violation) to plan for extra resources if needed. This type of prediction is referred to as *class-based* time series prediction (prediction ofan aggregatedmetric value and its class) and *static* optimization (the corresponding process instances have not started execution yet) is applied in this case (Castellanos et al., 2005c). While the first kind of prediction (i.e., instance-based), as its name suggests, is based on the instance properties (e.g., day of the week that the order was submitted, type of product, region, etc), the second one is based on the time series of previous values of the metric. In consequence, suitable techniques for instance-based prediction belong to data mining, while a relaxed form of time series forecasting is used for the second one (Castellanos et al., 2005c).

In instance-based prediction (Grigori et al., 2004) a model is generated from patterns mined from execution and business data associated to process instances. For example, a pattern may indicate that if an order was received on a Friday afternoon and step *check inventory* is performed by server S3, there is an 85% chance that the order won't get shipped in less than 24 hours. Figure 10 shows the display of predictions for instances of a process on the Business Cockpit platform.

Class-based time series prediction (Castellanos et al., 2005c) is a relaxed form of time series forecasting with the goal of predicting whether a given metric (i) will exceed a certain threshold or not, (ii) is within some specified range or not, or (iii) belongs to which one of a small number of specified classes. This relaxation enables complete automation of the forecasting process to enable the analysis of hundreds or even thousands or time series of business process metrics which otherwise would not be possible to incorporate in a BPI platform. The main idea is to characterize a time series according to its components (i.e.,

Figure 10. Screenshot of predictions for violation of wait time to Audit step for active cash out process instances

Metric: Wait time to audit

Number of Predictions 3363

Next Page Previous Reset

Instance ID	Current Active Node	Starting Time	Prediction	Confidence
26-1-1-11262	Vendor_mantainance	1/17/04 6:36 AM	Acceptable	0.90
26-1-1-1272	Vendor_mantainance	1/17/04 6:38 AM	Acceptable	0.97
26-1-1-1274	Vendor_mantainance	1/17/04 6:41 AM	Unacceptable	0.71
26-1-1-1274	Vendor_mantainance	1/17/04 6:44 AM	Acceptable	0.79
26-1-1-1275	Vendor_mantainance	1/17/04 6:47 AM	Unacceptable	0.70
26-1-1-1279	Vendor_mantainance	1/17/04 6:50 AM	Unacceptable	0.78
26-1-1-1281	Vendor_mantainance	1/17/04 6:53 AM	Acceptable	0.80
26-1-1-1287	Vendor_mantainance	1/17/04 6:56 AM	Unacceptable	0.70
26-1-1-1289	Vendor_mantainance	1/17/04 6:59 AM	Acceptable	0.97
26-1-1-1292	Vendor_mantainance	1/17/04 7:01 AM	Unacceptable	0.99
26-1-1-1294	Vendor_mantainance	1/17/04 7:04 AM	Acceptable	0.82
26-1-1-1297	Vendor_mantainance	1/17/04 7:07 AM	Acceptable	0.84
26-1-1-1299	Vendor_mantainance	1/17/04 7:10 AM	Acceptable	0.95
26-1-1-1301	Vendor_mantainance	1/17/04 7:13 AM	Unacceptable	0.88
26-1-1-1303	Vendor_mantainance	1/17/04 7:16 AM	Acceptable	0.99
26-1-1-1305	Vendor_mantainance	1/17/04 7:19 AM	Acceptable	0.95
26-1-1-1306	Vendor_mantainance	1/17/04 7:22 AM	Acceptable	0.71
26-1-1-1316	Vendor_mantainance	1/17/04 7:24 AM	Unacceptable	0.71
26-1-1-1317	Vendor_mantainance	1/17/04 7:27 AM	Acceptable	0.92

trend and seasonality) and then apply the most appropriate technique(s) to create a good forecasting model (Castellanos et al., 2005d). Once the model is created it can be applied to obtain a numeric prediction which is mapped to the corresponding class (e.g., exceeds-threshold or not, within-range or not, low/medium/high, or others).

Once a prediction is obtained different actions can be taken to optimize the process to improve the predicted value. When the prediction is made for a specific instance, it is possible to dynamically change things that only affect that instance to improve its execution. Typical actions are to assign a specific resource for a given action, change the priority of the instance, or dynamically change a selected path. In contrast, when the prediction is made for an aggregated metric, the optimization is static in the sense that it changes aspects of the process that are common to all its instances, like the number of resources of a given type that are allocated to a process (cf. Section 3.4). As stated above, prediction opens up the opportunity to proactively optimize aspects of a process upon the alert of undesired predicted values. Furthermore, prediction also proves helpful to business impact analysis (cf. Section 3.3).

3.3 Business Impact Analysis

Business managers need support to assess the impact of malfunctions in the Information Technology (IT) infrastructure in high level business terms. Business Cockpit provides functionality to analyze the impact on business goals (expressed as process metrics) caused by performance degradations in the IT infrastructure. The idea is to leverage the linkage information between the IT and the business layers (part of a process model defined on Business Cockpit), the IT resource monitoring functionality (provided by some infrastructure monitoring tool), and the prediction functionality (cf. Section 3.2). As a failure or degradation in an IT resource is detected, the linkage information is used to identify which nodes (i.e., process steps) and consequently which processes are affected by the failure. For example, the link established between an Oracle database server and the *invoice validation* step of the cash out process makes it possible to identify this step (i.e., node) and this process as the ones affected when the server fails. Moreover, not only the impact of a resource failure can be done at the type process level, but also at the process instance level to indicate which active instances are or will be affected by the failure. Prediction models (cf. Section 3.2) are obtained beforehand to determine whether a node supported by the resource that has failed will be executed or not and whether the time interval to get to the node is larger than the average time that the resource linked to that node takes to recover from a failure. Upon a failure, the appropriate models are applied and if both predictions are positive and with high confidence values (i.e., most likely the process instance will execute that node and will do it before the resource failure is fixed), then the process instance is predicted to be affected by the failure. A confidence value for this prediction is computed as a function of the confidence of both predictions.

3.4 Resource Allocation

The allocation of resources to tasks can significantly affect the performance and outcome of the business processes, which in turn affects the quality of services and products of an enterprise. Identification of bottlenecks in a business process and proper allocation of resources to critical tasks can help a business meet the deadlines and SLA terms while delivering services and products at a desired quality. Business process simulation tools are used for analyzing the behavior of resources and their effect on the overall performance and outcome of processes. In particular, sensitivity analysis (what-if analysis) (Castellanos et al., 2005b) allows users to analyze outcomes of various simulated scenarios in which the effect of different parameter settings can be observed. For example, the effect of assigning two resources to a particular task, instead of only one, to know how much benefit such an additional resource allocation could bring. Possible parameters for simulation and sensitivity analysis could be not only resource pool sizes for individual tasks, but also inter-arrival rate of entities to be processed, resource behavior (response time to particular tasks), and cost of individual resources (per unit time or total).

Companies are interested not only in understanding the effect of changes in a business process but also in determining the best possible (optimal) allocation of resources in order to achieve certain performance and quality goals. Simulation leveraged with a search technique offers the solution in Business Cockpit (Castellanos et al., 2005b). Here, the objective is (i) to minimize the number of process instances that exceed a certain metric threshold (e.g., the number of invoice payments that are delayed more than 3 days) or (ii) to minimize or maximize the overall value of a given metric (e.g., minimize the average duration of processing an order). The objective is subject to constraints on the cost, other metric values and maximum number of resource elements for one or more resource pools.

Figure 11 shows an example where the goal is to determine the optimal number (within a range) of resources in the pools to minimize the average value of the metric "Wait time to Audit". A simulation is run for a possible configuration of resource allocation and the resulting simulation execution data are transformed and loaded into the simulation results database so that metric values can be computed on them (just as for execution data of actual processes). These values determine which configuration from the search space to try next. This continues until (i) adding or removing a resource to any pool does not improve the goal, or (ii) a maximum number of simulations is reached. At the end of the process, the best configuration is presented to the user, along with the values reached for the objective and constraint metrics. Other configurations are also presented,

Figure 11. Wait Time to Audit metric optimization

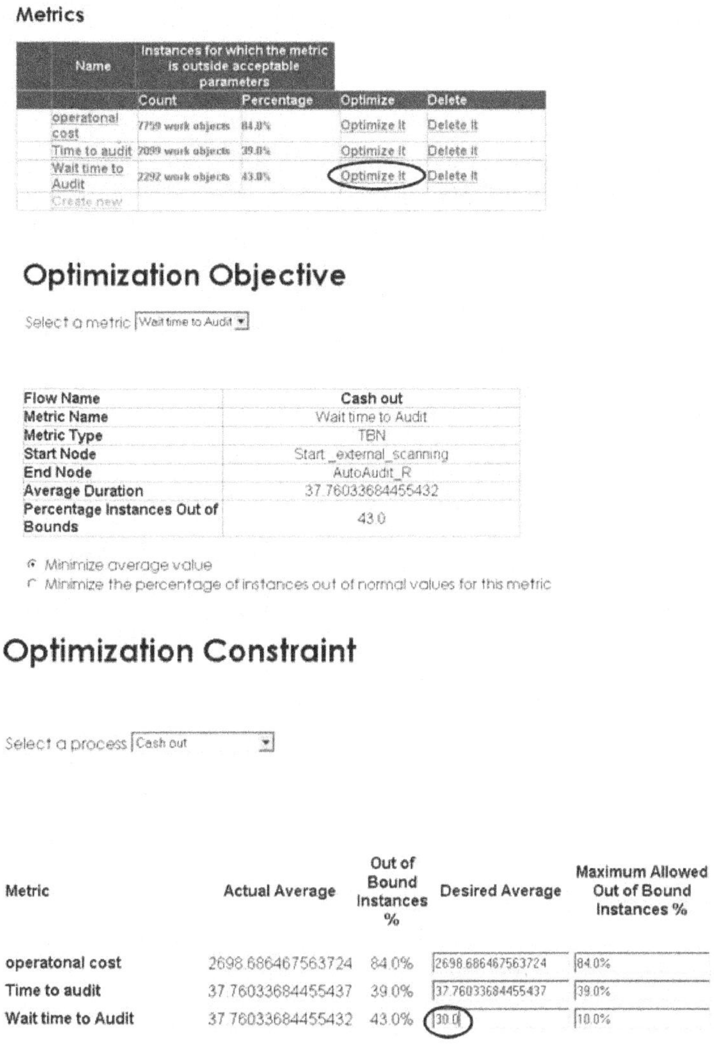

Metrics

Name	Instances for which the metric is outside acceptable parameters			
	Count	Percentage	Optimize	Delete
operatonal cost	7759 work objects	84.0%	Optimize It	Delete It
Time to audit	2099 work objects	39.0%	Optimize It	Delete It
Wait time to Audit	2292 work objects	43.0%	Optimize It	Delete It
Create new				

Optimization Objective

Select a metric Wait time to Audit

Flow Name	Cash out
Metric Name	Wait time to Audit
Metric Type	TBN
Start Node	Start _external_scanning
End Node	AutoAudit_R
Average Duration	37.76033684455432
Percentage Instances Out of Bounds	43.0

Minimize average value

Minimize the percentage of instances out of normal values for this metric

Optimization Constraint

Select a process Cash out

Metric	Actual Average	Out of Bound Instances %	Desired Average	Maximum Allowed Out of Bound Instances %
operatonal cost	2698.686467563724	84.0%	2698.686467563724	84.0%
Time to audit	37.76033684455437	39.0%	37.76033684455437	39.0%
Wait time to Audit	37.76033684455432	43.0%	30.0	10.0%

ranked by their objective metric value, for users to examine them. Figure 12 shows the results for the optimization request in Figure 11.

Finally, it is also important to automatically identify the resources that perform poorly in certain contexts. Data mining, and in particular classification algorithms, can be used for this purpose (cf. Section 3.1).

4. PRACTICAL CHALLENGES AND FUTURE TRENDS

The analysis of business processes with business process intelligence techniques and tools faces several challenges in practice. In this section, we focus in particular on three types of challenges: technical challenges (Section 4.1), interpretative challenges (Section 4.2), and pragmatic challenges (Section 4.3). These challenges have to be ad-

Figure 12. Optimal number of resources to minimize the Wait time to Audit metric average value

Optimal configuration

Optimization Requirement	Best Value	Desired
Objective metric value	29	30
Cost	2967	3000
Percentage of instances satisfying the optimization criteria	91	90

Resource Pool	Number of Units Required
Scan Assistant	3
Auditor	5

Detailed flow analysis for this configuration

Objective metric values achieved by other configurations

configuration #2	31
configuration #3	34

dressed with care in order to apply BPI successfully in an organization, and they are related to the challenges identified by the CRIPS-DM process which is an acronym for Cross Industry Standard Process for Data Mining (Shearer 2000). Finally, we discuss some future trends (Section 4.4).

4.1 Technical Challenges

Business process intelligence initiatives face several technical challenges, and some of them are analogous to data warehouse challenges (Brackett, 1996). Most importantly, business process intelligence has to cope with the *heterogeneous systems landscape* of large enterprises. While process discovery tools can be rather easily used on log data of business processes that are executed by a single workflow system (Aalst et al., 2007b), it becomes already difficult to project transactional log data of a single ERP system such as SAP back to high-level business events (Ingvaldsen and Gulla, 2008). Even worse, business systems, for instance, in some financial institutions have been growing over 40 years and contain diverse technologies and systems ranging from classical mainframe systems to message-oriented middleware and from implementation languages such as ancient COBOL to modern object-oriented .NET. The case of a German bank reported in (Genrich et al., 2008) summarizes some of the problems for business process intelligence associated with this systems heterogeneity. Beyond the diversity and sheer complexity of its applications, most of its applications were not developed with process-orientation in mind. This poses considerable challenges to definition and integration of case identifiers across systems, i.e. matching the data fields that uniquely identify the process instance. Furthermore, log files have to be transformed from various formats to one analysis format.

Some systems do not even record log files at all (or at least some human executed steps) such that they cannot be included in an analysis directly (Genrich et al., 2008). Finally, large scale business applications typically record heaps of data. In case of the German bank 40,000 database entries were generated each day. Accordingly, the analysis tools must be able to deal with such a high amount of data in an efficient manner.

4.2 Interpretative Challenges

When the technical challenges have been sorted out, it has to be kept in mind that BPI tools provide evidence to support or falsify certain hypotheses about the business operations. The generated pieces of evidence still have to be interpreted by the persons who understand the business. As van der Aalst et al. put it (Aalst et al., 2007b):

"It seems crucial to be closely involved with the people of the organization itself to carry out a meaningful analysis. As a small illustration of this point, it would have been impossible to determine the real value of the oddly connected activity 170_Parkeer [that] turned out not to be an activity at all, but rather a WfMS facility to suspend an operation. More importantly, it took the input of the [...] process owners to identify and prioritize four locations of the process that seemed of interest to subject to a closer analysis. This certainly helped to speed up the identification of relevant results."

This statement can hardly be underestimated. The interpretative challenge stems, among others, from the fact that BPI analysis techniques can only operate on the set of events that is actually recorded for a process. In practice, not all relevant events are actually logged, and people may find ways to work around the system (Aalst et al., 2007b). Even if data is available, the quality of it is often too poor to use it directly. Given these impediments, it is crucial to understand the mindset and motivations of the various agents involved in the execution of the process (Genrich et al., 2008). Accordingly, it can be recommended to interview process stakeholders to make sure that the data is interpreted correctly.

4.3 Pragmatic Challenges

As soon as technical and interpretative issues are resolved, pragmatic conclusions can be drawn from the interpretations. The findings must be presented in an appropriate manner such that decision makers can translate them into action. It appears that a poor selection of business metrics and performance indicators prevents the effective usage of BPI tools such as management dashboards (Corea and Watters, 2007). Even if the right analysis parameters have been found, they cannot be directly translated into business objectives for staff. The reason for this observation is that some objectives enforce undesired behavior of workforce (cf. Anderson and Oliver, 1987). This is, for example, the case when call center agents hang-up on callers in order to improve their number of handled calls. Therefore, the performance objectives concluded from the BPI analysis must be chosen such that they align the behavior of the workforce with the performance objectives of the business process.

4.4 Future Trends

While the technical challenges are currently addressed by tool vendors and academia, there is only little research around so far, e.g. (Corea and Watters, 2007), that investigates the interpretative and pragmatic challenges of BPI in a systematic way. This stream of research puts a stronger emphasis on behavioral research methods including qualitative interviews and quantitative survey analysis. It is likely that we will see more work following this research paradigm as technical tools and solutions mature, providing valuable feedback for creating new innovations in BPI.

To facilitate the automatic data integration and identification, as well as the interpretation of results, recently there is a trend to embed semantics in BPM systems, yield the Semantic BPM (SBPM) systems (Hepp et al., 2005). Such systems combine Semantic Web and SWS technologies with BPM. In a nutshell, SBPM targets accessing the process space (as registered in event logs) of an enterprise at the *knowledge level* so as to support reasoning about business processes, process composition, process execution, etc. The driving force behind SBPM is the use of ontologies (Gruber, 1993). Actually, the European project SUPER (European Project SUPER) is funding research in this field. In this context, first efforts have appeared for supporting BPI based on the semantic layer of SBPM systems. For instance, the work in (de Medeiros et al., 2007a) presents an outlook on the possibilities for *semantic process mining and monitoring*, and pointers to concrete implementations in the ProM framework.

5. CONCLUSION

In this chapter we introduced business process intelligence by giving an overview of its application areas and discussing its benefits. In particular, we showed how process discovery can be applied to extract information like control-flow or the organizational structure from event logs and illustrated the application of conformance checking to detect discrepancies between a process model and the corresponding event log. In addition to process discovery and conformance checking BPI gives enterprises functionality to optimize their business processes. We introduced techniques for identifying the main factors affecting malfunctions or bottlenecks and for pro-actively optimizing business processes. Although the benefits of BPI have been widely recognized, its application in practice still faces technical, interpretive and pragmatic challenges, which need to be resolved before BPI becomes mainstream. Recent trends focus on making use of Semantic Web technologies to bring the execution and analysis of processes to a semantic level.

REFERENCES

European Project SUPER - Semantics Utilised for Process Management within and between Enterprises. *http://www.ip-super.org/.*

Aalst, W. M. P. van der, Reijers, H. A., Weijters, A. J. M. M., van Dongen, B. F., Alves de Medeiros, A. K., Song, M., & Verbeek, H. M. W. (2007a). Business process mining: An industrial application. *Information Systems*, *32*(5), 713–732.

Aalst, W. M. P. van der, & de Medeiros, A. K. A. (2005). Process mining and security: Detecting anomalous process executions and checking process conformance. *Electronic Notes in Theoretical Computer Science*, *121*, 3–21.

Aalst, W. M. P. van der, Dongen, B. F. van, Herbst, J., Maruster, L., Schimm, G., & Weijters, A. J. M. M. (2003). Workflow Mining: A Survey of Issues and Approaches. *Data and Knowledge Engineering*, *47*(2), 237–267.

Aalst, W. M. P. van der, Weijters, A. J. M. M., & Maruster, L. (2004). Workflow Mining: Discovering Process Models from Event Logs. *IEEE Transactions on Knowledge and Data Engineering*, *16*(9), 1128–1142.

Aalst, W. M. P. van der, Beer, H. T. de, & Dongen, B. F. van. (2005a). Process Mining and Verification of Properties: An Approach Based on Temporal Logic. In R. Meersman, Z. Tari, M.-S. Hacid, J. Mylopoulos, B. Pernici, Ö. Babaoglu, H.-A. Jacobsen, J. P. Loyall, M. Kifer, & S. Spaccapietra (Eds.), *OTM Conferences (1)*, volume 3760 of *Lecture Notes in Computer Science*, (pp. 130–147). Springer, ISBN 3-540-29736-7.

Aalst, W. M. P. van der, Reijers, H. A., & Song, M. (2005b). Discovering Social Networks from

Event Logs. *Computer Supported Cooperative Work, 14*(6), 549–593.

Aalst, W. M. P. van der, Reijers, H. A., Weijters, A. J. M. M., Dongen, B. F. van, Alves, A. K., de Medeiros, Song, M., & Verbeek, H. M. W. (2007b). Business process mining: An industrial application. *Information Systems, 32*(1), 713–732,

Anderson, E., & Oliver, R. L. (1987, October). Perspectives on behavior-based versus outcome-based salesforce control systems. *Journal of Marketing, 51*(4), 76–88.

Brackett, M. H. (1996, July). *The Data Warehouse Challenge: Taming Data Chaos*. John Wiley and Sons.

Casati, F., Castellanos, M., Dayal, U., Hao, M., Shan, M. C., & Sayal, M. Business operation intelligence research at HP Labs. *Data Engineering Bulletin, 25*(4).

Casati, F., Castellanos, M., Dayal, U., & Shan, M.-C. (2006). A metric definition, computation, and reporting model for business operation analysis. In Y. E. Ioannidis, M. H. Scholl, J. W. Schmidt, F. Matthes, M. Hatzopoulos, K. Böhm, A. Kemper, T. Grust, & C. Böhm (Eds.), *Advances in Database Technology - EDBT 2006, 10th International Conference on Extending Database Technology, Munich, Germany, March 26-31, 2006, Proceedings*, volume 3896 of *Lecture Notes in Computer Science*, (pp. 1079–1083). Springer.

Casati, F., Castellanos, M., Dayal, U., & Salazar, N. (2007). A generic solution for warehousing business process data. In C. Koch, J. Gehrke, M.N. Garofalakis, D. Srivastava, K. Aberer, A. Deshpande, D. Florescu, C.Y. Chan, V. Ganti, C.-C. Kanne, W. Klas, & E.J. Neuhold (Eds.), *Proceedings of the 33rd International Conference on Very Large Data Bases, University of Vienna, Austria, September 23-27, 2007*, (pp. 1128–1137). ACM, 2007. ISBN 978-1-59593-649-3.

Castellanos, M., Casati, F., Sayal, M., & Dayal, U. (2005a). Challenges in business process analysis and optimization. In C. Bussler & M.-C. Shan (Eds.), *Technologies for E-Services, 6th International Workshop, TES 2005, Trondheim, Norway, September 2-3, 2005, Revised Selected Papers*, volume 3811 of *Lecture Notes in Computer Science*, (pp. 1–10). Springer, 2005a. ISBN 3-540-31067-3.

Castellanos, M., Casati, F., Shan, M.-C., & Dayal, U (2005). (2005b). iBOM: A platform for intelligent business operation management. In *Proceedings of the 21st International Conference on Data Engineering, ICDE 2005, 5-8 April 2005, Tokyo, Japan*, (pp. 1084–1095). IEEE Computer Society, ISBN 0-7695-2285-8.

Castellanos, M., Salazar, N., Casati, F., Dayal, U., & Shan, M.-C. (2005c). Predictive business operations management. In S. Bhalla (Eds.), *DNIS*, volume 3433 of *Lecture Notes in Computer Science*, (pp. 1–14). Springer, ISBN 3-540-25361-0.

Castellanos, M., Salazar, N., Casati, F., Shan, M. C., & Dayal, U.(2005d, July) Automatic metric forecasting for management software. In *Proceedings of the 12th HP Openview University Association (HP-OVUA) Workshop*, Porto, Portugal, July 2005d. Hewlett–Packard Corporation.

Cook, J. E., Du, Z., Liu, C., & Wolf, A. L. (2004). Discovering Models of Behavior for Concurrent Workflows. *Computers in Industry, 53*(3), 297–319.

Corea, S., & Watters, A. (2007). Challenges in business performance measurement: The case of a corporate it function. In G. Alonso, P. Dadam, & M. Rosemann (Eds.), *Business Process Management, 5th International Conference, BPM 2007, Brisbane, Australia, September 24-28, 2007, Proceedings*, volume 4714 of *Lecture Notes in Computer Science*, (pp. 16–31), Brisbane, Australia, 2007. Springer.

de Medeiros, A. K. A. (2006). *Genetic Process Mining*. PhD thesis, Eindhoven University of Technology, Eindhoven..

de Medeiros, A. K. A., Pedrinaci, C., van der Aalst, W. M. P., Domingue, J., Song, M., Rozinat, A., Norton, B., & Cabral, L. (2007a). An Outlook on Semantic Business Process Mining and Monitoring. In R. Meersman, Z. Tari, & P. Herrero (Eds.), *OTM Workshops (2)*, volume 4806 of *Lecture Notes in Computer Science*, (pp. 1244–1255). Springer. ISBN 978-3-540-76889-0.

de Medeiros, A. K. A. Weijters, A. J. M. M., & van der Aalst, W. M. P. (2007b). Genetic Process Mining: an Experimental Evaluation. *Data Mining Knowledge Discovery, 14*(2), 245–304.

van Dongen, B. F. (2007). *Process Mining and Verification*. PhD thesis, Eindhoven University of Technology, Eindhoven.

van Dongen, B. F., & van der Aalst, W. M. P. (2005_, A. K. A.). Multi-phase Process mining: Aggregating Instance Graphs into EPCs and Petri Nets. In *Proceedings of the Second International Workshop on Applications of Petri Nets to Coordination, Workflow and Business Process Management (PNCWB)*.

van Dongen, B. F., Mendling, J., & van der Aalst W. M. P. (2006). Structural Patterns for Soundness of Business Process Models. In *EDOC '06: Proceedings of the 10th IEEE International Enterprise Distributed Object Computing Conference (EDOC'06)*, (pp. 116–128), Washington, DC, USA. IEEE Computer Society.

Dumas, M., ter Hofstede, A. H. M., & van der Aalst, W. M. P. (Eds.), *Process Aware Information Systems*. Wiley Publishing.

Genrich, M., Kokkonen, A., Moormann, J., zur Muehlen, M., Tregear, R., Mendling, J., & Weber, B. (2008). Challenges for business process intelligence: Discussions at the BPI Workshop 2007. In A. H. M. ter Hofstede, B. Benatallah, & H.-Y. Paik, (Eds.), *Proceedings of the BPM 2007 Workshops*, volume 4928 of *Lecture Notes in Computer Science*, Brisbane, Australia. Springer-Verlag.

Greco, G., Guzzo, A., Pontieri, L., & Saccà, D. (2006). Discovering expressive process models by clustering log traces. *IEEE Transactions on Knowledge and Data Engineering, 18*(8), 1010–1027. ISSN 1041-4347.

Greco, G., Guzzo, A., Manco, G., & Saccà, D. (2007). Mining unconnected patterns in workflows. *Information Systems, 32*(5), 685–712.

Grigori, D., Casati, F., Castellanos, M., Dayal, U., Sayal, M., & Shan, M. (2004). Business process intelligence. *Computers in Industry, 53*(3), 321–343.

Gruber, T. R. (1993). A translation approach to portable ontology specifications. *Knowledge Acquisition, 5*(2), 199–220. ISSN 1042-8143.

Günther, C. W., & van der Aalst, W. M. P. (2007). Fuzzy mining - adaptive process simplification based on multi-perspective metrics. In G. Alonso, P. Dadam, & M. Rosemann, editors, *BPM*, volume 4714 of *Lecture Notes in Computer Science*, (pp. 328–343). Springer. ISBN 978-3-540-75182-3.

Hepp, M., Leymann, F., Domingue, J., Wahler, A., & Fensel, D. (2005). Semantic Business Process Management: a Vision Towards Using Semantic Web services for Business Process Management. In *IEEE International Conference on e-Business Engineering (ICEBE 2005)*, (pp. 535 – 540). ISBN 0-7695-2430-3.

Herbst, J., & Karagiannis, D. (2004). Workflow Mining with InWoLvE. *Computers in Industry, 53*(3), 245–264. ISSN 0166-3615. http://dx.doi.org/10.1016/j.compind.2003.10.002.

Hornix, P. T. G. (2007). *Performance Analysis of Business Processes Through Process Mining*. Master's thesis, Eindhoven University of Technology, Eindhoven.

Ingvaldsen, J. E., & Gulla, J. A. (2008). Preprocessing support for large scale process mining of sap transactions. In A. H. M. ter Hofstede, B. Benatallah, & H.-Y. Paik, (Eds.), *Proceedings of the BPM 2007 Workshops*, volume 4928 of *Lecture Notes in Computer Science*, Brisbane, Australia. Springer-Verlag.

G. Keller, M. Nüttgens, and A.W. Scheer. Semantische Processmodellierung auf der Grundlage Ereignisgesteuerter Processketten (EPK). Veröffentlichungen des Instituts für Wirtschaftsinformatik, Heft 89 (in German), University of Saarland, Saarbrücken.

Ly, L. T., Rinderle, S., Dadam, P., & Reichert, M. (2005). Mining Staff Assignment Rules from Event-Based Data. In *Business Process Management Workshops*, (pp. 177–190).

Pinter, S. S., & Golani, M. (2004). Discovering Workflow Models from Activities' Lifespans. *Computers in Industry*, *53*(3), 283–296.

Power, D. J. (2007, March). *A Brief History of Decision Support Systems*. dssresources.com, http://DSSResources.COM/history/dsshistory.html, version 4.0 edition.

Rozinat, A., & van der Aalst, W. M. P. (2008). Conformance checking of processes based on monitoring real behavior. *Inf. Syst.*, *33*(1), 64–95.

Rozinat, A., & van der Aalst, W. M. P. (2006). Decision Mining in ProM. In S. Dustdar, J. L. Fiadeiro, & A. P. Sheth (Eds.), *Business Process Management*, volume 4102 of *Lecture Notes in Computer Science*, (pp. 420–425). Springer, 2006. ISBN 3-540-38901-6.

Rozinat, A., de Jong, I. S. M., Günther, C. W., & van der Aalst, W. M. P. (2007). *Process Mining of Test Processes: A Case Study*. BETA Working Paper Series, WP 220, Eindhoven University of Technology, Eindhoven.

Sarbanes-Oxley Act. Sarbanes-Oxley Act of 2002. http://www.sarbanes-oxley-forum.com/.

Schimm, G. (2004). Mining Exact Models of Concurrent Workflows. *Computers in Industry*, *53*(3), 265–281. ISSN 0166-3615. http://dx.doi.org/10.1016/j.compind.2003.10.003.

Shearer, C. (2000). The CRISP-DM model: the new blueprint for data mining. *Journal of Data Warehousing*, *5*, 13-22.

Song, M., & van der Aalst, W. M. P. (2007). *Towards Comprehensive Support for Organizational Mining*. BETA Working Paper Series, WP 211, Eindhoven University of Technology, Eindhoven.

Wen, L., van der Aalst, W. M. P., Wang, J., & Sun, J. (2007). Mining process models with non-free-choice constructs. *Data Mining Knowledge Discovery*, *15*(2), 145–180.

KEY TERMS

Business Process Intelligence: Refers to the application of Business Intelligence (BI) techniques to business processes.

Conformance Checking: Compares an event log with a (process) model to check for undesired behavior.

Critical Factor Analysis: Analyses past process executions to identify the main factors determining specific process behaviors (with respect to the process metrics).

Event Log: An event log records business events from process-aware information systems (PAIS) such as WFM (Workflow Management), ERP (Enterprise Resource Planning), SCM (Supply Chain Management) and CRM (Customer Relationship Management) systems. Typically, event logs contain information about start and completion of activities, their ordering, resources which executed them and the process instance they belong to.

Prediction: It is the application of data mining and forecasting techniques to estimate future behaviors of a process.

Process Analysis: Refers to the analysis of past process executions with respect to process performance metrics.

Process Discovery: Refers to the analysis of business events recorded in event logs to discover process, control, data, organizational, and social structures.

Process Mining: Is the discovery of information based on event logs. Process discovery, conformance checking, critical factor analysis and prediction qualify as process mining techniques.

Process Monitoring: Refers to the monitoring of running process instances to inform users about critical events.

EXERCISES

Exercise 1: As illustrated in Section 1 BPI comprises several application areas. Recently most BPM vendors have extended their portfolio with BPI functionality, but not everyone is supporting the entire spectrum. Browse the website of selected vendors of BPM suites (e.g., IBM, SAP, Tibco, Oracle, Pallas Athena, Lombardi, webMethods, Savvion) and try to find out which BPI functionality they support. Which application areas are supported by which BPM suites?

Exercise 2: In the context of BPI a large number of buzzwords like Business Activity Monitoring (BAM), Business Operations Management (BOM), Business Process Intelligence (BPI), Process Mining, and Business Operations Intelligence (BOI) exist. Although these buzzwords all relate to BPI slight differences exist and they sometimes refer to different applications areas of BPI.

Browse the website of selected vendors of BPM suites (e.g., IBM, SAP, Tibco, Oracle, Pallas Athena, Lombardi, webMethods, Savvion).

a. Which buzzwords are used by which vendors?

b. Which application areas of BPI are usually covered by which buzzwords?

Exercise 3: In Section 1 different synonyms for BPI and different application areas are described. Create a mind map to organize all these terms and concepts. The mind map should have BPI in its center and the different synonyms and application areas should be organized around the central node in branches. In case you are not familiar with mind maps you can find a description of this technique as well as guidelines at http://en.wikipedia.org/wiki/Mind_Map. Examples for mind maps are provided at http://www.buzanworld.com/mindmaps/.

Exercise 4: To familiarize you with the analysis techniques provided by process mining tools, you will use the open source ProM tool that can be downloaded from www.processmining.org to analyze an event log for the running example used in this chapter: a Dutch rental housing organization. The event log is located at http://prom.win.tue.nl/research/wiki/_media/tutorial/EventLogDutchRentalHouseOrganization.zip Additionally, you may want to have a look at the ProM tutorial provided at the above URL. Your analysis should cover the following points:

What are the five most frequent paths for this process? How much of the log do they account for? What are their average throughput times?

How does the process model that describes the behavior in the log look like? Does this model completely fit the log? If not, how many instances fit this model and how many do not? Where are the problems for the non-fitting process instances?

What are the roles in the organization? Which employees can perform both immediate and internal repairs? Who is handing over work to whom? Who are the central employees for this process?

Is the rule "immediate repairs that could not be solved should be handled by an internal team again before being sent to an external team" being indeed obeyed? Which percentage of process instances complies with this rule? Which percentage does not comply with this rule?

What kind of repair is more common in the organization? Which percentage of repairs can be fixed in a first attempt?

Where are the bottlenecks in the system? Which bottlenecks are due to long waiting times and which are due to long execution times? Which three tasks have the longest average Sojourn times?

What are the business rules that usually apply for the moments of choice in the model? (Note: At least one rule should be reported!)

Exercise 5: The decision tree in the figure below shows the critical factors affecting the violation of an SLA on the maximum duration for processing an invoice. Notice that duration is the metric on which this SLA is defined. Interpret the decision tree and indicate which factors lead to the violation of the SLA, what could be a possible reason and how some of these violations could be eliminated. (note: Fiddo, Chatto and Eddie are Unix servers)

Exercise 6 (advanced): Think of a business process of your choice and model it with a simple diagram of nodes and arcs. Then, think of the

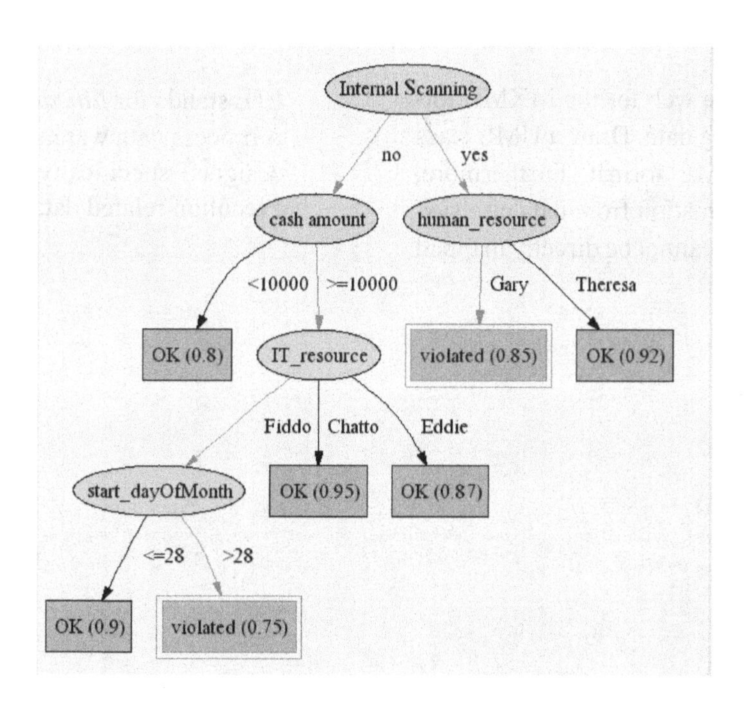

possible predictions that would be useful to have for this process and the opportunities that these predictions would open up for optimizing this process. Create a list of the predictions and the corresponding optimization actions to proactively eliminate the occurrence of the predicted behavior (assuming undesired behavior –metric values- is predicted) or at least to minimize its negative effect.

Exercise 7: A naïve way to do business impact analysis when a resource fails is to mark all the activities supported by the resource as potentially impacted. A smarter way to do it is using the technique explained in Section 3.3, where intelligence is injected to narrow down the set to only those activities with high probability of being impacted. What is the technique used to make business impact analysis more intelligent and what is the benefit of doing it in terms of the actions that need to be done to cope with the impact? (think as if you were the IT manager, what would you need to do to keep running your process and meeting SLAs while the resource's failure is solved? How would that be different if you get a long list of activities potentially impacted versus a short list of highly probable impacted activities?)

Exercise 8: Search the web for the MXML format for process mining data. Draw a UML class diagram of the MXML format. Furthermore, explain why log information from database systems and web servers cannot be directly mapped to MXML.

Exercise 9: The results of a process mining project show that the cases where employee Peter is involved take on average 50% longer than the other cases. Give four different explanations for this fact. Consider the different cases that Peter is a highly-qualified employee, a bottleneck of the process, a lazy employee, or an employee that only works at a certain time of the day. What does this variety of potential explanations imply for process mining?

Exercise 10: A process intelligence project reveals that the average call time in a call center of a bank takes 30% longer than the average across the financial industry. The bank plans to introduce a performance measurement system to keep track of the average call time. In a speech to the work force the CEO announces that in the next year the call center agents should reduce the average call time by 10%. What is the risk of taking average call time as a performance indicator for call center agents? Consider the different strategies a call center agent might consider to improve the performance in terms of this metric.

ENDNOTES

1. LTL stands for *Linear Temporal Logic.*
2. A process data warehouse is the repository designed specifically to store all process execution related data.

Chapter XXII
Applied Sequence Clustering Techniques for Process Mining

Diogo R. Ferreira
IST – Technical University of Lisbon, Portugal

ABSTRACT

This chapter introduces the principles of sequence clustering and presents two case studies where the technique is used to discover behavioral patterns in event logs. In the first case study, the goal is to understand the way members of a software team perform their daily work, and the application of sequence clustering reveals a set of behavioral patterns that are related to some of the main processes being carried out by that team. In the second case study, the goal is to analyze the event history recorded in a technical support database in order to determine whether the recorded behavior complies with a predefined issue handling process. In this case, the application of sequence clustering confirms that all behavioral patterns share a common trend that resembles the original process. Throughout the chapter, special attention is given to the need for data preprocessing in order to obtain results that provide insight into the typical behavior of business processes.

1. INTRODUCTION

The field of process mining (van der Aalst & Weijters, 2004) is a new and exciting area of research, whose purpose is to develop techniques to gain insight into business processes based on the behavior recorded in event logs. There are a number of process mining techniques already available and most of them focus on discovering control-flow models (van der Aalst et al, 2003). There are also techniques that take into account data dependencies (Rozinat et al, 2006), and techniques to discover other kinds of models such as social networks among workflow participants (van der Aalst et al, 2005).

Process mining techniques such as the α-algorithm (van der Aalst et al, 2004), the inference methods proposed by (Cook & Wolf, 1995), the directed acyclic graphs of (Agrawal et al, 1998), the inductive workflow acquisition by (Herbst & Karagiannis, 1998), the hierarchical clustering of (Greco et al, 2005), the genetic algorithms of (Alves de Medeiros et al, 2007) and the instance graphs of (van Dongen & van der Aalst, 2004), to cite only a few, are all techniques that aim at extracting the control-flow behavior of a business process and representing it according to different kinds of models. All of these techniques take an event log as input and as the starting point for the discovery of underlying process.

In many practical applications, however, the events that belong to a particular process can only be found among the events of other processes that are running within the same system. For example, events recorded in a CRM (Customer Relationship Management) system may belong to different processes such as creating a new customer or handling a claim submitted by an existing customer. Furthermore, even when focusing on a single process, the behavior in set of instances may be so diverse that it becomes appropriate to study different behaviors as separate workflows. Either way, the amount and diversity of activities recorded in an event log may be such that it becomes necessary to sort out the different existing processes before applying one of the above process mining techniques.

Sequence clustering is a particularly useful technique for this purpose, as it provides the means to partition a number of sequences into a set of clusters or groups of similar sequences. Although the development of sequence clustering techniques has been an active field of research especially in the area of bioinformatics—see for example (Enright et al, 2002), (Jaroszewski & Godzik, 2002) and (Chen et al, 2006)—its principles are equally applicable to other kinds of sequence data. For example, in applications such as user click-stream analysis it is possible to use sequence clustering to discover the typical navigation patterns on a Web site (Cadez et al, 2003). The same approach can be used to discover the typical behavior of different processes, or to distinguish between different behaviors within a single process, for example to identify what is considered to be the normal flow and what is deemed to be exceptional behavior.

The use of clustering algorithms in association with process mining techniques has received increased attention in recent years: in (Greco et al, 2004), the authors represent each trace in a vectorial space in order to make use of the *k*-means algorithm to cluster workflow traces; (Alves de Medeiros et al, 2008) make use of a similar approach in order to perform hierarchical clustering; (Jung et al, 2008) also address hierarchical clustering by means of a special-purpose algorithm based on a cosine similarity measure; in (Song et al, 2008) the authors make use of several clustering algorithms, including *k*-means and self-organizing maps; (Ceglowski et al, 2005) make use of self-organizing maps in order to cluster hospital emergency data. This means that there are several techniques available for clustering workflow traces. In this chapter we focus specifically on the use of sequence clustering techniques.

The chapter is organized as follows: Section 2 explains how sequence clustering works in order to find a set of clusters of similar sequences. Section 3 provides a word of caution regarding the need for preprocessing before actually applying sequence clustering to a given dataset. Section 4 presents a case study on the application of sequence clustering to an activity log that has been collected manually during the daily work of a software development team. Section 5 presents a second case study on the application of sequence clustering to the history recorded in a technical support system, in order to determine to what extent the recorded behavior complies with a standard incident management process. Section 6 concludes the chapter by highlighting how the case studies illustrate both the potential and limitations of sequence clustering as a process mining technique.

2. SEQUENCE CLUSTERING

The general purpose of clustering algorithms is to organize a given set of objects into a set of clusters, where each cluster contains objects that are similar by some kind of measure. This measure depends on the kind of objects or data being used. For example, if the objects are data points in two-dimensional space, then the measure of similarity can be formulated as the proximity between data points. In this case, points that are close together in space are more likely to belong to the same cluster than points that are farther apart.

The same concept can be extended to sequence data with some adaptations. As illustrated in Figure 1, given a set of input sequences and a set of clusters, the goal is to assign each sequence to one of the available clusters based on some similarity measure. In sequence clustering, each cluster is associated with a probabilistic model, usually a Markov chain. If the Markov chains for all clusters are known, then each input sequence is assigned to the cluster that can best produce such sequence. In general there can be more than one possible cluster, so the sequence is assigned to the cluster which can produce the input sequence with higher probability.

Since each cluster has its own Markov chain, the probability that an observed sequence belongs to a given cluster is the probability that the observed sequence was produced by the Markov chain associated with that cluster. For a sequence $\boldsymbol{x} = \{x_0, x_1, x_2, \ldots, x_{L-1}\}$ of length L this can be formalized as:

$$p(\boldsymbol{x} \mid c_k) = p(x_0; c_k) \cdot \prod_{i=1}^{L-1} p(x_i \mid x_{i-1}; c_k)$$

where $p(x_0;c_k)$ is the probability of x_0 occurring as the first state in the Markov chain associated with cluster c_k and $p(x_i|x_{i-1};c_k)$ is the transition probability of state x_{i-1} to state x_i in the same Markov chain.

Unfortunately, the Markov chains associated with each cluster [i.e. the probabilities $p(x_0;c_k)$ and

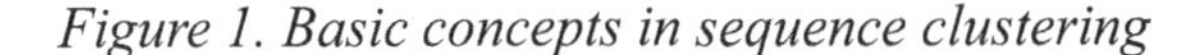

Figure 1. Basic concepts in sequence clustering

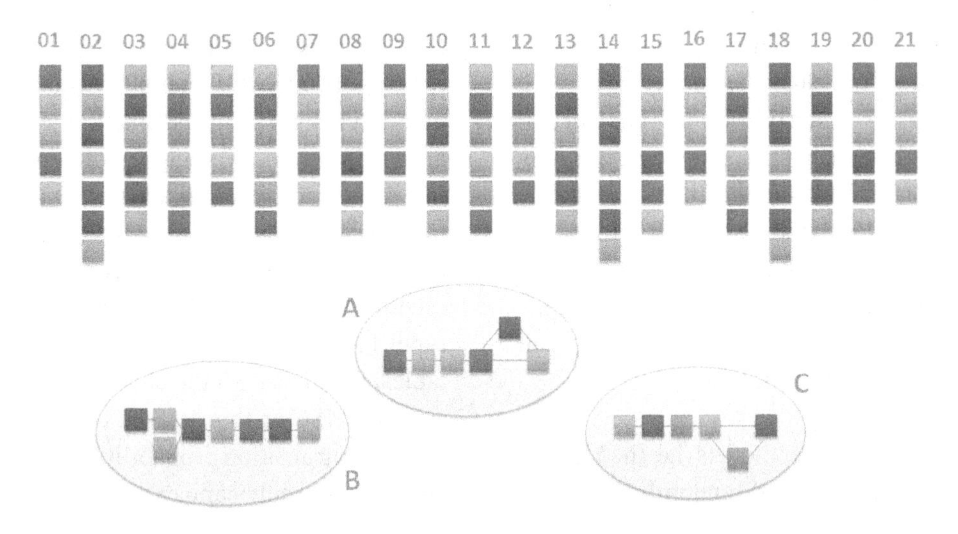

$p(x_i|x_{i-1};c_k)$ in the formula above] are not given, because they are the actual result being sought. These cluster models represent the behavioral patterns found in the input dataset. Sequence clustering can be seen as an approach to discover these behavioral patterns. To explain how this is achieved, we will focus on the particular algorithm proposed by (Cadez et al, 2003).

The sequence clustering algorithm described by (Cadez et al, 2003) is a model-based clustering technique (Han & Kamber, 2006) that relies on an iterative Expectation-Maximization procedure (Dempster et al, 1977). The idea can be described as follows. If the cluster models (i.e. the Markov chains) were known, then we could assign sequences to clusters in the way described above. Once the sequences have been assigned, it is possible to re-estimate the cluster models based on the actual population of each cluster, i.e., from the set of sequences that belong to a cluster it is possible to re-estimate the Markov chain for that cluster. After that estimation, we can re-assign the sequences to clusters and again improve the estimate for the cluster models. By repeating this procedure over and over again, the cluster models will eventually converge to a set of Markov chains that no longer change. These are the desired behavioral patterns.

Two difficulties arise from this approach. One is how to obtain a first estimate for the cluster models so that this iterative procedure can be applied. The simplest solution to this problem is to randomize the cluster models, i.e. using a random guess as a starting point. The second issue is whether such procedure will actually converge. Fortunately, this has been proved by (Dempster et al, 1977) for the general framework of Expectation-Maximization (EM), which is one of the cornerstones of model-based clustering.

The algorithm of (Cadez et al, 2003) can therefore be described as follows:

1. Initialize the cluster models (i.e. the Markov chain for each cluster) randomly.
2. Assign each input sequence to the cluster that is able to produce it with higher probability (by the equation above).
3. Estimate each cluster model from the set of sequences that belong to that cluster.
4. Repeat steps 2 and 3 until the cluster models, and hence the assignment of sequences to clusters, do not change.

This algorithm has been implemented in Microsoft SQL Server 2005® Analysis Services, where it is known as Microsoft Sequence Clustering (MSC), and is readily available for use either programmatically via a Data Mining API or manually via a user-friendly interface in Microsoft Visual Studio 2005®.

The MSC algorithm must be provided two input tables: a case table and a sequence table. The case table contains one record for each sequence; it conveys the number of sequences in the input dataset together with some descriptive information about each sequence. The sequence table contains the steps for all sequences, where each step is numbered and labeled. The number is the order of occurrence within the sequence, and the label is a descriptive attribute that denotes the state in a Markov chain. The case and sequence tables have a one-to-many relationship: each sequence in the case table is associated with several steps in the sequence table by means of a case id.

Figure 2 illustrates a simple example where the members of a family have different ways of zapping through TV channels according to their own interests. Let us assume that each member always finds the TV switched off, and after turning it on, goes through a set of channels before turning it off again. Every time it is turned on, the TV generates a session identifier (case id) and records the sequence of channels (by channel type). Figure 2 shows part of the case and sequence tables, together with the cluster models found by running MSC on this dataset. Each cluster model shows the transition probabilities between states, as well as the entry and exit probabilities that are

Figure 2. Input tables and cluster models for the simple TV usage scenario

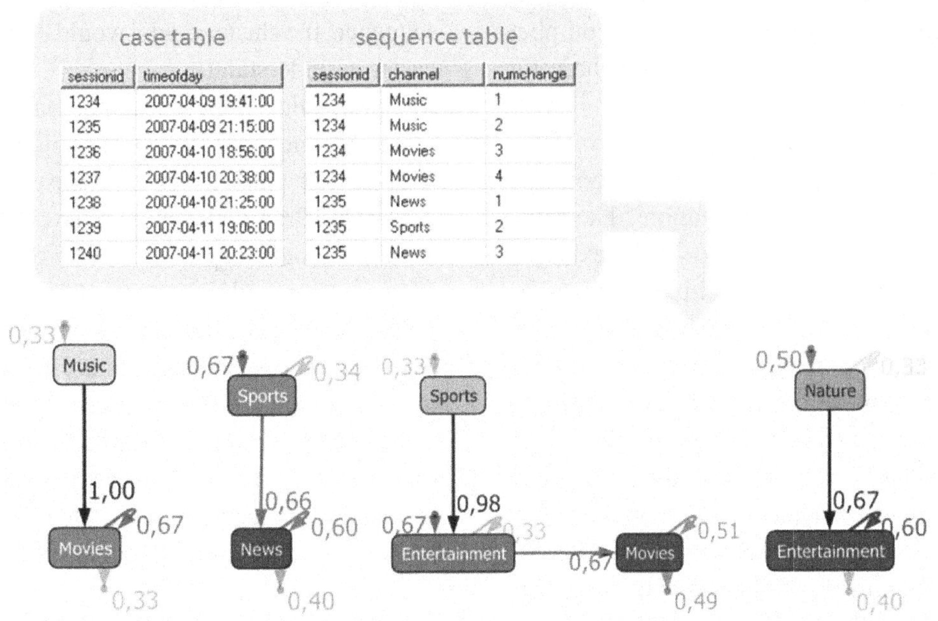

case table

sessionid	timeofday
1234	2007-04-09 19:41:00
1235	2007-04-09 21:15:00
1236	2007-04-10 18:56:00
1237	2007-04-10 20:38:00
1238	2007-04-10 21:25:00
1239	2007-04-11 19:06:00
1240	2007-04-11 20:23:00

sequence table

sessionid	channel	numchange
1234	Music	1
1234	Music	2
1234	Movies	3
1234	Movies	4
1235	News	1
1235	Sports	2
1235	News	3

determined from the beginning and ending states of the sequences that belong to that cluster.

Assuming that the case and sequence tables are already available in an existing database, the main steps to run such an example in Microsoft SQL Server 2005® Analysis Services are the following:

1. In the "Business Intelligence Development Studio", create a new "Analysis Services Project" – This creates a project that will contain several artifacts, namely data sources, mining models, etc., as described in the following steps.
2. Create a new "Data Source" and connect to the existing database – This step connects to the database that contains the input sequence data to be processed.
3. Create a new "Data Source View", add the case and sequence tables to that view, and create a one-to-many relationship based on the case id attribute – This step is necessary in order to specify which tables are the case table and the sequence table in the database that we connected to the previous step.
4. Create a new "Mining Structure" by specifying the table columns that will be the input for MSC – This step will specify which columns of the case and sequence tables will serve as input data for the algorithm to be chosen in the next step.
5. Create a new "Mining Model" and specify the use of sequence clustering – From the set of data mining algorithms available, the one to be chosen is Microsoft Sequence Clustering (MSC).
6. Configure the algorithm parameters, such as number of clusters and the minimum number of sequences in each cluster (minimum support) – Each data mining algorithm may have several parameters which can be adjusted to produce best results.
7. Run the mining model and wait until the processing is complete – This will take from a couple of seconds to a couple of minutes, depending on the size of the input dataset.

8. Browse through results using the "Mining Model Viewer" – With this component it is possible to study the results from a number of views, and to get the Markov chain for each cluster.

Each of these steps is explained in thorough detail in the product documentation[1]. The same steps can be done programmatically (for example in C#) by resorting to a class library known as Analysis Management Objects (AMO)[2] to create, configure and run the objects listed above. It is also possible to write a set of DMX (Data Mining Extensions) queries for the same purpose. The DMX language[3] is an extension to SQL that can be used to create and query mining models.

A key parameter to define when applying MSC (step 6) is the number of clusters to use, and this can be set either manually or automatically. In the later case, the algorithm will make use of heuristics to find the ideal number of clusters for the given data. On the other hand, even if the number of clusters is specified manually, the MSC algorithm may still increase or decrease this number slightly according to other parameters such as *minimum support*, i.e. the minimum number of sequences to be placed in each cluster.

3. DATA PREPROCESSING

The MSC algorithm described above relies on a database as its source of data and therefore it can deal with very large event logs. On the other hand, the algorithm is robust to noise in the sense that the probabilistic model associated with each cluster can accommodate several variations of the same sequence. It should be noted, however, that every given sequence will eventually be assigned to one of the available clusters. This means that if a sequence is very different or atypical and hardly fits any cluster, it will nevertheless be assigned to one of them. This, in turn, will have an effect on the probabilistic model estimated for that cluster. The effect is that an unusual sequence may actually distort the cluster model when, without that sequence, the cluster model would be simpler and easier to understand.

For the algorithm it does not matter what the input sequences are, but for the end user or business analyst who will interpret the results, it will be easier to draw conclusions if the cluster models are a meaningful representation of the typical sequences contained in that cluster. Therefore, when preparing the case and sequence tables for MSC, some preprocessing steps must be performed in order to ensure that behavioral patterns that are hidden in the input data will be more easily discovered. In practical applications such as the case studies presented ahead, the following preprocessing steps are usually performed:

1. **Dropping states with low support:** While some states may occur very often and be present in most of the sequences in the dataset, on the other hand there may be states that are so infrequent that their occurrence can only be attributed to pure ad-hoc behavior or even mislabeling. For the purpose of identifying typical behavior, these very infrequent states are usually removed from the input sequences.
   Example: If state "B" is found to occur very rarely in the input dataset, then the input sequence A→B→C→D turns into A→C→D.
2. **Dropping consecutive repetitions of the same state:** Some systems record multiple events caused by changes in attributes other than state. These changes may or may not be interesting to study under a control-flow point of view. In general, only events that pertain to changes in state are considered, and therefore events that do not change this state are usually discarded
   Example: the sequence A→C→C→D becomes A→C→D.

3. **Dropping single-step sequences:** Some cases actually contain no sequential behavior, as they comprise only a single step. These cases are usually removed from the dataset.
   Example: "A→B" is a sequence, but sequences with a single state, such as "A" or "B", are discarded.
4. **Dropping unique sequences:** Often there are sequences that are unique in the sense that they never happen twice. If after all the previous preprocessing steps there are still such sequences, they should be considered for removal, unless the set of all unique sequences is a significant portion of the whole input data. In general, unique sequences are undesirable as the MSC algorithm is forced to assign them to some cluster, possibly changing the cluster models in an unpredictable way.
   Example: if B→A→D→C is a sequence that happens just once in the entire dataset, then it is discarded.

Clearly, the order of these preprocessing steps does matter. By removing some rare states (step 1) there may be more consecutive repetitions in the remaining states (step 2); for example, if B is found to be rare state in step 1 and is removed from A→C→B→C→D, then the resulting sequence will be A→C→C→D and then step 2 will be applied to produce A→C→D, something that would not happen if the two steps be applied in reverse order. Also, removing states (steps 1 and 2) may increase the number of single-step sequences (step 3); consider for example the sequence A→B with B as a rare state, or the repetitive sequence A→A→A, both of which will be collapsed to a single state. Finally, unique sequences should not be dropped until the very end (step 4) as previous steps may produce identical sequences. For example, the sequence A→B→C→D becomes identical to A→C→D after step 1 if B is found to be a rare state; however, it could be the case that A→C→D was a unique sequence before step 1, which would have been dropped had step 4 been applied immediately.

4. CASE STUDY: MINING HUMAN ACTIVITIES

This case study is based on the work (Zacarias et al, 2006) in a banking institution, where a software development team was observed for three weeks. The team comprises four software developers and a project leader that performs both system development and project management tasks. The team develops web applications and performs systems analysis, design, programming, test and maintenance activities. During the three-week period of observation, the team performed tasks on the following applications: (1) Suppliers, (2) Claims, (3) Customer Correspondence (called Mail application), (4) Evictions and (5) Marketing Campaigns.

The purpose of the study was to collect a record of all activities taking place in daily work of that team. Those data would then be used to analyze the structure of work within the team and to devise a set of collaboration tools. The team members were asked to manually register their actions and interactions in chronological order during the observation period. To reduce the burden of such task, they were asked to register their actions and interactions by means of a simple summarizing sentence.

After the data have been collected, these sentences were first parsed using grammatical rules to separate the subject and predicate. Synonym verbs were replaced by a single verb to avoid inconsistencies. Each action description was augmented with a set of application, information and human resources involved. The results were further structured as described in (Zacarias et al, 2005) into an event table as shown in Figure 3. The table had 534 entries.

Figure 3. Example of actions collected during observation

#	Day	Actor Send.	Rec.	Action. Interacc.	Description	Tools	Information	Human competencies
8	6-01	Catarina		SOLVE	automatic table update problem	Sql Server, message management application	Sql Server and message management application documentation	programming & debugging skills
9	6-01	Catarina	Mariana	PROPOSE	solution to automatic table update problem			
10	6-01	Mariana	Catarina	ACCEPT	solution to automatic table update problem			

Figure 4. Total number of occurrences for each action, before (light column) and after eliminating repeating steps (dark column) ordered by decreasing number of the latter

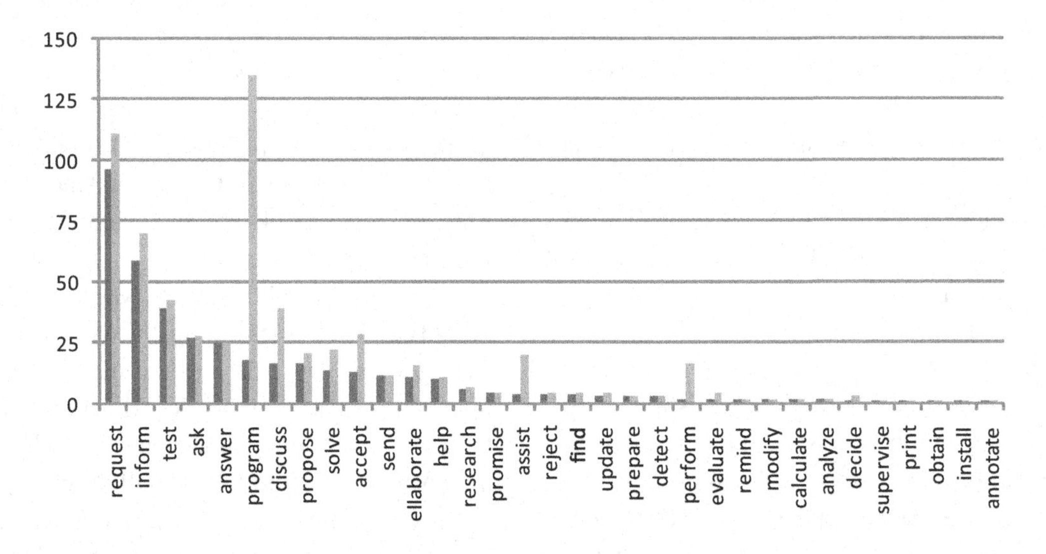

By analyzing this table it was possible to group events that belong to the same or to intimately related tasks. Given the chronological order of events for each team member, together with the interactions that took place between them, it was possible to determine the sequences of events that took place across actors. This led to a number of rather long sequences, which were then broken down into shorter, scope-delimited tasks. About 140 tasks were found.

A brief analysis of these task sequences revealed some issues. A first issue was that some of these tasks were not actually sequences, but just arbitrary repetitions of the same action. For example, all team members had at least one sequence in which they repeated the action "program" from 2 to 20 times. Therefore, consecutive repeating steps within each sequence were eliminated, and sequences ending up with just one single step were discarded. Figure 4 shows the total number of occurrences of each action, both before and after repeating steps were eliminated.

A second issue was that the relatively high number of different actions. This led to a set of very dissimilar sequences, despite the fact that most of them shared a limited set of common actions. For example, most tasks involve some form of "request", whereas the action "annotate" happened only once in the entire study. This suggests that the emphasis should be put on highly recurrent actions, which provide the basic structure for most sequences. The least recurrent actions (in the tail of Figure 4) represent ad-hoc variations that provide no real insight into the typical behavior. The last preprocessing stage was therefore to decide on a threshold for the number of occurrences; only actions above that threshold were allowed to remain in the sequences.

The case and sequence tables can then be built from the results of these preprocessing stages, and provided to the MSC algorithm for processing. In order to present and discuss a complete result set, here we will restrict our analysis to only the first five actions in Figure 4 (i.e. "request", "inform", "test", "ask" and "answer"). As a consequence, the sequences will also be rather short; there were 64 sequences with an average number of four events per sequence. Figure 5 shows the results of applying MSC to the input sequences. The sequences have been grouped into five clusters.

Despite using a limited set of actions, it is still possible to interpret these results in terms of the activities performed by the software team. In fact, it was only when the team was shown such kind of results that further insight into their activities emerged. From these results it is possible to identify the following:

Figure 5. Clusters models for a subset of actions

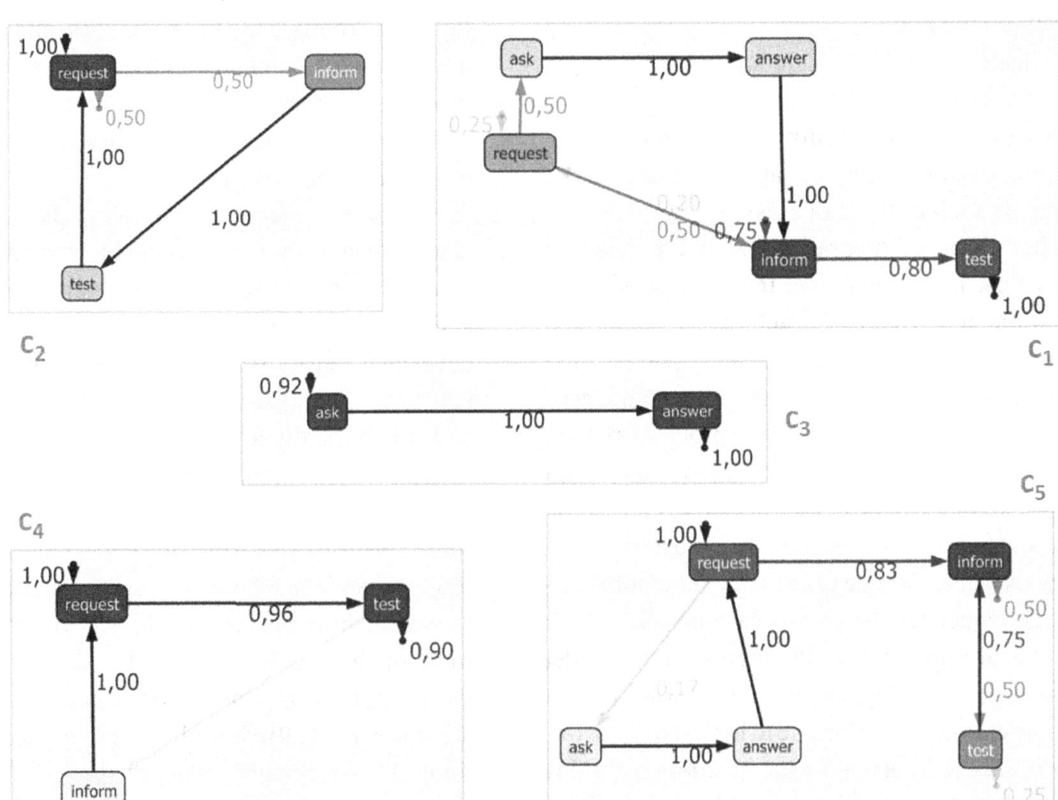

Clusters 1 and 4 concern software integration tests. The tests can be performed either upon explicit request or depending on the result of previous tests. Clusters 4 and 1 capture these two scenarios, respectively. Cluster 4 represents tests performed upon request, where sequences are typically in the form "request-test". Cluster 1 represents tests performed upon result of previous tests, where sequences have the form "inform-test". In this case, the typical sequence should include a third state to become "analyze-inform-test". However, the action "analyze" was not recorded since it is usually performed by an individual that was not observed in this study.

Clusters 2 and 5 concern software publishing activities. These include both forms, either "request-inform-test-request" (cluster 2) or "request-inform-test-inform" (cluster 5). This behavior should include an additional state to become "request-publish-inform-test-request" or "request-publish-inform-test-inform". However, the action "publish" is also performed by an unobserved member.

Cluster 3 contains common behavior in the form "ask-answer". This behavior occurs in several tasks and has to do mainly with team members helping each other. It also appears in particular contexts such as those of clusters 1 and 5.

In the case of integration tests and publishing activities, it is remarkable that it is possible to distinguish between these activities even though key actions such as "analyze" and "publish" are missing. On one hand, this suggests that sequences of actions that belong to different processes have a distinct signature, i.e. they have a basic sequential structure that can be distinguished even if some key states are missing; sequence clustering is a very useful technique to separate inherently different sequences which would otherwise seem similar or impossible to distinguish in the midst of a large event log. On the other hand, only a business analyst will be able to look at the clustering results and recognize the business activities being depicted in those results. This is especially true in practical applications where the users or systems being observed can provide only an incomplete view of the business processes within an organization. The kind of analysis that can be done via sequence clustering, or for that matter any other technique, is bound by the breadth and relevance of the input data that can be collected in the first place.

5. CASE STUDY: CONFORMANCE OF AN ISSUE HANDLING PROCESS

This case study involves a medium-sized IT company whose main product is an advanced software platform designed to accelerate the development of custom business applications. Using this platform, even complex applications can be developed in a graphical way without programming, and then deployed to a Web-based run-time environment. The platform is being improved continuously by successive release versions that add new functionality, improve existing features, and correct bugs. Besides extensive manual and automated in-house testing, end users also have an active role in pointing out desired improvements and problems to be solved.

Figure 6 illustrates the case study scenario, where customers report issues to the technical support team. To keep track of all reported issues and to handle them appropriately, the company developed a custom solution using its own software platform. The system is called Issue Manager and it is basically a database with a Web-based interface. The database stores information about each issue such as date, description, submitter, status, priority, risk, severity, etc., along with the product version where the issue was detected, as well as possible relationships to other issues. Most of these data can be filled with whatever the support team finds appropriate, except for the status field which is allowed to have one of a limited set of possible states.

Figure 6. Case study scenario

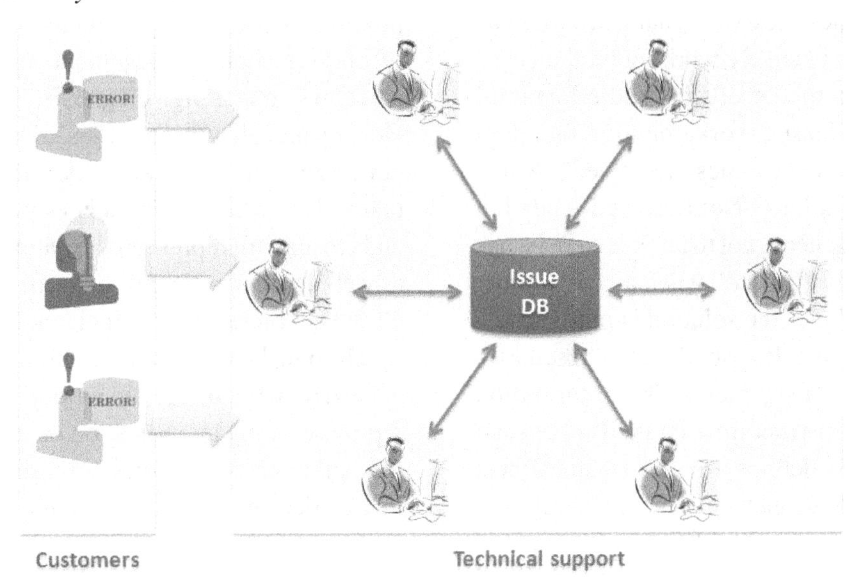

Figure 7. The issue handling process within the framework of ITIL

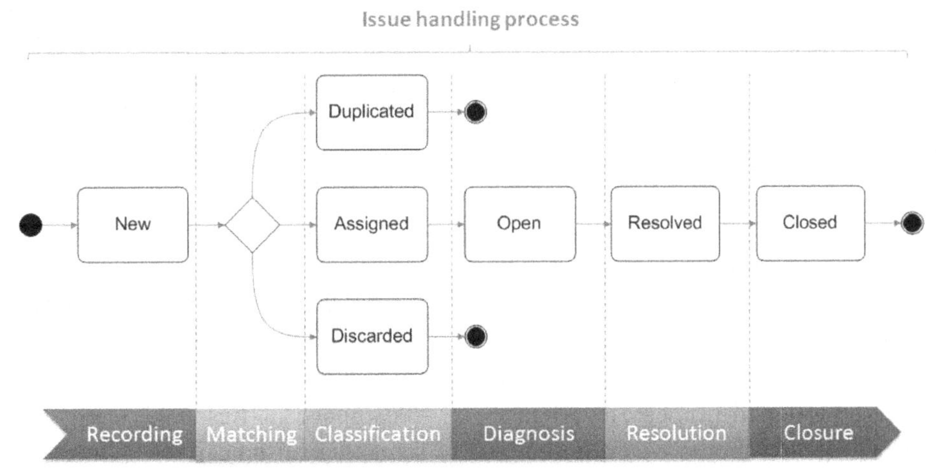

Figure 7 illustrates the typical set of states that an incident goes through. Regardless of the channel an issue comes from, it will be recorded in the system as "New". Then someone will look at it and check whether it is a duplicate issue, whether it is relevant, what priority level it should be assigned, whether there is enough information for the issue to be handled, whether there are other issues that could be related to this one, etc. In some cases, the issue may end up being "Discarded" if it is a non-issue; for example, it could be just a user mistake. In other cases it may be labeled as "Duplicated" if a similar issue is known and has been already recorded in the database.

In most cases, issues will follow the regular handling process. The issue may be "Assigned" either to a specific person, or collectively to the support team. The state will be changed to "Open" when someone is actively working on the issue. It will then be a matter of time and effort until a solution or at least a workaround is found; at this point the issue becomes "Resolved". A few issues may end up in a "Not Resolved" state but this result is, in general, not to be expected. Issues are automatically "Closed" when a new product version that includes the solution is released.

The process just described clearly resembles ITIL Incident Management. The Information Technology Infrastructure Library (ITIL) (van Bon et al, 2005) defines a set of standard best practices for IT service management, ranging several processes, and Incident Management is the ITIL process that focuses on the handling of events that disturb normal service operation. ITIL Incident Management defines the following steps to handle those events:

1. **Recording:** Upon reception, the incident must be recorded.
2. **Classification:** The incident is characterized in terms of type, impact and urgency, leading to a certain priority class.
3. **Matching:** A solution may already exist if the incident matches a known problem or error condition.
4. **Diagnosis:** All available information about the incident is gathered in order to investigate and determine a solution or workaround.
5. **Resolution:** The solution is applied in order to restore normal service or system operation.
6. **Closure:** The incident is closed once the service has been restored.

During incident diagnosis, successive levels of service support may be invoked until a solution or workaround is found. This behavior is known as *escalation* – if the current support level is unable to find a solution, then the incident escalates to the next (higher) support level.

As suggested in Figure 7, the issue handling process can be mapped directly to the structure of ITIL Incident Management: recording, classification, matching, diagnosis, resolution and closure are all present. Classification is being done between "New" and "Assigned"; diagnosis takes place when the issue is "Open"; resolution and closure are represented by appropriate states as well. Issue handling is, in itself, a process with all the characteristics of Incident Management.

Despite the fact that the issue handling process is clearly defined, the model depicted in Figure 7 provides only an indication of the sequence of states that an issue should go through. There is, in practice, no restriction being placed on the particular state of an issue, nor on the transition to other states. Members of the technical support team are free to use these or other states, and to change the issue state in any way as they see fit. The question now is to determine how far the behavior recorded in the system database actually complies with the original process depicted in Figure 7. This is a problem of conformance checking (Rozinat & Aalst, 2008).

In the database it was found that an issue can actually be in one of 15 possible states, in alphabetical order: "Approved", "Assigned", "Closed", "Discarded", "Duplicated", "Needs Approval", "Needs Specification", "Needs Verification", "New", "Not Approved", "Not Resolved", "Open", "Postponed", "Resolved", and "Waiting". The semantics of some of these states are not entirely clear, although their names provide some indication of their meaning. It was also found that the database contains many interrelated tables that aim at supporting a wide range of functionalities. An analysis of both the database schema and content revealed that there were two tables of interest to collect the state sequences:

- Table *issue*: Contains general information about an issue such as a unique identifier, name, description, product version and date of submission, but also about the priority, severity, present state and who is currently assigned to handle the issue. There were 14 982 issues in the database.

- Table *history*: keeps track of all events where an event is a change of some sort, including change of assignment, change of priority, and change in state. There were 143 220 events in the database, roughly ten times as much as the number of issues.

With the data contained in the history table it was possible to build a useful dataset for analysis. Basically, each sequence corresponds to the time-ordered list of state changes recorded for a given issue. Figure 8 shows that sequence length varies widely, from issues with a single recorded event to issues with over 50 events. In fact, the longest sequence had 75 events, most of which were just a repetition of the "Waiting" state. Figure 8 also shows that most issues had sequence lengths between 1 and 15.

The fact that the system allowed any kind of change to be freely made to an issue means that the sequences displayed an arbitrary repetition of states when the changes were being made to fields other than state. For this reason, the sequence length was often longer than it would have been obtained if only the change in the state would be considered. These and other preprocessing steps had to be done before applying MSC to the dataset. The following preprocessing steps were used:

1. *Dropping events with low support:* Figure 9 shows the number of occurrences of each state in the history table. The states in the bottom of Figure 9 have low support since they occur only very rarely. However, in this case study all states have been kept.
2. *Dropping consecutively repeated events*: Since many consecutive events were created by changes to fields other than state, they could be considered as a single event for our purposes. Around 63% of all events were eliminated in this step. The average sequence length also decreased dramatically, and there was a significant increase in the number of sequences with length between 1 and 5.
3. *Dropping sequences with either insufficient or excessive length*: Figure 8 shows that many sequences are actually non-sequences as they comprise a single event, so these

Figure 8. Number of issues vs. sequence length found in the history table

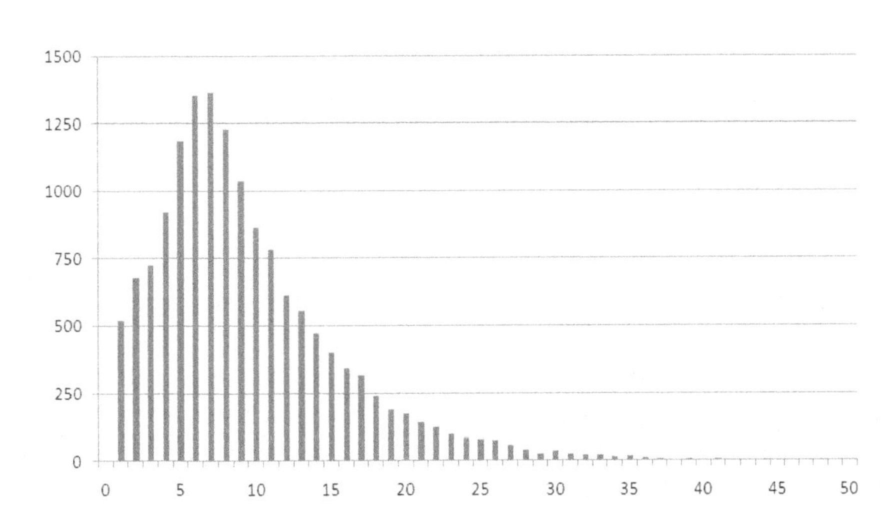

Figure 9. Number of occurrences of each state in the history table

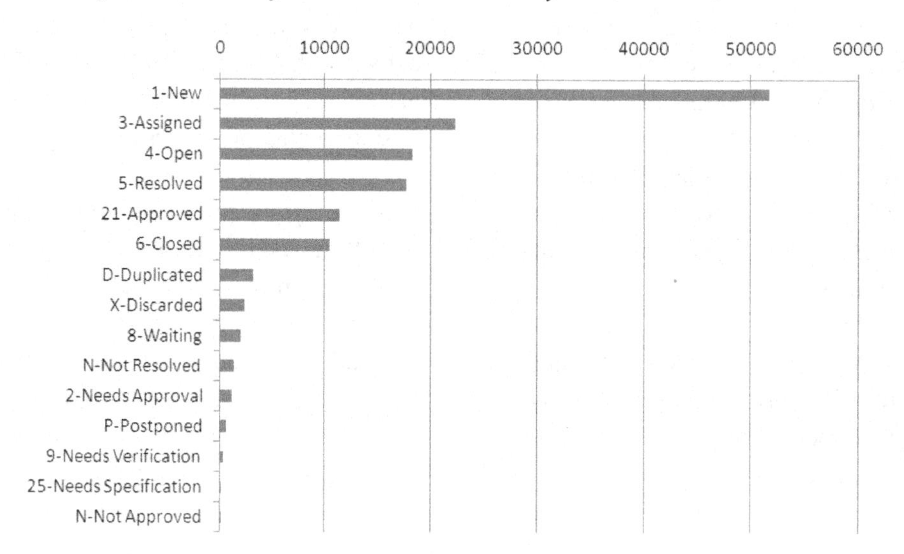

Figure 10. The most frequent sequences after preprocessing (top 20)

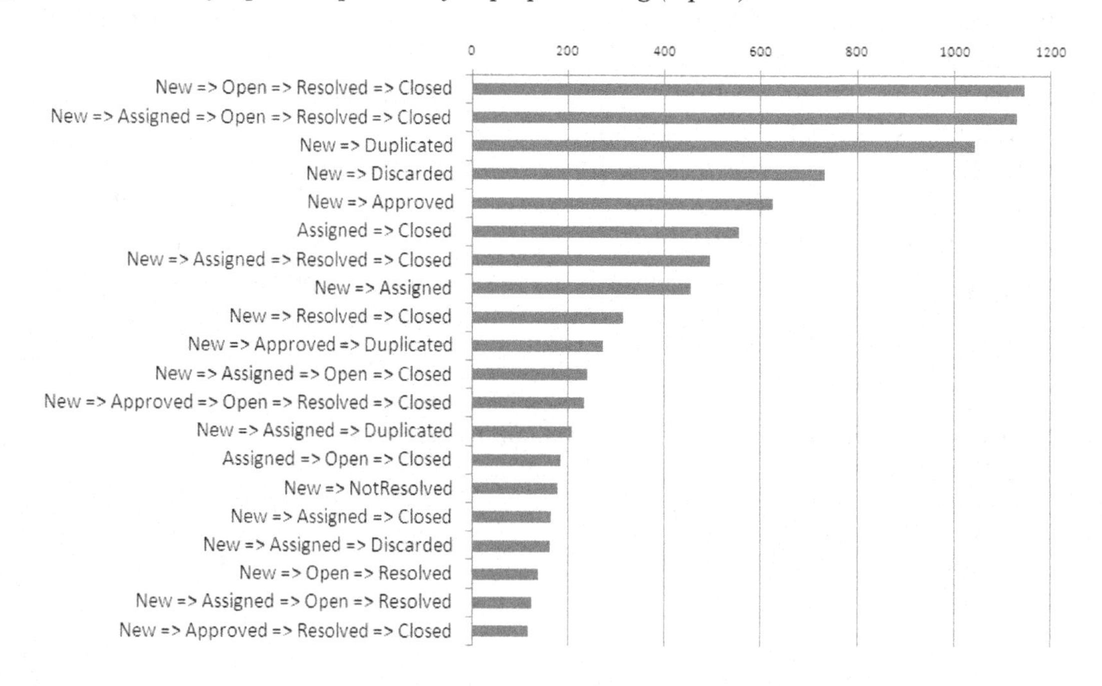

sequences were removed. About 1000 sequences were eliminated in this step.

4. *Dropping sequences with repeated events*: A sequence that contains a (non-consecutive) repetition in a state represents a case where the handling of an issue had to recede to a previous state. Sequences with such repetitions display a mixture of behavior, which makes them difficult to assign correctly to a single cluster. About 2500 sequences were eliminated in this step.

5. *Dropping unique, one-of-a-kind sequences*: Sequences that are unrepeatable are not interesting for the purpose of identifying typical behavior. About 300 unique sequences were removed from the dataset.

After these preprocessing steps 11 085 sequences remained, with a total of 35 778 events. Figure 10 shows the most frequent sequences after preprocessing of the input dataset. Although some of the expected behavior is immediately recognizable at the top of the figure, it should be noted that the most frequent sequence accounts for only about 10% of the total number of sequences. The total of 11 085 sequences includes 264 different sequences, of which only the top twenty are shown in Figure 10. We now turn to the application of sequence clustering to this dataset.

Judging by the kind of sequences found in the input dataset, a number of about 12 clusters seemed to be a good initial guess. After setting the parameters and running MSC on the dataset, 14 clusters were created. Figure 11 shows the top three most frequent sequences in each cluster. For cluster 14 only one sequence is shown, since this cluster has only one kind of sequence.

Some of these clusters display very similar behavior. For example, clusters 1 and 6 have sequences that could have been probably included in the same cluster. The same happens with clusters 4 and 9, and other clusters as well. The presence of similar sequences in different clusters suggests that the number of clusters should be decreased.

Running MSC again with different parameter settings, nine clusters were obtained. Figure 12 shows the most frequent sequences in each of these nine clusters. Again, cluster 9 shows fewer sequences because it has only two types of sequences. The top sequences in clusters 3, 4, 6 and 8 are clearly related, and other sequences within different clusters were also found to be similar. These results suggested that the number of clusters should be decreased even further.

Figure 11. Top sequences for 14 clusters

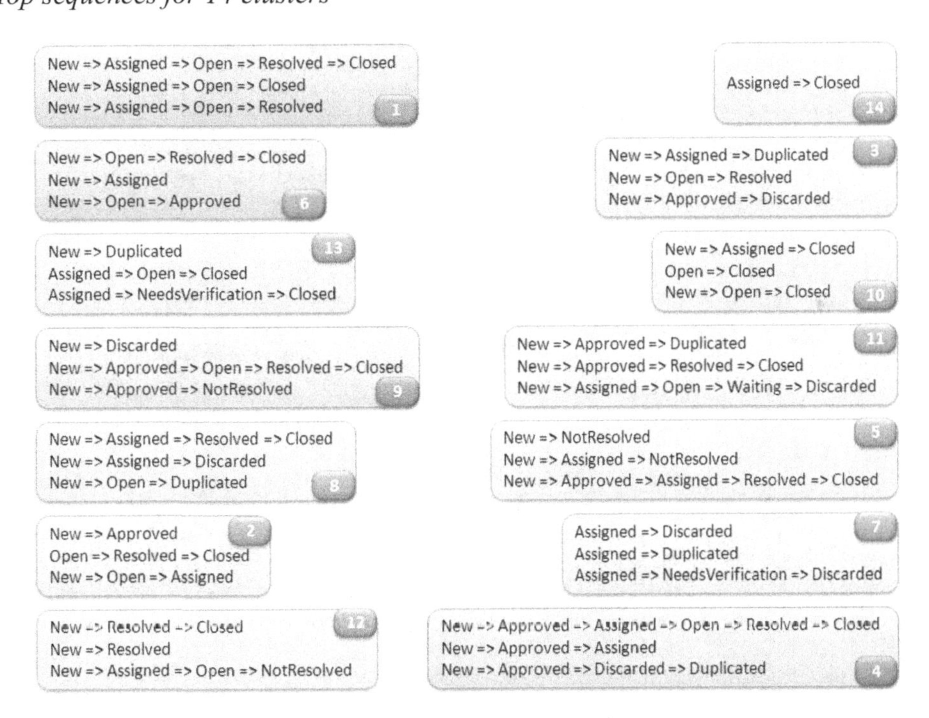

Figure 12. Top sequences for 9 clusters

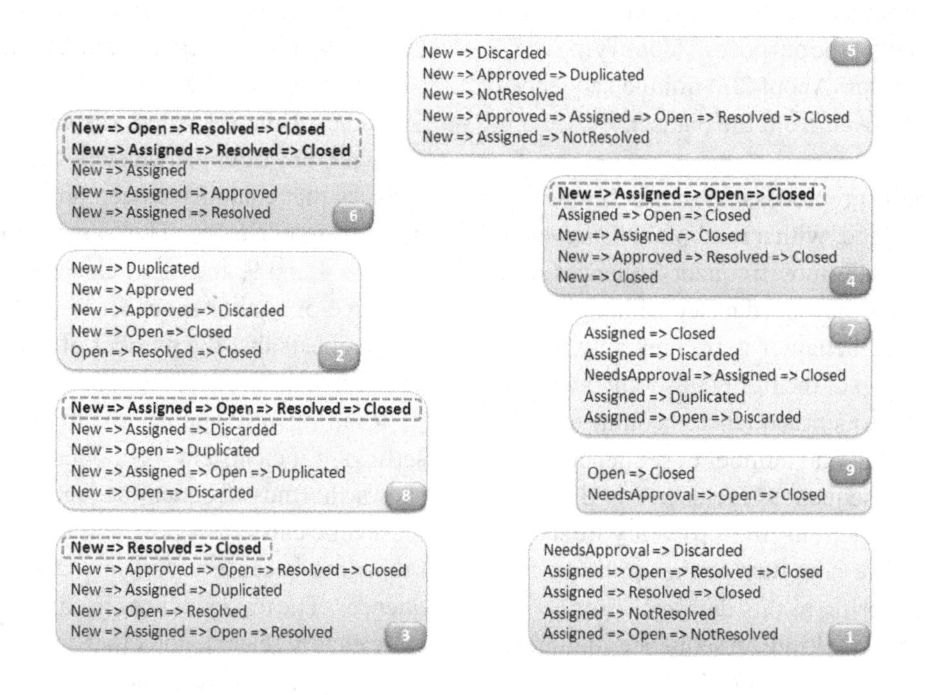

Figure 13. Top sequences and cluster models for 2 clusters

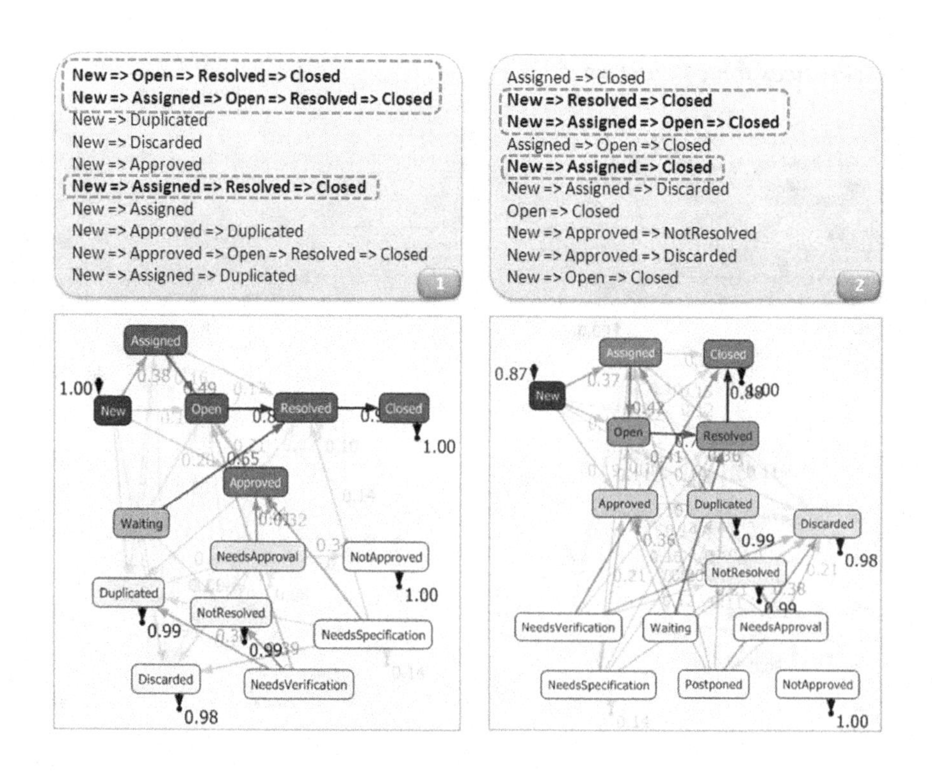

By setting the number of clusters to automatic, a surprising result emerged as the MSC algorithm produced only two clusters. Figure 13 shows the most frequent sequences for each cluster together with the corresponding cluster model. However, none of these models display clearly distinct behaviors. There are still similar sequences across the two clusters, and the cluster models do not help in establishing any meaningful difference. And yet, the dataset does contain very different sequences, as can be seen by manual inspection. These results suggest that the observed behavior, despite being quite heterogeneous, is evenly distributed in such a way that it is difficult to identify clearly distinct patterns.

We therefore turn to the study of the input dataset as a whole. If behavior cannot be separated into different clusters, then a single global model should suffice to identify typical behavior. Figure 14 depicts such model. Rather than transition probabilities, the actual state and transition counts are shown, providing an indication of the most frequent states as well as the most occurring transitions in absolute terms. Also, the node shading and line weight were made proportional to the state and transition counts, respectively. It is easy to see, for example, that "New" is the most recurring state, and that in most sequences the following state is "Assigned". However, some care must be taken when drawing conclusions about the most common sequences, as subsequent transitions may refer to different cases.

Looking up "New", "Assigned", "Open", "Resolved", "Closed", "Duplicated" and "Discarded" in Figure 14 reveals that the overall behavior in the input dataset actually resembles the original pro-

Figure 14. Global behavioral model for the preprocessed dataset (Only states with total count above 95 and transitions with total count above 35 are shown)

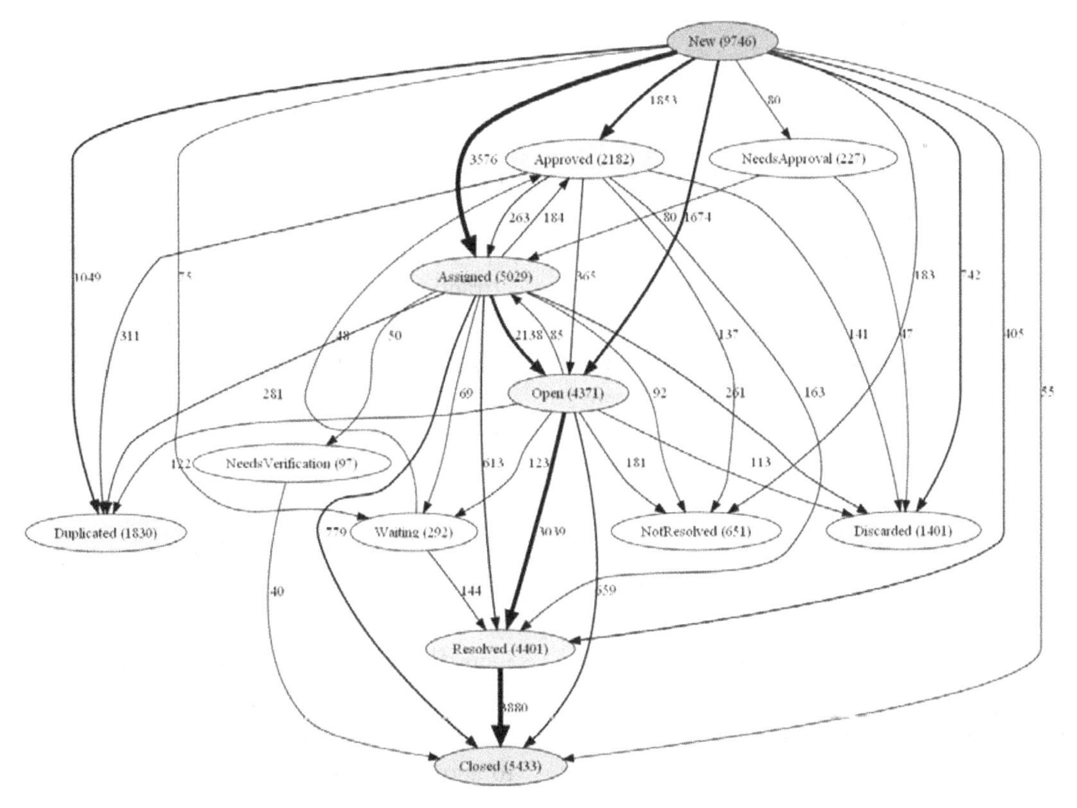

cess depicted in Figure 7. The main trend "New→Assigned→Open→Resolved→Closed" is clearly distinguishable in Figure 14, and the alternative branches are also apparent: "New→Duplicated" and "New→Discarded".

On the other hand, Figure 14 displays a lot of extra behavior that Figure 7 is unable to account for. When presenting the results to the company, some of this extra behavior was explained by business analysts as follows:

- About the transition: "New→Approved" – Some states are no longer being used. For example, in the past it was common to make new issues go through an approval process, and some of that behavior is still present in the database, as can be seen in Figure 14 in the transition from "New" to "Approved". Nowadays, that approval is implicit when the issue changes from "New" to "Assigned".
- About the transitions: "New→Open", "New→Resolved", "New→Closed" – The support team members usually skip steps when the solution to the issue is obvious. For example, the team member who registers a new issue may immediately recognize the problem and solve it, jumping directly to the "Resolved" state.
- About the transition: "Open→Assigned" – The state transitions may appear to be reversed as the result of arbitrary loops. For example, an issue may be assigned to and opened by a team member, just to find that it should have been assigned to someone else; in this case, a transition from "Open" to "Assigned" will be recorded. This kind of backtrack is also allowed by ITIL when there is escalation to a higher support level.
- About the transitions: "Assigned→Duplicated","Assigned→ Discarded", "Open→Duplicated", and "Open→Discarded" – The classification of an issue as a duplicate or the decision to discard it may come later in the process when more data about the issue has been collected or provided by the customer.

These special but relatively frequent cases explain most of the extra behavior shown in Figure 14. Overall, the event history recorded in the system database suggests that the issue handling process is being carried out in a way that is close to the originally intended process. The results of this study can now be used by business analysts to derive performance metrics, to investigate the causes of unusual behavior, or to devise new practices for the technical support team, to cite only a few of the potential benefits.

6. CONCLUSION

In both case studies, sequence clustering provided a useful result. Whereas in the first case study it showed that the work of the software team is structured according to a set of patterns, in the second case study the absence of distinct clusters suggests that the technical support team is indeed following the expected behavior for the issue handling process. This means that sequence clustering can become a useful technique both in the context of process discovery and in the context of process conformance.

What makes sequence clustering particularly attractive is its robustness to noise and its ability to deal with very large amounts of data. However, in practice it is often the case that some preprocessing must be applied before running the algorithm on the input dataset. This preprocessing is intended to build the input dataset in a way that the algorithm will produce results that can be easily interpreted by a business analyst. Allowing the presence of behavior that is known to be inadequate for processing will only make it more difficult to identify typical behavioral patterns.

In conclusion, sequence clustering with appropriate preprocessing is a powerful technique to acquire insight into the underlying structure of business processes. It can be used as a first approach to process mining, when the event log is large and must be partitioned into different behaviors. It is also useful when the presence of ad-hoc behavior makes it impossible for automated processing by deterministic algorithms. In these and other scenarios, sequence clustering becomes a valuable tool in the repertoire of available process mining techniques.

EXERCISES

1. Consider the following three cluster models, where states are represented by a single letter and arcs are labeled with the transition probabilities between states. Assume that a sequence may begin or end in any state.

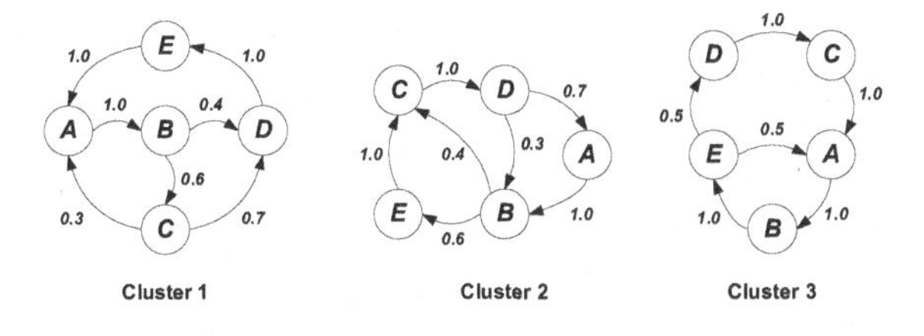

   For each of the following sequences, which cluster should it be assigned to? Why?
   (a) ABCD (b) CABE (c) EAB (d) BCDE
   (e) ABE (f) BCDB

2. Suppose that a cluster has been assigned the following four sequences: XWY, ZYXW, XWZY, and ZYXZ, where each letter stands for a state.
   Draw the cluster model and determine the transition probabilities.
   List three sequences of length 4 that are allowed by the cluster model but are not present in the original dataset.

3. Consider the following input dataset: {GBB, AAII, AEIIEBD, AEBBD, CCFCB, CFGFCBB, BBCD, BCDDD, DEEAC, AABCCD}
   With respect to the four preprocessing steps described in section 3:
   Apply step 1 assuming that any state that does not occur at least 3 times can be removed.
   Apply step 2 on the previous results.
   Apply step 3 on the previous results.
   Apply step 4 on the previous results.
   List the sequences in the preprocessed data-set.

4. Typically, the first step in preprocessing is to discard events with low support.
   In the first case study, only the first five actions in Figure 4 have been used to produce the results. Explain how the results would be affected if only the first three actions would have been used.
   In the second case study, all the states in Figure 9 have been used. Which states should be kept and which states could be discarded? Why? What would be the disadvantage of discarding those states?

SUGGESTED ADDITIONAL READING

For an introduction to the topic of model-based clustering and other data mining techniques, the book of (Han & Kamber, 2006) may serve as a general reference. A more formal account of Expectation-Maximization and related techniques can be found in (McLachlan & Krishnan, 1996). For sequence clustering in particular, the paper by (Cadez et al, 2003) describes the algorithm in detail together with an application to the discovery of navigation patterns on a Web site. The book of (Tang & MacLennan, 2005) as well as the online tutorials (Microsoft, 2007) explain how to use the MSC algorithm available in Microsoft SQL Server 2005® Analysis Services. The application of this algorithm in the context of process mining was first described in (Ferreira et al, 2007). For more information on the case studies presented here, we refer the reader to (Zacarias et al, 2005) and to (Ferreira & Mira da Silva, 2008). Regarding the problem of conformance checking of business processes, the work of (Rozinat & Aalst, 2008) is especially interesting and recommended.

REFERENCES

Aalst, W. M. P. van der, Dongen, B. F. van, Herbst, J., Maruster, L., Schimm, G., & Weijters, A. J. M. M. (2003). Workflow mining: A survey of issues and approaches. *Data and Knowledge Engineering, 47*(2), 237-267.

Aalst, W. M. P. van der, Reijers, H. A., Song, M. (2005).Discovering social networks from event logs *Computer Supported Cooperative work, 14*(6), 549-593.

Aalst, W. M. P. van der, Weijters, A. J. M. M. (2004). Process mining: A research agenda. *Computers in Industry, 53*(3), 231-244.

Aalst, W. M. P. van der, Weijters, A. J. M. M., & Maruster, L. (2004). Workflow mining: Discovering process models from event logs. *IEEE Transactions on Knowledge and Data Engineering, 16*(9), 1128-1142.

Agrawal, R., Gunopulos, D., & Leymann, F. (1998). Mining process models from workflow logs. In *Proceedings of the 6th International Conference on Extending Database Technology: Advances in Database Technology,* (LNCS 1377, pp. 469-483). Springer.

Medeiros, A. K. Alves de, Weijters, A. J. M. M., & Aalst W. M. P. van der (2007). Genetic process mining: An experimental evaluation. *Data Mining and Knowledge Discovery, 14*(2), 245-304.

Medeiros, A. K. Alves de, Guzzo, A., Greco, G., Aalst, W. M. P. van der, Weijters, A. J. M. M., Dongen, B. van, & Sacca, D. (2008). Process mining based on clustering: A quest for precision. In *Proceedings of the BPM 2007 International Workshops,* (LNCS 4928). Springer.

van Bon, J., Pieper, M., van der Veen, A. (2005). *Foundations of IT service management based on ITIL.* Van Haren Publishing.

Cadez, I., Heckerman, D., Meek, C., Smyth, P., White, S. (2003, October). Model-based clustering and visualization of navigation patterns on a Web site. *Data Mining and Knowledge Discovery, 7*(4), 399-424.

Ceglowski, A., Churilov, L., & Wassertheil, J. (2005). Knowledge discovery through mining emergency department data. In *Proceedings of the 38th Annual Hawaii International Conference on System Sciences (HICSS '05).*

Chen, Y., Reilly, K., Sprague, A., & Guan, Z. (2006). SEQOPTICS: A protein sequence clustering system. *BMC Bioinformatics, 7*(Suppl 4), S10.

Cook, J., & Wolf, A. (1995). Automating process discovery through event-data analysis. In *Proceedings of the 17th International Conference on Software Engineering,* (pp.73-82). ACM Press.

Dempster, A., Laird, N., & Rubin, D. (1977). Maximum likelihood from incomplete data via the EM algorithm. *Journal of the Royal Statistical Society, Series B, 39*(1), 1-38.

Dongen, B. F. van, & Aalst, W. M. P. van der (2004). Multi-phase process mining: Building instance graphs. In *Proceedings of the International Conference on Conceptual Modeling (ER 2004),* (LNCS, 3288, pp. 362-376). Berlin: Springer-Verlag.

Enright, A., Dongen, S. van, & Ouzounis, C. (2002). An efficient algorithm for large-scale detection of protein families. *Nucleic Acids Research, 30*(7), 1575-1584.

Ferreira, D., Zacarias, M., Malheiros, M., & Ferreira, P. (2007). Approaching process mining with sequence clustering: Experiments and findings. In *Proceedings of the 5th International Conference on Business Process Management (BPM 2007),* (LNCS 4714, pp. 360-374), Springer.

Ferreira, D., & Mira da Silva, M. (2008, April). Using process mining for ITIL assessment: A case study with incident management. In *Proceedings of the 13th Annual UKAIS Conference*, Bournemouth University.

Greco, G.,Guzzo, A., Pontieri, L., & Saccà, D. (2004). Mining expressive process models by clustering workflow traces. In *Procedings of the 8th Pacific-Asia Conference (PAKDD 2004),* (LNCS, 3056), Springer.

Greco, G., Guzzo, A., & Pontieri, L. (2005). Mining hierarchies of models: From abstract views to concrete specifications. In *Proceedings of the 3rd International Conference on Business Process Management (BPM2005),* (LNCS 3649). Springer.

Han, J., & Kamber, M. (2006). *Data mining: Concepts and techniques*, 2nd edition. Morgan Kaufmann.

Herbst, J., & Karagiannis, D. (1998). Integrating machine learning and workflow management to support acquisition and adaptation of workflow models. In *Proceedings of the 9th International Workshop on Database and Expert Systems Applications,* (pp.745-752).

Jung, J.-Y., Bae, J., & Liu, L. (2008). Hierarchical business process clustering. In *Proceedings of the IEEE International Conference on Services Computing (SCC '08),* (pp. 613-616).

Li, W., Jaroszewski, L., & Godzik, A. (2002, August). Sequence clustering strategies improve remote homology recognitions while reducing search times. *Protein Engineering, 15*(8), 643-649.

McLachlan, G., & Krishnan, T. (1996). *The EM algorithm and extensions.* John Wiley & Sons.

Rozinat, A., Mans, R. S., & Aalst, W.M.P. van der (2006, October). Mining CPN models: Discovering process models with data from event logs. In *Proceedings of the Seventh Workshop on the Practical Use of Coloured Petri Nets and CPN Tools* (CPN 2006), (DAIMI, 579, pp. 57-76), Aarhus, Denmark.

Rozinat, A., & Aalst, W.M.P. van der (2008). Conformance checking of processes based on monitoring real behavior. *Information Systems, 33*(1), 64-95.

Song, M., Günther, C., Aalst, W. M. P. van der (2008, September). Trace clustering in process mining. In *Proceedings of the 4th Workshop on Business Process Intelligence (BPI 08)*, Milan, Italy.

Tang, Z., & MacLennan, J. (2005). *Data mining with SQL Server 2005.* John Wiley & Sons.

Zacarias, M., Marques, A., Pinto, H., Tribolet, J. (2005, July). Enhancing collaboration services with business context models. *International Workshop on Cooperative Systems and Context, 5th International and Interdisciplinary Conference on Modeling and Using Context.*

Zacarias, M., Pinto, H., & Tribolet, J. (2006, October). A context-based approach to discover multitasking behavior at work. In *Proceeding of the 5th International Workshop on Task Models and Diagrams for User Interface Design.*

KEY TERMS

Behavioral Pattern: A behavior that has been observed to be common to multiple sequences.

Cluster Model: The model that represents the dominant behavior within a cluster.

Event Log: A file that contains recorded run-time behavior.

Parameters: A set of variables that can be configured in order to change the behavior of an algorithm.

Preprocessing: A series of steps applied to a dataset in order to facilitate its analysis.

Process Mining: Field of research that studies techniques to discover business process models automatically from recorded behavior.

Sequence Clustering: A data mining technique that groups sequences into clusters according to their similarity.

ENDNOTES

[1] A tutorial covering these steps is available at: http://msdn.microsoft.com/en-us/library/ms167167.aspx

[2] The documentation for AMO is available at: http://msdn.microsoft.com/en-us/library/ms124924.aspx

[3] A reference for DMX is available at: http://msdn.microsoft.com/en-us/library/ms132058.aspx

Chapter XXIII
A Data-Centric Design Methodology for Business Processes

Kamal Bhattacharya
IBM T.J. Watson Research Lab, USA

Richard Hull
IBM T.J. Watson Research Lab, USA

Jianwen Su
University of California at Santa Barbara, USA

ABSTRACT

This chapter describes a design methodology for business processes and workflows that focuses first on "business artifacts", which represent key (real or conceptual) business entities, including both the business-relevant data about them and their macro-level lifecycles. Individual workflow services (a.k.a. tasks) are then incorporated, by specifying how they operate on the artifacts and fit into their lifecycles. The resulting workflow is specified in a particular artifact-centric workflow model, which is introduced using an extended example. At the logical level this workflow model is largely declarative, in contrast with most traditional workflow models which are procedural and/or graph-based. The chapter includes a discussion of how the declarative, artifact-centric workflow specification can be mapped into an optimized physical realization.

1. INTRODUCTION

Most traditional workflow models are based on a procedural and/or graph-based paradigm for specifying how a business process or workflow is supposed to operate, and methodologies to design workflows in those models are typically founded on a process-centric perspective. This chapter describes a fundamentally different approach to workflow design, which is founded on a data-centric perspective, and which is especially useful for designing the detailed operation of business processes for enterprises in the modern era. The first major step in this data-centric approach is to identify the "business artifacts", which correspond to key (real or conceptual) business entities that are to be managed by the workflow. Examples include sales invoices, insurance claims, shipments, financing "deals", and customers. A business artifact includes both business-relevant data about the business entity, along with information about the macro-level lifecycle that the entity moves through, including the key stages of the processing of the entity and how they are or might be sequenced. The second major step is to develop a detailed logical specification of the data needed about each class of artifacts, the services (a.k.a. tasks) that will operate on the artifacts, and the associations between the services and the artifacts. In contrast with most workflow models used in industry today, the services and associations are described in a declarative manner, using pre-conditions and conditional effects for the services and Event-Condition-Action (ECA) rules for the associations. The third and final major step is to map the declarative workflow specification into a more procedural specification, which can be optimized and then mapped into a physical implementation. In addition to describing the data-centric design methodology, this chapter describes an artifact-centric workflow model which can be used as the target for data-centric workflow design activities. A business process is a set of (typically linked) activities executed by various stakeholders to provide value to a customer without exposing the customer to the costs and risks involved in delivering value. With enterprises of today shifting their business strategies from the more traditional product focus to a customer focus, it is important to be specific about how to organize business operations to deliver business value and enable growth. Business processes are a means to operationalize a business strategy and have become an important aspect of gaining the leading edge in the market place over competitors. Business processes are thereby a key element of an enterprise's "survival kit" and a lever to ensure growth and most importantly, outperform competitors.

Business process modeling is the act of representing a business process in a format (often a graphical representation) that can be used to communicate the intent of a process to different business stakeholders. The level of detail included in a business process model is determined by how the model is being used. For example, providing guidance about process execution may only require a step-by-step description whereas using a business process model as a driver for implementing a complete workflow may require a much greater level of detail.

Using process models as a driver for implementing workflow systems that will support business process execution poses significant design challenges. In most current approaches, activity-flows are designed to specify the how processing is organized. Data is incorporated, but usually at a limited level that focuses on the inputs and outputs of individual services. As a result, it is hard to obtain an understanding of the overall possible effects of the overall sequence of processing steps on key business entities. In contrast, data modeling is a crucial aspect of virtually all software design approaches. The emerging "business artifact" paradigm described in this chapter gives data a foundational role in the context of business process design. In particular, the notion of business artifact introduces data as a first-class modeling primitive that will drive the process modeling. A business artifact holds all of the business-relevant data and lifecycle information of concerning a key business entity. A business artifact-centered modeling approach first identifies these artifacts and specifies their information models (i.e., database schemas) and their macro-level lifecycles. For example, a withdrawal request in a bank can serve as the basis for an artifact, which specifies all the information required for a certain bank transaction. The lifecycle describes the various steps for how a withdrawal request artifact might be processed (from initially filling out the form to make the request to close of transaction). The data in the withdrawal request artifact should be necessary and sufficient to execute all the processing steps without any ambiguity. The completion of each service (task) that works on the withdrawal request can be viewed as a milestone of the overall end-to-end transaction.

This chapter is focused primarily on business artifacts and how these can be used to provide core elements of an overall design methodology for business operations. As such, many important aspects of business process management are not discussed here. For example, while the notion of business artifact is an extremely useful conceptualization for business process designers, the chapter does not discuss user interfaces or tools to help the designers with documenting or viewing a design. Similarly, user interfaces and their automatic generation for performing individual services (tasks) managed by the workflow are not considered. The important area of exceptions is not discussed. Support for monitoring business processes, including the tracking of key performance indicators (KPIs) and creating "dashboards" for high-level managers, is not covered. Management of the overall lifecycle of business processes, including the evolution of the business process designs is not addressed. And the use of "business rules", which might express high-level goals and constraints on the business operations, and might be specified using the SBVR standard, are not discussed. In all of these cases, and for many other aspects of business process, we believe that the design methodology and constructs described here provide a natural and robust foundation for their incorporation.

In this chapter, we present a data-centric methodology for business process design. In Section 2, the methodology is outlined in brief. Section 3 demonstrates the key design steps and techniques of this methodology using an example application. Section 4 briefly discusses the benefits of using a data-centric methodology and workflow model. Section 5 offers a summary and conclusions.

2. THE DATA-CENTRIC DESIGN METHODOLOGY

This section provides an overview of the data-centric design methodology. This methodology is based on a three-level framework, which is provides the structure for how high-level declarative business process models can be mapped faithfully into implemented, procedural workflows. In Section 2.1, a rich family of possible artifact-centric workflow models is described. In Section 2.2, the design methodology itself is outlined.

At the core of the data-centric design methodology is a three-level framework for business processes (Figure 1). At the top level, a Business Operations Model (BOM) provides a detailed *logical specification* of business process execution. In the running example used in this chapter, in addition to business artifacts, the BOM includes services specified in terms of their semantics (including pre-conditions and conditional effects), and ECA rules. At the bottom level is the *executable* workflow system in which executable services communicate with each other through messages and manipulate artifacts. At the middle is the *conceptual flow* that captures essentially the BOM in a procedural manner, while hiding implementation details. This level is suitable for

Figure 1. Three logical levels of BPM

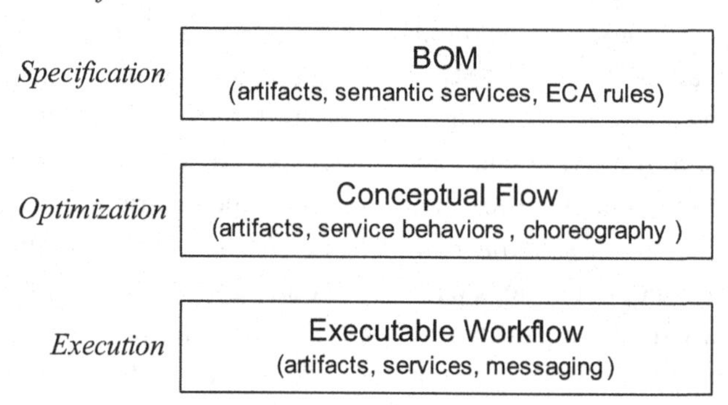

optimization since it allows for efficient reasoning in the context of the physical requirements for implementation, including possibly legacy systems and distribution of the workflow across organizations.

2.1. A Family of Possible Artifact-Centric Business Process Models

There are many ways that the central notion of business artifact can be used as the basis for a workflow model. Although the chapter is focused on a specific artifact-centric workflow model, this section provides a more general overview of possible artifact-centric workflow models.

There are four key elements in an artifact-centric workflow model: *business artifact information model, business artifact macro-level lifecycle, services* (*tasks*), and the *association* of services to business artifacts. We use the term 'association' here to indicate that the association might be specified in a largely declarative way using rules or a much more procedural manner using a flowchart or conventional workflow model. When it is clear from the context, we sometimes use the term 'artifact' to mean 'business artifact.'

In the following, we give a brief explanation of these four concepts, while noting that the concepts may take different (syntactic and semantic) forms in different steps of design.

Business Artifact Inormation Model. The information model (or database schema) of a business artifact is intended to hold all of the information needed in completing business process execution in connection with a given business entity. The artifact data should incorporate the information needed to (i) capture business process goals, and (ii) allow for evaluating how thoroughly these goals are achieved. Example data found in artifacts include data that are received during the business process execution from the external world, data that are produced by the execution, and data that record the decisions taken in the execution.

A business artifact has an *identity* and can be tracked as it progresses through the workflow. It can have a set of *attributes* to store the data needed for the workflow execution; in the general setting, both attributes and their values can be created, updated, or deleted by the services in the workflow. The attributes may be simple scalars or richly nested data structures. A good approach to modeling artifacts is to make them *self-contained*, in that all data needed by the artifact is present in the artifact. A subtlety arises when one artifact needs to refer to another one. For example, an order artifact typically refers to a customer, which may also be represented by an artifact. While it is appropriate to use the customer ID as a way to refer to a given customer, specific order-relevant data such as the shipping address of the customer, at the time the order was made, should be stored (either physically or virtually) as a part of the order.

In business terms, an artifact represents the explicit knowledge concerning progress toward a business operational goal at any instant. Operational goals, such as processing a customer order, are measurable results that individually and in the aggregate satisfy the purpose of the business. The information contained in the set of artifacts records all the information about the business operation. Hence, at any time of execution, the "runtime state" of a business process is determined by the snapshot of all artifacts.

Business Artifact (Macro-Level) Lifecycle. In the data-centric methodology, business artifacts combine, at a fundamental level, the information model for key business entities along with their macro-level lifecycle. In most cases the business stakeholders can describe this macro-level lifecycle in terms of stages in the possible evolution of the artifact, from inception to final disposition and archiving. In the artifact-centric workflow model presented in Section 3, the macro-level lifecycle of a given class of artifacts is represented using a variant of finite state machines, where each state of the machine corresponds to a possible stage in the life-cycle of an artifact from this class. In this variant of state machines, little or nothing is indicated about why or how an artifact might move from one stage to another, although conditions may be attached to transitions in the machine.

Artifacts may have differing "life expectancies." In some cases the artifact is relatively short-lived (e.g., a customer order), in other cases relatively long-lived (e.g., a customer, including an ongoing log of services to a customer, their preference level for the enterprise, their perceived level of satisfaction), and in yet other cases the artifact is essentially permanent (e.g., an artifact which holds the information about a product type, including product description, availability, and purchasing trends).

Services. A service in an artifact-centric business process encapsulates a unit of work meaningful to the whole business process in at least two aspects. First, the potential changes made by the service should reflect a measurable step (or steps) of progress towards the business goal. Second, the division of the business process into some collection of services should be able to accommodate (expected) administrative organization structures, IT infrastructures, customer-visible status, etc. Technically, a service makes changes to one or more business artifacts, and the changes should be transactional, i.e., a service should have (the effect of having) exclusive control over the involved artifacts when making these changes.

The term "service" rather than "task" is used here, to emphasize the close correspondence between the kind of services used here and the kinds of services found in the Services Oriented Architecture (SOA) and in web services in general. This is especially relevant as workflows will become increasingly distributed in the future, both across sub-organizations of a single organization, and via the web across multiple independent organizations.

In the design methodology, services are introduced in Step 2 as semantic services (in the spirit of OWL-S). In Step 3, the service specifications are extended to include a specific implementation (typically expressed as an algorithm or in a programming language). The executable services are then developed in Step 4.

Associations. In a business process services make changes to artifacts in a manner that is restricted by a family of constraints. These constraints might stem from a procedural specification (e.g., a flowchart) or from a declarative specification (e.g., a set of rules and logical properties that must be satisfied). Some common types of constraints include precedence relationships among the services, between services and external events (e.g., receiving a request), and between services and internal events (e.g., timeout). In many cases the constraints involve relative or absolute times, and are thus temporal constraints.

Association takes different forms in the three logical levels of BPM. In Section 3, at the BOM level, the association is expressed in a largely declarative fashion, using Event-Condition-Action (ECA) rules (e.g., when inventory falls below 10%, if there are orders from good customers in the queue, then replenish inventory quickly). At the Conceptual Flow level, the association is refined into a global "choreography", which provides at a logical level a more procedural specification of how data is distributed across "containers" and how service execution will occur (when and what actions to be taken on artifacts resident in which containers, based on what internal or external events and/or other considerations). At the Workflow level, the association is expressed as a procedural workflow that is implemented as executable services that communicating among each other and externally.

We use the acronym "BALSA" (for "Business Artifacts with Lifecycle, Services, and Associations") to refer to data-centric workflow models that combine these basic building blocks. The BOM for the running example presented in Section 3 shall use a particular variant of such models, called here BALSA^{basic}. As will be seen, the BALSA^{basic} model uses the Entity-Relationship data model to specify the format of artifacts, a framework for specifying services stemming from the Semantic Web Services literature, and (logical-level) Event-Condition-Action (ECA) rules for specifying the associations between services and artifacts.

A variety of other BALSA models can be obtained by varying the paradigm used in specifying the information model, lifecycle, services, and associations are specified. The artifact information model might be specified as attributes with scalar values, attributes with scalar or nested relation values, attributes stemming from ER schemas as in BALSA^{basic}, or XML, to name a few. The lifecycle might be specified using flowcharts (with or without parallelism), finite state machines as in BALSA^{basic}, state charts, or declarative mechanisms based on ECA or CA, among other choices. The services might be specified by giving details about their internal functioning (e.g., using flowcharts, state machines, BPEL), or in a more black-box manner by specifying only their I/O properties, or in a gray-box manner—as in BALSA^{basic}—using I/O and also pre- and post-conditions, among other possibilities. There is a fuzzy boundary between the paradigm used for specifying lifecycles and the paradigm used for specifying associations. For example, generalization of BALSA^{basic} could be obtained by using ECA rules to specify the lifecycles, and letting the designer decide whether to use a state machine paradigm or something else for lifecycle of artifacts in a particular BOM. Further, the distinction between lifecycle and association is fuzzy—in some variations of BALSA the lifecycle might be extremely detailed, in essence encompassing all aspects of the association level. The choice among the different paradigms in constructing a BALSA workflow model will depend on the intended areas of application.

2.2. Overview of Design Methodology

The design methodology is firmly centered on the data being manipulated as a business is managed. Data-centeredness is specifically reflected in two design principles. One is the *data first principle*, which demands that at each step, data consideration, specification, and design should precede that of other components. The other is the *data centered principle*, which suggests that the specification and design of tasks and workflow should be formulated using the data design obtained at each step.

Figure 2 summarizes the methodology for business process design. The design methodology consists of four major steps: (1) *business artifact discovery*, (2) *business operations modeling*, and

Figure 2. Design methodology at a glance

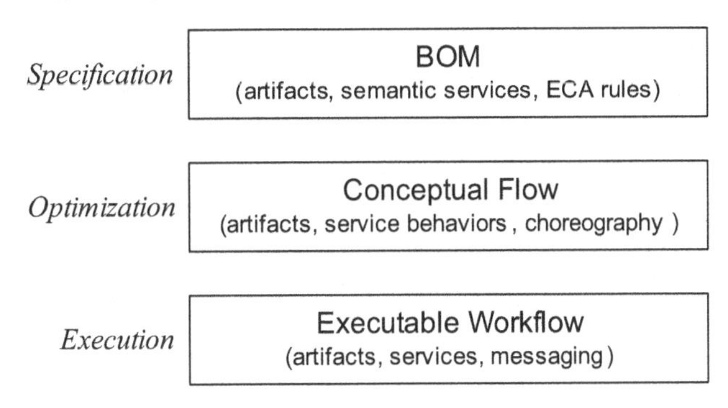

(3) *conceptual workflow design*, and (4) *workflow realization*. The first two steps aim at formulating a BOM as a logical specification of the business operations meaningful to business stakeholders, and with sufficient details to allow technical analysis and verification. The BOM provides a basis for system implementation. The last two steps focus on translating the BOM into an executable composition of services and sub-systems that faithfully "realizes" the BOM, in the sense that the execution of the underlying workflow corresponds to the intentions expressed using the ECA rules in the BOM.

We now consider the methodology in more detail. The goal of Step 1 is to develop a high level specification of the business operations through discovering key artifacts and important stages in their life cycles. Identifying artifacts requires an understanding of the whole business process, how data are changed and shared through the process, and what data hold critical business process information. This is done through a combination of top-down analysis and by examining typical scenarios (normal business cases and exceptional cases). Example scenarios could include, e.g., approving a qualified loan application, cancellation of an existing application, situations when credit-checking is unnecessary. A scenario does not have to be complete. Scenarios are useful as they are concrete examples of what should happen under some circumstance and how. Step 1(b) is to discover and develop scenarios.

Based on the top-down analysis and scenarios, in Step 1(b) important business stages are formulated and then the processing constraints on artifacts from the scenarios are synthesized to form an artifact *life cycle* representing possible ways for artifacts to complete in the business process. One possible form of representing an artifact life cycle is a directed graph with nodes representing stages and edges reflecting the sequencing requirements. Each graph defines a life cycle state machine. It is interesting to note that the machine is in many cases an abstraction of business processes in which hardcopy documents move between places.

In Step 2, the preliminary design produced in Step 1 provides the basic skeleton around which the BOM can be constructed. In particular, Step 2(a) focuses on data design of artifacts; in particular, the details of the artifact schemas are specified using ER diagrams, which provide a natural framework for specifying these designs at an appropriate level of detail. In Step 2(b), the business activities are examined with respect to the logical artifact schemas. Using the life cycle state machines to provide a macro-structure, abstract services are developed for the various business activities which operate on the artifacts. Finally in step 2(c) the associations between the services and the artifacts are specified.

Figure 3. Key artifacts for DES example, and primary relationships between them

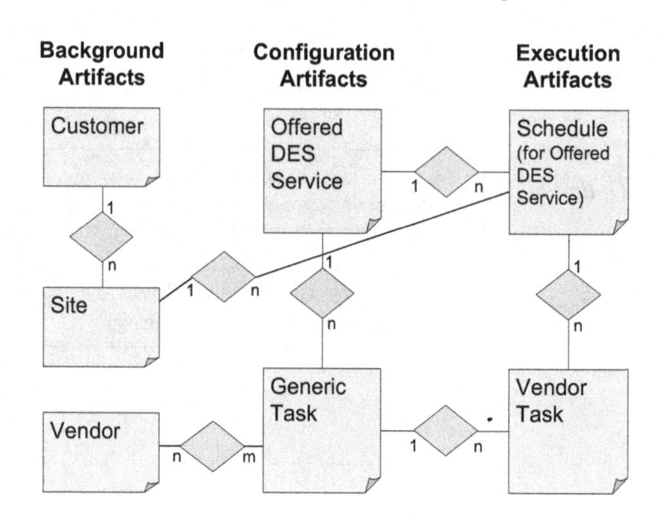

Steps 3 and 4 start from the BOM developed in Step 2 with the goal of obtaining an executable workflow system. This chapter is focused on workflow realizations for which there is a lack of central control, with components (artifacts and services) distributed both geographically and administratively. This is motivated by the increasing trend for outsourcing and globalization as enabled by the internet. For this context, a conceptual flow diagram is first developed in Step 3 that describes globally how different data and service components should be coordinated to fulfill the business operational requirements as specified in the BOM. The conceptual flow diagram can be viewed as another variant of the BALSA framework, in which the associations between services and artifacts are procedural in nature. In the methodology, the conceptual flow diagram is further modified to satisfy the service behavioral constraints, and optimized according to performance metrics. In Step 4, individual components as well as the workflow are turned into software systems with less or clear dependency.

3. ILLUSTRATION OF THE DESIGN METHODOLOGY

This section will illustrate the key elements of the data-centric design methodology using an example from the IT service provider business, called *Distributed Enterprise Services (DES)*. First the example is described, after which three subsections discuss steps 1, 2, and 3 (respectively) of the data-centric design methodology outlined in Section 2.

The DES example focuses on an IT service provider that provides IT services to one or more enterprises, each of which comprise a large number of geographically distributed "small sites". To avoid confusion, when it is not clear from the context we shall refer to the IT services in the DES example as 'DES services', and refer to the services used to manage the business operations of the IT service provider as 'BOM services'.

In the DES example, provided DES services include IT provisioning, installation, and maintenance as well as general support. Typical examples for small sites are individual hotels that are part of a larger chain, or fast food restaurants that are part of a franchise. The IT service provider typically signs a contract with a given chain or franchise corporation, which determines the service level agreements (SLAs) for each request for a given DES service. For example, a hotel corporation might sign a contract with the IT service provider that allows the provider to perform any kind of IT systems-related services at individual hotel sites. The DES services provided at the sites may be performed by the IT service provider themselves or by one or more sub-contracted vendors, the latter being rather typical due to the highly distributed nature of the problem.

3.1. Business Artifact Discovery for DES

In managing the business operations of an IT service provider of Distributed Enterprise Services, the artifact-centered approach focuses on the key business entities that keep track of how the business (in this case the IT service provider) reaches its operational goals. The first step of the design methodology is to identify, at a high level, these entities, along with the key stages of their life-cycle. The process used is typically a combination of top-down consideration along with scenario-based requirements gathering. Scenarios are often easy for the business stake-holders to create and understand, and should include both "sunny day" and exceptional cases.

The main operational goal in DES is the completion of a (possibly complex) DES service or installation at a site. The key kind of artifact that measures progress towards the operation goal for this case is called a *Schedule* artifact. It contains the planned and actual content of the installation project plan, including any mid-stream modifications to the plan and the working documents transferred between tasks as part of the execution. Note that the term "schedule" for this business case was derived from the fact that an outline project plan is generally attached as a schedule to the contract statement of work (SOW). A second important class of artifacts is called *Vendor Task*. Each artifact in this class corresponds to an individual (DES) task to be performed, by the IT service provider or one of its sub-contractors, as part of an overall schedule. In general a single *Schedule* artifact will refer to several *Vendor Task* artifacts.

Figure 3 shows at a high level the key artifacts for the DES example. Shown on the right-hand side are the two artifacts already described, which are used primarily during the "execution" of DES services. In the middle of the diagram are two artifact classes used during the "configuration" or set-up of a DES service. Specifically, the *Offered DES Service* artifact class holds templates for the different kinds of DES services that can be provided. In general, an actual *Schedule* artifact will be created by starting with an *Offered DES Service* artifact and then instantiating various components of it. Similarly, the *Generic Task* artifact class holds descriptions of (DES) tasks that are available to the IT service provider, including information on the vendors that provide them and the geographic regions for which they are available. Finally, on the left-hand side are some key artifact classes that provide on-going background information, including about the *Customers* of the IT service provider, along with the *Sites* that those customers have, and also about the *Vendors* that the IT service provider uses as sub-contractors.

It should be emphasized that an *Offered DES Service* artifact will include data that is essentially a high-level script or program, which will be referred to by the BOM services that work on individual *Schedule* artifacts. A *Schedule* artifact, in turn, will also essentially hold a script that is interpreted during the second phase of the execution of the BOM. This gives some indication of the richness of data that an artifact might hold, and how that data might be used.

As suggested above, the naming of artifacts is typically domain specific. The discovery of artifacts is usually a process that involves discussions with business stakeholders and subject matter experts (SMEs). The focus in these discussions is not on the BOM services executed to run the business, but rather on the entities that are used to manage the business operations. This includes identifying the key information related to these entities and also the high-level stages of their lifecycles. Figure 4 illustrates the high-level lifecycles for artifacts from the *Schedule* and *Vendor Task* classes.

In BALSA^{basic}, the high-level lifecycle of artifacts is specified using finite-state machines, typically with conditions on the transitions. Each state of the machine corresponds to a *stage* in the lifecycle of the artifact; these stages typically correspond to business-relevant phases in the overall artifact lifecycle. In Figure 4, the stages are shown using rounded rectangles with solid line boundaries. The dashed-line rectangles are included to suggest how the finite state machines extended to incorporate hierarchy. Although not formally included into BALSA^{basic}, these dashed-line "states" might be to provide a mechanism that permits substitution of one workflow component by another workflow component (e.g., by swapping the contents of a high-level state such as *Planning* for another version of it). This mechanism might be useful during BOM evolutions, or if a generic BOM is used to represent a global business, and specializations of it are used as the BOMs for different regions.

As shown in Figure 4, there are six stages in the lifecycle of a *Schedule* artifact, and four in the lifecycle of a *Vendor Task* artifact. The *Schedule_planning* phase includes BOM services that select and then flesh out an *OfferedDES Service* artifact, to create a *Schedule* artifact for a given IT service engagement. At some point during execution the schedule may move into the *Schedule_approvals* stage, where various management approvals (and perhaps external approvals from client and/or government) may be obtained. The condition governing this transition might state that all generic tasks needed to fulfill the schedule have

Figure 4. Representative artifact type lifecycles

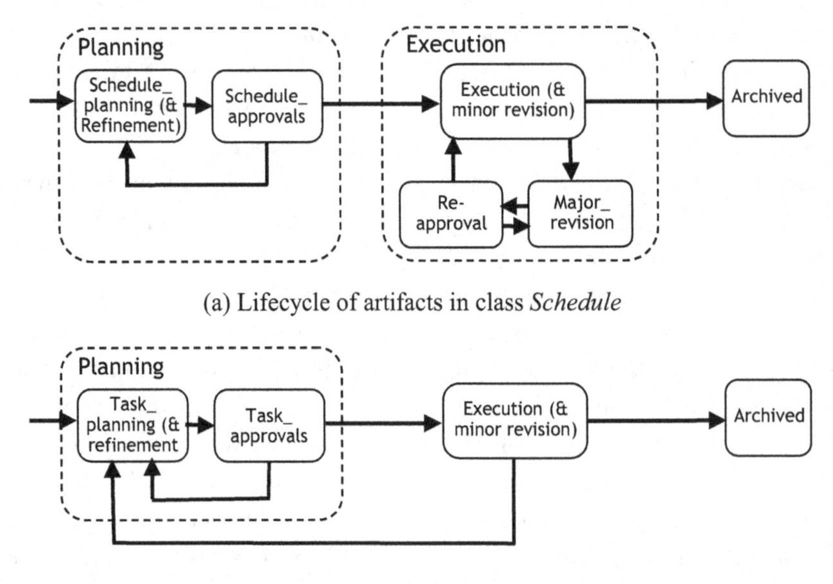

(a) Lifecycle of artifacts in class *Schedule*

(b) Lifecycle of artifacts in class *Vendor Task*

been associated to a specific *Vendor Task* artifact, with all dates and task-level government approvals established. Once in the *Schedule_approvals* stage, if the approvals are successful, the schedule moves onto the *Execution* stage; otherwise it goes back to *Schedule_planning*. (An alternative semantics would be to allow some stages to operate in parallel, in a controlled manner. This is not studied here, but is certainly an important topic for future investigation.) Minor plan revisions may occur in the *Execution* phase, but if more significant revisions are needed then the installation will pass into the *Major_revision* and *Re-approval* stages. Eventually, hopefully after a successful engagement, the schedule is *Archived*. The lifecycle of *Vendor Task* artifacts is similar. Not shown for either artifact class are transitions used if a schedule or vendor task is aborted (and archived) before successful completion.

As a general design principle, the conditions on transitions between artifact stages should be focused on the minimal business requirements needed to pass between them. As will be seen below, additional conditions governing when an artifact can pass from one stage to another can be incorporated at the level of associations. This provides rich flexibility in terms of specializing the basic artifact lifecycle to fit with a variety of contexts, e.g., resulting from government regulations in different regions, DES offerings provided at different budget points or for different classes of customers, or even occasional sales promotions or other special offerings.

As noted in Section 2.1, artifacts may have different life expectancies. In the DES example, the *Schedule* and *Vendor Task* artifacts may have lives of a month to a year, but have a definite beginning, middle, and end. The artifacts of other classes shown will typically have longer lives, but may individually be retired as they become obsolete. Allowing for artifact classes with these varying life expectances provides considerable flexibility while keeping the number of constructs in the BALSA workflow framework to a minimum.

3.2. Design of the Business Operations Model for DES

Creating a Business Operations Model (BOM) from the high-level artifact class and lifecycle specifications involves three primary steps, namely detailed specification at the logical level of: (a) the artifact information models and macro-level lifecycles, (b) the BOM services that will help move artifacts through their lifecycles, and (c) the ECA rules that associate the services to the artifact classes. These three steps typically occur simultaneously, although conceptually the artifact design leads naturally to the service design, and from there to the association step. This subsection considers each of these steps in turn, and also provides some comments on the operational semantics of the ECA rules used here.

Specification of artifact information models and lifecycles. As just mentioned, a primary step in the process of designing the BOM is to created specifications for the key artifacts, including both their information models and macro-level lifecycles. The discussion here will focus only on the information models for key artifacts, because representative macro-level lifecycles for them have already been described in Section 3.1 (see Figure 4).

Figure 5 shows portions of the information models for four of the key artifacts in the DES example. Entity-Relationship (ER) diagrams provide a convenient framework for specifying the information models, and tools are available to map such diagrams into relational database schemas. Each ER diagram is centered around its key artifact class; in essence all of the information held by the ER schema can be thought of as providing information about individual artifacts in this class. While the information models use ER paradigms for artifact classes discussed here, the artifacts might be physically stored using, e.g., relational or XML-based databases. In these ER diagrams the focus is on the "current" values that can be associated with an artifact. One typically thinks of an artifact information model in terms of providing storage for a variety of *attributes* of the artifact, e.g., for a *Schedule* artifact attributes such as associated the current stage, start-/end-dates, and references to associated *Vendor Tasks*, etc. In general, it is also useful to retain a log of values that have been overwritten over the course of an artifact's lifecycle.

When an artifact is created, many of its attributes have *undefined* or null values. As the artifact progresses through its lifecycle, the attributes may be assigned values, i.e., become *defined*, they may be overwritten (or in the case of set- or list-valued attributes they may obtain or lose elements). In addition, some attribute values may become *invalidated.* Intuitively, a service (task) might switch an attribute value to "invalid" as a way to indicate the existing value violates a constraint and should be repaired by some subsequent service invocation. This might arise, for example, because the *start_date* of one vendor task t_1 should be after the *end_date* of some other vendor task t_2, but the *end_date* of t_2 has just be re-assigned to a value which is after the assigned *start_date* of t_1. The use of these three types of values (*undefined, invalidated, defined*) is optional although convenient in many practical settings.

Key aspects of the four ER schemas in Figure 5 are now highlighted. Not all attributes for the artifacts are shown; rather the portions of the schemas shown are to suggest what might be included. The *Offered DES Service* schema provides scalar attributes for an *ID*, for the current *stage* the artifact is in, for a *description*, and for

Figure 5. Details of portions of ER diagrams for selected artifacts in DES example

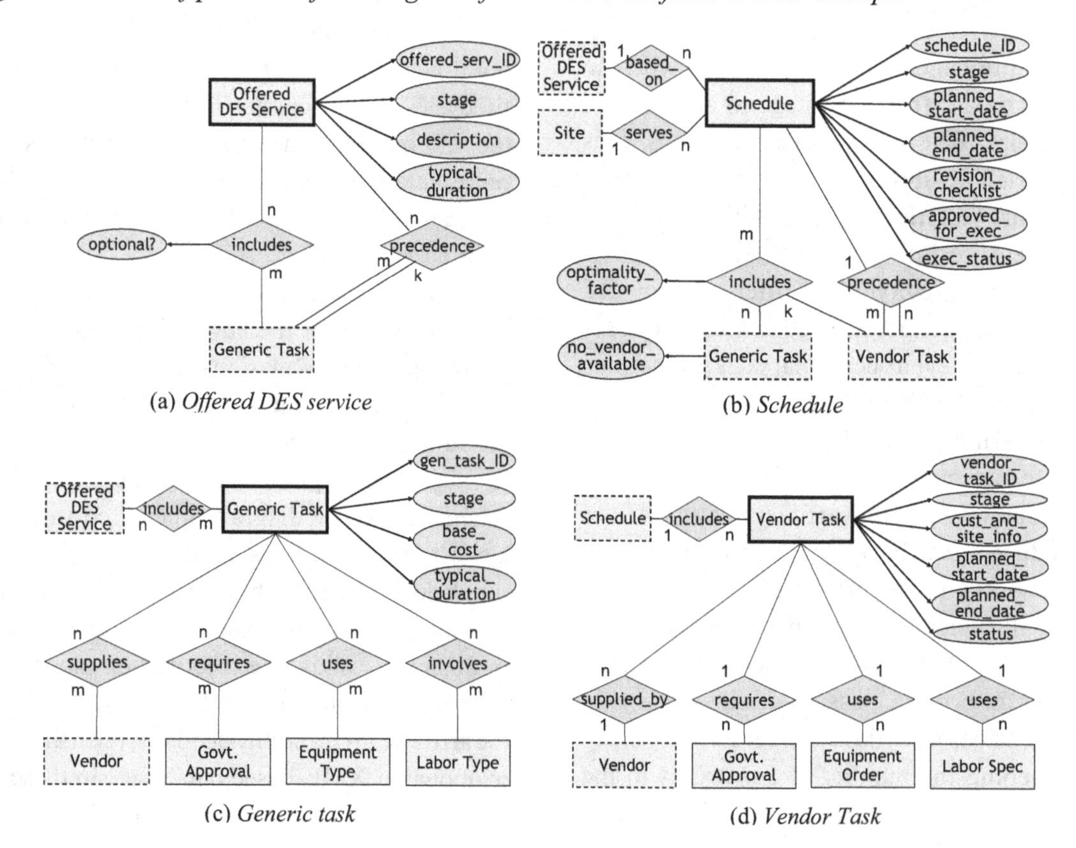

information on *typical_duration* of the given offered DES service. Each offered DES service may also "*contain*" a number of *Generic Task* artifacts – these would correspond to the individual tasks that must be performed during the course of the offered service. The rectangle enclosing *Generic Task* here is shown as dashed, to indicate that this entity type is defined elsewhere (namely in the schema for the *Generic Task* artifact class). The Boolean attribute *optional?* can be used to indicate some level of possible variation between instances (i.e., schedules) of an *Offered DES Service*. *Precedence* between the generic tasks is also included. For the example described here, a simple notion of precedence is used, based on start- and end-dates of the tasks, but richer forms of precedence could be used.

The *Schedule* schema includes various scalar attributes. The *revision_checklist* provides a structured value that is used to keep track of the revisions of the schedule that must be performed; this is useful as individual vendor tasks get modified, which may have impact that ripples to other, already planned vendor tasks. A schedule also has specific scalar values for *approved_for_exec(ution)* and *exec(ution)_status*, which can be used both to record how an artifact is progressing, and in the events and conditions of ECA rules. The *includes* relationship is used to connect a schedule to the generic tasks which must be performed, and as the planning process progresses, the specific vendor tasks that will be used to instantiate those generic tasks.

The schemas for *Generic Task* and *Vendor Task* should be self-explanatory. In those schemas several of the subordinate entity types are shown with solid rectangles, since in this example artifact classes are not associated with them.

There are two primary considerations in designing the artifact schemas. The first is driven by the basic axiom of the data-driven approach to workflow, specifically that an artifact *A* should hold, at any given time, all of the business-relevant information about *A*. The second consideration is that the logs of artifact instance histories should enable rich and flexible monitoring of current workflow performance, and analysis of past workflow performance. The artifact-centric approach lends itself to this, because the artifact life-cycles typically cross multiple sub-organizations (or organizations, in the case of out-sourcing). Even if the data for an artifact is physically stored in different places, the artifact schemas provide a unifying view against which to define Key Performance Indicators and dashboards, and to perform both systematic and *ad hoc* data mining and reporting. Although not at the same level as the artifact attributes included into the business operations model, it may be useful to incorporate into the artifact schemas additional attributes to store information about the provenance of the artifacts, that is, how and why they evolved as they did. This could include information about which services were used and details about how and why they were invoked.

Specification of BOM services. The discussion now turns to the second main activity in specifying a BOM: the specification of the BOM services that will help move artifacts through their life-cycles. If the artifact schemas are defined well, it should be relatively straightforward to identify BOM services that correspond to both (a) natural business activities, and (b) update coherent groups of artifacts and attributes. In the discussion here, each BOM service is associated with a primary artifact class; the action of the service will be focused on a single artifact of this class (including possibly creation of a new artifact of this class), and the service might read or write attributes of other artifacts (from the same and/or other artifact classes).

Recall that in the BALSA^{basic} workflow model, the family of BOM services for an application domain is typically specified in a manner largely independent of the anticipated sequencing of those services. In general, one might have a large library, or "soup", of BOM services associated with a family of artifact class schemas. For different realizations of an application domain (e.g., for different IT service providers offering DES) one might associate different subsets of this library to the artifact classes. This permits considerably more flexibility than is typical in workflow frameworks that specify the sequencing of services using exclusively procedural and/or graph-based formalisms.

To illustrate key points about BOM services and their specification the *Schedule* and *Vendor Task* classes are used. In the DES example there could be over 50 BOM services centered around the processing of artifacts in these classes. The focus here is on the group of BOM services that are relevant when a schedule is in the *Schedule_planning* stage (although some of them might also be used in the *Execution* and *Major_revisions* stages). A small but representative subset of these BOM services is listed below.

- *create_schedule* (*Offered DES Service*: *o*, *Customer*: *c*, *Site*: *si*): This service has the effect of creating a schedule artifact for *o*, *c*, and *si* (where *si* is a site of *c*).
- *create_vendor_task* (*Schedule*: *sch*, *Generic Task*: *g*): This service has the effect of creating a vendor task artifact that will be associated with *g* in *sch*.
- *adjust_task_general* (*Vendor task*: *t*, *Vender*: *v*, *Schedule*: *sch*, *list*[*Task*, *start_date*, *end_date*]): This service is used to revise any and all aspects of a vendor task *t* during the *Task_planning* stage. The vendor task serves as the primary artifact for this service and the following ones; the other artifacts that are used as input are all reachable from the primary artifact. The list of tasks with start- and end-dates is intended to hold all tasks that are immediate successors of *t* according to *sch*.
- *adjust_task_date* (*Vendor task*: *t*, *Vender*: *v*, *Schedule*: *sch*, *list*[*Task*, *start_date*, *end_date*]): This service is used to revise the date-related attributes of vendor task *t* (and possibly touch other artifacts that are impacted, e.g., by invalidating attributes of dependent vendor tasks and updating the *revision_checklist* attribute of the schedule *sch* that *t* belongs to). This service and the next two, while somewhat redundant with *adjust_task_general*, are included to illustrate how services might overlap in their function. Also, these three services might be executed in parallel, whereas if *adjust_task_general* is working on a vendor task *t*, it will typically block the other services from manipulating *t*.
- *request_govt_approval* (*Vendor task*: *t*, *Vender*: *v*, *Schedule*: *sch*): This service is used to create and transmit a request for one or several government approvals for a vendor task.
- *adjust_task_govt* (*Vendor task*: *t*, *Vender*: *v*, *Schedule*: *sch*, *list*[*Task*, *start_date*, *end_date*]): This service is used for manipulation of a task when information is received about pending government approvals.

In the BALSA^{basic} workflow model, at the level of the Business Operations Model, BOM services are specified using four key properties, namely,

- **I**nput artifacts and attributes,
- **O**utput artifacts and attributes,
- **P**re-conditions, and
- (Conditional) **E**ffects.

These combine to form the *IOPE* (pronounced I-O-P-E) specification of the service. The focus here on the logical properties of a service allows for a significant separation of concerns—at the BOM level the focus is on the logical properties and effects of invoking a service, whereas at the Realization level the focus can be on the more procedural and implementation aspects of a service. This follows the spirit of research in the past few years on OWL-S and more generally,

Semantic Web Services. It allows for rich forms of automation in the specification and realization of workflows. For example, *synthesis* algorithms have been developed for specialized settings, to automatically create compositions of services that satisfy high-level business goals (expressed using logical formulas) and government regulations (also expressed as logical formulas). Also, *analysis* algorithms, which can verify properties of workflows such as reachability or constraint satisfaction, are sometimes developed more easily if services and other components are specified using high-level logical properties rather than lower-level procedural ones. The use of logical specification of BOM services can also be viewed as providing a partition of specification information: analysis of a BOM at the macro level uses the logical specification of the BOM services, and then analysis of individual BOM services to check whether their detailed specification complies with the IOPE specification can occur separately.

In an IOPE specification of a BOM service, the input and output artifacts and attributes identify, respectively, the data values that will be read and that may be updated by the service. The pre-conditions must be satisfied before the service can be invoked. As a design guideline it is generally recommended to keep the pre-conditions as minimal as possible, focusing primarily on conditions needed by the service in connection with the specific artifacts. Additional information about when the service can be applied, which is specific to a given BOM design context, may be incorporated by the ECA rules for that domain. Finally, the conditional effects provide information about the possible effects that applying the service will have.

The IOPE specifications are now described for two of the BOM services, namely, *create_schedule* and *adjust_vendor_task*. The descriptions are provided in English, although in practice a formal notation would be used. The *create_schedule* service has an IOPE specification with the following properties.

- Inputs:
  - An *OfferedDESService* artifact *o*, and specifically the listing of used *Generic Tasks*, along with whether they are optional, and information about the *Precedence* relationships between them.
  - A *Customer* artifact *c*, and specifically information about specific requirements for *c*, e.g., levels of quality and service to be followed; implications around government regulations; etc.
  - A *Site* artifact *si* for *c*, and specifically information about specific requirements for *si*, including government-related issues based on location, municipality, state; information useful in determining vendor availability, shipping costs, etc.
- Outputs:
  - A new *Schedule* artifact *sch*. The data written will include attributes *schedule_ID*, *stage*, *planned_start_date*, and the *Generic Task* portion of the *includes* relationship. (The concrete *Vendor Task* values will be filled in by executions of the *assign_vendor_task* service.)
  - The *Site* artifact *si* is updated to record the fact that a new *Schedule* artifact has been created for *si*.
- Pre-conditions
  - *Offered DES Service* artifact *o* must be compatible with the infrastructure and needs of site *si*.
- Conditional effect
  - If true, then *sch* is in stage *Schedule_planning*.
  - If true, then *sch* holds a schedule skeleton (i.e., appropriate portions of the relationship *includes* are filled in).
  - If true, the *Site* artifact *si* is updated to reflect the creation of *sch*.

- If true, then for each *Generic Task* artifact *g* that is required to accomplish *o* for *si* for which there is not at least one qualified *Vendor* serving the region of the *Site*, then the *no_available_vendor* flag is set for *g*.

The IOPE specification for *adjust_task_dates* has the following properties:

- Inputs:
  - A *Vendor Task* artifact *t*, information about specific requirements for the customer and site associated with *t*'s schedule, and about the current status of various steps (government approvals, equipment availability, etc.).
  - A *Vendor* artifact *v*, and specifically information about *v*'s availability, about the cost for re-scheduling the task, etc., for the vendor assigned to perform *t*.
  - A *Schedule* artifact *sch*, and specifically information about immediate predecessors and successors of *t* in *sch*.
  - A list *T* of triples of form (*Task*, *date*, *date*).
- Outputs:
  - Updates to start and/or end dates of *t*.
  - (Possibly) updates to the *revision_checklist* of *sch*.
  - (Possibly) updates to the *status* fields of each *Vendor Task* artifact *t'* that is a successor of *t* in *sch*, if the modification to *t* impacts *t'*, and invalidating the dates of each such artifact.
- Pre-condition
  - Vendor task *t* is assigned to supplier *v*.
  - Vendor task *t* occurs in Schedule *sch*.
  - *T* is the list of tuples (t', $s^{t'}$, $e^{t'}$), where *t'* is a task that succeeds *t* in *sch* according to the *Precedence* relationship, and $s^{t'}$, $e^{t'}$ are the start- and end-times of *t'*, respectively.
- Conditional effects
  - If true, then the start and/or end dates of *t* may have been overwritten
  - If the start date of *t* is overwritten, then it is after the end date of each predecessor of *t*.
  - If the start or end date of *t* is overwritten and this impacts the timing of any successor *t'* of *t* (i.e., any task occurring in *T*), then the dates for *t'* are invalidated and the *revision_checklist* of *sch* is updated accordingly.

There is a *circumscription* condition on the semantics associated with conditional effects. Specifically, in the application of a BOM service each attribute that is not mentioned in the consequent part of a conditional effect with condition that evaluates to true must not change its value, and likewise, the state of an artifact must not change unless that is specifically called for by a conditional effect with condition that evaluates to true.

One might expect that the *adjust_task_dates* should include in the pre-condition a restriction permitting the service to run only if a vendor task's schedule is in stage *schedule_planning*, *execution*, or *major_revision*, since those are the stages where schedules might be modified. However, in the overall design of the BOM presented here, this restriction is incorporated into the ECA rule that governs when *adjust_task_dates* can be invoked. In general, there are trade-offs concerning whether conditions are included into the pre-condition for a service or the ECA rules that govern when it can be invoked. One advantage of keeping a service's pre-condition minimal is that it allows the service to be used in a broader variety of application domains and contexts.

Specification of ECA rules. The discussion now turns to the third major phase of specifying a BOM in BALSA^{basic}, namely, the specification of how services are associated to artifacts, or in other words, the specification of the "micro-level" of artifact lifecycles. The model uses Event-Condition-Action (ECA) rules. In general these rules have the form "if some event occurs, and if a condition is true about the objects that witness the event occurrence, then take a particular action." In some cases there are also "CA" rules in which the event portion is not specified; this means that the rule can be applied at essentially any time. The ECA rules used in BALSA^{basic} are focused at the conceptual level of the model; in particular the events are specified in terms of the BOM services being invoked or terminating; artifacts being created or modified, or changing stage; and operations-level external messages being received into the workflow system.

The ECA paradigm has been used in workflow (and other) contexts for several decades, and provides a very flexible mechanism for specifying system behaviors. On the one hand, it can be used to faithfully simulate flow-charts and other highly procedural styles of behavior specification. At the other extreme, by exclusively using CA rules the paradigm can take on a very declarative style reminiscent of logic programming and deductive database systems. Between these extremes, ECA can be used to simulate the paradigms of expert systems and production rule systems. Different "macros" can be constructed on top of an ECA basis to make it easy for ruleset creators and business users to think in terms of the various paradigms just mentioned. Further, a "hybrid" framework can be constructed on top of the ECA basis, combining for example a flowchart specification for certain stages of an artifact class and a much more free-form, declarative specification for some other stages of the class. BALSA^{basic} focuses on ECA because it provides a minimal set of constructs that can form the basis for this rich family of variations for associating services to artifacts in the data-centric workflow setting.

In the example ECA rules presented here, a fourth field is included. This "By" field is used to list the properties and qualifications of the people who may perform the associated action. These "performers" might include customer service representatives, clerks, managers, etc. This field is included here primarily to provide a brief illustration of how information about the process users and their participation can be associated to artifact lifecycles. In a full solution, it will be useful to include a substantial meta-model for representing all of the people that might be involved with a BOM, and the ways that they might interact with it. In addition to the actual performers, it will be useful to model teams of users, experts that provide consulting advice to the people actually performing the BOM services, etc.

The basic building blocks for the ECA rules used here are as follows.

Events:

- An attribute value just assigned
- An attribute value just assigned and satisfies a predicate involving other current artifacts and attribute values
- An artifact has just moved into a stage
- A service has been launched or completed on an artifact
- An incoming message (e.g., from a government agency)
- A performer request

Conditions

- Formulas written in first-order logic (or, more-or-less equivalently, a relational database query language). Typically the conditions come from a targeted subset of first-order logic, such as the quantifier-free fragment, or the fragment which does not permit quantifier alternations.

Actions

- Invoke a service
- Move an artifact to a stage

By

- Roles and qualifications needed by the performer of the action

A small family of representative ECA rules for the DES example is now presented, followed by a discussion of the semantics associated with ECA rules.

R1: *Initiate schedule*

event request by performer *p* to create a schedule instance for *Offered DES Service* artifact *o*, *Customer* artifact *c*, and *Site* artifact *si*
condition: the appropriate non-disclosure agreements (NDAs) are in place for *c*
action invoke *create_schedule(o, c, si)*
by performer *p* where *offer_manager* **in** *role(p)* and *qualification(p, o, region: si.region)* ≥ 5

The above rule is used to create a new schedule. It is triggered when a performer requests this. Note that the request includes the offered DES service, the customer, and the customer site where the service will be given. The *qualification* function is used in this rule and below as a mechanism for indicating the skill set needed by the performer that will actually perform the service being invoked. For these examples the values of *qualification* range from 1 (not very qualified) to 10 (a guru). The input argument *si.region* illustrates how we use the "." notation to navigate through one or more artifacts to find values of interest. This in-place function is viewed as being polymorphic–depending on the number and types of the input arguments it will evaluate appropriately. This function could be supported by a family of relational database tables.

R2: *Initiate vendor task*

condition for *Schedule* artifact *sch* and *Generic task* artifact *g* contained in *sch*, each predecessor of *g* in *sch* has an associated vendor task artifact with defined start and end dates; *sch* is in stage *Schedule_planning* or *Major_revision*; and *g* does not have an associated vendor task.
action invoke *create_vendor_task(s,g)*
by performer *p* where *qualification(p, sch.offered_service, g)* ≥ 2 and *qualification(p, g, sch.customer.site.region)* ≥ 6.

Note that this rule has no triggering event, which means that the rule can be fired at essentially any time that the condition becomes true. In practice, the rule might be triggered when the final predecessor of *g* in *sch* obtains defined start- and end-dates. In the example, the *create_vendor_task* will, among other things, set the intended start and end dates for the created vendor task. This is why the predecessor tasks of *g* in *sch* must already have dates assigned. Here the performer must be somewhat knowledgeable about the overall offered DES service that underlies schedule *sch*, and also well-qualified on the generic task *g* for the region where *sch* will be installed. There may be other rules that enable invocation of *create_vendor_task*, e.g., if a performer requests it.

R3: *Adjust vendor task dates*

condition for *Vendor Task* artifact *t* occurring in *Schedule* artifact *sch*, *sch* is in stage *Schedule_planning*, *Execution* or *Major_revision*; the start- and/or end-date of *t* is invalid; and each predecessor of *t* in schedule *sch* (according to the *precedence* relationship in *sch*) has defined start and end dates.
action invoke *adjust_task_dates(t, v, sch, T)*, where *v* is the vendor supplying *t*, and *T* is a list of triples holding, for each task *t'* that succeeds *t* in *sch*, the triple (*t'*, *s*, *e*) where *s*, *e* are the start- and end-times of *t'*, respectively.
by performer *p* where *qualification(p, o, g)* ≥ 4, where *o* is the offered DES service

associated with *sch*, and *qualification(p, g, region: sch.customer.site.region)* ≥ 8.

Performing the service *adjust_task_dates* under this rule requires more qualifications than performing *create_vendor_task*. This rule can be fired whenever the dates of a vendor task are invalid.

R4: *Request task government approval*
condition for *Vendor task* artifact *t* occurring in schedule *sch*, *sch* is in stage *Schedule_approvals* or *Re_approval*; if government approval is needed for *t* and not yet requested; and the required values for *t* are defined.
action invoke *request_govt_approval(t, v, sch)*, where *v* is the vendor providing *t*.
by performer *p* where *qualification(p, sch.offered_service, g)* ≥ 2 and *qualification(p, g, t.schedule.customer.site.region, aspect*: "government") ≥ 6.

R5: *Modify task government information*
event receive government response to a request approval of *Vendor task* artifact *t* which is owned by schedule *sch*.
condition *sch* is in stage *Schedule_approvals* or *Re_approval*.
action invoke *adjust_task_govt(t, v, sch, T)*, where *v* is the vendor supplying *t*, *sch* is the schedule that *t* participates in, and *T* is a list of triples holding, for each task *t'* that succeeds *t* in *sch*, the triple (*t'*, *s*, *e*) where *s*, *e* are the start- and end-times of *t'*, respectively.
by performer *p* where *qualification(p, sch.offered_service, g)* ≥ 2 and and *qualification(p, g, region: t.schedule.customer.site.region, aspect*: "government") ≥ 6.

The above two rules focus on government approvals for vendor tasks.

R6: *Launch schedule approval*
condition for *Schedule* artifact *sch*, *sch* is in stage *Schedule_planning*; *sch.revision_checklist* is empty; and for each *Generic task* artifact *g* of *sch*, *g* has an associated *Vendor task* artifact *t* which has *t.status* = *ready_for_execution.*
action move_to(*sch, Schedule_approvals*)
by automatic

The above rule permits a schedule to move from the *Schedule_planning* stage to the *Schedule_approvals* stage. This illustrates how the set of ECA rules associated with an application domain can specialize the conditions about stage transitions that are incorporated into the finite state machine for the macro-level life-cycle of an artifact. Note the use of a universal quantification ("for each *Generic task* artifact g …), which in this case is "bounded" to range over artifacts associated with *sch*.

R7: *Launch schedule execution*
event for *Schedule* artifact *sch*, *sch.approved_for_exec* := *true*
condition *true*
action move_to(*sch, Execution*)
by automatic

The final example rule permits a schedule to move to the *Execution* stage. This is triggered when the attribute *approved_for_exec* is set to true. This illustrates that there can be a close relationship between attribute values and stages in the macro-level lifecycle. Indeed, in a formal sense the state machine for stages can be simulated by extra attributes and some ECA rules. However, the stages and state machine are explicitly incorporated into the model to make BALSA^{basic} BOMs more readily understood by business managers, and to permit the specification of an intuitive structure for lifecycles at the macro level.

Execution Semantics of ECA rules. A simple, representative, *logical* execution semantics for ECA-based rules is now described. We emphasize that these are at the logical rather than implementation level – many optimizations can be incorporated when implementing a given ruleset while nevertheless obeying the logical semantics. The logical semantics is based on the following concepts.

1. **Non-determinism:** In the semantics presented here, non-determinism is permitted in two ways. The first concerns the order that eligible rules are fired. Thus, if more then one rule is triggered by the same event, or more generally, if more than one rule is eligible for firing at a given point, then the system will pick one of them non-deterministically for execution. This kind of assumption is common in declarative frameworks; once a designer is used to the non-determinism it can provide more flexibility in the design of an ECA ruleset. Alternatively, an ECA ruleset might incorporate mechanisms that restrict the non-determinism by requiring that rules happen in a more deterministic fashion (e.g., by adding conditions that help to narrow the set of rules eligible at any given point in time). The non-determinism offers many opportunities for optimization in the implementation. Importantly, an implementation that enables any one of the non-deterministically specified executions of the ECA ruleset is considered to be valid; the implementation does not itself have to support the non-determinism nor enable all possible valid execution sequences. The assumption of non-determinism is also quite useful in connection with formal verification and automated construction of ECA rulesets. The second form of non-determinism is discussed in item (3) below.
2. **Rule triggering:** This applies to rules with explicitly specified event. Such a rule is *triggered* if the event becomes true for some particular binding (assignment) β of the variables occurring in the event. The rule can be triggered only once for a given event and binding.
3. **Rule firing:** A rule is considered to be *eligible* for a given variable binding β if its event has been triggered with binding β, or if it has no event (in which case β is empty). The rule firing for an eligible rule has two phases. First, the condition of the rule is tested. The condition is considered to be true if there is some binding β' which extends β to the unbound variables occurring in the condition, so that the condition is true under β'. This choice of β' is the second form of non-determinism in the logical semantics for ECA ruleset execution. For a given eligible rule only one of the bindings β' that makes the condition true is considered when firing the rule. If an appropriate performer is not available to perform the action, then the action is parked until a performer becomes available.
4. **Heap of eligible rules:** As suggested in point (1) above, an unordered heap is maintained that holds eligible rules. Each time a rule event for some binding, the rule with binding is placed on the heap. Also, whenever a rule without event has a binding for which the condition is true, it is put on the heap with that binding. At any point in time a rule with binding in the heap can be selected and fired.
5. **No starvation:** The actual processing of the rules cannot indefinitely "starve" an eligible rule from firing.
6. **Serializability:** While the actual processing of the rules and their action might be interleaved and/or parallel, the net effect of the firing of rules must be equivalent to some serial firing of the rules with the same bindings. (This is analogous to the serializability requirement typically placed on sets of updates to a database.)

With any ECA-based semantics there are several issues that must be considered. At the logical level, these include the following.

- **Reachability:** Given a set of rules, is a given predicate (e.g., a certain stage in the macro lifecycle, an attribute reaching a given value, etc.) reachable through firings of the rules?
- **Deadlock:** Can the system reach a deadlock? How can all deadlocks be prevented?
- **Termination:** For each artifact type with a bounded lifecycle, does each execution of the rules for artifacts of this type end in a finite number of steps?

There are also questions that arise for implementations of the ECA logical semantics. Issues here include the following.

- **Conformance:** The implementation should provably conform with, i.e., satisfy, all of the requirements in the semantics, including no starvation and serializability.
- **Optimization:** How can the rule system be implemented to avoid testing rule conditions unnecessarily (especially for the rules whose event equals "anytime").

While simplistic implementations for the ECA semantics can be developed, there are still significant research challenges in developing approaches for highly optimized implementations.

3.3. Workflow Realization for DES

Artifact schema, services, and ECA rules in a BOM provide a logical design of both the business process (services and ECA rules) and data (artifact schema) with a clear semantics. The goal of realization is to develop an executable workflow system that *conforms* to the BOM specification. A naïve approach could be to simply develop a "rule engine" to manage and fire ECA rules, along with necessary databases for storing all artifacts, implementations for abstract services. The rule engine could serve as the "central controller" that coordinates databases, services, events, and possibly other components. This approach may be feasible for business processes that permit centralized control (but could be very inefficient). When centralized control is impossible (as in most of business process management applications including our DES example), realizing a BOM could become somewhat challenging, and in fact raises interesting research questions. The current practice is to outline a detail workflow and to include the important details (e.g., mechanism of fetching/storing artifacts). The workflow is then examined and reasoned about. And finally the workflow is implemented. These constitute the main design activities in Steps 3 and 4.

In an attempt to bring some rigor in the design steps, we sketch a few notations and use them to explain and illustrate the design activities (that are mostly done manually). In particular, we combine the two steps into a 3-phase approach to realization, which are *conceptual flow diagrams*, *operational optimization*, and *individual component implementation*.

ECA rules concern primarily the logical aspect of business processes. To coordinate a distributed array of services and components, a natural approach is to specify the global behaviors of the components as a *choreography*. The focus of the first phase of realization is to develop a choreography that implements the control structure of the ECA rules. The outcome is a *(conceptual) flow diagram*. Figure 6 shows pieces of a flow diagram where each artifact class is assumed to have a single *(logical) container* for storing artifacts in this class. Figure 6(a) shows a (disk shaped) container for the class *Schedule*. Event handlers (E_{11}, E_{31}) are shown as nodes in the diagram. The third type of node in the diagram correspond to rule actions and are either service execution or change of stage, represented as labeled rounded-corner boxes. An edge linked to the

Figure 6. Representing behaviors: services, actions, and events

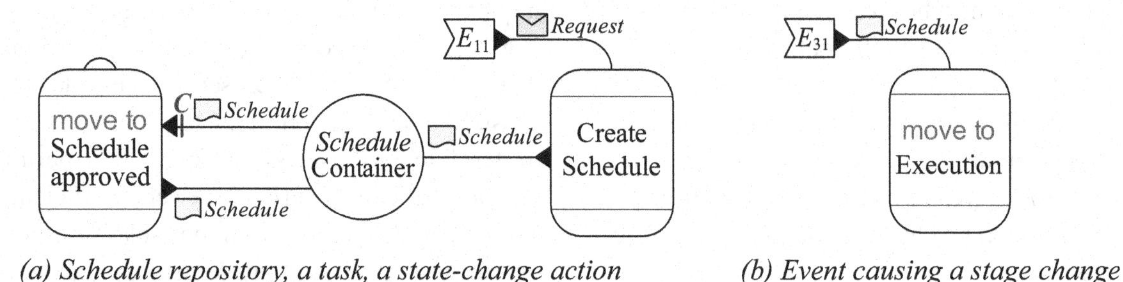

(a) Schedule repository, a task, a state-change action *(b) Event causing a stage change*

Figure 7. Writing flow diagram: split the repository, adding an event

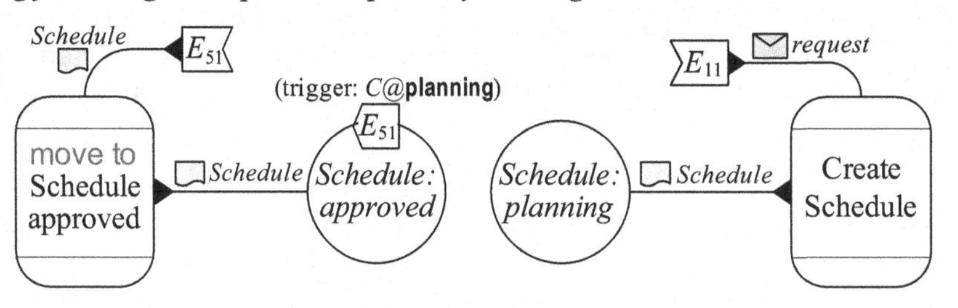

top indicates an invocation. A small half-circle on the top indicates that the service is proactive (i.e., always running and *cannot* be invoked). Edges are directed and represent flow of information. Edge labels indicate the information type being either an artifact, or a message (e.g., request in the figure). A novel aspect of conceptual flow diagrams is that behaviors of the nodes are explicitly shown through the shapes at edge endpoint. A solid triangle attached to a node signifies the communication action this node will take. For example, the event handler E_{11} emits a request message and invokes the "Create Schedule" service, which in turn emits a new *Schedule* artifact and stores it in the container. Also, change of stage "move to Schedule approved" pulls a *Schedule* artifact, the small vertical line labeled *C* denotes a filter with the condition *C*.

The conceptual flow diagram may be verified in at least two aspects. *Behavior type checking* focuses on the behavior interface well-formedness (e.g., reachability, free of deadlocks). *Behavior consistency checking* ensures that all possible "paths" permitted by the conceptual flow diagram are also permitted by the ECA rules of the BOM.

Obtaining a conceptual flow diagram is only a beginning. It is likely that the diagram is not ideal. We consider two examples below to demonstrate how the flow diagram can be modified. Consider the container for *Schedule* artifacts. It turns out that *Schedule* artifacts in the planning stage have an identifiable set of attributes that are modified and controlled by one department, while after the approval, new attributes may be added and a set of attributes are not allowed to be changed. The associations of control and updatability of attribute sets and stages may be important for the DES example. A natural solution is to split the *Schedule* container into two containers labeled with *planning* and *approved*, respectively. A careful examination of the ECA rules shows that "Create Schedule" only generates artifacts that are in planning stage. Therefore, we can associate links properly as shown in Figure 7. As another example, we realize that the filter condition C cannot be checked easily by stage changing component due to read restrictions on attributes and inaccessibility of *Generic task* artifacts. Thus the flow diagram in Figure 6 cannot be directly implemented. One solution is to define an event generator as a trigger in the container for *Schedule* artifacts in planning stage. (Another kind of event generator, not illustrated here, corresponds to the completion of a service execution.) The modified flow diagram is shown in Figure 7. The proactive action "move to Schedule approved" is replaced with a filtered pull with a database trigger, a reactive service, an event generator, an event handler, and an invocation.

The two examples above show how the changes of the flow diagram can help organizing services better and avoid implementation limitations. Other reasons may include performance metric, monitoring needs, etc. The second group of activities is then to "optimize" the flow diagram through local replacement or rewriting. The goal of *operational optimization* is to find the "best" flow diagram in terms of behavior constraints of the services and the cost metrics.

After a desirable flow diagram is obtained, the final group of activities is to turn each of the nodes in the diagram into an implementation. Many current software development techniques are applicable in this phase. We illustrate some of the implementation decisions for the DES example. Prior to implementing individual components, the initial decisions need to be made on how components should communicate with each other. Although in reality each edge in the flow diagram could have a different protocol considering the software systems used for each component, here we simply assume the SOA framework and allow only WSDL interactions (in cases legacy systems are involved, appropriate WSDL "wrappers" should be developed). We now turn to individual component implementation.

Consider the two containers for the Schedule artifact class in Figure 7. We first finalize their ER diagrams (they may have different attributes). For the *planning* container, we decide to implement it as a new relational database system. In this case, its ER diagram is mapped into relations using database design tools. Once the tables are created, we will develop web services to support the store/fetch actions on *Schedule* artifacts by other services (components). From Figure 7, "Create Schedule" will deposit artifacts to the *planning* container, thus a WSDL operation is needed. We also need to implement the event generator in the *planning* container, e.g., event E_{51} (Figure 7) is implemented as a trigger. We now consider the *approved* container. It turns out that the primary consumer of the approved *Schedule* artifacts already has a database that stores similar (but different) *Installation Plan* artifacts. For reasons, it is desirable that *Schedule* artifacts share some of the services on *Installation Plan* artifacts (including progress monitoring services that does not change these artifacts). To accommodate this, we change the database design for *Schedule* artifacts to decide which attributes of *Schedule* artifacts will be stored in the same relation(s) as *Installation Plan* artifacts. The remaining decisions are similar to the *planning* container. In general, the implementation of a container should not have significant impact on the business operations requirements.

For each event in the flow diagram, the key considerations are (1) where the event is generated, and (2) where should the handler be located. In Figure 7, E_{51} is generated by a trigger in *planning*, and the event handler could also be located there. E_{11}, however, is originated from another software system. Thus we need to implement a handler for E_{11} that invokes "Create Schedule" when the external message arrives. If E_{11} is the only invoker, we could consider merging the service and the handler.

The last types of nodes are services (and change of stages). Service may be implemented from scratch, or orchestrations from existing services; many service composition techniques are applicable here. We omit the details here.

4. DISCUSSIONS

In Figure 1, we show the three-level model for business processes. In this section, we give a brief discussion on two key benefits of the three-level model in the design and management of business processes.

At the top of the three-level model, BOM captures the logical semantics of the business processes, the conceptual flow and workflow levels provides the abstract and detailed (respectively) system design that preserves the BOM semantics. An important property is *realization independence* that permits changes to the conceptual flow and business workflow implementation (e.g., change of data management tools, software/hardware, service providers, etc.) while preserving the same BOM. Such a freedom to make changes allows improvements and optimization to the business processes. Considers a situation where the current service for *Schedule* planning is replaced with an outsourced service. In this case, there is no change in the BOM since the new service is just a logically equivalent replacement. However, changes must be made on the conceptual flow diagram since the new service may not have the exact same behaviors. For example, the new service will not be able to access the (internal) database that stores the *Schedule* artifacts. A solution is then to create another container which will be maintained by the out-sourced service provider. We then need to examine all other control (invocation) and artifact transmission edges in the flow diagram and make necessary changes. When the new conceptual flow diagram is obtained, we can identify current components (events, actions invoked by rules) and make change to those that affected. In this case, the conceptual flow diagrams provide a better tool to reason about the potential service replace.

Separation into three levels can also make it easier to manage mappings between the levels and reduce the complexity of making changes at the BOM level. Consider as an example in DES where some vendor tasks require government approval. Suppose that a new rule became effective that requires the approval to be obtained before the start date for selected types of tasks. To reflect this change, rule R_3 needs to be adjusted to include in its condition the approval status and the task types. Considering the complaints that the approval process took too long, the government relaxed the rule by allowing a task to start if the approval does not arrive 7 days after the submission was received. Assuming the government always sends an acknowledgement for a request, in DES each acknowledgement causes an event E. The event E will start a 7-day countdown event E_1; when E_1 happens, the Vendor task artifact needs to record that dates cannot be adjusted if the approval is not received (otherwise, E_1 is ignored). It is easy to see that the use of ECA rules allows the changes to be made easily.

5. CONCLUSION

One of the key challenges to business process management is to enable business managers to understand, design and easily make changes to their business operations, with confidence that their goals are accurately reflected in the underlying IT-level workflows. This chapter presents a promising modeling framework and methodology for addressing this challenge, which is fundamentally centered around data rather than activity flows. More specifically, the framework is based on the notion of "business artifact," which is used to capture both the information models and the lifecycles of key business entities. The artifact-centric approach has been successfully applied in business process design. We expect that the multi-leveled modeling framework for business workflows described here will further expand the usefulness of the artifact-centric approach to support business process design and evolution.

Many aspects of the modeling approach need further study. For example, one area of interest is to develop techniques and tools to aid the design process, specifically, static and dynamic analysis and verification tools. A related topic concerns monitoring workflow executions, in particular, it is desirable to automatically generate monitoring mechanisms from desired metrics given as input. Another area focuses on tools that help to automate design and modification of workflows. While full automation in the most general case is not achievable, we expect that substantial progress can be achieved in constrained but well-motivated settings.

SUGGESTED ADDITIONAL READING

The design methodology presented in this chapter is based on earlier work in several different areas, in particular, artifact-centric business process modeling, active databases and other ECA systems, and semantics web services.

The concept of business artifact and the idea of modeling business processes in terms of artifact lifecycles were first articulated by Nigam and Caswell in their seminal paper (Nigam, A. & Caswell, N. S., 2003). This paper formed the basis of a substantial effort at IBM Research, which resulted in the "Model-Driven Business Transformation (MDBT)" method and toolkit (Kumaran, S., 2004). This was subsequently incorporated as the "Business Entity Lifecycle Analysis (BELA)" (Strosnider, J. K., Nandi, P., Kumaran, S., Ghosh, S., & Arsanjani, A., 2008) capability pattern into IBM's Service-Oriented Method and Architecture (SOMA) (Arsanjani, A., Ghosh, S., Allam, A., Abdollah, T., Ganapathy, S., & Holley, K., 2008). The meta-models of (Nigam, A. et al., 2008) and of MDBT (Kumaran, S., 2004; Strosnider, J. K., Nandi, P., Kumaran, S., Ghosh, S., & Arsanjani, A., 2008) can be viewed as lying within the BALSA framework. Reference (Nigam, A. et al., 2008) uses an information model based on (possibly nested) attribute-value pairs, while (Kumaran, S., 2004; Strosnider, J. K., Nandi, P., Kumaran, S., Ghosh, S., & Arsanjani, A., 2008) use ER diagrams for the artifact information model. Both meta-models use detailed finite state machines for the artifact lifecycles. In MDBT, the states of these machines correspond to business-relevant conditions that an artifact can arrive into, and the transitions are annotated with the BOM services that can move the artifact from one state to another one. (This differs from the state machines used in the $BALSA^{basic}$ meta-model described in the current chapter, where the states correspond to stages of an artifact's lifecycle, within which numerous BOM services might be applied.)

Although the design methodology presented in the current chapter creates BOMs in an ECA-based meta-model, it is nevertheless largely inspired by the methods developed in the MDBT and BELA work. Also, several aspects of the meta-model in reference (Nigam, A. et al., 2008) are used in the Conceptual Flow level (see Section 3.3) of the design methodology presented here.

The MDBT modeling technique was applied to enable business transformation in several application contexts involving customer engagements in the areas of finance, supply chain, retail, banking, and pharmaceutical research. Experiences from some of these efforts are reported in (Bhattacharya, K., Caswell, N. S., Kumaran, S., Nigam, A., & Wu, F. Y., 2007; Bhattacharya, K., Guttman, R., Lyman, K., Heath III, F. F., Kumaran, S., Nandi, P., Wu, F., Athma, P., Freiberg, C., Johannsen, L., & Staudt, A., 2005; Strosnider, J. K., et al., 2008). The business managers and subject matter experts involved in these transformations said that the use of artifacts as the basic modeling primitive gave them a kind of "bird's eye" of their operations that they were not obtaining from the traditional activity-flow based approaches, and that it enabled substantially improved communication between the various stakeholders. Reference (Bercovici, A., Fisher, A., Fournier, F., Rackham, G., Razinkov, N., & Skarbovsky, I., 2008) describes how IBM's Component Business Modeling approach, used to develop a partitioning of business functions into clusters appropriate for organizing the operations and assigning accountability, can be enhanced by using an artifact-centric perspective to guide the partitioning into components. References (Kumaran, S., 2004; Kűster, J., Ryndina, K., & Gall, H., 2007; Wahler, K. & Küster, J. M., 2008) develop approaches for showing correspondences between process-centric views and artifact-centric views of a workflow model.

The BALSA framework presented here offers a new perspective on the meta-models developed in (Kumaran, S., 2004; Nigam, A. et al., 2008; Strosnider, J. K., et al., 2008), by permitting the study of a broad number of meta-models based on the underlying premise of making business artifacts the starting point of business operations modeling. The IBM Research teams behind (Skarbovsky, I., 2008; Nigam, A. et al., 2008)and the MDBT and BELA work have now joined with others to form Project ArtiFact™, which is focused on creating a next-generation artifact-centric meta-model, that can better address emerging challenges such as enabling rich flexibility within a BOM, gracefully handling numerous BOM versions as a business evolves, enabling the coherent specification of a generic BOM with many specializations (as might arise in a global organization with regional variations), and incorporating rich capabilities for representing how people are involved with business operations.

The ECA approach for specifying system behavior first appeared in (Dayal, U., 1998; Hsu, M., Ladin, R., & McCarthy, D. R., 1998) where it was used to specify the behavior of "active" database management systems. Reference (Ghandeharizadeh, S., Hull, R., & Jacobs, D., 1996) provides a general framework for specifying a variety of execution semantics for ECA and other kinds of active database systems. A variety of ECA workflow systems have been developed; for example, reference (Műller, R., Greiner, U., & Rahm, E., 2004) describes how ECA rules can be used to enable rich flexibility in dynamic adaptability for workflows. Unlike the meta-model presented here, however, none of these previous works place a strong focus on business artifacts as a key construct in their meta-model.

Reference (van der Aalst, W. M. P., & Pesic, M., 2006) describes a highly declarative approach for specifying constraints on how tasks in a workflow should be sequenced. This work is based on Linear Temporal Logic rather than ECA. It will be useful to explore a combination of this declarative approach with the artifact-centric paradigm.

Describing the semantics of services with input, output, precondition, and effects is formulated in the OWL-S (Martin, D., et al., 2004; McIlraith, S. A., Son, T. C., & Zeng, H., 2001); in fact OWL-S permits preconditions and effects to refer to an underlying "real world". More details on semantic web services and compositions can be found in (Hull, R. & Su, J., 2005). Reference (Su, J., Bultan, T., Fu, X., & Zhao, X., 2008) discusses several choreography languages as well as research issues concerning service choreography. The artifact-centric paradigm provides a natural setting for applying semantic web service perspectives and techniques to business process management, where the artifact information models can be viewed as an underlying "real world."

Work on formally analyzing artifact-centric business process models were recently reported in (Bhattacharya, K., Gerede, C. E., Hull, R., Liu, R., & Su, J., 2005; Gerede, C. E., & Su, J., 2007; Gerede, C. E., Bhattacharya, K., & Su, J., 2007). Properties investigated in these studies include reachability (Gerede, C. E., & Su, J., 2007; Gerede, C. E., et al., 2007), general temporal constraints (Gerede, C. E., 2007), and existence of complete execution or dead-end [5]. It was shown that in the general case, the verification problems are undecidable. Decidability results were obtained when rather severe restrictions are placed, e.g., an upper bound on the number of artifacts used during the entire execution.

The Vortex model of (Hull, R., Llirbat, F., Simon, E., Su, J., Dong, G., Kumar, B., & Zhou,

G., 1999) shares some key notions with the artifact-centric framework presented here. In particular, the focus of processing in Vortex is on "objects", which correspond closely to artifacts, and the flow of control is governed essentially by condition-action (CA) rules. Unlike the BALSA models, Vortex does not have an explicit concept of an object's macro-level lifecycle, and Vortex requires attribute assignment to be monotonic and acyclic. Reference (Dong, G., Hull, R., Kumar, B., Su, J., & Zhou, G., 1999)develops optimization techniques for Vortex, with an emphasis on data-intensive Vortex workflows.

ACKNOWLEDGMENT

The authors are grateful to all of the IBM Research community that is working on the artifact-centric approach, for conducting the research that forms the basis for this chapter and providing an environment for continued research. The authors thank Nanjangud C. Narendra, Mark Linehan, and two anonymous reviewers for detailed suggestions on the presentation of this chapter. Hull and Su are also grateful for partial support by NSF grants IIS-0415195, CNS-0613998, and IIS-0812578 for the development of this chapter.

REFERENCES

Arsanjani, A., Ghosh, S., Allam, A., Abdollah, T., Ganapathy, S., & Holley, K. (2008). SOMA: A method for developing service-oriented solutions. *IBM Systems Journal*, *47*(3), 377-396.

Bercovici, A., Fisher, A., Fournier, F., Rackham, G., Razinkov, N., & Skarbovsky, I. (2008). A method for service center architecture based on industry standards. In *Proc. IEEE Int. Conf. on Services Computing* (pp. 433-440). IEEE Press.

Battle, S., et al. (2005). *Semantic Web Services Ontology* (SWSO), W3C Member Submission. http://www.w3.org/Submission/SWSF-SWSO/

Bhattacharya, K., Caswell, N. S., Kumaran, S., Nigam, A., & Wu, F. Y. (2007). Artifact-centered operational modeling: Lessons from customer engagements. *IBM Systems Journal*, *46*(4), 703-721.

Bhattacharya, K., Gerede, C. E., Hull, R., Liu, R., & Su, J. (2007). Towards formal analysis of artifact-centricbusiness process models. In *Proc. 5th Int. Conf. on Business Process Management* (pp. 288-304). Berlin / Heidelberg: Springer.

Bhattacharya, K., Guttman, R., Lyman, K., Heath III, F. F., Kumaran, S., Nandi, P., Wu, F., Athma, P., Freiberg, C., Johannsen, L., & Staudt, A. (2005). A model-driven approach to industrializing discovery processes in pharmaceutical research. *IBM Systems Journal*, *44*(1), 145-162.

Dayal, U. (1988). Active database management systems. In *Proc. 3rd Int. Conf. on Data and Knowledge Bases: Improving Usability and Responsiveness* (pp. 150-169). Morgan Kaufmann.

Dong, G., Hull, R., Kumar, B., Su, J., & Zhou, G. (1999). A framework for optimizing distributed workflow executions. In *Proc. Int. Workshop on Database Programming Languages* (pp. 152-167). Berlin / Heidelberg: Springer.

Gerede, C. E., & Su, J. (2007). Specification and Verification of Artifact Behaviors in Business Process Models. In *Proc. Int. Conf. on Service Oriented Computing* (pp. 181-192). Berlin / Heidelberg: Springer.

Gerede, C. E., Bhattacharya, K., & Su, J. (2007). Static analysis of business artifact-centric operational models. In *Proc. IEEE Int. Conf. on Service-Oriented Computing and Applications* (pp. 133-140). IEEE Press.

Ghandeharizadeh, S., Hull, R., & Jacobs, D. (1996). Heraclitus: Elevating deltas to be first-class citizens in a database programming languages. *ACM Trans. Database Syst.*, *21*(3), 370-426.

Hsu, M., Ladin, R., & McCarthy, D. R. (1988). An Execution model for active data base management systems. In *Proc. 3rd Int. Conf. on Data and Knowledge Bases: Improving Usability and Responsiveness* (pp. 171-179). Morgan Kaufmann.

Hull, R., Llirbat, F., Simon, E., Su, J., Dong, G., Kumar, B., & Zhou, G. (1999). Declarative workflows that support easy modification and dynamic browsing. In *Proc. Int. Joint Conf. on Work Activities Coordination and Collaboration* (pp. 69-78). New York: ACM Press.

Hull, R. & Su, J. (2005). Tools for composite Web services: A short overview. *SIGMOD Record, 34*(2), 86-95.

Kumaran, S. (2004). Model-driven enterprise. In *Proc. Global Enterprise Application Integration (EAI) Summit* (pp. 166-180).

Kumaran, S., Liu, R., & Wu, F. Y. (2008). On the duality of information-centric and activity-centric models of business processes. In *Proc. Int. Conf. on Advanced Information Systems Engineering* (pp.32-47). Berlin / Heidelberg: Springer.

Kűster, J., Ryndina, K., & Gall, H. (2007). Generation of BPM for object life cycle compliance. In *Proc. 5th Intl. Conf. on Business Process Management (pp. 165-181)*. Berlin / Heidelberg: Springer.

Liu, R., Bhattacharya, K., & Wu, F. Y. (2007). Modeling business contexture and behavior using business artifacts. In *Proc. Int. Conf. on Advanced Information Systems Engineering* (pp. 324-339). Berlin / Heidelberg: Springer.

Martin, D., et al. (2004). *OWL-S: Semantic markup for Web services*, W3C Member Submission. http://www.w3.org/Submission/OWL-S/

McIlraith, S. A., Son, T. C., & Zeng, H. (2001). Semantic Web services. *IEEE Intelligent Systems, 16*(2), 46-53.

Műller, R., Greiner, U., & Rahm, E. (2004). AGENTWORK: A workflow system supporting rule-based workflow ddaptation. *Data & Knowledge Engineering, 51*(2), 223-256.

Nigam, A. & Caswell, N. S. (2003). Business artifacts: An approach to operational specification. *IBM Systems Journal, 42*(3), 428-445

Kobayashi, T., Ogoshi, S., & Komoda, N. (1997). A business process design method for applying workflow tools. In *Proc. IEEE Int. Conf. on Systems, Man, and Cybernetics, Computational Cybernetics and Simulation* (pp. 2314-2319). IEEE Press.

Strosnider, J. K., Nandi, P., Kumaran, S., Ghosh, S., & Arsanjani, A. (2008). Model-driven synthesis of SOA solutions. *IBM Systems Journal, 47*(3), 415-432.

Su, J., Bultan, T., Fu, X., & Zhao, X. (2008). Towards a theory of Web service choreographies. In *Proc. 2007 Workshop on Web Services and Formal Methods* (pp. 1-16). Berlin / Heidelberg: Springer.

van der Aalst, W. M. P. (2004). Business process management demystified: A tutorial on models, systems and standards for workflow management. In *Lectures on Concurrency and Petri Nets* (pp. 1-65). Berlin / Heidelberg: Springer.

van der Aalst, W. M. P., & Pesic, M. (2006). DecSerFlow: Towards a truly declarative service Flow Language. In *Proc. 2007 Workshop on Web Services and Formal Methods* (pp. 1-23). Berlin / Heidelberg: Springer.

Wahler, K. & Küster, J. M. (2008). Predicting Coupling of object-centric business process implementations. In *Proc. 6th Int. Conf. on Business Process Management* (pp. 148-163). Berlin / Heidelberg: Springer.

KEY TERM

Artifact: In the context of data-centric workflow, a synonym for "business artifact"

Artifact-Centric Workflow or Business Process Model: A workflow model that is based on the use of business artifacts, where each business artifact type includes both the data schema and specification of possible lifecycles for a key class of business entities.

Business Artifact: A business artifact type holds information about a key class of (real or conceptual) business entities, including both the information model (data schema) of the business-relevant data that can be associated with entities of this type over time, and specification of the possible macro-lifecycles of these entities. A business artifact is an instance of this type.

Business Operations Model (BOM): A detailed logical specification of the business artifacts (including both information models and lifecycle specifications) that are used to describe the business-level operation of a (portion of a) business or other organization.

Conceptual Flow (Diagram) of an Artifact-Centric Workflow: A conceptual flow is a specification that represents in abstract but procedural form how a Business Operations Model can be implemented. It does not include low-level physical implementation details. A conceptual flow is typically specified as a graph, which is called a 'conceptual flow diagram.'

Lifecycle (of a Business Artifact): A specification of the key business-relevant stages of the processing of an artifact, the tasks that are used to evolve the artifact between these stages, and (using procedural and/or declarative constructs) the possible sequencings of these tasks.

Chapter XXIV
Measurement and Maturity of Business Processes

Laura Sanchez
University of Castilla-La Mancha, Spain

Andrea Delgado
University of the Republic, Uruguay

Francisco Ruiz
University of Castilla-La Mancha, Spain

Félix García
University of Castilla-La Mancha, Spain

Mario Piattini
University of Castilla-La Mancha, Spain

ABSTRACT

The underlying premise of process management is that the quality of products and services is largely determined by the quality of the processes used to develop, deliver and support them. A concept which has been closely related to process quality over the last few years is the maturity of the process and it is important to highlight the current proposal of Business Process Maturity Model (BPMM), which is based on the principles, architecture and practices of CMM and CMMI for Software and describes the essential practices for the development, preparation, deployment, operations and support of product and service offers from determining customer needs. When maturity models are in place, it is important not to forget the important role that measurement can play, being essential in organizations which intend to reach a high level in the maturity in their processes. This is demonstrated by observing the degree of importance that measurement activities have in maturity models. This chapter tackles the Business Process Maturity Model and the role that business measurement plays in the context of this model. In addition, a set of representative business process measures aligned with the characteristics of BPMM are introduced which can guide organizations to support the measurement of their business processes depending on their maturity.

INTRODUCTION

As stated in (OMG, 2007), "the underlying premise of process management is that the quality of products and services is largely determined by the quality of the processes used to develop, deliver and support them". Regardless of what the business of an organization is, whether software development, government business or manufacturing, the need to explicitly define, manage, measure, control, analyze and improve its business processes is the same. A concept which has been closely related to process quality over the last few years is the maturity of the process, especially in the context of software processes.

Process maturity is based on the first ideas of (Crosby, 1979) and (Humphrey, 1987) and represents the degree of explicit definition, management, measurement, control and effectiveness a process has. The works of Humphrey (Humphrey, 1987) were carried out in the context of the development of CMM (Paulk et al., 1993) and later CMMI (CMMI Product Team, 2002 and 2006), and have become important reference models for improving the capability of software organizations. Since then, many similar standards have been developed for other processes, for example the People CMM (Curtis, 1995) which applied process maturity to the management and development of an organization's workforce.

In a mature organization, processes are defined, performed and managed and accurately communicated to the staff, and work activities are carried out according to planned processes. These processes are documented and usable with roles and responsibilities that are clearly defined and understood by the people performing the associated activities. The needed improvements in selected processes are developed and controlled and aligned with business objectives. The quality of products and services are monitored, as well as the processes that produce them (OMG, 2007). Thus, the importance and benefits of process maturity in an organization are clear.

Recently, earlier proposals which have shown themselves to be useful in the context of software processes have been applied to business processes. The main example of this is the current proposal for a Business Process Maturity Model (OMG, 2007), which is based on the principles, architecture and practices of CMM and CMMI for Software and describes the essential practices for the development, preparation, deployment, operations and support of product and service offers from determining customer needs. The BPMM, like other maturity models, is expected to benefit organizations in terms of rework reduction, consistency and improvements in quality (OMG, 2007).

When maturity models are in place, it is important not to forget the important role that measurement can play. As a matter of fact, measurement is essential in organizations which intend to reach a high level in the maturity in their processes. This is demonstrated by observing the degree of importance that measurement activities have in maturity models. Measurement provides objective information about and a view of project performance, process performance, process capability and product and service quality. Moreover, measurement helps to provide objective insight into issues in order to identify and manage risks and to provide the early detection and resolution of problems.

The use of measures and other information makes it possible for organizations to learn from the past in order to improve performance and achieve better predictability over time. It also provides information that improves decision-making in time to affect the business outcome. Therefore measurement activities are fundamental for the improvement of process, product and service quality, since they provide objective information that can be used for decision making. An organization with a mature approach in this area will have confidence in its abilities to deliver products or services that meet its customers' needs (Goldenson et al., 2003)

According to the issues identified above, this chapter tackles the Business Process Maturity Model (OMG, 2007) and the role that measurement plays in the context of this model. In addition, a set of representative business process measures aligned with the characteristics of this maturity model are introduced to illustrate how measurement can be applied to organizations in relation to each maturity level. The chapter is organized as follows: Section 2 describes the BPMM, including its maturity levels and Process Areas. Section 3 presents measurement and analysis activities in BPMM by each maturity level, including those with defined guidelines and those without them. Section 4 enumerates and discusses measurable concepts and measures aligned with BPMM maturity levels, and finally, Section 5 presents some conclusions and reflections.

BUSINESS PROCESS MATURITY MODEL

The Business Process Maturity Model (BPMM) (OMG, 2007) is one of the Object Management Group (OMG) (OMG,1989) business process standards, released in July of 2007 in its first version 1.0. Conceptually it follows the approach of the maturity models for software: Capability Maturity Model (CMM) (Paulk et al., 1993) and Capability Maturity Model Integration (CMMI) (CMMI Product Team, 2002) and was developed by the co-authors of these models. "The BPMM can be mapped to CMMI, but has been written to guide improvement of business processes which tend to be more transactional and are better characterized as workflows across organizational boundaries rather than the more bounded project orientation of CMMI" (OMG, 2007). Like the CMMI, it defines five process maturity levels to assess the achievement of specific characteristics that make it possible to determine the maturity level that the processes of the organization present.

It is important to define and establish the different meanings of the terms process capability, process performance and process maturity. Process capability describes the range of expected results that can be achieved by following a process, providing one means of predicting the most likely outcomes to be expected from the next effort undertaken. The Process Areas and maturity levels of the BPMM are indicators of process capability. On the other hand, process performance describes the actual results achieved by performing a process. The implementation and institutionalization of BPMM Process Areas incrementally improve this performance, where institutionalization refers to the infrastructure and culture built into the organization to support methods and practices that become the method of working. Finally, process maturity is the extent to which processes are explicitly defined, managed, measured, controlled and are effective. Process maturity implies that process capability has improved over time, so, as an organization matures, the institutionalized methods, practices and procedures endure even after those who defined them have left.

The continuous improvement of processes is based on taking small but evolutionary and innovative steps in the processes. BPMM provides a reference framework to organize these steps and innovations at the five maturity levels, which establishes the basis for the continuous improvement of the processes. The priorities in BPMM, expressed for those levels, are not focused on the (individual or group) work units, but on the processes that are of value to the whole organization. A work unit is a well-defined collection of people, managed as a single unit within the organization, who work closely together on tasks specifically related to developing, preparing, maintaining and delivering the organization's products and services or performing internal business functions. Figure 1 shows the five maturity levels of BPMM including for each: its name, a brief description and its main objectives.

An organization that implements the BPMM could obtain the advantages associated with using this kind of model, which include:

- Standardization of its processes and best practices and more knowledge and control of processes;
- Record of good practices and identified problems which would improve the instances of new processes or projects to perform;
- History of data on the processes executed, both qualitative and quantitative, which contributes to the definition of the improvements to make, and makes it possible to assess the impact of the changes made and the achievement of the planned improvements.

Thus, improving the organization can be based on sound practices implemented at each maturity level, making progress possible at the various existing levels.

The Five Maturity Levels of BPMM

Each maturity level is composed of a set of Process Areas, each containing a cluster of related practices for that area that when implemented collectively, provide a process capability that is an important component of its maturity level. Each Process Area is composed of various elements: area purpose, specific and institutionalization objectives of the area and specific and institutionalization practices which may contain subpractices. Each one also has practice guidelines for selected practices, such as the guidelines for Measurement and Analysis which are presented in the following section. There are thirty Process Areas in total: nine for level two, ten for level three, five for level four and six for level five. It is also possible to create a domain-specific BPMM, such as the Services Operations or Marketing, which have already been defined, adding domain Process Areas at level three to extend the BPMM for the specific domain with the aid of domain experts.

An organization at maturity level one or Initial shows inconsistent process practices and results.

Figure 1. The five maturity levels of BPMM from (OMG, 2007)

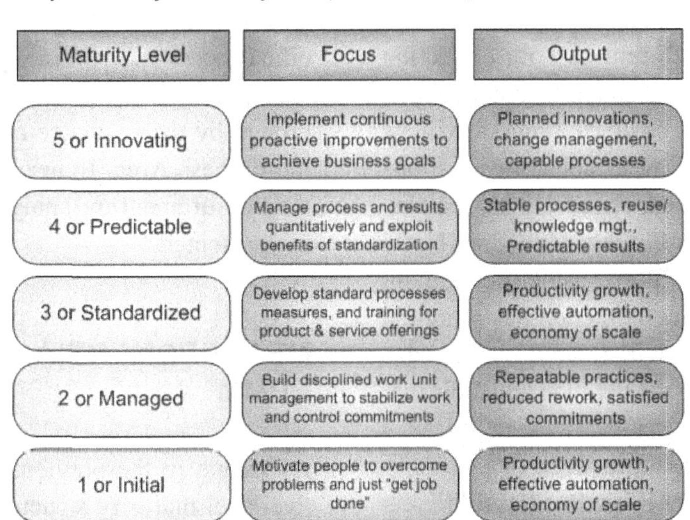

There are no specific defined objectives, so, the success of the organization depends on personal competence and heroics, and not on the use of proven processes. Some processes and/or projects may work well but there is no knowledge of how the positive results are achieved and the rest of the processes and/or projects, which in general, are the majority, are not usually successful. So, at this level there are no defined Process Areas.

Moving to **maturity level two or Managed**, each work unit and/or project has established basic processes for planning and management, control and management of its requirements and performs all essential activities to prepare, distribute, operate and support its products and services. The procedures which describe those processes are defined and repeatable, i.e., they can be used again in another project with similar results. At this level the organization, through its work units, achieves the expected results both in products and services, in planned schedule and budget and according to the requirements.

At **maturity level three or Standardized**, the organization's standard processes to prepare, distribute, operate and support its products and services are documented for their use through the entire organization. These standard processes include work, support and management processes, which are defined at an abstract level that makes it possible to apply them to different sections and projects. Thus, the standard processes will be instantiated by each unit of work or section making the necessary adaptations. For example, the process to model business process will be defined in a standard way, establishing notations and tools to use to make the model, which can be, for example, Business Process Modelling Notation (BPMN) (OMG, 2006) using a compliant tool. When a work unit or section has to model a business process, it will follow the standard process defined, using the notation and tools that it established. At this level the organization takes full advantage of its best practices.

Maturity level four or Predictable, sets achievable quantitative targets for performance and quality results to obtain in the business process of the organization -- for example to develop a product or provide a service -- and they are used as criteria to manage the associated effort. At this level, the main objective is to manage and take full advantage of the organizational processes, infrastructure capability and associated process assets, established at level three, to achieve predictable results with controlled variations.

At **maturity level five or Innovating**, the organization has knowledge about its critical business characteristics or areas of interest, for example, competitiveness, and sets quantitative improvement objectives to deal with them. The improvements are identified, evaluated, put into practice in pilot experiences and distributed in order to achieve the defined improvement objectives. The main objective at this level is the continuous improvement of the organization's processes and the resulting products and services, through defect and problem prevention, continuous capacity and innovating planned improvements.

Like CMM (Paulk et al., 1993), BPMM does not have a specific Process Area for measurement and analysis and the associated activities can be found spread across the Process Areas defined. This fact means that the process of measurement and analysis instead of being explicit is implicit in the model. In subsequent versions of CMM, CMMI v1.1 (CMMI Product Team, 2002) and CMMI v1.2 (CMMI Product Team, 2006), a specific Process Area for measurement and analysis is included, thus making the process explicit and guided by the sequence of activities defined by the Process Area. In next section, the activities for measurement and analysis included in BPMM are presented.

MEASUREMENT ACTIVITIES IN BPMM

As shown in the previous section, BPMM is a five-level maturity structure model where each maturity level is composed of various Process Areas. Measurement activities are defined in the different Process Areas to satisfy their goals. For example, in the Process Area "Organizational Process Management", some practices for defining organizational measures can be found and a set of guidelines are provided. These guidelines are optional, but facilitate some difficult activities for reaching higher maturity levels. The measurement activities must be done by a different work group than the decision making group, to assure objectivity. They consist of seven steps, and some of them generate artefacts for improving the measurement repository, for creating measurement plans and a list of measurement indicators. These guidelines are shown in Figure 2.

As can be observed in Figure 2, the first activity defined in the guidelines is to establish and maintain a description of the information needs. This refers to the identification and documentation of measurement-related objectives and issues. The next activity is to establish and maintain a specification of measures and this refers to specifying the operational definition of the measures.

The third activity concerns establishing and maintaining a specification of the information package. This refers to defining the measurement information package, which includes the measures, indicators, criteria and other information that the users of the data need to understand and use the data in making decisions. The fourth activity, establish and maintain measurement plans and procedures, refers to defining how the measures will be collected, verified and stored. The fifth activity, collect and verify measurement data, refers to obtaining and verifying base measures, and then generating derived measures and indicators under change management. The next activity concerns assembling an information package, meaning that the measurement data are assembled into a measurement information package as defined in the measurement plans and procedures for improving the measurement repository. The last activity concerns analyzing the measurement data for making decisions as defined in the measurement specifications, plans and procedures.

Figure 2. The measurement and analysis guidelines steps

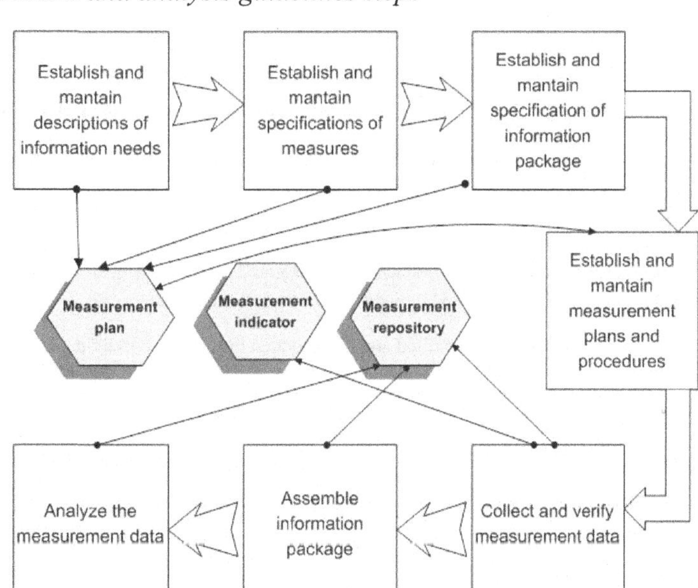

Process Areas with Guidelines for Measurement

At maturity level two, the relationship between business measurement and the business process is undefined. The reason for this is that the organization at this level does not have any explicit business processes, it is said that the "business process has still not been discovered". At this level, it is possible to create workflow measures for monitoring the performance of the business units and business activities. A business unit is a single well-defined organizational component within an organization and an activity is an element of work performed as part of a planned effort. Table 1 shows the Process Areas and corresponding activities for using guidelines for measurement and analysis and a brief description of each one.

While maturity level two defines measures at a work unit level for showing the performance of the work units, at maturity level three measures are defined at a process level. So, from the second to the third level, the measures are defined with two different levels of granularity: work unit level and process level. Table 2 shows the Process Areas and corresponding activities for using guidelines for measurement and analysis.

Table 1. Process Areas and activities at maturity level two for using guidelines for measurement and analysis

Process Areas and activities with guidelines at maturity level two
Organizational Business Governance (OBG)
SP2-Define business measures: Definitions of the business outcome measures related to the organization's near-term and long-term business goals are established and maintained
SP8 - Maintain definition of workflow measures: Definitions of the workflow measures used to monitor the performance of the units and business activities are established and maintained
Work Unit Planning and Commitment (WUPC)
SP5 - Maintain definitions of measures: Definitions of the measures used to plan and manage a work unit are established and maintained
Work Unit Monitoring and Control (WUMC)
SP6 - Monitor and adjust work assignments: The work assigned to individuals and workgroups in a work unit is monitored on a regular basis, and adjustments are made as needed
SP7 - Analyze measures: Measures defined in the plans for a work unit are collected, analysed, and used to manage the work
SP8 - Review performance and status: The performance and the status of the activities, work products, and services for a work unit are reviewed against its requirements, plans, and commitments on a regular basis
Work Unit Performance (WUP)
SP8 - Measure work performance: Measurements of the work activities performed by the individuals and work groups within a work unit and the work products produced are collected and analyzed to understand the performance and results
SP9 - Improve work performance: Improvements are identified and incorporated into the way individuals and workgroups within a work unit perform their work
Sourcing Management (SM)
SP5 - Maintain sourcing agreement: The sourcing agreement for a selected supplier is established and maintained
SP7 - Maintain supplier work orders: Work orders are established and maintained with a supplier to provide specified products and services
SP8 - Resolve planning conflicts: A supplier's plans and commitments are balanced with a work unit's internal plans and commitments

At **maturity level four**, the organization compares the previous results to make an analysis. This maturity level does not include any new measures since it only compares results. There are no guidelines for measuring and analysing the practices implemented at this level, but it provides some activities for performing statistical control and analysis of the results which are shown in next section.

At **maturity level five**, measures are performed about the clients' satisfaction and to give insight into the improvements made to the selected processes. The most important measures were developed at the third maturity level. Table 3 shows the Process Areas and corresponding activities for using guidelines for measurement and analysis.

The Implicit Process of Measurement and Analysis in BPMM

As mentioned in the earlier sections, there is no specific Process Area for measurement and analy-

Table 2. Process Areas and activities at maturity level three for using guidelines for measurement and analysis

Process Areas and activities with guidelines at maturity level three
Organizational Process Management (OPM)
SP7 - Maintain definitions of organizational measures: Definitions of measures are established and maintained to characterize the organization's standard processes and process assets
SP9 - Maintain process repositories: Repositories for storing and making available the organization's process descriptions and measures and information on their use are established and maintained
SP11 - Collect process assets: Process-related work products, measures, and improvement information derived from performing the organization's processes are collected, packaged, and maintained in the organizational repositories
SP12 - Analyze process information: Information, work products, and measures derived from performing the organization's processes are analyzed to provide insight into and improve the organization's standard processes and related process assets
Organizational Competency Development (OCD)
SP8 - Monitor competency development activities: Status and performance in meeting the organization's competency development plans are monitored, and significant deviations are identified
SP9 - Measure competency development effectiveness: The effectiveness of the organization's competency development activities is measured and evaluated, and significant deficiencies are identified
Product and Service Work Management (PSWM)
SP4 - Maintain definitions of measures: Definitions of the measures used to plan and manage the product and service work for an offer and to satisfy organizational measurement requirements are established and maintained.
SP9 - Manage product and service work: Definitions of the measures used to plan and manage the product and service work for an offer and to satisfy organizational measurement requirements are established and maintained
SP11 - Report utilization of organization's resources: The amount of each type of resource needed to perform the product and service work for an offer is determined and reported to executive management for use in managing the organizational resources
SP12 - Contribute to organization's process assets: Work products, measures, documented experiences, and improvements from the product and service work for an offer are contributed to the organization's process assets
Products and Service Deployment (PSD)
SP15 - Support parallel operations: Each terminated or replaced product and service offer is continued as needed to allow the customers and users to transition off the terminated or replaced offer.

Table 3. Process Areas and activities at maturity level five for using guidelines for measurement and analysis

Process Areas and activities with guidelines at maturity level five
Organizational Improvement Planning (OIP) SP3 - Maintain improvement goals Quantitative improvement goals for the organization and their priorities are established and maintained SP7 - Maintain organizational improvement plans Plans for improvement efforts that the organization will perform are established and maintained SP8 - Monitor improvement activities and results The organization's improvement activities and results are monitored against the organization's improvement strategies and quantitative improvement goals SP9 - Compare improvement measures to goals Measures and quantitative projections of the organization's improvements are monitored against the organization's quantitative improvement goals
Organizational Performance Alignment (OPA) SP1 - Allocate business goals and responsibilities to units The allocation of the organizational quantitative business goals and responsibilities to the organization's product and service offers and units is established and maintained. SP2 - Adjust unit plans for overall results The responsibilities, plans and commitments of the units are evaluated and aligned to ensure that, individually and in aggregate, they provide the best fit for the organization's business strategies and goals SP3 - Align work assignments within units The work assignments of workgroups and individuals in the work units are established and maintained to support the achievement of the business goals for the units SP4 – Monitor local Alignment and results The performance and results of the individuals, workgroups, units and product and service offers are monitored on a regular basis against their business goals SP6 – Monitor Organizational Alignment and results The overall performance and results of the organization are monitored on a regular basis against the organization's quantitative improvement goals and strategies
Defect and Problem prevention (DPP) SP8 – Measure effects of preventive actions The effects of the work unit's workgroup's defect and problem prevention actions on its plans and quantitative improvement goals are measured and analyzed.
Organizational Innovative Improvement (OII) SP4 - Evaluate candidate improvements Candidate innovative improvements are rigorously evaluated to determine their costs, impacts, and contribution to achieving the quantitative improvements goals assigned to an improvement workgroup SP5 - Prepare improvement solution A set of changes that makes up a complete improvement solution are prepared and evaluated to determine if the solution will achieve the assigned quantitative improvement goals

sis in BPMM like in CMM; thus, the activities are spread across the defined Process Areas. There are some activities with guidelines as presented in the previous section and there are some other activities related to this topic that do not have guidelines to perform them, which are presented in this section. Table 4 shows the Process Areas and activities for maturity level two for measurement and analysis without guidelines.

Table 4 shows the activities without guidelines for measurement and analysis defined in the Process Area "Organizational Process Leadership", which aim to guide the process improvement program in the organization. It involves the definition of measures for planning, managing and evaluating the results of the program, and reviewing the results obtained from the values registered for the defined measures.

In maturity level three there are no Process Areas that contain activities without guidelines for measurement and analysis. Table 5 shows the activities without guidelines for measurement and analysis for maturity level four.

Table 5 shows the activities without guidelines for measurement and analysis for maturity level four, which are defined in three different Process Areas. In the Process Area "Organizational Capability and Performance Management" the critical process elements, attributes and measures that characterize these aspects of the standard processes established for maturity level three are defined. Also the techniques that are going to be used for the quantitative control of the process are identified and selected, and the measures collected and stored in the organization's measurement repository for further analysis.

In "Product and Service Process Integration" the definitions of measures for integrated processes are defined. In "Quantitative Process Management" the definition of measurable attributes for understanding and controlling the variation in the processes is established, and the quantitative and analytic techniques that are used to understand and control this variation are determined. Also the performance, quality goals, capability measures, analysis and results of corrective actions to be used in the organization are recorded.

Table 6 shows the Process Areas and activities without guidelines for measurement and analysis for maturity level five.

Table 6 shows the only activity without guidelines for measurement and analysis at maturity level five, which is in the Process Area "Organizational Improvement Planning" and refers to the collection and analysis of measures on a regular basis to identify areas that need improvement.

From all the Process Areas and activities related to measurement and analysis practices (with or without guidelines), we can identify four principal aspects which must be taken into account in the implicit process with its corresponding

Table 4. Process Areas and activities at maturity level two for measurement and analysis without guidelines

Process Areas and activities without guidelines at maturity level two
Organizational Process Leadership (OPL)
SP7 – Maintain definition of improvement measures:
Definitions of the measures used to plan, manage, and evaluate results of the organization's process improvement program are established and maintained
SP10 – Review Process improvement results:
Progress in achieving the organization's process improvement goals is reviewed by executive management on a periodic basis

Table 5. Process Areas and activities at maturity level four for measurement and analysis without guidelines

Process Areas and Activities without guidelines at maturity level four
Organizational Capability and Performance Management (OCPM) SP2 – Maintain Process attribute measures The critical process elements, attributes, and measures that are used to quantitatively characterize the performance of the organization's standard processes are identified SP3 – Maintain Capability Analyses Definition of statistical and other quantitative techniques for evaluating the capability of organization's product and services processes for achieving performance and quality goals are established and maintained SP4 – Collect measures Measures of process attributes and performance and quality results emerging from the organization's product and service work are collected on a periodic basis and stored in the organizational measurement repository
Product and Service Process Integration (PSPI) SP3 – Define measures for integrated processes Definitions of measures used to plan and manage the product and service work using functionally integrated processes are established and maintained
Quantitative Process Management (QPM) SP2 – Maintain definitions of measures The definitions of the measurable attributes of a work effort that are relevant for understanding and controlling the variation in the work processes and managing the achievement of the work effort's quantitative performance and quality goals are established and maintained SP3- Determine quantitative and analytic techniques Quantitative and other analytic techniques needed to understand and control the variation in the work processes and manage the achievement of a work effort's quantitative performance and quality goals are identified and adapted for use SP10- Record work effort results The performance and quality goals, performance and capability measures, analyses, and the results of corrective actions for a work effort are recorded for local use and organizational use

Table 6. Process Areas and activities for maturity level five for measurement and analysis without guidelines

Process Areas and activities without guidelines at maturity level five
Organizational Improvement Planning (OIP) SP4 – Analyze measures to identify improvements Measures of the organization's processes, activities, performance, and results are analyzed on a regular basis to identify areas that are most in need of improvements

activities as defined in BPMM. Figure 3 proposes a summary of the activities logically grouped according to these criteria by maturity level.

As can be observed in Figure 3, the grouping of activities involves the definition of high level concepts that all the activities share, in the first one, to define and maintain the definition of objectives, measures, procedures and techniques, in second one to collect measures, monitor and review status, in third one to store and analyze measures and results and in fourth one to review results and needed improvements.

When comparing this proposal with the specific goals and associated practices in the CMMI family for Process Area measurement and analysis, it can be noted that it defines only two logical concepts for grouping the activities which correspond to Specific Goal 1: "Align measurement and analysis activities" and Specific Goal 2: "Provide measurement results". The former is equivalent to the first defined in our proposal, and the latter is equivalent to the other three together in our proposal. We think that to explicitly state the goals identified with fewer specifics shows better insight in the process and the objectives of each one can be better understood.

MEASURABLE CONCEPTS AND MEASURES ALIGNED WITH BPMM

First of all, it is necessary to establish a definition for a measurable concept and a measure. For this purpose, the Software Measurement Ontology (SMO) defined in (García et al., 2005) is used. The SMO aims to contribute to the harmonization of the different software measurement proposals and standards by providing a coherent set of common concepts used in software measurement. It is believed (Rolón et al., 2006b) that software

Figure 3. Grouped activities identified in the implicit process for measurement and analysis ordered by maturity level

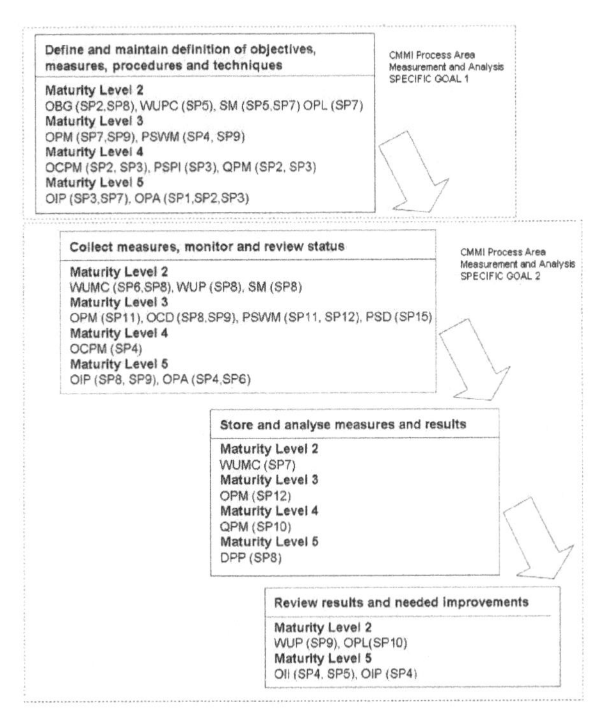

processes and business processes present some similarities including the fact that both seek to capture the main characteristics of a group of partially ordered activities that are carried out to achieve a specific goal. Based on that, the SMO can be used to define concepts also related to the measurement of business processes, as was done by (Rolón et al., 2006a;2006b).

The main features and characteristics of the SMO as mentioned in (García et al., 2005) are the following: "it uses the term 'measure' instead of 'metric', it differentiates between 'measure', 'measurement', and 'measurement result', and it distinguishes between base measures, derived measures, and indicators, but considering them all as measures and generalizing their respective measurement approaches (measurement method, measurement function and analysis model), and integrates the software measures with the quality model that defines the information needs that drive the measurement process". Some of the concepts defined in SMO are described below, especially those on which the presentation of the concepts included in this section rely.

The concept of "information need" refers to the information needed to manage a project (for example, goals and risks, among others). An "entity" is an object characterized by the measurement of its attributes as defined in (ISO/IEC-15939, 2002), e.g. a software or business processes model. An "attribute" is a measurable property, physical or abstract, shared by all entities of an entity category, e.g. activities or nodes in a software or business process model. A "measurable concept" is an abstract relationship between attributes and information needs, so, it is ultimately what is wanted to be measured or what makes it possible to make the measurements. Finally, a "measure" is defined with a measurement approach, which can be a measurement function, measurement method or an analysis model and the measurement scale. Measures are applied to measurable attributes of the entities. The SMO defines more concepts related to measurement, which are not presented here; the interested reader is referred to (García et al., 2005).

State of the Art of Measures for Business Process

The current literature includes some different classification measures for business processes. For example, according to (Vanderfeesten et al., 2008a), business process measures can be inspired by software measurement and experimental work on process model measures. However, in this section, measures are classified in design measures and execution measures based on Tjaden (1999) which defines operative measures and structural measures. Operative measures measure how the process is executing over time and are directly related to the dynamic properties of business processes. Structural measures treat the static properties of business processes and are defined upon the business process model at the design time.

Design measures quantify the quality of business processes related to some measurable attributes of the model. These measures are made before the business process is executed. Moreover, such measures could inform about if the model has an appropriate size, is clearly structured or is easy to comprehend. The great majority of these measures are independent from the modeling languages because they use only high-level information from the business process models.

For example, a design measure could measure the complexity of a business process model, expressed in terms of BPMN and it could measure the number of elements of a particular type. Table 7 shows some important measures for business process models. The goal is to highlight some of the most important measurement initiatives in the current literature and not to provide a complete state of the art about the measurement of business processes. For further information the interested reader is referred to the sources listed.

For each measurable concept, there are different initiatives. Each author has interpreted complexity, cohesion and coupling from different perspectives, as can be seen in Table 8.

As can be observed in Table 8, there is high heterogeneity in measuring complexity for business processes. Some of them could be used to complement others. For example, some authors have proposed the measure number of activities for calculating complexity, but this measure is rather simple and it is necessary to complement it with others. Tables 9 and 10 present coupling and cohesion measures are presented.

Coupling is related to cohesion, because the ideal situations are a business process model that

Table 7. Measurable concepts for business process models

Measurable Concept	Description
Complexity	Hard to separate, analyze or solve. (Latva-Koivisto, 2001) Complexity measures the simpleness and understandability of a design (Vanderfeesten et al, 2007). The degree to which a process is difficult to analyze, understand or explain. It may be characterized by the number and intricacy of activity interfaces, transitions, conditional and parallel branches, the existence of loops, roles, activity categories, the types of data structures and other process characteristics (Cardoso, 2005).
Cohesion	Relationship of the elements within the design. It is hypothesized that a design with low cohesion will contain more errors than a design with higher cohesion (Vanderfeesten et al, 2007).
Coupling	Number of interconnections among modules of a design. The degree of coupling depends on how complicated the connections are. It is hypothesized that a design with a high coupling will contain more errors (Vanderfeesten et al, 2007).

Table 8. Complexity measures in the design stage

Complexity	
Author	**Measure**
J. Cardoso (Cardoso, 2007)	**NOA**: number of activities in a process. This measure is highly criticized because of its simplicity. It could be used as a complement of other measures
J. Cardoso (Cardoso, 2007)	**CFC**: control-flow complexity. This is measured considering the complexity of the splits (AND, XOR,OR), joins, loops and ending and starting points It considerers the number of mental states that have to be taken into account when a designer develops a process.
V. Gruhn and R. Laue (Gruhn and Laue, 2006)	**Cognitive complexity**: cognitive effort to understand a model. This means how easy or difficult it is to comprehend a design. **Nesting depth**: information about the structure of the design. Number of decisions in the control flow that are necessary to perform this action. **Antipatterns**: counting the usage of antipatterns in a design can help to detect poor modeling. An antipattern is a design pattern that appears obvious but is ineffective or far from optimal in practice. **Fan-in/Fan-out**: this is the count of all other modules that calls the module under investigation and are called from it. **Number of handles**: measure of well-structuredness. This is always 0 for well-structured models.
J. Mendling (Mendling, 2006)	**Testing Density**: number of arcs for a given set of function, event and connector nodes.
E. Rolón (Rolón et al., 2006a)	**Structural Complexity**: depending on two aspects of maintainability and usability: understandability and modifiability, measures elements of a business process model modeled with BPMN (OMG, 2006).

is strongly cohesive and weakly coupled, the same desirable properties defined for the design of software systems. A coupling/cohesion ratio is defined to enable the comparison between various design alternatives. The design with the minimal process coupling/cohesion ratio is the most favourable design.

Regarding the execution of business processes, measures that can be obtained from it are going to be used to obtain insight into the execution of processes primarily for making improvements in business processes. In the literature of business process and workflows measures, there are not as many works about execution measures as about design measures. We think this is due to the fact that execution measures can be seen from two viewpoints which have their own type of defined measures: general execution measures that can be applied to processes of any kind (for example, software processes) and execution measures specific to the business process domain.

In the case of general execution measures, all of them refer to process attributes such as progress, duration, cost and quality, among others, with no reference to the type of processes they are measuring. Measures such as in the Project Management Book of Knowledge (PMBOK) Guide (Project Management Institute, 2004) for project management can be used to measure and control the execution of the processes. In the case of execution measures specific to the business process domain, the attributes could be, for example, the quantity of products delivered in the process or by activity, the total price of products delivered, average time to deliver a product, among others, which are defined as Process Key Indicators (PKI) for business processes by business analysts or managers with specific knowledge of the business of the organization, and presented in scorecards (Kaplan et al., 1996).

The BPMM provides examples of the information needs for the process improvement program and the measures to address them in Process Area Organizational Process Leadership at maturity level two in activity SP7. It can also be used to measure business process execution attributes even if this process is not part of the improvement program, since they also refer to attributes such as progress, cost, quality and customer satisfaction. These are shown, slightly adapted to be general for any process, in Table 11.

Table 9. Cohesion measures in the design stage

Cohesion	
Author	**Measure**
I. Vandersfeesten (Vanderfeesten et al., 2008b)	**Process cohesion**: coupling focuses on how strongly the activities in a workflow process are related or connected to each other. A certain activity is connected to another one if and only if they share one or more information elements

Table 10. Coupling measures in the design stage

Coupling	
Author	**Measure**
I. Vandersfeesten (Vanderfeesten et al., 2008b)	**Process coupling**: Number of interconnections among modules of business process model
M. Latva-Koivisto (Latva-Koivisto, 2001)	**Coefficient of connectivity**: average number of connections that a node has with other nodes of the process graph

Table 11. Measurable concepts for execution stage of business processes

Measurable concept	Description
Progress	Provides information about • Progress against the plans for process; • Progress toward achieving the related goals.
Cost	Provides information about the progress compared with savings and benefits.
Customer satisfaction	Provides information about changes in customer satisfaction.
Quality – trouble reports	Provides insight into the quality of the product and processes and the quality of the model being executed.

Measures for Business Processes at Each Maturity Level

Tables 12a and 12b provide a general insight into measurement in BPMM. These tables show the relationship between measurement, process and product. This relationship is based on (Pfleeger, 1996), which presents this relationship in the context of CMM and in an adaptation from (Lee et al., 2007).

As can be observed in Tables 12a and 12b, at level 2, business processes are shown as a black box at maturity level 2. Execution measures are applied because the organization only knows the inputs and outputs of the processes. At maturity level 3, the business processes are viewed as a white box and defined from an organizational perspective, instead of the work unit perspective used at maturity level 2. At this level it is possible to apply design measures to the defined processes because the process visibility makes it possible to have a consciousness of the intermediate products.

At maturity level 4 it is possible to apply techniques such as Business Process Mining (van der Aalst et al., 2007) to establish conformance between models and processes (the process is executed following the steps described in the model), to extend the business process models with new information extracted from event logs for improving models and even to register execution measures of the business processes in event logs files to analyse and improve the business processes. At this level, statistical control of the processes is used to control their variation. At maturity level 5, process quantitative management helps to achieve a continuous improvement of the processes.

In the next section, a more detailed vision about measures for business process modelling and execution is provided, along with the illustration of its usage based on an adaptation of the very well known example of a business process for trip reservations in a travel Agency (Singh et al., 2004).

Measures for Business Process Modeling

Design measures cannot be applied for organizations at the second maturity level. The main reason is shown in Tables 12a and 12b. It is possible that some work units can have visual descriptions of their processes, but not in a standardized way, so it is possible to analyze their attributes but with isolated efforts. On the other hand, at maturity level three some intermediate products are known. Work units are white boxes, so it is possible to apply design measures. The results of these measures could help business processes in facilitating maintainability and some potential points of errors would not be continued in later stages of the business process life cycle. The business process model for the travel agency is shown in Figure 4 expressed in BPMN (OMG, 2006).

Table 12 a. Relationship between measurement, process and product with respect to maturity

Maturity process and measurement		
Maturity	**Characteristics**	**Related measurement activities**
Initial	Ad hoc manner	
Managed	•Not defining or partially defining process •Measuring process performance partially •Monitoring and controlling process performance for a work unit in an ad hoc manner 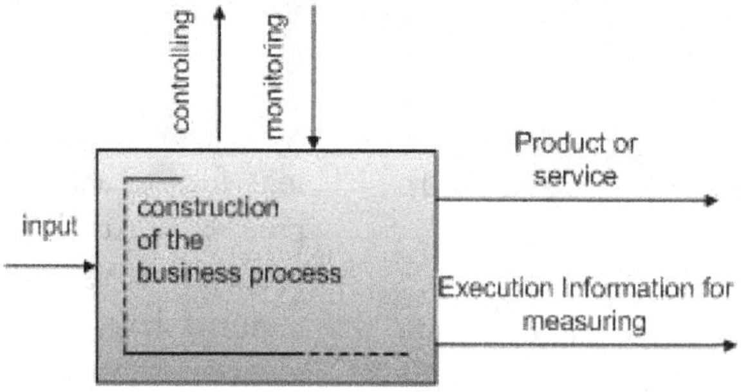	Execution measures
Standardized	•Defining process •Monitoring and controlling process performance for overall organization •Processes are monitoring in a systematic manner and controlled in a ad hoc manner 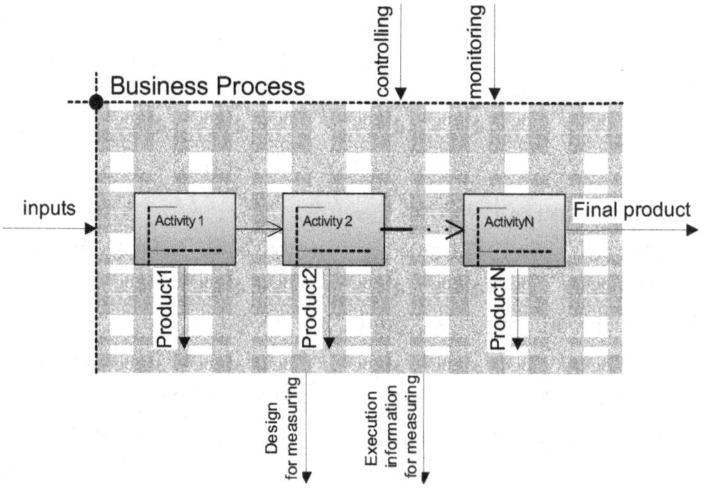	Design measures

Figure 4 shows the workflow of elements that define the business process for the travel agency, which starts when a client sends a request to the travel agency with information concerning the trip, including place, dates, and payment data. Meanwhile, the travel agency asks its partners to carry out the flight, hotel and car rental reservations; if a positive result is obtained a message is sent to the client with the information concerning the reservations and payment, while the travel agency

Table 12 b. Relationship between measurement, process and product with respect to maturity

Maturity process and measurement		
Maturity	**Characteristics**	**Related measurement activities**
Predictable	•Measuring process performance quantitatively •Systematically controlling and monitoring process performance 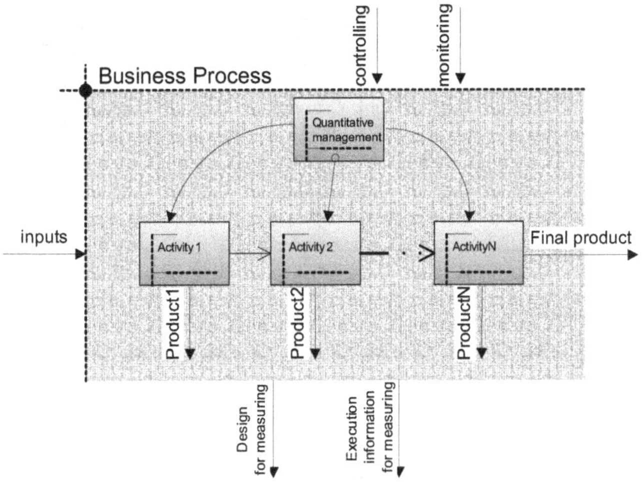	Quantitative management
Innovating	•Monitoring and controlling process performance in a proactive way 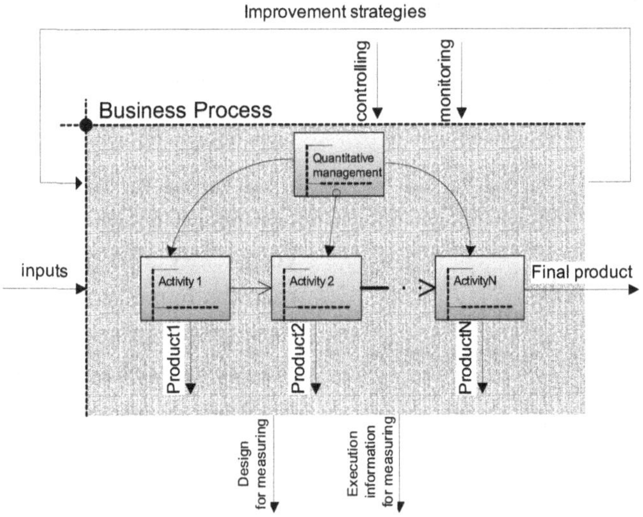	Improvement of processes

registers the successful booking, otherwise the reason of the failure is sent to the client.

To exemplify the use of the measures for business process modelling, we present the calculation of the CFC (Control Flow Complexity) (Cardoso, 2007) of the business process presented. This measure takes into account the quantity and characteristics of the gateways the business process

Figure 4. Business process for the travel agency

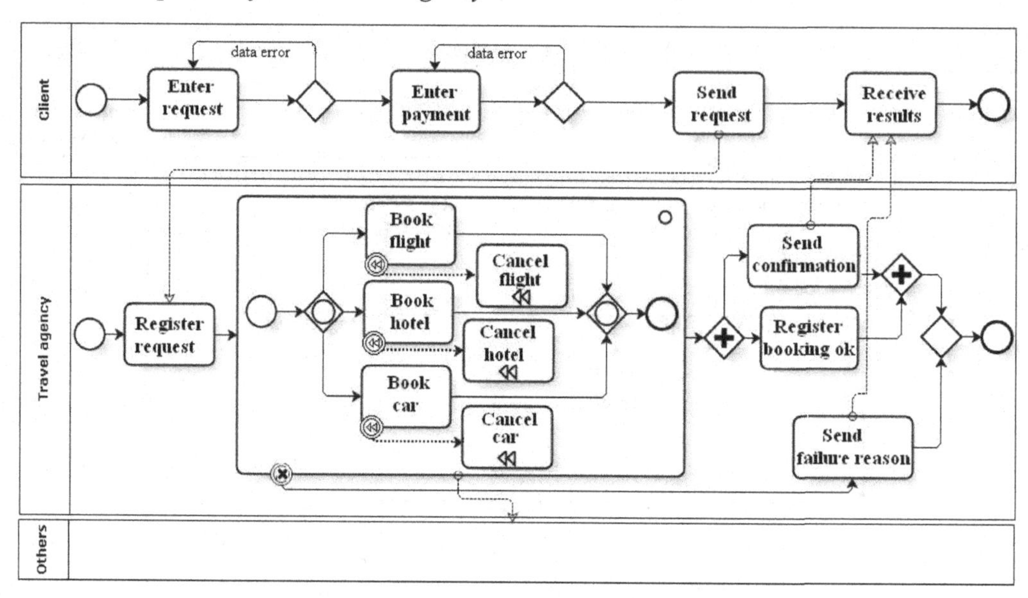

presents, in order to give a numerical indication of the complexity of the business process flow. This is based on the McCabe's cyclomatic complexity for software programs expressed as graphs, but semantics have been added to the gateways according to their type. The formula for the measure is as follows:

$$CFC(P) = \sum_{i \in \{AND\text{-splits of } P\}} CFC_{AND\text{-split}}(i) + \sum_{j \in \{XOR\text{-splits of } P\}} CFC_{XOR\text{-split}}(j) + \sum_{k \in \{OR\text{-splits of } P\}} CFC_{OR\text{-split}}(k)$$

where the value of CFC AND-Split is 1 for each AND-Split in the process (since all the transitions from the gateway are executed in parallel thus reaching the same state space when they are finalized), the value of CFC XOR-Split is calculated as the fan out of the split (since only one transition can be executed from it but could be any of the possibilities, so the reachable state space is therefore the sum of all the transitions) , and the CFC OR-Split is the result of calculating $2^n - 1$ where n is the fan out of the split (since the execution of the transitions could correspond to one, some, or all, so the state space corresponds to all the possible combinations between the transitions to be executed). The fan out of the split corresponds to the number of transitions that start from it.

For the calculation of the CFC for the business process of the travel agency the quantity and type of the gateways involved has to be counted, the definitions applied in order to obtain a number for each type of gateway and all must then be added up to obtain the final number for the complexity of the model. Although the McCabe's cyclomatic complexity also defines a range with which to map the numeric result to the complexity of the program, with the CFC measure this range has not yet been defined. Although it is interpreted as the highest value of the CFC it indicates greater global architectonic complexity of the process modelled. The numeric result of the calculation could, therefore, give an approximate idea of the complexity of the model, which could help to improve it. In the case of the example shown, the calculation is as follows:

CFC = AND result + XOR result + OR result = total number

$$CFC = (1) + (2+2) + (2^{(n=3)} - 1) = 1 + 4 + 7 = 12$$

Based on the number obtained for the travel agency business process, the complexity of the model could be associated with neither a very simple nor a highly complex model, but with a model of medium complexity.

Let us consider another example, in which the business process measures defined by Rolón et al. (2007; 2008) are calculated on the model shown in Figure 4. These measures are divided into two main groups: base measures and derived measures. There are 46 base measures, which are calculated by counting the different types of elements in a BPMN model. Derived measures are obtained as a result of applying measurement functions to another base and/or derived measures. There are 14 derived measures. This initiative evaluates the structural complexity of these models at a conceptual level. The goal is to obtain evidence with regard to the influence that the structural complexity of business models may have on their maintainability. Tables 13 and 14 show the calculation results of some base and derived measures applied to the model in Figure 4.

It is important to note that the most fundamental differences in applying design business process measures lie between the second and third maturity level, since the organization undergoes an important change in establishing the standard business processes to be measured. The purpose of the design measures at the fourth and fifth maturity levels is the same.

Measures for Business Process Execution

In this section some examples of business process execution measures are presented, adapted from the Process Areas "Organizational Process Leadership" and "Organizational Business Governance" of (OMG, 2007) and from (Baumert et al., 1992). In each table the formulas associated with the defined measures are presented and the maturity level in which they apply is proposed. Table 15 shows some examples for maturity levels two and three, and Table 16 shows some examples for maturity levels four and five.

The measures presented in Tables 15 and 16 are examples of general execution measures which can be applied to processes of any kind. For the business process of the travel agency presented in the previous section (see Figure 4), some execution measures specific to the business

Table 13. Base measures applied to the model in Figure 4

Base measures			
Start events		**Inclusive decision**	
NSNE: number of simple start events	2	NID: number of inclusive decision	2
End events		**Parallel decision**	
NENE: number of simple end events	2	NPF: number of parallel forks/joins	2
Tasks		**Participants**	
NT: number of simple tasks	11	NP: number of participants	3
NTC: number of compensation tasks	3		
Exclusive decision (data-based)		**Message flow**	
NEDDB: number of exclusive decisions/joins	3	NMF: number of message flows	4
		Sequence flow	
		NSF: number of sequence flows	28

Table 14. Derived measures applied to the model in Figure 4

Derived measures	
TNT: total number of tasks of the model TNT=NT+NTL+NTMI+NTC	15
CLA: connectivity level between activities CLA= TNT/NSF	0.54
CLP: connectivity level between pools CLP=NMF/NP	1.3

Table 15. Measurable concepts, measures and formulae for process business execution at maturity levels two and three

Measurable concept	Repeatable level (2)	Defined level (3)
Progress	• Actual vs. planned completion of task and milestones (Gantt chart) • Actual vs. planned consumption of resources	• Actual vs. planned completions with ranges (Gantt chart, PERT chart)
Cost	• Actual vs. planned cost • Cost and schedule variances	• Actual vs. planned costs with ranges • Cost and schedule performance indices
Customer satisfaction		• Range of customer satisfaction with the organization's products and services
Quality **Trouble reports**	• Status of trouble reports • Number of trouble reports opened, closed, unevaluated during reporting period • Trouble report density • Comparison of trouble reports and test cases passed	• Status of trouble reports • Number of trouble reports compared with historical data • Length of time trouble reports remain open • Number of trouble reports per process
Process stability		• Number of process changes • Number of process waivers

process domain can also be defined. For example, it could be interesting for the travel agency business to measure:

- Quantity of request received per hour and/ or per day
- Quantity of successful request including payment authorization
- Quantity of reservations cancelled due to failures in booking

Business goals provide a defined foundation for guiding the implementation and evaluation of business processes. The relation between business measures and business processes can be imprecise at maturity level two, but these measures can provide guidance for the results the organization wants to achieve through its business processes. In the presence of standard business processes, a set of standard organizational measures can be defined and collected. It is important to note, also, that many of the measures needed for the organization's process improvement program will have to be obtained from the units, so they need to understand the requirements for collecting and reporting them and how they will be used in the organization (OMG, 2007).

Table 16. Measurable concepts, measures and formula for process business execution at maturity levels four and five

Measurable concept	Managed level (4)	Innovating level (5)
Progress	• Actual vs. planned completions with control limits (Gantt chart, PERT chart)	• Ratio of rework time to total project time per project • Rate of time spent in activities undergoing process change
Cost	• Actual vs. planned costs with control limits • Cost and schedule performance indices. • Return on investment (ROI) of the process	• Comparative costs and benefits of alternative process improvement and defect prevention activities and technologies
Customer satisfaction	• Percent of customers that rate their satisfaction with the organization's products and services as satisfied or very satisfied	• Same as Managed level
Quality trouble reports	• Causes of trouble reports. • Testing, development and implementation efficiency	• Same as Defined and Managed levels
Process stability	• Same as Defined level	• Same as Defined level

CONCLUSION

In this chapter the importance of measurement activities in the maturity of business processes was analyzed. A Business Process Maturity Model (BPMM) was presented, which aims to guide the organizations in the maturity of its business processes, providing the benefits associated with this kind of models. By following the steps defined for each maturity level, an organization can take a path between ad hoc defined processes to continuous improving ones, where objective defined measures and the analysis of the processes results gives insight into the various aspects that have to be taken into account in decision making to achieve the defined business goals. In addition, a guide to help an organization to support the measurement of business processes depending on maturity was provided.

Creating the BPMM as a specific maturity model for business processes has led to some discussions. Although the importance of measurement when improving the organization and maturing its processes was presented in the introduction section, BPMM does not have a specific area for this purpose, following the CMM approach instead of the CMMI one. We strongly believe that the CMMI approach, which has a specific Process Area for measurement and analysis activities, explicitly defining the process, goals and specific practices to achieve them, is clearly better. Having this Process Area supports the activities for measurement and analysis that should be performed in all the other Process Areas to define, manage, measure, control, analyze and improve the business processes. The importance of having a defined measurement process to support the related activities is clear.

Regarding the existing literature on business process measurement, we found that a classification of design and execution measures is appropriate, and provides the foundation to improve both the models of the business processes prior to deploying automated systems, and their operation at the time of execution. Although design measures are a relatively new area of research, we believe that their importance is becoming well-known, making it possible to correct problems detected in early stages of the development process, with the associated benefits. On the other hand, even though execution measures have been defined for a long time, their use and benefits are not always understood and put into practice as they could be. We believe that an organization that follows the directives stated in BPMM to improve and mature its business processes, should make use of both types of measures to gain knowledge about its business processes and achieve its business goals with certainty.

ACKNOWLEDGMENT

This work has been partially financed by the INGENIO Project (Junta de Comunidades de Castilla La Mancha, Conserjería de Educación y Ciencia, PAC 08-0154-9262), ESFINGE Project (Ministerio de Educación y Ciencia, Dirección General de Investigación/Fondos Europeos de Desarrollo Regional(FEDER), reference IN2006-15175-C05-05).

REFERENCES

Alden, J., & Curtis, A. (2007). *The business process maturity model (BPMM): What, why and how.* http://www.bptrends.com/publicationfiles/02%2D07%2DCOL%2DBPMMWhatWhyHow%2DCurtisAlden%2DFinal%2Epdf

Baumert, J., & McWhinney, M. (1992). *Software measures and the capability maturity model. Software Engineering Insttitute (SEI),* CMU/SEI-92-TR-25.

Curtis, B., Hefley, W. E., & Miller, S. (1995). *People capability maturity model.* (Technical Report CMU/SEI-95-MM-02.) Software Engineering Institute/Carnegie Mellon University.

Cardoso, J. (2005). How to measure the control-flow complexity of Web processes and workflows. In *Workflow Handbook 2005.*

Cardoso, J. (2007). *Complexity analysis of BPEL Web processes.* Software Process Improvement and Practice

CMMI Product Team. (2002). Capability maturity model (CMM) for software engineering, Version 1.1. In *S. I. I. (SEI)* (Ed.): CMMI Product Team.

CMMI Product Team. (2006). *Capability maturity model integration (CMMI) for development,* Version 1.2. In *S. I. I. (SEI)* (Ed.): CMMI Product Team.

Crosby, P. B. (1979). *Quality is free.* McGraw-Hill. ISBN: 0-07-014512-1

Curtis, B. (2004). *Overview of the business process maturity model (BPMM).* Teraquest.http://www.dfw-asee.org/0501meet.pdf

García, F., Bertoa, M., Calero, C., Vallecillo, A., Ruiz, F., Piattini, M., et al. (2005). Towards a consistent terminology for software measurement. *Information and Software Technology, 48,* 631-644.

Goldenson, D., Jarzombek, J., & Rout, T. (2003). Measurement and analysis in capability maturity codel: Integration models and software process improvement. *Crosstalk the Journal of Defense Software Engineering, 6*(7), 20-24

Gruhn, V., & Laue, R. (2006). Complexity metrics for business process models. *International Conference on Business Information Systems.*

Humphrey, W. (1987). *Characterizing the software process: A maturity framework.* Software Engineering Insttitute (SEI), CMU/SEI-87-TR-11, DTIC Number ADA182895.

ISO/IEC 15939. (2002). *Software engineering - Software measurement process.* International Standards Organization: ISO/IEC 15939.

Kaplan, R., & Norton, D. (1996). *The balanced scorecard.* McGraw-Hill. ISBN: 978-0875846514.

Latva-Koivisto, A. M. (2001). *Finding a complexity measure for business process models.* Individual Research Projects in Applied Mathematics

Lee, J., Lee, D., & Kang, S. (2007). An overview of the business process maturity model (BPMM). Advances in data and Web management,. *Joint ninth Asia-Pacific Web Conference APWeb/ WAIM.*

Mendling, J. (2006). *Testing density as a complexity metric for EPCs.* Technical Report JM-2006-11-15.

OMG. (1989). *Object Management Group.* from http://www.omg.org

OMG. (2006). *Business process modeling notation (BPMN), Final adopted specification.* dtc/06-02-0, BPMI 2004 from http://www.omg.org/bpm

OMG. (2007). *Business process maturity model (BPMM), Beta 1 adopted specification.* dtc/2007-07-02, from http://www.omg.org/docs/dtc/07-07-02.pdf

Paulk, M., Curtis, B., Chrissis, M., & Weber, C. (1993). *Capability maturity model (CMM) for software, version 1.1.* Software Engineering Insttitute (SEI), CMU/SEI-93-TR-024.

Pfleeger, S. L. (1996). Integrating process and measurement. In A. Melton (Ed.), *Software measurement.* International Thomson Computer Press, (pp 53-74).

Project Management Institute. (2004). A *guide to the project management body of knowledge (PMBOK).* Project Management Institute.

Rolón, E., García, F., & Ruiz, F. (2006a). Evaluation measures for business process models. *Symposioum on Applied Computing SAC06.*

Rolón, E., García, F., & Ruiz, F. (2006a). Evaluation measures for business process models. In *21st Annual ACM Symposium on Applied Computing (SAC'06),* Dijon (France), (pp. 1567-1568).

Rolón, E., Ruiz, F., García, F., & Piattini, M. (2006b). Applying software metrics to evaluate business process models. *CLEI-Electronic Journal, 9*(1, Paper 5).

Rolón, E., García, F., Ruiz, F., & Piattini, M. (2007, April 23-26). An exploratory experiment to validate measures for business process models. *First IEEE International Conference on Research Challenges in Information Science (RCIS'07).* Ouarzazate, Marruecos: IEEE.

Rolón, E., Garcia, F., Ruiz, F., Piattini, M., Vissagio, A., & Canfora, G. (2008, May 4-7). Evaluation of BPMN models quality: A family of experiments. *3rd International Conference on Evaluation of Novel Approaches to Software Engineering (ENASE'08).* Funchal, Madeira.

Singh, I., Brydon, S., Murray, G., Ramachandran, V., Violleau, T., & Stearns, B. (2004). *Designing Web services with the J2EE 1.4 Platform: JAX-RPC, SOAP, and XML technologies.* Addison-Wesley , ISBN: 0-321-20521-9.

Tjaden, G. S. (1999). *Business process structural analysis.* Georgia Tech Center for Enterprise Systems. http://www.ces.gatech.edu/research.htm

van der Aalst, W. M. P., Reijers, H. A., & Medeiros, A. (2007). *Business process mining: An industrial application.* Information Systems

Vanderfeesten, I., Cardoso, J., Mendling, J., Reijers, H. A., & van der Aalst, W. M. P. (2007). Quality metrics for business process models. In *BPM and workflow handbook 2007.*

Vanderfeesten, I., Reijers, H. A., Mendling, J., van der Aalst, W. M. P., & Cardoso, J. (2008a). On a quest for good process models: The cross conectivity metric. *International Conference on Advanced Information Systems Engineering.*

Vanderfeesten, I., Reijers, H. A., & van der Aalst, W. M. P. (2008b*). Evaluating workflow process designs using cohesion and coupling metrics.* Computer in Industry.

Weske, M. (2007). *Business process management, concepts, languages, architectures.* Springer-Verlag ISBN 978-3-540-73521-2.

KEY TERMS

Activity: An element of work performed as part of a planned effort. An activity is often the lowest level work element in a work breakdown structure. It normally has an expected duration, an expect cost, and expected resource requirements, (BPMM, 2007).

Business Process Execution: Business process execution refers to the actual run of a process by a process engine, which is responsible for instantiating and controlling the execution of business processes. Process models are used by the process engine to instantiate and control the enactment of process instances, (Weske, 2008).

Business Process Model: A Business process model is a model of a business process of an organization, where a business process describes one of the standard sets of activities the organization needs to do to address one or more business requirements, (BPMM, 2007).

Guidelines: They are a list of advices that can be used to support the implementations of practices of the process areas. They cover topics that are applicable for many practices, but they are considered to be optional for the practices, (BPMM, 2007).

Maturity Level: A maturity level is a defined evolutionary plateau of process improvement. Each maturity level stabilizes an important part of the organization's processes, (BPMM, 2007).

Maturity Model: A maturity model is an evolutionary roadmap for implementing the vital practices from one or more domains of organizational process. (BPMM, 2007)

Measurement and Analysis: A list of activities which principal objective is to use quantitative information (obtained with measurement activities) to guide management decisions. Moreover, they involve planning and preparing for measurement, specifying the measures and measurement activities and performing them. Later, measurement results are studied to offer utility for organizations. Examples of the types of analyses that are performed include: a) estimation to support planning, b) analyzing feasibility of plans and alternatives, c) monitoring work performance, and d) monitoring performance of products, (BPMM, 2007).

Process Improvement: A program of activities designed to improve the performance and maturity of the organization's processes, and the results of such a program, (CMMI, 2002).

Process Maturity: Is the extent to which processes are explicitly defined, managed, measured, controlled and effective. Process maturation implies that process capability is improved over time, (BPMM, 2007).

Compilation of References

Abbott, K. R., & Sarin, S. K. (1994). Experiences with workflow management: Issues for the next generation. In *CSCW'94 (USA), Chapel Hill, 1994,* (pp.113-120).

Abramowicz, W., Filipowska, A., Kaczmarek, M., & Kaczmarek, T. (2007, June). Semantically enhanced business process modelling notation. In *Proceedings of the Workshop on Semantic Business Process and Product Lifecycle Management (SBPM-2007)*, (CEUR-WS, 251), ISSN 1613-0073.

Active BPEL execution engine (2008). Retrieved August 2008, from http://www.activevos.com/community-open-source.php

Active Endpoints (2006). ActiveBPEL Open Source Engine. http://www.active-endpoints.com.

Active Endpoints, Adobe, BEA, IBM, Oracle, SAP AG (2007): *WS-BPEL Extension for people.* Retrieved March 30, 2008 from IBM's Web site: http://www.ibm.com/developerworks/webservices/library/specification/ws-bpel4people/

ActiveBPEL (2008). Active BPEL Web Site. www.activebpel.org.

Adams, M., ter Hofstede, A. H. M., Edmond, D., & van der Aalst, W. M. P. (2006). Worklets: A service-oriented implementation of dynamic Flexibility in workflows. In R. Meersman & Z. Tari et al. (Eds.), *Proceedings of the 14th International Conference on Cooperative Information Systems* (pp. 291-308). Montpellier, France: Springer-Verlag.

Adams, M., ter Hofstede, A., Edmond, D., & van der Aalst, W.M.P. (2006). A service-oriented implementation of dynamic flexibility in workflows. In *Proceedings of the 14th Int'l Conf. on Cooperative Information Systems (CoopIS'06)*, Montpellier, France, (LNCS 4275, pp. 291-308).

Adams, M., ter Hofstede, A. H. M., van der Aalst, W. M. P., & Edmond, D. (2007). Dynamic, extensible and context-aware exception handling for workflows. In R. Meersman & Z. Tari et al. (Eds.), *Proceedings of the 15th International Conference on Cooperative Information Systems* (pp. 95-112), Vilamoura, Portugal: Springer- Verlag.

Adlassnig, K. P., Combi, C., Das, A. K., Keravnou, E. T., & Pozzi, G. (2006). Temporal representation and reasoning in medicine: Research directions and challenges. *Artificial Intelligence in Medicine*, *38*(2), 101-113.

Agostini, A., & De Michelis, G. (2000). A light workflow management system using simple process models. *Computer Supported Cooperative Work, 9*(3-4), 335-363.

Agrawal, A., Amend, M., Das, M., Keller, C., Kloppmann, M., König, D., Leymann, F., Müller, R., Pfau, G., Ploesser, K., Rangaswamy, R., Rickayzen, A., Rowley, M., Schmidt, P., Trickovic, I., Yiu, A., & Zeller, M. (2007). *WS-BPEL extension for people (WS-BPEL4People), Version 1.0.* http://download.boulder.ibm.com/ibmdl/pub/software/dw/specs/ws-bpel4people/BPEL4People_v1.pdf

Agrawal, A., Amend, M., Das, M., Keller, C., Kloppmann, M., König, D., Leymann, F., Müller, R., Pfau, G., Ploesser, K., Rangaswamy, R., Rickayzen, A., Rowley, M., Schmidt, P., Trickovic, I., Yiu, A., & Zeller, M. (2007). *Web services human task (WS-HumanTask), Version 1.0.* http://download.boulder.ibm.com/ibmdl/pub/software/dw/specs/ws-bpel4people/WS-HumanTask_v1.pdf

Agrawal, R., Gunopulos, D., & Leymann, F. (1998). Mining process models from workflow logs. In *Proceedings of the 6th International Conference on Extending Database Technology: Advances in Database Technology,* (LNCS 1377, pp. 469-483). Springer.

Agrawal, R., Johnson, C. M., Kiernan, J., & Leymann, F. (2006). Taming compliance with sarbanes-oxley internal controls using database technology. In L. Liu, A. Reuter, K.-Y. Whang, & J. Zhang (Eds.), *ICDE*, (pp. 92). IEEE Computer Society.

Alberti, M., Gavanelli, M., Lamma, E., Chesani, F., Mello, P., & Torroni, P. (2006). Compliance verification of agent interaction: a logic-based software tool. *Applied Artificial Intelligence, 20*(2-4), 133–157.

Alden, J., & Curtis, A. (2007). *The business process maturity model (BPMM): What, why and how.* http://www.bptrends.com/publicationfiles/02%2D07%2DCOL%2DBPMMWhatWhyHow%2DCurtisAlden%2DFinal%2Epdf

Aldred, L., van der Aalst, W. M. P., Dumas, M., & ter Hofstede, A. H. M. (2007). Communication abstractions for distributed business processes. In *Proceedings of the 19th International Conference on Advanced Information Systems Engineering* (pp. 409-423). Springer-Verlag.

Alonso, G., Dadam, P., & Rosemann, M. (Eds.) (2007, September 24-28). In *Proceedings, Business Process Management, 5th International Conference, BPM 2007, Brisbane, Australia, (LNCS*, 4714). Springer.

Alonso, G., Fiedler, U., Hagen, C., Lazcano, A., Schuldt, H., & Weiler, N. (1999). WISE: Business to business e-commerce. In *Proceedings of the 9th International Workshop on Research Issues on Data Engineering* (pp. 132-139).

Alonso, G., Hagen, C., Schek, H. J., & Tresch, M. (1997). Distributed processing over stand-alone systems and applications. In *Proceedings of the 23rd International Conference on Very Large Databases* (pp. 575-579).

Alves de Medeiros, A. K., Pedrinaci, C., ., von der Aalst, W. M. P., ., Domingue, J., ., Song, M., ., Rozinat, A., ., Norton, B., ., & Cabral, L. (2007). An outlook on semantic business process mining and monitoring. In *Proceedings of the 3rd International IFIP Workshop On Semantic Web & Web Semantics (SWWS '07) at On The Move Federated Conferences and Workshops.*

Alves de Medeiros, A. K., van der Aalst, W. M. P., & Pedrinaci, C. (2008). Semantic process mining tools: Core building blocks. In *Proceedings of the 16th European Conference on Information Systems,* Galway, Ireland.

Alves, A., Arkin, A., Askary, S., Barreto, C., Bloch, B., Curbera, F., Ford, M., Goland, Y., Guizar, A., Kartha, N., Liu, C.K., Khalaf, R., Koenig, D., Marin, M., Mehta, V., Thatte, S., van der Rijn, D., Yendluri, P., & Yiu. A. (2007). *Web Services Business Process Execution Language - Version 2.0.* OASIS.

Anderson, E., & Oliver, R. L. (1987, October). Perspectives on behavior-based versus outcome-based salesforce control systems. *Journal of Marketing, 51*(4), 76–88.

Andrews, T., Cubera, F., Dholakia, H., Goland, Y., Klein, J., Leymann, F., Liu, K., Roller, D., Smith, D., Thatte, S., Trickovic, I., & Weerawarama, S. (2003). *Business process execution language for web services specification.* Technical Report Version 1.1, May 5.

Antoniou, G., Billington, D., Governatori, G., & Maher, M. J. (2006). Embedding defeasible logic into logic programming. *Theory and Practice of Logic Programming, 6*(6), 703–735.

Antoniou, G., Billington, D., Governatori, G., & Maher, M. J. (2001). Representation results for defeasible logic. *ACM Transactions on Computational Logic, 2*(2), 255–287.

Arsanjani, A., Ghosh, S., Allam, A., Abdollah, T., Ganapathy, S., & Holley, K. (2008). SOMA: A method for developing service-oriented solutions. *IBM Systems Journal, 47*(3), 377-396.

Axenath, B., Kindler E., & Rubin, V. (2007).AMFIBIA: A meta-model for the integration of business process modelling aspects. *International Journal on Business Process Integration and Management, 2*(2), 120-131.

Axenath, B., Kindler, E., & Rubin, V. (2005). An open and formalism independent meta-model for business processes. In *Proc. of the Workshop on Business Process Reference Models* (pp. 45–59).

Baeten, J. C. M., & Weijland W. P. (1991) Process Algebra, Cambridge University Press, New York, Ny.

Bair, J. H. (1990). Contrasting workflow models: getting to the roots of three vendors. *Proceedings of International CSCW Conference.*

Bakera, M., & Renner, C. (2007). *GEAR - A model checking plugin for the jABC framework.* Retrieved May 2008, from http://www.jabc.de/modelchecking/

Ballinger, K., Ehnebuske, D., Ferris, C., Gudgin, M., Liu, C., Nottingham, M., & Yendluri, P. (2004). *Basic Profile Version 1.1.* WS-I Specification. http://www.ws-i.org/Profiles/BasicProfile-1.1.html

Ballou, D. P., Wang, R. Y., Pazer, H. L., & Tayi, G.K. (1998). Modelling information manufacturing systems to determine information product quality. *Management Science, 44*(4), 462–533.

Baresi, L., Bianchini, D., Antonellis V.D., Fugini, M.G., Pernici, B., & Plebani, P. (2003). Context-aware composition of e-services. In *Proceedings of the Third VLDB Workshop on Technologies for E-Services.*

Bassil, S., Benyoucef, M., Keller, R., & Kropf, P. (2002): Addressing dynamism in e-negotiations by workflow management systems. In *Proceedings DEXA'02 Workshops*, (pp. 655-659).

Bassil, S., Keller, R., & Kropf, P. (2004). A workflow-oriented system architecture for the management of container transportation. In *Proceedings of the 2nd Int'l Conf. on Business Process Management (BPM'04)*, Potsdam, Germany, (LNCS 3080, pp. 116-131).

Batory, D. S. (2005) Feature Models, Grammars, And Propositional Formulas. *Proceedings Of The 6th International Conference On Software Product Lines (Splc), 3714*, 7-20.

Battle, S., et al. (2005). *Semantic Web Services Ontology* (SWSO), W3C Member Submission. http://www.w3.org/Submission/SWSF-SWSO/

Bauer, T., Reichert, M., & Dadam, P. (2003). Intra-subnet load balancing in distributed workflow management systems. *Int'l Journal Cooperative Information Systems (IJCIS), 12*(3), 295-323.

Baumert, J., & McWhinney, M. (1992). *Software measures and the capability maturity model. Software Engineering Insttitute (SEI),* CMU/SEI-92-TR-25.

Becker, J., Delfmann, P., & Knackstedt, R. (2006) Adaptive Reference Modeling: Integrating Configurative And Generic Adaptation Techniques For Information Models. *Reference Modeling Conference 2006.*

Becker, J., Delfmann, P., Dreiling, A., Knackstedt, R., & Kuropka, D. (2004) Configurative Process Modeling - Outlining An Approach To Increased Business Process Model Usability. *Proceedings Of The 15th Irma International Conference.*

Bellman, R. (1958). *Dynamic programming and Stochastic Control Processes Information and Control, 1*(3), 228-239.

Bercovici, A., Fisher, A., Fournier, F., Rackham, G., Razinkov, N., & Skarbovsky, I. (2008). A method for service center architecture based on industry standards. In *Proc. IEEE Int. Conf. on Services Computing* (pp. 433-440). IEEE Press.

Berners-Lee, T., Hendler, J., & Lassila, O. (2001). The Semantic Web. *Scientific American -American Edition, 284,* 28-37.

Bernstein, A. (2000). How can cooperative work tools support dynamic group process? Bridging the specificity frontier. In *CSCW '00 (USA), Philadelphia,* (pp. 279-288).

Bernus, P., Nemes, L., & Williams, T. J. (Eds.) (1996). *Architectures for enterprise integration.* Chapman & Hall.

Bhattacharya, K., Caswell, N. S., Kumaran, S., Nigam, A., & Wu, F. Y. (2007). Artifact-centered operational modeling: Lessons from customer engagements. *IBM Systems Journal, 46*(4), 703-721.

Bhattacharya, K., Gerede, C. E., Hull, R., Liu, R., & Su, J. (2007). Towards formal analysis of artifact-centricbusiness process models. In *Proc. 5th Int. Conf. on Business Process Management* (pp. 288-304). Berlin / Heidelberg: Springer.

Bhattacharya, K., Guttman, R., Lyman, K., Heath III, F. F., Kumaran, S., Nandi, P., Wu, F., Athma, P., Freiberg, C., Johannsen, L., & Staudt, A. (2005). A model-driven approach to industrializing discovery processes in pharmaceutical research. *IBM Systems Journal, 44*(1), 145-162.

Bierbaumer, M., Eder, J., & Pichler, H. (2005). Calculation of delay times for workflows with fixed-date constraints. In *Proceedings of the CEC (Conference on E-Commerce Technology)* (pp. 544-547).

Bobrik, R., Bauer, T., & Reichert, M. (2006) Proviado – personalized and configurable visualizations of business processes. In *Proceedings 7th Int'l Conf. on Electronic Commerce and Web Technologies (EC-WEB'06)*, Krakow, Poland, (*LNCS 4082,* pp. 61-71).

Bobrik, R., Reichert, M., & Bauer, T. (2007). View-based process visualization. In *Proceedings of the 5th Int'l Conf. on Business Process Management (BPM'07)*, Brisbane, Austalia.

Boehm, M. (2000). *Design of workflow types, (in German).* Berlin: Springer-Verlag.

Born, M., ., & Doerr, F., & Weber, I. (2007). User-friendly semantic annotation in business process modeling. In *Proceedings of the Workshop on Human-friendly Service Description, Discovery and Matchmaking (Hf-SDDM) held in conjunction with the 8th International Conference on Web Information Systems Engineering (WISE 2007).*

Born, M.,Hoffmann, J.,Kaczmarek, T., Kowalkiewicz, M., Markovic, I., Scicluna, J.,Weber, I., & Zhou, X. (2008, June 1-5). Semantic annotation and composition of business processes with maestro. In *Proceedings of the 5th Annual European Semantic Web Conference* (ESWC 2008), (LNCS, 5021). Springer.

Bosch, J. (2007). *Towards mobile services: Three approaches.* IEEE Computer

Bowers, J., Button, G., & Sharrock, W. (1995). Workflow from within and without: Technology and cooperative work on the print industry shopfloor. In *ECSCW'95, (Sweden), Stockholm,* (pp. 51-66).

BPEL specifications website (2008). Retrieved August 2008, from http://www.ibm.com/developerworks/library/specification/ws-bpel/

BPM (2008). *Business process management conference series.* Retrieved 2008-04-01, from http://bpm08.polimi.it/

Brackett, M. H. (1996, July). *The Data Warehouse Challenge: Taming Data Chaos.* John Wiley and Sons.

Brogi, A., & Popescu, R. (2006). From BPEL Processes to YAWL workflows. In M. Bravetti, M. Nunez, & G. Zavattaro (Eds.), *Proceedings of the 3rd International Workshop on Web Services and Formal Methods* (pp. 107-122). Springer-Verlag.

Bunke, H. (2000) Recent Developments In Graph Matching. *International Conference On Pattern Recognition (Icpr).* Barcelona, Spain, Ieee Computer Society.

Burbeck, S. (2000). *The Tao of e-business services: The evolution of Web applications into service-oriented components with Web services.* IBM developerWorks. Available at http://www.ibm.com/developerworks/webservices/library/ws-tao/

Burlton, R. T. (2001). *Business process management: Profiting from processes*. Sams Publishing.

Business Process Modeling Notation Specification (2006). *OMG final adopted specification*. Retrieved February 6, 2006, from http://www.bpmn.org/Documents/OMG%20Final%20Adopted%20BPMN%201-0%20Spec%2006-02-01.pdf

Bussler, C. (2003). *B2B integration. Concepts and architecture*. New York: Springer

Bussler, C., & Jablonski, S. (1994). An approach to integrate workflow modeling and organization modeling in an enterprise. In *Proceedings 3rd IEEE Workshop on Enabling Technologies: Infrastructures for Collaborative Enterprises (WET ICE).*

Cabral, L., Domingue, J., Motta, E., Payne, T., & Hakimpour, F. (2004, May 10-12). Approaches to Semantic Web services: An overview and comparisons. In *Proceedings of the 1st European Semantic Web Symposium,* Heraklion, Greece.

Cadez, I., Heckerman, D., Meek, C., Smyth, P., White, S. (2003, October). Model-based clustering and visualization of navigation patterns on a Web site. *Data Mining and Knowledge Discovery, 7*(4), 399-424.

Cardoso, J. (2005). How to measure the control flow complexity for Web processes and workflows. In Layna Fisher (Ed.), *2005 workflow handbook*, (pp. 199-212). Light Point, FL: Future Strategies Inc.

Cardoso, J. (2007). *Complexity analysis of BPEL Web processes.* Software Process Improvement and Practice

Carmo, J., & Jones, A. J. (2002). Deontic logic and contrary to duties. In D. Gabbay & F. Guenther (Eds.), *Handbook of philosophical logic, 2nd Edition, 8*, (pp. 265–343). Dordrecht: Kluwer.

Casati, F. (1998). Models, semantics, and formal methods for the design of workflows and their exceptions. Unpublished doctoral thesis. Politecnico di Milano, Italy.

Casati, F., Ceri S., Paraboschi S., & Pozzi G. (1999). Specification and implementation of exceptions in workflow management systems. *ACM Transactions on Database Systems, 24*(3), 405-451.

Casati, F., & Cugola, G. (2001). Error handling in process support systems. In A. Romanovsky, C. Dony, J. Lindskov Knudsen, & A. Tripathi (Eds.), *Advances in exception handling techniques*, (LNCS, 2022, pp. 251-270). Springer-Verlag.

Casati, F., & Pozzi, G. (1999). *Modeling exceptional behaviors in commercial workflow management systems.* CoopIS, (pp. 127-138).

Casati, F., Castano, S., Fugini, M.G., Mirbel, I., & Pernici, B. (2000). Using patterns to design rules in workflows. *IEEE Trans. Software Eng., 26*(8), 760-785.

Casati, F., Ceri, S., Pernici, B., & Pozzi, G. (1996). Deriving production rules for workflow enactment. Database and expert systems applications (pp. 94-115).

Casati, F., Ceri, S., Pernici, B., & Pozzi, G. (1996). *Workflow evolution.* ER (pp. 438-455).

Casati, F., Ceri, S., Pernici, B., & Pozzi, G. (1998). Workflow evolution. *Int. Journal Data and Knowledge Engineering, 24*(1), 211-239.

Casati, F., Castellanos, M., Dayal, U., Hao, M., Shan, M. C., & Sayal, M. Business operation intelligence research at HP Labs. *Data Engineering Bulletin, 25*(4).

Casati, F., Castellanos, M., Dayal, U., & Salazar, N. (2007). A generic solution for warehousing business process data. In C. Koch, J. Gehrke, M.N. Garofalakis, D. Srivastava, K. Aberer, A. Deshpande, D. Florescu, C.Y. Chan, V. Ganti, C.-C. Kanne, W. Klas, & E.J. Neuhold (Eds.), *Proceedings of the 33rd International Conference on Very Large Data Bases, University of Vienna, Austria, September 23-27, 2007*, (pp. 1128–1137). ACM, 2007. ISBN 978-1-59593-649-3.

Casati, F., Castellanos, M., Dayal, U., & Shan, M.-C. (2006). A metric definition, computation, and reporting model for business operation analysis. In Y. E. Ioannidis, M. H. Scholl, J. W. Schmidt, F. Matthes, M. Hatzopoulos, K. Böhm, A. Kemper, T. Grust, & C. Böhm (Eds.), *Advances in Database Technology - EDBT 2006, 10th International Conference on Extending Database Technology, Munich, Germany, March 26-31, 2006, Proceedings*, volume 3896 of *Lecture Notes in Computer Science*, (pp. 1079–1083). Springer.

Castellanos, M., Casati, F., Sayal, M., & Dayal, U. (2005). Challenges in business process analysis and optimization. In C. Bussler & M.-C. Shan (Eds.), *Technologies for E-Services, 6th International Workshop, TES 2005, Trondheim, Norway, September 2-3, 2005, Revised Selected Papers*, volume 3811 of *Lecture Notes in Computer Science*, (pp. 1–10). Springer, 2005a. ISBN 3-540-31067-3.

Castellanos, M., Casati, F., Shan, M.-C., & Dayal, U (2005). iBOM: A platform for intelligent business operation management. In *Proceedings of the 21st International Conference on Data Engineering, ICDE 2005, 5-8 April 2005, Tokyo, Japan*, (pp. 1084–1095). IEEE Computer Society, ISBN 0-7695-2285-8.

Castellanos, M., Salazar, N., Casati, F., Dayal, U., & Shan, M.-C. (2005). Predictive business operations management. In S. Bhalla (Eds.), *DNIS*, volume 3433 of *Lecture Notes in Computer Science*, (pp. 1–14). Springer, ISBN 3-540-25361-0.

Castellanos, M., Salazar, N., Casati, F., Shan, M. C., & Dayal, U.(2005, July) Automatic metric forecasting for management software. In *Proceedings of the 12th HP Openview University Association (HP-OVUA) Workshop*, Porto, Portugal, July 2005d. Hewlett–Packard Corporation.

Ceglowski, A., Churilov, L., & Wassertheil, J. (2005). Knowledge discovery through mining emergency department data. In *Proceedings of the 38th Annual Hawaii International Conference on System Sciences (HICSS '05)*.

Chappell, D. A.(2004). *Enterprise service bus: Theory in practice.* O'Reilly Media.

Chen, J., & Yang, Y. (2008). *Temporal dependency based checkpoint selection for dynamic verification of fixed-time constraints in grid workflow systems.* ICSE, (pp. 141-150).

Chen, Y., Reilly, K., Sprague, A., & Guan, Z. (2006). SEQOPTICS: A protein sequence clustering system. *BMC Bioinformatics, 7*(Suppl 4), S10.

Chittaro, L., & Montanari, A. (2000). Temporal representation and reasoning in artificial intelligence: Issues and approaches. *Ann. Math. Artif. Intell., 28*(1-4), 47-106.

Chiu, D. K., Li, Q., & Karlapalem, K. (2001). WEB interface-driven cooperative exception handling in ADOME workflow management system. *Information Systems, 26*(2), 93-120.

Chopra, A. K., & Sing, M. P. (2007, May 8, 2007). Producing compliant interactions: Conformance, coverage and interoperability. In M. Baldoni & U. Endriss (Eds.), *Declarative agent languages and technologies IV*, (LNAI, 4327, pp. 1–15). Berlin Heidelberg. Springer-Verlag.

Cingil, I., Dogac, A., Tatbul, N., & Arpinar, S. (1999). An adaptable workflow system architecture on the Internet for electronic commerce applications. In *Proceedings of the International Symposium on Distributed Object Applications.*

Clark, T., Sammut, P., & Willians, J. (2008). *Applied metamodelling – A foundation for language driven development, 2nd Edition.* Retrieved 2008-04-01, from http://www.ceteva.com/book.html

Clarke, E. M., Grumberg, O., & Peled, D.A. (2001). *Model checking.* MIT Press.

Clevé, B. (2006). *Film production management.* Burlington, Oxford.

CMMI Product Team. (2002). Capability maturity model (CMM) for software engineering, Version 1.1. In *S. I. I. (SEI)* (Ed.): CMMI Product Team.

CMMI Product Team. (2006). *Capability maturity model integration (CMMI) for development,* Version 1.2. In *S. I. I. (SEI)* (Ed.): CMMI Product Team.

Combi, C., & Pozzi, G. (2002). Towards temporal information in workflow systems. *ER Workshops*, (pp. 13-25).

Combi, C., & Pozzi, G. (2003). Temporal conceptual modeling of workflows. *ER,* (pp. 59-76).

Combi, C., & Pozzi, G. (2004). Architectures for a temporal workflow management system. *ACM SAC*, (pp. 659-666).

Combi, C., & Pozzi, G. (2006). Task scheduling for a temporal workflow management system. *TIME*, 61-68.

Combi, C., & Pozzi, G. (2006). Temporal representation and reasoning in medicine. *Artificial Intelligence in Medicine*, *38*(2), 97-100.

Combi, C., Daniel, F., & Pozzi, G. (2006). A Portable approach to exception handling in workflow management systems. *OTM Conferences*, (1), 201-218.

Combi, C., Daniel, F., & Pozzi, G. (2008). XPDL Enabled Cross-Product Exception Handling for WfMSs. In L. Fisher (Ed.), *2008 BPM and workflow handbook*. Light Point, FL: Future Strategies Inc. in collaboration with Workflow Management Coalition.

Combi, C., Gozzi, M., Juàrez, J. M., Oliboni, B., & Pozzi, G. (2007). Conceptual modeling of temporal clinical workflows. *TIME*, (pp. 70-81).

Combi, C., Montanari, A., & Pozzi, G. (2007). The T4SQL temporal query language. *CIKM*, (pp. 193-202).

Console, L., Fugini, M. G., & the WS-Diamond Team (2007). WS-DIAMOND: An approach to Web Services – DIAgnosability, MONitoring and Diagnosis. In *Proceedings of the E-Challenges Conference*.

Cook, J. E., Du, Z., Liu, C., & Wolf, A. L. (2004). Discovering Models of Behavior for Concurrent Workflows. *Computers in Industry*, *53*(3), 297–319.

Cook, J., & Wolf, A. (1995). Automating process discovery through event-data analysis. In *Proceedings of the 17th International Conference on Software Engineering*, (pp.73-82). ACM Press.

Corea, S., & Watters, A. (2007). Challenges in business performance measurement: The case of a corporate it function. In G. Alonso, P. Dadam, & M. Rosemann (Eds.), *Business Process Management, 5th International Conference, BPM 2007, Brisbane, Australia, September 24-28, 2007, Proceedings*, volume 4714 of *Lecture Notes in Computer Science*, (pp. 16–31), Brisbane, Australia, 2007. Springer.

Crosby, P. B. (1979). *Quality is free*. McGraw-Hill. ISBN: 0-07-014512-1

Curbera F. (2007). *Policy and service contracts in SOA*. IEEE Computer

Curran, T., & Keller, G. (1997) *Sap R/3 Business Blueprint: Understanding The Business Process Reference Model*, Upper Saddle River.

Curtis, B. (2004). *Overview of the business process maturity model (BPMM)*. Teraquest.http://www.dfw-asee.org/0501meet.pdf

Curtis, B., Hefley, W. E., & Miller, S. (1995). *People capability maturity model*. (Technical Report CMU/SEI-95-MM-02.) Software Engineering Institute/Carnegie Mellon University.

Czarnecki, K., & Helsen, S. (2003, October). Classification of Model Transformation Approaches. *Proc. of the OOPSLA'03 Workshop on Generative Techniques in the Context of Model-Driven Architecture*, Anaheim, California.

Dadam, P., Reichert, M., & Kuhn, K. (2000). Clinical workflows - the killer application for process-oriented information systems? In *Proceedings of the 4th Int'l Conf. on Business Information Systems (BIS'2000)*, (pp. 36-59),Poznan, Poland. Springer, .

Davenport, T. H. (1993). *Process innovation: Reengineering work through information technology*. Boston: Harvard Business School Press.

Davis, J. (2003). *GME: Generic modeling environment, demonstration session*. OOPSLA 2003 (pp. 82-83). Anaheim, CA, ACM.

Davulcu, H., Kifer, M., Pokorny, L. R., Ramakrishnan, C. R., Ramakrishnan, I. V., & Dawson S. D. (1999). Modeling and Analysis of Interactions in Virtual Enterprises. In *Proceedings of the Ninth International Workshop on Research Issues on Data Engineering: Information Technology for Virtual Enterprises*.

Dayal, U. (1988). Active database management systems. In *Proc. 3rd Int. Conf. on Data and Knowledge Bases: Improving Usability and Responsiveness* (pp. 150-169). Morgan Kaufmann.

De Antonellis, V., Melchiori, M., De Santis, L., Mecella, M., Mussi, E., Pernici, B., & Plebani, P. (2006). A layered architecture for flexible Web service invocation. *Software – Practice and Experience, 36*(2), 191-223.

de Medeiros, A. K. A. (2006). *Genetic Process Mining*. PhD thesis, Eindhoven University of Technology, Eindhoven..

de Medeiros, A. K. A. Weijters, A. J. M. M., & van der Aalst, W. M. P. (2007). Genetic Process Mining: an Experimental Evaluation. *Data Mining Knowledge Discovery, 14*(2), 245–304.

de Medeiros, A. K. A., Pedrinaci, C., van der Aalst, W. M. P., Domingue, J., Song, M., Rozinat, A., Norton, B., & Cabral, L. (2007). An Outlook on Semantic Business Process Mining and Monitoring. In R. Meersman, Z. Tari, & P. Herrero (Eds.), *OTM Workshops (2)*, volume 4806 of *Lecture Notes in Computer Science*, (pp. 1244–1255). Springer. ISBN 978-3-540-76889-0.

Decker, G., Kopp, O., Leymann, F. and Weske, M.(2007, July) BPEL4Chor: Extending BPEL for Modeling Choreographies. In *Proceedings of the IEEE 2007 International Conference on Web Services* (ICWS), Salt Lake City, Utah. IEEE Computer Society.

Deiters, W., & Gruhn, V. (1994). The Funsoft Net approach to software process management. *International Journal of Software Engineering and Knowledge Engineering, 4*(2), 229-256.

Dellarocas, C., & Klein, M. (1998). A knowledge-based approach for handling exceptions in business processes. In *WITS'98, Helsinki, Finland.*

Dempster, A., Laird, N., & Rubin, D. (1977). Maximum likelihood from incomplete data via the EM algorithm. *Journal of the Royal Statistical Society, Series B, 39*(1), 1-38.

Desai, N., Mallya, A. U., Chopra, A. K., & Singh, M. P. (2005). Interaction protocols as design abstractions for business processes. *IEEE Trans. Software Eng., 31*(12), 1015–1027.

Desai, N., Narendra, N. C., & Singh, M. P. (2008). Checking correctness of business contracts via commitments. In L. Padgham, D. C. Parkes, J. Müller, & S. Parsons (Eds.), *AAMAS*, (pp. 787–794). IFAAMAS.

Dong, G., Hull, R., Kumar, B., Su, J., & Zhou, G. (1999). A framework for optimizing distributed workflow executions. In *Proc. Int. Workshop on Database Programming Languages* (pp. 152-167). Berlin / Heidelberg: Springer.

Dongen, B. F. van, & Aalst, W. M. P. van der (2004). Multi-phase process mining: Building instance graphs. In *Proceedings of the International Conference on Conceptual Modeling (ER 2004),* (LNCS, 3288, pp. 362-376). Berlin: Springer-Verlag.

Dumas, M., ter Hofstede, A. H. M., & van der Aalst, W. M. P. (Eds.), *Process Aware Information Systems*. Wiley Publishing.

Eclipse EMF. (2006). *Eclipse Modeling Framework*. http://www.eclipse.org/emf/.

Eclipse Foundation. (n.d.). *The Eclipse BPEL designer.* Web Site: http://www.eclipse org/bpel

Eder, J., & Liebhart, W. (1995). The Workflow Activity Model WAMO. In *Proceedings of CoopIS* (pp. 87-98).

Eder, J., & Pichler, H. (2005). Probabilistic calculation of execution intervals for workflows. *TIME,* (pp. 183-185).

Eder, J., Eichner, H., & Pichler, H. (2006). A Probabilistic approach to reduce the number of deadline violations and the tardiness of workflows. *OTM Workshops,* (1), 5-7.

Eder, J., Panagos, E., & Rabinovich, M., (1999). Time constraints in workflow systems. *CAISE,* (pp. 286-300).

Eder, J., Pichler, H., & Vielgut, S. (2006). An architecture for proactive timed Web service compositions. *Business Process Management Workshops,* (pp. 323-335).

Ellis, C. A. (1983). Formal and informal models of office activity. *Proceedings of the 1983 Would Computer Congress.*

Ellis, C. A., & Nutt, G. J. (1980). Office information systems and computer science. *ACM Computing Surveys, 12*(1).

Ellis, C. A., & Nutt, G. J. (1993). The modeling and analysis of coordination systems. *University of Colorado/Dept. of Computer Science Technical Report, CU-CS-639-93.*

Ellis, C., & Nutt, G. J. (1993). Modeling and enactment of workflow systems. In *Application and Theory of Petri Nets, Chicago, USA*, (pp. 1-16).Springer-Verlag.

Ellis, C., Keddara, K., & Rozenberg, G. (1995). Dynamic change within workflow systems. In *Proc. of conf. on Organizational computing systems,* Milpitas, USA, (pp. 10-21).

Elmasri, R., & Navathe, S.B. (2006). *Fundamentals of database systems. Fifth Edition.* Amsterdam: Addison Wesley.

Enright, A., Dongen, S. van, & Ouzounis, C. (2002). An efficient algorithm for large-scale detection of protein families. *Nucleic Acids Research, 30*(7), 1575-1584.

European Project SUPER - Semantics Utilised for Process Management within and between Enterprises. *http://www.ip-super.org/.*

Farrell, A. D. H., Sergot, M. J., Sallé, M., & Bartolini, C. (2005). Using the event calculus for tracking the normative state of contracts. *International Journal of Cooperative Information Systems, 14*(2-3), 99–129.

Ferraiolo, D. F., & Kuhn, D. R. (1992). Role-based access controls. *Proceedings of the 15th NIST-NSA National Computer Security Conference.*

Ferraiolo, D. F., Cugini, J. A., & Kuhn, D. R. (1995). Role-based access control: Features and Motivations. *Proceedings of the 11th Annual Computer Security Applications.*

Ferraiolo, D. F., et al. (1995). *An introduction to role-based access control.* NIST/ITL Bulletin.

Ferraiolo, D., Barkley, J., & Kuhn, D. R.. (1999). A role-based access control model and reference implementation within a corporate intranet. *ACM Transactions on Information and System Security* (TISSEC), 2(1), 34-64.

Ferreira, D., & Mira da Silva, M. (2008, April). Using process mining for ITIL assessment: A case study with incident management. In *Proceedings of the 13th Annual UKAIS Conference*, Bournemouth University.

Ferreira, D., Zacarias, M., Malheiros, M., & Ferreira, P. (2007). Approaching process mining with sequence clustering: Experiments and findings. In *Proceedings of the 5th International Conference on Business Process Management (BPM 2007),* (LNCS 4714, pp. 360-374), Springer.

G. Keller, M. Nüttgens, and A.W. Scheer. Semantische Processmodellierung auf der Grundlage Ereignisgesteuerter Processketten (EPK). Veröffentlichungen des Instituts für Wirtschaftsinformatik, Heft 89 (in German), University of Saarland, Saarbrücken.

García, F., Bertoa, M., Calero, C., Vallecillo, A., Ruiz, F., Piattini, M., et al. (2005). Towards a consistent terminology for software measurement. *Information and Software Technology, 48*, 631-644.

Genrich, M., Kokkonen, A., Moormann, J., zur Muehlen, M., Tregear, R., Mendling, J., & Weber, B. (2008). Challenges for business process intelligence: Discussions at the BPI Workshop 2007. In A. H. M. ter Hofstede, B. Benatallah, & H.-Y. Paik, (Eds.), *Proceedings of the BPM 2007 Workshops*, volume 4928 of *Lecture Notes in Computer Science*, Brisbane, Australia. Springer-Verlag.

Gerede, C. E., & Su, J. (2007). Specification and Verification of Artifact Behaviors in Business Process Models. In *Proc. Int. Conf. on Service Oriented Computing* (pp. 181-192). Berlin / Heidelberg: Springer.

Gerede, C. E., Bhattacharya, K., & Su, J. (2007). Static analysis of business artifact-centric operational models. In *Proc. IEEE Int. Conf. on Service-Oriented Computing and Applications* (pp. 133-140). IEEE Press.

Ghandeharizadeh, S., Hull, R., & Jacobs, D. (1996). Heraclitus: Elevating deltas to be first-class citizens in a database programming languages. *ACM Trans. Database Syst., 21*(3), 370-426.

Ghezzi, C., Jazayeri, M., & Mandrioli, D. (1991). *Fundamentals of Software Engineering.* Prentice Hall

Ghose, A., & G. Koliadis (2007). Auditing business process compliance. In *Service Oriented Computing, ISOC 2007*, LNCS, (pp. 169–180). Springer.

Giblin, C., Müller, S., & Pfitzmann, B. (2006, October). *From regulatory policies to event monitoring rules: Towards model driven compliance automation*. (Technical report, IBM Research Report). Zurich Research Laboratory.

Goedertier, S., & Vanthienen, J. (2006). Designing compliant business processes with obligations and permissions. In *Business Process Management (BPM) Workshops*, (pp. 5–14).

Golani, M. & Gal, A. (2006). Optimizing exception handling in workflows using process restructuring. In *Proceedings of the 4th Int'l Conf. Business Process Management (BPM'06)*, Vienna, Austria, (LNCS 4102, pp. 407-413).

Goldenson, D., Jarzombek, J., & Rout, T. (2003). Measurement and analysis in capability maturity codel: Integration models and software process improvement. *Crosstalk the Journal of Defense Software Engineering, 6*(7), 20-24

Gottschalk, F., Aalst, Van Der W. M. P., & Jansen-Vullers, M. H. (2007) Configurable Process Models - A Foundational Approach. *Reference Modeling. Efficient Information Systems Design Through Reuse Of Information Models*, (pp. 59-78).

Gottschalk, F., van der Aalst, W. M. P., Jansen-Vullers, M. H., & La Rosa, M. (2008). Configurable workflow models, *International Journal of Cooperative Information Systems 17*(2), 177-221.

Governatori, G. (2005). Representing business contracts in RuleML. *International Journal of Cooperative Information Systems, 14*(2-3), 181–216.

Governatori, G., & Rotolo, A. (2006). Logic of violations: A Gentzen system for reasoning with contrary-to-duty obligations. *Australasian Journal of Logic, 4*, 193–215.

Governatori, G., Hulstijn, J., Riveret, R., & Rotolo, A. (2007). Characterising deadlines in temporal modal defeasible logic. In *20th Australian Joint Conference on Artificial Intelligence, AI 2007*, (pp. 486–496).

Gray, J., & Reuter, A. (1993). *Transaction processing: Concepts and techniques*. Morgan Kaufmann.

Greco, G., Guzzo, A., & Pontieri, L. (2005). Mining hierarchies of models: From abstract views to concrete specifications. In *Proceedings of the 3rd International Conference on Business Process Management (BPM 2005)*, (LNCS 3649).Springer.

Greco, G., Guzzo, A., Manco, G., & Saccà, D. (2007). Mining unconnected patterns in workflows. *Information Systems, 32*(5), 685–712.

Greco, G., Guzzo, A., Pontieri, L., & Saccà, D. (2006). Discovering expressive process models by clustering log traces. *IEEE Transactions on Knowledge and Data Engineering, 18*(8), 1010–1027. ISSN 1041-4347.

Greco, G.,Guzzo, A., Pontieri, L., & Saccà, D. (2004). Mining expressive process models by clustering workflow traces. In *Procedings of the 8th Pacific-Asia Conference (PAKDD 2004)*, (LNCS, 3056), Springer.

Grefen, P., & Vonk, J. (2006). A taxonomy of transactional workflow support. *International Journal of Cooperative Information Systems, 15*(1), 87–118.

Grefen, P., Aberer, K., Hoffner, Y., Ludwig, H. (2000). CrossFlow: Cross-organizational workflow management in dynamic virtual enterprises. *Computer Systems Science & Engineering, 15*(5), 277-290. CRL Publishing.

Grefen, P., Ludwig, H., & Angelov, S. (2003). A Three-level framework for process and data management of complex e-services. *International Journal of Cooperative Information Systems, 12*(4), 487-531. World Scientific.

Grefen, P., Mehandjiev, N., Kouvas, G., Weichhart, G., & Eshuis, R. (2007). Dynamic business network process management in instant virtual enterprises. *Beta Technical Report WP198*. Eindhoven University of Technology.

Grefen, P., Pernici, B., & Sánchez, G. (1999). *Database support for workflow management: The WIDE Project*. Kluwer Academic Publishers.

Griffel, F. et al. (1998). Electronic contracting with COSMOS - How to establish, negotiate and execute electronic contracts on the Internet. In *Proceedings of the 2nd International Enterprise Distr. Object Comp. Workshop* La Jolla.

Grigori, D., Casati, F., Dayal, U., & Shan, M. C. (2001). Improving business process quality through exception understanding, prediction, and prevention. In *VLDB'01*, Rome, Italy.

Grigori, D., Casati, F., Castellanos, M., Dayal, U., Sayal, M., & Shan, M. (2004). Business process intelligence. *Computers in Industry*, *53*(3), 321–343.

Gruber, T. R. (1993). A translation approach to portable ontology specifications. *Knowledge Acquisition*, *5*(2), 199–220. ISSN 1042-8143.

Gruhn, V., & Laue, R. (2006). Complexity metrics for business process models. *International Conference on Business Information Systems.*

Gschwind, T., Koehler, J., & Wong, J. (2008). Applying patterns during business process modeling. In *Proceedings of the 6th Int'l Conf. Business Process Management (BPM'08)*, Milan, Italy, (*LNCS 5240*, pp. 4-19).

Guimarães, N., Antunes, P., & Pereira, A. P (1997). The integration of workflow systems and collaboration tools. In *Advances in Workflow Management Systems and Interoperability, Istanbul, Turkey.*

Günther, C. W., & van der Aalst, W. M. P. (2007). Fuzzy mining - adaptive process simplification based on multi-perspective metrics. In G. Alonso, P. Dadam, & M. Rosemann, editors, *BPM*, volume 4714 of *Lecture Notes in Computer Science*, (pp. 328–343). Springer. ISBN 978-3-540-75182-3.

Günther, C. W., Rinderle-Ma, S., Reichert, M., van der Aalst, W. M. P., & Recker, J. (2008). Using process mining to learn from process changes in evolutionary systems. *Int'l Journal of Business Process Integration and Management*, *3*(1), 61-78.

Günther, C.W., Rinderle, S., Reichert, M., & van der Aalst, W.M.P. (2006). Change mining in adaptive process management systems. In *Proceedings of the 14th Int'l Conf. on Cooperative Information Systems (CoopIS'06)*, Montpellier, France. (LNCS 4275, pp. 309-326).

Hagen, C. (1999). *A Generic kernel for reliable process support.* (Doctoral dissertation, Swiss Federal Institute of Technology Zürich). ETH Nr. 13114 .

Hallerbach, A., Bauer, T., & Reichert, M. (2008). Managing process variants in the process lifecycle. In: *Proceedings of the 10th Int'l Conf. on Enterprise Information Systems (ICEIS'08)*, Barcelona, Spain, (pp. 154-161).

Hamadi, R., & Benatallah, B. (2004). Recovery nets: Towards self-adaptive workflow systems. In *Proceedings of the International Conference on Web Information Systems Engineering (WISE)*, (LNCS 3306, pp. 439-453). Springer.

Hammer, M., & Champy, J. (1993). *Reengineering the corporation – A manifesto for business revolution.* New York: Harper Business.

Hammer, M., & Champy, J. (2005). *Reengineering the corporation: A manifest for business revolution.* Collins Business Essentials.

Han, J., & Kamber, M. (2006). *Data mining: Concepts and techniques*, 2nd edition. Morgan Kaufmann.

Han, Y., Sheth, A. P., & Bussler, C. (1998). A taxonomy of adaptive workflow management. In *Proceedings of the CSCW'98, Seattle, WA.*

Harmon, P. (2003). *Business process change: A manager's guide to improving, redesigning, and automating processes.* Morgan Kaufmann Publishers.

Harrington, H. J. (1991). *Business process improvement: The breakthrough strategy for total quality, productivity, and competitiveness.* Mc Graw Hill.

Hauser, R., & Koehler, J. (2004, October). *Compiling process graphs to executable code. Proc. of the 3rd Int'l Conf. on Generative Programming and Component Engineering (GPCE2004)* , (pp. 317-336).

Heinl, P. (1998). Exceptions during workflow execution. In *Proceedings of the EDBT'98, Valencia, Spain.*

Heinl, P., Horn, S., Jablonski, S., Neeb, J., Stein, K., & Teschke, M. (1999). A comprehensive approach to flexibility in workflow management systems. *SIGSOFT Softw. Eng. Notes, 24*(2), 79-88

Hendler, J., Berners-Lee, T., & Miller, E. (2002, October). Integrating applications on the Semantic Web. *Journal of the Institute of Electrical Engineers of Japan, 122*(10), 676-680.

Hentrich, C., & Zdun, U. (2006). Patterns for Process-oriented integration in Service-Oriented Architectures. In *Proc. of 11th European Conference on Pattern Languages of Programs (EuroPLoP'06).* Irsee, Germany.

Hepp, M., & Roman, D.(2007, Feb. 28-March 2). An ontology framework for semantic business process management. In *Proceedings of Wirtschaftsinformatik*, Karlsruhe, Germany.

Hepp, M., Leymann, F., Domingue, J., Wahler, A., & Fensel, D. (2005, Oct. 18-25). Semantic business process management: A vision towards using Semantic Web services for business process management. In *Proceedings of the IEEE International Conference on e-Business Engineering* (ICEBE 2005), (pp. 535-540), Beijing, China.

Herbst, J., & Karagiannis, D. (1998). Integrating machine learning and workflow management to support acquisition and adaptation of workflow models. In *Proceedings of the 9th International Workshop on Database and Expert Systems Applications,* (pp.745-752).

Herbst, J., & Karagiannis, D. (2004). Workflow Mining with InWoLvE. *Computers in Industry, 53*(3), 245–264. ISSN 0166-3615. http://dx.doi.org/10.1016/j.compind.2003.10.002.

Hoffner, Y., Ludwig, H., Gülcü, C., & Grefen, P. (2000). Architecture for cross-organisational business processes. In *Proceedings of the 2nd International Workshop Adv. Issues of E-Commerce and Web-Based Information Systems.*

Hollingsworth, D. (1995, January). *The workflow reference model.* (Technical Report TC00-1003). The Workflow Management Coalition (WfMC).

Hörmann, M., Margaria, T., Mender, T., Nagel, R., Steffen, B., & Trinh, H. (2008, October). The jABC approach to rigorous collaborative development of SCM applications. In *Proceedings of the ISoLA 2008, 3rd Int. Symp. on Leveraging Applications of Formal Methods, Verification, and Validation, Chalkidiki (GR).* CCIS N.17, Springer Verlag.

Hornix, P. T. G. (2007). *Performance Analysis of Business Processes Through Process Mining.* Master's thesis, Eindhoven University of Technology, Eindhoven.

Hsu, M., & Kleissner, K. (1996). ObjectFlow: Towards a process management infrastructure, *Distributed and Parallel Databases*, 2, 169-194.

Hsu, M., Ladin, R., & McCarthy, D. R. (1988). An Execution model for active data base management systems. In *Proc. 3rd Int. Conf. on Data and Knowledge Bases: Improving Usability and Responsiveness* (pp. 171-179). Morgan Kaufmann.

Hull, R. & Su, J. (2005). Tools for composite Web services: A short overview. *SIGMOD Record, 34*(2), 86-95.

Hull, R., Llirbat, F., Simon, E., Su, J., Dong, G., Kumar, B., & Zhou, G. (1999). Declarative workflows that support easy modification and dynamic browsing. In *Proc. Int. Joint Conf. on Work Activities Coordination and Collaboration* (pp. 69-78). New York: ACM Press.

Humphrey, W. (1987). *Characterizing the software process: A maturity framework.* Software Engineering Insttitute (SEI), CMU/SEI-87-TR-11, DTIC Number ADA182895.

Hwang, S. Y., Ho, S. F., & Tang, J. (1999). Mining exception instances to facilitate workflow exception handling. In *Proceedings of the 6th Int. Conf. on Database Systems for Advanced Applications, Hsinchu, Taiwan.*

IBM, Systems, Microsoft, SAP AG, & Systems Siebel. (2003). *Business Process Execution Language for Web services.* ftp://www6.software.ibm.com/software/developer/library/ws-bpel.pdf.

IEEE. (2000). Recommended Practice for Architectural Description of Software Intensive Systems (Tech. Rep. No. IEEE-std-1471-2000). IEEE.

Ingvaldsen, J. E., & Gulla, J. A. (2008). Preprocessing support for large scale process mining of sap transactions. In A. H. M. ter Hofstede, B. Benatallah, & H.-Y. Paik, (Eds.), *Proceedings of the BPM 2007 Workshops*, volume 4928 of *Lecture Notes in Computer Science*, Brisbane, Australia. Springer-Verlag.

Intelligent Reasoning for Integrated Systems (IRIS)http://rsws.deri.org/index.html

Internet Reasoning Service http://kmi.open.ac.uk/projects/irs/

ISO. (1998). Open Distributed Processing Reference Model (IS 10746). http://isotc.iso.org/.

ISO/IEC 15939. (2002). *Software engineering - Software measurement process*. International Standards Organization: ISO/IEC 15939.

Jablonski, S. (1994). MOBILE: A modular workflow model and architecture.In *Proc. International Working Conference on Dynamic Modelling and Information Systems*.

Jablonski, S., & Bussler, C. (1996). *Workflow management - Modeling concepts, architecture and implementation*. New York: International Thomson Computer Press

Jablonski, S., & Götz, M. (2007) Perspective oriented business process visualization. *3rd International Workshop on Business Process Design (BPD) 5th International Conference on Business Process Management (BPM 2007)*.

Jablonski, S., Volz, B., & Dornstauder, S. (2008) A meta modeling framework for domain specific process management. In *Proceedings 1st International Workshop on Semantics for Business Process Management*.

Jaeger, M. C., & Ladner, H. (2005). Improving the QoS of WS compositions based on redundant services". In *Proceedings of the International Conference on Next Generation Web Services Practices*.

Jansen-Vullers, M. H., Van Der Aalst, W. M. P., & Rosemann, M. (2006) Mining Configurable Enterprise Information Systems. *Data And Knowledge Engineering, 56*, 195-244.

Jensen, C., & Snodgrass, R. T. (1999). Temporal data management. *TKDE, 11*(1), 36-44.

Jeston, J., & Nelis, J. (2006). *Business process management: Practical guidelines to successful implementations*. Elsevier.

Jimenez, G., & Espadas, J. (2007). Visual Environment for Supply Chain Integration Using Web Services. In W. Lam & V. Shankararaman (Eds.), *Enterprise architecture and integration: Methods, implementation, and technologies*. Hershey, PA: Information Science Reference.

Jimenez, G., Ocampo, M.,Galeano, N.,& Molina, A. (2006). "Business process based integration of dynamic collaborative organizations. In W. Shen (Ed.), *Information technology for balanced manufacturing systems*. Springer.

Jordan, D., & Evdemon, J. (2007). *Web services business process execution language (WS-BPEL) – version 2.0*. Committee Specification. OASIS WS-BPEL TC. Available via http://www.oasis-open.org/committees/download.php/22475/wsbpel-v2.0-CS01.pdf

Jörges, S., Kubczak, C., Nagel, R., Margaria, T., & Steffen, B. (2006). Model-driven development with the jABC. *In HVC 2006 - IBM Haifa Verification Conference, Haifa, Israel, October 23-26 2006. LNCS 4383*. IBM, Springer Verlag.

JSR 208: Java™ Business Integration (JBI) http://www.jcp.org/en/jsr/detail?id=208

Jung, G., Margaria, T., Nagel, R., Schubert, W., Steffen, B., & Voigt, H. (2008, October). SCA and jABC: Bringing a service-oriented paradigm to Web-service construction. In *ISoLA'08, Proc. 3rd Int. Symp. on Leveraging Applications of Formal Methods, Verification, and Validation, Chalkidiki (GR), Oct. 2008*. CCIS N. 017, Springer Verlag.

Jung, J.-Y., Bae, J., & Liu, L. (2008). Hierarchical business process clustering. In *Proceedings of the IEEE International Conference on Services Computing (SCC '08)*, (pp. 613-616).

Kaiser, M. (2007) From composition to emergence - Towards the realization of policy-oriented enterprise management. *IEEE Computer, 40*(11), 57-63. IEEE Press.

Kaplan, R., & Norton, D. (1996). *The balanced scorecard.* McGraw-Hill. ISBN: 978-0875846514.

Karastoyanova, D., Leymann, F., Nitzsche, J., Wetzstein, B., & Wutke, D. (2006, September). Parameterized BPEL processes: Concepts and implementation. In *Proceedings of the Fourth International Conference on Business Process Management (BPM 2006)*, Vienna, Austria. Springer-Verlag.

Karastoyanova, D., van Lessen, T., Leymann, F., Ma, Z., Nitzsche, J., Wetzstein, B., Bhiri, S., Hauswirth M., Zaremba M. (2008, Feb. 26-28). A Reference Architecture for Semantic Business Process Management Systems. Track "Semantic Web Technology in Business Information Systems". In *Proceedings of the Multikonferenz Wirtschaftsinformatik. (MKWI 2008).* Munich, Germany.

Karastoyanova, D., van Lessen, T., Leymann, F., Nitzsche, J., & Wutke, D. (2008). *WS-BPEL Extension for Semantic Web services* (BPEL4SWS), Version 1.0.

Karastoyanova, D., van Lessen, T., Nitzsche, J., Wetzstein, B., Wutke, D., & Leymann, F. (2007, April 16). Semantic service bus: Architecture and implementation of a next generation middleware. In *Proceedings of the 2nd International Workshop on Services Engineering (SEIW) 2007, in conjunction with ICDE 2007.* Istanbul, Turkey.

Karbe, B.. & Ramsperger, N. (1991). Concepts and implementation of migrating office processes. *Wissensbasierte Systeme,* (pp. 136-147).

Kavantzas, N., Burdett, D., Ritzinger, G., Fletcher, T. and Lafon, Y.(2005). *Web Services Choreography Description Language* Version 1.0, W3C Candidate Recommendation. Web Site: http://www.w3.org/TR/ws-cdl-10/

Keller, G., Nüttgens, M., & Scheer, A. W. (1992). *Semantische Prozessmodellierung auf der Grundlage "Ereignisgesteuerter Prozessketten (EPK)".* Technical Report 89, Institut für Wirtschaftsinformatik Saarbrücken, Saarbrücken, Germany.

Keller, G., Nüttgens, M., & Scheer, A.W. (1992) *Semantische Prozess-modellierung.* Veröffentlichungen des Instituts für Wirtschaftinformatik, Nr 89, Saarbrücken, Germany.

Khalaf, R., Keller, A., & Leymann, F. (2006). Business processes for web services: Principles and applications. *IBM Systems Journal, 45*(2), 425-446.

Khatri, V., Ram S., & Snodgrass, R. T. (2004). Augmenting a conceptual model with geospatiotemporal annotations. *TKDE, 16*(11), 1324-1338.

Kim, K. (1999). Actor-oriented Workflow Model. *Proceedings of the 2nd international symposium on Cooperative Database Systems for Advanced Applications.*

Kim, K. (2003). Workflow dependency analysis and its implications on distributed workflow systems. *Proceeding of the AINA*, (pp. 677-682).

Kim, K. (2003). Workflow reduction for reachable-path rediscovery. *IEEE Proceeding of the ICDM Workshop.*

Kim, K. (2004). Cooperative fragment-driven workflow modeling methodology and system. *WfMC Workflow Handbook,* (pp. 189-207).

Kim, K. (2005). A process-driven e-business service integration system and its application to e-logistics services. *Lecture Notes in Computer Science, 3762*, 485-494.

Kim, K. (2005). A Process-Driven Inter-organizational Choreography Modeling System. *Lecture Notes in Computer Science, 3762*, 485-494.

Kim, K. (2006). A XML-based workflow event logging mechanism for workflow mining. *Lecture Notes in Computer Science, 3842,* 132-136.

Kim, K. (2006). An enterprise workflow Grid/P2P architecture for massively parallel and very large scale workflow systems. *Lecture Notes in Computer Science, 3842,* 472-476.

Kim, K. (2006). Beyond Workflow Mining. *Lecture Notes in Computer Science, 4102,* 49-64.

Kim, K. (2007). A layered workflow knowledge Grid/P2P architecture and its models for future generation workflow systems. *Future Generation Computer Systems, 23*(3), 304-316.

Kim, K. (2007). Signal-Algorithm: structured workflow process mining through amalgamating temporal workcases. *Lecture Notes in Artificial Intelligence, 4426,* 119-130.

Kim, K., & Ahn, H. (2005). An EJB-based very large scale workflow system and its performance measurement. *Lecture Notes in Computer Science, 3739*, 526-537.

Kim, K., & Ellis, C. A. (2001). Performance analytic models and analyses for workflow architectures. *Journal of Information Systems Frontiers, 3*(3), 339-355.

Kim, K., & Kim, H. (2005). A Peer-to-Peer workflow model for distributing large-scale workflow data onto Grid/P2P. *Journal of digital information management, 3*(2), 64-70.

Kim, K., & Kim, I. (2002). The Admon-Time workflow client: why do we need the third type of workflow client designated for administration and monitoring services? *Lecture Notes in Computer Science, 2419,* 213-224.

Kim, K., & Paik, S. (1996). Practical experiences and requirements on workflow. *Lecture Notes Asian '96 Post-Conference Workshop: Coordination Technology for Collaborative Applications, the 2nd Asian Computer Science Conference.*

Kim, K., & Ra, I. (2007). e-Lollapalooza: a process-driven e-Business service integration system for e-Logistics services. *KSII Transactions on Internet and Information Systems, 1*(1), 33-52.

Kim, K., Ahn, H., & Kim, C. (2005). SCO control net for the process-driven SCORM content aggregation model. *Lecture Notes in Computer Science, 3483,* 38-47.

Kim, K., et al. (1996). Practical experience on workflow: hiring process automation by FlowMark. *IBM Internship Report, IBM/ISSC Boulder Colorado.*

Kim, K., et al. (2003). Role-based model and architecture for workflow systems. *International Journal of Computer and Information Science, 4*(4).

Kim, K., Lee, J., & Kim, C. (2005). A real-time cooperative swim-lane business process modeler. *Lecture Notes in Computer Science, 3483,* 176-185.

Kim, K., Won, J., & Kim, C. (2005). A fragment-driven process modeling methodology. *Lecture Notes in Computer Science, 3483,* 817-826.

Kim, K., Yoo, H., & Won, J. (2004). The e-Lollapalooza global workflow modeler: a registry-based e-Logistic. *Lecture Notes in Computer Science,* (pp. 419-430).

Kindler, E. (2004, June). On the semantics of EPCs: Resolving the vicious circle. In J. Desel, B. Pernici, & M. Weske (Eds.), *Business Process Management, Second International Conference, BPM 2004*, (*LNCS*, 3080 pp. 82–97). Springer.

Kindler, E. (2006, January). On the semantics of EPCs: Resolving the vicious circle. *Data and Knowledge Engineering, 56*(1), 23-40.

Kobayashi, T., Ogoshi, S., & Komoda, N. (1997). A business process design method for applying workflow tools. In *Proc. IEEE Int. Conf. on Systems, Man, and Cybernetics, Computational Cybernetics and Simulation* (pp. 2314-2319). IEEE Press.

Koetsier, M., Grefen, P., & Vonk, J. (2000). Contracts for cross-organizational workflow management. In *Proceedings 1st International Conference on Electronic Commerce and Web Technologies.* (pp. 110-121). London.

Kozen, D. (1983). Results on the Propositional mu-Calculus. *Theoretical Computer Science, 27,* 333-354.

KPMG Advisory (2005). *The Compliance Journey: Balancing Risk and Controls with Business Improvement.* KPMG Advisory.

Krafzig, D., Banke, K., Slama, D. (2004). *Enterprise SOA. Service oriented architecture best practices.* Prentice Hall International.

Kumaran, S. (2004). Model-driven enterprise. In *Proc. Global Enterprise Application Integration (EAI) Summit* (pp. 166-180).

Kumaran, S., Liu, R., & Wu, F. Y. (2008). On the duality of information-centric and activity-centric models of business processes. In *Proc. Int. Conf. on Advanced Information Systems Engineering* (pp.32-47). Berlin / Heidelberg: Springer.

Küster, J. M., Ryndina, K., & Gall, H. (2007). *Generation of business process models for object life cycle compliance.* See DBLP:conf/bpm/2007, (pp. 165–181).

Kűster, J., Ryndina, K., & Gall, H. (2007). Generation of BPM for object life cycle compliance. In *Proc. 5th Intl. Conf. on Business Process Management (pp. 165-181).* Berlin / Heidelberg: Springer.

La Rosa, M., Lux, J., Seidel, S., Dumas, M., & Ter Hofstede, A. H. M. (2007) Questionnaire-Driven Configuration Of Reference Process Models. *19th International Conference On Advanced Information Systems Engineering (Caise).* Trondheim, Norway, Springer-Verlag.

La Rosa, M., Van Der Aalst, W. M. P., Dumas, M., & Ter Hofstede, A. H. M. (2008) Questionnaire-Based Variability Modeling For System Configuration. *International Journal On Software And Systems Modeling.*

Lamprecht, A.L., Margaria, T., & Steffen, B. (2008). Seven variations of an alignment workflow – an illustration of agile process design/management in BiojETI. *In: ISBRA 2008: 4th Int. Symp. on Bioinformatics Research and Applications* (pp. 445–456). LNCS 4983, Springer.

Lamprecht, A.L., Margaria, T., Steffen, B., Sczyrba, A., Hartmeier, S., & Giegerich, R. (2008). Genefisher-p: Variations of genefisher as processes in biojeti. *BioMed Central (BMC) Bioinformatics 2008; Supplement dedicated to Network Tools and Applications in Biology 2007 Workshop (NETTAB 2007)* ISSN 1471-2105. Published online 2008 April 25. 9 (Suppl. 4) S13

Lankhorst, M. et al., (2005). *Enterprise architecture at work: Modeling, communication, and analysis.* Springer.

Latva-Koivisto, A. M. (2001). *Finding a complexity measure for business process models.* Individual Research Projects in Applied Mathematics

Lazcano, A., Schuldt, H., Alonso, G., & Schek, H. (2001). WISE: Process based e-commerce. *IEEE Data Engineering Bulletin, 24*(1), 46-51.

Leban, B., McDonald, D., & Forster, D. (1986). A representation for collections of temporal Intervals. *AAAI86,* (pp. 367-371).

Lee, J., Lee, D., & Kang, S. (2007). An overview of the business process maturity model (BPMM). Advances in data and Web management,. *Joint ninth Asia-Pacific Web Conference APWeb/WAIM.*

Lenz, R., & Reichert, M. (2007). IT support for healthcare processes – premises, challenges, perspectives. *Data and Knowledge Engineering, 61*(1), 39-58.

Leontiev, A. N. (1978). *Activity, consciousness and personality.* Englewood Cliffs, NJ: Prentice Hall.

Leymann, F. (2005, December 13-16). The (service) bus: Services penetrate everyday life. In *Proceedings of the 3rd International. Conference on Service Oriented Computing ICSOC'2005,* Amsterdam. (LNCS, 3826), Berlin/Heidelberg: Springer-Verlag.

Leymann, F., & Roller, D. (1999). *Production workflow: Concepts and techniques.* Upper Saddle River, NJ: Prentice-Hall PTR.

Leymann, F., & Roller, D. (2000). *Production workflow.* Prentice Hall.

Li, C., Reichert, M., & Wombacher, A. (2008). On measuring process model similarity based on high-level change operations. In *Proceedings of the 27th Int'l Conf. on Conceptual Modeling (ER'08),* Barcelona, Spain. Springer, (LNCS, 2008).

Li, C., Reichert, M., & Wombacher, A. (2008). Discovering reference process models by mining process variants. In *Proceedings of the 6th Int'l Conference on Web Services (ICWS'08),* Beijing, China. IEEE Computer Society Press.

Li, C., Reichert, M., & Wombacher, A. (2008). Mining based on learning from process change logs. In *Proceedings BPM'08 workshops – 4th Int'l Workshop on*

Business Process Intelligence (BPI'08), Milan, Italy. LNBIP (to appear).

Li, W., Jaroszcwski, L., & Godzik, A. (2002, August). Sequence clustering strategies improve remote homology recognitions while reducing search times. *Protein Engineering, 15*(8), 643-649.

Lienhard, H. (1998). IvyBeans - Bridge to VSH and the project WISE. In *Proceedings of the Conference of the Swiss Priority Programme Information and Communication Structures,* Zürich, Switzerland.

Lindland, O. I., Sindre, G., & Sølvberg, A. (1994). Understanding quality in conceptual modelling. *IEEE Software, 11*(2), 42-49.

Liu, J., Zhou, C., & Chen, J. (2008). WdCM: A workday calendar model for workflows in service grid environments. *Concurrency and Computation: Practice and Experience, 20*(4), 377-392.

Liu, J., Zhou, C., Chen, J., Liu, H., Wen, Y. (2007). A job scheduling optimization model based on time difference in service grid environments. *GCC (Grid and Cooperative Computing),* 283-287.

Liu, R., Bhattacharya, K., & Wu, F. Y. (2007). Modeling business contexture and behavior using business artifacts. In *Proc. Int. Conf. on Advanced Information Systems Engineering* (pp. 324-339). Berlin / Heidelberg: Springer.

Liu, Y., Müller, S., & Xu, K. (2007). A static compliance-checking framework for business process models. *IBM Systems Journal, 46*(2), 335–362.

Lu, R., Sadiq, S. W., & Governatori, G. (2007). Compliance aware business process design. In *Business Process Management Workshops*, (pp. 120–131).

Luo, Z. (2001). Knowledge sharing, coordinated exception handling, and intelligent problem solving for cross-organizational business processes Unpublished doctoral thesis, Dep. of Computer Sciences, University of Georgia.

Ly, L. T., Rinderle, S., Dadam, P., & Reichert, M. (2005). Mining Staff Assignment Rules from Event-Based Data. In *Business Process Management Workshops*, (pp. 177–190).

Ly, L.T., Göser, K., Rinderle-Ma, S., & Dadam, P. (2008). Compliance of semantic constraints – A re-quirements analysis for process management systems. In *Proceedings 1st Int'l Workshop on Governance, Risk and Compliance - Applications in Information Systems (GRCIS'08)*, Montpellier, France.

Ly, L.T., Rinderle, S., & Dadam, P. (2008). Integration and verification of semantic constraints in adaptive process management systems. *Data and Knowledge Engineering, 64*(1), 3-23.

Ly, L.T., Rinderle, S., Dadam, P., & Reichert, M. (2005) Mining staff assignment rules from event-based data. In *Proceedings of the BPM'05 workshops*, Nancy, France. Springer (LNCS 3812, pp. 177-190.

Ma, Z., Wetzstein, B., Anicic, D., Heymans, S., & Leymann. F. (2007, June). Semantic Business Process Repository. *Proceedings of the Workshop on Semantic Business Process and Product Lifecycle Management (SBPM-2007)*, (CEUR-WS, 251).

Magedanz, T., Blum, N., & Dutkowski, S. (2007). *Evolution of SOA concepts in telecommunications.* IEEE Computer Nov. 2007.

Margaria, T., & Steffen, B. (2004). Lightweight coarse-grained coordination: A scalable system-level approach. *STTT*, 5(2-3), 107-123. Springer Verlag.

Margaria, T., & Steffen, B. (2006). Service engineering: Linking business and IT. *IEEE Computer, issue 60th anniv. of the Computer Society, (pp 53–63)*

Margaria, T., (2008). The Semantic Web services challenge: Tackling complexity at the orchestration level. *Invited paper ICECCS 2008 (13th IEEE Intern. Conf. on Engineering of Complex Computer Systems), Belfast (UK), April 2008,* (pp.183-189). IEEE CS Press.

Margaria, T., Steffen, B., & Reitenspieß, M. (2005). Service-oriented design: The roots. *ICSOC 2005: 3rd ACM SIG-SOFT/SIGWEB Intern. Conf. on Service-Oriented Computing, Amsterdam (NL), Dec. 2005* (pp.450-464). LNCS N. 3826, Springer Verlag.

Marjanovic, O., & Orlowska, M. E. (1999). On modeling and verification of temporal constraints in production workflows. *Knowl. Inf. Syst., 1*(2), 157-192.

Marjanovic, O., & Orlowska, M. E. (1999). Time management in dynamic workflows. *CODAS,* (pp. 138-149).

Martens, A., Moser, S.(2006, September). Diagnosing SCA components using WOMBAT. In P*roceedings of BPM'06, 4th International Conference on Business Process Management,* Vienna, Austria (LNCS 4102).

Martin, D., et al. (2004). *OWL-S: Semantic markup for Web services*, W3C Member Submission. http://www.w3.org/Submission/OWL-S/

McIlraith, S. A., Son, T. C., & Zeng, H. (2001). Semantic Web services. *IEEE Intelligent Systems, 16*(2), 46-53.

McLachlan, G., & Krishnan, T. (1996). *The EM algorithm and extensions.* John Wiley & Sons.

Medeiros, A. K. Alves de, Guzzo, A., Greco, G., Aalst, W. M. P. van der, Weijters, A. J. M. M., Dongen, B. van, & Sacca, D. (2008). Process mining based on clustering: A quest for precision.In *Proceedings of the BPM 2007 International Workshops,* (LNCS 4928). Springer.

Medeiros, A. K. Alves de, Weijters, A. J. M. M., & Aalst W. M. P. van der (2007). Genetic process mining: An experimental evaluation. *Data Mining and Knowledge Discovery, 14*(2), 245-304.

Mendling, J. (2006). *Testing density as a complexity metric for EPCs.* Technical Report JM-2006-11-15.

Miller, T., E. & Berger, D. W. (2001). *Totally integrated enterprises: A framework and methodology for business and technology improvement.* St. Lucie Press.

Minor, M., Schmalen, D., Koldehoff, A., & Bergmann, R. (2007). Structural adaptation of workflows supported by a suspension mechanism and by case-based reasoning. In *Proceedings of the WETICE'07 workshops,* (pp. 370-375). IEEE Computer Press.

Modafferi, S., & Conforti, E. (2006). Methods for enabling recovery actions in Ws-BPEL. In *Proceedings of OTM Conferences (1)*, 219-236.

Modafferi, S., Benatallah, B., Casati, F., & Pernici, B. (2005). A methodology for designing and managing context-aware workflows. In *Proceedings of IFIP TC 8 Working Conference on Mobile Information Systems (MOBIS).*

Mourão, H. R. (2008). *Supporting effective unexpected exception handling in workflow management systems within organizational contexts.* Unpublished doctoral thesis, University of Lisbon.

Mourão, H. R., & Antunes, P. (2003). Supporting direct user interventions in exception handling in workflow management systems. In *Proceedings of CRIWG 2003,* Autrans, France, (pp. 159-167).Springer-Verlag.

Mourão, H. R., & Antunes, P. (2004). Exception handling through a workflow. In *CoopIS 2004,* Agia Napa, (pp. 37-54). Springer-Verlag.

Mourão, H. R., & Antunes, P. (2005). A collaborative framework for unexpected exception handling. In *Proceedings of CRIWG 2005,* Porto de Galinhas, Brasil, (pp. 168-183). Springer-Verlag.

Müller, D., Herbst, J., Hammori, M., & Reichert, M. (2006). IT support for release management processes in the automotive industry. In *Proceedings of the 4th Int'l Conf. on Business Process Management (BPM'06),* Vienna, Austria. (LNCS 4102, pp. 368-377).

Müller, D., Reichert, M., & Herbst, J. (2007). Data-driven modeling and coordination of large process structures. In *Proceedings of the 15th Int'l Conf. on Cooperative Information Systems (CoopIS'07),* Vilamoura, Algarve, Portugal (LNCS 4803, pp. 131-149).

Müller, D., Reichert, M., & Herbst, J. (2008). A new paradigm for the enactment and dynamic adaptation of data-driven process structures. In *Proceedings of the 20th Int'l Conf. on Advanced Information Systems Engineering (CAiSE'08),* Montpellier, France (LNCS 5074, pp. 48-63).

Muller, R., Greiner, U., & Rahm, E. (2004) AGENTWORK: A workflow system supporting rule-based workflow adaptation. *Journal of Data and Knowledge Engineering, 51*(2), 223-256.

Müller-Olm, M., Schmidt, D.A., & Steffen, B. (1999). *Model-checking: A tutorial introduction* (pp. 330-354). Proc. SAS, LNCS.

Murata, T. (1989). Petri nets: Properties, analysis and applications. *Proceedings of the IEEE, 77*(4), 541–580.

Mutschler, B., & Reichert, M. (2008). On modeling and analyzing cost factors in information systems engineering. In *Proceedings of the 20th Int'l Conf. on Advanced Information Systems Engineering (CAiSE'08)*, Montpellier, France (LNCS 5074, pp. 510-524).

Mutschler, B., Bumiller, J., & Reichert, M. (2006). Why process-orientation is scarce: an empirical study of process-oriented information systems in the automotive industry. In *Proceedings of the 10th Int'l Conf. on Enterprise Computing (EDOC '06)*, Hong Kong, 433-440. IEEE Computer Press.

Mutschler, B., Reichert, M., & Bumiller, J. (2008): Unleashing the effectiveness of process-oriented information systems: problem analysis, critical success factors and implications, *IEEE Transactions on Systems, Man, and Cybernetics, 38*(3), 280-291.

Mutschler, B., Reichert, M., & Rinderle, S. (2007). Analyzing the dynamic cost factors of process-aware information systems: a model-based approach. In *Proceedings of the 19th Int'l Conf. on Advanced Information Systems Engineering (CAiSE'07)*, Trondheim, Norway (LNCS 4495, pp. 589-603).

Mutschler, B., Weber, B., & Reichert, M. (2008). Workflow management versus case handling: results from a controlled software experiment. In *Proceedings of the 23rd Annual ACM Symposium on Applied Computing (SAC'08)*, Fortaleza, Brazil, (pp. 82-89).

Nigam, A. & Caswell, N. S. (2003). Business artifacts: An approach to operational specification. *IBM Systems Journal, 42*(3), 428-445

Nitzsche, J. (2006). *Entwicklung eines Monitoring-Tools zur Unterstützung von parametrisierten Web Service Flows*, Diplomarbeit, Universität Stuttgart.

Nitzsche, J., Lessen, T. van, Karastoyanova, D., & Leymann, F. (2007, September). BPEL^{light}. In *Proceedings of 5th International Conference on Business Process Management (BPM 2007)*, Brisbane, Australia, 24-28 September 2007

Nitzsche, J., Lessen, T. van; Karastoyanova, D., & Leymann, F. (2007). WSMO/X in the context of business processes: Improvement recommendations. *International Journal on Web Information Systems (ijWIS)*.

Nitzsche, J., van Lessen, T., Karastoyanova, D., & Leymann, F. (2007, November). BPEL for Semantic Web services. In *Proceedings of the 3rd International Workshop on Agents and Web Services in Distributed Environments* (AWeSome'07).

Nitzsche, J., Wutke, D., & Lessen, T. van (2007, June 7). An Ontology for Executable Business Processes. *Workshop on Semantic Business Process and Product Lifecycle Management (SBPM2007), in conjunction with ESWC 2007.* Innsbruck, Austria.

Nute, D. (1994). Defeasible logic. In *Handbook of Logic in Artificial Intelligence and Logic Programming, 3.*

Nüttgens, M., & Rump, F. J. (2002). Syntax und Semantik Ereignisgesteuerter Prozessketten (EPK). In *PROMISE 2002, Prozessorientierte Methoden und Werkzeuge für die Entwicklung von Informationssystemen*, volume P-21 of *GI Lecture Notes in Informatics*, (pp. 64–77). Gesellschaft für Informatik.

OASIS (2007): *Web Service Business Process Execution Language (WS-BPEL)* Version 2.0, OASIS Standard, April 2007, OASIS Technical Committee, http://docs.oasis-open.org/wsbpel/2.0/OS/wsbpel-v2.0-OS.pdf

oAW. (2002) openArchitectureWare Project. http://www.openarchitectureware.org.

Object Management Group (2005). *Unified modeling language: Superstructure version 2.0 formal/05-07-04.* Technical report, http://www.omg.org/cgi-bin/doc?formal/05-07-04

Object Management Group (2006). *Business process modeling notation specification.*

Object Management Group (2006). *Meta object facility core specification* (Version 2.0)

Object Management Group/Business Process Management Initiative (2006). *BPMN 1.0: OMG Final adopted specification.* http://www.bpmn.org

OMG (2008). *Business Process Modeling Notation (BPMN),* Version 2.0, Request For Proposal, February 2008, http://www.bpmn.org/Documents/BPMN%20 2-0%20RFP%2007-06-05.pdf

OMG. (1989). *Object Management Group.* from http:// www.omg.org

OMG. (2004). Unified Modelling Language 2.0 (UML). http://www.uml.org

OMG. (2006). *Business process modeling notation (BPMN), Final adopted specification.* dtc/06-02-0, BPMI 2004 from http://www.omg.org/bpm

OMG. (2007). *Business process maturity model (BPMM), Beta 1 adopted specification.* dtc/2007-07-02, from http:// www.omg.org/docs/dtc/07-07-02.pdf

Open Applications Group (1994). *Open applications group.* Retrieved April 15, 2008. Web site: http://www. openapplications.org/

OSOA (2007). *Service Component Architecture Specifications - Open SOA collaboration.* Retrieved March 21, 2007 from OSOA's Web Site: http://www. osoa.org/display/Main/Service+Component+Architecture+Specifications

Ould, M. A. (2005). *Business process management: A rigorous approach.* Meghan-Kiffer Press.

Ouyang, C., Dumas, M., van der Aalst, W. M. P., ter Hofstede, A. H. M., & Mendling, J. (2008). From business process models to process-oriented software systems. Accepted for publication. *ACM Transactions on Software Engineering and Methodology.*

OWL-S (2004). *Semantic markup for Web services.* W3C Member Submission, 22 November 2004http://www. w3.org/Submission/OWL-S/

Padmanabhan, V., Governatori, G., Sadiq, S., Colomb, R. M., & Rotolo, A. (2006). Process modelling: The deontic way. In M. Stumptner, S. Hartmann, & Y. Kiyoki (Eds.), *Conceptual Modelling 2006. Proceedings of the Thirds Asia-Pacific Conference on Conceptual Modelling (APCCM2006),* (pp. 75–84). Australian Computer Science Communications.

Pall, G. A. (1987). *Quality press management.* Eaglewood Cliffs, NJ: Prentice-Hall.

Papazoglou, M., & Van den Heuvel, W.-J. (2006). Service-oriented design and development methodology. *Int. J. on Web Engineering and technology,* 412-442.

Park, M., & Kim, K. (2008). Control-path oriented workflow intelligence analyses. *Journal of information science and engineering, 34*(3).

Paulk, M., Curtis, B., Chrissis, M., & Weber, C. (1993). *Capability maturity model (CMM) for software, version 1.1.* Software Engineering Insttitute (SEI), CMU/ SEI-93-TR-024.

Pautasso, C. *JOpera: Process Support for more than Web services.* http://www.jopera.org

Pautasso, C., & Alonso, G. (2004). The JOpera Visual Composition Language. *Journal of Visual Languages and Computing, 16*(1–2), 119–152.

Pautasso, C., & Koehler, J. (2008, September). *Proc. of the 1st Int'l BPM Workshop on Model-Driven Engineering for Business Process Management*, Milan, Italy. (LNBIP). Springer.

Pautasso, C., Heinis, T., & Alonso, G. (2005) Autonomic execution of Web service compositions. In *Proceedings of the Third IEEE International Conference on Web Services.*

Pedrinaci, C., Domingue, J., & Alves de Medeiros, A. K. (2008). A core ontology for business process analysis. In *Proceedings of the 5th European Semantic Web Conference.*

Pelz, C. (2003). Web services orchestration and choreography. *IEEE Computer, 36*(8), 46-52.

Penker, M., & Eriksson, H. (2000). *Business modeling with UML: Business patterns at work*. Wiley.

Perez, J. M., Ruiz, F., Piattini, M. (2006, September). MDE for BPM: A systematic review. *Proceedings of the 1st Int'l Conf. on Software and Data Technologies (ICSOFT 2006)*, Setúbal, Portugal, (pp. 118-124).

Pernici, B., & Rosati, A. M. (2007). Automatic learning of repair strategies for web services. In *Proceedings of the European Conference on Web Services (ECOWS)*, (pp. 119-128).

Pesic, M., & van der Aalst, W. M. P. (2006). A declarative approach for flexible business processes management. In J. Eder & S. Dustdar (Eds.), *Business Process Management Workshops*, Volume 4103 of *Lecture Notes in Computer Science*, (pp. 169–180). Springer.

Pesic, M., Schonenberg, M., Sidorova, N., & van der Aalst, W.M.P. (2007). Constraint-based workflow models: change made easy. In *Proceedings of the 15th Int'l Conf. on Cooperative Information Systems (CoopIS'07)*, Vilamoura, Algarve, Portugal (LNCS 4803, pp. 77-94).

Petrie, C., Margaria, T., Zaremba, M., & Lausen, H. (Eds.) (in press) (2008). *Semantic Web services challenge: Results from the first year (Semantic Web and beyond)*, to appear Nov. 2008. Springer Verlag.

Pfleeger, S. L. (1996). Integrating process and measurement. In A. Melton (Ed.), *Software measurement*. International Thomson Computer Press, (pp 53-74).

Pinter, S. S., & Golani, M. (2004). Discovering Workflow Models from Activities' Lifespans. *Computers in Industry, 53*(3), 283–296.

Power, D. J. (2007, March). *A Brief History of Decision Support Systems*. dssresources.com, http://DSSResources.COM/history/dsshistory.html, version 4.0 edition.

Project Management Institute. (2004). A *guide to the project management body of knowledge (PMBOK)*. Project Management Institute.

Puhlmann, F., Schnieders, A., Weiland, J., & Weske, M. (2005) Variability Mechanisms For Process Models. Process Family Engineering In Service-Oriented Applications (Pesoa). Bmbf-Project.

Queille, J.-P., & Sifakis, J. (1982). Specification and verification of concurrent systems in CESAR. *Proc. 5th Colloquium on International Symposium on Programming* (pp.337-351). Springer-Verlag London.

Redman, T. C. (1996). *Data quality for the information age*. Artech House.

Reichert, M. (2000). Dynamische Ablaufänderungen in Workflow Management Systemen. *Dissertation*, Universität Ulm, Fakultät für Informatik.

Reichert, M., & Bauer, T. (2007): Supporting ad-hoc changes in distributed workflow management systems. In *Proceedings of the 15th Int'l Conf. on Cooperative Information Systems (CoopIS'07)*, Vilamoura, Algarve, Portugal (LNCS 4803, pp. 150-168).

Reichert, M., & Dadam, P. (1997). A framework for dynamic changes in workflow management systems. In *Proc. 8th Int'l Workshop on Database and Expert Systems Applications*, Toulouse, (pp. 42-48).

Reichert, M., & Dadam, P. (1998). ADEPTflex - Supporting dynamic changes of workflows without losing control. *Journal of Intelligent Information Systems, 10*(2), 93-129.

Reichert, M., & Rinderle, S. (2006). On design principles for realizing adaptive service flows with BPEL. In *Proceedings EMISA'06*, Hamburg (Lecture Notes in Informatics (LNI), P-95, pp. 133-146).

Reichert, M., Bauer, T., & Dadam, P. (1999). Enterprise-wide and cross-enterprise workflow-management: challenges and research issues for adaptive workflows. In *Proceedings of the Informatik'99 Workshop on Enterprise-wide and Cross-enterprise Workflow Management*, CEUR Workshop Proceedings, *24*, 56-64.

Reichert, M., Dadam, P., & Bauer, T. (2003). Dealing with forward and backward jumps in workflow management systems. *Int'l Journal Software and Systems Modeling, 2*(1), 37-58.

Reichert, M., Hensinger, C., & Dadam, P. (1998). Supporting adaptive workflows in advanced application environments. In *Proceedings of the EDBT Workshop on Workflow Management Systems (in conjunction with EDBT'98 conference)*, Valencia, Spain, (pp. 100-109).

Reichert, M., Rinderle, S., & Dadam, P. (2003). On the common support of workflow type and instance changes under correctness constraints. In *Proc. 11th Int'l Conf. Cooperative Information Systems (CoopIS '03)*, Catania, Italy (LNCS 2888, pp. 407-425).

Reichert, M., Rinderle, S., Kreher, U., & Dadam, P. (2005). Adaptive process management with ADEPT2. In *Proceedings of the 21st Int'l Conf. on Data Engineering (ICDE'05)*, Tokyo.

Reijers, H., & van der Aalst, W. M. P. (2005). The effectiveness of workflow management systems: predictions and lessons learned. *Int'l Journal of Information Management*, *5*, 457–471.

Rinderle, S., & Reichert, M. (2005). On the controlled evolution of access rules in cooperative information systems. In *Proceedings of the 13th Int'l Conf. on Cooperative Information Systems (CoopIS'05)*, Agia Napa, Cyprus. Springer (LNCS 3760, pp. 238-255).

Rinderle, S., & Reichert, M. (2006). Data-driven process control and exception handling in process management systems. In *Proceedings of the 18th Int'l Conf. on Advanced Information Systems Engineering (CAiSE'06)*, Luxembourg (LNCS 4001, pp. 273–287).

Rinderle, S., & Reichert, M. (2007). A formal framework for adaptive access control models. *Journal on Data Semantics,* IX, (LNCS 4601) 82-112.

Rinderle, S., Jurisch, M., & Reichert, M. (2007). On deriving net change information from change logs – the DELTALAYER algorithm. In *Proceedings of the 12th Conf. on Database Systems in Business, Technology and Web (BTW'07)*, Aachen, (Lecture Notes in Informatics, LNI-103, pp. 364-381).

Rinderle, S., Reichert, M., & Dadam, P. (2003). Evaluation of correctness criteria for dynamic workflow changes. In *Proceedings of the 1st Int'l Conf. on Business Process Management (BPM '03)*, Eindhoven, Netherlands. Springer (LNCS 2678, pp. 41-57).

Rinderle, S., Reichert, M., & Dadam, P. (2004). Correctness criteria for dynamic changes in workflow systems - A survey. Data and knowledge engineering. *Special Issue , Advances in Business Process Management 50*(1), 9-34.

Rinderle, S., Reichert, M., & Dadam, P. (2004). Flexible support of team processes by adaptive workflow systems. *Distributed and Parallel Databases*, *16*(1), 91-116.

Rinderle, S., Reichert, M., & Dadam, P. (2004). Disjoint and overlapping process changes - challenges, solutions, applications. In *Proceedings of the 12th Int'l Conf. Cooperative Information Systems (CoopIS'04)*, Agia Napa, Cyprus (LNCS 3290, pp. 101-120).

Rinderle, S., Reichert, M., & Dadam, P. (2004). On dealing with structural conflicts between process type and instance changes. In *Proceedings of the 2nd Int'l Conf. Business Process Management (BPM'04)*, Potsdam, Germany (LNCS 3080, pp. 274-289).

Rinderle, S., Reichert, M., Jurisch, M., & Kreher, U. (2006). On representing, purging and utilizing change logs in process management systems. In *Proceedings of the 4th Int'l Conf. Business Process Management (BPM'06)*, Vienna, Austria (LNCS 4102, 241-256).

Rinderle, S., Weber, B., Reichert, M., & Wild, W. (2005). Integrating process learning and process evolution - a semantics based approach. In *Proceedings of the 3rd Int'l Conf. Business Process Management (BPM'05)*, Nancy, France (LNCS 3649, pp. 252-267).

Rinderle, S., Wombacher, A., & Reichert, M. (2006). Evolution of process choreographies in DYCHOR. In *Proceedings of the 14th Int'l Conf. on Cooperative Information Systems (CoopIS'06),* Montpellier, France (LNCS 4275, pp. 273-290).

Rinderle-Ma, S. & Reichert, M. (2008) Managing the lfe cycle of access rules in CEOSIS. In *Proceedings of the 12th IEEE Int'l Enterprise Computing Conference (EDOC'08)*, Munich, Germany.

Rinderle-Ma, S., Reichert, M., & Weber, B. (2008). Relaxed compliance notions in adaptive process management systems. In *Proceedings of the 27th Int'l Conference on Conceptual Modeling (ER'08)*, Barcelona, Spain. Springer, LNCS.

Rinderle-Ma, S., Reichert, M., & Weber, B. (2008). On the formal semantics of change patterns in process-aware information systems. In *Proceedings of the 27th Int'l Conference on Conceptual Modeling (ER'08)*, Barcelona, Spain. Springer, LNCS.

Rolón, E., García, F., & Ruiz, F. (2006). Evaluation measures for business process models. In *21st Annual ACM Symposium on Applied Computing (SAC'06)*, Dijon (France), (pp. 1567-1568).

Rolón, E., García, F., Ruiz, F., & Piattini, M. (2007, April 23-26). An exploratory experiment to validate measures for business process models. *First IEEE International Conference on Research Challenges in Information Science (RCIS'07)*. Ouarzazate, Marruecos: IEEE.

Rolón, E., Garcia, F., Ruiz, F., Piattini, M., Vissagio, A., & Canfora, G. (2008, May 4-7). Evaluation of BPMN models quality: A family of experiments. *3rd International Conference on Evaluation of Novel Approaches to Software Engineering (ENASE'08)*. Funchal, Madeira.

Rolón, E., Ruiz, F., García, F., & Piattini, M. (2006). Applying software metrics to evaluate business process models. *CLEI-Electronic Journal, 9*(1, Paper 5).

Roman, D., & Kifer, M. (2007). Reasoning about the behaviour of semantic web services with concurrent transaction logic. In *VLDB*, (pp. 627–638).

Roman, D., Scicluna, J., & Nitzsche, J. (2007). *D14v1.0. Ontology-based choreography*. WSMO Final Draft, 15 February.

Rosemann, M., & van der Aalst, W. M. P. (2007). A configurable reference modelling language. *Information Systems, 32*(1), 1-23.

RosettaNet (1998). *RosettaNet*. Retrieved April 15, 2008. Web site: http://www.rosettanet.org/cms/sites/RosettaNet/

Rozinat, A., & Aalst, W.M.P. van der (2008). Conformance checking of processes based on monitoring real behavior. *Information Systems, 33*(1), 64-95.

Rozinat, A., & van der Aalst, W. M. P. (2006). Decision Mining in ProM. In S. Dustdar, J. L. Fiadeiro, & A. P. Sheth (Eds.), *Business Process Management*, volume 4102 of *Lecture Notes in Computer Science*, (pp. 420–425). Springer, 2006. ISBN 3-540-38901-6.

Rozinat, A., de Jong, I. S. M., Günther, C. W., & van der Aalst, W. M. P. (2007). *Process Mining of Test Processes: A Case Study*. BETA Working Paper Series, WP 220, Eindhoven University of Technology, Eindhoven.

Rozinat, A., Mans, R. S., & Aalst, W.M.P. van der (2006, October). Mining CPN models: Discovering process models with data from event logs. In *Proceedings of the Seventh Workshop on the Practical Use of Coloured Petri Nets and CPN Tools* (CPN 2006), (DAIMI, 579, pp. 57-76), Aarhus, Denmark.

Rozinat, A., Wynn, M., van der Aalst, W. M. P., ter Hofstede, A. H. M., & Fidge, C. (2008). Workflow Simulation for Operational Decision Support using YAWL and ProM. In *Proceedings of the 6th International Conference on Business Process Management*. Milan, Italy: Springer-Verlag.

RUP - Rational Unified Process (2008). Retrieved August, 2008, from http://www-306.ibm.com/software/awdtools/rup/

Russell, N. (2007). *Foundations of process-aware information systems*. Doctoral Thesis, Queensland University of Technology, Brisbane, Australia.

Russell, N., & van der Aalst, W. M. P. (2007). *Evaluation of the BPEL4People and WS-HumanTask Extensions to WS-BPEL 2.0 using the Workflow Resource Patterns*. BPM Center Report BPM-07-10, http://www.bpmcenter.org

Russell, N., & van der Aalst, W. M. P. (2008). Work distribution and resource management in BPEL4People: Capabilities and opportunities. *20th International Conference CAiSE 2008, Proceedings*, (LNCS, 5074, pp. 94-108).

Russell, N., ter Hofstede, A. H. M., Edmond, D., & van der Aalst, van der, W. M. P. (2005). Workflow data patterns: Identification, representation and tool support. In *Proceedings of the 24th International Conference on Conceptual Modeling* (pp. 353-368). Springer-Verlag.

Russell, N., van der Aalst, W. M. P., & ter Hofstede, A. H. M. (2006). Workflow exception patterns. In *Proceedings of the 18th International Conference on Advanced Information Systems Engineering* (pp. 288-302). Springer-Verlag.

Russell, N., van der Aalst, W. M. P., ter Hofstede, A. H. M., & Edmond, D. (2005). Workflow resource patterns: Identification, representation and tool support. In O. Pastor & J. Falcão e Cunha, (Eds.), *17th International Conference CAiSE 2005, Proceedings,* (LNCS, 3520, pp. 216-232). Springer-Verlag.

Russell, N., van der Aalst, W. M. P., ter Hofstede, A. H. M., & Wohed, P. (2006). On the suitability of UML 2.0 Activity diagrams for business process modeling. *APCCM (Asia-Pacific Conference on Conceptual Modeling),* (pp. 95-104).

Russell, N., ter Hofstede, A. H. M., van der Aalst, W. M. P., & Mulyar, N. (2006). *Workflow control-flow patterns: A revised view.* (Technical Report Report BPM-06-22). BPM Center, BPMcenter.org.

Saastamoinen, H. (1995). On the handling of exceptions in information systems. Unpublished doctoral thesis, University of Jyväskylä.

Sadiq, S. W. (2000). On capturing exceptions in workflow process models. In *Proceedings of the 4th International Conference on Business Information Systems,* Poznan, Poland.

Sadiq, S. W., Orlowska, M. E., & Sadiq, W. (2005). Specification and validation of process constraints for flexible workflows. *Inf. Syst., 30*(5), 349–378.

Sadiq, S., Governatori, G., & Naimiri, K. (2007). *Modelling of control objectives for business process compliance.* See DBLP:conf/bpm/2007, (pp. 149–164).

Sadiq, S., Sadiq, W., Orlowska, M. (2001). Pockets of flexibility in workflow specifications. In *Proceedings of the 20th Int'l Conference on Conceptual Modeling (ER'01),* Yokohama, Japan, *(LNCS 2224, pp.* 513-526).

Sadiq, W. and Orlowska, M.E. (2000). Analysing process models using graph reduction techniques. *Information Systems 25*(2), pp. 117–134

Sarbanes-Oxley Act of 2002, Public Law 107-204, 107th Congress, Senate and House of Representatives of the United States of America in Congress, 2002. http://frwebgate.access.gpo.gov/cgi-bin/getdoc.cgi?dbname=107_cong_public_laws&docid=f:publ204.107

Sarbanes-Oxley Act. Sarbanes-Oxley Act of 2002. http://www.sarbanes-oxley-forum.com/.

Sartor, G. (2005). *Legal reasoning.* Dordrecht, THe Netherlands: Springer.

Scheer, A. W. (2000). *ARIS - Business process modelling.* Berlin: Springer

Schimm, G. (2004). Mining Exact Models of Concurrent Workflows. *Computers in Industry, 53*(3), 265–281. ISSN 0166-3615. http://dx.doi.org/10.1016/j.compind.2003.10.003.

Schmidt, K. (1997). Of maps and scripts - The status of formal constructs in cooperative work. In *GROUP '97,* Phoenix, USA, (pp. 138-147).

Schnieders, A., & Puhlmann, F. (2006) Variability Mechanisms In E-Business Process Families. *Proceedings Of The 9th International Conference On Business Information Systems (Bis'06),* (pp. 583-601).

Schobbens, P.-Y., Heymans, P., Trigaux, J.-C., & Bontemps, Y. (2006) Feature Diagrams: A Survey And A Formal Semantics. *14th International Conference On Requirements Engineering.* Minneapolis, Minnesota, Usa.

Schonenberg, H., Mans, R., Russell, N., Mulyar, N., & van der Aalst, W. (2008). Process flexibility: A survey of contemporary approaches. In *Proceedings CIAO!/EOMAS Workshop.* (pp. 16-30).

Schonenberg, H., Weber, B., van Dongen, B., & van der Aalst, W.M.P. (2008). Supporting flexible processes by recommendations based on history. In *Proceedings of the 6th Int'l Conf. on Business Process Management (BPM'08).* Milan, Italy (LNCS 5240, pp. 51-66).

Schreder, B., Bhiri, S., Cekov, L., Konstantinov, M., & Evenson, M. (2008). *Use-case based component integration.* D7.4 of EU-Project SUPER.

Seidewitz, E. (2003) What models mean. *IEEE Software, 20*(5), 26-31

Semantic Annotations for WSDL and XML Schema, W3C Recommendation, 28 August 2007http://www.w3.org/TR/sawsdl/

Semantic Execution Environment http://www.oasis-open.org/committees/tc_home.php?wg_abbrev=semantic-ex

Service Component Architecture Website (2008). Retrieved October 2008, from http://www-128.ibm.com/developerworks/library/specification/ws-sca/

Shan, M. (1999). FlowJet: Internet-based e-Service Process Management. In *Proceedings of the Int. Process Techn. Workshop*, Villard de Lans, France.

Shan, M-C., Davis, J., Du, W., & Huang, Y. (1997). *HP Workflow research: Past, present, and future.* (Technical Report HPL-97-105). HP Labs.

Shankaranarayan, G., Wang, R. Y., & Ziad, M. (2000). Modeling the manufacture of an information product with IP-MAP. In *Proceedings of the 6th International Conference on Information Quality.*

Shearer, C. (2000). The CRISP-DM model: the new blueprint for data mining. *Journal of Data Warehousing, 5*, 13-22.

Sheth, A. P., Georgakopoulos, D., Joosten, S. M., Rusinkiewicz, M., Scacchi, W., Wileden, J., & Wolf, A. L. (1996). *ACM SIGMOD Record, 25*(4), 55-67.

Singh, I., Brydon, S., Murray, G., Ramachandran, V., Violleau, T., & Stearns, B. (2004). *Designing Web services with the J2EE 1.4 Platform: JAX-RPC, SOAP, and XML technologies.* Addison-Wesley , ISBN: 0-321-20521-9.

Smith, H., & Fingar, P. (2003). *Business process management: The third wave.* Mehan-Kiffer Press.

Snodgrass, R. T. (Ed.) (1995). *The TSQL2 Temporal Query Language.* Boston: Kluwer Academic Publisher.

Snodgrass, R. T., & Ahn, I. (1985). A taxonomy of time in databases. *SIGMOD Conference,* (pp. 236-246).

Song, M., & van der Aalst, W. M. P. (2007). *Towards Comprehensive Support for Organizational Mining.* BETA Working Paper Series, WP 211, Eindhoven University of Technology, Eindhoven.

Song, M., Günther, C., Aalst, W. M. P. van der (2008, September). Trace clustering in process mining. In *Proceedings of the 4th Workshop on Business Process Intelligence (BPI 08)*, Milan, Italy.

Steffen, B., & Narayan, P., (2007). Full Life-Cycle Support for End-to-End Processes. *IEEE Computer, Vol. 40(11), (pp. 57-63).* IEEE Press.

Steffen, B., Margaria, T., Nagel, R., Jörges, S., & Kubczak, C. (2006, October). Model-Driven Development with the jABC. *Proc. HVC'06, IBM Haifa Verification Conference,* Haifa (Israel), LNCS 4383, Springer.

Steiner, A. (1999). TimeDB, Timeconsult. *http://www.timeconsult.com.* accessed April 4th, 2008

Stephens, S. (2001) The Supply Chain Council And The Scor Reference Model. *Supply Chain Management - An International Journal,* 1, 9-13.

Strong, D. M., & Miller, S. M. (1995). Exceptions and exception handling in computerized information systems. *ACM Transactions on Information Systems, 13*(2).

Strosnider, J. K., Nandi, P., Kumaran, S., Ghosh, S., & Arsanjani, A. (2008). Model-driven synthesis of SOA solutions. *IBM Systems Journal, 47*(3), 415-432.

Su, J., Bultan, T., Fu, X., & Zhao, X. (2008). Towards a theory of Web service choreographies. In *Proc. 2007 Workshop on Web Services and Formal Methods* (pp. 1-16). Berlin / Heidelberg: Springer.

Suchman, L. A. (1983). Office procedure as practical action: Models of work and system design. *ACM TOIS, 1*(4), 320-328.

Suchman, L. A. (1987). *Plans and situated actions.* MIT Press.

Tang, Z., & MacLennan, J. (2005). *Data mining with SQL Server 2005*. John Wiley & Sons.

Taylor, F. W. (1911). *The principles of scientific management*. New York: Harper Bros..

The Business Process Modeling Notation, http://www.bpmn.org, accessed April 4th, 2008.

The OpenSymphony project. (2006), Retrievel November 11, 2006, from Http://www.opensymphony.com

Thom, L., Reichert, M., Chiao, C., Iochpe, C., & Hess, G. (2008). Inventing less, reusing more and adding intelligence to business process modeling. In *Proceedings of the 19th Int'l Conference on Database and Expert Systems Applications (DEXA '08)*, Turin, Italy (LNCS 5181, pp. 837-850).

Tilab (2008). *Java agent development framework*. http://jade.tilab.com/

Tjaden, G. S. (1999). *Business process structural analysis*. Georgia Tech Center for Enterprise Systems. http://www.ces.gatech.edu/research.htm

UN/CEFACT (1996). *United Nations Centre for Trade Facilitation and Electronic Business*. Retrieved April 15, 2008. Web site: http://www.unece.org/cefact/

University of Eindhoven (2008). *Workflow patterns*. Retrieved 2008-04-01, from http://www.workflowpatterns.com/

van Bon, J., Pieper, M., van der Veen, A. (2005). *Foundations of IT service management based on ITIL*. Van Haren Publishing.

van der Aalst, W.M.P. (1996). Three good reasons for using a Petri-net-based workflow management system. In S. Navathe & T. Wakayama (Eds.), *Proceedings of the International Working Conference on Information and Process Integration in Enterprises* (pp. 179-201), Cambridge, MA: Kluwer Academic Publisher.

van der Aalst, W. M. P. (1997). Verification of workflow nets. In *Proceedings of the 18th International Conference on Application and Theory of Petri Nets* (pp. 407-426). Springer.

van der Aalst, W. M. P. (2004). Business process management demystified: A tutorial on models, systems and standards for workflow management. In *Lectures on Concurrency and Petri Nets* (pp. 1-65). Berlin / Heidelberg: Springer.

van der Aalst, W., & Basten, T. (2002). Inheritance of workflows: An approach to tackling problems related to change. *Theoretical Computer Science, 270*(1), 125-203.

van der Aalst, W., & Berens, P. (2001). Beyond workflow management: Product-driven case handling. In *GROUP 2001, Boulder, USA*.

van der Aalst, W. M. P. , & de Medeiros, A. K. A. (2005). Process mining and security: Detecting anomalous process executions and checking process conformance. *Electronic Notes in Theoretical Computer Science, 121*, 3–21.

van der Aalst, W. M. P., & Pesic, M. (2006). DecSerFlow: Towards a truly declarative service Flow Language. In *Proc. 2007 Workshop on Web Services and Formal Methods* (pp. 1-23). Berlin / Heidelberg: Springer.

van der Aalst, W. M. P., & ter Hofstede, A. H. M. (2002). Workflow patterns: On the expressive power of (Petri-net-based) workflow languages (invited talk). In *Proceedings of the 4th Workshop on the Practical Use of Coloured Petri Nets and CPN Tools* (pp. 1-20). Denmark: University of Aarhus.

van der Aalst, W. M. P., & ter Hofstede, A. H. M. (2005). YAWL: Yet another workflow language. *Information Systems, 30*(4), 245-275.

van der Aalst, W. M. P., & van Hee, K. (2004). *Workflow management models, methods, and systems*. Boston: MIT Press.

van der Aalst, W. M. P., & van Hee, K. M. (2002). *Workflow management: models, methods, and systems*. MIT Press.

van der Aalst, W. M. P. , Beer, H. T. de, & Dongen, B. F. van. (2005). Process mining and verification of properties: An approach based on temporal logic. In R. Meersman, Z. Tari, M.-S. Hacid, J. Mylopoulos, B. Pernici, Ö. Babaoglu, H.-A. Jacobsen, J. P. Loyall, M. Kifer, & S. Spaccapietra (Eds.), *OTM Conferences (1)*, (LNCS, 3760, pp. 130–147). Springer, ISBN 3-540-29736-7.

van der Aalst, W.M.P., Desel, J., & Oberweis, A. (Eds.). (2000). *Business process management: Models, techniques, and empirical studies,* (LNCS, 1806). Springer-Verlag.

van der Aalst, W. M. P. , Dongen, B. F. van, Herbst, J., Maruster, L., Schimm, G., & Weijters, A. J. M. M. (2003). Workflow mining: A survey of issues and approaches. *Data and Knowledge Engineering, 47*(2), 237-267.

van Der Aalst, W. M. P., Dreiling, A., Gottschalk, F., Rosemann, M. & Jansen-Vullers, M. H. (2006) Configurable process models as a basis for reference modeling. *Bpm 2005 Workshops (Workshop On Business Process Reference Models),* (LNCS, 3812, pp. 512-518).

van der Aalst, W. M. P., Reijers, H. A., & Medeiros, A. (2007). Business process mining: An industrial application. *Information Systems, 32*(1), 713-732.

van der Aalst, W. M. P. , Reijers, H. A., & Song, M. (2005). Discovering social networks from event logs. *Computer Supported Cooperative Work, 14*(6), 549-593.

van der Aalst, W. M. P., Rosemann, M., & Dumas, M. (2007). Deadline-based escalation in process-aware information systems. *Decision Support Systems 43*, 492-511.

van der Aalst, W. M. P., ter Hofstede, A. H. M., Kiepuszewski, B., & Barros, A. P. (2003). Workflow patterns. *Distributed and Parallel Databases, 14*(1), 5-51.

van der Aalst, W. M. P., van Dongen, B. F., Günther, C. W., Mans, R. S., Alves de Medeiros, A. K., Rozinat, A., Rubin, V., Song, M., Verbeek, H. M. W., & Weijters, A. J. M. M. (2007). ProM 4.0: Comprehensive Support for Real Process Analysis. In *Proceedings of the 28th International Conference on Applications and Theory of Petri Nets and Other Models of Concurrency* (pp. 484-494). Springer-Verlag.

van der Aalst, W. M. P., Weijters, A. J. M. M., & Maruster, L. (2004). Workflow mining: Discovering process models from event logs. *IEEE Transactions on Knowledge and Data Engineering, 16*(9), 1128–1142.

van der, Aalst, W. M. P. Weijters, A. J. M. M. (2004). Process mining: A research agenda. *Computers in Industry, 53*(3), 231-244.

van der Aalst, W. M. P., Weske, M., & Grünbauer, D. (2005). Case handling: A new paradigm for business process support. *Data and Knowledge Engineering, 53*(2), 129-162.

van Dongen, B. F. (2007). *Process Mining and Verification.* PhD thesis, Eindhoven University of Technology, Eindhoven.

van Dongen, B. F., & van der Aalst, W. M. P. (2005_, A. K. A.). Multi-phase Process mining: Aggregating Instance Graphs into EPCs and Petri Nets. In *Proceedings of the Second International Workshop on Applications of Petri Nets to Coordination, Workflow and Business Process Management (PNCWB).*

van Dongen, B. F., Mendling, J., & van der Aalst W. M. P. (2006). Structural Patterns for Soundness of Business Process Models. In *EDOC '06: Proceedings of the 10th IEEE International Enterprise Distributed Object Computing Conference (EDOC'06)*, (pp. 116–128), Washington, DC, USA. IEEE Computer Society.

van Lessen, T. (2006). *Konzipierung und Entwicklung eines Repository für Geschäftsprozesse*, Diplomarbeit, Universität Stuttgart.

van Lessen, T., Nitzsche, J., Dimitrov, M., Konstantinov, M., Karastoyanova, D., Cekov, L., & Leymann, F. (2007, September). An Execution Engine for Semantic Business Process. In *Proceedings of the 2nd International Workshop on Business Oriented Aspects concerning Semantics and Methodologies in Service-oriented Computing (SeMSoC), in conjunction with ICSOC*. Vienna, Austria.

van der Aalst, W. (1998). The application of Petri nets to workflow management. *The Journal of Circuits, Systems and Computers, 8*(1), 21-66.

van der Aalst, W. M. P., van Dongen, B. F., Herbst, J., Maruster, L., Schimm, G., & Weijters, A. J. M. M. (2003). Workflow mining: A survey of issues and approaches. *Data Knowl. Eng., 47*(2), 237–267.

van der Aalst, W., & van Hee, K. (2002). *Workflow management: Models, methods, and systems.* Cooperative Information Systems. The MIT Press.

van der Aalst, W., Desel, J., & Kindler, E. (2002, November). On the semantics of EPCs: A vicious circle. In M. Nüttgens & F. J. Rump (Eds.), *EPK 2002, Geschäftsprozessmanagement mit Ereignisgesteuerten Prozessketten,* (pp. 71–79).

Van Dongen, B., de Medeiros A., Verbeek, H., Weijters, A., & van der Aalst, W. M. P. (2005). The ProM framework: A new era in process mining tool support. In *Proceedings 26th Int'l Conf. on the Applications and Theory of Petri Nets (ICATPN'05),* Miami, FL (LNCS 3536, pp. 444-454).

Vanderfeesten, I., Cardoso, J., Mendling, J., Reijers, H. A., & van der Aalst, W. M. P. (2007). Quality metrics for business process models. In *BPM and workflow handbook 2007.*

Vanderfeesten, I., Reijers, H. A., & van der Aalst, W. M. P. (2008*). Evaluating workflow process designs using cohesion and coupling metrics.* Computer in Industry.

Vanderfeesten, I., Reijers, H. A., Mendling, J., van der Aalst, W. M. P., & Cardoso, J. (2008). On a quest for good process models: The cross conectivity metric. *International Conference on Advanced Information Systems Engineering.*

Vanhatalo, J., Völzer, H., and Leymann, F. (2007): *Faster and more focused control-flow analysis for business process models through SESE decomposition,* Service-Oriented Computing (ICSOC 2007), (Lecture Notes in Computer Science, 4749). Springer.

Vanhatalo, J., Völzer, H., & Leymann, F. (2007). Faster and more focused control-flow analysis for business process models though SESE decomposition. In *5th International Conference on Service-Oriented Computing (ICSOC),* (pp. 43–55).

Verma, K. (2006, August). *Configuration and adaptation of Semantic Web processes.*Unpublished doctoral thesis, Department of Computer Science, The University of Georgia.

Verma, K., Doshi, P., Gomadam, K., Miller, J. A., & Sheth, A. P. (2006). Optimal adaptation in Web processes with coordination constraints. In *Proceedings of the Fourth IEEE International Conference on Web Services,* Chicago, IL.

Vernadat, F. (1996). *Enterprise modeling and integration: Principles and applications.* London: Chapman & Hall.

Vinoski, S. (2008). *Convenience Over Correctness - Internet Computing.* IEEE Volume 12(4), (pp 89-92).

Völter, M. & Stahl, T. (2006). *Model-Driven Software Development: Technology, Engineering, Management.* Wiley.

Vonk, J., & Grefen, P. (2003). Cross-organizational transaction support for e-services in virtual enterprises. *Distributed and Parallel Databases, 14*(2), 137-172.

Vonk, J., Wang, T., & Grefen, P. (2007). A dual view to facilitate transactional QoS. In *Proceedings of the 16th IEEE International Workshops on Enabling Technologies: Infrastructure for Collaborative Enterprises* (pp. 381-382). Paris, France.

Vonk, J., Wang, T., van Aarle, J., Brugmans, S., & Grefen, P. (2008). *An analysis of contractual and transactual aspects of a cardiothoracic surgery process.* Beta Technical Report, Eindhoven University of Technology.

W3C (2008). *Web services description language (WSDL) Version 2.0 Part 0: Primer.* Retrieved 2008-04-01, from http://www.w3.org/TR/wsdl20-primer/

W3C. (2001). Web Services Description Language 1.1. http://www.w3.org/TR/wsdl

W3C. (2001). XML Schema Part 1: Structures http://www.w3.org/TR/xmlschema-1/ and Part 2: Datatypes http://www.w3.org/TR/xmlschema-2/

Wächter, H., & Reuter, A. (1992): The ConTract Model. In Ahmed K. Elmagarmid (Eds.), *Database transaction models for advanced applications* (p. 219-263). San Francisco: Morgan Kaufmann

Wahler, K. & Küster, J. M. (2008). Predicting Coupling of object-centric business process implementations. In *Proc. 6th Int. Conf. on Business Process Management* (pp. 148-163). Berlin / Heidelberg: Springer.

Wainer, J., Kim, K., & Ellis, C. A. (2005). A workflow mining method through model rewriting. *Lecture Notes in Computer Science, 3706,* 184-191.

Wand, Y., & Wang, R. Y. (1996). Anchoring data quality dimensions in ontological foundations. *Communication of the ACM, 39*(11), 86-95.

Wang, R. Y., & Strong, D. M (1996). Beyond accuracy: What data quality means to data consumers. *Journal of Management Information Systems, 12*(4), 5-34.

Wang, T., Vonk, J., & Grefen, P. (2006). *Building a business transaction framework based on abstract transaction constructs.* Beta Technical Report WP187, Eindhoven University of Technology.

Wang, T., Vonk, J., & Grefen, P. (2007). TxQoS: A contractual approach for transaction management. In *Proceedings of the 11th IEEE International EDOC Enterprise Computing Conference* (pp. 327-338). Annapolis, MD.

Web Service Modeling Ontology (WSMO), WSMO Final Draft 2, October 2006http://www.wsmo.org/TR/d2/v1.3/#goals

Web Service Modelling eXecution environment. http://www.wsmx.org/

Web Services Description Language (WSDL) 1.1, W3C Note 15 March 2001http://www.w3.org/TR/wsdl

Web Services Reliable Messaging (WS-ReliableMessaging) (2007). *OASIS Web Services Reliable Messaging (WSRM) TC.*http://www.oasis-open.org/committees/tc_home.php?wg_abbrev=wsrm

Weber, B. & Reichert, M. (2008). Refactoring process models in large process repositories. In *Proceedings of the 20th Int'l Conf. on Advanced Information Systems Engineering (CAiSE'08)*, Montpellier, France (LNCS 5074, pp. 124-139).

Weber, B., Reichert, M. Wild, W., & Rinderle, S. (2005). Balancing flexibility and security in adaptive process management systems. In *Proceedings of the 13th Int'l Conf. on Cooperative Information Systems (CoopIS'05)*, Agia Napa, Cyprus (LNCS 3760, pp. 59-76).

Weber, B., Reichert, M., & Rinderle-Ma, S. (2008). Change patterns and change support features - Enhancing flexibility in process-aware information systems. *Data and Knowledge Engineering, 66*(3), 438-466.

Weber, B., Reichert, M., & Wild, W. (2006) Case-base maintenance for CCBR-based process evolution. In Proceedings of the 8th European Conf. on Case-Based Reasoning (ECCBR'06), Ölüdeniz/Fethiye, Turkey (LNCS 4106, pp. 106-120.

Weber, B., Reichert, M., Rinderle, S., & Wild, W. (2005). Towards a framework for the agile mining of business processes. In *Proceedings of the BPM'05 Workshops*, Nancy, France (LNCS 3812, pp. 191-202).

Weber, B., Reichert, M., Wild, W., & Rinderle-Ma, S. (2008). Providing integrated life cycle support in process-aware information systems. *Int'l Journal of Cooperative Information Systems (IJCIS)*, World Scientific Publ. (to appear).

Weber, B., Rinderle, S., & Reichert, M. (2007). Change patterns and change support features in process-aware information systems. In *Proceedings of the 19th Int'l Conf. on Advanced Information Systems Engineering (CAiSE'07)*, Trondheim, Norway (LNCS 4495, pp. 574-588).

Weber, B., Rinderle, S., Wild, W., & Reichert, M. (2005) CCBR–driven business process evolution. In Proceedings of the 6th Int'l Conf. on Case-Based Reasoning (ICCBR'05), Chicago (LNCS 3620, pp. 610-624).

Weber, B., Wild, W., & Breu, B. (2004). CBRFlow. enabling adaptive workflow management through conversational case-based reasoning. In *Proceedings of the ECCBR'04 conference.* Madrid, Spain (LNCS 3155, pp. 434-448).

Weber, I., Hoffmann, J., Mendling, J., & Nitzsche, J. (2007, September). Towards a methodology for semantic business process modeling and configuration. In *Proceedings of the 2nd International Workshop on Business Oriented Aspects concerning Semantics and Methodologies in Service-oriented Computing.*

Weber, I., Markovic, I., & Drumm, C. (2007). A Conceptual framework for composition in business process management. In *Proceedings of the 10th International Conference on Business Information Systems.*

Weerawarana S., Curbera, F., Leymann, F., Storey, T., & Ferguson D. F. (2005). *Web services platform architecture: SOAP, WSDL, WS-Policy, WS-Addressing, WS-BPEL, WS-Reliable Messaging, and More.* Upper Saddle River, NJ: Prentice Hall PTR.

Weerawarana, S., Curbera, F., & Leymann, F. (2005). *Web services platform architecture: Soap, WSDL, WS-Policy, WS-Addressing, WS-BPEL WS-Reliable Messaging and More.* Prentice Hall International.

Weijters, A. J. M. M., van der Aalst, W. M. P., van Dongen, B., Günther, C., Mans, R., Alves de Medeiros, A. K., Rozinat, A., Song, M., & Verbeek, E. (2007). Process mining with ProM. In M. Dastani, & E. de Jong(Eds.), *Proceedings of the 19th Belgium-Netherlands Conference on Artificial Intelligence (BNAIC).*

Wen, L., van der Aalst, W. M. P., Wang, J., & Sun, J. (2007). Mining process models with non-free-choice constructs. *Data Mining Knowledge Discovery, 15*(2), 145–180.

Weske, M. (2000). *Workflow management systems: Formal foundation, conceptual design, implementation aspects.* University of Münster, Germany, Habilitation Thesis.

Weske, M. (2001). Formal foundation and conceptual design of dynamic adaptations in a workflow management system. In *International Conference on System Sciences,* 2579-2588.

Weske, M. (2007). *Business process management: Concepts, languages, architectures.* Berlin, Heidelberg, Germany: Springer-Verlag

Wetzstein, B., Ma, Z., & Leymann, F. (2008, May). Towards measuring key performance indicators of semantic business processes. In *Proceedings of 11th International Conference on Business Information Systems (BIS 2008),* Innsbruck, Austria.

WFMC (1999). *Workflow Management Coalition - Terminology & Glossary* TC00-1011.

WfMC. (2005). XML Process Definition Language (XPDL). http://www.wfmc.org/standards/XPDL.htm

Wikipedia (2008). *Business process management.* Retrieved 2008-04-01, from http://en.wikipedia.org/wiki/Business_Process_Management.

Worah, D., & Sheth, A. P. (1997). Transactions in Transactional Workflows. In S. Jajodia & K. Larry (Eds.), *Advanced transaction models and architectures.* Kluwer Academic Publishers.

Workflow Management Coalition (1995). *Reference model - The workflow reference model.* Technical Report WFMC-TC-1003, 19-Jan-95, 1.1, http://www.wfmc.org/standards/docs/tc003v11.pdf

Workflow Management Coalition (1999). *Terminology and glossary.* Technical Report Document Number WFMC-TC-1011, Issue 3.0. Available at http://www.wfmc.org/standards/ docs/TC-1011_term_glossary_v3.pdf (Latest access: 08 September 2008)

Workflow Management Coalition (2002). *Workflow standard: Workflow process definition interface – XML process definition language (XPDL) WFMCTC-1025).* (Tech. Rep.). Lighthouse Point, FL: Workflow Management Coalition.

Workflow Management Coalition (2005). *Process Definition Interface - XML Process Definition Language Version 2.00.* WFMC-TC-1025, (Tech. Rep.). Lighthouse Point, FL: Workflow Management Coalition. Available at http://www.wfmc.org/standards/docs/TC-1025_xpdl_2_2005-10-03.pdf

Workflow Management Coalition: Terminology & glossary. (1999, February). (Technical Report WFMC-TC-1011). The Workflow Management Coalition (WfMC).

WS-Diamond Deliverable 3.1. *Specification of execution mechanisms and composition strategies for self-healing Web services.* Technical report, WS-DIAMOND European project, 2006. Available on line at: http://wsdiamond.di.unito.it/

WS-Diamond Deliverable 4.1.*Characterization of Diagnosis and Repair for Web Services.* Technical report, WS-DIAMOND European project, 2006. Available on line at: http://wsdiamond.di.unito.it/

WS-Diamond Deliverable 4.4. *Specification of repair/reconfiguration algorithms for Web Services.* Technical report, WS-DIAMOND European project, 2006. Available on line at: http://wsdiamond.di.unito.it/

WS-Diamond Deliverable 5.1. *Characterization of diagnosability and repairability for self-healing Web Services. Technical report,* WS-DIAMOND European project, 2006. Available on line at: http://wsdiamond.di.unito.it/

Wutke, D. (2006). *Erweiterung einer Workflow-Engine zur Unterstützung von parametrisierten Web Service Flows*, Diplomarbeit, Universität Stuttgart.

Wynn, M. T., Edmond, D., van der Aalst, W. M. P., & ter Hofstede, A. H. M. (2005). Achieving a general, formal and decidable approach to the OR-join in workflow using reset nets. In *Proceedings of the 26th International conference on Application and Theory of Petri nets and Other Models of Concurrency* (pp. 423-443). Springer-Verlag.

Wynn, M. T., Verbeek, H., van der Aalst, W. M., ter Hofstede, A. H., & Edmond, D. (2007). Business process verification - finally a reality! *Business Process Management Journal.*

Zacarias, M., Marques, A., Pinto, H., Tribolet, J. (2005, July). Enhancing collaboration services with business context models. *International Workshop on Cooperative Systems and Context, 5th International and Interdisciplinary Conference on Modeling and Using Context.*

Zacarias, M., Pinto, H., & Tribolet, J. (2006, October). A context-based approach to discover multitasking behavior at work. In *Proceeding of the 5th International Workshop on Task Models and Diagrams for User Interface Design.*

Zachman, J. A. (1987). A framework for information systems architecture. *IBM Systems Journal, 26*(3), 276-292.

zur Muehlen, M. (1999). Resource modeling in workflow applications. In *Proceedings of the Workflow Management Conference,* (Münster, 1999), (pp. 137-153). University of Münster, .

zur Muehlen, M., & Rosemann, M. (2005). Integrating risks in business process models. In *Proceedings of 16th Australasian Conference on Information Systems.*

zur Muehlen, M., Indulska, M., & Kemp, G. (2007). Business process and business rule modeling languages for compliance management: A representational analysis. In *Proc ER 2007: Tutorials, Poster, Panels, and Industrial Contribution.*

About the Contributors

Michael Adams is a lecturer and senior researcher within the BPM group at the Queensland University of Technology in Brisbane, Australia, and was awarded his PhD in 2007. His research interests focus on dynamic and adaptable workflows. He is currently directly responsible for the ongoing development and maintenance of the YAWL environment, and is the primary developer of YAWL Release 2.0.

Ana Karla Alves de Medeiros is a research fellow of Information Systems at the Department of Industrial Engineering at the Eindhoven University of Technology (TU/e). Her research interests include process mining, business process management, business intelligence, data mining, genetic algorithms, semantic web and web services, and Petri nets. She has published several articles on these topics.

Pedro Antunes is Associate Professor at the University of Lisbon's Department of Informatics. His main research interests are the design, development and assessment of collaborative technologies; complex socio-technical interactions; group decision and negotiation; and the technology support to awareness, safety, flexibility and resilience. He received his PhD in electrical and computer engineering from the Technical University of Lisbon.

Kamal Bhattacharya is a Research Staff Member and Manager leading the business-driven IT management group in the Services Research division at IBM Research. He received his PhD degree in Theoretical Physics from the Goettingen University, Germany. His research interest include IT management, cloud computing and business transformation.

Christoph Bussler (http://www.real-programmer.com) is Senior Staff Software Engineer at Merced Systems, Inc. His interests include workflow and process management, Business-to-Business and Enterprise Application Integration, as well as Semantic Computing. He is author of several books and journal articles on integration, workflow management and semantics. He is active in the professional community as keynote speaker, conference and workshop organizer as well as program committee member. Christoph has a PhD in Computer Science from the University of Erlangen, Germany, and worked in several organizations, including BEA Systems, Cisco Systems, Digital Enterprise Research Institute, Oracle Corporation, The Boeing Company and Digital Equipment Corporation.

Cinzia Cappiello received her Masters degree in Computing Engineering and a PhD in Information Engineering, both from Politecnico di Milano. Her PhD thesis focuses on data quality issues in multichannel services. Since 2005, she is research assistant at Politecnico di Milano and currently, her research interests regard data quality and service engineering. Her research contributions have been published in international journals and conferences.

Malu Castellanos is a senior researcher in the Intelligent Information Management Laboratory at Hewlett-Packard Laboratories in Palo Alto, CA, USA. Since 1998 she has been applying data mining, text mining and other technologies to develop intelligent solutions to different kinds of business related problems. She has also worked on integrating novel techniques in the development of a platform for business process intelligence and on design automation for different stages in the lifecycle of a data warehouse. She received a B.S. in Computer Engineering at the National University of Mexico and a PhD in Computer Science from the Polytechnic University of Catalunya where she spent 6 years as a professor at the Information Systems Department of the Informatics School. She has more than 40 publications in international conferences, journals and book chapters and has participated in the organization and program committees of prestigious conference including VLDB, SIGMOD, ICDE, ICWS, ICSOC and BPM. She has moderated panels and organized workshops related to business intelligence and business process intelligence at a number of conferences.

Carlo Combi received the Laurea degree in E.E. from Politecnico di Milano in 1987 and the PhD in 1993, respectively. He is now full professor of Computer Science and head of the Computer Science Department at the University of Verona, Italy. Additional information is available at the web site http://profs.sci.univr.it/~combi. Carlo Combi and Giuseppe Pozzi are co-authors of the paper "Architectures for a temporal workflow management system", which has been accepted for presentation and published in the proceedings of the ACM SAC Conference, Cyprus, 2004. The paper has been included into the monthly rankings of the "Top 10 Downloads from the ACM Digital Library" for 36 months from January 2005 to December 2007 (http://home.dei.polimi.it/pozzi/listpub.html#TopDownload).

Peter Dadam has been full professor at the University of Ulm, Germany and director of the Institute of Databases and Information Systems since 1990. Before he started his work at the University of Ulm he had been director of the research department for Advanced Information Management (AIM) at the IBM Heidelberg Science Center (HDSC). At HDSC he managed the AIM-P project on advanced database technology and applications. Current research areas include distributed, cooperative information systems, workflow management and database technology as well as their use in advanced application areas. Together with Manfred Reichert and other partners he is co-founder of the AristaFlow GmbH – a company which will provide a commercial version of the ADEPT2 technology. Peter was PC Co-chair of the BPM'07 conference in Brisbane, Australia. Together with Manfred Reichert he will be General Co-chair of the BPM'09 conference in Ulm.

Andrea Delgado is a PhD student in the Alarcos Research Group of the University of Castilla-La Mancha. She has an MSc(2003) and a Master degree(2007) in Computer Science from the University of the Republica in Uruguay, where she is a professor. Her research interests include business processes modeling, measurement and improvement, service oriented computing, model driven development, processes and methodologies for software development and design.

Marlon Dumas is Professor of Software Engineering at University of Tartu, Estonia and part-time Associate Professor at Queensland University of Technology, Australia. He obtained a PhD from University of Grenoble, France in 2000. His research interests are in the areas of Service-oriented Computing and Business Process Management. He has published over 100 publications in these and related fields and he is co-editor of a textbook on Process-Aware Information Systems.

Schahram Dustdar is a Full Professor for Internet Technologies at the Distributed Systems Group, Institute of Information Systems, Vienna University of Technology (TU Wien) where he is director of the Vita Lab and Honorary Professor of Information Systems at the Department of Computing Science at the University of Groningen (RuG), The Netherlands. He received his M.Sc. (1990) and PhD. degrees (1992) in Business Informatics (Wirtschaftsinformatik) from the University of Linz, Austria. In April 2003 he received his habilitation degree (venia docendi).

Clarence A. Ellis is professor of computer science and co-director of the collaboration technology research group at the University of Colorado at Boulder. At Colorado, he is a member of the Systems Software Lab, and the Institute for Cognitive Science. He is involved in research and teaching of workflow and process-aware information systems, groupware, coordination theory, and operating systems. Dr. Ellis received his PhD Degree in Computer Science from the University of Illinois, and has worked as a researcher and developer at MCC, Xerox PARC, Bull Corp, Bell Telephone Labs, IBM, Los Alamos Scientific Labs, and Argonne National Lab. His academic experience includes teaching at Stanford University, MIT, University of Texas, Stevens Institute of Technology, Johannes Kepler Institute in Austria, and at Chiaotung University in China. Clarence (Skip) Ellis is on the editorial board of numerous journals, and has been an active instigator and leader of a number of computer associations and functions; he has been a member of the National Science Foundation Computer Science Advisory Board; chairman of the NSF Information Technology and Organizations working committee; and chairman of the ACM Special Interest Group on Office Information Systems (SIGOIS). His interests include groupware, workflow systems, CSCW, collaboration theory, distributed systems, modeling and simulation, and humane interfaces to computers. Dr. Ellis has published over 200 technical papers and reports, written several books, lectured in more than two dozen countries, and was selected, in 1998, as a Computer Society ACM Fellow.

Diogo R. Ferreira is assistant professor of information systems at the Technical University of Lisbon. He is an active researcher on BPM systems since 1998 when he joined INESC to develop workflow-based solutions for teleworking, total quality management, enterprise application integration and supply chain management. He holds a PhD from the University of Porto where he worked on workflow systems to support business networking. In 2005 he received a best paper award for the application of learning and planning techniques to business process discovery. His current interests are centered on the application of sequence clustering to process mining. He has taught several courses at BSc, MSc and PhD levels and is currently in charge of the main database systems course and also the systems integration course at the Technical University of Lisbon.

Félix García. MSc (2001) and PhD (2004) in Computer Science at the University of Castilla-La Mancha (UCLM). Associate Professor in the Department of Information Technologies and Systems at the UCLM. His research interests include business process management, software processes, software measurement, and agile methods.

Guido Governatori received his PhD from the University of Bologna on Legal Informatics in 1997. Since then he has held academic and research positions at Imperial College, Griffith University, Queensland University of Technology, the University of Queensland, and NICTA. His research interests include non-classical logics, artificial intelligence, non-monotonic reasoning and rule technology with a particular focus on applications in normative reasoning, business process modelling, semantic web and common sense reasoning. He is the author of over 150 scholarly publications.

Paul Grefen is a full professor in the Department of Technology Management at Eindhoven University of Technology, where he chairs the Information Systems subdepartment. He received his PhD from the University of Twente. He held assistant and associate professor positions in the Computer Science Department at the University of Twente and was a visiting researcher at Stanford University. He was involved in a number of projects, among which WIDE, CrossFlow, CrossWork, and XTC. He is the main editor of the WIDE book and has published a book on workflow management. He is a member of the editorial boards of the International Journal of Cooperative Information Systems and the International Journal of Service Oriented Computing and Applications. His current research interests include architectural design of complex information systems, interorganizational workflow management, high-level transaction management, and contract support in electronic business.

Ta'id Holmes is a PhD student at the Distributed Systems Group, Institute of Information Systems, Vienna University of Technology, Austria. Ta'id received a Dipl.-Ing. from the Vienna University of Technology in Software Engineering/Internet Computing (2006) and a D.E.A. in Chimie Organique Fine from the Université Claude Bernard Lyon 1 (2004). Ta'ids research interests include distributed systems, model driven development and collaborative development environments.

In 2008, **Richard Hull** joined the IBM T.J. Watson Research Center in New York, USA, as a Research Staff Member and Manager. He leads a group conducting research on data-centric services and workflows. Before IBM, Hull spent 12 years at Bell Labs Research, a division of Alcatel-Lucent, and before that he was a Professor of Computer Science at the University of Southern California. Hull has broad research interests in the areas of data and information management, workflow and business processes, and web and converged services.

Since 2006 **Stefan Jablonski** is full professor for Applied Informatics at the University of Bayreuth. Before that he was professor for computer science at the University of Erlangen (1994 to 2005). Between 1991 and 1994 he was managing an advanced development group at Digital Equipment Corporation in Palo Alto, California. His major research interests are process management and meta modeling. One goal of his research is to apply these concepts in domains like quality management and knowledge management. Another goal is to provide integrated solutions for application domains like healthcare, engineering and manufacturing, biology and ecology which are based on these concepts. He has published more than 150 papers, mostly in international journals and conference/workshop proceedings. He has chaired more than a dozen workshops and conferences and was a reviewer for many national and international journals, conferences and workshops.

Guillermo Jimenez holds a PhD in Computer Science from the Tecnológico de Monterrey (www.itesm.mx). He participated as research leader in two international research projects: Ecolead (www.ecolead.org) and PyME CREATIVA (www.pymecreativa.com) in which business processes for e-enterprises played an essential role. At ITESM he teaches courses on enterprise integration engineering, business process management, component based software development, and software engineering. His current involvement is in how BPM could be implemented in different enterprises and the role service oriented computing (SOC) plays. Currently he is research leader in an enterprise-academia project involving innovation, knowledge management, end-to-end business processes, and collaboration addressed to introduce research practices in the involved concepts inside a global industry.

Dimka Karastoyanova is an associate professor at the Institute of Architecture of Application Systems and at the Cluster of Excellence "Simulation Technology" at the University of Stuttgart, Germany. Her research interests include service-oriented computing and architecture, Web Services, service middleware, workflow management, reusability and flexibility of workflows and service compositions, as well as applying the workflow technology for scientific computing and simulation. She received a PhD in Computer Science from the Technische Universtitaet Darmstadt, Germany, in 2006.

Kwang-Hoon Kim is professor of computer science department and director of the collaboration technology research laboratory at Kyonggi University, South Korea. At Kyonggi, he is involved in research and teaching of workflow, BPM, groupware, coordination theory, computer networks, software architectures, and database systems. Dr. Kim received B.S. degree in computer science from Kyonggi University in 1984. And he received M.S. degree in computer science from Chungang University in 1986. He also received his M.S. and PhD degree from the computer science department of University of Colorado at Boulder, in 1994 and 1998, respectively. His dissertation was entitled "Architectures for Very Large-scale Workflow Management Systems" and it was supervised by Professor Clarence A. Ellis. Dr. Kim had worked as a researcher and developer at Aztek Engineering, American Educational Products Inc., and IBM in USA, as well as at Electronics and Telecommunications Research Institute (ETRI) in South Korea. In present, he is a vice-chair of the BPM Korea Forum, a chair of the Workflow Project Group in TTA, and an ERC vice-chair of the Workflow Management Coalition. He has also been on the editorial board of the journal of KSII, and the committee member of the several conferences and workshops. His research interests include groupware, workflow systems, BPM, CSCW, collaboration theory, Grid/P2P distributed systems, data warehousing and mining, software architecture modeling and simulation, e-commerce, and computer networks. Dr. Kim has published over 200 technical papers and reports, and was selected as a winner of Sosung prize awarded by Kyonggi University and an awardee of Korea e-Business Awards, in 2003 and 2006, respectively.

Ekkart Kindler is an associate professor in Software Engineering at the Technical University of Denmark (DTU). He received his master degree and his PhD in Computer Science from the Technische Universtität München in 1990 and 1995. He received his Habilitation in Computer Science from the Humboldt-Universität zu Berlin in 2001. Later, he was visiting professor in theoretical as well as in practical computer science at different German Universities and was an assistant professor (Hochschuldozent) in Software Engineering at Paderborn University from 2002 to 2007. His research interests include formal methods and their application in software and systems engineering and business process management. Currently, he is working on unifying the concepts of business process modelling and on techniques and tools for the automatic analysis and verification of system and process models. He is also working in the area of Model-based Software Engineering, which includes techniques for interpreting models as well as for code-generation.

Matthias Kloppmann is a Distinguished Engineer with IBM Software Group. He has overall architectural responsibility for IBM's business process technology and is the chief architect of IBM's business process engine. He is involved in workflow standardization, working on the BPEL-* set of standards, and on BPMN 2.0.

Dieter König is a Senior Technical Staff Member with IBM Software Group's laboratory in Böblingen and architect for IBM WebSphere Process Server. He is a member of several OASIS Technical Committees for the standardization of WS-BPEL and Service Component Architecture. He has published many articles and has given talks at conferences about Web services and workflow technology, and is co-author of two books about Web services.

Marcello La Rosa is PhD student in the Business Process Management research group, Faculty of Science and Technology, Queensland University of Technology, Australia. He obtained his laurea degree in Computer Engineering at Politecnico di Torino, Italy in 2005. His research interests include configurable process modeling, collaborative process modeling and service-oriented computing. Marcello is one of the developers of the YAWL open-source workflow engine.

Frank Leymann, head of IAAS, is a Former IBM Distinguished Engineer and has twenty years of experience in software development at IBM. For example, he was lead architect of IBM's workflow products, co-architect of IBM's entire middleware stack (especially co-architect of MQSeries, a message queuing middleware used by most of the top fortune 1000 companies of the world), IBM lead architect for Web service Technology, lead-architect "On Demand computing" for IBM Software Group, and he is co-author of many Web service standards specifications. For many companies from all over the world, Prof. Leymann worked as technology consultant on architecture of large application systems.

Zhilei Ma is a researcher at the Institute of Architecture of Application Systems (IAAS) at the University Stuttgart in Germany. Since 2006 he is working in the European Union funded integrated project "SUPER", which tries to exploit the power of Semantic Web technologies to bridge the gap between the business and IT worlds in enterprises. His research interests are in business process modeling, enterprise content management, business knowledge reuse, and corporate performance management. Before 2006 he got his Bachelor of Science in Computer and Information Science at Qingdao University in the P.R. China and his Diplom-Informatiker in computer science at University Stuttgart in Germany.

Tiziana Margaria is chair of Service and Software Engineering at the Institute of Informatics, Universität Potsdam, Germany. Her research focuses on model-based system and service engineering as well as biologically inspired computing. Margaria received a PhD in computer and systems engineering from the Politecnico di Torino, Italy. She is a member of the IEEE, the ACM, the International Federation for Information Processing (IFIP), and the German Association for Computer Science (GI) as well as president of the European Association of Software Science and Technology (EASST). Contact her at margaria@cs.uni-potsdam.de.

Simon Moser is a Software Engineer and Architect with the Business Process Solutions Group at IBM's Software Laboratory in Böblingen, Germany. He holds a M. Eng. in Computer Science and Engineering and has been a member of the WS-BPEL standardization committee. He has published many articles and has given talks at conferences about Web services and workflow technology.

Hernâni Mourão is Professor at the Information Systems Department of the School of Business and Administration from Polytechnic Institute of Setúbal. His main research interests are in the field of Business Process Management and, in particular, their adequacy to concrete organizational scenarios where exception handling plays an essential role. He received is PhD in Informatics at the University of Lisbon in 2008 on Supporting Effective Unexpected Exception Handling in Workflow Management Systems Within Organizational Contexts.

Joerg Nitzsche is a senior researcher at the Institute of Architecture of Application Systems at the University of Stuttgart. He obtained a diploma in Computer Science at the University of Stuttgart in 2006. His research interests include business process management in an SOA environment where he focuses on the utilization of service technology, ontologies, and message exchange patterns, in order to increase reusability of services and processes. In the scope of the EU funded integrated project SUPER which aims at bridging the business/IT gap using semantic web technologies and techniques, he has been main contributor of the BPEL light and BPEL4SWS specifications. He has a huge experience in workflows management systems and middleware for service-oriented computing.

Chun Ouyang received her PhD from the University of South Australia in 2004. She currently works as a postdoctoral research fellow within the BPM Group at the Queensland University of Technology in Australia. Her research interests are in the areas of workflow management and its application, process modelling and analysis, workflow languages, and formalisation.

Cesare Pautasso is assistant professor in the new Faculty of Informatics at the University of Lugano, Switzerland. Previously he was a researcher at the IBM Zurich Research Lab and a senior researcher at ETH Zurich. His research focuses on building experimental systems to explore the intersection of model-driven software composition techniques, business process modeling languages, and autonomic/Grid computing. Recently he has developed an interest in Web 2.0 Mashups and Architectural Decision Modeling. He is the lead architect of JOpera, a powerful model-driven process management tool for Eclipse. His teaching and training activities both in academia and in industry cover advanced topics related to Web Development, Middleware, Service Oriented Architectures and emerging Web services technologies. For more information, visit www.pautasso.info.

Barbara Pernici is full professor of Computer Engineering at the Politecnico di Milano University. Her research interests include workflow information systems design, cooperative information systems, adaptive information systems, service engineering and web services, data quality, and computer based design support tools. She has published more than 40 papers in international journals, co-edited 12 books, and published about 140 papers at international level. She participated in many ESPRIT and IST European projects, among which WIDE (Workflow on Intelligent Distributed database Environment, 1995-1999), WS-Diamond (2005-2008) on selfhealing web services and the European research network on software service S-Cube (2008-2011). She has been chief scientist of the Italian MIUR-MURST FIRB research project MAIS (Multichannel Adaptive Information Systems). She serves as elected chair of TC8 Information Systems of the International Federation for Information Processing (IFIP) and of IFIP WG 8.1 on Information Systems Design.

Mario Piattini has an MSc. and PhD in Computer Science from the Technical University of Madrid, an MSc. in Psychology from UNED, and is a Certified Information System Auditor, Certified Information Security Manager and Certified in Governance Enterprise IT by ISACA. CSQE by ASQ. He is a professor in the Department of Computer Science at the University of Castilla-La Mancha (UCLM), in Ciudad Real, Spain. Author of several books and papers on software engineering, databases and information systems, he leads the ALARCOS research group at the UCLM and he is the Scientific Director of Alarcos Quality Center, S.L. a spinoff of the research group. His research interests are: software process improvement, metrics, maintenance and security in information systems.

Karsten Ploesser has several years of industry experience as a software engineer developing BPM products in SAP's NetWeaver division. Karsten is a member of the authoring team of a number of industry standards in the business process modelling space including BPMN 2.0, WS-BPEL4People and WS-HumanTask. He currently holds the position of senior researcher at the SAP Research centre in Brisbane, Australia, where he explores both the technological and organisational aspects of BPM. Next to his industry commitments, he conducts doctoral studies in the BPM group of Queensland University of Technology.

Giuseppe Pozzi received the Laurea degree in E.E. from Politecnico di Milano in 1986 and the PhD in 1992, respectively. He is now associate professor of Computer Engineering at the Politecnico di Milano, Italy. Additional information is available at the web site http://home.dei.polimi.it/pozzi Carlo Combi and Giuseppe Pozzi are co-authors of the paper "Architectures for a temporal workflow management system", which has been accepted for presentation and published in the proceedings of the ACM SAC Conference, Cyprus, 2004. The paper has been included into the monthly rankings of the "Top 10 Downloads from the ACM Digital Library" for 36 months from January 2005 to December 2007 (http://home.dei.polimi.it/pozzi/listpub.html#TopDownload).

Manfred Reichert has been full professor at the University of Ulm, Germany since January 2008. From 2005 to 2007 he worked as Associate Professor at the University of Twente (UT) where he was coordinator of the strategic research initiatives on E-health (2005 - 2006) and Service-oriented Computing (2007). At UT he was also member of the Management Board of the *Centre for Telematics and Information Technology* which is the largest ICT research institute in the Netherlands. Manfred has worked on advanced issues related to process management technology and service-oriented computing for ten years. Together with Peter Dadam he pioneered the work on the ADEPT process management system which currently provides the most advanced technology for realising flexible process-aware information systems. Manfred was PC Co-chair of the BPM'08 conference in Milan and will be General Co-chair of the BPM'09 conference in Ulm.

Francisco Ruiz. PhD in Computer Science for the University of Castilla-La Mancha (UCLM) in 2003, and MSc in Chemistry-Physics for the University Complutense of Madrid in 1982. He is associate professor of the Department of Information Technologies and Systems at UCLM in Ciudad Real (Spain). He has been Dean of the Faculty of Computer Science between 1993 and 2000. His current research interests include: business processes modeling and measurement, software process technology and modeling, software maintenance, and methodologies for planning and managing of software projects.

Nick Russell has over 20 years experience in the Australian IT industry in a series of technical and senior management roles. He received his PhD from Queensland University of Technology in 2007 and is currently a Postdoctoral Researcher at Eindhoven University of Technology in The Netherlands. Nick has been the driving force for the development of the workflow data and resource patterns and the recent revision of the control-flow patterns. He is also responsible for the development of the newYAWL business process reference language.

Shazia Sadiq is currently working in the School of Information Technology and Electrical Engineering at The University of Queensland, Brisbane, Australia. She is part of the Data and Knowledge Engineering (DKE) research group and is involved in teaching and research in databases and information systems. Shazia holds a PhD from The University of Queensland in Information Systems and a Masters degree in Computer Science from the Asian Institute of Technology, Bangkok, Thailand. Her main research interests are innovative solutions for Business Information Systems that span several areas including business process management, governance, risk and compliance, data quality management, workflow systems, and service oriented computing.

Laura Sánchez has an MSc(2007) in Computer Science from the University of Castilla-La Mancha. He is currently a PhD student and a member of the Alarcos Research Group at the School of Computer Science at the University of Castilla-La Mancha (Spain), and her research activity is in the field of Business Processes, especially in measurement topics.

Bernhard Steffen is chair of Programming Systems in the Department of Computer Science, Universität Dortmund (Germany) and Director of the Center of Innovation on Service Centered Continouus Engineering (SCCE). His research interests include program analysis and optimization, model-based analysis of distributed systems, and service-oriented computing. Steffen received a PhD in computer science from the Christian-Albrechts-Universität zu Kiel, Germany. He is a member of the IEEE, the ACM, IFIP, the GI, and EASST. Contact him at steffen@cs.uni-dortmund.de.

Jianwen Su is a Professor in the Department of Computer Science at the University of California, Santa Barbara. His received his PhD degree in Computer Science from the University of Southern California. His research interests include databases (data modeling, scientific data, data manipulation languages, data intensive systems, and applications) and web services (composition, verification and analysis, discovery, semantics).

Arthur H. M. ter Hofstede received his PhD in Computer Science from the University of Nijmegen in The Netherlands in 1993. Currently he is Professor at the Faculty of Science and Technology of Queensland University of Technology, Australia. He is co-leader of the Business Process Management research group in this faculty. His main research interests are in the conceptual and formal foundations of workflow. He is co-founder of the Workflow Patterns initiative (http://www.workflowpatterns.com) and of the YAWL foundation (http://www.yawlfoundation.org).

Huy Tran is a PhD student at the Distributed Systems Group, Institute of Information Systems, Vienna University of Technology, Austria. Huy received his Bachelor (2002) at Ho Chi Minh City University of Technology in Computer Science and Engineering. His research interests include service-oriented computing, model-driven engineering and business process modeling.

Tammo van Lessen is a senior researcher at the Institute of Architecture of Application Systems at the University of Stuttgart. He obtained a diploma in Software Engineering at the University of Stuttgart in 2006. His research interests include conversational Web services, message exchange patterns as well as business process management and modelling. He has been working in the EU funded integrated project SUPER which aims at bridging the business/IT gap using semantic web technologies and techniques. He has a huge experience in workflows management systems and middleware for service-oriented computing.

Kunal Verma is a research manager at Accenture Technology Labs. His research interests include Requirements Engineering, SOA, the Semantic Web, Semantic Web services, and adaptive Web processes. He has authored over 50 technical papers in these areas and served on over 20 program committees of conferences and workshops.

Barbara Weber obtained her PhD in Economics at the Institute of Information Systems, University of Innsbruck (Austria). Since 2004, she is researcher at the Department of Computer Science at the University of Innsbruck where she currently works on her habilitation. Barbara is a member of the Quality Engineering (QE) research group and head of the research cluster on business processes and workflows at QE. Her main research interests are agile and flexible processes and intelligent user support in flexible systems. This spans several technology areas including workflow management systems, process mining, case-based reasoning, process-oriented knowledge management, enterprise information systems, and agile software development.

A.J.M.M. (Ton) Weijters is associate professor at the technology management department of the Eindhoven University of Technology (TUE), and member of the BETA research group. Currently working on (i) the application of Knowledge Engineering and Machine Learning techniques for process mining, planning and scheduling (ii) fundamental research in the domain of Machine Learning and Knowledge Discovering. He is the auteur of many scientific publications in the mentioned research fields.

Branimir Wetzstein is researcher at the Institute of Architecture of Application Systems at the University of Stuttgart. He obtained a diploma in Software Engineering at the University of Stuttgart. He is working in the area of Business Process Management and Service Oriented Architecture focusing on monitoring and analysis of Business Process Performance. Currently, he is involved in the EU-funded Project SUPER which deals with Semantic Business Process Management.

Uwe Zdun is an assistant professor at the Distributed Systems Group, Institute of Information Systems, Vienna University of Technology, Austria. Prior to that, Uwe has worked as an assistant professor in the Department of Information Systems at the Vienna University of Economics and BA, Austria. His research interests include software patterns, software architecture, SOA, distributed systems, language engineering, and object orientation. He received his doctoral degree in computer science from the University of Essen in 2002, and his habilitation degree (venia docendi) from Vienna University of Economics and BA in 2006. He is coauthor of the books Remoting Patterns (John Wiley & Sons, 2004) and Software-Architektur (Elsevier/Spektrum, 2005).

Index

A

B

C

D

E

F

G

H

Q

R

S

T

U

V

W

X

Y